COMMUNICATION
AND THE
LAW

Communication and the Law

2017 Edition

Communication Law Writers Group
W. Wat Hopkins, Editor

ISBN 978-1-885219-56-5

Vision Press
4195 Waldort Drive
P.O. Box 1106
Northport, Alabama 35476

On the cover: *Scene at the Signing of the Constitution of the United States,* by Howard Chandler Christy (1940), depicts the signing of the U.S. Constitution at Independence Hall in Philadelphia. The painting hangs in the House wing of the Capitol building in Washington.

Printed in the United States of America

Communication Law Writers Group

COMMUNICATION
AND THE
LAW
2017 Edition

W. Wat Hopkins, Editor

VISION PRESS

Preface

The law is ever-changing.

While the guarantees of the First Amendment are provided in clear, succinct language, jurists, attorneys and free-speech advocates have come to learn that interpreting that language is often complicated. Communication law draws upon virtually every type and source of the law — from regulations to statutes, from contract law to constitutional law, from administrative law to the common law. In addition, each year Congress, regulatory agencies, state governments and the U.S. Supreme Court provide a wealth of information that those who follow communication law must locate, digest and come to understand.

So the law — and the interpretation of the law — continues to change.

The publication of the first edition of *Communication and the Law* in 1998 marked the beginning of an effort to keep up with that change in a concise, readable way. Sixteen authors — among them some of the leading communication law scholars in the country — agreed to update the text annually and to work for its continued improvement.

While authorship has changed — indeed, the number of authors has increased from sixteen to nineteen — the commitment to the comprehensive review of the law and to the continuing improvement of the textbook has not changed, as this, the twentieth, edition of *Communication and the Law* reflects.

In addition to its comprehensive overview of communication law, this edition of the text discusses significant events that have had an impact on communication law over the past year. And it continues to follow the evolution of changes that occurred in recent years.

For example, this edition contains a new section on the use of portable electronic devices in courtrooms and a new box focusing on the issue of Facebook threats that grew out of *Elonis v. United States*. There is also new information on net neutrality, possible changes in the management of the broadcast spectrum, expressive conduct, and other issues.

This edition of the textbook is better than the first, but it can be better still. We continue to need the help of our readers. This edition was barely in the mail to the publisher before we began planning the 2018 edition. If you have comments or if there are changes you would like to see, don't wait — let us know now. Our goal is to provide a comprehensive, readable text that is concise but complete. The e-mail address of each author accompanies that author's biography at the end of the book. If you have comments, please let us know.

A number of people played a big part in making *Communication and the Law* possible. I would like to thank longtime friend and colleague David Sloan of the University of Alabama and Joanne Sloan of Vision Press for suggesting the project to me, for encouraging its completion and for their continued support. The eighteen people who, with me, make up the Communication Law Writers Group have been a pleasure to work with. I thank them for their willingness to engage in this venture and for their willingness to work hard to see it through.

As always, I am thankful for my colleagues in the Department of Communication at Virginia Tech, a wonderfully supportive group that makes it a pleasure to go to work each day. Finally, I owe special thanks to the members of my family, especially to my wife, Roselynn, for continued love and support. They make it a pleasure to go home each day.

W. Wat Hopkins
November 2016
Blacksburg, Virginia
whopkins@vt.edu

Table of Contents

Expanded Table of Contents

CONTENTS

CONTENTS

1

The Law in Modern Society

By Cayce Myers

➡ **Headnote Questions**

- What is law?
- What are the sources of U.S. law?
- What is the difference between a trial court and an appellate court?
- What are the basic steps in a court case?
- How are judges chosen?

"The language of the law," the American jurist Learned Hand said in 1929, "must not be foreign to the ears of those who are to obey it."[1] Judge Hand thought the law ought to be clearly written and that, in a democracy, everyone should know the law. Unfortunately, Americans today can hardly be expected to "know" the law, given its amount and density. Also of concern, they tend to know little about the nature and process of law and the officials and institutions that create, administer, interpret and enforce it.

To understand communication law or any other area of the law, students need an introduction to the law generally. That is the purpose of this chapter. Although the law is a complex subject, its basics will be presented here so readers will have a framework within which to put any particular aspect of communication law.

Like the society it serves, law is dynamic. It is important to come to terms with the fundamentals of communication law, but it is also important to understand the forces that create and sustain the law, forces that inevitably will change the law, and how legal change comes about.

This chapter first offers some definitions and probes some of the assumptions of the legal system. The chapter then discusses how law is organized and the institutions that make, apply and interpret the law.

THE NATURE OF LAW

"Law" seems to have an unusual number of meanings. It is usually defined as the rules of conduct established and enforced by authority in a society. The law of a society is one of its most fundamental characteristics; the kind and amount of behavior a society prescribes and proscribes for its members reveal much about the nature of that society. It is the recognition of the law's authority that allows society to function.

The term "law" is also frequently used to refer to a variety of types of law including statutes, court decisions, administrative rulings or private contracts. When people say, "It's the law," they are referring to any sort of official policy. When they use the word "law," people may also mean jurisprudence, the theory of law. Law in this sense refers to a variety of legal philosophies including private ownership, civil liberties, government redress and human rights.

THE SOURCES OF LAW

All American law can be organized according to its sources. Any particular policy affecting communication may be categorized, roughly in the order in which the categories evolved, as common law, equity law, statutory law, constitutional law, administrative law, international law or contract law. These sources work together to inform what is "the law" in the American legal system. Virtually every law examined in this book can be categorized into one of these seven sources of law. When thinking

---

[1] Learned Hand, *Is There a Common Will?, in* THE SPIRIT OF LIBERTY: PAPERS AND ADDRESSES OF LEARNED HAND 56, 56 (1952).

about any particular law, you should consider where it fits in the larger scheme of the law.

Common Law

One of the most important and complex areas of law is "case law." In the American legal system case law is a body of law in which courts have applied the principles established in previous court decisions. These previous decisions are commonly referred to as precedent. The use of these previous court decisions, or precedents, is the basis for common law.

The roots of common law are found in twelfth century England, where local courts created a system for resolving disputes between common people. Judges assigned to these courts were charged to determine and apply local customs and values to resolve the conflicts. Consistency became a prized feature of the common law. In the name of fairness, a kind of conflict resolved one day naturally should be resolved the same way the next day, the next year and, perhaps, indefinitely. For a community to be stable, law should be stable, too.

Thus developed the powerful common law principle known as *stare decisis*, part of a Latin phrase meaning that once established, a legal decision should not easily be changed. When a common law court makes a decision, it sets a precedent. Courts within the same jurisdiction are required to apply that precedent in deciding similar cases. Today, one of the main functions of courts is to decide which precedents are applicable and how they apply to particular cases. Lawyers find precedent and argue that it should be construed in favor of their clients. Judges must analyze precedent and decide how it applies to a particular case. In a common law system there is a strong preference for following precedent. In fact, when lower courts fail to follow precedent, appellate courts frequently overturn the decision.[2]

Colonial America was subject to English common law, and a reformed system continues in modern American courts. Many American judicial precedents are rooted in older British interpretations of law. Today, several areas of law are controlled principally by common law or "judge made" law. Other branches of government generally leave the development of this law, obviously very important in society, to the courts. Other sources of law usually are not specific enough to handle each aspect of every dispute that arises in courts. Thus, judges have to make law to fill in the gaps.

The decisions and accompanying opinions — written rationales for court decisions — are recorded and maintained chronologically. The reports of some trial courts and almost all appellate courts are continuously published according to jurisdiction in consecutive volumes of books called "reports" or "reporters." These bound volumes constitute the seemingly endless rows of books on shelves in law libraries, law offices and courtrooms. Because these reports are organized by jurisdiction and chronologically, they would be impractical for use without the work of researchers who organize the law according to subject matter.

A number of these important analyses of English common law were performed near the turn of the eighteenth century. For instance, Sir William Blackstone, the first professor of law at Oxford University, collated English common law. The resulting set of volumes, which became known as *Blackstone's Commentaries*, organized the law according to subject matter, including the law of freedom of speech and the press. These scholarly collections and analyses of the law for use by lawyers and judges are referred to as legal "treatises," authoritative books on a particular legal subject. Certain treatises, notably the American Law Institute's *Restatements*, are highly influential on lawmakers and judges, and assist them in defining what the law should be in a particular area.

As readers will discover, the common law plays a central role in the law of communication, probably most prominently in the areas of libel and invasion of privacy.

Equity Law

In addition to producing precedent, American courts also issue orders, sometimes referred to as writs.[3] The United States inherited the law of equity from England, where equity courts were established as early as the fourteenth century. Judges in equity courts, unlike common law judges, were empowered to use general principles of fairness, rather than custom or precedent, in resolving problems. Equity solutions to problems brought to these courts, however, were to be supplemental to the common law, not to supersede it.

It is from these equity laws that we get what is commonly referred to as court orders or "writs." The best known is the writ of *habeus corpus*, provided for in Article I of the U.S. Constitution. It is an order from a court to determine the status of a person whom authorities have detained. Extraordinary writs, most commonly in the forms of temporary or permanent injunctions or restraining orders, are judicial orders requiring people to do something that they do not want to do or stopping them from doing something that they want to do. Violation of a court

---

[2] It is not a given that *stare decisis* will always govern a Court's decision. Sometimes appellate courts may decide to overturn their previous decisions because the court thinks the legal rationale for the decision was wrong.

[3] The term "writ" has largely been removed from the vocabulary of federal American jurisprudence. The *Federal Rules of Civil Procedure* did away with the term. However, the writ of *certiorari* (the petition used to ask the U.S. Supreme Court to hear a case) and the writ of habeas corpus (a prisoner's petition to be released from illegal imprisonment) remain in use. Some state systems still use the term "writ" for a few specific areas of law.

order would be a serious matter that can result in severe punishment.

Readers will see the law of equity at work in a number of cases in this book. For example, the Pentagon Papers case was instigated by an injunction a U.S. district court judge issued requiring the *New York Times* to discontinue publishing a classified history of American involvement in the Vietnam War.[4]

Statutory Law

America is a republican democracy. A pure democracy, frequently called a direct democracy, is a political system where citizens vote in regular elections on all governmental issues. The United States is a republican democracy in which the majority rules through officials whom the voters elect to represent them in political institutions. Representatives at the municipal, county, state and national levels meet regularly to enact legislation that reflects the will of the electorate. This legislation is called "statutory law."

Legislative bodies, city councils, county commissions, state assemblies and Congress, for example tend to follow strict procedures to create statutory law. Students of politics have a good sense of how ideas typically become laws. In Congress, a representative or senator may propose a law in the form of a bill, which congressional leadership may refer to an appropriate committee for consideration. The committee may refer the bill to a subcommittee. The subcommittee examines the bill, perhaps by holding hearings or undertaking other studies. After this review, the subcommittee may vote on whether to recommend to the full committee that the bill be amended or not be enacted as a statute. If the majority of the subcommittee members vote in favor of the bill, the committee may conduct additional deliberations before voting on whether to recommend the bill to the full chamber of Congress.

The full chamber may have additional discussion of the bill before voting on whether to enact it as law. In a bicameral legislature, such as Congress, a similar bill has usually followed a similar process in the other chamber. If the legislation is approved in the other chamber but in a different form, representatives of each chamber meet to work out the differences in a conference committee. Both the House of Representatives and the Senate must approve any compromises made in the conference committee. Upon adoption of these changes, a bill is referred to the president, who has the power to veto it. Congress can override the veto by a two-thirds vote of each chamber.[5] Rescinding laws requires the same process. All states except Nebraska have bicameral legislatures, while local governments tend to have unicameral councils or commissions.

Other sources of law are apt to be deferential to statutory law because it is seen as the will of the people in a democracy. Statutory law, however, must be consistent with the Constitution and applied, enforced and interpreted by the executive and judicial branches of government. Statutory law sometimes leaves room for interpretation. Sometimes courts give legal interpretations of statutory law in case law. In these situations case law and statutory law work together to constitute "the law" on a particular issue. A state statute applies only to people in the state wherein it was adopted and must be consistent with both the federal and the state's constitutions; a federal statute applies to all people in the United States and must be consistent with the federal Constitution.

Statutory law plays an important role in communication law. State and federal legislation is key to understanding the law of obscenity, electronic media, intellectual property, marketing and journalistic privilege.

Constitutional Law

America's most important contribution to thought about law in society is the written constitution. From 1781 to 1789 the colonies operated under the Articles of Confederation. This document placed the colonies in a loose confederation with a weak centralized government. After the American Revolution, each of the thirteen states wrote and ratified a document that was intended to be a kind of powerful contract between the people and government. Carrying the idea of democracy to a new and original extreme, the state constitutions vested sovereignty in the people through the constitutions and designated public officials and government bodies as public servants.

Based on the model of the early state constitutions and the desire for a stronger central government, the U.S. Constitution — written in 1787 and ratified in 1789 — became a model for constitutions of other nations and for states that subsequently joined the union. The Constitution is made up of the Preamble, seven articles and twenty-seven amendments. The most important parts are the first three articles and the Bill of Rights, the first ten amendments.

Important to understanding American constitutional law is the concept of "limited government." The colonial experience with Great Britain taught America's constitutional framers not to trust centralized power. They intended to create governments that would be explicitly excluded from almost all aspects of an individual citizen's life. Governments would be assigned only those functions in society that citizens could not perform for themselves. The Constitution was the device for the assignment of specific powers to government. The assumption was that government was powerless to do anything that it was not entitled

---

[4] New York Times Co. v. United States, 403 U.S. 713 (1971).

[5] *See* U.S. CONST. art I, § 7, cl. 3.

to do in the Constitution.

Article I of the Constitution establishes Congress and enumerates its powers, including the powers to tax and mint money, declare war and regulate interstate commerce. Article II establishes the presidency and enumerates its powers, including leading the military, establishing foreign policy and appointing government officers. Article III establishes the federal judiciary and enumerates its powers, including hearing cases involving federal and international matters and disputes between states and between citizens of different states. According to the theory of limited government, the states retain all other powers, or no government can exercise those powers.

FEDERAL JUDICIAL POWER

Article III, Section 2 of the Constitution provides that "the judicial Power shall extend to all Cases ... and Controversies":

1. "arising under this Constitution, the Laws of the United States, and Treaties made, ..."
2. "affecting Ambassadors, other public Ministers and Consuls, ..."
3. "of admiralty and maritime jurisdiction, ..."
4. "to which the United States shall be a Party, ..."
5. "between two or more States, ..."
6. "between a State and Citizens of another State, ..."
7. "between Citizens of different States" [also known as "diversity-of-citizenship" cases], ...
8. "between Citizens of the same State claiming Lands under the Grants of different States, ..."
9. "between a State, or Citizens thereof, and foreign States, Citizens or Subjects, ..."

All other matters are reserved for state courts. Most cases in federal courts involve items 1, 4 and 7.

The framers, particularly Alexander Hamilton and James Madison, believed the federal government could not exercise any powers not enumerated in the Constitution, so they rejected efforts to include a listing of individual rights and liberties, including freedom of speech and of the press, that the government should be forbidden to abridge. Including such provisions in the Constitution was politically popular. In its first session, Congress approved twelve constitutional amendments, ten of which were ratified as the Bill of Rights, including the famous First Amendment provisions for freedom of religion and expression.[6]

The Constitution, according to Article VI, is "the supreme Law of the Land," which has come to mean that any conflicting

source of law must yield to constitutional law. Because the Constitution is brief and often ambiguous, however, its provisions are subject to multiple interpretations. What one person considers an exercise of First Amendment protected "freedom of speech" may not be to another person.

Through their assertion of the power to declare statutory law inconsistent with constitutional law,[7] the courts, especially the U.S. Supreme Court, are decisive in explaining and applying the Constitution. When reviewing a challenge to the constitutionality of a government action, the Court explains what the Constitution means, thus producing constitutional law. As Chief Justice Charles Evans Hughes once observed, the "Constitution is what the judges say it is."[8]

The Constitution can be amended either by calling a new constitutional convention, which has never happened, or by a vote of two-thirds of each of the houses of Congress and three-fourths of the state legislatures.[9]

Constitutional law, of course, provides the theoretical umbrella for all law. Virtually every law affecting communication is ultimately answerable in some form to constitutional law. Most important are the Supreme Court's constitutional theories based on the First Amendment clauses protecting the rights of free speech, free press, assembly and petition. This terse constitutional language has generated countless court decisions and opinions explaining what those words mean.

Administrative Law

The nature of American life changed dramatically during the Industrial Revolution. In the decades following the Civil War, the national economy became dependent less on agriculture and more on manufacturing. Business saw the introduction of large-scale manufacturing, corporations and market speculation. Large cities now had to provide public services for growing populations of workers who left farms for factory jobs. These changes occurred in tandem with increased public consumption of manufactured goods, and technological innovations in mass communication and transportation.

As the economy became centralized, industrialists and financiers came to dominate society. They amassed great wealth and used their money to influence politics and government. Farmers, small business owners and workers became increasingly agitated over monopolies that dictated wages and prices. A

---

[6] Madison clearly changed his mind on the protection of individual rights because he was the congressman who introduced the original bill of rights. *See* Cayce Myers & W. Wat Hopkins, MASS COMMUNICATION LAW IN VIRGINIA 3-8 (2016).

[7] Perhaps the most famous decision in U.S. constitutional history is *Marbury v. Madison*, 1 Cranch 137 (1803). In his opinion for the Court, Chief Justice John Marshall asserted the power of the U.S. Supreme Court to deem congressional enactments unconstitutional. At best, Article III of the Constitution is ambiguous as to whether the framers meant that the Court should have such power.

[8] Speech at Elmira, N.Y., May 3, 1907.

[9] *See* U.S. CONST. art V.

wealthy few seemed to control markets and governments. Political groups calling themselves "Populists" and "Progressives" emerged around the end of the nineteenth century to seek political change. Frustrated in its appeals to corrupt legislatures, executives and courts, the reform movement pushed the concept of administrative law for reforming government.

The reformers reasoned that if unregulated capitalism resulted in reduced competition in the marketplace of goods and services, then the government should regulate the economy to ensure free enterprise. Some midwestern states first experimented with the idea of administrative law by regulating aspects of intrastate commerce. Then, in 1887, Congress created the first federal administrative agency, the Interstate Commerce Commission, to regulate commerce between states. Beginning in the 1910s, Congress created dozens of so-called "independent" agencies to regulate specific aspects of commerce. Among these agencies are the Federal Communications Commission, the Federal Trade Commission and the Securities and Exchange Commission.

Framers of federal administrative law meant for commissioners to be apolitical experts in the fields they regulate. Instead of being elected in a political process that the regulated industries might control, a commissioner is appointed by the president to a fixed term, although the Senate can veto appointments. Congressional legislation attempts to restrict politics in the appointment process by limiting the number of members of one political party on a commission. On the five-member FCC, for example, a maximum of three may be from the same political party. Administrative law was to be created by people trained and experienced in the frequently complex issues of finance and technology that the appointees would address. These administrative agencies proliferated during the twentieth century at both the federal and state level.

Administrative law is a creature of administrative agencies, most of which, unlike other political institutions, have quasi-legislative, quasi-executive and quasi-judicial powers. In short, an administrative agency can pass its own laws, execute those laws and adjudicate disputes over enforcement, unrestricted by considerations of the separation of powers that limit Congress, the president and the courts. The FCC can enact regulations affecting broadcasting licensees, punish an offending licensee and hear and resolve a licensee's challenge to the regulations or enforcement. The sum total of the rules, regulations, decisions and other policy-making of these agencies make up the body of administrative law.

Also important is how Congress, the president and the courts affect administrative law. Congress empowers the agencies through enabling statutes. An agency can exercise only the power the enabling statute grants. Federal agencies also are governed by the Administrative Procedures Act of 1946, which requires that agencies be fair and reasonable.[10] In addition, congressional legislation funds the agencies, and Congress sometimes threatens what it considers agency misbehavior with budget cuts. The agencies are accountable to the president most directly through the appointment of agency members. Decisions of the agencies can be appealed to federal courts, which usually are deferential to the expertise of the agencies but also can rule agency actions to be unconstitutional.[11]

Administrative law has a prominent place in the study of communication law. As examples, the FCC broadly regulates electronic media, the FTC regulates advertising and other marketing practices, and the SEC regulates communication by publicly held companies. Virtually every communication business must attend to at least some administrative law.

International Law

Beginning in the nineteenth century there was a movement toward creating a comprehensive international law. At the end of World War II, the United Nations was formed, and new international laws were created, such as those governing human rights. However, for centuries treaties have governed formal relationships between independent nations. Treaties are agreements that establish policies for how societies interact politically and economically. Designated the Commander in Chief and head of state by Article II of the U.S. Constitution, the president has much unilateral authority to conduct American relations with other nations, but Article I empowers Congress to fund transnational initiatives, declare war and approve treaties. Article III grants federal courts exclusive jurisdiction to hear cases involving U.S. foreign affairs.

The United States has entered into numerous world and regional covenants subjecting it and its citizens to policies of various multinational organizations, the most important of which is the United Nations. The U.N. Charter commits member nations to participate in efforts to foster peace and prosperity throughout the world. The Universal Declaration of Human Rights, International Covenant on Civil and Political Rights, European Convention for the Protection of Human Rights, and American Convention on Human Rights are examples of international and regional agreements that governments should protect human rights such as freedom of expression.

Treaties such as the North American Free Trade Agreement between Canada, Mexico and the United States have important

---

[10] 5 U.S.C. § 551 (1994).

[11] This deference to administrative agencies is found in the Supreme Court's decision in *Chevron USA. Inc. v. Natural Resources Defense Council,* 467 U.S. 837 (1984). In that case the Court held that federal courts should give great deference to an agency's interpretation of its own rules and regulations. The practical result from this decision is federal courts rarely overturn agency rules or regulations.

implications for both the amount and kind of communication between nations and the protection of freedom of expression in each nation. Agreements such as the Berne Convention for the Protection of Literary and Artistic Works and the Agreement on Trade-Related Aspects of Intellectual Property Rights attempt to establish harmonious policies for the international treatment of intellectual and creative property. (Intellectual property is discussed in Chapter 13.)

The development of new communication technology breaks down political and other barriers between nations, raising questions about international communication far faster than policy-making bodies can provide satisfactory answers. There is no doubt that international law will become increasingly influential as a source of communication law. (The regulation of new communication technologies is discussed in Chapter 12.)

Contract Law

One of the most common sources of law that affects both individuals and businesses is contract law, sometimes referred to as "private law." Since ancient times, contracts have been present in almost every legal system. Contracts include a variety of agreements between parties such as purchase agreements, employment contracts and the transfer of ownership. In the American legal system, case laws and statutes have regulations that dictate what constitutes a legal contract. These laws prohibit contracts made for illegal purposes, disallow contracts that unjustly enrich one party at the expense of another and require that both contracting parties willingly enter the contract. Modern American contract law requires three essential elements of all contracts. They must contain an offer, acceptance and consideration. Basically this means that during the formation of a contract there must be a meeting of the minds between all of the contracting parties in which one party pays the other for a good or service. Under most state laws, contracts can be written or oral. However, some states require contracts over a certain amount, usually $500, to be written.

While states have general regulations about contracts, the parties involved usually have unfettered discretion in selecting the terms of their contract. A contract can contain provisions that do not follow a specific state or federal law. In fact, contract terms can even include an election of laws that will govern any future contract disputes. Courts only become involved in contract terms when one party breaches his or her part of the contract. In that situation the wronged party can sue the breaching party in court. Absent a breach, courts almost never become involved with regulating or interpreting contracts.

When courts do become involved in contract disputes, they are frequently asked to interpret vague components of contracts. Over the years, legal conventions have developed that assist courts in determining the meaning of a contract in dispute. Courts usually resolve disputes by first examining what is written in a contract. This process is sometimes referred to as examining the "four corners" of the contract. In cases where the contract is vague or a meaning cannot be determined by the "four corners," most courts resolve the ambiguity in favor of the party with the fewest financial resources. In addition to interpreting contracts, courts sometimes are asked to issue orders requiring parties to fulfill their contractual obligation or pay the non-breaching party money damages.

In communication law, contracts are frequently at issue. This is because contracts are a part of daily management governing the sale of goods, employment and other obligations between private parties. Contract issues emerge in a variety of communication laws including intellectual property ownership, licensing agreements and employment contracts for journalists and public relations practitioners. When examining a contract issue a student needs to know the terms of the contract, how the contract is to be interpreted and what remedies the law provides if there is a breach.

COURTS

The focus of most interest in the law is the courtroom. Law schools train lawyers principally for careers in courts. To practice law in most American courts, a person must have graduated from a law school, be licensed and be admitted to a state or jurisdiction's bar.

Courts are at the center of the study of U.S. law for many reasons. Unlike judges of almost every other nation, American judges are vested with wide political authority. Through the power of judicial review and the ability to rule laws unconstitutional (and to have their decisions taken seriously), courts are the ultimate forums for the resolution of disputes, whether between private or public parties. In theory at least, even the most powerful must answer to the least powerful in courts. Congress, the president and the states have largely acceded to the courts the ability to square other laws with the Constitution. "In truth, few laws can escape the searching analysis of judicial power for any length of time," asserted Alexis de Tocqueville, the prescient French observer of early America, "for there are few which are not prejudicial to some private interest or other, and none which may not be brought before a court of justice by the choice of parties, or by the necessity of the case."[12]

As primary guardians of the Bill of Rights, the courts are protectors of individual rights and liberties, perforce an anti-majoritarian responsibility. The courts, however, tend to be cau-

---

[12] ALEXIS DE TOCQUEVILLE, DEMOCRACY IN AMERICA 75 (New American Library 1956) (1835, 1840).

THE AMERICAN JUDICIAL SYSTEM

FEDERAL COURTS		STATE COURTS
	Courts of Last Resort	
Supreme Court		Supreme Court[*]
	Intermediate Appellate Courts	
Courts of Appeals		Courts of Appeal[**]
	Trial Courts of General Jurisdiction	
District Courts		Circuit Courts[***]
	Trial Courts of Limited Jurisdiction	
Court of Federal Claims		*Examples:*
Court of International Trade		Family Court
Court of Appeals for Veterans Claims		Juvenile Court
Rail Reorganization Court		Small Claims Court
Tax Court		Traffic Court

* In Maryland and New York, this court is called the Court of Appeals, and in Maine and Massachusetts, the Supreme Judicial Court. Texas and Oklahoma have both supreme courts and courts of criminal appeals as courts of last resort. State supreme court decisions can be appealed to the U.S. Supreme Court. However, like any other appeal to the U.S. Supreme Court the court first must grant a writ of *certiorari.*

** Eleven states do not have intermediate courts of appeal. Twelve states call these courts by variations on this name, e.g., the Maryland Court of Special Appeals, the Florida District Court of Appeals and the Pennsylvania Superior Court.

*** Names of state trial courts include Circuit Court (18 states), District Court (16 states), Superior Court (13 states), Court of Common Pleas (Ohio and Pennsylvania), Supreme Court (New York) and Trial Court (Massachusetts). Vermont has both a District Court and a Superior Court.

---

tious in exercising judicial review. In its history, the Supreme Court has declared unconstitutional only about 170 acts of Congress and 1,200 acts of state and local governments. The courts seem sensitive to the undemocratic image of an un-elected body invalidating a law passed by elected representatives. Judges may also be aware, at least subconsciously, that their existence and funding depend on legislatures. The power of the courts is sometimes called "the judicial myth" because courts actually have few resources to require obedience to their decisions. They generally have only public esteem as political capital.

A court hearing a case is supposed to resolve a carefully framed question in a genuine dispute between two or more parties. The court should be apolitical, fair and principled in making a decision. The court is expected to follow strict legal procedure to ensure impartiality for all parties and fully to explain the rationale for the decision in a public document called the court's opinion. These decisions and opinions of American courts are not only important sources of law guiding everyday life but also of authoritative American political philosophy.

Jurisdiction

Perhaps the most important way to distinguish between courts is by their jurisdiction, that is, their power to hear and rule in a case. "Jurisdiction" usually refers to the subject matter (the kinds of legal issues) on which a court is entitled to rule, or to geography, places or types of parties over whom a court has authority. One fundamental distinction to be made in considering court jurisdiction is between trial courts and appellate courts; almost all American courts are either courts of original jurisdiction or appellate jurisdiction.

There are two ingredients in a court case: the facts and the law. Trial courts find facts and apply the law. An appellate court reviews only the trial court's application of the law; the appeals court is generally powerless to seek new evidence or directly apply the law to the case under review. Appeals courts affirm or reverse trial court verdicts; they do not issue new verdicts. Most American court systems consist of trial courts ("law-applying and fact-finding" courts), intermediate appellate courts ("law-reviewing" courts) and courts of last resort. As courts of last resort, the federal and state supreme courts usually have limited, if any, original jurisdiction. They mainly deal with peti-

THE U.S. COURT CIRCUITS AND DISTRICTS

FIRST CIRCUIT — The districts of Maine, Massachusetts, New Hampshire, Rhode Island and Puerto Rico

SECOND CIRCUIT — The districts of Connecticut, Eastern New York, Northern New York, Southern New York, Western New York and Vermont

THIRD CIRCUIT — The districts of Delaware, New Jersey, Eastern Pennsylvania, Middle Pennsylvania, Western Pennsylvania and Virgin Islands

FOURTH CIRCUIT — The districts of Maryland, Eastern North Carolina, Middle North Carolina, Western North Carolina, South Carolina, Eastern Virginia, Western Virginia, Northern West Virginia and Southern West Virginia

FIFTH CIRCUIT — The districts of Eastern Louisiana, Middle Louisiana, Western Louisiana, Northern Mississippi, Southern Mississippi, Eastern Texas, Northern Texas, Southern Texas and Western Texas

SIXTH CIRCUIT — The districts of Eastern Kentucky, Western Kentucky, Eastern Michigan, Western Michigan, Northern Ohio, Southern Ohio, Eastern Tennessee, Middle Tennessee and Western Tennessee

SEVENTH CIRCUIT — The districts of Central Illinois, Northern Illinois, Southern Illinois, Northern Indiana, Southern Indiana, Eastern Wisconsin and Western Wisconsin

EIGHTH CIRCUIT — The districts of Eastern Arkansas, Western Arkansas, Northern Iowa, Southern Iowa, Minnesota, Eastern Missouri, Western Missouri, Nebraska, North Dakota and South Dakota

NINTH CIRCUIT — The districts of Alaska, Arizona, Central California, Eastern California, Northern California, Southern California, Hawaii, Idaho, Montana, Nevada, Oregon, Eastern Washington, Western Washington, Guam and Northern Mariana Islands

TENTH CIRCUIT — The districts of Colorado, Kansas, New Mexico, Eastern Oklahoma, Northern Oklahoma, Western Oklahoma, Utah and Wyoming

ELEVENTH CIRCUIT — The districts of Middle Alabama, Northern Alabama, Southern Alabama, Middle Florida, Northern Florida, Southern Florida, Middle Georgia, Northern Georgia and Southern Georgia

DISTRICT OF COLUMBIA CIRCUIT — District of Columbia

FEDERAL CIRCUIT — National jurisdiction in certain cases in administrative law, intellectual property and monetary claims against the U.S. government

---

tions to review decisions by other appellate courts.

Courts will have either general or limited subject-matter jurisdiction. A general jurisdiction court handles a wide array of criminal and civil matters. A limited-jurisdiction court may be created to handle only, for example, tax issues, bankruptcy issues or juvenile issues.

Federal Courts

Article III of the Constitution says little about the number and sorts of federal courts, mentioning "one supreme Court" and "such inferior courts as the Congress may from time to time ordain and establish." With the Judiciary Act of 1789, as amended, and other legislation, however, Congress has developed an elaborate federal judiciary.

When Congress creates courts under Article III, a resulting court is called an "Article III court." When a federal court is created by way of other constitutional provisions, it is called a "non-Article III court." Article III provides that judges assigned to Article III courts have lifetime tenure, meaning they hold office until they die, are impeached and convicted, or choose to retire (at age 65 with at least fifteen years of service or age 70 after at least ten years of service). A non-Article III judge may serve a term specified in the law that established the judge's court. Examples of non-Article III courts are the Court of Federal Claims, the Court of Appeals for the Armed Forces and Administrative Law Judges. These courts have specific jurisdiction suggested by their names. Article III courts include the district courts, courts of appeals and U.S. Supreme Court.

U.S. District Courts

The ninety-four district courts are the federal courts of original jurisdiction. At least one is located in each state, Puerto Rico, the Virgin Islands, Guam and the District of Columbia. As many as four are located in each of the most populous states.

The number of judges assigned to each court ranges from two to twenty-eight, depending on the amount of work in the court. Normally, one judge presides in a case, with or without a jury, but a three-judge panel may be assigned to decide a case in special circumstances.

There are 677 judgeships in the fifty states and territories and fifteen in the District of Columbia. Each district also is assigned at least one magistrate, bankruptcy judge, marshal, clerk, U.S. attorney (federal prosecutor), probation officer and reporter. One of the judges in each district is appointed the chief judge to handle administrative matters. The district court judge is nominated by the President of the United States and confirmed by the Senate. Other judges in federal districts, such as magistrate and bankruptcy judges, are appointed by appellate and district court judges.[13]

In recent years, the district courts have heard an annual average of about 280,000 civil cases and 78,000 criminal cases. About half the civil cases involve contract and liability law. Half of the criminal cases involve narcotics, fraud, drunk driving and other traffic offenses.

U.S. Courts of Appeals

Congress established the current system of federal courts of appeal in 1891.[14] These courts take appeals of decisions of the district courts and federal agencies. Except when the Supreme Court agrees to review decisions of appeals courts, the lower decisions are final. Since the Supreme Court in recent years has been granting full review to fewer than 100 of about 9,000 petitions it gets each term, the courts of appeals are, as a practical matter, the courts of last resort in the federal judiciary.

There are 179 judgeships in eleven numbered multi-state circuits, the Federal Circuit, and the District of Columbia Circuit. Each circuit has one appeals court with six to twenty-nine permanent judgeships, depending on the docket size. All federal court of appeals judges are nominated by the president and confirmed by the Senate.

Rather than involve all of the judges in every decision, an appeals court normally assigns a case to a three-judge subcommittee, called a "panel." When the entire court assembles to decide a case, it is said to act *en banc*. *En banc* hearings are rare. They usually are reserved for special appeals cases. While an attorney may request an *en banc* hearing, holding such a hear-

ing is ultimately the federal appellate courts' decision.

About 53 percent of the 56,000 appeals court petitions each year involve civil matters. About 23 percent are criminal cases, and 14 percent are administrative cases. Only about 15 percent result in formal hearings before the appeals courts.

A chief judge is assigned in each appeals court to handle administrative work for the circuit. In addition, a Supreme Court justice is chosen to be the supervising "circuit justice" for each circuit.

U.S. Supreme Court

The Supreme Court of the United States, the federal court of last resort, is the only court specifically mentioned in Article III of the Constitution, and the Constitution says little else about how it was to be structured or how it was to conduct its work. Through legislation, Congress established the office of the Chief Justice of the United States and determined the number of justices, which was set at nine in 1869. A Supreme Court term opens on the first Monday in October, according to statute, and usually concludes at the end of June.

In the past thirty years, the annual number of petitions reaching the Court has grown from about 1,000 to about 10,000. The Court gave full-dress treatment to a peak of 174 cases in each of the 1982 and 1983 terms, but in recent terms it has decided fewer than 100 cases per term this way.

Notice that the title of the federal judiciary's chief administrative officer is the "Chief Justice of the United States," not the "Chief Justice of the U.S. Supreme Court." The associate justices do not regard the chief justice as their boss. Rather, the chief justice is head of the federal judiciary, chair of the Federal Judicial Conference (the policy-making body for the federal courts), and in charge of administrative matters for the Supreme Court, including its building. Also, the justices have agreed, the chief justice chairs the conferences of the justices in deciding cases and presides at public hearings for the Court. The chief justice is in a better position than anyone to set the Court's agenda, but the justices are not answerable to the chief justice, who, like each of them, has only one of the nine votes.

State Courts

Article III gives broad authority to the federal courts to handle legal issues, but the vast majority of American judicial work is done in the state courts. Federal jurisdiction is actually limited, leaving most matters of civil and criminal law to states. Although the most important constitutional issues seem eventually to reach the federal courts, state courts actually produce the law most directly affecting citizens on a day-to-day basis.

State court systems are generally organized like the federal

---

[13] Federal magistrate judges are appointed by a majority of the district court judges in a particular district. Bankruptcy judges are appointed by the judges of the federal court of appeals of a specific circuit.

[14] Everts Act of 1891, 28 U.S.C. ch. 3 (1994).

court system, with trial and intermediate appellate courts and courts of last resort. Names of these courts vary in the states. Sixteen states call their general jurisdiction trial court the "district court," but New York calls it the "supreme court." Most intermediate appellate courts are called "appeals courts," but in Pennsylvania, this court is called the "superior court." Most courts of last resort are "supreme courts," but in Maryland it is called the "court of appeals."

Each state court system is independent of other state court systems and the federal system. A state supreme court is the ultimate authority on that state's law. Just as a state court cannot correct the U.S. Supreme Court in its interpretation of federal law, federal courts cannot correct a state supreme court in its interpretation of state law. The U.S. Supreme Court can overrule a state supreme court on a state law question only when the two courts disagree over whether state law violates federal law. The U.S. Constitution, as the supreme law of the land, prevails whenever a law, even a state constitution, violates it. On the other hand, a state constitution can provide more and different rights than the federal constitution can. "State constitutions, too, are a font of individual liberties," U.S. Supreme Court Justice William J. Brennan Jr. noted, "their protections often extending beyond those required by the Supreme Court's interpretation of federal law."[15]

State court systems have created a large number of courts in special subject-matter jurisdiction. Probate, traffic, domestic relations and juvenile courts are common, as are courts dealing in only minor crimes, such as justice of the peace courts, and in minor civil matters, such as small-claims courts.

LEGAL PROCEDURE

Law is either substantive or procedural. Most of what this book describes is the substance of communication law, for instance, whether a particular communication is defamatory or obscene.

Procedural law, on the other hand, includes the rules for how substantive law is created, administered and adjudicated. In essence these laws enumerate the procedures used in the practice of law. To protect against governmental abuse, the federal and state constitutions require that authorities treat individuals fairly, equally and decisively. Mandating that a criminal suspect be represented by legal counsel and be given an impartial trial by peers are examples of procedural law. In federal courts, the *Rules of Civil Procedure* and *Rules of Criminal Procedure* establish details as specific as the cost of filing records and the dimensions of the paper permitted to be submitted as court documents. States have similar procedural laws. A case that is likely

to be won on the merits may be lost for failure to follow procedure. If a plaintiff's lawyer does not file an action within the statute of limitations, the legal deadline that procedural law establishes, the court will probably dismiss the action. That may be cause for the client to sue the lawyer for malpractice.

The procedure for a legal action depends on many factors, the most fundamental of which are whether the action is civil, criminal or administrative and where the action is brought. A civil action generally involves a dispute between private parties usually over money damages. Civil due process applies; the standard of proof is a "preponderance of the evidence"; and remedies in equity, such as an injunction, or in law, such as monetary damages, are available.

An administrative action is also a type of civil lawsuit. It typically involves a case over compliance or lack thereof with an administrative rule or regulation. An administrative agency's decision can be appealed through the agency's appeals process. Rules of administrative procedure are applied. Decisions by an agency's bureaucracy on fines and orders may be upheld, adjusted or dismissed by an agency's judges or by the agency's policy-making commissioners, acting as a kind of internal court of appeals. The administrative process is also subject to external judicial review only when all agency appeals are exhausted.

A criminal action is brought by the federal or state government against an individual for committing a crime designated in legislation. Criminal due process applies, the standard of proof is "beyond a reasonable doubt," and remedies include fines and imprisonment.

Legal procedure also depends on where an action is brought. Although procedural rules in different systems resemble each other, each state has its own specific procedures for its courts and agencies. Federal courts and agencies have separate sets of procedures. Procedures will also differ depending on whether the action is in a trial court or appellate court.

Trial Court Procedure

Courts are in the business of remedying or punishing social wrongs. Civil law was established to correct civil wrongs, such as torts or breaches of contracts, but has also become a way to achieve constitutional rights. Civil courts are intended to be places where civilized people will resolve their disputes rather than through violence or other inappropriate behavior. Criminal law was established to punish criminal wrongs, such as arson or larceny, although a major part of criminal law is devoted to protecting the constitutional rights of suspects.

Civil Procedures

The victim of a civil wrong will first consult an attorney who

---

[15] William J. Brennan Jr., *State Constitutions and the Protection of Individual Rights,* 90 HARV. L. REV. 489, 491 (1977).

may specialize in a particular area of law, such as torts or contract disputes. The attorney tries to determine whether the client has a cause for action based on the facts and the law and, if so, whether the law provides a remedy in equity or damages. The two major branches of civil law are torts and contracts. A tort is a non-criminal wrong committed by one party against another. Libel and invasion of privacy are torts. However, tort law covers many different scenarios including medical malpractice, defective products and personal injuries. A contract is an agreement between two parties. If one party violates the agreement, the other may seek a remedy for breach of contract.

A typical civil case seeks monetary damages to help the plaintiff recover from various kinds of losses, for example, harm to reputation, shame and ridicule resulting from defamation. Generally, a plaintiff has to present evidence that the defendant was at fault for causing the harm to the plaintiff and that the plaintiff suffered as a result. The defendant can prevail by contradicting the plaintiff's evidence or introducing other evidence. The judge and jury decide on whether the plaintiff succeeds in the action by proving their claim by a "preponderance of the evidence."

The plaintiff's attorney, once satisfied that a client has a case, may begin to collect evidence to support the claim. An example of evidence would be affidavits — sworn statements by potential witnesses. The attorney will also conduct legal research. One initial decision will be deciding in which court to bring the case. If the case involves state law and both parties are in the state, then the case should be filed in a court in that state. If the case involves federal law, then the case should be filed in the federal district of the legal wrong. If the parties are in different states and the case involves a controversy in excess of $75,000, the case may be brought in a court in either state or in a federal district court. If the case involves state law, the law of the state in which the case is brought prevails, including in a federal court. The law in one state might be more favorable to the plaintiff than the law in another state. These variables figure into "forum shopping," the process of picking a court for an action. The parties must have at least some connection to the court district where the case is brought.

Other initial legal issues for the plaintiff's attorney are the statute of limitations and standing to sue. The statute of limitations is the deadline for initiating a suit. A plaintiff must also establish "standing" – the right to bring the action; that is, does the plaintiff have a legally established interest in the litigation? For example, survivors of a libel plaintiff who dies generally do not have standing to sue on behalf of the deceased.

The legal system tries to encourage litigants to settle the case out of court. After the initial investigation, the plaintiff's attorney may ask the defendants for an amount of money to settle the case before legal action is filed. A defendant may also volunteer to settle at any stage of the process. Settlements account for a much larger proportion of the dispositions of civil actions than do trials. Part of the reason for this is the expense of trial. As attorney's fees, expert witness fees, and the length of time it takes to prepare for trial have increased, settlement in civil cases sometimes is the most cost efficient option.

The pre-trial process consists of two stages: pleadings and discovery. The basic pleadings are the complaint and answer. The first formal document filed in a case is the complaint, in which the plaintiff states the grounds for the action and jurisdiction of the court and demands judgment. Upon receipt of the complaint and a filing fee, the clerk of the court puts the case on the docket. The clerk issues a summons to be served on the defendant, notifying the defendant of the action. This step is called "service of process." The defendant is given a deadline within which to respond to the summons.

The defense attorney analyzes the complaint and researches other facts and law that may be relevant. If the defense does not challenge the complaint on the grounds of lack of jurisdiction or specificity, a document called an "answer" is prepared. The defendant's answer can admit, deny, or neither admit nor deny the facts in the complaint. The defendant's attorney strategically selects these possible answers to the complaint. The answer may deny the allegations in the complaint and establish the defense, even if the defendant denies the plaintiff has a cause of action. The answer is delivered to the clerk of courts and sent to the plaintiff. At this stage and in subsequent pre-trial stages, the defendant can ask the court summarily to dismiss the case on the grounds that the plaintiff's case is insufficient as a matter of law.

The next stage of the civil process is discovery, during which each side of a case obtains information from the other side. In civil discovery, the parties have wide latitude in seeking this information. Refusal to cooperate can result in a citation for contempt of court. Discovery includes interrogatories, depositions and requests for documents or other evidence.

An interrogatory is a list of written questions by one party of the other party. The answers are admissible as evidence in court. A deposition is a transcript of a formal interview by an attorney of a witness who answers questions under oath. The transcript is prepared by a court reporter, and the deponent is allowed to read it before signing it as an accurate account of the interview. A deponent, as a potential witness in a case, is served a subpoena, a court order that the person appear at a time and place to give evidence. A subpoena *duces tecum* requires that the person also produce any documents or other evidence relevant to the issues in the case. All of this evidence, filed at court, is available to both parties.

After completion of the discovery stage, the attorneys for both sides meet to discuss where the case stands and whether a settlement is possible. If a settlement isn't possible, they will try to produce a stipulation, an agreement on which facts both sides consider settled and which facts are still at issue. After requesting a trial, the attorneys meet with the judge in the case. The judge may review the record of the case, encourage settlement and request that the attorneys file briefs on legal issues. A trial date is scheduled.

The first step in the trial stage of civil procedure is *voir dire*, the selection of the jury, assuming a jury is used. In certain kinds of cases, a jury may not be used, perhaps at the request of the parties to the case. A case without a jury is called a "bench trial." When used, a civil jury's job is to determine the facts, that is, to determine from the competing versions of the truth exactly what happened. If a jury is not used, the judge determines the facts as well as applies the law. Otherwise, the function of the judge is solely to apply the law to ensure a fair trial.

Juror selection usually follows a standard procedure. Court clerks select potential jurors from drivers' registration or voter lists. Failure to report for a call for jury duty can result in a citation for contempt of court. In *voir dire*, the judge and attorneys may question the members of the preliminary *venire*, seeking information that might prevent them from being fair and effective. After this questioning, the attorneys can ask the judge to remove some of the jurors "for cause," that is, for a reason that the judge finds acceptable. In addition, the attorneys are given an opportunity to remove a set number of jurors through "peremptory challenges," or without justifying the removals.

After the jury is impaneled, the trial begins. The judge normally gives preliminary instructions to the jury about the conduct of the trial. The plaintiff's opening statement and then the defendant's opening statement follow. They are presentations by the attorneys of what they intend to show.

Next is the presentation of evidence, first by the plaintiff and then by the defendant. The lawyer who calls the witnesses conducts direct examination of them. The opposing lawyer conducts cross-examination. Throughout the presentation of evidence, the attorneys may invoke various rules of evidence. Arguments over these rules are directed at the judge, not the jury, because these are questions of law, not facts. One side may object that the other side is violating some rule of evidence. For example, lawyers are not allowed to ask leading questions during direct examination — that is, to frame questions in such a way as to encourage specific answers. A lawyer also may not use hearsay evidence — evidence of a statement made out of court and, therefore, of questionable validity. In determining the proper application of the rule, the judge may sustain or overrule the objection. The side that loses these arguments may use them as bases for an appeal that the trial court judge misapplied the law.

At the conclusion of the plaintiff's presentation of the evi-

dence, the defense may move that the judge dismiss the case on the grounds that the plaintiff failed to show with sufficient evidence a *prima facie* case, that is, a case that would likely prevail before a reasonable jury. This is called a "directed verdict" because the case ends at that point and does not go to the jury. Assuming the plaintiff has not failed to present a *prima facie* case, the defense presents its evidence and witnesses, subject to cross-examination by the plaintiff. Since the burden of proof is on the plaintiff, the defendant is not required to produce evidence but generally will do so. When the defense rests, the plaintiff's attorney presents closing arguments, followed by the defense attorney's closing arguments. Like the opening statements, closing arguments do not include presentation of evidence but are summaries of the evidence and arguments as to how the evidence should be interpreted.

After the closing arguments, the judge orally instructs the jury on the law as it applies to the case. These instructions to the jury are carefully written, sometimes in consultation with the attorneys in the case. The judge explains how a jury is supposed to use evidence, the plaintiff's burden of proof, the requirements necessary for the defense and any other law applicable to the jury's deliberations.

The jury retires to the jury room, selects a chairperson (often called a "foreman" or "forewoman") and deliberates until reaching a verdict in favor of one of the parties. In civil actions, depending on the jurisdiction, a party to the case sometimes can request that the jurors be unanimous in their decision. Sometimes only a majority vote is necessary for one side to prevail. The jury is usually asked not only to rule for one side of a civil action but also to determine how much in damages should be given to the plaintiff if the plaintiff wins. A jury is not expected to explain its decision.

After the jury decision is announced, the losing side is normally given a deadline within which to file a petition arguing that the jury's verdict should be set aside as a matter of law. In most jurisdictions, a judge has the power to order a judgment as a matter of law. The judge is expected to explain any decision that contradicts a jury's determination.

Criminal Procedure

The legal system sees crimes as wrongs committed against society, not just against the victims of those crimes. As a result, an elaborate criminal justice system, including police, prosecutors, defense attorneys, judges and jailers, has been constructed with tax money to deal with crime. Crimes are usually categorized as felonies or misdemeanors. Felonies are serious crimes — such as treason, murder and rape — with penalties of capital punishment, lengthy prison terms and large fines. Misdemeanors are less serious crimes — such as reckless driving, marijuana possession and disorderly conduct — that carry penalties of lower fines and shorter jail terms.

Some assumptions of criminal law procedure resemble those in civil law procedure, but because the liberty and perhaps life of the criminal defendant may be at stake, criminal law procedure tends to be much more strict and specific than those of civil law. Criminal rights in the Fourth, Fifth, Sixth and Eighth amendments of the U.S. Constitution have been the subject of great interest to the Supreme Court and other courts whose decisions on criminal procedure have had a great impact on the work of police, prosecutors, courts and prisons.

Criminal law procedure includes the police investigation, arrest, complaint, initial appearance, preliminary hearing, prosecutorial investigation, indictment, arraignment, plea, defense investigation, discovery, trial, verdict, sentencing and punishment.

Police must follow certain procedures when investigating a crime. They must find and preserve physical evidence and question witnesses and others with information relevant to the crime. They are restricted by the Fourth Amendment prohibition against unreasonable search and seizure. They can obtain a search warrant by satisfying a judge that they have probable cause to believe that evidence related to a specific crime can be obtained at a location specified in the warrant. Before an interrogation police must be careful to "Mirandize" suspects, that is, to advise them of their rights to have attorneys and not to speak to the police.[16] Police must know when to discontinue custodial interrogation and arrest a suspect.

TYPICAL STAGES OF LEGAL PROCEDURE

CIVIL CASE
Complaint filed • Answer • Discovery • Hearings and motions • Settlement conference • Trial • Appeal

CRIMINAL CASE
Investigation • Arrest • Arraignment • Complaint • Preliminary hearing • Grand jury indictment • Hearings and motions • Trial • Sentencing • Appeal

An arrest occurs when a person suspected of a crime is taken into custody. An arrest is usually made with an arrest warrant, which is based on reasonable evidence that the suspect committed a crime. The suspect is taken before a judge for an initial appearance and further advised of his or her rights. The suspect, who is legally presumed innocent until proven guilty, may ask to be released from custody until required to appear at sub-

sequent proceedings. The judge considers whether to grant bail and, if so, how much the bail should be, based on the seriousness of the charge and the likelihood the suspect will appear at future court proceedings.

A criminal defendant has the right to an attorney. If the defendant is indigent, the court will assign one, probably a public defender. The defense attorney represents the defendant at the preliminary hearing before a judge to determine whether there is probable cause to believe the suspect committed a crime. Depending on evidence presented, a judge can dismiss the case or "bind it over" for further proceedings.[17]

Next, the prosecution is expected to file an accusation or seek a grand jury indictment. An accusation, normally used in a less serious case, is a document read at a public hearing outlining the charges and evidence. Accusations do not require the presentation in front of a grand jury. More commonly, especially in serious cases, an indictment is issued by a grand jury, a panel of citizens assembled in secret to determine whether there is sufficient evidence to support further prosecution.[18]

The arraignment is another court hearing at which the defendant is expected to enter a plea to the charges filed by the prosecutor, generally guilty or not guilty. A suspect may also plead *nolo contendere,* which essentially means that the defendant will not contest the charges. If the defendant pleads guilty, the judge will set a date for sentencing. If the defendant pleads not guilty, the judge will set a date for trial.

The criminal discovery process differs from that of a civil case. Depositions are rare in criminal discovery; they are used only when a witness is unable to appear at a trial. Defendants have the Fifth Amendment right not to make any statements to the prosecution; but if they do, they probably will be required to respond under oath at the trial to a cross-examination by the prosecutor. In addition, the criminal record of a defendant may be suppressed as evidence against the defendant if it would unnecessarily prejudice the jury against the defendant. The police and prosecutor are required to share evidence they obtain that may help the defendant. Each side is free to ask the other for evidence, but not all evidence is required to be presented before trial. Each side is required to reveal to the other a list of witnesses expected to be called and exhibits to be presented.

The prosecutor will develop a theory about the criminal case and explain how the crime itself was committed. In response, the defendant develops a defense strategy. To have enough time to gather evidence and otherwise develop a sound strategy, the defense may ask for additional time through a motion for a continuance. Other pretrial motions might include a motion to sup-

---

[16] *See* Miranda v. Arizona, 384 U.S. 436 (1966).

[17] It is important to note that there is no right to an attorney in civil lawsuits.

[18] Accusations are typically used to charge defendants with misdemeanor crimes. A grand jury indictment is used to charge defendants with felonies.

press evidence illegally obtained, a motion to change the place of the trial because of adverse publicity and a motion to remove the judge because of prejudice.

Prosecution and defense strategies are often dependent on what are called "aggravating" and "mitigating" circumstances. Aggravating circumstances are often named and defined in legislation as factors that must be shown in order to convict a defendant of a certain crime. In a death penalty case, for example, the prosecutor might be required by state law to show that the defendant killed a police officer or a minor, had previously been convicted of a violent crime or was unusually cruel in committing the murder. Mitigating circumstances may be argued by the defense attorney to convince the jury to convict a guilty defendant of a lesser crime or to decide on less punishment than the prosecutor seeks. For example, evidence may show that the defendant played a small role as an accomplice to the principal perpetrator of the crime, that the victim consented to the conduct leading to the murder or that the defendant felt the murder was morally justified.

Voir dire in criminal cases works the same as with civil cases. In trials involving felonies, twelve jurors are typically empaneled. In an attempt to avoid mistrials, additional jurors may be chosen as alternates in the event regular jurors, once seated, become sick or are disqualified. Lawyers usually get more peremptory challenges in criminal cases than in civil cases. Jury selection in criminal cases can be lengthy and complicated. Behavioral experts may be hired as consultants to the lawyers in choosing jurors.

At the trial, the prosecutor makes an opening statement, followed by one by the defense attorney. The prosecutor presents the evidence with cross-examination by the defense. When the prosecution rests, the defense may ask the judge to dismiss the case on the grounds that as a matter of law, the prosecution failed to present evidence that the defendant was guilty "beyond a reasonable doubt." If the motion fails, the defense may present evidence, attempting to raise serious doubts about the defendant's guilt. The prosecutor's closing statement is followed by the defense attorney's.

After the judge gives the jury instructions, the jurors retire to the jury room and, in almost all jurisdictions, must reach a unanimous vote on a verdict of guilty or not guilty. If a unanimous vote cannot be achieved, the judge generally declares a mistrial. The jury forewoman or foreman announces the verdict in court. The defendant is free of custody from the moment of a verdict of not guilty. If found guilty, the defendant will be held for sentencing, which is normally a separate proceeding, sometimes involving the jury. The judge may request a report from a probation officer on the defendant's background and seek recommendations on sentencing from witnesses, the prosecution and the defense. Ranges of possible sentences for convictions of

crimes are established in legislation. Once sentenced, a convict is turned over to law enforcement and later prison authorities.

Plea bargaining in criminal procedure is important because the vast majority of the dispositions of prosecutions end when deals are reached between the defense and prosecutor. In exchange for pleading guilty to a crime, the defendant may be charged with a lesser offense or be offered a lesser punishment than if the defendant pleads not guilty and is found guilty at a trial. A judge must approve a plea bargain. Plea bargaining is used in about 95 percent of cases in pretrial stages in American courts.

Appellate Court Procedure

New Hampshire, West Virginia and Virginia are the only states where appellate courts have virtually complete discretion over the kinds of cases they accept. In most states, appellate courts are required to consider appeals in some kinds of cases and have discretion in accepting appeals in other kinds of cases.

In most jurisdictions, a notice of appeal must be filed within thirty days of a trial court's decision. The appellant, the party bringing the appeal, must take responsibility for providing the appeals court with the entire record of the lower court case. The appellant must also satisfy the appeals court that the case contains a legal issue that can be appealed. The appellant can raise only questions of law, not fact, and must show not only that the trial court erred in applying the law but also that the error was prejudicial, that is, an error that actually harmed the appellant's ability to win the trial.

An appeals court will require that the appellant file its argument, called a "brief," within thirty to sixty days after the appellant delivers the trial court record. The brief of the appellee is due thirty to sixty days after the appellant's brief is filed. Since an appeals court cannot overturn a jury's determination of the facts, the goal of the appellant is often to convince the appeals court that the record on which the jury based its decision was inadequate or unfair.

Appeals courts do not re-try cases but sometimes conduct oral arguments, allowing the parties to the case to supplement their briefs with public presentations before the judges. The judges usually ask questions of the attorneys during the arguments.

The appeals court can affirm or reverse the lower court decision. If ruling in favor of the appellant, an appeals court may nevertheless find that the error was not serious enough to have altered the outcome of the case. Further, an appeals court ruling in favor of an appellant is less likely to reverse the lower court than to remand the case to the lower court with directions on how to handle the legal issue that was appealed. This may require a new trial.

In most state systems and in the federal system, losers of

court decisions get a second opportunity to appeal to a court of last resort, usually called a supreme court. Cases may arrive in the form of what are called appeals, but often they are technically petitions to the court to have the court review the lower court decision. As a result, many parties bringing the cases are called petitioners rather than appellants and those responding to the petitions are called respondents rather than appellees.

Appellate jurisdiction is sometimes subdivided into categories of mandatory and discretionary jurisdiction. Mandatory jurisdiction means the constitution or legislation requires the court to take cases, either all cases brought to the court or cases addressing certain matters. Discretionary jurisdiction means the court can make the decision itself about whether to take a case.

U.S. Supreme Court Procedure

A brief overview of procedure at the U.S. Supreme Court can foster understanding of the law for three reasons: (1) the Court is an example of a court of last resort, (2) the Court's procedures are models for other courts of last resort, and (3) the Court is the most important of all courts in shaping law in the United States. Although the Court does not enact or carry out laws, it is an important national policy maker through its interpretation of law. The Supreme Court has been the most influential source of constitutional law.

The Court receives about 7,000 petitions a year. There are a number of different ways of obtaining permission to have the Court review a lower court decision. One famous way, though it is rarely accepted by the Court, is through an *in forma pauperis* affidavit, a "pauper's petition." Even when an individual may not be able to afford a lawyer or use a formal process to get the Court's attention, the petitioner might be able to bring the case forward with a simple letter to the Court and no filing fee.

The Court is also required by Article III of the Constitution and by congressional legislation to hear certain cases. For example, when state or federal laws are declared by lower courts to be unconstitutional, the Court has mandatory jurisdiction. Over time, however, the justices have successfully sought more and more discretion over what cases are put on the docket. Almost every case the Court decides is accepted by grant of a petition for a writ of *certiorari*, an order to a lower court requiring that the records of the case be brought to the Supreme Court.

The clerk, using guidelines established by the Court, sorts the petitions into groups called "frivolous" and "nonfrivolous." Both groups are transmitted to the office of the chief justice, whose law clerks screen the petitions, agreeing or disagreeing with the clerk. Petitions deemed frivolous by the chief justice are "deadlisted." Nonfrivolous petitions are put on the agenda for discussion by the justices and a vote on acceptance. Clerks for all the justices review all the petitions, even those deadlisted.

Members of the Court have established criteria for granting or denying *certiorari*. For example, the Court will reject a petition unless the petitioner has exhausted all other legal remedies. In short, if it is possible to take the case to another court, the petitioner must do so before the Supreme Court will consider hearing the case. Unlike some state supreme courts, the U.S. Supreme Court will not give advisory opinions to anyone, including other branches of government. It deals in only *bona fide* disputes between real parties, not hypothetical situations or moot cases. The Court, however, has an exception to its mootness doctrine: When an important issue repeatedly arrives before the Court but cannot be decided because of mootness, the Court may agree to hear the case. The Court also rejects what it calls political questions, that is, issues presented in the form of cases when they should be resolved in the political branches of government. Some issues are not resolvable in the courts. Many disputes between branches of government and between the federal and state governments, according to the Court, should be solved in the political process, not the legal process.

Also influential in shaping the Court's docket is the Office of the Solicitor General in the U.S. Department of Justice. The solicitor general, representing the federal government when it is a litigant before the Supreme Court, is given considerable independence by the president and attorney general in deciding which cases the government should ask the Court to review. Since the federal government — the most frequent and important litigant in the federal courts — loses dozens of cases in U.S. appeals courts each year, the solicitor general has recently asked the Court to hear only about thirty cases. The Court, respecting this advice and the restraint shown by the solicitor general, usually grants review to most of these cases.

Only about 10 percent of all of the petitions survive to be formally presented by the chief justice at regular meetings of the nine justices in the conference room of the Supreme Court building. At this conference, the justices may agree that some cases can be decided summarily, for example, simply affirming or reversing a lower court decision with a brief explanation or with no explanation. Most of the cases are dismissed without explanation. The justices may agree to decide a case without an oral hearing. This is usually done when the justices are unanimous or nearly so on what they see as a fairly straightforward question. Normally, a short unsigned opinion — called a *per curiam* — accompanies such a decision.

If at the conference four of the nine justices agree that a case should be heard, then the case is accepted for review. This happens in only about 100 cases a year. Written briefs by each side addressing the merits of the case are submitted to the Court within forty-five days. The Court may also accept briefs from other parties interested in the case — *amici curiae*, or "friends of the court." Political scientists call these parties "judicial lobbies." State governments, corporations and political organizations frequently file *amici* briefs.

The Court also holds a public oral argument for each case. Before the justices hear a case, they meet in the cloak room adjacent to the hearing room. In a ceremonial tradition, they help each other don their robes, shake hands with each other, line up in order of seniority and walk into the courtroom. At the raised bench in the courtroom, the chief justice — who is always considered the senior-most justice, no matter how long his or her tenure — sits in the middle. The senior-most justice sits to the chief justice's right, the next most senior justice sits to the chief justice's left and so forth, so that the junior-most justices are sitting at the outer wings of the bench.

The chief justice presides at the hearing, calling the cases for argument and controlling a red light that, when lit, means a lawyer representing one side may speak. When the light is shut off, the lawyer's time has ended. Each side is normally allocated thirty minutes to present arguments. Soon after a lawyer's presentation begins, however, the justices start asking the lawyer questions, which are often pointed and difficult. Most of the hearing is an exchange between the lawyer and the justices. After one side finishes, the other side presents. After one case is argued, the next case is called. When the scheduled cases have been heard, the chief justice adjourns the hearing, and the justices rise and leave the courtroom, again in order of seniority. The justices "de-cloak" and return to their respective chambers.

The private conferences of the justices are held not only to decide on which cases the Court ought to accept for review but also to discuss and vote on the cases that have been heard. The chief justice brings up each case, beginning the discussion and indicating his vote. In order of seniority, the justices offer their perspectives on the case and vote, although any justice may change her or his mind anytime between the conference and the time the decision is announced to the public. The chief justice keeps track of the votes. After the conference vote on a case, one member of the prevailing side is assigned to write the Court's opinion, explaining the decision. The senior-most member of the majority assigns the authorship of the Court opinion. Since the chief justice tends to vote with the majority in most cases, the chief justice makes the assignments much more often than do associate justices. This is considered the most significant power of the chief justice because writing the Court's opinion and explaining the law, especially in important cases is a prized assignment among the justices.

Once assigned, a justice will draft an opinion and circulate it among the justices who react with comments. The author is under pressure to be responsive to these comments because, if not, the author risks losing the support of the other justices. Besides having a vote in each case, a justice has the option of writing a separate opinion and/or joining other opinions.

Members of the prevailing side in a case resulting in a split vote among the justices realize that the strength of the Court's decision and opinion depends on the size of the majority. If a justice, however, agrees with the outcome of the case but disagrees with the rationale in the opinion of the Court, the justice can choose not to join the opinion and write what is called an opinion concurring in judgment or result, explaining why the justice disagrees. The ethic of the justices is to strive for unanimous opinions, but the cases often produce split votes and separate opinions. A majority opinion of the Court is one with which at least five justices concur. A plurality opinion is an opinion of the Court that attracts more agreement than any other opinion written by the justices in the absence of a majority opinion. Obviously a majority opinion is stronger than a plurality opinion. In some instances, such as with the sudden death of a justice or if a justice recuses him or herself, the U.S. Supreme Court can be evenly deadlocked 4-4. When this situation occurs, U.S. Supreme Court procedure states that the court's decision affirms the lower court's ruling, but does not set any precedent.

Concurring and dissenting justices have a number of options regarding the writing and joining of opinions. If in agreement with the opinion of the Court, a concurring justice can simply join that opinion. The justice may join the opinion of the Court and write a concurring opinion to clarify certain points the justice thinks necessary. Or, as indicated, the justice can write an opinion concurring in the judgment. These separate writings may or may not be joined by other justices.

Dissenting justices are less systematic than majority justices in the opinion process. Dissenters do not normally try to produce a single opinion that they then "sign." To make matters more complicated, justices sometimes write opinions concurring in part and dissenting in part. This variety of writings can cause confusion over the strength and endurance of an opinion of the Court.

Once the justices have settled their votes and opinions, the record of the case is given to the branch of the Government Printing Office located in the basement of the Supreme Court building. Because Court decisions might have undue influence for some people if the decisions are leaked, the decisions and opinions are kept under tight security until the Court is ready to announce them to the public. At separate public proceedings, the justices again parade into the hearing room, and, with the chief justice presiding, announce the outcome of each case and summarize its opinions. At the same time, the printed versions of the judgments and opinions are distributed to the parties to the cases and journalists covering the court.

JUDGES

Judges, through their decisions and opinions, are important in

SYSTEMS FOR THE SELECTION OF JURISTS IN STATE COURTS OF LAST RESORT

MERIT SELECTION

Alaska, Arizona, Colorado, Connecticut, Delaware, District of Columbia, Florida, Hawaii, Indiana, Iowa, Kansas, Maryland, Massachusetts, Missouri, Nebraska, New Hampshire, New Mexico, New York, Oklahoma, Rhode Island, South Dakota, Tennessee, Utah, Vermont, Wyoming

NONPARTISAN ELECTIONS

Arkansas, Georgia, Idaho, Kentucky, Michigan (but with partisan nominations), Minnesota, Mississippi, Montana, Nevada, North Carolina, North Dakota, Ohio (but with partisan primaries), Oregon, Washington, Wisconsin

PARTISAN ELECTIONS

Alabama, Illinois, Louisiana, Pennsylvania, Texas, West Virginia

GUBERNATORIAL APPOINTMENT

California, Maine, New Jersey

LEGISLATIVE APPOINTMENT

South Carolina, Virginia

Set terms for these jurists range from six to fifteen years. The term in Massachusetts and New Hampshire is until the age of 70. In South Carolina and federal courts, a justice has lifetime tenure. The number of jurists on each of these courts is five (nineteen courts), seven (twenty-five courts), eight (only Louisiana) or nine (eight courts).

---

the creation of law affecting communication. The interpretations of the free speech and press clauses by the U.S. Supreme Court are especially crucial to understanding the system of freedom of expression in America. A sense of who these decision-makers are and how their decisions are affected by less formal influences is important to a complete understanding of communication law.

States commonly require that a judge have a law degree and legal experience, but neither Article III of the Constitution nor federal statute requires that federal judges have either. There never has been a federal judge, however, who has not been trained in the law. State systems for choosing judges vary considerably. A plurality of states use what is called the "Missouri Plan." When a judicial seat becomes vacant, a judicial commission — usually made up of representatives of the legislature, judiciary, bar association and other constituencies — creates a short slate of candidates. The governor fills the seat with one of the candidates on the slate. After a substantial period in office, perhaps ten years, the judge runs not against another candidate, but in a retention election in which the voters are asked whether the judge should return to office for ten years. Given the low visibility of judicial elections, it is highly likely that, unless the judge's performance has been extraordinarily poor, the judge will remain in office indefinitely. Proponents of the Missouri Plan argue that it protects honest judges from partisan politics and other electoral influences but provides voters with some opportunity to make judges accountable.

Next most common among state judicial selection systems are elections. Eight states hold partisan elections. Judges, like candidates for non-judicial offices, campaign for election for terms with endorsements of political parties. Fourteen states hold nonpartisan elections, forbidding party labels of judicial candidates on voter ballots. Four states provide for gubernatorial appointments of judges, usually requiring legislative approval of those appointments.

The framers of the Constitution intended to insulate federal judges from political influences by providing for nominations of judges by the president "with the Advice and Consent of the Senate,"[19] which has come to mean essentially that the president appoints them, but the Senate can veto the appointments. Article III further distances federal judges from political considerations by giving them lifetime tenure and protecting their salaries from being reduced.[20] Federal judges can be removed from office only by impeachment in the House of Representatives and conviction in the Senate.[21]

The countervailing forces that create judicial selection systems that range from partisan elections to executive appointments are the concerns for judicial accountability to the public, on the one hand, and judicial independence from undue influences, on the other hand. The results of comparisons of the quality of the judiciary resulting from these different selection

---

[19] U.S. CONST. art II, § 2, cl. 2.

[20] U.S. CONST. art III, § 1.

[21] U.S. CONST. art II, § 4.

systems are mixed.

How divorced federal judges are from politics may depend at least in part on how they are chosen for nomination by the president for approval by the Senate. When a district court judge retires or dies, the president normally consults with the highest ranking members of Congress in the president's party from the state that contains the district court. Members of Congress consult with party leaders in the state on the person who should be recommended to the president. If the president nominates this candidate, the nomination is unlikely to meet resistance from other members because they will want similar support when they make recommendations to the president. In the Senate, this norm is called "senatorial courtesy." The Senate Judiciary Committee makes recommendations to the Senate concerning judicial appointments. This process is frustrated, however, when the Senate is controlled by the party opposite of the president's party, as was the case throughout the Clinton administration. President Bill Clinton had difficulty in the Republican-controlled Senate obtaining consideration, much less confirmation, of his nominations to fill judgeships. President George W. Bush had difficulty because of Democratic maneuvering despite the fact that until 2006 Republicans held a majority in the Senate.

A similar kind of politics plays a role in the filling of U.S. appeals court seats. Members of Congress from states in a federal circuit expect to be able to place an equitable share of judges from each of those states on the appeals court.

Because it is a national court and the most politically important court, the U.S. Supreme Court is subject to different levels of politics. There are examples in Court history of presidents appointing senators, cabinet members and other politicians not experienced as judges to Court seats. Chief Justice William Rehnquist, formerly an assistant attorney general, had no judicial experience when President Richard Nixon nominated him to be an associate justice in 1972. Nor did other justices: Louis Brandeis, Felix Frankfurter, Charles Evans Hughes, Harlan Fiske Stone and Earl Warren.

Presidents tend overwhelmingly to appoint judges from their own political parties. This is not surprising because state party leaders ultimately choose most judges. Recently presidents have attempted to increase the number of minorities and women on the federal bench. A nominee is subject to an official FBI background check and lobbying by a variety of special interest groups. In addition, a president is not likely to recommend a candidate whose credentials are poor. Although political litmus tests of federal nominees are seen as an overt politicization of the federal bench, presidential candidates often campaign for their election by promising that through judicial appointments, the candidate will remake federal courts that produce unpopular decisions.

There are stories of how disappointed presidents have been in the nominations they have made to the Supreme Court. Eisenhower, a conservative Republican, said his biggest mistake as president was naming Earl Warren the chief justice. Warren, also a Republican, led what historians consider to be a constitutional revolution at the Supreme Court by aggressively taking cases and pronouncing decisions to advance civil liberties and other liberal causes. Nevertheless, most judges, because of their political histories and perhaps interests in advancing to higher courts, perform predictably once on the bench.[22]

Discussion of judicial ideology tends to dwell not only on whether judges develop voting patterns consistent with conservative or liberal perspectives on the issues but also on their attitudes toward the role the courts should play in the political system. Judges called "activists" believe the courts have an active role to play in the political system. Judicial restraintists believe the courts should play a modest role. Paragons of these opposing views were William O. Douglas and Felix Frankfurter, both named to the Supreme Court in 1939 by President Franklin Roosevelt.

Douglas, a former chair of the Securities and Exchange Commission, and Frankfurter, a former Harvard law professor, were widely known liberals in support of Roosevelt's New Deal program. But once on the Court, these two justices frequently disagreed, not only on how broad a Supreme Court decision should be, but even on whether the Court should be hearing a case. Douglas championed the courts as constitutional crusaders, equal partners with Congress and the president in running the country. He was unafraid to assume power for the Supreme Court to advance a sweeping political vision he saw in the Constitution. Frankfurter, on the other hand, felt that no constitutional history or theory supported Douglas' activism. He urged the Court to be deferential to the political branches of government and to treat each case as narrowly as possible.

Most of the 112 justices in Supreme Court history would be properly labeled "conservative restraintists." Only during the Warren Court era of the 1950s and 1960s did liberal activists become a majority. In recent years, the court has frequently been split 5-4, and liberals have accused the majority of the Rehnquist and Roberts Courts of being conservative activists.[23] The conservatives favor limited government, including a modest role for the Court in the political system. In short, the idea of judicial politics should be kept in mind when trying to understand the law, including communication law.

---

[22] *See* JEFFREY A. SEGAL & HAROLD J. SPAETH, THE SUPREME COURT AND THE ATTITUDINAL MODEL REVISITED (2002).

[23] *See* DAVID M. O'BRIEN, STORM CENTER: THE SUPREME COURT IN AMERICAN POLITICS (7th ed. 2005).

THE JUSTICES OF THE SUPREME COURT OF THE UNITED STATES

NAME	BORN	APPOINTED	IDEOLOGY
Anthony M. Kennedy	1936	1988 by Reagan	Conservative

Born in Sacramento and appointed from California, Associate Justice Kennedy is a former private practitioner, law professor and judge on the U.S. Court of Appeals for the Ninth Circuit. Harvard Law School, 1961.

Clarence Thomas	1946	1991 by Bush I	Conservative

Born in Pinpoint, Ga., and appointed from Georgia, Associate Justice Thomas is a former chairman of the U.S. Equal Employment Opportunity Commission and judge on the U.S. Court of Appeals for the District of Columbia Circuit. Yale Law School, 1974.

Ruth Bader Ginsburg	1933	1993 by Clinton	Moderate

Born in Brooklyn and appointed from New York, Associate Justice Ginsburg is a former law professor and judge on the U.S. Court of Appeals for the District of Columbia Circuit. Columbia Law School, 1959.

Stephen G. Breyer	1938	1994 by Clinton	Moderate

Born in San Francisco and appointed from California, Associate Justice Breyer is a former law professor and chief judge of the U.S. Court of Appeals for the First Circuit. Harvard Law School, 1964.

John G. Roberts, Jr.	1955	2005 by Bush II	Conservative

Born in Buffalo, N.Y., and appointed from Maryland, Chief Justice Roberts is a former private practitioner, lawyer in the Reagan and Bush I administrations, and judge on the U.S. Court of Appeals for the District of Columbia Circuit. Harvard Law School, 1979.

Samuel A. Alito, Jr.	1950	2006 by Bush II	Conservative

Born in Trenton, N.J., and appointed from New Jersey, Associate Justice Alito is a former lawyer in the Justice Department of the Reagan and Bush I administrations, U.S. attorney for New Jersey and associate judge for the U.S. Courts of Appeals for the Third Circuit. Yale Law School, 1975.

Sonia M. Sotomayor	1954	2009 by Obama	Moderate

Born in New York City and appointed from New York, Associate Justice Sotomayor is a former assistant district attorney in New York and judge on the U.S. District Court for the Southern District of New York and U.S. Court of Appeals for the Second Circuit. Yale Law School, 1979.

Elena Kagan	1960	2010 by Obama	Moderate

Born in New York City and appointed from New York, Associate Justice Kagan is a former law professor at the University of Chicago, former professor and dean at Harvard Law School, former associate White House counsel in the Clinton Administration, and former Solicitor General in the Obama Administration. Harvard Law School, 1986.

Antonin Scalia died Feb. 13, 2016, leaving the Court with eight justices. March 16, 2016, President Barrack Obama nominated Merrick Garland, a Harvard Law School graduate and a judge on the U.S. Court of Appeals for the District of Columbia Circuit. Republican leadership in the Senate said the president could fulfill his constitutional mandate to nominate justices but that the Senate would take no action on the nomination.

Roberts is the 17th Chief Justice. Kagan is the 112th justice to serve on the Court. The Judiciary Act of 1789 provided for a Chief Justice and five associate justices. The number of seats at the Court varied from five to ten until 1869 when Congress established the present number of nine.

Identifying the ideologies of Supreme Court justices is no simple matter. Justices Bader Ginsberg and Breyer are often considered liberals in the popular view, for example. The reference to them as "moderate" is used here to distinguish their views from such 1950s-1970s liberals as William Douglas, Thurgood Marshall and Abe Fortas. Generally, in First Amendment cases, a "conservative" justice gives more weight to the government's interest, and a "liberal" justice favors claimants' interests. A "moderate" justice has a mixed voting record.

ALTERNATIVE DISPUTE RESOLUTION

Between 90 and 95 percent of all civil law disputes are settled out of court before trial but often not until years after the disputes arose. In the meantime, parties to the cases suffer prolonged delays and mounting legal costs that perhaps force un-satisfactory resolutions of the disputes. As dissatisfaction with the clogged courts has risen, some legislatures, courts, attorneys' groups, business leaders and other reformers have been encouraging, with considerable success, alternatives to courts for the resolution of disputes.

Alternative dispute resolution is a broad term encompassing

a number of ways that litigants can avoid courts: negotiation, mediation, arbitration, private judging, expert fact-finding, mini-trials and summary jury trials.

Mediation is a formal version of negotiation. A third party is engaged by the disputants to facilitate communication and reach a solution. The mediator need not be legally trained but should be knowledgeable in the area of dispute and effective at helping identify the problem and creating a resolution for the conflict. Mediation has been used in labor disputes for many years and has also become popular in the commercial world. A mediator may meet with the parties separately before bringing them together. The parties may stipulate that the proceedings are secret, not to be used as evidence in litigation should that follow the attempt to mediate. Mediators may charge hourly fees, but sometimes communities offer trained mediators at neighborhood dispute centers for free or at low cost. Mediation is strictly voluntary and does not foreclose the possibility of litigation if one or both parties are unhappy with the outcome.

Arbitration is more formal than mediation. A neutral third party, called the arbitrator, is chosen by the parties, called disputants. The arbitrator acts with the authority of a judge, issuing a decision that is legally binding on the disputants. Arbitrators often are lawyers, sometimes retired judges, who charge fees. Arbitration is common in resolving contractual disputes between businesses, even at the international level. Contracts increasingly include provisions for arbitration should contractual disputes arise.

Although state law may prescribe procedures for arbitration, often the procedures of the American Arbitration Association are used. The disputants, likely to be represented by lawyers, may also agree to their own procedures. In any case, the procedures normally are more relaxed than those used in courts.

Generally, an arbitration case proceeds like a court case, and the arbitrator issues a decision, called an award, within thirty days after the proceeding ends. Arbitration has many advantages over courts. Cases can be conducted in secret, avoiding exposure of information that the parties would rather keep out of public court documents. Arbitration is speedier than court procedure. Finally, it is less expensive than a court case.

Variations on arbitration include issue arbitration, non-binding arbitration and court-annexed arbitration. Issue arbitration means the disputants agree that an arbitrator will handle only a specific part of their dispute, not all of it. Non-binding arbitration, as its name suggests, is used when the disputants want the formality of arbitration but also want to reserve the right to take their dispute to court. Court-annexed arbitration is when a part of a court proceeding is referred to an arbitrator, either with the consent of the parties or as a state law requirement that certain kinds of civil actions go to arbitration before they are permitted to enter the courts. Courts have the power to enforce arbitration awards. Losers in arbitration can appeal the awards in courts, but judges tend to be deferential to the arbitration decisions.

Private judging is another ADR trend. Parties to a dispute, invoking state law, may hire a retired judge whose decision in what amounts to a private court is as final as that of a judge in a public court. Some states have provisions for rent-a-juries as well. Decisions in some states can be appealed to state appellate courts. Unlike other ADR choices, private judging is likely to be more expensive than regular court proceedings.

Expert fact-finding may be used when the parties to a case want to resolve only factual conflicts in a dispute. The expert investigates and produces a report attempting to establish the truth. This determination is not binding on the parties but can obviously influence their decisions about litigation.

Short of going to court, other ways for potential litigants to try to sort out their arguments over who is right about the nature of their dispute is to conduct a "mini-trial" or a "summary jury trial." Sometimes businesses will conduct an informal mini-trial with corporate officers from both companies acting as the jury. Parties in a summary jury trial, unlike in a mini-trial, will hire private citizens as potentially "typical" jurors to act as mock petit jurors. Lawyers can present as much of a case as they wish and allow the mock jury to reach a verdict. The lawyers may interview the mock jury to anticipate how an actual jury might react to their arguments. Whether mini-trials or summary jury trials are binding on the parties depends on whether they agree to it.

ADR has no application in the criminal justice system, but there is no doubt that it has helped reduce the number of civil cases in court dockets.

LEGAL RESEARCH

Law is highly codified and organized in surprisingly sophisticated ways. Law libraries at major universities require considerable physical space for the vast published collections of all the sources of laws at the international, federal and state levels. On-line access to the law is helping to ease the strain of the ever increasing size of legal collections.

Most law libraries are organized consistent with the structure of government. The national collection will include the primary legal materials generated by the federal legislative, executive and judicial branches of government. Using similar systems of organization, parallel materials from each of the states, in alphabetical order, are stacked behind the national materials. Separate from these primary materials of research are the secondary materials — for example, legal dictionaries, encyclopedias, treatises and law journals.

Legislation is maintained in multi-volume sets of books,

called "codes" or "revised statutes," according to topics, usually named "titles" or "chapters." Congressional legislation is officially published in the *United States Code*, organized in alphabetical order of fifty titles. Each enactment of Congress is assigned a title, and each part of the legislation is given a section number. When Congress enacts new legislation, it is assigned to the appropriate title and given new section numbers. If Congress amends statutes, it can specify exactly which sections are affected. If Congress rescinds legislation, the section numbers and text are removed.

In legal research, a citation to the *United States Code* looks like this: Federal Freedom of Information Act of 1976, 5 U.S.C. 552 (1994). The name of the act, which usually includes the year in which the act was passed, is followed by a series of numbers and abbreviations. This act is located in Title 5 of the *United States Code* beginning at section 552. The year "1994" was when the Code book was published. Private publishers issue annotated versions of the *United States Code*, including not only all that is in the *Code* but also citations to court decisions that have interpreted provisions in it. Sets of codes and revised statutes usually have elaborate indexes to help users find laws.

Court decisions are maintained in continually published volumes of books called "reports" or "reporters." Official reports of court decisions are organized by jurisdiction, and the decisions and opinions of the court are reported in chronological order. For example, the U.S. Government Printing Office prints and publishes the official reports of the U.S. Supreme Court as *United States Reports*. The citation to a Supreme Court case looks like this: *Chaplinsky v. New Hampshire*, 315 U.S. 568 (1942). The case name includes the names of the parties to the case. In almost all jurisdictions, the first-named party is the party initiating the action, and the second-named party is the party against whom the first-named party initiated the action. At the trial court level, the action initiator is called the "plaintiff," and the reactor is called the "defendant." In an appellate case, they are, respectively, the "appellant" and the "appellee." When an appellate court, usually a court of last resort, takes the case, in the form of a petition, the parties are called the "petitioner" and "respondent." The "v." is an abbreviation common in law for the word "versus." The legal community has assigned the abbreviation "U.S." to *United States Reports*. The first number refers to the number of the volume of *U.S.* in which the case appears. The second number is the first page of the report of the case in that volume. The parenthetical is the year in which the court made this decision. Thus, the case of *Chaplinsky v. New Hampshire*, decided in 1942, begins on page 568 in volume 315 of *United States Reports*. All reports of other courts also have been assigned unique abbreviations.

Administrative law is organized in several ways. Rules, decisions and other documents may be published officially or by private publishers in reports resembling court reports. For example, the Federal Communications Commission officially publishes its materials in *Federal Communications Commission Reports*. Citations to an agency's reports follow the format of a citation to a court case. To promulgate formal rules affecting the public or subjects of regulation, however, an agency must publish notice of its intention to do so and invite the public to participate in the process in the *Federal Register*, an official daily public accounting of the activities of the agencies. If a rule is approved, it must be published in the *Federal Register* and then in the *Code of Federal Regulations*. Each agency is assigned a title like a title in the *United States Code*. Each part of a regulation is assigned a section number. Citations to the *C.F.R.* resemble citations to the *U.S.C.* Like the *U.S.C.*, the *C.F.R.* has detailed indexes to facilitate finding regulations.

Although legal research emphasizes using original primary sources of law, comprehensive banks of legal materials are increasingly accessible on-line. Highly useful organizations of the law on-line are those provided by LEXIS-NEXIS and WEST-LAW. These services are extremely expensive, designed for researchers in law offices and government. See the list of law-related Web sites at the end of the chapter for other services.

SUMMARY

Law is a system of rules established and enforced by authority in a society. Law can be organized according to its sources: (1) common law, which is law made by judges in deciding cases; (2) equity law, which consists of orders by courts to resolve legal problems expeditiously; (3) statutory law, which is law enacted by legislative bodies; (4) constitutional law, which is documents containing the supreme rules for a society and the interpretation of the documents by courts; (5) administrative law, which is the rules and decisions of administrative agencies; (6) international law, which is mainly treaties between nations; and (7) contract law, which is the law created between individuals in a contract.

Trial courts find facts and apply the law. Appellate courts review the application of the law by trial courts. Civil and criminal legal procedure differs at both the trial and appellate court levels. A civil case usually consists of the complaint, the answer, discovery, hearings and motions, the settlement conference, the trial and appeals. A criminal case usually consists of an investigation, the arrest, an arraignment, the complaint, a preliminary hearing, a grand jury indictment, hearings and motions, the trial, sentencing and appeals.

Federal judges are nominated by the president with the "advice and consent" of the Senate in order to protect the judiciary from politics, but the process of choosing a federal judge is political. States use variations on the appointive and electoral systems to choose state judges.

FOR ADDITIONAL READING

Barkan, Steven M., Roy M. Mersky & Donald J. Dunn. *Fundamentals of Legal Research,* 9th ed. Eagan, Minn.: Westlaw, 2009.

Baum, Lawrence. *The Supreme Court,* 11th ed. Washington, D.C.: Congressional Quarterly Press, 2012.

Berch, Michael A., Rebecca White Berch & Ralph S. Spritzer. *Introduction to Legal Method and Process: Cases and Materials,* 5th ed. St. Paul, Eagan, Minn.: Westlaw, 2010.

Bonsignore, John J., et al. *Before the Law: An Introduction to the Legal Process,* 8th ed. Boston: Houghton Mifflin, 2006.

Greenburg, Jan Crawford. *Supreme Conflict: The Inside Story of the Struggle for Control of the United States Supreme Court.* New York: Penguin Press, 2008.

Harr, J. Scott & Karen M. Hess. *Constitutional Law and the Criminal Justice System,* 5th ed. Independence, Ky.: Cengage Learning, 2012.

Kerwin, Cornelius M. & Scott R. Furlong. *Rulemaking: How Government Agencies Write Law and Make Policy,* 4th ed. Washington, D.C.: CQ Press, 2010.

Magleby, David B., Paul C. Light & Christine L. Nemacheck. *Government by the People,* 24th ed. New York: Pearson, 2010.

Rehnquist, William H. *The Supreme Court.* New York: Knopf, 2001.

Scheb, John M. & John M. Scheb II. *An Introduction to the American Legal System,* 2nd ed. Albany, N.Y.: West/Thompson Learning, 2009.

Siegel, Larry J. & John J. Worrall. *Introduction to Criminal Justice,* 14th ed. Independence, Ky.: Cengage Learning, 2014.

SELECT LAW-RELATED INTERNET SOURCES

American Law Resources on-Line, http://www.lawsource.com, has links to legal materials in all states, Canada and Mexico.

Congress, https://www.congress.gov, is the Library of Congress server for legislative information, including bills, the *Congressional Register* and legislative histories.

Constitution of the United States of America, http://www.arc hives.gov/exhibits/charters/constitution includes text, analysis and annotations of court interpretations.

CSPAN America and the Courts, http://www.cspan.org/series/America-and-The-Courts.aspx, includes thoughtful television reports and documents on issues concerning courts and law.

FedWorld, http://www.fedworld.gov, offers through the Commerce Department access to thirty million government Web pages, including the *Statistical Abstract.*

GPO Access, http://www.gpo.gov, is the searchable home site for the Government Printing Office, offering dozens of federal resources, including presidential materials, public and private laws, *Congressional Record, Code of Federal Regulations, Federal Register* and *U.S. Code.* Includes search system for U.S. court opinions.

HG.Org, http://www.hg.org, is a multi-purpose legal resource containing legal news and hundreds of links to other law-related sites.

Jurist, http://www.jurist.org, has many helpful features, including legal news, forums, video, research and commentary mainly from and about the United States.

National Center for State Courts, http://www.ncsc.org, is a source for information about state courts.

OYEZ, http://www.oyez.org, contains, among a wide variety of other material, audio of Supreme Court hearings, Court trivia and video tours of the Court's building.

SCOTUSblog, http://www.scotusblog.com, blogging on the Supreme Court, including commentary and analysis; new orders, filings and opinions; multimedia; and stories from major and legal news media.

U.S. Federal Judiciary, http://www.uscourts.gov, is the site of the Administrative Office of the U.S. Courts.

U.S. House of Representatives, http://http://www.house.gov, is a site especially useful for following current activity in the House of Representatives.

U.S. Senate, http://http://www.senate.gov, contains useful information about Senate actions and committees.

U.S. Supreme Court, http://http://www.supremecourt.gov, includes the dockets, journal, calendar, oral argument transcripts, rules, *U.S. Reports,* maps and photographs of the Supreme Court building and related links.

2

The First Amendment in Theory and Practice

By Kathleen K. Olson

➡ **Headnote Questions**

- What are the guarantees of the First Amendment?
- How did freedom of the press and speech develop in the United States?
- What is the value of free expression?
- Why are the protections offered by the First Amendment not absolute?
- Why do individual First Amendment protections vary from person to person?
- How do the courts balance the right of expression against other personal rights or social interests?
- What is incorporation? Strict scrutiny? First Amendment due process?

In March 2016, a deadlocked U.S. Supreme Court let stand a lower court's ruling that public-sector unions may force non-union workers to pay fees supporting collective bargaining efforts on their behalf. The workers claimed the fees were a form of unconstitutional compelled speech. At oral argument in January, the five conservative justices on the Court were seen as supporting the workers' First Amendment arguments. But after Justice Antonin Scalia died in February, the vote was tied at 4-4. So the Ninth Circuit Court of Appeals' ruling became final.[1]

In 2015, the Court decided two important free speech cases. In one involving inflammatory Facebook posts, it gave the lower courts guidance on how to draw the line between protected speech and speech that constitutes an illegal threat to another person.[2] In the other, the Court ruled that states have the right to ban the Confederate flag from specialty license plates.[3]

The First Amendment played a central role in each of these cases, because what was at stake was the fundamental right to speak — or not to speak — free of government interference. In each of the cases, the debate centered on how to balance individual free speech rights with the rights of others — the right of labor unions to have every worker who benefits from their efforts pay his fair share, and the right of states to protect their citizens from threatening or offensive speech. Understanding First Amendment law requires an understanding of the differ-

ent factors that play a part in interpreting and applying constitutional protections.

The First Amendment and the rights it guarantees are fundamental parts of American democracy, but they are not absolute. Sometimes they must yield to other values society has determined are more important. Sometimes the level of protection the Constitution provides depends on the status of the person involved, or even the medium being used to communicate. The rest of the chapters in this book discuss these different factors and the balance that has been struck between free expression, on the one hand, and other important values, such as privacy or protecting a reputation from libel, on the other.

The American Constitution's emphasis on individual rights stands in contrast to other democratic countries that emphasize community and the common good over the individual. Stark differences can be seen in the treatment of hate speech, for example. In the United States, the First Amendment prevents the government from prohibiting speech just because it may be offensive to some people, whereas Canada and some European countries ban such speech.[4] France and Germany have laws that make it a crime to deny the Holocaust — restrictions that would be unconstitutional in the United States.

Still, the debate continues over the proper balance between individual First Amendment rights and other important government interests. How do we balance free speech and rules

---

[1] Friedrichs v. California Teachers Ass'n, 136 S.Ct. 1083 (2016).

[2] Elonis v. United States, 135 S.Ct. 2001 (2015).

[3] Walker v. Texas Division, Sons of Confederate Veterans, 135 S.Ct. 2239 (2015).

[4] *See* Robert A. Sedler, *Freedom of Speech: The United States versus the Rest of the World*, 2006 MICH. ST. L. REV. 377, 383 n.23. (2006).

against sexual or racial harassment? When can a public university tell a professor what not to say in the classroom or in his blog? What limits on newsgathering are appropriate to prevent paparazzi from recklessly endangering others in order to get a photo? Should the law ensure that protesters not bother mourners at military funerals? These and other questions are part of the task that the courts, including the Supreme Court, have in interpreting the First Amendment in the twenty-first century.

One of the most important and difficult questions concerns the need to limit individual rights in order to protect national security. The September 11, 2001, terrorist attacks began an unprecedented shift in the balance that has tested the country's commitment to basic constitutional principles. "We're in a new world where we have to rebalance freedom and security," Missouri congressman Richard Gephardt said after the attacks. "We're not going to have all the openness and freedom we have had."[5]

Among the immediate responses to the attacks were FBI agents monitoring private citizens' email, high schools and museums curtailing expressive activity, and police and National Guard troops confiscating film from journalists and tourists. Hundreds of thousands of public documents were removed from government Web sites and public libraries. Attorney General John Ashcroft issued a directive to government agencies that made it easier for government agencies to deny requests for public records under the Freedom of Information Act,[6] and governmental oversight suffered as deportation hearings for hundreds of people detained after 9/11 were closed to the press and public.[7]

Congress acted swiftly to pass the USA PATRIOT Act, in October 2001, to help the government in its fight against terrorism.[8] Among other measures, the act greatly expanded the government's intelligence-gathering capabilities, in part by easing restrictions on the ability to conduct surveillance and search records, including telephone, email and financial records.

Fifteen years later, most of the act's provisions are still in place, and in 2013, the public discovered the "monumental scope" of some of the surveillance programs instituted under the act.[9] Press reports revealed that while not listening to individual conversations, the National Security Agency has kept a record of most of the phone calls made in the United States on a daily basis. The public also learned of another government surveillance program called "PRISM" that allows officials to collect electronic communications data from the servers of Facebook, YouTube, Microsoft, Google and other companies.[10]

In 2013, federal prosecutors filed espionage charges against Edward Snowden, the former NSA contractor responsible for leaking the classified material that exposed those programs, and his passport was revoked. Snowden, who currently lives in Russia, was part of a growing list of federal or government contract workers prosecuted by the Justice Department for media leaks in recent years. In fact, the administration of Barack Obama has used the Espionage Act of 1917 against leakers more often than all prior administrations combined.[11]

In 2010, for example, the Justice Department charged former NSA official Thomas A. Drake with providing classified information to a reporter for *The Baltimore Sun* through hundreds of email messages. "The whole point of this prosecution is to have a chilling effect on reporters and sources, and it will," said Lucy Dalglish, former executive director of the Reporters Committee for Freedom of the Press.[12] The charges were later dropped.

That year the Justice Department also began a criminal investigation into WikiLeaks and its founder, Julian Assange, after it released 250,000 classified U.S. diplomatic cables on the Internet. Chelsea (born Bradley) Manning, the Army private who admitted leaking the documents, was court-martialed and convicted in 2013 of violating the Espionage Act and was sentenced to thirty-five years in prison. Some called for Assange to be prosecuted under the Espionage Act as well, but there was no apparent evidence that he obtained the cables illegally.[13]

Public opinion is divided over whether government leakers and sites like WikiLeaks are positive or destructive forces. Some called Snowden a traitor, for example, while others praised him for exposing the surveillance programs and for sparking a debate on the proper limits of the government's power.[14] In 2015, a federal appeals court ruled that the NSA's

---

[5] Paul McMasters, *Freedom Flees in Terror From Sept. 11 Disaster*, Sept. 19, 2001, http://www.freedomforum.org.

[6] *See* Mary Jacoby, *War on Terror Spurs Secrecy, Experts Say*, ST. PETERSBURG TIMES, Mar. 28, 2003, at 10A.

[7] *See* Edward Walsh, *High Court Stays Out of Secrecy Fray*, WASH. POST, May 23, 2003, at A04.

[8] Uniting and Strengthening America by Providing Appropriate Tools Required to Intercept and Obstruct Terrorism Act, Pub. L. No. 107-56, 115 Stat. 272 (2001).

[9] *See* Donna Cassata & Nancy Benac, *Monumental Phone-Records Monitoring is Laid Bare*, ASSOCIATED PRESS, June 6, 2013, http://www.ap.org.

[10] *See* Barton Gellman & Laura Poitras, *U.S., British Intelligence Mining Data From Nine U.S. Internet Companies in Broad Secret Program*, WASH. POST, June 7, 2013, *available at* http://www.washingtonpost.com.

[11] *See* Phil Mattingly & Hans Nichols, *Obama Pursuing Leakers Sends Warning to Whistle-Blowers*, BLOOMBERG, Oct. 17, 2012, http://www.bloomberg.com.

[12] Scott Shane, *Former N.S.A. Official Is Charged in Leaks Case*, N.Y. TIMES, Apr. 15, 2010, *available at* http://www.nytimes.com. Dalglish is now dean of the Philip Merrill College of Journalism at the University of Maryland.

[13] *See* Massimo Calabresi, *The War on Secrecy*, TIME, Dec. 13, 2010, at 30-37.

[14] Former Attorney General Eric Holder said Snowden "performed a public service" by raising the debate that led to changes, although he still thought Snowden should face trial for his actions. *See* Amanda Holpuch, *Eric Holder Says Edward Snowden Performed 'Public Service' With NSA Leak*, THE GUARDIAN, May 30, 2016, *available at* http://www.theguardian.com.

surveillance of telephone metadata was illegal. Congress passed legislation the next month that imposed limits on the government's ability to collect such data while still allowing access to it through the phone companies.

Free expression is essential to a free government and society. "The First Amendment is not just another phrase, another document in American history," said Ken Paulson, executive director of the Freedom Forum's First Amendment Center. "It is a binding contract with the American people. It is the heart of what we are as a nation."[15] His colleague Paul McMasters agreed: "As much as we wish to be safe forever from the horrors [of the attacks], we simply cannot protect freedom by forsaking freedom. As much as we want relief from this time of national duress, we simply cannot make ourselves more secure by making fundamental freedoms less secure."[16]

The First Amendment is not absolute, however, and others, including Judge Richard Posner, have argued that the Constitution is "not a suicide pact" and must, during times of national emergency, bend so that it does not break.[17] How far it must bend, and what constitutes a national emergency, are subjects of continuing and intense debate.

In a survey taken in 2002 after the events of 9/11, 49 percent of the respondents said they believed the First Amendment goes too far in the rights it guarantees. In 2015, only 19 percent said the First Amendment goes too far.[18] Other findings from the annual surveys conducted by the First Amendment Center suggest Americans continue to embrace freedom of speech, even while they maintain some misgivings.

"The year 2001 was a pivotal time at every level of government for free speech, from national security concerns in the wake of Sept. 11 to the actions of city councils and state governments," wrote Richard T. Kaplar, vice president of The Media Institute. "But the First Amendment survived, which is a tribute to journalists, government officials and the American people."[19]

FIRST AMENDMENT PROTECTIONS

Congress shall make no law respecting an establishment of religion, or prohibiting the free exercise thereof; or abridging the freedom of speech, or of the press; or the right of the people peaceably to assemble, and to petition the Government for a redress of grievances.

U.S. Constitution, amend. 1

The First Amendment protects five fundamental freedoms: religion, speech, press, assembly and petition. While freedom of religion is beyond the scope of this book, expression of one's religious beliefs may also be a free speech issue. Freedom of speech gives individuals the right to express themselves without interference from the government, as does freedom of the press.

The right to petition the government for redress of grievances gives individuals the right to complain to or seek the assistance of the government without fear of reprisal. This may include seeking help from the legislature, either state or federal, or from the courts. Freedom of assembly allows people to gather for peaceful and lawful purposes in public spaces — for protest rallies, for example, or for parades. In fact, some places are considered, because of their history, to be particularly suited for expressive purposes. These are called public forums, and they include public parks, streets and sidewalks — places that have been designated for public use and have long been used for that purpose. Other types of public spaces include designated or limited public forums, which are open to the public for expressive purposes in a limited way — such as state fairgrounds, a city-owned theater or a public school auditorium — and nonpublic forums, which are public spaces not open for public expression, such as military bases or prisons.

Implicit as part of the right of assembly is the right to associate, for First Amendment purposes, with like-minded individuals. When people band together for expressive purposes, the government cannot require the group to register or disclose its membership. As Justice John Harlan wrote in 1958 in *NAACP v. Alabama*:

Effective advocacy of both public and private points of view, particularly controversial ones, is undeniably enhanced by group association, as this Court has more than once recognized by remarking upon the close nexus between the freedoms of speech and assembly.... It is beyond debate that freedom to engage in association for the advancement of beliefs and ideas is an inseparable aspect of "liberty" assured by the Due Process Clause of the Fourteenth Amendment, which embraces freedom of speech.[20]

THE DISTINCTION BETWEEN "SPEECH" AND "PRESS"

The First Amendment includes both "speech" and "press" in its text. Almost from the time it was drafted, however, there has been debate over what those terms mean. Although the First Amendment says nothing about either "expression" or "conduct," for example, the Supreme Court has held that some ex-

---

[15] Kenneth A. Paulson, 1999 Speech, Mar. 17, 1999, *available at* http://www.freedomforum.org.

[16] McMasters, *supra* note 6.

[17] RICHARD A. POSNER, NOT A SUICIDE PACT: THE CONSTITUTION IN A TIME OF NATIONAL EMERGENCY 1 (2006).

[18] *State of the First Amendment 2015*, July 3, 2015, http://www.newseum.org.

[19] The Media Institute, *Unprecedented Events Created New First Amendment Challenges in 2001*, July 16, 2002, http://www.mediainst.org.

[20] 357 U.S. 449, 460 (1958).

pressive conduct is protected as speech. Chapter 3 covers conduct and speech in greater detail.

In a 1989 case, Justice William Brennan, an ardent supporter of the First Amendment who retired a year later, wrote: "The First Amendment literally forbids the abridgment only of 'speech,' but we have long recognized that its protection does not end at the spoken or written word."[21] Government restriction, he wrote, "is not dependent on the particular mode in which one chooses to express an idea."[22]

In the colonial period, speech manifested itself in meetings, on street corners, from pulpits and through traveling balladeers. The press produced bills of sale, advertisements, poetry, promotions, books, essays and newspapers. Colonists found value in their freedom to listen to the speechmakers and to read the output of the printers.

When the First Amendment was drafted, was there a clear sense of what "speech" and "press" meant? Scholars disagree. It may seem clear that "speech" is the spoken word and "press" is the written word, but as technology developed, the distinctions between these two have increasingly blurred. The blurring continues to challenge the courts to develop new interpretations of "speech" and "press." Computer technology has made it cheaper to provide information to a broad audience. We can publish *and* speak *via* the Internet. We can use computers to produce small special-interest publications cheaply and quickly. Blogs, Twitter, Facebook and assorted other electronic messaging systems blur the line between speech and press even more.

The word "press" no longer applies to only traditional newspapers and magazines. The term also must be applied to television shows such as *Extra*, tabloids such as the *National Enquirer*, documentaries and docudramas, and every special interest group or individual with the means to send a message. Some officials throughout history have reacted to each new technology — books, photographs, movies, radio, television, the Internet — with an urge to regulate.[23]

The Supreme Court has had to interpret the words "speech" and "press" in a variety of ways. Do bloggers have the same rights as journalists who work for mainstream publications? What are the other expressive activities that may fall under the broad categories of oral and printed words? Do they include pictures, gestures, dances, tattoos?

The Court has been required to go beyond the verbal and written communication of ideas based on what the framers were thinking — or what we think they were thinking — to issues involving the development of modern technology. Thomas Jef-

ferson predicted as much in 1816 when he wrote, "I know also that laws and institutions must go hand in hand with the progress of the human mind.... As new discoveries are made, new truths disclosed, and manners and opinions change with the change of circumstances, institutions must advance also, and keep pace with the times."[24] The founders had no concept of film, computers, DVDs or tweeting when they wrote the First Amendment.

In a broad sense, the courts have provided First Amendment protection to *expression*, a term that incorporates speech, press and some conduct. Expression also incorporates many forms of entertainment such as theater performances, movies, dancing and YouTube videos — even clicking on a "Like" button on Facebook.[25]

Still not fully answered is the question of whether the protection of expression includes the right to gather information. The Court has said newsgathering deserves some protection but has never backed up that *dicta* by providing constitutional protection.[26] The Court also has limited access to some public places and information. Chapters 16, 17 and 18 cover access to information and places in greater detail.

THE HERITAGE OF FREE EXPRESSION

The history of free expression is a long one — as long as rulers have tried to control their people, the ability to speak out has been an important antidote. One key development came in the mid-fifteenth century, when Johann Gutenberg developed movable type, and, shortly thereafter, William Caxton introduced the printing press to England. The concept of printing was new, so Caxton faced few, if any, restrictions. But that quickly changed. The British government recognized the power of the printed word and sought to control it.

The sixteenth and seventeenth centuries in England saw battles that mixed politics and religion. Dissent was a capital offense. The monarchy and the Church of England wanted opposition silenced. Religious and political fighting was linked to economic differences between the aristocracy, a rising middle class and the poor. All sides in these battles came to understand the importance of the printing press.

Government became involved early, implementing a system of licensing in 1520. The licensing allowed officials to preview material, thus controlling both content and distribution. A license became a coveted commodity, so much so that licensed printers often protected their own self-interests by exposing those who

---

[21] Texas v. Johnson, 491 U.S. 397, 404 (1989).

[22] *Id.* at 414.

[23] *See* David Hudson, *Government Regulation of New Technology is an Old Tale,* Mar. 16, 1999, http://www.freedomforum.org.

[24] Letter from Thomas Jefferson to Dr. Priestly (1802), *in* THOMAS JEFFERSON ON DEMOCRACY 67 (Saul K. Padover ed., 1939).

[25] Bland v. Roberts, 730 F.3d 368, 386 (4th Cir. 2013).

[26] *See* Branzburg v. Hayes, 408 U.S. 665 (1972).

published without government approval. Often the government engaged in heavy-handed means to censor ideas it considered dangerous. People were jailed, tortured and executed. Presses were wrecked, publications destroyed and buildings burned.

But the period was not without support for free expression. Poet John Milton wrote a forceful condemnation of censorship in *Areopagitica* in 1644, calling for open debate as the only way for people to discern the truth and reject falsehood. In the late seventeenth century, other philosophers advocating freedom of expression emerged. John Locke argued that government should answer to the people, instead of the people to the government.[27] People have natural rights, he wrote, including life, liberty and property ownership; government, through its grant by the people, should safeguard those rights, to which freedom of expression is central.

Free expression, of course, is linked to a free press. The ability to write one's thoughts and then pass them on to others is a foundation of free-speech theory. The development of the theory continued into the eighteenth century. Perhaps the most quoted representative of that period is the English jurist William Blackstone, who wrote that freedom of the press was "essential to the nature of a free state."[28] Blackstone's idea of a free press was limited to prior restraints — that is, to the government implementing restrictions on speech *before* it was published, rather than punishing speech after the fact. Freedom of the press, to Blackstone, "[C]onsists in laying no previous restraints upon publications, and not in freedom from censure for criminal matter when published."[29] This limited notion of freedom of the press would survive in the American colonies and even into the twentieth century.

During the colonial period in America, censorship was part of the way of life, because colonial governors loyal to the British crown exerted control over the press in the New World. In the eighteenth century, punishment for seditious libel — criticism of the government — grew as the prevailing form of censorship. What made the crime especially objectionable to the American colonists was that the truth was no defense — in fact, because accurate attacks were harder to refute and more likely to cause instability among the ruled, it was said that "the greater the truth, the greater the libel."[30]

The trial of John Peter Zenger for seditious libel in 1734 was a landmark case for free expression in America. Zenger was the printer of *The New York Weekly Journal*, which ran editorials that were highly critical of New York governor William Cosby. Because the authors used pseudonyms and could not be identified, Cosby had Zenger arrested in 1734 for seditious libel for printing material "tending to raise factions and tumults among the people of this Province, inflaming their minds with contempt of His Majesty's government, and greatly disturbing the peace thereof."[31]

Because seditious libel was defined under English law as any criticism of government, even if true, the only issue for the jury at Zenger's trial was whether he had in fact printed the editorials. But Zenger's attorney argued that English law should not be applied to the colonies in this case, urging the jury to send a message supporting freedom of the colonies from Britain's tyrannical rule.

His plea worked: The jury disregarded the facts and found Zenger not guilty. While the case did not set any legal precedent, it led to a decline in seditious libel prosecutions and sparked a greater awareness of the importance of freedom of speech and press in the colonies. One of the drafters of the Constitution, Gouverneur Morris, called the case "the germ of American freedom, the morning star of that liberty which subsequently revolutionized America."[32]

The Constitution and the Bill of Rights

The First Amendment was not part of the original Constitution; instead, it became part of the Bill of Rights, the first ten amendments that were added three years after ratification. Historians have little to go on regarding the discussions that took place at that constitutional convention, because no official record was kept, and the public was not admitted. But it seems clear that a bill of rights was not a high priority at the time.

At least partly because of the absence of provisions protecting fundamental, individual rights, supporters of the Constitution had a difficult time winning ratification by three-quarters of the states. Some delegates wanted the protections listed first, others wanted them included somewhere in the document, and still others didn't want them included at all. In the end, the Constitution was ratified without a bill of rights, but legislators in some states supported the document only upon promises that attempts would be made in the first Congress to approve such a bill.

James Madison, who made some of those promises in Virginia, introduced a bill of rights during the first session of the First Congress. His original amendment dealing with free expression read: "The people shall not be deprived or abridged of

---

[27] JOHN LOCKE, *Concerning the True Original Extent and End of Civil Government*, 35 GREAT BOOKS OF THE WESTERN WORLD 25-81 (Robert Maynard Hutchings ed., 1952).

[28] WILLIAM BLACKSTONE, COMMENTARIES OF THE LAWS OF ENGLAND, 1765-1769 152 (William Carey Jones ed. 1916) (1769).

[29] *Id.* at 112-13.

[30] 1 RODNEY A. SMOLLA, SMOLLA AND NIMMER ON FREEDOM OF SPEECH §1:4 (2013).

---

[31] WILLIAM LOWELL PUTNAM, JOHN PETER ZENGER AND THE FUNDAMENTAL FREEDOM 74-75 (2014).

[32] *Id.* at 63.

their right to speak, to write or to publish their sentiments and freedom of the press, as one of the great bulwarks of liberty, shall be inviolable."[33] That wording did not survive congressional committees, however. Though it is impossible to tell how the courts over time would have interpreted Madison's original amendment, its wording seems to provide more broad-based protection for both speech and the press than the version eventually adopted.

It's tempting to assign more importance to the protections of speech and press because they come first in the Bill of Rights, but, in fact, the First Amendment wasn't always first. When Madison's proposed bill of rights came out of a joint conference committee, there were twelve amendments. What would eventually become the First Amendment was third, behind two amendments that were not ratified. So the third amendment came to be first. Even had the amendment been listed first originally, however, there is no indication that courts would or should consider it more important than other rights. As Justice Harry A. Blackmun once wrote, "The First Amendment, after all, is only one part of an entire Constitution."[34]

The First Amendment, unlike Madison's original proposal, applied only to Congress. The wording clearly represented the founders' fear that the new federal government might overpower the states. They wanted to ensure that states' rights came first by preventing Congress from interfering with the protection of speech or press found in state constitutions. Consequently, if newspaper publishers wanted to seek recourse from attempts to muzzle them by state governments, they would have to do so through state constitutions. There was no help in the federal Constitution. It would take nearly 140 years for that interpretation to change.

And while the protections afforded by the First Amendment were unprecedented at the time, the passage of the Alien and Sedition Acts in 1798 showed that the country's first leaders were not above their own self-protective actions. The acts made it a crime to "write, print, utter or publish ... any false, scandalous and malicious writing or writings against the government of the United States," including the president and Congress, or to bring them "into contempt, or disrepute; or to excite against them ... the hatred of the good people of the United States."[35] The acts were in force only a few years, but they would not be the last attempt by the government to suppress political dissent.

The First Amendment in the Twentieth Century

The nineteenth century was a relatively quiet time for First Amendment doctrine. The early part of the twentieth century brought new pressures and new ways of thinking about free speech. Soon after the United States entered World War I, Congress passed the Espionage Act of 1917, followed by the Sedition Act of 1918. These statutes were wide-ranging and aimed in part at political dissent and antiwar activities. They made it a felony to "convey false reports or false statements with intent to interfere" with military efforts or to "obstruct the recruiting or enlistment service of the United States."[36]

The laws were vigorously enforced, and several appeals of convictions under the acts made their way to the Supreme Court, where they sparked an eventual shift in how the Court viewed speech restrictions. In the first case, *Schenck v. United States*,[37] the Court upheld the conviction of a man who had distributed anti-draft pamphlets. The case is important because Justice Oliver Wendell Holmes, while in the majority, set forth what became the "clear and present danger" test for determining when the government can restrict speech that may cause harm:

> The character of every act depends upon the circumstances in which it is done. The most stringent protection of free speech would not protect a man in falsely shouting fire in a theatre and causing a panic. It does not even protect a man from an injunction against uttering words that may have all the effect of force. The question in every case is whether the words used are used in such circumstances and are of such a nature as to create a clear and present danger that they will bring about the substantive evils that Congress has a right to prevent.[38]

Despite Holmes's strong wording, the Court upheld the convictions of the defendants in this and similar cases merely because their actions had a tendency to cause harm, not because of a real and imminent danger. In *Abrams v. United States*[39] in 1919, however, Holmes' thinking had changed enough that he was part of the dissent. The free exchange of ideas was too important, he said, to allow even repugnant opinions to be repressed, "unless they so imminently threaten immediate interference with the lawful and pressing purposes of the law that an immediate check is required to save the country."[40]

The clear and present danger test was a significant improve-

---

[33] 1 ANNALS OF CONGRESS 434 (1789).

[34] New York Times Co. v. United States, 403 U.S. 713, 761 (1971) (Blackmun, J., dissenting).

[35] Act of July 14, 1798, ch. 74, 1 Stat. 596 (*quoted in* SMOLLA, *supra* note 30, at §1:2 n.4).

[36] Act of June 15, 1917, 50 Stat. 217, codified as amended, 18 U.S.C. §2388(a).

[37] 249 U.S. 47 (1919).

[38] *Id.* at 52.

[39] 250 U.S. 616 (1919).

[40] *Id.* at 630 (Holmes, J., dissenting).

ment over the bad tendency test, for it provided a judge with a narrower window for restricting expression. In theory, speech would have to pose a serious and immediate danger for the government to restrict it. In later cases, however, the Court continued to uphold the convictions of defendants whose crimes consisted of mere advocacy of violence or illegal acts and no more.

In 1969, in *Brandenburg v. Ohio*, the Court ruled that the First Amendment protects the mere advocacy of illegal activity.[41] In what some scholars interpret as a variation of the clear and present danger test and others call "the *Brandenburg* test," the Court held that only when there is an imminent danger of incitement of illegal activity can authorities step in to stop speech. In a *per curiam* decision, the Court found unconstitutional the 1919 Ohio Criminal Syndicalism Statute, which was used to convict a Ku Klux Klan leader. In doing so, the Court established a two-part test to evaluate the likelihood that speech will lead to illegal activity:

• Who is the speaker? Does the person have a history of illegal activity or affiliation with an organization that does so? Do people take the speaker seriously?

• Is there a likelihood that the espoused actions will be carried out?

Brandenburg essentially put an end to the use of sedition as a threat against anti-government speech. The Court upheld the standard in a 1973 case involving an anti-Vietnam War street protester.[42] The *Brandenburg* test continues to be used. In *Nebraska Press Association v. Stuart*, for example, the Court invalidated a gag order that was intended to restrict reporting of a murder trial. Quoting appellate Judge Learned Hand, Chief Justice Warren Burger wrote that the Court had to determine whether "the gravity of the 'evil,' discounted by its improbability, justifies such invasion of free speech as is necessary to avoid the danger."[43]

Another important development in First Amendment doctrine occurred in the years after World War I. In *Gitlow v. New York*, the Supreme Court upheld the conviction of a man charged with criminal anarchy under a state law. In doing so, however, the Court reversed more than a century of precedent and applied the First Amendment to the states through the Fourteenth Amendment: "We may and do assume that freedom of speech and of the press — which are protected by the First Amendment from abridgment by Congress — are among the fundamental personal rights and 'liberties' protected by the due process clause of the Fourteenth Amendment from impairment by the States."[44]

This statement was a precursor to changes in the way of thinking about the Constitution that would have an enormous impact on expressive rights. In effect, Justice Edward Sanford found that state governments, just like the federal government, are bound by the Constitution. While judges and scholars recognized that state constitutions could provide more expansive rights than those provided in the federal Constitution — and indeed, some do — the idea that state laws and constitutions could not grant fewer rights was relatively new. This is called the "concept of incorporation." It didn't help Benjamin Gitlow, but it provided a touchstone that has protected expressive rights ever since.

While the Court in *Gitlow* assumed the Fourteenth Amendment protected fundamental rights, it wasn't until 1931 that the Court actually struck down a state statute that it said violated the press clause of the First Amendment, doing so in *Near v. Minnesota*,[45] a prior restraint case discussed in more depth in Chapter 4 of this book.

Incorporation also gives federal courts authority to review the constitutionality of state laws, allowing them to be the final interpreters of freedom of expression. After *Gitlow* and incorporation, the wording of the First Amendment was no longer strictly accurate — "Congress shall make no law" didn't mean Congress only. Today any "state action" — meaning local, state or federal government — that restricts freedom of speech or press will trigger scrutiny under the First Amendment.

The Supreme Court would prefer not to rule on issues from states involving fundamental rights. If legislation does not affect these fundamental rights, the Court assumes the legislation is constitutional. It tries to avoid political battles and counteracting majority rule, though it is often accused of doing just that. But if legislation — state or federal — is seen to infringe First Amendment rights, the Court will not defer to the legislature. In First Amendment cases, the Court examines the whole record of a lower court decision to determine whether the decision handicaps freedom of expression.

THE PURPOSE OF FREE EXPRESSION

While courts look to history and tradition for guidance as to what the First Amendment means, legal scholars have also attempted to categorize the philosophical values inherent in First Amendment protections. In deciding cases, judges may allude to any of a number of inherent purposes of free speech to support

[41] 395 U.S. 444 (1969).

[42] Hess v. Indiana, 414 U.S. 105 (1973).

[43] 427 U.S. 539, 562 (1976).

[44] 268 U.S. 652, 666 (1925). The Fourteenth Amendment provides that no state shall

"deprive any person of life, liberty, or property, without due process of law; nor deny to any person within its jurisdiction the equal protection of the laws." U.S. CONST. amend. XIV, §1.

[45] 283 U.S. 697 (1931). After *Near*, the Court, on a case-by-case basis, brought other clauses of the Bill of Rights under Fourteenth Amendment protection.

their findings. According to legal scholar Thomas Emerson, protecting free expression is necessary for four main purposes: "(1) as assuring individual self-fulfillment, (2) as a means of attaining the truth, (3) as a method of securing participation by the members of the society in social, and especially political, decision-making, and (4) as maintaining the balance between stability and change in the society."[46]

Individual self-fulfillment. This model of free expression is based on the inherent worth of every individual and the right of each person to form — and express — his or her beliefs and opinions. Philosopher John Locke argued that rather than being a means to an end, freedom of expression is valuable as a good in itself. Locke's view is based on the belief that expressing opinion is part of human nature. We want to express ourselves; indeed, we need to express ourselves. This helps each of us discover what it means to be human. Freedom of expression is needed, therefore, both to promote individual self-realization and as a way for the individual to communicate his ideas as an equal member of society. Protection for artistic expression — music, dance and art — is based in part on this model of free expression.

A means of attaining the truth. Often called the "marketplace of ideas" model, this idea can be traced at least as far back as John Milton's *Areopagitica* (1644), in which he wrote: "Though all the winds of doctrine were let loose to play upon the earth, so Truth be in the field, we do injuriously by licensing and prohibiting to misdoubt her strength. Let her and Falsehood grapple; who ever knew Truth put to the worse in a free and open encounter?" This model sees value in open debate as a way to gain knowledge and discover the truth. Justice Holmes is credited with coining the marketplace metaphor, writing that "the ultimate good desired is better reached by free trade in ideas — that the best test of truth is the power of the thought to get itself accepted in the competition of the market, and that truth is the only ground upon which their wishes safely can be carried out."[47] The theory is that, just as consumers search for the best products in a market, a system of free expression ensures a wide variety of ideas in circulation and allows them to succeed or fail based on their own value, with the faith that the best ideas will prevail. Under this theory, censorship is not only obnoxious, it is impractical. Still, critics question whether the current model of the marketplace gives equal access to all speakers — First Amendment scholar Jerome Barron says if the marketplace of ideas ever worked, it has long ceased to do so because

"there is an inequality in the power to communicate ideas just as there is inequality in economic bargaining power."[48] The marketplace may mean little to minorities, dissidents and fringe groups who do not have access to the media. Others dispute the notion that there is any objective notion of truth that the model can help us reach.

Participation in social and political decision-making. Also called the self-government model, this model of free expression is concerned with the individual's role in an open community and in a democratic system of government. If, in a democracy, the government acts on behalf of and with the consent of the governed, then the people must have the freedom to share information and ideas in order to have fully informed consent, to express their beliefs and needs to the government, and to criticize the government's actions and advocate for change. According to First Amendment scholar Alexander Meiklejohn, free speech

is not, primarily, a device for the winning of new truth, though that is very important. It is a device for the sharing of whatever truth has been won. Its purpose is to give to every voting member of the body politic the fullest possible participation in the understanding of those problems with which the citizens of a self-governing society must deal.[49]

Some scholars and judges have regarded this model as the most important, with a few going so far as to argue that only political speech should have full First Amendment protection.[50] But most see this model as encompassing non-political subjects, such as education, philosophy, science, literature and the arts — that is, any speech relating to public affairs broadly defined. This model also recognizes the importance of the press's role as an important check on government power. This role is so essential that the press has become known as the "fourth estate"; that is, as an unofficial fourth branch in the American system of self-government. Thomas Jefferson wrote in 1787 that people should have full information about public affairs through the press:

The basis of our government being the opinion of the people, the very first object should be to keep that right; and were it left to me to decide whether we should have a government without newspapers, or newspapers without government, I

---

[46] Thomas I. Emerson, *Toward a General Theory of the First Amendment*, 72 YALE L.J. 877, 878-89 (1962-63).

[47] Abrams v. United States, 250 U.S. 616 (1919) (Holmes, J., dissenting).

[48] Jerome Barron, *Access to the Press — A New First Amendment Right*, 80 HARV. L. REV. 1641, 1647 (1967).

[49] ALEXANDER MEIKLEJOHN, FREE SPEECH AND ITS RELATION TO GOVERNMENT 88-89 (1948).

[50] *See, e.g.,* Robert Bork, *Neutral Principles and Some First Amendment Problems*, 47 IND. L.J. 1 (1971).

essential for democracy

should not hesitate a moment to prefer the latter.[51]

Former Supreme Court Justice Brennan subscribed to this model of free expression, seeing its primary value for society, not individuals. In a democratic society, he argued, "[T]he government, the press, and the people all have roles to play in the operation of society. Self-government of a society requires a communications process, and it is that process the First Amendment is designed to protect."[52] His philosophy was manifested in the landmark case *New York Times Co. v. Sullivan*. In a unanimous opinion, Brennan wrote that a libel suit against a newspaper must be considered "against the background of a profound national commitment to the principle that debate on public issues should be uninhibited, robust, and wide-open."[53]

A free press, therefore, is essential to bringing to light abuses of power. From Tammany Hall to Watergate, citizens depend on the press to investigate and report on what the government is doing in their name. During the Watergate scandal, *The Washington Post* was instrumental in uncovering political dirty tricks, wiretapping, money laundering and obstruction of justice committed by the administration of Richard Nixon in the 1970s.[54] The *Post* also exposed the NSA surveillance programs that Edward Snowden's leaked documents revealed in 2013, winning the Pulitzer Prize for public service for its efforts.[55] Without the freedom to act aggressively as a watchdog of government at all levels, the press would not be able to uncover these governmental abuses.

Balance between stability and change. This is sometimes called the "safety valve model," because it sees free expression as a way to express disagreement with government or social policy and work for change within the system and without violence. Those in power often see public criticism as obstructionist, but the constitutional protection for government criticism demonstrates that the framers believed flexibility and stability work together. Stable change occurs because problems can be dealt with incrementally, reducing the need for drastic change, which could be disruptive. If speech is suppressed, frustrations can build up and become more violent when they are finally released. Open debate, on the other hand, allows citizens to "let

off steam" and effect change by debate and persuasion rather than by more violent means.

THE HIERARCHY OF PROTECTED EXPRESSION

The rights of all people to speak and publish are fundamental. So are the rights to engage in symbolic speech and to associate with others. And, the Supreme Court has said, because of the right to speak and disseminate ideas, there may be an implied right to receive some kinds of information.

Freedom of expression also guarantees some right to remain silent. In 1769 an English judge named Abraham Yates wrote, "It is certain every man has a right to keep his own sentiments, if he pleases. He has certainly a right to judge whether he will make them public or commit them only to the sight of his friends."[56] Yet, there is a debate among legal scholars about whether the Constitution affords individuals a broad right not to speak. Courts have held that a person cannot be compelled to salute the flag, affirm a belief in God, or associate with a political party or particular ideology.[57] New Hampshire, for example, lost its bid to require all car owners in the state to bear license plates with the slogan "Live Free or Die." The Supreme Court upheld the right of a Jehovah's Witness to block out the slogan because the Witness said it violated his religious beliefs.[58] The Court also invalidated a Missouri constitutional amendment that compelled its federal delegation and candidates for Congress to work and vote for a federal constitutional amendment setting term limits.[59]

It is important to remember that the First Amendment's prohibitions apply only to government, not to private people and institutions. Another constant theme throughout this chapter — indeed, throughout this book — is that the First Amendment is not absolute. There are instances in which speech — and speakers — can be restricted, and restrictions may vary based on the type of speech, the type of speaker, and even the medium of communication.

A constant theme throughout this chapter — indeed, throughout this book — is that the First Amendment is not absolute. There are instances in which speech — and speakers — can be restricted, and restrictions may vary based on the type of speech, the type of speaker and even the medium of communication.

In some cases, broad categories of speech have been judged to

---

[51] Letter from Thomas Jefferson to Edward Carrington (1787), *in* THOMAS JEFFERSON ON DEMOCRACY, *supra* note 24, at 93.

[52] Karen Green, "Uninhibited, Robust and Wide-Open" — But Informed: Justice Brennan's Structural Model of the First Amendment 2 (Mar. 1998) (unpublished paper presented at the AEJMC Southeast Colloquium, New Orleans, La.).

[53] 376 U.S. 254, 270 (1964).

[54] *See* CARL BERNSTEIN & BOB WOODWARD, ALL THE PRESIDENT'S MEN (1974).

[55] *See* Paul Farhi, *Washington Post Wins Pulitzer Prize for NSA Spying Revelations; Guardian also Honored*, WASH. POST, Apr. 14, 2014, *available at* http://www.washingtonpost.com.

[56] Miller v. Taylor, 4 Burr. 2301, 2302 (1769).

[57] *See, e.g.*, Wooley v. Maynard, 430 U.S. 705 (1977); Elrod v. Burns, 427 U.S. 347 (1966); Torcaso v. Watkins, 367 U.S. 488 (1961); West Virginia Bd. of Ed. v. Barnette, 319 U.S. 624 (1943).

[58] *Wooley*, 430 U.S. 705 (1977).

[59] Cook v. Gralike, 531 U.S. 510 (2001).

deserve little or no First Amendment protection. These are considered low-value speech because they do not implicate any of the functions, discussed above, that the First Amendment was designed to serve. Among these low-value categories of speech are obscenity, child pornography, fraud, defamation, false advertising and fighting words, which are explained in Chapter 3.

An intermediate level of protection is given to commercial speech, such as advertising. The Supreme Court has recognized that advertising and other forms of commercial speech have value and should be protected. Commercial speech, however, is a particularly sturdy form of speech; that is, it has a tendency to survive despite restrictions. Because, though, the speaker has a vested interest, the Court has ruled that the government may impose stricter regulations on commercial speech. Chapter 8 discusses this category more fully.

The highest level of protection afforded speech under the First Amendment goes to political speech. Core political speech consists of speech that is directly related to public debate about a particular political issue or candidate, but the definition has often been expanded beyond speech about government and politics to include topics as varied as education, health, agriculture and culture.

Because this type of speech is so important, laws that restrict political activities must have a compelling purpose that outweighs First Amendment rights. In the past, limits on campaign contributions, because they guard against corrupting influences, have been considered such a purpose. In several recent cases, however, the Supreme Court struck down some of these rules based on the First Amendment. In *Citizens United v. Federal Election Commission*,[60] the Supreme Court struck down parts of the Bipartisan Campaign Reform Act of 2002,[61] usually called McCain-Feingold after its primary sponsors, which restricted corporations and labor unions from using their own money for campaign purposes. The decision overruled longstanding precedents that had upheld campaign finance restrictions. In 2014, the Court overturned limits on the total amount of money any one person can give during an election.[62] In the majority opinion, Chief Justice John Roberts wrote, "The government may no more restrict how many candidates or causes a donor may support than it may tell a newspaper how many candidates it may endorse."[63]

Restrictions Based on the Medium of Expression

Why are television networks fined for broadcasting profanity

but swearing abounds on cable? Why is nudity allowed on cable channels but not NBC or ABC? Different media are afforded different levels of speech protection, based on a number of factors. Broadcasting — television and radio programming delivered over the public airwaves — is the most heavily regulated medium. The Federal Communications Commission has set up rules that restrict the content of programming, including banning obscenity, indecency and profanity. Courts have largely deferred to the commission in this regard, in part because stations receive licenses in return for agreeing to serve the public interest. Cable channels, for a variety of reasons, are not subject to the same level of content regulation. Chapters 10 and 11 explore the regulation of broadcasting and cable in more depth.

Newspapers, books, magazines and other print media receive the highest level of First Amendment protection. In 1974, the Supreme Court struck down a Florida law that required newspapers to give a right of reply to those who had been attacked in the newspaper's editorials, even though the Court had unanimously upheld an FCC rule that required the same right of reply of broadcast licensees just five years earlier.[64]

In 1997, the Supreme Court was faced with a historic decision: Should the Internet be regulated like broadcasting, or should it enjoy the same First Amendment freedoms as print? In a landmark decision regarding provisions of a federal law restricting indecency in cyberspace, the Court ruled that the Internet should enjoy the same level of First Amendment protection as print. The Court reviewed the "special factors" that had served to justify broadcast regulation in past cases and decided they were absent online: "[T]hese cases provide no basis for qualifying the level of First Amendment scrutiny that should be applied to the Internet," Justice John Paul Stevens wrote for a unanimous Court.[65]

Restrictions Based on the Status of the Speaker

Levels of protection attach to different types of people, just as they do to different types of speech. No particular type of person has absolute protection, and all types of people have some free speech rights. There is no language in the Bill of Rights that distinguishes categories of people and their levels of protection. Yet, over the years the courts have realized there are relevant distinctions, some based on age. Courts have also classified people by their employment status — in the public versus the private sector — as well as whether they are in prison. Adult private citizens enjoy the most rights. And, while many of those same rights apply to students, children and government em-

[60] 558 U.S. 310 (2010).

[61] 2 U.S.C. § 431 (2002).

[62] McCutcheon v. Fed. Election Comm'n, 134 S.Ct. 1434 (2014).

[63] *Id.* at 1448.

[64] *See* Miami Herald v. Tornillo, 418 U.S. 241 (1974); Red Lion Broadcasting v. Federal Communications Commission, 395 U.S. 367 (1969).

[65] Reno v. ACLU, 521 U.S. 844, 870 (1997).

ployees, the level of protection is not the same.

College students. Because state universities and colleges are run by the government, the First Amendment applies to them, and the Court has said it generally has the same force as in the community at large: "Mere dissemination of ideas — no matter how offensive to good taste — on a state university campus may not be shut off in the name alone of 'conventions of decency.'"[66] Free speech controversies continue, however, on public college campuses. For example, the Sixth U.S. Circuit Court of Appeals overturned a holding that the same restrictions that applied to public high schools could be applied to the college and university press.[67] The Seventh Circuit, though, ruled that a college student newspaper could be subject to administration control if it had been created as a certain type of public forum and the school funded it.[68]

Students at private colleges and universities have even fewer expressive rights because, as we have seen, the First Amendment is aimed only at the government — it has no bearing on private entities. While the administrations at public colleges and universities are tantamount to the government, private college and university administrations are not considered "state actors" under the law, so the First Amendment does not apply. Some state laws, such as one in California, provide greater protection to student speech on both public and private campuses. Students on a private college campus also may find support for free expression in the institution's own mission statement.

··· or could not !

High school students. Public high school students, like adults, have some fundamental expressive rights. But while students are at school, administrators and teachers may more easily restrict those rights in order to keep order and further their educational mission. A public school district may not prevent students from symbolically protesting a war — by wearing black armbands, for example — as long as the symbolic expression does not disrupt school activities.[69] The Supreme Court has recognized, however, that schools have specific functions that may be protected. School-sponsored publications may be restricted if they don't support the pedagogical mission of the school.[70] And speech can be curbed if it disrupts class work, involves substantial disorder, invades the rights of others or is interpreted as advocating illegal activity, even if the speech occurs off campus,

FOR SENIOR PROJECT

but at a school-sponsored event.[71] Student expressive rights at both the college and high school level are discussed in greater detail in Chapter 7.

Government employees. The protections afforded individuals under the First Amendment against government restrictions do not apply the same way when the government is acting as an employer. Government employees have the right to speak and publish, but with limitations. They may speak as private persons on public issues, just as they may vote for whomever they want. They cannot be fired, for example, for remarks hostile to the government or even to their own governmental agency, unless those remarks are likely to impede the agency's operations.

The Supreme Court ruled in 2006 that statements made by government employees in the course of their official duties are outside protection of the First Amendment.[72] "When a public employee speaks pursuant to employment responsibilities," the Court held, "there is no relevant analogue to speech by citizens who are not government employees."[73] The Court was expected to rule soon on how this precedent would apply to a public employee's employment-related testimony in court.[74]

For more than fifty years, federal government employees could not participate in political campaigns. That changed, however, when Congress passed, and President Bill Clinton signed, the Hatch Act Reform Amendments of 1993.[75] Most government employees still may not solicit campaign funds from the public and may not run for partisan office, but they may, if they choose, take active roles in campaigns.[76] The same law also states that employees cannot be forced to participate in a campaign.

Prisoners. Prisoners have fewer rights to speak, publish and receive information than free adults. Prison officials may enact reasonable restrictions to control their access to people and information in order to keep order or for other legitimate penal interests. Officials may prohibit, for example, the possession of

---

[66] Papish v. Bd. of Curators, 410 U.S. 667, 670 (1973).

[67] Kincaid v. Gibson, 236 F.3d. 342 (6th Cir. 2001).

[68] Hosty v. Carter, 412 F.3d 731 (7th Cir. 2005).

[69] *See* Tinker v. Des Moines Indep. Sch. Dist., 393 U.S. 503 (1969).

[70] *See* Hazelwood v. Kuhlmeier, 484 U.S. 260 (1988).

[71] *See* Morse v. Frederick, 551 U.S. 393 (2007). *See also* Nat Hentoff, *Saving Free Speech and Jesus*, VILLAGE VOICE, May 26, 2007, *available at* http://www.village voice.com.

[72] Garcetti v. Ceballos, 547 U.S. 410 (2006).

[73] *Id.* at 424.

[74] *See* Lane v. Cent. Ala. Cmty. College, 523 Fed. Appx. 709 (11th Cir. 2013), *cert. granted* 134 S.Ct. 999 (2014).

[75] Pub. L. 103-94, Sec. 2(a), Oct. 6, 1993, 107 Stat. 1001 (1993).

[76] Employees of the following federal agencies may not participate in politica' campaigns: Federal Election Commission; FBI; Secret Service; CIA; National Secur' Council; National Security Agency; Defense Intelligence Agency; Merit Systems' tection Board; Office of Special Counsel; Office of Criminal Investigations of ternal Revenue Service; Office of Investigative Programs of the U.S. Custom' Office of Law Enforcement of the Bureau of Alcohol, Tobacco and Firear' tral Imagery Office; and the Criminal Division of the Department of J' tion, FEC employees cannot contribute financially to political camp'

gang-related materials, including newspaper articles. But prisoners in a federal penitentiary successfully challenged a 1996 federal law that banned NC-17, R and X-rated movies, saying their First Amendment rights were violated.[77]

INTERPRETING THE FIRST AMENDMENT

Some First Amendment scholars and jurists, because of the clear language of the First Amendment, argue for absolute protection for all speech — regardless of content, motive of the speaker or consequences of the speech. Former Supreme Court Justice Hugo Black had what some call an "absolutist" view of the First Amendment. Because freedom of speech and press is explicitly mentioned, he argued that those forms of expression are absolutely protected. He believed no expressive conduct was protected, however, because the First Amendment does not explicitly mention conduct.

Former Supreme Court Justice William O. Douglas, also very nearly absolutist, took a broader view than his colleague. He believed symbolic speech — wearing armbands, burning draft cards — fell within the protection of the First Amendment. He was opposed to weighing the First Amendment against other values because, he said, doing so ran counter to the intent of the framers and the express language of the First Amendment. Despite the views of Justices Black and Douglas, nothing close to an absolute interpretation of the First Amendment has ever commanded a majority of the Supreme Court.

Because most speech is not absolutely protected, courts have used a variety of tests to balance freedom of expression against other rights or values to determine which must give way. In some cases, as we have seen, broad categories of speech have been judged to deserve little or no First Amendment protection. For other types of speech, general rules have been fashioned to help courts decide cases within a specific category of speech — the rules governing privacy, for example, have been developed in a way that reflects what is seen as the proper balance between privacy and free expression. for a certain purpow

Finally, when courts look to decide other types of cases, they may rely on "ad hoc" balancing, looking at the competing interests at stake and making a decision as to which interest — the government's or the individual's free speech rights — should prevail in the particular circumstances. In this type of case-by-case balancing, courts have a number of analytical tools they use to make their decision.

One tool is the strict scrutiny test, used when the government is attempting to regulate expression based on its content. "If there is a bedrock principle underlying the First Amendment,"

wrote Justice Brennan in 1989, "it is that the government may not prohibit the expression of an idea simply because society finds the idea itself offensive or disagreeable."[78]

Courts employ strict scrutiny when confronted with governmental actions specifically aimed at restricting the content of expression. Under the strict scrutiny test, the government must show a compelling reason for instituting a regulation that restricts speech. The reason, in fact, must be so compelling it requires free expression to take a subordinate role. Some of the government interests that have been found to be sufficiently important to justify content-based restrictions are national security and public safety. Strict scrutiny is discussed further in Chapter 3.

In addition, the government must demonstrate the regulation is necessary and narrowly tailored to meet a specific goal without restricting speech that is not related to the goal. The courts often will examine the circumstances of a case to see if the government could have taken action that was less destructive of First Amendment rights. If such a method exists, the courts will rule in favor of the First Amendment and strike down the regulation. In many cases, the burden is so great the government cannot meet it.

Other types of speech restrictions are considered "content neutral" — they are based on factors other than the content or underlying idea of the message. Often these regulate the time, place or manner in which messages are expressed. Time, place and manner regulations allow a local, state or federal government, for example, to require permits for parades, specifying the route the parade will follow and the time of day the parade can take place. The government can ban the parade because it would go down Main Street during rush hour, but cannot ban the parade because of the message being espoused by the marchers. Time, place and manner restrictions are constitutional as long as they are not arbitrary — for example, it might be unconstitutional to ban all messages without a valid reason — and as long as they are neutral — that is, they treat all messages the same way. Constitutional time, place and manner restrictions have included a New Hampshire state law that required a permit for parades,[79] a Colorado statute that created a moving "no-protest zone" around people entering abortion clinics,[80] and a New York City regulation requiring city employees to control the sound mix of performances in Central Park.[81]

---

[77] Wolf v. Ashcroft BOP, 297 F.3d 305 (3d Cir. 2002).

---

[78] Texas v. Johnson, 491 U.S. 397, 414 (1989).

[79] Cox v. New Hampshire, 312 U.S. 569 (1941).

[80] Hill v. Colorado, 530 U.S. 703 (2000).

[81] Ward v. Rock Against Racism, 491 U.S. 781 (1989).

Overbreadth, Vagueness and the Chilling Effect

Regulations that restrict protected as well as unprotected speech are called overbroad, and courts may strike them down as unconstitutional on their face. In *Board of Airport Commissioners of Los Angeles v. Jews for Jesus*, for example, the Supreme Court struck down a regulation banning First Amendment activities in the airport as overbroad.[82] While the rule may have helped the airport control pedestrian traffic by preventing groups from distributing religious literature in the terminal, it would also have prohibited protected speech such as talking or wearing a political button in the airport.

Many of the rules described elsewhere in this book are specific ways to keep the restrictions on speech narrowly tailored so they retain their constitutionality. The Supreme Court implemented the actual malice requirement in libel law, for example, as a way to limit libel suits from targeting constitutionally protected speech.

Another defect in some speech restrictions is when the rule is not specific enough for people to understand what exactly is being prohibited. A statute may be "void for vagueness" if it is so unclear that persons of common intelligence must guess at its meaning and will differ in their interpretation of what it means. An example of such a law was one making it a crime if a person "publicly mutilates, tramples upon, defaces or treats contemptuously the flag of the United States."[83] The word "contemptuously" was not defined, making it difficult to know what kind of treatment might be a crime. Burning the flag — the focus of the statute — may be "contemptuous," but so may be wearing a scarf that appears to be a flag or using a flag as a rug in an art gallery. In *Smith v. Goguen*, the Supreme Court struck down the statute as too vague and overturned the conviction of a man who had worn a small American flag on the seat of his pants.

A related problem is speech restrictions that leave government authorities with broad discretion to decide what speech will be permitted and what will not. In *Lovell v. Griffin*, for example, the Supreme Court struck down an ordinance that prohibited the distribution of literature without the written permission of the city manager.[84] Requiring a permit may be allowed under the First Amendment, but there must be specific — and constitutional — criteria for the granting of the permit, not just tradition or custom. Specific and narrowly tailored rules are needed because vague and overbroad laws make speakers unnecessarily cautious. They are not likely to fully exercise their free speech rights because they are not certain what

speech is or is not allowed. This is called a "chilling effect," because protected speech is "chilled" and not expressed. Courts will look closely at any regulation that may tend to cause this effect.

Suppressing speech is not an easy task. The courts require a specific legal procedure be followed that allows them to decide what expression is protected. The procedure, called "First Amendment due process," requires certain safeguards to protect individual rights. Those safeguards include requiring the government to notify individuals when action is being taken against them and providing an opportunity to be heard in court.

The process is left to the courts, which are seen as unbiased interpreters of government legislation and individual rights. This is part of the system of checks and balances of power. By following due process, the courts require the government to bear the burden of proving legislation does not violate individual rights. That is, the courts assume expression is protected unless the government proves otherwise.

The courts, in their examination of First Amendment cases, apply rules and principles that have been developed over time, primarily from legal precedent established in earlier cases. When First Amendment due process is involved, courts usually expedite the decision-making process, because the impact is much broader than in other types of cases.

SUMMARY

The First Amendment is essential to a free government and to American society. Without it, there is no protection from frivolous libel or invasion of privacy suits; there is no right of access to government proceedings; there is no protection from prior restraint; there is no right to investigate or criticize government. Without the First Amendment, newspapers, magazines, broadcast stations and other media would not exist as we know them.

The First Amendment's guarantees of free speech and press are not absolute. Courts throughout the country continue to interpret its language as new issues arise. Arguments and justifications for free expression are found in our English heritage in the words of John Milton, William Blackstone and others, who challenged the authority of government under threat of sometimes brutal punishment.

The First Amendment was the result of debate and political maneuvering among colonists. It was not always first. Thus, an argument can be made that it has no more weight than any of the other nine amendments that make up the Bill of Rights. Though it was initially interpreted to apply only to the federal government, the First Amendment became applicable to the states in 1925.

The rights found in the First Amendment manifest them-

---

[82] 482 U.S. 569 (1987).

[83] Smith v. Goguen, 415 U.S. 566, 573 (1974).

[84] 303 U.S. 444 (1938).

selves in a variety of ways. People often claim a right of expression — a right to speak or publish — without understanding the limits on those rights. The Supreme Court has placed those limits as it balances conflicting rights. However, the Court has made it clear that any regulation of expression that targets the content of speech must pass strict scrutiny. And the government — whether federal, state or local — must be able to justify its action to control expression by demonstrating that it used the means least damaging to the First Amendment.

There is value in the First Amendment because it allows us to discover the truth, continue to govern ourselves, promote stable change and enrich ourselves. While not everyone enjoys the same level of protection under the First Amendment, everyone has some protection.

FOR ADDITIONAL READING

Bezanson, Randall P. *Too Much Free Speech?* Urbana, Ill.: University of Illinois Press, 2012.

Epps, Garrett (ed.). *Freedom of the Press: Its Constitutional History and the Contemporary Debate.* Amherst, N.Y.: Prometheus Books, 2008.

Farber, Daniel A. *The First Amendment.* New York: Foundation Press, 2003.

Hentoff, Nat. *Free Speech for Me — But Not for Thee.* New York: Harper Collins Publishers, 1992.

Kennedy, Sheila Suess (ed.). *Free Expression in America: A Documentary History.* Westport, Conn.: Greenwood Press, 1999.

Lewis, Anthony. *Freedom for the Thought That We Hate: A Biography of the First Amendment.* Philadelphia: Basic Books, 2009.

Russomanno, Joseph. *Speaking Our Minds: Conversations with the People Behind Landmark First Amendment Cases.* Mahwah, N.J.: Lawrence Erlbaum Associates, 2002.

Smolla, Rodney A. *Free Speech in an Open Society.* New York: Vintage, 2011.

Stewart, David O. *The Summer of 1787.* New York: Simon & Schuster, 2007.

Willis, Clyde E. *Student's Guide to Landmark Congressional Laws on the First Amendment.* Westport, Conn: Greenwood Press, 2002.

SELECTED INTERNET SOURCES

American Civil Liberties Union, http://www.aclu.org

American Library Association, http://www.ala.org

Electronic Frontier Foundation, http://www.eff.org

First Amendment Center, http://www.firstamendmentcenter.org

Free Expression Policy Project, http://www.fepproject.org

Media Institute, http://www.mediainstitute.org

Media Law Resource Center, http://www.medialaw.org

National Coalition Against Censorship, http://ncac.org

National Freedom of Information Coalition, http://www.nfoic.org

Thomas Jefferson Center for the Protection of Freedom of Expression, http://www.tjcenter.org

3

Conduct and Speech

By W. Wat Hopkins

➡ **Headnote Questions**

- How does the Supreme Court determine whether conduct is expressive?
- How does the Supreme Court determine whether expressive conduct is constitutionally protected?
- What are the intermediate and strict scrutiny tests?
- What is the constitutional status of threatening speech, fighting words and intimidating speech?

As readers of this book will no doubt learn — if they haven't already — much First Amendment jurisprudence depends upon interpretation and, beyond that, degrees of interpretation. One man's art is another's obscenity; one woman's opinion is another's libel; one author's fair use is another's copyright infringement.

One of the best examples of the divergence of attitudes toward free speech might be the battle waged in the 1960s and '70s between Justice Hugo Black and some of his brethren on the U.S. Supreme Court. Justice Black took the position that the government cannot restrict the distribution of material because that material is obscene, defamatory, indecent, or even because it might harm the national security. "I read 'no law ... abridging'" freedom of speech and press, Justice Black wrote, "to mean *no law* abridging."[1] Speech, he maintained, was absolutely protected.

The great free-speech advocate, however, had a very narrow definition of "speech." Just as "no law" meant "no law," in Justice Black's view, "speech" meant "speech" and nothing more. He disagreed, therefore, when the Court ruled that students could not be punished for wearing black arm bands to school, or that a protester could not be punished for wearing a jacket with an offensive slogan on the back. These cases, Justice Black contended, involved conduct and did not implicate the First Amendment; no "speech" was involved.

Fortunately for picketers, flag-burners and dozens of others who have chosen over the years to express their views by doing rather than saying, a majority of the Supreme Court has never

agreed with Justice Black's definition of "speech." Indeed, a majority of the Court has always recognized that "speech" is more than talking. Justice Abe Fortas, for example, wrote that those students who wore armbands to school to protest the Vietnam War were participating in activity that was "closely akin to 'pure speech.'"[2] Justice Fortas' characterization was momentous. If something that was so clearly an action could be considered "pure speech," many other types of conduct could be recognized as speech as well and, therefore, eligible for First Amendment protection. Under such a construction, expression, which is not mentioned in the First Amendment, is protected alongside "speech" and "press."

That has long been the case in First Amendment jurisprudence. Indeed, the Court has recognized a variety of activities as being speech: carrying or displaying a flag; marching or picketing; burning a flag, cross or draft card.[3] The Court has also said that a sit-in is a form of expression, as is the "silent, reproachful presence" of a group of African Americans who refused to leave an all-white library.[4] In fact, in some circumstances, even sleeping could be described as "speech."[5]

This is not to say, however, that the First Amendment protects all expressive or symbolic conduct. Conduct, after all, may intrude on individual rights more than other forms of speech. It may literally do what a 1980s advertisement for a long-distance telephone company once suggested consumers figuratively do:

---

[1] Smith v. California, 361 U.S. 147, 157 (1959) (Black, J., concurring).

[2] Tinker v. Des Moines Indep. Sch. Dist., 393 U.S. 503, 505-06 (1969).

[3] *See, e.g.,* cases cited in footnote 10.

[4] Brown v. Louisiana, 383 U.S. 131, 141-42 (1966).

[5] *See* Clark v. Cmty. for Creative Non-Violence, 468 U.S. 288, 293 (1984); *id.* at 302 (Marshall, J., dissenting).

Reach out and touch someone. The Court has said, therefore, that there must be some balance between the rights of the actor and the rights of others present when conduct is used as a means of expression. This tension between rights has been at the heart of expressive conduct cases since the 1960s, when the Court's first substantive analysis in this area of the law began.

CONDUCT AS SPEECH

For First Amendment purposes, there are three kinds of conduct: (1) conduct that has no communicative value, (2) conduct that is purely communicative and (3) conduct that has a mix of communicative and non-communicative elements.

Sometimes it's easy to tell the difference. One spring, for example, a homeowner noticed that his U.S. flag had become frayed and moth-eaten. He decided to replace the flag and learned from the U.S. Code that the preferred way of disposing of a damaged flag is by burning.[6] He took the flag into the back yard, dropped it into the grill, doused it with lighter fluid and set it ablaze. No one saw the action, and the flag burner later disposed of the cold ashes by spreading them in the flower bed. The act had no communicative value. Its purpose was solely to dispose of a damaged U.S. flag as suggested by the U.S. Code.[7]

Come summer, the homeowner replaced the damaged flag and, on July 4, put it on a flag pole attached to the garage. The act is purely communicative: The homeowner displayed the flag to demonstrate patriotism on Independence Day.

But when fall arrived, the homeowner became dismayed. An incumbent president had taken actions with which the homeowner bitterly disagreed. He had a series of arguments with a neighbor, who happened to be the local chairman of the president's political party. The homeowner's irritation was inflamed even more because the president was using hundreds of flags in his re-election campaign, even using the flag as a background on campaign posters, bumper stickers and other paraphernalia. To demonstrate his distaste, the homeowner doused his recently purchased flag with lighter fluid, set it ablaze and tossed it on the neighbor's front porch. The burning flag destroyed a "Welcome" mat and left a large, sooty spot, requiring the porch to be repainted.

The homeowner's action contains both communicative and non-communicative elements. He communicated displeasure with presidential politics but also caused property damage.

Under Supreme Court rulings, the government may regulate purely communicative conduct only in extremely rare circumstances. Conduct that has both speech and non-speech elements, however, may be regulated more readily. Courts must balance the rights of an individual to express viewpoints through action against the rights of individuals who may be impacted by the action. The balancing is complex and often controversial.

Over the years, the Supreme Court has developed a series of tests it applies in adjudicating cases in which individuals or groups claim constitutional protection for symbolic speech. First, the Court asks, is the conduct expressive? If not, the First Amendment is not implicated, the inquiry ends, and the government may regulate the conduct. If the conduct *is* expressive, however, the Court then asks the more difficult question: Is the expressive conduct protected by the First Amendment?

Is the Conduct Expressive?

If conduct is expressive, it is "speech." The expressive nature of the conduct is the element that moves action from simply doing to communicating. The homeowner is no longer burning a damaged flag in his grill; he is burning it in public for the express purpose of communicating a message.

To determine whether conduct is purely utilitarian or has some communicative elements, the Court asks two questions: (1) Is there an intent to express a message? (2) Is there a likelihood the message will be understood by a witness? If there is no intent to express a message, or if it is not likely that a witness will understand the intended message, the conduct is not expressive; and the First Amendment does not apply.[8] Figure 1 demonstrates the flow of this inquiry.

The Court does not require that a viewer of expressive conduct understand the exact message the actor intends. Only a general understanding of the message is necessary. For example, when spectators watched in 1984 as Gregory Lee Johnson burned an American flag outside the meeting place of the Republican National Convention in Dallas, it was unnecessary that they knew Johnson was demonstrating his distaste for President Ronald Reagan, who was seeking re-nomination. It was sufficient that the spectators understood that Johnson was dissatisfied with some aspect of the United States or of the U.S. government — those entities symbolized by the flag.

Even though Johnson's action could be interpreted as a demonstration of disgust with President Reagan, the Republican Party, the U.S. government *or* the United States itself, Justice William Brennan, upholding Johnson's right to burn the flag, wrote in *Texas v. Johnson*, "The expressive, overtly political na-

---

[6] Respect for the U.S. flag is covered in the U.S. Code, Title 4, Chapter 1, § 8. Paragraph k of that section reads: "The flag, when it is in such condition that it is no longer a fitting emblem for display, should be destroyed in a dignified way, preferably by burning."

[7] Sometimes, however, ritualistic burnings of damaged flags are held as part of patriotic celebrations. *See, e.g.,* Keisha Stewart, *An Extra-Special Fourth of July,* ROANOKE TIMES, July 5, 2002, at B1, B6.

[8] This test was first enunciated in *Spence v. Washington,* 418 U.S. 405, 410-11 (1974), but was refined significantly in *Texas v. Johnson,* 491 U.S. 397, 404-06 (1989).

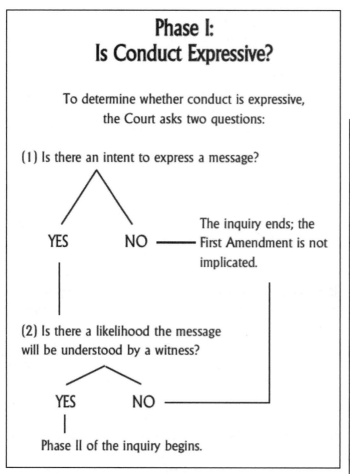

Phase I:
Is Conduct Expressive?

To determine whether conduct is expressive,
the Court asks two questions:

(1) Is there an intent to express a message?

YES   NO — The inquiry ends; the
First Amendment is not
implicated.

(2) Is there a likelihood the message
will be understood by a witness?

YES   NO

Phase II of the inquiry begins.

Figure 1

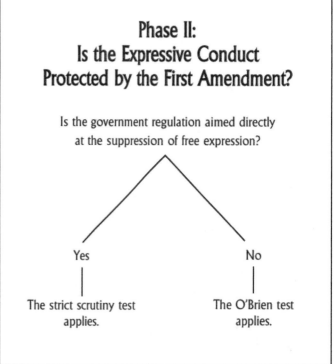

Phase II:
Is the Expressive Conduct
Protected by the First Amendment?

Is the government regulation aimed directly
at the suppression of free expression?

Yes   No

The strict scrutiny test   The O'Brien test
applies.   applies.

Figure 2

volvement in Vietnam was expressive conduct, but ruled that other concerns outweighed David Paul O'Brien's right to burn the card.[11] In *O'Brien,* the Court, for the first time, delineated the test for determining whether expressive conduct is protected by the First Amendment.

Is the Expressive Conduct Protected?

At first glance, O'Brien's burning of his draft card is remarkably similar to Johnson's burning of a U.S. flag. Both men had audiences, both were expressing distaste with political agendas, and both were using an age-old method of destruction to demonstrate that distaste. In both cases, there was an intent to express a message, and there was a likelihood that the message would be understood by witnesses.

But the Court found significant differences in the two acts. Ironically, the differences were based primarily upon the intent of the government rather than the intent of the actors.

After the Court finds conduct to be expressive, it determines whether the conduct may be regulated by examining the rationale behind the government regulation being applied. The Court must determine whether the regulation is directed at the suppression of speech or at some other goal. If the purpose of the regulation is to restrict speech, the Court applies what it calls a

ture of this conduct was both intentional and overwhelmingly apparent."[9]

The Court has recognized a wide array of conduct to be expressive: burning a cross, nude dancing, displaying a license plate, burning a draft card, saluting a flag, displaying a flag.[10]

Not all these activities, however, are constitutionally protected. Once an action has been determined to be expressive, the Court must determine whether the First Amendment protects the expressive conduct. Cases involving expressive conduct date to the early twentieth century, but the Court's first substantive treatment of it was in 1968. In *United States v. O'Brien,* the Court recognized that burning a draft card as a means of protesting the Selective Service system and U.S. in-

---

[9] 491 U.S. at 406.

[10] *See* Virginia v. Black, 538 U.S. 343 (2003) (cross burning, in many instances, is intimidating speech); Barnes v. Glen Theatre, 501 U.S. 560 (1991) (nude dancing, though expressive, may be regulated); Wooley v. Maynard, 430 U.S. 705 (1977) (a person cannot be forced to display a license plate that contains an ideological message with which the person disagrees); United States v. O'Brien, 391 U.S. 367 (1968) (burning of draft card is not constitutionally protected); West Virginia Bd. of Educ. v. Barnette, 319 U.S. 624 (1943) (students cannot be forced to salute the flag); Stromberg v. California, 283 U.S. 359 (1931) (a regulation prohibiting the display of a red flag is not constitutional).

---

[11] 391 U.S. 367 (1968).

"strict scrutiny test" to determine whether the regulation is constitutional; if the regulation is not directed at the suppression of speech, but at some other goal, the Court applies a test of intermediate scrutiny. Figure 2 demonstrates the flow of this inquiry.

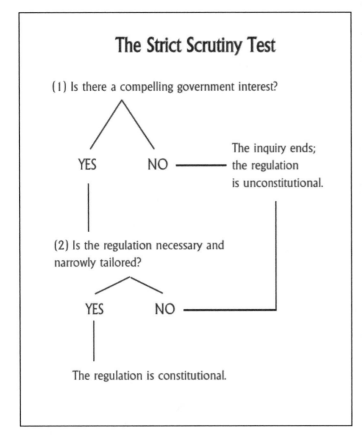

The Strict Scrutiny Test

(1) Is there a compelling government interest?

YES   NO ——— The inquiry ends; the regulation is unconstitutional.

(2) Is the regulation necessary and narrowly tailored?

YES   NO ———

The regulation is constitutional.

Figure 3

Strict Scrutiny. Attorneys for Texas argued to the Texas and U.S. supreme courts that the state's purpose in adopting its flag desecration act was to protect the U.S. flag as a symbol of patriotism and unity. And, the attorneys argued, the state had the right to do so. The Supreme Court agreed that protecting the flag is a noble cause. The method used to protect the flag, however, was directed at the suppression of free speech; the statute would allow expression supporting the state's goals, but would not allow expression contrary to those goals. Because the statute was directly related to the suppression of speech, therefore, strict scrutiny was required to determine whether the statute was constitutional. Figure 3 demonstrates the flow of the strict scrutiny test, which requires the resolution of two questions:

• *Is there a compelling government interest for the regulation?* The government interest advocated by the regulation must be more than a passing interest; it must be vitally important to governmental operations. In *Texas v. Johnson,* Justice Brennan recognized that there may be a compelling government interest

in protecting the flag as a symbol of national unity. National unity is important, Justice Brennan wrote, and the flag may be the single best symbol of the United States and that unity.

• *Is the regulation necessary and narrowly tailored to advance the government interest?* A necessary regulation is one that is essential, rather than optional, for the advancement of the government's interest. To survive strict scrutiny, a regulation must be necessary; but it must also be narrowly tailored. Being narrowly tailored means that the regulation goes as far as necessary to advance the government interest but does not overstep its bounds. In the area of speech, a narrowly tailored regulation is one that does not encompass protected speech in its prohibitions. Justice Brennan said the Texas act was not narrowly tailored. Even though protecting the flag is a compelling government interest, an individual's right to criticize the government is powerful. The government may promote the flag, Brennan wrote, but may not control messages critical of the government simply because the flag is the medium of that criticism. "If there is a bedrock principle underlying the First Amendment," he wrote, "it is that the government may not prohibit the expression of an idea simply because society finds the idea itself offensive or disagreeable."[12]

Intermediate Scrutiny: The O'Brien Test. The Court came to a different conclusion in *United States v. O'Brien.*

When David Paul O'Brien burned his draft card, he was, like Johnson, voicing his discontent with government policy, specifically, with Selective Service. At the time, federal law required all men in the United States who were eighteen or older to carry draft cards until they surrendered them to government officials upon induction into the armed forces or until they were no longer eligible for the draft.

O'Brien did not deny burning his draft card but contended that the law prohibiting the destruction or mutilation of the card was unconstitutional because it inhibited free speech and served no legitimate legislative purpose. A federal district court in Massachusetts found him guilty of violating the law. The First U.S. Circuit Court of Appeals found the statute unconstitutional but affirmed the conviction on grounds that O'Brien should have been convicted of the less serious offense of not having possession of the draft card.[13] Both the government and O'Brien appealed to the Supreme Court.

Chief Justice Earl Warren, writing for a seven-member majority, did not dispute O'Brien's contention that the burning of a draft card was expressive conduct. Instead, based upon the assumption that the conduct was sufficient to implicate the First Amendment, he took issue with O'Brien's argument that free-

---

[12] Texas v. Johnson, 491 U.S. at 414.

[13] O'Brien v. United States, 376 F.2d 538 (1st Cir. 1967).

dom of expression includes all modes of "communication of ideas by conduct." Wrote Warren: "We cannot accept the view that an apparently limitless variety of conduct can be labeled 'speech' whenever the person engaging in the conduct intends thereby to express an idea." When speech and non-speech elements combine in some form of expression, Warren wrote, a sufficiently important governmental interest in regulating the non-speech element of the communication can justify incidental limitations of First Amendment freedoms.[14] Warren delineated a four-part test for determining when the government regulation is justified:[15]

• *Is the regulation within the constitutional power of the government?* The government has a right to raise and support armies, the Court noted, and to make all necessary and proper laws to that end; therefore, the Selective Service Act was within the power of the government.

• *Does the regulation further an important or substantial government interest?* Because the draft card and other Selective Service documents further the smooth and proper functioning of the system, Congress has a legitimate and substantial interest in preventing their wanton and unrestrained destruction and assuring their continuing availability by punishing people who knowingly and willfully destroy them.

• *Is the governmental interest unrelated to the suppression of free expression?* The non-destruction requirements of the law were aimed at the continued smooth operation of the Selective Service system, the Court held. That is, they were aimed at the non-communicative aspects of O'Brien's conduct and nothing else.

• *Is the incidental restriction of free expression no greater than is essential to the furtherance of the stated governmental interest?* The Court noted that the restriction O'Brien violated was narrowly drawn.

O'Brien's conviction was upheld, therefore. More importantly, however, the Court established a test to be applied in cases involving expressive conduct. The flow of the O'Brien Test is demonstrated in Figure 4.

Flag Burning Revisited

Members of Congress — and of a number of state legislatures — were not happy with the Court's ruling in *Texas v. Johnson* and a follow-up case a year later.[16] Legislators began seeking ways to circumvent the Court's ruling, and those efforts continue.

Indeed, in 2006, Congress came as close as it has ever come of

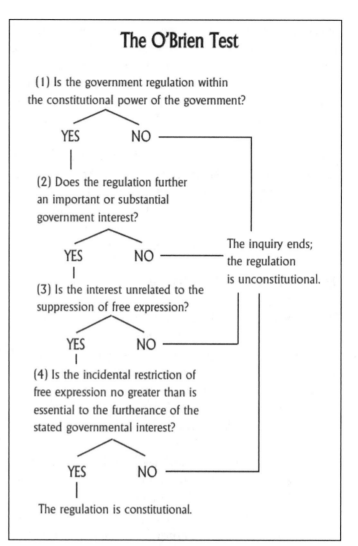

The O'Brien Test

(1) Is the government regulation within the constitutional power of the government?

YES / NO — The inquiry ends; the regulation is unconstitutional.

(2) Does the regulation further an important or substantial government interest?

YES / NO — The inquiry ends; the regulation is unconstitutional.

(3) Is the interest unrelated to the suppression of free expression?

YES / NO — The inquiry ends; the regulation is unconstitutional.

(4) Is the incidental restriction of free expression no greater than is essential to the furtherance of the stated governmental interest?

YES / NO — The inquiry ends; the regulation is unconstitutional.

The regulation is constitutional.

Figure 4

clearing the first hurdle in amending the Constitution to prevent flag desecration. The Senate came one vote short of approving a constitutional amendment that had already been approved by the House of Representatives.[17] The House, for the sixth time since *Texas v. Johnson,* approved a proposed constitutional amendment by a vote of 286-130, well beyond the two-thirds vote required before an amendment can be submitted to the states for consideration.[18] An amendment must be approved by a two-thirds vote in each house of Congress, however, and a Senate vote had never surpassed that margin.

In 1990, fifty-eight senators voted in favor of the amendment, and in 2001 sixty-three did so.[19] Some observers of Congress be-

---

[14] 391 U.S. at 376-77.

[15] *Id.* at 377-82.

[16] United States v. Eichman, 496 U.S. 310 (1990).

[17] *See* Carl Hulse, *Flag Amendment Narrowly Fails in Senate Vote,* N.Y. TIMES, June 28, 2006, at 1A.

[18] H.J. Res. 10, 109th Cong. (2005). The earlier votes came in 1995, 1997, 1999, 2001 and 2003.

[19] *See* Phillip Taylor, *House Approves Flag Amendment for Fourth Time in 6 Years,* FREEDOM FORUM ONLINE (July 18, 2002), http://www.freedomforum.org.

lieved that the Senate would approve the measure in 2006, and were nearly correct. In June, the Senate voted 66-34 in favor of the amendment, one vote shy of the 67 votes needed to achieve a two-thirds majority. The proposed amendment also failed in 2007, but the House keeps trying. Early in 2009, two other resolutions were introduced in the House and were referred to committee.[20]

Ironically, all this activity is apparently taking place absent a strong mandate from the citizenry. A poll the Freedom Forum released in 2005 indicated that 63 percent of the respondents opposed such a constitutional amendment, up from 53 percent in 2004. Only 35 percent of the respondents favored the amendment — down from 45 percent a year earlier.[21]

The Strange Case of Nude Dancing

Dancing, most people will agree, is a form of expression, at least in those contexts in which professionals perform for audiences. And it would seem just as obvious that whether a professional dances with or without clothing is irrelevant to whether the dancer is attempting to express a message, and the message is apparent to an observer. The Supreme Court, however, has reached such conclusions begrudgingly and remains unwilling to grant constitutional protection to nude dancing.

The Court most recently faced the issue in 2000 in *Erie v. Pap's A.M.*[22] The case began when the operator of a nightclub featuring nude dancing challenged an Erie, Pennsylvania, ordinance that prohibited public nudity. The nightclub owner claimed that the ordinance infringed his First Amendment free expression rights by prohibiting expressive conduct in the form of nude dancing. The Pennsylvania Supreme Court agreed,[23] but the U.S. Supreme Court overturned that opinion, ruling that the ordinance was constitutional. The Court was splintered in its rationale, however.

Writing for four justices, Sandra Day O'Connor found that, since the ordinance prohibited all nudity, not just nude dancing, it was not a content-based restriction and was constitutional under the four-part O'Brien Test.[24] Justice O'Connor admitted that nude dancing is expressive conduct — though "it falls only

within the outer ambit of the First Amendment's protection."[25] The two justices who concurred in the judgment, thereby allowing the ordinance to stand, were not willing to go that far. Antonin Scalia, joined by Clarence Thomas, wrote that nude dancing could be regulated as conduct, unless there was evidence that an ordinance aimed at the dancing was aimed specifically at the "communicative character" of the dancing rather than the nudity itself.[26]

Only Justices John Paul Stevens and Ruth Bader Ginsburg recognized that nude dancing is, indeed, expressive conduct, and regulations such as those enacted in Erie must face strict scrutiny. Discounting the Court's argument that the ban was aimed at the secondary effects of nude dancing — increased sex crimes, for example — Justice Stevens wrote that the Court held, for the first time, that such effects "may justify the total suppression of protected speech."[27]

What seems clear from the Court's opinion in *Erie* — as well as earlier nude dancing cases[28] — is that the justices are willing to allow certain types of expressive conduct to be regulated, not because the conduct is not expressive, but because they don't like the message the conduct is communicating.

SPEECH AS CONDUCT

Before the discussion of conduct and speech is complete, two special cases must be addressed: threatening speech and picketing.

Threatening Speech

Thus far, this discussion has centered on conduct that takes on the role of speech, that is, conduct that is expressive. Another area of law with which the Court has wrestled is the regulation of speech that takes on additional characteristics, that is, when the speech takes on the role of conduct. This occurs with fighting words, threatening speech and intimidating speech.

Fighting words are words that are so vile or obnoxious that they are likely to prompt a physical reaction. For example, what might happen if, during a hotly contested football game between two bitter rivals — say the University of Virginia and Virginia Tech — a Tech fan wandered into the U.Va. student section wearing a sweatshirt that read "Fuck the Cavaliers"?

The result might seem obvious, and the example is not as far-fetched as it might first appear. In 1968, Paul Robert Cohen

---

[20] H.J.Res. 8, 11th Cong. (2009) was referred to the House Committee on the Judiciary, and H.J.Res. 47, 11th Cong. (2009) was referred to the House Subcommittee on the Constitution, Civil Rights and Civil Liberties. Both bills would amend the Constitution to give Congress the power to prohibit the desecration of the U.S. flag.

[21] Press Release, First Amendment Center, 63% Oppose Flag-Burning Amendment, New Survey Shows (June 10, 2005), *available at* http://www.firstamendmentcenter.org.

[22] 529 U.S. 277 (2000).

[23] Pap's A.M. v. Erie, 719 A.2d 273 (Pa. 1998).

[24] 529 U.S. at 296-97 (plurality opinion).

[25] *Id.* at 289 (citing Barnes v. Glen Theatre, 501 U.S. 560, 565-66 (1991)) (plurality opinion).

[26] *Id.* at 310 (Scalia, J., concurring in judgment).

[27] *Id.* at 317-18 (Stevens, J., dissenting).

[28] *See, e.g.,* Barnes v. Glen Theatre, 501 U.S. 560 (1991); Renton v. Playtime Theatres, 475 U.S. 41 (1986).

walked into the Los Angeles County Courthouse wearing a jacket bearing the slogan "Fuck the draft." He was arrested and convicted of violating that portion of the California Penal Code that prohibited maliciously and willfully disturbing the peace or quiet of any neighborhood or person by offensive conduct.

The Supreme Court, however, found that the conduct was speech and was protected.[29] Three justices disagreed. Harry Blackmun, Warren Burger and Hugo Black argued, in a dissent drafted by Blackmun, that "Cohen's absurd and immature antic ... was mainly conduct and little speech."[30] They said Cohen should have found another way of expressing his opinion.

In the majority opinion, however, Justice John Marshall Harlan pointed out the importance of the emotive as well as the cognitive force of speech:

We cannot overlook the fact, because it is well illustrated by the episode involved here, that much linguistic expression serves a dual communicative function: it conveys not only ideas capable of relatively precise, detached explication, but otherwise inexpressible emotions as well. In fact, words are often chosen as much for their emotive as their cognitive force. We cannot sanction the view that the Constitution, while solicitous of the cognitive content of individual speech, has little or no regard for the emotive function which, practically speaking, may often be the more important element of the overall message sought to be communicated.[31]

Even though the Court found Cohen's "absurd and immature antic" to be protected speech, the antic demonstrates the type of speech that can take on the role of conduct: The words become like actions. A person willing to respond to the words with physical violence could have confronted either Cohen or the reckless Virginia Tech football fan.

The Court first recognized the so-called "fighting words" doctrine in 1942 in *Chaplinsky v. New Hampshire.*[32] A Jehovah's Witness was arrested for calling a police officer a "damned fascist" and a "God damned racketeer." The Court upheld the conviction, calling the verbal assault an attack of fighting words, that is, words "which by their very utterance inflict injury or tend to incite an immediate breach of the peace." Such utterances, the Court said, "are no essential part of any expression of ideas, and are of such slight social value as a step to truth that any benefit that may be derived from them is clearly outweighed by the social interests in order and morality."[33]

Not only must the words be particularly violent or obnoxious, they must be aimed directly at an individual for the fighting-words doctrine to apply, as the Court demonstrated seven years later in *Terminiello v. Chicago.*[34] A well-publicized speech by a right-wing anti-Semite was met by a crowd of protesters, some of whom were able to break into the meeting hall where the speech was held. The speaker, Arthur Terminiello, repeatedly referred to the protesters as "scum" or "slimy scum." The speech so stirred members of the crowd that police indicated they feared unrest. Like Walter Chaplinsky, Terminiello was convicted of breaching the peace by using language that would stir the public to anger. In Terminiello's case, however, the Court reversed. Justice William O. Douglas, in one of his few free-speech majority opinions, wrote that free speech is designed to invoke dispute:

It may indeed best serve its high purpose when it induces a condition of unrest, creates dissatisfaction with conditions as they are, or even stirs people to anger. Speech is often provocative and challenging. It may strike at prejudices and preconceptions and have profound unsettling effects as it presses for acceptance of an idea. That is why freedom of speech, though not absolute ... is nevertheless protected against censorship or punishment, unless shown likely to produce a clear and present danger of a serious substantive evil that rises far above public inconvenience, annoyance, or unrest. There is no room under our Constitution for a more restrictive view.[35]

What's the difference in the two cases? *Terminiello* did not involve a face-to-face confrontation. In an important lower court case, the Illinois Supreme Court upheld the rights of neo-Nazis to march in Skokie, Illinois, displaying the swastika, which an appellate court ordered removed because of the fighting-words doctrine.[36] The state supreme court recognized, however, that the march removed the speech from that one-on-one dialogue to a more abstract insult. Ironically, after winning the right to march in Skokie, the neo-Nazis never did.

The confrontational nature of language has been important to the Supreme Court as well. The Court has consistently struck down as vague and overbroad state laws prohibiting the use of abusive, menacing, insulting or profane language, if those statutes had not been narrowed by state courts to focus on fighting words.[37] Though the Court has upheld convictions for the use of abusive language when there was a threat of a riot, the threat

---

[29] Cohen v. California, 403 U.S. 15 (1971).

[30] *Id.* at 27 (Blackmun, J., dissenting).

[31] *Id.* at 25.

[32] 315 U.S. 568 (1942).

[33] *Id.* at 571.

[34] 337 U.S. 1 (1949).

[35] *Id.* at 4.

[36] Vill. of Skokie v. Nat'l Socialist Party of Am., 373 N.E.2d 21 (Ill. 1978).

[37] *See, e.g.,* Lewis v. New Orleans, 415 U.S. 130 (1974); Plummer v. City of Columbus, Ohio, 414 U.S. 2 (1973); Gooding v. Wilson, 405 U.S. 518 (1972).

must be relatively direct. A speaker's shout that "We'll take the fucking streets," for example, was found not to be fighting words, nor did it tend to incite a riot, because the speaker was obviously not referring to an imminent action, but, rather, to some possible future action.[38]

The Court has faced few fighting words cases, but did so in 1992. In *R.A.V. v. St. Paul*,[39] it held that a conviction for burning a cross in the yard of an African-American couple who had moved into a predominantly white neighborhood could not stand under the fighting-words doctrine. The cross that the juvenile burned didn't cause much of a fire — it was made from broken chair legs — but the Minnesota Supreme Court said the act amounted to fighting words. It upheld the conviction for violating a city ordinance prohibiting the burning of a cross, the placing of a Nazi swastika, or other similar action for the purpose of arousing anger, alarm or resentment "on the basis of race, color, creed, religion or gender."

The Supreme Court reversed. It said St. Paul could prohibit fighting words but that the ordinance allowed fighting words unless they were aimed at a member of one of the classes specified. It would be acceptable under the ordinance, the Court said, to use fighting words against someone based on political affiliation, union or non-union membership or sexual preference: "The First Amendment does not permit St. Paul to impose special prohibitions on those speakers who express views on disfavored subjects."[40] The Court recognized that the conduct was reprehensible but ruled that the subject was being unconstitutionally punished under an ordinance that advanced what amounted to viewpoint discrimination.

Revisiting the issue of cross burning during its 2002-03 term, the Supreme Court carved out a new category of speech that is not protected by the First Amendment — intimidation. In *Virginia v. Black*,[41] it held that when cross burning achieves the status of intimidating speech, it can be proscribed and punished, but the Court also held that not all instances of cross burning are intimidating. It found a Virginia state law to be unconstitutional because, in addition to banning cross burning that is designed to intimidate "any person or group," the law stated that the act of burning a cross was *prima facie* evidence of an intent to intimidate. The clause making cross burning automatically intimidating, the Court held, also made the law unconstitutional.[42] While cross burning can be "a particularly virulent

form of intimidation,"[43] Justice Sandra Day O'Connor wrote for the majority, and it always can be considered "a symbol of hate," it has also been used to communicate "messages of shared ideology."[44] Therefore, to be proscribed, cross burning must cross the line from being a symbol representing some ideology, celebration or ritual and must become intimidating.

The Court had previously indicated that, in addition to fighting words, speech that constituted what it called a "true threat" could be proscribed.[45] Some scholars and advocates had argued that cross burning constituted threatening speech. The Court in *Virginia v. Black* agreed and held that intimidating speech as a type of threat could be proscribed and punished. Wrote Justice O'Connor: "Intimidation in the constitutionally proscribable sense of the word is a type of true threat, where a speaker directs a threat to a person or group of persons with the intent of placing the victim in fear of bodily harm or death."[46]

The Court did not elaborate on what kinds of speech might be intimidating, what the distinctions are between intimidating speech and true threats or how lower courts can make such determinations. But that is the way of the Court. Because it only answers questions put to it, the process of establishing tests can be long and arduous. The Court, for example, held in 1957 that the First Amendment does not protect obscenity, but it was 1973 before a majority of the Court agreed upon a test for obscenity.[47] The Court has taken similar paths in the area of expressive conduct[48] and commercial speech.[49]

It may be years, however, before the Court develops a test for determining when speech in general and cross burning in particular become intimidating. Indeed the Court has already turned down one request to expand the scope of so-called intimidating speech. The Seventh U.S. Circuit Court of Appeals cited *Virginia v. Black* in denying First Amendment protection to a prison inmate's statements that he planned to bomb a federal office building in Milwaukee.[50] The court, however, rather

---

the burning of an object automatically *prima facie* evidence of an intent to intimidate, however. VA. CODE ANN. 18.2-423.01 (2002).

[43] 538 U.S. at 363.

[44] *Id.* at 356-57.

[45] *See* Watts v. United States, 394 U.S. 705, 707 (1969).

[46] 538 U.S. at 360.

[47] The Court held that obscene material lies outside the protection of the First Amendment in *Roth v. United States,* 354 U.S. 476 (1957) and established the test of obscenity in *Miller v. California,* 413 U.S. 15 (1973). *See* the discussion of obscenity in Chapter 5.

[48] *See* the cases cited in footnote 10.

[49] The Court held that commercial speech is protected by the First Amendment in *Bigelow v. Virginia,* 421 U.S. 809 (1975) and *Virginia State Board of Pharmacy v. Virginia Citizens Consumer Council,* 425 U.S. 748 (1976), and established a test to determine when commercial speech may be regulated in *Central Hudson Gas & Electric Co. v. Public Service Commission of New York,* 447 U.S. 557 (1980). *See* the discussion of commercial speech in Chapter 8.

[50] United States v. Parr, 545 F.3d 491, 499-500 (7th Cir. 2009).

---

[38] Hess v. Indiana, 414 U.S. 105, 107 (1973). *Compare with,* Feiner v. New York, 340 U.S. 315 (1951) (finding that speech constituted a clear and present danger of unrest).

[39] 505 U.S. 377 (1992).

[40] *Id.* at 391.

[41] 538 U.S. 343 (2003).

[42] The unconstitutional law remains on the books in Virginia, VA. CODE ANN. 18.2-423 (1950), but Virginia has also made it illegal to burn any object, either on public or private property, with the intent of intimidating someone. The law does not make

than recognizing that Justice O'Connor was recasting intimidating speech as unprotected, reported that she had established a new definition of "true threats."[51] It rejected the government's argument that the inmate's discussion of a potential bombing of a federal building was either a true threat or intimidating speech under *Virginia v. Black*, and the Supreme Court refused to hear the case.[52]

Picketing

The Court has recognized that picketing is a time-honored method of expressing a message. People who cannot afford to publish their complaints often use it, and it is generally aimed at a narrow problem. Therefore, the Court has granted picketers broad protection, still balancing their rights against those of other individuals and against public peace and safety. It has held that peaceful picketing cannot be licensed, that restrictions on picketing must be content-neutral and that picketing cannot be banned from public property.

One of the Court's most important rulings on picketing came near the middle of the twentieth century. In striking down Alabama's statute prohibiting picketing a place of business, the Court noted that freedom of speech and press "are among the fundamental personal rights and liberties which are secured to all persons" by the Constitution and that picketing is one of the activities that "may enlighten the public on the nature and causes" of public debate.[53]

The rights of individuals to picket or distribute information often depend upon where the picketing occurs and the rationale behind government regulations restricting the picketing. Picketing in an area designated a public forum — like a park or sidewalk — is almost always protected, if the picketing is peaceful and if it does not interfere with other valid uses of the public forum.[54] Even in the absence of a public forum, the Court has held that absolute bans on First Amendment activity — including picketing — may be unconstitutional because the government cannot justify such bans.[55]

The Court reaffirmed the constitutional protections for picketing on public property in 2011. *Snyder v. Phelps*[56] involved intentional infliction of emotional distress, but the Court did not decide the case on that issue. Instead, it held that members of the Westboro Baptist Church had a constitutional right to protest at the funeral of a serviceman killed in the line of duty because their speech involved matters of public concern and because the protest took place on public property. "Simply put," Chief Justice John Roberts wrote for the Court, "the church members had the right to be where they were."[57] Under the Court's ruling, the right to picket on public property trumped the right of a private person to be free from verbal attacks that cause severe emotional distress.[58]

The Court, however, let stand a ruling that limited picketing activities near Saint John's Church in the Wilderness, in Denver. The church was successful in seeking an injunction that prohibited anti-abortion picketing that inhibited worship services.[59] In addition to their shouting, picketers displayed placards that contained pictures of aborted fetuses. The Colorado Court of Appeals distinguished the case from *Snyder* because, the court found, the disturbance caused by the picketers interfered with the church's worship services. The court upheld most of the restrictions, and the Supreme Court denied certiorari.[60]

The Court also took action in June 2013 to protect its own grounds from public expressive displays. Two days after a federal judge struck down the restrictions as being counter to the First Amendment,[61] the Marshal of the Court, with the approval of Chief Justice Roberts, instituted a restriction to "maintain suitable order and decorum" on the Court grounds.[62] In 2015, a federal circuit court reversed the ruling of the district court and held that the restrictions on picketing are constitutional because they apply to the Court's plaza, not the adjacent sidewalks.[63] The court upheld the restrictions in order to maintain a tranquil environment around the Supreme Court building and to preserve the appearance of a judiciary immune to public pressure.[64]

The restriction against picketing does not apply to the public sidewalks around the Court building, but only to the courthouse plaza. The Supreme Court has held that restrictions on picketing on the public sidewalks are unconstitutional.[65]

A year later, the Court also upheld restrictions on picketing that the U.S. Secret Service said were required to protect the president. During President George Bush's campaign for a second term, Secret Service agents made arrangements to allow

---

[51] *Id.* at 499.

[52] Parr v. United States, 556 U.S. 1181 (2009) (denying certiorari).

[53] Thornhill v. Alabama, 310 U.S. 88, 95 & 104 (1940).

[54] *See, e.g.,* Bachellor v. Maryland, 397 U.S. 564 (1970); Gregory v. Chicago, 394 U.S. 111 (1969); Cox v. Louisiana, 379 U.S. 536 & 559 (1965); Henry v. Rock Hill, 376 U.S. 776 (1964).

[55] *See* Bd. of Airport Comm'rs v. Jews for Jesus, 482 U.S. 569 (1987).

[56] 562 U.S. 443 (2011).

[57] *Id.* at 457.

[58] *See* W. Wat Hopkins, Snyder v. Phelps *and the Unfortunate Death of Intentional Infliction of Emotional Distress as a Speech-Based Tort,* 3 J. OF MEDIA LAW & ETHICS 1 (2012).

[59] Saint John's Church in the Wilderness v. Scott, 296 P.3d 273 (Colo. App. 2012).

[60] Scott v. Saint John's Church in the Wilderness, 133 S.Ct. 2798 (2013), *denying cert.*

[61] Hodge v. Talkin, 949 F. Supp. 2d 152 (D.D.C. 2013).

[62] Regulation Seven (June 13, 2013), http://www.supremecourt.gov/publicinfo/buildingregulations.aspx.

[63] Hodge v. Talkin, 799 F.3d 1145 (D.C.Cir. 2015).

[64] *Id.* at 1163.

[65] United States v. Grace, 461 U.S. 171 (1983).

both supporters and opponents of the president to have an equal opportunity to picket in Jacksonville, Oregon. When the president made a sudden change in his plans, however, the Secret Service was required to alter the placement of his opponents. The new position put them outside the view of the president, and they claimed a viewpoint-based First Amendment violation. Justice Ruth Bader Ginsburg, for a unanimous court, wrote that in the absence of any decision by the Court or other "clearly established law," there was no liability on the part of the Secret Service for its on-the-spot action.[66]

Picketing on private property is more problematic. Often, however, even the private property rights of individuals and corporations must give way when individuals choose to express themselves by picketing. While the Court has recognized that owners have certain rights over their property, when the property is used for a public purpose and when it's obvious that the picketers are expressing their own viewpoints and are not speaking for the property owners, the Court has allowed picketing on private property.[67]

It has also held that towns may not restrict access to private homes to disseminate information. The Village of Stratton prohibited persons from distributing information door-to-door without first receiving a "Solicitation Permit." Apparently the issuance of the permit was *pro forma*, but the Jehovah's Witnesses of New York complained that the process of applying for the permit infringed their First Amendment rights. The Court agreed, ruling in 2002 that persons engaging in door-to-door advocacy could not be required to identify themselves through an application and permit procedure.[68]

The Court, however, has also allowed some picketing to be restricted, including in shopping malls and at private residences. And it allowed the military to restrict picketing and the distribution of literature on military bases — even those portions of the bases open to the public.[69]

Finally, the Court has balanced the free-speech rights of persons who picket abortion clinics with the rights of women who want abortions to have free access to the clinics. The Court has upheld the use of zones in which picketing could be banned but held that 300-foot buffer zones were unreasonable and burdened more speech than necessary to serve the government's interest in guaranteeing the free flow of traffic.[70] It also held that a so-

called "floating buffer zone" requiring picketers to stay at least fifteen feet from people or vehicles entering or leaving the clinics violated the First Amendment because it overburdened speech.[71] In its most recent term, the Court continued that balancing approach. In *McCullen v. Coakley*,[72] it struck down as overbroad a thirty-five-foot buffer zone around abortion clinics from which individuals were categorically excluded unless they were traveling through those zones to reach an abortion clinic or some other establishment. The Court ruled that the law establishing the zone failed the intermediate scrutiny test and unconstitutionally restricted the speech rights of persons who wanted to communicate with potential patients.[73]

In a related matter, the Court held in 2003 that a First Amendment challenge to a law prohibiting trespassing could not stand absent a showing that freedom of speech was being inhibited.[74] The case began when the city of Richmond and the Richmond Redevelopment and Housing Authority devised a plan to help reduce unwanted traffic in Whitcomb Court, a low-income housing project. The town gave to the housing authority the streets within and adjacent to the project, thereby closing those streets to public use. The housing authority then developed a set of rules governing foot traffic on those streets and authorized the Richmond Police Department to enforce the new trespass laws.[75]

Kevin Lamont Hicks was convicted of violating the trespassing law and appealed his conviction on grounds that his First Amendment rights had been violated.[76] He won before the Virginia Court of Appeals and the Virginia Supreme Court,[77] but the U.S. Supreme Court disagreed. The Virginia Supreme Court held that the law gave too much discretion to the manager of the housing project who, the court said, had "the unfettered discretion to determine not only who has a right to speak on the Housing Authority's property," but may also prohibit speech "she finds personally distasteful or offensive even though such speech may be protected by the First Amendment."[78]

The Supreme Court, however, held that the manager's discretion in allowing or prohibiting speech within Whitcomb Court was irrelevant, because there was no evidence that Hicks was attempting to speak. He had been barred from returning to the housing project, the Court noted, and, therefore, his challenge related solely to the rule that those barred could not reenter. He did not show and did not attempt to show that his banishment

---

[66] Wood v. Moss, 134 S.Ct. 2056 (2014).

[67] *See, e.g.,* Pruneyard Shopping Ctr. v. Robins, 447 U.S. 74 (1974); Lloyd Corp., Ltd. v. Tanner, 407 U.S. 551 (1972); Amalgamated Food Employees Union v. Logan Valley Plaza, Inc., 391 U.S. 308 (1968).

[68] Watchtower Bible and Tract Soc'y of New York v. Vill. of Stratton, 536 U.S. 150 (2002).

[69] *See, e.g.,* Greer v. Spock, 424 U.S. 828 (1976). *But see also,* United States v. Albertini, 472 U.S. 675 (1985); Flower v. United States, 407 U.S. 197 (1972).

[70] *See* Madsen v. Women's Health Clinic, Inc., 512 U.S. 753 (1994).

[71] Schenck v. Pro-Choice Network of Western New York, 519 U.S. 357 (1997).

[72] 134 S.Ct. 2518 (2014)

[73] *Id.* at 2540-41.

[74] Virginia v. Hicks, 539 U.S. 113 (2003).

[75] Hicks v. Commonwealth, 548 S.E.2d 249, 251-52 (Va. App. 2001).

[76] *Id.* at 252.

[77] Commonwealth v. Hicks, 563 S.E.2d 674 (Va. 2002).

[78] *Id.* at 681.

was related to speech.[79]

License Plates and Symbolic Speech

The Supreme Court determined Paul Robert Cohen's display of words to be a form of conduct. Similarly, other courts have determined the obscuring of words also to be a form of conduct.

In 1974, George Maynard, a Jehovah's Witness living in New Hampshire, was charged under state law with obscuring the words "Live Free or Die" on his license plate. Maynard said he found the slogan violated his faith, and, therefore, he objected to being forced to advocate that message.[80] A federal three-judge district court found Maynard's action to be symbolic speech. The Supreme Court, however, did not resolve the symbolic speech question, finding that Maynard could not be required by the government to advocate a message with which he disagreed.[81]

Speech by means of license plate returned to the Supreme Court — in a different context — in its 2015 term.

When the Texas Division of the Sons of Confederate Veterans was refused its request for a specialty license plate displaying the Confederate Battle Flag, it filed suit claiming its First Amendment free speech rights had been violated.[82] Members of the group argued that the license plate would constitute private speech — the speech of those who purchased and displayed it — and the refusal by the state amounted to constitutionally forbidden viewpoint discrimination.[83] The Court, however, ruled that the issuance of specialty license plates constituted government speech and ruled for the state. "When government speaks, it is not barred by the Free Speech Clause from determining the content of what it says,"[84] the Court held in a 5-4 opinion.

The cases are very different. One involves speech a private individual is required — or not required — to display. The other involves the murky area of government speech. They demonstrate, however, the continuing complexity of the issue of speech as conduct.

SUMMARY

The speech/conduct conundrum consists of parallel issues: conduct that takes on the role of speech and speech that takes on the role of conduct.

Based on *United States v. O'Brien, Texas v. Johnson* and other Supreme Court cases, the Court has established a care-

fully delineated course in dealing with expressive conduct. That course is described in Figure 5.

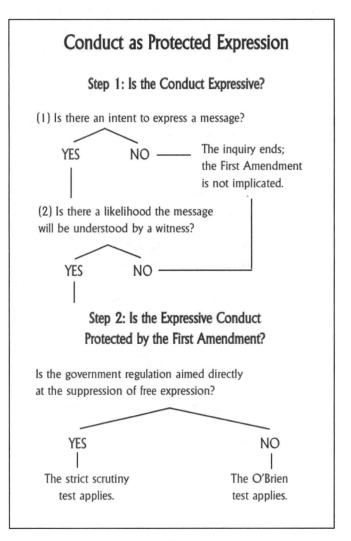

Figure 5

In traveling that course, the Court must answer some specific questions.

Is the conduct expressive? The conduct is expressive if there is an intent to express a message and if there is a likelihood the message will be understood. If there is either no intent or no likelihood of understanding, the conduct is not expressive, the First Amendment is not implicated, and the inquiry is over. If the conduct is expressive, however, the inquiry continues.

Is the expressive conduct protected? The path to determining whether conduct is protected begins with the rationale behind the government regulation. The Court first determines whether the regulation is aimed directly at speech. If it is, the Court applies a strict scrutiny test by asking two questions: (1) Does the regulation advance a compelling government interest? and (2) Is the regulation necessary and narrowly tailored? If the answer to either question is no, the regulation is unconstitutional. If the

[79] 539 U.S. at 118-19.

[80] Wooley v. Maynard, 430 U.S. 705, 707-08 (1977).

[81] *Id.* at 713.

[82] Walker v. Texas Division, Sons of Confederate Veterans, 135 S.Ct. 2239 (2015).

[83] *Id.* at 2245.

[84] *Id.*

answer to both questions is yes, the regulation is constitutional.

If the Court finds that the regulation is not aimed specifically at speech, it applies a test of intermediate scrutiny, called the "O'Brien Test," to determine whether the regulation is constitutional. Under the test, a regulation is required to meet four points: (1) The activity regulated must be within the constitutional power of the government; (2) the regulation must advance an important government interest; (3) the government interest must be unrelated to the suppression of free expression; and (4) the incidental restriction on speech must be no greater than necessary to advance the government interest.

Just as conduct can take on the role of speech, speech can sometimes become like conduct. Words can be so vile or obnoxious that they prompt a physical response. Courts allow such words to be regulated but take care to ensure that governments don't trammel free expression in their efforts to protect other individual rights. Statutes prohibiting offensive or abusive language, for example, have routinely been held to be unconstitutional unless they have been narrowed so they only prohibit fighting words. In addition, the Supreme Court has ruled that intimidation is a category of what it calls "true threats" and may be banned.

Finally, courts have recognized the value of picketing and have allowed individuals to picket on both private and public property. Picketing in areas traditionally held to be a public fo-rum is almost always allowed. Picketing on private property is more problematic, but the Supreme Court has often allowed such picketing.

FOR ADDITIONAL READING

Belmas, Genelle I. "Pushing Patriotism: Why Flag Encouragement Doesn't Fly," 14 *Communication Law and Policy* 341 (2009).

Goldstein, R.J. *Saving "Old Glory": The History of the American Flag Desecration Controversy.* Boulder, Colo.: Westview Press, 1996.

Haiman, Franklyn S. *Speech and Law in a Free Society.* Chicago: University of Chicago Press, 1981.

Hopkins, W. Wat. "Cross Burning Revisited: What the Supreme Court Should Have Done in *Virginia v. Black* and Why it Didn't," 26 *Hastings Communication and Entertainment Law Journal (COMM/ENT)* 269 (2004).

Katsh, M. Ethan, ed. *Taking Sides — Clashing Views of Controversial Legal Issues.* Guilford, Conn.: Dushkin, 1995.

Russomanno, Joseph. *Defending the First.* Mahwah, N.J.: Lawrence Erlbaum Associates, 2005.

Smolla, Rodney A. *Free Speech in an Open Society.* New York: Vintage, 1993.

4

Prior Restraint

By Steven Helle

➡ **Headnote Questions**

- What is the origin of the doctrine against prior restraint?
- Did the framers of the First Amendment intend for the amendment to ban only prior restraint, or did they intend something more?
- What are the characteristics of prior restraint, historically and currently?
- Why is a doctrine against prior restraint important?
- What are the critical principles that courts consider in applying the doctrine?

"Censorship" is a word casually used in editorials or angry speeches to denounce everything from postal rate increases, to obscenity prosecutions, to theft of campus newspapers. But the term meant something specific in historical usage, and it is rarely what writers or speakers mean today. Those who denounce contemporary attempts to control speech, however, are taking advantage of the considerable distaste that became associated with the historical form of censorship.

Therein lies the dilemma that runs throughout this chapter. The battles against the historical form of censorship have been won, and an extensive body of law seems to have extinguished the prospect of future censorship as long as the First Amendment retains any vitality. But is it advisable to expand the notion of censorship and the extent of protection available under the First Amendment in order to combat innovative forms of regulation that accomplish much the same thing as historical censorship? Or would stretching the First Amendment to offer the same degree of protection against more types of control ultimately dilute and weaken the protection, just as a balloon that expands becomes thinner — and more susceptible to breaking?

HISTORICAL BACKGROUND

Much of U.S. law has its roots in English law. England, of course, imposed its law on its American colonies. But even after the American Revolution, twelve of the thirteen states expressly adopted the common law of England as their own. Lawyers on this side of the Atlantic educated themselves primarily by reading Sir William Blackstone's *Commentaries on the Law of Eng-*

land. "In the first century of American independence, the *Commentaries* were not merely an approach to the study of law; for most lawyers they constituted all there was of the law," wrote Daniel J. Boorstin, librarian of Congress emeritus.[1] Because English law influenced not only U.S. law, but the framers of the U.S. Constitution as well, it is important to trace the English experience with censorship to better understand how and why U.S. law on the subject evolved the way it did.

Printing on a press was introduced to England in 1476, and not long afterward the Roman Catholic Church attempted to impose controls. It wanted to suppress what it considered heretical opinions. In 1501, Pope Alexander VI attempted to require printing to be licensed. In 1517, Martin Luther posted his *95 Theses* on the door of the Castle Church in Wittenberg, Germany, questioning the practice of contributing to the church as a means of buying forgiveness for sins. The Church burned the writings of Luther and others who questioned its authority, dismissed them from the Church, prohibited the faithful from reading their works and issued rebuttals. But the demand — and profit — for publishing the works only grew.

King Henry VIII

King Henry VIII of England, at the request of the Church, used this religious debate as the impetus for asserting the Crown's control over printing. Henry, in fact, secretly encouraged the reformers while publicly condemning them, even publishing his

---

[1] DANIEL J. BOORSTIN, THE MYSTERIOUS SCIENCE OF THE LAW 3 (1941).

own response to Luther. By appearing to lead the effort to defeat the heretics, he hoped to win the favor of Rome and the pope's blessing for his divorce from Queen Catherine.

When the clergy was unable to control the heretics' speech, Henry issued his first list of prohibited books in 1529, and several booksellers and others who possessed the banned books were executed. In 1530, he issued a proclamation establishing a licensing system, the first such system outside the Church. He decreed that no person could print any religious book until it was examined and approved by the clergy, and every printer would obey or "answere to the kinges highnes, at his uttermost peryll." Executions, fines and imprisonment followed. When Henry did not get the dispensation he desired from Rome, he switched sides and began executing the Catholic faithful.

As historian Fredrick Siebert noted, Henry was fully aware of the influence of the printing press in easing his break with Rome. He was an early and excellent master of manipulating public opinion by controlling the press, and he certainly had the tools and will to exercise that control to its fullest. "His policy henceforth was not only to eliminate undesirable reading matter but to stimulate the circulation of that which would strengthen his cause," Siebert wrote.[2]

Thus, the Proclamation of 1538 extended the king's censorship to all printing, not just religious writings, including "errors and seditious opinions." Sedition, or criticism of government, had no ecclesiastical foundation. The matter is muddled because Henry had made himself the head of the Church of England. Therefore, an attack on the church could be considered an attack on the state, or vice versa. But for the first time, speech that was expressly political was subject to censorship through a licensing system; and Henry's political appointees, not the Church, would decide what violated the regulations and deserved the king's displeasure. As Siebert noted: "The shift in the administration of the licensing regulations from the clergy to state officers was one of Henry's contributions to the regulation of the press. The method was subsequently adopted on the continent, even in Catholic countries."[3]

Henry also instituted the practice of requiring printers to post bonds, which would be forfeited if their publications offended him. He offered printers "privileges" — or copyrights — in certain works, which protected them from piracy. And the Tudor sovereigns who followed him engaged in a brilliant maneuver by recognizing a Stationer's Company, or organization of officially sanctioned printers. Just as broadcasters in this country did in the 1920s, these early printers actually sought government regulation. In the same way that the broadcasters favored by the U.S. government gained monopolies on the use of radio fre-

quencies, the favored English printers obtained monopolies on the printing of certain works, such as the Bible, which were very profitable.

But the monopolies served the interests of the government, as well, because the economic interests of the printers ensured that they would do nothing to alienate the government and risk losing their monopolies. Furthermore, the government gained an ally in controlling unlicensed printing. The members of the Stationer's Company were given broad powers of search and seizure to protect their monopolies from renegade printers. Their zealousness in exercising these powers led directly to the enactment of the Fourth Amendment to the U.S. Constitution, prohibiting unreasonable searches and seizures and requiring warrants based on probable cause.

Henry's licensing system endured until the close of the seventeenth century; and it was more or less successful, depending on how aggressively it was enforced or evaded at any given time. It took a brave printer to risk forfeiture of property, fines, imprisonment, torture, amputation and execution for flouting the system. The Stationer's Company sniffed out the trail of a press in 1589 that had been secretly moved all over England to avoid capture. John Hodgkins was finally arrested and charged with printing unlicensed Puritan tracts critical of the Church of England. He refused to confess, was tortured, jailed for a year and then put on the rack. There is no record of his fate after that.

Ingenious printers and authors attempted to circumvent the regulations — forging censors' signatures, changing manuscripts after they had been approved or writing ostensibly fictional dramas whose characters everybody understood to represent real people. But the stakes, depending on the political temper of the times and one's choice of patrons, could be high.

Parliament took control of the licensing system from the crown in 1643, but the structure of censorship remained essentially what it had been in 1538. Publication came to be subject to other forms of governmental regulation, primarily prosecutions for seditious libel and taxation, and the penalties associated with those forms of regulation could be just as severe. The licensing system was distinctive not only because it was first; but, because it applied to every publication, it gave the government complete discretion regarding the content of each publication, and it occurred in advance of publication. This latter feature indicates why this censorship was called "prior restraint."

Understandably, members of the Stationer's Company did not object to licensing (unless, as sometimes happened, some members obtained licenses that others did not). Objections came from those without licenses — and the philosophy and value of freedom of the press began to take shape. Two Puritans who wrote an unlicensed religious pamphlet in 1572 argued that they had presented the tract to Parliament and, in doing so,

---

[2] FREDRICK S. SIEBERT, FREEDOM OF THE PRESS IN ENGLAND, 1476-1776 47 (1965).

[3] *Id.* at 49.

they should have the privilege of "writing and speaking freely." This, according to Siebert, was the first time that the ancient right of Englishmen to petition Parliament was translated into an argument for a free press.[4] The pair, however, was sentenced to a year in prison.

Milton and Areopagitica

In 1644, John Milton presented in *Areopagitica,* which was itself unlicensed, what law professor Vincent Blasi has labeled the classic attack on prior restraint. Ironically, the impetus for this great treatise arose from Milton's having been cited for an earlier unlicensed tract on divorce, which was no easier for him to obtain than it had been for King Henry VIII. Milton framed his argument broadly:

> And though all the windes of doctrin were let loose to play upon the earth, so Truth be in the field, we do injuriously by licencing and prohibiting to misdoubt her strenth. Let her and Falshood grapple; who ever knew Truth put to the wors, in a free and open encounter.... [I]t is not possible for man to sever the wheat from the tares, the good fish from the other frie; that must be the Angels Ministery at the end of all mortall things. Yet if all cannot be of one mind, as who looks they should be? This doubtles is more wholsome, more prudent, and more Christian that many be tolerated, rather than all compell'd.[5]

Although it is an eloquent tribute to diverse expression without government suppression or endorsement of any one opinion, there is the view that Milton really was more interested in his divorce than in freedom of expression because he became a government censor just seven years after *Areopagitica.* In his defense, however, Professor Jeffrey Smith noted that Milton's role as censor primarily involved overseeing publication of the government's own newsletter — and, as censor, he had to recall his arguments from *Areopagitica* when he was questioned for approving a catechism that Parliament afterward condemned. Smith noted that, although Milton's arguments showed up in a few other tracts in his time, he probably had more impact in later centuries as philosophers, statesmen and jurists crafted libertarian theory.[6]

An abridged version of *Areopagitica* was published in 1693, but when the Licensing Act came up for renewal in 1694, the treatise apparently had no influence on the House of Commons'

decision to let the act lapse. A list of eighteen reasons for not renewing the act was presented in the House of Commons. The reasons, thought to be written by John Locke, had to do with the vagueness of the licensing standards, the impediments to free trade, the ineffectiveness of the system, and other objections unrelated to the philosophy of freedom of the press.

Under the two-party political system that had evolved, censors risked offending somebody important whether they licensed a publication or not. Important people did not want to undertake the task of censoring, and they did not trust unimportant people to do it. As Thomas Macaulay wrote in his *History of England* nearly two centuries later, "On the great question of principle, on the question whether the liberty of unlicensed printing be, on the whole, a blessing or a curse to society, not a word is said."[7] After more than a century and a half, licensing was dead in England.

The American Experience

Licensing continued in the American colonies until the 1720s. In 1723, the Massachusetts General Court (the colony's legislative body), stung by constant criticism from James Franklin, publisher of the *New England Courant,* ordered him never to publish the *Courant* or any other publication, "Except it be first Supervised, by the Secretary of this Province." Franklin published a new, unlicensed edition but identified his brother Benjamin as publisher. The General Court had not prohibited his soon-to-be-famous brother from publishing without a license.

James was eventually arrested, and the General Court sought an indictment from the grand jury, which historian Leonard Levy described as a mistake. The grand jury refused to indict, "probably motivated by a detestation of the licensing system which had ended a generation earlier in England.... Thus, Franklin went luckily free, and prior restraint of the press was at an end in Massachusetts," Levy wrote.[8]

Blackstone accurately summarized the law on both sides of the Atlantic when, in the late 1760s, he wrote in his *Commentaries* perhaps the most famous lines regarding the prior restraint doctrine:

> The *liberty of the press* is indeed essential to the nature of a

---

[4] *Id.* at 96.

[5] JOHN MILTON, AREOPAGITICA 74-76 (Eng. Rep. 1972) (1st ed. n.p. 1644).

[6] JEFFREY A. SMITH, PRINTERS AND PRESS FREEDOM — THE IDEOLOGY OF EARLY AMERICAN JOURNALISM 33-35, 40 (1988).

[7] 5 THOMAS B. MACAULAY, THE HISTORY OF ENGLAND FROM THE ACCESSION OF JAMES II 16-17 (1889). Macaulay observed that the event produced no excitement and was little noted, probably because Parliament was preoccupied with the funeral for Queen Mary. But the vote by the House of Commons not to renew the Licensing Act did "more for liberty and for civilisation than the Great Charter or the Bill of Rights." *Id.* at 15-16. The House of Lords did not object, probably because it assumed a different bill for regulating the press would be introduced — and, indeed, one was, but it did not clear committee before the session ended. Macaulay noted that "petty grievances did what Milton's *Areopagitica* failed to do."

[8] LEONARD W. LEVY, EMERGENCE OF A FREE PRESS 32 (1985).

free state; but this consists in laying no *previous* restraints upon publications, and not in freedom from censure for criminal matter when published. Every freeman has an undoubted right to lay what sentiments he pleases before the public: to forbid this is to destroy the freedom of the press: but if he publishes what is improper, mischievous, or illegal, he must take the consequences of his own temerity.[9]

Freedom from prior restraint seemed great when measured against the lack of any freedom at all just a few generations before. If subsequent punishment remained an option, that may only seem to be meager progress when viewed from the vantage point of today. But there were voices, even as Blackstone wrote, who argued that freedom *did* mean more, that subsequent punishments such as seditious libel prosecutions were also inconsistent with the notion of freedom of the press.

The Framers' Intent

What did the framers intend in 1791 — a little more than two decades after Blackstone's pronouncement — with the drafting of the First Amendment? Did they intend just to prohibit prior restraint, or did they mean to ban subsequent punishment as well? Professors Smith and Levy lead the opposing camps on this question. The arguments of Levy and the narrow constructionists — those who think the framers were only thinking of banning prior restraint — can be summarized this way:

• Blackstone's definition of the law was the notion of free speech and press commonly accepted at the time; so it must be what the framers were contemplating. If they were departing from the common understanding or common law of the time, they presumably would have said something.

• If the framers thought they were banning subsequent punishment such as seditious libel prosecutions, then how could many of those same members of Congress, just seven years later, enact the Alien and Sedition Acts of 1798 with the express intent of punishing people who criticized government?

• Prosecutions for seditious libel may have ended with the John Peter Zenger trial in 1735, but state legislatures brought citizens up on contempt charges for criticizing government at least twenty times after that date and before passage of the First Amendment, thus indicating endorsement of subsequent punishment as an alternative to prior restraint.

The broad constructionists, who think the First Amendment went beyond banning prior restraint, counter:

• Blackstone may have summarized the English common law that had been practiced up to his time, but he was not summa-

rizing U.S. law, and, indeed, why have a First Amendment at all if it was only intended to commemorate the common law supposedly already in place?

• The American experience with free press far exceeded the English common law. Not only were there no prosecutions for seditious libel after 1735 and no legislative contempt charges after independence in 1776, but politicians, printers and others exercised considerable freedom and espoused a distinctly libertarian theory of a free press in the century before the First Amendment. In short, how could there be so much freedom in practice if the law was so repressive?

• James Madison, author of the First Amendment, passionately proclaimed that the Sedition Act violated the First Amendment and criticized the Federalist party members of Congress for returning America to "ancient ignorance and barbarism." The act expired by its own terms three years later, which was also the time that Republican Thomas Jefferson became president and pardoned the twenty-five or so Republican printers and journalists convicted under the act. Thus, it can be argued that Congress, as it has demonstrated many times since, was not invoking constitutional principles in enacting the Sedition Act, but petty party politics.

• Why was a Sedition Act necessary if the common law already contemplated prosecution for seditious libel?

• Finally, the theme of the entire Constitution, not just the Bill of Rights, concerns limiting the power of government — in the words of Madison, "fortify[ing] the rights of the people against the encroachments of the government." A broad conception of freedom of speech and press is fundamental to limiting government and placing power in the people, and a narrow conception of the First Amendment would be inconsistent with the rest of the document. A freedom to criticize government without fear of subsequent prosecution is implicit in self-governing; so the First Amendment must have encompassed more than mere freedom from prior restraint.

It is impossible to provide a definitive answer to the question of whether the framers intended the First Amendment to go beyond freedom from prior restraint. Not only was there little debate on the question at the time, but the very issue of "framers' intent" is chimerical because there is no single way to gauge that intent. Whose intent? Do you look to Madison because he wrote the First Amendment, or to a poll of the legislators who voted on the measure, or to the sentiment in the states that ratified it? At what moment is the intent assessed? When proposed, when voted on, or when the framers first spoke on the meaning, which may be many years later? Does it matter if their understanding may be a bit different, more refined, or even contrary a few years later?

It may even be that the legislators actually had no "intent" in

---

[9] 4 WILLIAM BLACKSTONE, COMMENTARIES ON THE LAWS OF ENGLAND 151-52 (1769).

mind at the time of passage. They may have deliberately left the First Amendment — and the rest of the Bill of Rights — vague to reduce controversy and facilitate passage. Who can be opposed to freedom of speech and press at that level of abstraction? The legislators may even have been forward-thinking enough to want to leave the interpretation to later generations, which would face problems the framers could not anticipate.

The answer is relevant because interpretation of the Constitution often begins with an inquiry into the framers' intent, and several Supreme Court justices seemingly would end the inquiry there. But most jurists and scholars believe that the framers' intent is only one factor and that the Constitution is an evolving document that must take into account changing circumstances. So, even if we could determine what the framers intended regarding the First Amendment, and even if they only meant it to prohibit prior restraint, that would not necessarily bind current interpretation. Of course, once you break free from the historical intent, current interpretation could yield less as well as more freedom than the framers had in mind.

The strength of the doctrine against prior restraint, dating as it does to well before the First Amendment, is that it carries a certain cachet, a reminder of the baseline of individual freedom. The historical record of suppression and manipulation of the press by governments eager to promote their self-interest serves as evidence of what can happen in the absence of a prior restraint doctrine. The doctrine was created to serve two needs: individual freedom and limited government. At a minimum, the First Amendment was created to serve the same needs, with the same doctrine.

Historical Prior Restraint Defined

A number of other conclusions can be drawn regarding the historical record. The nature of prior restraint that Blackstone, Milton and Henry VIII had in mind involved a licensing system. Prior restraint, historically understood, involved (1) submitting *all* proposed publications (2) to government censors (3) who exercised considerable discretion regarding the content to be approved for publication, and it was (4) imposed in advance of publication.

Prior restraint did not refer to isolated efforts by government officials to suppress speech — a judge's order not to print a libelous tract, for example. Historically, the all-inclusiveness of the regulatory system, the fact that *every* proposed publication must be reviewed and approved, defined prior restraint. Therefore, even the works ultimately approved would still have been subject to prior restraint. "Prior review" is a phrase synonymous with "prior restraint."

Prior restraint meant suppression only by the government, al-

though employers, parents and others obviously suppress speech regularly. Indeed, the historical system of prior restraint did not apply to speech at all, because licensing was a reaction to the introduction of the printing press, although speech in the form of parades or theatrical productions, for example, could conceivably be subjected to licensing or a permit system. But any interference with publication, even if it entirely precluded publication, did not constitute prior restraint if undertaken by individuals or institutions not associated with government.

If the standards for what could be published could ever be delineated clearly enough, then a censor's discretion would have been unnecessary, because the violations could be handled easily through subsequent punishment of individual violators. The considerable discretion exercised by censors is a critical objection to a system of prior restraint.

Of course, the aspects of prior restraint most commonly associated with it had to do with its narrow focus on controlling the actual publication, in advance of publication. Other government restrictions that might have the effect of inhibiting or entirely foreclosing publication would still not be included within the scope of prior restraint, even if they occurred in advance of publication. Restrictions on news gathering, for example, or punishment for not revealing a journalist's confidential source would not qualify as prior restraint because they were not directed specifically at stopping publication.

Consider the 1664 case of printer John Twyn. He was caught with proofs for a book claiming the government was accountable to the people and the people were entitled to revolt. Setting the standard for current journalists, Twyn refused to name the author. For his temerity he was hanged, drawn and quartered — a vicious and ultimate penalty that certainly precluded his publication. Technically, however, it was not prior restraint because the government did not specifically target publication.

A more recent U.S. Supreme Court case is less brutal in its outcome but just as illustrative in its narrow conception of what constitutes prior restraint. In *Alexander v. United States,*[10] the government had prosecuted the owner of more than a dozen stores and theaters dealing in sexually explicit magazines and videotapes. Four magazines and three videotapes in the inventory were found to be obscene. Under a statute that allows the state to seize any property connected to a pattern of criminal behavior, the court ordered Ferris Alexander to forfeit his adult entertainment businesses and their inventories. The government then burned all of the magazines and videotapes.

Alexander maintained that the seizure and destruction of all his magazines and videotapes — which had *not* been found to be obscene and were therefore protected speech — constituted prior restraint. How could a ban on speech be more total than by de-

---

[10] 509 U.S. 544 (1993).

stroying the speech, he argued? But the Court noted that the term "prior restraint" applied only to orders that forbid certain communications in advance of the communications; this, on the other hand, was only punishment for his obscenity convictions. Prior restraints, by their nature, stop the speech completely and perpetually, Chief Justice William Rehnquist wrote for the Court. Alexander could theoretically open another adult entertainment store the next day, restock with new inventory, and sell videotapes and magazines, all without obtaining prior approval from any court, Rehnquist wrote. The statute that allowed the government to seize property connected with criminal activity did not differentiate between expressive and non-expressive property, he noted, and to do so would encourage criminals to invest their ill-gotten gains in expressive property to protect them from forfeiture. He added:

> By lumping the forfeiture imposed in this case after a full criminal trial with an injunction enjoining future speech, petitioner stretches the term "prior restraint" well beyond the limits established by our cases. To accept [Alexander's] argument would virtually obliterate the distinction, solidly grounded in our cases, between prior restraints and subsequent punishments.[11]

RATIONALES FOR PRIOR RESTRAINT

The doctrine against prior restraint can be considered merely a stepping-stone in the evolution of free speech and press. Having served its purpose, it arguably can now be relegated to the dustbin of history. But distinguishing prior restraint from subsequent punishment still makes sense. The extent to which the First Amendment prohibits subsequent punishment is a different question than whether prior restraint should be prohibited. The doctrine against prior restraint accords so wholly with the premises of limited government that disregarding the doctrine can be considered antithetical to the very form of government the Constitution prescribes.

Why Distinguish Subsequent Punishment?

Distinguishing prior restraint from subsequent punishment is a matter of some significance. The Supreme Court has said the First Amendment offers some protection from subsequent punishment. But the Court has also maintained that prior restraint is the most odious and least tolerable infringement of free speech. It would help to have some justification for the differential treatment beyond the venerable age of the prior restraint doctrine. After all, the point of subsequent punishment is to re-

strain speech in advance, too. Legislatures enact laws not to fill some prison quota, but to deter conduct; and laws punishing speech are no different. So how does the fact that the governmental force is applied prior to publication make it worse?

Professor Thomas Emerson attempted to answer that question more than fifty years ago in an important essay.[12] First, he noted the *breadth* of prior restraint. Because all publications are subject to prior restraint, necessarily more communication is affected than when individual publications are targeted for subsequent punishment.

Second, Emerson emphasized the temporal aspect implicit in the two forms of regulation. With prior restraint, *timing and delay* are in the government's hands. With subsequent punishment, the publication at least reaches the marketplace of ideas, and the timing is at the publisher's discretion. But the requirement of prior review imposes an obvious hitch in the editorial process, and sometimes mere delay can undermine the impact of a story, a factor of which the government is quite aware.

Third, a system of prior restraint has a *propensity toward an adverse decision.* To obtain a judgment after publication, no matter how stacked the trial may be, is still more bother than a system of censorship, which entails, as Emerson wrote, "a simple stroke of the pen." The publisher has practical advantages after publication that are missing beforehand, when the advantages favor government. Thus, Emerson concluded, a system of prior restraint by its very nature makes it easier and more likely that the result will be adverse to the expression.

Similarly, matters of *procedure* favor the government in prior restraint. Prior restraint is an administrative procedure rather than a criminal procedure. In the latter, there are presumptions of innocence, burdens of proof, stricter rules of evidence — all of the trappings that are intended to make courts more deliberative and fairer forums than administrative agencies. Juries are available in criminal proceedings, but in an administrative proceeding the case is heard only by a minor bureaucrat.

Fifth, subsequent punishment provides an opportunity for *public appraisal and criticism.* Administrative proceedings can avoid the glare of publicity, but court hearings have a rich history of openness, which can be said to be more consistent with democracy and the goal of informing public opinion.

Sixth, the *dynamics of prior restraint* are such that absurd and unintelligent administration is foreordained. Emerson noted that the personality of a person willing to be a censor tends toward overzealousness. Not only that, but quite bluntly, "The function of the censor is to censor," Emerson wrote. The job title does not include promotion of expression: When in doubt, excise.

---

[11] *Id.* at 549-50.

[12] Thomas I. Emerson, *The Doctrine of Prior Restraint,* 20 LAW & CONTEMP. PROBS. 648 (1955).

The risk is far greater if the censor approves something that later meets with disapproval than if the censor censors. "The long history of prior restraint reveals over and over again that the personal and institutional forces inherent in the system nearly always end in a stupid, unnecessary, and extreme suppression," Emerson wrote.

Seventh, a system of prior restraint favors *certainty over risk*. Scholars and publishers sometimes note that the advantage of a licensing system is that there is a seal of approval if the work passes review, and the work is presumably immune from further sanction. But in a system of subsequent punishment, a publisher could be punished even if the publisher intended to remain within the law; the publisher may have made an error in interpretation and faced punishment for that error. Prior restraint reduces risk, Emerson agreed, but he added that favoring such a system implies a "philosophy of willingness to conform to official opinion and a ... timidity in asserting rights that bodes ill for a spirited and healthy expression of unorthodox and unaccepted opinion."

Finally, prior restraint systems have greater *effectiveness* going for them. When it comes to enforcement, the question is only whether the publication received prior approval. Everybody understands the rules of prior restraint. Indeed, the virtue of the system is its simplicity, at least from government's perspective. Cases are open and shut. Publishers either obey or they don't, and most do. Thus, prior restraint can be distinguished from subsequent punishment, not only definitionally, but rationally.

"These ... considerations which underlie the doctrine of prior restraint ... are the reasons why the doctrine is not simply an arbitrary historical accident, but a rational principle of fundamental weight in the application of the First Amendment," Emerson concluded.

Premises of Prior Restraint

Apart from the definition, differentiation or appropriate treatment of subsequent punishment, prior restraint would be contrary to the First Amendment simply because it is inconsistent with a constitutional system of limited government. Professor Vincent Blasi, with a nod to Milton's *Areopagitica,* identified three premises underlying any system that endorses prior restraint, all of which are inconsistent with limited government and the libertarian theory inherent in the First Amendment:[13]

1. Prior restraint implies trust in the state rather than in the individual and public.

2. Speech is too risky in a democracy.

3. Individuals should have no autonomy from the state.

Blasi believed censorship to be an indignity to both writers and readers because the inherent paternalism of the state associated with censorship implies a general distrust of speakers and audiences. The state is a "suspicious, omnipresent tutor" if it must oversee and approve everything that is disseminated. "No system of political authority premised on the consent of the governed can admit the state to that role, whatever the behavioral consequences," Blasi wrote.

Preoccupation with government power is a trademark of the prior restraint doctrine and libertarian theory generally. Some contemporary free speech theorists are less skeptical of government and more concerned with what they see as the exercise of power by speakers, particularly the media and other corporations engaging in expression. They also are suspicious of the rational capacities of the public and propose a need for a "particularly active and absolute form of intervention by the state" that Blasi noted would be consistent with prior restraint.

Blasi responded that we may distrust the rationality of citizens, but the lesson of the First Amendment is that we distrust the state more. "To trust the censor more than the audience is to alter the relationship between the state and citizen that is central to the philosophy of limited government," Blasi wrote.

The second "troublesome premise" implicit in prior restraint is that speech is no different than other hazardous activities that are licensed or enjoinable, such as driving a vehicle or the practice of medicine. But licensing, Blasi explained, is a method of enforcing social norms. Free speech, by its nature, does not observe such norms; social conformity distorts public discourse. Speech — like democracy — is risky, but that is its virtue. "Only when the public views controversial speakers as normal people, with a legitimate role to play in the social system, can the fragile state-individual balance be maintained," Blasi noted.

The third and perhaps most obvious premise of prior restraint is its subordination of individual autonomy. Blasi contended that prior restraints such as

licensing systems and injunctions coerce or induce speakers to relinquish full control over the details and timing of their communications. These regulatory systems must be premised, therefore, on the notion that either such control is not an essential attribute of the autonomy of speakers, or that such autonomy need not be respected. Either premise is objectionable.[14]

Thus, prior restraints cannot be consistent with the implementation of limited government. Those cases in which the Court has condemned the regulation as a prior restraint aptly illustrate the libertarian principles providing the intellectual

---

[13] Vincent Blasi, *Toward a Theory of Prior Restraint: The Central Linkage,* 66 MINN. L. REV. 11, 69-82, 85 (1981).

[14] *Id.* at 85.

foundation for the doctrine against prior restraint: distrust of government, acceptance of the risk inherent in speech and individual autonomy from government.

CASE LAW AND PREMISES

A review of the major cases embracing the prior restraint doctrine yields a treasure trove of commentary and rulings illustrating Blasi's premises.

Distrust of Government

In 1931, the Supreme Court in *Near v. Minnesota*[15] for the first time explicitly adopted the doctrine against prior restraint as constitutional law. In its decision, it referred time and again to the danger of government regulation as a means of deterring criticism of government. The Court expressed concern about governmental abuse of its authority, with regard to both official misconduct and the exercise of the discretion necessary to implement the statute, which was intended to quell seditious libel. In striking the statute, the Court served notice that the prior restraint doctrine had broken free from its historical moorings.

The case involved a ban on speech in advance of publication, based on content; but the ban was in the form of a nuisance statute enforced by judicial injunction. Jay M. Near had published in his *Saturday Press* malicious and scandalous libels adjudged to be nuisances. As partial punishment, he was ordered not to publish any more under threat of contempt of court.

Some Supreme Court justices argued that the law was not a licensing system within the historical meaning of previous restraint but a remedy for past transgressions. The majority disagreed, however, arguing that the scheme "must be tested by its operation and effect." Thus understood, the Minnesota law was the "essence of censorship." Writing for the Court, Chief Justice Charles Hughes interpreted the statute as directed, not just at libels of private citizens, but "at the continued publication by newspapers and periodicals of charges against public officers of corruption, malfeasance in office, or serious neglect of duty."

This was a somewhat remarkable conclusion, given that the Court cited no specific language in the statute or in Minnesota Supreme Court opinions to support its conclusion that the statute concerned primarily libels of public officers. The Minneapolis mayor, a chief of police and a county attorney had been libeled by the defendant, but so had grand jurors, two newspapers and the "Jewish race." The Court, however, emphasized the "operation and effect" of the law when it noted that the newspaper had been targeted because its principal content was criticism of government. Seventeen times in the opinion, the Court ex-

pressed concern for protecting expression about official misconduct. Skepticism of government's capacity to oversee publications critical of government was hardly ameliorated by allowing a judge to determine if future issues of the *Saturday Press* were consistent with the "public welfare," the Court noted. If the statute operated to suppress expression critical of official misconduct, the doctrine against prior restraint was designed to thwart its operation as well as its effect.

The majority's expansion of the notion of prior restraint to include judicial injunctions, as well as administrative licensing systems, initiated an academic debate that continues to this day. It is significant, however, that in the Court's first pronouncement on prior restraint, it signaled its intention not to be bound by classical conceptions. Not coincidentally, it is also significant that this first opinion stands as tribute to the checking function, which the framers held dear and which presupposes governmental abuse of its authority.

The Court continued its concern for governmental exercise of discretion in matters relating to speech in a line of prior restraint cases, many of which were closer in kind to the licensing system contemplated by Blackstone. But a prior restraint case five years after *Near* illustrated that the Court considered taxation of the press as well as systems to suppress seditious libel as within the scope of prior restraint. The characteristic that was constant was a concern for government's abuse of its authority.

Grosjean v. American Press Co., Inc.[16] involved a Louisiana tax on selected newspapers that on its face did not even seem to qualify as a subsequent punishment. The tax was imposed, not on content, but on the basis of circulation, with all newspapers that circulated more than 20,000 copies weekly to pay a tax of 2 percent on gross receipts. The tax was imposed by statute, and the penalty for failure to pay the tax was a possible fine of up to $500 as well as imprisonment not exceeding six months.

The Court traced the history of "taxes on knowledge" to the English experience, taking judicial notice of the framers' familiarity with that legacy. Writing for the unanimous Court, Justice George Sutherland observed that stamp taxes and taxes on advertising historically had not been intended to gain revenue, but to control the flow of information regarding government. They shared that characteristic with prior restraint, but of course, the same might have been said of seditious libel laws, which constituted subsequent punishments and which operated concurrently with the English system of taxes on the press. Justice Sutherland concluded his survey of English repression of the

---

[15] 383 U.S. 697 (1931).

[16] 297 U.S. 233 (1936). Professor Emerson was particularly critical of the Court's application of the prior restraint doctrine in the tax cases. The doctrine could only be relevant to tax cases, he wrote, if it applied to any regulation that inhibited First Amendment freedom. "When employed in this way the concept becomes so broad as to be worthless as a legal rule," Emerson wrote. THOMAS I. EMERSON, THE SYSTEM OF FREEDOM OF EXPRESSION 511 (1970).

press with a quote from eighteenth century scholar and attorney Thomas Erskine, who said, "The liberty of opinion keeps governments themselves in due subjection to their duties." The quote, although it is not clear from Sutherland's opinion, dates from the year after the First Amendment was enacted — and was made in defense of freedom from seditious libel.

The *Grosjean* case articulates quite nicely the checking function of the press and the threat that governmental abuse of its authority poses to that essential value of freedom of the press. Using the British government as its example, the Court assailed the "persistent effort" to curtail any criticism, true or false. The "predominant purpose" of the First Amendment was "to preserve an untrammeled press as a vital source of public information." The Court described public opinion as "the most potent of all restraints upon misgovernment." The key to informed public opinion is a free press performing the vital function of the Fourth Estate. "To allow it to be fettered is to fetter ourselves," the Court wrote.

From this emphasis on government's sensitivity to criticism and the importance of insulation for critics, the Court concluded that the First Amendment was meant to preclude "any form of previous restraint upon printed publications, or their circulation, including that which had theretofore been effected by these two well-known and odious methods," referring to a stamp tax and a tax on advertising.

A virtue of the prior restraint doctrine as it has come to be construed is that it puts a heavy burden, indeed an insurmountable burden if case outcomes are any indication, on government. While tests and even balancing have been advocated in the same breath as the doctrine against prior restraint, a great strength of the doctrine is that it brings historical weight to bear in asserting outright skepticism of government. Prior restraints are presumed unconstitutional, and it is up to government to bear the heavy burden of attempting to overcome that presumption. The doctrine has a pedigree that no test of compelling or overriding interests can match. The lessons embodied in the doctrine against prior restraint should not be forgotten, but they can easily be lost through mere balancing.

Acceptance of Risk

Worst-case scenarios are integral to the second premise implicit in a system of prior restraint identified by Blasi: risk aversion. In imposing prior restraint, government is attempting to avert the consequences of speech that has yet to be uttered. This necessarily involves the government — including the courts that are passing on the constitutionality of the prior restraint — in gazing into crystal balls. Rationalizing the need for prior restraint thus lends itself to posing the worst possible conse-

quence of the speech if it were to occur.

The only antidote to threats of worst-case scenarios is straightforward acknowledgment that speech does involve risk and that freedom includes freedom for the potent as well as the impotent. "That at any rate is the theory of our Constitution," Justice Oliver Wendell Holmes wrote. We "wager our salvation," he added, "upon imperfect knowledge." He addressed the penchant for concocting worst-case scenarios head-on when he then observed that we must be "eternally vigilant against attempts to check the expression of opinions that we loathe and believe to be fraught with death."[17] Freedom is not for the faint of heart.

Holmes' caveat against caution was tested in the Pentagon Papers case. There, if documents the government had classified as secret were published in the newspapers, then the alleged resultant danger would be "the death of soldiers, the destruction of alliances, the greatly increased difficulty of negotiation with our enemies, the inability of our diplomats to negotiate," as well as prolonging the Vietnam War and extended delay in freeing U.S. prisoners.[18] Possible dangers just do not get any worse.

One might have wondered at this characterization of the danger, however, given that the Pentagon Papers were historical documents relating to U.S. involvement in the Vietnam War. They not only did not give away any planned troop movements or strategic objectives, but they contained nothing the North Vietnamese did not already know. Indeed, the people most ignorant of their content were the constituents of the government that was attempting to conceal them.

The papers, for example, revealed that the U.S. government had engaged in a manipulative public relations campaign aimed at U.S. citizens and foreign allies with little relation to the actual war effort or negotiations, of which the North Vietnamese were, of course, intimately aware. Justice Hugo Black, voting with the majority to allow the *New York Times* and other newspapers to continue publication of a series based on the documents, identified what might have been the real danger that the U.S. government perceived: its own embarrassment.

In the last opinion he was to write before he died, Black zeroed in on the government's use of "national security" as a cover for censorship in the case. The phrase demonstrates the government's felicitous choice of words. Advocating "security" is meant to be comforting, an appeal to our natural tendency to avoid risk. It also put the newspapers that would disclose these papers in the role of exposing us to hazards. But Black cautioned that the phrase was "a broad, vague generality." He seemed to be suggesting that a government whose capacity for deception in conducting war was revealed in the papers would not hesitate to

---

[17] *Abrams v. United States*, 250 U.S. 616, 630 (1919) (Holmes, J., dissenting).

[18] *New York Times Co. v. United States*, 403 U.S. 713, 763 (1971) (Blackmun, J., dissenting).

deceive in promising security to its citizens. Free speech does involve risks, but the framers of the First Amendment, who fully appreciated what it took to defend a nation, nevertheless understood that free speech provided the only real security, Black wrote.[19]

This paradox of security through risk is only one of many associated with the First Amendment: a freedom to espouse no freedom, freedom for the speech we hate, a right to be wrong. All, however, share an implicit acknowledgment of the risk of free speech. Such paradoxes perhaps explain why Professor Emerson wrote that the theory of freedom of expression "does not come naturally to the ordinary citizen, but needs to be learned."[20] One does not ordinarily choose the more hazardous course, much less associate risk with security. Prior restraint appeals to that impulse favoring the safer path. But the doctrine against prior restraint teaches not only that the government's worst-case scenarios seem not to come true when information is ultimately published, but that attempts to achieve security through suppression pose the greater risk. The risk is not in speech being published, but in it *not* being published. That, as Holmes said, is the theory of our Constitution.

Regard for Individual Autonomy

The final premise of prior restraint that also conflicts with a constitutional system of limited government is a depreciation of individual autonomy. The Court in *Schneider v. State*,[21] for example, recognized that the police had power to promote the public interest in regulating the public streets. But when municipal ordinances sought to license the dissemination of leaflets on those thoroughfares, the Court found that they infringed not only on individual speech but on a system of government:

> This court has characterized the freedom of speech and that of the press as fundamental personal rights and liberties. The phrase is not an empty one and was not lightly used. It reflects the belief of the framers of the Constitution that exercise of the rights lies at the foundation of free government by free men. It stresses, as do many opinions of this court, the importance of preventing the restriction of enjoyment of these liberties.... Mere legislative preferences or beliefs respecting matters of public convenience may well support regulation directed at other personal activities, but be insufficient to justify such as diminishes the exercise of rights so vital to the maintenance of democratic institutions.[22]

If speaking in a public forum imposes burdens or inefficiencies on the state, such is the price of maintaining individual autonomy. The Court said the ordinance in *Schneider* was particularly odious because it allowed a police officer to act "as a censor," determining what literature could be distributed and who would distribute it, and required pamphleteers to submit to an inquisition, photographing and fingerprinting. Such censorship struck at the heart of free expression because it placed discretion with the officer rather than the speaker. Moreover, the Court made clear that individual autonomy extended not only to the message but to the site of the speech: "[O]ne is not to have the exercise of his liberty of expression in appropriate places abridged on the plea that it may be exercised in some other place."[23]

The concept of individual autonomy answers the fundamental question in each prior restraint case: "Who is to decide?" The choice of what, when and where to speak is either left to the discretion of the speaker or overruled by the state. Autonomous speech is the condition precedent to the autonomous citizenship contemplated in the democratic model.

First Amendment doctrine, with its focus on individual autonomy, may seem quaint in the eyes of those who advocate that individuals must yield to the public interest, whether the issue involves mandatory motorcycle helmets, zoning or bans on racist speech. But the First Amendment, as exemplified by the prior restraint doctrine in particular, is one of the last areas of constitutional law to uphold the democratic tradition as it was historically understood. If autonomy in speech is rejected, Robert Post observed, the implications go to the core of our belief in self-government, and "beguiling visions of progressive reform" should not obscure the fact that democratic legitimacy, and not just autonomous speech, is at issue.[24]

RECENT CASES

The doctrine against prior restraint shows amazing vitality despite having roots stretching back more than three centuries. Perhaps even more amazing is that cases involving prior restraint persist and questions still emerge. Drawing on those three centuries of history seems to facilitate answering the questions, however.

Origin of a Test

The case in which the Supreme Court most recently employed the prior restraint doctrine shows evidence of distrusting gov-

---

[19] *Id.* at 719 (Black, J., concurring).

[20] EMERSON, *supra* note 16, at 12.

[21] 308 U.S. 147 (1939).

[22] *Id.* at 161.

[23] *Id.*

[24] Robert Post, *Meiklejohn's Mistake: Individual Autonomy and the Reform of Public Discourse,* 64 U. COLO. L. REV. 1109, 1137 (1993).

ernment, embracing risk and prizing individual autonomy; and it contains the Court's most thorough analysis, which ironically was borrowed from some of its earliest First Amendment cases. Those early cases did not even involve prior restraint, and the analysis was taken not from the majority opinions, but from a dissent and a concurring opinion.

The first early case, *Abrams v. United States*,[25] involved a prosecution for publishing two leaflets in 1918 containing objections to U.S. military intervention against the Bolsheviks, who would ultimately form what came to be known as the Soviet Union. In an earlier opinion he had written for the Court, Justice Holmes had framed the issue as "whether the words used are used in such circumstances and are of such a nature as to create a clear and present danger that they will bring about the substantive evils that Congress has a right to prevent."[26] He had endorsed the conviction of speakers in that case, but Harvard Law Professor Zechariah Chafee Jr. prevailed upon Holmes to impart more meaning to the clear and present danger test,[27] which Holmes did in *Abrams*.

When he circulated his dissent to the majority opinion in *Abrams* and defended it at the justices' Saturday conference, Chief Justice Edward White, his long-standing friend and daily companion on the long walk home, asked him not to issue it. When he persisted, three justices took the highly unusual step of calling on him at his home, where his wife joined them in attempting to persuade him not to publish the dissent. Holmes did not relent, and the effect was electric. "A great noise of vilification and praise went up all over the country," wrote biographer Sheldon M. Novick.[28]

In his famous dissent, which has eclipsed the majority opinion and become the law of the land, Holmes stiffened the meaning of a "present danger." "[N]obody can suppose," he wrote, "that the surreptitious publishing of a silly leaflet by an unknown man, without more, would present any immediate danger." Opinions should be allowed "unless they so imminently threaten immediate interference with the lawful and pressing purposes of the law that an immediate check is required to save the country," he wrote. Holmes's stress on the immediacy of the danger before speech should be unprotected presents a nearly impossible hurdle to regulation, but, curiously, it also seems to protect only speech that is unimportant or ineffective. Still, it was a major milestone in the evolution of the First Amendment.

Justice Holmes and Justice Louis Brandeis had a forty-year friendship before Brandeis was appointed to the Court, and they collaborated on some of the great opinions of their era. Brandeis joined in Holmes' dissent in *Abrams*, and Holmes joined Brandeis' concurrence in *Whitney v. California*,[29] a case in which a woman was convicted of criminal syndicalism for joining the Communist Labor Party. Brandeis's opinion concurring in the majority decision seemed to favor her acquittal, but because she did not raise at trial the argument that Brandeis presented, she could not do so on appeal, Brandeis wrote.[30]

This judicial restraint probably left Anita Whitney unimpressed, but Brandeis simply did not have the votes on the Court to overturn her conviction. So whether he labeled his lesson on First Amendment law a concurrence or a dissent seems less important than the fact that it fleshed out the clear and present danger test in a way that lower courts could apply it.

Brandeis pointed out that the Court had not yet determined "when a danger shall be deemed clear; how remote the danger may be and yet be deemed present; and what degree of evil shall be deemed sufficiently substantial to justify resort to abridgement of free speech." First, he turned the question around and suggested that the real danger lay in repression of speech and "that the path of safety lies in the opportunity to discuss freely supposed grievances and proposed remedies."

Brandeis believed that mere fear of serious injury did not justify suppression of speech. "Those who won our independence were not cowards.... They did not exalt order at the cost of liberty," he wrote. In the same libertarian vein, Brandeis indicated that the limited role of the state was to make individuals free to develop their faculties and to avoid "silence coerced by law — the argument of force in its worst form." He continued:

> To justify suppression of free speech there must be reasonable ground to fear that serious evil will result *if free speech is practiced*. There must be reasonable ground to believe that the danger apprehended is *imminent*. There must be reasonable ground to believe that the evil to be prevented is a *serious* one.[31]

To summarize, the speech must cause the alleged danger, the danger must be immediate, and it must be grave.

Nebraska Press Association

Nearly a half century later, the Court expanded on these themes in its most recent major press prior restraint case, *Ne-*

---

[25] 250 U.S. 616 (1919).

[26] Schenck v. United States, 249 U.S. 47, 52 (1919).

[27] *See* DONALD L. SMITH, ZECHARIAH CHAFEE JR., DEFENDER OF LIBERTY AND LAW 30 (1986); Fred D. Ragan, *Justice Oliver Wendell Holmes Jr., Zechariah Chafee Jr., and the Clear and Present Danger Test for Free Speech: The First Year, 1919*, 58 J. AM. HIST. 42-43 (1971).

[28] SHELDON M. NOVICK, HONORABLE JUSTICE — THE LIFE OF OLIVER WENDELL HOLMES 332 (1989).

[29] 274 U.S. 357 (1927).

[30] *Id.* at 379-80 (Brandeis, J., concurring).

[31] *Id.* at 375-76 (Brandeis, J., concurring) (emphasis added).

braska Press Association v. Stuart.[32] Erwin Simants had been arrested for the murder of six people in a small Nebraska town. Three days later, Judge Hugh Stuart issued an order prohibiting the public dissemination of any testimony or evidence. The Nebraska Press Association appealed the prior restraint.

The Supreme Court granted *certiorari* and used the case to review its decisions involving the "heavy presumption" against the constitutional validity of prior restraint, including *Near v. Minnesota* and the Pentagon Papers case. That heavy presumption translated into a nearly impossible burden on government to justify the exercise of such authority and implicit trust in the state rather than speakers. "The thread running through all these cases is that prior restraints on speech and publication are the most serious and the least tolerable infringement on First Amendment rights," wrote Chief Justice Warren Burger for a unanimous Court.

He distinguished prior restraint from subsequent punishment, noting that penalties for violating a criminal statute or libel judgments do not become effective until after trial and all appeals are ended. "A prior restraint, by contrast and by definition, has an immediate and irreversible sanction," Burger wrote. "If it can be said that a threat of criminal or civil sanctions after publication 'chills' speech, prior restraint 'freezes' it at least for the time."

Burger noted the possible risk that pre-trial publicity posed for a defendant's Sixth Amendment right to a fair trial by unbiased jurors. But he also quoted from an earlier case praising the press as the "handmaiden" of justice, because it "guards against the miscarriage of justice."[33] As Brandeis might have put it, the risk of free speech is real, but the risk of enforced silence is greater. In particular, an effective check on governmental abuse would be missing.

In the Pentagon Papers case, Burger was one of three dissenters voting in favor of prior restraint. He had seemed particularly bothered by the fact that the *New York Times* had three to four months to review and edit the classified documents, but the Court had very few days to digest the case. Why, he asked, after months of deferral, must the right to publish be vindicated so precipitously? He answered his own question five years later in *Nebraska Press Association*, noting it was a matter of the speaker's autonomy:

Of course, the order at issue ... does not prohibit but only postpones publication. Some news can be delayed and most commentary can even more readily be delayed without serious injury, and there often is a self-imposed delay when responsible editors call for verification of information. But such delays are normally slight and they are self-imposed. Delays imposed by governmental authority are a different matter.[34]

As Brandeis had observed — and Milton before him — thinking and speaking are private, individual matters sensitive to governmental interference. If speakers are to maintain their autonomy, the choice not only of what to say, but when to say it, must be left to individual discretion.

To uphold the prior restraint, Burger wrote:

[W]e must examine the evidence before the trial judge when the order was entered to determine (a) the nature and extent of pre-trial news coverage; (b) whether other measures would be likely to mitigate the effects of unrestrained pre-trial publicity; and (c) how effectively a restraining order would operate to prevent the threatened danger. The precise terms of the restraining order are also important. We must then consider whether the record supports the entry of a prior restraint on publication, one of the most extraordinary remedies known to our jurisprudence.[35]

First, Burger wrote, the trial judge had reasonably concluded that there would be intensive local and national press coverage. Judge Stuart had found "a clear and present danger that pre-trial publicity *could* impinge upon the defendant's right to a fair trial," the Court observed (emphasis added by the Court). But Stuart was wrong. As Holmes and Brandeis had postulated, a clear and present danger requires immediacy; mere conjecture is insufficient.

Burger wrote that the trial judge's "conclusion as to the impact of such publicity on prospective jurors was of necessity speculative, dealing as he was with factors unknown and unknowable." Nobody could tell what would be disseminated, who would read or view it, what impact it would have, who would be picked as jurors, or whether they would be able to decide the case based solely on the evidence introduced in court. One could not even be certain there would be a trial. Simants could plead guilty — or have a heart attack. When the Court referred to factors unknown and unknowable, the case was over. Once the burden of proof is assigned, that party loses, because it is impossible to prove factors "unknown and unknowable." Because the government has a heavy burden to overcome the presumption of unconstitutionality, it loses.

Likewise, in the second step of the analysis, Burger noted that the government has the burden of proving no other measures would mitigate the effects of publicity. That, too, is unknown and unknowable, without actually implementing the

---

[32] 427 U.S. 539 (1976).

[33] *Id.* at 560 (quoting Sheppard v. Maxwell, 384 U.S. 333, 350 (1966)).

[34] *Id.* at 559.

[35] *Id.* at 562.

measures. Multiple options exist: change of venue to a jurisdiction with less publicity, postponement of a trial to allow the effects of publicity to subside, intensive questioning of prospective jurors to determine possible bias, instructions to jurors to avoid publicity and consider only evidence presented in court, sequestration of jurors, restraints on leaks by trial participants, and, of course, a new trial. The obligation to provide a fair trial is on the state, not the press, and if the state holds an unfair trial, it must hold another, fair trial or not try the defendant. The press cannot deny defendants their Sixth Amendment rights.

Third, the Court questioned the effectiveness of the prior restraint. As Brandeis put it, would the danger result if the free speech in question were *not* stopped? Or would the danger only stop if the speech were stopped? In *Nebraska Press Association,* the Court said any danger would exist despite the restraint. The trial court, for example, might have had difficulty implementing its order regarding media outside the court's jurisdiction.

Even more difficult would be stopping a whole community of 850 people from discussing the case and probably generating rumors more damaging to the defendant than publicity would be. Although everybody was restrained from spreading information, the order was hardly enforceable. The townspeople — who constituted the pool of prospective jurors — would gossip no matter what the court decreed. If the restraint would be ineffective, that by itself is a reason for invalidating it.

Finally, the Court noted that the order was defective because it was vague and overbroad. Vague speech regulations inhibit speakers who cannot be sure if they will violate them. A regulation might be constitutional if narrowly crafted, but a regulation that proscribes protected speech as well as unprotected speech is constitutionally suspect. This court order, as modified by the Nebraska appellate court, banned "information strongly implicative of the accused." Would saying Simants had been arrested for six murders be "strongly implicative"? Too vague. If the order covered such an allegation, then it would cover speech that would not prejudice the outcome of a trial because the jury would learn the allegation as soon as the trial began anyway. Therefore, the order was overbroad as well as vague.

Applying the Test

So the case left a blueprint for how the Court would likely approach future prior restraint cases, regardless of whether the restraint involves fair trials. The Court is not willing, apparently, to merely determine if the government regulation qualifies as a prior restraint and declare it unconstitutional on those grounds alone, as it did in *Near v. Minnesota.*

First, the regulation must fit the definition of prior restraint, which has relaxed since the days of King Henry VIII, but is not

so elastic to include every restraint on publishing, as the Court illustrated in *Alexander v. United States.*[36] Today, a licensing system would still qualify as prior restraint, unless the government imposed it on its own employees (as with CIA agents), a condition of accepting a government subsidy (although this area is still developing and the case law is somewhat inconsistent), or involved broadcasting or the high school or elementary press. As well, though, (1) a government prohibition (2) of a specific publication (3) based on its content (4) after the exercise of discretion and (5) in advance of publication would constitute prior restraint today.

When a regulation is defined as prior restraint, it is presumed unconstitutional, and the government bears a heavy burden to overcome that presumption. This aspect cannot be emphasized too strongly, because the tendency is to give the government the benefit of the doubt and avoid the asserted risk of speech. It is easy to concoct worst-case scenarios and hard to favor an abstract concept such as free speech, but the presumption weights the balance solidly in favor of free speech. To overcome the presumption of unconstitutionality, the government must prove that the danger is serious *and* imminent; that the speech is the cause of the danger and that stopping the speech will stop the danger; that no alternatives to prior restraint will work; and that the terms of the prior restraint are neither vague nor overbroad. The prior restraint can fail at any of these steps and need fail only one to remain unconstitutional.

A danger can be serious without being imminent, as in the *Nebraska Press Association* case. Likewise, as Brandeis noted, a danger can be imminent without being serious. Advocacy of trespassing could be so persuasive that the speaker's audience immediately sought out backyards to traverse, but even so, it would not rise to the level of a serious danger justifying prior restraint. Seriousness is usually the easiest element of the test to meet, because the government's asserted danger is taken at face value and the government is always able to posit a danger of some magnitude.

Imminence, on the other hand, is generally the element least likely to be demonstrated. Proving something will immediately and inevitably occur is almost impossible. Nobody can know what will happen in the future. The *Nebraska Press Association* Court echoed Brandeis' observation that fear of serious injury alone will not justify suppression when it wrote that the trial judge's conclusions regarding the impact of publicity were necessarily speculative. Conjecture is *always* possible; evidence of imminence rarely so.

But even if the danger is imminent, it need not be caused by the speech. If the danger occurs regardless of whether the speech is practiced, then the rationale for the restraint fails.

---

[36] *See* text accompanying *supra* note 10.

This element of the test often comes into play when the proscribed speech is already in the public domain, as it was in the Pentagon Papers case where historical data was being suppressed. If the content of the speech is already available elsewhere, even if it poses an imminent danger, then there is no reason to stop the speech in a given case. The question is whether *the speech at issue in the case* causes the danger.

Alternatives to the prior restraint are almost always available to deal with the danger. The question here is not whether an alternative, narrower form of prior restraint would be preferable. That is an overbreadth question. Alternatives to regulating speech altogether are at issue in this context. Even if alternatives would impose substantial costs on government, as in moving the entire trial, regulating speech must be the last resort, not the first.

In any event, to preserve individual autonomy from government, the burden is on government to prove that no means other than infringing on the speaker would adequately address the problem. Publishing something different or at a later time is not an alternative because it shifts the burden to the speaker, when government must do everything possible to defer to the speaker's discretion. The question is not why the speaker wishes to speak, but why the government wants to censor; and the burden is heavy.

Legacy of Nebraska Press Association: CNN

Although the Supreme Court has not considered a prior restraint against the press in recent years, it did have the opportunity in 1990 and declined to do so. The case began when prison officials made tape recordings of conversations between the imprisoned former Panamanian leader Manuel Noriega and his attorney. Cable News Network obtained copies, but Noriega asked a judge to impose a prior restraint on the dissemination of the tapes to preserve his right to a fair trial.

The judge asked CNN to turn over the tapes so he could listen to them and decide whether they imperiled Noriega's fair trial right, but CNN refused. The judge imposed the ban, and CNN appealed. The case is muddied because the refusal to turn over the tapes became the issue that seemed to become more important in the court's mind than the constitutionality of the prior restraint. The case illustrates the legacy of *Nebraska Press Association* in the sense that the judge believed he had to have access to the tapes before he could apply the test. If the *Near v. Minnesota* approach had been in place, it would only have been necessary to define the regulation as a prior restraint and find it unconstitutional, without applying any test. Even though the burden seems impossible to meet after *Nebraska Press Association*, the fact that there is a test suggests that some prior re-

straints will pass the test; otherwise, why have a test?

As Professors Sigman Splichal and Matthew Bunker have noted, however, even if the trial judge had assumed the dissemination of the conversations on the tape posed a threat to Noriega's fair trial, without actually obtaining the tapes or hearing them, he could still have applied the test, and the prior restraint would have been unconstitutional. Indeed, the prior restraint would have failed at every step of the test because of the questionable imminence, ineffectiveness of the restraint and availability of alternatives.[37]

In any event, the Supreme Court met and discussed the case on a Sunday morning, which it had not done in forty years, before deciding not to hear it. The denial of *certiorari* provoked a passionate dissent from Justice Thurgood Marshall, joined by Justice Sandra Day O'Connor. He considered the case to be "of extraordinary consequence for freedom of the press." Marshall noted the presumed unconstitutionality of prior restraint and that the proponent of "this drastic remedy" carries a heavy burden to justify it. He continued:

I do not see how the prior restraint imposed in this case can be reconciled with these teachings. Even more fundamentally, if the lower courts in this case are correct in their remarkable conclusion that publication can be automatically restrained pending application of the demanding test established by *Nebraska Press,* then I think it is imperative that we re-examine the premises and operation of *Nebraska Press* itself. I would grant the stay application and the petition for certiorari.[38]

Justice Marshall is no longer on the Court, and the fact that the Court declined to hear the case means it still has never actually decided in favor of a prior restraint against the press. Perhaps the best that can be said about this case is that it has not served as precedent for any other cases. Yet.

Tory v. Cochran

The Supreme Court in 2005 decided a prior restraint case that introduced no new law but raises questions.

In the case, Ulysses Tory had been a client of attorney Johnnie L. Cochran Jr. (O.J. Simpson's lawyer), but he was dissatisfied with Cochran's work. He then engaged in several high-profile criticisms of Cochran, including writing letters to the bar association, picketing Cochran's office and pursuing him in public while chanting threats and insults. As an example of his

---

[37] Sigman L. Splichal & Matthew D. Bunker, *The Supreme Court and Prior Restraint Doctrine: An Ominous Shift?,* 3 MEDIA L. & POL'Y 11 (1994).

[38] Cable News Network, Inc. v. Noriega, 498 U.S. 976 (1990) (Marshall, J., dissenting from denial of *certiorari*).

criticisms, one of the signs he used in the picketing read "Hey Johnnie, How Much Did They Pay $$ You to Fuck Me?"[39]

Cochran sued for libel in California, and the court ruled that not only were the libels false and intended to extort money from Cochran, but that damages were an inadequate remedy because Tory said he would continue the campaign of defamation. So the court enjoined Tory and his agents or representatives from uttering, in the form of picketing or otherwise, any statements about Cochran in any public forum.[40]

The decision, the U.S. Supreme Court ruled, was a prior restraint and unanimously found it unconstitutional. It couched its nine-paragraph ruling in terms of causation and overbreadth. Tory's speech no longer represented any threat to Cochran because Cochran had died before the ruling came down. If the speech was not the cause of any danger, then it could not be restrained. Additionally, the terms of the restraint were so broad that the justices noted in oral argument that it prohibited Tory's lawyer from criticizing Cochran — and even prevented Tory and his representatives from saying anything, including praise, regarding Cochran. Thus, the restraint was fatally overbroad.

If the Court had said no more, one might have been satisfied. Indeed, one might even wonder why it had taken the case, because it added nothing to the law, and the California appeals court's opinion upholding the ruling had not even been published. Instead, the Court said the ruling left several questions unanswered, almost inviting further litigation.

Because Cochran had died, the Court said it did not resolve whether a permanent injunction could ever be issued in a defamation case against a public figure (a question First Amendment scholars had assumed had been resolved — in the negative — long ago).[41] Furthermore, the Court said it did not resolve whether the injunction would have been valid before Cochran's death, which was the essential issue in the case. Unless the Court was interested in rewriting decades of prior restraint law, there could only be one outcome to this case. For it to say that unsettled questions remained is, well, unsettling.

Business Week

In 1996, the U.S. Court of Appeals for the Sixth Circuit offered a ringing endorsement of the prior restraint doctrine.[42] Procter

& Gamble had sued Bankers Trust, alleging fraud in a business deal. The trial judge authorized the parties before trial to interview each other and collect evidence that would be kept secret, although on file with the court. The secrecy order was intended to protect trade secrets and other confidential information.

The parties later notified the judge that *Business Week* magazine had obtained a copy of documents that the parties wanted to keep secret and asked the judge to order *Business Week* not to publish them. He sent a facsimile to McGraw-Hill, publisher of *Business Week,* imposing a prior restraint three hours before the presses would have rolled and without any chance for McGraw-Hill to contest the order.

The next day, McGraw-Hill's lawyers asked the judge to withdraw his order and also filed a request for an expedited appeal with the Sixth Circuit. The Sixth Circuit turned McGraw-Hill down on procedural grounds, as did Supreme Court Justice John Paul Stevens when McGraw-Hill asked him for an emergency stay of the order. McGraw-Hill was effectively at the mercy of the trial court.

The trial judge conducted hearings off and on for three weeks, during which he was most interested in learning how *Business Week* had obtained the documents in violation of the secrecy order. It turned out that someone in the Procter & Gamble public relations office had notified a *Business Week* reporter that some fascinating documents had been filed in the case, and another *Business Week* reporter had obtained them from an acquaintance at a New York law firm representing Bankers Trust. Apparently neither the reporter who obtained the documents nor the New York lawyer who provided them knew anything about the secrecy order.

Upset that his order had been violated, the trial judge issued a permanent prior restraint ordering *Business Week* not to publish any of the documents it had obtained. But, at the same time, he held that the parties to the case had not given any good reason why the documents should be secret, and he made copies of them public — enabling *Business Week* and everybody else to obtain copies from the courthouse that could be published.

The Sixth Circuit panel concluded that the trial judge was trying to keep his prior restraint order from being appealed when he put the documents on the public record and allowed everybody, including *Business Week,* to publish them. But the Sixth Circuit was not fooled. Chief Judge Gilbert S. Merritt wrote that "appellate courts cannot allow themselves to be done out of their jurisdiction so cleverly.... So long as the permanent injunction remains technically in effect, we will review it as an injunction just as technically."

Merritt then turned to the First Amendment analysis, observing that the order was a "classic prior restraint" and therefore presumed unconstitutional. He applied textbook post-

---

[39] Tory v. Cochran, 544 U.S. 734, 735 (2005).

[40] *Id.* at 735-36.

[41] *See* ROBERT D. SACK, LIBEL, SLANDER AND RELATED PROBLEMS 361-63 (1980) ("One general rule long adhered to in defamation cases is that courts will not enjoin libels.... The absoluteness of this rule is crucial.").

[42] Procter & Gamble Co. v. Bankers Trust Co., BT Securities Corp., 78 F.3d 219 (6th Cir. 1996).

Nebraska Press Association analysis, beginning with a heavy burden on the proponent of prior restraint. The interests of Procter & Gamble and Bankers Trust fell vastly short of the "exceptional circumstances" required to justify prior restraint. According to the Sixth Circuit:

> Far from falling into that "single, extremely narrow class of cases" where publication would be so dangerous to fundamental government interests as to justify a prior restraint ... the documents in question are standard litigation filings that have now been widely publicized. The private litigants' interest in protecting their vanity or their commercial self-interest simply does not qualify as grounds for imposing a prior restraint. It is not even grounds for keeping the information under seal, as the District Court ultimately and correctly decided.... The permanent injunction, therefore, was patently invalid and should never have been entered.[43]

The court addressed three other bothersome aspects of the case. First, it criticized the trial judge for his extensive investigation into how *Business Week* obtained the documents. Not only did the trial court fail to conduct any First Amendment inquiry before sending the facsimile to *Business Week,* "but it compounded the harm by holding hearings on issues that bore no relation to the right of *Business Week* to disseminate the information in its possession," wrote the appeals court.

Preoccupation with the speaker's motive or knowledge seems to cast the speaker in the role of suspect, when it is government (here, the judge) whose motives are presumed suspect in prior restraint. Inquiring into how *Business Week* obtained the documents shifts the burden from the government to the magazine. In the Pentagon Papers case, the newspaper stories were based on documents that were not only classified, but stolen. Yet the origin of the stories was irrelevant to the outcome.

Second, the appeals court chided the trial court for relying on the Supreme Court opinion in *Seattle Times Co. v. Rhinehart*[44] as authority for its prior restraint. In that case, the Court ruled that if one litigant could be required to disclose confidential information to the opposing litigant, the opposing litigant could be required not to disseminate the information, at least until it was revealed in open court. The Sixth Circuit said *Rhinehart* only applied to the actual parties to a case. *Business Week* was not involved in this case and was not using a court to obtain information from another party — quite the opposite.

Third, the Sixth Circuit disapproved of the temporary prior restraint that stopped the *Business Week* presses and continued while the judge held hearings until the permanent prior re-

straint was issued. Temporary restraining orders, known in the legal trade as TROs, are common as a means of maintaining the status quo while a court gathers evidence and reaches a decision. Chief Judge Merritt quoted from a First Circuit case involving the *Providence Journal:* "This approach is proper in most instances, and indeed to follow any other course of action would often be irresponsible. But, absent the most compelling circumstances, when that approach results in a prior restraint on pure speech by the press it is not allowed."[45]

A temporary prior restraint is still a prior restraint. As the Sixth Circuit noted in considering if the situation was capable of recurring, there is no three-week exception to the prior restraint rule. Indeed, the court quoted from an opinion by Supreme Court Justice Harry Blackmun that "each passing day may constitute a separate and cognizable infringement of the First Amendment."[46]

The *Providence Journal* case, though, should not be taken too far as authority. The First Circuit held that the newspaper could disobey a prior restraint order that was "transparently invalid" as long as it made a "good faith" effort to appeal it. That was contrary to earlier authority holding that the press should ordinarily abide by an order and work within the judicial system to overturn it, which is what McGraw-Hill did. The Supreme Court soon granted certiorari to hear the *Providence Journal* case.

"I have read the oral argument before the Supreme Court and there is no doubt in my mind that the Supreme Court granted cert to reverse *Providence Journal,*" noted Ken Vittor, senior vice president and general counsel for McGraw-Hill.[47] Perhaps fortunately for the press, media lawyer Floyd Abrams (who also argued the *Nebraska Press Association* case before the Supreme Court) was able to convince the Supreme Court to dismiss the *Providence Journal* case because of a procedural problem with the prosecutor who had been assigned to the case.

Prior Restraint — of Terrorism?

Cryptography, the practice of coding messages so that only the intended receiver can decipher them, dates to at least Julius Caesar. Decrypting, or attempts by unintended receivers to uncover the right "key" to break the code, probably dates back just as far. With the advent of computers, the science has taken a huge leap. The number of possible keys to today's encryption

---

[43] *Id.* at 225.

[44] 467 U.S. 20 (1984).

[45] In re Providence Journal, 820 F.2d 1342, 1351 (1st Cir. 1986), *modified on rehearing,* 820 F.2d 1354 (1st Cir. 1987).

[46] Nebraska Press Ass'n v. Stuart, 423 U.S. 1327, 1329 (1975) (Blackmun, J., in chambers).

[47] Speech during panel discussion at Practicing Law Institute Seminar on Communication Law in New York City (Nov. 8, 1996).

codes is 1 followed by 77 zeroes, a number thought to be approximately equal to the number of atoms in the universe, making the codes virtually unbreakable.[48]

Purchases made over the Internet are encrypted so that credit card data will be secure. Individual or corporate users can have other legitimate uses for encryption. Encryption can even be understood as the digital-age equivalent of the First Amendment right to be anonymous.[49] However, governments are greatly concerned about the use of encryption by terrorists, criminals and spies. For example, Ramzi Yousef, who masterminded the bombing of the World Trade Center in 1993, apparently encrypted files that contained plans to crash eleven airliners; but the National Security Administration was able to crack his password and foil the plot. Al-Qaida operatives have used encryption in their communications, although it is not clear that any encrypted messages were used when they planned the September 11, 2001, attack on the World Trade Center.[50]

In the 1990s, in an effort to keep encryption techniques out of foreign hands, the U.S. government ruled that encryption technology was a "munition." Export of such technology had to be reviewed and licensed — and export included posting on the Internet if foreign nationals might access the technology. Under Department of Commerce regulations, license applications could be held indefinitely, appeals of denials were to be decided "within a reasonable time," and there was no judicial review.[51]

Daniel Bernstein, then a computer science professor at the University of Illinois in Chicago, developed a method of encryption, which he called "Snuffle." When informed he would need a license to distribute his source code within the general academic and scientific communities, he sued, claiming prior restraint.

The Court of Appeals for the Ninth Circuit determined that source code for encryption software was "speech." Computer programmers can read source code, and it expresses ideas little different from equations or graphs used in other fields. This was a controversial finding, to which the dissent objected because source code was "functional" rather than expressive. Computers translate source code into machine language (object code) — ones and zeroes — that then causes computers to work. Because source code controlled a computer without conveying information to humans during this translation, the dissent contended it could not be speech.[52]

But once the majority concluded that source code was, in fact, protected by the First Amendment, the court then found the regulations to be unconstitutional prior restraint. The regulations placed too much discretion in government officials and did not take into account the need for judicial oversight. "To the extent the government's efforts are aimed at interdicting the flow of scientific ideas — these efforts would appear to strike deep into the heartland of the First Amendment," the court wrote.

But what might have happened if this case had occurred after September 11, 2001? A year after the Bernstein case, a professor at Case Western Reserve University wanted to post source code to his Web site, which would constitute exporting the code under the regulations. The Court of Appeals for the Sixth Circuit first overturned the lower court finding that the code was not speech. But, although the expressive elements were protected, the court said the government's interest in regulating the functional elements must also be considered. In language that was prescient of 9/11, the court wrote that the exercise of presidential power on behalf of national security interests could sometimes outweigh free speech interests.[53]

The court returned the case to the lower court because changes in the encryption export regulations had just made it much easier to export source code, but the court's sensitivity to the balance of interests is mindful of a conclusion Professor Fredrick Siebert drew after surveying 300 years of English press law:

> The area of freedom contracts and the enforcement of restraints increases as the stresses on the stability of the government and of the structure of society increase.[54]

Prior restraint doctrine does not exist in a vacuum. Judges interpret it, and they are subject to the same anxieties and pressures as anybody else. It follows that judicial opinions are a product of their times. Sensitivity to First Amendment interests might well be waning in this period post-9/11 as people seem willing, even enthusiastic about trading freedom for what they hope to be security. Even the doctrine against prior restraint might not be adequate to protect speech in such a climate.

---

[48] *See* Barak Jolish, *The Encrypted Jihad*, http://dir.salon.com/story/tech/feature/2002/02/04/terror_encryption/index.html (Feb. 4, 2002).

[49] *See* McIntyre v. Ohio Elections Comm'n, 514 U.S. 334 (1995); Talley v. California, 362 U.S. 60 (1960) (anonymous leafleting protected).

[50] *See* Lisa M. Krieger, *How Technology Is Used to Mask Communications*, SAN JOSE MERCURY-NEWS, Oct. 2, 2001, at 1F; Jolish, *supra* note 48; Jake Tapper, *Don't Blame it on Reno*, http://archive.salon.com/politics/feature/2002/01/02/reno/index_np.html (Jan. 2, 2002).

[51] Bernstein v. United States, 176 F.3d 1132, 1138 (9th Cir. 1999), *reh'g en banc granted and opinion withdrawn*, 192 F.3d 1308 (9th Cir. 1999).

[52] *Id.* at 1142. *See also* Junger v. Daley, 209 F.3d 481 (6th Cir. 2000) (also finding source code to be speech). Apparently, no rehearing was ever held in the *Bernstein* case because the government in 2000 changed its regulations to allow most exports of encryption products and software.

[53] Junger v. Daley, 209 F.3d 481 (6th Cir. 2000).

[54] SIEBERT, *supra* note 2, at 10.

SUMMARY

Questions remain in this age-old area of the law. If even temporary restraints are so disdained and obviously unconstitutional, should the speaker be able to maintain autonomy and speak at will? Can the judiciary effectively censor the press through TROs in a way that it would not allow the executive branch to do? Are speakers better off to sacrifice principles for pragmatism and obey the prior restraint so they can appear before the appellate court with "clean hands"? It probably helped *Business Week* that it could point out that the only party who had violated the court order was one of the litigants, and it obviously hurt CNN when it refused to turn over the tapes so the judge could review them. And finally what does the future hold for this doctrine?

The prior restraint doctrine will not survive simply because it has a venerable pedigree. The government will continue to attempt to control and manipulate expression, and the doctrine may have to adapt to remain viable. That's what happened in *Near v. Minnesota* when the Court expanded the doctrine to include judicial orders as well as administrative licensing. But the test that the Court used in *Nebraska Press Association* to test the constitutionality of a judicial prior restraint might be considered a step back, because the *Near* Court, and even Blackstone, contemplated a clear rule rather than a balancing test, albeit one heavily weighted in favor of speech. But substituting a test for a clear rule suggests there will be an occasion on which the test will be met and the restraint upheld; otherwise, why not have a clear rule? A test seems to open the door to temporary prior restraints at a minimum, and it may significantly diminish the strength of the doctrine in the long run.

Requiring proof of an imminent danger is the cornerstone of the doctrine against prior restraint, in that it is the component most difficult for the government to prove and thus provides much of the doctrine's force. But there is constant pressure to diminish the imminence requirement in a terrorist-filled world with incessant threats on the Internet against everyone from jurors to presidents.

A recent case is troubling in that regard, although it involves a federal criminal statute and therefore is subsequent punishment and not prior restraint. Harold Turner was upset with an appellate court ruling limiting the right to bear firearms, and he blogged, "These Judges deserve to be killed." He quoted Thomas Jefferson, who wrote that the "tree of liberty must be replenished … with the blood of tyrants," and posted names, pictures, and addresses of the judges, along with pictures of the federal courthouse in which they worked, noting with red arrows the anti-truck bomb barriers.

The Court of Appeals for the Second Circuit affirmed Turner's conviction, rejecting any need for proof that Turner actually intended to carry out an assassination.[55] Notably, the Second Circuit specifically rejected any requirement that the threat posed an immediate danger. It was enough that Turner intended to intimidate the judges and that the judges had a reasonable "apprehension of impending injury." If this inquiry into the fearfulness of people targeted by speech, along with a repudiation of any imminence requirement, were to cross over into prior restraint law, the doctrine might not be dead, but it surely would be crippled.

The Supreme Court has not had a significant prior restraint case before it for almost forty years, which might be proof by itself of the doctrine's continued vitality. Or it might presage a fresh look at that doctrine when that case eventually does arrive before the Court in a world vastly different from the one confronting John Milton, the framers, or even the newspapers that published the Pentagon Papers. Ultimately, the future of the doctrine depends on those who understand its roots and its rationale and can explain both, whether in editorials, blogs, court papers or coffee shops.

FOR ADDITIONAL READING

Abrams, Floyd. "Prior Restraints," *in* 1 *Communications Law in the Digital Age 2009,* New York: Practising Law Institute, 2009.

Anderson, David A. "The Origins of the Press Clause," 30 *UCLA Law Review* 455 (1983).

Barnett, Stephen R. "The Puzzle of Prior Restraint," 29 *Stanford Law Review* 539 (1977).

Bezanson, Randall P. *How Free Can the Press Be?* Urbana: University of Illinois Press, 2003.

Bickel, Alexander. *The Morality of Consent.* New Haven: Yale University Press, 1975.

Blanchard, Margaret A. "Filling in the Void: Speech and Press in State Courts Prior to Gitlow," in *The First Amendment Reconsidered — New Perspectives on the Meaning of Speech and Press,* Bill Chamberlin & Charlene Brown, eds. New York: Longman, 1982.

Cain, Butler. "Freedom of the Press, 1500-1804," in *The Media in America: A History*, 9th ed., Wm. David Sloan, ed. Northport, Ala.: Vision Press, 2014.

Carter, Edward L. & Brad Clark. "Death of Procedural Safeguards: Prior Restraint, Due Process and the Elusive First Amendment Value of Content Neutrality," 11 *Communication Law and Policy* 225 (2006).

Friendly, Fred W. *Minnesota Rag: The Dramatic Story of the Landmark Supreme Court Case That Gave New Meaning to*

---

[55] United States v. Turner, 720 F.3d 411 (2d Cir. 2013).

Freedom of the Press. New York: Vintage Books, 1981.

Helle, Steven. "Prior Restraint by the Backdoor," 39 *Villanova Law Review* 817 (1994).

Helle, Steven. "Publicity Does Not Equal Prejudice," 85 *Illinois Bar Journal* 16 (January 1997).

Jeffries, John C. "Rethinking Prior Restraint," 92 *Yale Law Journal* 409 (1983).

Kalven Jr., Harry. "The Supreme Court, 1970 Term — Forward: Even When a Nation is at War," 85 *Harvard Law Review* 3 (1971).

Knoll, Erwin. "National Security: The Ultimate Threat to the First Amendment," 66 *Minnesota Law Review* 161 (1981).

Litwack, Thomas R. "The Doctrine of Prior Restraint," 12 *Harvard Civil Rights-Civil Liberties Law Review* 519 (1977).

Mayton, William T. "Toward a Theory of First Amendment Process: Injunctions of Speech, Subsequent Punishment, and the Costs of the Prior Restraint Doctrine," 67 *Cornell Law Review* 245 (1982).

Meiklejohn, Alexander. *Free Speech and its Relation to Self-Government.* New York: Harper & Brothers, 1948.

Morland, Howard. "The H-Bomb Secret — How We Got It, Why We're Telling It," *The Progressive,* November 1979, p. 14.

Redish, Martin H. "The Proper Role of the Prior Restraint Doctrine," 70 *Virginia Law Review* 53 (1984).

Rudenstine, David. *The Day the Presses Stopped: A History of the Pentagon Papers Case.* Berkeley: University of California Press, 1996.

Scordato, Martin. "Distinction Without a Difference: A Reappraisal of the Doctrine of Prior Restraint," 68 *North Carolina Law Review* 1 (1989).

Strong, Frank R. "Fifty Years of 'Clear and Present Danger': From *Schenck* to *Brandenburg* — and Beyond," *The Supreme Court Review* 41 (1969).

Ungar, Sanford J. *The Papers & the Papers: An Account of the Legal and Political Battle Over the Pentagon Papers.* New York: Dutton, 1972.

Regulating Pornography

By John C. Watson

➡ **Headnote Questions**

- How are issues of taste and morality tied to the laws regulating pornography, obscenity and indecency?
- How do obscenity, pornography and indecency differ?
- How are federal, state and local governments involved in the legal issue of obscenity?
- How has the Supreme Court defined speech that is obscene and, therefore, not protected by the First Amendment?
- How does the law shield children from inappropriate messages?
- How are zoning laws used to regulate sex-themed material?
- How have ratings systems evolved?

Purveyors of sexual messages and speech otherwise deemed socially inappropriate always have found receptive audiences as well as censors empowered by morality and law. This was true thousands of years ago when cave walls were a primary medium of communication, and it is equally true in the twenty-first century when the Internet has emerged as a top-tier medium for pornography. Societies have been persistent in constraining and punishing speech they found morally offensive or inappropriate. It does not matter whether these messages are carved in stone, written on paper, or measured in bytes.

Even though the U.S. Constitution has given freedom of expression a hallowed place in the First Amendment, restrictions on pornography, indecency and obscenity have grown in fits and starts to become a substantial body of law. These laws, perhaps because they are so closely tied to morality and evolving social mores, are sometimes enforced unevenly and often lack clear, objective rationales and justifications.

Scholars widely agree that all law was originally derived from precepts of morality that condone behavior supporting the peaceful and cooperative survival of society and condemning behaviors inimical to these basic goals. Condemnable behaviors are labeled immoral, evil or bad. Law renders them illegal. Laws regulating sexual expression and offensive messages remain closely tied to morality. This is often reflected in written court rulings that espouse rationales grounded in morality and other determinations of what is good or bad for society.

As with other moral judgments, there are greater and lesser evils in this area of law. Legal restrictions and protections vary accordingly. The most morally offensive categories of communication are those that incite violence and those with sexual content. The most evil of these two categories are fighting words and obscenity. They get no First Amendment protection, and legal restrictions on them can be as rigorous as those imposed on any behavior.[1] Anyone who creates, sells or conveys obscene messages can be convicted of felonies and sentenced to lengthy prison terms. In a highly publicized 2008 case, for example, Paul F. Little, a pornographer known in the business as Max Hardcore, was sentenced to nearly four years in prison for distributing obscenity on the Internet and through the mail.[2] He served less than three years.[3]

Pornography, which is less sexually offensive than obscenity, gets some First Amendment protection and is in the continuing process of losing some of its moral stigma. This was illustrated to some degree by the words of a federal prosecutor in the Max Hardcore case who reportedly said of the defendant: "What he

---

[1] Fighting words — speech highly likely to provoke a violent response — and words that incite violence or advocate a violent overthrow of the government are denied First Amendment protection. It may not be incidental that these types of communication also violate morality's goals of peace and cooperation in society. *See* Chaplinsky v. New Hampshire, 315 U.S. 568 (1942).

[2] *See* Elaine Silvestri, *Filmmaker Receives 46-month Sentence,* TAMPA TRIB., Oct. 4, 2008, at Metro 1.

[3] The Federal Bureau of Prisons reports Little was released July 19, 2011. *See* http://www.bop.gov/iloc2/LocateInmate.jsp (last visited May 23, 2016). *See also* Susannah Breslin, *Adult Director Max Hardcore Released From Prison,* http://www.forbes.Com/sites/susannahbreslin/2011/07/21/adult-director-max-hardcore-released-from-prison-2/ (last visited May 14, 2015).

creates gives mainstream pornography a bad name."[4]

So-called "mainstream pornography" does not include depictions of children. The inclusion of children in sexual communication that would be merely pornographic if adults were depicted, often is transformed into obscenity as a matter of law. A man convicted of trafficking in online child pornography was given a thirty-year federal prison sentence in 2014.[5]

American social mores increasingly label depictions of violence as inappropriate when children are the audience. But the level of public opprobrium as expressed in law remains below the scorn enforced against sexual depictions. In response to public pressure, purveyors of music, movies and video games with violent themes have implemented voluntary rating systems, but efforts to raise the level of legal excoriation to match that of sex-themed speech have failed. In 2011, a seven-justice majority of the U.S. Supreme Court found a California law unconstitutional, in part, because the state sought to impose the same limitations on violent speech that the law allows for sex-themed speech directed at children.[6]

Increasing moral condemnation of specific types of violence and invasions of privacy have led to the colloquial linking of the suffix "porn" to some socially and politically unacceptable communication behaviors.[7] For example, the term "revenge porn" refers to depictions of intimate situations that are not necessarily overtly sexual, but usually include nudity in an apparently private circumstance. The term "animal crush porn" has been applied to depictions of the killing of small animals, even when there is no overt sexual content. And "war porn" is the generically applied label for videos of graphic violent military or terrorist attacks. The courts have declined to treat these types of communication as pornography, but legal restrictions have been imposed sometimes on other grounds.[8]

The intensely moral nature of sexual communication law may have contributed to its murkiness and dearth of bright-line definitions. Moral judgments are often gut-level determinations that something is wrong or inappropriate. Such conclusions are not necessarily explicable through a clear path of reasoning. Justice Potter Stewart once famously confessed his inability to intelligibly define hard-core pornography. "But," he said, "I know it when I see it."[9]

When legal determinations are tied to morality and issues of taste, they lack some of the long-term predictability common in other areas of law. One of the purposes of written law is to provide the public with behavioral guidelines and notice of what is acceptable and what is not. But morality and taste change in response to a wide variety of cultural, political and religious influences. Victorian influences in the United States in the 1890s, for example, condemned the public display of a woman's naked ankle as indecent and scandalous. During the mid-1960s, television broadcasters would not expose the bellybutton of the era's most popular female genie for about five years because they were afraid of viewer backlash or a federal fine for indecency. Not until the 1980s did television commercials show women in bras for the first time. In the twenty-first century, television commercials for products to treat male erectile dysfunction became common fare.

PORNOGRAPHY AND THE LAW

Despite its obscurities, the law of morally offensive expression does have a traceable path of development and fundamental legal parameters to guide those who convey or receive such messages. An examination of this body of law must necessarily begin with an explanation of the basic terms: "obscenity," "pornography" and "indecency."

Indecency is the broadest of the three terms and is applied to perhaps the least morally offensive expression. It refers to — sexual and non-sexual — messages that are considered clearly offensive. Indecency, does not necessarily have any of the sexual content of obscenity or pornography, but is otherwise considered morally offensive or socially inappropriate. It receives substantial First Amendment protection in the print media and online, but is subject to legal restriction in the broadcast media. Indecency is often as much a question of taste, morality and social mores as it is an issue of law. It is nonetheless, a routinely used legal term at the heart of federal legal restrictions in the broadcast media and on the Internet. Broadcast stations, for example, are prohibited from transmitting indecent messages except during selected hours of the day.[10]

Indecency was also the term used to refer to the word "fuck" when it was used in a non-sexual, but apparently highly offensive epithet: "Fuck the Draft." Paul Cohen was convicted of disturbing the peace in 1968 because he wore a jacket inscribed with those words. The Supreme Court found no sexual meaning in the words as used and reversed the conviction. Justice John

---

[4] Id.

[5] See Associated Press, *Major Child Porn Distributor Sentenced to 30 Years*, NY TIMES, June 17, 2014, *available at* http://www.nytimes.com/aponline/2014/06/17/us/ap-us-child-porn-website-operator.html?_r=0 (last visited May 30, 2015).

[6] Brown v. Entm't Merchants Assoc., 564 U.S. 786 (2011).

[7] See HELEN HESTER, BEYOND EXPLICIT: PORNOGRAPHY AND THE DISPLACEMENT OF SEX (2014).

[8] See Rebecca Leber, *Is Revenge Porn Legal in Your State*, NEW REPUBLIC, Sept. 3, 2013, *available at* http:// www.newrepublic.com/article/119295/revenge-porn-laws-state-map-shows-theyre-rare-us (last visited May 23, 2016). *See also* United States v. Stevens, 559 U.S. 460 (2010) (crush videos).

[9] Jacobellis v. Ohio, 378 U.S. 184, 197 (1964) (Stewart, J., concurring).

[10] Indecency on the Internet is discussed further in this chapter and in Chapter 12. Broadcast indecency is discussed further in Chapter 10.

Marshall Harlan observed that the message was distasteful to many people but noted that "it is nevertheless often true that one man's vulgarity is another's lyric."[11] Profanity is often a synonym for indecency in that it also can have no sexual meaning but usually is considered vulgar and offensive expression that can be regulated by law in some contexts. The First Amendment protects indecency in print media, movies and CDs.

"Pornography" is a term used to label sexually explicit expression. It is indistinguishable from what is euphemistically identified as "erotica." "Pornography" is often used as a term of criticism indicating crass sexual expression. While erotica and pornography may be equally sexual, erotica conveys a somewhat literary nuance. "Pornography" generally indicates a decided lack of delicacy. It is not truly a legal term, but "pornography" often means sexual expression that gets some First Amendment protection. "Hardcore pornography" usually means obscenity.

"Obscenity" is a legal term that refers to material that has been deemed illegal by a court. It refers to sexual expression that is disgusting to the senses or abhorrent to morality and to graphic portrayals of sex acts intended to arouse lustful thoughts. The term is often used generically to express disgust or moral outrage in non-sexual contexts; but legally, material must meet a specific test to be deemed obscene.

Supreme Court rulings in the law of sexual expression and morally inappropriate speech fall into two basic areas. First, the Court interprets federal statutes and regulations that control or prohibit the creation and distribution of sexual expression. This body of law includes the Federal Communications Act, rules and regulations of the Federal Communications Commission and U.S. Postal Service, laws controlling imports and exports, and regulations governing interstate commerce. Obscenity laws, like statutes on almost any subject, contain vague provisions that courts must interpret. For example, if U.S. Customs agents in New York City intercept pornographic films shipped from Germany to New Hampshire, the courts must determine whether to apply the laws and standards to New York, Germany or New Hampshire. If federal statutes are silent on such issues, federal appellate courts must divine rules of law by relying on other legal precedents.

More importantly, the Supreme Court decides how far federal and state governments may go in restricting sexual expression. The Court indicated in 1931 that obscenity was one of a few, narrow classes of expression that is unprotected by the First Amendment. This ruling in the case, *Near v. Minnesota,* provided no guidelines about this narrow class.[12] Twenty-six years later, the Court began the difficult task of drawing the line between expression that was obscene (and therefore subject to government bans and criminal prosecution), and expression that was non-obscene (and protected by the First Amendment).

The creation and enforcement of anti-obscenity laws are primarily left to the states. The Supreme Court has determined that the states retain broad police power to prohibit all behavior deemed inimical to the comfort, safety, health and welfare of society. Police power authorizes states to enact laws to protect the peace, good order, morals and health of their communities.

Congress and federal agencies also have created legal restrictions on obscenity, but state supreme courts and legislatures are the sources of the greatest number of obscenity regulations. Local police and prosecutors handle the enforcement of state obscenity law or sometimes choose not to enforce it for political or practical reasons. Neither the First Amendment nor federal statutes mandate that states enact obscenity laws. Some state judges have effectively exercised their option to decriminalize the sale of obscenity to adults. And in some metropolitan areas, a liberal political environment and a thriving consumer market for sexual material have discouraged the enforcement of anti-obscenity laws. Some jurisdictions, however, vigorously prosecute obscenity. Anyone prosecuted always has, of course, recourse to the defenses provided by the First Amendment. Some state constitutions and state court rulings provide protection greater than the First Amendment provides.

PORNOGRAPHY AND SOCIETY

Whether pornography is a threat to public safety, health and morality remains a matter for debate. Critics claim the creation and sale of pornography are associated with illicit activities such as gambling, prostitution and illegal drugs. But businesses that provide sexually explicit imagery have thrived in malls and suburban neighborhoods and on the Internet largely without the accompanying taint of illegal drugs and prostitution.

Sociologists and political activists are divided on whether adult pornography is harmful. Two presidential commissions have studied the issue. President Lyndon Johnson created the Commission on Obscenity and Pornography in 1968. Two years later, during the Nixon Administration, the commission concluded that neither hard-core nor soft-core pornography leads to antisocial behavior and thus should not be prohibited. Eighteen years later, however, U.S. Attorney General Edwin Meese's Commission on Pornography, the "Meese Commission," concluded that pornography is pervasive in society and recommended vigorous enforcement of obscenity laws.

Many people, including some social scientists, oppose obscenity laws. They argue that moderate consumption of pornography — like wine, ice cream or even marijuana — is compatible with

---

[11] Cohen v. California, 403 U.S. 15, 25 (1971). *See also* W. Wat Hopkins, *When Does F*** Not Mean F***?: FCC v. Fox Television Stations and a Call for Protecting Emotive Speech,* 64 FED. COMM. L.J. 1 (2011).

[12] 283 U.S. 697 (1931).

physical and mental health. Sallie Tisdale, a journalist and so-cial commentator, defended pornography for women in a 1992 *Harper's* magazine article and in a 1994 book.[13] She wrote: "I want never to forget the bell curve of human desire, or that few of us have much say about where on the curve we land."

Proponents of strict enforcement of obscenity laws cite his-tory and research findings to defend their position. They point out that many cultures traditionally have controlled sexual ex-pression. The *Bible* may include bawdy tales of prostitutes and adulterers, but it tells them discretely without close-ups of geni-tals. They point to studies finding that men exposed to explicit videos become more callous toward women and that there is a strong correlation between consumption of men's girlie maga-zines and the incidence of sex crimes against women. Two femi-nists, Catherine MacKinnon and Andrea Dworkin, have been particularly active in fighting pornography, which they define as the graphic, sexually explicit subordination of women. They ar-gue that it presents women "as sexual objects for domination, conquest, violation, exploitation, possession, or use, or through postures or positions of servility or submission or display."[14] A 1984 ordinance in Indianapolis adopted this argument, but a federal court of appeals found it to be unconstitutional.[15]

Some federal judges, however, support attempts by states to restrict pornography and public nudity. Supreme Court Justice Antonin Scalia observed in 1991 that Indiana's nudity law would be violated "if 60,000 fully consenting adults crowded into the Hoosier Dome to display their genitals to one another, even if there were not an offended innocent in the crowd."[16] In 2000, the Court upheld an Erie, Pennsylvania, ordinance that banned public nudity and thus prohibited erotic dancers in bars from performing nude.[17] The majority gave state and local govern-ment broad latitude for creating and implementing such laws. Two justices said governments need no justification other than public morality to ban nude dancing in public. And four justices insisted on only the slimmest of justifications for such bans, stating that local government could justify the regulations by citing studies from other states and cities that documented sec-ondary effects of nude, barroom dancing. The cited effects often include sex crimes, prostitution and harm to property values.

PORNOGRAPHY AND THE SUPREME COURT

Justice Scalia's colorful observation — part of a lively history of Supreme Court jurisprudence in this area — is from a concur-ring opinion in a case involving nude dancing. Darlene Miller, a dancer at the Kitty Kat Lounge in South Bend, Indiana, argued that nude dancing was a form of protected expression. Indiana, however, said the state had a right to require all public per-formers at least to wear pasties and G-strings, and the Supreme Court agreed in a decision that is representative of the Court's history in pornography law.

In his majority opinion, Chief Justice William Rehnquist con-ceded that nude dancing was indeed "expressive conduct within the outer perimeters of the First Amendment," but insisted that Indiana had a right to combat public nudity. He observed, how-ever, "It is possible to find a kernel of expression in almost every activity a person undertakes."[18] Byron White, joined by three other justices, dissented and argued that non-obscene, nude dancing performed before consenting adults was protected expression. Justice David Souter joined Scalia in his attack on the concept that consent should affect the outcome of the case.

This kind of fragmentation dominated Supreme Court juris-prudence for more than thirty years. In *Manual Enterprises v. Day,*[19] the Court clearly indicated for the first time that gay-themed sexual expression was not in and of itself patently of-fensive or necessarily obscene. The case arrived at the Supreme Court after the U.S. Postal Service seized and refused to deliver copies of magazines that it judged obscene because they dis-played pictures of nude men. A fractured majority allowed the magazines to be delivered but reached that result on a variety of rationales. Two justices found the photographs to be no more patently offensive than those in the *Playboy* and *Esquire* maga-zines of the time. "[T]hese portrayals of the male nude cannot fairly be regarded as more objectionable than many portrayals of the female nude that society tolerates,"[20] Justice Harlan wrote. Three other justices indicated that only a court of law and not postal officials could determine whether expression is obscene. One justice claimed the First Amendment protected the magazines even if they were obscene.

Scattered rationales also were provided in the 1966 case *Memoirs v. Massachusetts,* for which Justice William Brennan presented a three-part test to determine whether a work was obscene.[21] Two other justices signed Brennan's plurality opinion

---

[13] SALLIE TISDALE, TALK DIRTY TO ME: AN INTIMATE PHILOSOPHY OF SEX (1994); Sallie Tisdale, *Talk Dirty to Me: A Woman's Taste in Pornography,* HARPER'S, Feb. 1992, at 37.

[14] ANDREA DWORKIN & CATHERINE MACKINNON, PORNOGRAPHY AND CIVIL RIGHTS: A NEW DAY FOR WOMEN'S EQUALITY 113-14 (1988).

[15] Am. Booksellers Ass'n v. Hudnut, 771 F.2d 323 (7th Cir. 1984).

[16] Barnes v. Glen Theatre, 501 U.S. 560, 575 (1991) (Scalia, J., concurring).

[17] Erie v. Pap's A.M., 529 U.S. 277 (2000).

[18] *Barnes,* 501 U.S. at 570.

[19] 370 U.S. 478 (1962).

[20] *Id.* at 490.

[21] 383 U.S. 413 (1966). Under the test, a work was obscene if (1) the dominant theme of the material taken as a whole appealed to a prurient interest in sex; (2) the material was patently offensive because it affronted contemporary community standards relating to the representation of sexual matters; and (3) the material was utterly

holding that the 1749 novel *Memoirs of a Woman of Pleasure* was not obscene; two justices concurred and voted to overturn the conviction for reasons articulated in other Court opinions; another judge wrote his own concurrence; and three justices filed separate, dissenting opinions.

Justice William Douglas, who advocated a strict interpretation of the First Amendment, concurred in the judgment. The First Amendment absolutely protected obscene speech, he wrote: "Publications and utterances were made immune from majoritarian control by the First Amendment, applicable to the States by reason of the Fourteenth. No exceptions were made, not even for obscenity."[22]

Justice Tom Clark disagreed with Douglas and Brennan. The new test, he wrote, "gives the smut artist free rein to carry on his dirty business" and "preying upon prurient and carnal proclivities for its own pecuniary advantage."[23]

The *Memoirs* ruling produced a definition of obscenity that was an expansion of the definition the Court developed in the 1957 case *Roth v. United States*.[24] The ruling made it hard to prosecute sex-themed works because this new legal definition required a finding that works were "utterly without redeeming social value." Most films or books contain a kernel of a story line or smidgen of non-sexual plotting that amount to some social value. Pornographers took pains to make sure this was so.

The social value test was suggested in *Roth* and formally adopted in *Memoirs*. Under the combined *Roth/Memoirs* test, other appellate courts found most sex-themed materials to be non-obscene and thus protected by the Constitution. Adult bookstores and theaters proliferated from the late 1960s through the 1980s, two presidential commissions studied pornography, and the Supreme Court generally ruled in favor of free speech when obscenity cases were brought to court. Justices on the Supreme Court, however, were divided on how to define obscenity and whether they should be spending so much time perusing sexual expression. For example:

• In 1964, the Court invalidated the $2,500 fine levied against a Cleveland Heights theater manager who was convicted of obscenity charges for showing *Les Amants*, a French film about an unfaithful wife. It was in this case that Justice Stewart conceded that he could not intelligibly improve on the legal definition of obscenity. "But I know it when I see it, and the motion picture involved in this case is not that,"[25] he wrote.

• In 1966, Justice Hugo Black objected to "saddling this Court with the irksome and inevitably unpopular and unwholesome task of finally deciding by a case-by-case, sight-by-sight personal judgment of the members of this Court what pornography (whatever that means) is too hard core for people to see or read."[26]

• In 1967, the Court reversed obscenity convictions from New York, Kentucky and Arkansas for distribution of the publications *High Heels, Gent, Swank, Lust Pool* and *Shame Agent* magazines. The justices disagreed on what rule of law to apply, but deemed the material protected "whichever of these constitutional views is brought to bear."[27]

• In 1968, Justice Harlan noted that the Court had published fifty-five separate opinions for 130 obscenity cases since *Roth*, creating a "chaotic state of affairs" that was "unmatched in any other course of constitutional adjudication." Harlan concluded: "[A]nyone who undertakes to examine the Court's decisions since *Roth* which have held particular material obscene or not obscene would find himself in utter bewilderment."[28]

• And, in 1970, Chief Justice Warren Burger complained about assuming the role of a "supreme and unreviewable board of censorship for the 50 states."[29]

The struggles the Court had in defining and regulating obscenity were mirrored throughout the judicial system. Some scholars, attorneys and judges joined Justices Black and Douglas in opposition to all obscenity laws, but most jurists and observers agreed that the task was unavoidable. Indeed, many so-called absolutists who insist that consenting adults have a right to view whatever they desire, agree that lines must be drawn for material aimed at children or that is obtrusive and unavoidable, such as billboards.

If limits must be imposed for materials that are available to children, the central question becomes, "Where are those lines drawn?" In 1973, in *Miller v. California*,[30] the fragmentation on the Supreme Court abated when five justices, for the first time since *Roth*, agreed where some lines should be set. The decision established the legal definition of obscenity in effect today.

MILLER V. CALIFORNIA

Marvin Miller sent a mass mailing to California residents, promoting four illustrated books — *Intercourse, Sex Orgies Illustrated, Man-Woman* and *An Illustrated History of Pornography* — and a film, *Marital Intercourse*. A restaurant owner and his

---

without redeeming social value.

[22] *Id.* at 427 (Douglas, J., concurring).

[23] *Id.* at 441-42 (Clark, J., dissenting).

[24] 354 U.S. 476 (1957).

[25] Jacobellis v. Ohio, 378 U.S. 184, 197 (1964) (Stewart, J., concurring).

[26] Mishkin v. New York, 383 U.S. 502, 516-17 (1966) (Black, J., dissenting).

[27] Redrup v. New York, 386 U.S. 767, 771 (1967).

[28] Interstate Circuit v. Dallas, 390 U.S. 676, 707, 704-05, 707 (1968) (Harlan, J., concurring and dissenting).

[29] Walker v. Ohio, 398 U.S. 434, 443 (1970) (Burger, C.J., dissenting).

[30] 413 U.S. 15 (1973).

mother in Newport Beach who received copies of the brochure complained to police. Miller was eventually charged with violating California's obscenity statute.

The Supreme Court described the brochure as consisting primarily of "pictures and drawings very explicitly depicting men and women in groups of two or more engaged in a variety of sexual activities, with genitals often prominently displayed."[31] Five justices, in an opinion written by Chief Justice Burger, found the brochure obscene under the Court's new definition:[32]

(1) whether the average person, applying contemporary community standards, would find that the work, taken as a whole, appeals to the prurient interest;
(2) whether the work depicts or describes, in a patently offensive way, sexual conduct specifically defined by applicable state law;
(3) whether the work, taken as a whole, lacks serious literary, artistic, political, or scientific value.

The first two parts of the *Miller* test were quite similar to the first two parts of the *Memoirs* test. In part three, however, the Court rejected the requirement that a work be utterly without redeeming social value and replaced it with the more restrictive requirement that the work lack serious value as determined by the "average person." In addition, the *Memoirs* definition had used the broad adjective "social" to qualify value; the *Miller* test specified that the value be literary, artistic, political or scientific, omitting, for example, entertainment value. The *Miller* test was a significant alteration of the third part of the *Memoirs* test by setting aside the implied social or moral expertise of an average person for the actual expertise of a "reasonable person" in areas such as the arts and sciences. The actual expertise requirement was made explicit by a Court ruling in 1987.[33]

On the same day that the Court decided *Miller*, it decided four other obscenity cases, all by 5-4 votes, clarifying a variety of constitutional provisions in obscenity law. Justice Douglas dissented in each case, insisting that the First Amendment protects even obscene material; Justice Brennan, joined by Thurgood Marshall and Potter Stewart, dissented, arguing that "obscenity" could not be defined sufficiently to give effective notice to guide producers of sexual material in the acceptable directions and, therefore, should be decriminalized.[34]

In *Kaplan v. California*, the Court ruled that images were not necessary for a work to be obscene; words alone are sufficient.[35]

Kaplan involved *Suite 69*, a book sold by the Peek-A-Boo Bookstore, one of 250 adult bookstores in Los Angeles. The Court described it as consisting "entirely of repetitive descriptions of physical, sexual conduct, 'clinically' explicit and offensive to the point of being nauseous."[36] The Court said the book contained almost every conceivable variety of sexual contact, homosexual and heterosexual, regardless of whether a reader sampled every fifth, tenth or twentieth page, and regardless of the page upon which the reader started.

In *Paris Adult Theatre I v. Slaton*,[37] the Court confirmed that adult movies could be found obscene, even when they were marketed discreetly. The Court described the Atlanta adult movie house as having a "conventional, inoffensive theatre entrance, without pictures." And the entrance door had the sign, "Adult theatre — you must be 21 and able to prove it. If viewing the nude body offends you, please do not enter." The fact that the theater had a tasteful, non-exploitative exterior and that it restricted its clients to interested adults did not exempt it from obscenity prosecution.

Finally, the Court upheld two federal prosecutions for importing obscene material into the United States for private, personal use and for the transportation of obscene material in common carriers in interstate commerce.[38]

Miller Part 1: The Prurient Interest Test

The first prong of the *Miller* test — "Whether the average person, applying contemporary community standards, would find that the work, taken as a whole, appeals to prurient interest" — is the easiest to satisfy. It requires that sexual expression be judged according to average persons — not particularly susceptible and sensitive persons or totally insensitive persons. And the work is judged according to local, contemporary standards, which may vary from community to community. Wrote the *Miller* majority:

It is neither realistic nor constitutionally sound to read the First Amendment as requiring the people of Maine or Mississippi to accept public depiction of conduct found tolerable in Las Vegas or New York City.... People in different states vary in their tastes and attitudes, and this diversity is not to be strangled by the absolutism of imposed uniformity.[39]

The first part of the *Miller* test requires that the overall work

---

[31] *Id.* at 18.

[32] *Id.* at 24.

[33] Pope v. Illinois, 481 U.S. 497 (1987).

[34] Paris Adult Theatre I v. Slaton, 413 U.S. 49, 103 (1973) (Brennan, J., dissenting).

[35] 413 U.S. 115 (1973).

[36] *Id.* at 116-17.

[37] 413 U.S. 49 (1973).

[38] United States v. 12 200-Ft. Reels of Super 8mm Film, 413 U.S. 123 (1973); United States v. Orito, 413 U.S. 139 (1973).

[39] 413 U.S. 15, 32-33 (1973).

have a prurient appeal, that is, the work arouses an immoderate or unwholesome interest in sex. The work, however, is judged on its entirety, not on isolated or fleeting passages or scenes that contain sexual descriptions or images. When a Cincinnati art museum was prosecuted for exhibiting photographs by Robert Mapplethorpe, the judge required the 175-photo exhibit to be judged on the basis of seven controversial photos that had been isolated from the others in the exhibit, violating the intent of the *Miller* test.[40]

Judges have conducted crude content analyses to determine the appeal of the overall work. A federal district court judge in Georgia concluded that an issue of *Penthouse* magazine satisfied the first part of the *Miller* test because most pages were devoted to photos emphasizing the genitals of nude women. The judge noted: "The magazine's overwhelming effect, obviously planned, is to create sexual excitement and stimulation, to scratch the itch — or to create the itch itself — of prurient interest."[41]

Miller Part 2: The Patent Offensiveness Test

The second prong of the *Miller* test is "Whether the work depicts or describes, in a patently offensive way, sexual conduct specifically defined by the applicable state law."

The same federal judge who found that *Penthouse* appealed to a prurient interest in sex also found that it satisfied the second part of the *Miller* test: The sexual portrayal was sufficiently graphic to be considered patently offensive. Ordinary photographs or drawings of nudes would not satisfy such a requirement, but the 108 photographs in the five photo features went beyond nudity. The judge noted that eighty-seven photos included exposed breasts, buttocks or genitals; nine included actual or simulated lesbian, oral sex; seven alluded to masturbation through the location of fingers in or near genitals; and sixteen photos showed legs spread to expose genitals, with six "close-up photographs showing nothing but women's groins."[42]

The patent offensiveness requirement separates hard-core sexual portrayals from other sexual expression. For a sexual portrayal to be obscene, it must be specifically enumerated in a state obscenity statute. In *Miller*, the Court said such portrayals were of ultimate sexual acts, normal or perverted, actual or simulated, including masturbation, excretory functions and the lewd exhibition of genitals. State statutes that define the behaviors whose portrayals may be obscene read like a catalog of sexual practices for heterosexual and homosexual couples and individuals. In Virginia, for example, obscene material contains content that appeals to "a shameful or morbid interest in nu-

dity, sexual conduct, sexual excitement, excretory functions or products thereof or sadomasochistic abuse."[43]

Thus, communities must restrict obscenity prosecutions to works containing explicit portrayals of hard-core sex acts. One year after *Miller*, the city of Albany, Georgia, fined theater manager Billy Jenkins $750 and sentenced him to twelve months of probation for showing the movie *Carnal Knowledge*. Some critics listed the film as among the ten best movies of 1971, and Ann-Margret received an Academy Award nomination for her performance. The Supreme Court reversed the obscenity conviction and pointed out that juries do not have "unbridled discretion in determining what is 'patently offensive.'" Sexuality may have been the major theme of the movie, the Court said, but it was not obscene: "There is no exhibition whatever of the actors' genitals, lewd or otherwise, during these scenes. There are occasional scenes of nudity, but nudity alone is not enough to make material legally obscene under the *Miller* standard."[44] The case, *Jenkins v. Georgia*, is a strong reminder to those individuals who mistakenly believe that *Miller* gave communities unlimited power to regulate erotic material.

Subjectivity, imprecision and unpredictability occur in all three parts of the *Miller* test. Complicating this subjectivity, tolerance for sexual-themed materials varies from community to community. The concepts of patently offensive and prurient interest vary according to community norms, which the law apparently assumes are reflected in the attitudes of jurors.

Miller Part 3: The Serious Value Test

The third and final determinant of obscenity is "Whether the work, taken as a whole, lacks serious literary, artistic, political or scientific value." Even if a work appeals to the prurient interest and is patently offensive under state law, it must satisfy the third part of the *Miller* test to be obscene and to lie outside the protection of the First Amendment. In effect, the third part forces judges to play the role of artistic or social critics and evaluate the aesthetic merit of works containing sexual content. Prosecuting and defense attorneys may call expert witnesses to characterize the social value of the work for the jury.

The presence of a substantial amount of serious, non-sexual material may salvage a work that contains graphic sex, but the amount of non-sexual material must be substantial. One judge has cautioned: "A quotation from Voltaire in the flyleaf of a book will not constitutionally redeem an otherwise obscene publication."[45] Although some judges have classified *Penthouse* as

---

[40] Cincinnati v. Contemporary Arts Ctr., 566 N.E.2d 214 (Ohio Mun. 1990).

[41] Penthouse v. Webb, 594 F. Supp. 1186, 1198 (N.D. Ga. 1984).

[42] *Id.*

[43] VA. CODE § 18.2-372 (1950).

[44] Jenkins v. Georgia, 418 U.S. 153, 161 (1974).

[45] Kois v. Wisconsin, 408 U.S. 229, 231 (1972) (*quoted in Miller*, 413 U.S. 15, 25 n.7 (1973)).

obscene because of the quantity of explicit, erotic photographs, others have judged it non-obscene because of its serious articles. The Louisiana Supreme Court in 1980 found that the 228-page, June 1980 issue of *Penthouse* satisfied the first two parts of *Miller,* and that ninety-six pages of photo essays of women satisfied the third part because they constituted hard-core sexual conduct. However, the magazine as a whole was redeemed by sixty-seven pages of articles that had serious value: "These articles convey ideas, and purport to convey serious information. They do not lack serious political and scientific value, nor even serious literary value."[46]

Similarly, in 1979, a Boston Municipal Court judge upheld First Amendment protection for the film *Caligula* by a legal thread. He found that the film lacked social value because it "does not lift the spirit, does not improve the mind, nor does it enrich the human personality or develop character." But a political scientist had testified that the film had a serious political theme about absolute power corrupting absolutely, and no witness rebutted the point. The judge ruled that the movie was protected because the government had failed to prove beyond a reasonable doubt that the film lacked serious political value.[47]

Judges are not free to serve as their own fact finders on the issue of social value. A federal district court judge found the lyrics of the 2 Live Crew album *As Nasty As They Wanna Be* obscene, but he ignored the testimony of critics that the music had political significance and literary conventions, and the government presented no evidence on the issue of artistic value. The Eleventh U.S. Court of Appeals reversed the ruling, rejecting the argument that "simply by listening to this musical work, the judge could determine that it had no serious artistic value."[48]

A federal district judge determined in 1991 that a modicum of political or literary value can salvage a work. The judge ruled that a truck driver's bumper sticker, "How's my driving? Call 1-800-EAT-SHIT," had serious literary value because it parodied bumper stickers that encouraged drivers to call truck companies with comments about the driving habits of truck drivers. The judge also said the bumper sticker had serious political value because it protested the "Big Brother" mentality that is promoted by serious versions of the sticker, and it did not satisfy the first two parts of *Miller* because it was not erotic.[49]

Other judges have not been so quick to find redeeming value in sexually explicit material. In 1977, the Kentucky Supreme Court upheld an obscenity conviction and $4,000 fine against the Paducah Fourth Street Cinema for showing *Deep Throat.*

The Transition of the Obscenity Test

The Rationale:

" [I]mplicit in the history of the First Amendment is the rejection of obscenity as utterly without redeeming social importance."

Prurient Interest:

Roth (1957): The average person, applying contemporary community standards must find that the dominant theme of the material, taken as a whole, appeals to the prurient interest.

Roth-Memoirs (1966): The dominant theme of the material, taken as a whole, must appeal to the prurient interest in sex.

Miller (1973): An average person, applying contemporary, local community standards, must find that the work, taken as a whole, appeals to the prurient interest.

Patent Offensiveness:

Roth (1957): The material is patently offensive because it affronts contemporary community standards.

Miller (1973): The work depicts in a patently offensive way sexual conduct specifically defined by applicable state law.

Value of the Work:

Roth (1957): The material is utterly without redeeming social value.

Miller (1973): The work lacks serious literary, artistic, political or scientific value.

The court held that the movie lacked serious value: "The story line consists entirely of the sexual activities of Miss Linda Lovelace. We failed to find any serious literary, artistic, political or scientific value in this motion picture."[50] A federal district court, four years later, similarly failed to find serious value in the film *Cinderella-96,* which was described as a translation of the fictional character Cinderella into a bawdy, lusty tale of recurring homosexual and heterosexual encounters. The judge said the "sum and substance of the movie is the almost unbroken string of sexual acts depicted." He concluded that the movie was obscene even though it contained no sexual penetration or ejaculation. And he said it lacked serious literary and artistic value even though it may be entertaining and enjoyable to some viewers.[51]

[46] Louisiana v. Walden Book Co., 386 So. 2d 342, 346 (La. 1980).

[47] Massachusetts v. Saxon Theatre Corp., 6 Media L. Rep. (BNA) 1979 (Boston Mun. Ct. 1980).

[48] Luke Records, Inc. v. Navarro, 960 F.2d 134, 138 (11th Cir. 1992).

[49] Baker v. Glover, 776 F. Supp. 1511 (N.D. Ga. 1991).

[50] Western Corp. v. Kentucky, 558 S.W.2d 605, 607 (Ky. 1977).

[51] Septum, Inc. v. Keller, 7 Media L. Rep. (BNA) 1664 (N.D. Ga. 1981).

OBSCENITY AND PUBLIC OPINION

After *Miller v. California*, obscenity convictions decreased, and more sexual materials became available. This may be because the public doesn't want obscenity laws to be strictly enforced. Some prosecutors and judges — those people responsible for enforcing obscenity law — are elected, and members of the public serve on the juries that decide criminal obscenity cases. Studies show that many people use erotica or tolerate its use by others. A 1994 study, for example, reported that 41 percent of men and 16 percent of women questioned said they had purchased auto-erotic materials during the previous twelve months. Twenty-three percent of the men had watched sexually explicit movies, 22 percent had visited clubs with erotic dancers, and 16 percent had purchased sexually explicit books or magazines. Only 34 percent of all subjects said they believed there should be laws prohibiting the sale of pornography to adults.[52]

Other studies report similar results. An Indiana survey found that 54 percent of adults questioned had watched adult videos or movies at least once.[53] A 1991 Gallup Poll found that 53 percent of adults either opposed tightening standards in their communities for the sale of sexually explicit material or wanted the standards to be less restrictive. In addition, more than 50 percent of adults said magazines with nudity or that show adults having sexual relations, theaters showing adult movies and sexually explicit video rentals should be available to adults without restrictions or without public displays.[54] Tolerance has no doubt increased in the years since the study.

These attitudes translate into high demand for sex-themed material. The Kinsey Institute estimated in 1990 that 35 million copies of "girlie" magazines are sold each month.[55] Reliable statistics on the sale of X-rated movie tickets or the rental of adult videos are unavailable, but the proliferation of home video and access to the Internet have played a major role in making sexual films more available to interested adults. The number of households with VCRs increased from less than 1 percent in 1978 to 73 percent in 1992. In 2002, more than 40 million American homes had DVD players, and the availability of sex videos has skyrocketed. In 2001, a producer of pornographic videos estimated the size of the U.S. porn industry at $10 billion. This included 25,000 video outlets, 10,000 new adult video titles a year and 711 million rentals of hard-core sex films.[56]

The proliferation of girlie magazines, increased explicitness of the major men's magazines, and growing availability of DVDs and sex videos are developments that reflect a public that consumes more sex-themed material and is increasingly tolerant of it. This is a public that balks at obscenity prosecutions. Law professor Robert Riggs counted the number of obscenity cases appealed to higher courts before and after *Miller* and found a sharp upward trend from 1969 to 1974, the year after the decision, and an "almost equally sharp down turn" after 1974.[57] Political scientist Harold Leventhal detected similar trends when he surveyed local prosecuting attorneys about obscenity enforcement before and after *Miller*. Although prosecutors reported an increase in the quantity of obscenity in their communities after 1973, they reported a lower priority for prosecuting obscenity and a drop in the number of obscenity cases. Leventhal concluded that *Miller* failed to spur more obscenity prosecutions.[58] Similarly, former University of Chicago law professor Cass Sunstein observed in 1993 that "realistically speaking, most people involved in the production of sexually explicit work have little to fear from the *Miller* test."[59]

So, while the three-part *Miller* test and the wording of some local obscenity statutes theoretically have made it easier to prosecute obscenity, the public has grown increasingly tolerant of sexual expression and has reduced political pressures on elected officials to enforce obscenity laws. And some members of that public have difficulty when they serve as jurors and are asked to restrict magazines or films that are similar to materials that the jurors may have rented or purchased themselves.

THE SCANT PROTECTION OF OBSCENITY

Miller and its companion cases were aimed at restricting the transportation and sale of explicit sexual expression, but what of the possession of sexually explicit material? Coexisting with the doctrine that obscenity may be regulated is a second doctrine at the core of which is the concept that when people are in the privacy of their homes, the government may not interfere with their personal thought process or their perusal of words or pictures. Under this doctrine, the private possession of objectionable material is legal in nearly every case.

Justice Marshall, in *Stanley v. Georgia,* a 1969 case, articulated this concept that the mere possession of obscenity for private use is generally beyond the reach of government.[60] When police searched the home of Robert Eli Stanley for bookmaking

---

[52] ROBERT MICHAEL ET AL., SEX IN AMERICA: A DEFINITIVE SURVEY (1994).

[53] JUNE REINISCH & RUTH BEASLEY, THE KINSEY INSTITUTE NEW REPORT ON SEX (1990).

[54] THE GALLUP POLL MONTHLY, October 1991.

[55] SAMUEL JANUS & CYNTHIA JANUS, THE JANUS REPORT ON SEXUAL BEHAVIOR (1993).

[56] *See* Mark Cromer, *Porn's Compassionate Conservatism,* THE NATION, Feb. 26, 2001, at 25.

[57] Robert Riggs, Miller v. California: *An Empirical Note,* 1981 BYU L. REV. 247.

[58] Harold Leventhal, *An Empirical Inquiry into the Effects of* Miller v. California *on the Control of Obscenity,* 52 N.Y.U. L. REV. 810 (1977).

[59] CASS SUNSTEIN, DEMOCRACY AND THE PROBLEM OF FREE SPEECH 211 (1993).

[60] 394 U.S. 557 (1969).

equipment, they found no gambling devices but discovered three reels of sexually explicit 8mm film.

In his majority opinion overturning Stanley's conviction, Justice Marshall found that the mere private possession of obscene matter could not be a crime under the Constitution. The state has no right "to control the moral content of a person's thoughts," he wrote, and the right to receive information and ideas is critical. Wrote Marshall:

If the First Amendment means anything, it means that a state has no business telling a man, sitting alone in his own home, what books he may read or what films he may watch. Our whole constitutional heritage rebels at the thought of giving government the power to control men's minds.[61]

Stanley was as much a victory for home sanctity as for free expression. A year later the Supreme Court upheld homeowners' prerogatives in another case involving pornography. In *Rowan v. U.S. Post Office,* it gave homeowners "complete and unfettered discretion" to prohibit a pornography distributor from mailing sex-themed material to a homeowner's address. "[W]e are often 'captives' outside the sanctity of the home and subject to objectionable speech," the Court noted. But that does not mean "we must be captives everywhere." The homeowner has sole discretion in deciding whether mailed material is sexually arousing or sexually provocative and can require the postal service to notify the mailer to stop sending the material to the homeowner.[62] Theoretically, a homeowner could judge a gun catalog or jewelry brochure, even one lacking human models, as erotic and order the distributor to cease mailings.

The reach of the *Stanley* ruling, however, was substantially diminished in subsequent cases, perhaps most notably in 1990 when the Court found the possession of child pornography, even at home, was subject to criminal prosecution.[63] The ruling in *Osborne v. Ohio* reemphasized the Court's finding of a compelling government interest in protecting child victims of pornography as elaborated in *New York v. Ferber.*[64]

State legislatures and supreme courts have minimized obscenity prosecutions. A state high court can do so by finding an obscenity statute unconstitutional as the Wisconsin Supreme Court did in 1980.[65] As long as the legislature remains inactive in redrafting a statute, obscenity prosecution is stymied. Similarly, in 1979, the Arkansas Supreme Court reversed a $1,000 fine and one-month jail term for the possession of one obscene

film in a home.[66] And, as the result of decisions by the Iowa Supreme Court, the dissemination and ownership of obscene material was legal for adults in Iowa from 1973 to 1977. In 1973, the court ruled that the state's obscenity statute was inconsistent with *Miller v. California.*[67] And, in 1977, the court ruled that state obscenity law restricted obscenity for minors but not for adults.[68] For twelve years, 1973 to 1985, there were no obscenity prosecutions in North Carolina because of the complexity of that state's law. A specific work could not be the target of a criminal obscenity prosecution until it first had been declared obscene in an advisory hearing.[69]

It is difficult for state legislators to get elected on a platform of decriminalizing obscenity. In 1990, a federal district court judge in Florida told opponents of obscenity laws: "In sum, if persons subscribe to the view that obscenity should be legalized, they should take their petitions to Tallahassee, the Florida capital, not to the steps of the U.S. courthouse."[70] But most state legislatures have been unsympathetic.

Most actions to abolish obscenity laws come from state supreme courts, which are more independent of voters than legislatures are. The most dramatic example is Oregon. In 1987, the Oregon Supreme Court voted unanimously to decriminalize the sale or ownership of obscenity for adults, though sale of sexually explicit material to minors remained illegal.[71] The court reversed the conviction of Earl Henry, the operator of an adult bookstore in Redmond, ruling that the state constitution's free-expression clause was broader than the First Amendment and protected obscenity. The court reasoned that territorial law existing in 1857, when the constitution was adopted, only prohibited the distribution of obscenity to minors. The court concluded: "In this state any person can write, print, read, say, or sell anything to a consenting adult even though the expression may be generally or universally considered 'obscene.'"[72]

Obscenity protection made other inroads in western states. The Hawaii Supreme Court ruled that the right of privacy, which had been incorporated in its state constitution nine years earlier, protected adult possession of obscenity. "Since a person has the right to view pornographic items at home," the court said in a unanimous opinion, "there necessarily follows a correlative right to purchase such materials for this personal use, or the underlying privacy right becomes meaningless."[73] The

---

[61] *Id.* at 565.

[62] 397 U.S. 728, 737 (1970).

[63] Osborne v. Ohio, 495 U.S. 103 (1990).

[64] 458 U.S. 747 (1982). This case is discussed accompanying *infra* note 106..

[65] Wisconsin v. Princess Cinema, 292 N.W.2d 807 (Wis. 1980).

[66] Buck v. Arkansas, 578 S.W.2d 579 (Ark. 1979).

[67] State v. Wedelstedt, 213 N.W.2d 562 (Iowa 1973).

[68] Chelsea Theater Corp. v. Burlington, 258 N.W.2d 372 (Iowa 1977).

[69] *See* Samuel Currin & Robert Howers, *Regulation of Pornography — The North Carolina Approach,* 21 WAKE FOREST L. REV. 263 (1986).

[70] Skywalker Records, Inc. v. Navarro, 739 F. Supp. 578, 587 (S.D. Fla. 1990).

[71] State v. Henry, 732 P.2d 9 (Or. 1987).

[72] *Id.* at 18.

[73] State v. Kam, 748 P.2d 372, 380 (Haw. 1988).

court indicated in a footnote that it was not deciding the issue of child pornography, the sale to minors, the obtrusive public display of pornography, the showing of obscenity to a captive audience, or films that depicted actual killings.

The Oregon obscenity doctrine almost crossed the Columbia River into Washington. There, the state's supreme court voted 5-4 that Washington's constitution did not afford obscenity greater protection than the federal constitution. The four-judge minority favored Oregon's approach.[74] One vote made the difference in public policy.

An effort to use a state constitution to expand protection for pornography occurred in Wisconsin in 1999. The Crossroads News Agency, an adult bookstore located along Interstate 94, was fined $4,000 and court costs for the sale of the obscene videotape, *Anal Vision No. 5*. The Wisconsin Supreme Court unanimously rejected the argument that the Wisconsin constitution provided greater protection for obscenity than the U.S. Constitution. The court observed that Oregon was the only state that had created this kind of protection of the roughly one-third of the state jurisdictions that had interpreted their state constitutional speech clauses to protect obscenity.[75]

PROTECTING CHILDREN AND JUVENILES

Even when obscenity is decriminalized for consenting adults, courts recognize the need to restrict sexually explicit material from view by juveniles and children. The exception has two manifestations. First, federal and state laws prohibit the sale of sexual materials to minors. Second, federal and state law prohibits the distribution of materials portraying children or juveniles in sexually explicit situations.

Variable Obscenity

State and federal laws don't merely ban the sale of legally obscene materials to minors; they also ban the sale of sexual materials that would be legal if sold to adults. This approach to regulating material has been called "variable obscenity." The government may be stricter in prohibiting the sale of sexual materials to juveniles than to adults.

In 1968, the Supreme Court upheld a New York statute that made it a crime to sell materials containing nudity to anyone under the age of 16. Sam Ginsberg, the owner of a Bellmore, Long Island, luncheonette, sold two girlie magazines to a 16-year-old boy on two different occasions. The magazines contained pictures of nude women that were clearly not obscene.[76]

The Court upheld the conviction and denied that the statute lacked a rational justification, even though studies neither proved nor disproved a causal link between sex-themed material and the ethical and moral development of youths.

Events three decades later demonstrate that the doctrine of variable obscenity remains very much alive. In 1996, a panel of the U.S. Court of Appeals for the Ninth Circuit upheld a California statute banning the sale of sexually oriented publications from unsupervised news racks. The court held that the California legislature had a compelling interest in shielding juveniles from sexual material that was not obscene for adults.[77] The next year, Phoenix police used a similar Arizona statute to justify seizure of fifteen coin-operated news racks for a local, sexually oriented weekly, *Beat*, which had been published for thirty-three years and had a circulation of 8,500. The publisher, Jerry Evenson, commented: "We're not pornographic. We have no full nudity, there is no profanity. The only thing we have is bare nipples." Simply reporting on the Phoenix event caused a controversy for the trade magazine *Editor & Publisher*. Its Richmond, Virginia, printer refused to include a two-inch reproduction of an ad from *Beat* showing bare-breasted dancers.[78]

The FCC has applied the same logic in prohibiting the use of indecent language on commercial radio. The Supreme Court has said radio may be restricted more than print media because of its intrusiveness and its accessibility to children.[79] The case began when WBAI broadcast a twelve-minute monologue by George Carlin, "Filthy Words," at 2 p.m. His satire was an analysis of the seven words — crude references to sex, excrement, body parts, and so forth — that were banned from broadcasting. Although the station preceded the monologue with an advisory that it contained offensive language, a man who was driving with his young son missed the advisory and tuned in to the middle of the monologue. He complained to the FCC.

The Supreme Court voted 5-4 to uphold possible civil sanctions against the station, but its decision was based on the fact that radio is uniquely available to children. The majority said the decision balanced the significant interests of listeners in their homes against broadcasters' interests. A concurring opinion indicated that the ruling did not apply to the isolated use of an offensive word in a broadcast. Eleven years later, in 1989, the Court underscored the importance of the intrusiveness factor and invalidated a ban on telephone indecency. The FCC was attempting to control the dial-a-porn business that made sexually oriented telephone messages available to people who paid for calls that began with the numbers 900. The Court indicated that the telephone was not nearly as intrusive as the radio:

---

[74] State v. Reece, 757 P.2d 947 (Wash. 1988).

[75] County of Kenosha v. C & S. Mgmt., Inc., 588 N.W.2d 236 (Wis. 1999).

[76] Ginsberg v. New York, 390 U.S. 629 (1968).

[77] Crawford v. Lungren, 96 F.3d 380 (9th Cir. 1996).

[78] *See* Mark Fitzgerald, *News Racks Seized,* EDITOR & PUBLISHER, Oct. 11, 1997, at 8.

[79] FCC v. Pacifica Found., 438 U.S. 726 (1978).

"Placing a telephone call is not the same as tuning in a radio and being taken by surprise by an indecent message."[80]

From 1989 to 1993, while Alfred Sikes was FCC chairman, the commission actively enforced radio's prohibition against indecency and levied fines ranging from $2,000 to $600,000. Most notorious was radio shock-jock Howard Stern, who paid a total of $1.7 million in fines for his off-color morning commentaries. He was cited for his numerous and explicit references to masturbation, fornication, excretory functions and sexual organs. A study of broadcast indecency fines for 1987-1997 found that the FCC issued thirty-six fines. The study concluded that the FCC tended to fine stations "when humor is combined with patently offensive descriptions of sexual or excretory activities or organs, expletives, or sexual innuendo."[81]

In 2001, the FCC attempted to clarify its indecency ban that is in effect daily from 6 a.m. to 10 p.m. on AM and FM radio and commercial television. The FCC said that it applies three criteria to determine indecency: (1) explicitness or graphic nature of the depiction of sexual or excretory organs or activities; (2) whether the materials dwell on or repeat at length such sexual depictions; (3) the context and whether the depiction appears to pander or titillate, or is presented for shock value. The heart of the FCC statement was thirty-two explicit examples from FCC indecency cases, twenty-three of which were ruled indecent. The indecent examples included the *Howard Stern Show* and songs with titles like "Uterus Guy," "You Suck," "Sit on My Face" and "Penis Envy." The nine segments that were found not to be indecent were from the *Oprah Winfrey Show,* the *Geraldo Rivera Show,* the film *Schindler's List* and the National Public Radio show *All Things Considered.*[82]

In addition, in 2005, Congress passed and a year later President George W. Bush signed a bill providing for a ten-fold increase in fines the FCC could levy on broadcast stations for airing indecent material. Apparently fed up with sexual references and incidents like the brief exposure of singer Janet Jackson's breast in 2004 Super Bowl half-time performance, Congress set the maximum possible fine for each incident at $325,000. The president signed the Broadcast Decency Enforcement Act of 2005 in June 2006.[83]

Two years later, the Third U.S. Circuit Court of Appeals held that the FCC's fine against CBS was improper because the agency had failed to give adequate notice as to why it was changing its method of determining on-air indecency.[84] The FCC had abandoned its policy of insulating what it called "fleeting expletives" from sanction. The court's ruling was short-lived, however. A year after the CBS ruling, the Supreme Court held in *FCC v. Fox Television Stations*[85] that the FCC did not act improperly when it changed its policy. The Court remanded the CBS case for reconsideration in light of its ruling in the *Fox Television* case.[86] To further complicate matters, the reversal of *Fox Television Stations* gave the Second Circuit an opportunity to reconsider the case on constitutional grounds. The case was originally considered only on whether the FCC had followed administrative law correctly when it changed the indecency policy. In 2010, the Second Circuit held that the FCC's policy related to indecency violated the First Amendment,[87] and the Supreme Court granted *certiorari.* In 2012, the Court held that the FCC did not give adequate notice to Fox Television Stations and ABC for the broadcast of an episode of *NYPD Blue* and, therefore, the standards as applied to the broadcasts were vague.[88] The Court set aside the FCC's orders.

The Supreme Court indicated in 1975 that there were limits to how far it would go to shelter children and disinterested adults from offensive speech that was not legally obscene. It ruled that a city ordinance prohibiting the showing of films with nudity in drive-in theaters with screens visible from streets or public places was unconstitutional.[89] The theater was prosecuted for the R-rated film *Class of '74.* The screen was visible from two city streets and a church parking lot. The Court majority said the censorship was not justified by the limited privacy interests of persons on public streets who could simply look away when confronted by offensive material. It said that "all nudity cannot be deemed obscene even as to minors."[90] Such a rule would bar films with pictures of baby's buttocks, nude bodies of war victims, cultures in which nudity is indigenous, the opening of art exhibits and bathers on a nude beach.

The Supreme Court applied similar logic when it invalidated the Communications Decency Act of 1996. The act made it a crime to communicate indecent material on the Internet to anyone 17 or younger. It defined "indecency" as patently offensive descriptions of sexual or excretory activities or organs. The Supreme Court said in *Reno v. American Civil Liberties Union* that the act would violate the First Amendment because it would allow Internet users to be punished for disseminating

---

[80] Sable Commc'ns v. FCC, 492 U.S. 115, 128 (1989).

[81] Milagros Rivera-Sanchez & Michelle Ballard, *A Decade of Indecency Enforcement: A Study of How the Federal Communications Commission Assesses Indecency Fines (1987-1997),* 75 JOURNALISM & MASS COMM. Q. 143, 147 (1998).

[82] In the Matter of Indecency: Guidance on the Commission's Case Law Interpreting, 18 U.S.C. 1464 (2000); Enforcement Policies Regarding Broadcast Indecency, *available at* http://www.fcc.gov.

[83] Pub. Law 109-235 (2006).

[84] CBS v. FCC, 535 F.3d 167 (3d Cir. 2008).

[85] 556 U.S. 502 (2009).

[86] FCC v. CBS, 556 U.S. 1218 (2009).

[87] Fox Television Stations v. FCC, 613 F.3d 317 (2d Cir. 2010).

[88] FCC v. Fox Television Stations, 132 S.Ct. 2307 (2012).

[89] Erznoznik v. Jacksonville, 422 U.S. 205 (1975).

[90] *Id.* at 212.

such things as the seven "dirty words" of the George Carlin monologue, discussions of prison rape or safe sexual practices, nude artistic images or, arguably, the card catalog of the Carnegie Library.[91] The Court concluded that the Internet was not as available to children as radio and television and that it was unconstitutional to deprive adults of sexual matter that was indecent but not obscene. The Court said banning such material "threatens to torch a large segment of the Internet community" and was like "burning the house to roast the pig."[92]

In 2000, the Supreme Court again invalidated a provision of the Telecommunications Act of 1996 that had restricted the dissemination of indecent and erotic material.[93] Two sections of the act had restricted the broadcasting by cable television of sexually oriented programming such as Playboy Television and Spice. The act required cable systems to fully scramble such programs so that the occasional and accidental bleeding of sexual images would not be available to children, or to delay the broadcasts to the safe harbor time period of 10 p.m. to 6 a.m., when children were less likely to be watching. Most cable systems opted for the delayed broadcasting because the technology for effective scrambling of signals was too expensive. Five justices agreed that the regulation unconstitutionally burdened the disseminators of programs that were indecent and sexual but not obscene. The majority favored the less restrictive and less intrusive alternative of requiring cable systems to inform their subscribers of a blocking option that would entirely block such sexual channels from their home televisions.

The *Reno v. ACLU* ruling provided First Amendment protection for indecency on the Internet but not for obscenity. Distributors of obscenity on the Internet have been successfully prosecuted. Robert and Carleen Thomas were sentenced to more than two years in federal prison and forfeited their computer system for operating a sex Internet site that they called "The Nastiest Place on Earth," from their Milpitas, California, home. A U.S. postal inspector in Memphis, Tennessee, paid $55 to copy their files. The two defendants were prosecuted on the basis of community standards in the recipient community of Memphis. A panel of a federal appeals court agreed that there was no need to adopt a new definition of community for obscenity prosecutions involving electronic bulletin boards.[94]

In addition, in 2006, the Supreme Court let stand a ruling by a federal three-judge panel for the Southern District of New York holding the obscenity provision of the Communications Decency Act was not overbroad.[95] The federal court held that the plaintiff failed to meet its burden proving that the community standards prong of the *Miller* test was not applicable to the widespread scope of the Internet.[96]

Congress has not given up in its attempt to protect children from sexual materials on the Internet. In 1998, following the *Reno* decision, it passed a statute that was narrower than the former Communications Decency Act. The new act, the Child Online Protection Act, prohibited easily accessible, commercial sexual materials on the World Wide Web that were harmful to minors. The law provided a three-part test, similar to the *Miller* test, to determine what content was harmful. Two of the three prongs were based on the application of community standards, which could mean local standards.

A U.S. court of appeals ruled that this use of community standards rendered the law substantially overbroad. The Supreme Court reversed the holding and ruled that it was just as valid to apply local standards to the Internet as to films, magazines and dial-a-porn telephone conversations, as the Court had in previous cases.[97] A dissenting Justice John Paul Stevens wrote that in the context of the Internet "community standards become a sword, rather than a shield." He argued, "If a prurient appeal is offensive in a Puritan village, it may be a crime to put it on the World Wide Web."[98]

In 2004, in its second opinion in the case — *Ashcroft v. ACLU* — the Supreme Court found unconstitutional the COPA provision that required Internet providers of porn to verify the age of customers. A five-justice majority found the age verification was not the least restrictive means of shielding minors from Internet pornography. The Court concluded that filters and blocking software on home computers were more effective methods.[99]

Congress' third attempt to shield children from Internet sexual expression met with success before the Supreme Court. In 2000, Congress passed the Children's Internet Protection Act, which required libraries that received federal subsidies to place filters on all their computers connected to the Internet. The purpose of the filters was to block child pornography and overtly sexual material that was inappropriate for children.

In a plurality opinion by Chief Justice Rehnquist, the Court upheld CIPA. It held: "Because public libraries have traditionally excluded pornographic material from their other collections, Congress could reasonably impose a parallel limitation on its Internet assistance program."[100] It noted that the statute allowed libraries to disconnect the filters for adults: "When a patron encounters a blocked site, he need only ask a librarian to

[91] 521 U.S. 844 (1977).

[92] *Id.* at 882.

[93] United States v. Playboy Entm't Group, Inc., 529 U.S. 803 (2000).

[94] United States v. Thomas, 74 F.3d 701 (6th Cir. 1996).

[95] Nitke v. Gonzales, 547 U.S. 1015 (2006).

[96] Nitke v. Gonzales, 413 F. Supp. 2d 262, 268-69 (S.D.N.Y. 2005).

[97] Ashcroft v. Am. Civil Liberties Union, 535 U.S. 564 (2002).

[98] *Id.* at 603 (Stevens, J., dissenting).

[99] Ashcroft v. Am. Civil Liberties Union, 542 U.S. 656 (2004).

[100] United States v. Am. Library Ass'n, 539 U.S. 194, 212 (2003) (plurality).

unblock it or disable the filter."[101] Justices Anthony Kennedy and Stephen Breyer wrote concurring opinions. Kennedy said the protection of minors was compelling and legitimate,[102] and Breyer said the law posed a comparatively small burden similar to the traditional library practice of isolating some materials in closed stacks where access required a wait and a signature for a patron.[103] In two dissenting opinions, Justice Stevens called the act a blunt nationwide restraint on adult access,[104] and Justice Souter, joined by Ruth Bader Ginsburg, said Congress could have protected children without restricting adults.[105]

The availability of sexual material on the Internet continues to trouble many people, especially parents and lawmakers. One solution to the problem that does not involve government or the courts is for parents to install software on home computers that filters out most sexual images and messages. Cyber Patrol, Net Nanny and X-Stop Librarian are examples of such software.

Child Pornography

The Constitution protects many portrayals of adults in sexual situations. But material that portrays minors is another matter. The Supreme Court, Congress, state supreme courts and legislatures have been unequivocal in authorizing criminalization of child pornography. In 1982, the Supreme Court upheld a state statute that prohibited the dissemination of material with sexual performances by children under the age of 16. *New York v. Ferber*[106] involved a Manhattan store that sold films of young boys masturbating. The Court conceded that material depicting children in sexual situations could be prosecuted even if it would not be obscene had it depicted adults in the same situation. But, in reversing the state's highest appellate court, the Court said the paramount concern in such cases was protecting children who were portrayed in such materials from psychological, emotional and mental harm. This was clearly a compelling state interest that justified some limits on expression.

Eight years later, the Supreme Court upheld an Ohio law that prohibited the possession of materials depicting nude children unless they served a *bona fide* artistic, scientific or educational purpose.[107] Clyde Osborne was sentenced to six months in prison for possession of four photographs of juvenile, nude males in sexually explicit positions. The Court said the gravity of the state interest in protecting victims of child pornography

justified the limits on free expression. The Ohio Supreme Court specifically limited its ruling to the lewd exhibition or graphic focus on genitals to prevent punishment for possession of innocuous photographs of naked children.

Child pornography, then, is one of the few categories of legally taboo speech in American society. However, during its 2001-02 term the Supreme Court found unconstitutional a federal law that criminalized images that did not involve real children but were computer images of fictitious children engaged in imaginary sexual conduct. The statute made illegal a visual depiction that appeared to be or "convey[ed] the impression" of a minor engaged in explicit sex. In a 6-3 opinion, the Court concluded: "The Government has shown no more than a remote connection between speech that might encourage thoughts or impulses and any resulting child abuse."[108]

In 2008, however, the Court upheld the constitutionality of a federal law that makes it a crime to advertise material as child pornography, regardless of whether actual children are involved.[109] Under the law, a crime occurs when an advertiser believes or intends for the customer to believe that the advertised material depicts real children.

PANDERING AND ZONING

Most of this chapter has analyzed the definitional approach for restricting inappropriate or sex-themed expression. Zoning laws and the concept of pandering are other approaches for controlling such material. The more obscure of the two is pandering.

Pandering

The classic pandering case is *Ginzburg v. United States*. Ralph Ginzburg was sentenced to five years in federal prison and fined $42,000 because of the method he used to promote his sex-themed but non-obscene books and periodicals. What was thought to be a liberal Supreme Court upheld the conviction by a 5-4 vote. Earl Warren and William Brennan voted to uphold the conviction because of Ginzburg's blatant pandering: "The business of purveying textual or graphic matter openly advertised to appeal to the erotic interest of their customers."[110]

Ginzburg — a former articles editor for *Esquire* and staff writer for NBC and *Reader's Digest* — mailed nine million copies of a brochure to promote the book, *The Housewife's Handbook on Selective Promiscuity;* the newsletter, *Liaison;* and the hardcover quarterly devoted to love and sex, *Eros.* The mailings generated 150,000, $25 subscriptions to *Eros.*

---

101 *Id.* at 209 (plurality).

102 *Id.* at 214 (Kennedy, J., concurring in judgment).

103 *Id.* at 215 (Breyer, J., concurring in judgment).

104 *Id.* at 220 (Stevens, J., dissenting).

105 *Id.* at 231 (Souter, J., dissenting).

106 458 U.S. 747 (1982).

107 Osborne v. Ohio, 495 U.S. 103 (1990).

---

108 Ashcroft v. Free Speech Coal., 535 U.S. 234, 254 (2002).

109 United States v. Williams, 553 U.S. 285 (2008).

110 383 U.S. 463, 467 (1966).

The Supreme Court said Ginzburg's method of promotion could be used to judge the content of the works: "Where the purveyor's sole emphasis is on the sexually provocative aspects of his publications, that fact may be decisive in the determination of obscenity."[111] Ginzburg had highlighted the erotic nature of his publications by mailing the promotions from cities whose names had sexual connotations: Intercourse and Blue Ball, Pennsylvania, and Middlesex, New Jersey.

Civil libertarians denounced the decision. They pointed out that none of Ginzburg's publications were even close to satisfying the court's own definition of obscenity. *Eros* had received a number of national graphics awards, including one from the National Society of Art Directors. In order to secure a conviction, federal prosecutors had moved the trial from New York City to more conservative Philadelphia, where the mayor had narrowly won election on a promise to rid the city of smut, and the police department's obscenity control squad recently had arrested twenty-two magazine dealers and confiscated seventeen vanloads of magazines. Ginzburg's appeal to the Supreme Court was supported by briefs of the American Civil Liberties Union, the Authors League of America and a group of writers that included literary icons Joseph Heller, James Jones, Norman Mailer and Arthur Miller.

Zoning

A decade after *Ginzburg,* the Supreme Court approved another non-content approach for the control of obscenity. In *Young v. American Mini Theatres, Inc.,* it allowed cities to use zoning laws to limit the location and concentration of businesses that specialize in sex-themed media.[112] The Pussy Cat, an adult theater in what had been a corner gas station, challenged a Detroit ordinance. The law said an adult business could not be located within 1,000 feet of two other adult businesses, or within 500 feet of a residential neighborhood. Adult businesses included pool halls, pawnshops and adult bookstores and theaters. The intent of the ordinance was to prevent the concentration of such businesses on one street.

In an opinion by Justice Stevens, the Court upheld the Detroit ordinance. Stevens wrote that the ordinance did not impose content limitations on the creators of adult movies or significantly restrict the viewing of such movies. He concluded that the impact of the ordinance on free expression was at most incidental and minimal. He attempted to create a doctrine granting sexual speech less protection than political speech, noting that "it is manifest that society's interest in protecting this type of expression is of a wholly different, and lesser, magnitude than the interest in untrammeled political debate."[113] But only a minority of justices joined him on that point.

In 2002, the Supreme Court again found it constitutional for cities to limit the geographic concentration of sex-themed businesses. It upheld a Los Angeles ordinance that prohibited the presence of more than one adult business in a building. The Court said that such uses of zoning laws must be backed up by studies that document a relationship between a concentration of adult business and undesirable secondary effects such as increases in crimes such as prostitution, robbery and assault.[114]

New York City Mayor Rudolph Giuliani used a Detroit-type ordinance to banish topless bars and X-rated peep shows from the Times Square area. And the state's highest court, the New York Court of Appeals, upheld the law. The unanimous decision noted that the number of adult establishments in New York City had grown from nine in 1965 to 177 in 1993; 107 of them were in Manhattan.[115]

DVDs, the advent of the Internet and the growth of cable television with adult networks have diminished the significance of the *Young* decision. In many cities adult theaters are a dying business.

RATINGS AND LABELING

Young helped to shield disinterested adults from unwanted sexual expression. It empowered cities to isolate adult businesses from homes, schools and churches and made it easier for disinterested adults to avoid such businesses. Offensive businesses that are unobtrusive and easily avoided are easier to tolerate. The voluntary labeling of movies, recordings and video games has had the same effect. It gives adults fair warning about the explicit content of media and assists them in avoiding material they find offensive for themselves or their children.

The Motion Picture Association of America initiated the most successful of the rating systems after Jack Valenti took over as president in 1966. That year a new kind of frankness emerged in movies. *Who's Afraid of Virginia Woolf* included the word "screw" and the phrase "hump the hostess." More movies contained nudity. Because of the fear of government censorship, the movie industry decided to create its own system for rating films. The system has changed over the years. As it exists today, the system has five categories:

• *G General Audiences.* All ages are admitted. The film contains nothing in language, nudity and sex, or violence that would offend parents whose children view the film. Snippets of language may go beyond polite conversation, but they are com-

---

[111] *Id.* at 470.

[112] 427 U.S. 50 (1976).

[113] *Id.* at 70.

[114] City of Los Angeles v. Alameda Books, Inc., 535 U.S. 425 (2002).

[115] Stringfellows of New York, Ltd. v. City of New York, 694 N.E.2d 407 (N.Y. 1998).

mon, everyday expressions.

• *PG   Parental Guidance Suggested.* Some material may not be suitable for children. There may be some profanity, violence or brief nudity, but these elements are not intense. There is no drug use content.

• *PG-13 Parents Strongly Cautioned.* Some material may be inappropriate for children under 13. The rating is required for drug use content or use of harsher, sexually derived words.

• *R   Restricted.* The admission of people under age 17 requires accompanying parent or adult guardian. The movie contains some adult material: hard language, tough violence, nudity within sensual scenes or drug abuse.

• *NC-17 No Children Under 17 Admitted.* The content of the movie is patently inappropriate for youngsters. The rating does not necessarily mean the content is obscene or pornographic. It can mean the presence of violence or sex or aberrational behavior or drug use that is too strong and therefore off-limits for viewing by children.

Leaders in the motion picture industry consider the movie rating system a success. The National Association of Theater Owners and the Video Software Dealers Association have embraced it. Polls conducted by the Opinion Research Corporation of Princeton, New Jersey, show that three-quarters of parents with children find the system very useful or fairly useful in selecting movies for their children.

The recording and video games industries have also adopted ratings, but in a more limited way. In 1985 the Recording Industry Association of America agreed to encourage its members to place the warning "Explicit Lyrics – Parental Advisory" on recordings containing references to explicit sex, violence or substance abuse. Instead of the warning, song lyrics may be printed on the back of the album cover. In 1994 the Software Publishers Association, following threats from Congress, agreed to encourage its members to label computer and video games. Games are labeled for age appropriateness and for the explicitness of violence, nudity or sex, and language.

The major advantage of such ratings is that, because they alert consumers to content, they tend to discourage the involvement of government in controlling that content. Congress has not been fully satisfied with the actions of the software industry, however, and several bills aimed at the industry were introduced but did not pass the 107th Congress.[116]

And in 1996, with pressure from Congress, most TV networks agreed to a voluntary rating system. The six classifications are:

• *TV-Y* Children's programs acceptable for kids of all ages.

• *TV-Y7* Children's programs for ages seven and older that might have material upsetting to younger kids.

• *TV-G* Appropriate for audiences of all ages.

• *TV-PG* Parental guidance suggested, may contain violence, sexual material or offensive language.

• *TV-14* Inappropriate for kids under fourteen because of more intense violence and sexual content.

• *TV-MA* Not for children under seventeen, may contain sex, profane language or graphic violence.

Additional rating subcategories were the following: V – violence, S – sexual situations, L – coarse language, D – suggestive dialogue and FV – fantasy violence. Television sets with "V-chips" may be programmed to restrict access to different categories of programs.[117]

SUMMARY

The landmark Supreme Court ruling in *Miller v. California* was not greatly heralded by either side of the sexual expression divide. In its aftermath, sexual-themed materials have become more available. Some of this may be attributed to technological developments that have provided easy access to the materials in private dwellings instead of public places. Increased access has occurred despite the ongoing efforts of virtually every state legislature to draft restrictive statutes. Sex-themed materials also have become quite commonplace in Canada. Under Canadian supreme court rules, portrayals of explicit sex are legal if they do not include degradation or violence.

Social mores are also arguably responsible because they clearly have grown quite tolerant of unobtrusive erotica. This often translates into less pressure on prosecutors and police to enforce obscenity laws and jurors who are less easily offended.

Nonetheless, the divide over sexual expression remains. It is part of what some have termed the culture wars.

FOR ADDITIONAL READING

Howitt, Dennis. *Crime, Media and the Law.* New York: John Wiley & Sons, 1998.

Lasky, Melvin J. *Profanity, Obscenity and the Media.* Somerset, N.J.: Transaction, 2004.

Linz, Daniel. "Estimating Community Standards: The Use of Social Science Evidence in an Obscenity Prosecution," 55 *Public Opinion Quarterly* 80-112 (Spring 1991).

Semonche, John. *Censoring Sex.* Lanham, Md.: Rowman & Littlefield, 2007.

Strossen, Nadine. *Defending Pornography: Free Speech, Sex, and the Fight for Women's Rights.* New York: Scribner, 1995.

---

[116] *See* Kyonzte Hughes, *Rating & Labeling Entertainment,* FIRST AMENDMENT CENTER, June 13, 2006, http://www.firstamendmentcenter.org. *See also,* Associated Press, *"Grand Theft Auto" Makers Settle With FTC Over Sex Content, available at* http://www.firstamendmentcenter.org.

[117] *See* Kelvin Childs, *No Rush to New TV Ratings,* EDITOR & PUBLISHER, Nov. 1, 1997, at 14.

Defamation

By Kyu Ho Youm

➡ **Headnote Questions**

- Why is libel considered an occupational hazard for media professionals?
- What are the key functions of libel law?
- What is the principal distinction between libel and slander?
- What must a plaintiff prove to win a libel case?
- What is the definition of "actual malice" in libel law?
- Why are state constitutions and common law important to libel law?
- What kinds of damages are recognized in a libel action?
- What kinds of defenses are available to libel defendants?
- Why is it a crucial libel defense issue to determine whether a plaintiff is a public official, public figure or private person?
- What comes closest to being an ironclad libel defense?
- When can "opinion" be used as a libel defense?
- Where does the law stand with regard to libel on the Internet?
- What is "republication" on the Internet?
- When is the anonymous online speaker subject to disclosure?
- When do U.S. media face transborder libel litigation, and what are the implications of foreign libel judgments?

Freedom of speech is not absolute. It must be balanced against other competing social interests. One area in which such balancing must occur is that of defamation. As the U.S. Supreme Court has noted: "[A]bsolute protection for the communications media requires a total sacrifice of the competing value served by the law of defamation."[1]

The libel law of a society indicates to a large extent how the society balances the importance of reputational interests with freedom of speech. Harm to reputation has been a criminal offense or a civil wrong since civilization's earliest days, but the social and cultural approach to reputation as a value varies from society to society. Professor Robert C. Post elaborates:

Defamation law would operate differently in a deference society than in a market society. In the latter, reputation is a quintessentially private possession; it is created by individual effort and is of importance primarily to those who have cre-

ated it. Reputation's claim to legal protection is neither greater nor less than the claim to public protection of similar private goods. The preservation of honor in a deference society, on the other hand, entails more than the protection of merely individual interests. Since honor is not created by individual labor, but instead by shared social perceptions that transcend the behavior of particular persons, honor is "public good, not merely a private possession."[2]

In the United States, defamation was one of the earliest legal actions available against the press, and it is still the most common legal danger to the media. Libel is clearly an occupational hazard for professional communicators: 70 percent of all libel actions are filed against the mass media; at least two-thirds of those are brought against newspapers.[3]

---

[1] Gertz v. Robert Welch, Inc., 418 U.S. 341, 341 (1974).

[2] Robert C. Post, *The Social Foundations of Defamation Law: Reputation and the Constitution,* 74 CAL. L. REV. 691, 702 (1986).

[3] *See* DONALD M. GILLMOR, POWER, PUBLICITY AND THE ABUSE OF LIBEL LAW 133 (1992).

Libel, then, has the very real possibility of chilling speech, particularly when one considers the ramifications of a libel suit. As attorney Barbara Dill writes:

Libel law in the United States is at a critical juncture. The old broken formula of sue-and-be-sued is not working well for anyone but lawyers. It costs too much, takes too long, and clogs the courts with fencing matches that end most often in technical decisions that bypass the fundamental issues and satisfy neither side.[4]

The chill caused by libel law is clearly an irony in the United States, where press freedom is protected as a constitutional right, but reputation is not. In many ways, First Amendment scholar Frederick Schauer writes, "[T]he American approach ... reflects a society in which the press is considered to occupy a much more important role in the resolution of public issues. The press occupies a special position in the American system, a position that accounts for its strong protection against inhibiting defamation laws."[5]

Libel suits are common, and they are not limited to traditional mainstream media and professional communicators. So-called "citizen journalists" or bloggers on social media are often the targets of libel litigation.[6] In an important Internet libel case, the Ninth U.S. Circuit Court of Appeals held that under the First Amendment, bloggers with no institutional media connections are no different from professional journalists formally affiliated with the traditional press.[7] "In defamation cases," the court stated, "the public-figure status of a plaintiff and the public importance of the statement at issue — not the identity of the speaker — provide the First Amendment touchstone."[8]

Attorney Bruce Sanford identifies the following key cyberlibel issues:[9]

• Should courts treat the Internet like print media or television?
• Does the new forum impact the public official/public figure inquiry?

• When online "journalists" are not backed by editors and lawyers, should they be held to the same standards of care as traditional journalists?
• Can liability for defamation arise out of "linking" to a site with libelous content?

In any case, instead of being passive, traditional and new media practitioners can be proactive in an attempt to stay out of trouble and to provide themselves with more protection should they be sued.

This chapter first reviews defamation law from the plaintiff's perspective and then provides an overview of libel defense strategies. It focuses on the elements of a cause of action for libel and related areas, including the technological impact of cyberspace and the emerging legal issues confronting news media and individuals around the world. It also explores various libel defenses the media use in accomplishing a great social good by publishing allegedly defamatory material.

DEFAMATION DEFINED

Defamation — the publication of material that would tend to hold one up to hatred, ridicule, contempt or spite — consists of twin torts: libel and slander. In general, libel is the publication of defamatory matter by written or printed words or by some other physical form. Slander is defamatory communication by spoken words, gestures or other transitory means.[10]

The distinction between libel and slander originated when relatively few people could read, and the spoken word was more credible. Since then, the written word has gained more credibility, and defamation by writing is perceived to cause greater harm. More recently, however, new modes of communication have developed that often make the distinction between libel and slander obsolete. Defamation by means of television or radio, for example, might have more impact and greater reach than that by a small newspaper. Modern legal guides suggest that, instead of the form of medium, courts should consider the area of dissemination, the deliberate and premeditated character of a publication and the persistence of the defamation when classifying a defamatory statement as libel or slander.[11]

Jurisdictions disagree on whether defamation by electronic means should be defined as libel or slander. Most states do not distinguish libel from slander with regard to broadcasting; but

---

[4] Barbara Dill, *Libel Law Doesn't Work, But Can It Be Fixed?, in* MARTIN LONDON & BARBARA DILL EDS., AT WHAT PRICE? LIBEL LAW AND FREEDOM OF THE PRESS 35 (1993).

[5] Frederick Schauer, *Social Foundations of the Law of Defamation: A Comparative Analysis,* 1 J. MEDIA L. & PRAC. 1, 18 (1980). For a perceptive articulation of how and why freedom of the press under the First Amendment should be expanded globally, *see* Lee C. Bollinger, UNINHIBITED, ROBUST, AND WIDE-OPEN: A FREE PRESS FOR A NEW CENTURY (2010).

[6] *See* Dan Frosch, *Venting Online, Consumers Can Find Themselves in Court,* N.Y. TIMES, May 31, 2010, 1A.

[7] Obsidian Fin. Grp., LLC v. Cox, 42 Media L. Rep. (BNA) 1186, 1191 (9th Cir. 2014).

[8] *Id.*

[9] BRUCE W. SANFORD, LIBEL AND PRIVACY § 8.4.10 (2d ed. 2015).

[10] *See* RESTATEMENT (SECOND) OF TORTS §§ 568(1), 568(2) (1977). "Defamation by pantomime" is recognized in Iowa and Nevada. *See* Kiray v. Hy-Vee, Inc., 716 N.W.2d 193 (Iowa Ct. App. 2006); K-Mart v. Washington, 866 P. 2d 274 (Nev. 1993). In April 2012, the Sixth U.S. Circuit Court of Appeals held: "Even if Kentucky recognized the tort of 'libel by pantomime,' defendants would be entitled to a qualified privilege for statements related to the conduct of their employees." Linton v. Riddle, 477 F. App'x, 322, 323 (6th Cir. 2012).

[11] *See id.* § 568(3).

four, including California, treat defamatory radio and television broadcasts as slander; and thirteen states, including New York, treat it as libel. A New York court explained its rationale:

When account is taken of the vast and far-flung audience reached by radio today, often far greater in number than the readers of the largest metropolitan newspaper, it is evident that the broadcast of scandalous utterances is in general as potentially harmful to the defamed person's reputation as a publication by writing. That defamation by radio, in the absence of a script or transcription, lacks the measure of durability possessed by written libel, in nowise lessens its capacity for harm.[12]

Some states — Connecticut and Tennessee are two — make a distinction between a statement broadcast from a script — libel — and that which is ad-libbed — slander. An appellate court in Georgia, noting that television broadcasting contains both libel and slander, coined the word "defamacast" to describe broadcast defamation. The court said, "Perhaps the most perplexing problem is whether defamatory material shown on television should be classified as a libel, a slander or in some third category." The court decided to classify this type of material:

Believing as we do that the common law must adapt, and classically has adapted, to meet new situations, we now make that "frank recognition..." that defamation by radio and television falls into a new category, thus completing the triptych. In this category, defamation by broadcast or "defamacast" is actionable *per se*.[13]

While debate on the issue continues, an increasing number of jurisdictions are accepting the position that, because of the wide dissemination and the increased power of the broadcast media, defamation by electronic means is closer to libel than slander.

THE RATIONALE AND REACH OF LIBEL LAW

Libel law protects the reputational interests of individuals because it involves statements about them made by others. Legal scholar David Anderson has identified four types of reputational harm in the context of relational interest. The defamation may (1) interfere with the plaintiff's existing relationships with other people; (2) interfere with future relationships; (3) destroy a favorable public image; or (4) create a negative public

image for a person who previously had no public image at all.[14]

Libel law also serves other important societal interests. It attempts to compensate for economic and emotional injury and promotes human dignity by providing a civilized forum in which a dispute is settled.

More importantly, libel law acts as a deterrent on the publication of false and injurious speech through the award of damages. The Supreme Court has noted, for example, that a state "may rightly employ its libel laws to discourage the deception of its citizens."[15] In addition, libel law serves a vital social interest by providing a check on media power. It opens the newsgathering and decision-making process of the media to public scrutiny and accountability. A federal judge in a libel action against *Time* magazine explained:

Time has refused to issue any correction or to print plaintiff's denial. Only through the litigation process has plaintiff been able to uncover and publish the evidence from which *Time* claimed to have learned the contents of [a secret document relating to the Beirut massacre in 1982]. And only through this avenue has he been able to bring to light the process by which the allegedly offending statement came to be written, including evidence of the possible motivations and truthfulness of its author. That this process has proved enormously expensive, and painfully contentious, is as much the product of *Time's* all-out litigation strategy as of any plan by plaintiff to intimidate the press.[16]

Constitutional and State Law

Although the Constitution does not explicitly recognize reputational rights, courts have often noted the value of a good name. In an oft-quoted opinion, Justice Potter Stewart characterized an individual's right to protection of reputation as "a concept at the root of any decent system of ordered liberty." He explained: "The protection of private personality, like the protection of life itself, is left primarily to the individual States under the Ninth and Tenth Amendments. But this does not mean that the right is entitled to any less recognition by this Court as a basic of our constitutional system."[17] Therefore, the Supreme Court has recognized that "society has a pervasive and strong interest in preventing and redressing attacks upon reputation."[18]

The Constitution, of course, is not the only source of law to be

---

[12] Shor v. Billingsley, 158 N.Y.S.2d 476, 484 (N.Y. Sup. Ct. 1956).

[13] Am. Broad.-Paramount Theatres, Inc. v. Simpson, 126 S.E.2d 873, 876, 879 (Ga. Ct. App. 1962).

[14] David A. Anderson, *Reputation, Compensation, and Proof*, 25 WM. & MARY L. REV. 747, 765-66 (1984).

[15] Keeton v. Hustler, 465 U.S. 770, 776 (1984).

[16] Sharon v. Time, 599 F. Supp. 538, 556 (S.D.N.Y. 1985).

[17] Rosenblatt v. Baer, 383 U.S. 75, 92 (1966).

[18] Milkovich v. Lorain Journal Co., 497 U.S. 1, 22 (1990) (quoting *Rosenblatt*, 383 U.S. at 86).

used in balancing free speech and reputational rights. State constitutions and common law play a significant role in protecting press rights and in allowing individuals to protect their reputations. State statutes can also affect libel conflicts. Statutes of limitations — laws that prevent stale lawsuits from being adjudicated — and retraction statutes — which can mitigate or eliminate some damages — are examples of state laws that directly affect libel.

In addition, the First Amendment principle that prior restraint is presumptively unconstitutional applies to attempts to restrain material because it may be defamatory.[19] In 2005, the Supreme Court refused to rule on the question of whether the First Amendment ever may allow a permanent injunction against defamation relating to a public figure. In *Tory v. Cochran*,[20] the Court sidestepped the substantive First Amendment issues over the injunction attorney Johnnie L. Cochran Jr. had obtained to prevent his former client Ulysses Tory from his continuing defamation. When Cochran died while the Supreme Court reviewed the California court's injunction, the Court ruled that the injunction was an overbroad prior restraint upon speech because it lacked "plausible justification."

Regardless, several state supreme courts have addressed injunction as a possible option in libel law. They recognized a possibility of defamatory statements being subject to prior restraint in limited circumstances.

In 2007, for example, the California Supreme Court ruled that an injunction can be issued to prohibit repetition of defamatory statements. In *Balvoa Island Village Inn, Inc. v. Lemen*,[21] the California high court reasoned:

[P]reventing a person from speaking or publishing something that, allegedly, would constitute a libel if spoken or published is far different from issuing a post-trial injunction *after* a statement that already has been uttered has been found to constitute defamation. Prohibiting a person from making a statement or publishing a writing *before* that statement is spoken or the writing is published is far different from prohibiting a defendant from *repeating* a statement or *republishing* a writing that has been determined at trial to be defamatory and, thus, unlawful. This distinction is hardly novel.[22]

In 2010, the Kentucky Supreme Court followed suit in adopting the "modern rule" permitting injunctions against defa-

mation. In *Hill v. Petrotech Resources Corp.*,[23] it wrote:

[D]efamatory speech may be enjoined only after the trial court's final determination by a preponderance of the evidence that the speech at issue is, in fact, false, and only then upon the condition that the injunction be narrowly tailored to limit the prohibited speech to that which has been judicially determined to be false.[24]

But the Texas Supreme Court rejected the modern rule in 2014. The court held in *Kinney v. Barney*[25] that barring future speech because of an earlier judicial decision that the same or similar statements have been defamatory is an impermissible prior restraint. "Given the inherently contextual nature of defamatory speech," the Texas court explained, "the most narrowly crafted of injunctions risks enjoining protected speech because the same statement made at a different time and in a different context may no longer be actionable. Untrue statements may later become true; unprivileged statements may later become privileged."[26]

Criminal Libel

As the Media Law Resource Center noted, "[I]t is hard to square modern First Amendment principles with laws that purport to criminalize statements that allegedly harm reputation."[27] Colorado repealed its criminal libel law in 2012. But thirteen states have statutes that allow the government to prosecute people for libel.[28] In his in-depth study of criminal libel, journalism scholar David Pritchard stated that criminal libel is more frequently used than media law texts acknowledge.[29] He wrote that the Internet is an increasingly important factor that precipitates

---

[19] For an in-depth analysis of the "no-injunction rule" in American defamation law, see David S. Ardia, *Freedom of Speech, Defamation, and Injunctions*, 55 WM. & MARY L. REV. 1 (2013).

[20] 544 U.S. 734 (2005). For a detailed discussion of *Tory v. Cochran, see* Chapter 4.

[21] 156 P.3d 339 (Cal. 2007).

[22] *Id.* at 344-45. *See also* Evans v. Evans, 76 Cal. Rptr. 3d 859 (Ct. App. 2008).

[23] 325 S.W.3d 302 (Ky. 2010). The Kentucky Supreme Court's analysis of prior restraint of speech under the First Amendment in general and in defamation law in particular is refreshingly detailed and informative. For a comment on the Kentucky Supreme Court's opinion, *see* UCLA law professor Eugene Volokh's blog posting of Oct. 26, 2010, Preliminary Injunctions in Libel Cases Forbidden, Permanent Injunctions Allowed, http://bit.ly/p4ED0N.

[24] *Id.* at 309. *See also* McCarthy v. Fuller, 810 F.3d 456, 462 (7th Cir. 2015) (suggesting that a narrow injunction barring a judgment-proof defamer from repeating statements judicially held to be false and defamatory might be constitutional).

[25] 443 S.W.3d 87 (Tex. 2014).

[26] *Id.* at 97-98.

[27] Preface, *Criminalizing Speech About Reputation: The Legacy of Criminal Libel in the U.S. After* Sullivan & Garrison, MLRC BULLETIN, Mar. 2003. American criminal libel law stands in contrast with foreign law, in which libel is increasingly "antiquated and anachronistic." FREEDOM OF EXPRESSION, MEDIA LAW AND DEFAMATION: A REFERENCE AND TRAINING MANUAL FOR EUROPE 19 (Feb. 2015), *available at* http://goo.gl/mnlR1n.

[28] *See* Eric P. Robinson, *Another One Bites the Dust: Minnesota's Criminal Libel Law Struck Down*, BLOG LAW ONLINE, May 28, 2015, http://goo.gl/YiWftU.

[29] David Pritchard, *Rethinking Criminal Libel: An Empirical Study*, 14 COMM. L. & POL'Y 1, 3 (2009).

criminal libel prosecutions. A Wisconsin woman, for example, was sentenced to twenty days in jail, a $100 fine, and one year of probation under Wisconsin's criminal libel law for emailing a local school board claiming that a local teacher was having sex with her students and videotaping it.[30]

The U.S. Supreme Court has *not* repudiated criminal libel. Indeed, in *Garrison v. Louisiana*,[31] it extended the actual malice rule — knowledge of falsity or reckless disregard of the truth — to criminal libel.

Criminal libel had its genesis in *De Libellis Famosis,* an English case in which Lord Coke delineated the principal points of the action:

> Every libel is made either against a private man, or against a magistrate or public person. If it be against a private man it deserves a severe punishment, for although the libel be made against one, yet it incites all those of the same family, kindred or society to revenge, and so tends *per consequens* to quarrels and breach of the peace, and may be the cause of the shedding of blood and greater inconvenience; if it be against a magistrate, or other public person, it is a greater offense; for it concerns not only the breach of the peace, but also the scandal of Government; for what greater scandal of Government can there be than to have corrupt and wicked magistrates to be appointed by the King to govern his subject under him.[32]

Courts have approached criminal libel in various ways, usually based on the actual malice requirement. In 1991, for example, a U.S. district court struck down South Carolina's criminal libel statute, finding it unconstitutional because it based liability on common law malice — ill will, spite or hatred — rather than actual malice.[33] Four years later, however, the Tenth U.S. Circuit Court of Appeals upheld Kansas' criminal libel statute. The court held that the law is not unconstitutional on its face because it requires actual malice to be proved in libel cases involving matters of public concern.[34] Then, in 2001, the Alabama Supreme Court invalidated the state's criminal libel statute because it did not require a showing of actual malice. The statute required proof that a defamatory statement about a public official or public figure be made "falsely and maliciously."[35] More recently, the First U.S. Circuit Court of Appeals struck down

Puerto Rico's criminal libel law on the ground that it lacked the actual malice requirement and truth as a defense.[36] Likewise, in 2007, the Washington Court of Appeals held the Washington criminal libel statute unconstitutional because it punished a false defamatory statement made without actual malice or a true defamatory statement made with no good motives or intent. Further, the Washington appellate court found that the criminal libel law was fatally overbroad and vague. The court reasoned that the law allowed punishment of permitted speech and that it did not define "malice," so creating a possible confusion between the common law malice and actual malice.[37] Similarly, a California appeals court in 2012 struck down a 1917 state law that criminalized making false statements or disseminating false rumors about a bank's financial condition. The court found that the pre-actual malice statute did not clearly require that the prosecutor prove the defendant's knowledge of falsity or reckless disregard for the truth.[38]

Regardless, criminal libel is not necessarily an exercise in futility. Professor Pritchard's empirical research concludes:

> Criminal libel is a legitimate legal tool to use when the reputations of private figures have been harmed by defamatory comments that have nothing to do with public issues. Criminal libel can be especially useful for people of limited means, those who would have difficulty finding lawyers to pursue civil lawsuits for libel. Criminal libel may also be useful in curbing defamatory gossip on the Internet.[39]

THE PLAINTIFF'S CASE

Before the Supreme Court constitutionalized libel law in 1964 with *New York Times Co. v. Sullivan*,[40] the basic requirement for a plaintiff in making a case for defamation was proof that the defendant published a statement about the plaintiff that had a tendency to harm the plaintiff's reputation in the community or to discourage other people from associating or dealing with the plaintiff. The burden was on the plaintiff to prove three essential elements: identification of the plaintiff in the allegedly defamatory material, publication of the material by the defendant, and the defamatory nature of the material.

---

[30] *See* Jacob Parsley, *Libel: Criminal Charges in Colorado, Wisconsin,* BULLETIN, Winter 2009, at 32.

[31] 379 U.S. 64 (1964).

[32] 77 Eng. Rep. 250, 251 (1609).

[33] Fitts v. Kolb., 779 F. Supp. 1502 (D.S.C. 1991).

[34] Phelps v. Hamilton, 59 F.3d 1058 (10th Cir. 1995). *See also* State v. Carson, 95 P.2d 1042 (Kan. Ct. App. 2004).

[35] Ivey v. Alabama, 821 So.2d 937, 941 (Ala. 2001).

[36] Mangual v. Rotger-Sabat, 317 F.3d 45 (1st Cir. 2003).

[37] Parmelee v. O'Neel, 186 P.3d 1094 (Wash. Ct. App. 2008), *rev'd in part,* 229 P.3d 723 (Wash. 2010).

[38] Summit Bank v. Rogers, 142 Cal. Rptr. 3d 40, 52 (Ct. App. 2012) (citing New York Times Co. v. Sullivan, 376 U.S. 254, 278 (1964); Garrison v. Louisiana, 379 U.S. 64, 73 (1964). *See also* Minnesota v. Turner, No. A14-1408, 2015 WL 2456991 (Minn. Ct. App. May 26, 2015) (holding the Minnesota criminal libel statute of 1963 "unconstitutionally overbroad"). For a case comment on this Minnesota libel case, *see* Robinson, *supra* note 28.

[39] Pritchard, *supra* 29, at 37.

[40] 376 U.S. 254 (1964).

But the requirements in a modern libel action are not that simple. To win damages, especially in libel actions against the media, a plaintiff must establish that: (1) a false *and* defamatory statement of fact concerning the plaintiff was published to a third party, (2) the publication was not privileged and was made with fault on the part of the publisher, and (3) the publication caused actual injury.

For cyberlibel, a plaintiff has to identify the originator(s) of libel who posted anonymously on the Internet. The plaintiff asks a court to order ISPs to identify the original online defamer. For a number of years, many courts have followed a test established by a New Jersey appellate court in a case called *Dendrite International, Inc. v. Doe*.[41] Applying the so-called "Dendrite Test," for example, a Tennessee circuit court held that to determine whether a plaintiff is entitled to discover the identity of an anonymous defendant, the plaintiff must:[42]

[1] Attempt to notify an anonymous online defendant that he or she is the subject of a subpoena or application for order of disclosure.

[2] Give the defendant a reasonable time to file opposition to the application.

[3] Identify the exact statements purportedly made by each anonymous online defendant that give rise to each claim.

[4] Make a prima facia [sic] or substantial showing of proof for each element of each cause of action.

[5] If a plaintiff has successfully complied with the first four requirements and the court concludes that a substantial showing of proof has been made, the fifth and final step is for the court to balance the First Amendment interests of the anonymous defendant against the strength of the plaintiff's prima facie case and the need for disclosure to allow the claims to proceed.

Falsity

Under the common law, when a libel action was filed, statements upon which the action was based were presumed to be false. As a matter of constitutional law, however, that presumption of falsity has been rejected. Libel plaintiffs now must prove the statements are false, even if they were made with ill will.

Judge Robert Sack of the Second U.S. Circuit Court of Appeals, in the highly acclaimed *Sack on Defamation*, wrote that under the constitutional rule, "Truth is usually now not a *defense*. Proof of falsity is instead part of the plaintiff's case, at least in defamation suits brought by public officials, or involving

communications about public issues, or both."[43]

Meanwhile, the falsity requirement should not concern the trivial inaccuracies of the challenged statement. As the U.S. Court of Appeals for the Tenth Circuit observed in 2011, the plaintiff must establish that the defamatory statement is not only false but material as well.[44] "To qualify as *material* the alleged misstatement must be likely to cause reasonable people to think 'significantly less favorably' about the plaintiff than they would if they knew the truth," the federal appeals court explained. "[A] mistatement is not actionable if the comparative harm to the plaintiff's reputation is real but only modest."[45]

Defamation

In addition to being false, offending material must be defamatory. Identifying defamatory language is the first order of business in libel law. As one scholar wrote, however, "[W]ords are not single faced. They have many facets and may have many interpretations. Their values change with time, with place, and with association. Whether a word has a libelous connotation will therefore require analysis and perception in terms of its milieu and period."[46] Earlier, Supreme Court Justice Oliver Wendell Holmes observed: "A word is not a crystal, transparent and unchanged; it is the skin of a living thought and may vary greatly in color and content according to the circumstances and the time in which it is used."[47] Thus, the same words may communicate different meanings in different contexts.

Words can be ambiguous. Love, democracy, communism and other words are capable of many connotations and interpretations. One cannot say with assurance that a word is or is not defamatory without placing it in time, in location, and in association so that its meaning can be determined. As the Hawaii Supreme Court said, whether a statement is defamatory "depends, among other factors, upon the temper of times, the current of contemporary public opinion, with the result that a word, harmless in one age, in one community, may be highly damaging to reputation at another time or in a different place."[48] In *Yonaty v. Mincolla*,[49] for example, a New York appellate court held in 2012 that falsely calling someone lesbian, gay or bisexual is not defamatory *per se*. It reasoned: "[P]rior cases categorizing state-

---

[41] 775 A.2d 756 (N.J. Super. Ct. App. Div. 2001).

[42] Swartz v. Doe, 37 Med. L. Rep (BNA) 2485, 2490 (Tenn. Cir. Ct. 2009) (citations omitted).

[43] ROBERT D. SACK, SACK ON DEFAMATION § 3-1 (4th ed. 2016).

[44] Bustos v. A&E Television Networks, 646 F.3d 762, 764 (10th Cir. 2011).

[45] *Id.* at 765.

[46] PHILIP WITTENBERG, DANGEROUS WORDS: A GUIDE TO THE LAW OF LIBEL 11 (1947).

[47] Towne v. Eisner, 245 U.S. 418, 425 (1918).

[48] Beamer v. Nishiki, 670 P.2d 1264, 1271 (Haw. 1983).

[49] 945 N.Y.S.2d 774, (N.Y. App. Div. 2012). For a detailed discussion of *Yonaty v. Mincolla, see* John Caher, *Panel Finds False "Gay" Label Is No Longer Per Se Defamation,* N.Y.L.J., June 1, 2012, http://www.newyorklawjournal.com/PubArticleNY.jsp?id=1202556645479&the page=1.

ments that falsely impute homosexuality as defamatory *per se* are based on the flawed premise that it is shameful and disgraceful to be described as lesbian, gay or bisexual."[50]

Compendiums of words cannot be considered a foolproof formula to divining how courts will rule on similar language, but they can often be warning signs for possible trouble. In addition, there are categories of words that are especially sensitive. Words are defamatory, for example, if they

- impute to another a loathsome disease;
- accuse another of serious sexual misconduct;
- impugn another's honesty or integrity;
- accuse another of committing a crime or of being arrested or indicted;
- allege racial, ethnic or religious bigotry;
- impugn another's financial health or credit-worthiness;
- accuse another of associating with criminals or others of unsavory character;
- assert incompetence or lack of ability in one's trade, business, profession or office.[51]

Interpreting Defamation. Defamation is recipient-oriented. That is, it hinges on how the language is interpreted by its recipients. Thus, the first step in analyzing the defamatory nature of a statement is determining whether the readers could interpret the words to be defamatory and whether they did so. The value judgments, knowledge and background of recipients will affect their interpretations of statements. For example, people who support abortion as a constitutional right of privacy would not consider it defamatory for a person to be depicted as being "pro-choice," while those who view abortion as morally reprehensible might lose their reputations among a certain group by being so depicted. So, whose understanding of a defamatory statement is used in establishing the defamatory nature of the statement?

The *Restatement (Second) of Torts,* a tract designed to explain the law, states, "It is enough that the communication would tend to prejudice [the plaintiff] in the eyes of *a substantial and respectable minority*" of the community, and "it is not enough that the communication would be derogatory in the view of a single individual or a very small group of persons, if the group is not large enough to constitute a substantial minority."[52]

As an example, a prison inmate was unsuccessful in maintaining a libel action when he was identified as an FBI informant because, the court said, he was not accused of unlawful or improper conduct. Noting that the defamatory statement must expose the plaintiff to public ridicule "in the minds of 'right

thinking persons' or among 'a considerable and respectable class of people,'" the court stated:

> It is true that a charge of informing may bring opprobrium from one's fellow inmates in the prison community. However, it is not one's reputation in a limited community in which attitudes and social values may depart substantially from those prevailing generally which an action for defamation is designed to protect.[53]

Rules of Construction. Most states use the reasonable construction rule to determine the defamatory nature of a statement. The meaning of a communication, according to the *Restatement,* "is that which the recipient correctly, or mistakenly but reasonably, understands it was intended to express."[54] The rule does not allow a strained interpretation. The Alabama Supreme Court provided a good explication of the rule:

> [T]he printed words are to be taken in their natural meaning, and according to the sense in which they appear to have been used and the idea they are adapted to convey to those who read them. A forced construction is not to be put upon them in order to relieve the defendant from liability, nor are they to be subjected to the critical analysis of a trained legal mind, but must be construed and determined by the natural and probable effect on the mind of the average lay reader.[55]

By contrast, the innocent construction rule, which is applied in Illinois and Ohio, requires a statement "to be considered in context, with the words and the implications there from given their natural and obvious meaning; if, as so construed, the statement may reasonably be innocently interpreted or reasonably be interpreted as referring to someone other than the plaintiff it cannot be actionable *per se.*"[56] The innocent construction rule has been under considerable attack over the years, but in 2006 the Illinois Supreme Court upheld it because, the court said, it advances free speech interests and promotes the robust discussion of daily affairs.[57]

The *Restatement* declares that a report of a single act of misconduct in the course of a person's business, trade, profession or office may be sufficient to support a libel action, even though the charge does not imply a habitual course of conduct. A number of states, however, have adopted the single-instance rule, which provides that a charge of ignorance or a mistake on a

---

[50] *Id.*

[51] NEIL J. ROSINI, THE PRACTICAL GUIDE TO LIBEL LAW 9 (1991).

[52] RESTATEMENT (SECOND) OF TORTS § 559 cmt. e (emphasis added) (1977).

[53] Saunders v. WHYY, 382 A.2d 257, 259 (Del. Super. Ct. 1978).

[54] RESTATEMENT (SECOND) OF TORTS § 563 (1977).

[55] Kelly v. Arrington, 624 So. 2d 546, 548-49 (Ala. 1993).

[56] Chapski v. Copley Press, 442 N.E.2d 195, 199 (Ill. 1982).

[57] Tuite v. Corbitt, 866 N.E.2d 214 (Ill. 2006).

single occasion is not actionable unless special damages can be shown. The rule is based on the common-sense premise that people make mistakes, and to state that a professional has made a mistake in a specific instance should not cause damage because the statement only implies that the person is human.

"RED-FLAG WORDS"

Attorney and libel expert Bruce Sanford has listed a number of so-called "red-flag words" that courts often consider defamatory. They are the following:

addict, adulteration of products, adultery, AIDS, alcoholic, altered records, atheist, bad moral character, bankrupt, bigamist, blacklisted, blackmail, booze-hound, bribery, brothel, buys votes, cheats, child abuse, collusion, con artist, confidence man, corruption, coward, crook, deadbeat, defaulter, divorced, double crosser, drug abuser, drunkard, ex-convict, fawning sycophant, fraud, gambling den, gangster, gay, graft, groveling office seeker, herpes, hit-man, hypocrite, illegitimate, illicit relation, incompetent, infidelity, informer, insider trading, intemperate, intimate, intolerance, Jekyll-Hyde personality, kept woman, Ku Klux Klan, Mafia, manipulate, mental illness, mobster, moral delinquency, mouthpiece, Nazi, neo-Nazi, paramour, peeping Tom, perjurer, plagiarist, pockets public funds, profiteering, prostitute, rape/rapist, scam, scandalmonger, scoundrel, seducer, sham, sharp dealing, shyster, slacker, smooth and tricky, smuggler, sneaky, solid influence, sold out, spy, stool pigeon, stuffed the ballot box, suicide, swindle, taken, thief, unethical, unmarried mother, unprofessional, unsound mind, unworthy of credit, vice den, villain.

From Bruce W. Sanford, *Libel and Privacy* § 4.13 (2d ed. 2014).

Implication. Defamation by implication occurs when false impressions arise from truthful statements. It demonstrates the larger problem of determining the meaning of an allegedly defamatory communication by examining the words in context. The Texas Supreme Court, for example, held: "A publication can convey a false and defamatory meaning by omitting or juxtaposing facts, even though all the story's individual statements considered in isolation were literally true or non-defamatory."[58] One example of such defamation by omission is a story the *Memphis Press-Scimitar* published. It reported that Mrs. Ruth A. Nichols was treated for a bullet wound she received when another woman found her with the woman's husband in the Nichols home. According to witnesses, the woman fired at her husband and then at Mrs. Nichols. The story was true. The Tennessee Supreme Court held, though, that the story was defamatory because it omitted crucial facts.[59] What the paper did not report was that Mrs. Nichols and the suspect's husband were not alone

in the home. Mrs. Nichols' husband and two neighbors were also there, and Mr. Nichols had attempted to prevent the shooting.[60]

Defamation through implication often arises in one of three contexts: (1) when a writer tries to guide a reader to a conclusion without stating the conclusion; (2) when a writer is ambiguous, offering multiple meanings, at least one of which is defamatory; (3) when a writer juxtaposes one message with another, creating an implication that is not necessarily intended.

An important tract on the law of torts has explained that proof of defamation by implication requires a combination of elements, defined by the terms "inducement," "innuendo" and "colloquium," explained here:

If the plaintiffs themselves are not directly named they must show by "colloquium" that the statements were "of and concerning" them. If it is still not clear how the plaintiffs have been defamed, they must plead extrinsic facts that would permit a defamatory meaning to be applied to defendants' words. This allegation of extrinsic facts is called the "inducement...." Where a statement is not clearly defamatory on its face it is the function of the innuendo to assert the meaning that plaintiff attaches to the passage and any additions by colloquium and inducement. The innuendo is not a fact but is the plaintiff's assertion of how the passage would be understood by those who heard the defendant's words and knew the additional unstated facts.[61]

To state, for example, that John Doe ran his car into a utility pole is not defamatory since he has every right to do so. But when it is specifically pleaded as "inducement" that Doe insured the car and, as "innuendo," that the statement is construed to mean that he was defrauding the insurance company, a charge of property damage is clearly implied, which is defamatory.

The Supreme Court has not addressed the issue of whether those who defame through implication are liable for damages. Several lower courts, however — including courts in Connecticut, the District of Columbia, Louisiana and Michigan — have declined to recognize liability for defamatory implications. The basis for the rulings appears to be this premise:

If unrestrained ... the theory of libel by implication would allow a jury to draw whatever inferences it wished, truthful or otherwise, from statements of fact. It would thereby permit liability for the mere tone of a publication, for statements that are in substance opinion or true, or for statements about

---

[58] Turner v. KTRK Television, Inc., 38 S.W.3d 103, 114 (Tex. 2000).

[59] Memphis Publ'g Co. v. Nichols, 569 S.W.2d 412 (Tenn. 1978).

[60] For a more recent federal case of defamation by omission, *see* Tomblin v. WCHS-TV8, 434 F. App'x. 205 (4th Cir. 2011).

[61] T. BARTON CARTER ET AL., THE FIRST AMENDMENT AND THE FOURTH ESTATE 92 (10th. ed. 2008).

public persons that do not pass the "actual malice" test because they do not constitute knowing falsity or "reckless disregard" for the truth.[62]

The California Supreme Court, for example, has noted that a false and defamatory meaning cannot be based on "the fact that some person might, with extra sensitive perception, understand such a meaning.... Rather, the test ... is whether by reasonable implication a defamatory meaning may be found in the communication."[63] On the other hand, an increasing number of jurisdictions have recently accepted libel by implication. In 2007, the Iowa Supreme Court expressly adopted the principle of defamation by implication. "Otherwise," the court stated, "by a careful choice of words in juxtaposition of statements in a publication, a potential defendant may make statements that are true yet just as damaging as if they were actually false."[64]

Libel *per se* and libel *per quod*. A statement that is libelous *per se* is defamatory on its face. That is, the defamation is apparent in the statement. If additional information is required before a statement is defamatory, the statement is libelous *per quod,* and a plaintiff must prove special damages — that there was, in fact, a loss of money — before the plaintiff can recover.

The distinction between libel *per se* and libel *per quod* was weakened in 1974 when, in *Gertz v. Robert Welch, Inc.,*[65] the Supreme Court required plaintiffs to prove damages before recovering. For example, the Missouri Supreme Court no longer recognizes a distinction between libel *per se* and libel *per quod.* That court stated that the rule created unjustifiable inequities by requiring a higher standard of proof for certain defamations:

> [I]n defamation cases the old rules of *per se* and *per quod* do not apply and plaintiff need only to plead and prove the unified defamation elements. In short, plaintiffs need not concern themselves with whether the defamation was *per se* or *per quod,* or with whether special damages exist, but must prove actual damages in all cases.[66]

In twenty-six jurisdictions, however, the *per se/per quod* distinction remains as a rule of law. Iowa is one of them. In *Bierman v. Weier,*[67] the Iowa Supreme Court refused to abrogate libel *per se.* Beth Weier and her father, Gail Bierman, sued Scott Weier and Author Solutions, Inc., a vanity press. In his memoir,

Scott Weier said his former wife, Beth, as a child had been molested by Bierman. In granting the plaintiffs summary judgment, the trial court ruled that the allegations by the non-media defendants were defamatory *per se.* Iowa defamation law distinguishes media from non-media defendants: "[L]ibel *per se* is available only when a private figure plaintiff sues a non-media defendant for certain kinds of defamatory statements that do not concern a matter of public importance."[68]

Noting that neither the First Amendment nor the Iowa Constitution compelled abolition of the libel *per se/per quod* distinction, the Iowa Supreme Court found that the libel *per se* doctrine was "useful" when actual damages are difficult to prove. The court further stated that "[w]e are not persuaded ... that the Internet's ability to restore reputations matches its ability to destroy them."[69]

Statements of Fact

For an allegedly defamatory statement to be actionable — that is, for a lawsuit to be based upon the statement — the statement must be one of fact rather than of opinion. In *Gertz,* the Supreme Court held:

> Under the First Amendment there is no such thing as a false idea. However pernicious an opinion may seem, we depend for its correction not on the conscience of judges and juries but on the competition of other ideas. But there is no constitutional value in false statements of fact.[70]

And in *Milkovich v. Lorain Journal*[71] the Court held that for a statement to be actionable, it must be provably false.

The threshold question facing the opinion defense is how to distinguish fact from opinion. The judge decides whether a statement is a statement of fact or opinion. If the judge cannot determine whether a particular statement constitutes fact or opinion, the jury makes the determination. (Opinion as a defense is discussed later in this chapter.)

Identification

In order to win a libel action, a plaintiff must prove that he or she was identified, that is, that the defamation was "of and con-

---

[62] SACK, *supra* note 43, § 2.4.5.

[63] Forsher v. Bugliosi, 608 P.2d 716, 723 (Cal. 1980).

[64] Stevens v. Iowa Newspapers, Inc., 728 N.E.2d 823, 828 (Iowa 2007).

[65] 418 U.S. 323 (1974).

[66] Nazeri v. Missouri Valley College, 860 S.W.2d 303, 313 (Mo. 1993) (en banc).

[67] 826 N.W.2d 436 (Iowa 2013).

[68] *Id.* at 448.

[69] *Id.* at 454. Libel law authority Rodney Smolla convincingly observed: "When a defamatory message is posted on the Internet, once [sic] can view and track and permanently document the echo boom of comments, posts, tweets, and repetitions of the defamatory story as the falsehood spreads like a virulent virus across digital space." RODNEY A. SMOLLA, LAW OF DEFAMATION § 1:27.50 (2016) (citation omitted).

[70] 418 U.S. at 339-40.

[71] 497 U.S. 1 (1990).

cerning" the plaintiff. Identification has nothing to do with the intent of the publisher of the defamation. As one writer put it, "The test is not whom the story intends to name but who a part of the audience may reasonably think is named — 'not who is meant but who is hit.'"[72]

Identification does not always mean that the plaintiff must be named. The plaintiff can be identified by other information within the published material or by extrinsic facts not included in the published material. And the plaintiff need not show every viewer or reader of the material identified the plaintiff, but that some significant number did.

A landmark Illinois case, *John v. Tribune Co.*,[73] provides a good example of how identification can cause unique problems. The case began when the *Chicago Tribune* reported about a police raid on a prostitution operation in an apartment house. Two articles about the raid identified the arrested owner as Dorothy Clark, also known as "Dolores Reising, 57, alias Eve Spiro and Eve John." By sheer coincidence, a woman whose maiden name was Eve Spiro and whose name at the time of the raid was Eve John was living in the basement of the raided building. She was a practicing psychologist and was not involved with the prostitution operation. She sued for libel. The Illinois Supreme Court held that the alias names could not be read as identifying Eve Spiro John as the "target" of the publication.[74] Thus, there was no identification of the plaintiff in the *Tribune* story.

Pictures of persons identified by fictitious names can also create headaches for the media. In 1982, *TV Guide* published an ad for an upcoming television documentary series on teenage pregnancy. The ad's heading asked in large, bold letters: "GUESS WHAT LORI FOUND OUT TODAY." In the middle of the advertisement was a photograph of a diary that contained the handwritten entry: "Dear Diary: I found out today that I'm pregnant. What will I do now?" Directly below the diary was a photograph of a teenager embracing a young man.

Libby Sue Chumley sued *TV Guide* for a false implication that she was pregnant. She claimed she was the girl in the picture and that she was not and had never been pregnant. She further asserted that she never engaged in sexual relations with the young man in the photograph or with anyone else.

In 1984, the Georgia Supreme Court ruled that the ad was "of and concerning" Chumley. It rejected the argument that the ad did not identify Chumley because "Lori" was the name used in the ad even though the photograph was of Chumley. The court reasoned that the bold print of the advertisement and the strategic placement of the photo made it possible for people to in-

terpret Chumley to be "Lori," a pregnant teenager.[75]

In addition, the Supreme Court has said that races or other large groups of people cannot win libel actions because individual members of the groups must be identified. The *Restatement* delineates the "group libel doctrine" this way:

One who publishes defamatory matter concerning a group or class of persons is subject to liability to an individual member of it if, but only if: (a) the group or class is so small that the matter can reasonably be understood to refer to the member; or (b) the circumstances of publication reasonably give rise to the conclusion that there is a particular reference to the member.[76]

The rationale for the rule is that, "First, defamatory statements do little damage to the reputation of any member of a group larger than twenty-five if the defamation refers to all members of the group.... Second, the price to be paid by making such statements actionable is simply too high" for freedom of expression.[77]

The cut-off point for identification probably ranges from about twenty-five to about one hundred. Indeed, a class of 637 commercial net fishermen was certainly too large for any individual fisherman to sustain a libel action against two television stations. The Florida Circuit Court noted in the case that the group libel doctrine is "deeply entrenched" in the common law and "almost never operates to create liability when the allegedly defamed group is greater than twenty-five individuals.... No case has been reported that has ever applied the principle to a group larger than 60 individuals."[78]

While members of groups can be defamed if the groups are small enough, it is almost impossible for family members to be defamed based on the activities of other members of the family. A father cannot be defamed, for example, because of a report that his son was charged with some crime.[79]

Publication

Publication is essential to a libel plaintiff's case. It is probably the easiest element to prove when the lawsuit involves the media. Legally, "publication" occurs when defamatory material is intentionally or negligently disseminated to someone other than the person defamed. As one court put it, "A defamatory writing

---

[72] PAUL P. ASHLEY, SAY IT SAFELY 30 (4th ed. 1969).

[73] 181 N.E.2d 105 (Ill. 1962).

[74] *Id.* at 108.

[75] Triangle Publ'ns v. Chumley, 317 S.E.2d 534, 537 (Ga. 1984).

[76] RESTATEMENT (SECOND) OF TORTS § 5645a (1977).

[77] REX S. HEINKE, MEDIA LAW 101 (1994).

[78] Adams v. WFTY, Inc., 24 Media L. Rep. (BNA) 1350, 1351 (Fla. Cir. Ct. 1995).

[79] Apparently only one Puerto Rico case violated this tenet of libel law. *Compare* Torre-Silva v. El Mundo, Inc., 3 Media L. Rep. (BNA) 1508 (P.R. 1977), *with* Rodriguez v. El Vocero De Puerto Rico, Inc., 22 Media L. Rep. (BNA) 1495 (P.R. 1994).

is not published if it is read by no one but the one defamed. Published it is, however, as soon as read by anyone else."[80]

The form of publication is irrelevant. Defamatory material can be published in written or spoken form or on computer bulletin boards. Especially noteworthy, however, is the congressional attempt to immunize online publication of defamatory statements from liability. In 1996, Congress enacted the Communications Decency Act, which provides, in part, that, "No provider or user of an interactive computer service shall be treated as the publisher or speaker of any information provided by another information content provider."[81] Thus, the federal law protects online service providers from state law causes of action for defamation. And, while repetition of a defamation generally consists of a new and separate libel, repetition by the defamed person does not constitute publication. Similarly, while each person involved in the publication of defamatory material may be sued, unless the involvement is direct, there is not likely to be liability. News vendors, book sellers and libraries, for example, are not subject to liability for "publishing" defamatory material if they had no reason to suspect that the material was defamatory.

The accurate republication of defamatory statements within quotation marks is automatically a republication. And, since accuracy is not necessarily the equivalent of truth, simply reporting what another person has said is no defense except where the neutral-reportage doctrine or the "third-party allegation" defense[82] or the fair report privilege is recognized. (The defenses of neutral reportage and the fair report privilege are discussed later in this chapter.[83])

At one time, each separate publication of a defamatory statement could prompt a cause of action. For example, if a newspaper sold 500,000 copies of an edition containing a libelous statement, a plaintiff could bring 500,000 different lawsuits. But courts have recognized the inherent unfairness of such a rule, and many have adopted the single-publication rule. The rule requires a plaintiff to recover all damages suffered from a libel published in any one edition of a magazine or newspaper in one action. This, of course, does not necessarily foreclose multiple causes of action against several defendants for a defamatory statement. Each person who is responsible for publication of the defamatory statement may be held liable for the publication.

The date of publication of an alleged libel is important because courts do not like to hear old lawsuits. Therefore, each jurisdiction has a statute of limitations, which bars legal actions after certain periods of time. The statute of limitations for libel actions in most states is one or two years. The key, therefore, is determining the actual date of publication of the libel. If each republication constitutes a new publication, therefore, a new statute of limitations applies to each republication.

Courts that have applied the single-publication rule, however, have held that the statute of limitations begins to run with the first publication. This single-publication rule applies to Internet postings. That is, "[D]espite the continued public availability," Judge Sack wrote, "there is a single publication at the time the posting is made, and the statute of limitations begins to run then."[84] In addition, courts have distinguished between a "republication" and a "repetition" of the libel, the latter not being a publication for purposes of a lawsuit. An example of a repetition would be the distribution of a syndicated column. The publication occurred, one court held, with the distribution of the column, and each printing of the column thereafter was a repetition, not a republication. The statute of limitations of the state where the column first appeared should apply, the court held.[85]

Fault

U.S. libel law is exceedingly complex, and one of the best examples of that complexity might be the various degrees of fault that are applied. Public figures and public officials are required to prove actual malice — knowledge of falsity or reckless disregard for the truth — before they can win libel actions. Private persons, on the other hand, must only prove negligence in most states in order to win, but must prove actual malice if they want to win punitive damages or presumed damages.

The actual malice rule, which originated for constitutional purposes in *New York Times Co. v. Sullivan*,[86] is derived from the constitutional right to express oneself about matters of public concern. Against the background of "a profound national commitment to the principle that debate on public issues should be uninhibited, robust, and wide-open," the Supreme Court declared, "erroneous statement is inevitable in free debate, and ... it must be protected if the freedoms of expression are to have the 'breathing space' that they 'need to survive.'"[87]

Times v. Sullivan arose from an advertisement published in the March 29, 1960, issue of the *New York Times*. The full-page

---

[80] Ostrowe v. Lee, 175 N.E. 505, 505 (N.Y. 1931).

[81] 47 U.S.C. 230(c) (Supp. 1996).

[82] In May 2015, Texas Gov. Gregg Abbot signed a "third-party allegation" bill into law that protects journalists against liability for libel in *accurately* quoting third-party sources who make allegations of wrongdoing. *See Laura Prather in the Texas Press Association Legislative Report*, HANESBOONE, June 4, 2015, http://goo.gl/ZaFLQu.

[83] For a discussion of various defenses against liability for libelous republications in U.S. libel law, *see* Chris Healy, *Libelous Truth?: Fifteen Years Later, a Libel Suit Finally Ends*, NEWS MEDIA & L., Winter 2012, *available at* http://goo.gl/EP6Cuf.

[84] SACK, *supra* note 43, § 7:2.2 (citations omitted). *See also* McCandliss v. Cox Enters., Inc., 593 S.E.2d 856 (Ga. 2004) (holding that the single-publication rule applies to archived stories on the newspaper's Web site).

[85] Givens v. Quinn, 877 F. Supp. 485, 490 (W.D. Mo. 1994).

[86] 376 U.S. 254 (1964).

[87] *Id.* at 270-72.

ad, "Heed Their Rising Voices," was placed by the Committee to Defend Martin Luther King and the Struggle for Freedom in the South and, among other things, solicited funds for the legal defense of Dr. King. It started thus:

As the whole world knows by now, thousands of Southern Negro students are engaged in widespread non-violent demonstrations in positive affirmation of the right to live in human dignity as guaranteed by the U.S. Constitution. In their efforts to uphold these guarantees, they are being met by an unprecedented wave of terror by those who would deny and negate that document which the whole world looks upon as setting the pattern for modern freedom.

The advertisement alleged repressive actions taken by local authorities against civil rights demonstrations in the South:

In Montgomery, Alabama, after students sang "My Country, 'Tis of Thee" on the State Capitol steps, their leaders were expelled from school, and truckloads of police armed with shotguns and tear-gas ringed the Alabama State College Campus. When the entire student body protested to state authorities by refusing to re-register, their dining hall was padlocked in an attempt to starve them into submission.

The advertisement, without naming any individuals or organizations, asserted that "the Southern violators of the Constitution" were "determined to destroy the one man who, more than any other, symbolizes the new spirit now sweeping the South — the Rev. Dr. Martin Luther King Jr., world-famous leader of the Montgomery Bus Protest." It continued:

Again and again the Southern violators have answered Dr. King's peaceful protests with intimidation and violence. They have bombed his home almost killing his wife and child. They have assaulted his person. They have arrested him seven times — for "speeding," "loitering" and similar "offenses." And now they have charged him with "perjury" — a felony under which they could imprison him for ten years.

L.B. Sullivan, a commissioner of public affairs for Montgomery, sued the New York Times Co. for libel. He claimed that because he was the commissioner responsible for supervision of the Montgomery police, the advertisement's allegations of police wrongdoing libeled him. He sought damages of $500,000, and a jury awarded him the entire amount. The Alabama Supreme Court affirmed the judgment, holding that the *Times* was irresponsible in publishing the false advertisement because the paper could have verified the allegations in the advertisement by checking its own files prior to publication. The Alabama court

curtly rejected the *New York Times'* argument that the U.S. Constitution protected the advertisement. It reasoned in a single sentence that "[t]he First Amendment of the U.S. Constitution does not protect libelous publications."[88]

The New York Times Co. appealed the decision to the U.S. Supreme Court. In 1964, the Court reversed the Alabama court decision unanimously. It was a stunning victory for free press and free speech in America. Alexander Meiklejohn, who had argued for years that political expression relating to the government should be immune from punishment, characterized the *Times* decision as "an occasion for dancing in the streets."[89]

Justice William Brennan, who wrote the opinion for the Court, began with the "general proposition that freedom of expression upon public questions is secured by the First Amendment." Noting the First Amendment's guarantee of freedom of expression as a right of American citizens, Justice Brennan wrote that the *Times* case should be examined "against the background of a profound national commitment to the principle that debate on public issues should be uninhibited, robust, and wide-open, and that it may well include vehement, caustic, and sometimes unpleasantly sharp attacks on government and public officials." Justice Brennan wrote that the advertisement in question was "an expression of grievance and protest on one of the major public issues of our time" and thus entitled to the constitutional protection. However, "The question is whether it forfeits that protection by the falsity of some of its factual statements and by its alleged defamation of respondent."[90]

Justice Brennan answered by stating that "the First Amendment guarantees have consistently refused to recognize an exception for any test of truth." He recognized the flexibility of the concept of truth and warned against the chilling effect of penalizing honest mistakes: "A rule compelling the critic of official conduct to guarantee the truth of all his factual assertions — and to do so on pain of libel judgment virtually unlimited in amount — leads to a comparable 'self-censorship.'"[91]

Therefore, the Court established that a public official could win a libel action based upon criticism of official conduct only if the official could prove actual malice, defined as knowledge of falsity or reckless disregard for truth or falsity. "Actual malice" does not mean hatred, ill will or spite, which is the definition of common law malice.

The Supreme Court has specifically said that actual malice is a subjective rather than objective standard. That means that the standard reflects an attempt by a publisher to, as Justice

---

[88] *Id.* at 264 (quoting New York Times Co. v. Sullivan, 144 So. 2d 25, 40 (Ala. 1962)).

[89] Harry Kalven Jr., *The New York Times Case: A Note on "The Central Meaning of the First Amendment,"* 1964 SUP. CT. REV. 199, 221 n.125.

[90] 376 U.S. at 271.

[91] *Id.* at 279.

Brennan said in *New York Times,* injure through knowing or reckless falsehood. Thus, the conduct of a libel defendant is often examined to determine whether there is objective evidence of the subjective standard. One way a plaintiff can prevail in a libel action, therefore, is to demonstrate that there was knowledge of falsity or reckless disregard for the truth.

Knowledge of Falsity. Actual malice is proved much more often by showing reckless disregard on the part of the defendant than by showing knowing falsity. One reason — perhaps the foremost reason — is that professional communicators rarely publish anything knowing it is false. But there are exceptions. One was when Ralph Ginzburg published in *Fact* magazine that some psychiatrists he surveyed found Republican presidential candidate Barry Goldwater to be mentally unstable. Goldwater sued for libel, and his attorneys were able to show that the survey results were actually very favorable toward Goldwater, but Ginzburg ignored the positive comments and focused only on the negative. In addition, there was evidence that the publisher of the article knew before the survey was distributed what the tenor of the article would be. Goldwater was able to meet the actual malice standard by showing that, although the statements Ginzburg made were true individually, collectively they misrepresented the truth; that is, they were false and that the author knew this but published them anyway.[92]

While knowledge of falsity can be easily applied, it's not easily proved. Because "[t]he knowledge of falsity prong of Times Rule Actual Malice is based on a determination of what the publisher knew or did not know at the time of publication," one scholar wrote, the defendant's state of mind at the time of publication is key.[93] Proving state of mind with convincing clarity can be challenging at the least. Rarely will a libel defendant admit knowledge of falsity, so, most often, plaintiffs must use objective evidence. That's difficult, but it can be done. When editorial writers at a newspaper asserted that a public official was a liar, for example, but articles in the same newspaper demonstrated that the official had not lied, the editorial writers were found to have acted with actual malice, for they *knew* their statements were false.[94]

A plaintiff's claim that a publication is false, while signaling that a publisher should investigate further, is not sufficient, standing alone, to show knowledge of falsity, particularly in the face of evidence from reliable, objective sources. If the evidence from those reliable sources raised questions about the truth of the material to be published, it's a different story. As one scholar wrote, "To publish in the face of such evidence would be to publish with knowledge of falsity. Similarly, to publish charges with little or no support for those charges has also been determined to be publishing with knowledge of falsity, as has the selective use of information to the detriment of the plaintiff."[95] Thus, the determination of knowledge of falsity rests on what the libel defendant knew at the time of publication. And what the publisher knew often rests on the extent of the investigation before publication, along with the interpretation, editing and presentation of the material. In *Herbert v. Lando,*[96] for example, the Supreme Court concluded that a plaintiff could inquire as to a defendant's state of mind while preparing a report. Questions about why the defendant believed and disbelieved certain sources, why the defendant used some material over other material and like issues were permissible, Justice Byron White wrote for the majority.

Former Army Col. Anthony Herbert contended that he was defamed in a *60 Minutes* segment. Producer Barry Lando and correspondent Mike Wallace argued that the First Amendment protected them from testifying as to their thought processes or state of mind in editing and producing the program. The Supreme Court disagreed, finding that state of mind was central to actual malice. In a previous case, the Court had held, "There must be sufficient evidence to permit the conclusion that the defendant in fact entertained serious doubts as to the truth of his publication."[97] The assertion by a defendant that he or she believed the publication to be true is inadequate standing alone, but may be sufficient when not refuted by the plaintiff.

What a libel defendant knew at the time of publication was also central to the 1984 case *Bose Corporation v. Consumers Union of United States.*[98] Bose filed suit against the publisher of *Consumer Reports* magazine for statements critical of stereo speakers developed by the company. Bose convinced a jury that the magazine had published false statements with actual malice. The U.S. Court of Appeals for the First Circuit reversed, however, and the Supreme Court upheld the reversal. Bose had succeeded in showing that the author of the critical report might not have expressed himself well and might have attempted at trial to cover up for that poor expression. That proof, the Court said, however, was irrelevant. What was important was the author's "state of mind when he wrote his initial report, or when he checked the article against that report."[99]

In short, it becomes essential to explore the libel defendant's state of mind at the time of the preparation and publication of

---

[92] Goldwater v. Ginzburg, 414 F.2d 324 (2d Cir. 1969).

[93] W. WAT HOPKINS, ACTUAL MALICE TWENTY-FIVE YEARS AFTER TIMES V. SULLIVAN 144 (1989).

[94] Costello v. Capital Cities Comm'ns, 505 N.E.2d 701 (Ill. Ct. App. 1987).

[95] HOPKINS, *supra* note 93, at 138.

[96] 441 U.S. 153 (1979).

[97] St. Amant v. Thompson, 390 U.S. 727, 731 (1968).

[98] 446 U.S. 485 (1984).

[99] *Id.* at 495.

the defamation in order to learn whether actual malice existed. The libel defendant should recognize that these are likely to be probed and should be prepared to justify both the actions and the state of mind that led to the choices made.

The publisher's state of mind toward the investigation and the material that is eventually published is also key to the question of knowledge of falsity. Indeed, the publisher's state of mind toward the *subject* of the report may be irrelevant because ill will toward the plaintiff is not sufficient to demonstrate actual malice. Ill will, however, may be introduced to demonstrate a defendant's motive for lying or publishing with reckless disregard for the truth. As one court noted, while "the concepts underlying malice and actual malice are not the same ... this does not preclude a relationship between them."[100] When courts permit evidence of ill will, hatred or spite to be introduced, they usually admonish juries that those elements, standing alone, can never establish actual malice.

Courts have also indicated that knowledge of falsity can be demonstrated by the way material is written, edited or presented. This may be particularly true with headlines. Wrote First Amendment scholar W. Wat Hopkins:

When large headlines are not literally defamatory, for example, but raise the implication of wrongdoing not supported by the texts of the articles over which they appear, a libel verdict for a public official can stand because of sufficient evidence that the headlines were published with actual malice. When the headlines are merely ambiguous, however, there is no knowledge of falsity. Similarly, ambiguous language or internal inconsistencies in news stories, standing alone, are insufficient evidence of actual malice.[101]

In addition to a media defendant's state of mind, the editorial policies that govern or guide actions can play a role in the determination of predisposition. The idea that a media defendant preconceived a story line, and then proceeded to skew reporting to fit that preconception, is evidence of knowledge of falsity. In *Burnett v. National Enquirer,* for example, the trial court suggested that the *Enquirer's* editorial predisposition may have contributed to its judgment. Entertainer Carol Burnett argued that the *National Enquirer* had falsely portrayed her as being "drunk, rude, uncaring, and abusive" in a Washington restaurant.[102] At trial, a reporter for the *Enquirer* testified that the article about Burnett was published even though he was unable to verify its accuracy.

Similarly, *Tavoulares v. Washington Post Co.*[103] resulted in an opinion that troubles journalists but that courts may believe they need to follow. A *Washington Post* article implied that William Tavoulares, the president of Mobil Oil Co., misused his corporate position by setting up his son to head an international tanker fleet. A federal jury awarded Tavoulares $2 million in damages. Before the full Court of Appeals for the District of Columbia overturned the verdict,[104] a panel of that court had held that the *Post's* predisposition toward "hard-hitting investigative journalism" could be considered as evidence relevant to actual malice.[105] The suggestion that a practice generally revered in journalism could be used against a libel defendant sent shock waves through the field. Those feelings were eased, however, when a full-panel rehearing by the District of Columbia Circuit reversed, throwing out the verdict and ruling that actual malice had not been proven. Adding to the relief was the court's assertion that a media organization's reputation for aggressive reporting was not to be taken as evidence of actual malice.

Pressure exerted by newsroom supervisors to produce high-impact stories may also be construed as a predisposition toward certain kinds of stories with specific plot lines. Such pressure may contribute to reporters skewing facts to fit such predilections. Libel expert Rodney Smolla places this phenomenon within the context of freedom of expression:

At the very core of our first amendment jurisprudence lies the elemental wisdom that government has no business prescribing what is orthodox, genteel, or polite in politics and culture. A publication or broadcast outlet is not to be penalized because of its unique boldness, style, or flair. Indeed, in an era in which one of the great *economic* tendencies in the media is toward consolidation and centralization, often resulting in "play it safe" editorial styles that make all news sound the same, the first amendment's protection for those media outlets with special courage or uniqueness is more vital than ever. To actually preconceive a story is one thing — such an act is quite properly probative of actual malice — but merely to have an editorial image or slant is quite another.[106]

Thus, when circumstances permit, proving falsity can be easier than exploring a defendant's state of mind. It simply stands to reason that it is much more difficult to prove a particular state of mind compared to presenting evidence that suggests reckless oversights. But what happens when a defendant admits to altering an interviewee's quotations? Arguably, that is an ex-

---

[100] DiLorenzo v. New York News, 432 N.Y.S. 2d 483, 486 (App. Div. 1981).

[101] HOPKINS, *supra* note 93, at 141-42.

[102] 193 Cal. Rptr. 206, 221 (Cal. Ct. App. 1983).

[103] 759 F.2d 90 (D.C. Cir. 1985).

[104] Tavoulares v. Wash. Post Co., 817 F.2d 762 (D.C. Cir. 1987) (en banc).

[105] Tavoulares v. Wash. Post Co., 759 F.2d 90, 121 (D.C. Cir. 1985).

[106] SMOLLA, *supra* note 69, § 3:73.

ample of knowing falsity. That is, if quotations were knowingly altered to the extent that their meaning was materially transformed, then the journalist must have been aware of the fact that they were false. Traditionally, journalistic practice suggests that words bracketed by quotation marks are the exact words of the person to whom they are attributed. When a journalist knowingly changes this material, the quoted information arguably has been knowingly falsified.

While that might be the case, publishing knowing falsehoods is only one element of a public figure's burden of proof. In *Masson v. New Yorker Magazine, Inc.*, the Supreme Court ruled that even the deliberate misquotation of a public figure cannot be libelous unless the wording materially changes the meaning of what was really said.[107] It stated that in *Masson* the meaning had not been transformed. On remand, a federal district court jury ruled in favor of the journalist, even though she had admitted to condensing certain statements by the plaintiff.[108]

In a non-media libel case in 2014, the Supreme Court applied the "material falsity" standard of actual malice. In determining that Air Wisconsin was not liable under a federal law for reporting to the Transportation Security Administration with no actual malice that one of its pilots was possibly armed and "mentally unstable," the Court said statements will not be considered materially false unless they would have affected the intended recipient of them in a different way than the truth.[109]

Reckless Disregard. Reckless disregard for whether material is true or false, like knowledge of falsity, is a subjective test. But it can often be determined by the publisher's rather than by thought processes, state of mind or predisposition at the time of publication.[110] Knowledge of falsity focuses on what the publisher knew; reckless disregard focuses on what the publisher reasonably *should have known*. The focus of the actual malice inquiry, as one scholar has written, "is on a defendant's attitude toward the truth or falsity of the publication," on "subjective awareness of its probable falsity" and on "actual doubts as to its accuracy." The "inquiry in 'actual malice' focuses largely on the defendant's belief regarding truthfulness."[111]

For recklessness to rise to the level of actual malice, it must be significant — it must be tantamount to lying; it must be obvious that the publisher did not care about the truth of the information. When publishers have demonstrated adequate inves-

tigation of potentially libelous charges, courts have typically ruled that there was no reckless disregard. Therefore, a plaintiff cannot prove reckless disregard if the defendant can show the statements were adequately investigated prior to publication.

The seriousness of the charges being made is also weighed. The more serious the material in question, the more detailed an investigation into its truth should be. In this connection, the "recklessness" of the actual malice rule is a concept of relativity in American tort law on reckless behavior. Judge Richard Posner of the Seventh Circuit stated in 2007 that if a person publishes a defamatory false statement recklessly, "[T]he potential harm that it creates [to reputation] … is wildly disproportionate to any benefits that the activity might be expected to confer."[112] In addition, reckless disregard is more likely to be found when sources for published material are anonymous, biased or of questionable reputation. Courts look to the number of reputable sources when determining whether a sufficient investigation was conducted.

The Supreme Court has provided guidance as to the meaning of reckless disregard. It has, for example, called reckless disregard publishing with a "high degree of awareness of their probable falsity."[113] And it has said, for reckless disregard to exist, "[T]here must be sufficient evidence to permit the conclusion that the defendant in fact entertained serious doubts as to the truth of his publication."[114] Whether a defendant had such serious doubts can be established by circumstantial evidence including determining what the defendant's thoughts were leading up to publication of the challenged statements.

The mere failure to investigate charges is not sufficient, standing alone, to prove reckless disregard. Publishers often rely on the work of reputable writers. If there is no reason to doubt the truth of material those writers submitted, publishers don't have to conduct independent investigations. If plaintiffs can show that publishers had doubts about the truth of such material or reasonably should have had doubts, however, that's a different story. In such cases, the question of reckless disregard may be open. In short, a publisher must be able to demonstrate a reasonable belief in the truth of the published material. That may sometimes require an investigation into the facts, but the belief may also be based on the reputation of the original author. To establish actual malice, plaintiffs must go beyond proving that "a reporter failed to show significant initiative in corroborating, verifying, or further investigating the defamatory story at issue." Rodney Smolla wrote:

[T]he mere failure to investigate, even when that failure to

---

[107] 501 U.S. 496, 516 (1991). For a libel case involving a TV broadcaster's out-of-context quotation of a televangelist's video clip, *see* Price v. Stossel, 620 F.3d 992 (9th Cir. 2010).

[108] Masson v. New Yorker, 832 F. Supp. 1350 (N.D. Cal. 1993).

[109] Air Wis. Airlines Corp. v. Hoeper, 134 S. Ct. 852, 861 (2014).

[110] *See, e.g.,* W. Wat Hopkins, *Good News or Bad for the Press? Actual Malice as Purposeful Avoidance of the Truth,* 14 NEWSPAPER RES. J. 99 (Summer/Fall 1993).

[111] SMOLLA, *supra* note 69, § 3:43.

[112] United States v. Boyd, 475 F.3d 875, 877 (7th Cir. 2007).

[113] Garrison v. Louisiana, 379 U.S. 64, 74 (1964).

[114] St. Amant v. Thompson, 390 U.S. 727, 731 (1968).

investigate is less than reasonable or responsible journalism, does not in and of itself meet the actual malice test. There must be some evidence of subjective suspicion that further investigation is needed. That evidence, of course, can be met by circumstantial data, including such things as the reliability or unreliability of the source or the inherent implausibility of the allegation, but something other than the stark failure to pursue investigation must be established.[115]

Negligence. At a minimum, the Supreme Court said in *Gertz v. Welch,* private persons seeking damages for the publication of false defamations related to matters of public interest must prove negligence. As a result, most states have ruled that negligence is the standard of fault for private-person libel plaintiffs.

Negligence has been defined in a variety of ways, but it is generally defined as failure to act as a reasonably or ordinarily careful person would under similar circumstances. A second definition — known as "journalistic malpractice" — is failure to adhere to standards of reporting and writing that are common to the news industry.

The reasonable care standard requires a libel plaintiff to establish that a libel defendant did not operate in a reasonable way, that is, that a reasonable person would have operated in a way significantly different from that of the defendant. The Arizona Supreme Court, for example, defined negligence this way:

[C]onduct which creates an unreasonable risk of harm. It is the failure to use that amount of care which a reasonably prudent person would use under like circumstances. The question which the jury must determine from the preponderance of the evidence ... is whether the defendants acted reasonably in attempting to discover the truth or falsity or the defamatory character of the publication.[116]

Most states have adopted the reasonable person definition of negligence, but some — including Iowa, Kansas and Oklahoma — define negligence as journalistic malpractice. The *Restatement* defines journalistic malpractice this way:

The defendant, if a professional disseminator of news, such as a newspaper, a magazine or a broadcasting station, or an employee, such as a reporter, is held to the skill and experience normally possessed by members of that profession.... Customs and practices within the profession are relevant in applying the negligence standard, which is, to a substantial degree, set by the profession itself, though a custom is not controlling.... If the defendant is an ordinary citizen, customs of the commu-

nity as a whole may be relevant.[117]

Regardless of the definition of negligence, some factors seem common when courts have ruled that defendants published material negligently. In his in-depth study of negligence as an actionable standard in post-*Gertz* cases, media law scholar W. Wat Hopkins identified three general negligence rules:

(1) [I]f there is a discrepancy between what a reporter says he was told by a source and what the source said he told the reporter, the court is more likely to believe the source and find that negligence is likely; (2) courts are likely to rule that negligence could be established if media representatives make little or no effort to contact a person against whom accusations are made or if a medium bases a story later found to be false upon a single source; (3) courts are likely to rule that negligence could be established if media fail to get all the information they should.[118]

Actual Injury

Even if libel plaintiffs can prove they were identified in false, defamatory publications, and even if they can prove the requisite degree of fault, they must still prove actual injury to reputation in order to recover damages, especially when the challenged statement relates to a matter of public concern. The New Mexico Supreme Court held: "Injury to reputation is the very essence of the tort of defamation. Evidence of humiliation and mental anguish, without evidence of actual injury to reputation, is insufficient to establish a cause of action for defamation."[119]

Warning against the "danger of media self-censorship" resulting from jury discretion in assessing punitive damages, the Supreme Court said that "punitive damages are wholly irrelevant to the state interest that justifies a negligence standard for private defamation actions. They are not compensation for injury. Instead, they are private fines levied by civil juries to punish reprehensible conduct and to deter its future occurrence." The Court noted, however, that the private libel plaintiff who establishes liability under a less demanding standard than actual malice may be limited to recovery of "only such damages as are sufficient to compensate him for actual injury."[120]

In a libel action, five types of damages are recognized: *Nominal damages* are awarded to plaintiffs who have not suffered from provable injury to their reputations. They are granted in

---

[115] SMOLLA, *supra* note 69, § 3:49.

[116] Peagler v. Phoenix Newspapers, Inc., 560 P.2d 1216, 1222 (Ariz. 1977).

[117] RESTATEMENT (SECOND) OF TORTS § 580B cmt. G (1977).

[118] W. Wat Hopkins, *Negligence Ten Years After Gertz v. Welch,* 93 JOURNALISM MONOGRAPHS 19 (Aug. 1985).

[119] Smith v. Durden, 276 P.3d 943, 943 (N.M. 2012).

[120] Gertz v. Robert Welch, Inc., 418 U.S. 341, 350 (1974).

very small amounts, usually $1, and are awarded where a plaintiff does not seek compensation for loss, but a vindication of reputation in the form of a declaration that a published statement is false.

Compensatory damages are awarded for actual injury. They compensate, not for out-of-pocket loss, but for harm to a reputation, humiliation, suffering and mental anguish. Awards must be based upon the evidence, but if the damages are not outrageous, a jury can award damages in its own discretion. Corporate defamation plaintiffs, unlike natural person plaintiffs, cannot recover damages for internal emotional distress. Compensatory damages are sometimes called "general damages."

Presumed damages, a form of compensatory damages, aim to "further … the state interest in providing remedies for defamation by ensuring that those remedies are effective."[121] They may be awarded without any actual proof of reputational injury. Recently, the New Jersey Supreme Court noted the heightened value of presumed damages to a private victim of non-public-concern online defamation who cannot prove actual damages.[122]

Special damages are designed to compensate for actual pecuniary loss. Evidence must demonstrate an actual amount of money the plaintiff lost as a result of the defamation.

Punitive or exemplary damages are designed to punish the defendant for outrageous and willful defamation. They are designed to deter the defendant and others from repeating similar actions. Actual malice must be proved for recovery of punitive damages. Four states — Massachusetts, Michigan, Oregon and Washington — do not recognize punitive damages, and others have capped the amount of punitive damages a plaintiff can win. Some states require that both actual malice and common law malice be established in seeking punitive damages for libel.

PUBLIC PERSONS

The Supreme Court has established that two categories of libel plaintiffs — public officials and public figures — must prove actual malice in order to win libel actions.

Public Officials

Public officials for purposes of the actual malice rule are persons in government who are in or appear to be in policy-making roles. The Supreme Court has indicated that "the 'public official'

designation applies at the very least to those among the hierarchy of government employees who have or appear to the public to have, substantial responsibility for or control over the conduct of governmental affairs."[123] The trial judge determines whether a plaintiff is a public official.

Determining just who qualifies as a public official is reasonably, but not entirely, clear-cut. In a 1979 case, the Supreme Court made it clear that "public official" is not synonymous with "public employee."[124] Whether a public employee is in or appears to be in a position to make policy and whether the employee has ready access to the media are key factors in determining his or her status.

A public official must establish that a defamatory statement was directed at the official rather than at his or her government unit. This is at the heart of First Amendment philosophy — that under the Constitution there is no such thing as seditious libel: that is, libel of the government. As the Texas Court of Appeals stated in 2007, "An impersonal attack criticizing the actions of a governmental agency without referring specifically to its agents, without more, will not support a claim of libel by the head of that agency."[125]

A person remains a public official for the purposes of the actual malice rule even after leaving office, at least with regard to stories that refer to conduct while in office. The passing of time, however, eventually may erode public interest in the office-holder's conduct so that the *New York Times* rule would no longer apply. There may be cases "where a person is so far removed from a former position of authority that comment on the manner in which he performed his responsibilities no longer has the interest necessary to justify the *New York Times* rule."[126] But this exception is rare.

Any statement that touches on an official's fitness for office — even if the statement is about the official's private life — is considered protected. Said the Supreme Court:

> The *New York Times* rule is not rendered inapplicable merely because an official's private reputation, as well as his public reputation, is harmed. The public-official rule protects the paramount public interest in a free flow of information to the people concerning public officials, their servants. To this end, anything which might touch on an official's fitness for office is relevant.[127]

---

[121] Dun & Bradstreet, Inc. v. Greenmoss Builders, Inc., 472 U.S. 749, 761 (1985).

[122] W.J.A. v. D.A., 43 A.3d 1248 (N.J. 2012) (per curiam) (holding, "[P]rivate persons face the real risk of harm through the modern ease of defamatory publications now possible through use of the Internet. Presumed damages vindicate the dignitary and peace-of-mind interest in one's reputation that may be impaired through the misuse of the Internet. Permitting reputational damages to be presumed in a defamation action arising in that setting serves a legitimate interest, one that ought not be jettisoned from our common law.").

[123] Rosenblatt v. Baer, 383 U.S. 75, 85 (1966).

[124] Hutchinson v. Proxmire, 443 U.S. 111, 119 n.8 (1979).

[125] Cox Texas Newspapers L.P. v. Penick, 219 S.W.3d 425, 435 (Tex. App. 2007) (citing New York Times v. Sullivan, 376 U.S. 254, 289 (1964)).

[126] *Rosenblatt*, 383 U.S. at 87 n.14.

[127] Garrison v. Louisiana, 379 U.S. 64, 77 (1964). *See also* Greer v. Abraham, 44 Media L. Rep (BNA) 1617, 1622 (Tex. 2016) (noting that the U.S. Supreme Court's interpretation of "official conduct" as a concept was "very broad").

Public Figures

In 1967, the actual malice rule was expanded to include public figures. In *Curtis Publishing Co. v. Butts,*[128] the Supreme Court ruled that there was little legal difference between persons who have widespread fame and notoriety — public figures — and public officials. "Many who do not hold public office at the moment," wrote Chief Justice Earl Warren, "are nevertheless intimately involved in the resolution of important public questions or, by reason of their fame, shape events in areas of concern to society at large."[129]

The rule was established in a roundabout way. Justice John Marshall Harlan had written a plurality opinion differentiating between public officials and public figures, but he also differentiated between the rules that should apply to the two categories. Chief Justice Warren wrote that the actual malice rule should apply to both categories of libel plaintiffs, and a sufficient number of justices joined his opinion so as to establish that rule.

The actual malice rule was extended in 1971 to any defamatory story involving matters of public or general interest, but the expansion was short-lived. In *Rosenbloom v. Metromedia, Inc.,*[130] a plurality of the Court had favored a rule that required private people involved in matters of public interest to prove actual malice when suing for libel based upon discussion of those matters. But the "Rosenbloom Rule" lasted only three years. In 1974, a 5-4 Court majority definitively rejected the rule by overruling *Rosenbloom* in *Gertz v. Robert Welch, Inc.*[131]

The *Gertz* case started in 1969 when *American Opinion,* a monthly periodical published by the John Birch Society, a far-right organization founded by Robert Welch, published an article critical of a Chicago civil liberties lawyer, Elmer Gertz. Gertz had been retained by the family of an African-American man who had been shot and killed by Chicago policeman Richard Nuccio. The article charged that Gertz, who was hired to initiate a wrongful death suit against Chicago and Nuccio, was the architect of the "frame-up" in the earlier prosecution of Nuccio for second-degree murder. It claimed that the prosecution was part of a Communist effort to discredit the Chicago police. The article declared, in part:

The file on Elmer Gertz in Chicago Police Intelligence takes a big Irish cop to lift.... He has been an official of the Marxist League for Industrial Democracy, originally known as the Intercollegiate Socialist Society, which has advocated the violent seizure of our government.... In fact, the only thing Chi-

cagoans need to know about Gertz is that he is one of the original officers, and has been Vice President, of the Communist National Lawyers Guild ... which probably did more than any other outfit to plan the Communist attack on the Chicago police during the 1968 Democratic Convention.

Gertz sued Robert Welch, Inc., publisher of *American Opinion,* for libel. He said the statements about him were false. He had no criminal record, contrary to the implications of the article. He was not a member of the Marxist League for Industrial Democracy. Further, although he had been a member of the National Lawyers Guild fifteen years earlier, the Guild was not a Communist organization. Neither had he anything to do with the prosecution of Nuccio for murder.

Gertz claimed he was injured both as an individual and as an attorney. He sought $100,000 in actual damages and $500,000 in punitive damages.[132] In 1970, a jury awarded him $50,000 in damages, but the trial judge set aside the verdict because, he said, since the article discussed Gertz's public activity, the actual malice rule should apply. Gertz appealed, but the U.S. Court of Appeals for the Seventh Circuit applied *Rosenbloom* and affirmed the trial judge's ruling, stating that there was no clear and convincing evidence of actual malice.[133]

In his appeal to the Supreme Court, Gertz argued in part:

Is every attorney, representing a client, to be exposed to the most scurrilous attacks, with absolutely no recourse? May a defamer concoct wholly fictitious stories about such an attorney which have no legitimate connections with the matter at hand? Are the members of the legal profession such public figures that they imperil their very livelihood to all unfounded attacks with absolutely no recourse? These issues must be considered very carefully and fully, not in an offhand manner.[134]

The Supreme Court agreed, holding that the actual malice rule applies to private-person libel plaintiffs only when they seek presumed or punitive damages. Other than that, the Court said, states could determine the fault standard for private-person libel plaintiffs, so long as states did not allow liability without some degree of fault. The Court explained the distinction between public and private persons:

Public officials and public figures usually enjoy significantly greater access to the channels of effective communication and

---

[128] 388 U.S. 130 (1967).

[129] *Id.* at 163 (Warren, C.J., concurring).

[130] 403 U.S. 29 (1971).

[131] 418 U.S. 323 (1974).

[132] Elmer Gertz, Gertz v. Robert Welch, Inc.: The Story of a Landmark Libel Case 40 (1992).

[133] Gertz v. Robert Welch, Inc., 471 F.2d 801 (7th Cir. 1972).

[134] Gertz, *supra* note 132, at 85-86.

hence have a more realistic opportunity to counteract false statements than private individuals normally enjoy. Private individuals are therefore more vulnerable to injury, and the state interest in protecting them is correspondingly greater. More important than the likelihood that private individuals will lack effective opportunities for rebuttal, there is a compelling normative consideration underlying the distinction between public and private defamation plaintiffs. An individual who decides to seek governmental office must accept certain necessary consequences of that involvement in public affairs. He runs the risk of closer public scrutiny than might otherwise be the case.[135]

In *Gertz,* the Court also differentiated between three types of public figures. General or all-purpose public figures are persons who have achieved pervasive fame or notoriety in their communities or are pervasively involved in the affairs of society. It is not easy to become an all-purpose public figure. The category is generally reserved for those people who have become so-called "household names" — that is, celebrities.

Far more common than the all-purpose public figure is the limited-purpose public figure. Limited-purpose public figures have "thrust themselves to the forefront of particular controversies in order to influence the resolution of issues involved."[136] This means, first, a public controversy must exist and, second, the nature and extent of the plaintiff's participation in that controversy must be determined. While it is clear that newsworthiness and public figure status are not synonymous, some courts have held that a person who creates a public controversy in order to affect the outcome of some public issue has met the limited-purposes criteria.

The Court also acknowledged that involuntary public figures may exist — at least in theory — but that such cases would be rare. Yet, an individual could be thrust into a matter of public controversy not merely through voluntary actions but also through bad luck. It is possible to become a public figure through no purposeful action. Meanwhile, as one media law scholar has noted:

While the Supreme Court has provided at least some guidance for lower courts attempting to identify public officials, all-purpose public figures, and limited-purpose public figures, the Court has provided little guidance in defining involuntary public figures. Indeed, some lower appellate courts have held that the Supreme Court has only established two categories of public figures status — all purpose and limited purpose —

ignoring the language of *Gertz* to the contrary.[137]

The *Gertz* Court saw a relationship between public figures and public officials, in part, because individuals in both groups tend to have access to the media and, therefore, have the ability to set the record straight when inaccuracies occur. Private figures, on the other hand, usually have limited access to the media and are, therefore, more vulnerable to irreparable injury. In addition, there is a certain degree of risk that accompanies those in the public eye. While public officials "must accept certain necessary consequences [regarding their] involvement in public affairs," they also "run the risk of closer public scrutiny than might otherwise be the case.... Those classified as public figures stand in a similar position.... [T]he communications media are entitled to act on the assumption that public officials and public figures have voluntarily exposed themselves to increased risk of injury from defamatory falsehoods concerning them."[138] The Court noted that society's stake in news about private figures is not as great as when public people are involved. Society places a high value in protecting private figures against libel, so the level of fault they are required to meet is less demanding than it is for public people.

Distinguishing between public and private figures, however, is not easy. As one court reported, it "is much like trying to nail a jelly fish to the wall."[139] Being in the public eye and being a public figure are not the same. The case of Mary Alice Firestone is an example. She was married to the heir to the Firestone Rubber Co. fortune, was a prominent member of Palm Beach society and even subscribed to a clipping service so she could keep track of news published about her. In addition, when she and her husband became involved in a notorious divorce proceeding, she held daily press conferences. When she sued *Time* for incorrectly reporting that her husband was granted a divorce because of her adultery and extreme cruelty — rather than because "neither party is domesticated" — it seemed certain that she would be categorized as a public figure for libel purposes. But the Supreme Court said no. The Court said that a large number of people might be interested in the problems of the extremely wealthy, but those were not the kinds of matters the Court had in mind when it referred to a public controversy.[140]

A plaintiff cannot be made public merely by the actions of the media. This bootstrapping occurs when media defendants attach themselves to the protection of the actual malice standard by pointing to their own allegedly libelous media coverage of the

---

[135] 418 U.S. at 344-45.
[136] *Id.* at 345.

[137] W. Wat Hopkins, *The Involuntary Public Figure: Not So Dead After All,* 21 CARDOZO ARTS & ENT. L.J. 1, 44 (2003).
[138] 418 U.S. at 345.
[139] Rosanova v. Playboy Enterprises, 411 F. Supp. 440, 443 (S.D. Ga. 1976).
[140] Time, Inc. v. Firestone, 424 U.S. 488 (1976).

plaintiff as evidence that the plaintiff is a public figure. The Supreme Court has said, "Clearly, those charged with defamation cannot, by their own conduct, create their own defense by making the claimant a public figure."[141] As a result, courts have noted that the public controversy at issue must have existed prior to the publication upon which the defamation claim is based. However, a court that rigidly applies the pre-existing controversy requirement may punish legitimate reporting that uncovers specific acts of wrongdoing. Courts, therefore, attempt to strike a delicate balance between which came first — the controversy or the story about the controversy.

Just as a media organization is not permitted to bootstrap itself into creating its own defense, a plaintiff may not avoid the actual malice standard by claiming that the attention was unwanted. The proper question is not whether the plaintiff volunteered for the publicity but whether the plaintiff volunteered for an activity from which publicity would foreseeably arise.

Even if an individual is not active within a particular sphere, mere presence within the sphere may satisfy a court's public-figure requirements. Where a person has

chosen to engage in a profession which draws him regularly into regional and national view and leads to fame and notoriety in the community, even if he has no ideological thesis to promulgate, he invites general public discussion.... If society chooses to direct massive public attention to a particular sphere of activity, those who enter that sphere inviting such attention overcome the *Times* standard.[142]

Thus, voluntary entry into a sphere of activity, the court reasoned, is sufficient to satisfy this element of the public figure inquiry.

Because the Supreme Court has said that someone with widespread fame or notoriety is a public figure, the individual's prominence is important in determining public-figure status. Moreover, that prominence may apply to a narrowly drawn context. Merely being an executive within a prominent and influential company does not by itself make a person a public figure. Professionals are typically not public figures, but under certain circumstances they can be. For example, voluntary use of controversial or unorthodox techniques may be enough to confer public-figure status. Publicly defending such methods or adopting other controversial stands also tends to bring about public status. Thus, a doctor who had written extensively on health issues as a newspaper columnist, who was also the author of various journal articles, and who had appeared on at least one nationally broadcast television program discussing health and nutrition issues was held to be a public figure for a limited range of issues — those pertaining to health and nutrition.[143]

An individual may assume public-figure status within small publics but may revert to being a private figure in larger spheres. For example, a professor may be a public figure on campus and in the adjacent academic community but a private person beyond those boundaries. The professor, therefore, may be a public figure for purposes of an article in the university newspaper but not for purposes of a regional newspaper or a national magazine. Thus, the professor's public-figure status is restricted. Similarly, an individual can attain the status of an all-purpose public figure within a particular geographical area.[144]

The passage of time may theoretically permit some people who were once public figures to regain private-figure status. To revert to private-figure status, it is likely that a plaintiff would need to demonstrate that the original status as a public figure was not connected to events or controversies that have become part of the permanent historical consciousness of the country.

Gertz, the most important libel case since *New York Times Co. v. Sullivan,* established a new set of guidelines for balancing the constitutional right of free speech against concerns for reputational interests.

First, the Court reaffirmed that public figures, along with public officials, must prove actual malice in libel cases involving matters of public concern.

Second, the Court held that "so long as they do not impose liability without fault, the states may define for themselves the appropriate standard of liability for a publisher or broadcaster of a defamatory falsehood injurious to a private individual," at least where the content of the defamatory statement "makes substantial danger to reputation apparent."[145]

Third, the Court stated that presumed or punitive damages may not be awarded absent a showing of actual malice. Those who cannot prove actual malice, the Court said, may be compensated only for actual injury.[146] In a later case, the Court held that the actual malice requirement for punitive damages does not apply to material "of purely private concern."[147]

As a result of *Gertz,* more than forty jurisdictions, including the District of Columbia, Puerto Rico and Virgin Islands, have established negligence as the private-person fault standard; five states — Alaska, Colorado, Indiana, Kansas and New Jersey — have apparently adopted a variation of the Rosenbloom Rule; and one state, New York, requires "gross irresponsibility" when

---

[141] Hutchinson v. Proxmire, 443 U.S. 111, 135 (1979).

[142] Chuy v. Philadelphia Eagles Football Club, 431 F. Supp. 254, 276 (E.D. Pa. 1977).

[143] Renner v. Donsbach, 749 F. Supp. 987 (W.D. Mo. 1990).

[144] *See, e.g.,* Williams v. Pasma, 656 P.2d 212 (Mont. 1982).

[145] 418 U.S. 323, 347-48 (1974).

[146] *Id.* at 349-50.

[147] Dun & Bradstreet, Inc. v. Greenmoss Builders, Inc., 472 U.S. 249, 759 (1985).

THE LIBEL PLAINTIFF'S BURDEN OF PROOF

1. **Publication**
2. **Identification**
3. **Defamation**

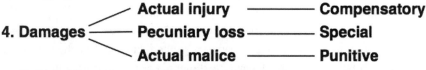

4. **Damages**
   - **Actual injury** —— **Compensatory**
   - **Pecuniary loss** —— **Special**
   - **Actual malice** —— **Punitive**

5. **Falsity *(in matters of public concern)***

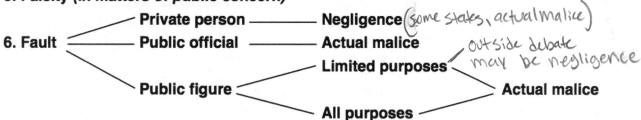

6. **Fault**
   - **Private person** —— **Negligence** *(some states, actual malice)*
   - **Public official** —— **Actual malice**
   - **Public figure**
     - **Limited purposes** *outside debate may be negligence* —— **Actual malice**
     - **All purposes**

---

matters of public concern are involved. The New York Court of Appeals held in *Chapadeau v. Utica Observer-Dispatch* that when the content of the article is arguably within the sphere of legitimate public concern, which is reasonably related to matters warranting public exposition, the party defamed may recover if he or she can establish "by a preponderance of the evidence, that the publisher acted in a grossly irresponsible manner without due consideration for the standards of information gathering and dissemination ordinarily followed by responsible parties."[148] The "gross irresponsibility" standard in New York for private-figure libel plaintiffs is considered closer to "actual malice" than to negligence when it comes to difficulty of proof. Indeed, Judge Sack of the Second Circuit noted: "It is almost as difficult as 'actual malice' for plaintiffs to meet in most cases and more difficult in some."[149]

DEFENSE STRATEGIES

The libel defendant is by no means defenseless. Any of a number of defenses or defense strategies is available to help prevent liability, depending on the circumstances of a case.

In libel law, the rights of individuals to be secure in their reputations are weighed against the rights of publishers to be heard on issues important to self-government. Broadly speaking, libel defenses assert that important issues of public concern should be debated in a free, open and uninhibited manner. A libel suit today, thanks to the precedent that *New York Times Co. v. Sullivan*[150] established, can be defended on constitutional grounds as well as through the common law.

Libel defenses begin by attempting to defeat the plaintiff's case. By refuting any of the plaintiff's claims, a defense may be successful. For example, the Tenth U.S. Circuit Court of Appeals upheld a federal district court's dismissal of a libel suit because the plaintiff had suffered no reputational harm from two news stories.[151] The federal appeals court reasoned that he had too tarnished a reputation as a convicted murderer to be further damaged when the stories were published.

If defeating an element of the plaintiff's case doesn't work, defendants then may try to assert affirmative defenses.

THE CONSTITUTIONAL DEFENSE

The First Amendment protects the freedoms of speech and press. Therein lies the heart of the so-called "constitutional defense" in libel law. The Supreme Court has recognized that free speech is vital because it ensures individual self-fulfillment and

---

[148] 341 N.E.2d 569, 571 (N.Y. 1975).

[149] SACK, *supra* note 43, § 6-4.

[150] 376 U.S. 254 (1964).

[151] Lamb v. Rizzo, 391 F.3d 1133 (10th Cir. 2004).

that it is a social good because it contributes to the search for truth. The First Amendment "rests on the assumption that the widest possible dissemination of information from diverse and antagonistic sources is essential to the welfare of the public."[152] Moreover, as Justice Louis Brandeis wrote during the era in which the Court truly began to interpret the meaning and scope of the First Amendment, "[F]reedom to think as you will and speak as you think are means indispensable to the discovery and spread of political truth."[153]

Thus, a libel defense, of sorts, has developed out of the notion that contributing significantly to public knowledge and information is important, and freedom of expression is a key element in that process.

The question becomes, does the speech contribute to the "profound national commitment to the principle that debate on public issues should be uninhibited, robust, and wide-open?"[154] At a base level, a media organization's defense on constitutional grounds is a claim that limiting its ability to convey information is an abridgment of the First Amendment guarantees of free speech and press. Carrying this argument to its logical conclusion, then, finding a media defendant responsible for libel is unconstitutional because doing so limits constitutionally protected freedoms. Moreover, knowing that such a verdict is possible in the wake of critical or less-than-positive statements about an individual may also limit freedom by producing a chilling effect. That is, the media may be less inclined to publish information containing critical statements knowing the dangers that may lie ahead in a libel trial.

The ability to criticize the government and government officials was central to *Times v. Sullivan*. At the root of Justice Brennan's opinion was the notion that statements about public officials — people who hold government positions — are most deserving of constitutional protection. The freedom to be critical of government and government officials, after all, was the basis and justification for the First Amendment's protection of speech and the press from interference by the state. Some scholars, in fact, have taken an unconditional approach to the issue. Alexander Meiklejohn, for example, has written that speech relevant to self-government is absolutely protected under the First Amendment.[155] Harry Kalven Jr. wrote that the central meaning of the First Amendment is uninhibited discussion of governmental affairs: "Political freedom ends when government can use its powers and its courts to silence its critics."[156]

It was the critical nature of the ability of citizens to criticize government and government officials that prompted Justice Brennan to appropriate the actual malice standard from state libel law and establish it as a constitutional rule. Unless a defendant's statement about a public plaintiff was made knowing it was false, or with reckless disregard for its truth, the defense will be successful. The scope of the standard was soon thereafter expanded to apply to more than public official plaintiffs.

As previously indicated, the Supreme Court, in *Curtis Publishing Co. v. Butts*, applied the actual malice standard to public figures, that is, individuals who either possess widespread fame or notoriety or who have thrust themselves into a public controversy in order to influence its outcome.

Chief Justice Warren justified the extension, writing that the "differentiation between public figures and public officials and adoption of separate standards of proof for each have no basis in law, logic, or First Amendment policy."[157] The case established the principle that many people who do not hold governmental office are nevertheless intimately enough involved in the resolution of public issues that, like public officials, they should be required to prove the defendant acted with actual malice.

Because of the dramatic difference in the level of fault required of public and private libel plaintiffs, defendants often try hard to demonstrate that a plaintiff is a public person. This effort, of course, while not purely a defense, is considered part of the so-called "constitutional defense" given that it stems from the actual malice concept. It is certainly an issue that libel defendants should consider as they formulate their strategies. How a libel suit unfolds hinges on this determination.

The Nature of the Statement

Not only is the categorization of the plaintiff important, but the nature of the statement at issue can be also. In *Dun & Bradstreet v. Greenmoss Builders*[158] a private-person plaintiff contended that material the Supreme Court said was a matter of private concern defamed him. A Dun & Bradstreet credit report sent to five subscribers inaccurately reported that Greenmoss Builders had declared bankruptcy. Justice Lewis Powell, for the majority, wrote that the purpose of the speaker and the nature and size of the audience are among the criteria for determining when speech involves matters of public concern.[159] Thus, the Court sought to establish minimal standards of fault not only depending on the status of the plaintiff but also according to the nature of the subject matter.

---

[152] Citizen Publ'g Co. v. United States, 394 U.S. 131, 139-40 (1969).

[153] Whitney v. California, 274 U.S. 354, 375 (1927) (Brandeis, J., concurring).

[154] *Sullivan*, 376 U.S. 254, 270 (1964).

[155] *See* ALEXANDER MEIKLEJOHN, POLITICAL FREEDOM 20-27 (1960).

[156] Kalven, *supra* note 89, at 205.

[157] 388 U.S. 130, 163 (1967) (Warren, C.J., concurring in the result).

[158] 472 U.S. 749 (1985).

[159] *Id.* at 783. For a fascinating backstory about *Dun & Bradstreet, see* LEE LEVINE & STEPHEN WERMIEL, THE PROGENY: JUSTICE WILLIAM J. BRENNAN'S FIGHT TO PRESERVE THE LEGACY OF *NEW YORK TIMES V. SULLIVAN* 237-77 (2014).

Opinion

The opinion defense has both constitutional and common law elements, causing discussion of this complex area of the law to become muddled. Traditionally, opinion as a defense stemmed from the common law. But the ability to voice opinions, particularly about issues of public concern, is now recognized as also being at the heart of the First Amendment's protection of expression. Constitutional derivations of the opinion defense are analyzed here; the common law components of opinion follow.

To attempt to separate statements of fact from statements of opinion is to venture onto one of the law's most slippery of slopes, yet to do so is vital in establishing the boundaries of the protection. In addition, state-to-state variations make the distinction all the more difficult.

In *Gertz*, the Supreme Court stated: "Under the First Amendment there is no such thing as a false idea. However pernicious an opinion may seem, we depend for its correction not on the conscience of judges and juries but on the competition of other ideas."[160] The question remained, however, just what is an opinion, and how is it different from a statement of fact?

The defining case in this area is *Ollman v. Evans*.[161] The 1984 ruling was by the D.C. Circuit Court of Appeals. A college professor sued newspaper columnists Rowland Evans and Robert Novak, who wrote that he had no status within the profession and that he used his classroom as an instrument to prepare for a Marxist revolution. The court split in its decision. Judge Antonin Scalia decided that the columnists wrote a "classic and coolly crafted libel,"[162] but the majority, led by Judge Kenneth Starr, found the column to be opinion protected by the First Amendment and the principles enunciated in *Gertz*. Judge Robert Bork concurred. Moreover, Judge Starr noted the difficulty in distinguishing opinion from fact and attempted to simplify the task by establishing a four-part test, now known as the *Ollman* test:[163]

1. The inquiry must analyze the common usage or meaning of the words.

2. Is the statement verifiable — "objectively capable of proof or disproof"? In other words, can the statement be proven either true or false?

3. What is the linguistic or journalistic context in which the statement occurs? The article or column must be considered as a whole: "The language of the entire column may signal that a specific statement that, standing alone, would appear to be factual, is in fact a statement of opinion."

4. What is the "broader social context into which the statement fits?"

Opinion was initially granted a wide berth of protection. Then — six years after *Ollman* and sixteen years after *Gertz* — came *Milkovich v. Lorain Journal*.[164] It reframed the opinion defense. It also forced recognition of the idea that where pure opinion may not exist, mixed opinion may. In *Milkovich*, a high school wrestling coach sued when a local newspaper columnist indicated that the coach lied under oath about his role in a brawl during a match. For the first time, the Supreme Court addressed the "false idea" statement from *Gertz*. "[W]e do not think this passage from *Gertz* was intended to create a wholesale defamation exemption for anything that might be labeled 'opinion,'" Chief Justice William Rehnquist wrote. "Not only would such an interpretation be contrary to the tenor and context of the passage, but it would also ignore the fact that expressions of 'opinion' may often imply an assertion of objective fact."[165] He said that facts can disguise themselves as opinions and that, when they do, they imply a knowledge of hidden facts that led to the opinion. While *Milkovich* holds that opinion is not protected as a category of speech, it provides a framework in which opinion *is* protected. That is, since an opinion cannot be proved false, it cannot be the basis for a successful libel action.

As noted above, opinion defenses are not limited to the constitutional category. "Fair comment and criticism" and "letters to the editor" are common law defenses.

Neutral Reportage

Neutral reportage is another defense with a constitutional foundation. It was first enunciated in 1977 in *Edwards v. National Audubon Society, Inc.*[166] Neutral reportage protects accurate, unbiased reporting of accusations by prominent, responsible persons about public figures. Courts that have adopted the neutral reporting rule have done so because news value attaches when public persons make such statements. The Second U.S. Circuit Court of Appeals, in *Edwards*, overturned a jury verdict against the *New York Times*, saying it was constitutionally impermissible to hold the newspaper liable:

[W]hen a responsible, prominent organization ... makes serious charges against a public figure, the First Amendment protects the accurate and disinterested reporting of those charges, regardless of the reporter's private views of their validity.... We do not believe that the press may be required under the First Amendment to suppress newsworthy statements

---

[160] 418 U.S. 323, 339-40 (1974).

[161] 750 F.2d 970 (D.C. Cir. 1984).

[162] *Id.* at 1038 (Scalia, J., dissenting in part).

[163] *Id.* at 979-83.

[164] 497 U.S. 1 (1990).

[165] *Id.* at 18.

[166] 556 F.2d 113 (2d Cir. 1977).

merely because it has serious doubts regarding their truth.[167]

Since the Supreme Court had said that serious doubts about a statement's truth constitutes actual malice, *Edwards* seemed to carve out an exception within the definition of actual malice. Neutral reportage, it seemed, would create even greater breathing space for a media industry already provided latitude *via* the actual malice standard.

In the three decades since its inception, several states — Alabama, Florida, Georgia, Illinois, Louisiana, New York, Oklahoma, Vermont and Washington — and the District of Columbia have accepted neutral reportage in some form. In addition, on the federal appeals level, the Fourth, Seventh and Tenth Circuit Courts have joined the Second in recognizing the privilege. Yet the judiciary has hardly embraced it. Indeed, a significant number of courts have rejected the libel defense, reasoning that it is neither First-Amendment-mandated nor justifiable on policy grounds. The rejection by the Pennsylvania Supreme Court of neutral reportage is illustrative. In *Norton v. Glenn,* the court held that the First Amendment creates no special rights for the news media in libel law over and above those enjoyed by ordinary citizens.[168] The court also stated that unless the Supreme Court changes the actual malice standard further in favor of the media, there is no public policy justification for adoption of the neutral reportage privilege.[169]

The Supreme Court has had virtually nothing to say about neutral reportage. While it remains an option in the libel defendant's strategy, the inconsistent manner in which courts have accepted neutral reportage makes it an unreliable defense.[170] (For a discussion of neutral reportage as a libel defense in foreign law, see the "Globalization of U.S. Libel Law" section later in this chapter.)

COMMON LAW DEFENSES

Libel defendants may also utilize defenses that originate with the common law. Traditional state rules governing libel law largely stem from laws and principles handed down through generations of legal precedent, mainly from English law. Early in the sixteenth century, the common law courts began to recognize a claim for defamation and, with it, various defenses. These grew out of the recognition that there is sometimes an interest in the free flow of information that is so important that

some allowance for error must be made.

Fair Comment and Criticism

Imagine a situation in which a newspaper writes a highly critical review of a local theater production. Should the subjects of the review be able to file a libel claim? At the turn of the century, the *Des Moines Leader* republished a review of an act by "The Cherry Sisters." Among other statements, the reviewer described one sister as "an old jade," a second as "a capering monstrosity," and the three of them as "strange creatures." When the sisters sued for libel, the Iowa Supreme Court accepted the *Leader's* defense:

> One who goes upon the stage to exhibit himself to the public, or who gives any kind of a performance to which the public is invited, may be freely criticised [sic].... [E]ntire freedom of expression is guarantied [sic] to dramatic critics, provided they are not actuated by malice or evil purpose in what they write.[171]

Thus began the development of the fair comment and criticism doctrine. Originally the privilege provided only modest coverage, protecting commentary only when it was based on true facts, but over time it has expanded. Still, to qualify for the privilege, commentary must be fair, it must be made without common law malice (that is, ill will), and it must accurately reflect the opinion of the commentator.

Fair comment and criticism is a common law privilege that protects critics from lawsuits brought by individuals in the public eye. A "critic" can be anyone who comments on the individuals. A person in the public eye is anyone who enters a public sphere: artists, entertainers, dramatists, writers, members of the clergy, teachers — anyone who moves in and out of the public eye, either professionally or as an amateur. The privilege also protects commentary on institutions whose activities are of interest to the public or where matters of public interest are concerned.

Fair comment and criticism protects criticism based on facts that are stated, privileged or otherwise known to be available to the public. If the challenged statement conveys or implies a defamatory message, this defense may be lost and the implication may be the basis of a libel suit.

The statement-of-fact requirement for the plaintiff raises challenges to Twitter users given that "tweets" are limited to 140 characters. As FindLaw columnist Julie Hilden noted: "[T]he limit may ... have a serious — and probably unanticipated — downside: It may make Twitter a trap for the unwary

---

[167] *Id.* at 120.

[168] 860 A.2d 48, 53 (Pa. 2004).

[169] *Id.* at 57.

[170] For a trenchant criticism of neutral reportage as a libel defense, *see* David A. Elder, *Truth, Accuracy and Neutral Reportage: Beheading the Media Jabberwock's Attempts to Circumvent* New York Times v. Sullivan, 9 VAND. J. ENT. & TECH. L. 551 (2007).

[171] Cherry v. Des Moines Leader, 86 N.W. 323, 325 (Iowa 1901).

when it comes to libel suits."[172] Given that the word limit offers not enough space to allow supporting facts for an opinion, Twitter users should be wary of potentially defamatory comments.

Truth

American defamation law protects "a good reputation honestly earned," not an undeserved reputation that has been damaged by the disclosure of hidden facts.[173] Thus, truth is a complete defense in a libel case. If it can be proved, there can be no liability. If a statement must be false for liability to attach, it cannot be the basis of a successful libel suit if, in fact, it is true. Truth can be asserted as a libel defense even where a person's criminal conviction was expunged but that conviction was subsequently publicized. "Although our expungement statute generally permits a person whose record has been expunged to misrepresent his past," the New Jersey Supreme Court stated, "it does not alter the metaphysical truth of his past, nor does it impose a regime of silence on those who know the truth."[174] In 2009, however, a federal appellate court, applying the Massachusetts libel law, held that true but defamatory statements about a private person relating to a matter of private concern can be actionable if published maliciously.[175]

Meanwhile, a number of misconceptions exist about the truth defense, and it is not easy to prove. For years, truth was considered a noble defense. After all, the media are supposed to be in the business of rooting out and publishing the truth. Modern libel law, however, has turned the truth-falsity distinction on its ear. The burden of proof in this area now lies with the plaintiff, not the defendant, especially when the news media are sued for defamation relating to a matter of public interest.[176]

Just because the burden of proof lies with the plaintiff, however, a libel defendant does not stand idly by. The defendant's attorneys will attempt to demonstrate that the disputed material is true. The attorneys will do this by cross-examining the plaintiff's witnesses and, possibly, by producing evidence of truth. In such circumstances — and even when a defendant advances a defense of truth — the defendant need not demonstrate that a defamatory statement is completely true in order to maintain the defense. Substantial truth is all that is re-

quired. As one court said, "Slight inaccuracies of expression are immaterial provided that the defamatory charge is true in substance."[177] The Supreme Court has agreed, saying that substantial truth would absolve a defendant even if the defendant cannot justify every word of the alleged defamatory matter; it is sufficient if the substance of the charge be proved true, irrespective of the slight inaccuracy in the details. Minor inaccuracies do not amount to falsity so long as the substance, the gist, the sting of the libelous charge can be justified.[178]

Substantial truth means, for example, that if a newspaper reported that an individual was in police custody when, in fact, the individual had been released on bail, the story would be substantially true, because the individual had been in custody and it was only a quirk in time that had caused the mistake. If, however, a newspaper published that an individual had been charged with a crime when the individual had only been questioned and released, the story would not be substantially true. In short, the substantial truth defense can protect a libel defendant when *minor* inaccuracies appear in a report.

A phenomenon unique to the broadcast media may play a role in libel cases and, in turn, may have a bearing on the truth defense. Broadcasters have the ability to alter a message — and its believability, that is, its perceived "truth" — with voice inflections. A libel suit was filed against a Chicago television station claiming that one of its reporters gave a false impression of what had actually occurred, and thereby defamed the plaintiffs, with his skeptical tone of voice. That is, while his words themselves were innocent enough, the tone with which they were delivered was at the root of the libel claim. The judge, however, agreed with the defendant's position that the tone alone could not support the defamation suit, and he dismissed it.[179]

It is worthwhile to note a growing trend in lawsuits against media defendants. Plaintiffs are circumventing the issue of truth in the defendant's stories by filing suit for transgressions other than libel. A good example is *Food Lion v. Cap Cities/ ABC*,[180] in which a supermarket chain that was unhappy with a television news magazine segment on its food preparation practices sued, not for libel, but because of the techniques used in gathering the information. This strategy enabled Food Lion to entirely bypass any obligation of proving that the broadcast was false.[181] Thus, whereas libel may have been the preferred sword for plaintiffs in cases like this, lawyers are more frequently advising their clients to avoid the realm in which media defen-

---

[172] Julie Hilden, *Libel by Twitter?: The Suit Against Kim Kardashian Over the "Cookie Diet,"* FINDLAW, http://bit.ly/5gB3kc.

[173] Bustos v. A&E Television Networks, 646 F.3d 762, 764 (10th Cir. 2011).

[174] G.D. v. Kenny, 15 A.3d 300 (N.J. 2011). *See also* Martin v. Hearst Corp., 777 F.3d 546 (2d Cir. 2015).

[175] Noonan v. Staples, Inc., 556 F.3d 20 (1st Cir. 2009), *rehearing en banc denied,* 561 F.3d 4 (1st Cir. 2009). *See generally* Samantha Fredrickson, *Truth Defense Dinged; Now What?,* NEWS MEDIA & L., Spring 2009, at 23.

[176] *See* Philadelphia Newspapers, Inc. v. Hepps, 475 U.S. 767 (1986) (holding that private persons, when suing the news media, must prove falsity if the defamation at issue relaters to a matter of public interest).

[177] Liberty Lobby v. Dow Jones, 838 F.2d 1287, 1296 (D.C. Cir. 1988).

[178] *See* Masson v. New Yorker Magazine, 501 U.S. 496, 516-17 (1991).

[179] Hanash and Yousef v. WFLD, 1998 U.S. Dist. Lexis 17738 (N.D. Ill. 1998).

[180] 964 F. Supp. 956 (M.D.N.C. 1997).

[181] A divided federal appeals court ultimately ruled that the newsgathering techniques used were not unlawful. *See* Food Lion, Inc. v. Capital Cities/ABC, 194 F.3d 505 (4th Cir. 1999).

dants have the shield of both constitutional and common law protection at their disposal. (The *Food Lion* case also is discussed in Chapter 18.)

Fair Report Privilege

Within some spheres of society, it is so vitally important that people be allowed to speak without fear of being sued for libel that they are granted immunity from liability. This privilege — called "absolute privilege" — typically occurs within the context of carrying out the business of government. Nothing a government official says that is relevant to the official's duties can be the subject of a successful libel suit. A corporation is no different in its absolute privilege when it provides an allegedly defamatory investigatory report to a government agency. As the Texas Supreme Court held in 2015, compelled cooperation by companies with the federal Department of Justice will not expose them to liability for defamation.[182] Moreover, an open society demands that members of the public have access to information relating to government proceedings. It logically follows, then, that people reporting on these proceedings or other absolutely privileged information also have the protection of privilege. This privilege, however, is often conditioned or qualified on the fair and accurate reporting of the proceeding and is generally known as "qualified privilege."

The privilege may be lost if the allegedly defamatory material is published with common law malice, if it is not fair, if the gist of the article is not substantially correct, or if the author draws conclusions or adds comments to the official report. According to the Supreme Court of Illinois, however, it is not defeated by either common law malice or *New York Times* actual malice.[183] Sometimes also referred to as the "fair report" or "official report" privilege, what is recognized by common law or statute in at least forty-seven states and the District of Columbia,[184] it proves to be an exception to the rule of republication,[185] discussed later in this chapter. The fair report privilege protects media reports of official government actions, regardless of possible defamatory elements in those reports. The rationale is that citizens in a participatory democracy are entitled to such information. But that entitlement rarely extends to official reports issued by governments other than those in the United States.[186]

Hyperlinking to a defamatory source is protected by the fair report privilege. In 2013, a federal district court in New York applied the fair report privilege in holding hyperlinking nonac-

tionable.[187] This hyperlink libel case arose from allegations made in a separate wrongful termination suit by an ex-employee against Sheldon Adelson, a Las Vegas businessman. Adelson was alleged to have approved "prostitution strategy" for his casino business. The National Jewish Democratic Council posted an article on its Web site claiming that Adelson "personally approved" of prostitution in his Macau casinos and hyperlinked to an Associated Press story.[188]

In connection with the source attribution as a requirement for the fair report privilege, the federal court said: "The hyperlink is the twenty-first century equivalent of the footnote for purposes of attribution in defamation law, because it has become a well-recognized means for an author or the Internet to attribute source."[189] The court added that shielding libel defendants from liability for hyperlinking to their sources is "good public policy," since it helps facilitate access to information of public interest.[190]

The privilege covers officials and proceedings in the executive, judicial and legislative branches of local, state and federal governments and, often, private individuals communicating with the government.

Executive Branch. Reports on the official statements and proceedings of people in the administrative — or executive — branch of government are typically privileged. The reports and hearings administrators are required by law to prepare and conduct are covered, particularly when the information contained therein has been made available to the public.

Meanwhile, the fair report privilege is not always confined to reports of official statements or of official actions. It may apply to news reports based on information provided by nonofficial sources, if the reports are fair and accurate. In 2010, the Massachusetts Supreme Judicial Court stated:

The privilege to report official actions would mean very little, … if to qualify for its protection, the media were limited to reporting such [official] actions solely on the basis of on-the-record statements by high-ranking (authorized to speak) officials or published official documents. Consequently, the privilege extends to reports of official actions based on information provided by nonofficial third-party sources. It should be of no moment that a reporter's source is, in fact, a high official, a low official, or a mere witness who overheard the proceedings, so long as it is official action that is reported.[191]

---

[182] Shell Oil Co. v. Writt, 464 S.W.3d 650 (Tex. 2015).

[183] *See, e.g.,* Solaia Technology LLC v. Specialty Publ'g Co., 852 N.E.2d 825 (Ill. 2006).

[184] *See* Salzano v. North Jersey Media Group Inc., 993A.2d 778, 787 n.2 (N.J. 2010).

[185] *See* Howell v. Enterprise Publ'g Co., 920 N.E.2d 1 (Mass. 2010).

[186] *See, e.g.,* Lee v. Dong-A Ilbo, 849 F.2d 876 (4th Cir. 1988).

[187] Adelson v. Harris, 973 F. Supp. 2d 467 (S.D.N.Y. 2013).

[188] *Id.* at 486.

[189] *Id.* at 484.

[190] *Id.* at 485.

[191] *Howell,* 920 N.E.2d 1, 18-19 (Mass. 2010) (citations omitted).

Law enforcement agencies are included as part of the executive branch of government. Thus, reports of police activity are conditionally privileged. Official reports and statements by police officials and officers qualify. A 2009 Arkansas case illustrates how the privilege can work. A man who was mentioned in a police report about an alleged rape sued the *Courier News* for libel after the newspaper published a story based on the inaccurate report. He argued that the newspaper's story was not fair and unprivileged. The Arkansas Supreme Court disagreed, holding that the news story about the rape allegations comprised the information from the report as recounted to the police by the victim's cousin. The court found that if the gist of the publication is in essence accurate, "some minor conflicts in what was alleged will not eliminate the privilege."[192]

Not every statement by a police officer is privileged, however. The Idaho Supreme Court, for example, refused to apply the privilege to statements a police officer made to a reporter during an interview.[193] These were not considered to be part of the officer's official duties, which is a key determinant in deciding whether the privilege applies.

Legislative Branch. Reports about the proceedings of Congress, state legislatures and local governing bodies are privileged. In addition, reports on documents — petitions and complaints, for example — that are filed with or submitted to these bodies are also privileged. It is important to remember, however, that documents coming from legislative meetings are not privileged until officials take possession of them.

Judicial Branch. Reports about judicial activities — the courts — are conditionally privileged unless otherwise codified.[194] So media accounts of testimony, depositions, arguments, trials, verdicts, opinions and orders — those aspects that are typically open or available to the public — are among the proceedings covered. Also, documents that relate to the judicial branch are also typically privileged. Conversely, those parts of the judicial process that are closed are not privileged.

As a Massachusetts judge, Oliver Wendell Holmes was among those who reasoned that the public should be provided with information about judicial proceedings because "those who administer justice should act under a sense of public responsibility."[195] Nearly a century later, another Massachusetts court echoed

Holmes and held that the value of granting privilege to media reports about the courts is "the security which publicity gives for the proper administration of justice."[196]

Non-Publication and Republication

Since a plaintiff in a libel case must prove that a defamatory statement was published, a defendant may prevail by showing he or she did not publish the statement, that the statement was not understood by a third party, or that it was published so long ago (one year or more, depending on the state) that the statute of limitations expired.

Since republication, a narrow exception to the single publication rule, is generally considered tantamount to publication, there is virtually no defense in arguing that the defendant merely repeated a defamatory statement. As one court ruled, "[O]ne who republishes a defamatory statement 'adopts' it as his own and is liable in equal measure to the original defamer."[197] Moreover, media are especially prone to libel suits for repeating defamatory statements, because plaintiffs tend to sue defendants who are best able to pay damages. Neither the original publisher nor a reporter is as likely to be as financially capable as a media organization.

Meanwhile, does the posting of new articles referencing or hyperlinking to a previously published defamatory story constitute republication? A federal district court in Kentucky answered no. The court held that a mere reference to a defamatory article "does not present the *defamatory contents* of the article to [a] new audience," while it may bring "the *existence*" of the article to the attention of the audience.[198] Further, the court found that the hyperlink, a new method of access to the referenced article, did not republish the article. For the hyperlink neither restated the defamatory article nor changed the contents of that article.[199] From a policy perspective, the court reasoned, finding republication by hyperlink would undercut the single publication rule:

> Websites are frequently, if not constantly, updated. Methods of access to portions of the website can change on a regular basis and links to previous posts on a website are constantly added and taken away from sites. Therefore, to find that a new link to an unchanged article posted long ago on a website

[192] Whiteside v. Russellville Newspapers, Inc., 295 S.W.3d 798, 804 (Ark. 2009).

[193] Weimer v. Rankin, 790 P.2d 347 (Idaho 1990).

[194] *See* N.Y. Civ. Rights Law § 74 (McKinney 2014) (providing that "[a] civil action cannot be maintained against any person, firm or corporation, for the publication of a fair and true report of any judicial proceeding"). For the recent interpretation on the fair report privilege in New York law, *see Alf v. Buffalo News, Inc.*, 995 N.E.2d 168 (N.Y. 2013).

[195] Cowley v. Pulsifer, 137 Mass. 392, 394 (1884).

[196] Liquori v. Republican Co., 396 N.E.2d 726, 728 (Mass. App. 1979).

[197] Liberty Lobby v. Dow Jones & Co., 838 F.2d 1287, 1298 (D.C. Cir. 1988).

[198] Salyer v. Southern Poverty Law Ctr., Inc., 701 F. Supp. 2d 912, 916 (W.D. Ky. 2009). For a similar reasoning in a recent landmark Internet libel case of the Canadian Supreme Court, *see* Crookes v. Newton, [2011] 3 S.C.R. 269 (holding that hyperlinking to defamatory material does not constitute (re)publication of defamation).

[199] *Id.* at 918.

republishes that article would result in a continual retriggering of the limitations period.[200]

Letters to the Editor

While the publication of letters to the editor represents a form of republication, letters are typically viewed as expressions of opinions rather than statements of fact. For that reason, newspapers and magazines have won most cases based on the publication of letters. Courts have sought to provide protection for their publication, often viewing them as part of an open forum for the general public.

The placement of a letter can have a bearing in determining whether it qualifies as opinion. That is, by appearing in a section of a newspaper or magazine that is clearly set aside for letters expressing opinions, a letter is much more likely to be viewed by a court as an expression of opinion.

Courts have held that some letters to the editor have been expressions that combined opinion and facts. Often cases based on such expressions end in favor of libel plaintiffs. For example, a Florida appellate court ruled that a letter questioning a child psychologist's qualifications was defamatory because it was this sort of mixed expression and, therefore, not privileged.[201] On the other hand, the Ohio Supreme Court, in 2001, supported the notion that writers of letters to the editor enjoy the same constitutional protection for opinions as journalists do: "The robust exchange of ideas that occurs each day on the editorial pages of our state's newspapers could indeed suffer if the non-media authors of letters to the editor published in these forums were denied the same constitutional protections enjoyed by the editors themselves."[202] Thus, the authors of letters that the news media publish are as shielded as the media themselves.

The Wire Service Defense

Another exception to the republication rule is the publication of information from a business that expressly provides information to news organizations. This "wire service defense" is available to libel defendants if four factors are met:

(1) The defendant received the copy in which the defamatory statements are contained from a reputable news gathering agency;

(2) The defendant did not know the story was false;

(3) Nothing on the face of the story could have reasonably alerted the defendant that it may have been incorrect; and

(4) The original wire service story was republished without substantial change.

In short, the wire service defense holds that the accurate republication of a story that a reputable news agency provided does not constitute fault as a matter of law.

The wire service defense originated with a 1933 case, *Layne v. Tribune Co.*[203] The Florida Supreme Court held that republication of wire service reports could not be libelous unless the publisher acted in a negligent, reckless or careless manner. "No newspaper could ... assume in advance the burden of specially verifying every item of news reported to it by established news gathering agencies," the court held.[204]

The wire service defense has succeeded even when a newspaper published a story that relied on past wire-service articles[205] and when a CBS affiliate broadcast network news reports.[206] Though by no means universally accepted, at least thirteen jurisdictions have adopted the wire service defense: Alaska, the District of Columbia, Florida, Georgia, Hawaii, Kentucky, Louisiana, Massachusetts, Missouri, New York, North Carolina, Wisconsin and Puerto Rico.

But what happens if the Associated Press republishes defamatory articles from reputable newspapers? The "reverse wire service defense" protects the AP from liability. The Massachusetts Court of Appeals, calling the relationship between the AP and its member newspapers and other media outlet members "symbiotic," noted that the AP employs its own staff to report original news stories but also often relies upon member newspapers as additional wire sources.[207]

Online Republication

Publication of online material by Internet service providers is related to publication and republication. The issue in libel law is whether an online service can be held liable for defamatory statements that are published through that service.

The defining case in this area is *Zeran v. America Online.*[208] This case dealt with the issue of an ISP as publisher, but did so in light of the passage of the Communications Decency Act in 1996. One section of the act provides that "no provider or user of an interactive computer service shall be treated as the publisher or speaker of any information provided by another information content provider."

Kenneth Zeran sued America Online when the company in-

---

[200] *Id. But cf. In re* Perry, 423 B.R. 215 (Bankr. S.D. Tex. 2010) (holding that individuals can be liable for linking defamatory blogs to a blog).

[201] Madsen v. Buie, 454 So. 2d 727, 729 (Fla. Dist. Ct. App. 1984).

[202] Wampler v. Higgins, 752 N.E.2d 962, 975 (Ohio 2001).

[203] 146 So. 234 (Fla. 1933) (en banc).

[204] *Id.* at 239.

[205] McKinney v. Avery Journal, 393 S.E.2d 295 (N.C. App. 1990).

[206] Auvril v. CBS, 140 F.R.D. 450 (E.D. Wash. 1991).

[207] Reilly v. Associated Press, 797 N.E.2d 1204 (Mass. Ct. App. 2003).

[208] 129 F.3d 327 (4th Cir. 1997).

cluded his name and telephone number in a series of bulletin board notices that advertised t-shirts and other items glorifying the 1995 bombing of a federal building in Oklahoma City. The inclusion of his name was part of a hoax by an unknown individual. A relevant section of the CDA stipulates that no provider of an interactive computer service may be treated as the publisher of information provided by some entity other than the provider. A U.S. district court ruled that while the CDA does not preempt all state law actions of this nature, it did preempt Zeran's claim of negligence by AOL because it conflicts with both the language and purposes of the CDA.[209] On appeal, the Fourth U.S. Circuit Court of Appeals ruled that this section of the CDA "plainly immunizes computer service providers like AOL for liability for information that originates with third parties."[210] Thus, an online libel defendant may be able to utilize the CDA when similar circumstances present themselves.

The California Supreme Court's application in 2006 of the CDA on the basis of the *Zeran* precedent is illustrative. Adopting *Zeran*'s ruling that the CDA protects both "publishers" and subsequent "distributors" against defamation liability for online republication, the California court stated that there is no practical distinction between active and passive use of interactive computer services.[211] Hence, the court concluded that Internet users cannot be held liable for posting defamatory statements prepared by someone else.

On the other hand, the Ninth U.S. Circuit Court of Appeals, in a 2008 *en banc* decision, held that Roommates.com was ineligible for immunity as a "developer" under the CDA when it "materially" contributed to creating the allegedly illegal content relating to housing discrimination under the federal Fair Housing Act.[212] In a recent Internet libel case, however, the New York Court of Appeals did not find the kind of "material" change that had deprived Roommates.com of CDA immunity in the Ninth Circuit's ruling. New York's highest court held in *Shiamili v. Real Estate Group of New York, Inc.*[213] that the defendant blog operators did not materially alter a defamatory comment by a user when they moved it to a stand-alone post and gave it a heading.[214] The court said: "Reposting content created and initially posted by a third party is well-within 'a publisher's traditional editorial functions.'"[215]

The Libel-Proof Plaintiff

A libel defendant may be able to invoke the concept of the "libel-proof plaintiff." When an individual's reputation is so bad that even a false accusation could not further harm it, the individual is considered to be libel-proof and cannot win a defamation suit. The libel-proof doctrine was first articulated as a libel defense in *Cardillo v. Doubleday Co., Inc.*, a 1975 case.[216] Since then, two separate prongs of the libel-proof doctrine have developed — incremental harm and issue-specific publication.

Incremental Harm. If an individual is identified in an article as a thief, child molester and tax evader, and if all of the charges are true, does it make any difference if the individual is also identified falsely as a kidnapper? The doctrine of incremental harm says no. In such a case, the publisher could probably win, arguing that the single false statement causes harm that is merely incremental beyond what already exists and, therefore, is not grounds for a libel suit. In short, in such circumstances the false statement causes no significant harm to the reputation beyond that caused by the true statements, which are protected.

One of the leading incremental harm cases is *Herbert v. Lando*.[217] Anthony Herbert, a retired Army officer, sued over statements made about him during a segment of *60 Minutes*. The segment questioned the validity of his claim that the U.S. Army had punished him for trying to disclose information about massacres by American forces in South Vietnam. The Second U.S. Circuit Court of Appeals ruled that if the charge that Herbert lied about reporting war crimes was not actionable, "[O]ther statements, even those that might be found to have been published with actual malice should not be actionable if they merely imply the same view, and are simply an outgrowth of and subsidiary to those claims upon which it has been held there can be no recovery."[218]

In several cases, however, the incremental harm doctrine has failed as a libel defense. A particularly noteworthy example was the outright rejection of the doctrine in *Liberty Lobby, Inc. v. Anderson*.[219] Journalist Jack Anderson described the founder of Liberty Lobby as a racist, fascist, anti-Semitic and neo-Nazi, and wrote that Liberty Lobby was founded to pursue his goals. Anderson argued that previous publications had already so ir-

[209] Zeran v. America Online, 958 F. Supp. 1124, 1135 (E.D. Va. 1997).

[210] Zeran v. America Online, 129 F.3d 327, 328 (4th Cir. 1997).

[211] Barrett v. Rosenthal, 146 P.3d 510 (Cal. 2006).

[212] Fair Housing Council of San Fernando Valley v. Roommates.com LLC, 52 F.3d 1157 (9th Cir. 2008) (en banc).

[213] 952 N.E.2d 1011 (N.Y. 2011).

[214] *Id.* at 1020.

[215] *Id.* at 1019.

[216] 518 F.2d 638 (2d Cir. 1975) (ruling that the passages of a book whose authors wrote that a habitual criminal was involved in various other criminal activities were not published with actual malice).

[217] 781 F.2d 298 (2d Cir. 1986), *aff'g, in part, rev'g, in part,* and *remanding,* 596 F. Supp. 1178 (S.D.N.Y. 1984). The case and its facts had been thoroughly explored by the courts on several previous occasions. *See* Herbert v. Lando, 73 F.R.D. 387 (S.D.N.Y.), *rev'd,* 568 F.2d 974 (2d Cir. 1977), *rev'd,* 441 U.S. 153 (1979).

[218] *Id.* at 312.

[219] 746 F.2d 1563 (D.C. Cir. 1984), *rev'd on other grounds,* 477 U.S. 242 (1986).

reparably tarnished the plaintiff's reputation that the libel-proof doctrine should apply. In an opinion written by Judge Antonin Scalia, the court rejected the claim, ruling that "we cannot envision how a court would go about determining that someone's reputation had already been 'irreparably' damaged — i.e., that no new reader could be reached by the freshest libel."[220]

Nevertheless, the doctrine, which the First Amendment does not mandate, remains a valuable defense weapon, particularly against frivolous libel suits, and especially given the Supreme Court's opinion that states are free to adopt the doctrine as they see fit.[221]

Issue-Specific Publication. Courts recognizing the issue-specific doctrine have found that libel plaintiffs with tarnished reputations with regard to a particular issue are libel-proof *only with respect to that topic area.* Libel claims pursued in the issue-specific context, the New Hampshire Supreme Court held in 2007, require proof not only

> that the plaintiff engaged in criminal or anti-social behavior in the past, but also that his activities were widely reported to the public. The evidence on the nature of the conduct, the number of offenses, and the degree and range of publicity received must make it clear, as a matter of law, that the plaintiff's reputation could not have suffered from the publication of the false and libelous statement.[222]

In one case, for example, the defendant had published an article that said the plaintiff had used his relationship with actress Elizabeth Taylor for financial gain.[223] The court held that the plaintiff had a "reputation for taking advantage of women generally, and of Miss Taylor specifically." It ruled that "[a]n individual who engages in certain anti-social or criminal behavior and suffers a diminished reputation may be 'libel-proof' as a matter of law, as it *relates to that specific behavior.*"[224]

More recently, however, Howard K. Stern, the former attorney and companion of the late Anna Nicole Smith, was found not to be libel-proof. A federal district court judge held that Stern's bad reputation as Smith's "principal enabler," could still be further damaged by the false "promiscuous homosexual sex" or "pimping" assertions in defendant Rita Cosby's book *Blonde Ambition: The Untold Story Behind Anna Nicole Smith's Death.* Judge Denny Chinn stated: "That someone has been falsely called a thief in the past does not mean that he is immune from

further injury if he is falsely called a thief again."[225]

Thus, the doctrine of the libel-proof plaintiff may serve a defendant who has published otherwise defamatory statements about an individual whose reputation is already so sullied as to render additional accusations moot, regardless of their falsity. The doctrine may apply to accusations of any nature or to those that relate only to a specific issue.

OTHER DEFENSE ISSUES

While not defenses *per se*, several other issues can have a bearing on — and even strengthen — a libel defense.

Responsible Reporting

As part of a defense strategy, a libel defendant may attempt to demonstrate that it conducted itself in a responsible way. Within the context of a media organization, responsible reporting may be demonstrated through attempts to show that journalists acted without negligence or reckless disregard of the truth.

In attempting to prove that a libel defendant acted with reckless disregard, a plaintiff is likely to attempt to build a case bit by bit, demonstrating irresponsibility or carelessness in publishing. Courts have said that no single element is sufficient to prove clearly and convincingly that a defendant acted with actual malice, but each can be used as evidence. A libel defendant who is aware of certain claims of irresponsibility or carelessness, therefore, can be prepared to refute them. Some of the claims might be the following:

- failure to investigate sufficiently;
- failure to interview parties who have knowledge of facts related to the story, including the subject of the report;[226]
- reliance on previously published material;
- reliance on biased stories or sources;
- inaccurate reporting;
- reporting from a specific point of view in an investigative story;
- refusal to retract or correct if facts warrant;
- absence of a fixed deadline;
- ill will or hatred toward the plaintiff, that is, common law malice.

Even if media defendants are unable to escape liability altogether, by refuting these points, and demonstrating responsible reporting, they are likely to mitigate damages.

A case in Ohio illustrates how a court may consider one or more of these elements. Within the context of a libel suit, a

---

[220] *Id.* at 1568.

[221] *See* Masson v. New Yorker Magazine, 501 U.S. 496, 523 (1991).

[222] Thomas v. Telegraph Publ'g Co., 929 A.2d 993, 1005 (N.H. 2007).

[223] Wynberg v. Nat'l Enquirer, 564 F. Supp. 924 (C.D. Cal. 1982).

[224] *Id.* at 928 (emphasis added).

[225] Stern v. Cosby, 645 F. Supp. 2d 258, 271-72 (S.D.N.Y. 2009).

[226] *See* Harte-Hanks Commc'ns, Inc. v. Connaughton, 491 U.S. 657 (1989); Tatum v. Dallas Morning News, Inc., 2015 WL 9582903 (Tex. App. 2015).

state appellate court concluded that a reporter's failure to interview one of the police officers accused of brutality in a series of reports could be regarded as negligent behavior. The court ruled, however, that that irresponsibility alone did not support the officer's claim that the reporter had acted with actual malice.[227] Conversely, a television journalist argued that his reporting methods were responsible by maintaining that he spent four days interviewing thirty people and reviewing 500 pages of court records in preparing the story. That contributed to an appellate court overturning a libel judgment against him.[228]

Retractions, apologies and corrections for reputation-damaging reports can also be considered examples of "responsible reporting." In the eyes of the law, their impact varies greatly from state to state. In some states, a prompt and complete apology, correction and retraction will protect a defendant from punitive damages. In other states, jurors merely consider retractions in determining the amount of damages.

While a retraction or apology is not a libel defense, a potential libel defendant is often advised to correct possibly libelous errors due to the correction's ability to alleviate the statement's defamatory sting in the eyes of a court. Admitting errors in such circumstances may be regarded as an aspect of responsible reporting.[229] Moreover, many states have retraction laws that provide varying degrees of protection. Typically, they require a plaintiff to give a publisher an opportunity to retract a libelous statement prior to initiating a libel suit. If the publisher honors the request in a timely manner, the retraction may reduce the damages that the plaintiff may later seek should a lawsuit be filed. It should be noted, however, that the plaintiff may use a retraction, apology or correction as a defendant's admission of liability.

Summary Judgment

A judge may summarily decide certain points of a case and issue a judgment dismissing the case. Summary judgment can occur at any of several junctures in litigation.

A judge may issue a summary judgment on grounds that there is no genuine issue as to any material fact. Generally, this is a result of a plaintiff clearly being unable to meet at least one element in the plaintiff's burden of proof. On numerous occasions, the Supreme Court said that when considering motions for summary judgment, courts "must view the facts and inferences to be drawn from them in the light most favorable to the

opposing party."[230] The rationale is that, if the summary judgment is granted, the plaintiff's opportunity to prove a case is ended, but if the defendant's motion for summary judgment is denied, the defendant still has an opportunity to prove its case.

Summary judgments are seen as important tools for protecting free expression, particularly in an environment in which plaintiffs have harassed the media by filing frivolous lawsuits. Allowing judges to dismiss claims without merit tackles the chilling effect on media coverage that these lawsuits can have. As one federal judge explained:

> In the First Amendment area, summary procedures are even more essential. For the stake here, if harassment succeeds, is free debate. One of the purposes of the [*New York*] *Times* [actual malice] principle, in addition to protecting persons from being cast in damages in libel suits filed by public officials, is to prevent persons from being discouraged in the full and free exercise of First Amendment rights with respect to the conduct of their government. The threat of being put to the defense of a lawsuit brought by a popular public official may be as chilling to the exercise of First Amendment freedoms as fear of the outcome of the lawsuit itself, especially to advocates of unpopular causes.[231]

Until 1979, summary judgment was a preferred method of dealing with libel cases involving actual malice. When the defense submitted a motion for summary judgment — based on the contention that the plaintiff could not prove actual malice — the judge would either grant or deny it. If granted, the case was over; if denied, the case went to trial.

In 1979, Chief Justice Warren Burger cast doubt on the appropriateness of summary judgment in libel cases because, he argued, any examination of actual malice "calls a defendant's state of mind into question." Such a circumstance, he argued, "does not readily lend itself to summary disposition."[232] While some lower courts took Burger's admonition to heart — using it as a basis for denying summary judgment — motions for summary judgment are granted more often than not. Then, in 1986, Justice Byron White wrote that in deciding whether to grant motions for summary judgment, trial judges should decide whether public plaintiffs can meet the actual malice standard by "clear and convincing evidence." If not, summary judgment should be granted.[233] In short, this tempered Burger's words, suggesting that summary judgment remains a viable option.

---

[227] Early v. Toledo Blade, 720 N.E.2d 107 (Ohio App. 1998).

[228] Dolcefino and KTRK Television, Inc. v. Turner, 987 S.W. 2d 100 (Tex. 1998).

[229] It should be acknowledged that retractions and/or apologies are sometimes discouraged by those who advise potential media defendants. To retract or apologize, they say, is tantamount to an admission of guilt, thus increasing the challenge of mounting a successful defense.

[230] Mourning v. Family Publ'ns Serv., 411 U.S. 356, 382 (1973). *See also* United States v. Diebold, 369 U.S. 654, 655 (1979); Adickes v. Kress & Co., 389 U.S. 144, 157 (1970).

[231] Washington Post Co. v. Keogh, 365 F.2d 965, 968 (D.C. Cir. 1966).

[232] Hutchinson v. Proxmire, 443 U.S. 111, 120 n.9 (1979).

[233] Anderson v. Liberty Lobby, 477 U.S. 242, 244, 256 (1986).

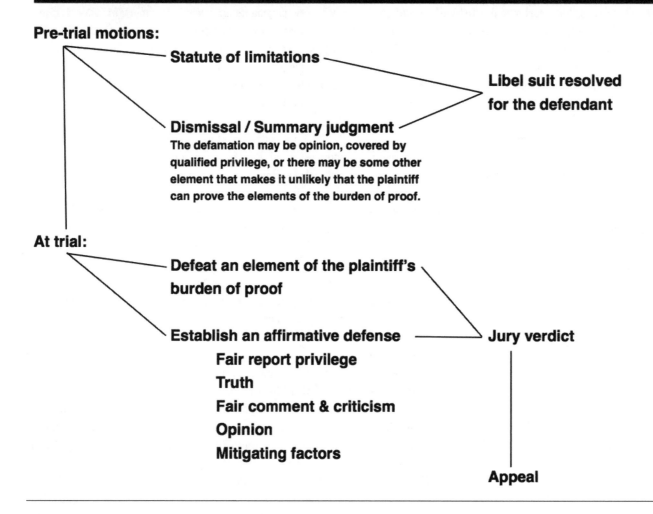

THE DEFENDANT'S CASE

Pre-trial motions:

Statute of limitations

Libel suit resolved for the defendant

Dismissal / Summary judgment
The defamation may be opinion, covered by qualified privilege, or there may be some other element that makes it unlikely that the plaintiff can prove the elements of the burden of proof.

At trial:

Defeat an element of the plaintiff's burden of proof

Establish an affirmative defense
Fair report privilege
Truth
Fair comment & criticism
Opinion
Mitigating factors

Jury verdict

Appeal

Today, judgment in an effort to curtail the increasing cost of defending libel suits, judges may be more apt to grant motions for summary. About 80 percent of libel insurance costs are incurred, not through the compensation of injured plaintiffs, but merely in defense costs. Estimates regarding the average defense cost vary but typically range from $100,000 to $200,000. In major cases, defendants have spent millions of dollars. Moreover, they have discovered that juries are increasingly unsympathetic toward them. The median jury award increased from $200,000 in the early 1980s to an average of $1.5 million over the decade. The Media Law Resource Center found that libel judgments against the media averaged $1.8 million in 2001.[234] In fact, juries seem to be punishing some defendants — those whose content or newsgathering techniques they find dis-

tasteful — particularly hard with punitive damages. Verdicts can reach into the millions, making it appear that juries base their decisions at least in part on a defendant's perceived unsavory nature. In the wake of these awards, one scholar wrote, such awards "[fly] in the face of the First Amendment which protects unorthodox as well as mainstream speech."[235]

While approximately two-thirds of jury verdicts in media libel cases are rendered against media defendants, about 75 percent are reversed or reduced on appeal. The bottom line — and not necessarily a reassuring one — for those facing a libel suit may be that media defendants tend to win on the law rather than having to rely on the often emotion-based conclusions of jurors.

[234] Press Release, Libel Defense Resource Center, Media Defendants' Win Rate Higher ... But So Are Damage Awards, *available at* http://www.ldrc.com/Press_Releases/bull2002-1.html.

[235] Nicole B. Casarez, *Punitive Damages in Defamation Actions: An Area of Libel Law Worth Reforming*, 32 DUQ. L. REV. 667, 687 (1994).

GLOBALIZATION OF U.S. LIBEL LAW: JURISDICTION AND CHOICE OF LAW ISSUES

Now broadcasters and publications transcend the boundaries of one state, or even one country, causing complicated problems for potential libel plaintiffs and defendants. Such is increasingly the case with Internet communicators, both institutional and individual.[236] The site where a lawsuit is adjudicated is — in legal parlance — the "place of wrong," that is, the place where the alleged injury occurred. In past years, the place of wrong for libel actions was the jurisdiction where the defamatory publication was made, regardless of where it originated. More recently, however, libel actions have been adjudicated in the place with the most significant relationship to the case. Generally, the place with the most significant relationship to the case is the jurisdiction in which the plaintiff lives or works.[237]

The determination of which law should govern in multi-state or multi-nation lawsuits is called the "choice of law" issue. Transnational media litigation, which often involves libel cases in foreign countries against media defendants in the United States, is growing. This is especially true of libel involving the Internet. A good illustration is the High Court of Australia's 2002 decision in *Dow Jones & Co. v Gutnick*.[238] Australian businessman Joseph Gutnick sued the U.S. company Dow Jones & Co. in the Supreme Court of Victoria for defamation in connection with online material published in *Barron's Online* magazine. Noting that Victoria residents downloaded the material at issue, the Australian court held that when a defamatory statement is accessible to and read by ISP subscribers in an Australian state, a court of that state has jurisdiction to hear an action for defamation relating to the statements.

In a 2005 Internet libel case, however, a Canadian appellate court refused to exercise jurisdiction over an American newspaper. In *Bangoura v. Washington Post*,[239] the Ontario Court of Appeal held that there was "simply no real and substantial connection" between the libel action and Ontario. Cheickh Bangoura, a native of Guinea, who moved to Ontario in 2000, sued the *Washington Post* and three reporters for defamation. In 1997, the *Washington Post* had published two articles claiming that Bangoura, then a U.N. official in Kenya, engaged in sexual harassment, financial improprieties and nepotism.

Generally, American courts hold that the First Amendment protects U.S. libel defendants from such foreign judgments if they are brought to the United States for enforcement.

In *Bachchan v. India Abroad Publications, Inc.*,[240] for example, an Indian national living in London asked a New York state court to enforce a libel verdict the plaintiff won in England against the publisher of a newspaper and news service for Asian Indians in the United States. Judge Shirley Fingerhood found that England's lack of an equivalent to the First Amendment to be significant and ruled that enforcing a foreign libel judgment would seriously jeopardize the First Amendment protections of speech and the press.

The Maryland Court of Appeals reached a similar conclusion five years later. A U.S. citizen was successfully sued in England for a letter he had written to the editor of the London *Daily Telegraph*. When the writer returned to Maryland, the plaintiff asked American courts to enforce the libel judgment.[241]

The Maryland Court of Appeals, however, noting England's adherence to strict liability in libel actions, the presumptive falsity of alleged defamations, the lack of distinction between private and public figures and differences in defenses, concluded that defamation law was totally different in England "in virtually every significant respect." The principles of libel law applied to the suit in England, the court held, were "so contrary to Maryland defamation law, and to the policy of freedom of the press" that the judgment should not be recognized.[242]

In 2006, a federal district judge in California held the French court's order against Yahoo! unenforceable in the United States. U.S. District Judge Jeremy Fogel stated in *Yahoo! Inc. v. La Ligue Contre le Racisme et l'Antisemitisme*, "Although France has the sovereign right to regulate what speech is permissible in France, this Court may not enforce a foreign order that violates the protections of the U.S. Constitution by chilling protected speech that occurs simultaneously within our borders."[243] The 2006 Internet hate speech case involved civil lawsuits filed by two French human rights groups against Yahoo! in a French court. The French court ordered Yahoo! to prevent France-based access to Yahoo!'s Internet auction service that displays Nazi artifacts and to any other site or service defending Nazism or contesting Nazi crimes.

In an effort to preempt various free speech issues arising from "libel tourism" abroad,[244] state and federal lawmakers have taken legislative initiatives. In 2008, the New York legis-

---

[236] *See, e.g.,* Joseph Weiler, *In the Dock, in Paris — The Judgment,* http://bit.ly/gNo1Bf (describing a French court's ruling in a criminal libel complaint by an Israeli academic against an American book review editor for publishing a German scholar's review of her book).

[237] *See* RESTATEMENT (SECOND) OF CONFLICT OF LAWS § 150 (1971).

[238] 194 A.L.R. 433 (2003).

[239] 258 D.L.R.4th 341 (Ont. Ct. App. 2005).

[240] 585 N.Y.S.2d 266 (1992).

[241] Telnikoff v. Matusevitch, 702 A.2d 230 (Md. 1997).

[242] *Id.* at 247-48.

[243] 145 F. Supp. 2d 1168, 1192 (N.D. Cal. 2001), *rev'd en banc,* 433 F.3d 1199 (9th Cir.), *cert. denied,* 547 U.S. 1163 (2006).

[244] "Libel tourism" refers to "a phenomenon that they variously describe as the use of libel judgments procured in jurisdictions with claimant-friendly libel laws — and little or no connection to the author or purported libelous material — to chill free speech in the United States." Ehrenfeld v. Bin Mahfouz, 881 N.E.2d 830, 834 (N.Y. 2007).

lature passed the Libel Terrorism Protection Act, which requires New York courts to dismiss foreign libel judgment as unenforceable if the foreign laws underlying the judgments are less protective of speech and the press than the First Amendment or the state constitution.[245] California, Florida, Illinois, Maryland and Utah have also enacted similar laws.[246]

In 2010, President Obama signed federal legislation that bars domestic enforcement of foreign libel judgments against Americans if the judgments are inconsistent with the First Amendment. The SPEECH (Securing the Protection of our Enduring and Established Constitutional Heritage) Act, modeled on the New York libel tourism law, was designed to protect American news media, journalists, ISPs, and others from libel litigation overseas. The SPEECH Act, which an Australian legal commentator has criticized for being a flawed response to a nonissue in U.S. law,[247] would enable a U.S. publisher or author sued abroad for libel to collect attorneys' fees if the foreign judgment is successfully opposed.[248] Libel tourism is not necessarily limited to the traditional media. Postings on Facebook, Twitter and other social media can be subject to libel tourism abroad.[249]

In 2013, the Fifth U.S. Circuit Court of Appeals held that the SPEECH Act barred enforcement of a Canadian defamation judgment.[250] Canadian residents sued a Mississippi-based blogger in a Nova Scotia court for defamation. They won a default judgment against the blogger, which included injunctive relief, in addition to $252,000 in damages and costs.[251] When they sought to enforce their Canadian judgment, the federal district court in Mississippi refused, citing the SPEECH Act. The Fifth Circuit, affirming the district court ruling, reasoned that Canadian law, an offshoot of U.K. law, was less protective of free speech than American law[252] and that a Mississippi court would not have found defamation on the facts and circumstances involved.[253] The blogger, as the prevailing party under the

SPEECH Act, was awarded an attorney's fee of $48,000.[254]

The gap between the United States and the rest of the world remains considerable. American libel law is decidedly more media-friendly than other laws. Nonetheless, free speech defenses, including the *Sullivan* actual malice standard, for the news media against liability for libel are increasingly accepted in other countries.[255] In *Jameel v. Wall Street Journal Europe*,[256] the United Kingdom House of Lords, a body that functions as the highest appellate court in England, held that responsible news reporting on a matter of public interest should preclude liability although it resulted in false defamatory stories. More importantly, the Law Lords in *Jameel* recognized neutral reportage as a libel defense in a similar way that the Second Circuit in *Edwards* did in 1977.[257] Especially Lord Leonard H. Hoffmann's comment on reportage in *Jameel* is provocative. "[T]here are cases ('reportage') in which the public interest lies simply in the fact that the statement was made, when it may be clear that the publisher does not subscribe to any belief in its truth," Lord Hoffmann stated. "[Here] the defense is not affected by the newspaper's inability to prove the truth of the statement at the trial."[258] More recently, the Canadian Supreme Court embraced "reportage" as part of its new "responsible communication" defense in libel law. The Court in *Grant v. Torstar* held:

> If a dispute is itself a matter of public interest and the allegations are fairly reported, the publisher should incur no liability even if some of the statements made may be defamatory and untrue, provided: (1) the report attributes the statement to a person, preferably identified, thereby avoiding total unaccountability; (2) the report indicates, expressly or implicitly, that its truth has not been verified; (3) the report sets out both sides of the dispute fairly; and (4) the report provides the context in which the statements were made. [259]

Further, Argentina and Spain are other countries that incorporate neutral reportage,[260] although the libel defense is increas-

---

[245] N.Y.C.P.L.R. § 302 (McKinney 2008). For a discussion of the Libel Terrorism Protection Act, *see* Yasmine Lahlou, *Libel Tourism: A Transatlantic Quandary*, 2 J. INT'L MEDIA & ENT. L. 199 (2009).

[246] *See* Laura R. Handman et al., *U.S. Congress Passes Historic Libel Tourism Bill*, Aug. 3, 2010, http://bit.ly/pXgRgD.

[247] *See generally* HARRY MELKONIAN, DEFAMATION, LIBEL TOURISM, AND THE SPEECH ACT OF 2010: THE FIRST AMENDMENT COLLIDING WITH THE COMMON LAW (2011).

[248] Securing the Protection of Our Enduring and Established Constitutional Heritage Act, 28 U.S.C. §§ 4101-4105 (2010). For a succinct discussion of the SPEECH Act, *see* Handman, *supra* note 246.

[249] *See* Pontigon v. Lord, 340 S.W.3d 315 (Mo. Ct. App. 2011) (applying the SPEECH Act in reversing the trial court decision to grant registration of a Canadian libel judgment relating to a Missouri resident's Internet "life story").

[250] Trout Point Lodge, Ltd. v. Handshoe, 729 F.3d 481 (5th Cir. 2013).

[251] *Id.* at 485.

[252] *Id.* at 488.

[253] *Id.* at 494.

[254] Trout Point Lodge, Ltd. v. Handshoe, No. 1:12CV90—LG—JMR, 2013 WL 6524650 (S.D. Miss. Dec. 11, 2013).

[255] Kyu Ho Youm, *"Actual Malice" in U.S. Defamation Law: The Minority of One Doctrine in the World?*, 4 J. INT'L MEDIA & ENTER. L. 1 (2011-12).

[256] [2006] U.K.H.L. 44.

[257] Surprisingly, the Law Lords have made not a single reference to *Edwards v. National Audubon Society*, undoubtedly the seminal U.S. neutral reportage case. For a discussion of "reportage" as a libel defense in U.K. law, *see* Alastair Mullis, *Qualified Privilege*, *in* CARTER-RUCK ON LIBEL AND PRIVACY 366-73 (Alastair Mullis & Cameron Doley eds., 6th ed. 2010).

[258] [2006] U.K.H.L. at ¶ 62 (opinion of Lord Hoffmann).

[259] 2009 S.C.C. 61 at ¶ 120 (citations omitted).

[260] *See* Pablo Crescimbeni et al., *Argentina, in* MEDIA, ADVERTISING & ENTERTAINMENT LAW THROUGHOUT THE WORLD § 1:15 (Andrew B. Ulmer ed., 2015); Miquel Martín-Casals & Josep Solé Feliu, *The Protection of Personality Rights Against Invasions by Mass Media in Spain*, *in* THE PROTECTION OF PERSONALITY RIGHTS

ingly questionable in U.S. law.

SUMMARY

Defamation law is designed to protect reputations so that individual interests are not harmed, while the guarantees of free expression are designed to promote the gathering and dissemination of information. Reputational rights are recognized in every society as a significant interest, but the degree of protection by law or custom varies greatly from country to country.

In the United States, though free expression is vigorously protected, libel law is one of the most visible legal restraints on expression. In recent years, the chill on expression caused by libel law has been a growing concern for the media. On the other hand, those critical of the excesses of the press welcome some degree of press chill. Notwithstanding the debate, there is no denying that libel law serves as a necessary mechanism for the balance between reputational rights and press freedom.

There are two types of defamation: libel, or written defamation, and slander, or spoken defamation. The traditional distinction between libel and slander is not as clear-cut as it once was because of new modes of communication. Broadcast defamation, for example, is more often than not treated as libel.

Nearly all libel cases are civil actions, in which plaintiffs claim monetary damages for reputational harm from defamatory statements. Libel is still recognized as a crime in some jurisdictions, but criminal libel statutes are rarely invoked.

To establish a cause of action against a non-media libel defendant, a plaintiff must prove that he or she was identified in a statement that was published to a third person, and that the statement was defamatory. When a media organization is the defendant, the plaintiff must establish two additional elements: (1) that the publication resulted from fault on the part of the defendant and (2) that the plaintiff suffered actual injury from publication of the defamatory statement. But the Ninth Circuit ruling of 2013 on the First Amendment right of bloggers questions the media and non-media distinctions.

Libel as a tort — a civil wrong — is premised on the requirement that a statement be false and defamatory. Thus, falsity is essential to a libel claim. Therefore, a libel claim for a statement of opinion — which cannot be proved to be true or false — cannot stand.

"Truth" in libel law is not synonymous with "accuracy." Verbatim quotations in a news story may be accurate but may not necessarily be true. "Truth" means that the substance of the quoted statement is factually verifiable.

It is difficult to determine when some language is defamatory; other language is clearly defamatory. The meanings of words change with the time, place and manner in which they are used. In the majority of jurisdictions, the libel *per se* and libel *per quod* rules are still followed. Libel *per se* refers to words and phrases that are defamatory on their face and need no additional information. Libel *per quod* refers to a statement that is not defamatory in and of itself but that can be made defamatory if additional facts are known.

Family members or relatives of libel plaintiffs can rarely claim damages for libels unless they can individually establish that they suffered from damage to their reputations because of the publication of defamatory statements about them. Identification is not necessarily the specific reference to a plaintiff by name. If a plaintiff is identifiable to those who were exposed to the publication, the identification requirement is met. Individuals who are members of groups have increasing difficulty proving they were identified as the size of the group grows.

Publication has little to do with the ordinary meaning of printing or broadcasting a defamatory statement. Instead, it means that material is disseminated to someone other than the defamed person. Publication is rarely an issue in media libel actions because defamatory statements are usually disseminated to a wide audience when media publish them. Republication of a libelous statement can constitute a cause of action separate from the original publication. Whoever is substantially and directly involved in publishing a defamatory statement is liable and thus can be sued.

Libel plaintiffs must prove fault, but the degree of fault depends upon the status of the plaintiff. In most jurisdictions, private persons are required to prove negligence in order to win compensatory damages. Public figures and public officials must prove actual malice in order to win compensatory damages. In addition, every libel plaintiff must prove actual malice in order to win punitive or presumed damages.

Libel defendants have at their disposal a variety of tools to use to defend themselves. Typically, their first option is to seek summary judgment. If there is reason to believe that the plaintiff is unable to prove all the elements of the burden of proof — whether on constitutional or common law grounds — a defense attorney may be able to prevail with a summary judgment.

When a case goes to trial, libel defendants can use both constitutional and common law defenses. Among the defenses in the latter category, truth is regarded as the most definitive, given that it refutes any claim that a statement is false. Other common law defenses for media defendants include the privilege of reporting the proceedings of all government branches. The privilege is qualified on the reporting being fair and accurate.

At the heart of the constitutional defense is the notion that there is a First Amendment value embedded in the media's freedom to express themselves. The creation of actual malice

AGAINST INVASIONS BY MASS MEDIA 294-95 (Helmut Koziol & Alexander Warzilek eds., 2005).

was designed to provide an additional layer of protection for media defendants in reporting about public officials. The doctrine was later extended to public figures. Thus, establishing the nature of the plaintiff is key. Libel defendants seek to have plaintiffs categorized as public because they then have to prove the defendant acted with actual malice— knowledge of falsity or reckless disregard for the truth.

Media organizations and their employees have the right to express opinions, and that right has its roots in the First Amendment freedom of the press. However, defining what qualifies as opinion has been a challenge, and largely rests with the four-part *Ollman* test. The protection of opinion is also derived from the common law. Those who are in the public eye subject themselves to fair comment and criticism by the media.

To some extent, defending against a libel accusation involves refuting the elements of the plaintiff's case — that is, contesting the plaintiff's attempts to prove that the definition of libel was met. Given that one of those elements is that the statement at issue is false, if the defendant can prove that it is true, the defense is successful. Similarly, because publication is an element of the plaintiff's case, a defendant may attempt to prove that its publication qualifies as one of the exceptions to the republication rule — neutral reportage, the wire service defense, or online republication. With regard to the latter, the Communication Decency Act of 1996 offers protection to computer service providers.

Finally, media defendants want to portray themselves as reliable and trustworthy organizations that conduct themselves responsibly. While not a defense, *per se*, this representation can only help the defendant's image in the eyes of the court and jury. Moreover, journalistic integrity is simply the proper way to conduct business, and often tends to be the best way to avoid libel suits in the first place — and that is often the best defense.

Libel actions resulting from multi-state publications of defamatory statements create various choices of law questions for plaintiffs. The law of the state with "the most significant relationship" to the libel action is generally applied. Foreign libel judgments against transnational U.S. media cannot be enforced in the United States when they are found to violate First Amendment standards on freedom of speech and the press. New York and other states have passed "libel terrorism" laws intended to protect American journalists, writers and publishers from foreign defamation judgments.

FOR ADDITIONAL READING

Ardia, Davis S. "Freedom of Speech, Defamation, and Injunctions," 55 *William and Mary Law Review* 1 (2013).

Collins, Matthew. *The Law of Defamation and the Internet*, 3d ed. Oxford: Oxford University Press, 2010.

Collins, Matthew. *Collins on Defamation*. Oxford: Oxford University Press, 2014.

Elder, David A. *Defamation: A Lawyer's Guide*. Deerfield, Ill.: Clark Boardman Callaghan, 2014.

Glasser, Charles J., Jr., ed. *International Libel & Privacy Handbook: A Global Reference for Journalists, Publishers, Webmasters, and Lawyers*, 4th ed. New York: LexisNexis, 2016 (in press).

Jones, William K. *Insult to Injury: Libel, Slander, and Invasions of Privacy*. Boulder, Colo.: University Press of Colorado, 2003.

Levine, Lee & Stephen Wermiel. *The Progeny: Justice William J. Brennan's Fight to Preserve the Legacy of New York Times v. Sullivan*. Chicago: American Bar Association, 2014.

Lewis, Anthony. *Make No Law: The* Sullivan *Case and the First Amendment*. New York: Random House, 1991.

Lisby, Gregory C. "No Place in the Law: The Ignominy of Criminal Libel in American Jurisprudence," 9 *Communication Law and Policy* 433 (2004).

Melkonian, Harry. *Defamation, Libel Tourism, and the SPEECH Act of 2010: The First Amendment Colliding with the Common Law*. Amherst, NY: Cambria Press, 2011.

Mullins, Alastair & Cameron Doley, eds. *Carter-Ruck on Libel and Privacy*, 6th ed. London: LexisNexis, 2010.

Pritchard, David. "Rethinking Criminal Libel: An Empirical Study," 14 *Communication Law and Policy* 1 (2009).

Sack, Robert D. *Sack on Defamation: Libel, Slander, and Related Problems*, 4th ed. New York: Practising Law Institute, 2016.

Sanford, Bruce W. *Libel and Privacy*, 2d ed. Englewood Cliffs, N.J.: Aspen Law & Business, 2015.

Smolla, Rodney A. *Law of Defamation*, 3d ed. St. Paul, Minn.: W Thomson Reuters, 2016.

Wimmer, Kurt A. "International Law and the Enforcement of Foreign Judgments Based on Internet Content," http://www.ldrc.com/Cyberspace/cyber12.html#_ftn1.

Youm, Kyu Ho. "The Interface Between American and Foreign Libel Law: U.S. Courts Refuse to Enforce Libel Judgments," 49 *International and Comparative Law Quarterly* 131 (2000).

Youm, Kyu Ho. "The 'Actual Malice' of *New York Times Co. v. Sullivan*: A Free Speech Touchstone in a Global Century," 19 *Communication Law and Policy* 185 (2014).

7

Regulating Student Expression

By Dan V. Kozlowski

➡ **Headnote Questions**

- How do the free expression rights of students differ from those of other citizens?
- How are the free expression rights of high school and college students different?
- Why is it important that high school and college publications be identified as public forums?
- How and why do student press freedoms differ from those of the professional media?
- Under what circumstances can school or college officials restrict the free expression rights of students?

Public schools have changed in the years since the U.S. Supreme Court said that students do not "shed their constitutional rights to freedom of speech or expression at the schoolhouse gate."[1] Today we know that not all schoolhouse gates are the same. Some have narrow passages. Over-protective gatekeepers guard others.

Yet the Supreme Court's premise remains: Students are citizens even when they're on school property. The Court has said that no mental detector should prevent students from bringing their beliefs to school or to college and expressing them. Educational institutions, the Court implied, can be laboratories for young citizens trying to grasp the First Amendment's meaning and applications.[2]

But just as all citizens discover that freedom of expression has strings attached, students quickly learn that they do not have the absolute freedom to say anything they want, anywhere they want. Courts have ruled that the First Amendment lets government officials regulate in a reasonable way where, when and how citizens speak, as long as those officials have valid reasons and are not suppressing ideas only because the government does not like them.

Student journalists, especially those on university publications, have many of the freedoms accorded their professional counterparts. Both groups face similar legal obligations and are subject to the same standards regarding libel, privacy, copyright and even the more peripheral student media concerns of broadcast regulation and confidentiality of sources.

Because the education of young people is of paramount concern in society, educators have some latitude when regulating speech on school property. But differences among high school and college experiences and educational objectives often lead judges to rule differently in the two settings. Because the learning environments are different, as are the age and maturity of the students and the responsibilities of those in charge, the freedom available and officials' ability to restrict that freedom generally vary from high school to college.

Some free-speech concerns — especially prior restraint and access to information — pose special problems for the student press. Denial of access to crime statistics and disciplinary proceedings, among other information, has led to conflicts with college administrators. Censorship has been more of a problem for the high school press, primarily because courts give public officials latitude when protecting children from potentially harmful material, and administrators often interpret "harmful" broadly.

Following the 1999 shootings at Colorado's Columbine High School, through more recent violence at an elementary school in Newtown, Conn., and at college campuses (Virginia Tech and Northern Illinois University, for example), parents and the public seem more willing to give authorities latitude in controlling

---

[1] Tinker v. Des Moines Indep. Cmty. Sch. Dist., 393 U.S. 503, 506 (1969).
[2] *See* Jamin Raskin, *No Enclaves of Totalitarianism: The Triumph and Unrealized Promise of the* Tinker *Decision,* 58 AM. U.L. REV. 1193 (2009).

the school environment.[3] Some high school officials, increasingly vigilant when monitoring offensive speech, are quick to punish students for what they've said online while at home. How far administrators' hands can reach off campus remains an unresolved — though increasingly litigated — question.

To complicate matters, Supreme Court rulings of the past two decades demonstrate both support for free speech in the schools and reluctance to curb administrative authority. In 2007, the Court seemingly extended that power, upholding punishment of one student's expression at a community event outside the high school.[4] And although a federal appellate court, in 2001, strongly rebuked arguments that college publications share the same free-speech constraints as the high school press, the appellate court in a neighboring circuit, in 2005, suggested a 1988 Supreme Court case limiting speech rights in the high school could be applied to colleges and universities.[5]

This chapter reviews principles of free expression as they extend to students. Court cases affecting student media reveal legal arguments used to limit students' freedom of speech and how the physical environment, the age of young citizens, societal interests, communication technology and public-forum theory affect the expressive rights of students.

A FRAMEWORK FOR STUDENT EXPRESSION

Most Americans understand that citizens are not free to speak or publish anything they wish, that there are limits and penalties, that circumstances affect constitutional liberties. To understand that concept better, college students only have to think back to their high school days. Whether individually or as student journalists, they have experienced some of the societal tensions that influence free expression.

School as Society

At least in public colleges and high schools, a microcosm of American society exists that can help young citizens learn and appreciate what "free speech" and "free press" mean. We have organizations and social classes, rules established to benefit all citizens, various outlets for free expression and government officials who make and enforce regulations.

When the abstract principle of free expression becomes real in the educational laboratory, student journalists learn what professionals know — the press has no special free-speech privilege. By balancing legal rights and ethical responsibilities, journalists maintain credibility and earn public support.

The college campus more closely parallels society than does the high school, where students today often must express themselves responsibly or risk losing freedoms. Adults, including college students, generally have not faced that limitation. In fact, as will be demonstrated, courts historically have considered college campuses to be public forums where students' freedom to exchange ideas is central to the educational mission. Just as government officials have little power to stop or punish professional journalists who express unpopular or embarrassing ideas, college administrators historically have had little control over content of the student press.[6] But there still are efforts to control expression — by citing campus speech codes, by creating speech zones on campus, by denying the student press access to information, by not punishing those who steal or destroy student newspapers and by refusing to recognize student publications as public forums.

The Legal Foundation

Students and educators have asked the courts to address two central questions: How does one balance the competing interests of individual freedom and institutional responsibility, and how much freedom do young citizens have while in school?

In 1943, the Supreme Court told students that they bring the right of free expression with them to school. In *West Virginia State Board of Education v. Barnette*,[7] the Court applied the long-standing concept that government may neither require nor suppress expression. A school policy requiring students to pledge allegiance to the flag, the Court ruled, unconstitutionally forced them to express beliefs they did not hold. When sitting in

---

[3] Public support for the rights of high school students has traditionally been low. The First Amendment Center's 1999 State of the First Amendment report, for instance, indicated that 70 percent of adults surveyed believe students should not be allowed to wear t-shirts with messages or pictures "that others may find offensive." In 2004, 72 percent agreed with this statement; in 2007, 74 percent agreed. In 2001, the center's results showed that 71 percent of high school teachers and administrators believe student journalists should not be allowed to report on controversial issues without school officials' approval. That year, 58 percent of American adults surveyed also agreed with that sentiment. But in 2014, 68 percent of American adults surveyed said they agreed that high school journalists should *not* need prior approval to explore controversial subjects, an "encouraging" change in public opinion. Ken Paulson, *Young Americans Have Free-speech Rights, Too*, FIRST AMENDMENT CTR. ONLINE, June 24, 2014, http://www.firstamendmentcenter.org/young-americans-have-free-speech-rights-too.

[4] Morse v. Frederick, 351 U.S. 393 (2007). *See also* discussion accompanying *infra* notes 33-34.

[5] *See* discussion accompanying *infra* notes 60-76.

---

[6] Less freedom exists for broadcast journalists than for print journalists on the university campus. *See First Amendment on the Air*, STUDENT PRESS L. CTR. REP., Spring 2000, at 29. But editorial discretion survives. *See* Knights of the Ku Klux Klan v. Curator of the Univ. of Missouri, 203 F.3d 1085 (8th Cir. 2000).

[7] 319 U.S. 624 (1943). A circuit court recently echoed *Barnette*, invalidating a Florida law that required public school students to stand and recite the Pledge of Allegiance. Frazier v. Winn, 535 F.3d 1279 (11th Cir. 2008).

silent protest does not interfere with other students' rights, school officials may not punish such expression. "If there is any fixed star in our constitutional constellation," Justice Robert Jackson wrote for the Court, "it is that no official, high or petty, can prescribe what shall be orthodox in politics, nationalism, religion, or other matters of opinion or force citizens to confess by word or act their faith therein."[8]

Despite the ruling in *Barnette*, the prevailing judicial sentiment for the next quarter century would be that public school officials have a parent-like role that entitles them discretion in their control of students. First Amendment cases with a college setting did not reflect this attitude, however. Differences in the environment, maturity of the students and educational function led courts to view public college administrators as facilitators rather than parents.

Strengthening the Foundation

Students, including young journalists, received a boost when the high Court revisited the situation in public schools twenty-six years after *Barnette* and stated more emphatically that constitutional rights extend to students, even on public school property. *Tinker v. Des Moines Independent Community School District*[9] focused on the limits that public school officials have in the regulation of student expression. What the Court said about students, administrators and the educational environment had sweeping implications that touched all young citizens.

Mary Beth and John Tinker and their friend Christopher Eckhardt wore black armbands to school in 1965 to express their opposition to the Vietnam War. Their form of silent protest clashed with a hastily prepared school policy. Officials thought such conduct would disrupt the school. When the students refused to remove the armbands, they were suspended and sent home.

Legal action that challenged the suspensions raised larger questions about whether First Amendment principles that the Court applied outside of the school setting would pertain in school as well.

Officials obligated to maintain an orderly learning environment may control student behavior inside the school. The U.S. Supreme Court in *Tinker*, however, ruled that wearing an armband is not conduct but a symbolic form of speech that can be stopped or punished only when educators can show that such expression would "materially and substantially disrupt the work and discipline of the school."[10]

Tinker tells us that public officials are not to stop or punish speech solely because they find it offensive. In the words of Justice Abe Fortas, writing for the Court:

Students in school as well as out of school are "persons" under our Constitution.... In our system, students may not be regarded as closed-circuit recipients of only that which the State chooses to communicate. They may not be confined to the expression of those sentiments that are officially approved. In the absence of a specific showing of constitutionally valid reasons to regulate their speech, students are entitled to freedom of expression of their views.[11]

The Supreme Court placed the burden on school officials but acknowledged that they may have valid reasons that would justify regulation. The most common, and the one most often challenged in court, is the claim that expression can be regulated because it disrupts the educational process. A "material and substantial disruption" justifies suppression of speech, as does a reasonable forecast of such a disruption — provided that officials show a factual basis for their prediction.

Another argument used to restrict expression is that *Tinker* does not protect speech that invades the rights of others.[12] High school officials have used the argument to justify censorship of defamatory material or, as in *Hazelwood School District v. Kuhlmeier*,[13] because of fear that content invades someone's privacy. Because libel and privacy are defined no differently inside the school than outside, the student press and professional media are equally vulnerable but share the same legal defenses.

The Tinker Philosophy

The Supreme Court suggested in *Tinker* that educational institutions are appropriate laboratories for learning the marketplace of ideas philosophy. "Freedom of expression would not truly exist," the Court said, "if the right could be exercised only in an area that a benevolent government has provided as a safe haven for crackpots."[14]

The Court knew the risks of free speech, but was willing to take those risks with young people. As Justice Fortas wrote:

Any word spoken in class, in the lunchroom, or on the campus, that deviates from the views of another person may start an argument or cause a disturbance. But our Constitu-

---

[8] 319 U.S. at 642.
[9] 393 U.S. 503 (1969).
[10] *Id.* at 513.

[11] *Id.* at 510.
[12] At one point in *Tinker*, Justice Fortas wrote that "conduct by the student, in class or out of it, which for any reason...materially disrupts classwork or involves substantial disorder or invasion of the rights of others" is unprotected. *Id.* at 513. Few reported cases have explored the "rights-of-others" justification for regulation.
[13] 484 U.S. 260 (1988). *Hazelwood* is discussed in detail later in this chapter.
[14] 393 U.S. at 513.

tion says we must take this risk.... Our history says that it is this sort of hazardous freedom — this kind of openness — that is the basis of our national strength and of the independence and vigor of Americans.[15]

The Student Press Law Center, a Virginia-based nonprofit that provides legal advice for student journalists, considers *Tinker* "undoubtedly the most important student First Amendment case in the nation's history."[16] Little wonder. State and federal courts have cited *Tinker* in hundreds of school cases. Free-speech advocates value the Court's emphasis on individual liberties and its assertion that speech — even on school property — is protected unless officials can demonstrate a reason to restrict it. With *Tinker*, a free-speech philosophy applied to all citizens clearly embraced students too. And the case provided a solid foundation for a long line of higher-education cases that declare college students to be adults worthy of rights accorded citizens off campus.

Tinker was a student-rights case but not a student-press case. During the 1970s and 1980s, however, many lower courts adopted the *Tinker* philosophy and applied it to cases involving student publications. Courts saw public school students as citizens and officials in all public institutions as arms of the government.

Limitations in Private Schools

It's different in private institutions. The First Amendment does not tell citizens that they must speak or what they must say if they do; it tells government not to interfere with citizens' expressive rights. The First Amendment applies, therefore, when there is government involvement or what is called "state action." When taxpayers are not heavily funding an educational institution or dictating its policies — and when those making decisions for it are not elected by, paid by or working for taxpayers — there is no state action. The assumption is that private school officials are not obligated to abide by First Amendment constraints on government.

Students in private institutions, then, do not have First Amendment protection within those institutions.[17] But that does not mean that students cannot be given the right to express themselves. Where a private school's promotional material or written philosophy, policies and practices promise certain freedoms, students may argue that reneging on those promises

constitutes breach of contract.[18]

A state's constitution and legislature may be additional vehicles for private school students to obtain free-speech rights. In 1995, a California court upheld what then was the only state law in the country that extended First Amendment protection to students at private, post-secondary schools. In *Corry v. Stanford University*,[19] it found Stanford's speech code unconstitutional and rejected its argument that as a private school it was not bound by the First Amendment. The state's 1992 Leonard Law extended First Amendment protection to more California citizens (those on private college campuses), the court said. The law does not require a university to express ideas or provide a platform for speech, the court added, nor would it lead the public to associate a college with ideas expressed on its campus.[20]

Despite the ruling, the reality is that, other than in California, First Amendment protection extends to private school students only when those who operate schools and colleges allow it or a state constitution provides it.[21] If private school practices and stated policies permit expression, students can benefit from them.[22] If restrictions abound, students may stay at the school and abide by its rules or transfer to a public institution or a more permissive private school.

THE COLLEGE ENVIRONMENT

The California court's unwillingness to distinguish between First Amendment protection on and off campus did not surprise those familiar with free-speech cases involving college students. With some exceptions, courts have equated the university campus with a public forum open to as far-reaching a collection of ideas as one might expect in a public park, and judges have given post-secondary students the adult-citizen status they would have if they were not in college.

Trying to meet their obligation to control disruptive student conduct, yet at the same time allow students the right to express themselves on campus, officials at many universities have established what they call "free speech zones." In these designated places, individuals may distribute literature, give

---

[15] *Id.* at 508.

[16] LAW OF THE STUDENT PRESS 25 (3rd ed. 2008).

[17] *See Legal Guide for the Private School Press*, STUDENT PRESS L. CTR. REP., Winter 2002-03, at 33, *available at* http://www.splc.org/legalresearch.

[18] LAW OF THE STUDENT PRESS, *supra* note 16, at 86-89. *See, e.g., Judge Rules Valdosta State Student Handbook a Binding Contract; University Appeals*, STUDENT PRESS L. CTR. NEWSFLASH, Aug. 2, 2012, http://www.splc.org/news/newsflash_archives.asp.

[19] No. 740309 (Cal. Super. Ct., Santa Clara Cty., Feb. 27, 1995).

[20] The Leonard Law — California Education Code Section 48950 (1992) — was the basis of a lawsuit filed by Jason Antebi, who claimed his firing as a host on KOXY, Occidental College's student radio station, violated his constitutional rights as a student at the California private college. California courts dismissed his case under the Leonard Law — narrowing the scope of Leonard Law protection — but he received a cash settlement from the college to resolve a related defamation suit in 2007. *See Ineffective Protections*, STUDENT PRESS L. CTR. REP., Winter 2006-07, at 24.

[21] *See, e.g.,* Mercer Univ. v. Barrett, 610 S.E.2d 138 (Ga. Ct. App. 2005) for a rationale precluding application of Georgia's Open Records Law to a private college.

[22] *See* Kelly Sarabyn, *Free Speech at Private Universities*, 39 J.L. & EDUC. 145 (2010).

speeches or stage demonstrations without college interference. Schools have come under fire, however, when they either impose restrictions on speech elsewhere on campus or deny speech zone use to non-students. Courts have also told university officials they cannot narrowly define campus locations that operate as public forums, but they have more leeway to deny non-students access to a limited public forum.[23]

Distinguishing Student Expression

The concerns that courts normally consider when addressing student expression make it easier to distinguish high school and college cases than to differentiate between cases involving college students on campus and citizens in non-campus settings.

Three factors have been central to a court's reasoning in cases concerning regulation of student expression.

1. The Age of the Speaker and Audience.

When calls to protect children accompany efforts to regulate cyberspace and computer access to sexual material, the courts are asked to reconcile a legal dilemma that has distinguished high school and college students.[24] Courts for years have ruled that children are more vulnerable and deserve more protection than adults. This has led to different legal standards for sexual material and indecent, over-the-air broadcasts. Judges have said that high school students more comfortably qualify for the special protection of children than do college students, who are legally adults.

Both a three-judge federal court in Pennsylvania, when it enjoined the enactment of the Communications Decency Act in 1996, and the Supreme Court, when it held the act unconstitutional a year later, were careful not to refute the notion that children deserve to be shielded from indecency. Both courts held that regulation must not be so sweeping that it prohibits adults from obtaining or disseminating material that is legally protected for adults.[25] This is particularly true, the Court has said, when alternative means are available to shield children from objectionable material.[26] In 1999, a federal district court blocked enforcement of the Child Online Protection Act, meant to address constitutional defects in the CDA. The Third U.S. Circuit Court of Appeals affirmed the ruling.[27] In 2004, the Su-

preme Court agreed in a 5-4 ruling that COPA likely is overbroad because it denies adults access to material protected for adults. But the Court asked the lower court to see if the latest technology could allow enforcement of the law in a way that both protects children and allows adults access.[28] The Third Circuit ruled again in 2008 that despite existing technology, COPA still is not the least restrictive way to protect children from harmful Internet content.[29]

2. Where the Speech Occurs.

The public high school is a different setting than either a college campus or a public street. High school students are closer to a captive audience, with less freedom to come and go. Because the university is more open and enrollment is voluntary, judges have generally been reluctant to give college officials more authority over students than city officials have over a public demonstration or parade. Recent decisions, however, suggest that reluctance fades in the context of curricular speech in the college setting. In 2012, the Sixth U.S. Circuit Court of Appeals ruled that the *Hazelwood School District v. Kuhlmeier* decision, which resulted from censorship of a high school newspaper, applied to a case involving a graduate student who sued after she was expelled from her counseling program when she refused to counsel a gay client as part of a practicum course. The Sixth Circuit concluded that "*Hazelwood* respects the latitude educational institutions — at any level — must have to further legitimate curricular objectives."[30]

Judges have generally given broad latitude to public high school officials, and even more to elementary and middle school officials,[31] who argue that discipline and control of behavior are necessary to provide an effective learning environment. Complicating matters is the growing willingness of judges and school officials to regulate and punish online expression students generate off campus but about school-related issues and individuals. And public sentiment supports such restrictions. The First Amendment Center found that 50 percent of Americans sur-

---

[23] *See Zoning Free Speech*, STUDENT PRESS L. CTR. REP., Winter 2004-05, at 32. *See also* Thomas J. Davis, *Assessing Constitutional Challenges to University Free Speech Zones Under Public Forum Doctrine*, 79 IND. L.J. 267 (2004).

[24] *See* Leora Harpaz, *Internet Speech and the First Amendment Rights of Public School Students*, 2000 BYU EDUC. & L.J. 123. *See also* D.F. v. Bd. of Educ. of Syosset Cent. Sch., 386 F. Supp. 2d 119 (E.D.NY 2005), *aff'd*, 180 Fed. Appx. 232 (2nd Cir. 2006).

[25] Reno v. ACLU, 521 U.S. 844 (1997), *aff'g* 929 F. Supp. 824 (E.D. Pa. 1996).

[26] *See* Sable Commc'ns v. FCC, 492 U.S. 115 (1989).

[27] ACLU v. Reno, 31 F. Supp. 2d 473 (E.D. Pa. 1999), *aff'd* 217 F.3d 162 (3rd Cir. 2000).

[28] Ashcroft v. ACLU, 542 U.S. 656 (2004).

[29] ACLU v. Mukasey, 534 F.3d 181 (3rd Cir. 2008).

[30] Ward v. Polite, 667 F.3d 727, 733 (6th Cir. 2012). In the 2015 case *Oyama v. University of Hawaii*, the Ninth U.S. Circuit Court of Appeals ruled that a university justifiably removed a student from his teaching program based on comments he made both to instructors and in class assignments. The court ruled that the decision to deny the student's teaching application did not infringe the First Amendment "because it related directly to defined and established professional standards, was narrowly tailored to serve the University's foundational mission of evaluating [the student's] suitability for teaching, and reflected reasonable professional judgment." Oyama v. Univ. of Haw., 813 F.3d 850, 868 (9th Cir. 2015).

[31] *See, e.g.*, Muller v. Jefferson Lighthouse Sch., 98 F.3d 1530, 1538 (7th Cir. 1996) ("The 'marketplace of ideas,' an important theme in the high school student expression cases, is a less appropriate description of an elementary school, where children are just beginning to acquire the means of expression."). *But see* K.A. v. Pocono Mountain Sch. Dist., 710 F.3d 99, 111 (3d Cir. 2013) ("[T]he *Tinker* analysis has sufficient flexibility to accommodate the educational, developmental, and disciplinary interests at play in the elementary school environment.").

veyed in 2008 agreed that school officials should be able to discipline students who, while off-campus, post on social networking sites entries that "may be disruptive to school classes."[32]

Where expression occurs has become even more of an issue since the Supreme Court's 2007 ruling in *Morse v. Frederick*.[33] In that 5-4 decision (discussed later in this chapter), the Court upheld punishment of a student who displayed a banner that read "BONG HiTS 4 JESUS." Although the student stood across the street from his high school, watching an Olympic Torch Relay, the Court said Joseph Frederick was participating in a "school-sanctioned and school-supervised event" that gave the principal authority to restrict what could be perceived as a message advocating the use of illegal drugs.[34]

More officials are punishing out-of-school expression — especially when off-campus expression implies violent action.[35] Punishment has not been limited to online speech threatening violence, however. After an Indiana high school student called a school administrator an "ass" on a Facebook group site in 2007, he was punished. The superintendent in West Lafayette said that whether students are punished is determined on a case-by-case basis. Political and idea speech are protected, he said, but a student conduct code is applied when students write online about administrators, teachers or other students.[36]

Two recent Pennsylvania cases show how courts are struggling to identify school boundaries in cyberspace. In *Layshock v. Hermitage School District,* a district court judge in 2007 said a student's vulgar language and name-calling on a MySpace page targeting his high school principal was protected speech because there was insufficient disruption in school.[37] But in 2008, in *J.S. v. Blue Mountain School District,* a federal judge upheld punishment of a student who created a fictitious MySpace profile of her middle school principal, with words and images the court found lewd and offensive.[38] Both rulings were appealed, and, in 2010, two three-judge panels of the Third U.S. Circuit Court of Appeals issued seemingly conflicting rulings on the same day, one favoring student Justin Layshock, the other supporting Blue Mountain school officials.[39] The Third Circuit va-

cated both opinions and ordered en banc review, and, in 2011, the full Third Circuit ruled in favor of the students.[40] Both cases are discussed in more detail later in this chapter.

Though seemingly not to the same degree and with the same frequency as middle and high school officials, college administrators also have regulated, and are regulating, their students' online speech.[41]

3. The Educators' Responsibilities. The Supreme Court has given school officials some discretion when regulating speech they believe is inconsistent with educational goals and moral values.[42] Afterwards, the gap widened between freedom of speech in high school and college because courts consistently held that universities should be forums for exchanging ideas and that college officials should encourage, not interfere with, that process. This view was strongly stated in the Sixth Circuit's *Kincaid v. Gibson* ruling,[43] analyzed in more detail later in this chapter.

The Legal Arguments

In general, five topics must be addressed in determining the status of speech in the college environment.

1. Lack of Disruption. *Tinker* has been cited to support college free-speech positions because it solidified the "substantial disruption" standard that was applied even earlier in a college press case. In the 1967 case *Dickey v. Alabama State Board of Education*, editor Gary Dickey was suspended from Troy State College for his published protest of student newspaper censorship. The Alabama federal district court judge who lifted the suspension said that only reasonable regulations needed to maintain order and to operate "in a manner conducive to learning" are appropriate.[44]

After the Supreme Court reinforced the disruption standard in *Tinker*, the Court applied it to the college setting with two decisions in the early 1970s. In *Healy v. James*[45] and *Papish v. Board of Curators of the University of Missouri*,[46] the Court found there is no less need for order in universities than else-

---

[32] *See State of the First Amendment 2008*, Sept. 11, 2008, http://www.firstamend mentcenter.org.

[33] 551 U.S. 393 (2007).

[34] *Id.* at 396.

[35] *See, e.g.,* Wisniewski v. Weedsport Cent. Sch. Dist., 494 F.3d 34 (2nd Cir. 2007).

[36] *See Ind. High School Student Punished for Calling Administrator an "Ass" on Facebook*, STUDENT PRESS L. CTR. NEWSFLASH, Oct. 13, 2007, http://www.splc.org/news /newsflash_archives.asp. *See also Ill. High School Suspends 10 for Tweets,* STUDENT PRESS L. CTR. NEWSFLASH, Oct. 27, 2012, http://www.splc.org/news/newsflash_ar chives.asp.

[37] 496 F.Supp. 2d 587 (W.D. Pa. 2007).

[38] 2008 U.S. Dist. LEXIS 72685 (M.D. Pa. Sept. 11, 2008).

[39] Layshock v. Hermitage Sch. Dist. 593 F.3d 249 (3rd Cir. 2010); J.S. v. Blue Mountain Sch. Dist. 593 F.3d 286 (3rd Cir. 2010) (rehearing *en banc* granted, opinions vacated, Apr. 9, 2010).

[40] J.S. v. Blue Mountain Sch. Dist., 650 F.3d 915 (3d Cir. 2011); Layshock v. Hermitage Sch. Dist., 650 F.3d 205 (3d Cir. 2011).

[41] *See, e.g., Central Okla. Journalism Student Forced to Delete and Apologize for Blog Post,* STUDENT PRESS L. CTR. NEWSFLASH, Mar. 20, 2013, http://www.splc.org/news /newsflash_archives.asp; *N.J. Community College Suspends Student For Tweets About Former Red Sox Pitcher's Daughter,* STUDENT PRESS L. CTR. NEWSFLASH, Mar. 3, 2015, http://www.splc.org/article/2015/03/n-j-community-college-suspends-student-for-tweet s-about-former-red-sox-pitchers-daughter.

[42] *See* Bethel Sch. Dist. v. Fraser, 478 U.S. 675 (1986).

[43] 236 F.3d 342 (6th Cir. 2001).

[44] 273 F. Supp. 613, 617 (M.D. Ala. 1967).

[45] 408 U.S. 169 (1972).

[46] 410 U.S. 667 (1973).

where in society, but that there also is no less First Amendment protection. That means, the Court held, that school officials may not silence a student organization just because it has a philosophy of disruption and violence (as in *Healy*) or suspend a graduate student just because the alternative newspaper she was distributing contained offensive language (as in *Papish*). In both instances, the Court ruled, such speech is consistent with the notion that universities are forums for exchanging ideas, and expression may be restricted only if officials can show that the learning process is substantially disrupted.

2. Public Forums. Sidewalks and parks traditionally have been public forums for sharing ideas, and the government has no authority to be selective about who speaks there. Not all public property is automatically a forum, but it may become one, as when a city-owned building becomes a civic center open to community groups. The purpose of utility poles is not to carry signs, for instance, but if a city lets citizens post notices, the poles have been designated a public forum, and officials may not arbitrarily allow some messages and prohibit others.[47]

The public-forum doctrine has been an important concept that has helped distinguish free-speech and free-press rights in high school and college. The Supreme Court underscored this point with three rulings. One involved a university,[48] and two concerned high schools.[49] A public high school is not traditionally a place for all citizens, or even all young people, to exchange ideas. Nor is all of a high school a public forum. And a student newspaper may not be a public forum because its function may not be to allow all students to express themselves. To qualify as a public forum, it must clearly be identified, by practice or policy, as such.

There was no public forum in the Santa Fe School District of suburban Houston, the Supreme Court reported. The Court rejected what school officials called private, voluntary, student-led prayer before football games. The district had not established a protected public forum for expression, the Court held, but instead had set guidelines that not only defined "appropriate" messages but also precluded minority viewpoints. Without "viewpoint neutrality," Justice John Paul Stevens wrote for the 6-3 majority, officials not only sanctioned and sponsored prayer, but they controlled its content.[50]

So as not to be accused of "sponsoring" religious worship, administrators in a New York school denied a private community group access to the Milford Central School facilities. The Good News Club argued that this action was discriminatory because the school had created a limited public forum when it allowed the 4-H Club, Boy Scouts and similar groups to use the school after hours. In a 6-3 ruling in 2001, the Supreme Court agreed that school officials were not deciding in a viewpoint-neutral way on the use of the established forum.[51]

The university press has not faced such rigid restrictions. Courts often have found the state university campus, by the nature of its mission and environment, to be a limited public forum. Remaining viewpoint-neutral is not only constitutionally required of administrators at public colleges and universities, but it is central to the role of higher education. That message from the Supreme Court in *Board of Regents v. Southworth* upheld the University of Wisconsin's system of using student fees to support organizations representing a range of ideologies.[52]

Scott Southworth was one of five conservative, Christian students who objected to the university's activities fee that supported almost twenty organizations with political or ideological perspectives the students opposed. The federal district court and the Seventh U.S. Circuit Court of Appeals agreed with the students, who argued that the required fee forced them to express ideas they did not hold.[53] But the Supreme Court viewed the regulation as beneficial to all students rather than a burden to some and unanimously overturned the circuit court ruling.

Justice Anthony Kennedy wrote that a fee-distribution system that is viewpoint neutral is constitutional. Wisconsin's program funded a range of controversial student organizations across the political spectrum, the Court ruled. Individual students may disagree with some of the funded organizations' ideas, it said, and a university could find a way to refund fee money to objecting students if it wished. But the system in place, operating as a public forum, was consistent with the mission of a university as a marketplace of ideas.[54]

The courts have long recognized that a university is by nature closely aligned with the notion of a public forum. A federal district court in Utah said as much when it allowed a student

---

[47] The Supreme Court has identified three kinds of forums: traditional, limited and nonpublic. As the Court said in *Hazelwood School District v. Kuhlmeier*, "The public schools do not possess all of the attributes of streets, parks, and other traditional public forums that 'time out of mind, have been used for purposes of assembly, communicating thoughts between citizens, and discussing public questions.'" 484 U.S. 260, 267 (1988) (quoting Hague v. CIO, 307 U.S. 496, 515 (1939)). A limited — sometimes called designated — public forum is property that the government intentionally opens up for speech. In contrast, a nonpublic forum is property that is not by tradition or designation a forum for expression.

[48] Bd. of Regents of Univ. of Wis. Sys. v. Southworth, 529 U.S. 217 (2000).

[49] Good News Club v. Milford Cent. Sch., 533 U.S. 98 (2001); Santa Fe Ind. Sch. Dist. v. Doe, 530 U.S. 290 (2000).

[50] *Santa Fe*, 530 U.S. at 308-09. *See also* Adler v. Duval County Sch. Bd., 250 F.3d 1330 (11th Cir. 2001). A school policy allowing the senior class to choose a classmate to deliver a graduation message was ruled constitutional because students made all decisions, even though each message for four years had been religious in nature.

[51] *Good News Club*, 533 U.S. 98 (2001).

[52] 529 U.S. at 234.

[53] Southworth v. Grebe, 151 F.3d 717 (7th Cir. 1998).

[54] 529 U.S. at 232-33. *See also* Christian Legal Society v. Martinez, 561 U.S. 661, 694 (2010) (upholding a law school's policy for recognizing registered student groups as viewpoint neutral because it required "all student groups to accept all comers").

group to construct shanties on the grounds of the University of Utah to protest apartheid and the university's South African investment policies.[55] A federal appellate court in 1992 ruled that policy and practice at Southwest Texas State University clearly established all outdoor grounds "owned or controlled by the university" as a public forum.[56] Similarly, courts have said that once a university has established a newspaper, it has created a limited forum for the exchange of ideas[57] — a forum where student editors retain control over content.[58] Even a public radio station on a state university campus is free to reject an organization's request to sponsor programming.[59]

A Kentucky federal district court judge, in 1997, took a different position in a case of great concern to the collegiate press. The judge ruled that administrators at Kentucky State University could refuse to distribute about 2,000 copies of the student-produced yearbook and could remove the faculty adviser who would not force editors to print positive stories about the university. Students argued that university censorship based on dissatisfaction with negative newspaper stories and with the yearbook's content, grammatical errors, missing photo captions and the color of its cover abridged the students' First Amendment rights. In ruling for the university, Judge Joseph M. Hood became the first federal judge to apply to a college media case the Supreme Court's decision in the high school case of *Hazelwood School District v. Kuhlmeier*.[60]

Rejecting student arguments that the newspaper and yearbook were public forums, Judge Hood cited *Hazelwood* and deferred to the "intent of the publisher," in this case a university administration that the judge said did not intend to open the pages but retain them as "an educational tool."[61]

If collegiate journalists were upset that a federal judge ignored three decades of court rulings that generally equated press freedom on campus with that of the professional news media, they were stunned in 1999 when a three-judge panel of the Sixth U.S. Circuit Court of Appeals upheld the lower court decision.[62] Adding to the injury was the appellate court's reliance on the high school case of *Hazelwood* when it rejected public-forum arguments and found broad administrative censorship powers reasonable.

Writing for a 2-1 majority, Judge Alan Norris said that explicit administrative intent is necessary if a student publication is to function as a public forum. He concluded that school officials intended to manage their publications and thus could reasonably confiscate the yearbook or refuse to distribute any university publication "that might tarnish, rather than enhance" the school's image.[63]

Sixth Circuit Judge R. Guy Cole Jr. disagreed. He argued that different students and settings at the high school and college levels make it inappropriate to apply the *Hazelwood* ruling, and he asserted that the yearbook was indeed a public forum.[64] After the Sixth Circuit vacated the 2-1 ruling and reheard the case, Judge Cole presented his arguments again, this time for a 10-3 majority that overturned the district court decision.[65]

Staff members of university newspaper and yearbook staffs breathed a sigh of relief. They had escaped a threat that limited their freedom to that of their high school counterparts. The language of the Sixth Circuit's final ruling in *Kincaid v. Gibson* strongly reaffirmed the public-forum role of the student press, especially on a university campus. University policy and publication board practices at Kentucky State clearly identified student publications as limited public forums, Judge Cole wrote. The court made no distinction between the roles or content of yearbooks and newspapers. The appellate court considered KSU's written policy and its hands off practice as indices of the yearbook as a public forum. "The university environment is the quintessential 'marketplace of ideas,' which merits full, or indeed heightened, First Amendment protection," Judge Cole wrote. The court also found the age of the students relevant. Because readers likely are young adults, it said, the university has "no justification for suppressing the yearbook on the grounds that it might be 'unsuitable for immature audiences.'"[66]

Finally, the court ruled, officials "must not attempt to suppress expression based on the speaker's viewpoint." Confiscating a publication is among "the purest forms of content alteration," Judge Cole wrote; it is an unconstitutional way "to coerce speech that pleases the government" and an action that the court said it would not tolerate.[67] Regulation, he said, must be reasonable, not "a rash, arbitrary act" of censorship.[68] The university did not appeal the ruling.

But campus celebrations of the *Kincaid* ruling were short-lived. Despite the appellate court's strongly worded free-speech rationale and the court's refusal to apply the *Hazelwood* standard to the college press, the issue resurfaced almost immedi-

[55] Univ. of Utah Students Against Apartheid v. Peterson, 649 F. Supp. 1200 (D. Utah 1986).

[56] Hays County Guardian v. Supple, 969 F.2d 111, 117 (5th Cir. 1992).

[57] *See* Bazaar v. Fortune, 489 F.2d 225 (5th Cir. 1973).

[58] *See* Leeds v. Meltz, 85 F.3d 51 (2nd Cir. 1996); Sinn v. Daily Nebraskan, 829 F.2d 662 (8th Cir. 1987); Miss. Gay Alliance v. Goudelock, 536 F.2d 1073 (5th Cir. 1976); Lee v. Bd. of Regents of State Colleges, 441 F.2d 1257 (7th Cir. 1971).

[59] Knights of the Ku Klux Klan v. Curators of the Univ. of Missouri, 203 F.3d 1085 (8th Cir. 2000).

[60] Kincaid v. Gibson, Civ. No. 95-98 (E.D. Ky, Nov. 14, 1997), *applying* 484 U.S. 260 (1988).

[61] *Id.*

[62] Kincaid v. Gibson, 191 F.3d 719 (6th Cir. 1999).

[63] *Id.* at 729.

[64] *Id.* at 730-31 (Cole, J., dissenting).

[65] Kincaid v. Gibson, 236 F.3d 342 (6th Cir. 2001).

[66] *Id.* at 352 (internal citations omitted).

[67] *Id.* at 355.

[68] *Id.* at 356.

ately, this time before the Court of Appeals for the Seventh Circuit, consisting of Illinois, Indiana and Wisconsin. The Illinois Attorney General's Office, on behalf of Governors State University, argued that the restrictive *Hazelwood* decision justified administrative review and approval of the college student newspaper's contents prior to publication.[69]

The case followed telephone calls the university's dean of student affairs and services made to the printer of the student newspaper, the *Innovator*. Dean Patricia Carter said no issues should be printed until a university official reviewed the content. Editors filed suit, claiming that such action was unconstitutional prior restraint. University officials argued that university funding and the *Hazelwood* criteria should give administrators such discretionary authority.

In 2003, a three-judge panel unanimously rejected the university's arguments. In *Hosty v. Carter*, the court cited twenty years of legal precedent in holding that administrators may censor only when student media content is "legally unprotected or if they can demonstrate that some significant and imminent physical disruption of the campus will result from the publication's content." The court added that the *Hazelwood* rationale is "not a good fit" for university students. Obvious differences in the missions of high schools and colleges — as well as differing needs, ages and maturity levels of their students — also reveal why *Hazelwood* reasoning is inappropriate, the court noted.[70]

What the Student Press Law Center called a "major victory," two years after an equally strong decision in *Kincaid v. Gibson*, delighted student press supporters — temporarily. Because the ruling was clear and unanimous, few were prepared for the circuit court's decision to vacate the ruling and re-hear the case en banc. No one expected it would be two years before the full court would rule in the case.

High school journalists have been told that the best legal protection from censorship is designation of the student publication as a public forum.[71] The Supreme Court in *Hazelwood* gave officials more authority to regulate speech in school-sponsored venues than in public forums. Forum designation was important in the more controlled environment of a high school campus. At a university, however, where the exchange of ideas is encouraged, student publications presumably have been the public forums that the Sixth Circuit described in its *Kincaid* ruling. But the *Hosty* court disagreed with this reasoning.

Writing for the majority in a 7-4 ruling, Judge Frank Easterbrook said that one cannot assume that a student publication is a public forum.[72] He applied what he called the "framework" of *Hazelwood*, which gives administrators the authority to regulate expression if there is a reasonable pedagogical justification. However, such control exists only in a nonpublic forum, the court said, making it essential in every college free-speech case to first determine whether the ideas were expressed in a limited or designated public forum.

The court found it unclear whether the student newspaper at Governors State University was a public forum, either by practice or by policy. For that reason, Judge Easterbrook wrote, Dean Carter had qualified immunity from charges that she purposefully denied students their constitutional rights when she stopped the printing of the *Innovator*.

Mark Goodman, executive director of the Student Press Law Center at the time, said that most college student publications would remain protected because they had functioned as public forums for years. He was more concerned that college officials would incorrectly interpret the court's references to *Hazelwood* as justifications to restrict objectionable content without considering whether a public forum exists to permit such content.[73] Legal authorities agreed that all student publications — at the college or high school level — are better protected when clearly identified and officially recognized as public forums.[74] Though this is no guarantee of press freedom,[75] Illinois legislation in 2007 neutralized *Hosty* in that state by making public forums of all student media at public colleges there.[76]

3. Requiring Civil Discourse. With a few exceptions, then, courts have tended to protect college students and the collegiate press from administrative censorship.[77] Threats persist through newspaper theft, advocacy of politically correct speech and pressure that school officials mandate civility. But many courts continue to strike down sweeping, well-intentioned restrictions. For evidence, one need look no further than cases involving speech codes created to curb hate speech on campus or the free speech zones discussed earlier in this chapter.

When college officials were faced with incidents of bigotry and racism on campus, they tried to curb verbal harassment rather than do nothing and appear to condone such incidents.

---

[69] Hosty v. Governors State Univ., 174 F. Supp. 2d 782 (N.D. Ill. 2001), *rev'd* Hosty v. Carter, 325 F.3d 945 (7th Cir. 2003).

[70] *Hosty*, 325 F.3d at 948.

[71] A recent circuit court decision perhaps muddies this advice, however. *See infra* notes 213-17 and accompanying text.

[72] *Hosty*, 412 F.3d 731 (7th Cir. 2005) (en banc).

[73] *See U.S. Court of Appeals Upholds Censorship by Governors State University Officials*, STUDENT PRESS L. CTR. NEWSFLASH, June 20, 2005, http://www.splc.org/news/newsflash_archives.asp.

[74] *See Going Public*, STUDENT PRESS L. CTR. REP., Spring 2006, at 6; *SPJ Drafts Statement to Designate Student Media as Public Forums*, May 30, 2006, http://www.spj.org/news.

[75] *See* Derigan A. Silver, *Policy, Practice and Intent: Forum Analysis and the Uncertain Status of the Student Press at Public Colleges and Universities*, 12 COMM. L. & POL'Y 201 (2007).

[76] *See* College Campus Press Act, 110 ILL. COMP. STAT. 13 (2007).

[77] *See* LAW OF THE STUDENT PRESS, *supra* note 16, at 59.

Aware that courts had given broad protection to on-campus speech, officials attempted to equate verbal abuse with easier-to-control conduct and with unprotected fighting words. But the codes clearly focused on offensive expression, and when they were challenged, courts continued to hold that on-campus speech restrictions were no more permissible than off-campus restrictions.

A federal court, for example, found that a University of Michigan policy was so vague and sweeping that it punished constitutionally protected speech, even though the university's motive was to provide a comfortable learning environment for all students.[78] Even a more focused policy in the University of Wisconsin system was declared overbroad in 1991 and sent back to the board of regents for revision.[79]

When the Supreme Court unanimously ruled a city's hate speech ordinance unconstitutional in 1992, it seemed unlikely that any campus speech code could withstand a court challenge.[80] For a time, many schools abandoned efforts to draft speech codes, chose to keep them but not enforce them or decided to punish hate speech only when it was tied to a criminal action.[81] But the mood changed, and tension again increased over speech restrictions. During the 2002-03 academic year, for instance, the Student Press Law Center reported clashes over speech policies at nine universities in Texas, West Virginia, California, Illinois, Pennsylvania, Maryland and Wisconsin.[82]

Courts, however, continue to find most policies unconstitutionally overbroad when they are challenged. In 2003, a federal judge stopped a Pennsylvania university from enforcing what the court said was an unconstitutionally vague and overbroad code used to make students remove from dormitory-room doors anti-Osama bin Laden posters the university said were offensive. Shippensburg University rewrote its code in 2004, and threats of lawsuits challenging policies at the University of Texas-El Paso and Southwest Missouri State University led those schools to adopt less restrictive codes. Two universities — Georgia Tech and Penn State — changed their policies in 2006 after students filed lawsuits claiming both discrimination and harassment from policies violating freedom of speech. In 2008, the California State University system amended its student conduct code to resolve a court dispute over its constitutionality, and the Third U.S. Circuit Court of Appeals struck down Temple University's sexual harassment policy because it was over-

broad and encompassed protected speech.[83]

4. Access to Crime Reports and Other Records. College journalists face similar struggles as professional journalists in exercising First Amendment freedoms. One of the major battles continues to rage over access to campus crime information.

Professional journalists know that once they have information, the First Amendment makes it hard for government to stop publication. But it is just as clear that the First Amendment does not require that government agencies release information. State and federal freedom of information acts can require release of such information. Journalists use these tools to joust with public officials over access to information some government employees would prefer to keep quiet.

Some university officials react with the same reservations when student journalists seek details about the types and extent of crimes on campus. Traci Bauer, while editor-in-chief of the Southwest Missouri State University newspaper, was the first to win a federal court decision granting access to incident reports from the campus police. A Missouri judge rejected the university's argument that police reports were education records that the Family Educational Rights and Privacy Act (known as FERPA) required be closed to protect student privacy. Judge Russell Clark, in *Bauer v. Kincaid*, cited the First Amendment and the Missouri Sunshine Law when he granted students access to the same type of information other police departments in Missouri must provide.[84]

The *Bauer* ruling did not stop colleges and universities from resisting the release of crime information, and the U.S. Department of Education fueled this tension by rejecting the judge's interpretation in that case. It wasn't until the Student Press Law Center took the DOE to court and federal legislation was passed that crime records were released from the bonds of FERPA secrecy.[85] Or so it seemed.

The Federal Campus Security Act of 1990 requires that colleges and universities receiving federal aid publish annual figures for the number of crimes reported on campus. Instances of incomplete or misleading reports of campus crime prompted the U.S. House of Representatives to pass unanimously a resolution in 1996 urging the DOE to monitor crime reports more closely.

Matters did not improve, and in 1997 the DOE reported to Congress that 60 percent of post-secondary institutions required

---

[78] Doe v. Univ. of Mich., 721 F. Supp. 852 (E.D. Mich. 1989).

[79] UWM Post, Inc. v. Univ. of Wis. Bd. of Regents, 774 F. Supp. 1163, 1165 (E.D. Wis. 1991).

[80] *See* R.A.V. v. City of St. Paul, 505 U.S. 377 (1992).

[81] *See* Scott Jaschik, *Campus "Hate Speech" Codes in Doubt After High Court Rejects a City Ordinance*, CHRON. OF HIGHER EDUC., July 1, 1992, at A19.

[82] *See, e.g., Campus Speech Rules Scrutinized by Courts, Students, Advocates*, STUDENT PRESS L. CTR. REP., Winter 2002-03, at 6; *Free-Speech Zones Frustrate Students*, STUDENT PRESS L. CTR. REP., Fall 2002, at 8.

[83] *See* DeJohn v. Temple Univ., 537 F.3d 301 (3d Cir. 2008); Bair v. Shippensburg Univ., 280 F. Supp. 2d 357 (M.D. Pa. 2003). *See also Colleges Adopt New Policies on Free Speech*, STUDENT PRESS L. CTR. REP., Spring 2004, at 28; *Cal. State System Revises Conduct Code to Settle Free-Speech Suit*, STUDENT PRESS L. CTR. NEWSFLASH, Mar. 4, 2008, http://www.splc.org/news/newsflash_archives.asp; *Penn State, Georgia Tech Change Speech Policies*, STUDENT PRESS L. CTR. NEWSFLASH, Oct. 5, 2006, http://www.splc.org/news/newsflash_archives.asp.

[84] 759 F. Supp. 575 (W.D. Mo. 1991).

[85] *See* Student Press Law Ctr. v. Alexander, 778 F. Supp. 1227 (D.C.D.C. 1991).

to compile crime statistics did not follow federal guidelines. The report fueled additional congressional activity, and 1998 amendments to the Higher Education Act removed some loopholes and strengthened reporting requirements of the Campus Security Act, renamed the Jeanne Clery Disclosure of Campus Security Policy and Campus Crimes Statistics Act.[86] The new legislation also complemented and reinforced state open-records laws.[87]

These amendments require better disclosure of crime on campus — more access to campus police logs and student disciplinary records and proceedings. The law also requires universities to keep, and open to the public, records of all criminal incidents reported to campus police or security personnel. That information must be made public within two business days of authorities being notified.

After the assault and thirty-three deaths on the Virginia Tech campus in 2007, amendments to the Clery Act required universities to immediately notify college students and personnel about emergencies on campus. University officials now are told to compile and report a broader range of safety violations and threats related to hate crimes.[88]

Legislation was, in part, a response to an access battle college journalists have, with modest success, fought in court. University of Georgia student journalists spent more than five years in court seeking entry to university disciplinary board hearings and records. In 1993, the state supreme court cited Georgia's open meeting and open-records laws and released the records from a hearing involving fraternity hazing[89] and from a different hearing about a gay-bashing incident.[90] The Ohio Supreme Court ruled that Miami University of Ohio officials were wrong to consider disciplinary records from the campus court to be "education records" and thus deny student journalists access to them.[91] When Michigan State University officials sidestepped the state's Freedom of Information Act and refused to turn over to the student newspaper campus police records involving an assault in a dormitory, the university fought for three years before a trial verdict told officials they were wrong.[92]

Department of Education regulations that went into effect in 2000 require not just campus police and security personnel to report offenses as part of annual campus crime statistics; now

any administrator responsible for "student and campus activities," including coaches, housing officials and deans of students, must report incidents they're aware of, regardless of whether the campus police are involved.[93]

Despite these rulings and federal regulations, student journalists often have to go to court to gain access.[94] The DOE continued to oppose disclosure, even after the Miami University of Ohio case. In 1995, it said state open-meetings laws may provide access to campus judicial proceedings and colleges may open disciplinary proceedings. But, taking a position that would put it on a collision course with the state courts, the DOE also said that all disciplinary records, even those related to criminal misconduct, remain "educational records" subject to FERPA.[95]

In 1998, the DOE sought a court order to prevent Ohio State University and Miami University of Ohio from releasing unedited campus disciplinary records. In a surprise ruling inconsistent with previous court decisions, including those from the highest state courts in Ohio and Georgia, U.S. District Judge George Smith declared student disciplinary records to be "educational" and not akin to law-enforcement files subject to Ohio's Public Records Act.[96] The U.S. Court of Appeals for the Sixth Circuit upheld the decision, preventing the *Chronicle of Higher Education* from obtaining the same information that Miami University of Ohio student journalists had acquired *via* Ohio's open-records law.[97]

The Supreme Court offered some hope for easier access to campus crime information. In *Gonzaga University v. Doe*[98] it ruled 7-2 that individuals cannot sue colleges that release private student records protected by FERPA. It said that schools not complying with federal law face sanctions from the DOE, adding that no FERPA provisions allow students or their parents to sue the institutions.

But the battle for access to campus crime information continues.[99] The DOE has again made it easier to hide information

---

[86] 20 U.S.C. § 1092(f) (1990).

[87] The Student Press Law Center reports that many schools try to use state laws to justify their refusal to disclose campus crime information. When Arkansas State University did, the state's attorney general, in 2000, said that student disciplinary records are not "scholastic records" and that state law requires disclosure. *See Same Game, Different Rules*, STUDENT PRESS L. CTR. REP., Spring 2004, at 16.

[88] The Higher Education Opportunity Act, H.R. 4137, August 2008.

[89] Red & Black Publ'g Co. v. Bd. of Regents, Univ. of Ga., 427 S.E.2d 257 (Ga. 1993).

[90] John Doe v. Red & Black Publ'g Co., 437 S.E.2d 474 (Ga. 1993) (without opinion).

[91] Miami Student v. Miami Univ. of Ohio, 680 N.E.2d 956 (Ohio 1997).

[92] State News v. Michigan State Univ., No. 133682 (Ingham County Cir. Ct., May 20, 2009).

[93] The DOE has a database of college and university crime statistics at its Office of Postsecondary Education Web site, http://www.ope.ed.gov/security. *But see A Light in the Darkness*, STUDENT PRESS L. CTR. REP., Winter 2003-04, at 15; *Crime Under Wraps*, STUDENT PRESS L. CENTER REP., Fall 2003, at 16.

[94] *See* Cmty. College of Philadelphia v. Brown, 674 A.2d 670 (Pa. 1996). The Pennsylvania Supreme Court denied the student newspaper access to campus crime records. Pennsylvania's open records act did not apply to the state's educational institutions, the court said, because they are not agencies performing an "essential governmental function." Pennsylvania's Right-To-Know Law changed this in 2008.

[95] *See* Mac McKerral, *Changes to Buckley Amendment Keep Campus Crime Reports Hidden*, QUILL, May 1995, at 17.

[96] United States v. Miami Univ., 91 F. Supp. 2d 1132 (S.D. Ohio 2000).

[97] United States v. Miami Univ., 294 F.2d 797 (6th Cir. 2002). *See also Federal Appeal Court Prohibits Release of Student Disciplinary Records Under FERPA*, STUDENT PRESS L. CTR. NEWSFLASH, June 27, 2002, http://www.splc.org/news/newsflash _archives.asp.

[98] 536 U.S. 273 (2002).

[99] *See Privacy Rules Could Stunt Access*, STUDENT PRESS L. CTR. REP., Fall 2008, at 24. *See also* Frank LoMonte, *Secret Schools: The FERPA Rabbit Hole*, LAS VEGAS REV.-

under the guise of FERPA. In 2009, the DOE said colleges are to consider as a confidential "education record" any request for a document that could identify a student. Even if identification is removed from the document, disclosure should be denied if school officials reasonably believe that the person requesting the information could determine the identity of the student referred to in the document.[100] Everyone from scholastic press proponents to retired U.S. Senator James L. Buckley, who helped draft FERPA, criticized this sweeping, subjective exemption to disclosure.[101] The Iowa Supreme Court relied on the exemption in a controversial 2012 decision in ruling that FERPA prevented the release of records related to an investigation of an alleged sexual assault by University of Iowa football players in a dorm room.[102]

Using the Iowa decision as but one example, critics have argued generally that FERPA has become a "broken statute" that allows schools to hide behind "fictitious privacy interests."[103] As one more example, the Society of Professional Journalists announced in 2013 that Oklahoma State University was the recipient of its Black Hole Award, given out annually to "highlight the most heinous violations of the public's right to know." OSU received the award after university officials claimed that FERPA prevented them from even notifying police or the public about a series of alleged sexual assaults on campus.[104]

A few recent state court decisions, however, have rejected what judges say are schools' too-broad interpretations of what constitutes an "education record" under FERPA. In 2011, for instance, an Arizona judge ruled that FERPA did not prevent Pima Community College from releasing to news media internal college emails about Jared Loughner, the man who killed six people and injured thirteen others — including a congresswoman — in a shooting spree in Tucson, Arizona; Loughner had been a student at the college.[105] That same month, a North Carolina judge ruled that FERPA did not protect from disclosure the phone records of university athletic department offi-

cials and parking tickets given to student athletes. The judge in the case emphasized that "FERPA does not provide a student with an invisible cloak so that the student can remain hidden from public view while enrolled" at school.[106] And, in 2012, a Montana judge clarified that FERPA protects records "directly related" to a particular student but not records that incidentally mention students — and FERPA thus did not prevent Montana State University from releasing records concerning the school's investigation of a professor's misconduct.[107]

Students at private universities find it much harder to gain access than students at public universities.[108] Administrators at private universities in several states have stymied students' efforts to get campus crime information. When taken to court, officials have successfully argued that because they are private, not public, state open-records laws do not apply to them.[109] While federal law may stipulate that all colleges and universities record and release crime-related incident reports, state laws that call for release of details such as those in arrest records apply to government agencies. Private colleges have escaped obligatory disclosure, although laws have opened police records at private universities in Texas, North Carolina, Virginia and Georgia, with similar legislation proposed in Massachusetts and Illinois.[110] In 2015, the Ohio Supreme Court ruled that the police department at Otterbein University, a private institution, was "a public office for purposes of the [state's] Public Records

J., Mar. 19, 2009, *available at* http://www.reviewjournal.com; *Campus Crimes Slip Through Cracks,* STUDENT PRESS L. CTR. REP., Winter 2008-2009, at 11.

[100] 73 Fed. Reg. 74,806 (Dec. 9, 2008), codified at 34 C.F.R. § 99.31.

[101] *See Education Department Narrows Educational Privacy Laws,* STUDENT PRESS L. CTR. NEWSFLASH, Dec. 12, 2008, http://www.splc.org/news/newsflash_archives.asp. *See also FERPA Foibles,* QUILL, September/October 2009, at 18-23.

[102] *See* Press-Citizen Co., Inc. v. Univ. of Iowa, 817 N.W.2d 480 (Iowa 2012).

[103] *SPLC Calls for FERPA Reform After "Outlandish" Court Ruling Shielding Iowa Rape Records,* STUDENT PRESS L. CTR. NEWSFLASH, July 13, 2012, http://www.splc.org/news/newsflash_archives.asp.

[104] *SPJ Announces Winner of 2013 Black Hole Award,* Mar. 22, 2013, http://spj.org/news.asp?REF=1158. Critics continue to blast colleges for misusing FERPA to shield information about sexual assaults on campus. *See, e.g., University of Oregon Students Criticize University for Using FERPA to "Frivolously" Avoid Answering Questions About Sexual Assault Allegations Involving Athletes,* STUDENT PRESS L. CTR. NEWS-FLASH, May 8, 2014, http://www.splc.org/wordpress/?p=6266.

[105] Phoenix Newspapers Inc. v. Pima Cmty. Coll., No. C20111954 (Ariz. Super. Ct. May 17, 2011).

[106] The News & Observer Publ'g Co. v. Baddour, No. 10 CVS 1941 (N.C. Super. Ct. May 12, 2011). One year later, the same judge decided that FERPA also did not protect records pertaining to NCAA rule violations regarding impermissible benefits student athletes at the University of North Carolina received. "Just as in the case of parking tickets, this kind of behavior has nothing to do with education," the judge said in a memo. *N.C. State Judge Issues Decision in UNC FERPA Case,* STUDENT PRESS L. CTR. NEWSFLASH, Aug. 9, 2012, http://www.splc.org/article/2012/08/n-c-state-judge-issues-decision-in-unc-ferpa-case. In 2014, officials at the University of Oklahoma and Oklahoma State University announced that they would release parking ticket records, after university officials had argued for more than a year that the records were exempt from disclosure under FERPA. The decision at the University of Oklahoma to reverse course and release the records came after the student newspaper there threatened to join an ongoing lawsuit against the university over the records. *See U. of Oklahoma President Orders Release of Parking Ticket Records After Student Paper Joins Editor's Suit,* STUDENT PRESS L. CTR. NEWSFLASH, Nov. 12, 2014, http://www.splc.org/article/2014/11/u-of-oklahoma-president-orders-release-of-parking-ticket-records.

[107] Bozeman Daily Chronicle v. Montana State Univ., No. DV-11-581A (Mont. Jud. Dist. Ct. Mar. 1, 2012).

[108] *See Same Game, Different Rules,* STUDENT PRESS L. CTR. REP., Spring 2004, at 16.

[109] *See, e.g.,* Ochsner v. Elon Univ., 725 S.E.2d 914 (N.C. Ct. App. 2012) (concluding that the campus police department at Elon University, a private university, is not subject to the North Carolina Public Records Act).

[110] *See, e.g.,* Mercer Univ. v. Barrett, 610 S.E.2d 138 (Ga. Ct. App. 2005); Harvard Crimson, Inc. v. President & Fellows of Harvard College, 840 N.E.2d 518 (Mass. 2006); *North Carolina Legislature Approves Bill to Open Private School Police Records,* STUDENT PRESS L. CTR. NEWSFLASH, June 4, 2013, http://www.splc.org/news/newsflash_archives.asp; *Texas Legislature Votes for Transparency in Private University Police Departments,* STUDENT PRESS L. CTR. NEWSFLASH, May 20, 2015, http://www.splc.org/article/2015/05/texas-legislature-votes-for-transparency-in-private-university-police-departments.

Act"[111] and, thus, must disclose public records upon request. The case began when a student journalist sued after university officials denied her request for police reports. In March 2016, the Indiana Court of Appeals ruled that Notre Dame's police department is subject to that state's public records laws; frustrated by the decision, Notre Dame announced plans to appeal it to the state supreme court.[112] Yale University's police records are also open, thanks to a state commission's interpretation of Connecticut's Freedom of Information Act. It ruled in 2008 that Yale's police department is a public agency because it performs a public function that extends beyond the university's boundaries.[113]

Colleges can face fines as well as reprimands for ignoring their obligations under the law. Mount St. Clare College in Iowa paid $15,000 as the first school fined by the DOE for violating the Clery Act.[114] New Jersey's William Patterson University was threatened with a $55,000 fine for violating the act in 2003; Salem International University in West Virginia paid a $200,000 fine in 2005 for failing to maintain records and report campus crime from 1997 to 1999.[115] In 2007, the DOE recommended the largest fine ever — the maximum of $27,500 for each of thirteen violations of the act by Eastern Michigan University. The violations related to an attempt to cover up the murder of a 22-year-old student in her dormitory room. In 2008, the university agreed to pay $350,000 in federal fines and a large cash settlement to the family to resolve a civil lawsuit.[116] And, in 2010, Dominican College in New York paid the state $20,000 and agreed to take steps toward improved campus security and reporting of crime statistics.[117] The maximum fine for any violation under the Clery Act increased to $35,000 in 2012.

In 2013, a circuit court judge in Kentucky fined National College — a for-profit college based in Lexington — $1,000 per day for refusing to obey a subpoena issued by the state's attorney general. The college had argued, among other things, that FERPA prevented it from producing documents the attorney general sought in his investigation of alleged wrongdoing associated with deceptive advertising claims made by the school. The judge said that argument was meritless.[118]

The fight for access to campus records extends beyond information about crime. As one example, Louisiana State University drew the ire of journalists, on and off campus, in the 2012-13 academic year when it refused to release the names of candidates for the school's presidency. The school conducted the presidential search through a private foundation and, thus, argued the names were exempt from public records laws. In 2013, a state judge disagreed with the school and ruled that LSU had to disclose those names the search committee considered as finalists for the position.[119] But a state appeals court reversed that ruling in 2014. The legal fight came to an end in 2015 when LSU agreed to reveal the names of the four finalists it considered.[120]

5. Special Press Problems. College journalists face a few free-speech problems that professionals are spared. One that the Supreme Court has addressed concerns student fees, an essential revenue source for many campus publications. Student governments usually have a hand in dispersal of this money and occasionally try to place content requirements on the newspaper as a condition of funding.[121] So collegiate journalists closely watched the case involving University of Wisconsin students who challenged mandatory student fees as unconstitutional.

The Seventh U.S. Circuit Court of Appeals had said that the university should not force students to subsidize speech with which they disagree, ruling that students may refuse to pay activity fees that support organizations with ideologies they find objectionable.[122] Because student fees help to subsidize student publications on most campuses, and student newspapers carry editorials and opinion pieces that often are political or ideological, some collegiate journalists feared that an adverse Supreme Court ruling could mean that the content of their publication would determine their level of financial support.[123]

The Supreme Court emphatically reassured apprehensive stu-

---

[111] State ex rel. Schiffbauer v. Banaszak, 33 N.E.3d 52, 55 (Ohio 2015).

[112] *See Private Campus Police Forces' Records Should be Public, Indiana Court of Appeals Rules - But Legislation Seeks to Supersede Ruling,* STUDENT PRESS L. CTR. NEWSFLASH, March 15, 2016, http://www.splc.org/article/2016/03/indiana-court-of-appeals-espn.

[113] *See Commission: Yale Police Must Comply With Requests for Records,* STUDENT PRESS L. CTR. NEWSFLASH, Feb. 15, 2008, http://www.splc.org/news/newsflash_archives.asp. *See also Open Season: Private Police Facing Greater Public Scrutiny,* STUDENT PRESS L. CTR. REP., Spring 2008, at 19.

[114] *See College Pays $15,000 to Education Dept.,* STUDENT PRESS L. CTR. REP., Winter 2000-01, at 35.

[115] *See College Settles With DOE Over Clery Act Violations,* STUDENT PRESS L. CTR. REP., Fall 2005, at 32; *Record Fine Issued for Clery Act Violations,* STUDENT PRESS L. CENTER REP., Fall 2004, at 20.

[116] *See Eastern Mich. U. Agrees to Largest-Ever Fine for Violations of Crime Reporting Law,* STUDENT PRESS L. CTR. NEWSFLASH, June 6, 2008, http://www.splc.org/news/newsflash_archives.asp.

[117] *N.Y. College Must Pay $20,000 in Settlement Over Discrepancies in Campus Crime Statistics,* STUDENT PRESS L. CTR. NEWSFLASH, June 30, 2009, http://www.splc.org/news/newsflash_archives.asp.

[118] *For-Profit Kentucky College Sanctioned $126,000 After "Meritless" Claim of FERPA Secrecy,* STUDENT PRESS L. CTR. NEWSFLASH, Dec. 5, 2013, http://www.splc.org/wordpress/?p=5926.

[119] *See Names of LSU Presidential Finalists Must be Made Public, Judge Rules,* STUDENT PRESS L. CTR. NEWSFLASH, Apr. 25, 2013, http://www.splc.org/news/newsflash_archives.asp.

[120] *See LSU Unveils 3 Other Finalists in Secretive Presidential Search,* THE ADVOCATE, April 24, 2015, http://theadvocate.com/news/education/12196626-123/lsu-unveils-3-other-finalists.

[121] *See Who Controls the Purse Strings at Your Newspaper?,* STUDENT PRESS L. CTR. REP., Winter 2001-02, at 26.

[122] Southworth v. Grebe, 151 F.3d 717, 732 (7th Cir. 1998).

[123] *See Paying for Free Speech,* STUDENT PRESS L. CTR. REP., Spring 1999, at 30.

dents when it ruled unanimously that divergent views should be encouraged on a university campus. As long as its system of distributing student fees dealt with all student organizations in a viewpoint-neutral way, the Court said, the university could require fees of all students and determine how to allocate those resources.[124]

Concerns remain, however. Among them:

• University officials or student governments withholding funds from newspapers because of disagreement with content.[125]

• Student newspaper advisers increasingly finding their jobs at risk because administrators want fewer controversial stories and more positive news published.[126] Ron Johnson, adviser of the Kansas State *Collegian*, went to court when he lost his job based on the newspaper's content. Despite three decades of court rulings that call such action unconstitutional, a federal district court judge ruled that Johnson's First Amendment

rights were not denied.[127] But Karen Bosley received a $90,000 settlement and successfully retained her journalism teaching assignment and position as newspaper adviser in 2007 through legal action she and her students took in a censorship dispute with administrators at Ocean County (N.J.) College.[128]

• Students stealing and destroying copies of newspapers as a means of expressing dissatisfaction with content or policies. The Student Press Law Center continues to find many schools where campus newspapers are stolen.[129] The SPLC reported more than 129 thefts from 2000 to 2005. Twenty-one colleges in eighteen states reported thefts in 2006-07. The SPLC learned of thefts at twenty colleges during 2007-08 and another twenty-two from 2008-2010.[130] Twenty-seven thefts were reported in 2012, the most reported thefts in any one year in a decade. About ten thefts were reported each year in 2013, 2014 and 2015.

School officials have often been reluctant to bring criminal charges. Colorado, California and Maryland have state laws criminalizing the theft of free newspapers; San Francisco and Berkeley have ordinances punishing such theft; and students in Oregon, Indiana and Florida were among those fined or sentenced to community service as newspaper editors in increasing numbers put a price tag on the theft of their publications.[131] In 2012, Central Connecticut State University's president announced that he had suspended the men's soccer coach for sixty days without pay and sanctioned the athletic department after the coach dumped about 150 copies of the school's student newspaper. The coach was apparently unhappy with a story that reported the soccer team faced academic sanctions and would be disqualified from the next year's postseason play.[132]

• Government restrictions on advertising alcoholic beverages in college newspapers, in response to reports of binge

[124] Bd. of Regents of Univ. of Wisconsin Sys. v. Southworth, 529 U.S. 217 (2000). *See also* Rosenberger v. Rector & Visitors of the Univ. of Virginia, 515 U.S. 819 (1995).

[125] *See, e.g.*, Stanley v. Magrath, 719 F.2d 279 (8th Cir. 1983). In February 2016, current and former editors-in-chief of the student newspaper at the University of Kansas sued administrators there for reducing the newspaper's funding on the basis of content. *See Editors of the Daily Kansan Filed First Amendment Suit Against University Administrators for Funding Reduction*, STUDENT PRESS L. CTR. NEWSFLASH, Feb. 5, 2016, http://www.splc.org/article/2016/02/daily-kansan-lawsuit. *See also U. of Memphis Paper Faces Funding Cut After Tension with Administrators, Police*, STUDENT PRESS L. CTR. NEWSFLASH, July 30, 2012, http://www.splc.org/news/newsflash_ar chives.asp (the funding cut was eventually reversed); *New York Paper Stops Publishing After Student Court Cuts Off Staff Pay*, STUDENT PRESS L. CTR. NEWSFLASH, Apr. 10, 2013, http://www.splc.org/news/newsflash_archives.asp; *University Will Step In After Student Government Slashes Missouri Student Newspaper's Funding*, STUDENT PRESS L. CTR. NEWSFLASH, April 23, 2014, http://www.splc.org/news/newsflash.asp? id=2713; *Student Government at N.Y. College Freezes — Then Reinstates — Student Newspaper Funding After April Fool's Day Issue*, STUDENT PRESS L. CTR. NEWSFLASH, Apr. 3, 2015, http://www.splc.org/article/2015/04/student-government-at-n-y-col lege-freezes-then-reinstates-student-newspaper-funding-after-april-fools-day-issue; *Wesleyan Student Government Revokes Student Newspaper's Funds*, STUDENT PRESS L. CTR. NEWSFLASH, Mar. 24, 2016, http://www.splc.org/article/2016/03/wesleyan-argus-fund ing-revoked.

[126] *See, e.g., Adviser, in Need of Brain Surgery, Suddenly Fired at UT-Tyler*, STUDENT PRESS L. CTR. NEWSFLASH, Apr. 22, 2011, http://www.splc.org/news/newsflash_ar chives.asp; *Court Revokes Order That Blocked Kansas State from Removing Newspaper Adviser*, STUDENT PRESS L. CTR. NEWSFLASH, July 15, 2004, http://www.splc.org/ news/newsflash_archives.asp; *East Carolina Fires Newspaper Adviser in Wake of "Streaker" Controversy*, STUDENT PRESS L. CTR. NEWSFLASH, Jan. 4, 2012, http:// www.splc.org/news/newsflash_archives.asp; *Editors: Bridgewater State Adviser Forced Out, Newspapers Stolen*, STUDENT PRESS L. CTR. NEWSFLASH, Apr. 27, 2012, http://www.splc.org/news/newsflash_archives .asp; *Federal Lawsuit Alleges Northern Michigan U. Student Newspaper Board Violated Adviser's Free-speech Rights in Termination*, STUDENT PRESS L. CTR. NEWSFLASH, Apr. 16, 2015, http://www.splc.org/arti cle/2015/04/federal-lawsuit-alleges-northern-michigan-u-student-newspaper-board-viol ated-advisers-free-speech-rights-in-termination; *Mo. University Removes Award-winning Newspaper Adviser*, STUDENT PRESS L. CTR. NEWSFLASH, Apr. 26, 2011, http://www.splc.org/news/newsflash_archives.asp. *But see Adviser Settles with Ga. University*, STUDENT PRESS L. CTR. REP., Spring 2002, at 12 (fired Georgia newspaper adviser won $192,000 settlement from Fort Valley State University); *Judge Orders Chicago State to Reinstate Fired Newspaper Adviser*, STUDENT PRESS L. CTR. NEWS-FLASH, Mar. 14, 2012, http://www.splc.org/news/newsflash_ archives.asp.

[127] *See* Lane v. Simon, No. 04-4079-JAR, 2005 WL 1366521, 2005 U.S. Dist. LEXIS 11330 (D.C. Kan., June 2, 2005) (slip opin.).

[128] *See* Bosley v. Larson, 06-02747 (D.N.J. filed June 9, 2006). *See also Students, Adviser Reach Agreements With College*, STUDENT PRESS L. CTR. REP., Spring 2007, at 7.

[129] *See, e.g., Fraternity Member Accused of Stealing 250 Papers, Asking Students to Help Him*, STUDENT PRESS L. CTR. NEWSFLASH, Nov. 13, 2015, http://www.splc.org/arti cle/2015/11/fraternity-member-accused-of-stealing-papers-asking-students-to-help-him; *Student Election Endorsement Prompts Tennessee College Newspaper Theft*, STUDENT PRESS L. CTR. NEWSFLASH, Apr. 4, 2014, http://www.splc.org/news/newsflash.asp?id= 2707; *University of Vermont Newspapers Disappear From Stands*, STUDENT PRESS L. CTR. NEWSFLASH, Apr. 30, 2012, http://www.splc.org/news/newsflash_archives.asp.

[130] *See Newspaper Thefts Level Off*, STUDENT PRESS LAW CTR. REP., Spring 2007, at 4. *See also Despite April Spike, Theft Rate Steady*, STUDENT PRESS L. CTR. REP., Spring 2008, at 11.

[131] CAL. PENAL CODE § 490.7 (2007); COLO. REV. STAT. § 18-4-419 (2004); MD. CODE ANN., CRIM LAW § 7-106 (2009). *See also Concealing Newspapers Can Qualify as Theft*, STUDENT PRESS L. CTR. REP., Fall 2009, *available at* http://www.splc.org.

[132] *See CCSU Suspends Soccer Coach, Fines Athletic Department $100K Over Newspaper Theft*, STUDENT PRESS L. CTR. NEWSFLASH, May 15, 2012, http://www.splc.org/ news/newsflash_archives.asp.

drinking and increased use on campus.[133] Pennsylvania law allowed the Liquor Control Board to revoke the liquor license of any establishment advertising in a college newspaper. A federal district court and the Third U.S. Circuit Court of Appeals both initially rejected a request by the University of Pittsburgh's student newspaper to stop enforcement of the law. The appellate court said the burden may be economic, but the law was not so onerous as to threaten the publication's constitutional rights.[134] But after the Supreme Court remanded the case, the Third Circuit ruled the state ban unconstitutional.[135] Then, in 2013, newspapers at Virginia Tech and the University of Virginia successfully challenged a law banning alcohol advertising in that state's student media.[136] The Fourth U.S. Circuit Court of Appeals ruled that the ban was not "appropriately tailored" to the state's aim of reducing abusive drinking on campus.[137]

Notwithstanding these special concerns and the *Hosty* ruling, most college publications remain closer to equal First Amendment footing with the professional press than the high school press does. The 2001 *Kincaid v. Gibson* ruling strengthened the legal foundation for student expression at colleges and universities. It did so with language that should echo far beyond campus boundaries in the Sixth Circuit (Kentucky, Tennessee, Ohio and Michigan). It is not clear whether the *Hosty v. Carter* ruling is affecting college publications in and beyond the Seventh Circuit (Wisconsin, Illinois and Indiana), but collegiate journalists nationwide have become more assertive of press freedom and in establishing the public-forum status of their publications.[138]

Legislators in three states have taken steps to protect the college press and neutralize the potential chill of the *Hosty* ruling. In 2006, California became the first state with a law prohibiting censorship of college publications. Oregon went even farther in 2007 with a law that says that both high school and college student journalists "are responsible for determining content of school-sponsored media."[139] In Illinois, where the *Hosty* case originated, the College Campus Press Act, a bill similar to the one approved in California, took effect in 2008. It prohibits prior review by school officials and says that any student media outlet at a public college is "a public forum for expression by the student journalists and editors."[140] And California, in 2009, offered college and high school teachers additional free-speech support. The Journalism Teacher Protection Act protects all high school and college teachers in that state from retaliation for their expression or that of their students.[141] North Dakota, in 2015, and Maryland, in 2016, similarly passed laws that both protect student journalists – high school and college – as well as their advisers.

REGULATING HIGH SCHOOL EXPRESSION

During the 1970s and much of the 1980s, lower courts, with increasing regularity, relied on *Tinker* to protect individual expression. They made it hard for school officials to censor the student press, telling them to write guidelines before regulating expression. And courts rejected vague and overbroad guidelines that allowed administrators to suppress material that, while embarrassing or disturbing to school officials, neither was substantially disruptive nor infringed on the rights of others.[142] In the mid-1980s, however, the Supreme Court began signaling a shift that would make it far harder for high school journalists to exercise the rights acknowledged in the *Tinker* decision.[143]

Tinker, with its inspirational free-speech rhetoric, remains good law for individual expression in the high school. Meanwhile, the many students in supervised speech-related activities, such as student publications, now have less First Amendment protection. Indeed, in high school free-speech cases of the past thirty years, the Court has shifted its attention away from the rights of students.[144]

A Modified First Amendment Philosophy

Instead of viewing constitutional freedom as an instrument to help those in school learn societal values, the Supreme Court has focused on school officials and what they may do to meet their responsibility to instill those values in the young. Administrators now have more latitude. When school-sponsored activities are involved, the burden shifts to students, who more easily can be silenced in public schools because of who they are, where they are and why they're there.

A 1986 Supreme Court case introduced this philosophy, fore-

---

[133] *See Drinking in Victory*, STUDENT PRESS L. CTR. REP., Winter 2004-05, at 16.

[134] Pitt News v. Fisher, 215 F.3d 354 (3d Cir. 2000). The newspaper was no more successful when arguing that the law is a content restriction. The case was dismissed on summary judgment. CIV. NO. 99-529 (W.D. Pa., Feb. 14, 2003).

[135] Pitt News v. Pappert, 379 F.3d 96 (3d Cir. 2004).

[136] *See Fourth Circuit Says Virginia Ban on College Papers' Alcohol Advertisements Unconstitutional*, STUDENT PRESS L. CTR. NEWSFLASH, Sept. 25, 2013, http://www.splc.org/news/newsflash.asp?id=2609.

[137] Educ. Media Co. at Virginia Tech v. Insley, 731 F.3d 291, 302 (4th Cir. 2013).

[138] *See Hosty Q&A*, STUDENT PRESS L. CTR. REP., Spring 2006, at 26; *Hosty v. Carter: An Analysis*, STUDENT PRESS L. CTR. REP., Fall 2005, at 27; *Life After Hosty*, STUDENT PRESS L. CTR. REP., Spring 2006, at 24.

[139] ORE. REV. STAT. §351.649 (2007).

[140] *See Illinois Takes on Hosty*, STUDENT PRESS L. CTR. REP., Spring 2007, at 31. *See also* Leonard Law, CALIF. EDUC. CODE §66301 (2006); Student Free Expression Law, ORE. REV. STAT. §351.649 (2007); College Campus Press Act, 110 ILL. COMP. STAT. 13 (2007).

[141] *See* S.B. 1370, signed into law Sept. 28, 2008.

[142] *See* Gambino v. Fairfax County Sch. Bd., 564 F.2d 157 (4th Cir. 1977); Nitzberg v. Parks, 525 F.2d 378 (4th Cir. 1975).

[143] *See Sacking News Coverage*, STUDENT PRESS L. CTR. REP., Spring 2003, at 20.

[144] *See* Mark W. Cordes, *Making Sense of High School Speech After Morse v. Frederick*, 17 WM. & MARY BILL OF RTS. J. 657 (2009).

shadowed a landmark high school newspaper case two years later and heavily influenced the 2007 *Morse v. Frederick* ruling. *Bethel School District v. Fraser*[145] began when a student gave a two-minute campaign speech during a school assembly. Matthew Fraser used no four-letter words, but he did use sexual innuendo. He described the candidate as "firm — he's firm in his pants, he's firm in his shirt, his character is firm" and as one who "takes his point and pounds it in.... He doesn't attack things in spurts; he drives hard, pushing and pushing until finally — he succeeds."[146] Several students in the audience of 600 hooted during the speech, but when Fraser finished, the candidate spoke briefly, and the end-of-school assembly concluded. The next day, several teachers complained, and Fraser was suspended for three days. He filed suit and won when federal district and appellate courts agreed that because it was not substantially disruptive, his speech was protected.

But the Supreme Court disagreed. The disruption standard stemmed from *Tinker,* which dealt with students who wore armbands as individuals expressing political beliefs. Because circumstances were different in *Fraser,* the Court said, a different standard applies. First, school officials have more control over the content of a school-sponsored assembly than over what a student says in the corridors. Second, school officials should see that public education instills moral values and encourages civility. To do this, the Court said, school officials must be free to disassociate the school from "vulgar and lewd speech" that undermines the educational mission and is "inconsistent with the 'fundamental values' of public school education." The Court said it was more important that school officials have discretionary power to identify and inculcate "fundamental values" than that they establish and follow narrow regulations.[147]

Although the Court said *Fraser* did not overturn *Tinker,* it was unclear until two years later whether the Court intended the *Tinker* standard to remain in place for serious idea speech (such as a war protest) or whether *Tinker* was to apply only to speech not under the control of school officials. In 1988, the Court's *Hazelwood School District v. Kuhlmeier*[148] ruling clarified this: *Tinker* would apply when students spoke on their own in school, but a different set of rules applied to students using a school-sponsored vehicle such as the student newspaper.[149]

The Hazelwood Standard

The *Spectrum* was very much a part of Hazelwood East High School. Its adviser taught most staff members, who were in their second journalism course at the suburban St. Louis, Missouri, school. The student newspaper had covered serious topics in earlier issues and put together a spring edition that included two pages featuring stories on teenage concerns, including pregnancy and divorce.

It was established practice to let Hazelwood East principal R.E. Reynolds review page proofs before publication. He objected to two stories. In one, three unnamed students described their pregnancies. In the other, students were quoted discussing the impact of their parents' divorces. Concerned that these stories might offend young readers and invade students' and parents' privacy, Reynolds pulled the two pages that included the offending articles. Three staff members, who learned of the censorship when the printed paper was delivered, filed suit.

A federal district court said that the principal's actions were reasonable and that he had authority because the newspaper was part of the school curriculum instead of a public forum.[150] The Eighth U.S. Circuit Court of Appeals, however, disagreed and said the *Spectrum* was part of the curriculum but also a public forum. The appellate court built its decision on a number of student-press cases grounded in *Tinker* and concluded that school officials had no reason to forecast substantial disruption and no liability for any libel or invasion of privacy suit.[151]

The same day the Eighth Circuit overturned the district court decision and supported the Hazelwood East students, the Supreme Court handed down its *Fraser* ruling. Six months later, the Court agreed to review *Hazelwood.*

The Court's holding carved a large hole through *Tinker's* First Amendment shield. In reversing the Eighth Circuit, the Supreme Court described a high school setting and citizenry in stark contrast to those of the university or society at large.[152] As it had done two years before, it stressed the obligation school officials have and the authority they need to educate youth. The content of the censored *Spectrum* stories was less important than whether the principal's actions were reasonable.

The Educator's Role. A public school official doesn't quite have

[145] 478 U.S. 675 (1986).

[146] *Id.* at 687 (Brennan, J., concurring).

[147] *Id.* at 685-86.

[148] 484 U.S. 260 (1988).

[149] *See Rulings Emphasize Tinker Standard,* STUDENT PRESS L. CTR. REP., Winter 2003-04, at 9. *See also,* Justin Peterson, *School Authority v. Students' First Amendment Rights: Is Subjectivity Strangling the Free Mind at Its Source?,* 2005 MICH. ST. L. REV. 931.

[150] Kuhlmeier v. Hazelwood Sch. Dist., 607 F. Supp. 1450 (D. Mo. 1985).

[151] Kuhlmeier v. Hazelwood Sch. Dist., 795 F.2d 1368 (8th Cir. 1986).

[152] In footnote 7 of the *Hazelwood* decision, the Court noted: "We need not now decide whether the same degree of deference is appropriate with respect to school-sponsored expressive activities at the college and university level." Although the Court, then, did not foreclose that possibility, it was more than ten years before a federal judge applied the *Hazelwood* standard in a college press rights case. The Sixth Circuit refused to apply *Hazelwood* at the college level in *Kincaid v. Gibson,* 236 F.3d 342 (6th Cir. 2001), but the Seventh Circuit applied the *Hazelwood* "framework," if not the holding, to a college press case in *Hosty v. Carter,* 412 F.3d 731 (7th Cir. 2005).

the autonomy of a true publisher but does have more control over expression than do most government officials. The Court has come close to granting public school administrators the same unquestioned authority of a private newspaper's owner. It did so in a 2002 case that involved not student speech but drug use and personal safety and health concerns[153] — concerns prominent in the 2007 *Morse* ruling.

Principal Deborah Morse permitted staff and students to observe from the street in front of school the 2002 Olympic Torch Relay as it passed through Juneau, Alaska. When camera crews went by, high school senior Joseph Frederick and his friends unfurled a fourteen-foot banner with the phrase "BONG HiTS 4 JESUS."[154] Morse demanded the banner be taken down. When Frederick refused, she pulled it down and suspended Frederick from school for ten days.

Frederick said his banner's words "were just nonsense meant to attract television cameras."[155] His legal argument rested on *Tinker* and its protection for individual expression that is not disruptive. School officials said, however, that their actions were consistent with school policy because Frederick's message "was not political," but instead "appeared to advocate the use of illegal drugs."[156] The Ninth U.S. Circuit Court of Appeals agreed with Frederick, saying that officials cannot censor non-disruptive speech simply because what is said is inconsistent with the school's mission. The ruling applied *Tinker* instead of *Hazelwood* or *Fraser*.[157]

The Supreme Court agreed that *Tinker* governs individual student expression on political issues but found this not to be such a statement. Chief Justice John Roberts, for the majority, wrote that the banner, regardless of ambiguous wording, made "undeniable reference to" and "advocated the use of illegal drugs."[158] *Hazelwood* does not apply here, Roberts wrote, because no one would reasonably believe the school endorsed the banner's message. But the Court held that *Fraser* allows limitations on student expression in a "school setting" (including this school-monitored trip outside to view the torch relay), especially when there is a compelling "governmental interest in stopping student drug abuse."[159]

The dissenters in *Morse* had the most trouble with the majority's assumption that Frederick's "oblique reference to drugs"

constituted advocacy of illegal behavior.[160] Justice John Paul Stevens argued that even in school there should not be viewpoint-based restrictions or punishment for mention of drugs when no illegal action is likely to occur.

Disappointed with the vote, student press advocates stressed the *Morse* decision's narrow focus.[161] Justice Samuel Alito, joined by Justice Anthony Kennedy, wrote that the problem in *Morse* was that the banner seemed to advocate illegal drug use — and drug use presents "a grave and in many ways unique threat to the physical safety of students."[162] They opposed viewpoint-based regulation by public school officials ("agents of the State") and "any restriction of speech that can plausibly be interpreted as commenting on any political or social issue."[163] Such sentiments are closely aligned with those of the dissenters in *Morse*. Some lower courts, though, have latched onto Justice Alito's physical safety rationale and have expanded the ruling to uphold punishment for speech not involving illegal drugs.[164] Two such decisions will be discussed later in this chapter.[165]

The high Court issued an early sign that *Morse* did not prevent all student expression in school. Four days after its ruling, it refused to hear an appeal from a Williamstown, Vermont, high school where a student was suspended for wearing a t-shirt that called then-President George W. Bush "Chicken-Hawk-in-Chief" and showed him with pictures of cocaine and a martini glass. The Second U.S. Circuit Court of Appeals said the school could not censor what obviously was a political message and, as per *Tinker*, caused no disruption in the school.[166]

State or local government officials have strict limits on their censorship power and must justify restrictions. High school officials also have to defend any censorship, but today that is easier to do. The *Hazelwood* decision encourages close scrutiny of student expression. Officials may regulate "in any reasonable manner" the content of any "supervised learning experience," the Court held. In the words of Justice Byron White: "[E]ducators do not offend the First Amendment by exercising editorial control over the style and content of student speech in school-sponsored expressive activities so long as their actions are reasonably related to legitimate pedagogical concerns."[167] These concerns include "speech that is ... ungrammatical, poorly written, inadequately researched, biased or prejudiced, vulgar or

---

[153] Bd. of Educ. of Pottawatomie County v. Earls, 536 U.S. 832 (2002). This 5-4 Supreme Court decision allowing broad drug testing in public high schools is evidence that the rights of students must defer to administrative decisions and an overriding health and safety concern related to drug use.

[154] Frederick was late to school, and when he arrived, he joined his friends standing on the sidewalk across the street from the school, off school grounds.

[155] Morse v. Frederick, 551 U.S. 393, 401 (2007).

[156] *Id.* at 398.

[157] Frederick v. Morse, 439 F.3d 1114 (9th Cir. 2006).

[158] 551 U.S. at 402 (Alito, J., concurring).

[159] *Id.* at 395.

[160] *Id.* at 420 (Stevens, J., dissenting).

[161] *See Experts Say Alito Key Factor in "Bong Hits" Decision*, STUDENT PRESS L. CTR. NEWSFLASH, June 26, 2007, http://www.splc.org/news/newsflash_archives.asp.

[162] 551 U.S. at 425 (Alito, J., concurring).

[163] *Id.* at 411 (Alito, J., concurring).

[164] *See, e.g.,* Clay Calvert, *Misuse and Abuse of Morse v. Frederick by Lower Courts: Stretching the High Court's Ruling Too Far to Censor Student Expression*, 32 SEATTLE UNIV. L. REV. 1 (2008).

[165] *See infra* notes 191-92 and accompanying text.

[166] Guiles v. Marineau, 461 F.3d 320 (2nd Cir. 2006).

[167] 484 U.S. 260, 273 (1988).

profane, or unsuitable for immature audiences."[168] The Court also said schools have the authority to refuse to sponsor student speech that might be perceived to advocate "irresponsible sex" or "conduct otherwise inconsistent with the shared values of a civilized social order."[169] Moreover, the Court ruled, schools can control school-sponsored speech that would "associate the school with any position other than neutrality on matters of political controversy."[170] The Court said school officials do not need specific written guidelines in order to control school-sponsored publications, and they violate the First Amendment only when censorship serves no valid educational purpose.

Numerous subsequent lower court rulings suggest that administrators' sphere of authority is expanding. The U.S. Court of Appeals for the Ninth Circuit held in *LaVine v. Blaine School District*, for example, that school officials justifiably expelled a student who asked a teacher to comment on a poem he wrote about a fictitious shooting in a school.[171] The school's safety concerns superseded the student's First Amendment rights, the court said.

In *Fleming v. Jefferson County School District*, the U.S. Court of Appeals for the Tenth Circuit let Columbine High School administrators prevent the display of decorative tiles with religious symbols.[172] Relying on *Hazelwood*, the court said the school's decision was legitimately related to the need to create a safe environment for Columbine High's students.

Safety, security and substantial disruption remain the primary justifications school officials use to curtail the expression of individual students.[173] A California student was told he could not wear in school a t-shirt that said "Homosexuality is Shameful," and a New Hampshire high school student was prevented from wearing a "No Nazis" patch with a line through a swastika. In both cases the courts sided with school officials who warned of disruptive consequences.[174] Indeed, recent research has shown that courts overall seem increasingly willing to defer to schools when they forecast or predict disruption.[175]

A recent controversy involves whether the First Amendment protects students who wear to school breast cancer awareness bracelets bearing the phrase "I ♥ Boobies." Students have worn the bracelets, which are sponsored by the Keep A Breast Foundation, to honor a family member or friend who has battled breast cancer. Several school districts have banned the bracelets, arguing they are inappropriate. In 2011, a federal district judge in Pennsylvania struck down a middle school's ban and ruled that the bracelets were not vulgar or lewd under *Fraser*, nor did they substantially disrupt the school under *Tinker*.[176] But, in 2012, a federal district judge in Wisconsin reached the opposite conclusion and upheld a middle school's ban on the bracelets in that state, ruling that the bracelets "can reasonably be interpreted as vulgar."[177] A high school student in Indiana filed a third lawsuit, and a federal district judge in that state also ruled in favor of a school's ban on wearing the bracelets.[178]

The losing school district in the Pennsylvania case appealed to the Third U.S. Circuit Court of Appeals, but, in 2013, the court sided with the students. The Third Circuit ruled that "because the bracelets…are not plainly lewd and because they comment on a social issue, they may not be categorically banned."[179] The school appealed the decision to the Supreme Court, with several prominent education groups — including the National School Boards Association — filing friend-of-the-court briefs siding with the school and urging the Court to overturn the Third Circuit's ruling. But, in 2014, the Supreme Court denied cert in the case.[180]

The Learning Environment. In *Hazelwood*, the students argued successfully at the circuit court level that the *Spectrum* was a public forum that should be free of content-based regulation, but the Supreme Court disagreed. It ruled that because the newspaper had not been clearly designated as a public forum, school officials were free to oversee its content.

The Court did not assume what lower courts had come to accept — that the ideas exchanged in the student newspaper made it a public forum. Although it covered controversial issues and carried letters to the editor, *Spectrum* had not become a public forum because no school board policy clearly stated such intent, and the practice of submitting the newspaper for administrative review indicated the school wanted to retain control.

---

[168] *Id.* at 271.

[169] *Id.* at 272 (internal quotations and citation omitted).

[170] *Id.*

[171] 257 F.3d 981 (9th Cir. 2001).

[172] 298 F.3d 918 (10th Cir. 2002).

[173] *See, e.g.,* Cuff v. Valley Cent. Sch. Dist., 677 F.3d 109, 114 (2d Cir. 2012) ("Courts have allowed wide leeway to school administrators disciplining students for writings or other conduct threatening violence.").

[174] Harper v. Poway Unified Sch. Dist., 445 F.3d 1166 (9th Cir. 2006), *vacated as moot* 549 U.S. 1262 (2007) (Harper was no longer a high school student.); Governor Wentworth Reg'l Sch. Dist. v. Henderson, No. 05CV-133-SM, 2006 WL 658936 (D.N.H. Mar. 15, 2006). *See also* BWA v. Farmington R-7 Sch. Dist., 554 F.3d 734 (8th Cir. 2009) (upholding suspension of student who wore depiction of the Confederate flag in violation of a school ban; Brown v. Cabell County Bd. of Ed., 605 F. Supp. 2d 788 (S.D. W.Va. 2009) (justifying suspension of student who wrote on his hand "Free A-Train" in support of a local man charged with shooting a police officer); Miller v. Penn Manor Sch. Dist., 588 F. Supp. 2d 606 (E.D. Pa. 2008) (allowing the ban of a t-shirt displaying images of automatic handguns and the phrase "Volunteer Homeland Security").

[175] *See, e.g.,* Dan V. Kozlowski, *Toothless* Tinker: *The Continued Erosion of Student Speech Rights*, 88 JOURNALISM & MASS COMM. Q. 352 (2011).

[176] B.H. v. Easton Area Sch. Dist., 827 F. Supp. 2d 392 (E.D. Pa. 2011).

[177] K.J. v. Sauk Prairie Sch. Dist., No. 3:11-cv-00622-bbc, 2 (W.D. Wis. 2012).

[178] J.A. v. Fort Wayne Cmty Sch., 2013 U.S. Dist. LEXIS 117667 (N.D. Ind. 2013).

[179] B.H. v. Easton Area Sch. Dist., 725 F.3d 293, 298 (3d Cir. 2013).

[180] *Supreme Court Won't Hear "Boobies" Bracelet Case; Third Circuit Ruling Siding With Students Stands*, STUDENT PRESS L. CTR. NEWSFLASH, Mar. 10, 2014, http://www.splc.org/news/newsflash.asp?id=2690.

While acknowledging that a student newspaper functioning as a public forum is harder to censor, the Court implied that stated school policy would be the only sure way to establish such a forum.[181] Federal judges have ruled in two relatively recent cases that school policy can be revealed in a number of ways, and a publication allowed to function as a forum can gain legal standing as a limited public forum.[182]

Age and Maturity. When it supported school officials, the Supreme Court in *Hazelwood* applied a legal philosophy built on the premise that government decision-makers may deny children, for legitimate reasons, constitutional rights that adults have. The age and maturity of high school students put their rights of free expression second to the rights of adults responsible for advancing the school's educational goals.

The Court held that school officials could use censorship to protect students from a newspaper story on coping with teenage pregnancy. Then it applied the legal rationale it had used in previous rulings to protect children from sexual material.

The Court earlier had defined and defended "variable obscenity" as a permissible way for the government to protect minors from the potential harm of sexual content. In *Ginsberg v. New York*,[183] the Court held that when evaluating sexual material available to minors, the test for judging a work as obscene for adults can be modified and the material restricted if it meets a lesser standard. In 1982, the Court unanimously upheld a state law directed at material not obscene for adults but illegal because it involved minors.[184] The rationale was a valid state interest in protecting vulnerable youth. In *Hazelwood*, the Court again decided that the First Amendment permits government — in this case, high school officials — to consider the "emotional maturity of the intended audience" when determining "whether to disseminate speech on potentially sensitive topics."[185] The high Court offered a variation of this protective role in its 2007 *Morse* ruling, holding that "schools may take steps to safeguard those entrusted to their care from speech that can reasonably be regarded as encouraging illegal drug use."[186]

As computers and Internet resources have entered the classroom and become tools for research and learning, school officials have had the added burden of protecting the young from adult material online. Even in decisions citing the unconstitutionality of the Communications Decency Act and the Child

Online Protection Act, federal courts have acknowledged the valid government interest in protecting minors.[187] Yet some overly protective school administrators are denying student journalists access to Internet resources useful in reporting, and publication staffs have to resolve privacy concerns before their newspapers are allowed to go online.[188] Schools' reliance on filters to deny students access to some online material poses problems, as a panel of federal judges determined in 2002, declaring the Children's Internet Protection Act unconstitutional. The Supreme Court saw no problem, ruling that the state interest in protecting children from pornography is more persuasive when adults can gain access to online library materials by removing the filters.[189] Infrequent but highly publicized incidents of school violence and acute apprehension about national security and online predators also have made administrators quick to respond to insensitive student behavior and youthful impulse.[190]

Arguing for Free Speech

The Supreme Court has not left students powerless to speak in the public schools. Valid legal arguments for free expression remain, as students learned in several recent student press-rights cases. Some questions relating to the most persuasive of those arguments are addressed here.

Is There a Legitimate Reason to Regulate? In general, the government must show that a legitimate public good will occur as a result of any regulation of an individual's speech. It's no different in public educational institutions. In high schools, it is easier for officials to find valid reasons, especially when regulations are closely linked to educational objectives. Two federal appellate courts in 2007 cited the Supreme Court's *Morse v. Frederick* decision in upholding school officials' punishment of students writing about violence.

A Georgia ninth-grader was suspended from school after a teacher saw the student's notebook with a section marked "Dream" and her journaled thoughts about shooting a math teacher. The Eleventh U.S. Circuit Court of Appeals upheld the district court ruling. Not only could Rachel Boim's writings cre-

---

[181] *See* Andrew D.M. Miller, *Balancing School Authority and Student Expression*, 55 BAYLOR L. REV. 623 (Fall 2002).

[182] Dean v. Utica Cmty. Sch., 345 F. Supp. 2d 799 (E.D. Mich. 2004); Draudt v. Wooster City Sch. Dist., 246 F. Supp. 2d 820 (N.D. Ohio 2003).

[183] 390 U.S. 629 (1968).

[184] New York v. Ferber, 458 U.S. 747 (1982).

[185] 484 U.S. 260, 272 (1988).

[186] 551 U.S. 393, 408 (2007).

[187] *See* ACLU v. Reno, 31 F. Supp. 2d 473 (E.D. Pa. 1999.), *aff'd*, 217 F.3d 162 (3d Cir. 2000), *aff'd* Ashcroft v. ACLU, 535 U.S. 564 (2002), *aff'd on remand* 322 F.3d 240 (3d Cir. 2003), *aff'd* 542 U.S. 656 (2004).

[188] *See Off-Campus Web Sites Endure Censorship*, STUDENT PRESS L. CTR. REP., Winter 2004-05, at 15. *See also*, Student Press L. Ctr. White Paper: Legal Tips to Know Before You Post, http://www.splc.org/resources/websitelegalguide.pdf.

[189] United States v. American Library Ass'n, 539 U.S. 194 (2003), *rev'g* 201 F. Supp. 2d 401 (E.D. Pa. 2002). *See also* Candace Perkins Bowen & John Bowen, *First Amendment Also Protects Right to Hear*, ADVISER UPDATE, Spring 2005, at 18A.

[190] *See, e.g., FERPA Fundamentalism*, STUDENT PRESS L. CTR. REP., Spring 2001, at 35-39 (discussing how schools use this federal privacy law to require parental permission before student publications can publish the names or photographs of students).

ate a "substantial disruption" in school, the court said, but students have no First Amendment right on school property during the school day to make written or oral comments that reasonably could be perceived as a threat of school violence.[191]

Morse was again cited four months later when the Fifth U.S. Circuit Court of Appeals overturned a district court ruling and reinstated a three-day school suspension for a high school sophomore. A student notebook again was the focus — a first-person diary account headed "My Nazi Diary Based on a True Story." Authorities looked at the diary, which was an account of a growing neo-Nazi party in the district's schools, leading to a Columbine-like assault during graduation. Despite claims that it was a "model student's" creation, the court of appeals said that, as in *Morse*, school officials could reasonably believe that such writing advocates behavior that could harm students, and such speech is not protected.[192]

As discussed previously, school-sponsored student speech is controlled by *Hazelwood* and is subject to what can be a broad judicial interpretation of the school's "legitimate pedagogical concerns" justifying censorship. In fact, when a court rules that *Hazelwood* controls a case, the First Amendment claimant is almost always about to lose because courts generally apply the "legitimate pedagogical concerns" standard so deferentially. On rare occasions, though, students have successfully challenged administrators to demonstrate in court that restrictions on school-sponsored speech are reasonably related to educational goals. One student victory came from the New Jersey Supreme Court, which ruled unanimously in 1994 that the principal of Clearview Junior High School had not met the *Hazelwood* standard when he censored two movie reviews by Brien Desilets. The principal had no problem with the content of the eighth-grader's reviews for the student newspaper but censored them because the films — *Rain Man* and *Mississippi Burning* — are R-rated, which school officials said meant that the subject matter was inappropriate for junior-high students. The state supreme court disagreed and concluded that there were insufficient educational grounds to justify the censorship.[193]

A Michigan judge in a later federal case noted that the quality of journalism that editor Katy Dean and the *Arrow* staff of Utica High School practiced overshadowed any censorship justifications that administrators offered. Officials tried to stop publication of an investigative story about a lawsuit that two community members filed against the school district, claiming that diesel fumes from idling buses constituted a nuisance, violated their privacy rights and harmed their health. Ruling for the students, Judge Arthur Tarnow noted the thoughtful and thorough

investigation of a story that "was relevant to the school community." He reviewed each of *Hazelwood's* bases for reasonable censorship and concluded that there was no evidence that censorship of the student newspaper story in Utica High School was "reasonably related to any stated pedagogical concern."[194]

School officials also have used the *Hazelwood* ruling and a low-tolerance atmosphere in schools to exercise more control over what teachers say. Often school authorities link sanctions to a teacher's performance in the classroom and justify their actions as properly related to administrative oversight of the curriculum. The Fourth U.S. Circuit Court of Appeals upheld sanctions of a North Carolina drama teacher whose selection of a controversial play led school officials to remove the production from state competition and transfer the teacher to another school. The court said that although the teacher always selects the play, the drama is part of the curriculum that administrators can legitimately control as school-sponsored speech.[195] Publication advisers do much of their work with journalism students outside of the classroom, but these teachers also risk losing their jobs as advisers or being abruptly transferred to different schools if their performance dissatisfies administrators.[196] In 2009, the Journalism Teachers Protection Act began offering California college and high school teachers (including advisers) protection from retaliation for engaging in protected expression, defending student expression or refusing to engage in unlawful censorship.[197]

Is It School-sponsored Speech That's Being Regulated? The *Hazelwood* Court clearly gave high school officials more control than they had before over expression that is school-sponsored or supervised by faculty members. Before 1988, pre-publication review of school newspapers was permitted in most of the country, as long as constitutional procedural guidelines existed. The *Hazelwood* majority removed the requirement of guidelines for school-sponsored speech.

Speech that has not come through a faculty-supervised activity has had more protection because it is subject to the *Tinker* standard and must be permitted unless school officials can show the speech is, or will be, substantially disruptive. Post-*Hazelwood* cases that supported this view dealt with students wanting to distribute religious materials or publish alternative student newspapers.

[191] Boim v. Fulton County Sch. Dist., 494 F.3d 978 (11th Cir. 2007).

[192] Ponce v. Socorro Ind. Sch. Dist., 508 F.3d 765 (5th Cir. 2007).

[193] Desilets v. Clearview Regional Bd. of Educ., 647 A.2d 150 (N.J. 1994). *See also In re* George T, 93 P.3d 1007 (Cal. 2004).

[194] Dean v. Utica Cmty. Sch., 345 F. Supp. 2d 799, 809 (E.D. Mich. 2004).

[195] Boring v. Buncombe County Bd. of Educ., 136 F.3d 364 (4th Cir. 1998).

[196] *See* Amanda Lehmert, *Advisers Removed — But is it Censorship?*, QUILL, July-Aug. 2002, at 22. *See also Advisers in Limbo*, STUDENT PRESS L. CTR. REP., Fall 2002, at 23; *Silencing the Rebellion*, STUDENT PRESS L. CTR. REP., Fall 2002, at 20.

[197] *See* S.B.1370 amending sections 48907, 48950, 66301 and 94367 of the California Education Code. *See also Bill Would Protect Journalism Advisers*, STUDENT PRESS L. CTR. NEWSFLASH, Feb. 22, 2008, http://www.splc.org/news/newsflash_archives.asp.

The same year as *Hazelwood*, the Ninth U.S. Circuit Court of Appeals ruled that school officials were wrong to discipline five students who distributed their newspaper at a class picnic without getting prior permission. The court said that the school's broad control over curriculum does not extend to a policy controlling content of non-school-sponsored speech.[198]

Three recent high school cases reflect how the *Tinker* disruption standard still prevails, to the benefit of individual student expression. In a case remindful of *Tinker*, the Eighth U.S. Circuit Court of Appeals ruled that school officials could not punish students who wore black armbands as a protest of a school's dress code.[199] A student punished for wearing a T-shirt saying "Be Happy, Not Gay" was allowed to wear the shirt while the case against the school district proceeded, the Seventh U.S. Circuit Court of Appeals ruled in 2008.[200] The court ruled in the student's favor again in 2011 when the case came back to the court on appeal.[201] And a Florida district court judge issued an injunction preventing school officials from punishing students or denying them the right to wear messages or symbols advocating gay rights. Students were told they could not write "Gay Pride" on their arms or wear rainbow belts or t-shirts saying "I support gays." The judge also ordered the school board to pay $325,000 in attorney fees for violating the students' rights.[202]

In *Owasso Independent School District v. Falvo*[203] the Supreme Court did not address a student press issue, but instead the federal privacy law that school officials have used to prevent publication or Web posting of student names and photos. FERPA, discussed above, requires schools to get parental consent before releasing a student's "educational records." Administrators have applied FERPA to the student media, requiring parental approval before publishing identification of students or even conducting student surveys.

Kristja Falvo's parents sued the Oklahoma school district, claiming that the classroom practice of having students exchange and grade quizzes and then read the results aloud violated FERPA. But the Supreme Court unanimously disagreed. Writing for the Court, Justice Anthony Kennedy said that students are not "acting for" the school when they grade quizzes at a teacher's request, nor does reading grades aloud meet the FERPA requirement of a school-maintained educational record.[204] The ruling makes it easier for student journalists to argue that they are not "agents" of the school, and their published work will not open the district to a charge of violating FERPA.

Is the Publication a Public Forum? A city is not required to create a public park or stock one with benches where people can share ideas. But if there is a park, public officials can't decide which political ideas may be expressed on a park bench and which may not. Students have used this public forum principle to defend their right to express ideas on school property. The *Hosty* ruling notwithstanding, courts consistently have found a public university's campus and student newspaper to be public forums, certainly for the university's students and faculty. The courts have not said that about high school corridors and publications. High school students and publication staffs will have more legal right to freedom of expression if school officials acknowledge that the newspaper and yearbook are public forums,[205] but today neither high school nor college students can assume that their publications are forums.[206]

The Ninth U.S. Circuit Court of Appeals has clarified what it means for a school to designate a public forum. A Nevada school district gave principals the authority to set guidelines for advertising in student publications and reject ads that did not meet them. The school set a review procedure and refused to run Planned Parenthood ads considered unsuitable. Before deciding whether the broad administrative discretion of *Hazelwood* applied to the case, the court had to decide whether the publications were public forums, thus limiting administrative control. It said the publications did not become public forums just because they accepted advertising or reported on controversial issues. It ruled the publications were not forums because school officials, with their policy and practice of prior review, clearly retained control and had not turned them over to the staff.[207]

Even when school officials allow students to make editorial decisions, it does not mean that the student publications are public forums open to anyone who wants access to the newspaper or yearbook. When the Supreme Court refused in 1998 to hear his case, a Massachusetts businessman lost his argument that a high school newspaper had to accept his political advertisement encouraging sexual abstinence. Douglas Yeo wanted the ad in the newspaper and yearbook, but the student editors said no. Yeo rejected the students' offer to write a letter to the editor after they cited an unwritten policy not to accept political or advocacy ads. The First U.S. Circuit Court of Appeals initially ruled for Yeo, but a six-judge panel of the appellate court reheard the case and unanimously ruled for the students. The

[198] Burch v. Barker, 861 F.2d 1149 (9th Cir. 1988).

[199] Lowry v. Watson Chapel Sch. Dist., 540 F.3d 752 (8th Cir. 2008).

[200] Nuxoll v. Indian Prairie Sch. Dist. #204, 523 F.3d 668 (7th Cir. 2008).

[201] Zamecnik v. Indian Prairie Sch. Dist. #204, 636 F.3d 874 (7th Cir. 2011).

[202] Gillman v. Sch. Bd. for Holmes City, Fla., 567 F. Supp. 2d 1359 (N.D. Fla. 2008).

[203] 534 U.S. 426 (2002).

[204] *Id.* at 434.

[205] *But see* R.O. v. Ithaca City Sch. Dist., 645 F.3d 533 (2d Cir. 2011).

[206] *See* Hills v. Scottsdale Unified Sch. Dist., 329 F.3d 1044 (9th Cir. 2003); Draudt v. Wooster City Sch. Dist., 246 F. Supp. 2d 820 (N.D. Ohio 2003). *See also Going Public*, STUDENT PRESS L. CTR. REP., Spring 2006, at 6; Hosty v. Carter: *An Analysis*, STUDENT PRESS L. CTR. REP., Fall 2005, at 27; Frank LoMonte, *Shrinking* Tinker: *Students are "Persons" Under Our Constitution — Except When They Aren't*, 58 AM. U.L. REV. 1323 (2009).

[207] Planned Parenthood v. Clark County Sch. Dist., 887 F.2d 935 (9th Cir. 1989).

court said in *Yeo v. Lexington* that where high school officials (here under the mandate of a Massachusetts statute) grant editorial control to students, there is "no legal duty here on the part of school administrators to control the content of the editorial judgments of student editors of publications."[208]

In New Hampshire, a student sued his school district because the student yearbook would not publish a senior photo of him posing with a shotgun over his shoulder. A district court judge ruled that the student's First Amendment rights were not denied because the yearbook staff, not school officials, made the decision. Judge Steven McAuliffe implied that the student may have had a claim if the administration had banned the photo.[209]

An Ohio federal judge offered useful guidance on the public-forum issue when deciding a newspaper censorship case in 2003. Noting that a student newspaper is not always a public forum, Judge James Gwin discussed and weighed nine factors that he said should be used to determine whether a student publication is protected as a limited public forum. When he found that six of the nine criteria were met, he declared the Wooster High School newspaper a limited public forum. The school district then settled the case, agreeing to pay the students' legal fees of $30,000 and to donate $5,000 to charities of the students' choice.[210]

In *Dean v. Utica*, a case that former SPLC Executive Director Mark Goodman called "[t]he most important student-newspaper censorship case since *Hazelwood*,"[211] the judge noted how both practice and policy identified the publication as a limited public forum. Among other things, he brought attention to the school's description of the journalism class, the course's curriculum guide and the newspaper's printed masthead as evidence that the publication was a forum.[212]

For more than two decades, free press advocates have encouraged high school journalists to clearly establish their publications as public forums. Where school authorities clearly have sanctioned the newspaper as a limited public forum, or where administrators have given students editorial control over content, it is likely that the standard from *Tinker*, not *Hazelwood*, will apply. The newspaper or yearbook can become a forum through state law, school board policy, curriculum materials or an agreement with school officials, reinforced by practice and a staff policy that demonstrate the newspaper is used for an exchange of opinions.

A 2011 decision by the Second U.S. Circuit Court of Appeals, however, complicates the advice free press advocates have given high school journalists. In *R.O. v. Ithaca City School District*, the Second Circuit ruled that *The Tattler*, the student newspaper of Ithaca High School, was a limited public forum — but the school's speech restrictions were still permissible under *Hazelwood*, the court said.[213] *The Tattler*'s staff wanted to print a political cartoon, which depicted stick figures in various sexual positions, alongside an article headlined "How is Sex Being Taught in Our Health Class?" The paper's adviser permitted the article but not the cartoon, and the principal upheld the adviser's decision when the students appealed. The students then sued. Supreme Court precedent has established that limited public forums receive more First Amendment protection than nonpublic forums.[214] The Second Circuit, however, labeled *The Tattler* a limited public forum, but then nevertheless ruled the paper was school-sponsored, analogous to *Spectrum* in *Hazelwood*. The court said the cartoon could be censored because it was lewd and because publishing it would have undermined the school's efforts to stress to students "the seriousness of sexual relations."[215] SPLC Executive Director Frank LoMonte criticized the court for "just fundamentally misunder[standing] what it means to be a limited public forum."[216] In light of the decision, LoMonte argued that student journalists in Connecticut, New York and Vermont — for whom *R.O.* is binding precedent — should advocate for specific publications policies that do not rely simply on the limited public forum label and instead robustly explain the freedoms publications have.[217]

Do Officials Know That Editorial Control Brings Liability? Whether a student newspaper is, by policy or practice, a public forum is generally important to students. But school officials also can benefit when they decide not to review copy before publication and give the staff responsibility for content.[218]

Officials at a high school or college who fear they will be held responsible for harmful expression should be reassured that they will be as liable as a private publisher if they routinely re-

---

[208] 131 F.3d 241, 253 (1st Cir. 1997).

[209] Douglass v. Londonderry Sch. Bd., 413 F. Supp. 2d 1 (D.N.H. 2005). *See also N.H. Court Rejects Student's Claim That School Unfairly Banned Photos*, STUDENT PRESS L. CTR. REP., Spring 2005, at 9.

[210] Draudt v. Wooster City Sch. Dist., 246 F. Supp. 2d 820 (N.D. Ohio 2003). *See also School Board Pays $35,000 to Settle* Wooster Blade *Censorship Lawsuit*, STUDENT PRESS L. CTR. REP., Winter 2003-04, at 8.

[211] *Court Releases Opinion on Utica High School Censorship Case*, STUDENT PRESS LAW CTR. NEWSFLASH, Nov. 18, 2004, http://www.splc.org/news/newsflash_archives .asp.

[212] Dean v. Utica Cmty. Sch., 345 F. Supp. 2d 799, 807-08 (E.D. Mich. 2004).

[213] 645 F.3d 533 (2d Cir. 2011).

[214] *See, e.g.*, Cornelius v. NAACP Legal Def. & Educ. Fund, 473 U.S. 788 (1985).

[215] 645 F.3d at 542. After their adviser refused the cartoon, the students created *The March Issue*, an independent student publication that they hoped to distribute on school grounds. The district superintendent barred the students from distributing the paper on campus because it included the same stick-figure cartoon, and the Second Circuit upheld that decision under *Fraser*, ruling that the cartoon "clearly qualif[ied]" as lewd. *Id.* at 543.

[216] *Appeals Court: N.Y. School Can Censor Cartoon in "Forum" and Independent Newspapers*, STUDENT PRESS L. CTR. NEWSFLASH, May 18, 2011, http://www.splc.org/ news/newsflash_archives.asp.

[217] *Id.*

[218] *See Hold That Thought*, STUDENT PRESS L. CTR. REP., Fall 2003, at 36.

view and regulate publication content.[219]

Private publishers are legally responsible for defamatory content they print because they and their editors are free to decide what to publish. The Supreme Court, however, said that a television station carrying the defamatory comments of a political candidate was not responsible because the station had no editorial control. Broadcasters cannot be held accountable for content that Congress, through Section 315 of the Communications Act, denied station owners the power to edit, the Court said.[220] Section 230 of the Communications Decency Act of 1996 also protects from liability an educational institution or an individual re-posting someone else's content on an "interactive computer service" such as a student publication's Web site.[221]

School authorities may argue for the same immunity when the student newspaper at their school, by policy or by practice, has become a public forum and the administration does not review content. This was true when editors chose photos for the school yearbook[222] and may apply as well to a school-hosted Web site.[223] In public universities, where administrators have little control over student publication content, it is unlikely that a court would hold school officials legally liable for what is printed. In the high school, officials have more authority to oversee content but are not required by Hazelwood to do so. The more oversight and influence the administration exercises, the more likely it is that the school will be legally liable for what is published. By turning editorial decisions over to a staff and/or faculty adviser, school officials are in a better position to argue for the immunity that at least four courts have accorded state universities.[224] A state judge in Washington embraced that reasoning in 2011 when she ruled that a school district was not liable for the content of a student-run high school newspaper.[225] The Student Press Law Center reported that the decision was the first to explicitly establish liability protection at the high school level.[226]

At the college level, a Minnesota appeals court has protected university officials from liability in a libel suit against the student newspaper. The court said that the university did not have the liability of a private publisher when college policy and First Amendment constraints prevented the university from controlling newspaper content.[227]

Has Law or Policy Given Students More Free-Speech Rights? The Supreme Court has clearly indicated that lawmakers may give citizens more free speech protection than the Constitution provides. That's what students learned when the Court unanimously upheld their rights under the California Constitution to distribute literature at a privately owned shopping mall.[228]

California also passed a law in 1977 that codified the *Tinker* "substantial disruption" standard and protection for the speech and press rights of high school students.[229] By the early 1980s, federal courts regularly cited and applied *Tinker*, and some free-speech observers thought that the California law merely restated the Supreme Court precedent.

Then along came the *Hazelwood* decision, and within weeks a high school administrator tried to apply the ruling and censor a California student newspaper. But the censorship was challenged, and a judge ruled that the state law granting students more free-speech rights takes precedence over the *Hazelwood*-based argument that educational goals justified censorship.[230]

Since then, the Student Press Law Center reports, almost three dozen other states have considered or debated legislation on student expression. Massachusetts followed California's lead and enacted legislation in 1988. Then came Iowa, Colorado, Kansas and Arkansas. A celebrated 2011 decision by the Iowa Court of Appeals reaffirmed that the Iowa legislature passed its law in order to give student journalists "more robust free-expression rights than those articulated by the Supreme Court" in *Hazelwood*.[231] Between 1995 and 2007, no similar legislation was passed in other states, despite numerous attempts. During the years when no new legislation was passed, school personnel struggled with the aftermath of Columbine, and budget deficits preoccupied legislators.[232]

Two California laws protect the college press there. One guards college journalists from the censorship threat of *Hosty v. Carter*. The other makes it a misdemeanor to take more than

[219] *See* Gallo v. Princeton Univ., 656 A.2d 1267 (N.J. 1995); McEvaddy v. City Univ. of N.Y., 633 N.Y.S.2d 2 (N.Y. App. Div. 1995); LAW OF THE STUDENT PRESS, *supra* note 16, at 159. *See also* Ruth Walden, *The University's Tort Liability for Libel and Invasion of Privacy in the Student Press*, 65 JOURNALISM Q. 616 (Fall 1988).

[220] Farmers Educ. & Coop. Union of Am. v. WDAY, 360 U.S. 525 (1959).

[221] 47 U.S.C. § 230 (1996). *See also* Michael Beder, *Understanding Cybershield Law*, STUDENT PRESS L. CTR. REP., Fall 2009 at 37.

[222] *See* Douglass v. Londonderry Sch. Bd., 413 F. Supp. 2d 1 (D.N.H. 2005).

[223] *See Guide to Internet Law*, STUDENT PRESS L. CTR. REP., Fall 2004, at 40, 42. *See also Ask Frank: A Student Journalist's Guide to Instant Journalism and Media Law*, STUDENT PRESS L. CTR. REP., Winter 2008-09 at 33.

[224] *See* Milliner v. Turner, 436 So.2d 1300 (La. Ct. App. 1983); Lewis v. St. Cloud State Univ., No. C2-04-2244 (Dist. Ct. Ramsey County, June 9, 2004), *affd.*, 693 N.W.2d 466 (Minn. Ct. App. 2005); Mazart v. State, 441 N.Y.S. 2d 600 (N.Y.Ct.C1. 1981); Doe v. New York Univ., No. 109457/04 (N.Y. Sup. Ct., New York County, Dec. 8, 2004).

[225] Sisley v. Seattle Sch. Dist., No. 10-2-10522-1 SEA (Wash. Super. Ct. July 22, 2011).

[226] *See Seattle School Not Liable for Student Newspaper Story about Landlord*, STUDENT PRESS L. CTR. NEWSFLASH, July 26, 2011, http://www.splc.org/news/newsflash_archives.asp.

[227] *See* Lewis v. St. Cloud State Univ., 693 N.W.2d 466 (Minn. Ct. App. 2005). *See also Old Issues, New Questions*, STUDENT PRESS L. CTR. REP., Fall 2008, at 15.

[228] Pruneyard Shopping Ctr. v. Robins, 447 U.S. 74 (1980).

[229] California Student Free Expression Law, CAL. EDUC. CODE § 48907 (1977).

[230] Leeb v. DeLong, 243 Cal. Rptr. 494 (Cal. Dist. Ct. App. 1988). *But see Principals Censor Newspapers at Two Calif. Schools*, STUDENT PRESS L. CTR. REP., Spring 2000, at 24 (describing censorship incidents where administrators ignored the state law).

[231] Lange v. Diercks, 808 N.W.2d 754, *6 (Iowa Ct. App. 2011) (unpublished).

[232] *See Censorship on the Rise*, STUDENT PRESS L. CTR. REP., Spring 2002, at 20; *Sad State of Affairs*, STUDENT PRESS L. CTR. REP., Spring 2003, at 27.

twenty-five copies of a free newspaper. And in Illinois, the College Campus Press Act that took effect in 2008 essentially nullifies the *Hosty* ruling by making public forums of all student media at public colleges in the state.[233]

Legislatures in two western states worked on similar bills to protect both high school and college publications. Efforts succeeded in Oregon, where House Bill 3279 was signed into law in 2007, making Oregon the seventh state (the first since 1995) to give legislative protection to the high school press. A contentious battle in Washington saw an amendment remove from the bill protection of high school students, harsh criticism of the bill from professional journalists at the *Seattle Times* and eventual death of the legislation in 2007 when it failed to reach the floor of the state senate.[234] A similar bill that would have protected high school and college students was introduced in the state senate in 2008, but it died in the judiciary committee.[235]

In 2015 North Dakota became the eighth state to give legislative protection to the high school press. The governor signed the law after it received unanimous support in both the state house and senate. The law prevents officials at public high schools and colleges in the state from invoking the *Hazelwood* standard to justify censorship. The law also protects teachers against retaliation for work their students publish. The executive director of the North Dakota Newspaper Association celebrated that the "student free press movement has been reinvigorated" by legislation emerging from a "small, obscure, rural state like North Dakota."[236]

Indeed, the legislative success in North Dakota ignited movements across the country the following year to pass similar legislation. In April 2016, Maryland became the ninth state to reinforce high school students' First Amendment rights through legislation. Like the North Dakota law, the Maryland law applies to college student journalists, and it also protects student media advisers from retaliatory punishment. And at press time

for this book in 2016, a student press freedom bill had been passed by the Illinois house and senate and was on its way to the governor's desk. If the governor signs the law, Illinois would become the tenth state to give legislative protection to the high school press.

Nationwide, other legislative obstacles, such as the following, have also discouraged censorship:

• California's Leonard Law, discussed earlier in connection with campus speech codes, extends First Amendment protection to high school and college students in both public and private schools and, as of 2009, to advisers and all teachers.[237]

• Students in Oregon and New Jersey have argued that their state constitutions protect student expression.

• Two states — Pennsylvania and Washington — have added protection in "student rights" sections of their state education codes.[238] In its code, Pennsylvania's Department of Education used *Tinker* to build a standard for freedom of expression that the state's scholastic press association uses to help police censorship efforts in the schools. Student press advocates have had to monitor efforts to weaken the protection of those state codes. Pennsylvania successfully fought off such an assault in 2002, only to face and successfully thwart State Board of Education attempts again in 2004 and 2005.

ONLINE STUDENT SPEECH

The proliferation of social media and the relative ease with which students can communicate online and across school boundaries have given the term "underground press" a new dimension. Off-campus use of the Internet qualifies as individual expression, in the past subject to punishment by school officials only if it reaches school and meets the "substantial disruption" standard of *Tinker*.[239] But school administrators increasingly are defining "disruption" broadly, punishing students when off-campus, online speech carries offensive or crude attacks on someone in the school.[240]

Several courts have supported students' off-campus expression. While the public often seems willing to defer to administrators and tight regulations when children's health and safe-

[233] *See California Governor Signs College Student Press Freedom Bill,* STUDENT PRESS L. CTR. NEWSFLASH, Aug. 28, 2006, http://www.splc.org/news/newsflash_archives.asp; *California Governor Approves Newspaper Theft Law,* STUDENT PRESS L. CTR. NEWSFLASH, Sept. 11, 2006, http://www.splc.org/news/newsflash_archives.asp; *Illinois Lawmakers Approve Bill to Protect Rights of Student Journalists at College Newspapers,* CHRON. HIGHER EDUC., June 11, 2007, *available at* http://chronicle.com; *Ruling Affirms Ill. Campus Free-Press Act,* FIRST AMENDMENT CTR. ONLINE, Mar. 20, 2012, http://www.firstamendmentcenter.org/ruling-affirms-ill-campus-free-press-act.

[234] *See* Candace Perkins Bowen & John Bowen, *Protecting "Labs for Journalism Education,"* ADVISER UPDATE, Spring 2007, at 24; *Oregon Student Free Press Bill Signed Into Law,* STUDENT PRESS L. CTR. NEWSFLASH, July 13, 2007, http://www.splc.org /news/newsflash_archives.asp; *Pioneering Washington State Press Freedom Bill Dies in State Senate,* STUDENT PRESS L. CTR. NEWSFLASH, Apr. 18, 2007, http://www.splc.org/ news/newsflash_archives.asp.

[235] *See Wash. Free-Expression Bill Dies in State Senate,* STUDENT PRESS L. CTR. NEWSFLASH, Feb. 1, 2008, http://www.splc.org/news/newsflash_archives.asp.

[236] *N.D. House Approves 'Anti-Hazelwood' Student Press Freedom Bill,* STUDENT PRESS L. CTR. NEWSFLASH, Apr. 6, 2015, http://www.splc.org/article/2015/04/n-d-house-approves-anti-hazelwood-student-press-freedom-bill.

[237] *See* CALIF. EDUC. CODE § 66301 (2006).

[238] *See* Washington Administrative Code: Student Rights, WAC 392-40-215 (1997); Pennsylvania Administrative Code: Student Rights and Responsibilities, 22 PA. CODE § 12.9 (2005).

[239] *See* Mahaffey v. Aldrich, 236 F. Supp. 2d 779 (E.D. Mich. 2002).

[240] *See* Frank. D. LoMonte, Issue Brief: *Reaching Through the Schoolhouse Gate: Students' Eroding First Amendment Rights in a Cyber-Speech World,* AMERICAN CONSTITUTION SOCIETY FOR LAW AND POLICY, Mar. 2, 2009, https://www.acslaw.org/sites/ default/files/LoMonte_Issue_Brief.pdf. *See also* Clay Calvert, *Punishing Public School Students for Bashing Principals, Teachers and Classmates in Cyberspace: The Speech Issue the Supreme Court Must Now Resolve,* 7 FIRST AMEND. L. REV. 210 (2009); Rita J. Verga, *Policing Their Space: The First Amendment Parameters of School Discipline of Student Cyberspeech,* 23 SANTA CLARA COMPUTER & HIGH TECH. L.J. 727 (2007).

ty are at stake, the courts have not always been as willing to ignore infringements on the constitutional rights of students and
teachers. Some students who appeal their punishments by
overzealous administrators have found support in court. An
eighth-grader in New Jersey won a $117,500 settlement after
school officials punished him for using his personal Web site
(maintained at home) as a forum for students who found school
boring.[241] In 2010, a school agreed to remove any record of a
Florida high school student's punishment and pay $15,000 in at-
torney fees after a federal judge ruled in the student's favor and
refused to dismiss her lawsuit challenging her three-day suspension for creating a Facebook page that criticized one of her
teachers.[242] In 2015, a federal district court held that a middle
school violated a student's First Amendment rights when it
suspended him for calling a teacher a "bitch" who "needs to be
shot" on Facebook.[243] The judge in the case ruled that the Facebook posts did not cause a "material and substantial interference with appropriate school discipline."[244] Also in 2015, a student received a $425,000 settlement after a federal judge had
ruled his lawsuit challenging his punishment could go forward.[245] The student had been suspended for a sarcastic tweet
that hinted he "made out" with a teacher at the school. But the
student maintained he was joking, and there was no evidence
the student had any sort of inappropriate relationship with the
teacher. In refusing to dismiss the case, the judge said the
school had not shown that the tweet caused a substantial disruption.[246]

Student victories in cases involving punishment for off-campus, online speech are far from inevitable, however. One scholar
has rightly called the issue of how to treat students' online
speech a "pervasive and pernicious First Amendment problem."[247] Students today are electronically wired to one another
and the outside world everywhere they go, and judges are struggling to determine how far administrators' reach extends.[248]

A look at the path of three recent cases vividly reveals the
challenge to students and school officials seeking judicial guidance amid uncertainty about school boundaries and authoritative parameters.

In *Layshock v. Hermitage School District*, Judge Terrence Mc-
Verry's ruling reflected long-standing interpretations of the
Tinker protections.[249] Justin Layshock fabricated a MySpace
profile as a parody of his principal. It included a photo of the
principal and called him a "big steroid freak" and a "hard-ass"
who had an alcohol-abuse problem. Layshock was suspended for
ten days and moved to an alternative school. A federal district
court in Pennsylvania ruled the punishment a free-speech violation. Although vulgar and accessible in school, Judge McVerry
said, the MySpace profile was created off-campus and did not
substantially disrupt the school's work. Because two other federal district courts ruled differently in cases similar to Layshock, free-speech advocates closely followed Layshock when it
went before the Third U.S. Circuit Court of Appeals.

In a separate case, another fake MySpace profile of a Pennsylvania principal led to the ten-day suspension of a middle-
school student in 2008.[250] Again the profile and photo were
posted from home. But the judge asserted there was an "effect"
at school when the student used "vulgar" and "lewd" language to
characterize her principal as a pedophile who performed sexual
acts in his office. One factor the judge considered in *J.S. v. Blue
Mountain School District* was the ease and frequency with
which off-campus speech becomes on-campus speech through
the technology of instant messaging and social networking.[251]

Shortly before the district court ruled in *J.S.*, the Second U.S.
Circuit Court of Appeals affirmed a district court decision
against a Connecticut high school student. Avery Doninger was
barred from running for student government because online —
from home, on her commercial blog — she criticized school administrators. She called them douchebags and encouraged her
classmates to complain because the officials were preventing a
concert student government was planning for the student body.
Administrators said that Doninger was punished because her
speech, which the principal discovered two weeks after Doninger posted it, was disruptive. Doninger sued, seeking an injunction barring her discipline.

A panel of the Second Circuit said the online posting fueled
controversy over scheduling of the annual concert and thus substantially disrupted "work and discipline" within the school. The
school argued that Doninger's post was misleading because
school officials had informed her that the event would be re-
scheduled rather than canceled. The appellate court thus said

[241] Dwyer v. Oceanport Sch. Dist., No. 03-6005, slip. op. (D.N.J. Mar. 31, 2005).

[242] Evans v. Bayer, 684 F. Supp. 2d 1365 (S.D. Fla. 2010).

[243] Burge v. Colton Sch. Dist., 2015 U.S. Dist. LEXIS 50819, 3 (D. Or. July 21, 2015).

[244] *Id.* at 10.

[245] *See Student Suspended for Two-Word Sarcastic Tweet to Receive $425,000 in Set-
tlement,* STUDENT PRESS L. CTR. NEWSFLASH, Dec. 9, 2015, http://www.splc.org/article/
2015/12/student-suspended-for-two-word-sarcastic-tweet-to-receive-425000-in-settlemen
t.

[246] Sagehorn v. Indep. Sch. Dist., 122 F. Supp. 3d 842 (D. Minn. 2015).

[247] Calvert, *supra* note 240, at 211.

[248] *See* Kyle W. Brenton, *BONGHiTS4JESUS.COM? Scrutinizing Public School Authority Over Student Cyberspeech Through the Lens of Personal Jurisdiction,* 92
MINN. L. REV. 1206 (2008).

[249] 496 F. Supp. 2d 587 (W.D. Pa. 2007).

[250] North Carolina passed a law in 2012 that makes it illegal for students to create
fake social media profiles mocking school officials. Penalties could include as much
as sixty days in jail or a $1,000 fine for those as young as 16, who are treated as
adults under state law. *See N.C. Outlaws Fake Social Media Profiles of School Officials,* STUDENT PRESS L. CTR. NEWSFLASH, Aug. 1, 2012, http://www.splc.org/news/news
flash_archives.asp.

[251] 2008 U.S. Dist. LEXIS 72685 (M.D. Pa. Sept. 11, 2008).

that Doninger used "at best misleading and at worst false" information in an effort to solicit more calls and emails.[252] And because the post took place amidst already circulating rumors about the event's status, the Second Circuit concluded that "it was foreseeable in this context that school operations might well be disrupted further by the need to correct misinformation as a consequence of [the] post."[253] Frank LoMonte of the SPLC said the ruling teaches students a terrible civics lesson, adding that Doninger was merely urging citizens to get involved in a matter of public concern.[254]

After being denied the injunction that would have allowed her to be reinstated as a class officer, Doninger continued the case and argued in court that she deserved monetary damages because she was denied her First Amendment right to criticize school officials. In 2011, a new Second Circuit panel ruled unanimously that it did not need to decide whether Doninger's punishment in fact violated the First Amendment because the law surrounding off-campus speech is unsettled and school officials were thus entitled to qualified immunity.[255] The court concluded that administrators acted reasonably given that it was

> not clearly established at the time of these events that Doninger had any First Amendment right not to be prohibited from running for senior class secretary because of offensive off-campus speech, at least when such speech pertained to a school event, invited students to read and respond to it by contacting school administrators, and it was reasonably foreseeable that the speech would come on to campus and thus come to the attention of school authorities.[256]

As First Amendment advocate Ken Paulson wrote shortly after the decision, "Here's the takeaway for school officials: You can punish students for any off-campus speech that you reasonably believe could disrupt the school. You may be wrong, but you can't be sued for it."[257]

The Third Circuit added to the confusion in the case law when two separate panels issued conflicting rulings in the *Layshock* and *J.S.* cases in 2010. The *Layshock* panel upheld the decision that Justin Layshock's fake MySpace profile of his principal was offensive but protected speech because it did not materially or substantially disrupt the school.[258] In the *J.S.* case, however, an appellate court panel deferred to the school's argument that the administrator ridiculed in the fake online profile there could reasonably forecast that such a verbal assault would disrupt his work as a high school principal.[259] Two months later, the Third Circuit vacated both opinions and ordered en banc review.

Student speech advocates anxiously awaited word from the full Third Circuit for more than a year. Then, in 2011, the en banc court ruled in favor of the students in both cases. In *Layshock*, the court ruled unanimously that the First Amendment protected the profile. The school elected not to challenge the district court's ruling that no disruption occurred in the case, and the Third Circuit then held that *Fraser* was inapplicable to off-campus speech. "It would be an unseemly and dangerous precedent to allow the state, in the guise of school authorities, to reach into a child's home and control his/her actions there to the same extent that it can control that child when he/she participates in school sponsored activities," Chief Judge Theodore McKee wrote for the court.[260]

The Third Circuit divided in *J.S.*, however. An eight-judge majority ruled that it did not need to decide definitively whether *Tinker* governed off-campus, online speech because, even if it did, the profile caused no actual disruption, nor did the facts of the case support the conclusion that the school could reasonably forecast disruption. The court said that although the profile contained crude content, vulgar language, and "shameful personal attacks,"[261] the speech "was so outrageous that no one could have taken it seriously, and no one did."[262] Five judges concurred in the case, signing onto an opinion written by Judge D. Brooks Smith that urged the majority to go even farther. The concurrence argued that *Tinker* should not apply to off-campus speech at all because "the First Amendment protects students engaging in off-campus speech to the same extent it protects speech by citizens in the community at large."[263]

---

[252] Doninger v. Niehoff, 527 F.3d 41, 51 (2nd Cir. 2008).

[253] *Id.*

[254] *See Appeals Court Won't Reinstate Conn. Student to Class Office During Free-Speech Challenge*, STUDENT PRESS L. CTR. NEWSFLASH, May 30, 2008, http://www.splc.org/news/newsflash_archives.asp.

[255] Doninger v. Niehoff, 642 F.3d 334, 351 (2d Cir. 2011) ("Under the qualified immunity doctrine, government officials such as the school administrators here are shielded from liability for civil damages insofar as their conduct does not violate clearly established statutory or constitutional rights of which a reasonable person would have known.") (internal quotations and citation omitted).

[256] *Id.* at 350 (internal quotations and citation omitted). The court found the administrators also entitled to qualified immunity on a second issue in the case. School officials had prevented Doninger from wearing a T-shirt related to the controversy to a school election assembly. The shirt included the phrase "Team Avery" on the front and "Support LSM Freedom of Speech" on the back. The court held that, although "a reasonable fact-finder could conclude that [the school was] mistaken" because any disruption from the shirt would likely not have satisfied *Tinker's* standard, "[W]e conclude any such mistake was reasonable...the very sort of mistake for which the qualified immunity doctrine exists to shield officials against unwarranted liability." *Id.* at 351, 355.

[257] Ken Paulson, *2nd Circuit Sides with Conn. School in Dispute Over Off-campus Speech*, FIRST AMENDMENT CTR. ONLINE, Apr. 26, 2011, http://www.firstamendment center.org.

[258] 593 F.3d 249 (3d Cir. 2010).

[259] 593 F.3d 286 (3d Cir. 2010).

[260] Layshock v. Hermitage Sch. Dist., 650 F.3d 205, 216 (3d Cir. 2011).

[261] J.S. v. Blue Mountain Sch. Dist., 650 F.3d 915, 920 (3d Cir. 2011).

[262] *Id.* at 930.

[263] *Id.* at 936 (Smith, J., concurring).

Six judges dissented, arguing that *Tinker* applied and that disruption from the profile was reasonably foreseeable. The dissenting opinion chided the majority for "misconstru[ing] the facts" and allowing a student "to target a school official and his family with malicious and unfounded accusations about their character in vulgar, obscene, and personal language."[264]

The lawyer representing the students in both *Layshock* and *J.S.* said that although the Third Circuit decisions offered harmony between cases (and victories for the students), they did not bring clarity to a confused area of law, as neither decision clearly established which legal standard applies to off-campus speech.[265] That confusion remains.

Doninger, J.S., and *Layshock* involved middle or high school students, but college students also have found themselves entangled in legal disputes over their online speech — and courts have similarly wrestled with what standard to apply.

In one much-publicized case, Amanda Tatro, a student in the mortuary science department at the University of Minnesota, was punished for a series of Facebook posts she made in 2009. In one, she wrote that she "gets to play, I mean dissect, Bernie today" — which was the name she had given to the donated cadaver on which she was working. In another post, she wrote that she wanted to use an embalming tool "to stab a certain someone in the throat."[266] A fellow student reported the comments to university officials, who filed a formal complaint against Tatro, alleging she violated the school's student conduct code by engaging in "threatening, harassing, or assaultive conduct" and by engaging in conduct "contrary to university rules related to the mortuary-science program." As punishment, Tatro was given a failing grade in the course and required to enroll in an ethics course, write a letter of apology, and complete a psychiatric evaluation. She also was placed on academic probation for the remainder of her undergraduate career.

Tatro sued in state court. In 2011, the Minnesota Court of Appeals sided with the school. It relied on *Tinker* and ruled that Tatro's posts caused a material and substantial disruption and could be punished. The court said her posts worried school officials, necessitated an investigation and caused funeral directors and families who had donated cadavers to call the program and express concern about its professionalism.

Tatro then appealed to the state supreme court, arguing that *Tinker* should be inapplicable to a college student's online speech. The university, on the other hand, argued that *Hazelwood* actually should govern the case. In 2012, the Minnesota Supreme Court issued its decision and followed neither Tatro nor the university — nor did it apply *Tinker,* as the court of appeals had. Instead the state supreme court upheld Tatro's punishment on a different ground. It concluded that Tatro's posts violated the rules for her mortuary science program and she could thus be punished. "[W]e hold that a university does not violate the free speech rights of a student enrolled in a professional program," the court ruled, "when the university imposes sanctions for Facebook posts that violate academic program rules that are narrowly tailored and directly related to established professional conduct standards."[267] The court emphasized what it said were the unique circumstances of a case that involved "a program that gives students access to donated human cadavers and requires a high degree of sensitivity."[268] In the wake of the decision, student speech advocates said they hope the opinion is worded carefully enough that it will restrict other courts from applying it beyond fields "that have formalized standards, such as medicine and law."[269]

SUMMARY

In public institutions, students have many rights other citizens have, and administrators are considered public officials subject to some of the same constitutional restrictions all government officials face. But freedoms of speech and press have limits in the schools. The reach and power of cyberspace also blur some legal distinctions among and within educational institutions.

The legal springboard for student free-speech rights is the Supreme Court's 1969 ruling in *Tinker v. Des Moines Independent Community School District,* which stressed the value of free expression and held that school officials could stop student speech only by showing that the expression would substantially disrupt the school or infringe on the rights of others. Hundreds of public school cases during the next seventeen years were based on *Tinker* and its premise that free speech should be encouraged, even in school.

Some educators, especially in high schools, continued to argue for different regulatory standards based on school officials' responsibility to teach the young. That plus the relative immaturity of students and the need for an environment conducive to learning were reasons administrators gave for denying students freedom in school that they might have elsewhere.

The Supreme Court eventually agreed that free-speech distinctions and tighter restrictions may be appropriate when dealing with the health, safety and well-being of high school students. Until recently, students in post-secondary schools have been considered adults, with generally the same First Amend-

---

[264] *Id.* at 941 (Fisher, J., dissenting).

[265] *See Third Circuit Sides With Students in Online Speech Fight,* STUDENT PRESS L. CTR. NEWSFLASH, June 13, 2011, http://www.splc.org/news/newsflash_archives.asp.

[266] Tatro v. Univ. of Minn., 816 N.W.2d 509, 512 (Minn. 2012).

[267] *Id.* at 521.

[268] *Id.* at 524.

[269] *Minn. High Court: University Can Discipline Student for Online Cadaver Comments,* STUDENT PRESS L. CTR. NEWSFLASH, June 20, 2012, http://www.splc.org/news/newsflash_archives.asp.

ment rights accorded adults elsewhere in society. A lower court in Kentucky tried to apply *Hazelwood School District v. Kuhlmeier* to a yearbook at the college level before an appellate court overturned the ruling. *Kincaid v. Gibson* removed some uncertainty about the context for free expression on college campuses, distancing student publications there from the restrictive free-speech rationale of *Hazelwood*. The Seventh Circuit's 2005 ruling in *Hosty v. Carter* kept ties to *Hazelwood* alive and implied that college publications should clearly be identified as limited public forums to remain censorship-free, but that threat has not moved nationwide.

College students have successfully challenged speech and conduct codes that the courts ruled too broad and restrictive, and college journalists have had some success in the Congress and the courts during frequent battles for access to campus crime information. High school officials have found it easier to restrict expression, but student journalists have tried to curb censorship by getting their schools to recognize the student press as a public forum. Social media and the Internet, with their ease of access, wealth of information and potential for abuse and harm, have imposed added responsibility on school officials. As they gauge public opinion, balance the risk and reach of cyberspeech and consider their obligation to protect vulnerable youth, school authorities seem more willing to err on the side of close regulation, within and beyond the confines of the school. The courts, therefore, likely will remain the arbiter of the struggle for free expression.

FOR ADDITIONAL READING

Clery Center for Security on Campus, http://clerycenter.org/
College Media Association, http://www.collegemedia.org/
Journalism Education Association, http://jeasprc.org/
Law of the Student Press, 4th ed. Arlington, Va.: Student Press Law Center, 2013.
Student Press Law Center, http://www.splc.org/

8

Regulating Advertising

By Robert L. Kerr

➡️ **Headnote Questions**

- What is commercial speech?
- How has constitutional protection for commercial speech changed over the years?
- Why doesn't commercial speech get the same First Amendment protection as other forms of speech?
- What is the four-part test courts use to determine the constitutionality of government restrictions on commercial speech?
- What is the Federal Trade Commission's role in regulating advertising?
- How does the Federal Trade Commission define deceptive advertising?
- What remedies can the Federal Trade Commission use to stop deceptive ads from being disseminated?
- What other remedies are available to prevent the dissemination of deceptive ads?
- How does the advertising industry regulate itself?

In announcing some four decades ago the beginning of the age of First Amendment protection for advertising, Justice Harry Blackmun observed, "So long as we preserve a predominantly free enterprise economy, the allocation of our resources in large measure will be made through numerous private economic decisions. It is a matter of public interest that those decisions, in the aggregate, be intelligent and well informed."[1] Writing in 1976, Justice Blackmun could not have imagined the dizzying degree to which technology would soon make it possible for rapidly escalating advertising techniques to enter every nook and cranny of the private lives in which those economic decisions would be made.

When Blackmun died in 1994, he would have been familiar with a world in which advertising was widely present in consumers' lives *via* television and radio, in newspapers and magazines, on billboards and buses, selling everything from the latest movie to the next president. But he could have known nothing about the way social media like Facebook and countless other digital, cyber-networked entities would soon be able to collect and market infinitely more data than ever before on virtually every aspect of consumers' activities, making their economic decisions less private than ever, if indeed truly private at all. He could not have known of the imminent arrival of peer-to-peer

and viral marketing in which individuals would be paid to surveil and influence, often surreptitiously, the economic decisions of friends and neighbors in cyberspace, or of a blogosphere in which untold streams of apparent social commentary would actually be commercially purposed. He probably could not have imagined an age in which the story lines of so many tales told *via* film, television, Webcast, graphic novel, video game and even textbook would be shaped to one degree or another by product placements, or one when technology giants like Google would consider ways to advertise inside individuals' automobiles, on their wristwatches and eyeglasses, and in their homes via wired devices such as their thermostats. As Ronald Collins and David Skover have characterized it, advertising today often has "less to do with facts than image" and advances "more a total cultural system" in which "truth is that which sells."[2]

In an age when so much traditional advertising has morphed into forms more difficult to test for truth, advertising nevertheless remains a highly regulated field. Despite so many technological changes, the legal basis continues for commercial messages to be regulated at the federal level most directly by the Federal Trade Commission, but also by agencies such as the Food and Drug Administration and the Securities and Exchange Commission. Similar agencies at the state level also regulate

---

[1] Virginia State Bd. of Pharmacy v. Virginia Citizens Consumer Council, 425 U.S. 748, 765 (1976).

[2] Ronald K.L. Collins & David M. Skover, *Commerce and Communication*, 71 TEX. L. REV. 697, 710 (1993).

advertising. At the same time, advertising is protected from such regulation in more ways than ever by a First Amendment doctrine that has evolved dramatically over the years since the landmark ruling in which Justice Blackmun framed the matter in terms of the public interest.

That dramatic evolution of First Amendment doctrine on commercial speech since the 1970s and the parade of cases that have shaped it have generated extensive scholarly debate over whether the broadened protections have gone too far or not far enough. And the most recent ruling on the subject by the U.S. Supreme Court suggests it may be prepared to push the evolution of the doctrine considerably further.

Cases continue to test the Court's definition of commercial speech as expression that does "no more than propose a commercial transaction" or is "solely motivated by the desire for profit."[3] Scholars continue to debate whether it is paternalistic to provide consumers with some protection from unscrupulous advertisers or whether advertising techniques have largely surpassed consumers' abilities to detect deception. The tension in the debate is inherent in the reality of commercial speech's dual nature. It is speech that both conveys information and establishes transactional promises between buyer and seller. In the political-social context, informational speech receives almost absolute First Amendment protection from government restriction. But in the well established context of preserving the fair-bargaining process, expression involved in contractual arrangements "is not the sort of 'speech' to which the First Amendment Applies."[4] Thus, arguments that commercial speech should be treated identically to political speech face the enduring question of "why a government that can regulate an underlying commercial transaction should not be able to regulate speech promoting the same commercial transaction."[5]

CONSTITUTIONAL PROTECTION FOR COMMERCIAL SPEECH

While the debate continues, it is clear that the commercial speech doctrine today is a far different one from the mid-twentieth century era when the Supreme Court dispatched the question of First Amendment protection for advertising almost dismissively.[6] In *Valentine v. Chrestensen* in 1942, the Court deemed that its answer required only a four-page opinion and declared unanimously that no such protection was justified be-

cause the "Constitution imposes no ... restraint on government as respects purely commercial advertising."[7]

That challenge reached the Court through the creative efforts of F.J. Chrestensen to promote tours of a Navy submarine he had moored at a pier in New York City. Upon learning that passing out commercial fliers advertising his tours to pedestrians violated a city anti-litter code — which did not apply to political handbills — Chrestensen had his fliers reprinted with a message on the flip side criticizing the city law. Despite his assertion that his speech thus had been rendered political and protected, police officials said he was still violating the ordinance, and he sued to enjoin the government from interfering with his distribution of advertising that he argued was constitutionally protected. The Court rejected his challenge, declaring that the "affixing of the protest against official conduct to the advertising circular" was clearly only "for the purpose of evading the prohibition of the ordinance," but noting that future cases could well involve more complicated questions in this area of First Amendment law.[8]

And how they have. Over the course of a long series of cases moving far beyond some key elements of *Valentine*, the Court has focused on shaping a doctrine that continues to sharply distinguish commercial from political expression, but emphasizes protection for truthful advertising on the reasoning that it advances a public good for consumers to receive accurate commercial information.[9] At the same time, the Court's holdings in those cases have not wavered on the government's power to regulate false or deceptive advertising.

The Court first signaled the potential for a shift away from *Valentine*'s rejection of First Amendment protection for advertising in 1964's *New York Times Co. v. Sullivan*,[10] in the course of constitutionalizing libel law in that landmark ruling. The case involved a full-page advertisement for a civil rights organization published in the *New York Times* that criticized officials in Montgomery, Alabama, for their handling of civil rights protests and sought financial support for the civil rights movement. L.B. Sullivan, the Montgomery police commissioner, brought the libel action, contending that false assertions in the ad regarding police activity had defamed him. His attorneys maintained that *Valentine*'s holding meant the *Times* could argue no First Amendment defense in the case, because the alleged libel appeared in an advertisement.[11] But the Court found that argument "wholly misplaced" in that the speech in question in *Valentine* had amounted to an effort "to evade" a city ordinance in order to promote a commercial venture while the speech in *Sul-*

---

[3] Pittsburgh Press Co. v. Pittsburgh Comm'n on Human Relations et al., 413 U.S. 376, 385 (1973). *See also* Dun & Bradstreet v. Greenmoss Builders, Inc., 472 U.S. 749, 762 (1985).

[4] Daniel A. Farber, *Commercial Speech and First Amendment Theory*, 74 NW. L. REV. 372, 386-87 (1979).

[5] Reza R Dibadj, *The Political Economy of Commercial Speech*, 58 S.C. L. REV. 913, 930 (2007).

[6] *See* Valentine v. Chrestensen, 316 U.S. 52 (1942).

[7] *Id.* at 54.

[8] *Id.* at 55.

[9] *Virginia State Bd.,* 425 U.S. 748, 765 (1976).

[10] 376 U.S. 254 (1964).

[11] *Id.* at 265.

livan concerned "matters of the highest public interest and concern." It held that in the context of the facts of that case, the advertising format alone could not bar the speech involved from First Amendment protection,[12] which eventually offered the opening for other cases to make their way toward the Court on other commercial-speech questions.

Nine years later, in *Pittsburgh Press Co. v. Pittsburgh Commission on Human Relations*, the newspaper challenging a city regulation barring help-wanted advertisements segregated according to male or female interest, asked the Court to "abrogate the distinction between commercial and other speech."[13] The Court suggested that it might be willing to give constitutional protection to "an ordinary commercial proposal" but found that the facts of *Pittsburgh Press* did not warrant it because "discrimination in employment is not only commercial activity, it is illegal commercial activity."[14]

In rejecting the newspaper's argument, the Court said the help-wanted ads resembled the speech in *Valentine* more than that of *Sullivan* in that the help-wanted ads did not express a position on "whether, as a matter of social policy, certain positions ought to be filed by members of one or the other sex, nor ... criticize the ordinance." Because a help-wanted ad "is no more than a proposal of possible employment," it represented "classic examples of commercial speech."[15] The Court noted, however, that it might well consider some degree of First Amendment protection for advertising for an ordinary commercial proposal not tainted by illegality.[16]

The next year provided evidence of how difficult the Court found sorting out the questions involved in First Amendment protection for commercial speech to be when it was unable to form a majority for an opinion in a case involving a challenge to a ban on political advertising on city buses in *Lehman v. City of Shaker Heights*.[17] While a majority upheld the ban, only three justices joined the plurality opinion by Justice Harry Blackmun that declared the buses did not constitute a public forum for First Amendment purposes, so the city was free to allow commercial advertising on cards posted inside the buses while not accepting political advertising, because the city was only "engaged in commerce" in providing bus service.[18]

A year after that, seven justices found greater agreement in declaring unconstitutional a Virginia statute that banned publication of any advertisement for abortion services. In *Bigelow v.*

Virginia,[19] the Court distinguished the ad in question, noting that it contained truthful information for a service that was legal in the state where the abortion services were offered (New York) and of public interest in the state where it was published (Virginia), even though abortions were illegal there.[20] While once again holding that commercial speech was thus not without constitutional protection, the Court still declined to decide "the precise extent to which the First Amendment permits regulation of advertising that is related to activities the State may legitimately regulate or even prohibit."[21] *Bigelow* came just two years after the 1973 ruling in *Roe v. Wade* that abortion was part of the constitutionally protected right of privacy.[22]

Expanding Protection for Purely Commercial Speech

After that series of cases, in which the Court established its willingness to protect political ads as well as ads promoting legal activities in the public interest, it squarely addressed the issue of First Amendment protection for purely commercial advertisements in 1976 in *Virginia State Board of Pharmacy v. Virginia Citizens Consumer Council*.[23] In striking down a state prohibition on pharmacists advertising the price of prescription drugs, the Court focused on preventing government from blocking the dissemination of truthful information to citizens: "Virginia is free to require whatever professional standards it wishes of its pharmacists.... But it may not do so by keeping the public in ignorance of the entirely lawful terms that competing pharmacists are offering."[24] The pharmacy board had argued that the restriction was necessary to avoid pressure on pharmacists to participate in aggressive price competition rather than developing relationships with customers, possibly endangering consumers' health and harming the pharmacists' status as professionals, and potentially pushing some conscientious pharmacists out of business while raising advertising costs that would be passed on to consumers in the form of higher drug prices.

It was not pharmacists who challenged the regulation, but the non-profit Virginia Citizens Consumer Council, which was not actually barred from advertising pharmaceutical prices, as Justice William Rehnquist noted in a dissenting opinion.[25] The group argued, however, that consumers had a First Amendment right to *receive* information from pharmacists, which would allow them to find the drugs they needed at the best prices.

In agreeing, the Supreme Court recognized for the first time

---

[12] *Id.* at 266.
[13] 413 U.S. 376, 388 (1973).
[14] *Id.* at 388, 389.
[15] *Id.* at 385.
[16] *Id.* at 389.
[17] 418 U.S. 298 (1974).
[18] *Id.* at 303.

[19] 421 U.S. 809 (1975).
[20] *Id.* at 821-23.
[21] *Id.* at 824-25.
[22] 410 U.S. 113 (1973).
[23] 425 U.S. 748 (1976).
[24] *Id.* at 770.
[25] *Id.* at 781-84 (Rehnquist, J., dissenting).

that the First Amendment protects purely commercial advertising by focusing on "the free flow of commercial information," noting that a consumer's interest in commercial information "may be as keen, if not keener by far, than his interest in the day's most urgent political debate."[26] That free flow of information, the Court reasoned, is also crucial to the development of intelligent opinions about how to reform or regulate the economic system.[27]

It emphasized, however, that the government was still free to regulate ads that were false, misleading, deceptive or that promote illegal products or services, making clear that the First Amendment "does not prohibit the State from insuring that the stream of commercial information flow cleanly as well as freely."[28] The Court also detailed why "commonsense differences" between commercial speech and other, protected types of speech made government regulation of untruthful commercial speech more tolerable. First, advertisers may easily verify their commercial speech because they disseminate information about their own product or service and, therefore, know more about it than anyone else. In contrast, reporters and political commentators must rely on other sources as the basis for the information they distribute. Second, commercial speech is hardier than other types of speech because it is so necessary for generating profits that regulation would not chill an advertiser's speech.[29]

A year later, the Court emphasized its focus on preventing government from denying citizens truthful information in declaring unconstitutional a city ban on the posting of signs advertising homes for sale in *Linmark Associates v. Willingboro*.[30] The purpose of the ordinance was argued as promoting racial integration by preventing "panic selling ... by whites who feared that the township was becoming all black, and that property values would decline."[31] The Court declared, however, that if "dissemination of this information can be restricted, then every locality in the country can suppress any facts that reflect poorly on the locality," and that restricting government from denying citizens "information that is neither false nor misleading" was precisely the point of *Virginia Pharmacy*.[32]

The same year, the Court similarly relied on *Virginia Pharmacy* to invalidate an Arizona state bar regulation that prohibited lawyers from advertising prices for legal services in the mass media in *Bates v. State Bar of Arizona*.[33] The state bar had argued that advertising would make lawyers less dignified

and professional, stir up unnecessary lawsuits, and also result in higher costs for legal services. The Supreme Court rejected all of those arguments, asserting that *Virginia Pharmacy* made it clear that the "choice between the dangers of suppressing information and the dangers arising from its free flow was seen as precisely the choice 'that the First Amendment makes for us.'"[34] Because people who have a legitimate need for legal services may not know where to turn for advice or may be afraid that legal services will cost too much, advertising could help them in such situations, the Court noted.[35] It also emphasized its view that there was nothing inherently misleading about lawyers advertising the cost of routine legal services as important to its decision, because "the leeway for untruthful or misleading expression that has been allowed in other contexts has little force in the commercial arena."[36]

A year later, the Court found cause to qualify its holding on advertising by attorneys in *Ohralik v. Ohio State Bar Association*.[37] The case involved a First Amendment challenge to sanctions against an attorney who had utilized undue influence and misrepresentation in ways Justice Thurgood Marshall called "classic examples of 'ambulance chasing'" to induce two 18-year-old women to hire him to represent them in relation to an automobile accident in which they were injured.[38] In a unanimous ruling, the Court declared that in-person solicitation by attorneys "does not stand on a par with truthful advertising about the availability and terms of routine legal services, let alone with forms of speech more traditionally within the concern of the First Amendment." More broadly, the *Ohralik* opinion authored by Justice Lewis Powell reasserted why distinctions between advertising and more protected expression were justified. It emphasized that the Court's decisions had "afforded commercial speech a limited measure of protection, commensurate with its subordinate position in the scale of First Amendment values" and that requiring equal protection for commercial and non-commercial speech "could invite dilution, simply by a leveling process, of the force of the Amendment's guarantee with respect to the latter kind of speech."[39]

The Central Hudson Test

Two years later, Justice Powell went much further to formally establish the commercial-speech doctrine for maintaining the distinction between advertising and more protected expression. In *Central Hudson Gas & Electric Co. v. Public Service Com-*

---

[26] *Id.* at 763, 765.
[27] *Id.* at 765.
[28] *Id.* at 771-72.
[29] *Id.* at 772 n.24.
[30] 431 U.S. 86 (1977).
[31] *Id.* at 88.
[32] *Id.* at 96-97.
[33] 433 U.S. 350 (1977).

[34] *Id.* at 365 (quoting 425 U.S. at 770).
[35] *Id.* at 370.
[36] *Id.* at 372.
[37] 436 U.S. 447 (1978).
[38] *Id.* at 449-453, 469.
[39] *Id.* at 456.

mission of New York,[40] he enunciated a formal test for determining the extent of First Amendment protection for commercial speech. In striking down a New York state law that sought to conserve energy by banning all advertising that promoted the use of electricity, the Court put forth a standardized four-part test of intermediate scrutiny to determine whether a government regulation on advertising is constitutional.

The test, as articulated in *Central Hudson* and applied to the facts of that case,[41] unfolded in this manner:

(1) The test first asks *whether the advertising that is regulated is misleading and whether it concerns a legal product or service*. Neither a misleading ad nor one for an illegal product or service receives any First Amendment protection. In *Central Hudson*, the New York Public Service Commission did not claim that the advertising at issue was misleading, deceptive or for any illegal activity. So that meant the Court's analysis continued to the second question.

(2) The second part of the *Central Hudson* test asks *whether the asserted governmental interest is substantial*. This part of the test requires government to show that it has a substantial interest in protecting the health, safety, morals and aesthetics of the public — rather than a compelling interest, a much more rigorous standard which the Court considers very few government interests to meet. In *Central Hudson*, the government's asserted interest in energy conservation was certainly a substantial one, the Court concluded.

(3) Third, the *Central Hudson* test asks *whether the regulation directly advances the asserted governmental interest*. In *Central Hudson*, the Court found there must be an immediate connection between advertising and electrical consumption, because otherwise the company would not have been advertising. Therefore, a restriction on advertising would reduce electrical consumption, directly advancing the government's interest.

(4) Finally, the test asks *whether the regulation is "not more extensive than necessary" to serve the governmental interest*. In *Central Hudson*, the Court concluded that the regulation there failed the test, finding it to be more extensive than necessary because it banned ads even for electric services or devices that were energy efficient.

Thus, the Court ruled that because the challenged regulation reached "all promotional advertising, regardless of the impact ... on overall energy use ... the energy conservation rationale, as important as it is, cannot justify suppressing information" that could reduce total energy consumption.[42]

Three years later, the Court provided its most substantial guidance for distinguishing between commercial and noncommercial speech in 1983's *Bolger v. Youngs Drug Products Corp.*[43] To determine if a condom manufacturer's flyers and pamphlets promoting its products — but also discussing venereal disease and family planning — could be considered commercial messages subject to federal regulation, the Court developed a three-part test that considered the combination of the advertising format of the messages, reference to a specific product, and the economic motivation for disseminating the messages.[44] It stressed that one of those three factors by itself would not necessarily prove dispositive; but, when considered together, the messages in question were "properly characterized as commercial speech ... notwithstanding the fact that they contain discussions of important public issues."[45] Further, the Court emphasized advertisers' ability to separate commercial messages from noncommercial messages: "A company has the full panoply of protections available to its direct comments on public issues, so there is no reason for providing similar constitutional protection when such statements are made in the context of commercial transactions."[46]

In 1986, the Court applied the test in *Posadas de Puerto Rico Associates v. Tourism Company of Puerto Rico* and upheld a ban on casino ads in Puerto Rico.[47] The island had legalized gambling to promote tourism but banned casino ads because it did not want to encourage Puerto Ricans to gamble.

The majority applied the *Central Hudson* test and found the ban to be constitutional in that its restriction on a form of commercial speech advanced a substantial government interest (promoting the public welfare by reducing demand for gambling) in a manner that was no more extensive than necessary.[48] Writing in dissent, however, Justice William J. Brennan argued that *Posadas* had gone too far beyond the Court's prior commercial-speech cases that had accepted regulation of "dissemination of information that is false, deceptive, or misleading ... or that proposes an illegal transaction," but not restrictions "designed to deprive consumers of accurate information about products and services legally offered for sale."[49] Justice Rehnquist's majority opinion asserted that even though casino gambling was legal in Puerto Rico, "[T]he Puerto Rico Legislature surely could have prohibited casino gambling by the residents of Puerto Rico altogether. In our view, the greater power to completely ban casino gambling necessarily includes the lesser power to ban advertising of casino gambling."[50]

---

[40] 447 U.S. 557 (1980).
[41] *Id.* at 566-70.
[42] *Id.* at 570.

[43] 463 U.S. 60 (1983).
[44] *Id.* at 62-63, 65-68.
[45] *Id.* at 67-68.
[46] *Id.* at 68.
[47] 478 U.S. 328 (1986).
[48] *Id.* at 340-44.
[49] *Id.* at 350 (Brennan, J., dissenting).
[50] *Id.* at 345-46.

Three years later, a regulation by the State University of New York prohibiting private commercial activities in university facilities was upheld in *Board of Trustees, State University of New York v. Fox.*[51] The university said the regulation sought to prevent commercial exploitation of students, maintain an educational atmosphere on campus, promote student safety, and protect residential tranquility. In applying the *Central Hudson* test, the Court interpreted the meaning of the fourth part of the test as asking whether a reasonable fit existed between the asserted governmental interest and the challenged regulation — "a fit that is not necessarily perfect, but reasonable" or "narrowly tailored to achieve the desired objective."

Recent Cases and Trends

The potential weakening of protection for advertising in *Posadas* and *Board of Trustees* was counterbalanced by rulings in the 1990s that stiffened the government's burden in the *Central Hudson* test, particularly the third and fourth prongs. In 1993's *Cincinnati v. Discovery Network,*[52] the Court ruled unconstitutional a city ban on use of newsracks on city streets to distribute commercial handbills. It found a lack of reasonable fit between the city's purpose of promoting the safety and aesthetics of public streets and the banning of commercial, but not noncommercial, news racks.[53] It emphasized that the ban's distinction between commercial and noncommercial speech bore "no relationship whatsoever to the particular interests that the city has asserted" because "commercial newsracks are no greater an eyesore than the [noncommercial] newsracks permitted."[54]

The same year, in *Edenfield v. Fane,*[55] the Court ruled unconstitutional a state ban on certified public accountants' personal solicitation of prospective clients, declaring the state had not demonstrated that the regulation advanced the interests asserted. To the contrary, the Court found the rule threatened citizens' access to complete and accurate commercial information, because the speech in question sought "to communicate no more than truthful, non-deceptive information proposing a lawful commercial transaction."[56] The Court, also in 1993, upheld a federal law prohibiting lottery advertising by radio stations located in states where lotteries are not legal, applying the *Central Hudson* test to conclude that the regulation advanced North Carolina's anti-gambling policy without unduly interfering with lotteries sponsored by nearby States.[57]

In the mid 1990s, the Court began moving even more aggressively to strengthen the *Central Hudson* test, and to emphasize sharply its determination to protect the dissemination of truthful, factual information from government regulation that seeks to discourage activities that are otherwise legal. In 1995, the Court held a federal law prohibiting beer labels from advertising alcohol content to be unconstitutional because it failed both the third and fourth prongs of the *Central Hudson* test. In *Rubin v. Coors Brewing Co.,*[58] the government had asserted that allowing alcohol content on beer labels would lead to strength wars among brewers, which would in turn lead to an increase in alcoholism. The Court held that although preventing strength wars did represent a substantial interest, the government had failed to meet its burden of showing that the regulation advanced its interest in a "direct and material way."[59] The federal government allowed the labels of distilled spirits to disclose alcohol content, required the labels of some wine bottles to do so and did not prohibit brewers from indicating alcohol content in advertisements.[60] Additionally, the regulation failed the Court's application of the fourth prong, the Court concluded, because there were less restrictive alternatives that would have advanced the government's interest, such as directly limiting the alcohol content of beer or prohibiting marketing that emphasized strong alcohol content.[61]

The next year, in *44 Liquormart v. Rhode Island,* the Court unanimously struck down two Rhode Island statutes that prohibited the advertisement of alcohol prices anywhere in the state except at the point of purchase.[62] The state maintained that the ban served the substantial government interest of reducing alcohol consumption among its residents, because if alcohol retailers could advertise their prices, prices would fall and consumption would rise.

The Court was splintered in its reasoning, however, with no more than four justices agreeing on what test should be applied to the commercial-speech regulations and a majority agreeing only on the judgment and the application of the Twenty-First Amendment to the issue. Justice John Paul Stevens delivered the Court's opinion concerning the Twenty-First Amendment issue and the facts and procedure of the case, but no more than three justices joined him in any other parts of his opinion. On the question of the Twenty-First Amendment's grant to states of broad regulatory power over the commerce of alcohol, the Court held that the "Twenty-first Amendment does not qualify the constitutional prohibition against laws abridging the freedom of

---

[51] 492 U.S. 469 (1989).

[52] 507 U.S. 410 (1993).

[53] *Id.* at 417.

[54] *Id.* at 424-425.

[55] 507 U.S. 761 (1993).

[56] *Id.* at 765.

[57] United States v. Edge Broad., 514 U.S. 418 (1993).

[58] 514 U.S. 476 (1995) (striking down 27 U.S.C. § 205(e)(2)(1995)).

[59] *Id.* at 490.

[60] *Id.* at 488.

[61] *Id.* at 490-91.

[62] 517 U.S. 484 (1996).

speech embodied in the First Amendment."[63] Because the state presented no evidentiary support, the Court said it could not agree that the ban would significantly advance the state's interest in promoting temperance.[64]

Only two justices joined Stevens' argument that more rigorous scrutiny than *Central Hudson* intermediate scrutiny should be applied to regulations that entirely prohibit "the dissemination of truthful, nonmisleading commercial messages for reasons unrelated to the preservation of a fair bargaining process."[65] Four justices specifically rejected any such departure from the *Central Hudson* test for considering First Amendment protection of commercial speech, declaring that the challenged regulation would fail the fourth prong of the test because it was more extensive than necessary to serve its stated interest.[66]

In a part of Stevens' opinion joined by three other justices, the Court indicated that its earlier decision in *Posadas* was incorrect. "*Posadas* erroneously performed the First Amendment analysis," the Court held, declaring that the government "does not have the broad discretion to suppress truthful, non-misleading information."[67] A plurality declared that, henceforth, the Court would apply a more stringent constitutional review when the government completely suppresses truthful expression.[68]

In *Lorillard Tobacco v. Reilly*,[69] the Court noted that petitioners challenging state regulations on outdoor tobacco advertising urged the Court to "reject the *Central Hudson* analysis and apply strict scrutiny" on the grounds that some justices in the earlier cases had "expressed doubts about the *Central Hudson* analysis and whether it should apply in certain cases.[70] Pointing out that the same argument had been raised in *Greater New Orleans Broadcasting v. United States*[71] two years earlier, the *Lorillard* Court found, as in that case, "[N]o need to break new ground. *Central Hudson*, as applied in our more recent commercial speech cases, provides an adequate basis for decision."[72] So in *Lorillard*, the Court applied the *Central Hudson* test and concluded that the regulations involving advertising of cigars and smokeless tobacco failed the test as more extensive than necessary to advance the government's substantial interest

in preventing underage tobacco use.[73] It declared that while the government's interest in preventing minors' tobacco use was

[S]ubstantial, and even compelling ... it is no less true that the sale and use of tobacco products by adults is a legal activity. We must consider that tobacco retailers and manufacturers have an interest in conveying truthful information about their products to adults, and adults have a corresponding interest in receiving truthful information about tobacco products.[74]

In 2009, Congress enacted the Family Smoking Prevention and Tobacco Control Act, giving the Food and Drug Administration extensive regulatory control over tobacco.[75] Tobacco companies then challenged FDA guidelines that required a significant portion of tobacco packaging be reserved for health warnings, restricted commercial marketing of "modified risk tobacco products" (those promoted as representing relatively less risk of disease or harm than others), banned statements that convey the impression FDA regulation means that tobacco products are safer, limited the use of colorful tobacco displays and ads, barred the distribution of free samples of tobacco products in most locations as well as brand-name tobacco sponsorship of athletic and social events, and banned "continuity programs" (distribution of free items as rewards for tobacco purchase). A district court judge upheld most of the regulations, though not the limitations on use of colorful displays and ads and the ban on statements of relative safety.[76] A federal appeals court, in 2012, affirmed most of the lower court ruling, but reversed its striking down of the ban on statements of relative safety and its upholding of the ban on continuity programs.[77] Application of the *Central Hudson* test was central to both rulings. In a second challenge, brought against the FDA's newest guidelines under the act, which call for graphic warnings on cigarette packs and in advertising about the health consequences of tobacco use, another district court judge applied strict scrutiny rather than the *Central Hudson* test in striking down the regulation.[78] A federal appeals court held that the *Central Hudson* test was the appropriate standard, but that the government had failed to satisfy the test's burden of showing that the regulation directly advanced the government's interest in reducing smoking rates.[79]

In *Thompson v. Western States Medical Center*, the Court

---

63 *Id.* at 516 (plurality).
64 *Id.* at 505 (plurality).
65 *Id.* at 501 (plurality).
66 *Id.* at 528-34 (Thomas, J., concurring in part and in the judgment).
67 *Id.* at 509-10 (plurality).
68 *Id.* at 508 (plurality).
69 533 U.S. 525, (2001).
70 *Id.* at 554.
71 527 U.S. 173 (1999). The Court ruled unconstitutional federal regulations that prohibited casino gambling advertisements broadcast by stations located in states where such gambling was legal, holding that the government had failed to meet the *Central Hudson* burden of showing that the regulation directly advanced the government's interest in reducing harmful effects of gambling.
72 533 U.S. at 554-55.

73 *Id.* at 540-67.
74 *Id.* at 564.
75 Family Smoking Prevention and Tobacco Control Act, PL 111-31 (2009).
76 Commonwealth Brands Inc. et al. v. United States, 678 F. Supp. 2d 512 (W.D. Ky. 2010).
77 Discount Tobacco City & Lottery. et al. v. United States, 674 F.3d 509 (6th Cir. 2012), *cert. den.* 133 S.Ct. 1996 (2013).
78 R.J. Reynolds, et al. v. F.D.A., 845 F. Supp. 2d 266 (D.D.C. 2012).
79 R.J. Reynolds, et al. v. F.D.A, 696 F.3d 1205 (D.C. Cir. 2012).

struck down provisions of the federal Food and Drug Administration Modernization Act of 1997 that precluded pharmacists from advertising compounded drugs.[80] Under the FDAMA, compounded drugs — those custom-made for patients by pharmacists — did not have to comply with the FDA's drug approval process if providers refrained from advertising or promoting them. This restriction sought to balance the government's interests in protecting public health through the FDA approval process for manufactured drugs and continuing to permit pharmacists to compound drugs that had not been tested for safety or efficacy. After a group of licensed pharmacies challenged the limitation as a violation of their free-speech rights, the Supreme Court ruled 5-4 that the restriction was too broad. While acknowledging that protecting the integrity of the FDA's drug approval process was a substantial interest, the Court held that the interest could have been advanced by other means that did not include restrictions on speech: "We have made clear that if the Government could achieve its interests in a manner that does not restrict speech, or that restricts less speech, the Government must do so."[81]

Thus, over the years since it first enunciated a test for commercial speech cases, the Court has expanded protection for such speech, but no majority has found a need to depart from the *Central Hudson* test. Although some justices have argued for equal protection for noncommercial speech and truthful, non-misleading commercial speech, the Court's holdings have focused on preventing government from denying citizens truthful information while maintaining *Central Hudson* as an effective means for achieving that. Thus, the Court's commercial speech doctrine has placed a priority on protecting truth in advertising. Scholarship has asserted that the *Hudson*-centric doctrine has endured so long and despite challenges because of the way the Court's four-part test successfully institutionalized a difficult balancing between protecting the informational component of advertising and maintaining preservation of the fair-bargaining process in its contractual component.[82]

Questions Raised About the Future of the Doctrine

However, in its most recent major commercial-speech case, the Court raised considerable questions as to where its doctrine may be headed. In *Sorrell v. IMS Health Inc.*, decided in 2011, the Court ruled unconstitutional a Vermont statue that restricted the sale, disclosure and use of prescriber histories for marketing purposes without the physician's consent.[83] The act targeted the practice of collecting data on the prescriptions individual physicians write and selling that data to pharmaceutical companies who, in turn, use the information to better market their drugs to doctors. According to the majority, Vermont was essentially trying to curb the effective promotion of brand-name prescription drugs in favor of generic alternatives. Thus, it held that the statute restricted speech based on its content and on the identity of the speaker and, therefore, warranted heightened constitutional scrutiny under the First Amendment. Vermont argued that the speech involved was commercial speech and deserving of less protection. But the Court noted that the statute's restrictions on speech would not survive regardless of the scrutiny level used. Citing its *Bates* decision, the Court reaffirmed the strong interest consumers have in receiving free-flowing commercial information and said that interest is especially important "in the fields of medicine and public health, where information can save lives."[84]

The impact of the *Sorrell* case on the commercial-speech doctrine remains to be seen. The Court did not abandon its *Central Hudson* analysis as the constitutional test for restrictions, but it indicated it would scrutinize regulations more stringently if they disfavored particular speakers and messages. For the *Sorrell* Court, the Vermont law's placing of restrictions on marketing in that manner disfavored "speech with a particular content" and "specific speakers, namely pharmaceutical manufacturers"[85] and, thus, imposed "burdens that are based on the content of speech and that are aimed at a particular viewpoint."[86] The implications of *Sorrell* — that commercial speech potentially can be considered nothing more than a protected viewpoint, rather than part of a contractual offering between seller and buyer — along with the holding that government may not burden the expression of such viewpoints when non-commercial speakers are not similarly burdened,[87] appear to be potentially expansive. The ruling raises questions about further ramifications for a commercial-speech doctrine that long has permitted many regulations on commercial speakers that would not be permissible on noncommercial speakers. Justice Stephen Breyer argued in dissent that the *Sorrell* majority had at the least applied "an unforgiving brand of 'intermediate' scrutiny"[88] that if extended in future cases "would work at cross-purposes" with the Court's established commercial-speech doctrine.[89] Certainly future commercial-speech rulings will bear watching for indica-

[80] 535 U.S. 357 (2002).

[81] *Id.* at 371-72.

[82] *See* Robert L. Kerr, *A Justice's Surprise That Has Stood Its Ground: The Enduring Value of the Commercial Speech Doctrine's Powellian Balance*, 13 JOURNALISM & COMM. MONOGRAPHS 215 (2012).

[83] 564 U.S. 552, 580 (2011).

[84] *Id.* at 566.

[85] *Id.* at 564.

[86] *Id.* at 565.

[87] *Id.* at 579-80.

[88] *Id.* at 592 (Breyer, J., dissenting).

[89] *Id.* at 584 (Breyer, J., dissenting).

tions of just how unforgivingly the *Central Hudson* analysis may be applied.

One additional element of potential instability regarding the future of the commercial-speech doctrine may have been introduced *via* the Court's 2010 ruling in *Citizens United v. Federal Election Commission*.[90] In that case, a 5-4 majority, more sweepingly than ever, protected corporate political media spending from regulation aimed at preventing corruption of candidate campaigns, ruling for the first time that corporations may make unlimited political expenditures directly from their treasuries and declaring unconstitutional virtually any limits on spending of that type.[91] That extended First Amendment protection of such unlimited political expenditures (already in place for human beings) to corporate beings on the reasoning that "the First Amendment does not allow political speech restrictions based on a speaker's corporate identity."[92] Although *Citizens United* was not itself a commercial-speech case, the sweeping ruling freed a vast array of political advertising from government regulation and has raised questions of its potential impact on regulation of commercial speech by corporations. For example, if future challenges of such regulation should successfully advance arguments that "any speech by a commercial entity must be, to some degree, commercial" and thus establish that "corporate speech is also commercial speech," will the First Amendment then permit corporate commercial speech to be regulated as extensively as it has been to date?[93]

REGULATION OF DECEPTIVE ADVERTISING

Commercial speech can be regulated at both the federal and state levels, but the primary regulatory body is the century-old FTC. It has long been such an established fact of life for the advertising industry that, for example, an early episode of the acclaimed television drama *Mad Men* featured a discussion about dealing with the FTC in the 1950s at the fictional ad agency on which the show focused. In the episode, the agency's executives respond to the concerns of a client, frustrated at being unable to fight the FTC, by helping creatively craft a campaign strategy that will carefully walk as close as possible to the line of deceptive advertising without actually crossing it. Having a sense of where the FTC draws that line is crucial to advertising practitioners — and to consumers concerned about deceptive or misleading advertising.

The FTC in the Twenty-First Century

The FTC's regulation of deceptive advertising must be considered in the context of its broader mission to "prevent business practices that are anticompetitive or deceptive or unfair to consumers, ... enhance informed consumer choice, ... without unduly burdening legitimate business activity."[94] Established by Congress in 1914, the FTC is "the only federal agency with both consumer protection and competition jurisdiction in broad sectors of the economy."[95] An agency that was born when technologies like motion pictures and radio were transforming the nation's economy now operates in an age shaped by the transformative forces of wireless communications, the Internet, and Big Data. As the FTC enters its second century, it is actively interfacing its mission with rapidly evolving digital technological developments to advance a cyber-age understanding of Justice Blackmun's vision in which intelligent, well-informed consumer decision-making is prioritized as a matter of public interest.

In a world in which the "Internet of Things" means more and more aspects of consumer activity are constantly tracked by an ever increasing array of Internet-connected sensors, "Today's currency is data," said Edith Ramirez, chairwoman of the FTC, in 2014. She outlined a broad approach for the agency in which its activities are targeted at "areas where we can have the greatest impact for consumers" and "address the problems that affect them in their day-to-day lives."[96] To that end, the FTC in recent years has advanced its mandate to maintain competition and protect consumers with a creative and expansive cyber sensibility grounded in "tried-and-true tools of law enforcement, sound public policy, and consumer education."[97] Among recent manifestations of that approach:

• The agency has increasingly focused on the way that the media through which advertising is increasingly utilized can be intertwined with digital intrusions upon consumer privacy. In 2015, for example, Ramirez publicly pressed the makers of tech gadgets to make data security a priority and to give consumers more control over the data that is gathered on them digitally for advertising and other purposes in a growing market worth billions. The FTC has also recently increased its investigations and enforcement actions related to the collecting and selling of consumer data. "Your smart TV and Tablet may track whether you watch the History Channel or reality television, but ... will

---

[90] 558 U.S. 310 (2010).

[91] *Id.* at 365-66.

[92] *Id.* at 347.

[93] Robert Sprague & Mary Ellen Wells, *The Supreme Court as Prometheus: Breathing Life into the Corporate Supercitizen*, 49 AM. BUS. L.J. 507, 550 (2012).

[94] *About the FTC: Our Mission* (2015), *available at* https://www.ftc.gov/about-ftc (accessed June 12, 2015).

[95] 15 U.S.C. § § 41-48 (1999).

[96] Edward Wyatt, *Edith Ramirez is Raising the F.T.C.'s Voice*, N.Y. TIMES, Dec. 21, 2014, at B1.

[97] Edith Ramirez, *After 100 Years, Looking Ahead to Our Next Century*, Sept. 26, 2014, https://www.ftc.gov/news-events/blogs/competition-matters/2014/09/after-100-years-looking-ahead-our-next-century (accessed June 12, 2015).

this information be used to paint a picture of you that you won't see but that others will," Ramirez said in remarks at an international electronics trade show. "People who might make decisions about whether you are shown ads for organic food or junk food, ... and what offers of credit and other products you receive?"[98]

• In a 2014 example of FTC action concerning data collection that involved deceptive advertising, the mobile-messaging app Snapchat agreed to settle charges by the agency that user messages did not "disappear" in the way the company had represented the service — in fact, others could save the messages without being detected.[99] "If a company markets privacy and security as key selling points in pitching its service to consumers, it is critical that it keep that promise," Ramirez said of the case, in which the private data of millions of Snapchat users were accessed illegally. "Any company that makes misrepresentations to consumers about its privacy and security practices risks FTC action."[100] In settling, Snapchat agreed to be monitored by an outside privacy expert for twenty years in an arrangement similar to settlements Google, Facebook, and Myspace agreed to in recent years.[101]

• In the FTC's first case involving crowdfunding, it reached a settlement in 2015 with a project creator who deceptively raised money from consumers online through representations in a Kickstarter campaign that he planned to produce a board game — when in fact he spent most of the money on unrelated personal expenses such as rent payments and moving expenses and never produced a game. The settlement order with Erik Chevalier imposed a $111,793 judgment, suspended on the basis of his inability to pay it unless he were to be found to have misrepresented his financial condition.[102]

• In another 2015 settlement that demonstrated the agency's increased focus on so-called "revenge" Web sites, the FTC shut down the activities of a man who was deceptively advertising a legal service that would get nude photos of women posted online without their permission. The photos were actually from a revenge porn site that the man operated by obtaining photos from the women's former boyfriends. The settlement barred Craig Brittain, who had promoted his purported legal service as "Takedown Lawyer," from engaging in any further "revenge porn" activity and required that he destroy all the images and personal contact information he had collected.[103]

When Ramirez began her tenure at the agency in 2010, she observed that "most everyday Americans really don't know much about what the FTC does."[104] As part of the agency's efforts to raise awareness of its activities, it reaches out to the public via Twitter and Facebook, an online subscription service for its press releases and "complaint assistant" to aid in the reporting of fraud and abuse, and a toll-free help line. Despite its heightened cyber-profile and its intensified focus on maintaining competition and protecting consumers in the digital world, its fundamental tools for regulating deceptive advertising are well established and remain at the core of its activity.

The FTC and Deceptive Advertising

The FTC's five commissioners are nominated by the president and confirmed by the Senate for terms of seven years. No more than three may be of the same political party. The FTC administers a variety of federal statutes that "promote competition and protect the public from unfair and deceptive acts and practices in the advertising and marketing of goods and services."[105] Seven regional offices are responsible for enforcing regulations, investigating complaints and educating the public.[106] The FTC focuses on national advertising, referring purely local concerns to state and local government agencies. While the FTC staff itself monitors national ad campaigns for potentially deceptive claims, letters from consumers or businesses, congressional inquiries, or news stories on consumer or economic topics may also trigger FTC investigations.

The FTC is responsible for protecting consumers from both unfair and deceptive advertising: "When consumers see or hear an advertisement, whether it's on the Internet, radio or television, or anywhere else, federal law says that ad must be truthful, not misleading, and when appropriate, backed by scientific evidence." In enforcing truth-in-advertising laws, the FTC "applies the same standards no matter where an ad appears in newspapers and magazines, online, in the mail, or on billboards or buses."[107]

[98] Associated Press, *FTC Chief Says Gadget Industry Must Prioritize Privacy*, N.Y. TIMES Dec. 6, 2015, *available at* http://www.nytimes.com/aponline/2015/01/06/technology/ap-us-tec-gadget-show-ftc-privacy.html (accessed June 12, 2015).

[99] Snapchat, Inc., 2010 (No. C-4501) (F.T.C. Dec. 23, 2014) (consent order).

[100] *Snapchat Settles FTC Charges That Promises of Disappearing Messages Were False* (May 8, 2014), *available at* https://www.ftc.gov/news-events/press-releases/2014/05/snapchat-settles-ftc-charges-promises-disappearing-messages-were (accessed June 15, 2015).

[101] Associated Press, *FTC Says Snapchat Deceived Customers*, N.Y. TIMES May 8, 2014, *available at* http://www.nytimes.com/aponline/2014/05/08/technology/ap-us-tec-snapchat-ftc.html (accessed June 12, 2015).

[102] *Crowdfunding Project Creator Settles FTC Charges of Deception* (June 11, 2015), *available at* https://www.ftc.gov/news-events/press-releases/2015/06/crowdfunding-project-creator-settles-ftc-charges-deception (accessed June 12, 2015).

[103] *See Website Operator Banned from the "Revenge Porn" Business After FTC Charges He Unfairly Posted Nude Photos*, Jan. 29, 2015, https://www.ftc.gov/news-events/press-releases/2015/01/website-operator-banned-revenge-porn-business-after-ftc-charges (accessed June 12, 2015).

[104] Wyatt, *supra* note 96, at B1.

[105] FTC Policy on Deception, 16 C.F.R. § 0.1 (1999).

[106] The offices are in Atlanta, Chicago, Cleveland, Dallas, New York, San Francisco and Seattle.

[107] *Truth in Advertising* (2015), *available at* https://www.ftc.gov/news-events/media-resources/truth-advertising (accessed June 12, 2015).

The agency gives especially close attention to advertising claims that can affect consumers in terms of health or finances, such as claims about food, over-the-counter drugs, dietary supplements, alcohol, tobacco and technology. It also monitors and creates reports about advertising-industry practices regarding the marketing of food and violent media to children.

Unfairness is defined by the Commission as an act or practice that "causes or is likely to cause substantial injury to consumers, which is not reasonably avoidable by consumers themselves and not outweighed by countervailing benefits to consumers or to competition."[108] Unfairness arises more often in a business' relationship with a consumer than in advertising; for example, a company may be found to have acted unfairly if it coerces a customer to buy expensive unnecessary parts or services.

The FTC is more concerned with deception than with unfairness. The Commission defines a deceptive ad as one that contains a material representation, omission or practice that is likely to mislead a consumer acting reasonably under the circumstances. The definition, then, has three key parts:

• *The representation, omission or practice must be material.* "Material" means the representation, omission or practice "is likely to affect the consumer's conduct or decision with regard to a product or service." Types of material statements include those about the health, safety, cost, quality, durability, performance or efficacy of a product or service.[109] A claim such as "You will save 50 percent with our long distance service" would be material because it is a statement about price that is likely to influence a consumer's purchasing decision.

Express claims as to the attributes of a product are always considered material. Ads involving health and safety are usually presumed to be material, as are those containing information that pertains to a product's central characteristic. A Colgate-Palmolive claim that its Rapid Shave shaving cream was so good it could be used to shave sandpaper is an example of a material representation. In the TV commercial, Rapid Shave was apparently spread on sandpaper and then a few seconds later shaved off. The FTC complained that the ad was deceptive and a material misrepresentation because it used not sandpaper but sand sprinkled on glass. Colgate-Palmolive argued that the product really could shave sandpaper if left on long enough, but that on TV the sand and the paper were the same color. Glass had to be used to get the proper visual impression. The Supreme Court agreed with the FTC that this was a material misrepresentation.[110]

Not all fake demonstrations will result in an allegation of material misrepresentation. Only those that are used to suggest a product attribute will be. For example, a fake television could be used in an ad for satellite TV service because no claim about the quality of the television is being made. A fake television could not be used to advertise the television itself, especially if the ad were extolling the virtues of the sharp, clear quality of the screen image.

• *The representation, omission or practice must be likely to mislead.* An ad does not have to actually mislead or cause deception so long as it appears likely to do so. A deceptive statement may mislead expressly ("Using Listerine prevents colds," for example) or by implication, in which the ad suggests that the product contains certain elements or does certain things.[111] Omission of important or material information can make an ad deceptive. For example, if a company advertised that people could save 50 percent with its long distance service but failed to say that it required customers to spend at least $100 to get the savings, the omission would make the claim misleading.

• *The representation, omission or practice must be likely to mislead a reasonable consumer.* The FTC has said that the key question is "whether the consumer's interpretation or reaction is reasonable."[112] The FTC does not seek to protect people who are "foolish or feeble-minded."[113] In addition, the FTC will consider the intended audience for the ad in deciding whether an ad is deceptive. For example, for a claim in an advertisement targeting children, the agency would evaluate the ad from the perspective of how reasonable children of the age group targeted would be likely to respond. Similarly, the agency would evaluate a claim in a prescription drug ad directed to doctors taking into account the knowledge and sophistication of the highly educated target audience. Also, the FTC will evaluate the impact of the advertisement *as a whole* on reasonable consumers, rather than focusing on isolated, out-of-context words or imagery.

In addition to standards for deceptive advertising, since 1971 the FTC has required prior substantiation of advertising claims. Advertisers must be able to substantiate the explicit and implied statements in ads that make objective claims about products and services before the claims are made. That is, they must have "a reasonable basis" for their claims before they make them. Without such a basis, companies are deemed to have violated Section 5 of the FTC Act.[114] An advertiser must have at least the level of evidence the ad says exists.

In 2010, the FTC settled a lawsuit against the Dannon Company in which it alleged Dannon exaggerated the health benefits of its Activia yogurt and DanActive dairy drink. In its Ac-

[108] FTC Act Amendments of 1994, 15 U.S.C.A. § 45(n) (West Supp. 1995).

[109] Federal Trade Commission, *FTC Policy on Deception,* Oct. 14, 1983, http://www.ftc.gov/bcp/policystmt/ad-decept.htm.

[110] FTC v. Colgate-Palmolive Co., 380 U.S. 374 (1963).

[111] *See Warner-Lambert Co. v. FTC,* 562 F.2d 749 (D.C. Cir. 1977).

[112] *FTC Policy on Deception, supra* note 110.

[113] Heinz W. Kirchner, 63 F.T.C. 1282, 1290 (1963).

[114] Federal Trade Commission, *FTC Policy Statement Regarding Advertising Substantiation, available at* http://www.ftc.gov/bcp/guides/ad3subst.htm (accessed June 10, 2016).

tivia ads, Dannon claimed the yogurt relieved temporary irregularity because it contained probiotics. It did not, however, tell consumers that three servings a day of Activia were required to produce the benefit. As part of the settlement, Dannon agreed to stop making the irregularity claim unless it conveyed that three servings per day were required or it obtained scientific evidence to substantiate that the benefit can be achieved from a smaller amount. With respect to DanActive, Dannon agreed to stop claiming the drink would help people avoid catching colds and the flu unless the FDA approves the claim.[115]

Exaggerations or hyperbole in ads are considered *puffery* and are not generally deemed deceptive by the FTC. Puffery claims are considered to be ones that reasonable people do not believe are true qualities and are incapable of being proven true or false. They usually involve subjective matters such as taste or appearance. Examples of puffery would be describing a soft drink as the "World's Best" or "the perfect summer drink."

Testimonials and endorsements by experts, celebrities or even ordinary people, on the other hand, are regulated because they are considered to carry special weight with consumers. Under guidelines adopted by the FTC in 2009, ads featuring a customer who lost 100 pounds on a weight-loss program, for example, can no longer hide behind a disclaimer that "Results Are Not Typical" disclaimer. The ads must now show the results that consumers most likely can expect. The 2009 guidelines also reveal the FTC's concern about the use of fictitious consumer reviews online. Now "material connections" between a reviewer and a company must be disclosed.[116] One of the first complaints under the new guidelines was against Reverb Communications, a communications company that had its interns pose as ordinary customers posting game reviews on the iTunes store Web site.[117] In 2011, Legacy Learning Systems, a company that sells guitar-lesson DVDs, was ordered to pay $250,000 to settle charges that it used "Review Ad" affiliates to promote its courses through endorsements in articles, blogs and other online outlets. According to the FTC, the endorsements generated more than $5 million in sales for the company.[118]

The FTC engages in a number of activities to help prevent deceptive ads from appearing in the marketplace including:

• *Advisory opinions.* An advertiser may seek an advisory opinion from FTC commissioners or FTC staff on a proposed advertisement or specific issue of concern. An advisory opinion is a statement giving an informed judgment about a legal question or issue. The Commission may provide an advisory opinion if the request "involves a substantial or novel question of fact or law and there is no clear Commission or court precedent" and the request is a matter of significant public interest.[119] Because advisory opinions are only opinions and are not legally binding, the Commission may later reconsider the question and rescind or revoke its opinion. Advisory opinions become part of the public record after they are issued.[120]

• *Industry guides.* The FTC publishes detailed guides that tell advertisers how to avoid creating advertising that is deceptive. Some of the guides, for example, describe how advertisers may avoid deception in the use of the word "free." The Commission has also created industry guides specific to advertising for particular types of products, such as jewelry, dietary supplements and food. The FTC may take action against an advertiser who fails to comply with industry guides.[121]

• *Policy statements.* The FTC may publicly state its regulatory philosophy in a policy statement. For example, the FTC issued a policy statement about comparative advertising after examining the advertising industry's codes and standards on the subject.[122] Finding that its codes and standards seemed to discourage the use of comparative advertising, the FTC wanted to clearly state its position that "industry self-regulation should not restrain the use by advertisers of truthful comparative advertising." The FTC's policy on comparative advertising "encourages the naming of, or reference to, competitors, but requires clarity, and, if necessary, disclosure to avoid deception of the consumer.... Comparative advertising, when truthful and non-deceptive, is a source of important information to consumers and assists them in making rational purchase decisions."[123] An example of what the FTC considers deceptive in comparative advertising involved a Kentucky Fried Chicken ad, in which the company implied that eating two Original Recipe fried chicken breasts was better for an individual's health than eating a Burger King Whopper. In fact, while two KFC Original Recipe fried chicken breasts do have slightly less total fat and saturated fat than the Whopper, they have more trans fat, cholesterol, sodium and calories.[124]

• *Rulemaking.* The FTC may establish Trade Regulation Rules, which have the force of law, to address widespread deceptive practices. The commission holds informal hearings at which

---

[115] Dannon Co., Inc., 2010 WL 5199606 (No. 082-3158) (F.T.C. Dec. 15, 2010) (consent order).

[116] Guides Concerning the Use of Endorsements and Testimonials in Advertising 16 C.F.R. § 255 (1999), *available at* http://www.ftc.gov/os/2009/10/091005revisedendorsementguides.pdf (accessed July 5, 2010).

[117] Reverb Communications, Inc., 2010 WL 4897037 (No. C-4310) (F.T.C. Nov. 22, 2010) (consent order).

[118] Legacy Learning Systems, Inc., 2011 WL 2415390 (No. C-4323) (F.T.C. June 1, 2011) (consent order).

[119] 16 C.F.R. § 1.1 (1999).

[120] 16 C.F.R. § 1.1 (1999), 16 C.F.R. § 1.3 (1999), 16 C.F.R. § 1.4 (1999).

[121] 16 C.F.R. § 1.5 (1999).

[122] The FTC defines comparative advertising as "advertising that compares alternative brands on objectively measurable attributes or price, and identifies the alternative brand by name, illustration or other distinctive information." 16 C.F.R. § 14.15 (1999).

[123] 16 C.F.R. § 14.15 (1999).

[124] KFC Corp., 138 F.T.C. 422 (2004) (consent order).

interested parties and the public may participate and give their opinions about the proposed rule.[125]

If the FTC decides that an ad is deceptive, it has a number of remedies at its disposal. One problem the FTC has is that ad campaigns can be over long before the FTC catches up with the company and brings a complaint. On the other hand, the FTC does have publicity working in its favor. Companies do not like the negative publicity that comes with a charge of false advertising; so publicity can be a powerful sanction.

FTC remedies are:

• *Consent agreements.* If the FTC believes an ad is deceptive, it may issue a complaint to the advertiser detailing its charges. The advertiser may then choose to settle the charges with the FTC by signing a consent agreement. Generally, the advertiser does not admit liability but agrees to start or stop doing something, such as running a particular ad or making specific claims in an ad. The agreement also provides that the advertiser waives the right to judicial review. The FTC places proposed consent agreements on the record for sixty days to allow public comment before they become final.

• *Cease-and-desist orders.* If a consent agreement cannot be reached and the advertiser chooses to fight the charges, the FTC's complaint will be adjudicated before an FTC administrative law judge in a proceeding similar to a trial. At the end of this quasi-judicial proceeding, the judge will issue a decision stating findings of fact and conclusions of law and recommending either a cease-and-desist order or dismissal of the complaint. A cease-and-desist order is an order to start or stop doing something. The decision of the judge may be appealed to the full commission. The advertiser may appeal the commission's decision to a federal court of appeals, and either party may appeal that decision to the Supreme Court.

• *Corrective advertising.* In some cases the FTC will require a company to correct its advertising message in future ads to clear up any misleading impressions that were left from the deceptive ads. This remedy is usually reserved for long-running and successful ad campaigns where the FTC fears the public will be left with false information. For example, Novartis was ordered in 1999 to state in its future advertising for Doan's Pills that "there is no evidence that Doan's is more effective than other pain relievers for back pain."[126]

• *Court injunctions.* Rather than taking an administrative route first, the FTC may go directly to federal court to seek a preliminary or permanent injunction in cases of ongoing consumer fraud in an attempt to stop it before too many consumers are harmed.[127] In 2011, it sought such an injunction to stop the use of fake news sites to sell weight loss products. The FTC alleged that headlines such as "Acai Berry Diet Exposed: Miracle Diet or Scam?" on a Web site like "News 6 News Alert" were actually being used to promote the product by deceptively representing the article as an objective news report.[128]

• *Civil and criminal penalties.* The FTC can ask a federal district court to impose civil penalties for a number of reasons, including to reimburse all consumers who bought an advertiser's product, because an advertiser violated a federal statute that imposes fines on violators, or because an advertiser has violated an FTC order. To get consumer redress, the FTC must show that an advertiser demonstrated conduct that a "reasonable man would have known under the circumstances was dishonest or fraudulent."[129] The FTC can also refer cases to the Justice Department for criminal prosecution.

The FTC is active in regulating advertising and marketing practices on the Internet. Advertising on the Internet must conform to the same rules as advertising in other media.

Legal Liability

The basic defense against any false advertising complaint is truth, that is, providing evidence that proves the product does what the ad says it does or has the attributes the ad claims it does. Advertising agencies may be held legally liable, along with their clients, for deceptive claims, because they have a responsibility to independently check claims made in ads. Public-relations agencies have the same obligation, a Public Relations Society of America forum emphasized recently, even though many PR practitioners believe they are beyond FTC concerns because of the differences in what they and advertising practitioners do. However, it is advisable for PR firms to have a reasonable basis to support all claims made in content they disseminate for clients; include clear and conspicuous disclosures to ensure content is not false, deceptive or misleading; design content so it will specifically not mislead the audience for whom it is targeted; inform their clients of the need to comply with FTC guides and include disclosures when endorsers are paid to provide opinions in content.[130]

Lanham Act

At the federal level, the Lanham Act also provides redress for

[125] 15 U.S.C. § 57 (a)(b)(3) (1999).
[126] Novartis Consumer Health, Inc., 127 F.T.C. 580 (F.T.C. May 27, 1999).
[127] 15 U.S.C. § 53 (b) (1999).
[128] Federal Trade Commission, *FTC Seeks to Halt 10 Operators of Fake News Sites from Making Deceptive Claims about Acai Berry Weight Loss Products,* Apr. 19, 2011, http://www.ftc.gov/opa/2011/04/fakenews.shtm.
[129] 15 U.S.C. § 57 (b) (1999).
[130] Ann Willets, *PR & Advertising: The Lines Continue to Blur,* PRSAY, Sept. 17, 2014, http://prsay.prsa.org/index.php/2014//09/17/pr-advertising-the-lines-continue-to-blur (accessed June 12, 2015).

individuals and businesses harmed by false or deceptive advertising. The Lanham Act is the federal trademark protection law, but it contains a section dealing with advertising. Section 43(a) reads, in part:

> Any person who ... in commercial advertising or promotion, misrepresents the nature, characteristics, qualities, or geographic origin of his or her or another person's goods, services, or commercial activities, shall be liable in a civil action by any person who believes that he or she is or is likely to be damaged by such act.[131]

The section creates a "distinct federal statutory tort designed to afford broad protection against various forms of unfair competition and false advertising."[132]

Because of the Lanham Act's focus on protection of commercial interests, as opposed to consumers, courts have not generally given consumers standing to bring an action under Section 43(a). The act allows businesses or people to sue others for competitive harm arising from false advertising. For a claim, the plaintiff must establish that the advertiser made a false representation about a product or service; that the representation deceives, or has a tendency to deceive, a substantial segment of the target audience; that the representation is material; and that it resulted or is likely to result in injury to the plaintiff. Although the elements are similar to the FTC's standards for deceptive advertising, the biggest difference is the requirement of injury. In Lanham Act cases, the plaintiff must show that it has or is likely to have suffered commercial harm by the defendant's deceptive advertising claims. The plaintiff also must show that the claim was in fact false and not just that the advertiser lacked prior substantiation.

State Laws

All fifty states have enacted legislation similar to the Federal Trade Commission Act, prohibiting deceptive advertising. Unlike the federal law, however, most of the state statutes permit private lawsuits to be brought by consumers and competitors against advertisers and allow plaintiffs to sue for damages in addition to an injunction stopping the ads. Some national advertisers, such as tobacco companies and airlines, have sought to avoid state penalties by claiming the state law is pre-empted by federal law. Commercial speech is an area of law that is shared by the state and federal governments. When a conflict between the two arises, the federal law takes precedence.

When it was sued by smokers of its light cigarettes, Altria

Group, the parent company of Philip Morris, tried to argue that the Maine Unfair Trade Practices Act was pre-empted by the Federal Cigarette Labeling and Advertising Act. But the Supreme Court, in a 5-4 decision in 2008, held that the Labeling Act did not pre-empt a state-law fraud claim. The respondents claimed that light cigarettes were advertised as delivering less tar and nicotine than regular cigarettes, which the company knew was not true.[133]

A year earlier, Philip Morris had been foiled in a similar case in its attempt to remove to federal district court a state-court case brought against it in Arkansas. The suit claimed that the company violated Arkansas' unfair business practice laws by advertising some of its cigarettes as "light" when in fact the tests had been manipulated to register lower levels of tar and nicotine than were actually present in the cigarettes. The company, in turn, argued that the plaintiffs were challenging the use of the test, which was an approved FTC method, and therefore were suing the company for acting under the FTC. The Supreme Court unanimously held in 2007 that Philip Morris was not "acting under" the FTC, but was simply regulated by it. Therefore, the case was to stay in the Arkansas court.[134]

Industry Self-regulation

The advertising industry has developed a variety of methods for self-regulation. The Advertising Self-Regulatory Council establishes the policies and procedures of the National Advertising Division, the National Advertising Review Board and the Children's Advertising Review Unit. The Council of Better Business Bureaus administers this self-regulatory system.

The National Advertising Division. The NAD, which was created in 1971, "uses a unique, hybrid form of alternative dispute resolution, working with in-house counsel, marketing executives, research and development departments and outside consultants to decide whether [disputed advertising] claims have been substantiated."[135] Self-regulation allows advertisers to resolve disputes quickly and inexpensively, without government involvement and assessment of penalties.

The NAD reviews national advertising and investigates complaints about the truth or accuracy of claims. It focuses on product performance, superiority, and scientific and technical claims, and maintains, "National advertisers who use the NAD process find it to be significantly less expensive than litigation. By utilizing the NAD process, cost-conscious companies save hundreds of thousands of dollars typically spent seeking repara-

---

[131] 15 U.S.C. § 1125(a), § 43(a) (1999).
[132] Estate of Presley v. Russen, 513 F. Supp. 1339, 1376 (D.N.J. 1981).

[133] Altria Group, Inc. v. Good, et al., 55 U.S. 70 (2008).
[134] Watson v. Philip Morris Cos., Inc., 551 U.S. 142 (2007).
[135] Advertising Self-Regulatory Council, *About NAD,* http://www.asrcreviews.org/how-nad-works/.

tion through the courts."[136]

While the NAD cannot force an advertiser to comply with a recommendation or accept its findings, it exerts pressure on advertisers by publishing its conclusions in the *NAD Case Reports* and by issuing news releases announcing decisions. For example, in 2012 NAD released a statement recommending that Discover Financial Services more clearly disclose limitations on its cash-back promotions. It also recommended that Sonic disclose that its "Free Coffee with any Breakfast Burrito" promotional offer did not apply to the Junior Breakfast Burrito, but only to premium burritos.[137] The NAD will also refer cases to the FTC if a company does not comply with NAD recommendations.

The National Advertising Review Board. Either an advertiser whose claim is in question or a challenger of a claim may appeal a finding of the NAD to the National Advertising Review Board. The NARB is a group of advertising professionals who work in ad agencies, companies that advertise, academia and government, and who wotk in panels to decide NAD appeals. If an advertiser does not accept the NARB panel's decisions and recommendations, which the ASRC characterizes as "extremely rare," the NARB refers the case to an appropriate law-enforcement agency, such as the FTC.[138]

The Children's Advertising Review Unit. To combat misleading and socially irresponsible advertising aimed at children, the advertising industry created the Children's Advertising Review Unit in 1974. CARU "evaluates child-directed advertising and promotional material in all media to advance truthfulness, accuracy and consistency."[139] When such advertising is found to be "misleading, inaccurate, or inconsistent with CARU's guidelines, CARU seeks change through the voluntary cooperation of advertisers."[140] In 2016, for example, a CARU review recommended that the maker of Aquabeads (a child crafting product) revise an ad representation — "Spray with water, and the beads magically stick together" — to more accurately disclose that users must allow time for the beads to dry before they stick together after being sprayed with water.[141]

A section of CARU's guidelines highlights issues "including

---

[136] *Id.*

[137] Seller Beware, *NAD Deals a Double Whammy on Two Consumer Promotions,* June 26, 2012, http://http://www.consumeradvertisinglawblog.com/2012/06/nad-deals-a-double-whammy-on-two-consumer-promotions.html.

[138] Advertising Self-Regulatory Council, *NARB Process,* http://www.asrcreviews.org/how-the-narb-process-works/.

[139] Advertising Self-Regulatory Council, *About CARU,* http://www.asrcreviews.org/about-caru/.

[140] *Id.*

[141] Advertising Self-Regulatory Council, *CARU Recommends International Playthings Better Disclose Drying Time for 'Aquabeads' Product; Company Says it Will Do So,* http://caru-recommends-international-playthings-better-disclose-drying-time-for-aquabeads-product-company-says-it-will-do-so/.

children's privacy, that are unique to the Internet and online sites directed at children age 12 and under," which formed the basis of the federal Children's Online Privacy Protection Act (COPPA) of 1998.[142]

SUMMARY

Commercial speech can be defined as expression that proposes a commercial transaction or is related solely to the economic interests of a speaker and the speaker's audience. The saga of the development of constitutional protection for commercial speech began in 1942 with a Supreme Court pronouncement that commercial advertising received no First Amendment protection. The Court modified that initial view, saying in 1977 that the First Amendment does protect even purely commercial expression, though government remains free to constitutionally restrict advertising that is false, misleading or deceptive, or promoted illegal products or services. The Court has ruled that commercial speech receives a lower level of protection than other types of expression because the truth of its content is more easily verified and because it is an economic necessity for companies; thus, commercial advertising can better tolerate government regulation.

In 1980 the Court articulated a four-part test, commonly referred to as the "*Central Hudson* test," to determine whether a regulation on commercial speech is constitutional:

(1) Is the commercial speech true and not misleading, and does it advertise a legal product or service?

(2) Is the asserted governmental interest substantial?

(3) Does the regulation directly advance the governmental interest?

(4) Is the regulation no more extensive than necessary to serve the governmental interest?

The Court later clarified the fourth part of that test as requiring a reasonable fit between the regulation and the governmental interest. But within a few years after that, the Court further revised its application of the *Central Hudson* test so as to make it a more substantial burden for government to meet, in particular requiring greater proof to support government assertions that regulations pass the *Central Hudson* test. In its most recent commercial-speech ruling, the Court's application of *Central Hudson* suggested support for an even more stringent level of assessment of government regulation related to advertising. Although some justices have argued for the same broad protection accorded noncommercial speech to be extended to truthful, non-misleading commercial speech, the Court's holdings on balance have focused more sharply on preventing government from denying citizens truthful information while maintaining the

---

[142] Advertising Self-Regulatory Council, *supra* note 139.

Central Hudson test as an effective means for achieving that. Thus, the Court's commercial-speech doctrine has placed a high priority on protecting and maintaining truth in advertising and preserving the fair-bargaining process.

The FTC is the federal governmental agency that regulates deceptive advertising in the United States. Its definition of a deceptive ad is one that contains a representation, omission or practice that is material and likely to mislead a consumer acting reasonably in the circumstances.

The commission uses various tools — offering advisory opinions to advertisers, issuing policy statements, publishing industry guides, making rules and requiring substantiation — to try to prevent deceptive advertising from appearing in the marketplace. Once advertisers disseminate deceptive claims to consumers, the FTC seeks remedies — through a consent agreement, cease-and-desist order, injunction, or civil or criminal penalties — to stop such claims from continuing to deceive consumers and to seek redress for harms advertisers have inflicted on consumers.

Competitors and others harmed by false and deceptive advertising can seek redress through the Lanham Act. In Lanham Act cases, the plaintiff must show that it has suffered or is likely to suffer commercial harm by the defendant's false and deceptive claims. State laws also regulate advertising, and many allow consumers and competitors to sue for damages in addition to injunctive relief.

Self-regulation by the advertising industry can be an effective and quick way of addressing concerns about deceptive or unsupported claims in national advertising and about various issues relating to children's exposure to advertising. The National Advertising Division, Children's Advertising Review Unit, and National Advertising Review Board, which all operate as part of the Better Business Bureau, are the main industry groups involved in the self-regulatory process.

FOR ADDITIONAL READING

An, Soontae. "From a Business Pursuit to a Means of Expression: The Supreme Court's Disputes Over Commercial Speech," 8 *Communication Law and Policy* 201 (2003).

Better Business Bureau Advertising Review Programs Web site, http://www.bbb.org/advertising.

Browne, M. Neil, Lauren Frances Biksacky & Alex Frondorf. "Advertising to Children and the Commercial Speech Doctrine: Political and Constitutional Limitations," 58 *Drake Law Review* 67 (2009).

Federal Trade Commission Web site, http://www.ftc.gov.

Hoefges, Michael. "Protecting Tobacco Advertising Under the Commercial Speech Doctrine: The Constitutional Impact of Lorillard Tobacco Co.," 8 *Communication Law and Policy* 267 (2003).

McGeveran, William. "Disclosure, Endorsement, and Identity in Social Marketing," 2009 *University of Illinois Law Review* 1105 (2009).

Piety, Tamara. "'A Necessary Cost of Freedom?' The Incoherence of *Sorrell v. IMS*," 64 *Alabama Law Review* 1 (2012).

Piety, Tamara. *Brandishing the First Amendment: Commercial Expression in America* (Ann Arbor: University of Michigan Press, 2012).

Post, Robert. "The Constitutional Status of Commercial Speech," 48 *UCLA Law Review* 1 (2000).

Schwartz, Victor E., Cary Silverman, Michael J. Hulka & Christopher E. Appel. "Marketing Pharmaceutical Products in the Twenty-First Century: An Analysis of the Continued Viability of Traditional Principles of Laws in the Age of Direct-to-Consumer Advertising," 32 *Harvard Journal of Law & Public Policy* 333 (2009).

Sprague, Robert & Mary Ellen Wells. "The Supreme Court as Prometheus: Breathing Life into the Corporate Supercitizen," 49 *American Business Law Journal* 507 (2012).

Stern, Nat. "In Defense of the Imprecise Definition of Commercial Speech," 52 *Maryland Law Review* 55 (1999).

Tushnet, Rebecca. "It Depends on What the Meaning of 'False' Is: Falsity and Misleadingness in Commercial Speech Doctrine," 41 *Loyola Los Angeles Law Review* 227 (2007).

Vladeck, David C. "Lessons from a Story Untold: *Nike v. Kasky* Reconsidered," 54 *Case Western Reserve Law Review* 1049 (2004).

Regulating Public Relations

By Karla K. Gower

➡ **Headnote Questions**

- To what extent do corporations have constitutional protection for their speech?
- Why do public relations practitioners need to understand securities law?
- What is the role of the Food and Drug Administration and how does the agency impact public relations?
- What is required for a negligence action?
- What is required for a "no-compete" clause in a public relations practitioner's employment contract to be enforceable?

Public relations involves managing relationships through communication. As such, it requires knowledge of laws affecting communication and management. PR practitioners "speak" for their clients on a broad range of political, economic, technological, social and cultural issues. Like journalists, they inform, and like advertisers, they persuade. They seek to provide publics with knowledge about their clients, and to persuade them to think favorably about those clients, ultimately moving publics to action, whether voting in a particular way or buying a particular product or service. Thus, the practice of public relations crosses many legal categories, from the traditional media law areas of defamation, privacy and access to information, to the more business-oriented ones of commercial speech, contracts and regulation.

While nonprofits, religious organizations, political candidates, celebrities and activists — among others — all engage in PR activities, this chapter will focus on legal issues affecting the public relations endeavors of business entities. Specifically, it will discuss the law as it affects corporate speech, as opposed to commercial speech, which was described in Chapter 8. The Supreme Court has defined commercial speech as either speech that does "no more than propose a commercial transaction" or that is "solely motivated by the desire for profit."[1] Corporate speech, on the other hand, is speech by a corporation on issues of importance to society and that is not tied directly to the pro-

motion of the corporation's products or services.

CONSTITUTIONAL PROTECTION FOR CORPORATE SPEECH

Corporations have long had certain recognized rights under the Constitution. For example, they are considered "persons" for purposes of the equal protection and due process clauses of the Fourteenth Amendment.[2] And the Fifth Amendment protects them against double jeopardy.[3] But, as was seen in Chapter 8, the First Amendment historically did not protect what might be termed economic or commercial expression. The assumption was that only expression contributing to informed self-government, or political speech, was worthy of protection. Economic or commercial speech was considered a business activity, not an act of expression.[4] There was no fear, it was believed, that government regulation would chill companies' speech. Businesses would always find a way to communicate to consumers about their products or services.

In the 1978 case *First National Bank of Boston v. Bellotti*,[5] the Supreme Court for the first time ruled that the First Amendment protects corporate speech. First National had sought to inform Massachusetts citizens of the bank's position

---

[1] *See* Dun & Bradstreet v. Greenmoss Builders, Inc., 472 U.S. 749, 762 (1985); Pittsburgh Press Co. v. Pittsburgh Comm'n on Human Relations, 413 U.S. 376, 385 (1973).

[2] Corporations were first deemed "persons" entitled to the Constitution's equal protection guarantees in *Santa Clara County v. Southern Pac. R.R.*, 118 U.S. 394, 396 (1886), and to its due process guarantees in *Smyth v. Ames*, 169 U.S. 466, 522 (1898).

[3] *See* United States v. Martin Linen Supply Co., 430 U.S. 564 (1977).

[4] *See* Valentine v. Chrestensen, 316 U.S. 52 (1946).

[5] 435 U.S. 765 (1978).

regarding an upcoming state constitutional amendment refer-endum that would decide whether the state could impose a flat income tax rate. Massachusetts prohibited corporations from spending money on political referenda unless the issue directly impacted their business. In this case, it clearly did not. The sharply divided Court declared that the bank's "speech" was

> the type of speech indispensable to decision-making in a de-mocracy, and this is no less true because the speech comes from a corporation rather than an individual. The inherent worth of the speech in terms of its capacity for informing the public does not depend upon the identity of its source, wheth-er corporation ... or individual.[6]

In other words, the Court held that it was the speech that de-termined protection, not the nature of the speaker.

The *Belotti* decision was subsequently expanded to include ideological groups and entities — those formed to disseminate political ideas, rather than amass economic capital.[7]

Although *First National Bank v. Bellotti* is considered the "Magna Carta" of corporate speech doctrine,[8] the decision by no means settled all questions regarding the role of corporations in public life, their influence on the democratic process, and their involvement in the political sphere through monetary contribu-tions to campaigns and parties.

Two years prior to *Bellotti*, the Supreme Court, in *Buckley v. Valeo*, had upheld limits on contributions to candidates and po-litical parties on the grounds that large contributions create fears of improper influence on the political process and under-mine citizens' faith in government honesty and integrity.[9] Thus, limits were valid as long as a regulation was "closely drawn" and matched a "sufficiently important [governmental] interest," the Court held,[10] writing that "a limitation upon the amount that any one person or group may contribute to a candidate or political committee entails only a marginal restriction upon the contributor's ability to engage in free communication."[11] At the same time, the Court rejected limits on independent expendi-tures in support of candidates. Such expenditures did not repre-sent a corrupting influence the way that contributions did. More importantly, restrictions on "the amount of money a person or group can spend on political communication during a campaign necessarily reduces the quantity of expression by restricting the

number of issues discussed, the depth of their exploration, and the size of the audience reached."[12]

In 2002, Congress again tackled the issue of money and poli-tics, enacting the Bipartisan Campaign Reform Act,[13] called "the most ambitious effort since Watergate to reduce the influence of big donations on the political process."[14] The statute was imme-diately challenged in eleven separate lawsuits, which were con-solidated into a single action: *McConnell v. Federal Election Commission*.[15] A special three-judge panel upheld much of the statute but found that its two most important provisions were unconstitutional infringements of free expression: its restric-tions on large political donations from corporations and labor unions to political parties for "party-building activities," known as "soft money" contributions; and its prohibitions against those same entities using their general treasuries to pay for election-eering communications (communication that mentions a candi-date) within a month or so of an election. Concluding that the soft money restrictions only minimally affected free speech, the Supreme Court reversed the lower court's ruling, while uphold-ing its decision regarding electioneering communications.[16] Yet the Court overturned this provision, too, in 2007,[17] when it con-cluded that such election advertising by groups is "core political speech," which could not be censored[18] — effectively, though not explicitly, gutting its four-year-old *McConnell* ruling.

This evisceration of *McConnell* continued in 2010 with the Court's ruling in *Citizens United v. Federal Elections Commis-sion*,[19] which also overturned its twenty-year-old ruling in *Aus-tin v. Michigan Chamber of Commerce*.[20] In *Austin*, the Court upheld a ban on the use of corporate general treasury funds for expenditures in state elections. Such expenditures could only come from a segregated account set up specifically for political purposes and to which employees and stockholders could volun-tarily contribute. In *Citizens*, involving a 2008 film documentary

---

[6] *Id.* at 777.

[7] *See* Fed. Election Comm'n v. Massachusetts Citizens for Life, 479 U.S. 238 (1986).

[8] Norman Dorson & Joel Gora, *Free Speech, Property, and the Burger Court: Old Values, New Balances*, 1982 SUP. CT. REV. 195, 212.

[9] 424 U.S. 1 (1976).

[10] *Id.* at 25.

[11] *Id.* at 20.

[12] *Id.* at 19.

[13] 2 U.S.C. 441a *et seq.* (2009).

[14] Neil A. Lewis & Richard A. Oppel Jr., *U.S. Court Issues Discordant Ruling on Campaign Law*, N.Y. TIMES, May 3, 2003, at A14.

[15] 251 F. Supp. 2d 176 (D. D.C. 2002).

[16] McConnell v. Fed. Elections Comm'n, 540 U.S. 93 (2003). *See* Linda Greenhouse, *Justices, in a 5-to-4 Decision, Back Campaign Finance Law That Curbs Contributions*, N.Y. TIMES, Dec. 11, 2003, at A1; Glen Justice, *Even with Campaign Finance Law, Money Talks Louder Than Ever*, N.Y. TIMES, Nov. 8, 2004, at A16.

[17] Fed. Election Comm'n v. Wisconsin Right to Life, 551 U.S. 449 (2007).

[18] *See* Linda Greenhouse & David D. Kirkpatrick, *Justices Loosen Ad Restrictions in Campaign Law*, N.Y. TIMES, June 26, 2007, at A1.

[19] 558 U.S. 310 (2010). *See also* Adam Liptak, *Justices, 5-4, Reject Corporate Cam-paign Spending Limit*, N.Y. TIMES, Jan. 22, 2010, at A1; Adam Liptak, *Justices Turn Minor Movie Case into a Blockbuster*, N.Y. TIMES, Jan. 23, 2010, at A13; Adam Liptak, *Former Justice O'Connor Sees Ill in Election Finance Ruling*, N.Y. TIMES, Jan. 27, 2010, at A17; Adam Liptak, *A Justice Responds to Criticism from Obama*, N.Y. TIMES, Feb. 4, 2010, at A15.

[20] 494 U.S. 652 (1990).

critique of presidential hopeful Hillary Clinton, the Court allowed corporations and unions to spend monies directly from their treasuries to advocate political positions and outcomes, as long as the messages were produced independently and not associated with any candidate's campaign. The First Amendment, the Court said, "does not permit laws that force speakers to retain a campaign finance attorney, conduct demographic marketing research, or seek declaratory rulings before discussing the most salient political issues of our day."[21]

Most recently, the Supreme Court has held that the BCRA's aggregate limits on the amount of money a donor may contribute in total to all candidates are an unconstitutional restriction under the First Amendment because they have nothing to do with the prevention of quid pro quo corruption.[22]

Moreover, the lines separating corporate action from corporate expression, and corporate commercial speech from corporate political speech, are still uncertain and — some would say — artificial, in that giving money and spending money are essentially the same to a corporation.[23] As corporations can only "express" themselves by disbursing money, they would prefer that all expressive activity be deemed corporate speech, which the First Amendment protects, rather than action, which may be regulated. And, too, they would prefer that all corporate speech be deemed political speech, which requires a higher level of judicial scrutiny to justify regulation than does commercial speech. But the question of what is and is not corporate political or corporate commercial speech is not easily answered.

In an attempt to provide more predictability, the Court, in *Central Hudson Gas & Electric Corp. v. Public Service Commission*, differentiated between commercial and political advertising and established a four-part test for determining when commercial speech may be regulated.[24] As a result, the First Amendment protects commercial expression as long as it promotes lawful products and services and unless the regulation comes within certain narrow circumstances. But even the *Central Hudson* case has come under fire from legal scholars who

argue that it provides no real clarification on how to distinguish between corporate and commercial speech and that in any event such a distinction is unworkable.

The issue was presented to the California Supreme Court in a direct way in 2002. In *Nike v. Kasky*,[25] the court concluded that Nike's defense of its corporate reputation and controversial business and labor practices in Southeast Asia *via* traditional PR strategies and tactics constituted commercial expression because (1) Nike was a corporate speaker, (2) the expression was motivated primarily by pecuniary interests, and (3) the targets were consumers and potential consumers. The court also held that Nike's speech was not political speech because the debate was over Nike's own operations and not corporate America's labor practices in general. Having found the expression to be commercial and not political, the California court then held that the state's false advertising statute could regulate Nike's speech and penalize Nike for its falsity.

The decision is troubling because the test the court used to determine that the speech was commercial (nature of speaker, motivation and intended audience) makes most corporate speech, even on political and social issues, commercial and therefore subject to less First Amendment protection. It also ignores the reality of the public debate. Nike was responding to activists who had full First Amendment rights and who had intentionally targeted the company. Nike could not respond in general as the California court had suggested because the debate was not framed in general terms. The Supreme Court, however, refused to hear the case on the basis that the appeal was premature and sent it back for trial. The case was later settled out of court, leaving the important question of whether Nike's speech was political or commercial unanswered.[26]

REGULATING THE SPEECH OF CORPORATIONS

While the speech of corporations has First Amendment protection, it still is highly regulated. Some of the federal agencies that directly impact the practice of public relations are the Securities and Exchange Commission, the Food and Drug Administration, and the Federal Trade Commission, which is discussed in the previous chapter. While, arguably, it is impossible for a PR practitioner to have a complete knowledge of every federal and state law and regulation that impacts a particular corporate or public communication, the practitioner should be aware of certain important concepts and definitions regularly used by each administrative agency with which his or her client deals.

[21] 558 U.S. at 324.

[22] McCutcheon v. Fed. Elections Comm'n, 134 S.Ct. 1434 (2014).

[23] *See* Adam Liptak, *Sidebar: Viewing Free Speech Through Election Law Haze*, N.Y. TIMES, May 4, 2010, at A18.

[24] 477 U.S. 557, 566 (1980):

At the outset, we must determine whether the expression is protected by the First Amendment. For commercial speech to come within that provision, it at least must concern lawful activity and not be misleading. Next, we ask whether the asserted governmental interest is substantial. If both inquiries yield positive answers, we must determine whether the regulation directly advances the governmental interest asserted, and whether it is not more extensive than is necessary to serve that interest.

The Court modified the final part of the test to require only a reasonable fit between state interests and the regulatory methods used to protect them in *Board of Trustees of the State University of New York v. Fox*, 492 U.S. 469 (1989).

[25] 45 P.3d 243 (Cal. 2002).

[26] 539 U.S. 654 (2003) (per curiam). *See also* Illinois v. Telemarketing Assoc., 538 U.S. 600 (2003); Linda Greenhouse, *Justices Rule Charity May Be Charged with Fraud*, N.Y. TIMES, May 6, 2003, at A1. Fraud in advertising was determined by the Court to be without First Amendment protection in *FTC v. Colgate-Palmolive*, 380 U.S. 374 (1965).

Lobbying

Federal and state laws impact the way businesses do business. For example, acts to protect the environment can force corporations to engage in greener technologies and practices, potentially increasing production costs. Legislation can also protect businesses from the unscrupulous activities of competitors. Thus, corporations have an interest in what laws are passed and what regulations those laws impose.

To protect their interests, corporations, as well as associations and nonprofit organizations, lobby legislators. The goal is either to avoid legislation altogether or to help shape it in ways favorable to the organization. Lobbying politicians is not a new phenomenon. It dates from at least the early days of the British parliamentary system. In the United States, the First Amendment protects lobbying because it encompasses both freedom of speech and the right to petition government for grievances. However, the government is permitted to regulate lobbying activities to prevent corruption of the democratic process.

Lobbying is controlled by the Lobbying Disclosure Act of 1995, which defines lobbyists as individuals who made more than one contact with a legislator on behalf of a client and who spent at least 20 percent of their time during a six-month period providing that service to the client.[27] A contact is defined as "a communication, either oral or written, on behalf of a client to a covered executive or legislative branch official regarding legislation, rules, regulations, grants, loans, permits, programs, or the nomination of anyone subject to Senate confirmation."[28]

Grassroots lobbying, which attempts to influence public opinion to pressure the government to act on an issue, is generally not considered lobbying for the purposes of the act.

Lobbyists who make more than $5,000 in a six-month period for their services and in-house lobbyists who expect to spend more than $20,000 on lobbying activities in a six-month period must register with the government. They are also required to file statements identifying their clients and detailing the general areas and specific issues on which they have lobbied.[29]

Lobbyists who work for foreign clients also must disclose their activities. Prior to World War II, Congress became concerned with the distribution of pro-German and Communist literature in the United States. To control this "un-American propaganda," Congress passed the Foreign Agents Registration Act of 1938.[30] Under the act and its amendments, foreign agents must report their affiliations, the manner in which they carry out their activities, and how they disseminate their information to influence American public opinion. They also must attach the label "political propaganda" to any material they disseminate.

A foreign agent is any American who acts "as a public relations counsel, publicity agent, information-service employee or political consultant" for a foreign client. As of 1966, only agents who represent foreign governments are required to register under the Foreign Agents Registration Act.[31] Those who work for foreign companies and trade associations must register under the Lobbying Disclosure Act.

Securities and Exchange Commission

The Securities and Exchange Commission oversees financial markets and grew out of the stock market crash of 1929. Congress passed the Securities Act of 1933 and the Securities Exchange Act of 1934 in response to concerns that speculators partly caused the Great Depression. The 1934 Act created the SEC to "administer federal securities laws and issue rules and regulations to provide protection for investors and ensure that the securities markets are fair and honest."[32] President Franklin Roosevelt stated the SEC's guiding principle: "No essentially important element [may] be concealed from the buying public."[33] The purpose of the agency and the myriad of securities laws enacted in the early 1930s, the Supreme Court has said, is "to substitute a philosophy of full disclosure for the philosophy of *caveat emptor* and thus to achieve a high standard of business ethics in the ... industry."[34]

The SEC operates on the assumption that transparency leads to greater levels of trust. Thus, it seeks to level the playing field for all investors by requiring truthful, complete and timely disclosure to the public of information about publicly traded companies that could be important to an investor's decision to buy, sell or hold securities.

The 1933 Act, also called the "Truth in Securities Act," deals with new issues of stock. It requires that, before any security may be offered for sale to the public, a registration statement disclosing financial and other information about the issuing company be filed with the SEC. While the SEC reviews the material, no press releases, news conferences or other mass media publicity encouraging the sale of the new securities on behalf of

---

[27] 2 U.S.C.S. §1601 *et seq.* (2002).

[28] *Lawmakers Enact Lobbying Reforms*, CONGR. Q. 1995 ALMANAC: 104TH CONGRESS § 1, 40 (1996).

[29] *Id.*

[30] 22 U.S.C. §611 *et seq.* (1988).

[31] 22 U.S.C. §611(b) (2002).

[32] *See* http://www.sec.gov.

[33] Message of the President to Congress, House of Representatives Report No. 85, 73rd Congress, 1st Sess. 2 (Mar. 29, 1933).

[34] SEC v. Capital Gaines Research Bureau, 375 U.S. 180, 186 (1963). These laws include the Securities Act of 1933, 15 U.S.C. 78 (2009); the Securities Exchange Act of 1934, 15 U.S.C. 78 (2009); the Public Utility Holding Company Act of 1935, 15 U.S.C. 79 (2009); the Trust Indenture Act of 1939, 15 U.S.C. 77 (2009); the Investment Company Act of 1940, 15 U.S.C. 80 (2009).

the corporation are permitted, although the company may still publish regular information through its normal channels, such as a Website. The only advertisements allowed during this waiting period are "tombstone" ads, text-based ads with no graphics or persuasive techniques that simply identify the company and the number of securities to be issued.

After the SEC deems the registration effective, the stock is sold in an initial public offering. No earnings forecasts or research reports may be issued on behalf of the company, however, for forty days, the "quiet period," after the IPO.

The Securities Exchange Act of 1934, on the other hand, applies to stock already publicly traded. Its purposes are to ensure full disclosure of timely and pertinent information and to prevent deception or manipulation of prices. As a result, the SEC requires reports to be filed periodically detailing a company's financial state, its future plans and other information that could affect an investor's decision regarding that company's securities.

The best-known report is Form 10-K, which companies must file with the SEC annually. In it, a company discloses specific information about its financial status and direction. Form 10-K is the basis of the annual report that companies must give shareholders no less than fifteen days prior to the company's annual meeting. PR professionals are often involved in writing the narrative portion of annual reports, including the letter to the shareholders from the president/CEO, and thus need to be aware of the SEC rules to avoid liability.

In addition to the annual report, the SEC requires timely and accurate disclosure of material facts or claims impacting the company. A fact is material if it would influence an individual's decision to buy, sell or hold a particular stock. The claim need not actually influence an investor's decision to buy, nor must the investor actually lose money for the claim to be considered deceptive. The material fact must only have the capacity to affect an investor's choices. Such an omission — however inadvertent — makes the information false and misleading, according to the SEC. For the Supreme Court:

> An omitted fact is material if there is a substantial likelihood that a reasonable shareholder would consider it important in deciding how to vote.... Put another way, there must be a substantial likelihood that the disclosure of the omitted fact would have been viewed by the reasonable investor as having significantly altered the "total mix" of information available.[35]

Corporations traditionally considered material facts requiring disclosure as those that would affect a company's earnings by 5 percent or more. But for the SEC, the question is whether a reasonable investor would consider the information to be important or material in the context of the company's overall financial situation. Such extensive disclosure requirements reinforce Congress' belief that "there cannot be honest markets without honest publicity. Manipulation and dishonest practices of the marketplace thrive on mystery and secrecy."[36]

Failure or delay in disclosing material information can be evidence of a company's deceptive or misleading actions or even proof of intention to defraud. On the other hand, the information must be "available and ripe for publication" before there commences a duty to disclose. To be ripe under this requirement, the content must be verified sufficiently to permit the officers and directors to have full confidence in its accuracy.[37]

As in the area of advertising, corporate release of knowingly false and misleading information may be equated with fraudulent misrepresentation and may even give rise to private enforcement actions, as long as the misrepresentation actually caused a loss.[38] Information may be fraudulently misrepresentative when a corporation uses "indefinite and unverifiable" terms — such as "high value" or "fair" — in public communication. In fact, "such conclusory terms in an economic context are reasonably understood to rest on a factual basis that justifies them as accurate, the absence of which renders them misleading." Corporate expression "should be to inform, not to challenge, the reader's critical wits."[39] Disclosure that is made with honesty of purpose and freedom from fraudulent intent, without the knowledge of any circumstances that would cause a reasonable individual to inquire further, is good faith disclosure.

The courts and the SEC have made it clear that PR agencies cannot escape liability for misleading investors by saying they relied on the company's representations. A PR agency must undertake a reasonable investigation to satisfy itself that the representations are accurate.

Regulation FD (fair disclosure), an SEC rule that went into effect in 2000, is designed to make important corporate information available to individual investors by prohibiting unfair selective disclosure. The rule extended the duty to disclose information to include the practice of giving corporate news first to stock analysts and mutual fund managers before announcing it publicly, as well as to disclose corporate executives' cancellations of stock purchases.[40] Under Regulation FD, if the nonpub-

---

[35] TSC Indus. v. Northway, 426 U.S. 438, 449 (1976). The falsehood's materiality is its "natural tendency to influence, or [capacity for] influencing, the decision of the ... body to which it was addressed." Kungys v. United States, 485 U.S. 759, 770 (1988).

[36] House of Representatives Report No. 1383, 73rd Congress, 2d Sess. 11 (1934).

[37] Financial Indus. Fund v. McDonnell Douglas Corp., 474 F.2d 514, 519 (10th Cir. 1973).

[38] *See* J.I. Case Co. v. Borak, 377 U.S. 426 (1964). *See also* Dura Pharmaceuticals v. Broudo, 544 U.S. 336, (2005); Linda Greenhouse, *Securities Fraud Standards Upheld by Supreme Court*, N.Y. TIMES, Apr. 20, 2005, at C3.

[39] Virginia Bankshares v. Sandberg, 501 U.S. 1083, 1097 (1991).

[40] *See* Danny Hakim, *S.E.C. Approves Regulation Against Selective Disclosure*, N.Y.

lic, material information is disclosed intentionally, distribution of the same information to the public must be made simultaneously. If the disclosure is unintentional, the information must then be released to the public promptly, usually within twenty-four hours, *via* recognized channels of distribution.

In 2012, the SEC investigated whether Reed Hastings, the CEO of Netflix, violated Regulation FD when he posted on his personal Facebook page that Netflix had streamed one billion hours of content in June of that year. That was a record for the company, but Netflix had not disclosed it publicly. The SEC decided not to take action against Hastings, opting instead to clarify that companies must inform the public about which channels of communication, including social media sites, they will use to disseminate nonpublic, material information. As the SEC noted, "Without such notice, the investing public would be forced to keep pace with a changing and expanding universe of potential disclosure channels, a virtually impossible task."[41]

The SEC also prohibits insider trading. In modern corporate law, the term "insider" is generally defined as anyone who has company information that is not available to the general public. Corporate officers and directors obviously fall into this category.[42] PR professionals, at times, also may be so classified. An insider must act on the nonpublic information for personal gain in order to be in violation of the law. For example, in August 2016, the SEC charged a cardiologist who was the principal investigator of a drug trial, with insider trading because he sold all of his shares in the drug company when he learned the trial was being suspended because the drug was causing allergic reactions. By selling his stock before the news became public, he managed to avoid $160,000 in potential losses.[43] Individuals can still be guilty of insider trading, however, even if they did not act on the information but tipped off others, such as their family and friends, who in turn acted on the information.

At the heart of the ban on insider trading and tipping is the concept of fiduciary duty. Those who manage a corporation and their advisors owe a duty to the corporation's shareholders to act at all times in the best interests of the corporation. That fiduciary duty is breached when insiders use nonpublic material information to trade a corporation's shares and may well subject the corporation and its directors and officers to lawsuits by the SEC and individual investors.

The best known of the recent insider cases brought by the SEC involved Martha Stewart. She was accused of selling her shares in the biopharmaceutical firm ImClone Systems, Inc., in 2001. The SEC alleged that she did so after her broker told her that ImClone's CEO had sold his. ImClone at the time was seeking approval from the Food and Drug Administration for a new cancer drug. The actions of ImClone's CEO suggested that the FDA was going to deny the company's application, prompting Stewart to sell her shares, according to the SEC. It settled its civil lawsuit with Stewart when she agreed to a five-year ban on serving as a director of a public company and a five-year limitation on her services as an officer, and to pay a $195,081 fine.[44]

Food and Drug Administration

Congress initially enacted the Pure Food and Drug Act of 1906 after Upton Sinclair and other muckraking journalists exposed the hazardous conditions of the food and drugs being sold to the public.[45] The act prohibited the interstate transport of unlawful food and drugs. To be "unlawful," food could not include any ingredients "that would substitute for the food, conceal damage, pose a health hazard, or constitute a filthy or decomposed substance."[46] Drugs had to indicate the presence of certain dangerous ingredients on their labels. But according to the Supreme Court, the 1906 law did not apply to false therapeutic claims.[47] No testing of drugs for safety was required. Thus, products such as Radithor, a tonic that contained radium and subjected users to a slow and painful death, were protected.[48] It took a drug called "Elixir Sulfanilamide," marketed by a Tennessee company as a new wonder drug in the treatment of streptococcal infections, to prompt changes. Elixir Sulfanilamide contained the highly toxic compound antifreeze and killed 100 people, many of them children, in fifteen states over a two-month period in 1937.[49] The incident led to the enactment of the 1938 Food, Drug and Cosmetic Act, the basis of the current law. Today, the FDA regulates food, drugs, medical devices, vaccines, cosmetics, and radiation-emitting, veterinary and tobacco products.

Specifically, the FDA is concerned with claims on a product's packaging, which includes "all labels and other written, printed, or graphic matter upon any article or any of its containers or

---

TIMES, Aug. 11, 2000, at C7; Floyd Norris, *S.E.C. Tells Concerns to Disclose Cancellations of Stock Purchases*, N.Y. TIMES, Feb. 1, 2001, at C1.

[41] Report of Investigation Pursuant to Section 21(a) of the Securities Exchange Act of 1934: Netflix, Inc., and Reed Hastings, Release No. 69279 (Apr. 2, 2013), p. 7.

[42] *See* SEC v. Texas Gulf Sulfur Co., 401 F.2d 833 (2d Cir. 1968).

[43] "SEC Charges Cardiologist with Insider Trading on Confidential Drug Trial Developments," SEC 2016-156, Aug. 4, 2016.

[44] *See* Landon Thomas Jr., *Stewart Deal Resolves Stock Case*, N.Y. TIMES, Aug. 8, 2006, at C1.

[45] 34 Stat. 768 (1906).

[46] *FDA History, Part I: The 1906 Food and Drugs Act and Its Enforcement*, http://www.fda.gov/AboutFDA/WhatWeDo/History/Origin/ucm054819.htm (accessed May 21, 2014).

[47] United States v. Johnson, 221 U.S. 488 (1911).

[48] *See FDA History, Part II: The 1938 Food, Drug and Cosmetics Act.* http://www.fda.gov/AboutFDA/WhatWeDo/History/Origin/ucm054826.htm (accessed May 21, 2014).

[49] *See* Carol Ballentine, *Taste of Raspberries, Taste of Death: The 1937 Elixir Sulfanilamide Incident*, FDA CONSUMER MAGAZINE, June 1981, at 1.

wrappers, or accompanying such article,"[50] though it also regulates the advertising of all prescription drugs.[51] A product is deemed to be misbranded "unless its labeling bears adequate directions for use."[52] The regulation covers pharmaceutical trade and generic names, pesticides and similar products, and promotional materials.[53] The Federal Trade Commission, not the FDA, controls the contents of book, magazine, or non-label advertising of food and non-prescription drug products, and evaluates them under a "truthful and not misleading" standard.[54]

In general, the FDA bars all health claims from labels without prior approval.[55] The Food and Drug Administration Modernization Act of 1994 allowed health claims on food labels if supported by authoritative statements from certain health research and protection agencies, such as the National Academy of Sciences, provided that the FDA was given pre-marketing notice.[56] Out of "concern over excessive regulation of dietary supplements and the suppression of truthful information,"[57] Congress enacted the Dietary Supplement Health and Education Act of 1994, which allows certain health claims on the labels of dietary supplements without petitioning the FDA for approval.[58] The claims may include statements that dietary supplements restore nutrient deficiency, claims regarding how the human body uses the nutrient and proclamations that dietary supplements contribute to one's general well being.[59] Yet these may only be made if the manufacturer has substantiation that the claim is "truthful and not misleading," if the label expressly states that the FDA has not evaluated the claim, and if the FDA is notified thirty days before the marketing claim is made.

In response to congressional passage of the Nutrition Labeling and Education Act of 1990,[60] the FDA enacted regulations allowing health claims to be made only when it

determines, based on the totality of publicly available scientific evidence (including evidence from well-designed studies conducted in a manner which is consistent with generally recognized scientific procedures and principles), that there is significant scientific agreement, among experts qualified by scientific training and experience to evaluate such claims, that the claim is supported by such evidence.[61]

A lawsuit claiming that the requirements were an unlawful prior restraint of truthful commercial speech by the FDA was determined in 1998 to be without merit.[62]

In 2002, the FDA reviewed its rules about what corporations may say about products (specifically, food, drugs, cosmetics or supplements). The review came after the Supreme Court overturned a ban on pharmacies from advertising the availability of "compounded" pharmaceuticals (drugs pharmacists mix themselves for the specific needs of certain types of patients).[63] Scolding the government for its failure to consider alternatives to a complete advertising ban, the Court offered a ringing defense of free expression: "If the First Amendment means anything, it means that regulating speech must be a last — not first — resort."[64] Recognizing the challenge, the FDA stated:

> The FDA must continue to pursue regulation of products for purposes of protecting the public health with a full recognition of the evolving judicial landscape in areas that directly affect its ability to regulate words. . . . In particular, the FDA intends to defend [its regulations] against constitutional challenges [while seeking] to ensure ... that its regulations, guidances, policies, and practices comply with the First Amendment.[65]

This commitment has already been challenged. The 2009 Family Smoking Prevention and Tobacco Control Act gave the FDA extensive regulatory control over tobacco for the first time since the U.S. surgeon general declared smoking a health hazard in 1966.[66] In response, the FDA adopted regulations that restricted the advertising, sale and distribution of cigarettes and smokeless tobacco to minors. Even before those restrictions took effect in 2010, tobacco companies challenged the provision that prohibited the use of color on labels and in advertisements,

---

[50] 21 U.S.C. 321(m) (2009). *See also* Marian Burros, *U.S.D.A. Enters Debate on Organic Label Law*, N.Y. TIMES, Feb. 26, 2003, at D1; Joyce Cohen, *Amid a Lawsuit, Keeping Track of a Candy Wrapper's Fine Print*, N.Y. TIMES, Nov. 9, 2005, at D18; Andrew Martin, *Food Labels Lack Origins Despite Law*, N.Y. TIMES, July 2, 2007, at A1.

[51] FDA rules concerning the content of prescription drug ads may be found beginning at 21 C.F.R. 202.1.a (2009). *See, e.g.*, Stuart Elliott, *FDA Criticizes Viagra Ads, Prompting Pfizer To Halt Them*, N.Y. TIMES, Nov. 16, 2004, at C6.

[52] 21 U.S.C. 352(f) (2009). *See also* Heckler v. Chaney, 470 U.S. 821 (1985).

[53] *See* Ruckelshaus v. Monsanto, 467 U.S. 986 (1984) (applying the Federal Insecticide, Fungicide and Rodenticide Act of 1972, 7 U.S.C. 135FF (2009)); Abbott Labs v. Gardner, 387 U.S. 136 (1967); United States v. Exachol, 716 F. Supp. 787 (S.D. N.Y. 1989).

[54] 21 U.S.C. 343(a) (2009).

[55] *See* William Neuman, *F.D.A. Cracks Down on Nestlé and Others Over Health Claims on Labels*, N.Y. TIMES, Mar. 4, 2010, at B3.

[56] 21 U.S.C. 343(r) (2009).

[57] Nutritional Health Alliance v. Shalala, 953 F. Supp. 526, 528 (S.D. N.Y. 1997).

[58] 21 U.S.C. 343(r) (2009).

[59] *See* Donald G. McNeil Jr. & Sherri Day, *F.D.A. to Put New Rules on Dietary Supplements*, N.Y. TIMES, Mar. 8, 2003, at A13. *See also* Donald G. McNeil Jr., *Sometimes, the Labels Lie*, N.Y. TIMES, Sept. 9, 2003, at D7.

[60] 21 U.S.C. 301 (2009).

[61] 21 C.F.R. 101.14(c) (2009).

[62] Nutritional Health Alliance v. Shalala, 144 F.3d 220 (2d Cir. 1998).

[63] Thompson v. Western States Med. Ctr., 535 U.S. 357 (2002). *See also* Gina Kolata, *Stung by Courts, F.D.A. Rethinks Its Rules*, N.Y. TIMES, Oct. 15, 2002, at D1.

[64] *Id.* at 373. *See also* Linda Greenhouse, *Citing Free Speech, Justices Lift a Ban on Advertising Mixed-to-Order Drugs*, N.Y. TIMES, Apr. 30, 2002, at A20.

[65] 67 Fed. Reg. at 34943 (May 16, 2002). *See also* Gardiner Harris, *FDA Moves Toward More Openness with the Public*, N.Y. TIMES, Feb. 20, 2005, at A19.

[66] 123 Stat. 1776, Public Law 111-31 (June 22, 2009).

claiming it was more extensive than necessary to reduce minors' tobacco use. A U.S. district court agreed, finding that the ban on all uses of color demonstrated a lack of tailoring.[67]

Undeterred, the FDA decided to require color warnings that graphically depict the negative health consequences of smoking. The warnings were to occupy the top half of the front and back of all cigarette packages. The Sixth Circuit ruled that regulations requiring the warnings, which were to take effect in 2012, were constitutional.[68] The D.C. Circuit Court of Appeals, however, in a lawsuit brought by five tobacco companies, held the same requirements were unconstitutional, setting up a Supreme Court challenge.[69] The D.C. court applied the *Central Hudson* standard to the regulation because "this case ... involves a compelled commercial disclosure."[70] In concluding that the graphic warnings did not pass the *Central Hudson* test, the court noted:

> The FDA failed to present any data — much less the substantial evidence required ... — showing that enacting their proposed graphic warnings will accomplish the agency's stated objective of reducing smoking rates.[71]

In August 2016, the FDA finalized a rule extending its reach to all tobacco products,[72] including "hookah, e-cigarettes, dissolvables, smokeless tobacco, cigarettes, all cigars, roll-your-own tobacco, pipe tobacco, and future tobacco products."[73] The rule prevents the sale of such products to anyone under the age of 18 and requires FDA approval for the sale of all tobacco products that have come on the market since 2007. Not surprisingly, the rule was immediately the subject of lawsuits.[74] In one such case, Nicopure Labs, an e-cigarette company, asked a judge of the D.C. federal court to vacate the rule in part on the basis that the rule "violates the First Amendment in that the FDA bars manufacturers . . . from making truthful and non-misleading

statements about their e-cigarette devices."[75]

National Labor Relations Board

In 1935, Congress passed the National Labor Relations Act to protect the rights of both employees and employers, and to encourage collective bargaining.[76] The act was a formal recognition of the inequality of bargaining power between employees and employers and an attempt to balance that power. While labor law is a relatively settled legal area, social media are taking the National Labor Relations Board into uncharted waters. At issue before the NLRB most recently was a company's social media policy for employees.

In 2014, an administrative law judge ruled that four provisions of the social media policy of the Kroger grocery chain were unlawfully broad and violated the employees' speech rights. One of the provisions required workers to include a disclaimer that they did not represent the company if they identified themselves as Kroger employees and published "any work-related information online." The judge wrote that "the requirement that a disclaimer be posted by the employee every time he or she speaks on work-related issues and is identifiable as an employee of the employer, is unduly burdensome ... and will have a tendency to chill legitimate" speech about labor issues.[77]

The other provisions barred the use of Kroger's logo or insignia without permission; the discussion of confidential or proprietary information including "rumors, speculation or personnel matters;" and the engagement in "behavior that would be inappropriate at work." In each case, the judge found the restrictions to be overly broad. PR practitioners, who typically help develop such policies, should monitor the situation closely to ensure their clients' policies are in compliance.

TORT LAW

A tort is a legal wrong that results in damages to a person or property caused by the actions or omissions of another individual. Tort law has three purposes: compensation, justice and deterrence. It deals with fairly compensating individuals for losses that the actions of others caused. The harms, at a minimum, may be physical (such as battery, trespass to land or intrusion upon physical solitude), mental (such as infliction of emotional distress) or reputational (such as defamation or misappropria-

---

[67] Commonwealth Brands, Inc. v. United States, 678 F. Supp. 2d 512 (W.D. Ky. 2010).

[68] Discount Tobacco City & Lottery, Inc. v. United States, 674 F. 3d 509 (6th Cir. 2012).

[69] R.J. Reynolds Tobacco Co. v. FDA, 696 F.3d 1205 (D.C. Cir. 2012).

[70] *Id.* at 1217.

[71] *Id.* at 1222.

[72] Deeming Tobacco Products to Be Subject to the Federal Food, Drug, and Cosmetic Act, as Amended by the Family Smoking Prevention and Tobacco Control Act; Restrictions on the Sale and Distribution of Tobacco Products and Required Warnings Statements for Tobacco Products, No. FDA-2014-N-0189, 81 Fed. Reg. 28, 973 (May 10, 2016).

[73] *The Facts on the FDA's New Tobacco Rule.* http://www.fda.gov/ForConsumers/ConsumerUpdates/ucm506676.htm (accessed Aug. 9, 2016).

[74] *See* Right to Be Smoke-Free Coalition, et al. v. FDA, No. 1:16-cv-01210 (D.D.C. June 20, 2016); Cyclops Vapor 2, LLC, et al. v. FDA, et al., Co. 2:16-cv-556 (M.D. Ala. July 8, 2016); Cigar Association of America, et al. v. FDA, No. 1:16-cv-01460 (D.D.C. July 15, 2016).

[75] Nicopure Labs, LLC v. FDA, et al., No. 1:16-cv-00878-ABJ (D.D.C. May 10, 2016). Allison H. Semaya, *The FDA Faces Challenges to its New Regulations for E-Cigarettes,* PRODUCT LIABILITY MONITOR, Aug. 2, 2016. https://product-liability.weil.com/legislation/the-fda-faces-challenges-to-its-new-regulations-for-e-cigarettes (accessed Aug. 9, 2016).

[76] 29 U.S.C. §§ 151-169.

[77] Kroger Co. of Mich. v. Granger, NLRB, No. 07-CA-098566 (Apr. 22, 2014).

tion). There are three types of torts:
- negligent (the defendant did not intend to cause harm);
- intentional (the defendant caused harm intentionally); and
- strict liability (the defendant is liable regardless of intention or negligence).

A negligent tort has four elements, all of which must be present for a plaintiff to be successful:
- the defendant must owe the plaintiff a duty of care;
- the defendant must have breached that duty;
- the plaintiff must have been injured or harmed; and
- the breach of duty must have caused the harm.

Everyone has a duty to protect others from harms that his or her actions or omissions cause. The degree of required care varies, but it is always based on what a reasonable person would have done under the circumstances. Doctors, for example, are held to the standard of care expected of a reasonable member of the medical profession. Defendants breach their duty of care by falling short of what a reasonable person would have done.

The most important element of negligence is causation. Did the defendant's actions cause the harm? The actions must be the actual cause (the plaintiff would not have been injured but for the defendant's actions) and the proximate cause. Proximate cause operates as a policy limit to actual causation liability. The question the courts ask is, was the injury or harm foreseeable? For example, in a two-car collision, a passenger was ejected and thrown thirty feet. His leg was impaled on the remains of a municipal drainpipe. The passenger sued the village for negligence.[78] The court held that the accident was not foreseeable, describing the circumstances as "tragically bizarre" and possibly even a unique outcome.[79] The opposite result came in *Weirum v. RKO General*.[80] In that case a radio station held a promotion in which a disc jockey, popular with teens, drove to unspecified locations around the city. The first person to physically locate the DJ would receive a prize. Two teens in separate cars decided to follow the DJ. As they raced each other on the highway to get to the DJ first, one forced another car into the center divider, killing its driver. The deceased's family sued the radio station for negligence, arguing that it should have known teens would drive recklessly to win the contest. The court agreed that it was foreseeable that "defender's youthful listeners ... would race to arrive first at the next site and in their haste would disregard the demands of highway safety."[81]

Product Liability

Product liability is the liability of manufacturers and sellers for damages their defective products cause. A PR practitioner has a duty to warn consumers of dangerous conditions associated with a product.[82]

The general rule is that for a duty to warn to exist, a product must be dangerous beyond the extent to which a reasonable consumer, with common knowledge about the product's characteristics, would use it. To mitigate a product's inherent danger, a seller could be required to provide directions for use of the product. If a product contains a dangerous ingredient — or one whose danger is not widely known or that an average consumer would not reasonably expect to find contained in the product — a seller could be required to provide a warning with each sale of the product. For example, warnings as to appropriate use are generally required for poisonous drugs.

To determine the adequacy of directions or warnings, judges must balance "the likelihood that the product would cause the harm complained of, and the seriousness of that harm, against the burden on the manufacturer of providing an adequate warning."[83] Adequacy may be measured

> not only by what is stated, but also by the manner in which it is stated. A reasonable warning not only conveys a fair indication of the nature of the dangers involved, but also warns with the degree of intensity demanded by the nature of the risk. A warning may be found to be unreasonable in that it was unduly delayed, reluctant in tone, or lacking in a sense of urgency.[84]

Adequacy also requires resolving other questions: How explicit must the warning be?[85] In whose language must the warning be made?[86] At what point is a warning sufficient?[87]

When a product's label meets a federal statute's labeling requirements, the manufacturer is usually protected from tort lawsuits brought in state courts, although the Supreme Court

---

[78] Cunis v. Brennan, 308 N.E.2d 617 (Ill. 1974).

[79] *Id.* at 620.

[80] 539 P. 2d 36 (Cal. 1975).

[81] *Id.* at 40.

[82] *See* Albright v. Upjohn Co., 788 F.2d 1217 (6th Cir. 1986).

[83] Ayers v. Johnson & Johnson Baby Products Co., 818 P.2d 1337, 1346 (Wash. 1991).

[84] Seley v. G.D. Searle Co., 423 N.E.2d 831, 837 (Ohio 1981).

[85] In *Ayers*, the Court concluded that because Johnson & Johnson's Baby Oil was marketed as "pure and gentle," consumers could reasonably have concluded that it was safe even if accidentally inhaled and, therefore, a more explicit warning was required. 818 P.2d at 1346-47.

[86] *See* Ramierz v. Plough, 863 P.2d 167 (Cal. 1993) (holding that warnings in English only regarding the dangers of non-prescription drugs were adequate).

[87] *See* MacDonald v. Ortho Pharmaceutical Corp., 475 N.E.2d 65, 69 (Mass. 1985) (holding that warnings included with oral contraceptives must be given to all "who it is foreseeable will come in contact with, and consequently be endangered by" the product, except in certain, narrow circumstances when the manufacturer only has a duty to warn a "responsible, ... learned intermediary," such as a physician).

has ruled that neither federal regulatory approval nor advertising control completely shields drug companies and cigarette manufacturers from claims of fraudulent deception.[88]

The same rule applies to manufacturers' product warranties and marketing promises. A company that promoted its "Golfing Gizmo" as "completely safe" was held liable when a 13-year-old boy hit the ball in an unusual manner and was struck in the head when the ball bounced back. The device consisted of a golf ball attached to an elastic cord. It was supposed to allow users to improve their swings without having to retrieve balls. The company's promotional literature urged users to "drive the ball with full power" since the "ball will not hit player." The court upheld an award based on claims of breach of warranty and misrepresentation.[89]

Strict liability is often applied in cases involving dangerous or defective products. With strict liability, the manufacturers or sellers of a product are liable for damages that result from the use of the product even if they were not negligent in producing or selling it. The application of strict liability is a matter of public policy and is an attempt to protect consumers.

Misrepresentation

The core of the intentional tort of misrepresentation is a person's reliance on a false statement. Thus, fraudulent misrepresentation requires:

(1) a false statement that is material — substantially central to a person's decision,

(2) knowledge of that falsity on the part of the communicator,

(3) an intention to induce others to make economic decisions based upon the statement, and

(4) damages caused by reliance on the statement.

Negligent misrepresentation occurs when a PR practitioner makes a false representation of a material fact in his or her professional capacity, when the practitioner fails to use reasonable care to determine the statement's truth, and when the practitioner owes a duty to the person who justifiably relied on it, causing damages. However, the general rule is that nondisclosure, when two parties are dealing independently and knowingly, "at arm's length," is not grounds for a misrepresentation claim.[90] Third parties, such as PR agencies, are not generally li-

able for negligent misrepresentation unless they

(1) know their statements will be used for a particular purpose,

(2) know another specific party will rely on their statements, and

(3) are somehow linked to that party and understand the consequences of that party's reliance on their statements.[91]

Interference in a Business Relationship

Tortious interference in a business relationship is an example of an intentional tort. There are two types of tortious interference. The first occurs when an individual convinces another to breach a contract with a third entity. The second occurs when an individual acts to prevent another from successfully establishing or maintaining a business relationship. Such a claim requires that

(1) there was some sort of a contractual or beneficial business relationship between two parties,

(2) the defendant was aware of the relationship,

(3) the defendant intentionally caused a breach in that relationship, and

(4) damage resulted.

For example, if a PR practitioner working for Agency A learns that a competitor, Agency B, is pitching its services to a new company in town and the Agency A petitioner calls the company and says that PR Agency B does lousy work, causing the company not to hire Agency B, that action is unethical according to PRSA's Code of Conduct. In addition, the Agency A practitioner could be sued for tortious interference in a business relationship.

In the early twentieth century, corporations used the tort as a weapon to keep employees from joining labor unions.[92] More recently, in what ended up a PR fiasco for Texaco, Pennzoil filed a tortious interference claim when Texaco topped Pennzoil's offer for Getty Oil — interfering with the two companies' agreement. The result was a verdict of $7.53 billion in actual damages and $2.5 billion in punitive damages for Pennzoil, a final appeal to

---

[88] *See* Wyeth v. Levine, 555 U.S. 555 (2009); Altria Group v. Good, 555 U.S. 70 (2008); Adam Liptak, *No Legal Shield in Drug Labeling*, N.Y. TIMES, Mar. 5, 2009, at A1; Adam Liptak, *Top Court Lets Smokers Sue for Fraud*, N.Y. TIMES, Dec. 16, 2008, at B1. *See also* Cipollone v. Liggett Group, 505 U.S. 504 (1992) (holding that federal regulation of cigarette warning labels in the Federal Cigarette Labeling and Advertising Act of 1965, 15 U.S.C. 1331 (2009), and its successor, the Public Health Cigarette Smoking Act of 1969, 15 U.S.C. 1331-1340 (2009), preempted state labeling requirements).

[89] Hauter v. Zogarts, 534 P.2d 377 (Cal. 1975).

[90] *See* Swinton v. Whitinsville Sav. Bank, 42 N.E.2d 808 (Mass. 1942) (holding that a vendor who failed to disclose as a latent defect that the house was infested with ter-

mites did not commit misrepresentation). It is important to note that many jurisdictions by state statute require termite inspections by licensed inspectors before a house may be sold. For another type of transaction, *see Osborn v. Gene Teague Chevrolet*, 459 P.2d 988 (Or. 1969) (upholding a fraud verdict when a used car dealer had reset a vehicle's odometer from 100,000 miles to 62,000 miles, even in the absence of any verbal statement misrepresenting the vehicle's condition).

[91] *See* Credit Alliance Corp. v. Andersen & Co., 483 N.E.2d 110 (N.Y. 1985) (where the detrimental reliance on a report by certified public accountants was at issue).

[92] *See* Hitchman Coal & Coke Co. v. Mitchell, 245 U.S. 229 (1917). The miners' decision to join a labor union was ruled to have violated their "yellow dog" contracts in which they agreed not to join a union while employed by the mining company. The outcome was first changed by enactment of the Norris-Laguardia Act of 1932, 29 U.S.C. 101 (2009), which prohibited the enforcement of "yellow dog" contracts in federal courts. These type of contracts were finally outlawed by the National Labor Relations Act of 1935, 29 U.S.C. 151 (2009), which made it an "unfair labor practice" to discriminate against employees because of their union membership.

the Supreme Court, and an ultimate settlement of $3 billion.[93]

CONTRACT LAW

Because public relations involves the marketing of corporate ideas and ideals, as well as the defense of economic actions and transactions (such as contracts), a close, symbiotic relationship exists between business law and public relations law.

At its simplest, a contract consists of an offer, acceptance of the offer, and consideration. The offer must be specific, such as "I am offering my car for sale for $1,000." If someone agrees to the price, there is acceptance. If the person responds instead with "I'll pay you $900 for the car," that is a new offer and requires the seller's acceptance. For a valid contract, there must be consideration, an exchange of something of value by each party. In the car example, the car and the purchase price serve as consideration. If your friend says he will give you his car when he graduates, there is no consideration and his "promise" is not enforceable. He can do whatever he wants with the car after graduation, and you are out of luck.

Contracts do not need to be in writing to be valid although some are required by law to be so, and others should be written because of their complexity, the length of the contractual duration or their importance.

Contracts such as release forms and consent agreements are often used in public relations to secure the right to use the name or likeness of someone in public relations materials. Although releases may not be necessary in every situation, the basic rule of thumb is that if the use is commercial — if it is for purposes of trade — releases are necessary. An ideal consent release should be in writing and contain these elements:

1. consideration or exchange of value,

2. identification of parties' names and ages,

3. a statement as to the agreement's scope and duration,

4. words binding one's legal successors and representatives, and

5. a statement that the agreement is the full agreement, that no promises were made not plainly stated in the release.

It is also wise to keep the agreement broader than the specific purpose at hand to protect future uses of the material.

Under contract law, minors, usually under the age of 18, are considered too young to understand the significance of a contract. Therefore, they may disaffirm any contract they sign. Typically, PR practitioners have the parents or guardians sign on the behalf of the minor, but care must be taken whenever minors are being used in promotional materials.

Contracts with Clients

PR practitioners and their clients typically sign contracts stipulating:

- the terms of work to be produced, timeliness, deadlines, billing routines, the use of free-lancers through sub-contracting and other pertinent data;

- the terms of supplying information, timetables for review of work and payment schedules.

Once contracts are signed, both parties must satisfy their parts of the bargain. In other words, they must deliver the consideration provided for in the contract. In the case of the PR practitioner, that might mean a campaign plan, for example. But what if the client does not like the plan or considers it of inferior quality? As long as the client provides an honest evaluation of the work, the client can cancel the contract on the basis that the practitioner did not fulfill the terms of the contract to its satisfaction.[94]

Employment Contracts

Most new practitioners for organizations or PR agencies are required to sign an employment contract. Such a contract sets out the expectations of the employer and employee. Most employment contracts allow termination only for cause. Two other provisions typically found in employment contracts governing PR positions are non-compete covenants and confidentiality agreements.

Non-Compete Covenants. A covenant not to compete restricts the employment of a PR practitioner by a company's competitors in order to protect a company's trade secrets, customer contacts and other intellectual property.[95] The common law prohibition against contracts in restraint of trade is one of the oldest and most firmly established in the law.[96] Public policy concerns still generally disfavor such restraints and favor an individual's freedom of contract and right to work.[97] Essentially, non-compete clauses must not deny the practitioner the right to earn a living.

Thus, such clauses in employment agreements must be reasonable in both duration (time) and space (geography).[98] Is the

---

[93] *See* Texaco v. Pennzoil, 485 U.S. 994 (1988); Texaco v. Pennzoil, 729 S.W.2d 768 (Tex. App. 1987).

[94] *See* Ard Dr. Pepper Bottling Co. v. Dr. Pepper Co., 202 F.2d 372 (5th Cir. 1953).

[95] *See* David Koeppel, *Lose the Employee, Keep the Business*, N.Y. TIMES, May 5, 2005, at C5.

[96] *See* Dutch Maid Bakeries v. Schleicher, 131 P.2d 630, 634 (Wyo. 1942).

[97] For example, chapter 237 of the Acts of 1998 of the Commonwealth of Massachusetts (amending chapter 149 of the General Laws of the Commonwealth of Massachusetts) prohibits the use of such clauses in employment contracts in the broadcasting industry.

[98] For an example of such an agreement applied in a media business context, *see*

time or geographic limitation greater than required to protect the employer's interests? Do the limitations impose an undue hardship on the employee's ability to profit from his or her skills? Is either limitation injurious to the public's interest, which favors free competition in the market?

Because such agreements typically favor the employer, courts place the initial burden on the employer to prove that the non-compete clause is reasonable, is fairly related to and is necessary to protect the employer's business interests or activities.[99] The employer is not entitled to protection against ordinary competition in the market. For example, even if a business were national in scope, an agreement not to compete anywhere in the nation would be unreasonable.

Confidentiality Agreements. Most employment contracts for PR positions require a confidentiality or nondisclosure agreement because PR practitioners are often privy to their clients' confidential and proprietary information. Clients want to know that information is protected from disclosure to competitors and the public. PR professionals are not like doctors, ministers and attorneys who have a legally privileged relationship with patients and clients. Thus, the nondisclosure agreement is used to create a confidential relationship to protect nonpublic business information. It should be noted that the confidentiality agreement will not necessarily protect you from being required to disclose what you know before a judge.

Ownership of Work and Proposals

In most situations, the materials PR professionals prepare for an employer are "works for hire." We create them in the course of our employment and they belong to our employers. The case may be different, however, if we are freelancers or independent contractors, and not employees. The Supreme Court ruled in 1989 that, unless an express contractual agreement exists to the contrary, independent contractors own the copyright to works they create.[100] Historically, corporate clients assumed they owned such works-made-for-hire because they had contracted with PR practitioners to create particular campaigns, programs, projects or plans. A close look at the works-made-for-hire provisions of the Copyright Act of 1976, however, reveals that the corporation owns the finished work only if the creator is an employee acting "within the scope of his or her employment."[101] Other works, "specifically ordered or commissioned," require an express agreement "that the work is to be considered a work-made-for-hire."[102] Even then, the corporation may not own all rights to the work, because the Copyright Act defines a "work-made-for-hire" in a limited way, as "a contribution to a collective work, as a part of a motion picture or other audio-visual work, as a translation, as a supplementary work, as a compilation, as an instructional text, as a test, as answer material for a test, or as an atlas."[103]

Generally, PR campaigns, projects, programs or plans created by independent practitioners do not fit into any of these categories and, thus, continue to be owned by their creators even if the copyright is assigned to the corporation. So corporations and PR practitioners should carefully agree to the origin and ownership of PR plans in very specific contractual terms. Because prospective clients can easily use part or all of a proposal after having seen it during a presentation, a statement of ownership should be included on the proposal's title page.

SUMMARY

Public relations, which generally may be defined as the explanation of business or institutional concerns to the public, involves the communication of corporate ideas and ideals and the defense of economic actions and transactions. Public relations law has been described as plain, old business law polished with a veneer of First Amendment protections. In fact, it is not really an area of law — such as defamation and copyright — but a study of the application of other areas of law to the practice of public relations. Thus, a close, symbiotic relationship exists between public relations law and the general laws of business.

While corporations today have First Amendment speech rights, the level of protection for that speech depends on how the speech is classified. Corporate speech on issues of political and social importance tends to have greater protection than does commercial speech. But deciding what is political and what is commercial is not easy when it comes to corporate speech. Courts continue to struggle with the extent of the influence and power of corporate speech in the political process and how best to treat blended corporate and commercial speech.

In addition to the constitutional questions, however, PR professionals need an understanding of federal regulations impacting their clients' industries such as the SEC, the FDA and NLRB to ensure they and their clients do not run afoul of the law. Similarly, they must be careful not to misrepresent a com-

---

David Carr, *The Media Equation: Ethics Tenet Is on Trial in Minnesota*, N.Y. TIMES, July 9, 2007, at B1; Richard Perez-Pena, *Judge Orders Publisher To Leave Job for a Year*, N.Y. TIMES, Sept. 19, 2007, at C10; Mark Reilly, *Pioneer Press Sues S-Trib, Ex-Publisher Ridder*, MINNEAPOLIS-ST. PAUL BUS. J., Apr. 13, 2007, at 1.

[99] *See* Matt Villano, *The Noncompete Clause: Balk at Your Own Risk*, N.Y. TIMES, Jan. 21, 2007, at Sec. 3, p. 9.

[100] Cmty. for Creative Non-Violence v. Reid, 490 U.S. 730 (1989).

[101] 17 U.S.C. 101 (2009); 17 U.S.C. 201 (2009).

[102] 17 U.S.C. 101 (2009).

[103] 17 U.S.C. 101(A)(2) (2009).

pany's products or services to the public or they open the company and themselves up to litigation.

In the area of employment law, PR practitioners must understand who owns the plans they create and the extent of their non-compete clauses. Finally, PR practitioners should be aware of the potential legal consequences of their promises and agreements, whether written or oral.

FOR ADDITIONAL READING

Gower, Karla K. *Legal and Ethical Considerations for Public Relations*. Prospect Heights, Ill.: Waveland Press, 2008.

Kerr, Robert L. "Naturalizing the Artificial Citizen: Repeating Lochner's Error in Citizens United v. Federal Election Commission," 15 *Communication Law & Policy* 311 (2010).

Moore, Roy L., Carmen Maye & Erik L. Collins. *Advertising & Public Relations Law*. 2d ed. New York: Routledge, 2010.

Parkinson, Michael & Marie Parkinson. *Law for Advertising, Broadcasting, Journalism & Public Relations*. Mahweh, N.J.: Lawrence-Erlbaum, 2006.

Parkinson, Michael G. & L. Marie Parkinson. *Public Relations Law: A Supplemental Text*. New York: Routledge, 2008.

Broadcast Regulation

By Michael A. McGregor

➡️ **Headnote Questions**

- Why are broadcasting media regulated differently than print media?
- What are the powers of the Federal Communications Commission?
- What are the main structural regulations of the broadcast media?
- What are the main content regulations of the broadcast media?
- What role do the courts play in the regulation of broadcasting?

Broadcast regulation is one of the most complex and dynamic areas of communication law. To better understand how broadcasting came to be regulated as it is today, it is necessary to review some of its history. That history will be followed by a discussion of regulation as it affects broadcasting today. But first, it is crucial to understand exactly what a "broadcasting" service is, and what it is not. A broadcast service is one that is free to the public, is distributed over the air, and is intended for the general public. Thus, broadcasting refers to local radio and television stations serving specific communities across the country. "Broadcast" should not be used when referring to program networks distributed by cable or satellite services (ESPN or Comedy Central, for example) or programming distributed solely *via* the Internet (Netflix or Pandora, for example).

THE DEVELOPMENT OF BROADCAST REGULATION

Few people involved in radio's development, which began more than 100 years ago, foresaw its becoming a form of mass communication. "Wireless," as it was called, initially was considered an extension of the telegraph and the telephone. Only much later did it become a mass medium.

Broadcasting's Early History

Guglielmo Marconi, considered the first person to send radio

signals without wires, believed his "wireless radio," used for ship-to-shore and ship-to-ship radio transmissions, would be commercially successful. He competed fiercely with rival companies to retain rights to his invention. Employees of Marconi Wireless Company of America, for example, refused to recognize signals sent to shore from ships using equipment that other firms manufactured. Concern that distress signals might be ignored led Congress to adopt the Wireless Ship Act of 1910, which required large ships to have wireless equipment and radio operators on board. The law also made it illegal not to retransmit or answer wireless transmissions from ships. The 1910 law was the first American regulation of devices using the electromagnetic spectrum, a natural resource through which radio signals are transmitted.

When ships began using wireless equipment, many radio signals filled the spectrum. They would interfere with each other. So only static was heard, causing problems for ships throughout the world. In an effort to deal with the problem, representatives from a number of countries met to establish certain standards for radio use. They also insisted that individual nations adopt laws requiring that the standards be followed. This agreement and one tragic event led to the United States replacing the 1910 law with the Radio Act of 1912.

The Radio Act of 1912

The tragedy was the sinking of the *Titanic*. The supposedly unsinkable ship hit an iceberg in the Atlantic Ocean, and more than 1,500 people died. The irony that tied the *Titanic* tragedy to broadcast regulation was the fact that a ship only a few miles away could have saved many lives. No one on the nearby ship knew of the *Titanic's* desperate radio transmissions, however, because even though the ship met the provisions of the 1910 Act and possessed the required radio equipment, the radio operator had gone off duty. While the 1910 Act required radio equipment, it did not require a radio operator to be on duty.

The *Titanic* tragedy focused public and congressional attention on radio legislation. Congress adopted the 1912 Act, which, in addition to closing some of the loopholes of the earlier act, became the first law directly affecting commercial radio. Among other provisions, it allowed the U.S. Secretary of Commerce to award licenses for radio stations and to assign the spectrum frequencies those stations would use. In an era when wireless was considered a point-to-point medium, the 1912 Act worked well enough. Dramatic changes in the use of wireless, however, soon demonstrated the act's limitations.

Following World War I, rather than simply communicate with each other, wireless hobbyists began using their stations to deliver information and entertainment to a broader audience. This form of mass communication, which became known as "broadcasting," quickly became popular with listeners and caught the attention of major electronics manufacturers. General Electric, Westinghouse, the Radio Corporation of America and other companies, anticipating the revenue potential of broadcasting, began acquiring radio licenses around the country. The problems with the 1912 Act became apparent. Although the act gave the secretary of commerce the power to grant licenses, it did not allow him to reject license applications. All he could do was award a license to anyone who applied. The secretary faced other limitations as well. Station operators would unhesitatingly change frequencies and the height of transmission towers. An operator might even move a station from city to city. Under the 1912 statute, federal courts ruled, Secretary of Commerce Herbert Hoover had no power to control these actions.[1] The U.S. Attorney General agreed.[2]

So, as commercial radio began to develop, the government granted and registered licenses, but could neither refuse a license to an applicant nor limit the purposes for which radio stations were used. This inability to control the use of the spectrum led to serious interference problems. By 1920, many commercial broadcasters and hobbyists believed radio was doomed as a public medium unless the government could control both the number of radio stations on the air and the broadcast frequencies. In an attempt to deal with the chaos on the airwaves, Hoover convened several radio conferences between 1922 and 1926 but could not convince radio station owners to cooperate with one another. At first, Congress ignored calls to adopt legislation controlling radio broadcasting. In most major cities, interference constantly interrupted radio stations' signals. Eventually, the problem became so serious that Congress cooperated.

The Radio Act of 1927

Recognizing radio's importance to the public and the country's commerce, and realizing the need to control spectrum use, Congress adopted the Radio Act of 1927. The act established a five-member Federal Radio Commission, each commissioner representing a different region of the country. The FRC was given the power to grant and deny radio station licenses, assign frequencies and prevent spectrum interference, but it did not have the power to censor content.

The 1927 Act was important because it was the first law giving the U.S. government, through Congress and the FRC, control over radio broadcasting to the public. The act established definitively that the electromagnetic spectrum belonged to the public — it was not to be privately owned. In addition, it required the FRC to act in the "public interest, convenience or necessity," the standard the Federal Communications Commission still uses. The act also established that broadcast stations were not to be regulated as common carriers, that is, the licensee was responsible for the content of the station's transmissions. The 1927 law did not explicitly give the federal government exclusive jurisdiction over broadcast regulation, but the Supreme Court later interpreted it as doing so and as forbidding the states from interfering.[3] Each of these points continues to be an important element in broadcast regulation.

Communications Act of 1934

In adopting the 1927 Act, Congress expected that the FRC could be disbanded after completing its task of allocating licenses to radio stations, but it soon became apparent that the federal government would need to oversee broadcasting on a continuing basis. Another problem was that the 1927 Act had added yet another federal agency, the FRC, to the list of bureaucracies — including the Interstate Commerce Commission, the Department of Commerce and the Postmaster General's Office — with control over spectrum use and telephony. To continue jurisdic-

---

1 *See* United States v. Zenith Radio Corp., 12 F.2d 614 (N.D. Ill. 1926); Hoover v. Intercity Radio Co., 286 F. 1002 (D.C. Cir. 1923).

2 126 Op. Atty. Gen. (1)-(c) (1926).

3 Fed. Radio Comm'n v. Nelson Bros., 289 U.S. 266 (1933).

tion over broadcasting, but also to simplify the regulatory process, Congress adopted the Communications Act of 1934, establishing the Federal Communications Commission. The FCC had jurisdiction over "radio and wire communication service," that is, broadcasting and various aspects of telephone service. The 1934 Act replaced the 1927 law, and the FCC superseded the FRC.

In the nearly eighty years since the adoption of the act, the FCC has had to decide how to deal with satellites, cellular telephones, the Internet and other new technologies that use the spectrum but which, of course, were not mentioned in the act and were not imagined by any member of Congress in 1934. To address these new technologies, Congress has amended the act many times. The most recent major amendment came when Congress adopted the Telecommunications Act of 1996. The act significantly altered many rules regarding broadcasting, as well as cable, telephone service, satellite television transmission and other communications media. (Cable regulation is discussed in Chapter 11, and the Telecommunications Act is discussed in Chapters 11 and 12.)

RATIONALES FOR BROADCAST REGULATION

The First Amendment states that the government "shall make no law ... abridging the freedom of speech, or of the press." Does that mean broadcasters have the same First Amendment rights as publishers of the print media? The Supreme Court has said "No," holding that various mass media may be treated differently under the First Amendment, and that broadcasters' rights are not equal to those of the print media.[4]

Print v. Broadcast

When the Supreme Court began making rulings involving broadcasting, it had precedent for not treating the industry the same as the print media. From 1915 until 1952, the Court held that motion pictures were entertainment and, therefore, not entitled to First Amendment protection.[5] As radio developed into a major mass medium, it primarily offered entertainment. By the mid-1930s, First Amendment rights essentially had been applied only to the print media, and courts found no reason to extend the same type of protection to broadcasting. For example, just one year after the Supreme Court ruled in *Near v. Minnesota* that a state could not stop a newspaper from printing "malicious, scandalous, and defamatory" attacks on public officials,[6]

a federal appellate court upheld the FRC in denying a radio license renewal to a church whose minister, Dr. Robert Shuler, used the station to attack government officials, labor unions and religions other than his own.[7]

The Supreme Court took a similar approach in 1964, when a small Pennsylvania radio station carried a fifteen-minute program in which the Rev. Billy James Hargis attacked Fred J. Cook, the author of *Goldwater — Extremist on the Right.* Hargis said Cook was fired as a newspaper reporter because he made false charges against city officials and that he had worked for a Communist publication, denounced then FBI chief J. Edgar Hoover and the Central Intelligence Agency, and set out to "destroy Barry Goldwater," Republican presidential candidate in 1964. When Cook learned of the broadcast, he asked the station for free time to reply under the FCC's personal attack rule. It refused. Cook complained to the FCC, which ordered the station to offer him time. The station appealed to the courts.

In 1969, the Supreme Court found in *Red Lion Broadcasting Co. v. FCC* that "those who are licensed stand no better than those to whom licenses are refused. A license permits broadcasting, but the licensee has no constitutional right ... to monopolize a radio frequency to the exclusion of his fellow citizens." Therefore, the Court held, the First Amendment does not prohibit "requir[ing] a broadcaster to permit answers to personal attacks occurring in the course of discussing controversial issues."[8]

Five years later, the Supreme Court heard a case in which a newspaper refused to abide by a state statute that required the paper to provide free space for a candidate it had criticized. The *Miami Herald* had published an editorial highly critical of a candidate for the Florida House of Representatives. When the candidate demanded space for a response under Florida law and the newspaper refused, he sued. The Supreme Court, in *Miami Herald Publishing Co. v. Tornillo,* held that it is unconstitutional for the government to force a newspaper to publish anything it chooses not to. The Court said that a "responsible press is an undoubtedly desirable goal, but press responsibility is not mandated by the Constitution and like many other virtues it cannot be legislated."[9]

The Court apparently thought of "press" as "print media," not broadcasting. *Red Lion* required a radio station to provide a right of reply, while the Court held in *Tornillo* that the same requirement could not be applied to newspapers. This does not mean broadcasters have no First Amendment rights. The Court has found that they do. But it has said that "of all forms of communication, it is broadcasting that has received the most

---

[4] *See, e.g.,* Red Lion Broad. Co. v. FCC, 395 U.S. 367 (1969) (upholding limits on broadcasters' First Amendment rights).

[5] *See* Joseph Burstyn, Inc. v. Wilson, 343 U.S. 495 (1952); Mutual Film Corp. v. Indus. Comm'n of Ohio, 236 U.S. 230 (1915).

[6] 283 U.S. 697 (1931). See Chapter 4 for a discussion of *Near v. Minnesota.*

[7] Trinity Methodist Church, South v. Fed. Radio Comm'n, 62 F.2d 850 (D.C. Cir. 1932).

[8] 395 U.S. at 389, 392.

[9] 418 U.S. 241, 256 (1974).

limited First Amendment protection."[10] Courts have used several rationales for the proposition that print media have greater First Amendment rights than broadcasters. The rationales are spectrum scarcity, the concept of public trusteeship, pervasiveness and the special impact broadcast media can have, especially on children.

Spectrum Scarcity

The electromagnetic spectrum is the array of energy that includes radio waves.[11] Radio and TV stations use transmitters to send radio waves to receiving antennas. Transmitters radiate several thousands or millions of radio waves per second. This is the "frequency" at which the station broadcasts. The FCC assigns frequencies to stations and requires them to transmit only on those frequencies.

Groups of frequencies can be used only for certain types of broadcasting. Television, AM radio and FM radio are assigned frequencies within a certain portion of the spectrum. Because of the way the federal government has allocated the spectrum for broadcasters' use, only a limited number of radio and television stations can be on the air. Adding more would cause harmful interference. Therefore, only a relatively few people or companies may use the spectrum for broadcasting. So there is a spectrum scarcity; there are not enough frequencies to allow all who want to broadcast to do so. Courts have decided that Congress may impose certain obligations to serve the public on those fortunate enough to have broadcast licenses.

However, most cities have more radio and television stations than newspapers. Where, then, is the scarcity? As the courts see it, this is not simply a matter of numbers. There are so few newspapers because a newspaper is very costly to begin and operate, and advertisers and subscribers for competing newspapers are limited. This is an economic limitation, the courts say, while spectrum scarcity is a physical and technical limitation, that is, a limitation of nature. No matter how much money might be available to begin a new broadcast station, if there is no room on the spectrum — if a station cannot be added without causing signal interference with other stations — the new station may not go on the air.

Therefore, the award of a broadcast license is considered to be a grant of a privilege. Another person or company who wants to communicate by owning a broadcast station simply may not do so if no frequencies are available in the area.

The Supreme Court adopted the spectrum scarcity rationale

in 1943. The Court was straightforward, stating that radio's "facilities are limited; they are not available to all who may wish to use them; the radio spectrum simply is not large enough to accommodate everybody. There is a fixed natural limitation upon the number of stations that can operate without interfering with one another."[12] It echoed the point twenty-six years later in *Red Lion*: "[I]t is idle to posit an unabridgeable First Amendment right to broadcast comparable to the right of every individual to speak, write, or publish."[13]

The Concept of Public Trusteeship

Unlike some countries where the government owns and controls all broadcasting outlets, in the United States nearly all commercial stations are privately owned. But because the spectrum remains in the government's hands, those who are given licenses hold portions of the spectrum in trust for the public, that is, they are public trustees. The courts have said that Congress and the FCC may require them to operate in the public interest as part of the privilege of holding broadcast licenses. The Supreme Court has accepted this approach, stating in *Red Lion*:

> There is nothing in the First Amendment which prevents the Government from ... requiring a licensee to ... conduct himself as a proxy or fiduciary with obligations to present those views and voices which are representative of his community.... [T]he people as a whole retain their interest in free speech by radio and their collective right to have the medium function consistently with the ends and purposes of the First Amendment. It is the right of the viewers and listeners, not the right of the broadcasters, which is paramount.... Licenses to broadcast do not confer ownership of designated frequencies, but only the temporary privilege of using them.[14]

In 1973, just four years after deciding *Red Lion*, the Court refined this point. The CBS television network refused to accept advertisements from the Business Executives' Move for a Vietnam Peace, which, together with the Democratic National Committee, asked the FCC to rule that broadcasters could not "refuse to sell time to responsible entities ... for comment on public issues."[15] The FCC rejected the request. The Supreme Court ruled that broadcasters did not have to take any and all advertisements.

Red Lion, which held that a radio station must give time for an individual to reply to a personal attack, and the CBS case, which held that broadcasters need not sell time for commercials

---

[10] FCC v. Pacifica Found., 438 U.S. 726, 748 (1978).

[11] Other portions of the spectrum are identified as "infrared," "X-rays," "gamma rays" and "ultraviolet." For a discussion of broadcast technology, *see* MICHAEL A. McGREGOR, PAUL D. DRISOLL & WALTER McDOWELL, HEAD'S BROADCASTING IN AMERICA (10th ed. 2010).

[12] Nat'l Broad. Co. v. FCC, 319 U.S. 190, 213 (1943).

[13] 395 U.S. at 388.

[14] *Id.* at 394.

[15] Columbia Broad. Sys. v. Democratic Nat'l Comm., 412 U.S. 94, 98 (1973).

about public issues, may not be as contradictory as they appear. The two decisions suggest that there is no general right for the public to have access to broadcast stations. But Congress may require access under certain circumstances, such as when a political candidate running for federal office wants to purchase airtime to reach the public. This still leaves broadcasters less protected than the print media under the First Amendment.

The spectrum scarcity and public trustee rationales have been attacked often as unsupportable. By the mid-1980s, even the Supreme Court suggested that it would consider a "signal from Congress or the FCC that technological developments have advanced so far that some revision of the system of broadcast regulation may be required."[16] That is, the Court recognized that, since audiences may receive video signals from cable television, satellites, microwave transmissions and other new technologies, the scarcity of spectrum space may not limit communication with the public through the electronic media. Moreover, new technologies exist to put more signals on the broadcast bands without causing interference. For example, in 2000, the FCC authorized a new, low power FM radio service, which when fully implemented could add thousands of additional stations across the country.[17] Also, the move from analog to digital transmission (discussed later in this chapter) allows existing broadcast stations to deliver multiple programs simultaneously over their facilities.

A former chair of the FCC has argued that even if there is a spectrum scarcity, all goods are scarce to some degree.[18] Newsprint is scarce and increasingly expensive, for example. Does that justify government control of newspapers or limits on publishers' First Amendment rights?

Pervasiveness

Another rationale courts use to justify differential First Amendment treatment of broadcasters is that radio and television are ubiquitous — they are heard and seen in homes, stores and in many other places, and are constantly intrusive, especially on the lives of children. Further, a listener or viewer has no idea what is being broadcast until a receiver is turned on.

Exactly that kind of confrontation was at the center of a case in which the Supreme Court noted that broadcasting is different from other media. In *FCC v. Pacifica*,[19] a child inadvertently was exposed to indecent language when his father turned on the car radio. The Court said that with many forms of speech —

like movies or words on jackets[20] — people have a responsibility to avoid the communication; they can turn their heads or avert their eyes, for example. But, the Court said, radio and television are omnipresent; they are intruders rather than forms of communication people invite into their lives. The Court was particularly concerned that when radio or television comes into the home, children may be exposed to material their parents do not want them to see or hear. Broadcasting's intrusiveness and omnipresence make it unique among mass media, the Court said. These characteristics justify treating radio and television differently than print media under the First Amendment.

Special Impact

Congress and a few courts have articulated an additional rationale for broadcast regulation: that radio and television have a greater impact on audiences than do print media.[21] Considering a law forbidding cigarette and small cigar advertising on television, a federal appellate court in the 1960s, without clearly explaining the grounds for its assertion, stated:

> [A]n ordinary habitual television watcher can avoid these commercials only by frequently leaving the room, changing the channel, or doing some other such affirmative act. It is difficult to calculate the subliminal impact of this pervasive propaganda, which may be heard even if not listened to, but it may reasonably be thought greater than the impact of the written word.[22]

In 1996, Congress decided that televised violence presented enough of a threat to the well-being of children that it passed a law calling for a voluntary system that rated television violence, profanity and sexual content. The law — known as the "v-chip law" — will be discussed later in this chapter.

In addition, the Supreme Court has said that indecent broadcast programming can have a powerful impact on children. In *Pacifica*, it said that while parents may be able to shield their children from offensive books or motion pictures, broadcasting is "uniquely accessible to children, even those too young to read."[23] As a result, an indecent broadcast could instantly enlarge the vocabulary of very young children. The Court found that, in order to protect children, the FCC could constitutionally channel indecent broadcasts to times when children were less likely to be in the audience.

---

[16] FCC v. *League of Women Voters*, 468 U.S. 364, 376 n.11 (1984).

[17] In the Matter of Creation of Low Power Radio Service, 15 F.C.C.R. 2205 (2000).

[18] Mark Fowler & Daniel Brenner, *A Marketplace Approach to Broadcast Regulation*, 60 TEXAS L. REV. 207 (1982).

[19] 438 U.S. 726 (1978).

[20] *See* Erznoznik v. Jacksonville, 422 U.S. 205 (1975); Cohen v. California, 403 U.S. 15 (1971).

[21] *See, e.g.,* Robinson v. American Broad. Co., 441 F.2d 1396 (6th Cir. 1971); Banzhaf v. FCC, 405 F.2d 1082 (D.C. Cir. 1968).

[22] *Banzhaf*, 405 F.2d at 1101.

[23] 438 U.S. at 749.

THE FEDERAL COMMUNICATIONS COMMISSION

The FCC is responsible for regulating broadcasting, other spectrum uses such as satellite communications and amateur radio, and various aspects of telephone service.

Structure of the FCC

The FCC is one of the federal government's independent agencies, similar in that respect to the Securities and Exchange Commission and the Federal Trade Commission. But the FCC cannot be considered truly independent. Congress allocates the FCC's budget in a bill that the president must approve. Its five members are selected by the president and confirmed by the Senate. They serve five-year terms and can be reappointed.[24] The president decides which of the five commissioners will be chair. While the FCC is not intended to be political — only three of the five commissioners can be from the same political party — political considerations do play a part in the appointment process and in many of its decisions. In many ways, the FCC is imbued with politics, as evidenced by straight party-line votes on important policy issues.

The FCC employs more than 2,000 staff members across seven bureaus. Of these seven bureaus, two are particularly relevant to broadcasters:

- The Media Bureau administers the policy and licensing programs related to electronic mass media, including radio, television and cable television. It also handles post-licensing matters related to direct-to-home satellite services, for example, Direct TV and Sirius/XM.
- The Enforcement Bureau resolves complaints involving radio frequency interference, indecent communications, and false distress signals, among others.

As an independent regulatory agency, the FCC has judicial, legislative and executive powers.

Judicial Power

When the FCC makes decisions that affect individual licensees — taking action to revoke a license, for example — it acts much as a court does. Administrative law judges within the FCC initially decide cases that deal with individual parties. An ALJ will hold a hearing that might look much like a trial. Counsel represents the parties to the hearing. They present evidence and witnesses, and witnesses may be cross-examined. After all the evidence is presented, the ALJ weighs it and writes an opin-

ion, referred to as the "Initial Decision." A losing party may appeal the decision to the five commissioners.

Legislative Power

The FCC also acts much as a legislative body, adopting regulations affecting an entire industry. The FCC or an interested outside party may initiate the legislative process. When a decision is made to begin the process, FCC staff members prepare a Notice of Proposed Rule Making, stating what regulations the FCC is considering adopting, changing or rescinding, and explaining the reasons behind the proposed changes. When the commissioners agree on the NPRM's language, they make it public. Members of the public — although that usually means corporations and lobbying groups representing companies that may be affected by the rules — submit comments to the FCC. The Commission makes them public and then accepts reply comments — written arguments supporting or rebutting the initial comments. The staff and commissioners review the comments and replies, discuss the proposed rules and finally adopt a Report and Order. The regulations in the order may be the same as those originally proposed in the NPRM, or they may be different, based on the public comment or changes made by commissioners for other reasons. After an order is released, members of the public may ask the FCC to reconsider the decision, which it may or may not do.

Executive Power

The FCC may impose an array of penalties to enforce its decisions, rules, regulations and policies — from a letter of reprimand inserted into a licensee's file, to a fine, to renewing a license for less than a full term, to non-renewal or revocation of a license. Short-term license renewals and non-renewals are harsh penalties, and the FCC normally prefers to impose no more than a fine, called a "forfeiture," when it finds a licensee has violated the rules. But the threat of losing a license generally keeps broadcasters in line.

Final Commission decisions, whether adjudicative, legislative or enforcement in nature, may be appealed to a federal appellate court. That court's decision may then be appealed to the Supreme Court. An appellate court is to give deference to the FCC's interpretation of the Communications Act.[25] When the FCC rules on a factual matter — whether a licensee lied to the Commission, for example — a court may overturn the FCC's decision only if it was "arbitrary, capricious [or] an abuse of discretion."[26]

---

[24] The FCC initially had seven commissioners instead of the FRC's five, since the FCC had more responsibilities. Congress reduced the number of commissioners to five in 1982.

[25] *See* Chevron U.S.A., Inc. v. Natural Res. Def. Council, 467 U.S. 837 (1984).
[26] 5 U.S.C. § 706 (2)(A) (2012).

The Public Interest Standard

In both the 1927 and the 1934 acts, Congress required the FCC to regulate broadcast licensees so that they function in the "public interest, convenience and necessity."[27] The public interest standard, adopted from the 1890 Interstate Commerce Act, is the standard that is supposed to govern FCC decisions. The Communications Act does not define the term, leaving it to the FCC and the courts to give it substance — thus allowing flexibility in establishing policies and deciding cases. There are several problems with this scenario. The FCC may give the words different meanings at different times, for example, depending upon its make-up. It has used the standard both to adopt and later reject the same regulation, and the Commission and the courts cannot always agree on what the term means.

The FRC issued several statements providing technical and content guidelines for radio that it believed were required to meet the public interest.[28] These suggestions included ways to limit spectrum interference, provide radio signals to much of the country, limit the private use of commercial radio frequencies and provide well-rounded programming. The FRC also recommended that it would be in the public interest for stations to limit the "use of phonograph records" as program material.

In addition, the FRC applied the public interest standard when evaluating broadcast content. For example, in the 1920s Dr. John R. Brinkley aired a program called the

"Medical question box," devoted to diagnosing and prescribing treatment of cases from symptoms given in letters.... Patients are not known to the doctor except by means of their letters.... The doctor usually advises that the writer of the letter is suffering from a certain ailment, and recommends the procurement from one of the members of the Brinkley Pharmaceutical Association, of one or more of Dr. Brinkley's prescriptions.... [For instance,] "Sunflower State, from Dresden Kans[as]. Probably he has gall stones. No, I don't mean that, I mean kidney stones. My advice to you is to put him on Prescription No. 80 and 50 for men, also 64. I think that he will be a whole lot better. Also drink a lot of water."[29]

The FRC refused to renew the station's license, stating that Dr. Brinkley's programs did not serve the public interest. On appeal, the court agreed that Brinkley operated the station only to earn revenue for himself and that public health was being endangered. Brinkley argued that his First Amendment rights

were being abridged, but the court found that the FCC "has merely exercised its undoubted right to take note of appellant's past conduct, which is not censorship."[30]

Similarly, the FRC refused to renew a radio station licensed to a church. It found that the Rev. Robert Shuler used his access to the airwaves to issue attacks against public officials and various religious groups. On appeal, the court upheld the FRC's decision finding that

The evidence abundantly sustains the conclusion of the Commission that the continuance of the broadcasting programs is not in the public interest.... [I]t is manifest, we think, that it is not narrowing the ordinary conception of "public interest" in declaring his broadcasts — without facts to sustain or to justify them — not within that term.[31]

The interplay between the FCC and the courts often has helped define the public interest. For example, the Supreme Court agreed with the FCC that the Commission could not take into consideration any possible impact on an existing radio station's revenues when it granted a license for a new station in the same city.[32] The public interest meant being concerned with the public, not the licensee, the Court said. Three years later, the Court reinforced this interpretation in *National Broadcasting Co. v. FCC*: "The 'public interest' to be served under the Communications Act is ... the interest of the listening public."[33] The Court has held that judges have limited powers to overturn a public interest determination. If the FCC balances the various interests at stake, it is up to the Commission to define the public interest.[34]

In 1946, the FCC attempted to give station licensees better guidance about how to operate in the public interest. A set of informal programming guidelines — known as the "Blue Book" after the color of its cover — suggested that stations broadcast non-sponsored programs, live programs originated locally, and programs "devoted to public discussions."[35] The Blue Book also urged stations to limit the number of commercials and to be careful of their content. Although broadcasters feared the Blue Book was an attempt by the FCC to scrutinize programming practices, in fact, the Commission never denied the renewal of a station's license for violation of Blue Book guidelines.[36]

In 1960, the FCC replaced the Blue Book with a formal pro-

---

[27] 47 U.S.C. §§ 302(a), 307(d), 309(a) & 316(a) (2012).

[28] *See, e.g.,* Public Interest, Convenience, or Necessity, 2 F.R.C. Ann. Rep. 166 (1928); Great Lakes Broad. Co., 3 F.R.C. Ann. Rep. 32 (1929), *rev'd on other grounds,* Great Lakes Broad. Co. v. F.R.C. 37 F.2d 993 (D.C. Cir. 1930).

[29] KFKB Broad. Ass'n v. Fed. Radio Comm'n, 47 F.2d 670, 671 (D.C. Cir. 1931).

[30] *Id.* at 672.

[31] Trinity Methodist Church, South v. Fed. Radio Comm'n, 62 F.2d 850, 852 (D.C. Cir. 1932).

[32] Sanders Brothers v. FCC, 309 U.S. 470 (1940).

[33] 319 U.S. 190, 216 (1943).

[34] *See, e.g.,* FCC v. WNCN Listener's Guild, 450 U.S. 582 (1981).

[35] FCC, Public Service Responsibility of Broadcast Licensees (Mar. 7, 1946), *reprinted in* F. KAHN, DOCUMENTS OF AMERICAN BROADCASTING 132 (3d ed. 1978).

[36] *See, e.g.,* Hearst Radio, Inc. (WBAL), 15 F.C.C. 1149 (1951).

gramming statement that specified fourteen program categories as "the major elements usually necessary to meet the public interest."[37] The categories included children's, religious, educational, public affairs, agricultural, news, sports, entertainment and weather programs, and "opportunit[ies] for self-expression, ... the development and use of local talent" and "service to minority groups."

After decades of protecting the public interest by imposing regulations on broadcast stations and networks, the FCC, in the 1980s, moved toward an economic marketplace approach. It said that competition among stations and from other forms of electronic media would be sufficient to ensure that licensees operate in the public interest and that extensive regulation would be unnecessary.

The FCC took significant steps to deregulate radio in 1981[38] and television in 1984.[39] In these and other actions, it eliminated a number of programming guidelines; requirements for surveying community leaders, interest groups and individuals to ascertain programming needs and preferences; most limits on how much time could be used for commercials; complex license renewal processes; certain technical rules; and a number of other minor regulations. But it left many other rules in place.

Whether adding new regulations or deregulating, the FCC consistently tries to grapple with how to interpret the concept of public interest. In attempting to understand the meaning, it may be safe to say that "the public interest" means what the FCC says it means at any given time, subject to congressional oversight and judicial review.

STATION LICENSING

In large part, the Federal Radio Commission was created to ensure that stations broadcast without interfering with other stations' signals. That responsibility continues, but today the FCC's duties extend much farther. The Communications Act of 1934 gave the FCC the authority to allocate frequencies to individual communities around the country and then license those frequencies to companies that the Commission has decided may operate radio and television stations. The act requires that the FCC do this in a "fair, efficient and equitable" manner.[40]

The Commission first must decide which portions of the spectrum will be used for what purposes — satellite transmissions, AM or FM radio, cellular communications or for police and fire

department use.[41] As technology evolves and demand for the spectrum continues to grow, the FCC's job of allocating this valuable resource becomes more complex and demanding. For this reason, in 2010 a new spectrum task force was created to ensure that burgeoning mobile services will have sufficient spectrum for continued development and growth.[42] One controversial proposal regarding the allocation of spectrum will allow television broadcasters to give up part of their spectrum for use by mobile service operators.[43] As an incentive to relinquish a chunk of their spectrum, television broadcasters will receive a portion of the income generated when the spectrum is auctioned for other uses. In 2012, Congress gave the FCC the authority to conduct these "incentive auctions."[44] In 2014, the Commission adopted a Report and Order implementing the auctions,[45] which began in May 2016. At the time this text went to press, the results of the auction had not yet been announced.

License Requirements

The Communications Act of 1934 makes it illegal to operate a radio or television station in the United States without an FCC license. Stations operating without licenses — sometimes referred to as "pirate stations" — can be subject to civil fines, court injunctions, seizures of equipment, and even criminal penalties including jail time.[46] According to the Communications Act, all applicants for broadcast licenses must be technically, financially and legally qualified.[47]

To be technically qualified, an applicant must have access to technical expertise sufficient to operate the station. That means having sufficiently planned for the equipment and engineering personnel needed. To be financially qualified, an applicant must demonstrate sufficient financial backing, through funds on hand or loan commitments, to run the station for the first three months without advertising or other income.

There are several aspects to being legally qualified. The first criterion is U.S. citizenship. The Communications Act forbids

---

[37] En Banc Programming Inquiry, 44 F.C.C. 2303, 2314 (1960), aff'd sub nom., Henry v. FCC, 302 F.2d 191 (D.C. Cir. 1962).

[38] Deregulation of Radio, 84 F.C.C. 2d 968 (1981), aff'd in part, remanded in part sub nom., Office of Communication of the United Church of Christ v. FCC, 707 F.2d 1413 (D.C. Cir. 1983).

[39] Commercial Television Stations, 98 F.C.C. 2d 1076 (1984).

[40] 47 U.S.C. § 303 & § 307(b) (2012).

[41] The FCC shares spectrum allocation responsibilities with the National Telecommunications and Information Administration. NTIA allocates all spectrum used by the federal government, and the FCC allocates everything else.

[42] See Press Release, FCC, FCC Chairman Julius Genachowski Announces Launch of Spectrum Task Force (Apr. 26, 2010).

[43] See Chairman Julius Genachowski, Prepared Remarks at NAB Show 2011 (Apr. 12, 2011), available at http://transition.fcc.gov/Daily_Releases/Daily_Business/2011/db0412/DOC-305708A1.pdf.

[44] Middle Class Tax Relief and Job Creation Act of 2012, § 6402, Pub. L. No. 112-96, 126 Stat. 158 (2012).

[45] Expanding the Economic Innovation Opportunities of Spectrum Through Incentive Auctions, 29 F.C.C.R. 6567 (2014), available at http://transition.fcc.gov/Daily_Releases/Daily_Business/2014/db0602/FCC-14-50A1.txt.

[46] See Press Release, FCC, Rayon Sherwin "Junior" Payne Sentenced to Prison for Unlicensed Radio Operation (May 12, 2003).

[47] 47 U.S.C. § 308(b) (2012).

granting a license to foreign governments or alien individuals, or their representatives, or to foreign corporations.[48] In addition, foreign interests may own no more than 20 percent of the stock of a corporation holding a broadcast license. For a corporation that is controlled by another corporation, the controlling entity may not have more than 25 percent of its stock owned or voted by foreign interests.

A second criterion for licensure is that the applicant be of good character. Specifically, the FCC will not award licenses to companies run or controlled by individuals who have engaged in fraudulent conduct or been convicted of felonies or of violating antitrust laws involving the mass media.[49] It is particularly concerned with applicants who have lied or made misrepresentations to the Commission. For example, it revoked the licenses of Contemporary Media, whose sole shareholder, Michael Rice, was convicted of sexually abusing children.[50] Contemporary Media informed the FCC of Rice's arrest and told the Commission that he was removed from his managerial role of the company as a result of the arrest. However, the FCC later learned that Rice was actually involved in the affairs of his company after his conviction, and it revoked the company's licenses and construction permits. Contemporary Media appealed the FCC's decision, but the D.C. Circuit upheld it as reasonable.[51] While the fact that Contemporary Media lied to the FCC probably tipped the balance against the licensee, this case ratified the Commission's authority to base its licensing decisions on the issue of character.

The final aspect of being legally qualified to be a licensee relates to the FCC's media ownership rules. In certain instances, regulations forbid one company from owning more than a specified number of stations in a market.[52] If an applicant for a license is not eligible to own the station for which it is applying due to the ownership rules, it may not be awarded the license. These specific ownership regulations will be discussed below under the heading "Structural Regulation of Broadcasting."

Applying for a license

Before filing a broadcast application with the FCC, would-be broadcasters must ascertain whether a frequency is available for the area they wish to serve. To do that, they usually hire an engineering consulting firm. Assuming an appropriate frequency is available, applicants must wait for the FCC to announce that frequency's availability before submitting their applications.

The Commission makes these announcements periodically, on no apparent systematic schedule. These announcements are made several months before applications are due so that applicants have notice and time to prepare their applications.[53]

Mutually Exclusive Applications

If two or more entities apply for the same frequency, the FCC must choose among them. Prior to 1993, it held full-blown evidentiary hearings to determine which one of the applicants would best serve the public interest. To make such a determination, it applied a set of comparative standards that it developed in 1965.[54] These criteria included diversification of ownership (the FCC preferred applicants who did not already own broadcast stations), integration of ownership and management (whether station owners were involved in the station's day-to-day management), prior broadcast experience and the likely reach of a station's signal.

For many years the FCC's comparative hearing process for awarding licenses when there was more than one qualified applicant was heavily criticized. Even the FCC criticized its own method as one that "can be described most charitably as laborious, exceedingly time consuming, expensive and often resulting in choices based on, at most, marginal differences."[55]

Then, in the 1993 case of *Bechtel v. FCC*, a federal appellate court rejected one of the comparative factors the FCC had been using.[56] The court held that the FCC had offered no proof that the criterion favoring integration of ownership and management had led to better broadcast service than absentee ownership did. Consequently, there was no evidence that using the integration factor was in the public interest. Because of the *Bechtel* decision, the agency stopped using comparative hearings in these kinds of licensing cases.

As early as 1982, the FCC experimented with lotteries to grant certain kinds of licenses, including low-power television. But it moved away from lotteries shortly thereafter. It continued to search for ways to deal with mutually exclusive applications but took no final action.[57] Congress finally resolved the matter in the Balanced Budget Act of 1997, which required

[48] 47 U.S.C. § 310 (2012).

[49] Character Qualifications in Broad. Licensing, 5 F.C.C.R. 3252 (1990); Character Qualifications in Broad. Licensing, 102 F.C.C.2d 1179 (1986).

[50] In re Contemporary Media, Inc., 13 F.C.C.R. 14437 (1998).

[51] Contemporary Media, Inc. v. FCC, 214 F.3d 187 (2000).

[52] 47 C.F.R. § 73.3555 (2016).

[53] For example, on April 22, 2015, the Commission announced that 131 frequencies for FM radio stations were available for application, which were due May 28, 2015. Public Notice, FCC, Auction of FM Broadcast Construction Permits Scheduled for July 23, 2015, http://wireless.fcc.gov/auctions/default.htm?job=auctions_home.

[54] Policy Statement on Comparative Hearings, 1 F.C.C.2d 393 (1965).

[55] Amendment to the Commission's Rules to Allow the Selection from Among Competing Applications for New AM, FM and Television Stations by Random Selection (Lottery), 4 F.C.C.R. 2256, 2256 (1989).

[56] 10 F.3d 875 (D.C. Cir. 1993).

[57] Reexamination of the Policy Statement on Comparative Broadcast Hearings, 9 F.C.C.R. 2821 (1994) (seeking comment on the effect of the *Bechtel* decision on comparative hearings).

the FCC to use auctions to award licenses when there are mutually exclusive applications.[58] In order to assure that licenses do not always go to the applicant with the deepest pockets, and to help diversify the ownership of broadcast media, the FCC provides what it calls "bidding credits" to applicants who own three or fewer existing media outlets. The credits allow applicants to bid more money for the license than they have. Since the auction process took effect in 1998, more than 1,160 broadcast frequencies have been licensed to applicants who could bid the most, adding nearly $345 million to the U.S. treasury.[59]

License Renewals

Both radio and television station licenses are awarded for eight-year periods, after which the licenses must be renewed. The renewal application is much smaller and simpler than the application for the original license. Licensees who have engaged in serious misconduct during the license term may not have their licenses renewed, but the vast majority of license renewal applications are routinely granted.

The Telecommunications Act of 1996 requires the FCC to take a two-step approach to license renewal. First, it must decide whether to renew the current license holder, without considering whether the public interest would be better served by a different licensee. It must renew the license unless it finds that the incumbent broadcaster has not operated in the public interest, has committed serious violations of the Communications Act or FCC rules, or in any other way has shown a pattern of abusing the law or FCC regulations. The Commission also is to consider any comments submitted by the public to the station or the FCC about a licensee's performance. If it decides under these standards that a license should not be renewed, it then will move to the second step and put the license up for auction. While the Telecommunications Act of 1996 seems to ensure that most broadcast licenses will be renewed, the FCC still may refuse to renew a license on grounds that the station owner has not operated in the public interest.

Transferring Broadcast Licenses

A broadcast station's facilities — such as its transmitter, compact disk players, desks and trucks — belong to the station owner and can be sold to anyone at any time. But the facilities are useless without a license to broadcast. The license belongs to the federal government and is given to a licensee for a specified period of time. If the licensee — the station owner — wants to sell the station, it is unlikely anyone would purchase it

without also being able to use the station's license, and that requires asking the FCC to transfer the license. Generally, the FCC will transfer a license upon request if the new licensee meets the basic criteria.

Public Involvement in Licensing

It may seem obvious that since the FCC's standard is the public interest, the public should have a voice in the decision-making process. It took a court decision, however, to require the FCC to allow public involvement.

In 1964, a public interest group accused television station WLBT in Jackson, Mississippi, of selecting its programming based on racial bias. The FCC, presuming that it represented the public and, therefore, that the public need not be involved, would not allow the group to participate in the license renewal proceeding. But a federal appellate court held that members of the public had a right to be part of the process.[60] Then, after the FCC renewed WLBT's license, a court overturned the decision. The court said that when the public participates in FCC proceedings, it only has to draw the Commission's attention to pertinent issues; the public is not required to prove the charges are true.[61] The Commission must investigate the claims, if it decides they have credence.

Since 1966, then, members of the public have been able to participate in licensing proceedings. The FCC may set certain limits, such as allowing participation only by groups representing listeners or viewers who actually will be affected by the FCC's action. The usual method of public participation is the filing of what is called a "petition to deny" the granting of a construction permit, license renewal, or transfer application. The Commission may reject the petition or attempt to gather additional information needed to make a decision on the petition's complaint.

Another station may intervene in the process also, either because it believes its signal will be degraded if the FCC grants or renews a license, or because it claims it will suffer financially. But a claim that it will lose revenue is not sufficient grounds for denying or not renewing a license.[62] The FCC is not required to protect other broadcasters' economic interests from competition.

Regulatory Fees

For seven decades, broadcasters paid essentially nothing to the federal government, which did not charge fees for licenses. The

---

[58] Pub. L. No. 105-33, § 302(a)(1), codified at 47 U.S.C. § 309(j)(2012).

[59] *See generally* the FCC Auctions home page *at* http://wireless.fcc.gov/auctions/.

[60] Office of Commc'n of the United Church of Christ v. FCC, 359 F.2d 994 (D.C. Cir. 1966).

[61] Office of Commc'n of the United Church of Christ v. FCC, 425 F.2d 543 (D.C. Cir. 1969).

[62] FCC v. Sanders Bros., 309 U.S. 470 (1940).

costs of obtaining a license were substantial, but they were for engineering studies and attorneys' fees to assist with the application process. Beginning in 1989, Congress authorized the FCC to impose and collect application processing fees.[63] These fees, which range from around $5,000 for a new commercial television station construction permit to $200 for a renewal application, go directly to the U.S. Treasury and are not available to the FCC.[64] Beginning in 1993, in an effort to recover the FCC's costs, Congress required the Commission to collect additional regulatory fees.[65] These fees range from several hundred dollars to more than $60,000 per year, depending on the type of service — AM, FM, TV — and the size of the market in which the station operates. These regulatory fees, which Congress set at $384,012,497 for fiscal year 2016, covered nearly all of the agency's total costs.[66]

Broadcast Networks

Many programs that broadcast television stations carry are, or once were, network shows. The same was true of radio from 1930 to 1952. A "network" distributes programs to stations, and the stations broadcast the programs. For example, NBC sends *The Tonight Show* to more than 200 stations throughout the country, all of which receive the program the same evening, although networks send programs at several different times to accommodate the country's different time zones. That makes NBC a broadcast network, as are ABC, CBS, Fox, CW, and Univision, the nation's largest Spanish language network. Most of the stations receiving network programs are known as affiliates because they have contractual obligations to carry the programming the networks distribute. Some stations, however, are licensed to the networks and are known as "O & O's" — owned and operated by the networks.

The FCC licenses only broadcast stations. "Broadcasting" means sending a signal intended for general reception. The signals a network sends — *via* satellite today, formerly by a nationwide network of terrestrial microwave links — are meant only for the stations affiliated with the network, not for the general public. Therefore, networks do not broadcast and are not licensed by the FCC. Each of the major networks has licenses for several television stations it owns and operates. So the FCC, which licenses the stations, has indirect control over the networks. Also, courts have allowed the FCC to set rules for the networks because of their contractual relations with the sta-

tions, over which the FCC does have jurisdiction.[67]

STRUCTURAL REGULATION OF BROADCASTING

In order to fulfill its public interest goals without intruding on a licensee's programming discretion, the FCC often adopts rules regulating the structure of the broadcast industry. The rules, for example, set limits on the number of stations a company may own in a single market or restrict the kinds of businesses in which a licensee may engage.

The FCC long has acted on the assumption that the public interest is best served when many different licensees operate stations. Diverse ownership, it asserted, would lead to diverse viewpoints in programming and increased economic competition. For decades the FCC has limited the number of stations, as well as other media outlets, a single owner can control.[68]

The ownership restrictions were designed to prevent undue concentration of ownership at both the national and the local levels. The national rules first limited the number of stations that a company could own to seven AM, seven FM and seven TV (no more than five of which could be VHF stations).[69] In the 1980s and 1990s, the FCC modified the national ownership limits several times, finally setting the limits at twenty AM, twenty FM and twelve TV stations.[70] It also added a requirement for television group ownership: the stations could collectively cover no more than 25 percent of the nation's TV households.[71] Another rule prohibited one company from controlling two television broadcast networks. Networks were also not allowed to own cable television systems.

At the local level, the anti-duopoly rule limited a licensee to one station of the same service in a market. (AM radio, FM radio and television each is a "service.") The rule barred an entity from owning both a commercial television station and a radio station in the same market (although this rule was often waived to permit such combinations). There were also cross-ownership restrictions: A company could not, for example, own a cable system and a broadcast station in the same local market.

Over the years, the FCC significantly amended the rules. Moreover, Congress sharply modified some ownership limits in the Telecommunications Act of 1996.[72] The act further directed the FCC periodically to review whether the remaining own-

---

[63] 47 U.S.C. § 158 (2012).

[64] *See, generally*, FCC, Application Processing Fees, *available at https://www.fcc.gov/licensing-databases/fees/application-processing-fees*.

[65] 47 U.S.C. § 159 (2012).

[66] *See*, FCC, Assessment and Collection of Regulatory Fees for Fiscal 2016 (2016), *available at* https://www.fcc.gov/licensing-databases/fees/regulatory-fees.

[67] *See, e.g.*, Nat'l Broad. Co. v. FCC, 319 U.S. 190 (1943) (upholding the FCC Chain Broadcasting Rules which regulated the contractual relationships between broadcast networks and their affiliates).

[68] *See, e.g.*, Broadcast Services Other than Standard Broadcast, 6 Fed. Reg. 2282 (1941) (imposing national ownership restrictions on television broadcast stations).

[69] Rules and Regulations Relating to Multiple Ownership, 18 F.C.C. 288 (1953), *aff'd sub nom.* United States v. Storer Broad. Co., 351 U.S. 192 (1956).

[70] Radio Multiple Ownership Rules, 7 F.C.C.R. 2755 (1992).

[71] Multiple Ownership, 100 F.C.C.2d 74 (1985).

[72] Telecommunication Act of 1996, Pub. L. 104-104, 110 Stat. 136 § 202 (1996).

ership restrictions continued to serve the public interest.[73]

The FCC last updated its ownership rules in 2007.[74] Since then the Commission has initiated two further reviews of the rules,[75] but has made no further decisions on whether the rules continue to serve the public interest — decisions Congress mandated when it required periodic review of the rules. Consequently, in April of 2016, a federal appeals court criticized the agency for not following the directions of Congress and ordered the Commission to conclude the 2010 and 2014 Quadrennial Reviews no later than the end of 2016.[76] The following text explains the current ownership rules, but they may change when the Commission finishes its current deliberations as required by the court.

Radio

Congress, in the 1996 Act, rescinded the national ownership limits for radio stations.[77] Thus, one company may own as many stations throughout the country as it wants. Rules continue to restrict ownership within each local market. The limit depends on the number of stations in the market:

- In communities with up to fourteen radio stations, a licensee may have no more than five radio operations, no more than three of which may be AM or FM stations, and no single licensee may control more than half of the total radio stations in a market.

- In markets with fifteen to twenty-nine radio stations, one owner may control up to six radio stations, but no more than four AM or four FM stations.

- In communities with thirty to forty-four radio stations, one owner may control up to seven radio stations, but no more than four AM or four FM stations.

- In markets with forty-five or more radio stations, one owner may control up to eight radio stations, but no more than five AM or five FM stations.[78]

The FCC's 2007 Order did not change these numerical limitations on ownership, but the Commission amended its definition of local radio markets in an effort to make the rules more predictable and understandable.[79]

Television

The 1996 Act removed all limits on the number of television stations one company may own, but owners could not control stations collectively capable of reaching more than 35 percent of the country's households with television sets.[80] The FCC was forced to review the 35 percent rule after the D.C. Circuit Court ordered it to justify whether keeping the rule continued to serve the public interest.[81] The FCC then raised the coverage cap to 45 percent, finding that there was a need to retain some ownership limits but that increasing the limits would benefit the public by allowing large group owners, such as the broadcast networks, to expand their holdings and funnel increased revenues into expensive, high-quality programming.[82] Congress subsequently amended this provision so that group-owned stations could cover no more than 39 percent of U.S. television households.[83]

At the local level, rules allow common ownership of two stations within the same local television market (as defined by Nielsen Media Research) if eight full-power independent stations (commercial and non-commercial) remain in operation after the merger — the "eight-voices exception." The rule only allows common ownership if one of the stations is not among the

---

[73] *Id.* at § 202(h).

[74] 2006 Quadrennial Regulatory Review — Review of the Commission's Broadcast Ownership Rules and Other Rules Adopted Pursuant to Section 202 of the Telecommunications Act of 1996 (MB Docket No. 06-121); 2002 Biennial Regulatory Review — Review of the Commission's Broadcast Ownership Rules and Other Rules Adopted Pursuant to Section 202 of the Telecommunications Act of 1996 (MB Docket No. 02-277); Cross-Ownership of Broadcast Stations and Newspapers (MM Docket No. 01-235); Rules and Policies Concerning Multiple Ownership of Radio Broadcast Stations in Local Markets (MM Docket No. 01-317); Definition of Radio Markets (MM Docket No. 00-244); Ways to Further Section 257 Mandate and To Build on Earlier Studies (MB Docket No. 04-208); Public Interest Obligations of TV Broadcast Licensees (MM Docket No. 99-360), FCC 07-216, 23 F.C.C.R. 2010 (2007).

[75] 2010 Quadrennial Regulatory Review—Review of the Commission's Broadcast Ownership rules and Other Rules Adopted Pursuant to Section 202 of the Telecommunications Act of 1996 (MB Docket 09-182), 26 F.C.C.R. 17489 at ¶¶ 118-135 (2011); 2014 Quadrennial Regulatory Review — Review of the Commission's Broadcast Ownership Rules and Other Rules Adopted Pursuant to Section 202 of the Telecommunications Act of 1996 (MB Docket No. 14-50), 79 F.C.C.R. 28995 (2014).

[76] Prometheus Radio Project v. FCC, 2016 U.S. App. LEXIS 9688 (3d Cir. May 25, 2016).

[77] Telecommunications Act of 1996, Pub. L. 104-104, 110 Stat. 136, § 202(a) (1996).

[78] 47 C.F.R. § 73.3555(a) (2016).

[79] 2006 Quadrennial Regulatory Review, *supra* note 74, at ¶ 110. The FCC replaced its signal contour method of defining markets (i.e., the extent to which various stations' signals overlapped with other signals), with Arbitron's market method, in which radio stations are assigned to a single specific geographic market.

[80] Telecommunication Act of 1996, Pub. L. 104-104, 110 Stat. 136 § 202(b) (1996).

[81] Fox TV v. FCC, 280 F.3d. 1027 (D.C. Cir. 2002). The court also struck down an FCC rule that prohibited the common ownership of a broadcast television station and a cable television system in the same community. The court found that the FCC had failed to justify the retention of the rule as necessary to safeguard competition or the public interest. *Id.* at 1051.

[82] 2002 Biennial Regulatory Review — Review of the Commission's Broadcast Ownership Rules and Other Rules Adopted Pursuant to Section 202 of the Telecommunications Act of 1996 (MB Docket No. 02-277); Cross-Ownership of Broadcast Stations and Newspapers (MM Docket No. 01-235); Rules and Policies Concerning Multiple Ownership of Radio Broadcast Stations in Local Markets (MM Docket No. 01-317); Definition of Radio Markets (MM Docket No. 00-244), FCC 03-127, 18 F.C.C.R. 13620 (2003).

[83] Consolidated Appropriations Act of 2004, Pub. L. No. 108-199, Div. B, § 629, 118 Stat. 3, 99-100 (2004). Congress chose the 39 percent figure because two group owners, Viacom and News Corp., had already reached the 39 percent mark by virtue of the FCC's waiving the rules. Setting the cap at 39 percent thus foreclosed the possibility that these two companies would have to divest any of their television properties.

top four in the market based on audience share.[84]

Media Cross Ownership

The FCC maintains two separate cross-ownership restrictions — one regulating the common ownership of radio and television stations in the same market and the other regulating the common ownership of broadcast stations and newspapers in the same market. The regulations allow one owner to control up to two television stations and six radio stations in markets with twenty additional independent media voices. For purposes of this rule, independent media voices include full-power television stations, radio stations, daily newspapers and cable television systems. A company may own up to two television stations and four radio stations in markets with ten additional voices. There are no restrictions on owning one TV and one radio station in a market.[85] In its 2011 Notice of Proposed Rule Making, the FCC proposed to eliminate this rule and instead rely solely on the provisions of the radio and television multiple ownership regulations described above.[86]

The second cross-ownership restriction generally forbids the common ownership of a daily newspaper and any commercial broadcast station — radio or television — in the same community,[87] although over the years, the FCC has granted a handful of waivers. In its 2007 ruling, it rescinded the newspaper/broadcast cross-ownership ban in the largest twenty television markets. It also established a liberal waiver policy to consider such combinations in smaller television markets.[88] In 2011 a federal circuit court remanded this provision to the Commission due to procedural errors in its adoption.[89] Consequently, the agency is reconsidering this regulation in its current rule making proceeding.[90]

Broadcast Networks

At one time, broadcast networks could not own cable systems, but Congress ordered the rescission of the rule in 1996.[91] The dual network rule, which prohibits a company from owning two national television broadcast networks, still exists,[92] but the

FCC has interpreted the rule to prohibit only the merger of the four major networks, ABC, CBS, NBC and Fox.[93]

REGULATION OF BROADCAST PROGRAMMING

The Communications Act forbids the FCC from censoring broadcast programming, but that has not prevented the FCC and Congress from adopting a number of regulations and laws affecting broadcast content. Some broadcasters argue that these limitations amount to censorship, but courts generally have allowed content requirements and restrictions.

Formats

While most television stations offer a broad selection of programming, radio stations adopt formats with a relatively limited range of content. A radio station's format may be country-and-western music, adult-oriented albums, oldies or another subgenre of rock, sports or news and talk. Listeners tune to a station because of its particular programming and may be upset if the station changes formats. This is particularly true if the format is unusual — jazz, classical music or children's programming, for example. Indeed, at one time courts told the FCC that the public interest requires the Commission to give approval, and to allow citizens' groups to have an opportunity to express their views, before a station could change a unique format.[94]

Several years later, however, the Commission decided that stations should be able to choose their formats without FCC approval, based upon the rationale that market forces should determine the formats of the large number of stations on the air. The Supreme Court upheld that decision.[95] Stations now may change formats at will, no longer needing FCC permission, the rationale being that if a sufficient number of listeners will support a station offering a particular format, a station in the market will respond to that consumer demand.

Fairness Doctrine

Broadcasters have argued that many rules and laws affecting programming conflict with their First Amendment rights, but the fairness doctrine particularly nettled them. The FCC developed the doctrine in a number of decisions beginning in 1949. The doctrine required broadcasters to inform audiences about controversial issues of public importance in the stations' license areas and to present contrasting viewpoints about the issues.

[84] 2006 Quadrennial Regulatory Review, *supra*, note 74, at ¶ 87; 47 C.F.R. § 73.3555(b) (2016).

[85] *Id.* at ¶ 80; 47 C.F.R. § 73.3555(c) (2016).

[86] 2010 Quadrennial Regulatory Review—Review of the Commission's Broadcast Ownership rules and Other Rules Adopted Pursuant to Section 202 of the Telecommunications Act of 1996 (MB Docket 09-182), 26 F.C.C.R. 17489 at ¶¶ 118-135 (2011).

[87] 47 C.F.R. § 73.3555(d) (2016).

[88] 2006 Quadrennial Regulatory Review, *supra* note 74, at ¶ 13.

[89] Prometheus Radio Project v. FCC, 652 F.3d 431 (3d Cir. 2011).

[90] 2014 Quadrennial Regulatory Review, *supra* note 76, at ¶¶ 113-199.

[91] Telecommunications Act of 1996, Pub. L. 104-104, 110 Stat. 136 § 202(f)(1) (1996).

[92] 47 C.F.R. § 73.658(g) (2016).

[93] Dual Network Order, 16 F.C.C.R. 11115 (2001).

[94] *See* Citizens Comm. to Save WEFM v. FCC, 506 F.2d 246 (D.C. Cir. 1973); Citizens Comm. to Preserve the Voice of the Arts in Atlanta v. FCC, 436 F.2d 263 (D.C. Cir. 1970).

[95] FCC v WNCN Listeners Guild, 450 U.S. 582 (1981).

This was to be done in overall programming, not necessarily through any individual program.[96] The Supreme Court, in *Red Lion Broadcasting v. FCC*, effectively upheld the FCC's right to impose fairness requirements.[97]

By the mid-1980s, however, the FCC began to question whether it needed the doctrine, since the number of broadcast and other outlets available to most people for dissemination of news and opinions about controversial issues had grown significantly. The Commission also concluded that the doctrine in fact had a chilling effect on speech because broadcasters would often avoid controversial issues altogether rather than open themselves to complaints about presenting contrasting viewpoints. For these reasons, in 1987 the FCC rescinded the doctrine, a decision the courts upheld.[98]

Indecent Programming

No electronic media may carry obscene material. The First Amendment protects obscenity on radio or television no more than in any other mass medium. (Obscenity is covered in Chapter 5.) In addition to possibly violating criminal laws, broadcasters who air obscene material are subject to stiff fines for not complying with FCC rules. Broadcasters, however, are also forbidden from airing "indecent or profane" programs,[99] a restriction not placed on other mass media.

During broadcasting's first fifty years, no station was punished solely on grounds that it aired indecent material.[100] But in the 1970s, the face of radio was changing, and some stations allowed — indeed, encouraged — on-air personalities to discuss sexual topics in a joking way, often at times when children could be listening.[101] Reacting to complaints from the public, the FCC fined some stations and stated that it expected such programming to stop.[102]

Then, in 1973, the FCC was faced with what it considered an egregious example of indecent material. During a weekday midafternoon, a father and son driving through New York City turned on the radio and heard on WBAI, an FM station licensed to the Pacifica Foundation, a portion of an album by comedian George Carlin. Recorded live, the twelve-minute routine was based on Carlin's list of seven words "you can't say on the public ... airwaves." The father complained to the FCC, and, after a hearing, the Commission warned Pacifica that if it broadcast indecent programming again, the FCC could impose sanctions. Pacifica appealed, and the Supreme Court upheld the FCC.[103]

The Court adopted the FCC's definition of indecent communication as words that "describe, in terms patently offensive as measured by contemporary community standards for the broadcast medium, sexual or excretory activities and organs, at times of the day where there is reasonable risk that children may be in the audience."[104] The Court recognized that the restriction on indecent programming limited broadcasters' First Amendment rights but found it acceptable because (1) broadcasting is pervasive, and (2) the Carlin monologue was aired at a time children likely could be listening. Both points were important.

First, the Court assumed that people could be exposed to radio or television at any time, in any place, with little control over what they would hear or see. Because broadcasting differs in this regard from print media, which normally require a decision to purchase and a conscious effort to read, broadcasters' First Amendment rights could be narrowed. Second, since the primary concern was preventing children from being exposed to indecent programming, the FCC and Supreme Court did not hold that stations never could carry such material. Rather, they could not air indecent material when children were likely to hear or see it. Accordingly, the FCC has chosen 10 p.m. to 6 a.m. as a so-called "safe harbor" during which broadcasters are permitted to carry indecent programming.[105]

Until a few years ago, most indecency fines were levied against radio stations, usually for broadcasts involving live shows that featured sexually graphic or suggestive discussions, expletives or lewd songs. In an effort to help the broadcast industry avoid violating the indecency rules, the FCC issued a Policy Statement in 2001 that listed the various factors the Commission uses to determine whether material is indecent.[106]

Several notable events in 2003 and 2004 led both the FCC and Congress to reconsider the ways indecent and profane broadcasts are regulated. First came a string of high-profile violations involving radio shock jocks. One instance involved the "Opie and Anthony Show," during which descriptions of couples

---

[96] *See* Editorializing by Broad. Licensees, 13 F.C.C. 1246 (1949).

[97] 395 U.S. 367 (1969).

[98] Syracuse Peace Council v. FCC, 867 F.2d 654 (D.C. Cir. 1989). *See also* Arkansas AFL-CIO v. FCC, 11 F.3d 1430 (8th Cir. 1993).

[99] 18 U.S.C. § 1464 (a provision of the United States Criminal Code); 47 U.S.C. §§ 312(a)(6), 503 (b)(1)(D) (2012).

[100] *But see* Robinson v. FCC, 334 F.2d 534 (D.C. Cir. 1964) (in which the FCC found that a disk jockey told offensive jokes, capable of indecent meaning, on the air, but based its non-renewal of the station's license on grounds that the station management had lied to the FCC).

[101] *See* Sonderling Broad. Corp., 41 F.C.C.2d 777 (1973) (for example, a caller saying, "... I used to spread [peanut butter] on my husband's privates.... [W]omen should try their favorite...," and the announcer replying, "Whipped cream, marshmallow....").

[102] *See, e.g.*, Illinois Citizens Comm. for Broad. v. FCC, 515 F.2d 397 (D.C. Cir. 1974).

[103] FCC v. Pacifica Found., 438 U.S. 726 (1978).

[104] *Id.* at 732.

[105] New Indecency Enforcement Standards, 2 F.C.C.R. 2726 (1987).

[106] In the Matter of Industry Guidance on the Commission's Case Law Interpreting 18 U.S.C. § 1464 and Enforcement Policies Regarding Broadcast Indecency, 16 F.C.C.R. 7999 (2001). The factors are (1) the explicitness or graphic nature of the description or depiction of sexual or excretory organs or activities; (2) whether the material dwells on, or repeats at length, descriptions of sexual or excretory activities or organs; and (3) whether the material appears to pander, is used to titillate, or appears to have been presented for shock value.

having sex in St. Patrick's Cathedral were aired live.[107] Another involved a call-in show in which callers described in detail explicit sexual and excretory experiences.[108] The incident most credited with provoking Congress, however, was the famous "costume malfunction" during the 2004 Super Bowl halftime show in which Janet Jackson's breast briefly was revealed, which the FCC subsequently ruled was indecent.[109] In response to these and other violations and the resulting complaints from thousands of citizens, in 2006, Congress amended the Communications Act to raise the permissible penalty for airing indecent language from $32,500 to $325,000 per incident.[110]

In another development, the FCC, in a departure from long-established practice, announced that it would begin to act against stations airing what the FCC called "fleeting expletives." The issue arose when Bono, while accepting a Golden Globe award on live television, said the award was "fucking brilliant." After review, the FCC's Enforcement Bureau, citing precedent, declared that the one-time, fleeting use of the word — even though it was broadcast outside the safe harbor — was not indecent.[111] The word was used as an adjective, not as a reference to sexual activity. Congress responded with resolutions condemning the decision.[112] Several months later, the full Commission reversed the bureau's decision, finding the use of the word to be actionable and indicating that future use of such language outside the safe harbor will result in forfeitures.[113]

Based on this decision, many television licensees declined to carry the award-winning World War II movie *Saving Private Ryan* due to the film's strong language. Several stations did carry the program, and many complaints about the language were filed at the Commission. The FCC ruled that the program was not indecent because the language was integral to the film's objective of presenting the horror of war.[114] However, when musicians used the same language in a critically acclaimed documentary on the blues, the FCC ruled the language was illegal.[115] In 2006, the FCC declared that use of the word "shit" outside the safe harbor also was actionable and could lead to sanctions.[116] However, the agency decided that use of the word "bullshitter" during *The Early Show* was not actionable because the word was said in the context of a *bona fide* news interview.[117] Further complicating the matter, the FCC stated in the same proceeding that there is "no outright news exemption from our indecency rules."[118]

The broadcast networks challenged several of the FCC actions in court, citing both procedural errors and First Amendment concerns.[119] In 2010, the Second Circuit ruled that the FCC's policy was unconstitutionally vague and created a chilling effect on protected speech.[120] However, when the Supreme Court considered the case in 2012, it vacated the Second Circuit's First Amendment decision.[121] In a very narrow ruling, the Supreme Court concluded that the FCC's specific sanctions in the cases being appealed violated the broadcasters' Fifth Amendment due process rights because the broadcasts occurred before the FCC's announced change in its indecency policy; the broadcasters accordingly had no notice that the broadcasts would be actionable. The Supreme Court declined to address the First Amendment issue.

The Supreme Court decision essentially leaves the FCC's indecency policies intact. However, in 2013, the FCC opened a proceeding seeking comment on whether to continue its current enforcement policies (the ones that led to all the recent litigation) or go back to its pre-fleeting expletive policy by focusing only on "egregious" cases.[122] As of late 2016 no decision had been made in the proceeding.

Children's Programming

For decades Congress and the FCC have sparred with networks over children's programming. Early on, the battle involved excessive violence in shows children watched. Later, advocates for

---

[107] *See* Infinity Broadcasting Operations, Inc. et al., 18 F.C.C.R. 19954 (2004).

[108] *See* Infinity Broadcasting Operations, Inc., 18 F.C.C.R. 6915 (2003).

[109] Complaints Against Various Television Licensees Concerning Their February 1, 2004, Broadcast of the Super Bowl XXXVIII Halftime Show, 21 F.C.C.R. 2760 (2006). The case bounced around the courts for several years: CBS Corp. v. FCC, 535 F.3d 167 (3d Cir. 2008); FCC v. CBS Corp., 556 U.S. 1213 (2009). Ultimately the FCC's decision was reversed by a court of appeals on due process grounds because CBS had no prior notice that "fleeting indecencies" such as this would be actionable. CBS Corp. v. FCC, 663 F.3d 122 (3d Cir. 2011), *cert. denied* 132 S.Ct. 2677 (2012).

[110] Broadcast Decency Enforcement Act of 2005, Pub. Law 109-235 (2006).

[111] Complaints Against Various Broadcast Licensees Regarding Their Airing of the "Golden Globe Awards," 18 F.C.C.R. 19859 (Enforcement Bur. 2003).

[112] H. Res. 500, S. Res. 283, 108th Cong. (2003).

[113] Complaints Against Various Broadcast Licensees Regarding Their Airing of the "Golden Globe Awards," 19 F.C.C.R. 4975 (2004).

[114] Complaints Against Various Television Licensees Regarding Their Broadcast on November 11, 2004, of the ABC Television Network's Presentation of the Film "Saving Private Ryan," 20 F.C.C.R. 4507 (2005).

[115] Complaints Regarding Various Television Broadcasts Between February 2, 2002, and March 8, 2005, 21 F.C.C.R. 1664, ¶¶ 72-86 (2006).

[116] *Id.* at ¶¶ 100-145.

[117] Complaints Regarding Various Television Broadcasts Between February 2, 2002, and March 8, 2005 (Remand Order), 21 F.C.C.R 13299, ¶¶ 67-73 (2006).

[118] *Id.* at ¶ 71.

[119] Initially the U.S. Court of Appeals overturned the FCC's new policy, arguing that the agency had not adequately explained its policy changes. Fox TV Stations v. FCC, 489 F.3d 444 (2d Cir. 2007). The Supreme Court disagreed and remanded the case to the Second Circuit for consideration of the First Amendment issues. FCC v. Fox TV Stations, 556 U.S. 502 (2009).

[120] Fox TV Stations v. FCC, 613 F.3d 317 (2d. Cir. 2010).

[121] FCC v. Fox TV Stations, 132 S.Ct. 2307 (2012).

[122] Public Notice, FCC, FCC Reduces Backlog of Broadcast Indecency Complaints by 70% (More than One Million Complaints); Seeks Comment on Adopting Egregious Cases Policy, 28 F.C.C.R. 4082 (2013).

better children's programming convinced Congress that there simply were not enough shows that helped children learn about themselves and their world. Congress held a number of hearings about children's television and tried to convince broadcast network executives to pay more attention to the quality of children's programs.

Finally, in 1990, Congress adopted a law requiring stations to provide certain types of children's programs, which essentially meant that networks and syndicators would need to supply the shows.[123] The statute also limited the amount of commercial time that could be inserted before, during and after children's programming on broadcast stations and cable networks.

The Children's Television Act requires broadcast stations to provide programming intended for children 16 years old or younger that will serve their "educational and information needs."[124] The law also encourages stations to offer educational and information programming that is meant for families — adults, as well as children. Nature programming is an example. Additionally, the act suggests that stations could show their concern about children's programming in other ways. They could air announcements for children's shows on public television, for example, or help pay for study guides for educational and information programs.[125] The law did not specify how much programming aimed at children would be required for a station to be in compliance, but the voluntary activities could help convince the FCC that a station has met the requirements.

By the mid-1990s, several FCC commissioners and some members of Congress asserted that broadcasters were not fulfilling their responsibilities under the Children's Television Act. To give the law more teeth, in 1996, the FCC adopted rules making it clear what stations must do.[126] They are to broadcast three hours per week of programs designed to serve children's intellectual/cognitive and social/emotional needs. Programs are required to be at least thirty minutes long, regularly scheduled on a weekly basis and broadcast between 7 a.m. and 10 p.m. The rules establish what is termed "core programming," and stations' compliance with the rules is considered at license renewal. For broadcasters that multicast (provide more than one simultaneous program stream), an additional three hours of programming are required for every full-time free program stream. Program streams broadcast less than full time are required to provide children's programming on a pro rata basis.[127]

A station that does not broadcast quite three hours of core programming can still have its license renewed by airing public service announcements, programs fewer than thirty minutes in length and programs not scheduled weekly — all of which are designed to meet children's intellectual and emotional needs and which the station persuades the FCC are equivalent to meeting the three-hour requirement. Stations not coming within either of these categories will have to convince the FCC that they deserve to have their licenses renewed.

While the programming requirements apply to broadcast stations and not to cable networks, the Children's Television Act has commercial limits that apply to both. It restricts advertising time before, during and after programming directed at children 12 years old and younger. Commercials are limited to twelve minutes per hour during the week and ten and one-half minutes per hour on Saturdays and Sundays. These limits are prorated; a half-hour program may carry only six minutes of commercials on Thursday afternoon, for example. The FCC also has ruled that characters in children's programs may not appear in commercials before, during or after the programs.[128] In 2004, it added rules to deal with special considerations relating to children's Web sites. Television programs that target children 12 and younger may not display Web addresses that lead children to commercial sites that include e-commerce or advertising. Only sites that contain primarily program related and other noncommercial content may be listed in children's programs.[129]

V-Chip and Television Program Ratings

In the 1990s, rumblings from the public and politicians about the perceived amount of violence and sex on television rose to a roar. Congress addressed the complaints in the Telecommunications Act of 1996, which required that, beginning in 1998, all television sets sold in the United States include a means for viewers to prevent certain programs from being seen on the sets. A microprocessor chip — called a "v-chip" — within the set picks up an electronic signal embedded within certain television programs. The signal indicates the program's rating. The v-chip in a set may be instructed to prevent programs rated for mature audiences, for example, from being seen on that set.

In conjunction with the v-chip, Congress mandated the development of a voluntary rating system for TV programs. There are two sets of parental guidelines, as the ratings are known. One category applies to programs designed solely for children. A TV-Y rating means a program is appropriate for all children; TV-Y7 means a program is designed for children aged seven and

---

[123] Children's Television Act, Pub. L. No. 101-437, 104 Stat. 996 (1990) (codified at 47 U.S.C. § 303(a-b) (2012).

[124] 47 U.S.C. § 303(b) (2012).

[125] Children's Television Programming, 6 F.C.C.R. 2111 (1991); Children's Television Programming, 6 F.C.C.R. 5093 (1991).

[126] Policies and Rules Concerning Children's Television Programming, 11 F.C.C.R. 10660 (1996).

[127] Children's Television Obligations of Digital Television Broadcasters, 21 F.C.C.R. 11065 (2006).

[128] Children's Television Programming, 6 F.C.C.R. 7199 (1990).

[129] Children's Television Obligations of Digital Television Broadcasters, 19 F.C.C.R. 22943 (2004).

above. The second rating category applies to programs designed for the entire audience. TV-G means that most parents would find the program suitable for all ages. TV-PG means the program contains material that parents may find unsuitable for younger children. TV-14 means it contains some material that many parents may find unsuitable for children younger than 14. Finally, TV-MA means a program is specifically designed for an adult audience and is, therefore, unsuitable for children younger than 17. Additionally, the ratings include letters that identify various types of content. For example, "V" stands for violence, "FV" for fantasy violence, "S" for sexual material, "L" for strong language, and "D" for suggestive dialogue. Sports and news programs are not rated.

While the law does not require a rating to be applied to any individual program, once a program is rated, the rating must be imbedded on the signal carrying the show. In 2000, the FCC released a survey that indicated that all the broadcast networks and most of the basic cable networks were encoding their programming.[130]

Responding to public concern about the coarsening of television content, several members of Congress asked the FCC to study television violence and its impact on children. The Commission began its inquiry in 2004 and issued its report to Congress in 2007.[131] The report agreed with many commenters that there is strong evidence that exposure to violence in the media can increase aggressive behavior in children, but that existing devices for shielding children from such programming, such as the v-chip, are not effective. Consequently, the FCC recommended that Congress pass legislation requiring broadcasters to channel violent programming to time periods when children are less likely to be in the audience, much like the regulations that currently apply to indecent and profane programming.[132] As of late 2015, Congress had not formally reacted to the FCC's proposal.

Political Broadcasting

Under Section 315 of the Communications Act, once a legally qualified candidate for an elective office has used a station — has been given or sold time — all other legally qualified candidates for the same office must be given equal opportunities. That is, candidates for the same office have the right to approximately the same amount of time during a period of the day when they are likely to be seen or heard by the same size and

type of audience. Section 315 applies to candidates running for all types of elective office — local, state or federal.

While the FCC has held, essentially, that the public interest requires candidates to be given access to broadcast stations, Congress made certain of that for those running for federal offices. Section 312(a)(7) of the Communications Act requires broadcast stations to give federal candidates "reasonable access" to radio and television audiences. The term "reasonable access" is interpreted liberally. In 1980, the Carter-Mondale Committee asked ABC, NBC and CBS to sell it thirty minutes of time. The networks refused, and the Supreme Court upheld the FCC's decision that the refusal violated section 312(a)(7).[133] The Commission also has stated that "reasonable access" does not mean free time for federal candidates; stations may charge candidates for air time, a ruling also upheld in court.[134]

Section 312(a)(7) guarantees that a candidate for federal office cannot be denied time on broadcast stations. Otherwise, federal candidates are subject to the provisions of Section 315, just as are candidates for non-federal offices.

A point of contention between broadcasters and candidates for federal office has been the length of political ads. Broadcasters usually sell time to commercial advertisers in thirty- and sixty-second slots. But some candidates have sought to buy five-minute time slots in order to present a more detailed message. Consequently, the FCC issued an order stating that candidates may not be barred from purchasing advertising time in lengths most useful for their purposes simply because broadcasters traditionally sell time in thirty- and sixty-second slots.[135]

Legally Qualified Candidate. A legally qualified candidate is one who has announced publicly that she or he is running for an office. This means more than telling a few friends. The person must have made a widely disseminated statement. Second, the person must meet qualifications for the office — age or residency, for example. Third, the person must either (a) have qualified for a place on the ballot, usually by having a sufficient number of registered voters sign a nominating petition or being nominated by a political party, or (b) be a publicly committed write-in candidate. Independent candidates can be legally qualified, and even candidates with no reasonable chance of winning the election can insist upon equal opportunity.

A candidate claiming equal opportunity in reaction to another's appearance must be running for the same office. Clearly, two candidates seeking the mayor's seat or two seeking a Senate seat are running for the same office. But other scenarios are not so clear. Assume two Republicans are running in a primary

[130] News Release, FCC, FCC V-Chip Task Force Releases Updated Survey on the Encoding of Video Programming (Jan. 11, 2000), *available at* http://www.fcc.gov/Bureaus/Miscellaneous/News_Releases/2000/nrmc0004.html.

[131] Violent Television Programming and Its Impact on Children (MB Docket 04-261), FCC 07-50, 22 F.C.C.R. 7929 (2007).

[132] *Id.* at ¶ 5.

[133] CBS, Inc. v. FCC, 453 U.S. 367 (1981).

[134] Kennedy for President Comm. v. FCC, 636 F.2d 417 (D.C. Cir. 1980).

[135] People for the American Way and Media Access Project, FCC 99-231 (Sept. 7, 1999), *available at* http://ftp.fcc.gov/Bureaus/Mass_Media/Orders/1999/fcc99231.pdf.

election for mayor, as are two Democrats. A Republican buys a minute of time on a radio station, and one of the Democrats insists on a similar purchase. Under Section 315, the station need not sell time to the Democrat. The FCC has ruled that the Democrat and Republican are not running for the same office: The Democrat is running for the Democratic nomination, and the Republican for the Republican nomination. If both candidates were to win their primary races and face each other in the general election, they would be running for the same office, and so would any third-party or independent candidates for mayor.

A station could avoid all these problems by not selling advertising time to any candidates for state and local offices under Section 315, although the FCC has indicated it would frown on such action. But the requirement under Section 312(a)(7) that broadcast stations offer reasonable access for federal candidates essentially means that a station must sell time to even the first candidate for a federal office asking to run an advertisement.

Use. "Using" a station, which triggers Section 315 for competing candidates, happens when a candidate or the candidate's picture or identifiable voice appears on the air. This can be a campaign commercial, or it can be an appearance on a station's cooking show with no mention of the election. There is no use if the appearance is disparaging, which would occur, for example, if an opponent used the candidate's picture in a belittling way.

In 1959, Congress amended Section 315 by specifying four news exemptions to the use rule. In these instances, even if a candidate's voice or picture is used on the air, Section 315 does not apply because there has been no use under the law. Congress' intent was to be certain that Section 315 did not artificially limit news coverage of political campaigns and candidates. The exemptions are:

(1) On-the-spot coverage of a news event will not trigger Section 315. The FCC and courts have ruled that press conferences and speeches by candidates generally will be considered news events, and coverage of them will not constitute a use. Similarly, debates among candidates are news events and, therefore, exempted from Section 315 regardless of who sponsors them – the candidates, broadcasters or a nonpartisan group.[136] The FCC and the courts have said that it is not required that all candidates for an office be included in a debate, and those who are excluded cannot claim time under Section 315.[137] In 1998, the Supreme Court said that even state-owned public television stations may exclude minor political candidates from on-air debates. The 6-3 opinion held that public stations could exercise their journalistic discretion as long as the exclusion of minority

candidates was not based on the candidate's views.[138] In 1996, the FCC allowed ABC, Fox and the Public Broadcasting Service to provide free time for the major party presidential candidates.[139] It held that the candidates' appearances would be exempt from the equal opportunities requirement of Section 315 as coverage of a bona fide news event.

(2) An appearance on a regularly scheduled newscast is not considered a use. The appearance could be an interview with a candidate, coverage of a candidate's campaign activities or other such activities. Courts have interpreted this exception broadly. Candidates appearing on *The McLaughlin Group*, for example, a television program featuring discussions among panelists as well as presentations of news events, are considered to be involved in news coverage, even though the appearance was not in a typical newscast.[140] The FCC does not interpret the broadcast exemption broadly in relation to on-air personalities who are running for office. While it may seem, for example, that a news program anchor who is a political candidate would come under the newscast exemption, the FCC has held otherwise.[141] Congress recognized that the broadcasting of news about candidates for public office is important to viewers, so it amended Section 315 to exclude appearances by candidates in newscasts. Appearing in a news story, however, and appearing on a news program as a reporter or anchor are not the same. A person presenting the news does not help the public learn more about the campaign; it simply gives the candidate an unfair opportunity to become known. Therefore, an anchor on a Sacramento station who was a candidate for town council in a nearby community had to choose between being on the air or being a candidate during the campaign period. Had he been both, the station would have been required to offer more than thirty hours of free time to other candidates for the same office to comply with the requirements of Section 315.

(3) A candidate's appearance on a regularly scheduled news interview program is not a use and does not trigger Section 315. Interview programs like *Meet the Press* and *Issues and Answers* are exempt. The FCC has extended the definition of a "news interview program" to include *The Today Show, Entertainment Tonight* and similar programs.[142] Even interview segments of call-in talk shows can be exempt.[143] To fall under the exemption, the program must have been regularly scheduled beginning well before the election period, and the station must control the con-

[136] *See* League of Women Voters Educ. Fund v. FCC, 731 F.2d 995 (D.C. Cir. 1984) (without opinion).

[137] Johnson v. FCC, 829 F.2d 157 (D.C. Cir. 1987).

[138] Arkansas Educ. Television Comm'n v. Forbes, 523 U.S. 666 (1998).

[139] Fox Broad. Co., Public Broad. Serv. and Capital Cities/ABC, 11 F.C.C.R. 11101 (1996).

[140] Telecommunications Research and Action Center, 7 F.C.C.R. 6039 (1996).

[141] *See* Branch v. FCC, 824 F.2d 37 (D.C. Cir. 1987).

[142] *See, e.g.*, Paramount Pictures Corp., 3 F.C.C.R. 245 (1988) (*Entertainment Tonight*); Multimedia Entertainment, 56 Rad. Reg. 2d (P & F) 143 (1984) (*Donahue*).

[143] Request of Infinity Broadcasting Operations Inc. for Declaratory Ruling, DA 03-2865, 18 F.C.C.R. 18603 (2003).

tent, format and guests.

(4) A candidate's appearance on a news documentary program is not a use if the appearance is incidental to the campaign. For example, a water engineer running for governor could be in a documentary about water conservation in the state. But a documentary about the political views of a mayoral candidate would not qualify under the exemption.

Application Time of Section 315. Section 315 applies whenever there are two or more legally qualified candidates for the same elective office. That may be only a short time before an election, or months prior to an election.

Requesting Time and Public File Requirements. Under Section 315, a candidate whose opponent has used a broadcast station must ask for equal opportunity. Candidates must make requests for time within seven days of the appearance that triggered Section 315. The station has no obligation to notify candidates of prior uses. Stations, though, must keep public files with information about candidates who have appeared and those who have requested time.

Lowest Unit Rate. Section 315 provides that candidates purchasing time for political commercials must be charged no more than the station's most favored advertiser would pay. That is, whatever the rate would be for the advertiser who purchases the most minutes during the year on a station is the rate a candidate would be charged. This is true even if that minute is the only time the candidate will purchase during the entire campaign.[144] But if the appearance triggering Section 315 was free to the first candidate — a candidate appears on a local children's program only to read a story aloud — opponents may demand equivalent free time.

The lowest-unit-rate provision takes effect forty-five days before a primary election and sixty days before a general or special election. Outside those periods, stations may charge candidates what any other advertiser would be charged (not just their best advertiser) for comparable advertising time.

Content of Political Commercials. Broadcast stations cannot edit political advertisements, nor can they refuse to run a candidate's commercial because they believe the message will offend an audience. At the same time, stations are not liable for anything said or shown in political commercials. Broadcasters cannot be sued for libel, invasion of privacy or any other tort based on material in a candidate's presentation under Section 315.[145]

The general rule that political advertisements cannot be cen-

sored was severely tested in the 1990s when some candidates chose to show aborted fetuses as part of their commercials. A Georgia candidate for the U.S. House of Representatives included in a commercial depictions of "the actual surgical procedure for abortion ... [including] graphic depictions and descriptions of female genitalia, the uterus, excreted uterine fluid, dismembered fetal body parts, and aborted fetuses."[146] The FCC held that while such commercials are not indecent, stations and cable systems may decide to carry such advertisements only in the safe harbor hours used for indecent programming if they find that the commercials could be harmful to children.[147] But a federal appellate court found that this would permit "broadcasters to take the content of a political advertisement into account" in determining whether to confine the commercial to the safe harbor period, allowing broadcasters "standardless discretion."[148] The court said that, on balance, candidates' rights as specified in sections 315 and 312(a)(7) of the Communications Act took precedence over concerns about children being exposed to possibly offensive material.

Ballot Issues. Section 315 applies only to candidates for public offices but not to ballot issues. Supporters and opponents of such issues may purchase broadcast time if they wish, but there is no requirement that such time be sold or that equal opportunities be provided.

Other Programming Requirements

The FCC has imposed on broadcasters several other rules affecting program content. When those rules have been challenged as violating broadcasters' First Amendment rights, courts have generally upheld them.

Lotteries. A lottery is a contest that has a prize of more than token value, uses chance rather than skill to determine winners, and requires some form of consideration — like the purchase of a ticket — to enter. FCC rules and federal criminal laws have long restricted the information broadcasters may carry about lotteries. The exception has been state-run lotteries in states where the stations are located.

Congress changed all that in 1988. Broadcasters may carry information about certain lotteries. As before, they can provide facts about state lotteries if the station is located in a state that

[144] Political Programming Policies, 7 F.C.C.R. 678 (1991).

[145] *See* Farmers Educ. & Coop. Union of America v. WDAY, 360 U.S. 525 (1959).

[146] Gillette Commc'ns of Atlanta v. Becker, 807 F. Supp. 757, 763 (N.D. Ga. 1992) (finding the commercial to be indecent), *dismissed without opinion and remanded,* 5 F.3d 1500 (11th Cir. 1993).

[147] Petition for Declaratory Ruling Concerning Section 312(a)(7) of the Communications Act, 9 F.C.C.R. 7638 (1994) (disagreeing with the *Gillett* decision that such commercials are indecent).

[148] Becker v. FCC, 95 F.3d 75, 81 (D.C. Cir. 1996).

has a lottery. They may also carry news or advertisements for gaming conducted by American Indian tribes.[149] And they may provide information about a lottery legal in the state where it is conducted and that a governmental or nonprofit organization offers or is sponsored by a person or company not primarily in the business of sponsoring lotteries.[150] Thus, reports or advertisements for bingo games at churches or a cereal company giving away an automobile are acceptable if state law permits. But until recently, stations could not carry information or advertisements for private (non-American Indians) gambling casinos or sports betting. In 1999, the Supreme Court unanimously struck down the ban on television and radio advertising of private casino gambling in states where such gambling is legal, finding that the ban was "so pierced by exemptions and inconsistencies that the government cannot hope to exonerate it."[151]

Sponsorship Identification. Broadcasters must identify clearly any individual or group providing money, or anything else of value, in return for the dissemination of a message.[152] The purpose of the rule is to ensure that viewers and listeners will not confuse paid advertising with entertainment or news programs. If the sponsor is obvious — a cereal, a laundry detergent, a fast food restaurant — the requirement is met. Other messages are not so clearly identifiable. If, for example, a local company provides funds for a "Clean Up The Parks" ad campaign, the ads must carry the company's name as a sponsor.

Hoaxes and News Distortion. The FCC prohibits the broadcasting of hoaxes. Under the regulation, a hoax occurs when a station knowingly broadcasts false reports of crimes or catastrophes that "directly cause foreseeable — immediate, substantial and actual public harm."[153]

WALE-AM radio in Providence, Rhode Island, perpetuated a hoax in 1991 when the news director announced over the air that a WALE talk show host had been shot in the head while outside the station's studio. About ten minutes later, the station stated that the shooting had been a dramatization. Before the second announcement, several police officers rushed to the scene, as did several members of the media. WALE apologized and offered to repay the Providence Police Department for any costs resulting from the hoax. The FCC admonished the station's owner, citing the Commission's policy "requiring licensees

to program their stations in the public interest."[154]

The FCC also has a policy against news distortion. One example of distortion occurred when a Chicago television station had a group of people stage a gathering at which marijuana was smoked in order to film a "pot party." The FCC expressed its concern about manufacturing news but did not threaten action against the station.[155] In another instance, the CBS documentary *Hunger in America* showed a child said to be suffering from malnutrition but who was afflicted with a different illness.[156] The FCC took no action against CBS but used the case to establish a policy forbidding intentional news distortion. The Commission, however, distinguishes deliberate distortion from a mistake or negligent reporting.

Cigarette and Alcohol Advertising. Concerned with the costs to public health that cigarette smoking causes, Congress made it "unlawful to advertise cigarettes on any medium of electronic communication" after January 1, 1971.[157] The law was upheld despite a challenge based on broadcasters' First Amendment rights.[158] Contrary to popular belief, the advertising of alcoholic beverages on broadcast stations has never been illegal (at least since the end of Prohibition), though the distilled spirits industry voluntarily declined to purchase broadcast ads for many years. This voluntary ad ban was abandoned in the 1990s.

NONCOMMERCIAL BROADCASTING

Certain parts of the broadcast spectrum are set aside for use by noncommercial stations. Radio broadcasters were using the AM band before any government agency could consider whether to reserve frequency assignments for noncommercial uses. The FCC, however, was able to set aside portions of the FM band and reserve certain television frequencies for nonprofit organizations, usually educational institutions and state governments, but also religious groups. It recognized that some educational institutions might be tempted to sell their stations to commercial broadcasters, in part because of the high costs of keeping a station on the air, unless certain frequencies were reserved only for nonprofit, educational use.

In 1967, Congress aided noncommercial broadcasting by adopting the Public Broadcasting Act, which established the Corporation for Public Broadcasting, an agency through which government and other funding is used to produce programming for noncommercial stations. The FCC has no jurisdiction to en-

[149] Indian Gaming Regulatory Act, Pub. L. No. 100-497, § 21, codified at 25 U.S.C. § 2720 (2012).

[150] Charity Games Advertising Clarification Act of 1988, Pub. L. No. 100-625, § 2(b), codified at 18 U.S.C § 1307 (2012).

[151] Greater New Orleans Broad. Ass'n v. United States, 527 U.S. 173, 190 (1999).

[152] 47 U.S.C. § 317 (2012).

[153] Broadcast Hoaxes, 7 F.C.C.R. 4106, 4106 (1992).

[154] Letter to WALE-AM, 7 F.C.C.R. 2345, 2346 (1992).

[155] WBBM-TV, 18 F.C.C.2d 124 (1969).

[156] Hunger in America, 20 F.C.C.2d 151 (1969).

[157] 15 U.S.C. § 1335 (2012).

[158] Capital Broad. Co. v. Mitchell, 333 F. Supp. 582 (D.C. 1971), *aff'd without opinion*, 405 U.S. 1000 (1972).

force any provisions of the Public Broadcasting Act,[159] such as that requiring "strict adherence to objectivity and balance in all programs or series of programs of a controversial nature."[160]

One section of the act insisting on objectivity and another forbidding noncommercial stations from supporting political candidates raise questions of First Amendment protection for public stations. The Supreme Court rejected the provision forbidding public stations from supporting political candidates and the Public Broadcasting Act's ban on noncommercial stations editorializing. It said that First Amendment protection of journalistic freedom should also apply to public stations.[161]

Most public stations receive federal and possibly state funds, and government agencies own many of them. The tension between the public nature of noncommercial stations and First Amendment freedoms was reflected in the *Death of a Princess* case. The docudrama, intended for showing on public TV, portrayed the execution in Saudi Arabia of a woman and her lover accused of adultery. The government of Saudi Arabia objected strongly to it, and several public television stations decided not to carry it.[162] Viewers took government-owned stations in Alabama and Houston, Texas, to court, hoping to force them to broadcast the program.[163] In part, the suits claimed that the public stations were arms of the government and were engaging in censorship, as well as violating viewers' First Amendment rights. A federal appellate court found that, as licensees under the Communications Act, the stations were permitted to use their editorial judgment in selecting what programs to carry.[164]

Most of the regulations that apply to commercial stations also apply to non-commercial stations, but there are several differences. In comparative licensing situations, for example, Congress has forbidden the use of auctions in awarding noncommercial licenses. Accordingly, the FCC has developed a point system that compares objective criteria such as local diversity and technical superiority.[165] Another regulatory difference relates to the multiple- and cross-ownership limitations, which do not apply to noncommercial licensees.[166] Finally, as the name implies, noncommercial stations are not permitted to carry advertisements.[167] However, they are permitted to acknowledge

entities that contribute money to the station or underwrite programming. These underwriting announcements differ from commercial advertising in that they contain no qualitative statements about the underwriter's products or services, they cannot make comparisons among products, they cannot provide price information, and there can be no calls to action or inducements to purchase.[168]

THE MOVE TO DIGITAL

Following almost ten years of study and testing, the FCC, in consultation with various industry groups, adopted a new digital television transmission standard in 1996.[169] The new standard, which allows for transmission of multiple program streams as well as high definition television, replaced the analog transmission standard that broadcasters used since the 1940s. The Commission initially proposed a ten-year transition period during which broadcasters and consumers would replace their incompatible analog transmission and receiving equipment with new digital equipment. Every full-power television broadcaster was given a second six-megahertz channel on which to broadcast its digital signal. During the transition, all broadcasters sent out two signals, the old analog signal and the new digital signal. At the end of the transition period, which Congress extended to 2009,[170] all full-power television broadcasters ended their analog transmissions and broadcast solely using their digital signals. The spectrum no longer being used for analog broadcasting was auctioned for other uses.[171]

The transition to digital broadcasting for terrestrial radio has been much simpler than the television transition. For radio, the FCC has approved a digital transmission system that allows stations to provide both analog and digital signals on the same frequency simultaneously.[172] Accordingly, this system, known as In-Band On-Channel, does not require the allocation of additional frequencies. Digital radio, currently marketed as "HD Radio," provides much higher quality signals plus the ability to broadcast more than one program stream at the same time.[173]

[159] *See* Accuracy in Media, Inc. v. FCC, 521 F.2d 288 (D.C. Cir. 1975).

[160] 47 U.S.C. § 396(g)(1)(A) (2012).

[161] FCC v. League of Women Voters, 468 U.S. 364, 402 (1984).

[162] *See, e.g.,* Barnstone v. Univ. of Houston, KUHT-TV, 487 F. Supp. 1347, 1348 (S.D. Tex. 1980).

[163] In Alabama, all public stations operate under a statewide agency; in Texas, the public television stations operate independently of one another.

[164] Muir v. Alabama Educ. Television Comm'n, 688 F.2d 1033 (5th Cir. 1982) (en banc).

[165] In the Matter of Reexamination of the Comparative Standards for Noncommercial Educational Applicants, 15 F.C.C.R. 7386 (2000), *aff'd sub nom.* American Family Ass'n v. FCC, 365 F.3d 1156 (D.C. Cir. 2004).

[166] 47 C.F.R. § 73.3555(f) (2016).

[167] 47 U.S.C. § 399B (2012).

[168] Commission Policy Concerning the Noncommercial Nature of Educational Broadcast Stations, 7 F.C.C.R. 827 (1992).

[169] Advanced Television Systems and Their Impact Upon the Existing Television Broadcast Service, 11 F.C.C.R. 17771 (*Fourth Report and Order,* 1996).

[170] DTV Delay Act, Pub. L. No. 111-4 (2009).

[171] The auction, which was held in January 2008, netted the government nearly $20 billion. *See* FCC, Public Notice DA 08-595, Auction of 700 MHz Band Licenses Closes (Mar. 20, 2008), *available at* http://hraunfoss.fcc.gov/edocs_public/attachmatch/DA-08-595A1.pdf.

[172] Digital Audio Broadcasting Systems and Their Impact on the Terrestrial Radio Broadcast Service, 17 F.C.C.R. 19990 (2002).

[173] For more information on digital radio, *see* the FCC's digital radio page *at* http://www.fcc.gov/cgb/consumerfacts/digitalradio.html.

EQUAL EMPLOYMENT OPPORTUNITIES

The FCC, in conjunction with the Equal Employment Opportunity Commission, a federal agency established in 1964, requires that broadcasters not discriminate in hiring, promoting or firing on the basis of race, gender, religion, color or national origin. While the EEOC is expected to notify the FCC of any discrimination complaints filed against broadcast licensees, the FCC also enforces its own equal employment rules.

These regulations require licensees to widely disseminate information concerning full-time job vacancies, provide notice of full-time job vacancies to recruitment organizations, and complete a series of longer-term recruitment initiatives — such as job fairs, internships and mentoring programs — over a two-year period.[174]

SUMMARY

The broadcast media play an integral role in the dissemination of news and information, but the Supreme Court has said that of all forms of mass media, broadcasting has the least protection under the First Amendment. In other words, as long as the FCC issues licenses, broadcasters are required to serve the public interest, which subjects them to more regulation than other mass media. That is, of course, unless the Supreme Court reverses itself and rules that all media are entitled to the same rights under the First Amendment.

It will be interesting to see how the government deals with stations that purchased the right to use the spectrum — those that bid for a radio or a television license. Will they have more protection under the First Amendment? And, as new technologies emerge, will the FCC or the courts eventually change the definition of "scarcity"? Forecasting the answers to these questions is not easy, but at some point — as new technologies give the public more information and entertainment choices — the regulatory scheme under which broadcasting operates is likely to change.

While the FCC's role may change, for now it will continue issuing licenses, reviewing the transfer of licenses, making spectrum allocations, settling controversies among competing parties, issuing fines, and developing policy that will affect the broadcast media as well as other new technologies. But the FCC will not be doing all of this on its own. Regardless of whether its powers are changed or limited in any way, the FCC will always operate under the watchful eye of the courts and the Congress.

FOR ADDITIONAL READING

Benjamin, Louise. "Radio Comes of Age, 1900-1945," in *The Media in America: A History*, 9th ed., Wm. David Sloan, ed. Northport, Ala.: Vision Press, 2014.

Einstein, Mara. *Media Diversity: Economics, Ownership, and the FCC*. Mahwah, N.J.: Lawrence Erlbaum Associates, 2004.

Hopkins, W. Wat. "When Does F*** Not Mean F***? FCC v. Fox Television Stations and a Call for Protecting Emotive Speech," 64 *Federal Communications Law Journal* 1, December 2011.

Lipschultz, Jeremy H. *Broadcast Indecency: F.C.C., Regulation and the First Amendment*. Boston: Focal Press, 1996.

McCall, Jeffrey. *Viewer Discretion Advised: Taking Control of Mass Media Influences*, New York: Rowman & Littlefield Publishers, 2007.

Minow, Newton N. and Craig L. LaMay. *Abandoned in the Wasteland: Children, Television, and the First Amendment*. New York: Hill and Wang, 1995.

Powe, Lucas A., Jr. *American Broadcasting and the First Amendment*. Berkeley, Calif.: University of California Press, 1987.

Tillinghast, Charles H. *American Broadcast Regulation and the First Amendment: Another Look*. Ames, Iowa: Iowa University Press, 2000.

"The Vast Wasteland Revisited," 55 *Federal Communications Law Journal* 395, May 2003.

---

[174] 47 C.F.R. § 73.2080 (2016).

Regulating Cable Communication

By Matt Jackson

➡ **Headnote Questions**

- What is the legal history of cable television?
- What are the rationales for the government's regulation of the cable industry?
- What level of First Amendment protection does cable enjoy?
- Why do courts allow more stringent governmental structural regulations on cable than on the print media?
- What kinds of regulations are designed to protect each of the various cable-related interest groups — broadcasters, programmers, Internet content providers, competitors, consumers?

Cable is the primary communication pathway into the home, providing most Americans with their television programming, broadband (high speed) Internet access, and increasingly their telephone service as well. According to the latest government figures, at the end of 2014, more than 76 percent of all U.S. households subscribe to some form of pay television service. Of the 101 million households that pay for television, 52.8 percent subscribe to cable, 33.8 percent subscribe to direct broadcast satellite, and 13 percent receive TV programming from their telephone company.[1] Cable lost 1.4 million video subscribers in 2014 after a decline of two million video subscribers in 2013, with some switching to telephone companies and other "cord cutters" relying on a combination of over the air broadcasting and Internet video services such as Netflix and Hulu.

In addition, 75 percent of American households have wireline broadband Internet access at home. Of those residential broadband subscribers, more than half (58 percent) get their Internet access through their cable provider.[2] Beyond television and Internet access, almost thirty-one million homes now get their landline telephone service through their cable provider as

well.[3] Cable systems collect more than $107 billion per year in subscriber fees.[4] Given its size and central role in our culture, it is no surprise that the cable industry has drawn the attention of regulators, politicians and consumer advocates.

Cable originally was regulated because it posed a threat to over-the-air broadcasting. Regulators were concerned that cable would siphon away the audience for local TV stations. In time, cable regulations evolved in response to concerns about monopoly power, since initially just one cable operator served each local market. Today, regulators are trying to foster competition between the cable, satellite, telephone, broadcast and Internet industries to make sure consumers have adequate choices for television, telephone and Internet service.

Government regulators try to protect consumers and preserve competition in all large industries, but cable, broadcasting and other forms of telecommunications receive special attention because of their central role in transmitting speech. Policymakers recognize that these media are important to the proper functioning of democracy. A handful of corporations, such as Comcast and Time-Warner, control the infrastructure that citizens rely on for information and political participation. So, in addition to normal concerns regarding competition, cable regulation

---

[1] Seventeenth Report: Annual Assessment of the Status of Competition in the Market for the Delivery of Video Programming (DA 16-510) (May 6, 2016). These numbers represent a slight decline in the number of cable subscribers and a significant increase (almost 12 percent growth) in the households that receive television programming through their wireline telephone company.

[2] FCC Wireline Competition Bureau, Internet Access Services: Status as of Dec. 31, 2014, Chart 13, p. 21 (March 2016).

[3] National Cable and Telecommunications Association, Industry Data, http://www.ncta.com/industry-data (last visited June 10, 2016).

[4] Nick Petrillo, IBISWorld Industry Report 51711a: Cable Providers in the U.S. (May 2016). Cable networks and local cable systems generate another $30 billion annually in advertising revenues.

also is based on free speech principles and a desire to foster a marketplace of ideas. But regulators must avoid violating the First Amendment rights of cable operators in their attempt to promote the First Amendment rights of others.

The Constitution was written long before the invention of the electronic communication technologies that dominate our world today, so it is not always clear how the First Amendment should be applied to a new technology. The U.S. Supreme Court has recognized that the unique traits of each mass medium permit different constitutional standards.[5] Yet, the most important characteristics of a new technology often are not apparent until after the public has adopted it.

Convergence of the media industries also creates problems for policymakers. Originally, cable merely provided video programming. Today, cable operators offer Internet access, telephone service, interactive TV and other new services. As the distinctions between cable companies, telephone companies and broadcasters blur, their different regulatory schemes come into conflict. For example, phone companies have to share their wires with competing phone companies. Now that cable companies offer telephone and Internet service, should they have to share their cable wires as well? As another example, your telephone provider is not allowed to alter or interrupt the information transmitted during a phone call. Should Internet access providers also be prohibited from interfering with the content that consumers try to view online?

For First Amendment purposes, cable regulations can be classified broadly as either structural or content-based. Most content-based cable regulation is similar to content-based regulation of broadcasting and print. For example, the standards for defamation and invasion of privacy apply to cable the same way they apply to other media. Content-based cable regulations usually must pass strict scrutiny in order to be constitutional.

The structural regulation of cable is grounded in modern economic theory. As a general rule, economists believe companies behave best when faced with competition. Competition leads to efficient use of resources, a wide range of choices for consumers, and continual product innovation. When there is little or no competition, companies with market power can take advantage of consumers, suppliers and would-be competitors. Antitrust law, which is applied to all industries, is designed to preserve competition in the marketplace.

Some industries have unique characteristics that make competition more difficult to achieve or sustain. The large infrastructure costs and economies of scale involved in operating a cable system led many regulators to believe that cable, like the telephone industry, was a natural monopoly. In other words, it would be more efficient for one company to run a single cable down the street and serve every house than for two separate companies to run separate cables down the street with each company serving half the houses. Theoretically, one company could offer the service more cheaply than two competing companies. Therefore, most cities initially granted one cable company a monopoly franchise. But without a competitor, a company might raise prices since consumers would have no alternative. Similarly, a monopoly cable provider can take advantage of program suppliers (cable networks like Comedy Central and ESPN) because the program supplier has few other potential customers for its programming in that geographic location.

Because of this history of monopoly franchises, most homes are served by only one cable operator, typically a huge company that serves millions of subscribers. Thus, regulators impose special structural regulations on operators so that they cannot abuse their monopoly position. Today regulators are trying to promote competition between cable, telephone, DBS and wireless companies in the hope that it will reduce the need for regulation. Often the regulations created to encourage competition are just as complex as the regulations that apply when there is no competition. As discussed later in this chapter, cable structural regulations are usually evaluated under the First Amendment standard of intermediate scrutiny.

Sometimes the law contains elements of both content and structural regulation — for example, the access and must-carry requirements discussed later in this chapter. This creates special problems for First Amendment analysis. On the one hand, the purpose of these laws is to assure citizens have access to a robust marketplace of ideas. Lawmakers are concerned when one company has the ability to control much of what consumers see or hear. At the same time, the Supreme Court has said that companies have First Amendment rights.

To make matters even more complex, cable operators must negotiate franchise agreements with local communities for the right to run cables over (or under) city streets. Broadcasters, who don't need wires to distribute their signals, don't need permission to use the public rights-of-way. Thus, cable companies must deal with both federal and local regulations. As we shall see, many times this results in conflicting rules.

HISTORY OF CABLE TELEVISION REGULATION

When cable TV was introduced in the late 1940s, broadcasters welcomed it because it expanded the audience for local stations by physically extending the reach of broadcast signals. Cable providers erected tall antennas to pick up TV signals and strung coaxial cables to transmit them to homes unable to receive the broadcast signal clearly.

Beginning in the mid-1950s, these community antenna television — CATV — systems, as they were known, began using

---

[5] *See, e.g.,* Times Film Corp. v. Chicago, 365 U.S. 43 (1961).

microwave technology to import signals from distant TV stations. Cable subscribers now had more channels to choose from. Local broadcasters quickly realized that the new channels would siphon away parts of their audiences, ultimately reducing advertising revenues, so broadcasters asked the Federal Communications Commission to control the cable industry.

The FCC was caught in a bind. On the one hand, increased viewing choices clearly promoted its mandate to serve the public interest and foster diversity. But broadcasters argued that if cable viewers stopped watching local TV stations, the stations would go bankrupt, leaving those homes that did not subscribe to cable without any television at all. Broadcasters reminded the FCC that part of its mandate was to promote broadcasting.

One unanswered question was whether the FCC had the authority to regulate cable at all. When Congress adopted the Communications Act of 1934, it created a framework for regulating broadcasting and wire communications like telegraph and telephone. The act gave the FCC power over common carriers — companies that allow anyone to use their facilities and do not limit or control the content that can be transmitted — and over broadcasting. At that time, Congress could not have envisioned cable TV. Consequently, the FCC initially said the act did not grant it power to regulate cable, for its jurisdiction was limited to radio, broadcast television, other technologies using the electromagnetic spectrum and common carriers. Through the 1950s, the FCC refused to assume control over cable, even at the request of broadcasters.[6]

Early Federal Regulation of Cable Television

As cable grew, broadcasters continued to call for regulation. In the 1960s, the FCC decided it could regulate cable because of the effect cable had on broadcast TV. It said the general language of the Communications Act gave the FCC power over "interstate ... communication by wire" and the responsibility to adopt rules and regulations which were needed to "make available ... [an] efficient ... radio communication service..." in the "public interest, convenience and necessity." In 1962, the FCC decided it was required to regulate cable because cable involves interstate communication by wire and because cable might harm efficient TV service.[7] It was concerned that TV stations, particularly UHF stations (which had weaker signals than VHF stations) and stations in smaller markets, could be harmed financially, even driven off the air, if viewers switched from local stations to stations imported by cable from other cities.

In 1968, the Supreme Court supported that interpretation,

ruling that because the Communications Act of 1934 gave the FCC responsibility to foster the growth of broadcast television, the FCC could regulate cable as long as the regulation was "reasonably ancillary" to the Commission's jurisdiction over broadcast television.[8] Therefore, the FCC could regulate cable in order to protect broadcasting even though the Communications Act never mentions cable.[9] The Court's opinion did not mention the First Amendment at all.

As technology improved, national cable networks emerged, providing programming that was not available on broadcast stations. These new networks transmitted their signals to a satellite that retransmitted the signals to cable operators all over the country, which then distributed the signals to cable customers. At first, the FCC tried to restrict the growth of cable networks by creating complex rules that prevented cable companies from taking advantage of the new satellite technology. The rules prevented premium channels — channels for which a subscription is required, such as HBO — from carrying movies between three and ten years old or most major sporting events. The rules were designed to prevent premium channels from siphoning away popular programming from free, over-the-air broadcast stations. After the Court of Appeals for the District of Columbia struck down the Commission's pay cable rules, subscription-based premium channels like HBO began to prosper.[10]

Early Local Regulation of Cable Television

The number of cable subscribers skyrocketed between 1975 and 1985, and cable operators, local authorities, broadcasters and program producers disagreed about who should regulate cable and how it should be regulated. Each group lobbied the FCC and Congress for rules favoring its own interests. The FCC prevented city and state authorities from regulating pay TV. Yet states, counties and local governments imposed extensive requirements on cable systems through an elaborate franchising process. Local governments had authority over cable systems because cable systems must run their wires from the head end to subscribers' homes over streets and other public land. Local authorities control public rights-of-way and, therefore, can impose conditions, in the form of franchise agreements, on cable.

A franchise is essentially a contract between the two parties. Many franchising authorities wanted to control programming, the rates cable systems charged, the customer services they provided and other aspects of cable business. Franchising authori-

---

[6] *See* Frontier Broad. Co. v. Collier, 24 F.C.C. 251 (1958).

[7] *See* Carter Mountain Transmission Corp., 32 F.C.C. 459 (1962), *aff'd,* Carter Mountain Transmission Corp. v. FCC, 321 F.2d 359 (D.C. Cir. 1963).

[8] United States v. Southwestern Cable Co., 392 U.S. 157, 178 (1968).

[9] The FCC's ancillary power to regulate new technologies would be called into question by an appellate court in 2010. That court ruled in *Comcast v. FCC,* 600 F.3d 642 (D.C. Cir. 2010) that the FCC did not have unlimited authority to regulate cable Internet service.

[10] *See* Home Box Office v. FCC, 567 F.2d 9 (D.C. Cir. 1977).

ties also required cable systems to pay a portion of their revenues in return for permission to use public rights-of-way. Many of the early agreements imposed such a heavy burden on new cable operators that the systems failed. In 1984 the Supreme Court helped reduce this problem when it held that the FCC, not local authorities, had broad power regarding cable and that certain regulatory powers belonged to the commission alone.[11]

The Cable Acts and the Telecommunications Act

In 1984, thirty-five years after the introduction of CATV and fifty years after the adoption of the Communications Act, Congress decided the law needed to be amended to include cable regulation. It adopted the Cable Communications Policy Act of 1984[12] to distinguish the areas of responsibility of local and federal authorities. The 1984 Cable Act freed cable operators to determine the prices they would charge subscribers and forced cable systems to provide service to their entire franchise areas instead of ignoring low-income neighborhoods. The law also limited the fees local franchising authorities could charge cable operators and prevented franchisers from arbitrarily refusing to renew a cable operator's franchise. By deregulating cable television, the act permitted increased growth of cable.

But soon complaints arose that the cable industry was interested more in profits than service. Customers complained about rapidly rising prices. Localities complained about unfulfilled franchise obligations. So Congress, believing the 1984 Act had eliminated too much regulation, again amended the 1934 Communications Act with the Cable Television Consumer Protection and Competition Act of 1992.[13] Among other provisions, it gave local TV broadcast stations the choice of requiring cable systems to carry their signals (must-carry) or to insist on payment or other compensation for being carried (retransmission consent). The act also regulated rates for many cable services and required the FCC to adopt rules to allow cable television's competitors to have access to much of the programming cable TV carries. Federal courts have upheld several of the act's provisions.[14] While the 1984 Act was designed to *deregulate* the cable industry, the 1992 Act was passed to *re-regulate* the industry.

Four years later, again changing its mind, Congress passed the Telecommunications Act of 1996. It reduced some regulations and eliminated others affecting cable.[15] It focused on increased competition — rather than regulation — to assure

communications serve in the public interest. It reflected a belief among lawmakers and many economists that regulations were stifling, rather than protecting, competition. At the same time, rapid changes in technology (particularly wireless technology) made policymakers question the assumption that cable and telephone industries were natural monopolies. Instead, they reasoned that phone companies, terrestrial and satellite wireless companies, and even electric companies (which have wires into every home) could offer the same services as cable companies.

The Telecommunications Act sought to encourage competition by allowing local telephone companies, long distance phone companies and cable companies to enter each other's businesses. Instead of competition, though, the law initially prompted mergers and buyouts among the companies.[16] The Telecommunications Act maintained existing cable system content requirements but prohibited the FCC from imposing new content obligations on cable operators. It also requires the FCC to review its ownership rules every two years with a mandate to repeal or modify any rule that is no longer in the public interest.[17] Cable operators now face more competition than before. Direct Broadcast Satellite — DBS — companies control more than 30 percent of all subscribers. Telephone companies and Internet television sites are also winning over some cable TV customers. The number of households subscribing to cable peaked in 2001 at 66.9 million homes. By 2013 that number had declined to 54.4 million, a decrease of 18 percent. Many of those households switched to new services offered by Verizon and AT&T.[18]

CABLE AND THE FIRST AMENDMENT

In 1986, the Supreme Court held for the first time that cable operators clearly had First Amendment interests and enjoyed some level of constitutional protection. In *Los Angeles v. Preferred Communications, Inc.,* it said cable TV operators engage in "some of the aspects of speech and the communication of ideas as do the traditional enterprises of newspapers and book publishers."[19] A franchising authority could not use its franchising process to grant a cable monopoly, it ruled. Instead, it held that Los Angeles was required to show that its interests in refusing to issue a competing franchise outweighed the cable applicant's First Amendment interests.

In 1991, the Court said in *Leathers v. Medlock* that cable is

---

[11] *See* Capital Cities Cable, Inc. v. Crisp, 467 U.S. 691 (1984).

[12] Pub. L. No. 98-549, 98 Stat. 2779 (1984) (codified at 47 U.S.C. §§ 601-639).

[13] Pub. L. No. 102-385, 106 Stat. 1460 (1992).

[14] *See* Time Warner Entm't. Co. v. FCC, 93 F.3d 957 (D.C. Cir. 1996); Time Warner Entm't Co. v. FCC, 56 F.3d 151 (D.C. Cir. 1995).

[15] Pub. L. No. 104-104, 110 Stat. 56 (1996).

[16] *See* Jeffrey P. Cunard, *Cable Remains Dominant and Strong,* CABLE TV & NEW MEDIA L. & FINANCE, Jan. 1999, at 1; Andrea Foster, *Panels Will Study AT&T Cable TV,* NAT'L L.J., June 14, 1999, at B1; Tom McGhee, *Cable Industry Due for Mergers,* DENVER POST, Apr. 26, 2004, at C1; *Telecom Act in Action; Vision of Competition Blurred by Consolidation,* N.Y. L.J., Sept. 10, 1998, at 5.

[17] Pub. L. No. 104-104, § 202(h), 110 Stat. 56 (1996).

[18] *See* Sixteenth Report, *supra* note 1.

[19] 476 U.S. 488, 494 (1986).

"engaged in 'speech' under the First Amendment."[20] Nevertheless, it held that a state could tax cable system revenues, even if other mass media aren't taxed, so long as the tax is unrelated to speech and is a non-discriminatory, property and service tax applied to a large number of other businesses. In neither of these two cases did the Court specify what standards courts should use to determine whether a cable operator's First Amendment rights had been abridged.

The Court finally did so in *Turner Broadcasting System, Inc. v. FCC*.[21] In response to a First Amendment challenge to the must-carry provisions of the 1992 Cable Act, the Court drew a distinction between content-based and content-neutral regulations and upheld the constitutionality of the must-carry rules, which require cable systems to carry local broadcast programming. It held that the First Amendment must be applied to cable TV in two ways. First, regulations directed at programming content must pass the strict scrutiny test. That is, the government must show that the law directly advances the least restrictive means to protect a compelling governmental interest of the highest order. This is the same standard applied to content regulations of newspapers.[22]

If a cable regulation is not directed at content, however, and imposes only an incidental burden on a cable operator's speech, the Court held that the regulation need be tested only under the intermediate First Amendment standard established in *United States v. O'Brien* and *Ward v. Rock Against Racism*.[23] Intermediate scrutiny of content-neutral regulations requires the government to show that the regulation is a reasonable way to achieve an important or substantial government interest. Here again, the Court applied the same level of protection it would afford to core First Amendment speakers such as newspapers. In general, structural regulations of cable are treated as content-neutral and thus face only intermediate scrutiny.

CABLE STRUCTURAL REGULATIONS

Cable operators face many structural regulations. This stems in part from the government's early view of cable as a video delivery business that was not engaged in speech in the same way as a newspaper or broadcast station. Instead, cable was viewed as a threat to free speech since it threatened the viability of free, over-the-air broadcast stations, especially marginal TV stations. In addition, cable was assumed to be a natural monopoly. Congress and the FCC imposed ownership and rate regulations to protect consumers and program producers from unfair business practices on the part of large cable operators. However, many regulations are being rescinded as cable operators face more competition from DBS providers, telephone companies, and online video streaming services.

Cable Competition

Cable is the dominant multichannel television distribution technology in the United States. In 1992, it controlled 95 percent of the subscription TV marketplace. Yet by the end of 2014, its share of the market had declined to less than 53 percent. There are more than 5,000 individual cable systems, most of them are owned by a handful of large multiple system operators. At the end of 2014, the four largest MSOs (Comcast, Time Warner-Charter, Cox and Cablevision) reached more than 80 percent of all U.S. cable subscribers.[24] Comcast, the largest MSO with 27 million subscribers, controls television service for almost one out of every five homes with television.

Cable faces increasing competition from satellite TV, which serves more than thirty-four million homes (34 percent of total pay TV subscribers). Telephone companies like Verizon and AT&T also offer subscription TV services in some areas.[25] In addition, multiple Web sites offer streaming or paid downloads of TV shows. However, even including DBS and all other forms of subscription television, the top four cable companies still control more than 44 percent of all TV subscribers.[26] This has led to rate regulation, ownership size limits, and various access requirements on cable operators to promote competition.

Rate Regulation

For decades, cable TV operators, the FCC and franchising authorities have received complaints about cable rates. Attempts to limit rates have competed with concerns that cable's growth as a business would be stunted if government interfered by setting prices. In 1971, the FCC prohibited franchising authorities from regulating rates for pay-per-channel services but did not address rate regulation for other cable services.[27]

The 1984 Cable Act restricted the ability of local franchising authorities to regulate cable rates. Cable prices rose rapidly, and Congress reimposed rate regulation in the 1992 Cable Act. Under it, each local franchising authority regulated the basic tier of local broadcast and public access channels, and the FCC

---

[20] 499 U.S. 439, 444 (1991).

[21] 512 U.S. 622 (1994) (*Turner I*).

[22] *See, e.g.,* Miami Herald Publ'g Co. v. Tornillo, 418 U.S. 241 (1974) (applying strict scrutiny to content-based regulation of newspapers).

[23] 391 U.S. 367 (1968); 491 U.S. 781 (1989).

[24] Sixteenth Report, *supra* note 1, at para. 73.

[25] AT&T and Verizon are now the fifth and sixth largest MVPDs respectively, with more than five million subscribers each. *Id.*

[26] *Id.*

[27] *See* Time-Life Broad., Inc., 31 F.C.C. 2d 747 (1971).

regulated the cable tier (including the common package of cable networks such as CNN, MTV, ESPN and TBS). Premium channels such as HBO, Showtime and Cinemax, digital cable services and pay-per-view channels remained unregulated. The FCC's regulation of the cable tier expired in 1999. Currently, only the basic tier faces rate regulation by the franchise authority and only if the cable company has no effective competition. In 2015, the FCC issued a new order creating a presumption that all cable systems face effective competition.[28] Thus, any local franchising authority that wants to regulate the basic tier price must first demonstrate that the cable provider does not face effective competition. In other words, the burden now is on the local government to prove it should be allowed to regulate basic cable rates rather than on the cable operator to demonstrate that it should not be subject to rate regulation.

Cable rates rose an average of 3.1 percent in 2014 while the Consumer Price Index rose 1.6 percent that year. From 1995 to 2014, basic cable rates rose at a compound rate of 5.9 percent per year compared to a CPI increase of 2.4 percent during the same period. Cable rates thus rose more than twice as fast as the general rate of inflation.[29] Cable systems that face wireline competition charge an average of 14 percent less per channel than systems that have no wireline competition.[30] Analyzing cable rates can be difficult since most operators continue to add additional channels. When examining the price per channel for cable service, the average price per channel increased by 0.9 percent in 2014. When looking at long term cable prices, over 19 years the price per channel has remained relatively flat compared to the 2.4 percent increase in CPI.[31]

Ownership Restrictions

In addition to rate regulation, cable operators face various ownership and conduct restrictions. This is because the government historically has been concerned with cable's position as a monopoly bottleneck that controls consumers' access to video programming. At one time, federal law and FCC rules designed to prevent concentration of media ownership prohibited the owner of a broadcast TV station from owning a cable system in the same area. The purpose of the so-called "cross-ownership rule," adopted by the FCC in 1970 and made part of the 1984 Cable

Act, was to protect diversity of ownership and content. The ban on broadcast-cable cross-ownership was intended to prevent a broadcast owner from favoring the owner's station and refusing to carry competing broadcasters on the cable system.

In 1992, the FCC recommended that Congress repeal the cross-ownership ban, in part because the must-carry rules (discussed later in this chapter) would prevent discrimination against other local stations. Congress took that action in the Telecommunications Act of 1996, but the FCC never repealed its version of the rule. The U.S. Court of Appeals for the D.C. Circuit struck down the FCC cross-ownership ban in 2002.[32] It said the FCC had failed to justify why the rule should be kept, but it did not evaluate whether the rule violated the First Amendment. Cable systems now may own local TV stations.

Another cross-ownership rule imposed by the 1992 Cable Act generally prohibited a cable operator from owning a wireless cable or a satellite master antenna television system (both of which will be discussed in the next chapter) in the same area served by the cable system. The 1996 Act removed that joint ownership ban if the cable system faces competition from another company providing multi-channel video service. There are no legal restrictions on ownership of cable systems by citizens of other countries or owners of newspapers or other print media in the areas the cable system serves.

Horizontal and Vertical Ownership Limits

Some of the most contested ownership rules deal with horizontal and vertical integration. The 1992 Cable Act directed the FCC to impose ownership limits to make sure cable operators won't have so much power as gatekeepers that they are able to prevent unpopular views from being heard.[33] The primary purpose of the rules is to prevent large cable companies from discriminating against independent cable networks. The largest cable operators — MSOs Comcast, Time Warner and Cox, for example — own hundreds of cable systems.

During debate of the 1992 Cable Act, one issue was increased ownership of cable networks by cable system operators (vertical integration). Congress expressed concern that companies that own their own networks might exclude competing networks from reaching viewers. For example, Time Warner might refuse to carry MSNBC or Fox News because both of those networks compete with CNN, which Time Warner owns. In response to the potential for unfair competition, a provision of the 1992 Act ordered the FCC to adopt rules to limit the number of cable networks owned or partially owned by the MSO that the owner could carry on its cable systems.

---

[28] *In re* Amendment to the Commission's Rules Concerning Effective Competition, FCC 15-62, (Jun. 3, 2015). The FCC notes that almost all households have access to two DBS services and that cable also faces increased competition from Internet television services.

[29] Report on Cable Industry Prices, *In re* Implementation of Section 3 of the Cable Television Consumer Protection and Competition Act of 1992 (DA 14-1829), 29 F.C.C.R. 14895, ¶ 2 (Dec. 15, 2014).

[30] *Id.* at ¶ 4.

[31] *Id.* at ¶ 3.

---

[32] Fox Television Stations, Inc. v. FCC, 280 F.3d 1027 (D.C. Cir. 2002).

[33] 47 U.S.C. § 533, 613 (2000).

The FCC vertical ownership rules state that no more than 40 percent of a cable system's first seventy-five channels may be used for programming affiliated with the system's owner. The remaining 60 percent has to be made available for broadcast TV stations and cable programming in which the system's owner has no more than a 5 percent interest.[34] Slightly more of a system's channels may be used for programming in which the system owner has an interest if minority individuals or businesses control the services. (This rule is to help promote minority-owned networks to increase diversity in the marketplace of ideas). If a system has more than seventy-five channels, the regulation does not affect those additional channels.

For example, Comcast owns all of the NBC Universal cable networks (USA, MSNBC, Bravo, Golf Channel, SyFy, Comcast SportsNet and others). In communities where Comcast owns the local cable franchise, only 40 percent of the first seventy-five channels can be Comcast-owned networks. Regulators feared that otherwise the MSO would refuse to carry cable networks that competed with its own cable networks. For example, Comcast might refuse to carry ESPN or Fox News since they compete with Comcast Sportsnet and MSNBC respectively. The vertical ownership rule was designed to promote competition among program suppliers and ensure diversity of programming.

Congress also directed the FCC to establish horizontal ownership limits. The limits prevent one MSO from owning cable systems in too many cities. Policymakers wanted to prevent one MSO from becoming so large that it could take advantage of program suppliers. For example, assume that a new independent cable network is being launched. If one MSO controlled 60 percent of the nation's cable subscribers and refused to carry that network, the network would likely fail because it cannot reach 60 percent of the population.

The FCC initially imposed a 30 percent national limit on the number of subscribers one MSO may control. It assumed that a new cable channel would need the opportunity to reach at least 40 percent of the nation's homes to be viable. It reasoned that if each MSO was limited to a 30 percent reach, a new channel would have a chance to succeed even if the two largest MSOs refused to carry it. The FCC believed this would encourage diversity of programming and prevent the largest MSOs from refusing to pay a fair price to carry new cable networks.

In 2000, Time Warner and AT&T, the two largest MSOs at the time, challenged the horizontal and vertical ownership rules. The D.C. Circuit Court of Appeals ruled that the regulations were content-neutral and should be reviewed under intermediate scrutiny. It said Congress and the FCC could impose some ownership limits without infringing on the First Amend-

ment rights of cable operators.[35] In 2001, however, the same court ruled that the FCC had not provided adequate justification for the specific 30 percent horizontal limit or the 40 percent vertical limit that it had chosen.[36]

In 2007, the FCC issued an order using new calculations to justify maintaining the 30 percent horizontal ownership limit.[37] Comcast and other cable operators immediately challenged the justification for the rule.[38] In 2008, the D.C. Circuit vacated the 30 percent horizontal ownership limit again. It said the FCC's new formula for determining the horizontal ownership limit was arbitrary and capricious, in large part because it did not take into account increasing competition from DBS companies like Dish network and DirecTV.[39] The FCC likely will have to raise the ownership limit above 30 percent in order to pass judicial scrutiny. The FCC has not yet announced a new decision related to the 40 percent vertical limit that was rejected in 2001.

To further ensure that independent networks have access to cable subscribers, the 1992 Cable Act also gave the FCC the authority to review complaints about anticompetitive behavior when cable operators negotiate with cable networks. The FCC can intervene when the operator (1) demands a financial interest in the network, (2) requires exclusive rights or penalizes the network for not granting exclusive rights, or (3) discriminates against nonaffiliated networks in terms or conditions of carriage.[40] In 2011, for example, the FCC ruled that Comcast had unfairly discriminated against the Tennis Channel by placing it on a premium tier that subscribers had to pay extra to receive, resulting in a very small potential audience, while Comcast's own sports networks were available on a more popular programming tier with a much larger potential audience.[41]

Access to Cable Networks

The preceding horizontal and vertical ownership rules are designed to make sure independent networks have a fair chance at getting distributed by large cable MSOs. Congress was also concerned that MSOs would try to harm competition by not allowing other distributors to carry popular cable networks that are owned by the MSOs. The 1992 Cable Act required companies that supply affiliated cable systems with programming *via* satellite to offer such programming to cable's competitors as

---

[34] Development of Competition and Diversity in Video Programming Distribution and Carriage, 8 F.C.C.R. 8565 (1993); 47 U.S.C. § 536 (2000).

[35] Time Warner Entm't Co. v. United States, 211 F.3d 1313 (D.C. Cir. 2000).

[36] Time Warner Entm't Co. v. United States, 240 F.3d 1126 (D.C. Cir. 2001).

[37] *In re* the Commission's Cable Horizontal and Vertical Ownership Limits, Fourth Report and Order (FCC 07-219), 23 F.C.C.R. 2134 (Feb. 11, 2008).

[38] Comcast Corp. v. FCC, 579 F.3d 1 (D.C. Cir. 2009).

[39] *Id.* at 8-9.

[40] 47 U.S.C. § 536(a) (2010).

[41] Tennis Channel v. Comcast Cable Commnc's, FCC 12-78, 27 F.C.C.R. 8508 (July 24, 2012).

well.[42] The act prevents cable systems and programmers from entering into exclusive agreements or in other ways limiting access to programming by other multi-channel video distributors such as direct broadcast satellite systems or telephone companies. In other words, Comcast, which owns USA, must allow DBS provider DirecTV, telephone company Verizon, and other competitors to offer USA to their customers as well.

The purpose of this rule was to create more competition and reduce the power of large MSOs. If one cable company had the exclusive right to distribute the most popular cable networks like MTV and ESPN, few consumers would be willing to switch to a competing distributor. Notice that like the vertical and horizontal ownership rules discussed previously, the concern is potential anticompetitive behavior by large, vertically integrated cable operators. Whereas the vertical and horizontal ownership rules are primarily aimed at protecting content *producers* (cable networks) by making sure that cable operators carry networks they don't own, the access rules are primarily aimed at protecting competing *distributors* by making sure cable operators share the networks they do own.

The ban on exclusive agreements between cable programmers and cable operators was set to expire in 2002. The FCC twice extended the ban for five years, ultimately until 2012. Cablevision and other cable MSOs challenged the extension of the rule, arguing that it violated the First Amendment and the Communications Act.[43] The appellate court acknowledged that the industry is much more competitive than it once was, but ruled that it was reasonable for the FCC to decide that the extension of the rule until 2012 was necessary.[44] The FCC decided to let the program access rules expire in October 2012. While cable operators like Comcast and Time Warner are no longer preemptively banned from refusing to offer their affiliated networks to competing distributors, the FCC retains the right to approve or deny exclusive arrangements on a case-by-case basis.[45]

The ban on exclusive contracts between cable-affiliated networks and cable operators never covered networks that rely on terrestrial distribution. Many MSOs have regional sports or news channels that are not distributed *via* satellite. The MSOs do not normally have to share these networks with competitors. However, in 2010, the FCC passed a rule granting the agency the power to prohibit exclusive contracts for terrestrial deliv-

ered networks on a case-by-case basis.[46] The FCC was concerned that, if cable operators such as Comcast withhold their popular regional sports networks, the practice will put telephone and satellite competitors at a disadvantage. An appellate court upheld the new FCC rules in 2011.[47]

CABLE ACCESS REGULATIONS

As mentioned earlier, cable was initially regulated because local broadcasters felt threatened by cable's ability to import distant signals and add original, cable-only programming. Another aspect of this concern was that attaching a coaxial cable to the back of a television set effectively meant unplugging the antenna. If viewers wanted to watch a local station that the cable system didn't carry, they would have to switch back and forth between cable reception and antenna reception. Broadcasters and the FCC believed most viewers would not be willing to make the extra effort (this was before remote controls), meaning that local stations not carried by the cable system would lose that portion of their audience who subscribed to cable. The broadcasters wanted to make sure they had access to cable subscribers. The FCC and Congress were concerned that a local station could lose so many viewers that it might go out of business, leaving those viewers who *don't* subscribe to cable with fewer stations to choose from. This led to a long evolution of must-carry rules. The basic premise is that the local cable operator is a gatekeeper with the ability to determine which channels viewers can receive. Many observers believe this power threatens the marketplace of ideas. Regulators also feared that cable operators would have an incentive to not carry local broadcast stations because they compete with those stations for advertising revenues. If 60 percent of local homes subscribe to cable and station A is not available on cable, then station A is effectively cut off from 60 percent of the local audience. Advertisers then might stop advertising on station A and purchase commercial time directly from the local cable operator instead.

Must-Carry Rules

Although the FCC began in 1965 to adopt rules forcing cable to carry broadcast stations, federal appellate courts twice ruled that the so-called "must-carry rules" infringed on cable operators' First Amendment rights.[48] The courts did not say the rules could never be applied but that the FCC had not adequately

[42] 47 U.S.C. § 548 (1992). *See also* Time Warner Entm't Co. v. FCC, 93 F.3d 957 (D.C. Cir. 1996), *reh'ng denied*, 105 F.3d 723 (D.C. Cir. 1997).

[43] Cablevision Sys. Corp. v. FCC, 597 F.3d 1306 (D.C. Cir. 2010).

[44] *Id.* at 1314-15.

[45] Revision of the Commission's Program Access Rules (FCC 12-123), 56 C.R. 1271 (Oct. 5, 2012).

[46] 47 C.F.R. § 76.1001 (2010). *See also* Review of the Commission's Program Access Rules and Examination of Programming Tying Arrangements (First Report and Order) (FCC 10-17), 25 F.C.C.R. 746 (Jan. 20, 2010).

[47] Cablevision Sys. Corp. v. FCC, 649 F.3d 695 (D.C. Cir. 2011).

[48] *See* Century Commc'ns Corp. v. FCC, 835 F.2d 292 (D.C. Cir. 1987); Quincy Cable TV, Inc. v. FCC, 768 F.2d 1434 (D.C. Cir. 1985).

demonstrated why it favored broadcasters' concerns over cable operators' rights. In the 1992 Cable Act, Congress tried to resolve the problem by allowing a TV station either to choose must-carry status with the local cable system or to negotiate with the cable operator on the terms for retransmitting the station's signal. The latter option is called "retransmission consent." The rules implicate the First Amendment rights of cable system operators and cable networks. Operators are forced to carry local stations regardless of whether they want to. The rules affect the free speech rights of cable networks because they reduce the number of cable networks that a local system may carry. If a system has 100 channels and fifteen have to be set aside for local stations, the system won't be able to carry as many cable networks. Turner Broadcasting, owner of TBS, TNT and CNN, sued to have the rules declared unconstitutional.

In 1994, in *Turner Broadcasting System, Inc. v. FCC (Turner I)*,[49] the Supreme Court considered whether the must-carry rules were content-neutral. The Court found that the rules did not impermissibly favor broadcast programming but were a content-neutral means to protect the broadcast industry and enhance competition. The majority said the rules were content-neutral because they merely favored one mode of delivery (free, over the air broadcasting) over another mode of delivery (pay cable) without regard to the specific content being delivered:

It is true that the must-carry provisions distinguish between speakers in the television programming market. But they do so based only upon the manner in which speakers transmit their messages to viewers, and not upon the messages they carry: Broadcasters, which transmit over the airwaves, are favored, while cable programmers, which do not, are disfavored. Cable operators, too, are burdened by the carriage obligations, but only because they control access to the cable conduit. So long as they are not a subtle means of exercising a content preference, speaker distinctions of this nature are not presumed invalid under the First Amendment.

Our review of the Act and its various findings persuades us that Congress' overriding objective in enacting must-carry was not to favor programming of a particular subject matter, viewpoint, or format, but rather to preserve access to free TV programming for the 40 percent of Americans without cable.[50]

In contrasting the case to *Miami Herald v. Tornillo*,[51] in which the Supreme Court struck down a state right-of-reply law applying to newspapers, the majority noted that the Florida law punished newspapers based on the content of their editorial columns, while the must-carry law was not based on a cable operator's programming decisions. Cable systems had to adhere to the must-carry requirements regardless of which cable networks they picked, while the right-of-reply law was only enforced when a newspaper criticized a candidate for public office. Unlike the Florida papers, cable operators were not being punished for choosing specific programming to include on their systems.[52]

The Supreme Court remanded the case to the district court to determine if the rules were necessary and narrowly tailored.[53] The lower court found them constitutional,[54] and, in 1997, the Supreme Court agreed. By a 5-4 vote, it said in the second *Turner Broadcasting System v. FCC* case that the must-carry rules were a proper, content-neutral means to protect the broadcast industry from extinction[55] — an appropriate way the government could assure that cable operators would not force broadcasters out of business and deprive consumers of programming.

In a sharp dissent, Justice Sandra Day O'Connor wrote that the majority opinion actually supported the argument that the must-carry rules were an unconstitutional content-based means to promote the speech of broadcasters over cable operators. She noted that Congress stated that it specifically wanted to protect local and educational programming.[56] Therefore, the law was based at least in part on the content of the broadcasters' speech. Justice O'Connor — joined by Justices Antonin Scalia, Clarence Thomas and Ruth Bader Ginsburg — would have applied strict scrutiny to the must-carry rules and struck them down as favoring local (broadcast) speech over national (cable) speech.[57]

Generally, the must-carry rules apply to all except the smallest cable operations. All full-power commercial stations in a community served by a cable system may demand to be carried. Rules also require non-commercial stations to be carried, but they cannot choose to negotiate for carriage under the retransmission consent rules.[58] Every three years, commercial TV stations must decide whether to negotiate terms for carriage or to demand carriage under the must-carry standards. When the law was passed, local stations hoped cable operators would pay a monthly fee for their signals, just as they pay cable networks.

However, most cable operators refused to pay fees to carry local stations, believing the stations need cable more than the cable company needs the stations. Owners of multiple cable systems instead negotiated non-monetary deals with companies

---

[49] 512 U.S. 622 (1994).

[50] *Id.* at 645-46.

[51] 418 U.S. 241 (1974).

[52] *Turner I*, 512 U.S. at 654-56.

[53] *Id.* at 667.

[54] Turner Broad. Sys., Inc. v. FCC, 910 F. Supp. 734 (D.D.C. 1995).

[55] 520 U.S. 180 (1997) *(Turner II)*.

[56] *Id.* at 232-35 (O'Connor, J., dissenting).

[57] *Id.* at 234 (O'Connor, J., dissenting).

[58] 47 U.S.C. § 535 (2000).

that own a number of stations. For example, some cable operators agreed to carry the FX cable network if Fox would permit them to retransmit the TV stations Fox owned. Similarly, Disney agreed to allow carriage of the stations it owned in various cities in exchange for cable systems carrying ESPN2, the cable network. Retransmission agreements continue to foster controversy as companies that own broadcast stations demand cash or prime channel space for their cable networks in return for giving the cable operator permission to carry their local broadcast stations.[59] Over the past few years, cable operators have finally started paying cash to local stations, providing an important source of revenue as local advertising revenues decline.[60] In 2014, Congress passed a law limiting the ability of local stations to engage in joint negotiations for retransmission consent.[61]

Digital Must-Carry

In 2009, all full-power TV stations in the United States switched from analog to digital transmission, requiring over-the-air viewers to purchase either digital TV sets or converter boxes to watch the digital broadcast on older analog TV sets. But what about the millions of analog TV sets that are connected to cable? In 2007, the FCC ruled that cable operators with an analog tier had to provide their subscribers with an analog signal of local broadcast stations (or a converter box) until 2012 — when the rule expired — to ensure that all subscribers would still have access to local stations.[62]

With a digital signal, it is possible for a station to transmit more than one program at a time (multicasting) and to transmit other information as well (electronic program guides and Internet services, for example). Broadcasters want the FCC to require cable systems to carry all of their digital content, including programs sent on secondary channels. Should a cable operator be forced to carry all of a station's digital signal or just the primary program on the station's main channel? The FCC has ruled that for now, the cable operator only has to carry the primary video program and program-related content such as closed captioning or v-chip data. In addition, if a broadcast station provides a high definition signal to the cable provider, the cable

provider must deliver the signal to homes in the HD format.[63]

Leased-Access Channels

The must-carry rules grew out of a concern that a local cable system is usually a monopoly provider that controls the programming options for subscribers. As discussed earlier, this concern is alleviated in part by the vertical ownership restrictions that force cable operators to carry cable networks in which they don't have a financial interest. To foster competition and a marketplace of ideas, additional access requirements have been imposed on cable operators as well.

The 1984 Cable Act requires large cable systems to provide channels for purchase or lease by commercial users and allows franchising authorities to negotiate with cable systems to offer channel capacity for use by the public and by educational and governmental organizations (PEG channels). Requirements for commercial leased-access channels and PEG channels do not violate cable operators' First Amendment rights, according to a federal appellate court.[64]

Under the 1984 Act, cable systems with thirty-six to fifty-four channels must designate 10 percent of the channels for this purpose. Systems with fifty-five or more channels must set aside 15 percent for leased access. Anyone who wants to put programming on the cable system may lease these channels for a fee. The FCC has jurisdiction over the rates, terms and conditions of commercial leased-access contracts. Cable systems often use these channels for purposes other than leased access, such as carrying cable network programming, until they are requested for leased-access purposes. Under the 1992 Cable Act, a cable system may use up to one-third of its leased-access channels for certain educational or minority cable programming services and still count the channels as being used for leased access.

While the purpose of the leased-access provisions was to make sure alternative viewpoints could be heard on cable systems, as a practical matter few programmers can afford to lease a channel full-time. This severely limits the potential audience for any program transmitted on a leased-access channel. In 2008, the FCC adopted a new formula for determining the maximum rate a cable operator may charge for leased access in the hope that this would make leased access more affordable for programmers who want to start a commercial network.[65] The

---

[59] *See* Georg Szalai, *Broadcasters, Pay TV Firms Submit Comments for FCC Retrans Rules Review,* Hollywood Reporter, May 21, 2011, *available at* http://www.hollywoodreporter.com/news/broadcasters-pay-tv-firms-submit-192823.

[60] Steve Donohue, *Gannett, Media General Post Big Gains in Retransmission-Consent Revenue,* Fierce Cable, Apr. 24, 2013, *available at* http://www.fiercecable.com/story/gannett-media-general-post-big-gains-retransmission-consent-revenue/2013-04-24.

[61] STELA Reauthorization Act of 2014, Pub. L. No. 113-200, 128 Stat. 2059 (2014).

[62] Carriage of Digital Television Broadcast Signals: Amendment to Part 76 of the Commission's Rules, Fifth Report and Order (FCC 12-59), 77 Fed. Reg. 36178 (June 12, 2012).

[63] *In re* Carriage of Digital Television Broadcast Signals: Amendments to Part 76 of the Commission's Rules (FCC 05-27), 20 F.C.C.R. 4516 (Feb. 23, 2005). Very small cable systems that don't carry any HD programming are exempt from this requirement. However, once they offer any HD programming, they must offer local broadcast signals that are transmitted in an HD format. *In re* Carriage of Digital Television Broadcast Signals: Amendments to Part 76 of the Commission's Rules, Sixth Report and Order, FCC 15-65 (Jun. 10, 2015).

[64] *See* Time Warner Entm't Co. v. FCC, 93 F.3d 957 (D.C. Cir. 1996).

[65] Leased Commercial Access (FCC 07-208), 23 F.C.C.R. 2909 (Feb. 1, 2008).

new rule has been stayed while cable operators challenge the FCC decision in court.[66]

In 2016, the FCC opened a new inquiry to determine whether diverse and independent programming has the opportunity to thrive in the current marketplace.[67] Specifically, the FCC is exploring whether MVPDs impose onerous contractual conditions before agreeing to carry new programming and whether it is unfair for those contracts to restrict alternative distribution platforms. Both MVPDs and independent programmers argue that current bundling agreements, whereby large content providers require MVPDs to carry less popular programming in order to gain access to popular programs also limits the space available for new independent content. The inquiry is also looking into whether MVPDs adequately promote PEG content (see discussion of PEG channels below).

Leased-Access Content Restrictions

Cable operators generally act as common carriers of commercial, leased-access channels; they do not control the content they deliver. But the 1992 Cable Act gave cable systems the right to reject leased-access programming that the operator "reasonably believes describes or depicts sexual or excretory activities or organs in a patently offensive manner as measured by contemporary community standards."[68] The 1996 Act permits a cable system operator to refuse to carry a program or portion of a program "which contains obscenity, indecency or nudity" on a commercial, leased-access channel.

Congress also developed a complex method of segregating indecent leased-access material that operators carried. The Communications Decency Act of 1996 required cable operators to put all such programming on separate channels scrambled or blocked in some way. A subscriber was required to ask in writing for such a channel to be unblocked and, later, could also ask for it to be re-blocked. The cable operator has thirty days to comply with a written request for unblocking or re-blocking.

In 1996, a divided Supreme Court reviewed a First Amendment challenge to the law's indecency and obscenity restrictions and upheld the provision permitting cable operators to reject indecent programming.[69] But the Court rejected the parts of the law that required operators to segregate indecent material and force subscribers to request it. Several justices noted that, unlike obscenity, indecency is protected by the First Amendment. They said alternative means that would interfere less with

viewers' First Amendment rights could still protect children and sensitive viewers from the material. In addition, the justices expressed concern that cable customers who wanted access to some or all of the segregated programming might hesitate to request access in writing for fear their names would be released.

The U.S. Court of Appeals for the Second Circuit in 1999 dismissed a First Amendment challenge against Time Warner Communications for its refusal to transmit sexually explicit and violent sexual programming over its leased-access channels.[70] However, the court also ruled that Time Warner had infringed the free expression rights of programmers through its blanket refusal to consider future programming submissions from any programmer who had submitted programs Time Warner deemed indecent. The court enjoined Time Warner from applying its blanket refusal policy.

PEG Access Channels

The 1984 Cable Act permits, but does not require, franchising authorities to negotiate with cable operators to provide access channels for educational institutions, the public and governmental bodies. The agreements need not require all three types of programming, and a system may devote one channel to multiple purposes. For example, it could use one channel for educational access during daytime hours and for governmental access during the evening.

Access channels grew out of competitive offerings from cable operators attempting to land franchises in large cities. Beginning decades ago, cable operators promised PEG access and other features as a means to win franchises. Then, in 1969, the FCC encouraged cable operators to offer PEG channels[71] and in 1972 required systems to do so.[72] In 1979, the Supreme Court ruled that the Commission did not have the authority to require PEG channels,[73] but the ruling did not prevent cable systems and franchising authorities from voluntarily agreeing to have them. Finally, the 1984 Cable Act gave franchising authorities the right to negotiate with cable operators to have PEG channels. As more states adopt statewide franchising agreements, those laws are less likely to require PEG channels than the older, local franchising agreements.[74]

PEG Channel Content Restrictions

Cable operators have limited control over the content of PEG

---

[66] *See* John Eggerton, *Court Stays Leased-Access Rule Change*, BROADCASTING & CABLE, May 26, 2008, at 22.

[67] Promoting the Availability of Diverse and Independent Sources of Video Programming (FCC 16-19), 81 Fed. Reg. 10241 (Feb. 18, 2016).

[68] 47 U.S.C. § 532(h) (2000).

[69] Denver Area Educ. Telecomm. Consortium, Inc. v. FCC, 518 U.S. 727 (1996).

[70] Life Without Shame v. Time Warner Entm't Co., 191 F.3d 256 (2nd Cir. 1999).

[71] Community Antenna Television System, 20 F.C.C. 2d 201 (1969).

[72] Cable Television Report and Order, 36 F.C.C. 2d 143 (1972).

[73] FCC v. Midwest Video Corp., 440 U.S. 689 (1979) *(Midwest Video II)*.

[74] Fourteenth Report *supra* note 18, at 8639.

channels and are not liable for material they cannot prohibit. This means a cable system cannot eliminate specific programming or public-access provisions to exclude ideas it dislikes or disfavors. For example, when the Ku Klux Klan attempted to offer a program on the Kansas City, Missouri, cable system's public-access channel, the city council removed the public-access channel requirement from the city's cable franchise. With the requirement gone, the operator stopped providing the channel, and the Klan had no way to offer its program. It sued the cable system. A federal district court ruled in favor of the Klan because the city could not show that it had not eliminated the channel requirement as a way to limit the Klan's First Amendment rights to free speech.[75] The city re-established the public-access provision, and the Klan presented its program.

The 1984 Cable Act says franchising authorities and cable systems may agree that cable services — including PEG channels — will not present material that is "obscene or otherwise unprotected by the United States Constitution."[76] The 1992 Act went further. It allowed cable operators to prohibit "obscene material or sexually explicit content or material soliciting or promoting unlawful conduct" on PEG channels and withdrew operators' protection against lawsuits based on the presentation of such material. The Supreme Court found this provision violated the First Amendment.[77] It said both public and private groups provided sufficient oversight of public-access channels to exclude the type of material to which Congress objected. Moreover, the government had not provided sufficient evidence to demonstrate that further control by the cable operator was required to protect children from indecent material. The Court also said cable operators permitted to exclude programming from public-access channels might restrict borderline material that otherwise might be protected under the First Amendment.

In 1998, the U.S. Court of Appeals for the Second Circuit upheld the right of an independent program producer to broadcast a sexually explicit show on public-access channels. It said that although the 1984 Cable Act permits local authorities to enforce franchise agreements and control the operation of public-access channels, the law also prohibits cable operators from exercising editorial control over public-access programming and assures that cable systems provide the widest possible diversity of information services and sources to the public.[78]

In 1999, the U.S. Court of Appeals for the Fifth Circuit held a Houston franchise rule giving preference to locally produced programming on PEG access channels permissibly advanced the government interest in programming diversity.[79] The court said the city's practice of charging a fee for all non-locally produced programming was a constitutional, content-neutral rule that did not distinguish between favored and disfavored speech. Instead, the court said, the rule advanced the city's substantial interest in promoting localism. The court of appeals then remanded the case to the lower court to determine whether the general fee schedule was narrowly tailored to advance this interest.

Access Rules and the First Amendment

Notwithstanding the restrictions on obscene and indecent content discussed previously, the motivation behind the access rules is that, for the 50 percent of homes that subscribe to cable, the cable operator controls which programs and channels are available. Newspapers and other print publishers do not have the burden of must-carry, leased access or other access requirements. All of these structural access rules imposed on cable operators very likely would be struck down as unconstitutional if applied to newspapers. Why the different treatment between the two industries? The Supreme Court provided some insight in its *Turner I* decision:

Although a daily newspaper and a cable operator both may enjoy monopoly status in a given locale, the cable operator exercises far greater control over access to the relevant medium. A daily newspaper ... does not possess the power to obstruct readers' access to other competing publications.... The same is not true of cable. When an individual subscribes to cable, the physical connection between the TV set and the cable network gives the cable operator bottleneck, or gatekeeper, control.... A cable operator, unlike speakers in other media, can thus silence the voice of competing speakers with a mere flick of the switch.[80]

So while a local newspaper may have a larger monopoly than the local cable provider, you can have multiple newspapers delivered to your door whereas you could only have one cable system connected to your television. In a certain sense, the Court is justifying cable regulation based on the scarcity of inputs on the back of a TV set just as it justified broadcast regulation based on the scarcity of frequencies. Newer digital TV sets often have multiple inputs that viewers can easily select using a remote control device. If viewers can now easily switch between multiple content providers that are all plugged in to the back of the television, should that change the First Amendment analysis of these regulations? Does the availability of Internet streaming

[75] Missouri Knights of the Ku Klux Klan v. Kansas City, 723 F. Supp. 1347 (W.D. Mo. 1989).

[76] 47 U.S.C. § 544(d) (2000).

[77] Denver Area Educ. Telecomm. Consortium, Inc. v. FCC, 518 U.S. 727 (1996).

[78] McClellan v. Cablevision of Connecticut, Inc., 149 F.3d 161 (2nd Cir. 1998).

[79] Nationalist Television v. Access Houston Cable, 179 F.3d 188 (5th Cir. 1999).

[80] 512 U.S. 622, 656 (1994) (*Turner I*).

(Netflix and Hulu, for example) reduce the power of cable operators to control access to information?

LOCAL CABLE REGULATION

As previously indicated, cable operators must adhere to local as well as federal regulations because their cables are placed on public property. Congress has periodically given and then taken away the power of local authorities to regulate cable franchises. Local laws, also, cannot violate the First Amendment or other constitutional restrictions.

Cable System Franchises

The 1984 Cable Act made it clear that local and state authorities have a right to grant cable franchises and that a cable system must have a franchise in order to offer service. Traditionally, local municipalities awarded franchises, with a few states offering statewide franchises. As telephone companies attempt to get into the video distribution business, they have lobbied for statewide franchises, arguing that negotiating with hundreds of individual municipalities creates a barrier to entry that makes it harder to compete with incumbent cable operators. Twenty-seven states have passed statewide franchising laws.[81] In 2006, Congress considered but ultimately rejected a proposal to allow companies to obtain a national franchise to offer cable service.[82] In 2012, the Fifth Circuit ruled unconstitutional a Texas law allowing any company to obtain a statewide franchise except for two incumbent companies that already provided service in Texas' largest cities. Applying strict scrutiny because a small number of speakers were singled out for disparate treatment, the court held the law violated the First Amendment rights of the incumbent cable companies.[83] It added that the law would have been unconstitutional even under the more relaxed intermediate scrutiny standard.[84]

The 1992 Cable Act forbids authorities from awarding exclusive franchises. That is, they cannot agree to grant one, and only one, franchise. At first, communities liked awarding exclusive franchises because they could then ask for more in return from the cable operator. The prohibition on exclusive franchises is supposed to encourage competition. A city can also own a cable system, even in competition with a cable company offering service in the municipality.

Most communities have franchised only one company to offer cable service because other companies have not sought franchises. These companies do not want to invest the large amount of money necessary to build competing cable systems (known as "overbuilds"). This is in large part because of the economies of scale that led observers to refer to cable as a natural monopoly.

Courts have also ruled that technologies competing with cable generally are not required to obtain franchises from local government. The U.S. Courts of Appeals for the Seventh and Fifth circuits ruled in 1999 that neither satellite master antenna television systems nor telephone video systems are required to obtain franchises to offer video to consumers.[85]

In 2006, the FCC passed new rules to make it easier for cable companies to obtain local franchises. Local authorities now have to adhere to strict FCC-specified deadlines in making franchising decisions. The rules limit the ability of local franchise authorities to impose build-out requirements or to impose conditions that would exceed the 5 percent cap on franchise fees.[86]

Cable Franchise Provisions

Franchises can be short or hundreds of pages long, depending on the complexity of the agreement between the franchising authority and cable system. Certain provisions, however, will be found in most franchises.

Franchise fees. For decades, authorities have required cable systems to pay franchise fees as part of the agreement to use public rights-of-way. At one time, fees were set as high as 36 percent of a system's revenues. In 1972, the FCC limited the fees, and the 1984 Cable Act set a fee ceiling of 5 percent of gross annual revenues. The act does not define "gross annual revenues," allowing cable operators and authorities to negotiate definitions. Some cable operators have argued that having to pay any franchise fees violates their First Amendment rights, but most courts hearing such cases have decided that cable's use of public rights-of-way justifies imposing fees.[87] In 2005, a federal district court ruled that under federal law, the 5 percent fee could only be applied to revenues from cable services. Minneapolis wanted to include revenues from cable modem service as well. The court noted that the FCC had already declared that

---

[81] *See* Jay T. Spurgin, State Video Franchise Law: State of Art or State of War? (Aug. 29. 2008) (paper presented at the American Public Works Association), *available at* http://www.apwa.net/Documents/Meetings/Congress/2008/Handouts/4271.pdf.

[82] H.R. 5252, 109th Cong. (2006).

[83] Time Warner Cable Inc. v. Hudson, 667 F.3d 630 (5th Cir. 2012).

[84] *Id.* at 641.

[85] City of Austin v. Southwestern Bell Video Services, 193 F.3d 309 (5th Cir. 1999); City of Chicago v. FCC, 199 F.3d 424 (7th Cir. 1999).

[86] The FCC's initial ruling was expanded to cover incumbent franchisees in 2007. Implementation of Section 621(a)(1) of the Cable Communications Policy Act of 1984 as amended by the Cable Television Consumer Protection and Competition Act of 1992 (FCC 07-190), 22 F.C.C.R. 19633 (Nov. 6, 2007). The Sixth U.S. Circuit Court of Appeals upheld the FCC's new rules in July 2008. Alliance for Cmty. Media v. FCC, 529 F.3d 763 (6th Cir. 2008).

[87] *See, e.g.,* Group W Cable, Inc. v. City of Santa Cruz, 679 F. Supp. 977 (N.D. Cal. 1988).

cable modem Internet access did not constitute a cable service.[88]

Programming. The 1984 Cable Act allows franchising authorities to specify broad categories of video programming that the cable operator must carry, such as movies, children's programming, sports and public affairs. They, however, are not permitted to specify which programming services a cable system must provide (those such as CNN or ESPN) or to forbid a cable operator from offering specific services.

Duration. Franchises also specify the agreement's duration, which typically is from eight to fifteen years. Most franchises specify that the cable operator must ask the franchising authority's permission to transfer or sell to a new owner. Most cable owners invest heavily in the equipment needed to operate their systems and hope to renew franchises and continue providing service beyond the initial franchise period. The 1984 Cable Act established a franchise renewal process that creates renewal expectancy so that cable operators would be willing to invest in upgrading their systems. As we shall see in the next section, local governments have attempted to use the franchising process as a means to regulate new services offered by cable companies.

CABLE AND THE INTERNET

Perhaps no change within the cable industry has created as many problems for regulators as broadband (high speed) access to the Internet. As the Internet and the World Wide Web rapidly increased in popularity in the 1990s, consumers became interested in broadband access. Broadband access allows users to surf the Web and download Web pages, software, audio and video literally hundreds of times faster than a standard telephone modem.[89] For example, a ten-megabyte file that would take twenty-four minutes to download using a 56k modem can be downloaded *via* a cable modem in less than twenty seconds. Broadband speeds also are necessary to stream video from services such as Netflix, Amazon and Hulu.

There are many ways to achieve a broadband connection, including cable modems, digital subscriber line telephone service, known as DSL, wireless and satellite. The two most popular methods for Internet service to the home are cable modems offered by cable operators and DSL offered by telephone companies. In 2014, 75 percent of Americans had high speed Internet access at home. Of those, more than half used a cable modem.[90]

In the days of dial-up Internet connections, you would use a phone line to call your ISP every time you wanted to connect to the Internet. You could choose which ISP you wanted to use since each had its own set of phone numbers with which to call to connect. The phone company owned the telephone wire that went to your house, but it was not allowed to restrict what phone numbers you chose to dial.

With a cable modem, users connect to the Internet using a coaxial cable connection rather than a telephone wire. The cable company was not regulated as a common carrier; so it did not have to give you a choice of ISPs. Most cable companies own their own ISP service. So if you are a Comcast cable customer you are forced to use Comcast's Internet service. In 2005, the FCC ruled that telephone companies would not have to share their broadband DSL lines either, putting them on equal regulatory footing with cable operators.[91] This means whether you subscribe to broadband Internet access through your cable company or your telephone company, you might not get any choice regarding the company that provides the Internet access.

Open Access Requirements

As more Internet users switched to cable modems and DSL, competitors and consumer groups became afraid that cable-affiliated ISPs would favor cable-affiliated content providers. For example, if you get your broadband access through Comcast, maybe Comcast-owned Web sites like MSNBC.com will download faster than competing Web sites like Fox.com or Google news. This is similar to the previous discussion that cable operators would favor affiliated cable networks over competing networks. The horizontal and vertical ownership limits, leased access rules, and access to cable networks were all designed to prevent these types of anti-competitive practices in the provision of cable TV service. Independent ISPs and consumer groups want laws that require cable operators to provide open Internet access so that competing ISPs can lease the cable wires to reach customers as well.

Cable operators refer to such demands as "forced access." They argue that the cable wire is their private property and that they would have no incentive to spend the money to build broadband networks if they then have to share the networks with competitors. In addition, they argue that the current lack of regulation encourages investment in competing broadband technologies such as DSL and wireless access.

In 1999, the FCC released a report stating that it did not in-

---

[88] City of Minneapolis v. Time Warner Cable, Inc., 2005 U.S. Dist. Lexis 27743 (D. Minn. Nov. 10, 2005) (unpublished opinion). *See also,* City of Chicago v. Comcast, 900 N.E.2d 256 (Ill. 2008).

[89] *See* Deborah A. Lathen, FCC, Broadband Today, A Staff Report to William E. Kennard, Chairman (1999), *available at* http://www.fcc.gov/Bureaus/Cable/Reports/broadband.pdf.

[90] FCC Wireline Competition Bureau, Internet Access Services: Status as of Dec. 31, 2014, Chart 13, p. 21 (March 2016).

[91] Appropriate Framework for Broadband Access to the Internet over Wireline Facilities (FCC 05-150), 70 Fed. Reg. 6022 (Oct. 17, 2005).

tend to require open access.[92] At that time, telephone companies had to lease their DSL lines to competitors. In other words, an independent ISP like Earthlink could lease wires from a telephone company to offer broadband DSL service, but it could not lease wires from a cable company to offer broadband cable service. (As discussed above, the FCC stopped requiring telephone companies to share their DSL wires in 2005.)

Meanwhile, AT&T was completing its mergers with TCI and MediaOne, two large MSOs, and the new company was beginning to offer @Home broadband access through its cable lines. A number of ISPs, including AOL, lobbied the government to force AT&T to provide open access to its cable customers. The FCC refused to require open access, but consumers and competitors convinced some local franchise authorities to require open access as a condition of the franchise transfer or renewal. This resulted in court cases in three different cities where the local franchise was being transferred to AT&T. In all three cases, the courts held that cities could not require open access as a condition of the cable franchise agreement.

AT&T v. City of Portland began when AT&T sued the franchising authority for refusing to grant the franchise transfer.[93] The authority had included a requirement stating that the franchise could not be transferred unless AT&T agreed to provide open access for competing ISPs. The district court rejected AT&T's argument that Portland did not have the authority to impose such a requirement, but the Court of Appeals for the Ninth Circuit reversed the decision. It stated that cable Internet access is a telecommunications service, not a cable service, and that the Communications Act bars local franchising authorities from regulating telecommunications services.[94] In a Virginia case, the Fourth U.S. Circuit Court of Appeals reached a similar conclusion.[95]

In both cases, the courts distinguished between (1) the provision of Internet content and services (such as email access and Web storage space on the ISP's server) and (2) the provision of transmission services between the ISP and the subscriber. Both courts concluded that the connection between the subscriber and the ISP, whether *via* a copper telephone line operated by the local telephone company or a coaxial cable operated by the cable company, should be classified as a telecommunications service. While such a classification precluded local franchise authorities from demanding open access as a condition of franchise approval, it left the door open for the FCC to begin regu-

lating cable Internet access as a telecommunications service. This could result in the imposition of common carrier requirements and force cable companies to contribute to the universal service fund to support affordable telephone service unless the FCC chose to forebear from imposing those requirements.

In the Florida case of *Comcast Cablevision of Broward County v. Broward County,* a district judge held that the franchise authority's attempt to impose open access requirements violated the First Amendment.[96] The court reasoned that the open access requirement was a content-based regulation similar to that in *Miami Herald v. Tornillo*[97] because the cable operator is essentially punished if it chooses to offer Internet access. The court also said that even if the regulation were content-neutral it would fail intermediate scrutiny because the county did not conduct adequate fact-finding to establish that a substantial governmental interest was at risk.

After initially lobbying for regulations requiring open access to cable modems, AOL abruptly changed its position upon acquiring Time Warner.[98] Time Warner's holdings included Time Warner Cable, the second largest MSO in the nation with 12.7 million subscribers. After the merger was complete, AOL owned its own cable wires, and it began to oppose government regulation in this area. Ironically, the Federal Trade Commission and the FCC required AOL Time Warner to provide open access for competing ISPs as a condition of allowing the two companies to merge, even though there is no general requirement that other MSOs have to offer open access.[99] Thus, after AOL bought its own cable company and stopped lobbying for open access, it became the only cable company required to provide open access.[100]

In 2002, the FCC issued a ruling that cable modem service would be classified as an information service rather than as a telecommunications service or cable service.[101] This important decision prevented local governments from requiring open access to cable modems or regulating cable Internet service in any way. The ruling also meant that cable companies could avoid any of the common carrier regulations that telephone companies face. The FCC eliminated most of the open access regulations

---

[92] *In re* Inquiry Concerning the Deployment of Advanced Telecommunications Capability to All Americans in a Reasonable and Timely Fashion, and Possible Steps to Accelerate Such Deployment Pursuant to Section 706 of the Telecommunications Act of 1996 (FCC 99-5), 14 F.C.C.R. 2398 (1999).

[93] 43 F. Supp. 2d 1146 (D. Ore. 1999).

[94] AT&T v. City of Portland, 216 F.3d 871 (9th Cir. 2000).

[95] Media One Group, Inc. v. County of Henrico, 257 F.3d 356 (4th Cir. 2001).

[96] 124 F. Supp. 2d 685 (S.D. Fla. 2000).

[97] 418 U.S. 241 (1974).

[98] *See* Kathy Chen, *AOL Changes Tune in Debate on Cable Access,* WALL ST. J., Feb. 14, 2000, at B5.

[99] *See* Stephen Labaton, *FCC Approves AOL-Time Warner Deal, With Conditions,* N.Y. TIMES, Jan. 12, 2001, at C1.

[100] In 2010, AOL Time Warner split, creating three separate companies: AOL, Time Warner Entertainment and Time Warner Cable. Since the merger has been dissolved, the FCC has proposed eliminating the special open access requirements that were put in place in 2001. Commission Seeks Comment on Time Warner Cable's Request to Terminate Remaining AOL Time Warner Merger Condition, DA-12-921, June 12, 2012.

[101] *In re* Inquiry Concerning High-Speed Access to the Internet Over Cable and Other Facilities, Internet Over Cable Declaratory Ruling: Appropriate Regulatory Treatment for Broadband Access to the Internet Over Cable Facilities (FCC 02-77), 17 F.C.C.R. 4798 (2002) [hereinafter Internet Over Cable Ruling].

imposed on telephone DSL lines as well.[102]

In declaring cable modem service to be an information service, the commission ignored the *Portland* court analysis that cable modem service has two components: information service (such as Web pages and email) and telecommunications (the transmission of data between the cable headend and the home subscriber). Instead, the FCC said cable modem service is a "single, integrated service."[103] It also ruled that cable service is interstate because most Internet data cross state borders. This means that state regulators don't have jurisdiction to regulate cable modems. The FCC also issued a Notice of Proposed Rulemaking to decide what regulations (if any) should be imposed on cable modem service. Independent ISPs and consumer groups appealed the ruling to the Court of Appeals for the Ninth Circuit, the same court that ruled cable Internet access is a telecommunications service in the *Portland* case. In 2003, the court ruled that its *Portland* decision was binding precedent that controlled its review of the FCC's ruling.[104] Therefore, it stated that it was compelled to vacate the FCC's determination that cable modem service did not include a telecommunications service. In 2005, the Supreme Court resolved this conflict between the *Portland* decision and the FCC's ruling regarding the proper classification of cable modem Internet service. The Court held that the FCC's classification of cable modem service as an information service (rather than a telecommunications service) was reasonable.[105] Furthermore, it said that when a court precedent conflicts with an agency's interpretation, the court must accept the agency's interpretation *unless* the statute is unambiguous and contrary to the agency's interpretation.

Network Neutrality

Network neutrality is a more recent policy issue related to open access. Whereas open access would require a cable company or other broadband provider to share its wires with other ISPs, network neutrality requires commercial ISPs to treat all content and applications equally. In other words, network neutrality focuses on how an ISP manages the data that flows through its wires. Some policymakers are concerned that the companies that control the physical infrastructure of the Internet (mostly large cable and telephone companies) will discriminate against certain types of content by charging more, slowing the connection speed, or blocking access to that content entirely. Why would an ISP discriminate? It might want to promote its own

content, harm a potential competitor, favor a content partner, manage bandwidth, charge more money, or even block content with which it disagrees. Network neutrality advocates favor regulations requiring ISPs to treat all Internet content equally.

The issue gained prominence in 2008 when it was revealed that Comcast, the largest broadband ISP, was blocking its subscribers from connecting to BitTorrent, a popular P2P file sharing service. Comcast was using fake packets repeatedly to close the P2P connection. It claimed the move was necessary to prevent users from causing an online traffic jam. Critics argued that Comcast was really concerned that as P2P file sharing grew in popularity, it would threaten Comcast's cable revenues. In addition to its interference with P2P applications, Comcast began reducing the bandwidth available for customers who did the most downloading. In Florida, Comcast settled with the attorney general after complaints that it never notified customers what the bandwidth limit would be.[106]

The FCC ruled that Comcast was discriminating against some of its customers. This decision was significant, in part, because the FCC asserted its authority to enforce its Internet Policy Statement and regulate how companies manage their Internet networks.[107] It stated:

> Although Comcast asserts that its conduct is necessary to ease network congestion, we conclude that the company's discriminatory and arbitrary practice unduly squelches the dynamic benefits of an open and accessible Internet and does not constitute reasonable network management. Moreover, Comcast's failure to disclose the company's practice to its customers has compounded the harm.[108]

The FCC ordered Comcast to stop blocking BitTorrent and to publicly disclose all of its future network management policies. Comcast appealed the ruling. In a very important decision, the appellate court ruled that the FCC did not have jurisdiction to regulate Comcast's Internet management practices.[109] The Communications Act gives the FCC explicit authority to regulate telecommunications services (Title II), broadcast services (Title III), and cable services (Title VI). At times, the FCC can also use its ancillary authority under Title I to regulate information services. (See the section "History of Cable Television

---

[102] Press Release, FCC, FCC Adopts New Rules for Network Unbundling Obligations of Incumbent Local Phone Carriers (Feb. 20, 2003).

[103] Internet Over Cable Ruling, *supra* note 103, at 4823.

[104] Brand X Internet Serv. v. FCC, 345 F.3d 1120 (9th Cir. 2003).

[105] Nat'l Cable and Telecomm. Ass'n v. Brand X Internet Services, 545 U.S. 967 (2005).

[106] Press Release, Office of the Attorney General of Florida, Attorney General Reaches $150,000 Settlement with Comcast (Aug. 29, 2008), *available at* http://www.myfloridalegal.com/newsreel.nsf/newsreleases/D70311C8F60F2852574B400566134 (last visited June 22, 2009).

[107] Appropriate Framework for Broadband Access to the Internet over Wireline Facilities, FCC 05-151, 20 F.C.C.R. 14986 (Sep. 23, 2005).

[108] *In re* Formal Complaint of Free Press and Public Knowledge Against Comcast Corporation for Secretly Degrading Peer-to-Peer Applications, FCC 08-183, 23 F.C.C.R. 13028, at ¶ 1 (Aug. 20, 2008).

[109] Comcast Corp. v. FCC, 600 F.3d 642 (D.C. Cir. 2010).

Regulation" earlier in this chapter). However, in this case the court held that the FCC can only exercise its ancillary authority in conjunction with its "statutorily mandated responsibilities."[110] Regulating Comcast's network management practices was not tied to any of the specific provisions contained in the Communications Act. Therefore, the appeals court held, the FCC does not have jurisdiction over this aspect of Comcast's Internet access service.

Notwithstanding the court ruling against it, the FCC issued new network neutrality rules in 2010 for fixed broadband providers (wireline cable and telephone companies) and mobile broadband providers (cellular phone companies).[111] The rules had three key components: (1) transparency: all broadband providers (fixed and mobile) must be transparent about their network management practices; (2) no blocking: fixed broadband providers may not block any lawful content or applications, while mobile broadband providers can block some devices and applications (but not competing voice applications); and (3) no unreasonable discrimination: fixed broadband providers cannot discriminate in transmitting lawful traffic.[112]

The impetus for the rules was the concern that most homes get their broadband Internet access from either their cable company or their telephone company. The FCC was concerned that cable and telephone companies would discriminate against Internet services, applications and content that compete with their traditional video and telephone services. After all, Comcast does not want subscribers to sign up for Internet service and cancel their cable service, and Verizon does not want subscribers to cancel their telephone service.

As Netflix, Hulu Amazon and other companies offer online video streaming services, more and more consumers are "cord-cutting," that is canceling their cable or DBS video service and relying on streaming Internet services for all their television viewing. Internet providers like Comcast want to charge streaming companies like Netflix an additional fee to guarantee the necessary broadband speed for smooth viewing. Consumer groups complain that while Netflix and Hulu can afford to pay additional fees, a new company that wants to compete with Netflix or Hulu would be unable to afford the fee, resulting in less competition, which would harm consumers. In addition, if Comcast and other cable operators begin charging Netflix a higher fee for access to a fast lane, Netflix will ultimately pass the cost along to consumers in the form of higher subscription fees. The FCC and consumer groups fear that cable companies like Comcast will either slow or block access to content that competes with their own offerings, or extort higher fees from those companies.

After the FCC issued its new network neutrality rules in 2010, Verizon sued, arguing the FCC did not have the authority to impose the rules. In 2014, a federal appeals court again struck down the rules.[113] It held that the FCC could not impose common carrier style regulations on Internet access unless it first classifies Internet access as a telecommunications service.[114] Remember that in a series of decisions going back to the FCC's Broadband Over Cable ruling in 2002, the agency had explicitly rejected classifying Internet access as a telecommunications service subject to common carrier regulation. In response to the court decision, the FCC opened a new inquiry to develop network neutrality rules that would pass judicial scrutiny.[115]

The FCC's 2015 Open Internet Order

In 2015, the FCC issued a landmark network neutrality ruling known as the "Open Internet Order."[116] The Commission expanded the rules it had tried to implement in 2010 but which had been overturned by the appeals court. Recall that the court stated that some of the rules would only be valid if Internet access were classified as a telecommunications service. So in its new order, the FCC discarded its 2002 classification of Internet access as an "information service" and declared that Internet access would now be considered a "telecommunications service" and therefore subject to tighter regulation.[117]

The new open Internet rules expand upon the principles from the FCC's 2010 order that had been vacated by the courts. In the 2010 order, the FCC applied one set of rules to wireline broadband providers like Comcast, and a different set of rules to wireless broadband providers that use cellular networks like AT&T, Sprint, and Verizon. The new 2015 rules apply equally to wireline and wireless broadband providers.[118]

The new rules impose three restrictions on broadband providers: (1) no blocking of lawful content, applications or services; (2) no throttling — reducing the speed or quality on the basis of content, service or application; and (3) no paid prioritization — accepting or charging additional money for better or faster service for certain content, service, or applications.[119] In addition, the FCC maintained the transparency rule from the 2010 order that requires broadband providers to disclose their

---

[110] *Id.* at 646.

[111] Preserving the Open Internet, FCC 10-201, 25 F.C.C.R. 17905 (Dec. 23, 2010).

[112] *Id.* at ¶ 1.

[113] Verizon v. FCC, 740 F.3d 623 (D.C. Cir. 2014).

[114] *Id.* at 650.

[115] *In re* Protecting and Promoting the Open Internet, FCC 14-61, 29 F.C.C.R. 5561 (May 15, 2014).

[116] Protecting and Promoting the Open Internet (FCC 15-24), adopted Mar. 12, 2015, 80 Fed. Reg. 19737 (Apr. 13, 2015).

[117] *Id.* at ¶ 43.

[118] *Id.* at ¶ 14.

[119] *Id.* at ¶ 14-19.

network management and pricing practices.[120] To prevent broadband providers from using loopholes to get around the new rules, the FCC also added a catch all rule that prohibits unreasonable interference or disadvantage imposed on consumers or edge providers (the companies like Netflix, Facebook, Google and Twitter that provide the content, services and applications that consumers use).[121]

While the FCC has reclassified broadband access as a telecommunications service to justify its jurisdiction to impose these new rules, the agency has also chosen to forbear from enforcing other aspects of Title II telecommunications common-carrier regulation. For example, broadband providers are not required to provide open access to competing ISPs and they are not subject to rate regulation.[122]

Cable and telecommunications providers immediately challenged the new FCC rules in court.[123] In June 2016, the D.C. Circuit Court of Appeals ruled in favor of the FCC.[124] The court held that the FCC has the authority to reclassify broadband Internet access as a telecommunications service. Referring to the Supreme Court's *Brand X* decision, the appeals court stated that it is proper for the FCC to consider the end user's perspective when classifying a service and that the FCC was reasonable to assert that end users consider Internet access as a standalone service that "transmits messages unadulterated by computer processing."[125] In its earlier 2002 order classifying Internet access as an information service, the FCC had noted that the service combines information processing such as email with a transmission service to create one integrated service.[126] In its 2015 Open Internet Order, the FCC noted that many consumers consider access to third-party content and services as separate from the email and other add-on services offered by their Internet service provider.

Another area of controversy is broadband providers' desire to offer usage-based pricing. Comcast, the nation's largest broadband provider, in 2014 announced plans to charge extra to customers who use more than 300 gigabytes per month. Public interest groups are concerned that Comcast will put Internet video providers like Netflix at a disadvantage by metering customers' usage of Netflix while offering unlimited usage of Comcast's own video-on-demand offerings. The Department of Justice in 2012 began investigating whether such a policy is a violation of antitrust law.[127] However, the DOJ does not appear to be actively pursuing the issue at this time.

Pole Attachment Agreements

Cable operators need permission to attach cables to poles or run them through underground conduits that are owned by telephone or electric companies. To prevent the companies from charging unreasonably high rental prices or refusing cable use entirely, Congress adopted the Pole Attachment Act in 1978. Its purpose was to make sure new companies were able to compete. It gave the FCC authority to regulate the rates, terms and conditions of agreements between most pole owners and cable systems. In addition, the Telecommunications Act of 1996 *requires* pole owners to allow cable companies to rent pole or conduit space. It also extended the pole attachment provisions to cable operators' use of poles or conduits for non-video services — such as data or voice transmissions — that compete with telephone offerings.[128] The law permits a state, rather than the FCC, to oversee pole rental contracts within the state. Nearly twenty states have decided to do so.

The FCC is struggling to determine the fees cable Internet service providers should be charged for pole use and the status of wireless carriers that attach their equipment to poles. In 1998, the FCC established a formula for fees for pole attachments by cable and wireless telephone services unable to negotiate terms in states that do not regulate pole attachments.[129] Internet services carried by cable have been charged at the rate applied to cable services, which is less than half the rate applied to telephone services. Utility companies challenged these rules.

The Eleventh U.S. Circuit Court of Appeals ruled the FCC did not have the authority to require pole attachments for wireless providers or to set the rates for Internet service providers. The Supreme Court overturned the ruling and held that the FCC *does* have the authority to set rates for any pole attachment made by a cable company even if the attachment is used for purposes beyond providing cable services.[130]

In 2011, the FCC adopted an order that established new rules for setting pole attachment rates to reduce some of the disparity between the pole attachment rates paid by cable providers and telecommunications providers.[131] However, cable and small

[120] *Id.* at ¶ 23.

[121] *Id.* at ¶ 21.

[122] *Id.* at ¶ 37.

[123] Rebecca R. Ruiz, *Appeals Court Denies Delay of Net Neutrality Rules,* N.Y. Times, Jun. 12, 2015, at B2.

[124] U.S. Telecom Ass'n v. FCC, No. 15-1063, *slip op.* (D.C. Cir. Jun. 14, 2016).

[125] *Id.* at 24.

[126] See discussion of the FCC's Internet Over Cable ruling earlier in this chapter.

[127] *Fear and Loathing Over the Top,* MULTICHANNEL NEWS, June 18, 2012, at 12.

[128] 47 U.S.C. § 224 (2000). *See also* Texas Utilities Elec. Co. v. FCC, 997 F.2d 925 (D.C. Cir. 1993); Heritage Cablevision v. Texas Utilities Elec. Co., 6 F.C.C. Rcd. 7099 (1991).

[129] *In re* Implementation of Section 703(e) of the Telecommunications Act of 1996, 13 F.C.C.R. 6777 (1998) (codified at 47 C.F.R. §§ 1.1401 - 1.1418 (1999)).

[130] Gulf Power Co. v. United States, 208 F.3d 1263 (11th Cir. 2000), *rev'd sub nom.* Nat'l Cable & Telecomms. Ass'n v. Gulf Power Co., 534 U.S. 327 (2002).

[131] Implementation of Section 224 of the Act: A National Broadband Plan for Our Future (FCC 11-50) 26 F.C.C.R. 5240 (Apr. 7, 2011).

telephone providers complained that the new rules still allowed pole owners to charge higher rates for telecommunications services. They petitioned the FCC at the time to reconsider its pole attachment rules. The 2015 Open Internet Order that reclassified Internet access as a telecommunications service has created the possibility that utility pole owners can raise the rate they charge broadband providers (including cable companies) by as much as 70 percent. The NCTA has requested that the FCC reconsider its 2011 petition in order to prevent the potential rate increase for pole attachments.[132]

CONTENT AND PROGRAMMING REGULATIONS

Despite court decisions establishing that the First Amendment protects cable from content-based regulations, Congress has placed a variety of content-related and access regulations on cable TV. Courts have allowed many of the laws to stand.

Sexually Explicit Programming on Commercial Channels

In addition to the content restrictions on leased access and PEG channels discussed earlier, Congress has tried to regulate sexually explicit programming on cable. The 1996 Telecommunications Act required the FCC to establish rules regarding such programming on channels used primarily for such material (Playboy and other adult channels, for example).[133] The FCC issued a regulation that the channels must be fully scrambled or blocked, unless a subscriber chooses to receive them. The purpose was to address the problem of signal bleed whereby the audio or portions of the video are still viewable even though a channel has been scrambled. The rule required cable operators who do not completely scramble such channels to provide a safe harbor free of sexually oriented programming from 6 a.m. until 10 p.m. The Supreme Court applied strict scrutiny to strike down the rule as a content-based restriction that violated the First Amendment.[134] Its 5-4 decision said the law improperly singled out particular programmers. Since blocking methods were either very expensive or not completely effective, most cable operators had to limit the transmission of sexually oriented channels to between 10 p.m. and 6 a.m. Thus, many adult viewers, including those who do not have children, were being denied access. Another provision of the law already required cable operators to block access to channels for individual households on request — clearly a less restrictive alternative solution. The Court held the government had not demonstrated that the harm

was real or that a less restrictive alternative was unavailable.

Other Content Laws and Rules

Cable systems also must comply with certain federal laws and FCC rules that apply to broadcasters regarding political advertising, bans on carrying obscene material, limitations on information about lotteries and sponsorship identification rules. Cable systems must comply with the limits on commercial time during children's programs, but unlike broadcast stations, they do not have to provide three hours of children's educational programming per week.

OTHER CABLE REGULATION ISSUES

Cable operators face numerous other regulations, some of which are briefly covered here.

Interactive Television

Digital technology has created countless opportunities for interactive TV. Services include program guides, personal video recorders like TiVo and Replay, video on demand and other enhanced services like immediate product purchases while viewing TV. Many of the new interactive services are available through the Internet or sophisticated set-top boxes. In 2001, the FCC opened an inquiry to determine if large, vertically integrated cable operators might discriminate in favor of affiliated ITV providers.[135] This is similar to the concern that cable operators would favor affiliated networks that eventually led to the vertical ownership limits.

Another issue related to interactive TV is the provision of set-top boxes. Digital cable and video-on-demand are areas of huge growth for cable systems. Subscribers typically rent a set-top box from the cable provider to access these services. The boxes integrate digital video recorders and navigation features for changing channels with security features to prevent cable theft. To stimulate competition and give consumers more choices, in 2007, the FCC ordered cable companies to separate out the boxes' security function from the other features. Consumers could then buy a third-party box or digital TV from a local store and insert the cable company's security card (known as a CableCARD) into the box or TV to receive programming rather than being forced to rent a box from the cable company.[136] One problem with the rules is that the CableCARD standard only works with one-way cable signals. Video on demand and

---

[132] Parties Asked To Refresh Record Regarding Petition to Reconsider Cost Allocators Used to Calculate The Telecom Rate Pole Attachments, DA 15-542 (May 6, 2015).

[133] 47 U.S.C. § 561 (2000).

[134] United States v. Playboy Entm't. Group, 529 U.S. 803 (2000).

[135] *In re* Nondiscrimination in the Distribution of Interactive Television Services Over Cable (FCC 01-15), 66 Fed. Reg. 7913 (Jan. 26, 2001).

[136] *See* Ellen Sheng, *A Makeover for the Cable Box*, WALL ST. J., Mar. 8, 2007, at D6.

switched digital video both incorporate two-way signals between the customer and the cable company. Therefore, third-party boxes can't access these functions, forcing consumers to rely on the cable company's own set-top box. In 2009, the FCC held that cable companies may migrate channels to SDV technology even though it is incompatible with CableCARD technology and reduces the functionality of third party set-top boxes.[137]

In 2010, the FCC issued a Notice of Inquiry to develop a new policy regarding set-top boxes.[138] The CableCARD initiative had not achieved its intended effect of creating competition for set-top boxes. Since 2007, when the new rules took effect, more than 97 percent of consumers continued to rent their set-top boxes directly from their cable companies. Cable and satellite providers currently earn almost $20 billion per year renting set-top boxes to consumers.

The FCC began to consider new software-based set-top box rules in 2016.[139] The rules would create open technical standards for any third-party equipment manufacturer or software developer to access pay TV content. Cable providers vigorously oppose the new rules, which they claim would give large tech companies like Google and Apple an unfair advantage, by allowing them to collect consumer data, sell advertising, and integrate streaming services with traditional pay television. Cable companies and cable networks also assert the new rules would increase the problem of video piracy and threaten consumer privacy.[140] The cable industry recently proposed a compromise whereby the industry would develop an app that would replace the set-top box entirely.[141] With the cable industry strongly opposed to the FCC's proposal and consumer groups strongly opposed to the industry's alternative solution, it is unclear if any decision will be made in the near future.

Exclusivity and Non-duplication Rules

The FCC has adopted two rules in addition to must-carry designed to protect broadcast stations from cable competition: syndicated exclusivity and network non-duplication. Syndicated programming is sold by exclusive contract to individual stations in different cities. When cable systems import distant stations'

signals, the signals may include the same syndicated programming being shown by a local station under an exclusive contract. To address this duplication and protect local stations, the FCC adopted syndicated exclusivity rules in 1972.[142] The rules permit a local station to require a cable system to black out any syndicated program on an imported signal that the station also was carrying. The commission rescinded the rules in 1980 but reinstated them in 1988,[143] and they continue in force and have been upheld as content-neutral by the U.S. Court of Appeals for the D.C. Circuit.[144] Similar rules for network programs allow stations affiliated with a broadcast network to demand that a cable system black out network programming being carried on an imported station affiliated with the same network.[145]

Another FCC rule prohibited a cable or satellite operator from televising a local sporting event if the telecast has been blacked out on local broadcast stations.[146] The FCC repealed the rule in 2014, though a professional sports league can still require blackouts through its private contracts with broadcast stations and cable providers.[147] In 2012, the NFL relaxed its rule to allow the local team to decide if a game will be blacked out as long as 85 percent of the tickets have been sold.[148]

Cable and Copyright

Broadcast programming is protected under copyright law, which, as discussed in Chapter 13, requires that permission be granted for use of the material. Broadcast TV stations, or the networks with which the stations are affiliated, pay the producers of television programming for the right to broadcast their shows. Similarly, when cable systems began to retransmit local broadcast signals, program producers argued that cable TV was required to obtain permission as well. Producers said that they had sold their shows to broadcast television, not to cable. Broadcast stations also argued that cable should be required to obtain permission to carry local programming — like evening news shows — for which local stations held the copyrights.

In 1968 and again in 1974, the Supreme Court held that a cable system's retransmission of a broadcast station's signal did

---

[137] *In re* Oceanic Time Warner Cable, Order on Review (FCC 09-52), 24 F.C.C.R. 2716 (June 26, 2009).

[138] Video Device Competition; Implementation of Section 304 of the Telecommunications Act of 1996: Commercial Availability of Navigation Devices; Compatibility Between Cable Systems and Consumer Electronics Equipment (FCC 10-60), 25 F.C.C.R. 4275 (Apr. 21, 2010).

[139] Expanding Consumers' Video Navigation Choices (FCC 16-18), 81 Fed. Reg. 13997 (Feb. 18, 2016).

[140] Jim Puzzanghera, *FCC Move May Boost Options for Set-top Boxes,* L.A. TIMES, Feb. 19, 2016, at C1.

[141] Brian Fung, *Cable Firms Offer Plan to Ditch Boxes as Compromise to Regulations,* WASH. POST, June 18, 2016, at A13.

[142] Cable Television Report and Order, 36 F.C.C. 2d 143 (1972).

[143] Syndicated Exclusivity Rules, 79 F.C.C. 2d 663 (1980); *In re* Rules Relating to Program Exclusivity in the Cable and Broadcast Industries, 3 F.C.C.R. 5299 (1988).

[144] United Video, Inc. v. FCC, 890 F.2d 1173 (D.C. Cir. 1989).

[145] First Report and Order in Dockets 14895 and 15233, 38 F.C.C. 683 (1965); *In re* Rules Relating to Program Exclusivity in the Cable and Broadcast Industries, 3 F.C.C.R. 5299 (1988).

[146] 47 C.F.R. § 76.111 (2002).

[147] Sports Blackout Rules, FCC 14-141, 29 F.C.C.R. 12053 (Sep. 30, 2014).

[148] Stephen F. Holder, *NFL Changes Blackout Rules?,* TAMPA BAY TIMES, July 1, 2012, at C1.

not violate the copyright law in effect at that time.[149] Instead, the Court said the cable was simply an extension of the viewer's antenna. Program producers and broadcasters reached a compromise with cable operators that Congress adopted as part of the Copyright Act of 1976.[150] The law's compulsory copyright license for broadcast TV and radio programs permits cable operators to carry such programming for a fee without asking permission.[151] A complex formula determines the amount each cable system must pay, but the fee is less than what the system would pay if it negotiated separately with the copyright holder of each individual program. Cable payments are made to a fund administered through the U.S. Copyright Office, which distributes the money to the copyright holders. The broadcast stations and networks do not receive any of the money unless they are the copyright owners. In 2008, the Copyright Office issued a report recommending that the compulsory license be phased out, after which cable systems would have to negotiate directly with the copyright owners for the right to retransmit the programs carried on distant broadcast stations.[152] In 2010, Congress passed a law amending the compulsory license to cover payments when a cable system retransmits multiple video streams (multicasting) from a broadcast station.[153] The law also directs the Copyright Office to conduct a new inquiry into whether the compulsory licenses should be phased out.

A company called Aereo thought it found a loophole in the compulsory licensing law and began to offer low-cost subscriptions to local TV programming. It invented a tiny antenna less than an inch long that could receive local TV signals. Aereo installed thousands of the antennas at its office. A consumer could rent an antenna, and Aereo would send the TV programming to the consumer *via* the Internet. Program producers and local TV stations sued Aereo for copyright infringement for publicly performing their copyrighted content. Like the cable industry in the late 1960s and early 1970s, Aereo argued it should not have to pay local TV stations for programming because each subscriber was still using her own remote antenna, which the Supreme Court had said was permissible. The Supreme Court rejected Aereo's argument, noting that Congress had specifically closed that loophole when it passed the Copyright Act of 1976.[154]

As consumers and the various industries switched from analog to digital television, program producers were concerned that viewers would begin to trade movies and TV programs on the Internet the same way they trade MP3 music files. HBO would find it difficult to rent or sell DVD copies of *Game of Thrones* if consumers were trading the episodes for free. In addition, fewer viewers might subscribe to HBO if they could get the programs for free on the Internet. To prevent the illegal trading of copyrighted programs, cable companies, broadcast outlets, copyright owners and consumer electronics manufacturers began developing special encryption software and digital watermarks to prevent consumers from copying and/or distributing TV programs.

In order to speed the transition from analog to digital broadcasting, the FCC passed a rule in 2003 that would have required all digital TV receivers manufactured after July 1, 2005, to recognize a "broadcast flag" — a digital code inserted in the broadcast to prevent redistribution of the content. Thus, the FCC was requiring copyright protection measures be built into TV sets. In 2005, the Court of Appeals for the D.C. Circuit struck down the requirement and ruled that the FCC had exceeded its statutory authority. The court reasoned that the FCC can impose requirements related to the reception of TV signals, but that it could not impose requirements controlling TV sets *after* the transmission is complete.[155]

In yet another copyright battle, a group of cable networks sued Cablevision when it announced it would offer customers a remote digital video recorder feature. Currently, many households use Tivo or another type of DVR to record shows for later viewing. The Supreme Court has ruled that this form of time shifting is not a copyright infringement. Cablevision wanted to offer a service where the programs are recorded and stored at the company's head end rather than in the subscriber's set-top box. Copyright owners sued, claiming that if Cablevision stores the recordings at its offices, it is no longer considered a fair use and should instead be considered copyright infringement. An appeals court ruled in favor of Cablevision, holding that the new service does not constitute infringement.[156]

Cable Companies as Telephone Providers

The Telecommunications Act of 1996 opened local telephone service to competition. For nearly 100 years, a residential telephone user could obtain service from only one local company. But the 1996 Act permits any firm to offer local phone service and requires phone companies to make their facilities available, on a nondiscriminatory basis, to others who want to compete in the local telephone market. In return, local phone companies

[149] Teleprompter Corp. v. Columbia Broad. Sys., 415 U.S. 394 (1974); Fortnightly Corp. v. United Artists Television, Inc., 392 U.S. 390 (1968).

[150] Pub. L. No. 94-553, 94 Stat. 2541, 17 U.S.C.S. §§ 101 et seq. (1976).

[151] 17 U.S.C. § 111 (1976).

[152] Register of Copyrights, U.S. Copyright Office, Satellite Home Viewer Extension and Reauthorization Act § 109 Report, June 30, 2008, *available at* http://www.copyright.gov/reports/section109-final-report.pdf (last visited June 22, 2009).

[153] Satellite Television Extension and Localism Act 0f 2010, Public Law 111-175, 124 Stat. 1218 (2010).

[154] American Broad. Cos., Inc. v. Aereo, Inc., 134 S.Ct. 2498 (2014).

[155] American Library Ass'n v. FCC, 406 F.3d 689 (D.C. Cir. 2005).

[156] Cartoon Network LP v. CSC Holdings, Inc., 536 F.3d 121 (2d Cir. 2008).

are allowed to offer long distance service.

Congress incorrectly expected cable to seize the opportunity provided by the 1996 Act to rush into and provide competition in the lucrative local telephone market. After all, local telephone service providers earned more than $66 billion a year, nearly three times the $23 billion in revenues earned from cable TV service at the time. Moreover, cable lines — already in nearly two-thirds of American homes and passing more than 95 percent of homes — were permitted to carry a full range of communications services: local telephone, Internet access, cable video and other services such as online banking. But such communications packages require fiber optic cable, and many operators hesitated to make the major investment necessary to upgrade their coaxial lines. Other cable operators entered the telephone market carefully and selectively because they lacked experience or expertise in interactive services billed by usage.

In its 2009 annual report on competition, the FCC noted that most cable companies were waiting for improved Internet protocol telephony technology before trying to offer telephone service on a large scale. At that time, about 8.5 million customers got some form of telephone service through their cable company.[157] This number began to grow as cable companies marketed the "triple play" of cable, Internet access and telephone service more aggressively. Today, 31 million households subscribe to landline telephone service through their cable company.[158]

Cable Customer Privacy

In the 1984 Cable Act, Congress reacted to a concern that cable companies could collect private information about their customers and share that information with others without subscribers' permission. Congress particularly focused on cable company access to customer information through cable's two-way capabilities, such as banking-from-home. Most of these two-way services have not fully developed yet, but cable systems are limited in the information they can gather and release about their customers.

Such private information includes the customer's name, address, telephone number, cable services taken and other information that identifies a particular subscriber. Cable systems annually must inform customers in writing what private information the system collects, what use it makes of the information, to whom the information is disclosed and why, how long the information will be kept by the system, when and where the

customer may see the information, the limits placed by law on the system's right to collect and disclose private information, and what steps the customer may take if the cable system violates those limitations.

Without a customer's permission, a cable operator may collect only the private information needed to offer cable or other services ordered by the customer and to be certain customers are not stealing services. Similarly, a cable operator may not release the information to others without permission except as needed to provide services to the customer or for the system's legitimate business needs, such as giving information to a company that sends the cable system's monthly bills.

The foregoing rules, though, apply only to cable service, not to high speed Internet service. In 2006, a cable modem customer sued Comcast for collecting IP addresses and URLs from the Web sites that its customers visited. The U.S. Court of Appeals for the Sixth Circuit ruled that the privacy rules that restrict collecting personal data only apply to cable service and not to other services offered by the provider.[159]

In 2016, the FCC proposed new privacy rules for broadband providers.[160] The new rules would require providers to obtain opt-in consent from consumers before using customer information for certain purposes. The FCC proposed three categories of information: (1)ISPs would have implied customer consent to use information necessary to provide service and billing, (2) ISPs would be allowed to use customer data to market affiliated services unless consumers opt-out of sharing such data, and (3) consumers would have to opt-in before ISPs could use customer information for other purposes.[161] The rules would apply to broadband providers such as telephone and cable companies, but not edge providers such as Facebook, Twitter or Google.[162] These proposed rules follow from the FCC's recent classification of broadband providers as common carriers subject to Title II regulations.[163]

Another privacy issue concerns government wiretapping. In 1994, Congress passed the Communications Assistance for Law Enforcement Act, requiring telecommunications carriers to ensure that law enforcement can engage in electronic surveillance using their telecommunications networks.[164] In 2005, the FCC ruled that facilities-based ISPs and Voice over Internet Protocol (VoIP or "Internet telephony") providers also had to comply with CALEA, calling them telecommunications carriers even

---

[157] Thirteenth Annual Report: In Annual Assessment of the Status of Competition in the Market for the Delivery of Video Programming (FCC 07-206), 24 F.C.C.R. 542 at ¶ 67 (Jan. 27, 2009).

[158] National Cable and Telecommunications Association, Industry Data, http://www.ncta.com/industry-data (last visited June 10, 2016).

[159] Klimas v. Comcast Commc'ns Inc., 465 F.3d 271 (6th Cir. 2006).

[160] In re Protecting the Privacy of Customers of Broadband and Other Telecommunications Services (FCC 16-39), Apr. 1, 2016, 81 Fed. Reg. 23359 (Apr. 20, 2016).

[161] Id. at 18.

[162] Id. at 13.

[163] See discussion of the FCC's Open Internet Order accompanying notes 118-27.

[164] Pub. L. No. 103-414, 108 Stat. 4279 (1994).

though they are generally classified as information service providers by the FCC.[165] In 2006, the U.S. Court of Appeals for the D.C. Circuit upheld the FCC's ruling.[166]

Equal Employment Opportunity Requirements

The FCC has had equal employment opportunity rules for broadcasters and cable systems in place for twenty-five years, but the 1984 and 1992 cable acts codify these rules for cable systems and other multi-channel video programming providers. Generally, the law forbids cable systems and their corporate owners from discriminating on the basis of national origin, race, color, age, religion or gender in employment.

The rules also required that the employees in certain job categories, such as managers and technicians, reasonably reflect the makeup of the pool of possible employees in the cable system's area. Further, cable systems and their owners had to establish programs to ensure that no discrimination occurred in any phase of employment, including hiring, training, promotions and firing. However the validity of the rules were put into doubt when the D.C. Circuit Court of Appeals rejected similar rules which the FCC had put into place for broadcasters.[167]

The FCC created new rules in 2002 for broadcasters and cable companies that require them to conduct broad outreach when filling job vacancies and file an annual report concerning their EEO efforts. Under these new rules cable companies do not have to show that the racial makeup of their employees reflected that of the community.[168]

Theft of Cable Service

Cable companies lose millions of dollars each year because of theft of cable services. Individuals tap into cable wires to obtain service without being subscribers, or they may use illegal set-top boxes to receive premium channels. The 1984 Cable Act forbids intercepting or receiving any cable service, or assisting anyone in doing so. Violators face up to two years in jail, $50,000 in fines or both. The law also forbids the manufacture and distribution of equipment intended to be used to steal cable service. Another section of the Communications Act makes it illegal to intercept signals not intended for the general public and to manufacture or sell equipment used to intercept such signals. Additionally, more than forty states enacted laws that may be used to prosecute theft of cable service.

A la Carte Pricing

In recent years, consumer interest groups have called on Congress to require cable companies to offer all their channels *a la carte*, as opposed to the bundled tiers that consumers must now purchase. Advocates for *a la carte* argue that consumers should not have to pay for channels they don't watch. The FCC has supported this approach as one way to help deal with the issue of violent content, since consumers would have the option to purchase only family friendly networks.[169] The cable industry opposes a mandatory *a la carte* option, arguing that consumers won't save any money because each channel will be more expensive on an *a la carte* basis. Opponents of *a la carte* also argue that it will reduce diversity since many less popular and minority-oriented networks will go out of business.[170]

In 2012, the Ninth Circuit dismissed a lawsuit by consumers that programming deals between companies that own multiple networks and cable operators harmed competition and violated the Sherman Act. Companies like Disney operate multiple cable networks, some more popular than others. Disney sometimes requires a cable operator to carry all of its networks even though the operator might only want ESPN. The appeals court held that there was no evidence that bundling networks instead of offering each channel *a la carte* harmed competition.[171]

In an interesting twist, Cablevision, a large cable operator, sued Viacom for forcing Cablevision to carry Viacom's less popular channels in order to gain access to Viacom's popular channels, including Nickleodeon, MTV, BET and Comedy Central. Cablevision argued that this policy violated antitrust law by creating a tying arrangement. A classic example of tying occurred in the movie industry in the 1940s when film distributors forced theater chains into block-booking arrangements. The distributors required movie theaters to book less popular "B" movies in order to gain access to the most popular films. The Supreme Court ruled in 1948 that this practice violated antitrust law.[172] Cablevision argued that Viacom was engaging in a similar anticompetitive practice. In June 2014, a federal district court ruled that Cablevision's lawsuit against Viacom could proceed.[173] The two companies settled the lawsuit the following year without disclosing the terms of the agreement.[174] It was

---

[165] Communications Assistance for Law Enforcement Act (CALEA) and Broadband Access and Services (FCC 05-153), 70 Fed. Reg. 59704 (Oct. 13, 2005).

[166] American Council on Educ. v. FCC, 451 F.3d 226 (D.C. Cir. 2006).

[167] Md/DC/DE Broadcasters Ass'n v. FCC, 236 F.3d 13 (D.C. Cir. 2001).

[168] *In re* Review of the Commission's Broadcast and Cable Equal Employment Opportunity Rules and Policies (FCC 01-363), 67 Fed. Reg. 1704 (2002).

[169] Violent Television Programming and Its Impact on Children (FCC 07-50), 22 F.C.C.R. 2979 (Apr. 25, 2007), 47.

[170] National Cable and Telecommunications Association, *Government Mandated A La Carte*, http://www.ncta.com/DocumentBinary.aspx?id=562 (Feb. 2007).

[171] Brantley v. NBC Universal, Inc., 675 F.3d 1192 (9th Cir. 2012).

[172] United States v. Paramount Pictures, 334 U.S. 131 (1948).

[173] Cablevision Sys. Corp. v. Viacom Int'l Inc., 2014 U.S. Dist. Lexis 84498 (S.D.N.Y. June 20, 2014).

[174] *See* Meg James, *Viacom and Cablevision Settle Lawsuit Over Bundles*, L.A. Times, Oct. 17, 2015, *available at* http://www.latimes.com/entertainment/envelope/cotown/la-et-ct-viacom-cablevision-settle-lawsuit-over-channel-bundles-20141016-story.html.

ironic that Cablevision sued for the right to purchase cable channels from suppliers on an *a la carte* basis while simultaneously refusing to offer the same type of choice to its own customers. Senator John McCain had reintroduced legislation in 2013 that would have forced cable companies to offer *a la carte* channels, though the bill never became law.[175] The debate over *a la carte* pricing has receded somewhat as individual networks like HBO and CBS and third-party providers like Hulu and Sling TV offer alternatives to standard cable bundles.

Mergers and Competition

As discussed earlier, many structural regulations have been put in place to protect cable's competitors and consumers from unfair competition. When two large media companies merge, policymakers must weigh the costs and benefits of increased consolidation. The FCC and other government agencies often impose special conditions on the new company before allowing the merger to take place. For example, when Time Warner Cable acquired some of Adelphia's cable systems, the FCC ordered Time Warner to negotiate with unaffiliated regional sports networks. The FCC was concerned Time Warner would refuse to carry those networks to drive them out of business and then acquire their popular sports programming. The FCC determined that Time Warner treated one of those networks unfairly when it placed the network on a digital tier rather than the analog tier that had significantly more subscribers.[176]

In 2009, Comcast, America's largest cable company, announced plans to merge with NBC Universal, owner of two national broadcast networks, twenty-six TV stations, a production studio and multiple cable networks. Both companies were already vertically integrated, with each owning film and television production companies, national TV networks and local outlets. Comcast is also the nation's largest broadband provider.

Public interest groups opposed the merger, concerned that it would continue the trend of very large media conglomerates becoming even larger, making it harder for new independent voices to succeed. In addition, NBC is part owner of Hulu, an online TV service. Hulu, along with services like Netflix, competes with Comcast. Opponents of the merger feared that once Comcast acquired NBC, it would shut down Hulu and restrict other competitors from distributing NBC's popular content.

The FCC and the Department of Justice approved the merger in 2011.[177] Both imposed conditions on the new company. Comcast must make its online video content available to other distributors at nondiscriminatory rates, and Comcast cannot restrict online video content through its broadband Internet service. These conditions are to ensure that Comcast does not try to put Hulu or other online video services out of business.

In addition, Comcast agreed to offer stand-alone broadband service for customers who do not want to subscribe to cable TV. Comcast was also required to offer discounted Internet access to low income households and extend its high speed networks to more rural communities, schools and libraries. The NBC and Telemundo local TV stations owned by the newly merged company agreed to produce more local news and television programming. Comcast also agreed to add additional minority oriented cable networks to its lineup.

New mega-mergers are proposed almost every year. In 2014, Comcast sought to acquire Time Warner Cable, the country's second largest cable provider for $45 billion.[178] The merger would have given Comcast more than 30 million subscribers and merged the largest and third-largest ISPs in the country. The companies abandoned the proposed merger in the face of opposition by regulators in 2015.

In 2015, the FCC approved AT&T's acquisition of DirecTV, the nation's largest DBS provider with more than twenty million subscribers (second only to Comcast with twenty-two million). AT&T is the country's second largest wireless phone company and also the second largest Internet access company (behind Comcast). Even before acquiring DirecTV, AT&T provided pay TV service to more than 5.9 million households, making it the third largest wireline television provider behind Comcast and Time Warner. AT&T was competing with DirecTV for video subscribers in the markets where AT&T operates. The merger gave AT&T control of DirecTV's twenty million DBS subscribers.[179]

Much as Comcast argued in its failed attempt to merge with Time Warner, AT&T had argued that its proposed merger with DirecTV should be approved because the pay TV industry faces increasing competition from Netflix, Hulu, Amazon, and other Internet video providers. For example, Netflix has forty-one million subscribers, and Hulu 9 million.[180] Furthermore, more people now access the Internet through smartphones and other wireless devices than through fixed broadband access provided by cable and telephone companies.

The latest large merger occurred in 2016 when Charter Communications, the nation's third largest MSO, acquired both

---

[175] *See* Joe Flint, *McCain Targets Cable Channel Bundling,* L.A.TIMES, May 10, 2013, at B1

[176] Mid-Atlantic Sports Network v. Time Warner Cable Inc., DA 08-2441 (Media Bureau), 23 F.C.C.R. 15783 (Oct. 30, 2008).

[177] Joe Flint, *Comcast-NBC Universal Deal Gets Federal Approval,* CHICAGO TRIB., Jan. 19, 2011, at A18.

[178] David Gelles, *Comcast Deal Seeks to Unite Two Cable Giants,* N.Y. TIMES, Feb. 13, 2014, at A1.

[179] Brian Fund, *FCC approves AT&T's acquisition of DirecTV,* WASH. POST, July 24, 2015, at A9.

[180] National Cable and Telecommunications Association, Industry Data, https://www.ncta.com/industry-data (last visited June 13, 2015).

Time Warner (the second largest MSO) and Bright House Networks. The $65 billion merger gives Charter close to twenty-four million customers, making it the second largest cable company behind Comcast. The deal was approved by the Department of Justice and the FCC under the condition that Charter not impose data caps on broadband customers and not to prohibit content providers from distributing programming online.[181]

SUMMARY

Since cable television's commercial development in the 1950s, Congress, the FCC and the courts have vacillated about how it should be regulated. In general, Congress and the FCC have imposed regulation on cable operators when cable's growth and market dominance appeared to jeopardize over-the-air broadcasting or the public's interest in diverse content, quality service and fair pricing. Cable also has been regulated to protect the public, especially children, from indecent or obscene programming. Although the courts view cable systems as part of the media protected by the First Amendment, some regulations treat cable more like a common carrier and require that the public, government and educational institutions, and even competitors, have access to a cable system's delivery network. Cable operators face such a complex array of regulations in part because of their size and economic power and in part because of their central role in disseminating news and other content.

In the 1960s, the FCC asserted its authority to regulate cable TV as "reasonably ancillary" to its obligation to protect an efficient broadcast system. The Supreme Court agreed and generally has deferred to the power of Congress to regulate cable. In fact, the Court has affirmed the authority of the FCC, rather than local or state governments, to regulate many aspects of cable systems. However, local governments maintain some power through their franchising authority. Congress finally gave the FCC explicit authority to regulate cable in 1984.

While the Supreme Court and lower courts have generally deferred to the FCC's policy decisions with regard to cable, in a few instances they have blocked FCC regulations. The FCC still has not adequately justified its cable ownership rules. But in a major FCC win, in 2016, the D.C. Circuit said the FCC did have the authority to reclassify broadband Internet access as a telecommunications service subject to strict regulation.

In 1986, the Supreme Court said in *Los Angeles v. Preferred Communications* that cable operators enjoy some First Amendment protection. The Court has reviewed most structural regulation of the cable industry under intermediate scrutiny and generally has upheld content-neutral laws that advance the government's dedication to providing broad access, encouraging a diversity of programming, or controlling excessive market power. In 2000, however, the Court, in *United States v. Playboy Entertainment*, afforded cable full First Amendment protection and also applied strict scrutiny to strike down a federal law requiring cable operators to fully scramble indecent programming.

As consumers spend more time using the Internet and watching video entertainment through providers such as Netflix, Amazon and Hulu, cable companies are becoming more important as broadband Internet providers than as pay TV providers. Thus, the FCC's 2015 Open Internet Order is likely to have the most important long-term ramifications on free speech and a competitive communications marketplace. While some are calling for the FCC to repeal its landmark decision, polls suggest most Americans favor the new network neutrality rules.

Policymakers continue to be driven by the belief that competition serves the public interest and protects both competitors and consumers better than regulation. Most regulatory efforts are designed to be short-term measures to protect small competitors until they are strong enough to compete with large established ones. These regulatory efforts are complicated by the convergence of cable, telephone and Internet services; each with its own history of regulation. More than a decade after the passage of the Telecommunications Act of 1996, increases in competition have been modest at best. Cable operators now control only 52 percent of the subscription TV market, down from 95 percent just twenty years ago. As high speed Internet access becomes ubiquitous, traditional broadcast and cable TV providers will face increasing competition from Internet streaming services. Internet service will increase in importance as more consumers cancel their cable TV and watch video online. The debate over network neutrality will occupy policymakers for the foreseeable future.

Cable companies now offer two major products: subscription video programming and broadband Internet access. Competition continues to increase for both products. Online video services like Netflix, Hulu and Amazon Prime Video offer competing bundles of programming while individual content companies like HBO, Showtime and Viacom begin to offer their own stand-alone content services. At the same time, more Americans now connect to the Internet through their wireless carrier such as AT&T or Verizon, than through a wired service. Cable broadband still has an advantage in speed while the wireless carriers have the advantage of mobility. Both wired and wireless Internet providers and their relationship with edge providers like Netflix, Google, Facebook and Amazon will be the key focus for regulators going forward. Time will tell if the changing regulatory landscape serves to enhance competition and the marketplace of ideas.

---

[181] Max Lewontin, *Charter Finalizes Time Warner Purchase: Is Era of "Mega Cable" Here?*, CHRISTIAN SCIENCE MONITOR, May 18, 2016, *available at* http://csmonitor.com /Technology/2016/0518/Charter-finalizes-Time-Warner-purchase-is=era-of-mega-cable-here.

FOR ADDITIONAL READING

Aufderheide, Patricia. *Communications Policy and the Public Interest: The Telecommunications Act of 1996.* New York: Guilford Press, 1999.

Brock, Gerald W. *Telecommunication Policy for the Information Age: From Monopoly to Competition.* Cambridge: Harvard University Press, 1994.

Crandall, Robert W. *Cable Television: Regulation or Competition.* Washington, D.C.: Brookings Institution, 1996.

Crawford, Susan. *Captive Audience: The Telecom Industry and Monopoly in the New Gilded Age.* New Haven: Yale University Press, 2013.

Ferris, Charles D., et al. *Cable Television Law.* New York: Mathew Bender, 1984-1998.

Huber, Peter W., et al. *The Telecommunications Act of 1996: Special Report.* Boston: Little, Brown, 1996.

Parsons, Patrick. R. *Cable Television and the First Amendment.* New York: Free Press, 1987.

Pool, Ithiel de Sola. *Technologies of Freedom.* Cambridge, Mass.: Belknap Press, 1983.

12

New Communication Technologies

By Jeremy Harris Lipschultz

➡ Headnote Questions

- How has the Internet redefined communication law and regulation?
- How are new telephone and digital television services challenging existing law and regulation?
- What role have the courts played in interpreting digital law?
- How have recent U.S. Supreme Court and appellate decisions set cyberlaw precedents?
- How are social media changing the law, regulation and policy landscape?

From telecommunication to Internet searches, social media and mobile smartphones, new technologies are challenging traditional communication law. As newer media allow individuals to take on roles as publishers (through blogs, podcasts, Twitter, Facebook, Instagram, Vine, Snapchat and other social postings), there are new freedoms *and* responsibilities.[1] The Federal Trade Commission, for example, has warned bloggers to disclose financial interests when endorsing products or services.[2] While social media users have a lot of freedom, errors in judgment may spark lawsuits.

At the same time, from Wikileaks to the National Security Agency PRISM case, technologies may alter traditional norms of privacy, journalism and law.[3] The desire for open access to online information clashes with the need for counter-terrorism surveillance programs. The change can be examined against a broader backdrop of rapid diffusion, adoption and convergence of mobile, Internet and social communication technologies. Mobile apps, for example, make it easier for smartphone users to communicate from almost anywhere at any time. Smartphones also make it: (1) easier for the government to monitor and spy on citizens, including journalists;[4] (2) possible for retail apps to track consumer location and movement;[5] (3) more likely there will be patent disputes.[6]

A ubiquitous mobile media environment is giving rise to new interest in so-called "big data" privacy protection. For example, cloud-based computing — such as DropBox, Google Drive and Apple's Cloud (which store files at remote servers) — make it difficult to establish clear property rights over shared content. Popular social media sites ask users to guard their privacy but also collect and use personal data based upon Terms of Service agreements, with few legal restrictions in the United States.

The international distribution of unfiltered media across a mosaic of legal systems and structures means technological freedom as a trend is colliding with governmental, corporate and individual desires to control messages. At the dawn of the digital age, Irving Fang first observed that email empowered users for good or bad. While Internet headquarters was based in Reston, Virginia, nobody "controls this digital hydra" because it is too

---

[1] *See* Kaye D. Sweetser, Lance V. Porter, Deborah Soun Chung & Eunseong Kim, *Credibility and the Use of Blogs Among Professionals in the Communications Industry*, 85 JOURNALISM & MASS COMM. Q. 169 (2008). While anyone may blog and reach an international audience, the credibility of bloggers varies in the eyes of the public and media professionals. Harris Interactive found more than half of Americans never even read political blogs. The Harris Poll #25 (Mar. 10, 2008), http://www.harrisinteractive.com/harris_poll.

[2] *See #Bloggers, Vloggers, Instagrammers Beware: FTC May Be Coming After You*, SOCIAL MEDIA LAW TODAY, http://socialmedialawtoday.com/bloggers-vloggers-instagrammers-beware-the-ftc-may-be-coming-after-you/.

[3] *See NSA Surveillance is an Attack on American Citizens, Says Noam Chomsky*, GUARDIAN, *available at* http://www.guardian.co.uk/world/2013/jun/19/nsa-surveillance-attack-american-citizens-noam-chomsky.

[4] *See NSA Collecting Phone Records of Millions of Verizon Customers Daily*, GUARDIAN, *available at* http://m.guardiannews.com/world/2013/jun/06/nsa-phone-records-verizon-court-order (June 6, 2013).

[5] *See Mobile Social Media Marketing and Privacy in 2016*, HUFFINGTON POST, *available at* http://www.huffingtonpost.com/jeremy-harris-lipschultz/mobile-social-media-marke_b_8740154.html.

[6] *See, e.g.*, HTC Corp. v. IPCom GmbH & Co., 667 F.3d 1270 (Fed. Cir. 2012).

massive and ubiquitous.[7] This is a context for understanding disputes and current case law impacting the Internet, digital and mobile telecommunication, and social network sites. Overall global growth in active accounts and users translates into increasing legal complexities.

GLOBAL DATA SNAPSHOT (2015-16)

Description	2016 (2015) data	% Penetration
World Population, % urban	7.40 (7.21) billion	54 (53)%
-Unique Mobile Users	3.79 (3.65) billion	51 (51)%
-Active Internet Users	3.42 (3.01) billion	46 (42)%
-Active Social Media Accounts	2.31 (2.08) billion	31 (29)%
-Active Mobile Social Accounts	1.97 (1.69) billion	27 (23)%

Sources: Smart Insights. Global social media research summary 2016 (April 21, 2016), http://www.smartinsights.com/social-media-marketing/social-media-strategy/new-global-social-media-research/; The Next Web. 2015 worldwide Internet, mobile and social media trends: get into 376 pages of data (January 2015), http://thenextweb.com/socialmedia/2015/01/21/2015-worldwide-internet-mobile-social-media-trends-get-376-pages-data/.

Social media have spawned new litigation.[8] As Chip Stewart, a journalism law professor, observed: "Centuries of jurisprudence about media law provides a foundation for understanding the particular challenges we face when using social media. However, courts, lawmakers, and regulators have done little to keep up with these challenges, particularly for media professionals."[9]

In 2002, cases began to challenge a desire by some to remain anonymous online — even in the face of lawsuits. Some Internet service providers (ISPs), under pressure, removed controversial Web pages. In one early case, a lawsuit against a professor was dismissed when the court applied Louisiana's anti-SLAPP (strategic lawsuits against public participation) law, which granted First Amendment freedoms to Web publish-

ers.[10] By 2016, though, a D.C. Circuit Court of Appeals panel voted 2-1 to back the Federal Communications Commission (FCC) reclassification of wired and mobile ISPs as common carriers exercising no editorial control over Internet content.[11]

More broadly, sites such as RateMyProfessors.com offer students the opportunity to openly criticize instructors, evaluate them and compare them to others on campus. Further, the explosion of user-created Internet video is one important challenge to traditional norms about copyright and content property law.[12] YouTube and similar sites must police users in order to respond to media company complaints about copyright infringement in use of music and video.

Data suggest that Internet media freedom is spreading across the globe. New technologies spread adoption of new ideas. The diffusion of the Web was explosive after its introduction to the general public in about 1994. Today the number of users worldwide is estimated at nearly 3.5 billion, or nearly half of world population. Data, however, do not explain what social media theorist Jeremy Hunsinger describes as *how* technological changes transform "the legal system of torts from a punitive one to a profitable one," which may be "deeply problematic" for democracy.

Data painted enormous growth on every continent, and it was most dramatic in Asia. China had more broadband connections than the United States.[13] China took the lead in the number of Internet users in 2009.[14] However, freedom continued to be a concern, as China pressured computer manufacturers to preinstall filtering software and resist outside nudging to be more open.[15] The 2010 re-licensing of Google in China was contingent

---

[7] B. IRVING FANG, ALPHABET TO INTERNET, MEDIATED COMMUNICATION IN OUR LIVES 286 (2008).

[8] *See LaRussa v. Twitter, Inc.,* CITIZEN MEDIA LAW PROJECT, July 8, 2009, http://www.citmedialaw.org/threats/la-russa-v-twitter-inc. St. Louis Cardinals baseball manager Tony LaRussa dropped his case that came after an unnamed user created an account at twitter.com/TonyLaRussa and posted parody updates. LaRussa alleged cybersquatting, right of publicity, trademark infringement and trademark dilution following numerous postings that included his photograph. Earlier, *Hollywood Reporter* said designer Dawn Simorangkir, known as Boudoir Queen, claimed defamation, invasion of privacy and emotional distress after Courtney Love tweeted: "oi vey don't f--- with my wardrobe or you will end up in a circle of scorched earth hunted til your dead" [sic]. *See Simorangkir v. Love,* CITIZEN MEDIA LAW PROJECT, June 12, 2009, http://www.citmedialaw.org/threats/simorangkir-v-love.

[9] DAXTON R. STEWART, SOCIAL MEDIA AND THE LAW, A GUIDEBOOK FOR COMMUNICATION STUDENTS AND PROFESSIONALS VII (2013).

[10] *See* Dan Carnevale, *Professor Who Runs Web Site Can Remain Anonymous for at Least a While Longer,* CHRON. OF HIGHER EDUC., Feb. 6, 2002, *available at* http://chronicle.com/free/2002/02/2002020601t.htm. A University of Louisiana at Monroe professor on his Web site alleged administrators had mismanaged funds. At first, the professor sought to remain anonymous and appealed a lower court decision that ordered a California ISP to identify him so that a university vice president could sue for libel and slander. Associated Press, *Anonymous University Web Critic Steps Forward,* FIRST AMENDMENT CENTER, June 3, 2002, http://www.firstamendmentcenter.org/news.aspx?id=3823&printer-friendly=y. The professor later identified himself, and the ISP removed the page. *See also Web Site Defamation Suit Against Professor Dismissed,* REPORTERS COMMITTEE FOR FREEDOM OF THE PRESS, May 29, 2003, http://www.rcfp.org/news/2003/ 0529baxter.html.

[11] U.S. Telecomm V. FCC, No. 15-1063, slip. Op. 1619173 (D.C. Cir. June 14, 2016).

[12] *See* Viacom v. YouTube & Google, 253 F.R.D. 256 (S.D.N.Y. July 2, 2008).

[13] *See Internet World Stats,* http://www.internetworldstats.com/asia.htm, June 2, 2008. Broadband China Internet connections were 66,464,000 not counting Hong Kong and Macao. Usage and Population Statistics, June 7, 2007, http://www.internetworldstats.com/stats.htm. The report also reports 399 million users in Asia (10.7 percent market penetration), 315 million users in Europe (38.9 percent market penetration), 233 million users in North America (69.7 percent market penetration), 96 million users in Latin America (17.3 percent market penetration), 33 million users in Africa (3.6 percent market penetration), 19 million users in the Middle East (10 percent market penetration), and 18 million users in Australia/Oceana (53.5 percent market penetration).

[14] *See* Jeremy Reimer, China to Overtake US in Number of Internet Users in 2009, July 15, 2007, http://arstechnica.com.

[15] *See* Jacqui Cheng, China Hits Pause on Mandatory Filtering Software, July 6, 2009, http://arstechnica.com. Green Dam Youth Escort is a client software promoted as a

upon regulatory limitations. Meanwhile, in Germany and other countries, there was increased protection of user privacy and emergence of a "right to be forgotten" online.[16] So-called "law-based management" required Google to accept government filtering in various countries, such as China:

> In the application letter, Guxiang (Google) pledged to "abide by Chinese law," and "ensure the company provides no law breaking content as stipulated in the 57th statement in China's regulations concerning telecommunications."
>
> The statement says that any organization or individual is prohibited from using the Internet to spread any content that attempts to subvert state power, undermine national security, infringe on national reputation and interests, or that incites ethnic hatred and secession, transmits pornography or violence.
>
> Guxiang also accepted that all content it provides is subject to supervision of government regulators.[17]

NATIONAL INTERNET USERS (2016)

Country	Users	% Growth 2015-2016	% Penetration
1. China	721,434,547	2.2%	52.2%
2. India	462,124,989	30.5	34.8
3. United States	286,942,362	1.1	88.5
4. Brazil	139,111,185	5.1	66.4
5. Japan	115,111,595	0.1	91.1
6. Russia	102,258,256	0.3	71.3
7. Nigeria	86,219,965	5.0	64.1
8. Germany	72,016,605	0.6	88.0
9. United Kingdom	60,273,385	0.9	92.6
10. Mexico	58,016,997	2.1	45.1
World Total	3,424,971,237	7.5	46.1

Source: Internet Live Stats (June 2016), http://www.internetlivestats.com/internet-users-by-country/. Note: It took a decade to reach one billion Internet users, but the second billion was reached just five years later in 2010. Four years later, by the end of 2014, there were more than 3 billion global users.

As Internet use around the world has continued to increase, the Pew Internet & American Life project predicts that Internet usage will lead to more information and unity and potentially "might also increase domestic tensions" in the world.[18] As futurist David Mathison has observed: "Because of today's technology, almost anyone can be an author, musician, filmmaker, journalist, politician, blogger, cartoonist, podcaster, speaker, radio or TV host, or licensor."[19]

New technologies allow interactive collaboration. For example, the author of this chapter has used Twitter (@JeremyHL) to have ongoing discussions with sources and subjects and even plan formal presentations. The use of unfiltered channels also opens new avenues for social conflict that may trigger litigation: Facebook in 2013 sued a user allegedly posting deceptive spam messages promising pornographic video of celebrities Justin Bieber and Salena Gomez.[20] This may be called the social media decade, as disputes lead to more frequent case law and interpretation.

At the heart of the technological revolution is the empowerment of individuals to exercise free speech:

- In *Minnesota v. Tatro*, the state supreme court upheld discipline against a mortuary science student posting "satire" about a body on her Facebook wall.[21]
- A juror posting on Facebook a vague verdict announcement that violated a judge's instructions was not found to prejudice conviction of a state senator.[22]
- Facebook Live streamed a broadcast video of a suicide and a rape.[23]
- Facebook exercises "community standards" in defining pornographic content that it filters.[24]

CONVERGING VOICE, DATA AND VIDEO

The convergence of printed text, photographs, audio and video presents challenges across the legal spectrum, from libel and

---

way to block child access to pornography, but may also filter political messages.

[16] *See* Jane Kirtley, *"Misguided In Principle and Unworkable In Practice": It Is Time To Discard The Reporters Committee Doctrine Of Practical Obscurity (And Its Evil Twin, The Right To Be Forgotten)*, 20 COMMUNICATION L. AND POL'Y 91, 105 (2015) (Europeans appear to "have an affirmative right" to ask Google to remove Web links.).

[17] Xinhua, China Confirms Google's Operation License Renewed, http://news.xinhuanet.com/english2010/china/2010-07/11/c_13394498.htm (July 11, 2010), para. 4-6. Also reporting: "The official said the country will stick to the opening-up policy and welcome foreign investments in China, but the government will follow the principle of law-based management." *Id.* at para. 8.

---

[18] *See* Deborah Fallows, China's Population Explosion (2007), at para. 2, http://uploadi.www.ris.org/editor/1184918816China_Internet_July_2007.pdf.

[19] DAVID MATHISON, BE THE MEDIA XV (2009).

[20] Don't Spam Facebook With Fake Bieber Porn Unless You Want to Get Sued, http://techcrunch.com/2013/11/21/dont-spam-facebook-with-fake-bieber-porn-unless-you-want-to-get-sued/.

[21] 816 N.W.2d 509 (Minn. 2012). *See also*, Barbara A. Lee, *Student-Faculty Academic Conflicts: Emerging Legal Theories and Judicial Review*, 83 MISS. L.J. 837 (2014).

[22] United States v. Fumo, 655 F.3d 288 (3d Cir. 2011).

[23] *The (Very) Dark Side of Live Streaming That no One Seems Able to Stop*, WASH. POST, JUNE 5, 2016, *available at* http://www.washingtonpost.com/news/the-intersect/wp/2016/05/26/the-very-dark-side-of-live-streaming-that-no-one-seems-to-stop/.

[24] *See Who Defines Pornography? These Days, It's Facebook*, WASH. POST, MAY 25, 2016, *available at* http://www.washingtonpost.om/news/in-theory/wp/2016/05/25/who-defines-pornography-these-days-its-facebook/.

privacy to obscenity and copyright issues.[25] Technology scholar John Pavlik sees First Amendment protection of "public media" and its extension to online media on the one hand as differing in the video area in which fewer restrictions exist, but also "subject to restrictions from any country, regardless of whether that country is part of the video providers' intended audience."[26] Social media include photographs and video that may trigger cross-border regulation.

TOP DIGITAL MEDIA PROPERTIES (2016)

Internet and social media use are fragmented across dozens of popular sites and countless numbers of others. In the past year, Facebook moved into second place in the rankings behind Google. Microsoft, Comcast NBC Universal and CBS Interactive also moved up positions on the list of total unique visitors.

Property	TOT Unique Visitors By Platform (000s)
1. Google Sites	245,167
2. Facebook	207,654
3. Yahoo Sites	205,419
4. Microsoft Sites	196,320
5. Amazon Sites	183.020
6. AOL, Inc.	169,930
7. Comcast NBC Universal	161,020
8. CBS Interactive	156,475
9. Apple	139,812
10. Mode Media	139,168

Source: *comScore Ranks the Top 50 U.S. Digital Media Properties for April 2016*, comScore, February 24, 2016, *available at* http://www.comscore.com/Insights/Rankings/comScore-Ranks-the-Top-50-US-Digital-Media-Properties-for-January-2016.

Digital technology unleashed stiff competition among video services, and some regulatory battles were about which companies and media technologies would survive and prosper. Telecommunication deregulation allowed, for example, phone companies to provide video and cable companies to offer phone services. This form of cross-media competition came at a time of mergers and corporate consolidation. Some observers worried that telecommunications cartels threatened to monopolize

mass media and the Internet. Lawmakers and the FCC debated such issues as net neutrality, pricing, connection speeds and bandwidth concerns.[27] Net neutrality issues included the desire of cable companies to offer premium download speeds that could favor some content providers over others. Web and smart app phone speeds also vary, and regulators and courts must decide what constitutes fair competition.

Network Neutrality

The U.S. Court of Appeals for the D.C. Circuit rejected portions of the FCC Open Internet Order developed in 2010 addressing network neutrality and other issues. In *Verizon v. FCC* a three-judge panel relied upon a previous FCC definition of broadband cable as information service providers rather than telecommunications common carriers.

While the court upheld FCC authority to encourage broadband infrastructure deployment under the Telecommunication Act of 1996, the Open Internet Order went further in requiring disclosure of traffic speeds, anti-blocking and anti-discrimination requirements: "Even though the Commission has general authority to regulate in this arena, it may not impose requirements that contravene express statutory mandates."

The court distinguished legal issues of Internet backbone networks, broadband providers, edge providers (Amazon and Google, for example) and end users. Social media users of Facebook, though, "may often act as edge providers by creating and sharing content that is consumed by other end users." At the same time, broadband Internet Service Providers also may offer content and software applications.

In *National Cable & Telecommunications Ass'n v. Brand X Internet Services*, the Supreme Court upheld FCC classification of cable through its reasonable interpretation of vague language in the 1996 Act. When Comcast subscribers later complained about slowed peer-to-peer services, the FCC ordered disclosure in 2008. The D.C. Circuit, however, vacated the order, ruling the FCC failed to demonstrate regulatory authority over network management practices.

The FCC went forward with Open Internet proceedings in 2009 and 2010. Faced with a contrary Comcast decision, it then sought to reclassify broadband. The successful Verizon appeal was based upon (1) lack of FCC regulatory authority, (2) arbitrary and capricious rules, and (3) actions contrary to the 1996 Act. By attempting to reclassify broadband as a common carrier, the FCC did so without identifying its statutory authority.

The FCC's ISP common carrier re-classification in 2015 was first decided by a three-judge panel in 2016. Six months after the

---

[25] *See, e.g.,* Leibovitz v. Paramount, 137 F.3d 109 (2d Cir. 1998) (copyright); Zeran v. America Online, 129 F.3d 327 (4th Cir. 1997) (libel); ApolloMedia Corp. v. Reno, 19 F. Supp. 2d 1081 (N.D. Cal. 1998) (obscenity); Blumenthal v. Drudge and America Online, 992 F. Supp. 44 (D.D.C. 1998) (libel); Jessup-Morgan v. America Online, Inc., 20 F. Supp. 2d 1105 (E.D. Mich. 1998) (privacy); Cubby v. CompuServe, 776 F. Supp. 135 (S.D.N.Y. 1991) (libel).

[26] JOHN V. PAVLIK, MEDIA IN THE DIGITAL AGE 174-75 (2008). He concludes that history will judge whether the digital transition benefited individual media producers, large corporations or both.

[27] *See* Kim Hart & Kara Kehaulani Goo, *Tech Faceoff: Net Neutrality, in the Eye of the Beholder,* WASH. POST, July 2, 2006, at F4.

D.C. Circuit Court of appeals heard *United States Telecom Assoc. v. FCC*, the court voted 2-1 to deny a petition for review of the FCC Order. The government rules blocked ISPs from purposely slowing speeds from specific sites. In its motion to dismiss, the FCC told the court that the rules were "carefully-tailored" to favor Internet openness.

The FCC's "bright line" rules ban blocking lawful pages, throttling speeds, and paid prirotization of the Internet. Importantly, the D.C. Circuit panel addressed application of the rules to emerging mobile: The FCC "permissibly found that mobile broadband — like all broadband — is a telecommunication service subject to common carrier regulation under Title II of the Communications Act. The majority also recognized the mobile marketplace and a projection that 90 percent of broadband may be mobile and smart by 2019. The FCC "permissibly found that mobile broadband now qualifies as interconnected because it gives subscribers the ability to communicate to all users of the newly defined public switched network." The majority quoted the FCC Order: "Broadband users should be able to expect that they will be entitled to the same Internet openness protections no matter what technology they use to access the Internet" (citing 2015 Open Internet Order, 30 FCC Rcd. At 5638, para. 92).

The common carrier telecommunications service classification explicitly rejects First Amendment issues: "The absence of any First Amendment concern in the context of common carriers rests on the understanding that such entities, insofar as they are subject to equal access mandates, merely facilitate the transmission of speech of others rather than engage in speech in their own right." The majority observed that broadband providers provided no messages and little editorial control over content. Instead, the FCC views broadband as "mere conduits for the messages of others." The majority distinguished any case where a broadband provider also operates a news or weather channel, exercises content decisions and qualifies for First Amendment protection. However, most broadband providers do not exercise editorial judgment similar to a newspaper or cable TV operation. "In that regard, the role of broadband providers is analogous to that of telephone companies: They act as neutral, indiscriminant platforms for transmission of speech of any and all users."

While broadband providers may face network capacity issues, the majority concluded that these buffering issues are temporary. The FCC defined broadband in data marketing terms — mallowing end users to send and receive data across "all or substantially all Internet endpoints."

The decision of the panel may be heard *en banc* by the full D.C. Circuit Court of Appeals. If so, there also will be a review of the dissenting opinon. In it, the senior circuit judge for the court observed that the FCC failed to offer evidence and full analysis for changing broadband classification from an information to a telecommunications service. The dissenting opinion called for a thorough analysis of broadband competition, an accurate reading of regulatory history, and use of available data.

Early commentary on the decision observed that it may be the first battle to stop the FCC from discarding a long-held ISP distinction between wired and mobile, but for now the rules allow the FCC to consider online privacy and put a check on FTC broadband regulation. The rapid rise in mobile smartphone and tablet use to access rich media content is likely to spark new regulatory challenges.[28]

In 2014, the D.C. Circuit struck down a FCC attempt to address net neutrality. In 2015, however, the FCC voted to treat ISPs as common carriers similar to telephone companies, and a panel of the same court upheld the Order.[29] However, the full appeals court and U.S. Supreme Court are likely to offer future constitutional interpretation on net neutrality. By reclassifying broadband services as telecommunication, the FCC acknowledged rapid changes, including mobile access to video services. Congress could attempt legislative alternatives.

The First Amendment and Cyberspace

A review of new media begins with free expression theory and practice, but it must go beyond the law to view social change in an increasingly technological world. Defamation, as we saw in chapter 6, is one example of how law may be defined within unique cultural contexts around the world. Social media sites, such as Twitter, spark new cases and issues.

Tweets, which are messages of no more than 140 characters on Twitter.com, are receiving attention from lawyers. *The National Law Journal* reported in 2008 that micro-blogging is a quick way to get an employee or an employer in trouble. Such interaction could be subpeonaed during a case.

The tech Web site Mashable.com (@Mashable) identified four potential lawsuit areas: company secrets, invasion of privacy,

---

[28] Sources for this discussion of net neutrality include: United States Telecom Association v. FCC, No. 15-1063, slip. Op. 1619173 (D.C. Cir. June 14, 2016); Stuart N. Brotman, Tangled Up in The Legal Web of Net Neutrality, June 21, 2016, http://www.brookings.edu/blogs/techtank/posts/2016/06/21-tangled-legal-web-net-neutrality-brotman; Brendon Fowler, James Ianelli, Lawrence Robert Krevor & Marc Martin, Six Key Consequences of the D.C. Circuit Upholding Net Neutrality, June 21, 2016, http://www.jdsupra.com/legalnews/six-key-consequences-f-the-d-c-circuit-65623/; National Cable & Telecommunications Ass'n v. Brand X Internet Services, 545 U.S. 967 (2005); Verizon v. FCC, 740 F.3d 623 (D.C. Cir. 2014); D.C. *Appeals Court Strikes Down Net Neutrality Rules*, MASHABLE, Jan. 14, 2014 http://mashable.com/2014/01/14/fcc-net-neutrality-ruling/; Alex Vlisides, *D.C. Circuit Strikes Down FCC "Net Neutrality" Rules*, SILHA BULLETIN, Spring 2014, at 6-7; *New FCC Rules Spur Heated Debate anout Net Neutrality Regulation*, SILHA BULLETIN, Winter/Spring 2015, at 20.

[29] *Protecting and Promoting the Open Internet*, 80 Fed. Reg. 19,738 (Apr. 13, 2015), 47 C.F.R. 1.

defamation, trademark violations and wrongful employee termination claims. In 2009, for example, Horizon Group Management, which manages rental property in Chicago, sued tenant Amanda Bonnen for $50,000 after she tweeted: "You should just come anyway. Who said sleeping in a moldy apartment was bad for you? Horizon realty thinks it's okay." Bonnen had just twenty followers on Twitter. The libel lawsuit claimed the tweet damaged Horizon's reputation. A Cook County judge dismissed the case in finding the tweet was too vague.

FCC AND FTC ISSUE AGENDAS

Administrative law agencies, such as the FCC and FTC, derive delegated authority from the U.S. Congress to regulate areas based upon complexity and specialized knowledge.

FCC Key Issues
- Texting while driving
- Unwanted marketing calls
- Affordable phone service
- Caller ID and spoofing
- Telephone bills and charges
- Disability issues
- Broadband access
- Media ownership

FTC Key Issues
- Online privacy
- Email hacking
- Crowdfunding deception
- Illegal robocalls
- Deceptive auto advertising
- Consumer personal data protection
- Retail tracking opt our choices
- Mobile identity theft
- Marketing disclosure

Sources: FCC.gov and FTC.gov (July 2016).

The Twitter Law site (http://www.twitterlaw.net/) tracks developments in policies, law and ethics. Twitter has changed its Terms of Service in a number of important ways. Silha Center for the Study of Media Ethics & Law Research Assistant Scott Memmel reported in 2016 that Twitter sought to stop violent, harrassing and terroristic tweets. Twitter labels "hateful conduct" as tweets threatening to "race, ethnicity, national origin, sexual orientation, gender, gender identity, religious affiliation, age, disability, or disease." Among Twitter's concerns were attacks, such as rape threats, on women journalists. The future of First Amendment freedoms, in part, rests on the ability of speakers to use social media platforms. Twitter and other sites, however, exercise editorial judgment

and filtering.[30]

The First Amendment does not mention new technologies, but lawmakers, regulators and the courts have attempted a variety of strategies to apply it. For example, the U.S. Supreme Court recognized that the unique traits of each mass medium may permit different constitutional standards.[31] Yet new technology characteristics often are not apparent until long after an introduction. Congress, the FCC, the FTC, other regulators applying administrative law, and the courts must choose to (1) regulate an emerging technology before it is well understood or widely used; (2) regulate during the uncertain developmental and evolutionary period; (3) attempt to formulate logical and consistent regulatory models after the new technology is in general use; or (4) avoid regulation altogether.

Legislation frequently is challenged in the courts on First Amendment and other grounds. State privacy law, for example, remains an unsystematic set of measures related to arrest, banking, medical and school records, computer crime and justice, government data, employment and other issues.[32]

Adding to confusion is the FTC's implementation of the Children's Online Privacy Protection Act,[33] known as COPPA, originally part of congressional attempts to protect children in cyberspace.[34] Web sites had to require operators to post privacy policies, provide notice and obtain parental consent prior to collecting certain personal information from children.[35] The rule allowed Internet operators to submit individual regulatory plans for dealing with children under age 13, and many Web sites responded by restricting access. Legal scholars raised constitutional concerns about, among other aspects, the chat room restrictions of COPPA, which require parental consent and may not be narrowly tailored.[36]

Often, it is unclear whether, or how much, the technology of a medium should affect the legal protection of the message con-

---

[30] Simply Measured, The State of Social Marketing, 2016 Annual Report; Scott Memmel, *Twitter's Change in terms of Service to Limit "Harmful Speech" Garners Criticism*, SILHA BULLETIN, Winter/Spring 2016, at 25-27, *available at* http://conservancy .umn.edu/discover?query=Silha+Bulletin; Tresa Baldes, *Beware: Your "Tweet" on Twitter Could be Trouble*, NAT'L L.J., Dec. 22, 2008, *available at* http://www. law.com; Pete Cashmore, *Twitter Lawsuits: 4 Reasons Your Tweets Might be Trouble*, MASHABLE, http://mashable.com 2008; Twitter Lawsuit Dismissed, Jan. 21, 2010; http://chicagoist. com/2010/01/21/twitter_lawsuit_dismissed.php; Marian Wang, *UPDATED: Rounding up the Buzz*, CHICAGO NOW.COM (2009).

[31] *See, e.g.,* Times Film Corp. v. Chicago, 365 U.S. 43, 50 (1961).

[32] *See* Electronic Privacy Information Center, *Privacy Laws by State,* June 13, 2001, http://www.epic.org/privacy/consumer/states.html.

[33] 16 CFR 312.10(a) (2003). *See also* 65 F.R. 99 (May 22, 2000), at 32100.

[34] Federal Trade Commission, Children's Online Privacy Protection Rule, 15 U.S.C. § 6501 (1999).

[35] 65 F.R. 45 (Mar. 7, 2000), at 11947.

[36] *See* Charlene Simmons, *Protecting Children While Silencing Them: The Children's Online Privacy Protection Act and Children's Free Speech Rights,* 12 COMM. L. & POL'Y 119 (2007).

veyed. History of a technology — such as telephone service — appears to affect the courts' willingness to apply the First Amendment.[37] The result is a highly detailed, often inconsistent and confusing array of regulations and rulings.[38] Several state legislatures, for example, have passed a patchwork of data privacy laws,[39] while they and the federal government also became concerned about unwanted email, called "spam." A study by the FTC found deception in 66 percent of unsolicited commercial email.[40] Scholar Jasmine McNealy reported that since 2005 twenty states passed or amended criminal laws, and various federal proposals also have targeted "phishing" emails designed to steal private information.[41]

While state legislation may be designed to solve the nagging concern of email spam, this problem goes beyond the full reach of law and regulation. Even technological solutions, such as filtering software, fail to stop all unwanted email. The FTC continues to prosecute those who send spam — in one case winning a $2.5 million judgment for CAN-SPAM violations.[42]

The FTC rule was aimed at protecting identifiable information such as names, addresses, email addresses and phone numbers.[43] In response, about 147 individuals and corporations filed comments with the FTC. Retailer Amazon.com, for example, complained that the rule was "likely to interfere with the overall customer experience and inherent benefits of the Internet."[44] The FTC sought more authority over Internet consumer privacy because fewer than half of the Web sites in the study had implemented adequate privacy protections.[45] In the end, Internet e-commerce and shopping continued to grow under the new rules. The blending of such Internet new technology issues with converging questions about telephone and video regulation raised the prospect that the legal landscape would continue to be complex.

Video Services and Telephone Company History

Under the Communications Act of 1934, telephone companies were common carriers that had to provide non-discriminatory services at similar rates to anyone wishing to send and receive messages over their systems. Different portions of the act govern phone companies, broadcast stations and cable systems, making the law cumbersome. As fiber optic technologies developed, many government regulators believed phone companies would use their large size, universal penetration and economic power to drive other multi-channel video providers out of business. Of course, cable and broadcast lobbyists helped fuel these fears within the political, policy-making system.[46] Concerns about phone company behavior pre-date the break-up initiated in the 1970s and settled in the 1980s.

The problem of ownership concentration was known from the dawn of the telephone age. The dominance was so great that the federal government filed lawsuits against the original AT&T in 1914 and again in 1956. The government charged that AT&T violated antitrust laws by attempting to monopolize local and national telecommunications markets for service and equipment. Each time, AT&T would sign a consent decree, promising that it would no longer engage in the impermissible actions, but change was rarely seen.

Similar concerns arose during the early years of the cable industry, when many phone companies owned cable systems. They often needed to string above ground lines, but local governments sometimes refused to allow cable operators to erect their own poles, which was inefficient. So, cable operators rented or leased space on existing poles that telephone or power companies owned. From cable's earliest days and through the 1960s, though, the FCC heard many complaints that affiliated cable operators were not being allowed to rent space on telephone poles. In 1960, the FCC responded by adopting the telephone-cable cross-ownership ban to eliminate the incentive for phone companies to discriminate against cable competitors.

In 1974, the U.S. Department of Justice filed a third antitrust suit against AT&T, claiming that the 1956 consent decree had failed to prevent monopoly. Originally, there were twenty-two Bell Operating Companies, which were reorganized into seven Regional Bell Operating Companies. The new agreement, settled

---

[37] *See, e.g.,* Susan D. Ross, *A Decade After Divestiture: Regional Bells, Video Programming and the First Amendment,* 21 Rutgers Computer & Tech. L. J. 143 (1995).

[38] *See, e.g.,* AT&T v. Iowa Utilities Bd., 525 U.S. 366, 397 (1999) (noting that "it would be a gross understatement to say that the Telecommunications Act of 1996 is not a model of clarity").

[39] *See* Rachel Zimmerman & Glenn R. Si, *Lobbyists Swarm to Stop Tough Privacy Bills,* State, Apr. 21, 2000, http://www.djreprints.com.

[40] Federal Trade Commission, Internet Service Providers (ISPs) Reportedly Blocked 78-93% of Spam in a 2007 Survey, Spam Summit: The Next Generation of Threats and Solutions. Staff Report, Division of Marketing Practices, Nov. 2007, *available at* http://www.ftc.gov/os/woo7/12/071220spamsummitreport.pdf.

[41] Jasmine E. McNealy, *Angling for Phishers: Legislative Responses to Deceptive E-Mail,* 13 Comm. L. & Pol'y 275, 281 (2008).

[42] *See* FTC v. Sili Neutraceuticals, No. 07C 4541 (N.D. Ill., Feb. 4, 2008). The standards for commercial email are enforced by the FTC. CAN-SPAM is short for "Controlling the Assault of Non-Solicited Pornography and Marketing" — an act passed in 2003.

[43] The FTC Web site is http://www.ftc.gov.

[44] Children's Online Privacy Protection Rule, Public Comments Received, *available at* http://www.ftc.gov/privacy/comments/amazoncom.htm (June 11, 1999).

[45] *See* Robert L. Jackson, *FTC Seeks Online Privacy Law From Congress,* L.A. Times, May 23, 2000, at C3.

[46] Industry critics claim regulated industries exert too much influence through their frequent access to regulators. *See* Erwin G. Krasnow et al., The Politics of Broadcast Regulation (3d ed. 1982); Philip M. Napoli, *The Federal Communications Commission and Broadcast Policy-Making — 1965-1995: A Logistic Regression Analysis of Interest Group Influence,* 5 Comm. L. & Pol'y 203 (2000).

in 1982, became known as the "Modification of the Final Judgment."[47] It forced AT&T to sell off its local telephone service divisions, and AT&T then became only a long-distance provider. The newly formed regional and local phone companies were limited to local phone services.

THE REGIONAL BELL OPERATING COMPANIES (RBOCs) 2010-16

AT&T (including **SBC** and **BellSouth**) — Covering California, Texas, Illinois, Michigan and Ohio, SBC, formerly Southwestern Bell, acquired Ameritech (Michigan Bell, Ohio Bell and Wisconsin Bell) and Pacific Telesis (Pacific Bell and Nevada Bell). The BellSouth (South Central Bell and Southern Bell) territory in the southeast was renamed.

CenturyLink — It acquired all of the former Qwest and USWest (Montana Bell, Northwestern Bell and Pacific Northwestern Bell) territory in the upper midwest, west and northwest.

Verizon — Bell Atlantic purchased Nynex (New England Telephone and New York telephone) and later became Verizon. It now also includes what was GTE and MCI, as a $10.6 billion deal was completed in 2011.[48]

Congress adopted the FCC's cross-ownership ban as part of the 1984 Cable Act. It prevented all telephone companies — including approximately 2,500 independent phone companies not formerly affiliated with AT&T — from owning or operating cable systems.[49]

The original seven RBOCs (now merged to three — AT&T, CenturyLink and Verizon) became the nation's largest providers of local phone service: Ameritech, Bell Atlantic, Bell South, Nynex, Pacifio Telesis, Southwestern Bell and USWest. They chafed at many restrictions in the MFJ, including the ban on information services. In 1991, federal district judge Harold Greene oversaw the consent decree and essentially removed the information services ban.[50] However, that left in place the 1984 Cable Act ban on telephone-cable cross-ownership. Several RBOCs sued and argued that the ban abridged their First Amendment rights to free speech. Beginning in 1993, every court that heard such a case agreed and overturned the ban.[51]

While the RBOCs were challenging the Cable Act ban, the FCC also gave phone companies a way to be involved in video. In 1992, the Commission allowed the RBOCs to offer a common carrier video service called "video dialtone."[52] With it, a phone company used its wires and support services to provide video similar to television signal quality.

Telephone companies had to provide the service on a non-discriminatory, first-come-first-served basis. The companies, historically viewed as common carriers, provided households access to shared long distance lines. In this environment, the phone companies were not involved in content or editing. Still, video services seemed to redefine phone companies. A telephone company could offer its own video services over a VDT system on a limited basis. Unlike cable television, however, VDT systems did not require local city or county franchises — neither the telephone company nor the programming services met a legal definition of a cable system.[53] Cable companies opposed VDT systems and argued that the absence of franchising requirements gave VDT systems an unfair advantage.

The Telecommunications Act of 1996 eliminated the telephone-cable cross-ownership ban and allowed local phone companies to provide video programming in one of four ways:

- A firm offering local telephone service could also own a cable system as a subsidiary company. Telephone-owned systems would need to comply with all of the laws and local and state cable franchise requirements.

- A telephone company could operate a common carrier video service similar to VDT (although that term is no longer used) on a first-come-first-served basis. Under this approach, its video service would be regulated much as its common carrier telephone service.

- The "Open Video System" providers served both as common carriers of others' programming and as program providers. If outside demand for video carriage exceeds system capacity, then the OVS provider may program no more than one-third of its channels, with the remainder offered to other providers on a first-come-first-served basis. The systems were not required to obtain franchises, but local governments could require OVS fees equivalent to the franchise fees of a cable operator. By acting as video common carriers, OVS providers are absolved of some regulatory obligations.

- A phone company could offer video services through what is called "wireless cable." Wireless technology is further discussed later in the chapter and is perhaps the most important

---

[47] *See* United States v. Western Elec. Co., 552 F. Supp. 131 (D.D.C. 1982).

[48] The Telecommunications Act of 1996 allowed the so-called "Baby Bells" to compete in the long-distance market. At the same time, long-distance providers, such as AT&T and Sprint, were allowed to compete in the local telephone market.

[49] 47 U.S.C. § 613(b) (1984).

[50] *See* United States v. Western Elec. Co., 767 F. Supp. 308 (D.D.C. 1991); United States v. Western Elec. Co., 900 F.2d 283 (D.C. Cir. 1990).

[51] *See* Chesapeake & Potomac Tel. Co. v. United States, 830 F. Supp. 909 (E.D. Va. 1993), *aff'd* 42 F.3d 181 (4th Cir. 1994), *vacated and remanded,* 516 U.S. 415 (1996); Ameritech Corp. v. United States, 1994 U.S. Dist. LEXIS 4920 (Apr. 11, 1994). After adoption of the Telecommunications Act of 1996, 104 Pub. L. 104, the Supreme Court found this series of decisions moot, since Congress had answered the question

of whether telephone companies could offer video services. *See* United States v. Chesapeake & Potomac Tel. Co. of Virginia, 516 U.S. 415 (1996).

[52] *See* Telephone Company-Cable Television Cross-Ownership Rules, 7 F.C.C. Rcd. 5781 (1992).

[53] *See* Nat'l Cable Television Ass'n v. FCC, 33 F.3d 66 (D.C. Cir. 1994).

development in the new media technology area.

In 1999, the Fifth U.S. Circuit Court of Appeals overturned the law's exemption of OVS from local franchising in Dallas.[54] However, it found that Southwestern Bell Video Services, a subsidiary of SBC Communications that provided video to apartments, need not enter into a cable franchise agreement with Austin, Texas, because it was not a "cable operator" under federal and state law.[55] The FCC was left to reexamine its OVS rules. The 1996 Act seemed to permit, but not require, franchising of OVS.

In general, telephone companies prefer to compete with cable companies in the video business, but they would also like to avoid oversight and financial obligations imposed in franchising agreements.

In a case from Florida, a federal district court, citing the Dallas decision, held that state and federal regulations limited Palm Beach to narrow right-of-way regulation of BellSouth's services.[56] BellSouth failed to get the court to strike down the entire local ordinance as an unconstitutional violation of due process and the Commerce Clause, and Palm Beach was allowed to charge reasonable compensation for use of the public rights-of-way.[57] The court limited Palm Beach under Florida law to collect no more than 1 percent of gross receipts on local telephone services. Despite federal regulations, each state retains rights to delegate state regulatory authority to its local governments, if it so chooses.[58] A state could also preempt all home-rule by cities, towns, counties and other local units. In general, state public service commissions tend to exert a lot of control over these in-state telephone issues; and in many locations, telephone companies now compete side-by-side against cable companies for video customers.

In another case, a federal appeals court rejected Cablevision of Boston's claim that the city did not do enough to level the playing field when Boston Edison entered a joint venture to wire underground fiber optic cable for video services.[59] At issue was whether the cable company had been given a chance to participate.[60] The court held that under federal law the city was only required to manage disruption caused by the work. It had no obligation to monitor the fiber optic business deal. State or federal regulators, however, might concern themselves with such issues. State regulators may be concerned with service quality and consumer rights. In general, fiber optic cables dramatically expanded the number of available lines and the range of services. Long-distance phone calls, for example, went from an expensive proposition limited to the elite to a common and relatively inexpensive consumer use. The expansion of telephone services, however, is challenging for regulators applying traditional rules.

In the United States, a telephone company generally is not permitted to purchase an existing cable system located in the same service area, nor is a cable system allowed to buy a telephone company where both provide service. A rule the FCC adopted before passage of the 1996 Act prohibited any cable system operator from passing its wires by more than 30 percent of all homes passed by cable in the United States (and 35 percent if the company is minority-controlled).[61] A federal appellate court ruled that a challenge to this regulation was not yet ready to be heard by the courts.[62]

The RBOCs also challenged provisions of the 1996 law. They argued that it unfairly punishes them by requiring delays until competition exists before providing advanced services. In 1998, a federal circuit court upheld the FCC's effective competition standard before allowing a RBOC to offer long-distance services.[63] The court later rejected another RBOC's constitutional challenge to the Telecommunications Act's mandate that Bell companies provide electronic publishing only through separate affiliates.[64] It said the rule was a well-justified, content-neutral mechanism to prevent monopolies and unfair competition. The Supreme Court refused to review rulings that upheld special restrictions of the RBOCs.

Even before the 1996 Act was adopted, USWest (now Century Link) had invested in Time Warner. Shortly after the act's passage, USWest agreed to acquire Continental Cablevision for $5.3 billion. Through these two transactions, USWest had a potential reach of more than sixteen million customers, approximately one in every four cable subscribers. In 1997, the FCC approved another major merger between British Telecom and MCI Communications. The Supreme Court refused to review a circuit court of appeals ruling granting a small telephone provider $1.54 million and possible punitive damages as a result of

---

[54] City of Dallas v. FCC, 165 F.3d 341 (5th Cir. 1999).

[55] City of Austin v. Southwestern Bell Video Servs., 193 F.3d 309 (5th Cir. 1999).

[56] Bellsouth Telecomm. v. Town of Palm Beach, 127 F. Supp. 2d 1348 (S.D. Fla. 1999), aff'd in part, rev'd in part, 252 F.3d 1169 (11th Cir. 2001).

[57] See Federal Telecommunications Act of 1996, 47 U.S.C. § 253 (1999). The act preempted local control over telecommunications in general, but allowed for nondiscriminatory regulation of rights-of-way. See Bellsouth v. City of Coral Springs, 42 F. Supp. 2d 1304 (S.D. Fla. 1999).

[58] See AT&T Commc'ns v. City of Dallas, 8 F. Supp. 2d 582 (N.D. Texas 1998).

[59] Cablevision of Boston v. Public Improvement Comm'n., 184 F.3d 88 (1st Cir. 1999).

[60] Id. at 92-93.

[61] Horizontal and Vertical Ownership Limits, Second Report and Order, 8 F.C.C. Rcd. 8565 (1993).

[62] Time Warner Entm't. Co. v. FCC, 93 F.3d 957 (D.C. Cir. 1996).

[63] SBC Commc'ns v. FCC, 138 F.3d 410 (D.C. Cir. 1998).

[64] BellSouth v. FCC, 144 F.3d 58 (D.C. Cir. 1998) (challenging that the special provisions violate the phone company's First and Fifth Amendment rights and constitute illegal punishment without a trial).

AT&T's unfair and anti-competitive treatment of the company; a year later, though, the case was reversed.[65] The Telecommunications Act has granted the FCC legal authority on a variety of issues, including definition of "reasonable period of time" for wireless service facilities applications.[66]

Rates, Services and Access

Rates for service and competitor access to new marketplaces continue to be important issues. For example, the Supreme Court decided that the FCC methods for determining interconnection rates required new entrants to pay so-called "incumbent local telephone companies" (or "incumbent local exchange carriers," ILECs) fees in order to access a market and provide competitive services.[67] The D.C. Circuit Court of Appeals, however, after two previous interventions, refused to overturn the FCC method for determining fair charges for coinless pay telephone calls.[68] The same court vacated one FCC order that would have transferred licenses from Ameritech to SBC Communications as part of a merger and forced regulators to revisit the scope of services allowed to be included.[69] Companies and the Commission also have bickered over the release of required audit data that the FCC uses to determine fairness of rates.[70]

Merger mania abounded among the so-called "Baby Bells" and others, and, in 2000, the FCC reviewed a proposed merger between the nation's second and third largest long-distance providers. The merger would have placed 80 percent of the residential long-distance market in the hands, once again, of two companies, AT&T and MCI (WorldCom). However, they called off the $129 billion deal following regulatory challenges in the United States and Europe.[71]

By 2002, a national economic downturn and questionable business practices led to a dramatic shakeout of the more than 600 competing telecommunications companies. Global Crossing and McLeodUSA filed for bankruptcy.[72] WorldCom collapsed, admitted to $11 billion in fraud, agreed to pay shareholders $500 million, and signed on to a settlement that included a $1.5-billion Securities and Exchange Commission fine.[73] The deal allowed MCI to continue to operate the business.

From a regulatory perspective, two questions involving the mergers and telecommunication companies (known as "telcos") are (1) Is there a settling point between free-wheeling marketplace economics and regulatory limits on monopolization of the market? and (2) What role will the courts play in managing the telecommunication marketplace in such an environment?

The Supreme Court, in two important cases in 2002, began to address several key issues raised by expanding phone services and wireless delivery methods. In *National Cable & Telecommunications Association v. Gulf Power*, it held that the FCC had authority under the Pole Attachments Act to set reasonable rates and conditions for high-speed Internet, traditional cable and wireless services. It found that "the subject matter here is technical, complex, and dynamic; and as a general rule, agencies have authority to fill the gaps where the statutes are silent."[74]

Moreover, in *Verizon Communications v. FCC*, the Court upheld rules requiring large local phone companies to allow new competitors reasonably priced access to existing networks.[75] The decision was hailed as a victory for smaller competitors but was by no means the end of telephone powerhouses' attempts to retain a competitive advantage.[76] In *AT&T v. FCC*, the D.C. Circuit Court of Appeals said regulators may allow Bell operating companies to have expanded access to new long-distance customers, if the competitors have access to local networks that meet the public interest.[77] In *SBC v. FCC*, circuit judges denied review of $6 million in FCC fines for merger agreement violations.[78]

The three proposed remaining "Baby Bell" RBOC phone companies — the new AT&T, Qwest and Verizon — earlier had faced millions of dollars in fines because they withheld or delayed providing access for competitors to lines and equipment, a small price to pay to gain a competitive edge in a business worth billions of dollars.[79] By 2004, the FCC had to draft new rules promoting competition after the Supreme Court left standing an appeals court decision that tossed out government rules. The inability to create legal regulation at first threatened AT&T and MCI, long-distance companies "struggling ... to launch their own

---

[65] Central Office Tel. v. American Tel. & Tel., 108 F.3d 981 (D.C. Cir. 1997). *Certiorari* in the case was granted Dec. 12, 1997, but then denied three days later. 522 U.S. 1036 (1997). The case, however, was later reversed in *Am. Tel. and Tel. Co. v. Central Office Tel., Inc.,* 524 U.S. 214 (1998), *reh'g denied,* 424 U.S. 972 (1998).

[66] City of Arlington, Texas et al. v. FCC, 133 S.Ct. 1863 (2013). The FCC set ninety days for co-location application processing, and 150 days for all other applications.

[67] Verizon Commc'ns v. FCC, 531 U.S. 1124 (2001).

[68] American Public Commc'n Council v. FCC, 215 F.3d 51 (D.C. Cir. 2000).

[69] Ass'n of Commc'ns Enterprises v. FCC, 235 F.3d 662 (D.C. Cir. 2001).

[70] *See* Qwest v. FCC, 229 F.3d 1172 (D.C. Cir. 2000).

[71] *See* Matt Moore, *Sprint, WorldCom Call Off Merger,* AP ONLINE, July 13, 2002, http://wwwwire.ap.org.

[72] *See* Kenneth Gilpin, *The Strong Will Survive the Fallout In Telecom,* N.Y. TIMES, Feb. 3, 2002, *available at* http://www.nytimes.com.

[73] *See* Associated Press, *WorldCom's Settlement Closely Watched,* N.Y. TIMES, May 27, 2003, *available at* http://www.nytimes.com.

[74] 534 U.S. 327, 339 (2002).

[75] 535 U.S. 467 (2002).

[76] *See* Stephen Labaton, *Leasing Rules for Phone Start-Ups Are Upheld,* N.Y. TIMES, May 14, 2002, *available at* http://www.nytimes.com.

[77] 369 F.3d 554 (D.C. Cir. 2004).

[78] 373 F.3d 32 (D.C. Cir. 2004).

[79] *See* Peter J. Howe, *Rivals Question Impact of Financial Penalties on Baby Bells,* BOSTON GLOBE, May 20, 2002, at C1.

brands of local service."[80] However, the new mergers pushed MCI to Verizon, and the SBC deals assumed the AT&T brand. At stake were the huge profits to be made from wireless and high-speed Internet services. The U.S. House of Representatives voted, in 2007, to deregulate the business further and allow Baby Bells to offer DSL Internet service without being required to provide competitors with access to equipment and networks, but the issues remained unresolved. The proposed bill placed those promoting new technologies in opposition to lawmakers who viewed Baby Bells as too large.[81] Nevertheless, the business deals continued. Dell (the computer manufacturer) offered customers high-speed DSL Web access through BellSouth (FastAccess), SBC (Yahoo!) and Verizon (Online) in thirty-eight states.[82] One report suggested that SBC and Verizon "benefited immensely" by being the local telephone market incumbents: "In addition to their vast telephone networks, built over decades with ratepayer dollars, the companies have established relationships with loyal customers who are unlikely to jump ship to an unproven rival."[83]

One concern of journalists involves data and telephone privacy. In 2008, the director of the FBI apologized to the *New York Times* and *Washington Post* for not following DOJ rules in 2004, instead obtaining newspaper reporters' telephone records in violation of federal law. These were among apparently "hundreds of cases" that utilized an "exigent circumstance" exception.[84] Although the practice apparently has ended, little additional information was released. Clearly, telephone records provide information that reflects individuals' communication patterns. Thus, the telephone industry maintains databases worthy of exceptional levels of protection.

The 2013 disclosure by Edward Snowden of widespread NSA surveillance of telephone and computer records sparked media coverage and public debate. President Barack Obama maintained the post 9/11 programs developed in the George W. Bush administration. The spying aimed at protecting the nation from future enemy attacks has been funded by Congress and reviewed in the federal courts. There remains room, though, to debate boundaries within a free society.

NSA SURVEILLANCE PROS AND CONS

The political debate over NSA surveillance programs raises important issues in the balance between freedom and the desire to be safe from terrorist attacks. Despite some changes offered by President Barack Obama following the Edward Snowden disclosures, some say more reform is needed to protect U.S. citizens from electronic data collection.

David Cole, legal affairs correspondent for *The Nation*, writes: "Americans from the right and left have voiced concerns... But privacy advocates will have to keep pressing their cause if they want real reform... True reform would replace that mass surveillance with a more targeted approach, one that authorizes intrusive surveillance when the agency has reason to suspect a person of wrongdoing or of being a foreign agent, but not otherwise" (*Real NSA Reform Still Needed*, THE NATION, Feb. 10, 2014, at 3-4).

Arthur Herman and John Yoo, writing in the *National Review*, defended NSA "bulk collection" of telephone and email data: "President Obama could continue a program that takes advantage of America's technological superiority, meets the requirements of constitutional law, and has proven effective in stopping terrorist attacks... With an eleven-judge panel overseeing every step, NSA handles data with a lot more care than Facebook or Google" (*A Defense of Bulk Surveillance*, NAT'L REV., Apr. 7, 2014, at 31-33).

In *Smith v. Maryland*, 442 U.S. 735 (1979), the Supreme Court found no constitutional right to hide telephone numbers already available to telephone companies. They are considered third parties that weaken a case for individual privacy protection. The Court may need to revisit the issue based upon the new technologies for using computer algorithms to dissect big data in search of behavioral patterns across social networks.

Glenn Greenwald first reported the government snooping in *The Guardian* in 2013, and journalists James Risen and Laura Poitras followed a year later in *The New York Times*. Among the revelations from Snowden data was that the NSA was developing facial recognition systems from digital photographs.[85] The Electronic Frontier Foundation fought the data collection system. The passage of the USA Freedom Law in 2015 followed expiration of Section 215 PATRIOT Act provisions. The new instructions revert some provisions to the law in 2001. A commentator wrote: "[T]he government is seemingly back to only being able to request a court order to obtain business records from common carriers, public accommodation facilities, physical storage facilities, and vehicle rental facilities, per the pre-PATRIOT Act and current version of Section 1862(a)."[86] The EFF continues to challenge another law, Section 702 of the FISA Amendments Act, which the NSA has used to collect telephone and email big data from company computers through fiber optic cables without a warrant.[87]

---

[80] Christopher Sterling, *Local Phone Service Rules Left to Expire*, WASH. POST, June 10, 2004, at A01.

[81] *See* Susan Milligan, *House OKs Baby Bell-Backed Broadband Bill Plan*, BOSTON GLOBE, Feb. 28, 2002, at C2.

[82] *See* Colin C. Haley, *Dell Offers DSL Through Baby* Bells, INTERNETNEWS.COM, Jan. 8, 2003, http://www.internetnews.com/bus-news/article.php/1566111.

[83] Joelle Tessler, *Baby Bells Emerging as Winners In Telecom Wars*, MERCURY NEWS, Jan. 27, 2002, *available at* http://www.siliconvalley.com/mld/siliconvalley/3 560250.htm.

[84] *Journalists and Subpoenas, FBI Apologizes to Washington Post, New York Times over Phone Records Breach*, [Silha Center] BULLETIN, Fall 2008, at 11, 14.

[85] Fallout from NSA Surveillance Continues One Year After Snowden Revelations, *The Silha Bulletin* (Summer 2014), 1-5.

[86] Megan Graham, *What Did the USA Freedom Act Actually Amend?*, JUST SECURITY, June 4, 2015, at para. 7, http://justsecurity.org/23458/usa-freedom-act-amend/, para. 7.

[87] Richard Esguerra, *Fighting for Privacy, Two Years After Snowden*, June 5, 2015,

THE FCC AND SLAMMING

Slamming has been the single largest source of complaints to the Commission for several years. The number rose from 12,795 in 1996 to 23,484 in April 1999. FCC rules were at the core of the agency's efforts to eliminate slamming by giving consumers meaningful recourse against deceptive switching of carriers. Thereafter, there was a decline in slamming complaints the FCC received (with local phone companies also reporting similar declines) after April 1999.

The FCC has levied fines of more than $15 million for slamming violations. However, in 2006-07 there was only one $85,000 consent decree with Long Distance Consolidated Billing Co., and this followed a $4 million consent decree with Sprint Communications Company. In that case, it was alleged that consumers shopping at Sprint PC retail stores had their exchange services changed without authorization. Sprint could not provide the FCC with records showing that it had followed verification procedures before making changes. The FCC continues to encourage consumers to file complaints against companies that change service without their approval. In 2008 the FCC proposed a $5,084,000 fine against one carrier. *See* http://www.fcc.gov/eb/tcd/slam.html.

As of 2016, thirty-five states administer slamming rules, and the FCC continues to offer a form for consumer complaint. Many states now review slamming allegations through public service or utilities commissions. *See* FCC, Slamming — States Administering Slamming Rules, Jan. 1, 2016, https://www.fcc.gov/general/slamming-states-administering-slamming-rules.

Beyond government issues, consumers must deal with corporate providers of service. Early DSL high-speed Internet competition was one issue. Consumers sometimes found their interests at odds with those of the large corporations. Two days after FCC rules cracking down on slamming — *the illegal practice of switching long-distance service without permission* — were to go into effect in 1999, for example, the U.S. Court of Appeals for the D.C. Circuit halted enforcement,[88] but its order did not address the validity of the rules.[89] The FCC defined slamming as unauthorized changes in the preferred telephone carrier of a consumer, such as switching a consumer without an explicit request. While courts have upheld the FCC's regulation of slamming, fines have been vacated when imposed simply because a telephone company could not prove the actual line subscriber had agreed to the service charge.[90]

Similarly, there has been concern about telemarketing. When the public complained about the prevalence of unsolicited telephone sales calls, the FTC responded with a national "Do Not Call" list in 2003. In the first day alone, 735,000

numbers were registered. Still, consumers continue to complain about calls that skirt or violate the rules.

The 1984 AT&T divestiture left regional monopolies called Incumbent Local Exchange Carriers, but ILECs were left out of the long-distance market until deregulation in 1996.[91] Upstart Competitive Local Exchange Carriers, however, went to court to challenge what they insisted were antitrust and unfair trade practices.[92] The 1996 Act requires that ILEC's share network resources with competitors, but it is not a simple matter to guarantee access to fair pricing, open markets and reasonable compensation.[93]

The Supreme Court, in 2007, reviewed common carrier provisions of the Communications Act and mandated *just and reasonable* charges to customers *and* suppliers.[94] Congress has utilized public interest regulatory principles born in the Interstate Commerce Act of 1887 and the Communications Act of 1934 to consider reasonableness of rates and fairness of access.[95]

The telephone market continues to evolve, as regulators address new competition of voice over Internet protocol services, including requiring help in subsidizing rural, educational, library and low income access. Meaningful competition has produced cases between communication giants. In Omaha, for example, traditional telephone provider Qwest (now CenturyLink) saw its market impacted by Cox, the original cable TV provider, which now offers Internet and digital telephone services. In 2010, the company unveiled wireless business plans. Cox's market share led the FCC and courts to conclude that consumers are in fact protected by the competition, and those opinions should have an impact on the obligation to provide competitors unbundled network elements. A federal court agreed with the FCC.[96] Cox continues to bundle its cable TV, DVR and telephone services. It also markets a tablet app for mobile viewing of video content. Meanwhile, newer video players, such as AT&T, now market a broad array of Internet-based services, such as home security and automation. This is important, as companies innovate "the Internet of things" and leverage new technologies to disrupt traditional business models.

---

https://www.eff.org/deeplinks/2015/06/fighting-privacy-two-years-after-snowden.

[88] United States Telecom. Ass'n v. FCC, 295 F.3d 1326 (D.C. Cir. 2002).

[89] *See* Jeannine Aversa, *Appeals Court Halts Enforcement of FCC's New "Slamming" Rules,* LEGAL INTELLIGENCER, May 19, 1999, at 4.

[90] *See* AT&T Corp. v. FCC, 323 F.3d 1081 (D.C. Cir. 2003).

[91] *See* Bell Atlantic Corp., et al. v. William Twombly et al., 550 U.S. 544 (2007).

[92] Verizon Commc'ns Inc.. v. Law Offices of Curtis V. Trinko, LLP, 540 U.S. 398 (2004).

[93] *See* Sprint Commc'ns Co. v. APCC Services, Inc., 554 U.S. 269 (2008). The deregulated telephone business has produced many claims for payment across companies sharing services. *See also* Pacific Bell Telephone v. Linkline Commc'n., 555 U.S. 438 (2009) (dealing with Internet Service Provider sale of DSL access).

[94] Global Crossing Telecomm., Inc. v. Metrophones Telecomm., Inc., 550 U.S. 45 (2007).

[95] American Telephone & Telegraph Co. v. Central Office Telephone, Inc., 524 U.S. 214, 222 (1998).

[96] Qwest Corp. v. FCC, 482 F. 3d 471 (D.C. Cir. 2007).

OTHER NEW ELECTRONIC MASS MEDIA

A variety of emerging consumer technologies have raised numerous legal issues. Systems for delivering video into the home have been particularly problematic for regulators. As Internet video compression improved, though, consumers had amazing new options for watching news, entertainment and sports across a variety of mobile and fixed devices.

Direct-to-Home Services

Cable systems provided service to a majority of multichannel video consumers, but the industry is rapidly losing customers to Internet video. Netflix, Hulu, HBO, MLB, CBSN and others attracted gorwing audiences.

In 1934, when Congress passed the Communications Act, it did not envision satellites. Science fiction writer Arthur C. Clarke first advanced this concept — known as "geosynchronous orbit" — in 1945.[97] It is not surprising, then, that the Communications Act did not mention direct broadcast satellites that use modern technologies such as digital band compression to beam down hundreds of channels of video programming. For about thirty years, before the rapid rise of Internet streaming video, satellite TV was a very important delivery system.

The FCC has jurisdiction over direct broadcast satellites because they use the electromagnetic spectrum to send signals to receiving dishes. The FCC licenses all DBS operations. In 1982, when it faced the issue of how to regulate DBS, it realized that DBS could be seen as (1) a broadcasting service, distributing signals to terrestrial antennas, just as broadcast stations do, or (2) a service much like local phone companies, renting space on the satellite to anyone who wants to send signals. The Commission chose to adopt simplified, flexible regulations to allow DBS to develop.[98] Broadcasters challenged the fairness of the rules, and a federal appellate court disagreed, in part, with the FCC's strategy.[99] It found that DBS met many legal characteristics of a broadcast medium and could be regulated only to the extent that the FCC could justify distinctions. The court said DBS could be regulated as a non-local broadcast service without local programming obligations. A later court decision held that DBS was more like subscription services than broadcasting because it does not use the spectrum to transmit to the general public.[100] The

Commission used the term "direct-to-home" for services sending video signals to receivers in the United States, and required technical standard agreements with Mexico and other Latin American nations. Operators such as DirecTV and Dish Network formerly offered this service using high-power signals. Another company, Prime-Star, offered DBS service using medium power.

Under international agreements, the United States had eight positions for DTH satellites in the geosynchronous orbit. Each position used up to thirty-two transmission channels. Digital signal compression allowed for several signals to transmit in the portion of the spectrum previously needed for a single signal; hundreds of channels may fit on a single satellite. The FCC shifted from awarding these orbital positions through competitive hearings or by lottery to auctions for the slots.

Satellite operators must comply with federal laws and FCC regulations, but they also must operate under standards set by the International Telecommunications Union, the worldwide body overseeing spectrum use. U.S. satellite operators also need not strictly comply with ITU rules, but ultimately the ITU must approve the deviations from its standards, or the operators must come into compliance.

The 1992 Cable Act required the FCC to establish certain public interest obligations of satellite operators, such as rules regarding political communication, retransmission consent (but not the must-carry rules) and equal employment opportunities.[101] Broadcasters and cable operators argued that DBS had an unfair competitive edge and should have been subjected to government mandated must-carry rules. In 1998, the FCC adopted rules requiring DBS providers to set aside 4 percent of their channel capacity for noncommercial educational or informational programming, as required by the public interest section of the law.[102] The FCC has interpreted the 1992 Act to apply these requirements to DBS operators.

A federal appellate court held that satellite operators, like cable operators, may use the compulsory copyright license.[103] EchoStar, a leading DBS provider, brought a federal lawsuit against the television networks to obtain legal permission for a retransmission of programming to residents where over-the-air reception of local signals is marginal.[104]

The broadcast regulation system was originally designed to aid local broadcasters because it was believed they had an ability to serve the unique "public interest, convenience or necessity" of a

---

[97] Arthur C. Clarke, *Extra-Terrestrial Relays — Can Rocket Stations Give World-Wide Radio Coverage?*, WIRELESS WORLD, Oct. 1945, at 305.

[98] *See* Direct Broadcast Satellites, 90 F.C.C. 2d 676 (1982).

[99] Nat'l Ass'n of Broadcasters v. FCC, 740 F.2d 1190 (D.C. Cir. 1984).

[100] Nat'l Ass'n for Better Broad. v. FCC, 849 F.2d 665 (D.C. Cir. 1988).

[101] *See* Implementation of Section 25 of the Cable Television Consumer Protection and Competition Act of 1992, 8 F.C.C. Rcd. 1589 (1993).

[102] *See* Jeffrey P. Cunard, *DBS' Public Interest Duties Given Minimal Definition*, CABLE TV & NEW MEDIA L. & FIN., Dec. 1998, at 1.

[103] NBC v. Satellite Broad. Networks, 940 F.2d 1467 (11th Cir. 1991). *See also* Nat'l Ass'n for Better Broad. v. FCC, 849 F.2d 665 (D.C. Cir. 1988).

[104] *See* Michael L. Landsman, *EchoStar Takes on TV Networks*, CABLE TV & NEW MEDIA L. & FIN., Nov. 1998, at 8.

particular community.[105] Under the 1992 Cable Act, the FCC was instructed to determine whether DBS operators also should be subject to such "localism" rules. Under the Communications Act of 1934, the FCC employed its licensing power to promote local ownership and programming. The FCC, though, was unable to determine how a service that sends a signal nationally and offers a wide variety of programming options could be concerned with "localism" in the same way as a local broadcast station. Regardless, the general trend toward deregulation has led to declining emphasis on the concept of localism in the licensing process. The 1996 Act limited the ability of cities, home-owners' associations and others to restrict satellite dishes; Congress' intent was to ensure that DBS growth would not be stymied. By consolidating and streamlining DBS regulation, the FCC promoted more competition with cable, whose rates continued to climb.[106]

Satellite Master Antenna Television Systems

A satellite master antenna television system, also called "private cable," is essentially a cable system contained within an apartment building or several buildings. Similar to cable, a SMATV system collects local TV signals through an antenna and satellite signals through receiving dishes, all placed on top of the building. It sends the signals through wires that run through the building, into individual apartments. The SMATV system may serve other commonly owned buildings on the same plot of private land, and the system's wires will run to and through each building. If the wires go across public rights-of-way, such as a public street, the operation becomes a cable, not a SMATV, system.[107] The FCC and one court, however, have ruled that a SMATV may use telephone lines to transmit signals across rights-of-way without hurting its status as a non-regulated private cable system.[108]

The FCC has chosen to impose few regulatory burdens on SMATV systems, thus allowing them to develop into competition for cable. Further, it has held that there can be no local or state regulation of SMATV.[109] As a result, the systems must comply with the FCC's equal employment opportunity rules —

unless they serve fewer than fifty subscribers — but do not face rate regulation, franchise fees, customer service standards or most other regulations imposed on cable systems.

Wireless Cable

In 1970, the FCC dedicated a portion of the spectrum to a service for business communications. By 1974, it realized that part of the spectrum could be used to send video signals to subscribers and established the "Multipoint Distribution Service." The FCC permitted two video channels to be provided in the country's fifty largest markets and one video channel in other markets. It increased the number of available channels in 1983 and again in 1991.[110]

The business soon became known as "Multichannel Multipoint Distribution Service." Wireless cable sent as many as thirty-three channels by microwave signals to antennas on subscribers' homes. Since it used microwaves, part of the electromagnetic spectrum, the FCC licensed and regulated it. Because it did not cross public rights-of-way, it was not considered a cable system and didn't require a local franchise. Wireless cable became a viable business when the FCC permitted operators to combine their spectrum allocations with portions of the spectrum dedicated to other types of wireless services. By combining allocations, wireless cable systems could compete with cable systems in some cities. Wireless cable was helped by the 1992 Cable Act requirement that cable networks offer their programming to wireless cable and other multi-channel multi-point video providers.

The FCC did not permit cities or states to regulate wireless cable, and, as with satellite operators, the Commission allowed wireless operators to act as conduits for other video programmers or to themselves provide programming.[111] In either case, the Commission imposed very few regulatory requirements on wireless cable, but it must approve any non-subscription service supplied by MDS or MMDS.[112] As with DBS, wireless cable services must comply with the retransmission consent rules requiring operators to obtain permission from any broadcast stations that the wireless cable service carries.

In 1997, the FCC issued its first rulings preempting restrictions on the installation and use of satellite dishes imposed by local governments and homeowners associations in four states. It also began a proceeding to adopt more flexible regulation of wireless cable and to encourage its use for interactive services. In a 1998 decision intended to strengthen the foundering wireless ca-

---

[105] *See* CHRISTOPHER H. STERLING & JOHN M. KITTROSS, STAY TUNED, A CONCISE HISTORY OF AMERICAN BROADCASTING 236-37, 557-80 (2d ed. 1990). *See also,* Nat'l Broad. Co. v. United States, 319 U.S. 190 (1943).

[106] Policies and Rules for the Direct Broadcast Satellite Services, Notice of Proposed Rulemaking, FCC 98-26, IB Docket No. 98-21 (Feb. 26, 1998).

[107] *See* FCC v. Beach Commc'ns, Inc., 508 U.S. 307 (1993).

[108] *See* City of Austin v. Southwestern Bell Video Services, 1998 U.S. Dist. Lexis 16332 (Aug. 3, 1998). *See also* Frank W. Lloyd, *Litigation Update Court OKs Telco Video Service Without Cable Franchise,* CABLE TV & NEW MEDIA L. & FIN., Sept. 1998, at 8.

[109] *See* New York State Comm'n on Cable Television v. FCC, 669 F.2d 58 (2d Cir. 1982).

[110] Private Video Distribution Systems, 6 F.C.C. Rcd. 1270 (1991).

[111] Multipoint Distribution Service, 2 F.C.C. Rcd. 4251 (1987).

[112] Revisions to Part 21 of the Commission's Rules Regarding the Multipoint Distribution Service, Second Report and Order, FCC 98-70, CC Docket No. 86-179 (Apr. 14, 1998).

ble industry, the Commission adopted rules that allowed MDS operators to offer two-way digital services, such as Internet access and videoconferencing.[113]

The FCC used auctions to award hundreds of wireless cable licenses. As technological advances enabled wireless cable operators to offer a number of video signals on each of their thirty-three channels through digital signal compression, licenses became more valuable. Several phone companies expressed an interest in purchasing wireless cable operations because the 1996 Telecommunications Act permits telephone companies to provide video services through wireless cable.

In 1998, the FCC auctioned portions of the local MDS spectrum, which uses transmitters to send voice, data or video to within a six-mile radius. The FCC awarded more than 859 local MDS, or LMDS, licenses and raised approximately $580 million. The FCC did not permit local telephone or cable companies to bid for most licenses, hoping that other smaller companies would develop competitive LMDS services.[114] In recent years, digital and Internet video access replaced many of the older technologies that tend to persist in smaller, rural communities that still lack high-speed Internet access.

Digital Television

"Digital television" is a term applied to technological standards for advanced television, affecting both the transmission and widescreen display of signals. The first high-definition TV sets were introduced in 1998. Traditional analog sets can display HDTV only if they are used with an external ATSC tuner converter.[115] The conversion to digital from analog was slowed by the historic investment in traditional analog television systems. The transmission standard in use in the United States since 1941 is called NTSC (for the National Television System Committee, which suggested its adoption to the FCC).

DTV development, initially called HDTV, began in Japan in the 1960s. Later work was undertaken in Europe on a different DTV standard incompatible with the Japanese technology. The United States began work on DTV late, but the delay gave American companies a digital rather than an analog transmission scheme. In 1987, the FCC established the Advisory Committee on Advanced Television Systems to coordinate American research. After years of work, the "Grand Alliance," comprised of the companies that had been competing

to develop DTV, agreed upon a technical standard different from Japanese and European electronic engineering.

In 1996, the FCC approved an ATSC standard, which differed from that used in Europe and much of the rest of the world. ATSC addressed signal transmission protocols, giving TV manufacturers the confidence to build and sell sets able to receive DTV signals. Televisions compatible with both the Grand Alliance and the FCC standards reached the market, and broadcasters and cable companies began to provide digital programming while simulcasting existing analog programs. Most desktop and laptop computers today feature video cards and DVD drives capable of handling theater-quality digital video.

In 1997, the Commission gave current full-power television broadcasters a second channel to use for DTV. A decade later, DTV broadcasts became a reality in the United States. It was a challenging transition for broadcasters and the public. In 1998, the FCC affirmed its commitment that conversion to DTV be completed by 2006, when analog channels were first scheduled to go dark.[116] However, in early 2006, a provision of the Deficit Reduction Act delayed the death of analog television until February 2009.[117] Some analog signals went dark then, but the remainder finally made the transition in June 2009. Consumers wanting to watch broadcast television needed sets capable of receiving digital signals, or set-top converter boxes to make reception possible. The government offered coupons to help pay for the cost of converters and, additionally, some computer users purchased HDTV tuner cards.

Digital channels may be used for high definition television, or "multiplexing" — up to four TV signals, but not HDTV. Using compression, several signals, plus data and other services, such as paging, may be provided on the spectrum space previously devoted to one channel. The 1996 Act states that if broadcasters are given second channels, and they use them to provide services for which they charge a fee, they must compensate the federal government for using those channels.

Interactive Video and Data Services

Interactive Video and Data Services combine data transmission and interactivity to permit home shopping, banking and other services. Some IVDS providers entered the business by buying available portions of the spectrum through FCC auctions that

---

[113] See FCC Watch, CABLE TV & NEW MEDIA L. & FIN., Sept. 1998, at 6.

[114] Rulemaking to Establish Rules and Policies for Local Multipoint Distribution Service and for Fixed Satellite Services, Fourth Report and Order, FCC 98-77, CC Docket No. 92-297 (May 6, 1998).

[115] See HDTV BASICS, CNET, Mar. 14, 2005, http://reviews.cnet.com/4520-7608_7-1016109-3.html.

[116] See Advanced Television Systems and Their Impact Upon Existing Television Broadcast Service, Memorandum Opinion and Order, FCC 98-24, MM Docket No. 87-268 (Feb. 23, 1998).

[117] See Amy Schatz, Deadline in 2009 is Set for Digital-TV Switch, WALL STREET J., Dec. 20, 2005, at D1. See also Jim Barnett & Michelle Cole, Federal Cuts Sting Social Services, OREGONIAN, Feb. 3, 2005, at B01. The appropriated $7.5 billion from the sale of broadcast rights to assist consumers and public safety agencies make the costly switch from analog to digital signals.

offered preferences for women and minorities. In 1997, a federal circuit court ruled that a constitutional challenge to these preferences must be reviewed on its merits by the FCC.[118] An IVDS provider argued that the preferences unconstitutionally favored select groups and inflated auction prices.

These developments were less important than the low-cost access available with the World Wide Web. Anyone may launch a multimedia site and attempt to compete with major media players without approval from government regulators.

THE INTERNET

The Internet offers global email, information and entertainment. It has grown from a handful of sites in 1994, and global online advertising surpassed $33 billion early in the last decade.[119] These numbers grow dramatically each year, and the global trend is toward ubiquitous access.[120] The number of Web pages has surpassed one trillion,[121] and everyone seems to agree that the Internet will continue to expand and be a dominant force for years to come — particularly in Asia and in underdeveloped nations. To assure the continued strength and growth of this network, some Internet service providers are lobbying Congress for laws requiring local cable TV companies to provide access to their lines for Internet use. This policy is known as "unbundling" or "open access."

The Internet presents legal problems, some of which are familiar and others that are new. For example, communication through the Internet can be undertaken anonymously, copyrighted material can be distributed without the copyright holder's permission, and information stored on computers can be obtained by people with no right to it. In 2000, the world organization that registers trademarks and protects copyrights ruled that so-called "cybersquatters" may not buy and sell World Wide Web addresses using for-profit trade names such as the World Wrestling Federation.[122] Canadian and American broadcasters filed suit against iCraveTV.com, a Toronto com-

pany that had been re-transmitting network programs on the Web. Broadcasters maintained their rights to license Web broadcasts.[123] As time passed, it became clearer that the Web was less revolutionary than first predicted and more an extension of traditional media in terms of American communication law. One of the toughest challenges is how to define offensive material. For example, Senator Joseph Lieberman complained to Google about the existence of YouTube videos posted by terrorist organizations, such as al-Qaeda.[124] Google (YouTube) found, however, that legal, nonviolent and non-hate speech videos also mentioned the organization, and that the video-sharing site could not remove them.

The Internet and Indecency

A portion of the Telecommunications Act of 1996, called the Communications Decency Act, made it illegal to knowingly send or make available to minors any indecent or obscene material.[125] The CDA was one of four unsuccessful U.S. government attempts (under two presidents and three sessions of Congress) to restrict or filter access by children to pornography, particularly on the Internet. The CDA of 1996, the Child Pornography Prevention Act of 1996, and the Child Online Protection Act of 1998 all have failed a number of various legal challenges. In 2003, however, the Supreme Court reversed a lower court and upheld the Children's Internet Protection Act of 2000. (See the box "Five Key Court Cases.")

In 1997, the Supreme Court found part of the CDA's indecency provisions unconstitutional. In *Reno v. ACLU*,[126] it acknowledged Congress' concern with preventing children from being the targets of, or having access to, sexually explicit communications, but it said the CDA's ban on indecency was vague and overbroad. The law did not define indecency in a way that conformed to previous Court decisions.

In a ruling against the law that would have defined as criminal making such content accessible to children, the Court distinguished the Internet from broadcasting. The Internet does not use the limited public spectrum, and people are not as likely to be exposed inadvertently to sexually explicit material on the Internet as on broadcast stations. Accordingly, adult Internet users should not suffer the reduced First Amendment protections that apply to radio and television station operators, the Court reasoned. However, the Court concluded that obscene material may

---

[118] Graceba v. FCC, 115 F.3d 1038 (D.C. Cir. 1997).

[119] *See* First Quarter 2005 Highest Internet Ad Revenue in Nine Consecutive Growth Quarters. Interactive Advertising Bureau, http://www.iab.net/news/pr_2005_6_6.asp.

[120] *See* Internet World Stats, http://www.internetworldstats.com/stats.htm. From 2000 to 2009, the number of users more than quadrupled. The top five nations in terms of Internet use are China, the United States, Japan, India and Brazil. Among the fastest growing countries for Internet use are Estonia, Poland, Belgium, Ukraine and Sweden.

[121] *See* The Official Google Blog, http://googleblog.blogspot.com/2008/07/we-knew-web-was-big.html. The number of Internet users in Asia, which has more than half the world's population, is estimated to be more than 700 million.

[122] *See* WWF Wins Case Against Cyber-Squatter, CBC ARCHIVES, Jan. 23, 2000, http://cbc.ca.

[123] *See* CBC Among Broadcasters Launching Lawsuit Against iCraveTV, CBC ARCHIVES, Feb. 1, 2000, http://cbc.ca.

[124] *See* CNN, *Lieberman to YouTube: Remove al Qaeda Videos*, http://www.cnn.com/2008/POLITICS/05/20/youtube.lieberman/index.htm.

[125] 104 Pub. L. 104, tit. 5, 110 Stat. 56 (1996).

[126] 521 U.S. 844 (1997).

be banned from the Internet because the First Amendment does not protect any obscene messages, regardless of medium. Most importantly, the Court treated Web site operators as publishers: "Publishers may either make their material available to the entire pool of Internet users, or confine access to a selected group, such as those willing to pay for the privilege."[127] The Court has consistently called for narrowly tailored restrictions on Internet speech and application of traditional obscenity law. From a legal perspective, the Internet has been viewed as similar to print media with respect to the First Amendment. A somewhat recent broadcast indecency decision maintained divided law that continues to isolate broadcast regulation as a special case.[128]

The *Reno* decision reflected the Court's 1989 position in *Sable Communications v. FCC*, when it said Congress may prohibit obscene telephone communications but may not ban indecent "dial-a-porn" messages available *via* telephone for a fee.[129] Although the Court had ruled in *FCC v. Pacifica Foundation* that the FCC could restrict indecency on broadcast stations,[130] it found in *Sable Communications* that telephones are markedly different from broadcasting. Radio is ubiquitous, uniquely powerful and accessible to children, the Court held. On the other hand, a person must consciously choose to access a dial-a-porn service. Likewise, people pay to gain access to the Internet, and filtering software is available to assist parents in protecting their children from offensive messages. And pornography sites often are supported by additional user subscription fees. Congress later adopted a law requiring dial-a-porn businesses to make their services available only through a pre-subscription arrangement, credit card payment or other method that would make it difficult for children to gain access.[131] Attempts to enact similar restrictions for the Internet have been

more problematic.

While courts use the *Miller v. California*[132] definition of obscenity for print and visual media, questions existed about applying it to the Internet. For example, the Sixth U.S. Circuit Court of Appeals upheld the conviction on federal obscenity charges of two people who operated a computer bulletin board from their California home.[133] The subscriber service offered sexually explicit materials. The couple was charged in Memphis with transmitting obscene material. A postal official had obtained computer files and ordered six videotapes, all containing sexually explicit material. A jury found that the material violated the community standards of Memphis and convicted the couple of transporting obscene images across state lines *via* the Internet. The lower court rejected the argument that the ruling effectively established a national standard for obscenity, contrary to the Supreme Court's *Miller* test, or that upholding the conviction would mandate that all material sent over the Internet be no more explicit than permitted by the most restrictive community. It stated that the defendants could, and should, have made certain when screening subscribers that their materials would not be received in restrictive communities.

Concerned by the high Court's elimination of the CDA's online indecency ban, Congress enacted and President Bill Clinton signed the Child Online Protection Act in 1998 to help prevent children from accessing material harmful to minors. Six months later, the U.S. Department of Justice was in the U.S. Court of Appeals for the Third Circuit to challenge a district court order that enjoined enforcement of the new law.[134]

In 1999, a federal judge in Pennsylvania stopped application of Congress's second attempt to shield children from Internet pornography.[135] COPA would have required commercial Web sites to collect credit card numbers or some other proof of age before allowing users to access targeted materials. The law called for a $50,000 fine and up to six months in prison for any commercial provider who knowingly made harmful material available to minors under the age of 17. In 2000, an appeals court struck another blow to COPA by upholding the district court ruling.[136] The Third U.S. Circuit Court of Appeals held that the ACLU's attack on the constitutionality of the act would likely succeed.

In 2002, the Supreme Court held in *Ashcroft v. ACLU* that community standards may be used to identify material that is

---

[127] *Id.* at 853.

[128] *See* F.C.C. v. Fox Television Stations, Inc., 556 U.S. 502, 532 (2009) (Thomas, J., concurring):

> Highlighting the doctrinal incoherence of *Red Lion* and *Pacifica*, the Court has declined to apply the lesser standard of First Amendment scrutiny imposed on broadcast speech to federal regulation of telephone dial-in services, ...cable television programming, ...and the Internet. "There is no justification for this apparent dichotomy in First Amendment jurisprudence. Whatever the merits of *Pacifica* when it was issued[,] .... it makes no sense now." (Edwards, C.J. dissenting). "...The justifications relied on by the Court in *Red Lion* and *Pacifica* – 'spectrum scarcity, intrusiveness, and accessibility to children – neither distinguish broadcast from cable, nor explain the relaxed application of the principles of the First Amendment to broadcast" [Statement of Commissioner Furchtgott-Roth]. ('It is ironic that streaming video or audio content from a television or radio station would likely receive more constitutional protection, *see Reno* [v. ACLU, 521 U.S. 844, (1997)], ... than would the same exact content broadcast over-the-air').

[129] 492 U.S. 115 (1989).

[130] 438 U.S. 726 (1978).

[131] 47 U.S.C. 223(b) (1994).

[132] 413 U.S. 15 (1973).

[133] United States v. Thomas, 74 F.3d 701 (6th Cir. 1996). *See also* Pamela A. Huelster, *Cybersex and Community Standards,* 75 B.U.L. REV. 865 (1995).

[134] *See Recent and Pending Cases,* MULTIMEDIA & WEB STRATEGIST, Apr. 1999, at 8. *See also* Michael Rubinkam, *DOJ to Appeal COPA Injunction,* LEGAL INTELLIGENCER, Apr. 5, 1999, at 5.

[135] American Civil Liberties Union v. Reno, 31 F. Supp. 2d 473 (E.D. Penn. 1999).

[136] American Civil Liberties Union v. Reno, 217 F.3d 162 (3d Cir. 2000).

harmful to minors.[137] Ruling on COPA, the Court found the use of *Miller v. California* language distinguishable because all three prongs of the test must be used. While the earlier *Reno* decision failed because only the patently offensive standard was utilized, the COPA statute also employed *Miller's* "prurient interest" and "serious value" tests. Justice Clarence Thomas, writing for the 8-1 majority, reiterated that, unlike the first two prongs, the third allows a court to set aside community standards in favor of "whether a reasonable person would find ... value in the material, taken as a whole."[138]

The decision then remanded the case for further review by lower courts. Only Justice John Paul Stevens dissented: "In the context of the Internet ... community standards become a sword rather than a shield. If a prurient appeal is offensive in a puritan village, it may be a crime to post it on the World Wide Web."[139]

In 2004, the Supreme Court sided 5-4 with a lower court decision to block COPA, but it remanded the case to update evidence on the effectiveness of Internet filters, as well as other existing laws and technologies.[140] In an opinion written by Justice Anthony Kennedy, the Court held: "Content-based prohibitions, enforced by severe criminal penalties, have the constant potential to be a repressive force in the lives and thoughts of free people."[141] The Court noted that Congress passed two other laws, one prohibiting misleading domain names and another creating a "Dot Kids" domain.[142] The idea to create separate Internet domain space for children, however, has not become popular. A for-profit company owns .kids and the second-level kids.us project has been inactive since 2012.

The decision to return the case to the district court relied on the *Reno* decision and the idea that filtering software satisfies the least restrictive means test better than forcing commercial Web sites to verify user age. The Court, however, refused to accept the appellate court conclusion that use of community standards was overbroad. It distinguished the differences between the district court opinion, which held that the statute must be narrowly tailored to serve a compelling government

interest, and the appellate court's unconstitutional finding, which the majority refused to accept without fresh evidence.

FIVE KEY COURT CASES: NARROWLY TAILORING LAWS THAT RESTRICT INTERNET FREE SPEECH

Between 1997 and 2004 the Supreme Court addressed issues related to Internet pornography, obscenity and indecency in five important opinions:

• In *Reno v. ACLU* (1997), the Court found unconstitutional portions of the Communications Decency Act, which was part of the Telecommunications Act of 1996. It found the language too vague and rejected Justice Sandra Day O'Connor's call for zoning the Internet.

• In *Ashcroft v. ACLU* (2002), the Court voted 8-1 to remand the Child Online Protection Act of 1998 to lower courts to reconsider application of the obscenity test from *Miller v. California* (1973). The case appeared to apply the traditional obscenity test to Internet content. It was remanded again in 2004 on a 5-4 decision to seek fresh evidence comparing site age verification blocking to user-based filtering software. In 2007, District Judge Lowell Reed found that software filters "are far more effective than COPA would be at protecting children from sexually explicit material," and he struck down the law as "not narrowly tailored to Congress' compelling interest." He issued an injunction against enforcement. The law would have made it federally criminal to offer any commercial "harmful" communication to minors on the Web, punishable with fines and imprisonment. The ruling means that Congress is free to draft a narrower law that addresses constitutional concerns.

• In *Ashcroft v. Free Speech Coalition* (2002), the Court, by 6-3 vote, rejected a ban on "virtual" child pornography, as defined in the Child Pornography Prevention Act of 1996, as violating the First Amendment.

• In *United States v. American Library Association* (2003), a lower court decision was reversed in a 6-3 vote. The Children's Internet Protection Act of 2000, which requires libraries supported by federal funds to install filtering software on computers, was found to be a constitutional and effective measure to block pornographic images that are deemed harmful to children. The Supreme Court rejected First Amendment arguments that public libraries are a public forum subject to the strict scrutiny standard. Instead, libraries make content-based decisions.

• In *Ashcroft v. ACLU* (2004) (*Ashcroft II*), the Supreme Court, by a 5-4 vote, blocked the latest iteration of COPA. The Court remanded the case to a lower court and sought fresh evidence on filtering software effectiveness.

The Court's majority sought, by placing the burden on the government, to seek less restrictive alternatives: "The purpose of the test is to ensure that speech is restricted no further than necessary to achieve the goal, for it is important to assure that legitimate speech is not chilled or punished."[143] It reasoned that filters are less restrictive and more effective in blocking all porn sites, not just those in the United States. Minors may be able to obtain credit cards and access pornographic Web sites, and filters are not entirely effective. However, they go beyond Web sites and

---

[137] 535 U.S. 564 (2002).

[138] *Id.* at 579 (quoting Pope v. Illinois, 481 U.S. 497, 501 (1987)).

[139] *Id.* at 603 (Stevens, J., dissenting).

[140] Ashcroft v. ACLU, 542 U.S. 656 (2004).

[141] *Id.* at 664. The government has the burden to prove that user-based filters are not at least as effective as site-based age verification systems.

[142] *See* Doreen Carvajal & Brad Stone, *New Flavors For Addresses On the Web*, N.Y. TIMES, June 27, 2008, at C1; Michelle Kewssler, *Internet Group Opens Door to Domains Beyond.com*, USA TODAY, June 27, 2008, at B1. The Internet Corporation for Assigned Names and Numbers approved new Internet domain name suffixes, but .xxx and other words will be sent to an independent review board. Some argued a new variety of names would make it more difficult to filter pornography using software programs.

[143] 542 U.S. at 667.

may also be used to block email. The Court majority concluded that parents and libraries may be encouraged to use filters.

The Court was severely divided, though, on whether filters solve the problem, as well as how best to fit restrictions within the requirements of the First Amendment. Justices Stevens and Ruth Bader Ginsburg would have taken it further. Their concurrence supported the appellate court reasoning that use of community standards warranted striking down the law as unconstitutional. However, Justice Antonin Scalia dissented, arguing that restricting commercial pornography is consistent with existing law. Justice Stephen Breyer's dissent, meantime, argued that COPA advanced a compelling interest and followed the *Miller* test.

In 2007, District Court Judge Lowell Reed appeared to settle the question by ruling that software filters were more effective than COPA in protecting children from harmful material and that the legislation was "impermissibly vague and overbroad" when applying the strict scrutiny test:

Because COPA suppresses a large amount of speech that adults have a constitutional right to receive, under the strict scrutiny standard, COPA may only be upheld as constitutional if defendant meets the burden of proving that COPA is narrowly tailored to the compelling interest that COPA was enacted to serve and there are no less restrictive alternatives.[144]

In 1999, the Supreme Court had let stand a lower court ruling upholding another part of the Communications Decency Act.[145] The Court issued a one-sentence order that allowed the government to enforce a CDA ban on obscene and indecent email that is intended to harass or annoy a recipient. In *ApolloMedia Corp. v. Reno*, a San Francisco company challenged a provision that made it a felony to initiate "the transmission of, any comment, request, suggestion, proposal, image, or other communication which is obscene, lewd, lascivious, filthy, or indecent, with intent to annoy, abuse, threaten, or harass another person."[146] Annoy.com had allowed people to send anonymous and lewd electronic mail to public officials. Attorney William Bennett Turner argued that the provision unconstitutionally punishes indecent material under the *Miller* test:

There is no conceivable government interest that could justify 223's content prohibition of "indecent" speech.... The government cannot even advance the interest in protecting children from exposure to "indecent" material — the in-

terest that it unsuccessfully urged to support the other provisions of the Act held unconstitutional.... The provisions at issue here apply regardless of the age of the recipient, govern communications among adults, and have no safe harbor defenses.[147]

Nevertheless, the Supreme Court refused to revisit its earlier decision. Internet pornography and the profitable business that surrounds it have created First Amendment issues because of photographic artists such as Barbara Nitke, who sued the government in 2001. She argued that community judgments about obscenity could empower the most restrictive community, which would affect the entire Internet. In *Nitke v. Gonzalez*, however, the government won.[148] The court held:

There is insufficient evidence on the record to enable us to make a finding as to whether "the variation in community standards is substantial enough that the potential for inconsistent determinations of obscenity is greater than that faced by purveyors of traditional pornography, who can control the dissemination of their materials."[149]

The Supreme Court affirmed without comment.

In another case dealing with children's access to sexually explicit materials online, a federal judge enjoined enforcement of a Virginia library's policy to block public access to such Internet sites.[150] While recognizing a compelling government interest in reducing illegal access to pornography, the court ruled that the library had adopted an overbroad policy to address speculative concerns with no evidence of illegal access or citizen complaints. The lawsuit against the library alleged that the policy violated the First Amendment and was an unconstitutional prior restraint. An earlier ruling declared: "The First Amendment applies to, and limits, the discretion of a public library to place content-based restrictions on access to constitutionally protected materials within its collection."[151] The court held that receiving Internet information was consistent with the type of public forum the library routinely offered.[152]

---

[144] ACLU v. Gonzalez, 478 F. Supp. 2d 775, 809 (E.D. Pa. 2007).

[145] ApolloMedia Corp. v. Reno, 526 U.S. 1061 (1999) (without opinion).

[146] Communications Decency Act, 47 U.S.C. § 223(a)(1)(A)(ii); 47 U.S.C. § 223(a)(2).

[147] Brief for Appellant, ApolloMedia Corp. v. Reno, 526 U.S. 1061 (1999).

[148] 413 F. Supp. 2d 262 (S.D.N.Y. 2005), *affd.*, 547 U.S. 1015 (2006).

[149] *Id. at* 271-72 (citing Nitke v. Ashcroft (*Nitke I*), 253 F. Supp. 587, 383 (S.D.N.Y. 2004)). The court also rejected an overbreadth challenge to CDA.

[150] Mainstream Loudon v. Bd. of Trustees of the Loudon County Library, 24 F. Supp. 2d 552 (E.D. Va. 1998).

[151] Mainstream Loudon v. Bd. of Trustees of the Loudon County Library, 2 F. Supp. 2d 783, 794-95 (E.D. Va. 1998).

[152] *See* Perry Educ. Ass'n v. Perry Local Educators' Ass'n, 460 U.S. 37 (1983). There are three categories of fora, according to the Supreme Court: (1) a traditional forum, such as a public park; (2) a limited forum, such as a public meeting; and (3) a non-public forum, such as a public employee's mailbox. A library may not be open to all forms of free expression, but it has been designated as a place where the public goes to find in-

In another twist on the library issue, seven Minneapolis librarians claimed that the amount of pornography on Central Library computers created a "hostile, offensive, palpably unlawful working environment."[153] Library patrons downloading pornographic images prompted at least two bills in Minnesota to require blocking or filtering software on all school and library computers. Ultimately, the library director apologized to the public and announced plans to require sign-ins at workstations, as well as limiting computer use to thirty minutes.

A three-judge panel of the Third Circuit in Philadelphia at first rejected the Children's Internet Protection Act, which requires filtering software on computers at libraries supported by federal funds. The court unanimously ruled the law unconstitutional.[154] It said filters tend to overblock educational content:

> While most libraries include in their physical collection copies of volumes such as *The Joy of Sex* and *The Joy of Gay Sex*, which contain quite explicit photographs and descriptions, filtering software blocks large quantities of other, comparable information about health and sexuality.... One teenager testified that the Internet access in a public library was the only venue in which she could obtain information important to her about her own sexuality. Another ... witness described using the Internet to research breast cancer and reconstructive surgery for his mother.... Even though some filtering programs contain exceptions for health and education, the exceptions do not solve the problem of overblocking constitutionally protected material ... not only information relating to health and sexuality that might be mistaken for pornography or erotica, but also vast numbers of Web pages and sites that could not even arguably be construed as harmful.[155]

The district court found that the four most popular filtering software programs blocked thousands of Web sites that were not pornographic, and this raised First Amendment issues. The court rejected the government's argument that current technology is imperfect but effective in blocking most hardcore porn sites. The court accepted the plaintiff's argument against the government that libraries constitute a public forum subject to a strict scrutiny First Amendment analysis:

Because the filtering software mandated by CIPA will block access to substantial amounts of constitutionally protected speech whose suppression serves no legitimate government interest, we are persuaded that a public library's use of software filters is not narrowly tailored to further any of these interests. Moreover, less restrictive alternatives exist that further the government's legitimate interest in preventing the dissemination of obscenity, child pornography, and material harmful to minors, and in preventing patrons from being unwillingly exposed to patently offensive, sexually explicit content.[156]

The court noted that there are less restrictive options such as enforcing library rules prohibiting access to pornography or providing unfiltered computers in restricted areas. Instead, the measure would have restricted funds to any library that did not keep minors from visual depictions of obscene content, child pornography or content generally harmful to minors.[157]

Citing *FCC v. League of Women Voters of California* and other cases, the district court concluded that the government has no right to restrict speech for content reasons: "By interfering with public libraries' discretion to make available to patrons as wide a range of constitutionally protected speech as possible, the federal government is arguably distorting the usual functioning of public libraries as places of freewheeling inquiry."[158] CIPA, which would have been enforced through FCC actions and the provisions of the Library Services Technology Act, was enjoined from going into effect while the Supreme Court considered an appeal. The Court was faced with a series of arguments that the American Civil Liberties Union outlined. It contended:[159]

- It violates the First Amendment.
- Web site blocking is erratic and ineffective.
- It was passed against the advice of Congress' own experts.
- Web blocking is contrary to the mission of public libraries.
- It will widen the digital divide.

Nevertheless, six justices agreed to reverse the lower court and uphold the law. The plurality opinion, written by Chief Justice William Rehnquist, noted that Internet pornography has been a serious problem for public libraries: "Some patrons also expose others to pornographic images by leaving them displayed on Internet terminals or printed at library printers." The federal government provides two sources of funding to public libraries: (1)

---

formation. Under this reasoning, a court might be less sympathetic to someone using a library computer to send information.

[153] Paul Levy, *Complaints Filed Over Web Porn*, STAR TRIB., May 4, 2000, at 1B; Paul Levy, *Minneapolis Public Library Revises Internet Policy*, STAR TRIB., May 18, 2000, at 3B.

[154] American Library Ass'n v. United States, 201 F. Supp. 2d 401 (E.D. Pa. 2002).

[155] *Id.* at 406.

[156] *Id.* at 410.

[157] *Id. See also* Children's Internet Protection Act, 20 U.S.C.A. § 9134 (2003), at 342; 47 U.S.C.A. § 254 (2003), at 359.

[158] *Id.* at 490 n.36 (citing FCC v. League of Women Voters, 468 U.S. 364 (1984)).

[159] *American Civil Liberties Union, Blocking Programs On Trial: Why CIPA is Unconstitutional*, Mar. 30, 2002, http://www.aclu.org/court/CIPA_Intro.html.

discounted rates for Internet access and (2) technology grants for equipment. The Court considered filtering "reasonably effective."[160] Further, the law allows libraries to disable filters "to enable access for bona fide research or other lawful purposes."[161] The plurality rejected the First Amendment issues that the lower court raised but noted library decision-making and the need for broad discretion. Rehnquist found instead that "the government has broad discretion to make content-based judgments in deciding what private speech to make available to the public."[162]

Funding decisions typically use content-based criteria: "Public library staffs necessarily consider content in making collection decisions and enjoy broad discretion in making them."[163] Thus, a public library is not a public forum: It "does not acquire Internet terminals in order to create a public forum for Web publishers to express themselves, any more than it collects books in order to provide a public forum for the authors of books to speak."[164] Instead, the Court said library resources exist "to facilitate research, learning, and recreational pursuits by furnishing materials of requisite and appropriate quality."[165] Because Rehnquist found a library is not a public forum, he refused to apply a strict scrutiny standard:

A library's need to exercise judgment in making collection decisions depends on its traditional role in identifying suitable and worthwhile material; it is no less entitled to play that role when it collects material from the Internet than when it collects material from any other source. Most libraries already exclude pornography from their print collections because they deem it inappropriate for inclusion. We do not subject these decisions to heightened scrutiny; it would make little sense to treat libraries' judgments to block online pornography any differently, when these judgments are made for the same reason.[166]

The Court found no problem with the requirement that adults must ask librarians to unblock a Web site or disable a filter because "the Constitution does not guarantee the right to acquire information at a public library without any risk of embarrassment."[167] In a concurring opinion, Justice Breyer also rejected the strict scrutiny approach. "The statutory restriction in question," he wrote, "is, in essence, a kind of 'selection' restriction (a kind of editing)."[168]

This is especially true when there is a need to be "shielding" children from exposure.[169] In a dissenting opinion, Justice Stevens wrote that CIPA "operates as a blunt nationwide restraint on adult access to 'an enormous amount of valuable information' that individual librarians cannot possibly review."[170] He argued that government "may not suppress lawful speech" and reduce adult access to "only what is fit for children."[171] He wrote:

Unless we assume that the statute is a mere symbolic gesture, we must conclude that it will create a significant prior restraint on adult access to protected speech. A law that prohibits reading without official consent, like a law that prohibits speaking without consent, "constitutes a dramatic departure from our national heritage and constitutional tradition."[172]

Justice Stevens saw local library discretion as similar to academic freedom at a university, and penalizing funding violates the First Amendment: "An abridgment of speech by means of a threatened denial of benefits can be just as pernicious as an abridgment by means of a threatened penalty."[173]

In a strident separate dissent, Justice David Souter, joined by Justice Ginsburg, wrote that CIPA "says only that a library 'may' unblock, not that it must."[174] He criticized the statute:

Children could be restricted to blocked terminals, leaving other unblocked terminals in areas restricted to adults and screened from casual glances. And of course the statute could simply have provided for unblocking at adult request, with no questions asked. The statute could, in other words, have protected children without blocking access for adults or subjecting adults to anything more than minimal inconvenience, just the way (the record shows) many librarians had been dealing with obscenity and indecency before the imposition of federal conditions.[175]

---

[160] United States v. American Library Ass'n, 539 U.S. 194, 200 (2003).

[161] *Id.* at 201 (quoting 20 U.S.C. § 9134(f)(3) (2003); 47 U.S.C. § 254(h)(6)(D)).

[162] *Id.* at 204.

[163] *Id.* at 205.

[164] *Id.* at 206.

[165] *Id.* at 204 (holding, "To fulfill their traditional missions, public libraries must have discretion to decide what material to provide their patrons").

[166] *Id.* at 208.

[167] *Id.* at 209.

[168] *Id.* at 216 (Breyer, J., concurring) (citing Miami Herald Co. v. Tornillo, 418 U.S. 241, 256-58 (1974)).

[169] *Id.* at 219 (Breyer, J., concurring) (citing New York v. Ferber, 458 U.S. 747, 756-57 (1982)).

[170] *Id.* at 220 (Stevens, J., dissenting).

[171] *Id.* at 222 (Stevens, J., dissenting) (quoting Ashcroft v. Free Speech Coalition, 535 U.S. 234, 252, 255 (2002)).

[172] *Id.* at 225 (Stevens, J., dissenting) (quoting Watchtower Bible & Tract Soc. of N.Y. v. Vill. of Stratton, 536 U.S. 150, 166 (2002)).

[173] *Id.* at 227 (Stevens, J., dissenting).

[174] *Id.* at 233 (Souter, J., dissenting).

[175] *Id.* at 234 (Souter, J., dissenting).

Souter wrote that a local library could not, on its own, impose adult restrictions and that the opinion ignored that, when a library does not have a book, a patron may use interlibrary loan:

> [T]he Internet blocking here defies comparison to the process of acquisition. Whereas traditional scarcity of money and space require a library to make choices about what to acquire, and the choice to be made is whether or not to spend the money to acquire something, blocking is the subject of a choice made after the money for Internet access has been spent.... Thus, deciding against buying a book means there is no book (unless a loan can be obtained).... The proper analogy therefore is not passing up a book that might have been bought; it is either to buying a book and then keeping it from adults lacking an acceptable "purpose," or to buying an encyclopedia and then cutting out pages with anything thought to be unsuitable for all adults.[176]

Souter wrote that CIPA and the Court's support for it defied library history and reminded the Court that, by the time of McCarthyism, the American Library Association had explicitly opposed censorship in its own Bill of Rights. The American library tradition has favored adult access and adult inquiry:

> Quite simply, we can smell a rat when a library blocks materials already in its control, just as we do when a library removes books from its shelves for reasons having nothing to do with wear and tear, obsolescence, or lack of demand. Content-based blocking and removal tell us something that mere absence from the shelves does not.[177]

Souter concluded: "There is no good reason, then, to treat blocking of adult enquiry as anything different from the censorship it presumptively is."[178]

The Court has become increasingly interested in issues in Internet law, especially where there is concern about children accessing obscene or pornographic content and when the pornography industry victimizes them. The question of whether computer-animated "virtual child pornography" could be restricted came before the Court in 2001. An appeals court held that the Child Pornography Prevention Act of 1996 was unconstitutional in prohibiting computer images that do not involve real children but simply appear to be minors.[179] At issue

was whether there was a government interest beyond attempting to protect real victims of child pornography.[180] In a 6-3 decision, the Supreme Court ruled that CPPA violated the First Amendment.[181] It held that the statute's language was "overbroad and unconstitutional" because it defined images as "any visual depiction, including any photograph, film, video, picture, or computer-generated image or picture" that "is, or appears to be, a minor engaging in sexually explicit conduct."[182] The Court rejected government arguments that pedophiles could use virtual pornography to seduce children. Justice Kennedy's opinion said the law went beyond law the Court set forth in its child pornography case, *New York v. Ferber*: "As a general rule, pornography can be banned only if obscene, but under *Ferber*, pornography showing minors can be proscribed whether or not the images are obscene under the definition set forth in *Miller*."[183] However, restriction on computer-morphed images was found to be too sweeping.

By quoting the First Amendment, Justice Kennedy and the Court's majority made it clear that they found CPPA to be a disturbing intrusion on First Amendment rights:

> [A] law imposing criminal penalties on protected speech is a stark example of speech suppression. The CPPA's penalties are indeed severe. A first offender may be imprisoned for 15 years.... A repeat offender faces a prison sentence of not less than 5 years and not more than 30 years.... While minor punishments can chill speech, ... this case provides a textbook example of why we permit facial challenges to statutes that burden expression. With these severe penalties in force, few legitimate movie producers or book publishers, or few speakers in any capacity, would risk the distribution of images in or near the uncertain reach of this law. The Constitution gives significant protection from overbroad laws that chill speech within the First Amendment's vast and privileged sphere. Under this principle, the CPPA is unconstitutional on its face if it prohibits a substantial amount of protected expression.[184]

The articulation of a "vast and privileged sphere" of First Amendment protection is expansive in terms of the type of speech

---

176 *Id.* at 236-37 (Souter, J., dissenting).

177 *Id.* at 241 (Souter, J., dissenting).

178 *Id.* at 242 (Souter, J., dissenting).

179 Free Speech Coalition v. Reno, 198 F.3d 1083, 1086 (9th Cir. 1999) (reviewing the CPPA, 18 U.S.C. § 2556(8) (1996), definition prohibiting depictions that "convey the impression" that they are "sexually-explicit portrayals of minors").

180 *See* New York v. Ferber, 458 U.S. 747 (1982). Justice Stevens posed a hypothetical example: "If a child actor resided abroad, New York's interest in protecting its young from sexual exploitation would be far less compelling than in the case before us." *Id.* at 779. If a New York theater were offered a serious art film, which contained one lewd scene, a "federal interest in free expression" would be relevant. *Id.* Extended to virtual child pornography, there may be a weak state interest in stopping production and distribution of the content.

181 Ashcroft v. Free Speech Coalition, 535 U.S. 234 (2002).

182 *Id.* at 241 (quoting 18 U.S.C. § 2251, 2256(8)(B) and (D) (1996)).

183 *Id.* at 240 (citing New York v. Ferber, 458 U.S. 747 (1982); Miller v. California, 413 U.S. 15 (1973)).

184 *Id.* at 244.

under the umbrella of safety. Outside the safe zone are "defamation, incitement, obscenity, and pornography produced with real children."[185] By contrast, the Court was concerned that CPPA might render illegal Shakespeare's *Romeo and Juliet* or the popular movie *American Beauty*. CPPA, the Court found, failed to distinguish isolated sexual scenes from the *Miller* requirement to evaluate the "work as a whole." It rejected the argument that because virtual child pornography and real child pornography might soon be impossible to distinguish, prosecution would become difficult:

> The hypothesis is somewhat implausible. If virtual images were identical to illegal child pornography, the illegal images would be driven from the market by the indistinguishable substitutes. Few pornographers would risk prosecution by abusing real children if fictional, computer images would suffice.[186]

In his concurrence, Justice Thomas wrote that the government failed to provide evidence of any case in which someone charged with production of illegal child pornography had raised reasonable doubt by contending the images were virtual and not of real children.[187]

Justice O'Connor, writing for Chief Justice Rehnquist and Justice Scalia, offered a partial dissent. They disagreed that CPPA's virtual-child-pornography ban was overbroad: "Such images whet the appetites of child molesters, ... given the rapid pace of advances in computer-graphics technology, the Government's concern is reasonable."[188] Rehnquist added in a separate dissent that the CPPA statute had clearly defined explicit content as sex that was "genital-genital," "oral-genital," "anal-genital or oral-anal," "bestiality," "masturbation," "sadistic or masochistic abuse," or "lascivious exhibition of the genitals or pubic area."[189] Rehnquist and Scalia argued unsuccessfully that the definition relates only to hard-core child pornography and not to classic plays or movies.

At the time, Attorney General John Ashcroft responded to the decision by suggesting that it provided "a dangerous window of opportunity for child abusers ... left law enforcement at extreme disadvantage," and further opened a "thriving market for child pornography."[190]

---

[185] *Id.* at 246.

[186] *Id.* at 254.

[187] *Id.* at 259-60 (Thomas, J., concurring).

[188] *Id.* at 263-64 (O'Connor, J., concurring in judgment and dissenting in part). The government contended that advancing technology would allow a pornographer to hide behind the defense that there was no real victim to be found.

[189] *Id.* at 268 (Rehnquist, C.J., dissenting) (quoting 18 U.S.C. § 2256(2) (1996)).

[190] David Stout, *Ashcroft Pushes for Legislation to Ban Virtual Child Pornography*, N.Y. TIMES, May 1, 2002, *available at* http://www.nytimes.com.

Internet Libel

Portions of the Communications Decency Act not struck down by the *Reno v. ACLU* ruling have been used to protect Internet service providers from liability for libel.[191] A federal district court in 1998, for example, protected America Online from a libel suit by a Clinton administration official and his wife against the Drudge Report.[192] The report, republished on AOL's site, said the husband had a history of spousal abuse. The court ruled that the act protects providers of interactive services from liability for third-party materials. It said that, even though AOL exercises some editorial control and is more than a passive carrier, the law dictates that online providers be protected from liability. Internet gossip columnist Matt Drudge, as a result, was left to defend himself in the libel suit. In the years since the case, much remains unsettled about defamation on the free-wheeling Internet. As was noted earlier in the discussion of Twitter, the lack of a definable mass audience makes it difficult to measure economic impact of statements that *may* damage individual reputation.

Beyond libel law, the changing nature of the social Internet also renders problematic content owner rights. The emergence of a sharing culture, promoted by sites that encourage users the share content with online friends or fans, introduces a new media model. Content owners that benefit from advertising revenue generated by increased numbers of site visitors, must also try to protect property rights.

Copyright on the Internet

The Internet presents questions about protection of intellectual property rights. Copyright protects original material upon its creation, and the creator has exclusive rights to reproduce and distribute it, as well as the right to create other works derived from the original. Therefore, uploading a document or media file, copying an Internet posting and re-transmitting it without permission all could violate copyright and digital theft law.[193] Even browsing through material on a computer, which causes a copy of the digital information to be held in temporary memory, could possibly constitute illegal copying. Alternately, such use might be interpreted as the digital form of reading a book in a library or a magazine at a newsstand, and not a copyright infringement.[194]

The growth of Internet sites that link to or frame a small sec-

---

[191] *See* Zeran v. America Online, 129 F.3d 327 (4th Cir. 1997); Communications Decency Act, 47 U.S.C § 230.

[192] Blumenthal v. Drudge and America Online, 992 F. Supp. 44 (D.D.C. 1998).

[193] *See* Playboy Enters., Inc. v. Frena, 839 F. Supp. 1552 (M.D. Fla. 1993); Digital Theft Deterrence Act, 17 U.S.C. § 504(a), (c)(1)(1999).

[194] *See* Religious Technology Ctr. v. Netcom On-Line Commc'ns Servs., 907 F. Supp. 1361, 1378 n.25 (N.D. Cal. 1995).

tion of another site's content raised a new question of copyright infringement. In 1997, the *Washington Post* and five other news organizations charged a group of Internet news sites with copyright infringement for republishing and repackaging media Web pages for profit.[195] The organizations charged that the news sites copied trademarks for use as links and republished copyrighted material with advertising that generated revenue for the pirates rather than the copyright holders. The suit was settled out of court when the news sites agreed to provide links but not to frame any content from the news organization's sites. The *Los Angeles Times* won its case against FreeRepublic.com, a Web site that reprinted full-text online news stories and invited caustic reader reaction.[196]

Other copyright questions surround computer-generated material. To qualify for copyright protection, material must be fixed in a tangible medium and must be original. It remains to be determined whether material created and transmitted electronically is "fixed in a tangible medium." For example, a live broadcast is not fixed in a tangible medium and is not protected unless it is simultaneously put on videotape. In contrast, a document put on a hard drive disk, CD or DVD is fixed.[197] Thus, is material created on a computer, sent over the Internet and then not saved on the computer fixed in a tangible medium and subject to copyright protection? One court has held that material in a computer's random access memory is sufficiently fixed to be protected.[198]

In 1995 and again in 1998, Congress updated copyright laws in part to deal with such issues. It enacted the Digital Millennium Copyright Act of 1998 to eliminate an apparent loophole in the Digital Performance Rights in Sound Recordings Act that had permitted webcasters to digitally transmit recordings without copyright licenses or fees. The law grants webcasters a statutory license to transmit, with certain limitations, recordings at fees established voluntarily or by a Copyright Arbitration Royalty Panel.[199] The fees ended many webcasts. For example, some college radio stations ended webcasts when forced to pay as much as $20,000 in music licensing fees.[200]

In the meantime, the Supreme Court upheld the Sonny Bono Copyright Term Extension Act of 1998 as a constitutional

exercise of congressional powers.[201] The 7-2 decision dismissed concerns about free expression. However, Justices Stevens and Breyer wrote dissenting opinions. Breyer wrote: "The Copyright Clause and the First Amendment seek related objectives — the creation and dissemination of information."[202] In this view, the two should work together to promote free expression and dissemination of ideas. The law extended copyrights on, for example, Disney's Mickey Mouse for another twenty years to 2023.[203] Many twentieth century icons were kept out of the public domain. On another front, the rock music band Metallica sued the Napster.com site in 2000 for copyright infringement and racketeering over its free software that allowed users to trade MP3 copies of music on an unrestricted basis. The digital music format allowed CD quality songs to be converted into a personal computer format, and this made possible the easy distribution of pirated copies over the Internet. The software made it so easy that thousands of music bootleggers clogged university campus network systems.

International distribution of illegal copies *via* the Internet is a problem for Internet service providers and computer users. A German judge ruled that ISPs may be held liable for their roles in distributing illegal copies. However, the Supreme Court has let stand a New York Court of Appeals ruling that ISPs are not liable for transmissions but are akin to telephone and telegraph companies that are accorded common law qualified privilege against liability.[204] That ruling protected Prodigy from a defamation lawsuit. In the Metallica case, two of three universities — Yale and Indiana — blocked access to Napster.com in exchange for being dropped from the lawsuit. The band claimed large numbers of students were using campus computer systems to access the Napster site and trade pirated music. Metallica also identified 335,000 Napster screen names in 60,000 pages of documents.[205] Napster ultimately yielded to legal pressures by removing 317,377 users, a move that did not prevent the traders of bootleg music from returning.[206] At the same time, the company MP3.com settled its lawsuit by halting access to major label songs after a federal district court ruled its database of more than

---

[195] Washington Post Co. v. Total News Inc., No. 97 Civ. 1190 (S.D.N.Y., complaint filed Feb. 20, 1997).

[196] Los Angeles Times v. Free Republic, 2000 U.S. Dist. LEXIS 5669, No. 98-7840 (C.D. Cal. 1999).

[197] *See* Mai Sys. Corp. v. Peak Computer, Inc., 991 F.2d 511, 518 (9th Cir. 1993).

[198] *See id. See also* Triad Sys. Corp. v. Southeastern Express Co., 64 F.3d 1330 (9th Cir. 1995).

[199] Miscellaneous Provisions, Title IV of the Digital Millennium Copyright Act, H.R. 2281 (105th Cong., 2d Sess. 1998).

[200] *See* Mark L. Shahinian, *Why College Radio Fears the DMCA,* SALON, Dec. 18, 2001, http://www.salon.com.

[201] Eldred v. Ashcroft, 537 U.S. 186, 223 (2003), *reh'g denied,* 538 U.S. 916 (2003).

[202] *Id.* at 244 (Breyer, J., dissenting).

[203] *See* Lawrence Lessig, *Protecting Mickey Mouse at Art's Expense,* N.Y. TIMES, Jan. 18, 2003, at A17. Seven justices found that: "[T]he Constitution grants Congress an essentially unreviewable discretion to set the lengths of copyright protections however long it wants, and even to extend them." Linda Greenhouse, *Supreme Court to Intervene in Internet Copyright Dispute,* N.Y. TIMES, Feb. 19, 2002, *available at* http://www.ny times.com.

[204] Lunney v. Prodigy Servs. Co., 529 U.S. 1098 (2000). *See also* Richard Carelli, *Supreme Court Lets Stand Decision Freeing Internet Providers from Liability for E-Mail Content,* AP ONLINE, May 1, 2000, http://wire.ap.org.

[205] *See Metallica Delivers List of Alleged Music Pirates to Online Firm,* AP ONLINE, May 5, 2000, http://wire.ap.org.

[206] *See Napster Removes Users,* CNET NEWS, May 9, 2000, http://www.cnet.com.

80,000 songs was copyright infringement against Time Warner, Sony and others.[207] MP3 agreed to pay licensing fees to music companies. The Napster case, though, attracted much attention.

DIGITAL RIGHTS MANAGEMENT

Publishers and the entertainment industry have experimented with a variety of technologies designed to monitor, track, charge and restrict copying of copyrighted content. There is debate about the effectiveness of the DRM technologies. Additionally, research has found both positive and negative effects of file-sharing on sales and revenues.

Apple's Steve Jobs, arguing in 2007 that DRM does not work, pushed music companies to move away from the DRM model:

Imagine a world where every online store sells DRM-free music encoded in open licensable formats. In such a world, any player can play music purchased from any store, and any store can sell music which is playable on all players. This is clearly the best alternative for consumers, and Apple would embrace it in a heartbeat. If the big four music companies would license Apple their music without the requirement that it be protected with a DRM, we would switch to selling only DRM-free music on our iTunes store. Every iPod ever made will play this DRM-free music.

In 2006, music copies had sold about $2 million in DRM-protected music, but $20 million in unprotected songs. By 2010 the Apple iTunes store boasted more than 13 million songs available DRM-free at between 69 cents and $1.29 per legal download. With the exception of a relatively small number of artists and labels, Apple has been largely successful at moving the industry away from ineffective DRM systems, but DRM has been important for peotecting DVD and video game technologies.

Source: Steve Jobs, *Thoughts on Music*, Feb. 6, 2007, http://www.apple.com/hotnews/thoughtsonmusic/:Apple; *What is iTunes?*, http://www.apple.com/itunes/what-is/.

"Napster has built a business based on large-scale piracy," the complaint alleged.[208] The Recording Industry Association of America also sued over the distribution of MP3 music. A district court held that record companies and artists owned the music and issued an injunction prohibiting Napster from "engaging in, or facilitating ... copying, downloading, uploading, transmitting, or distributing ... copyrighted recordings."[209] The Ninth U.S. Circuit Court of Appeals agreed, holding that Napster infringed on music reproduction and distribution rights and that its sharing software went beyond a fair use.[210]

It distinguished Internet file sharing from the Supreme Court's ruling in *Sony Corp. v. Universal Studios, Inc.* that video cassette recorders constituted a fair use.[211] Following the decision, Napster was unable to reach an agreement with music companies to compensate them.[212] Subsequently, federal District Court Judge Marilyn Patel in San Francisco ordered Napster to curb trading of copyrighted music.[213] Napster went ahead with plans to develop a fee-based system, even though it had no initial agreement with record companies.[214] At the same time, alternative services such as Gnutella, Aimster, Grokster and Kazaa prompted new legal challenges, as record companies struggled to develop their own pay sites.[215] Ultimately, the controversy appeared to be moving toward resolution *via* business deals: Vivendi Universal (teaming with Sony and Yahoo! to form Duet) purchased MP3.com for about $372 million, and Bertelsmann aligned with Napster, EMI, AOL Time Warner and RealNetworks to form MusicNet.[216] agreed to pay $8 million for its assets.[217] In 2002 four of five record companies suspended legal action against Napster in order to avoid inquiries into their copyright actions; Napster continued to be threatened with bankruptcy; and Bertelsmann ultimately agreed to pay $8 million for its assets.[218]

The original Napster no longer exists; and Gnutella, Grokster, Madster, KaZaA and other services — after flourishing for awhile — faced various legal challenges in lower courts. In 2003,

---

[207] *MP3.com Settles Lawsuit*, REUTERS, May 10, 2000, http://www.reuters.com.

[208] John Borland, *Metallica Sues Napster, Colleges*, AP ONLINE, Apr. 14, 2000, http://wire.ap.org.

[209] A&M Records, Inc. v. Napster, Inc., 114 F. Supp. 2d 896, 927 (N.D. Cal. 2000).

[210] A&M Records, Inc. v. Napster, Inc., 239 F.3d 1004 (9th Cir. 2001).

[211] 464 U.S. 417 (1984).

[212] *See* Ron Harris, *Napster Offers Millions to Nix Case*, AP ONLINE, Feb. 21, 2001, http://wire.ap.org.

[213] *See* Matt Richtel, *Judge Orders Napster to Police Trading*, N.Y. TIMES, Mar. 7, 2001, at C1.

[214] *See* Matt Richtel, *Napster Planning Fees Starting in the Summer*, N.Y. TIMES, Feb. 21, 2001, at C6.

[215] *See* Hana C. Lee, *Aimster Gets the Napster Treatment*, THE STANDARD, May 24, 2001, http://www.thestandard.com; Rob Tedeschi, *E-Commerce Report: Record Labels Struggle With Napster Alternatives*, N.Y. TIMES, Apr. 23, 2001, at 7. Aimster, later known as Madster, used instant-messaging to allow file sharing between people on a buddy list. The company said it could not police private Internet exchanges. It was sued in New York. While it and Napster continued to operate, another firm called "Scour" declared bankruptcy.

[216] *See* Andrew Ross Sorkin, *Vivendi in Deal to Acquire MP3.com*, N.Y. TIMES, May 21, 2001, at C1.

[217] *See* Matt Richtel, *Judge Grants a Suspension of Lawsuit on Napster*, N.Y. TIMES, Jan. 24, 2002, at C4; Matt Richtel, *Plaintiffs Sought Timeout After Turn in Napster Case*, N.Y. TIMES, Jan. 31, 2002, at C5; Matt Richtel, *Turmoil at Napster Moves the Service Closer to Bankruptcy*, N.Y. TIMES, May 15, 2002, at C1; John Schwartz, *Bertelsmann, In a Reversal, Agrees to Acquire Napster*, N.Y. TIMES, May 18, 2002; Neil Strauss, *Record Labels' Answer to Napster Still Has Artists Feeling Bypassed*, N.Y. TIMES, Feb. 18, 2002, at A1. *See also* Perfect 10, Inc. v. Amazon.com, Inc., 508 F.3d 1146 (9th Cir. 2007); Atlantic Recording Corp. v. Brennan, 534 F. Supp. 2d 278 (D. Conn. 2008).

[218] *See* Matt Richtel, *Judge Grants a Suspension of Lawsuit on Napster*, N.Y. TIMES, Jan. 24, 2002, at C4; Matt Richtel, *Plaintiffs Sought Timeout After Turn in Napster Case*, N.Y. TIMES, Jan. 31, 2002, at C5; Matt Richtel, *Turmoil at Napster Moves the Service Closer to Bankruptcy*, N.Y. TIMES, May 15, 2002, at C1; John Schwartz, *Bertelsmann, In a Reversal, Agrees to Acquire Napster*, N.Y. TIMES, May 18, 2002; Neil Strauss, *Record Labels' Answer to Napster Still Has Artists Feeling Bypassed*, N.Y. TIMES, Feb. 18, 2002, at A1. *See also* Perfect 10, Inc. v. Amazon.com, Inc., 508 F.3d 1146 (9th Cir. 2007); Atlantic Recording Corp. v. Brennan, 534 F. Supp. 2d 278 (D. Conn. 2008).

THE MUSIC LABELS VERSUS FILE SHARING

Although the Recording Industry Association of America ceased filing lawsuits in December 2008, the industry group continues to pursue previous cases against individuals using peer-to-peer sites to share copyrighted songs and video. In a Boston case, four labels — Sony BMG, Warner Bros., Arista and UMG — won a $675,000 civil jury award in 2009 against a graduate student who "willfully engaged in thousands of copyright infringements," but it was subsequently reduced by a judge in 2010 to $67,500, or $2,250 per infringement (one-third of a federal statute minimum $750) from thirty songs illegally shared. District Judge Nancy Gertner, in a sixty-two-page order, rejected both the recording industry desire to tie the case to billions of dollars in claimed losses and a Harvard legal team argument of much lower actual damages based upon the iTunes price of 99 cents per legal download (the industry receives seventy cents "wholesale price"). Instead, Judge Gertner found that a jury award was higher than she would have ordered and "unconstitutionally excessive" damages, in part, because those who have settled paid so much less:

> This award is far greater than necessary to serve the government's legitimate interests in compensating copyright owners and deterring infringe-ment. In fact, it bears no meaningful relationship to these objectives.... I have merely reduced the award to the greatest amount that the Constitu-tion will permit given the facts of this case. There is no question that this reduced award is still severe, even harsh. It not only adequately com-pensates the plaintiffs for the relatively minor harm that Tenenbaum caused them; it sends a strong message that those who exploit peer-to-peer networks to unlawfully download and distribute copyrighted works run the risk of incurring substantial damages awards. Tenenbaum's behavior, after all, was hardly exemplary. The jury found that he not only violated the law, but did so willfully.

The industry sent thousands of claims letters over several years to alleged violators and settled out of court with most for payments of less than $5,000. A handful of people refused to settle, and these cases continue to go forward. In Minnesota, for example, one woman was hit with a $1.9 million jury award, which was later reduced to $54,000 in a second trial. In the Boston case, the Digital Theft Deterrence Act of 1999 was used against a graduate student who admitted he had freely shared copyrighted music. In 1999, the record showed, Joel Tenenbaum had used Napster to download songs and place them in a shared folder. After Napster closed, he used Kazaa and other services, such as LimeWire, through 2007. Under federal procedure, Tenenbaum could have received a new trial, but his legal team raised a constitutional challenge. At issue is the constitutionally permissible size of punitive damages and the statutory range provided under the digital theft law. On appeal in the First Circuit, Tenenbaum's lawyer argued in April 2011 that the jury verdict was excessive, unreasonable and in violation of due process. At oral arguments, judges seemed skeptical about the need to protect noncommercial copyright infringers.

Meanwhile, following a $105 million settlement with LimeWire, RIAA went after Box.Net copyright infringers. Using the Digital Millennium Copyright Act, Mashable.com reported that takedown notices were issued to copyright infringers. An attorney for plaintiffs pointed to congressional intent to punish willful conduct. Tennenbaum had been warned that what he was doing was wrong, and he persisted with the behavior on more than one site — even after one location was closed. The music industry said it needs to now stop noncommercial copies because Internet peer-to-peer technologies have a "viral nature" that empowers users to damage copyright holders: "Now, this technology turns home copiers into home distributors." The unprecedented nature of what the technology allows an individual to do, plaintiffs argued, forced music labels to protect their economic interests. Appellate judges, however, also heard that restrictive limits on noncommercial use also are harmful to libraries and archives.

Sources: Jonathan Saltzman, *Judge Slashes Downloading Penalty, Calls $675k Award in BU Student's Case "Excessive,"* Boston Globe, July 10, 2010, *available at* http://boston.com; Nancy Gohring, *Judge Cuts File-sharing Fine to $67,500,* It World, http://itworld.com/print/113554; Debbie Rosenbaum, *Gertner's Ruling on Damages*, Joel Fights Back, http://joelfightsback.com/; Sony BMG Music et al. v. Tenenbaum, 721 F. Supp. 2d 85 (D. Mass. 2010); Digital Theft Deterrence Act, 17 U.S.C. § 504(a), (c)(1) (1999); Brenna Erlich, *After LimeWire, the RIAA Cracks Down on Box.Net Infringers*, Mashable, http://mashable.com/2011/05/20/riaa-boxnet/.

---

the recording industry filed lawsuits against hundreds of people, including college students in campus housing and par-ents of teens who illegally shared music. However, it lost a case before the D.C. Circuit Court of Appeals that would have re-quired Verizon and other ISPs to comply with court subpoenas to turn over the names of customers.[219]

The copyright challenges raised the issue of whether Napster-like sites could survive economically by charging user fees to supplement advertising revenues. Napster was forced to show it was eliminating illegal file swapping and creating new software to monitor the behavior of users.[220] Thus, the one-time adver-

saries became partners.[221] One of the success stories is Apple's iTunes Music Store. It enables users to listen to thirty-second clips, legally download music for ninety-nine cents per song, and then create customized compact discs.[222]

In 2005, the Supreme Court overturned the Ninth Circuit Court summary judgments that had insulated Grokster and Streamcast Networks from copyright infringement liability. In *MGM v. Grokster*, the Court held that "one who distributes a de-vice with the object of promoting its use to infringe copyright, as

---

[219] RIAA v. Verizon, 351 F.3d 1229 (D.C. Cir. 2003).

[220] *See* Christopher Stern, *Napster Signs Deal to Offer Music from Record Giants,*

Wash. Post, June 6, 2001, at E1.

[221] *See* David D. Kirkpatrick & Matt Richtel, *Napster Near Accord on Music Sales,* N.Y. Times, June 5, 2001, at C1.

[222] *See* http://www.Apple.com/music/store.

shown by clear expression ... is liable."[223] The peer-to-peer networks featured the sharing of mostly copyrighted works, without any attempt to filter. The Court found that file sharing was not similar to VCR recording, which the 1984 *Sony* decision protected from liability. The number of downloads each day influenced the Court's decision, but the opinion stopped short of revisiting the earlier law: "It is enough to note that the Ninth Circuit's judgment rested on an erroneous understanding of *Sony* and to leave further consideration of the *Sony* rule for a day when that may be required."[224] Digital video recording devices, such as TiVo, however, may hasten the day when the Court will reconsider whether the VCR recording protection afforded in the *Sony* case for the purpose of time-shifting program viewing will survive.[225]

A 1995 committee report of the U.S. Patent and Trademark Office to consider copyright questions on the Internet failed to resolve the issues.[226] While it suggested that computer transmissions should be considered "copies" similar to photocopies of a book page, it decided that existing copyright law was generally adequate to deal with the Internet.[227]

Conditions changed quickly on the Web. If a subscriber uses a service to send copyrighted material, is the service as well as the user guilty of copyright violation? For example, a company could publish a magazine online. A user could copy a story and send it to millions of Internet users. Who is liable?[228] Two courts have found ISPs liable for their subscribers' copyright infringements,[229] and one has found to the contrary.[230] A key factor was whether the provider had, or should have had, prior knowledge of the infringement. Online providers who electronically screen or preview material may be held accountable for copyright infringements, although providers who act as common carriers may not.

Google, by uploading copyrighted book material, has become involved in what is known as the Google Book Search Settlement.[231] An administrator in the class-action lawsuit is creating a system to pay authors for use of their works.

DVD copying is also a problem. An engineering student faced a lawsuit for publishing on the Internet a code to unscramble encryption for copy protection.[232] Motion Picture Association of America representatives testified to Congress that an estimated 350,000 movies were being downloaded illegally each day at a cost of billions of dollars to the industry.[233]

A new problem has arisen from the theft of wireless network signals from homes and business. People have broken into private networks in order to facilitate illegal file transfers. In 2005, for example, St. Petersburg, Florida, police arrested a 41-year-old who had hacked into a home network by parking his SUV nearby and using a laptop computer.[234] The case was one of the first to raise significant legal issues about theft of online bandwidth. Further, in apartment complexes, a computer user might "see" more than one access point, and it is possible for there to be confusion over legal (with permission) and illegal access. Clearly, the convenience of wireless networking comes at a price — the availability of signals for potentially illegal activities and the possibility of invasion of privacy of legal and paying users. ISP liability continues to spawn new case law. For example, Craigslist — used by individuals to advertise — was found not liable for housing classifieds that discriminated in violation of federal law[235] and also entitled to immunity from gun violence that may have resulted from a weapon purchased online.[236] State attorneys general and lawmakers continued to target Craigslist and its inability to filter all illegal activities, including under-aged sex trafficking. Craigslist responded with changes — removing all adult advertising.[237]

The Internet and Privacy Issues

Workers using the Internet for personal reasons could find that employers have access to everything. People using the Internet from home for banking, shopping and email could find they have less privacy protection than when engaging in such activities by

---

[223] 545 U.S. 913, 914 (2005).

[224] *Id.* at 934.

[225] The Cartoon Network v. CSC Holdings & Cablevision Sys., 536 F.3d 121 (2d Cir. 2008). In a reversal of the lower court, Cablevision was not liable for direct copyright infringement when customers used their DVRs, which relied upon buffering and hard-drive storage at Cablevision rather than on private home recorders.

[226] Working Group on Intellectual Property Rights, Information Infrastructure Task Force, Intellectual Property and the National Information Infrastructure (1995) (White Paper).

[227] *See* Jeri Clausing, *Report Proposes Update of Copyright Act*, N.Y. TIMES, May 22, 2000, at C6.

[228] *See* Playboy Enters. v. Frena, 839 F. Supp. 1552 (M.D. Fla. 1993).

[229] *See id.;* Sega v. MAPHIA, 857 F. Supp. 679 (N.D. Cal. 1994).

[230] Religious Technology Ctr. v. Netcom On-Line Commc'ns Servs., 907 F. Supp. 1361 (N.D. Cal. 1995).

[231] *See* http://googlebooksettlement.com.

[232] *See* Andrea L. Foster, *Free-Speech Group Backs Former Purdue U. Student Accused in DVD-Decoding Case*, N.Y. TIMES, May 2, 2002, *available at* http://www.nytimes.com.

[233] *See* Press Release, Motion Picture Association of America, Valenti Testifies to Studios' Desire to Distribute Movies Online to Consumers (Apr. 23, 2002), *available at* http://www.mpaa.or/MPAAPress/.

[234] *See* Alex Leary, *WiFi Cloaks a New Breed of Intruder*, ST. PETERSBURG TIMES, July 4, 2005, at 1A.

[235] Chicago Lawyers' Committee v. Craigslist, 519 F.3d 1361 (7th Cir., 2008), aff'g Chicago Lawyers' Committee v. Craigslist, 461 F. Supp. 2d 681 (7th Cir. 2006), in which a district court found the predominance of user-generated content on the Web site meant Craigslist should not be treated as a publisher. Thus, the immunity from liability meant Craigslist, as the messenger, could not be sued.

[236] Gibson v. Craigslist, 2009 U.S. Dist. LEXIS 53246 (June 15, 2009).

[237] *See* Cecilla Kang, *Adult Ads Permanently Off U.S. Cites, Craigslist Says*, WASHINGTON POST, Sept. 16, 2010, at A22.

mail or in person. Additionally, social networking sites allow users to set privacy settings, but new users may skirt them.

A 13-year-old in 2005 lied about her age and then at 14 met a 19-year-old online. He sexually assaulted her when they met in person.[238] Her mother sued, claiming, "MySpace failed to implement basic safety features,"[239] but a lower court rejected negligence because findings were "barred by the CDA and Texas common law"[240] — a finding affirmed. In another MySpace case, criminal prosecution of Missouri mother was tentatively tossed by as U.S. District Judge. Lori Drew was convicted of violating MySpace terms of service by creating a false profile of a boy named "Josh Evans." It was used to get back at her daughter's former girlfriend Megan Meier, 13, who later committed suicide after online flirting exchanges with the fictitious boy, who dumped her in a message that said "the world would be better without [you] in it."[241] In other developments:

- A police search of a smartphone by arresting officers without a warrant generally violates the Fourth Amendment.[242]
- Google apologized for Street View vehicles collecting personal data from open WiFi networks, and Facebook reported conducting secret psychological content filtering experiments — a top company officer apologized that the routine product testing was "poorly communicated."[243]
- Facebook won an $873 million judgment against a Canadian spammer who flooded more than four million users with sexually explicit messages promoting penis enlargement products and illegal drugs.
- YouTube banned videos intended to incite violence or encourage dangerous, illegal activities.

Politwoops, a Web site that archived politicians' tweets, raised issues about the privacy rights of a user to delete content once published. The Open Foundation created the site at a 2010 meeting of computer hackers in the Netherlands. The Sunlight Foundation extended access to the United States in 2012. Because of legal issues, Politwoops faced closure in about 30 countries. Twitter disconnected access within the United States,

citing Terms of Service violations.[244] It was criticized for the action.

Walmart sent Jeph Jaques, author and cartoonist, a cease-and-desist letter for the Walmart.horse Web site. It featured only the image of a horse pasted in front of a store photograph. Walmart did not accept simple fair use parody instead of trademark infringement. It then filed a complaint with the World Intelectual Property Organisation under the Uniform Domain Name Dispute Resolution policy. Rather than litigate, the Web site was voluntarily removed.[245]

New technologies also threatened to erode traditional common law views about the sanctity of privacy in one's own home. Privacy becomes a question when law enforcement authorities tap into computer transmissions. While a court order is required, it may be possible for computer users to encrypt transmissions. In 1993 the National Security Agency proposed a clipper chip to allow decoding.

Web-based telephone services, such as Vonage, posed an interesting privacy problem for regulators and the courts. The U.S. Court of Appeals, D.C. Circuit, upheld the FCC decision that law enforcement agencies require wiretap compatibility. The court, though, exempted university and private computer networks, as well as instant messaging.[246] The clarification of the scope of the Communications Assistance for Law Enforcement Act, CALEA, meant that voice over Internet protocol was not exempt from telecommunication regulation under all circumstances.

Another privacy issue involves Web site content that is considered a threat. A federal jury in Portland, Oregon, ordered abortion protesters to pay $109 million in damages resulting from the Nuremberg Files site.[247] The site featured images of dripping blood and fetuses and was ordered to close. It resembled a hit list of abortion providers, some of whom were victims of violence, and listed names and towns of doctors providing abortions.[248] The case was appealed on First Amendment grounds. A legal scholar worried that the decision may be used in the future as a precedent to hold protesters liable for the violent acts of others."[249]

---

[238] Jane Doe v. MySpace, News Corp., 528 F.3d 413 (5th Cir. 2008).

[239] *Id.* at 416.

[240] *Id.* at 417 (citing Jane Doe v. MySpace, 474 F. Supp. 2d 843, 849 (W.D. Tex. 2007)).

[241] Tom McCarthy & Scott Michels, *Lori Drew MySpace Suicide Hoax Conviction Thrown Out,* ABC NEWS, July 2, 2009, http://abcnews.go.com/TheLaw/story?id=7977226&page=1.

[242] Riley v. California, 134 U.S. 2473 (2014).

[243] *See* Joshua Brustein, *Google's Street View Snooping Problems Aren't Going Away,* BLOOMBERG BUSINESSWEEK, July 1, 2014, *available at* http://www.buissiness week.com/articles/2014-06-30/googles-street-view-snooping-problems-arent-going-away; Nick Summers, *Facebook COO Sheryl Sandberg Apologizes for* Psychological *News Feed Experiment,* TNW, July 2, 2014, http://thenextweb.com/facebook/2014/07/02face book-coo-sheryl-sandberg-apologises-psychological-news-feed-experiment/.

[244] *Website That Saves Politicians' Deleted Tweets Faces Deletion,* AFP, June 4, 2015, *available at* http://www.thejakartapost.com/news/2015/06/05/website-saves-poli ticians-deleted-tweets-faces-deletion.html.

[245] Alex Hern, *Supermarket Giant Shuts Walmart.horse Website After Joke Has Bolted,* THE GUARDIAN, May 19, 2015, *available at* http://www.theguardian.com/tech nology/2015/may/19/jeph-jaques-walmart-horse-website.

[246] Am. Council of Educ. v. FCC, 451 F.3d 226 (D.C.Cir. 2006).

[247] *See* Planned Parenthood of Columbia/Willamette, Inc. v. Am. Coalition of Life Activists, 41 F. Supp. 2d 1130 (D.Or. 1999).

[248] *See* Ashley Packard, *Threats or Theater? Does* Planned Parenthood v. American Coalition of Life Activists *Signify That Tests for "True Threats" Need to Change?* 5 COMM. L. & POL'Y 234 (2000).

[249] *Id.* at 266.

PRIVACY AT WORK
Ontario v. Quon
560 U.S. 746 (2010)

The Supreme Court reversed the Ninth Circuit Court of Appeals in finding in favor of the Ontario, California, Police Department and its monitoring of on-duty officer text messages.

In 2001, the city had issued police officers pagers, which had limits on the amount of text sent and received each month. When some officers exceeded the limits, a review of two months found that SWAT team member Jeff Quon had many personal and sexual messages during work hours. After being disciplined, he and other officers alleged violation of privacy on Fourth Amendment grounds, as well as the Stored Communications Act.

A district court found that the city had conducted a reasonable audit of the text messages and that the officers' privacy had not been violated, but the appeals court reversed the decision. At issue was the nature of a reasonable expectation of privacy at work, the ability of employers to conduct legitimate investigations of work-related misconduct and the evolving nature of the technology.

In a narrow ruling, the Supreme Court found the police department's warrantless search was reasonable because it was motivated by a legitimate work-related purpose and was not excessive in scope. A city policy informed employees that all messages on city-owned equipment could be reviewed in connection with computer use, the Internet and email. The text messages, however, had been sent and received over radio frequencies. Still, police officers had been given verbal advance warning that the general policy applied to texting. A case-by-case precedent led Justice Anthony Kennedy to write: "The judiciary risks error by elaborating too fully on the Fourth Amendment implications of emerging technology before its role in society has become clear." Justice Antonin Scalia disagreed on that point: "The-times-they-are-a-changin' is a feeble excuse for disregard of duty."

Beyond the Internet and Future Regulatory Issues

The 106th Congress proposed at least fifty bills seeking to regulate various aspects of the Internet — pharmacy consumer protection, online investor protection, spam advertising limitations, email protection and e-commerce protection.[250] One bill sought to limit sales of prescription drugs by requiring Web sites to include a page that lists licensed pharmacists.[251] The mood to regulate was promoted by cases such as that of a Seattle doctor ordered to halt online prescribing of the sexual dysfunction drug Viagra after a 16-year-old boy and a woman posing as a man obtained prescriptions.[252] The Food and Drug Administration raised concerns about the rampant online sale of prescription drugs. State attorneys general, meanwhile, maintained that licensing and monitoring of health care professionals should continue to be a matter of state regulation. Nevertheless, former U.S. Senate Democratic Leader Tom Daschle of South Dakota concluded that Congress had not kept pace with technological change. He stated: "Internet users are often promised basic privacy protection, only to have their expectations disappointed and their personal information put up for sale or disseminated in ways to which they never consented."[253]

The global nature of telecommunications will pose new challenges. In the United Kingdom, for example, the government in 2000 planned for a spy center capable of tracking every email and Web site hit; but civil libertarians were outraged at the plan, even if its purpose was to crack down on cyber crime.[254]

In the last several years, a variety of telecommunication developments have provided a landscape for monitoring the years ahead, including:

- FCC government auction of Advanced Wireless Services in 2006 raised more than $13 billion from 104 bidders, but mostly from the nation's largest carriers.[255]

- Worldwide Interoperability for Microwave Access is leading to 3.5 and 4G high-speed broadband and video access.[256] Internet convergence is accelerating because of broadband deregulation, DSL and cable modem parity concerns, and telephone company regulatory relief requests.[257]

- In 2008, the FCC "furthered the ability of wireless service providers and public safety entities to make use of broadcast spectrum to be recovered" following the digital television transition.[258]

- The Internet is increasingly *the* method of access to public records and information, such as televison station public files.[259]

- Spectrum recovery means that wireless mobile technology will have a wider playing field for innovation and market development.[260]

- Web privacy issues increased, as online advertising posed questions about user data gathered, stored and sold.[261]

---

[250] *See* Thomas, 106th Congress (1999-2000), Bill Text, *at* http://thomas.gov.

[251] Internet Pharmacy Consumer Protection Act, H.R. 2763, § 503B (Aug. 5, 1999).

[252] *See* Carol M. Ostrom, *Doctor Told to Halt Internet Prescriptions,* SEATTLE TIMES, Jan. 29, 2000, at A9.

[253] Tom Daschle, Report Card of the 106th Congress on Privacy, United States Senate, Dec. 14, 2000, *available at* http://thomas.loc.gov.

[254] *See To Civil Libertarians, It Smacks of Big Brother.com,* AP ONLINE, May 11, 2000, http://wire.ap.org.

[255] *See* 25TH ANNUAL INSTITUTE ON TELECOMMUNICATIONS POLICY & REGULATION 95-96 (Richard E. Wiley, Kathleen Q. Abernathy & R. Clark Wadlow eds. 2007).

[256] *Id.* at 139-40.

[257] *Id.* at 259-60.

[258] *See* 1 BRUCE P. KELLER, LEE LEVINE & JAMES C. GOODALE, COMMUNICATIONS LAW IN THE DIGITAL AGE 2008 17 (2008).

[259] *Id.* at 61-62.

[260] *Id.* at 91-92.

[261] 2 BRUCE P. KELLER, LEE LEVINE & JAMES C. GOODALE, COMMUNICATIONS LAW IN THE DIGITAL AGE 2008 73-76 (2008).

ELONIS v. UNITED STATES
135 S.Ct. 2001 (2015)

The United States Supreme Court reversed and remanded a conviction of Anthony Elonis for making Facebook threats in violation of 18 U.S.C.S., Sec. 875(c). The Court rejected a reasonable-person standard — instead requiring that the jury consider a defendant's mental state. The Court voted 8-1 (partial dissenting opinion).

While a reasonable-person standard is common in civil liability of tort law, the Court refused to apply a negligence standard to a criminal case. The majority concluded that it matters what a defendant thinks.

Elonis' wife left him, and he had used the pseudonym "Tone Dougie" on Facebook "to post self-styled rap lyrics containing graphically violent language and imagery concerning his wife, co-workers, a kindergarten class, and state and federal law enforcement." He used disclaimers that the posts were ficticious and an exercise of his First Amendment rights. Still, the targets of the alleged attacks — including his wife and former boss who fired him — sought protection orders. The FBI began monitoring the posts and later charged Elonis under the federal statute with a "threat... to injure the person of another."

At trial, Elonis sought a jury instruction that the government was required to prove that his intent was to communicate a "true threat." However, the judge instead instructed jurors that Elonis "could be found guilty if a reasonable person would forsee that his statements would be interpreted as a threat." Elonis was convicted on four of five counts, and he appealed. The Third Circuit U.S. Court of Appeals affirmed the conviction under the reasonable-person standard of a threat, and Elonis appealed this point of law to the Supreme Court.

Chief Justice John Roberts wrote the opinion that reversed the conviction. He first noted a 2010 "Halloween Haunt" post of a photograph in which Elonis held a toy knife to a co-worker's neck with a caption that said, "I wish" — leading to his firing and a new post:

"Moles! Didn't I tell y'all I had several? Y'all sayin' I had access to keys for all the f***in' gates. That I have sinister plans for all my friends and must have taken home a couple. Y'all think it's too dark and foggy to secure your facility from a man as mad as me? You see, even without a paycheck, I'm still the main attraction. Whoever thought the Halloween Haunt could be so f***in' scary?"

After the firing, Elonis adapted a sketch about killing the president and substituted his wife, explaining that while it is illegal to threaten to kill someone, it is not illegal to explain the law.

"Hi, I'm Tone Elonis. Did you know that it's illegal for me to say I want to kill my wife? ... It's one of the only sentences that I'm not allowed to say.... Now it was okay for me to say it right then because I was just telling you that it's illegal for me to say I want to kill my wife.... Um, but what's interesting is that it's very illegal to say I really, really think someone out there should kill my wife.... But not illegal to say with a mortar launcher..... I also found out that it's incredibly illegal, extremely illegal to go on Facebook and say something like the best place to fire a mortar launcher at her house would be from the cornfield behind it because of easy access to a getaway road and you'd have a clear line of sight through the sun room.... Yet even more illegal to show an illustrated diagram. [diagram of the house]."

Elonis went on to ask about the protection order, "Is it thick enough to stop a bullet?" Among his rap lyrics were "Pull my knife, flick my wrist, and slit her throat... Leave her Bleedin' from her jugular in the arms of her partner [laughter]." The Court, though, concluded from precedent that, "'the crucial element separating legal innocence from wrongful conduct' is the threatening nature of the communication... The mental state requirement must therefore apply to the fact that the communication contains a threat."

Justice Clarence Thomas dissented. He concluded that the Court overturned nine circuits but failed to replace the reasonable-person standard. In his view these were "true threats" that lacked First Amendment protection: "Nothing in the statute suggests that Congress departed from the 'conventional *mens rea* element' of general intent.... I would not impose a higher mental-state requirement here." He added that the "departure from our precedents" makes "threats one of the most protected categories of unprotected speech." Fighting-words doctrine, for example, has not "generally ... required a heightened mental state under the First Amendment."

In the end, the majority decision found error in a reasonable-person jury instruction. Instead, a lower court must consider any evidence of mental state in concluding the nature of a social media or other online threat.

Internet television challenged the traditional government-broadcast regulation model.[262] Author Ken Auletta has observed that we live in a confusing time with respect to mass media: "I think we have to look at the world as a great paradox.... On the one hand, you've got growing concentration.... On the other hand, you've got this democratic instrument, this technology, that basically challenges companies."[263] Daschle's Electronic Rights for the Twenty-First Century Act was not given

---

[262] *See Couch Potatoes: Let Your Fingers Do the Talking,* NEWSWEEK, Jan. 17, 2000, at 57.

[263] Cable News Network, Millennium 2000: Media in the New Century (Jan. 1, 2000), Lexis-Nexis database, News/Transcripts/CNN.

serious consideration.

SUMMARY

This chapter focused on legal and regulatory issues involving new communication technology — telephones, digital television and the Internet. The predicted convergence of online and wireless media is leading to new cases in the courts. The struggle is to find legal and regulatory standards that will pass constitutional muster years after the technological developments are no longer new.

Changing social and political conditions created from the September 11, 2001, terrorist attacks presented a new level of complexity. New communication technologies may be used for good or evil, and regulators struggle to allow for advances without making it easier to harm people. Some social media sites warn users about data they collect on postings and user locations.[264] As Facebook tells users: "Remember, when you post to another person's timeline, that person controls what audience can view the post. Additionally, anyone who gets tagged in a post may see it, along with their friends." User settings may limit public viewing, but data are saved for use by the company for advertising purposes and the government, if subpoened.

The Web continues to present new issues: fraudulent business practices,[265] the sale of World Trade Center items on eBay auctions, and attempts by France to impose fines on Yahoo! for sale of Nazi memorabilia, in violation of French law.[266]

The boundaries and limitations of communication and business in cyberspace remain unsettled. As one scholar has noted, digital and Internet technologies present a paradox: "Utopian and dystopian views about the future of the Internet describe two very different future scenarios."[267] Faced with such uncertainty, we will likely see much action within the courts, as parties dispute the virtual landscape.

In the business world, communication technologies remain very important. AT&T and other giants expand markets at the same time as they improve consumer access. When AT&T in

2007 moved to acquire Dobson Communications, the $2.8 billion offer attempted to consolidate rural and suburban networks.[268]

EMERGING TECHNOLOGY ISSUES

The development of Internet and social media sites offered fertile ground for important developments to watch:

- Google removal of search results, such as revenge porn.
- Facebook content filtering and removal.
- Social media site responses to government data requests.
- Reduced Internet speeds based upon hugh usage.
- Net neutrality complaints.
- Illegal videotaping of subjects without consent.
- Social media employee policies and state laws.
- Regulation of small drone video cameras.
- Photographer image rights.
- The European right to be forgotten cases.[269]
- Yik Yak, Burn Book and other apps that may promote Internet threats.
- Mobile video blocking technology by Apple to protect live concerts, but also potentially useful during law enforcement and military operations.

Source: AEJMC Law & Policy Division, Facebook group, https://www.facebook.com/groups/2811061986617877/

Competition between previously separate industries, such as is happening with cable and telephone companies, has created unfair situations that may force future government intervention.[270] At the same time, advances in technology will continue to present new legal challenges to the First Amendment freedoms of speech and press. As Jacques Ellul observed decades ago, "The process of technological encroachment upon reality always consists in breaking up reality into malleable fragmentary units."[271] On the international front, what some are calling a "mobile Internet" is rapidly opening new behaviors at the expense of others.

As we enter 2017, among the many pressing issues are the following:

- Evolving Terms of Service social networking site user agreements and expectations about privacy protection.

---

[264] See Facebook Privacy, http://www.facebook.com/about/privacy/your-info ("We receive data about you whenever you interact with Facebook.").

[265] See Ashley Ingber, *Cyber Crime Control: Will Websites Ever Be Held Accountable for the Legal Activities They Profit From?*, 18 CARDOZO J.L. & GENDER 423 (2012). Craigslist and other sites find it difficult to eliminate all free advertising for illegal activities, such as prostitution. In contrast, a ticket-selling site, such as StubHub, profits from every sale and may be liable for sale of fake or misrepresented tickets, a court ruled. See id.

[266] See Michael Cooper, *eBay is Asked to Remove Trade Center Items*, N.Y. TIMES, Feb. 22, 2002, *available at* http://www.nytimes.com.; Carl S. Kaplan, *French Decision Prompts Questions About Free Speech and Cyberspace*, N.Y. TIMES, Feb. 11, 2002, *available at* http://www.nytimes.com; Jennifer Lee, *3 Web Sites Closed In Spam Inquiry*, N.Y. TIMES, Mar. 12, 2002, at C6, *available at* http://www.nytimes.com.

[267] SUSAN B. BARNES, COMPUTER-MEDIATED COMMUNICATION 331 (2003).

[268] See *AT&T to Acquire Dobson Communications, Expand Wireless Coverage*, PR NEWSWIRE, June 29, 2007, http://www.prnewswire.com/cgi-bin/stories.pl?ACCT=104&STORY=/www/story/06-29-2007/0004618462 &E DATE=.

[269] Kirtley, *supra* note 20, at 102-03 ("[P]olicy advocates" advanced a proposal in 2012 "based on the right to privacy, or personality" within the European Convention for the Protection of Human Rights, Article 8 — "the right to respect for his private life and family life, his home and his correspondence.").

[270] See Seth Schiesel, *Cable Giants Refuse to Sell Ads to Internet Competitors*, N.Y. TIMES, June 13, 2001, *available at* http://www.nytimes.com. Time Warner Cable in New York refused to sell advertising to Verizon Communications promoting high-speed DSL Internet service that competes with cable modem service, and no laws or regulations appeared to prevent the block on competitors.

[271] JACQUES ELLUL. THE TECHNOLOGICAL SYSTEM 44 (1980).

- Use of "big data" for commercial and other purposes.
- Differing national legal standards and expectations within a global Internet.
- Ongoing concern about use of online sites to promote terrorism.
- Interest by companies and governmental interests in creating social media user guidelines.
- FTC review of advertising and public relations in online consumer review sites.
- Student and employee social media rights state laws.[272]
- Redefinition of digital piracy.
- Impact of TV content cord-cutting.

The path ahead will be defined by discussion of online privacy, broadband access and privacy protection, big data and security, mobile speeds and prices, data retention rules, and promotion of new technologies.[273]

Among the many newer cases and issues to watch in the year ahead: labor law limitations on employer social media policy restrictions;[274] broader labor and employment law changes;[275] and revenge porn and other potential content restrictions.[276]

The study of new communication technology, cyberspace law and telecommunication issues on the Internet presents many challenges and many opportunities alike. Within the broader context of communication and the law, regulation and court challenges are literally redefining the field. From algorithm filtering by media companies to surveillance and outright government censorship, new communication technology law will be increasingly complex.

FOR ADDITIONAL READING

Albarran, Alan B., ed. *The Social Media Industries*. New York: Routledge, 2013.

Beckett, Charlie, with James Ball. *WikiLeaks, News in the Networked Era*. Cambridge: Polity Press, 2012.

Dencik, Lina & Oliver Leistert, eds. *Critical Perspectives on Social Media Protest, Between Control and Emancipation*. London: Rowman & Littlefield.

Ekstrand, Victoria Smith. *Hot News in the Age of Big Data*. El Paso: LFB Scholarly Publishing, 2015.

Hunsinger, Jeremy & Theresa Senft, eds. *The Social Media Handbook*. New York: Routledge, 2014.

Lipschultz, Jeremy Harris. *Social Media Communication: Concepts, Practices, Data, Law and Ethics*. New York and London: Routledge, 2015.

Mihailidis, Paul. *Media Literacy and the Emerging Citizen: Youth, Engagement and Participation in Digital Culture*. New York: Peter Lang, 2014.

Mills, Jon L. *Privacy in the New Media Age*. Gainesville: University Press of Florida, 2015.

Stewart, Daxton R., ed. *Social Media and the Law, A Guidebook for Communication Students and Professionals*. New York: Routledge, 2013.

Strangelove, Michael. *Post-TV: Piracy, Cord-Cutting and the Future of Television*. Toronto: University of Toronto Press, 2015.

Webster, James G. *The Marketplace of Attention, How Audiences Take Shape in the Digital Age*. Cambridge: The MIT Press, 2014.

Wiley, Richard E., Kathleen Q. Abernathy & R. Clark Wadlow, eds. *25th Annual Institute on Telecommunications Policy & Regulation*. New York: Practicing Law Institute, 2007.

---

[272] *See* Kelby Clark, *Maryland Law Grants Students Social Media Privacy Rights,* USA TODAY, June 5, 2015, *available at* http:/college.usatoday.com/2015/06/05/social-media-privacy-rights-maryland-law/; Linn Freedman, *Oregon social media law signed by Governor,* JDSUPRA, June 5, 2015, *available at* http://www.jdsupra.com/legalnews/orego-social-media-law-signed-by-46598/.

[273] *See, Tag Archives: Telecommunications,* PRIVACY & INFORMATION LAW BLOG, June 4, 2015, *available at* http://www.huntonprivacyblog.com/tag/telecommunications/.

[274] *See* Kroger v. Granger, NLRB 107-CA-098566 (2014).

[275] Gregory A. Hearing & Jeffrey L. Patenaude, *The Times Are Still A Changin': Technology's Continued Impact on Labor and Employment Law.* 90 FLA. BAR.J. 57 (2016).

[276] Layla Goldnick, *Coddling the Internet: How the CDA Exacerbates the Proliferation of Revenge Porn and Prevents a Meaningful Remedy for Its Victims.* 21 CARDOZO J.L. & GENDER 583 (2015).

13

Intellectual Property

By Greg Lisby

➡️ **Headnote Questions**
- What is the copyright duration of works created since 1978?
- How does intellectual property differ from other forms of personal property?
- What part of expression does copyright protect?
- What are the parts of the Fair Use Doctrine? Which part is most important?
- What exclusive rights does a copyright holder have?
- What is the public domain, and why is it important to the function of copyright?
- What one characteristic must all works have before they are copyrightable?
- What types of information are not copyrightable?
- What two things must be established to prove copyright infringement?
- What is "poor man's copyright"?
- What is time-shifting, and how is it considered a fair use of copyrighted materials?
- How long does a trademark last and under what circumstances may it be renewed?
- What one characteristic must all marks have before they may be used as trademarks?

The First Amendment and the constitutional protections afforded what has become known as "intellectual property" are two sides of the same coin, in that their legal functions advance and balance the societal purpose of each other.[1] While the First Amendment protects freedom of speech, the Constitution's protections of intellectual property — video, music, books and other artistic works — create the right to profit financially from one's creative abilities and resourcefulness. To help reach this end, the Constitution gives Congress the power "to promote the Progress of Science and useful Arts, by securing for limited Times to Authors and Inventors the exclusive Right to their respective Writings and Discoveries."[2]

The Copyright Act of 1976 is the primary federal statutory application of this power over copyrights.[3] In the realm of trademarks and service marks, the Trademark Act of 1946, also known as the Lanham Act,[4] is the principal implementation of the power.

COPYRIGHTS

The relationship between copyright law and the First Amendment is so strong and so essential to the role of communication in the United States (in both its political/democratic and economic/capitalistic aspects) that, in *Harper & Row Publishers v. Nation Enterprises*, the U.S. Supreme Court labeled copyright "the engine of free expression"[5] — though some have described it instead as "an engine of corporate censorship."[6] As the Court explained in an earlier case, "[T]he economic philosophy behind

---

[1] Intellectual property consists of copyright, trademarks and patents. Copyright law protects original, created works, such as those of authors and artists. Trademark law protects the symbols and images that signify the authenticity of commercial goods or services. Patent law protects inventions and discoveries (and is beyond the scope of this chapter). *See What Is Copyright?* at ¶ 1, COPYRIGHT (2015), *available at* http://www.benedict.com/ (last visited June 15, 2016).

[2] U.S. CONST., art. I, § 8, ¶ 8. The Supreme Court has interpreted the phrase "to promote" as having the same meaning as, "to encourage" and "to stimulate." Goldstein v. California, 412 U.S. 546, 555 (1973).

[3] 17 U.S. Code 101 *et seq.* (2016).

[4] 15 U.S.C. 1051 *et seq.* (2016). The act was named for its sponsor, Rep. Frederick G. Lanham (D-Texas).

[5] 471 U.S. 539, 558 (1985).

[6] Siva Vaidhyanathan, *Copyright Jungle*, COLUMBIA JOURNALISM REV., September/October 2006, 42, at 44.

the clause empowering Congress to [protect] copy rights is the conviction that the encouragement of individual effort by personal gain is the best way to advance [the] public welfare through the talents of authors and inventors."[7] This "encouragement" takes the form of a guarantee of a fair return for one's creative labor as a means of promoting "the general public good."[8] Yet, because copyright also "has the potential of locking up knowledge, insight, information and wisdom from the rest of the world ... it is ... fundamentally a *conditional* restriction on speech and print. Copyright and the First Amendment are in constant and necessary tension."[9]

Thus, there are competing and yet complementary philosophical foundations for the protection of created works — competing, in that works protected by copyright, as a result of the economic monopoly given the works' owners, are unavailable for unrestricted use by others; and complementary, in that the assumption is that works no longer protected by copyright serve as the basis for the creation of new copyrightable works. Thus, the twofold purpose of copyright is (1) "to protect the rights of artists to profit from and control the use of their work" and (2) "to preserve [the] public interest by guaranteeing that eventually the right to use the works will pass into the public domain."[10] As will be seen, the law has generally treated the first foundation as the more important.

Though copyright law in Great Britain in 1710 began as a way for government to track and censor printed material through the granting of a royal privilege and license to printers, copyright law in the United States has always aimed to encourage creativity by providing authors and artists with legal protection for their creative activities. The first federal copyright law in 1790, adapted from the British statute, offered legal protection for fourteen years for books, maps and charts.[11] Prints were added to this list in 1802; musical compositions in 1831; dramatic compositions and the public performance thereof in 1856; photographs in 1865; drawings, paintings, sculpture and designs and models for the creation of fine art in 1870; and the performance of musical compositions in 1897.[12] The Copyright Act of 1909 provided for the protection of unpublished works de-

signed for exhibition or performance,[13] and, as technological innovation progressed through the twentieth century, resulting in the invention of the motion picture, the phonograph record, and radio and television broadcasts, all these various forms of communication were deemed copyrightable, to one degree or another. The Copyright Act of 1976 goes so far as to protect all "original works of authorship fixed in any tangible medium of expression, now known or later developed, from which they can be perceived, reproduced, or otherwise communicated, either directly or with the aid of a machine or device."[14]

By continually expanding the subject matter of copyright, Congress attempted to encourage creativity and innovation. Works whose copyrights have expired are deemed to be in the "public domain," available for public use in further creativity and innovation.[15] Works that are not eligible for the legal protection of copyright have always been in the public domain.

What's Copyrightable — and What's Not

Copyright law protects only the form or style — that is, the way something is described — in which an idea is expressed or communicated. The federal statute extends copyright protection to "original works of authorship," some of which are:[16]

1. Literary works
2. Musical works, including any accompanying words
3. Dramatic works, including any accompanying music
4. Pantomimes and choreographic works
5. Pictorial, graphic and sculptural works
6. Motion pictures and other audiovisual works
7. Sound recordings

---

[7] Mazer v. Stein, 347 U.S. 201, 209 (1954). Advancement of the public welfare includes, "[T]he production of literary [or artistic] works of lasting benefit to the world." Washingtonian Pub. Co. v. Pearson, 306 U.S. 30, 36 (1939).

[8] Twentieth Century Music v. Aiken, 422 U.S. 151, 156 (1975).

[9] Vaidhyanathan, *supra* note 6, at 45 (emphasis in original).

[10] Sabra Chartrand, *Congress Has Extended Its Protection for Goofy, Gershwin and Some Moguls of the Internet*, N.Y. TIMES, Oct. 19, 1998, at C2.

[11] Copyright Act of May 31, 1790, 1 Stat. 124.

[12] Copyright Act of 1802, 2 Stat. 171; Copyright Act of 1831, 4 Stat. 436; Copyright Act of 1856, 11 Stat. 138; Copyright Act of 1865, 13 Stat. 540; Copyright Act of 1870, 16 Stat. 212, Rev. Stat. §§ 4948-4971; Copyright Act of 1897, 29 Stat. 481, Rev. Stat. § 4966.

[13] Copyright Act of 1909, 35 Stat. 1075.

[14] 17 U.S.C. 102(a) (2016). *But see, e.g.*, Conrad v. AM Comm'ty Credit Union, 750 F.3d 634 (7th Cir. 2014) (where a singing performance in a banana costume was not "fixed" and thus not copyrightable).

[15] For example, Sherlock Holmes and the story elements included by Arthur Conan Doyle in the more than fifty works he published before Jan. 1, 1923, are no longer covered by copyright in the United States. *See* Klinger v. Conan Doyle Estate, 755 F. 3d 496 (7th Cir. 2014). *See also* Jennifer Schuessler, *Appeals Court Affirms Sherlock Holmes Is in Public Domain*, N.Y. TIMES, June 17, 2014, *available at* http://artsbeat. blogs.nytimes.com/2014/06/17/conan-doyle-estate-loses-sherlock-holmes-copyrightappeal/ (last visited June 15, 2016); Jennifer Schuessler, *Mystery He Won't Face: U.S. Copyright Laws*, N.Y. TIMES, Dec. 28, 2013, at C3. With regard to films, *see* Nicolas Rapold, *Even Good Films May Go to Purgatory*, N.Y. TIMES, Feb. 16, 2014, Arts & Leisure, at 16-17.

[16] Issues of "authorship" are increasingly the topic of litigation. *See* Larry Rohter, *For a Classic Motown Song About Money, Credit Is What He Wants*, N.Y. TIMES, Sept. 1, 2013, at A1. Publishers are increasingly willing to give credit where credit is due. *See* Ben Sisario, *Who Wrote "Uptown Funk"? RCA Adds 5 to Credits*, N.Y. TIMES, May 2, 2015, at C3; Ben Sisario, *Petty to Get a Credit on Sam Smith Hit*, N.Y. TIMES, Jan. 27, 2015, at C3. Questions about the "what" and the "how" of art's protection by copyright (item 5 in the list) are also of increasing scholarly interest. *See, e.g.*, Kenneth Crews & Melissa Brown, *Control of Museum Art Images: The Reach and Limits of Copyright and Licensing*, *in* THE STRUCTURE OF INTELLECTUAL PROPERTY LAW 269-84 (A. Kur & V. Mizaras eds., 2011); Patricia Cohen, *Art Is Long; Copyrights Can Be Even Longer*, N.Y. TIMES, Apr. 25, 2012, at C1, C2.

8. Architectural works

Copyright does not protect any of the elements inherent in, underlying or part of the manner in which an idea is expressed or communicated. This distinction is known as the "idea/expression dichotomy." Copyright thus protects the expression, not the idea itself. What this means is that "copyright does not preclude others from using the ideas or information revealed by the author's work."[17] In *Baker v. Seldon,* the Supreme Court used this rule to distinguish between the copyrightability of a book (that is, the form of the expression of the idea) and the non-copyrightability of the "peculiar system [or method] of bookkeeping" explained in the book (that is, the idea itself),[18] noting that "there is a clear distinction between the book, as such, and the art which it is intended to illustrate."[19] The Court concluded: "The description of the art in a book, though entitled to the benefit of copyright, lays no foundation for an exclusive claim to the art itself. The object of the one is explanation; the object of the other is use."[20]

As a result, copyright law does not protect news, facts, ideas or theories,[21] procedures, concepts, processes, systems, methods of operation, principles,[22] history, works produced by the federal government,[23] standard calendars, height and weight charts, typography or blank forms, listings of ingredients or contents, formulas, compounds, recipes, titles, names, short phrases and slogans, other facts and works consisting entirely of information that is common property and contains no original authorship, useful articles and works of function or utility — including, clothing — whose design is generally one of style,[24] and anything not expressed in tangible form, such as narrated ideas.[25]

The leading case that delineates the distinction between what is and is not copyrightable is *Feist Publications v. Rural Telephone Service.*[26] The issue involved whether the alphabetical listing of names in the white pages of telephone books may be copyrighted. Though facts themselves are not copyrightable, a compilation — or the form — in which facts appear generally is.[27] Feist took the alphabetical listing of names in the Rural Telephone Service's telephone book after Rural refused to license the use of the names in a Feist-produced phone book.[28] The question was: Did Feist violate Rural Telephone Service's copyright?

The Supreme Court said, no, and sided with Feist. Works protected by copyright must be "original to the author," though not

---

[17] House of Representatives Report No. 94-1476, 94th Congress, 2d Session, 56-57 (1976). *See, also, e.g.,* Andy Newman, *Artist Challenges Genesis of Duke Riley's Illuminated-Pigeon Project,* N.Y. TIMES, May 27, 2016, *available at* http://nyti.ms/1U17 20m (last visited June 15, 2016).

[18] 101 U.S. 99, 100 (1879).

[19] *Id.* at 102.

[20] *Id.* at 105. Methods and processes, along with inventions and discoveries, may be protected by patent law.

[21] *See, e.g.,* Hoehling v. Universal City Studios, 618 F. 2d 972 (2d Cir. 1980) (where an author unsuccessfully claimed copyright infringement when his theory of sabotage was used as the central theme of a motion picture about the 1937 crash in New Jersey of the German airship, the Hindenburg). *See also* Dave Itzkoff, *Copyright Suit Dismissed,* N.Y. TIMES, Aug. 20, 2011, at C2 (where the work of two photographers was held to share only "the same fundamental idea").

[22] *See* U.S. Copyright Office, Ideas, Methods or Systems (2012), *available at* http://www.copyright.gov/circs/circ31.pdf (last visited June 15, 2016). *See also* Ian Lovett, *Court Rules "Hot Yoga" Isn't Entitled to Copyright,* N.Y. TIMES, Oct. 15, 2015, at A18.

[23] Exceptions include stamps and similar designs. On the other hand, works produced by state governments appear to be subject to copyright (in that no statute or court ruling states that they are not), though the U.S. Copyright Office takes the position that a state's laws may not be copyrighted. *See* U.S. Copyright Office, *Edicts of Government,* COMPENDIUM OF THE U.S. COPYRIGHT OFFICE PRACTICES § 313.6(C)(2), at 300:37 (3d ed., 2014), *available at* http://www.copyright.gov/comp3/ (last visited June 15, 2016). An "Edicts of Government" amendment to the Copyright Act has been proposed to clarify that such edicts are not copyrightable. *See The Edicts of Government Amendment,* PUBLICRESOURCE.ORG, May 7, 2013, https://law.resource.org/pub/edicts .html (last visited June 15, 2016). Whether non-government generated "official" annotations of government works are protected by copyright is now being litigated. *See also* Code Revision Comm'n of Georgia v. Public.Resource.org, No. 1:2015cv02594 (N.D. Ga., July 21, 2015); Martha Neil, *Georgia Sues Carl Malamud Group, Calls Publishing State's Annotated Code of Laws Online Unlawful,* ABA J., July 24, 2015, *available at* http://www.abajournal.com/news/article/State_of_Georgia_sues_Carl_Mala mud_says_he_published_its_annotated_code_of (last visited June 15, 2016).

[24] The Supreme Court is expected to determine when a useful article may be protected by copyright in its 2016-2017 term, when it rules in *Star Athletica v. Varsity Brands,* No. 15-866, *cert. granted,* May 2, 2016, 799 F. 3d 468 (6h Cir. 2015) (where the utility of uniform design elements was at issue). *See,* Eriq Gardner, *Supreme Court to Hear Fight over Cheerleader Uniforms,* HOLLYWOOD REPORTER, May 2, 2016, *available at* http://www.hollywoodreporter.com/thr-esq/supreme-court-hear-fight-cheerleader-889321 (last visited June 15, 2016). *Compare* Kurt S. Adler, Inc. v. World Bazaars, 897 F. Supp 92 (S.D. N.Y. 1995) (where stereotypical elements of Santa Claus are not protectable), *with* Barton Candy v. Tell Chocolate Novelties, 178 F. Supp. 577 (E.D. N.Y. 1959) (where the jolly elf in different arrangements is original and thus copyrightable). *Compare* Masquerade Novelty v. Unique Industries, 912 F. 2d 663 (3d Cir. 1990) (where animal nose masks were not "useful articles" and were thus copyrightable), *with* Whimsicality v. Rubie's Costumes, 721 F. Supp. 1566 (E.D. N.Y. 1989) (where animal and insect Halloween costumes were not copyrightable as their design was inseparable from their utilitarian function). Recently, imperial storm trooper costumes from the film *Star Wars* (1977) were determined to be "functional rather than artistic works and thus not fully subject to copyright law." Dave Itzkoff, *Artist Prevails in Lawsuit over "Star Wars" Costumes,* N.Y. TIMES, July 28, 2011, at C3. *See also* Great American Fun v. Hosung New York Trading, 960 F. Supp. 815 (S.D. N.Y. 1997) (where the fur covering of a monkey hand puppet was functional and not copyrightable); Warner Bros. v. Film Ventures, 403 F. Supp. 522 (C.D. Calif. 1975) (where a commonly accepted depiction of possession by an evil spirit involved no original authorship). Legal protections for such products, including furniture, "exist in the form of trade dress and trademark rights." Julie Lasky, *Once Again, Seeing Double,* N.Y. TIMES, Oct. 11, 2012, D1, at D9.

[25] *See* Foxworthy v. Custom Tees, 879 F. Supp. 1200 (N.D. Ga. 1995). For guidance on some of these issues, *see* U.S. Copyright Office, Blank Forms and Other Works Not Protected by Copyright (2015), *available at* http://www.copyright.gov/circs/circ32.pdf (last visited June 15, 2016); U.S. Copyright Office, Recipes (2011), *available at* http://www.copyright.gov/fls/fl122.html (last visited June 15, 2016); U.S. Copyright Office, COPYRIGHT BASICS 3 (2012), *available at* http://www.copyright.gov/circs/circ01 .pdf (last visited June 15, 2016).

[26] 499 U.S. 340 (1991).

[27] *Id.* at 345. ("It is beyond dispute that compilations of facts are within the subject matter of copyright.")

[28] Rural Telephone Service knew Feist Publications had taken the names for its use, as four of the listings in its book were fictitious, deliberately "inserted into its directory to detect copying." *Id.*

necessarily "novel."[29] Originality, thus, has two components: [30]

• "Independent creation" by the author (that is, not copied from another source),[31] and

• Some minimal degree of creativity.

In *Burrow-Giles Lithographic v. Sarony*, the Supreme Court ruled that even "the mere mechanical reproduction of the physical features" of a person in a photograph contained enough "selecting and arranging" as part of the posing of the subject to meet the required nominal originality standard.[32]

Thus, facts may not be copyrighted because they are not and cannot be original. A collation or compilation of facts "is eligible for copyright if it features an original selection or arrangement of facts, but the copyright is limited to the particular selection or arrangement. In no event may copyright extend to the facts themselves."[33] Thus, printed telephone directories, as a single unit, may be copyrighted, as they contain government listings in "blue pages," advertising in "yellow pages," and other original and subjective arrangements, selections, and decisions relating to the design and display of facts and other contact information, both print and visual.[34]

Copyright Ownership

Ownership of a created work belongs to the work's creator (or joint creators).[35] This is a general rule. An author or artist may not own a work, however, if it was created: (1) "within the scope" of one's employment,[36] (2) if a specific contract provision exists between two parties to the contract stating the conditions and extent of ownership, or (3) if the work was created as a commissioned "work for hire."

First, because employers have the right to benefit economically from the work that employees produce as part of their jobs, a worker's legal rights are greatly limited when he or she accomplishes or creates something within the scope of the worker's employment. This precept is central to the law of agency.[37] Thus, "[T]he employer ... is considered the author [of the created work] and ... owns all the rights comprised in the copyright."[38] Second, any copyright owner may transfer ownership, either as a whole or in part, to another by means of a written contract or agreement or through the provisions of a will. Thus, an employer's ownership rights may be transferred back to the employee who first created the work for the employer, or to anyone else.[39] Third, "a work specifically ordered or commissioned" may be deemed to be owned by the person or entity which "ordered or commissioned" it.[40]

This third situation served as the basis of the ownership claim in *Community for Creative Non-Violence v. Reid*.[41] In that case, a nonprofit group conceived the idea of a sculpture depicting homelessness in Washington, D.C. — and not just any sculpture but one whose attributes and characteristics the group extensively dictated to the artist it hired.[42] After the artist had been fully paid for his efforts, the two sides disagreed on future plans for the sculpture and each claimed sole ownership, the sculptor on the grounds that he created the work and the group on the grounds that the sculptor's efforts were a "work for hire."

---

[29] "Originality does not signify novelty [which may be defined as: 'new,' 'unusual,' or 'innovative']; a work may be original even though it closely resembles other works so long as the similarity is fortuitous, not the result of copying. To illustrate, assume that two poets, each ignorant of the other, compose identical poems. Neither work is novel, yet both are original and, hence, copyrightable." *Id.* at 345-46. Originality is an essential, indispensable element of copyright. *See* Bell v. E. Davis Int'l, 197 F. Supp. 2d 449 (W.D. N.C. 2002). And, as Justice Oliver Wendell Holmes wrote, "A very modest grade of art [such as, a poster advertising Ringling Brothers and Barnum & Bailey's circus] has in it something irreducible, which is one man's alone. That something he may copyright...." Bleistein v. Donaldson Lithographing Co., 188 U.S. 239, 250 (1903). Even Beatles' tribute bands may sue each other for copyright infringement claiming lack of originality, though some have asked, "How do you monopolize the ability to present an impersonation of the Beatles? How many different ways can you really do it?" Eric Grode, *Can't Buy Me Love? A Lawsuit Debates It*, N.Y. TIMES, July 16, 2013, at C1, C5.

[30] *Feist Publications*, 499 U.S. at 348. The Court held: "To be sure, the requisite level of creativity is extremely low; even a slight amount will suffice. The vast majority of works make the grade quite easily, as they possess some creative spark, 'no matter how crude, humble or obvious' it might be." *Id.* at 345 (internal references omitted).

[31] In the first copyright lawsuit involving comic books, Fox Publications' Wonder Man was found to have been copied from Action Comics' Superman: "[T]he only real difference between them is that 'Superman' wears a blue uniform and [Wonder Man] wears a red one." Detective Comics v. Bruns (Fox) Pubs., 111 F. 2d 432, 433 (2d Cir. 1940). *See also* Nat'l Comics v. Fawcett Pubs., 191 F. 2d 594 (2d Cir. 1951) (Superman vs. Captain Marvel). Similarly, producers of *Spider-Man: Turn Off the Dark* claimed that the Broadway musical's former director, Julie Taymor, "borrowed so many ideas from Spider-Man superhero lore that she was not entitled to copyright protection for her initial three-page script outline." Robin Pogrebin, *"Spider-Man" Lawyers Challenge Taymor*, N.Y. TIMES, June 2, 2012, at C3. *See also* Patrick Healy, *"Spider-Man" Legal Fight Ends in "Artistic Divorce*," N.Y. TIMES, Apr. 11, 2013, at C1, C6.

[32] 111 U.S. 53, 59-60 (1884). Even the push of a motion picture camera button by Abraham Zapruder, coincidentally at exactly the right moment, was sufficient for his film of the 1963 assassination of President John Kennedy to have the requisite originality to warrant copyright protection. Time, Inc. v. Bernard Geis Associates., 293 F. Supp. 130 (S.D. N.Y. 1968). *But see* Murray Hill Prods. v. ABC Comm's, 264 F. 3d 622 (6th Cir. 2001) (where a copy of the Ten Commandments drawn by a child was not sufficiently creative to be eligible for copyright protection).

[33] *Feist Publications*, 499 U.S. at 349.

[34] *See* Southern Bell Telephone & Telegraph v. Associated Telephone Directory Publishers, 756 F.2d 801 (11th Cir. 1985).

[35] *See, e.g.,* Doreen Carvajal, *Anne Frank Gains "Co-Author" in Copyright Move*, N.Y. TIMES, Nov. 14, 2015, at A3; Vikas Bajaj, *Who Wrote 'The Diary of Anne Frank'?* N.Y. TIMES, Nov. 17, 2015, *available at* http://nyti.ms/1S2mKc0 (last visited June 15, 2016).

[36] 17 U.S.C. 101(1) (2016).

[37] RESTATEMENT (SECOND) OF AGENCY § 228 (1958).

[38] 17 U.S.C. 201(b) (2016). *See also* ARTHUR MILLER & MICHAEL DAVIS, INTELLECTUAL PROPERTY IN A NUTSHELL 383 (3d ed. 2000).

[39] 17 U.S.C. 201(b) & (d) (2016).

[40] 17 U.S.C. 101(2) (2016).

[41] 490 U.S. 730 (1989).

[42] *See* Cmty. for Creative Non-Violence v. Reid, 652 F. Supp. 1453, 1454 (D. D.C. 1987).

The Supreme Court concluded that sculptor James Reid had been "an independent contractor,"[43] in that he had been paid by but not controlled or assisted by the nonprofit group in his artistic efforts, and that the sculpture did not fall within one of the copyright statute's nine, limited work-for-hire categories that would have allowed ownership by the group.[44] Despite the degree of its involvement, the nonprofit group was thus not the "author" of the work and did not own its copyright.

Copyright thus belongs to the creator/author of the work, at least, initially. Yet it is also important to note that "mere ownership" of an original work, much less a copy of an original work, "does not give the possessor the copyright."[45] A sale or transfer of the object may dispose of the artifact itself but does not include a sale or transfer of the copyright,[46] without an express, written agreement to the contrary.

Copyright Notice and Registration

At the moment a work is created, that is, "fixed in any tangible medium" for the first time, it is automatically copyrighted, without the author having to do anything.[47] As a result, official registration with the U.S. Copyright Office — which in 2012 registered more than 511,500 works, or roughly 2,000 per business day — is voluntary and not a legal requirement.[48] Yet, because all claims of copyright infringement start with accusations of illegal copying, the initial defense is proof that one's work was created prior to the creation of an accuser's similar work. Thus, official registration is highly recommended.[49] Registration establishes a public record of the copyright, and is required of works of U.S. origin before a lawsuit for copyright infringement may be filed in federal court to allow the copyright owner the right to collect statutory damages and possibly attorneys' fees.

At the very least, every work should prominently feature a proper copyright notice, which includes three elements:[50]

• © (the letter "c" in a circle) or the word "Copyright" or the abbreviation "Copr."[51]
• The year of first publication
• The name of the copyright owner

For example, then, a proper copyright notice could look something like this:

Copyright © 2017 Peter Panther

In addition, some have sought legal protection in what has been known as "poor man's copyright." In such situations, a copy of the created work is not officially registered, but rather sent to oneself through the mail — and keeping the package in one's possession, unopened — to establish its date of creation through the postmark on the package, in the expectation of saving the money spent on the registration fee while at the same time establishing authenticity of the work and protecting one's legal right to monetary damages in case of copyright infringement.[52] However, "poor man's copyright" is a myth.[53] As the Copyright Office states on its Web site: "There is no provision in the copyright law for any such type of protection, and it is not a substitute for registration."[54]

Legal Rights of Copyright Owners

Because intellectual property — such as a copyrighted work — is a form of personal property, yet property of a unique kind,[55] the

---

[43] 490 U.S. at 752. The Supreme Court analyzed a "non-exhaustive list" of relevant factors — from the RESTATEMENT (SECOND) OF AGENCY § 220(2) (1958) — to reach its determination. *Id.* at 751-53.

[44] For a work for hire by an independent contractor to be owned by the group which first commissioned it, the work must be "for use as a contribution to a collective work, as a part of a motion picture or other audiovisual work, as a translation, as a supplementary work, as a compilation, as an instructional text, as a test, as answer material for a test, or as an atlas." 17 U.S.C. 101(2) (2016).

[45] U.S. Copyright Office, *Two General Principles*, COPYRIGHT BASICS 2 (2012), *available at* http://www.copyright.gov/circs/circ01.pdf (last visited June 15, 2016).

[46] 17 U.S.C. 202 (2016).

[47] 17 U.S.C. 102(a) (2016).

[48] *See* U.S. Copyright Office, Copyright in General (undated), *available at* http://www.copyright.gov/help/faq/faq-general.html (last visited June 15, 2016).

[49] Forms may be obtained by writing: U.S. Copyright Office, Library of Congress, 101 Independence Ave. SE, Washington, D.C. 20559, or online through the Electronic Copyright Office (undated), http://www.copyright.gov/eco/ (last visited June 15, 2016). Online registration costs $35. *See, e.g.*, Bill Torpy, *Roswell Artist Alleges Copyright Infringement*, ATLANTA J.-CONSTITUTION, Nov. 18, 2012, at B1, B7.

[50] U.S. Copyright Office, *Notice of Copyright*, COPYRIGHT BASICS 4 (2012), *available at* http://www.copyright.gov/circs/circ01.pdf (last visited June 15, 2016). Works published before March 1, 1989, required a copyright notice to be attached to prevent copyright protection from being irrevocably lost. *Id.* at 1.

[51] For a sound recording, this should be ℗ (the letter "P" in a circle) designating a phono-record of a sound recording.

[52] *See* Nathan Boehme, *How to Get a "Poor Man's" Copyright*, EHOW.COM (2016), http://www.ehow.com/video_4467952__poor-man_s_copyright.html (last visited June 15, 2016).

[53] *See* Jonathan Bailey, *The Myth of Poor Man's Copyright*, PLAGIARISMTODAY.COM, Aug. 25, 2006, http://www.plagiarismtoday.com/2006/08/25/the-myth-of-poor-mans-copyright/ (last visited June 15, 2016).

[54] Copyright in General, *supra* note 48.

[55] In a classic definition of copyright as property, Oliver Wendell Holmes wrote:

The notion of property starts ... from confirmed possession of a tangible object, and consists in the right to exclude others from interference with the more or less free doing with it as one wills. But, in copyright, property has reached a more abstract expression. The right to exclude is not directed to an object in possession or owned.... It restrains the spontaneity of men where, but for it, there would be nothing of any kind to hinder their doing as they saw fit. It is a prohibition of conduct remote from the persons or tangibles of the party having the right. It may be infringed a thousand miles from the owner and without his ever becoming aware of the wrong. It is a right which could not be recognized or endured for more than a limited time, and therefore ... it is one which hardly can be conceived except as a product of statute.

legal rights of copyright owners differ from those of owners of all other types of property, which generally include the right to control and to exclude all others from the use of one's property, complete and unlimited ownership of the property itself, and the right to bequeath the property to one's heirs permanently and in perpetuity. Unlike physical property, however, intellectual property "is non-rivalrous [in that] the right to exclude is not essential to its enjoyment" by or its value to its owner.[56] In fact, others' use of the copyrighted work can actually enhance its overall worth.

Yet the evolution of the Internet has brought with it the reality that the custody or ownership of content is questionable, or problematic at best, in cyberspace. Some feel the risk is "that we may end up [producing] fewer and fewer original works [which] has created a growing sense of unease ... that the end of 'ownership' could eventually diminish the Web's value" and also harm the importance of and protections inherent in copyright.[57]

As a means of protecting the value of created works, copyright owners enjoy six exclusive, legal rights that provide unique protections to intellectual property:[58]

1. The right to reproduce the copyrighted work in copies and phono-records;

2. The right to prepare derivative works based upon the copyrighted work;

3. The right to distribute copies or phono-records of the copyrighted work to the public by sale or other transfer of ownership, or by rental, lease or lending;

4. The right to perform the copyrighted work publicly;

5. The right to display the copyrighted work publicly;

6. The right to perform the copyrighted work publicly by means of a digital transmission.

Copyright is, thus, essentially "the right to say no."[59] However, several mitigating points should be noted. First, while the last four of these six rights are public rights,[60] the first two may be violated either publicly or privately. Second, because federal law does not limit copyright infringement to commercial uses only, all uses of copyrighted material, not approved by the copyright holder, violate the copyright owner's rights, unless excused or mitigated by some defense or by other statutory limitation.[61] Third, this list of far-reaching legal rights is not comprehensive. As an example of a legal right not listed yet also included in the Copyright Act of 1976, authors and artists who have transferred or sold their rights to others, may now terminate those transfers — in effect, cancel the sale — and regain control over copyrighted works that they created thirty-five years after the date of the original transfer.[62] Victor Willis, lyricist of the disco group the Village People, has already had his termination rights upheld.[63] Others are expected to follow his lead.[64] Still others are demanding that Congress address the situation when the songs involved are works for hire.[65]

Of the six exclusive rights, the first is obviously the most fundamental and important. It allows copyright owners the right to prohibit all others from reproducing the work in the form of copies, recordings, adaptions and publishing. Thus, "[A] copyrighted work would be infringed by reproducing it in whole or in any substantial part, and by duplicating it exactly or by imitation or simulation."[66] For example, the well-known 2008 Barack Obama "HOPE" poster was created by the artist Shepard Fairey and subsequently licensed for use on clothing and other merchandise without permission from the original photo-

---

(1) to perform or display [a work] at a place open to the public or at any place where a substantial number of persons outside of a normal circle of a family and its social acquaintances is gathered; or (2) to transmit or otherwise communicate a performance or display of the work to a place specified [above] or to the public, by means of any device or process, whether the members of the public capable of receiving the performance or display receive it in the same place or in separate places and at the same time or at different times.

17 U.S.C. 101 (2016).

[61] For specific, detailed statutory limitations on a copyright owner's legal rights, beyond the Fair Use Doctrine, *see* 17 U.S.C. 108-122 (2015). *See also* MILLER & DAVIS, *supra* note 38, at 323.

[62] 17 U.S.C. 203, 304(c-d) (2016). This provision does not apply to works "made for hire." 17 U.S.C. 203(a) (2016). In addition, grants made through an author's testamentary disposition cannot be terminated. 17 U.S.C. 203(a)(5) (2016).

[63] *See* Leslie Gordon, *Jury Sides with "the Cop" in Copyright Question over a Village People Hit*, ABA J., July 1, 2015, *available at* http://www.abajournal.com/magazine/article/jury_sides_with_the_cop_in_copyright_question_over_a_village_people_hit/ (last visited June 15, 2016); Larry Rohter, *Copyright Victory, 35 Years Later*, N.Y. TIMES, Sept. 11, 2013, at C1, C7; Larry Rohter, *Lyricist of "Y.M.C.A." Wins Suit over Control of Songs*, N.Y. TIMES, May 9, 2012, at B1, B2.

[64] *See* Larry Rohter, *Record Industry Braces for Artists' Battles over Song Rights*, N.Y. TIMES, Aug. 16, 2011, at C1, C6; Matthew Belloni, *Tom Petty, Bob Dylan vs. Music Labels: The Industry's New Copyright War*, HOLLYWOOD REPORTER, Feb. 10, 2012, *available at* http://www.hollywoodreporter.com/news/tom-petty-bob-dylan-copyright-law-music-rights-289295 (last visited June 15, 2016).

[65] *See* Larry Rohter, *Legislator Calls for Clarifying Copyright Law*, N.Y. TIMES, Aug. 29, 2011, at C1, C3.

[66] H.R. Rep. No. 94-1476, 94th Cong., 2d Sess. 61 (1976).

White-Smith Music Publ'g v. Apollo Co., 209 U.S. 1, 19 (1908) (Holmes, J., concurring).

[56] Randy Barnett, *All We Need Is "Love"?*, ¶ 5, Mar. 6, 2007, VOLOKH CONSPIRACY, http://volokh.com/posts/1173221206.shtml (last visited June 15, 2016). Professor Barnett has explained the difference between tangible and intangible personal property this way: "With tangible property you control your stuff. With intangible property you control other people's stuff." *Id.*

[57] David Carr, *A Code of Conduct for Content Aggregators*, N.Y. TIMES, Mar. 12, 2012, at B1.

[58] 17 U.S.C. 106 (2016). As an example of an author's right to display a work publicly, Harper Lee sued her county museum over an unauthorized display featuring her book *To Kill a Mockingbird*. *See* Jennifer Howard & Serge Kovaleski, *Atticus, Here's Drama on Your Turf: "Mockingbird" Discord Lingers in Alabama*, N.Y. TIMES, Apr. 18, 2016, at C1, C5; Allan Kozinn, *Harper Lee Lawsuit Seems at an End*, N.Y. TIMES, June 7, 2014, at C3. On other occasions derivative works have been reworked to avoid copyright infringement claims. *See* Michael Cieply, *"Raging Bull" Suit Settled: Sequel Now a Non-sequel*, N.Y. TIMES, Aug. 3, 2012, at C3.

[59] Vaidhyanathan, *supra* note 6, at 44.

[60] The term "publicly" means:

THE CASE OF THE SMILING SIMIAN 'SELFIE'

If a monkey takes a selfie in the forest, who owns the copyright?

No, it's no joke. That was the focus of a story in the *Washington Post* (Aug. 6, 2014) that resulted in a 2016 federal court ruling (*Naruto v. Slater*, No. 15-cv-04324-WHO, N.D. Calif.), filed "by and through" his "next friends," People for the Ethical Treatment of Animals (PETA). The situation poses very real questions for intellectual property law.

Nature photographer David Slater was traveling in a national forest preserve in North Sulawesi, Indonesia, in 2011, looking to find a crested black macaque monkey to photograph. It's unclear whether a monkey managed to steal Slater's camera equipment as he has said, or whether Slater knowingly left the equipment unattended for the shy species to find as a way to get some unique pictures. However it happened, a female crested black macaque picked up the camera and in playing with it took hundreds of pictures, including some self-portraits. (PETA claims that the monkey is actually a 6-year-old male, whom Indonesian wildlife researchers recognized as Naruto, though the group presented no additional evidence to support this.) The resulting selfie of the smiling simian was posted online, went viral, and was more popular than one by Kim Kardashian, according to 2014 Google search statistics.

Since American law treats photographs the same as it does the writings specifically protected by the Copyright Clause of the U.S. Constitution (*Bridgeman Art Library v. Corel Corp.*, 36 F. Supp. 2d 191, S.D. N.Y. 1999), a key question arose.

Who owns the copyright to the photograph?

Answer: Copyright ownership generally belongs to the photographer, and not to the object of the photograph and not to the camera's owner (even if he's spent a lot of money to get the photograph or spent time setting up the equipment and creating the conditions that enabled the photograph to be taken), unless the owner is also the photographer.

As the Supreme Court unanimously noted in *Burrow-Giles Lithographic v. Sarony*, 111 U.S. 53 (1884), a photograph of British author Oscar Wilde was a "useful, new, harmonious ... and graceful picture ... made ... entirely from [the photographer's] own original mental conception, to which he gave visible form by posing Oscar Wilde in front of the camera, selecting and arranging the costume ... arranging the subject so as to present graceful outlines ... evoking the desired expression." The photographer thus owned the copyright.

Since the crested black macaque took her own picture here, does she own the copyright?

Answer: No, because she is not a "person" under the U.S. Constitution and has no legal rights. The U.S. Copyright Office announced in 2014 (in COMPENDIUM OF THE U.S. COPYRIGHT OFFICE PRACTICES, 3d ed., § 313.2, at 300:22) that it "will not register works produced by nature, animals or plants, [or any] work purportedly created by divine or supernatural beings."

So, who is a "person"?

Answer: Human beings are natural persons, though at different times in history different degrees of the legal rights of personhood were available to free, land-holding males, to free women, and to slaves. Since 1886 (in *Santa Clara County v. Southern Pacific Railroad*, 118 U.S. 394), the Supreme Court has expanded the concept of "person" to include corporations — called "artificial persons" by some — which are entitled to many of the rights that natural persons enjoy, including ownership of intellectual property.

So, who owns the selfie taken by the macaque with David Slater's camera?

Answer: No one. Monkeys can't own copyrights. Works from non-human sources aren't copyrightable, unless a person makes substantial changes and edits to the photograph, which would enable him to claim the copyright on the resulting, altered image — but still not to the original photograph. Here, the monkey can't own the copyright, and the photographer doesn't because he didn't actually create the photograph. Thus, the picture is in the public domain. "Monkey see, monkey sue is not good law," to use a short retort from the 2015 pleadings in the case.

graph's owner.[67] Thus, the medium in which the work is reproduced makes no difference.

In *New York Times v. Tasini*, the Supreme Court agreed with a group of freelance journalists that they had sold only first publication rights to the *New York Times* and that subsequent electronic reproduction first required an additional license from and another royalty payment to the writers.[68] Yet in *Greenberg v. National Geographic*, the court found that "an exact, unrevised digital replica of 1,200 pre-existing collective works (that is, magazines)" on a CD-ROM was not a new anthology or collective work, but only a republication of a copyrighted collection.[69] Still unanswered is how freelance journalists and photogra-

---

[67] *See* Randy Kennedy, *Probation and a Fine for Shepard Fairey*, N.Y. TIMES, Sept. 8, 2012, at C3.

[68] 533 U.S. 483 (2001).

[69] 533 F.3d 1244, 1270 (11th Cir. 2008), *cert. denied* 550 U.S. 1070 (2008).

phers, such as those in *Tasini*, can be fairly compensated.[70]

When phono-recordings are involved, this exclusive right is limited by the statutory license available to anyone wishing to record his or her own version of a musical composition or song, without the copyright owner's consent.[71] This is not the legal right to copy and sell the original but a compulsory license to "cover" the original, provided that proper licensing or royalty fees are paid.[72] Royalty rates are published annually in the *Code of Federal Regulations*.[73] Failure to obtain such a license before distribution is illegal copying and an infringement of copyright.[74] Penalties can include a court-ordered injunction forbidding further distribution and a recall of any or all phono-records already shipped.[75]

The second right gives copyright owners control over all subsequent uses of their works. Specifically, "A copyright owner holds the right to create sequels" and to keep all others from creating anything based on his own creation.[76]

As an example, Sylvester Stallone — movie star and screenplay author of *Rocky*, *Rocky II* and *Rocky III* — took a thirty-one-page film treatment by Timothy Anderson, which incorporated characters initially created by Stallone, and made the movie *Rocky IV*, that pitted Stallone's boxer, Rocky Balboa, against Ivan Drago, a "scientifically trained" Russian opponent. Stallone was not required to pay Anderson anything for tort claims of unjust enrichment, because Anderson's film treatment was an infringing derivative work, using characters so extensively developed that any subsequent use in any work automatically belongs to their creator, Sylvester Stallone.[77] As another example, Castle Rock Entertainment — which owns the copyright to comedian Jerry Seinfeld's television series, *Seinfeld* — was able to stop publication of *The Seinfeld Aptitude Test* by Beth Golub — a short book with trivia questions from the show

— on the grounds that it was an unauthorized derivative work.[78] Even though "Castle Rock … evidenced little if any interest in exploiting this market for derivative works based on 'Seinfeld,' such as by creating and publishing 'Seinfeld' trivia books," the appellate court ruled that "the … law must respect that creative and economic choice."[79] This legal right to control derivative works even includes re-compiling and assembling new works, comprised of newly bound articles (assembled according to subject matter) from legally purchased copies of *National Geographic* magazine.[80] It also includes Lucasfilm's recent attempts to control fan-filmed homages and unofficial sequels to its *Star Wars* series of films,[81] as well as J.K. Rowling's right to halt a fan's Harry Potter lexicon and E.L. James' retelling of *50 Shades of Grey* from the perspective of her male lead.[82] However, federal law does not include the power to prevent copyrighted images from being cropped and from being used in that altered form to advocate politically that federal funds not be used to subsidize art and any derivative work can be reworked into a new, stand-alone, original piece.[83]

The third right gives copyright owners the exclusive control over publication and distribution of their works, whether it be by sale, lease, lending or downloading.[84] This right is also known as "The First Sale Doctrine,"[85] in that it guarantees the copyright owner the legal right to prohibit others from any and all distribution of the work, prior to its first sale. At that point, the new owner of the work may choose to display the work publicly or to sell the work to someone else;[86] however, the owner does not have the right to do anything else with the work, including making additional copies of it or re-selling it in a different form, as the ownership rights involve only the mere possession of the work and not its copyright.[87] In addition, this right specifically does not include any renting, leasing or lending of

---

[70] *See* Reed Elsevier v. Muchnick, 559 U.S. 1237 (2010); Jeremy Peters, *Court Rejects Publishers' Deal with Writers*, N.Y. TIMES, Aug. 18, 2011, at B5.

[71] 17 U.S.C. 115(a) (2016). *See also* U.S. Copyright Office, Licensing (undated), *available at* http://www.copyright.gov/licensing/index.html (last visited June 15, 2016).

[72] 17 U.S.C. 115(c) (2016).

[73] 37 C.F.R. 255.3(m) (2016). For "covers" made and sold after 2006, the royalty rate is 9.1 cents per song or 1.75 cents per minute of playing time, whichever is greater.

[74] 17 U.S.C. 115(b) (2016); 17 U.S.C. 501 (2016). *See, e.g.*, Ben Sisario, *Clear Channel-Warner Music Deal Rewrites the Rules on Royalties*, N.Y. TIMES, Sept. 13, 2013, at B1, B6; Ben Sisario, *Record Labels Sue Sirius XM over the Use of Older Music*, N.Y. TIMES, Sept. 12, 2013, at B4.

[75] *See, e.g.*, Cherry River Music v. Simitar Entm't, 38 F. Supp. 2d 310 (S.D. N.Y. 1999).

[76] *See* Micro Star v. Formgen, 154 F.3d 1107, 1112 (9th Cir. 1998). When a copyright to a work has been sold or assigned to another entity, even the original author (now no longer the copyright holder) may be prohibited from creating derivative works. *See, e.g.*, Adam Kepler, *Publisher Objects to Sequel to Dendak's "Wild Things,"* N.Y. TIMES, July 8, 2013, at C3; Dave Itzkoff, *Paramount Sues Over "Godfather" Novel*, N.Y. TIMES, Feb. 23, 2012, at C3.

[77] Anderson v. Stallone, 11 U.S.P.Q. 2d 1161 (C.D. Calif. 1989).

[78] Castle Rock Entm't v. Carol Pub. Group, 150 F.3d 132 (2d Cir. 1998).

[79] *Id.* at 145-46.

[80] Nat.l Geographic Soc'y v. Classified Geographic, 27 F. Supp. 655 (D. Mass. 1939).

[81] *See* Amy Harmon, *"Star Wars" Fan Films Come Tumbling Back to Earth*, N.Y. TIMES, Apr. 28, 2002, Arts & Leisure, at 28.

[82] *See* Alexandra Alter, *Writer of 'Shades' Answers Her Fans*, N.Y. TIMES, June 20, 1015, at C1, C6; John Eligon, *Judge Rules for Rowling Against Writer of Lexicon*, N.Y. TIMES, Sept. 9, 2008, at C11.

[83] *See* Wojnarowicz v. American Family Ass'n, 745 F. Supp. 130 (S.D. N.Y. 1990) (where edited depictions, constituting derivative works, of artwork offensive to the Christian religion were sent to members of Congress, accompanied by letters arguing that arts grants not be awarded to artists for such works).

[84] *See, e.g.*, Playboy Enters. v. Frena, 839 F. Supp. 1552 (M.D. Fla. 1993) (where the availability of images for downloading from an online bulletin board was held to be a violation of the copyright owner's right to distribute).

[85] American Int'l Pictures v. Foreman, 576 F.2d 661, 661 (5th Cir. 1978).

[86] 17 U.S.C. 109(c) (2016).

[87] *See, e.g.*, Fawcett Publ'ns. v. Elliot Publ'g, 46 F. Supp. 717 (S.D. N.Y. 1942) (where the legal purchase of second-hand copies of a comic book, followed by their re-assembly into a separate work, and its subsequent sale were held to be a violation of the copyright owner's right to distribute).

phono-records or computer software for commercial purposes by any owner after the first sale.[88]

In 2013, the Supreme Court ruled in *Kirtsaeng v. John Wiley & Sons*[89] that the First Sale Doctrine has "no geographic boundaries," meaning that copyright owners cannot ban resale of physical copies of their works inside the United States at a lower price than intended by the copyright owners.[90] Textbook publishers criticized the decision as "a loss for the U.S. economy, and students and authors in the U.S. and around the world," while others saw the decision as "a necessary and vital balance between the interests of rights holders and the rights of the public, between commerce and learning."[91] What remains unsettled is the extent to which the First Sale Doctrine protects the resellers of electronic products, such as e-books and digital music files.[92]

The remaining three exclusive rights give the copyright owner the legal right to control the performance, display and digital transmission of copyrighted works, sometimes known as public performing rights.[93] Prior to congressional enactment of the Copyright Act of 1976, the broadcast reception in a public fast-food restaurant of songs being played as part of a radio station's programming was not understood to be a public performance, since the shop keeper did nothing more than turn on the radio for his patrons to enjoy.[94] Today, that act clearly is a public performance that must be licensed unless it is included in a list of statutory exemptions, which include face-to-face nonprofit educational activities and religious worship services. The performance (1) must involve no profit motive or private financial gain in that no one involved or responsible is paid any fee and (2) must include no admission charge, either direct or indirect.[95]

Other performances, displays and transmissions that require copyright permissions and licensing include: the online streaming to subscribers of freely available broadcast television programs,[96] the renting of motion pictures in combination with rooms in which they may be viewed,[97] the transmission of screen displays of a copyrighted work to subscribers,[98] satellite antenna television reception in a local bar of National Football League games that are blacked out in a particular media market,[99] Internet bulletin board displays of copyrighted *Playboy* photographs,[100] and the use of copyrighted songs by presidential candidates without permission of their copyright owners.[101] In fact, they even include those copyrighted songs — such as, "Puff, the Magic Dragon" — that Girl Scouts sing around the campfire,[102] and enforced by the Recording Industry Association of America; the American Society of Composers, Authors & Publishers; Broadcast Music, Inc., and the Society of European Stage Authors & Composers.[103] (See Figure 1.) Each organization has licensing agents whose job it is to "persuade every small-town bar, beauty parlor and diner to pay for their music."[104] And as the amount and dollar value of material reposted online have grown, private companies have become involved by buying copyrights and then initiating their own lawsuits.[105]

Copyright Duration

Copyright law in the United States has encouraged creativity by providing authors and artists ever-lengthening legal protection for their creative activities. The first federal copyright law, in

[88] 17 U.S.C. 109(b)(1) (2016). Noncommercial or nonprofit libraries are generally exempt from this restriction.

[89] 133 S. Ct. 1351 (2013). *See* Adam Liptak, *Justices Permit Resale of Copyrighted Imports*, N.Y. TIMES, Mar. 20, 2013, at B8.

[90] *See* Debra Weiss, *A Victory for Commerce? SCOTUS Rules for Student Who Bought Texts Abroad and Sold Them on eBay*, ABA J. DAILY NEWS, Mar. 19, 2013, at ¶ 3, *available at* http://www.abajournal.com/news/article/a_victory_for_commerce_scotus_rules_for_student_who_bought_texts_abroad_and/ (last visited June 15, 2016).

[91] *Quoted in id.*, at ¶ 11. *See* Maureen Sullivan, *Libraries and Authors*, N.Y. TIMES, Apr. 11, 2013, at A20. *See also* Scott Turow, *The Slow Death of the American Author*, N.Y. TIMES, Apr. 7, 2013, *available at* http://www.nytimes.com/2013/04/08/opinion/the-slow-death-of-the-american-author.html (last visited June 15, 2016).

[92] *See* Capitol Records v. ReDigi, Inc., 934 F. Supp. 2d 640 (S.D. N.Y. 2013). *See also* Ben Sisario, *A Setback for Resellers of Digital Products*, N.Y. TIMES, Apr. 2, 2013, at B3; Maria Pallante, *Copyright and the Music Marketplace* (February 2015), *available at* http://copyright.gov/policy/musiclicensingstudy/copyright-and-the-music-marketplace.pdf (last visited June 6, 2016).

[93] As such, they are limited by the definition of "publicly" contained in federal law. 17 U.S.C. 101 (2016). Public reception using "a single receiving apparatus of the kind commonly used in private homes" is exempted. 17 U.S.C. 110(5) (2016). *See, e.g.*, Edison Bros. Stores v. Broad. Music, Inc., 954 F. 2d 1419 (8th Cir. 1992).

[94] Twentieth Century Music v. Aiken, 422 U.S. 151 (1975).

[95] 17 U.S.C. 110(4)(A-B) (2016).

[96] ABC v. Aereo, Inc., 134 S. Ct. 2498 (2014). *See also* Adam Liptak & Emily Steel, *Supreme Court Rules Against Aereo, a TV Streaming Service*, N.Y. TIMES, June 26, 2014, at B1, B7; Farhad Manjoo, *The Cloud Roots for Aereo, But People Need Better*, N.Y. TIMES, Apr. 25, 2014, at B3; Keach Hagey, *A Death Knell for Aereo?*, WALL ST. J., June 25, 2014, *available at* http://blogs.wsj.com/law/2014/06/25/a-death-knell-for-aereo/ (last visited June 15, 2016).

[97] Columbia Pictures v. Aveco, Inc., 800 F.2d 59 (3d Cir. 1986); Columbia Pictures v. Redd Horne, 749 F.2d 154 (3d Cir. 1984).

[98] On Command Video v. Columbia Pictures, 777 F. Supp. 787 (N.D. Cal. 1991).

[99] National Football League v. McBee & Bruno's, 792 F.2d 726 (8th Cir. 1986).

[100] Playboy Enters. v. Webbworld, 991 F. Supp. 543 (N.D. Tex. 1997).

[101] *See* James McKinley, *G.O.P. Candidates Are Told, Don't Use the Verses, It's Not Your Song*, N.Y. TIMES, Feb. 4, 2012, at C1, C7; Ben Sisario, *In Choreographed Campaigns, Candidates Stumble over Choice of Music*, N.Y. TIMES, Oct. 13, 2015, at A19.

[102] *See* Elisabeth Bumiller, *ASCAP Asks Royalties from Girl Scouts, and Regrets It*, N.Y. TIMES, Dec. 17, 1996, *available at* http://www.nytimes.com/1996/12/17/nyregion/ascap-asks-royalties-from-girl-scouts-and-regrets-it.html (last visited June 15, 2016); Jonathan Zittrain, *The Copyright Cage*, LEGALAFFAIRS.ORG, July-August 2003, *available at* http://www.legalaffairs.org/issues/July-August-2003/feature_zittrain_julaug03.msp (last visited June 15, 2016).

[103] *See* http://riaa.com/; http://www.ascap.com/; http://www.bmi.com/; http://www.sesac.com/ (last visited June 15, 2016).

[104] John Bowe, *The Copyright Enforcers*, N.Y. TIMES MAG., Aug. 8, 2010, at 38.

[105] *See* Dan Frosch, *Enforcing Copyright, for a Profit*, N.Y. TIMES, May 2, 2011, at B1.

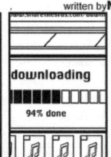

FIGURE 1
"Revenge of the Copyright Cops" by Neil Strauss / Copyright © 2003 Neil Strauss. Used with permission

TERMS OF COPYRIGHT PROTECTION
UNDER 1998 TERM EXTENSION ACT

DATE OF WORK	TERM OF PROTECTION
Created after January 1, 1978	Life of the author plus 70 years; 95 years from first publication or 120 years from creation, whichever is shorter, for works made for hire, anonymous, pseudonymous works or corporate authorship
Created but not published or registered before January 1, 1978	life of the author plus 70 years or December 31, 2002, whichever is longer
Created before January 1, 1978, and published before December 31, 2002	life of the author plus 70 years or December 31, 2047, whichever is longer
Pre-1978 works still in their original or renewal term of copyright	95 years from the date that copyright was originally secured

FIGURE 2

1790, offered legal protection for books, maps, and charts for fourteen years from the date of publication, with an option for a single fourteen-year renewal. The second federal statute, in 1831, extended this initial period of protection to twenty-eight years, with an option for a fourteen-year renewal period. The third statute, in 1909, extended the renewal term to twenty-eight years, and the fourth statute extended the term of protection for anything created before 1976 to forty-seven years, while providing anything created after 1976 copyright protection for the life of the author, plus an additional fifty years.[106] With the passage of the Copyright Term Extension Act of 1998,[107] copyright protection became available for the life of the author, plus seventy years.[108] Figure 2 shows the current copyright terms for the different types of owners. But how long is too long? At what point does the continuing expansion of copyright term limits violate the "limited times" constraint of the Constitution's copyright clause? Don't repeated term extensions effectively create never-ending copyrights? In addition, it's one thing to extend protection for future works but quite another to apply these new limits to existing works and thereby reduce the amount of content in the public domain, which is also a crucial piece of the American system of copyright. This was the challenge to the Copyright Term Extension Act in *Eldred v. Ashcroft.*[109] However, it proved to be a frail challenge. The Supreme Court ruled 7-2 that the federal statute was "a rational enactment" and concluded that the Court was "not at liberty to second-guess congressional determinations and policy judgments of this order, however debatable or arguably unwise they may be."[110]

The Court dealt with a similarly difficult question when it heard the appeal in *Golan v. Holder,*[111] which involved a challenge to the Uruguay Round Agreements Act of 1994,[112] enacted to bring the United States into compliance with international treaty obligations by extending copyright protection to works that are still protected in their country of origin. Was Congress thus "free to restore copyright protection to works that had entered the public domain and become public property," including paintings by the Spanish artist Pablo Picasso, films by the Italian director Frederico Fellini, books by the British author C.S. Lewis, and symphonies by the Russian composer Igor Stravin-

---

[106] Copyright Act of May 31, 1790, 1 Stat. 124; Copyright Act of 1831, 4 Stat. 436; Copyright Act of 1909, 35 Stat. 1075; Copyright Act of 1976, 90 Stat. 2541.

[107] 112 Stat. 2827 (1998). The statute is sometimes known as the "Mickey Mouse Protection Act." *See* Lawrence Lessig, *Copyright's First Amendment*, 48 UCLA LAW REV. 1057, 1065 (2001).

[108] 17 U.S.C. 302(a) (2016). *See* Peter Hirtle, *Copyright Term and the Public Domain in the United States* (2016), Cornell Copyright Information Center, *available at* http://copyright.cornell.edu/resources/publicdomain.cfm (last visited June 15, 2016).

[109] 537 U.S. 186 (2003).

[110] *Id.* at 208.

[111] 609 F.3d 1076 (10th Cir. 2010). The appellate court ruled that the statute did not violate the constitutional right to freedom of speech, in that it protected and advanced a substantial or important government interest — protecting both the economic and expressive rights of American copyright holders abroad.

[112] 17 U.S.C. 104A (2016).

sky? Did Congress have to act to remedy "past inequities of foreign authors who lost or never obtained copyrights in the United States," at the expense of American "orchestra conductors, educators, performers, publishers, film archivists, and motion picture distributors who have relied on artistic works in the public domain for their livelihoods"?[113] Must there "be a 'bright line' drawn around the public domain" to protect free speech rights and the public interest in continuing creativity and innovation?[114] Is there "a constitutional line Congress may not cross when it comes to the public domain"?[115] The Court ruled that Congress could, without violating the First Amendment, restore protected, copyrighted status to works already in the American public domain when it determined that national interests — including, "ensuring exemplary compliance with our international obligations, securing greater protection for U.S. authors abroad, and remedying unequal treatment of foreign authors" — were "best served by our full participation in the dominant system of international copyright protection."[116] Thus, there is no "constitutional significance to" or protection for "a work's public domain status," which appears to guarantee continued litigation over a work's copyright standing.[117]

Proving Infringement

From the moment a work is "fixed in any tangible medium of expression" — published or unpublished, officially registered or not — it is constitutionally protected by federal law, which effectively preempts state regulation and means that copyright infringement claims must be filed in federal court. Lawsuits claiming copyright infringement must be filed within three years of the alleged infringement.[118]

Infringement occurs when someone assumes, appropriates or usurps any of the exclusive rights granted copyright owners, without authorization. Infringement may be through the creation of an unauthorized derivative work. It may be the result of an unauthorized public display of copyrighted material. It may be a result of vicarious or indirect action, as when recorded music is performed publicly without a license. It may occur when a new work infringes on — in that it borrows from or copies portions of — another prior work, which is the most common form of copyright infringement.

It does not matter whether infringement is intentional. Legal liability for innocent — unknowing or non-deliberate or unconscious — plagiarism or copyright infringement is well recognized by the law.[119]

To prove copyright infringement, two essential conditions must be established.

First, the evidence must show proof of one's ownership of the copyrighted work. Without this there is no injury which can be remedied. This is the major benefit of official registration with the U.S. Copyright Office, which legally establishes both ownership and date of creation.

Second, the copyright owner must prove that the copyrighted work itself has been illegally copied. In some cases, this is not difficult — as with the use of boxer Mike Tyson's facial tattoo in the 2011 film, *The Hangover Part II*.[120] But because copying usually cannot be proven directly, courts allow it to be proven indirectly with evidence that: (1) the other person(s) had access to the copyrighted work, and (2) that the new work created or produced by the other person(s) is substantially similar to the original, copyrighted work.[121]

"Access," of course, may be defined as actually having seen or having had contact with an earlier work, having knowledge of, or having had the opportunity to see or have contact with the earlier work. The concept of "substantial similarity" is not as easily defined.[122] For example, is the storyline of the 2012 movie *Premium Rush*, about a Manhattan bicycle messenger with a

---

[113] *Golan*, 609 F.3d, at 1083, 1081-82.

[114] *Id.* at 1095.

[115] *See* Adam Liptak, *Once in the Public's Hands, Now Back in Picasso's*, N.Y. TIMES, Mar. 22, 2011, at A16.

[116] Golan v. Holder, 132 S.Ct. 873, 894 (2012). *See* Christopher M. Toula & Gregory C. Lisby, *Towards an Affirmative Public Domain*, 28 CULTURAL STUDIES 996 (2014).

[117] *Id.* at 891 n. 32. For example, after four years of litigation, courts have determined that the song, "Happy Birthday to You," is no longer under copyright, as it was first published in 1893 as "Good Morning to All". *See* Ben Sisario, *Details of "Happy Birthday" Copyright Settlement Are Revealed*, N.Y. TIMES, Feb. 10, 2016, at B3; Ben Sisario, *"Happy Birthday" Copyright Case Reaches a Settlement*, N.Y. TIMES, Dec. 10, 2015, at B8; Ben Sisario, *"Happy Birthday" Copyright Invalidated by Judge*, N.Y. TIMES, Sept. 22, 2016, *available at* http://nyti.ms/1YB9QGV (last visited June 15, 2016); Ben Sisario, *A Clue in the Case of "Happy Birthday,"* N.Y. TIMES, Aug. 5, 2015, at B1, B6; Daniel Victor, *New Evidence Should Free "Happy Birthday" from Copyright, Lawyers Say*, N.Y. TIMES, July. 28, 2015, *available at* http://nyti.ms/1IIrP9g (last visited June 15, 2016); Benjamin Weiser, *Birthday Song's Copyright Leads to a Lawsuit for the Ages*, N.Y. TIMES, June 14, 2013, at A24. As a result, other copyrights are also being challenged. *See* Ben Sisario, *"We Shall Overcome" Copyright Challenged*, N.Y. TIMES, Apr. 13, 2016, at B2.

[118] 17 U.S.C. 301 (2016); 17 U.S.C. 507 (2016). *But see* Petrella v. MGM, 134 S.Ct. 1962 (2014) (where a lawsuit filed in 2009 over a 1980 film based on a 1963 screenplay may proceed to allow the copyright owner to determine whether litigation is worth

---

the effort). *See also* Adam Liptak, *Justices Reinstate Copyright Lawsuit Over "Raging Bull,"* N.Y. TIMES, May 20, 2014, at B3.

[119] *See, e.g.,* Northern Music v. Pacemaker Music, 147 U.S.P.Q. 358, 359 (S.D. N.Y. 1965) (where the court held that copying "cannot be defended on the ground that it was done unconsciously and without intent to appropriate [another's] work").

[120] *See* Noam Cohen, *"Hangover 2" Settles Suit from Artist Over Tattoo*, N.Y. TIMES, June 22, 2011, at B9. The question of who owns the copyright to a tattoo has never been judicially determined. *See* Jacob Gershman, *Athletes' Tattoo Artists File Copyright Suits, Leaving Indelible Mark*, TATTOO ARTIST MAG., June 17, 2014, *available at* http://tattooartistmagazineblog.com/2014/06/17/athletes-tattoo-artists-file-copyright-su its-leaving-indelible-mark/ (last visited June 15, 2016).

[121] *See* Warner Bros. v. American Broad. Co., 654 F. 2d 204, 207 (2d Cir. 1981).

[122] "[T]he determination of the extent of similarity that will constitute a substantial and hence infringing similarity presents one of the most difficult questions in copyright law, and one that is the least susceptible of helpful generalization." MELVILLE B. NIMMER & DAVID NIMMER, 3 NIMMER ON COPYRIGHT §13.03[A].

mysterious envelope being pursued throughout New York City by a corrupt police officer, too similar to that of a 1998 novel, *Ultimate Rush*, about a San Francisco messenger on in-line skates pursued by Chinese assassins after delivering an opened package containing illegal stock information?[123]

Professor Melville Nimmer developed two sub-categories of the concept of "substantial similarity" to help with the definition: (1) "comprehensive nonliteral similarity" and (2) "fragmented literal similarity." The first is an example of non-infringing, legally permissible similarity, and the second is an example of infringing, impermissible similarity. Others see the distinction between the two as the difference between "inspiration" and "imitation," still others as the difference between "homage" and "theft" (or "plagiarism"), or between the "new way" and the "old way" of making music, or as the point where copyright ends and cultural appropriation begins.[124]

The first type of similarity could occur when two works share the same all-encompassing and central theme. For example, consider the narrative theme of star-crossed, unlucky lovers, cursed by destiny. William Shakespeare wrote the play *Romeo and Juliet* (1597) based on this theme. But assuming for a moment that the play is still copyrighted today — which it is not — would Robert Wise's 1961 film *West Side Story* violate Shakespeare's copyright? Does it matter that Shakespeare's "Juliet" character is named "Maria" in the film? What about Franco Zeffirelli's 1968 film *Romeo & Juliet*? What about James Cameron's 1997 film, *Titanic* — which is essentially *Romeo and Juliet* set on a boat? What about Jonathan Levine's 2013 film, *Warm Bodies*, in which "R," an unusual zombie with feelings, falls in love with the still-living Julie? What about the 2014 CW television series, *Star Crossed*, in which an alien hero is attracted to a human heroine? Or what about Andrzej Bartkowiak's 2000 film *Romeo Must Die* — which does not include any character named "Romeo" anywhere in the movie?

Based on this hypothetical fact situation, the Zeffirelli film could not be made without Shakespeare's agreement; certainly, the names of the characters are the same, but the film also includes the same characters and the same narrative transferred onto the motion picture screen. However, neither the CW television series nor the Wise, Cameron, Levine or Bartkowiak films would violate Shakespeare's copyright. They have a "comprehensive nonliteral similarity" to the original *Romeo and Juliet* in the most general, broadest, non-infringing sense. They are all about doomed lovers but they do not copy from the original.

On the other hand, Timothy Anderson's appreciation of Sylvester Stallone's *Rocky* films led him to write a film treatment for *Rocky IV*, which copied characters and their characteristics, as well as Rocky Balboa's back story — all of which demonstrated his admiration for and acknowledgement of Stallone's original work. Anderson's only original contribution was what happened to whom and what Rocky did next. His work demonstrated a "fragmented literal similarity" to Stallone's already copyrighted work and thus infringed Stallone's copyright.[125] Could Anderson have written his own story about some down-and-out athlete, even perhaps a boxer, who overcomes great obstacles to win a contest no one believes he can win? Yes, he could have, but he didn't. Could he have negotiated a license from/contract with Stallone for Anderson to write a *Rocky IV* film treatment for pay? Yes, he could have; but, again, he didn't.

A more complex example of a copyright infringement claim involved George Harrison — former member of the Beatles and himself an internationally known performing artist — and his 1970 hit song "My Sweet Lord." Harrison composed the song in 1969 with Billy Preston, though Harrison is credited as sole author. His music company, Harrisongs Music, held the copyright. In 1971, Bright Tunes Music, the owner of the copyright for the song "He's So Fine" — a 1963 hit for the Chiffons — sued him for plagiarism resulting in copyright infringement. Harrison lost. The court concluded that "it is perfectly obvious to the listener that in musical terms, the two songs are virtually identical except for one phrase."[126]

Bright Tunes was thus able to establish copyright infringement, first, by showing that it held the copyright to the song "He's So Fine," originally written by Ronald Mack. Second, it was able to prove copying by Harrison by establishing that he had access to the song and that the two songs were legally similar. "He's So Fine" had been on the top of the American music charts for five weeks in 1963 and had ranked in the top thirty in Great Britain for seven weeks. Harrison even conceded access, admitting that he "remembered hearing [the song] when it was popular."[127] The substantial similarity between the two

---

[123] *See* Elizabeth Stevens, *A Big Hollywood Movie Is Coming and a Novelist Cries Foul*, N.Y. TIMES, Aug. 20, 2011, *available at* http://www.nytimes.com/2011/08/21/us/21bcquirk.html (last visited June 15, 2016).

[124] *See* Ben Sisario, *Songwriters Sue to Defend a Summer Hit*, N.Y. TIMES, Aug. 17, 2013, at B6; Ben Sisario, *In Dispute over a Song, Marvin Gaye's Family Files a Countersuit*, N.Y. TIMES, Oct. 31, 2013, at B2. *See also* Toni Lester, *Blurred Lines - Where Copyright Ends and Cultural Appropriation Begins: The Case of Robin Thicke versus Bridgeport Music and the Estate of Marvin Gaye*, 36 HASTINGS COMM. & ENT. L.J. 217 (2014); Jon Caramanica, *A Verdict Based on an Old Way of Making Music*, N.Y. TIMES, Mar. 12, 2015, at C1; Ashby Jones, *Homage or Theft? A Closer Look at the 'Blurred Lines' Verdict*, WALL STREET J., Mar. 11, 2015, *available at* http://blogs.wsj.com/law/2015/03/11/homage-or-theft-a-closer-look-at-the-blurred-lines-verdict/ (last visited June 15, 2016); Ben Ratliff, *The Blurred Lines Between Homage and Plagiarism*, N.Y. TIMES, Mar. 13, 2015, *available at* http://nyti.ms/1Ao2rMt (last visited June 15, 2016).

[125] Anderson v. Stallone, 11 U.S.P.Q. 2d 1161 (C.D. Calif. 1989).

[126] Bright Tunes Music v. Harrisongs Music, 420 F. Supp. 177, 180 (S.D. N.Y. 1976).

[127] ABKCO Music v. Harrisongs Music, 722 F.2d 988, 998 (2d Cir. 1983). Similarly, Wonder Man creator Will Eisner had rejected purchase of the original *Superman* comic strip before its acquisition by DC Comics, thus establishing his access to the copyrighted material from which he developed Wonder Man in 1939. BOB ANDELMAN,

songs was discussed extensively and agreed upon — Harrison's own expert witness agreed with the court that he "had never come across this unique ... use of these materials,"[128] and Harrison himself "conceded ... that the two songs were 'strikingly similar' as played by a pianist during the ... trial."[129] As a result, the trial court "concluded that the substantial similarity coupled with access constituted copyright infringement,"[130] even though the judge stated that he believed that the impermissible infringement was "subconsciously accomplished."[131]

In 2010, the band Men at Work — whose 1982 hit song "Down Under" has served as the unofficial anthem for the country of Australia for thirty years — was found to have taken the song's distinctive flute solo from the 1932 children's campfire song "Kookaburra Sits in the Old Gum Tree." The group lost its last appeal in 2011, and the plagiarism cost it 5 percent of the royalties the song had earned during the past decade.[132] Yet the film documentary *The Agony and the Ecstasy of Phil Spector* used "a greatest-hits collection of twenty-one Spector songs, played or performed in their entirety ... without having obtained Mr. Spector's written permission,"[133] based on the argument that "Mr. Spector's records cannot be appreciated or assessed except in their entirety."[134] On the other hand, release of a documentary film about mostly anonymous studio musicians who actually recorded many of the biggest hits of the 1960s working as contract session labor for many different record labels, a group known as the Wrecking Crew, has been indefinitely delayed because the producer cannot afford to pay licensing fees for the 132 songs included in the film.[135] And an upcoming movie about rock guitarist Jimi Hendrix may not include any of his music, a result of licensing disagreements between the filmmaker and the Hendrix estate.[136]

An even more problematic legal situation arises when advertisers create "sound-alike tracks" — songs that "mimic a group's musical style." Artists complain that such music represents a way for advertising agencies to get around licensing requirements, that such songs copy artists' "feeling and ... sentiment and ... energy ... to sell something [the artist] didn't want to sell."[137] Yet because artists generally "cannot copyright an instrumental style, mood or an overall sound,"[138] it is very difficult to establish any actual violation of copyright laws.

The Fair Use Defense

The most important and far-reaching statutory limitation to the exclusive rights of copyright owners is the defense found in the Fair Use Doctrine.[139] The use of copyrighted works for "criticism, comment, news reporting, teaching (including multiple copies for classroom use), scholarship [and] research" is permitted by the rule, as is any other use which is determined to be "a fair use" as a result of the application of the rule's four factors:

1. The purpose and character of the use, including whether such use is of a commercial nature or is for nonprofit educational purposes;

2. The nature of the copyrighted work;

3. The amount and substantiality of the portion used in relation to the copyrighted work as a whole;

4. The effect of the use upon the potential market for or value of the copyrighted work.

The Supreme Court's ruling in *Harper & Row Publishers v. Nation Enterprises* demonstrates this analysis.[140] Harper & Row had contracted with former President Gerald Ford to publish his memoirs, *A Time to Heal*. The autobiography would focus on Ford's presidency, as well as the political aftermath of the resignation of President Richard Nixon, accused of orchestrating the 1972 burglary of the Democratic National Committee's offices in the Watergate office building, and Ford's pardon of the former president. Harper & Row had sold the rights to publish excerpts from the book to *Time* magazine, but even before the book was published in 1979, *The Nation* magazine scooped everyone and published an article using copyrighted materials it obtained from the unpublished book. When *Time*

WILL EISNER: A SPIRITED LIFE 43 (2005). *See also* Detective Comics v. Bruns (Fox) Pubs., 111 F. 2d 432 (2d Cir. 1940).

[128] *Bright Tunes*, 420 F. Supp. at 180.

[129] *ABKCO Music*, 722 F.2d at 998.

[130] *Id.* at 997.

[131] *Bright Tunes*, 420 F. Supp. at 181. *See also* Music Copyright Infringement Resource (2012), *available at* http://mcir.usc.edu/ (last visited June 15, 2016).

[132] *See* Kristen Gelineau, *Band Penalized for Copied Riff in "Down Under" Hit,* July 6, 2010, BOSTON.COM, http://archive.boston.com/ae/music/articles/2010/07/06/band_penalized_for_copied_riff_in_down_under_hit/ (last visited June 15, 2016).

[133] John Anderson, *In Documentary, Wall of Sound Meets Wall of Law*, N.Y. TIMES, June 27, 2010, Arts & Leisure, at 12. The filmmaker Vikram Jayanti, however, claimed that Spector verbally agreed to cooperate with him before Spector's 2009 conviction in the shooting death of an actress in his Hollywood home and had seen the film before its premiere and acquiesced to its distribution. *Id.*

[134] *Id.* at 20.

[135] *See* Larry Rohter, *Music Film Is Delayed by Fees for Songs*, N.Y. TIMES, Apr. 26, 2012, at C1, C7.

[136] *See* Dave Itzkoff, *A Hendrix Biopic with No Hendrix Songs*, N.Y. TIMES, July 4, 2012, at C4. Generally, the use of music in advertising always requires a license. *See* Dave Itzkoff, *Beastie Boys Settle Suit over Toy Company Ad*, N.Y. TIMES, Mar. 19, 2014, at C3.

[137] James McKinley, *To Singers, Ad Sounds Too Familiar*, N.Y. TIMES, June 9, 2012, at C1.

[138] *Id.* at C5.

[139] 17 U.S.C. 107 (2016). Yet application of the Fair Use Doctrine to works not easily divisible or susceptible to partial use, such as artwork, is not easy. For example, if fair use "allows artists to borrow from other works so long as they give a new expression or meaning to the original work," at what exact, legally ascertainable point does such borrowing — or "mash-up" — become improper appropriation? Michael Rips, *Fair Use, Art, Swiss Cheese and Me*, N.Y. TIMES, June 17, 2012, Week in Review, at 5.

[140] 471 U.S. 539 (1985).

magazine sought to get out of its contract with Harper & Row, the publisher sued *The Nation* for copyright infringement.[141]

The magazine agreed in court that its exact copying of between 300 and 400 words of direct quotations from Ford's original 200,000-word manuscript "and constituting some 13%" of the magazine's article "would constitute [copyright] infringement unless excused [as] fair use."[142] After analyzing and applying each of the four factors, the Supreme Court ruled in favor of Harper & Row.

First, the Court said, *The Nation* "went beyond simply reporting uncopyrightable information and actively sought to exploit the headline value of its infringement, making a 'news event' out of its unauthorized first publication of a noted figure's copyrighted expression."[143] Thus, its intended purpose was commercial in that it intended to "supplant … the copyright holder's commercially valuable right of first publication."[144] Second, the Court noted, "[T]he fact that a work [was] unpublished [was] a critical element of its 'nature,'" as pre-publication "confidentiality and creative control" were critical to the value and success of the project. As such, "The author's right to control the first public appearance of his expression weighs against [any] use of the work before its release."[145] Third, without regard to any exact number of words that may be considered "substantial," the Court agreed with the trial-level court that *The Nation* took "essentially the heart of the book."[146] The excerpts taken played "a key role in the infringing work." Finally — recognizing that the fourth factor "is undoubtedly the single most important element in fair use"[147] — the Court concluded that Harper & Row had "established a *prima facie* case of actual damage that respondents failed to rebut,"[148] especially given the "extensive prepublication quotations from an unreleased manuscript without the copyright owner's consent [which pose] substantial potential for damage to the marketability of first serialization rights."[149]

However, the Court reached a somewhat different conclusion in *Campbell v. Acuff-Rose Music*.[150] In that case, the rap music group, 2 Live Crew, parodied a well-known 1964 song, "Oh, Pretty Woman," written by Roy Orbison and William Dees, in express defiance of its owner's determination not to grant permission for the use. The 2 Live Crew 1989 version of the song, written by Luther Campbell, took the original song's opening snare drum beat and bass line but then created its own lyrical vision (or version) of a woman who is anything but attractive or feminine or faithful to her boyfriend. Because of its "fragmented literal similarity," if the use is not a "fair use," then the 2 Live Crew parody clearly infringes on the Acuff-Rose copyright.

In analyzing 2 Live Crew's use of the song, according to the Fair Use Doctrine's four factors, the Supreme Court acknowledged the commercial nature of the use up front but downplayed that first factor's determinative importance, saying only that the first "factor tends to weight against a finding of fair use."[151] After essentially dismissing the relevance of the second factor — both songs, after all, had already been published — the Court found itself in agreement with the trial-level court in its analysis of the third, substantiality/amount, factor and determined that "2 Live Crew had not helped themselves overmuch,"[152] contrary to the appellate court's conclusion that the parody had taken "the heart of the original and [made] it the heart of a new work."[153]

So how much is too much? The answer to this question is also at the heart of the $7.3 million jury verdict awarded to the Marvin Gaye estate in 2015 on the grounds that Robin Thicke's "Blurred Lines" (2013) was substantially similar to Gaye's "Got to Give It Up" (1977). The similarity between the two songs basically amounts to "atmospheric and textual elements … bass phrasing" and cowbell syncopation.[154] Thus, the song's authors "only seem guilty of stealing a vibe."[155] The issue, then, "is less

---

[141] Richard Nixon was president from 1969 until 1974, and Ford from 1974 to 1977. In the aftermath of what has become known as "the Watergate scandal" (1972-74), Nixon resigned the presidency rather than be impeached. *See* Carl Bernstein & Bob Woodward, All the President's Men (1974). The magazine's Apr. 3, 1979, article by Victor Navasky, "The Ford Memoirs — Behind the Nixon Pardon," was reprinted as an appendix to the Court's ruling. *Harper & Row*, 471 U.S. at 570.

[142] *Id.* at 548, 569.

[143] *Id.* at 561.

[144] *Id.* at 562. *See also* Sony v. Universal City Studios, 464 U.S. 417, 452 (1984) (where the Court ruled that "every commercial use of copyrighted material is presumptively an unfair exploitation of the monopoly privilege that belongs to the owner of the copyright").

[145] *Id.* at 564.

[146] *Id.* at 565 (quoting Harper & Row v. Nation Enters., 577 F. Supp. 1067, 1072 (S.D. N.Y. 1983)). *See also* Kelly v. Arriba Soft Corp., 336 F.3d 811, 820 (9th Cir. 2003) (where the appellate court noted that "while wholesale copying does not preclude fair use *per se*, copying an entire work militates against a finding of fair use").

[147] *Id.* at 566.

[148] *Id.* at 567.

[149] *Id.* at 569.

[150] 510 U.S. 569 (1994).

[151] *Id.* at 585 (quoting *Harper & Row*, 471 U.S. at 562). Previously, the Court had stated that "every commercial use of copyrighted material is presumptively … unfair." Sony v. Universal City Studios, 464 U.S. 417, 451 (1984).

[152] *Id.* at 587.

[153] Campbell v. Acuff-Rose Music, 972 F. 2d 1429, 1438 (6th Cir. 1992).

[154] Ben Sisario, *Side Issues Intrude in "Blurred Lines" Case*, N.Y. Times, Mar. 2, 2015, B1, at B3. *See also* Ben Sisario & Noah Smith, *Hit Single Plagiarized 1977 Song, Jury Rules*, N.Y. Times, Mar. 11, 2015, at B1.

[155] "And if vibes are now considered intellectual property, let us swiftly prepare for every idiom of popular music to go crashing into juridicial oblivion, because music is a continuum of ungovernable hybridity, a dialogue between generations where the aesthetic inheritance gets handed down and passed around in every direction. To try to adjudicate *influence* seems as impossible as it does insane" (emphasis in original). Chris Richards, *It's OK If You Hate Robin Thicke, But the "Blurred Lines" Verdict Is Bad for Pop Music*, Wash. Post, Mar. 11, 2015, at ¶ 8-9, *available at* http://www. washingtonpost.com/blogs/style-blog/wp/2015/03/11/the-blurred-lines-of-the-blurred-lines-verdict/ (last visited June 15, 2016). *See also* Ed Christman, *"Blurred Lines" Ver-*

about chords than about 'feel.' The 'Blurred Lines' groove hits the ear a lot like the [Marvin] Gaye [song], but when, exactly, does 'feel' become infringement?"[156]

In *Campbell*, the Supreme Court stated that "context is everything" and a "fair use" analysis "asks what else the parodist did besides go to the heart of the original." It found "that 2 Live Crew not only copied the first line of the original, but thereafter departed markedly from the Orbison lyrics for its own ends."[157] Finally, the Court warned against presuming economic harm in any analysis of the fourth, market, factor, as the appellate court had done. Rather, the Court ruled, "as to parody pure and simple, it is more likely that the new work will not affect the market for the original ... by acting as a substitute for it."[158]

Thus, the parody here targeted the original and transformed it into something entirely new and copyrightable — a separate, original work. Parody, the Court concluded, "has an obvious claim to transformative value.... Like less ostensibly humorous forms of criticism, it can provide social benefit, by shedding light on an earlier work, and, in the process, creating a new one."[159] Clearly, then, a transformative use is a fair use.

But what is a transformative use? Paramount Pictures took a well-known 1991 picture of actress Demi Moore, eight months pregnant and partially nude, from the cover of *Vanity Fair* magazine, doctored it — by taking a similarly posed photograph of a semi-nude, pregnant model and super-imposing the head of actor Leslie Neilson on the body and then used the resulting photograph to promote its 1993 movie, *The Naked Gun 33 1/3: The Final Insult*. The photographer, Annie Leibovitz, sued but

lost — because the movie poster was a parody of Leibovitz's earlier photograph.[160]

Yet the publication of a three-year-old nude photo of a TV news reporter participating in a wet T-shirt contest was not a transformative fair use, since by publishing it "clearly for commercial purposes" in an unaltered form, "*Hustler* was selling a [copyrighted] picture, and not a [news] story."[161] And the widow of Theodor Geisel — who wrote children's books as Dr. Seuss — won when she sued Penguin Books for its use of Dr. Seuss-like rhymes, meter and style in the book, *The Cat NOT in the Hat*, to tell the tale of the O.J. Simpson murder case. The appellate court concluded that the book was an infringement of copyright in that it did not specifically aim at Dr. Seuss' *The Cat in the Hat* as the target of any transformative parody.[162]

These cases suggest another unanswered question: Are there any other types of uses that qualify as transformative uses? Though only future court rulings can answer this, the question is at the heart of the many "Hitler Downfall" parodies now existing on YouTube, in which Adolph Hitler — in a scene from the 2004 German film *Der Untergang* — rages and rants not about his approaching doom but about new features on the Apple iPad; about the Adam Sandler film, *Jack and Jill* (2011); about the new features on Microsoft's Windows operating system; about the global financial crisis; and about the parodies themselves. There is even a YouTube channel devoted exclusively to such clips.[163] Or what about Randy Moore's 2013 movie, *Escape from Tomorrow*, about a father going insane at Walt Disney World? Could the filmmaker use Disney's copyrighted images in his "critique [of] Disney's style of mass entertainment"?[164] And what about artist Richard Prince's use of Patrick Cariou's photographs of Rastafarians as the basis for a 2008 series of paintings?[165] Whether such examples are transformative uses and thus protected by copyright is not clear.

So what do all these rulings tell us about what uses of copy-

dict: How It Started, Why It Backfired on Robin Thicke and Why Songwriters Should be Nervous, BILLBOARD, Mar. 13, 2015, *available at* http://www.billboard.com/articles/business/6502023/blurred-lines-verdict-how-it-started-why-it-backfired-on-robin-thicke-and (last visited June 15, 2016); Mark Swed, *"Blurred Lines" Verdict Would Rock Amadeus and Other Great Composers*, L.A. TIMES, Mar. 14, 2015, *available at* http://www.latimes.com/entertainment/arts/la-et-cm-blurred-lines-classical-notebook-20150314-column.html (last visited June 15, 2016); Jody Rosen, *Robin Thicke on "Blurred Lines" and Learning from His Mistakes*, N.Y. TIMES, July 1, 2015, *available at* http://nyti.ms/1C9T2iI (last visited June 15, 2016).

[156] Spencer Kornhaber, *The "Blurred Lines" Verdict Could Be Bad for Music*, THE ATLANTIC, Mar. 2015, at ¶ 3, *available at* http://www.theatlantic.com/entertainment/archive/2015/03/why-the-blurred-lines-verdict-could-be-bad-for-music/387433/ (last visited June 15, 2016). *See also* Ben Sisario, *Skirmishing Continues in "Blurred Lines" Case*, N.Y. TIMES, Mar. 20, 2015, at C2. This issue of a recording's "feel" is already being litigated further. *See* Ben Sisario, *Led Zeppelin Members Set to Defend 'Stairway,'* N.Y. TIMES, June 6, 2016, at B1, B4; Tim Kenneally, *'Stairway to Heaven' Lawsuit: Led Zeppelin Denies Copyright Claims, Admits Being 'One of the Greatest Bands in History,'* BOSTON.COM, May 24, 2015, *available at* http://archive.boston.com/entertainment/music/2015/05/24/stairway-heaven-lawsuit-led-zeppelin-denies-copyright-claims-admits-being-one-the-greatest-bands-history/22Ad9750vnSxnQJwsYaQsO/story.html (last visited June 15, 2016).

[157] 510 U.S. at 589.

[158] *Id.* at 591.

[159] *Id.* at 579. Playwright David Adjmi, for example, successfully claimed that his 2012 play, *3C*, was a parody of the 1977 television series, *Three's Company. See* John Koblin, *Play Reimagining 'Three's Company' Wins Case*, N.Y. TIMES, Apr. 2, 2015, at C3.

[160] *See* Leibovitz v. Paramount Pictures, 137 F. 3d 109 (2d Cir. 1998). *See also Annie Leibovitz & the Naked Gun*, COPYRIGHT (undated), *available at* http://www.benedict.com/visual/nakedgun/nakedgun (last visited June 15, 2016).

[161] Balsley v. LFP, Inc., 691 F.3d 747, 759 (6th Cir. 2012).

[162] Dr. Seuss Enters. v. Penguin Books, 109 F.3d 1394 (9th Cir. 1997).

[163] *Hitler Rants Parodies* (undated), YOUTUBE.COM, *available at* http://www.youtube.com/user/hitlerrantsparodies?feature=results_main (last visited June 15, 2016). *See also* Aaron Schwabach, *Reclaiming Copyright from the Outside In: What the Downfall Hitler Meme Means for Transformative Works, Fair Use & Parody*, 8 BUFF. INTELL. PROP. L.J. 1 (2012).

[164] *See* Brooks Barnes, *It's a Grim World, After All*, N.Y. TIMES, Jan. 21, 2013, at C1, C7.

[165] *See* Cariou v. Prince, 714 F. 3d 694 (2d Cir. 2013). *See also* Randy Kennedy, *Richard Prince Settles Suit over Photos*, N.Y. TIMES, Mar. 20 2014, at C3. Photographer Donald Graham has since also complained about Prince's use of his images. *See* Jennifer Schuessler, *Artist and Gallery Told to Cease and Desist*, N.Y. TIMES, Feb. 17, 2015, at C3; Patricia Cohen, *Photographers Band Together to Protect Work in "Fair Use" Cases*, N.Y. TIMES, Feb. 22, 2014, at C1, C6. *See also* Kelly Crow, *Court Says a Photo of a Photo Can Become Art, Too*, WALL STREET J., Apr. 25, 2013, at B6.

righted works are "fair"?

First, the question of "whose dime" is a very important issue. For a commercial use to be fair, it must be transformative, as the Court found that it was in *Campbell*. Even when the use involves teaching, including multiple copies for classroom use, if students must pay for a supplemental course packet that includes photocopied excerpts from books and other periodicals for use in class, it is not a fair use. This rule was established in *Basic Books v. Kinko's Graphics*.[166] One may argue that requiring students to purchase a large number of books in a given course makes the cost of higher education nearly prohibitive. Yet, because of the commercial interests involved — including the fact that Kinko's made a significant profit from the sales of these anthologies, which also themselves competed with the sale of the books from which the excerpts were taken — the company was guilty of copyright infringement in the making of unauthorized copies of copyrighted works.

Second, unpublished works not only have a higher degree of copyright protection than published ones, but they also are further protected in that possession of the work does not give the owner the right to use it otherwise. For example:

• May the letters of the late author J.D. Salinger be published because they are available to researchers in publicly accessible libraries? No: Salinger's estate still owns and controls copyright in the unpublished letters.[167]

• May the personal letters from George Steinbrenner, the late owner of the New York Yankees, written in 1949 to a female friend, be published by the recipient in a book she wants to write about their relationship? No: They may not be published although they may be sold.[168]

• May students record and subsequently post a professor's lectures online? Although students have a right to the private possession of such recordings, making the recordings available to others by online posting would violate the intellectual property rights of the professor.[169]

• May a journalist befriend acquaintances of author Harper Lee over a period of years and write a book based on this direct access? Yes: Despite the reclusive author's public statement denying that she had authorized any such book or that she willingly participated in the project, such a book may be published as long as it is based on the journalist's own observations and does not include any material in which Harper Lee's estate has a copyright claim.[170]

Possession may indeed be nine-tenths of the law, but not where the copyright owner's exclusive rights of copying and derivative works are concerned. Just ask Eva Gabrielsson, long-time partner of Swedish author Stieg Larsson. Despite having possession and ownership of the late writer's laptop computer containing an unpublished sequel to his *Millennium* series of novels featuring Lisbeth Salander — *The Girl with the Dragon Tattoo* — the copyright to the unpublished work (specifically, the right to publish a sequel as a derivative work) is owned by Larsson's family, since Gabrielsson and Larsson never married and she does not qualify as his legal heir.[171]

Third, "the amount and substantiality of the portion used in relation to the ... work as a whole" cannot be calculated to be a specific allowable percentage. There is no "20 percent rule" or "40-word rule."[172] There is no exact amount at all; whatever it is "remains a murky proposition."[173] How much constitutes "the heart" of a work is a question which cannot be answered in general terms, but only on a case-by-case, contextual basis and then only in relation to the fourth part of the Fair Use Doctrine.[174] "It is uncontested," however, that — had it not been legally excused as being transformative — 2 Live Crew's lifting of the opening snare drum beat and bass line of Roy Orbison's "Pretty Woman" would have been sufficient — because of the "fragmented literal similarity," however insignificant it was — to constitute illegal copying.[175]

Fourth, unless a work is transformative, the copyright owner has the right not only to exploit the market for his or her work but also to choose what potential markets to exploit in the future and which ones to avoid. It is solely the copyright owner's choice. In addition, it makes no difference whether the infringement is for or not for, with or without monetary gain. Castle Rock Entertainment, owner of the *Seinfeld* television series

[166] 758 F. Supp. 1522 (S.D. N.Y. 1991). *See also* Princeton Univ. Press v. Michigan Document Servs., 99 F.3d 1381 (6th Cir. 1996).

[167] Salinger v. Random House, 811 F.2d 90 (2d Cir. 1987). Essentially, the same issue was raised with regard to personal correspondence between Jacqueline Kennedy and the Rev. Joseph Leonard, which also involved questions of minister-parishioner privileged communication. *See* Katharine Seelye, *Jackie Kennedy's Letters Taken Off the Auction Block*, N.Y. TIMES, May 24, 2014, at A14. *See also* James McKinley, *Belafonte Sues the King Family*, N.Y. TIMES, Oct. 16, 2013, at C1, C6.

[168] *See* Richard Sandomir, *Yankees Want Steinbrenner Letters Kept Private*, N.Y. TIMES, Oct. 14, 2010, *available at* http://www.nytimes.com/2010/10/15/sports/baseball /15steinbrenner.html (last visited June 15, 2016).

[169] *See* Alexandra Rice, *Canadian Faculty Union Warns That Student Postings of Lectures Could Violate Copyright Law*, CHRON. OF HIGHER ED., Dec. 21, 2011, *available at* http://chronicle.com/blogs/wiredcampus/canadian-faculty-union-warns-that-student-postings-of-lectures-could-violate-copyright-law/34740 (last visited June 15, 2016).

[170] *See* Patricia Cohen, *"To Kill a Mockingbird" Author Repudiates Journalist's Memoir About Her*, N.Y. TIMES, Apr. 27, 2011, *available at* http://artsbeat.blogs.ny times.com/2011/04/27/to-kill-a-mockingbird-author-repudiates-journalists-memoir-abo ut-her (last visited June 15, 2016).

[171] *See* Charles McGrath, *The Girl Who Cast a Spell on Her Rivals*, N.Y. TIMES, June 22, 2011, at C1.

[172] *See* Vaidhyanathan, *supra* note 6, at 47.

[173] John Anderson, *In Documentary, Wall of Sound Meets Wall of Law*, N.Y. TIMES, June 27, 2010, Arts & Leisure, at 12.

[174] This is especially true when poetry is involved. *See* David Orr, *When Quoting Verse, One Must Be Terse*, N.Y. TIMES, Sept. 9, 2011, at A25.

[175] *Campbell*, 510 U.S. 569, 574 (1994).

copyright, could choose for whatever reason not to publish any "Seinfeld" trivia book, such as *The Seinfeld Aptitude Test*, and the law "must respect that creative and economic choice."[176] Similarly, author J.D. Salinger could stop publication of an unauthorized sequel — John David California's *60 Years Later: Coming Through the Rye* — to his own ground-breaking coming-of-age novel, *Catcher in the Rye*.[177] Although a federal appellate court required Salinger to prove harm from the publication, it did acknowledge the Salinger estate's control over the markets for all derivative works based on his writings and concluded "that Salinger is likely to succeed on the merits of his copyright infringement claim."[178]

The challenge of fair use, then, is to develop a centrist application of the doctrine, one that is not too narrow and restrictive and one that is not too broad and inclusive, yet one that is substantially more assertive and expansive than that which is regularly applied today.[179] To this end, the American University Center for Social Media has collected several codes of "best practices" to assist students and everyone else in the fair application of "fair use."[180]

Copyright's Digital Transformation

If the primary purpose of copyright law is to protect the copyright owner's right to make copies, then technological innovation has always been the enemy of copyright. For most of recorded history, "Copying was hard and expensive."[181] Yet, every invention since Johannes Gutenberg's printing press in 1436 has made it progressively easier to copy and, thus, has taken the physical ability to control one's creation ever further out of the hands of the copyright holder. Indeed, "As a duplicating machine, the printing press ... made texts cheaper and more accessible" and easier to disseminate, with or without the acquiescence or approval of the original author.[182]

As a result, copyright law has always viewed technological developments cautiously — whether the created expression takes the form of printed marks on a page or analog radio waves or digital bits of information. As innovations have developed and copyright owners have become increasingly aware of the profit potential in these new methods of "publication," there has at the same time developed a growing assumption of infringement, a belief by copyright holders that technological innovations will be used to their detriment. Today, the Internet enables the flouting of copyright "on a scale unfathomable" twenty years ago.[183]

A century ago, "The disruptive technology was player pianos," and the question before the Supreme Court was whether player piano rolls were copies of songs or something else.[184] If they were copies, then player piano manufacturers should pay copyright owners for each copy produced; if they were something else, then the manufacturers could continue to do what they were doing — which was to purchase a single piece of copyrighted sheet music legally, have someone create the "recording" of the music, and sell these rolls to consumers without any further royalty payment on the manufacturers' part. In *White-Smith Publishing v. Apollo*, the Court ruled that player piano rolls were mechanical reproductions and not copies of musical compositions — and, in fact, were not music at all, since most people could not read the perforations and/or otherwise gather musical thoughts from the rolls themselves — and that no additional royalty payments were required, according to then-current copyright law.[185]

Contributory Infringement. Thus, it should have surprised no one when several film production companies, looking at the new Sony Betamax video tape recorder, concluded that the sale of each machine must be taxed to pay the film production companies for the royalties they would lose from all the copying (and copyright infringement) that would result from their use and misuse by consumers. The fear of infringement was so real that some said "the VCR is to the American film producer and the American public as the Boston strangler is to the woman home alone."[186] In *Sony v. Universal City Studios*, however, the Supreme Court determined that time-shifting — the viewing of a recorded program at a time other than when it was first broadcast — was a fair use of the new technology,[187] in that it actually

---

[176] Castle Rock Entm't v. Carol Publ'g. Group, 150 F.3d 132, 145-46 (2d Cir. 1998).

[177] *See* Sewell Chan, *Ruling for Salinger, Judge Bans "Rye" Sequel*, N.Y. TIMES, July 1, 2009, *available at* http://cityroom.blogs.nytimes.com/2009/07/01/judge-rules-for-salinger-in-copyright-suit/ (last visited June 15, 2016).

[178] Salinger and Salinger v. Colting, 607 F.3d 68, 83 (2d Cir. 2010). John David California is the pseudonym of Fredrik Colting.

[179] *See* PATRICIA AUFDERHEIDE & PETER JASZI, RECLAIMING FAIR USE: HOW TO PUT BALANCE BACK IN COPYRIGHT (2011). *See also* Patricia Aufderheide, *Myths About Fair Use*, INSIDEHIGHERED.COM, Aug. 2, 2011, http://www.insidehighered.com/views/2011/08/02/essay_calls_on_academics_to_use_their_fair_use_rights (last visited June 15, 2016).

[180] *See* International Communication Association, Code of Best Practices for Scholarly Research in Communication (2010), *available at* https://www.natcom.org/uploadedFiles/More_Scholarly_Resources/Publishing_Primer/PDF-publishingprimer-fair_use.pdf (last visited June 15, 2016); Society for Cinema Studies, *Statement of Best Practices in Fair Use in Teaching for Film & Media Educators*, 47 CINEMA J. 155 (Winter 2008).

[181] Vaidhyanathan, *supra* note 6, at 45.

[182] JAMES GLEICK, THE INFORMATION: A HISTORY, A THEORY, A FLOOD 400 (2011).

[183] Michael Rustad, *Copyrights in Cyberspace: A Roundup of Recent Cases*, 12 SUFFOLK U. L. REV. 106, 107 (2011).

[184] Hal Varian, *Economic Scene: File-Sharing Is the Latest Battleground in the Clash of Technology and Copyright*, N.Y. TIMES, Apr. 7, 2005, at ¶ 5, *available at* http://www.nytimes.com/2005/04/07/business/07scene.html (last visited June 15, 2016).

[185] 209 U.S. 1 (1908).

[186] Eduardo Porter, *In a Ruling, the Legacy of Betamax*, N.Y. TIMES, Mar. 27, 2013, at B1 (quoting Jack Valenti, then head of the Motion Picture Association of America).

[187] 464 U.S. 417, 455 (1984).

increases the value of the copyrighted work by increasing the size of its audience through the option of what might be considered a deferred purchase. Further, the Court held that manufacturers of video cassette recorders cannot be held legally responsible for contributing to copyright infringement as long as the machines are "capable of substantial non-infringing uses."[188]

Twenty years later, Grokster, a peer-to-peer computer file-sharing service whose users downloaded copyrighted music files without permission, argued similarly that its software was also capable of innocent uses in that it could be used, for example, to download very large data files, such as the complete works of William Shakespeare. Was Grokster thus liable for the acts of those who used its software to download music illegally and violate copyright? In *MGM v. Grokster*, the Supreme Court concluded that the file-sharing service was legally liable, because of the company's intent in the marketing and sales campaigns for its software was to encourage customers to infringe copyright.[189]

The modern two-part test for contributory infringement thus seems to be: (1) Is the technology capable of substantial non-infringing uses? and (2) Is the manufacturer/seller's intent to encourage or induce others to violate copyright? This focus on capability and intent is also evident in the position that the Digital Millennium Copyright Act of 1998 takes in immunizing Internet service providers and not holding them legally liable for any copyright violations by their users.[190]

Digital Sampling and Mash-ups. The availability of almost all copyrighted works in digital format today — as computerized bits of binary data — is threatening the exclusive rights of copyright holders as never before, especially the right to reproduce a copyrighted work and the right to make derivative works from the original.[191] This threat is particularly evident in the area of musical composition — unsurprising in view of the "long tradition of musical borrowing"[192] — known as sampling, which may be loosely defined as the incorporation or re-purposing of a snippet, a recognizable portion of a song, into another song

through some digital means.[193] WhoSampled.com, the "ultimate database of sampled music, remixes, and cover songs," claims to have links to 99,000 songs by 39,000 artists.[194] So many examples are now available that lists and smartphone apps of sampled songs abound.[195]

An interesting example of video sampling is the short film *A Fair(y) Use Tale*, by Professor Eric Faden. The ten-minute film uses snippets of dialogue from characters in Disney animated films to create a critical parody to explain copyright law and fair use.[196] The film uses snippets of words and phrases, sometimes *ad nauseum*, from twenty-seven Disney cartoon feature films — from *Snow White and the Seven Dwarfs* to *Bambi* to *Sleeping Beauty* to *Jungle Book* to *The Little Mermaid* to *Toy Story* to *Finding Nemo* — to construct its educational narrative focus. Its transformative nature claim is based on the film's creative use of copyrighted Disney characters, despite Disney's well-known, highly restrictive attitude regarding the use of its characters by all others, including scholars engaged in the study of popular culture.

And, sometimes, whole albums are "mashed" together into something else entirely. A well-known example occurred in 2004 when the hip-hop group Danger Mouse took *a cappella* samples from the 2003 *Black Album* by rapper Jay-Z and combined them with instrumental loops from the Beatles' 1968 *White Album*, creating a musical mixture known as *The Grey Album*. Though legal problems quickly arose — Danger Mouse never sought copyright clearance for its use of the Beatles' songs, lawsuits were threatened, and nearly 200 Internet sites posted tracks from the bootleg album in support of Danger Mouse on what came to be known as Grey Tuesday — its release began the "mainstreaming of the mash-up," which continues today.[197] A recent example was the artist Baauer's surprise viral Internet hit, "Do the Harlem Shake," which subsequently climbed the pop charts in 2013 and included the voices of several uncredited — and unpaid — artists.[198] Yet "the joy of the mash-up lies in the

---

[188] *Id.* at 442. Another non-infringing use is to make a single, archival, back-up copy of a legally owned video.

[189] 545 U.S. 913 (2005). Grokster shut down shortly afterwards as part of the settlement of the lawsuit. *See* Jeff Leeds, *Grokster Calls It Quits on Sharing Music Files*, N.Y. TIMES, Nov. 8, 2005, at C1.

[190] 17 U.S.C. 512 (2015).

[191] *See, e.g.*, Gregory C. Lisby, *Web Site Framing: Copyright Infringement Through the Creation of an Unauthorized Derivative Work*, 6 COMM. LAW & POL'Y 541 (2001); Elina Lae, *Mashups — A Protected Form of Appropriation Art or a Blatant Copyright Infringement?* (U. Michigan Law Sch. Working Paper, Dec. 2011), *available at* http://papers.ssrn.com/sol3/papers.cfm?abstract_id=2003854 (last visited June 15, 2016).

[192] Ira Flatow, *Digital Music Sampling: Creativity or Criminality*, at ¶ 1, NPR.ORG, Jan. 28, 2011, http://www.npr.org/2011/01/28/133306353/Digital-Music-Sampling-Creativity-Or-Criminality (last visited June 15, 2016).

[193] *See, e.g., Music Sampling*, WHOSAMPLED.COM (2016), http://www.whosampled.com/sampling/ (last visited June 15, 2016).

[194] *See, e.g.*, Dave Izkoff, *Kanye West Is Sued over Song Sample*, N.Y. TIMES, Dec. 26, 2013, at C2.

[195] *See, e.g., Music Sampling Song List* (undated), POP CULTURE MADNESS, *available at* http://www.popculturemadness.com/Music/Lists/Samples.html (last visited June 15, 2016); *Top Rated Samples*, WHOSAMPLED.COM (2016), http://www.whosampled.com/browse/samples/top/1/ (last visited June 15, 2016).

[196] The 2007 film is available on the Internet site of the Stanford Fair Use Project, http://cyberlaw.stanford.edu/documentary-film-program/film/a-fair-y-use-tale (last visited June 15, 2016).

[197] In other words, the best mash-ups are always unauthorized, unlicensed ones. *See* William Ferguson, *The Mainstream Mash-Up*, N.Y. TIMES MAG., Dec. 12, 2004, at ¶ 2, *available at* http://www.nytimes.com/2004/12/12/magazine/12MAIN.html (last visited June 15, 2016).

[198] *See* James McKinley Jr., *Surprise Hit Was a Shock for Artists Heard on It*, N.Y. TIMES, Mar. 11, 2013, C1, C5.

certainty that no matter how many lawyers are involved, Madonna and the Sex Pistols could never coexist except in a flash of inspiration." But, of course, musicians and consumers are also "expected to pay for it."[199]

An early example of a mashed-up movie is Joe Dante's *The Movie Orgy* (1968), which is nothing more than discarded 16mm film footage, both amateur and professional, "creatively re-edited" into

> a hilarious meta-movie in which five or six stories seem to be going on at once (giant grasshoppers invade Chicago as flying saucers attack Washington), constantly interrupted by prom night do's and don'ts, stomach-churning commercials for laxative pills and disturbing excerpts from children's television shows (including a stuffed cat and mouse who perform "Jesus Loves Me" on piano and drums).[200]

More recently, fans have taken full seasons of television series, such as *Arrested Development*, downloaded them and re-edited them in an order different from that in which they were originally released.[201] With the digital format of modern film, "mash-ups and hybrids will rule; everything that can be mashed together will be,"[202] since "the Internet has created a mash-up culture."[203]

But the legal rule today is still simple and straightforward: "A sampling license [is] absolutely necessary when you are interested in using any portion of someone else's copyrighted music" or film.[204] A license "to use samples [is] standard practice in the music industry, and — in most cases — is needed from both the music publisher and the record label that made the master recording."[205] Do not believe the so-called "fair use rule" in the music industry that "says that as long as it is four notes or less, there is no penalty for copyright infringement."[206] That is

wrong, as the appellate ruling in *Bridgeport Music v. Dimension Films* demonstrates.[207]

There, three notes lasting two seconds were sampled from the 1975 Funkadelic song, "Get Off Your Ass and Jam," in the 1990 N.W.A. song, "100 Miles and Runnin'," which was included as part of the 1998 film, *I Got the Hook Up*. The three notes still were sufficient to constitute copyright infringement. The appellate court acknowledged that "advances in technology, coupled with the advent of the popularity of hip-hop or rap music, have made instances of digital sampling extremely common and have spawned a plethora of copyright disputes and litigation,"[208] but said that the solution was to "get a license or do not sample.... Sampling is never accidental.... When you sample a sound recording, you know you are taking another's work product."[209]

Though there are some specific limitations on the scope of copyright in sound recordings, when the question involves copying, "the only issue is whether the actual sound recording has been used without authorization."[210] If it has been, then that is infringement.

"Copyleft" and Future Challenges to Copyright. The ready availability (and easy manipulation) of digitized information on the Internet has created today's "instability of the copyright system."[211] This, in turn, has led to two results.

First, copyright has "become too strong for its own good. It protects more content and outlaws more acts than ever before. It stifles individual creativity and hampers the discovery and sharing of culture and knowledge."[212] Copyrights are being rigorously enforced, using the "jackboot" of IP law, "with a vengeance and in such a manner as to stifle rather than advance ... 'Science and the useful Arts.'"[213] This part of the problem is fur-

---

[199] Ferguson, *supra* note 197, at ¶ 5. For examples of other mash-ups, *see* the Web site of Mark Vidler's "Go Home Productions" (2015), *available at* http://www.gunkelweb.com/ghp.html (last visited June 15, 2016).

[200] Dave Kehr, *Saved from Extinction: Classics and Curiosities*, N.Y. TIMES, Oct. 14, 2011, at C1. *See also* Eric Grode, "*Alphaville*," N.Y. TIMES, Feb. 7, 2014, at C18.

[201] *See* Dave Itzkoff, *In a Twist on the Remix, Fans Recut TV Series*, N.Y. TIMES, June 10, 2013, at C1, C8.

[202] David Carr, *New Rules for the Ways We Watch*, N.Y. TIMES, Dec. 26, 2011, at C1, C2. *See* Teju Cole, *On Photography*, N.Y. TIMES MAG., Apr. 19, 2015, at 20.

[203] Noam Cohen, *A Store of Images, from a Time When "Cut & Paste" Meant Just That*, N.Y. TIMES, Oct. 31, 2011, at B3.

[204] *Sampling Music & Law Regarding Sampling*, at ¶ 4, MUSIC LAW (undated), http://www.music-law.com/sampling.html (last visited June 15, 2016). The music licensing company, Rumblefish, has introduced a service that allows creators of non-commercial YouTube videos to add music legally to their films. *See* Joseph Plambeck, *For $1.99, a (Legal) Song To Add to YouTube Videos*, N.Y. TIMES, June 28, 2010, at B6.

[205] McKinley, *supra* note 198, at C5.

[206] *Sampling Music, supra* note 204, at ¶ 6.

[207] 410 F.3d 792 (6th Cir. 2005); 401 F.3d 647 (6th Cir. 2004).

[208] *Id.* at 798-99. *See, e.g.,* Allan Kozinn, *Katy Perry Is Named in Lawsuit over Song*, N.Y. TIMES, Jul. 5, 2014, at C3; Allan Kozinn, *More Sampling Madness, as Seen on YouTube*, N.Y. TIMES, Sep. 13, 2014, at C3.

[209] *Id.* at 801.

[210] BRADLEY ROSEN, 22 CAUSES OF ACTION § 12 (2d ed. 2003). The single exclamation, "Oh!," sampled forty-two times in the background of Jay-Z's 2009 single, "Run This Town," has no essential significance to the original recording of Eddie Bo's "Hook and Sling - Part I" and is thus not protected by copyright law. *See* Joe Coscarelli, *Judge Dismisses a Suit Over Jay-Z's "Run This Town,"* N.Y. TIMES, Dec. 9, 2014, *available at* http://artsbeat.blogs.nytimes.com/2014/12/09/judge-dismisses-a-suit-over-jay-zs-run-this-town/ (last visited June 15, 2016). *See also* Lorne Manly, *Justin Bieber and Usher to Face a Copyright Trial*, N.Y. TIMES, June 20, 2015, at C3.

[211] Vaidhyanathan, *supra* note 6, at 43.

[212] *Id.*

[213] Randy Barnett, *Reds in Suits*, REGULATION, at 65 (Fall 2002) (quoting U.S. CONST., art I, § 8, ¶ 8), noting:

> [M]ore than a few view one person's use of his own physical property as "theft" of another's intangible property. Because of so-called intellectual property, the property owner cannot fully use what he reasonably thought was his; he cannot copy music from one of his CDs onto his computer and then move the files onto his MP3 player. He cannot make photocopies of a book that he owns, and then hand those

ther exacerbated and the positions of the different parties become even more inflexible and seemingly more confused when a corporate entity is involved.[214]

Second, some legal theorists — Professor Lawrence Lessig is one — are re-examining the very nature of intellectual property in non-physical cyberspace. The Internet, in Lessig's view, is a commons area and should be structured as "a common market of innovation," and its uses not structured, regulated or restricted as private property. Goods, such as intellectual property, in such common areas "are a resource for decentralized innovation. They create the opportunity for individuals to draw upon resources without connections, permission, or access granted by others. They are environments that commit themselves to being open. Individuals and corporations draw upon the value created by this openness. They transform that value into other value,"[215] since "*the digital world is closer to the* [Jeffersonian] *world of ideas than to the world of things.*"[216]

This philosophy has led to the development of the "copyleft" concept, a copyright licensing arrangement — sometimes known as a Creative Commons license — that gives all possessors and users of a work the same control over it as authors, including the right to copy and share it with others, and to modify and distribute derivative versions — rights exclusively reserved to copyright holders under copyright law. The "copyleft" symbol is a backwards "C" in a circle (see Figure 3) but has no legal significance or meaning. Though the concept obviously has potential application to other types of intellectual property, open source software development is the most common application of the concept today.[217]

Clearly, some new interpretation of (or, failing that, intensive education regarding) copyright law and its myriad of applications to what are no more than various combinations of digital bits in cyberspace needs to be developed. Previously unheard-of problems are now being confronted. For example:

• How can music best be made available to consumers, in a manner that properly credits and compensates copyright holders? Should artists charge for their music and thus limit their audience, or should they seek the widest possible audience, one

FIGURE 3

that uses their music without permission or remuneration?[218]

• Is using one's telephone to take pictures of housing diagrams, illustrations and pictures contained in a book available for purchase an infringement of a publisher's copyright? In all likelihood, yes, since "'documenting' a book ... bears many similarities to pirating music."[219] A definitive result would of course depend on the outcome of a judicial analysis of the fact situation using the Fair Use Doctrine.

• In its "quest for the universal library," does Google's book-scanning project create copyrighted works out of those already in the public domain or violate the rights of unknown owners of so-called "orphan works" or infringe on existing copyrights by digitizing them to make them easily accessible online?[220] Is Google trying to create "a single liquid fabric of interconnected words and ideas,"[221] or, is it really "trying to control ... access to virtually all information in the world"?[222] Publishers reached a

---

copies to a friend or a class of students. He cannot use his own guitar to play particular notes or his voice to sing particular lyrics in public.

[214] *See* Randy Cohen, *Hollywood Property Values*, N.Y. TIMES MAG., Feb. 20, 2011, at 17.

[215] LAWRENCE LESSIG, THE FUTURE OF IDEAS: THE FATE OF THE COMMONS IN A CONNECTED WORLD 85 (2001). Lessig has written two other books on related topics: CODE AND OTHER LAWS OF CYBERSPACE (1999); CODE: VERSION 2.0 (2006).

[216] *Id.* at 116 (emphasis in original). *See Thomas Jefferson to Isaac McPherson, Aug. 13, 1813*, AMERICAN HISTORY: FROM REVOLUTION TO RECONSTRUCTION AND BEYOND (undated), *available at* http://www.let.rug.nl/usa/presidents/thomas-jefferson/letters-of-thomas-jefferson/jefl220.php (last visited June 15, 2016).

[217] *See What Is Copyleft*, GNU OPERATING SYSTEM (2015), http://www.gnu.org/copyleft/copyleft.html (last visited June 15, 2016).

[218] *See* David Pogue, *Online Music, Unshackled*, N.Y. TIMES, July 28, 2011, at B1, B9; Ben Sisario, *Debate Over Music Piracy Writ Large, on Billboard*, N.Y. TIMES, Mar. 27, 2013, at C1, C4. *See also* Tim Arango, *Rights Clash on YouTube and Videos Disappear*, N.Y. TIMES, Mar. 23, 2009, at B1, B5; Roy Furchgott, *Free Music Downloads Without the Legal Peril*, N.Y. TIMES, Sept. 4, 2008, at C6.

[219] *See* Nick Bilton, *Ping: Can Your Camera Phone Turn You into a Pirate?*, N.Y. TIMES, Jan. 16, 2011, Week in Review, at 3.

[220] *See* Jeffrey Toobin, *Annals of Law: Google's Moon Shot*, NEW YORKER, Feb. 5, 2007, *available at* http://www.newyorker.com/reporting/2007/02/05/070205fa_fact _toobin (last visited June 15, 2015). *But see* Author's Guild v. HathiTrust, 755 F. 3d 87 (2d Cir., 2014) (where a searchable book database for the sight impaired was determined to be a transformative "fair" use which does not violate copyright).

[221] Vaidhyanathan, *supra* note 6, at 42.

[222] Miguel Helft, *Visual Artists to Sue Google over Vast Library Project*, N.Y. TIMES, Apr. 7, 2010, ¶ 9, *available at* http://www.nytimes.com/2010/04/07/technology/07

settlement with Google in 2012, a lawsuit by authors was dismissed in 2013, and appeals were exhausted in 2016.[223]

• Are "tweets" copyrightable?[224] If so, how much may be used, according to the Fair Use Doctrine, when the entire "tweet" is limited to 140 characters or less?

• Do musical scores in the public domain and available for free online unfairly hurt publishers' sales of "modern editions that may be entitled to copyright protection ... [which include] significant changes to the music ... based on years of scholarship about the composer's intentions"?[225]

• Can publishers electronically limit the readable "shelf life" of an electronic copy of a book in a public library's collection — an "e-book" — so it will wear out (and the library be forced to purchase an additional copy for lending to patrons) at some rate similar to that of print versions of the book? Can digital goods be "loaned" at all must they be transferred?[226]

• Does the Copyright Office have unilateral administrative power to permit copyright infringement of automobile or smartphone software to allow owners to use Internet applications (known as "apps") that have not been approved by the manufacturer – a practice known as "jail-breaking" — to recalibrate performance?[227]

• Which is better legislatively, to hold Internet sites and services, such as Kim Dotcom's Megaupload service, responsible for theft and piracy by their users or to hold individual users liable for unauthorized downloads of music and films and books?[228]

• As both professional and amateur sports organizers increasingly turn to claims of contractual copyright entitlements as a way of cornering the entertainment marketplace for themselves, how do the media and artists and others deal with the growing claims of "monopoly over ever broader swaths of the business of distributing information" about sporting events?[229]

• Should the conversion of academic publishers' copyrighted works into Adobe's public document format and the posting of PDF files on university-controlled Internet sites (such as, the Georgia State University library's electronic course reserves Web site) for educational purposes — for students to read, download and copy, all without paying royalty fees — be considered copyright infringement?[230] Whose dime must cover the costs, and to what degree must accessibility be restricted for this practice to qualify as "teaching (including [the right to make] multiple copies for classroom use)" and be protected as a fair use of copyrighted works?[231] The appellate court overturned a ruling that essentially set a 10 percent threshold for allowable online, educational posting, stating that a "fair use" analysis must not be applied "mechanistically."[232]

• Can YouTube be held legally liable for its own blindness to the uploading by some users of copyrighted videos, despite the safe harbor provisions of the Digital Millennium Copyright Act of 1998?[233]

• How will three-dimensional "printing," which can reproduce objects by spraying layers of plastic or ceramics into the shape of an item, change the nature of manufacturing and challenge

---

google.html (last visited June 15, 2015).

[223] *See* Alexandra Alter, *Google's Digital Library Wins Court of Appeals Ruling*, N.Y. TIMES, Oct. 17, 2015, at B2; Adam Liptak, *Challenge to Google Books Is Declined by Supreme Court*, N.Y. TIMES, Apr. 18, 2016, *available at* http://nyti.ms/1SpBCFZ (last visited June 15, 2016); Claire Miller, *Google Deal Gives Publishers a Choice: Digitize or Not*, N.Y. TIMES, Oct. 5, 2012, at B7; Claire Miller & Julie Bosman, *Siding with Google, Judge Says Book Search Does Not Infringe Copyright*, N.Y. TIMES, Nov. 15, 2013, at B7; Andrea Peterson, *Google Books Just Won a Decade-Long Copyright Fight*, WASHINGTON POST, Apr. 18, 2016, *available at* https://www.washingtonpost.com/news/the-switch/wp/2016/04/18/google-books-just-won-a-decade-long-copyright-fight/ (last visited June 15, 2016);

[224] *See* James Joyner, *Twitter Law: Are Tweets Copyrighted?*, OUTSIDE THE BELTWAY BLOG, Mar. 30, 2009, http://www.outsidethebeltway.com/twitter_law_are_tweets_copyrighted/ (last visited June 15, 2016).

[225] Daniel Wakin, *Free Trove of Music Scores on the Web Hits Sensitive Copyright Note*, N.Y. TIMES, Feb. 22, 2011, at A3.

[226] *See* David Streitfeld, *Imagining a Swap Meet for E-Books and Music*, N.Y. TIMES, Mar. 7, 2013, *available at* http://www.nytimes.com/2013/03/08/technology/revolution-in-the-resale-of-digital-books-and-music.html (last visited June 15, 2016). *See also* Julie Bosman, *Library E-Books Live Longer, So Publisher Limits Shelf Life*, N.Y. TIMES, Mar. 15, 2011, at A1; Philip Corbett, *To Mooch or Not to Mooch?*, N.Y. TIMES MAG., Apr. 15, 2012, at 27; Randall Stross, *Publishers vs. Libraries: An E-Book Tug of War*, N.Y. TIMES, Dec. 24, 2011, *available at* http://www.nytimes.com/2011/12/25/business/for-libraries-and-publishers-an-e-book-tug-of-war.html (last visited June 15, 2016).

[227] *See* Barry Meier & Jad Mouawad, *Car Buffs Get the Keys to Software*, N.Y. TIMES, Nov. 23, 2015, at B1, B2; Joelle Tessler, *Government Rules Allow Unapproved iPhone Apps*, MYRTLE BEACH SUN NEWS, July 27, 2010, at 9A. *See also* U.S. Copyright Office, Rulemaking on Anti-circumvention (2015), *available at* http://www.copyright.gov /1201/ (last visited June 15, 2016).

[228] *See* Nick Bilton, *Internet Pirates Will Always Win*, N.Y. TIMES, Aug. 5, 2012,

Sunday Review, at 5; Stuart Green, *When Stealing Isn't Stealing*, N.Y. TIMES, Mar. 29, 2012, at A23; Jonathan Hutchison, *A Year After the Closing of Megaupload, a File-Sharing Tycoon Opens a New Site*, N.Y. TIMES, Jan. 21, 2013, at B5; Roger Parloff, *Megaupload & the Twilight of Copyright*, FORTUNE, July 11, 2012, http://fortune.com/ 2012/07/11/megaupload-and-the-twilight-of-copyright/ (last visited June 15, 2016); Somini Sengupta, *U.S. Pursuing a Middleman in Web Piracy*, N.Y. TIMES, July 13, 2012, at A1, A3; Jenna Wortham & Amy Chozick, *The Piracy Problem: How Broad?*, N.Y. TIMES, Feb. 9, 2012, at B1, B7.

[229] Eric Johnson, *The NFL, Intellectual Property and the Conquest of Sports Media*, 86 N.D. L. REV. 759, 761 (2010). *See also* Daniel Grant, *Free Speech vs. Infringement in Suit on Alabama Artwork*, N.Y. TIMES, Jan. 31, 2012, at B12, B16.

[230] *See* Cambridge Univ. Press v. Patton, 769 F. 3d 1232 (11th Cir. 2014).

[231] 17 U.S.C. 107 (2016).

[232] *Cambridge Univ. Press*, 769 F. 3d, at 1283. For a book without chapter divisions, the district court ruled that 10 percent of its pages may be made available to students without royalty payments; for a book with ten or more chapters, the fair use copying of one chapter is permissible. *See* Cambridge Univ. Press v. Becker, 863 F. Supp. 2d 1190, 1243 (N.D. Ga. 2012).

[233] In the "dancing baby" case, copyright owners whose musical works are only incidental parts of online videos must now consider fair use in good faith before making takedown requests. *See* Lenz v. Universal Music, 801 F. 3d 1126 (9th Cir. 2015). *See also* Ben Sisario, *Copyright Ruling Aims at Fair Use on the Web*, N.Y. TIMES, Sept. 15, 2015, at B2. *And see* 17 U.S.C. 512(c) (2016). Assessments of fair use, of course, depend upon who is doing the using. *See* Jim Naureckas, *For NYT, Fair Use Depends on Who's Doing the Using*, FAIR & ACCURACY IN REPORTING, June 9, 2016, *available at* http://fair.org/home/for-nyt-fair-use-depends-on-whos-doing-the-using/ (last visited June 15, 2016).

the legal concepts of ownership and copyright?[234]

• Do online news aggregation Web sites that compile news stories without publishers' permission infringe copyright?[235]

• What implications do digital "reincarnations" or holograms have for copyright and the ownership of one's image?[236]

As is clear, the evolving technological landscape that is cyberspace promises that more issues such as these will arise in the future. Some believe that "more than ever, the law restricts what individuals can do with the elements of their own culture. Generally the exercise of copyright protection is so extreme these days that even the most innocent use of images or song lyrics ... can generate a legal threat,"[237] which will force "artists to get permission for every snippet they [use, thus creating] a logistical and financial nightmare."[238] Others fear that without a strong copyright law, the markets that copyright protects will be undermined by piracy, which is "a lucrative, innovative, global enterprise. Clusters of overseas [computer] servers can undermine much of the commercial basis for creative work around the world, offering users the speedy, secret transmission of stolen goods."[239] They also warn:

[S]ince the Enlightenment, Western societies have been lulled into a belief that progress is inevitable. It never has been. It's the result of abiding by rules that were carefully constructed and practices that were begun by people living in the long shadow of the Dark Ages. We tamper with those rules at our peril.[240]

Still others argue that we live in a "post-genius" world in which the ideas of "independent creation" and "originality" are cul-

tural myths that have long outlived their legal usefulness.[241] But, whether we like it or not, "As the most pervasive regulation of speech and culture, the copyright system will help determine the richness and strength of democracy in the twenty-first century."[242]

TRADEMARKS/SERVICE MARKS

If copyright is the "engine of free expression,"[243] then trademark law — along with the Commerce Clause,[244] which gives Congress the power to control trade among states — is the engine of economic expression and the means to protect the economic value of a company's brands, as well as its reputation.[245] Thus, words, designs or phrases — or any combination of the three — that denote a specific product, service or company may be registered with the U.S. Patent & Trademark Office and protected by the Lanham Act of 1946,[246] giving companies an exclusive right to use the mark in their dealings with the consuming public.[247]

A product's design or image, as part of its "trade dress," may

---

[234] *See* Nick Bilton, *Like That Vase? Print It. And, No, It's Not Stealing*, N.Y. TIMES, Nov. 14, 2011, at B8; Nick Bilton, *On the Fast Track to Routine 3-D Printing*, N.Y. TIMES, Feb. 18, 2013, at B4; Martha Mendoza, *3-D Printing Goes from Sci-Fi Fantasy to Reality*, YAHOO! NEWS, June 2, 2013, http://news.yahoo.com/3-d-printing-goes-sci-fi-fantasy-reality-133123371.html (last visited June 15, 2016); Amy O'Leary, *3-D Printers to Make Things You Need or Like*, N.Y. TIMES, June 20, 2013, at B1, B9; Elizabeth Royte, *The Printed World*, SMITHSONIAN MAG. (May 2013), at 50.

[235] Yes, if such Web sites resell the news stories they aggregate. *See* Associated Press v. Meltwater News, 106 U.S.P.Q. 2d (BNA) 1509 (S.D. N.Y. 2013).

[236] *See* Vera Chan, *Tupac's Resurrection and Questions over Raising the Dead*, YAHOO! NEWS, Apr. 19, 2012, http://news.yahoo.com/blogs/trending-now/y-big-story-tupac-resurrection-questions-over-raising-215806421.html (last visited June 15, 2016); Eriq Gardner, *Marilyn Monroe Estate Threatens Legal Action over Hologram*, HOLLYWOOD REPORTER, June 11, 2012, *available at* http://www.hollywoodreporter.com/thr-esq/marilyn-monroe-estate-hologram-legal-334817 (last visited June 15, 2016).

[237] Vaidhyanathan, *supra* note 6, at 45.

[238] Eduardo Porter, *Tech Suits Endanger Innovation*, N.Y. TIMES, May 30, 2012, at B1, B2.

[239] Scott Turow, Paul Aiken & James Shapiro, *Would the Bard Have Survived the Web?*, N.Y. TIMES, Feb. 15, 2011, at A27.

[240] *Id.* The issue can also be framed in moral terms. *See* Ben Sisario, *Defining and Demanding a Musician's Fair Shake in the Internet Age*, N.Y. TIMES, Oct. 1, 2013, at C1, C5.

[241] Joshua Shenk, *The End of "Genius*,*"* N.Y. TIMES, Jul. 20, 2014, Sunday Review section, at 6.

[242] Vaidhyanathan, *supra* note 6, at 43.

[243] Harper & Row Publishers v. Nation Enter., 471 U.S. 539, 558 (1985).

[244] U.S. CONST., art. I, § 8, ¶ 3.

[245] *See, e.g.,* Joe Drape, *Rolling in Cash, Crimson Tide Lifts All Boats*, N.Y. TIMES, Nov. 6, 2015, at A1, B12; Elizabeth Olson, *Burger Lawsuit Shows Value of Trademarks*, N.Y. TIMES, Oct. 29, 2015, at B4; Jack Ewing & Quentin Hardy, *Alphabet? Google Might Get Some Letters*, N.Y. TIMES, Aug. 12, 2015, at B3; James Stewart, *Alphabet with a Capital 'G'*, N.Y. TIMES, Aug. 14, 2015, at B1, B2. *See also* Stuart Elliott, *Technology Titans Lead Ranking of Most Valuable Brands*, N.Y. TIMES, Oct. 9, 2014, at B6.; Eric Taub, *Trademarks Can Protect Your Good Name*, N.Y. TIMES, Sep. 26, 2007, Special Section, at 2. A list of protected brands would also include the Hells Angels Motorcycle Club's "Death Head" logo. *See* Serge Kovaleski, *Despite Outlaw Image, Hells Angels Often Sue*, N.Y. TIMES, Nov. 29, 2013, at A1, A22. Similarly, from a legal standpoint, the U.S. Marines are proactively seeking to protect their image of dignity, recently seeking cease-and-desist orders against a toilet paper product called Leatherneck Wipes. *See* Helene Cooper, *As Wars End, Military Gives Its Trademarks New Vigilance*, N.Y. TIMES, May 25, 2014, at A13, A18. *But see* Christopher Coble, *Feds Want to Seize Biker Gang Logo*, FINDLAW BLOTTER, June 16, 2015, *available at* http: //blogs.findlaw.com/blotter/2015/06/feds-want-to-seize-biker-gang-logo.html (last visited June 15, 2016) (where the government seeks to seize a motorcycle club's trademarked logo as part of a racketeering prosecution).

[246] 15 U.S.C. 1051 *et seq.* (2016). *See, e.g.,* Adriana Gardella, *"Chanel's Salon" May Not Have Been Best Choice for a Name*, N.Y. TIMES, Oct. 9, 2014, at B8. Even without federal trademark protection, a mark may also be protected under common law or state statute. The URL for the Trademark Office is: http://www.uspto.gov/ (last visited June 15, 2016).

[247] For example, the Amateur Sports Act of 1978, 36 U.S.C. 380 (2016), gives the International Olympic Committee exclusive control over the games' multicolored, interlocking rings, as well as, the words "Olympic" and "Olympiad." *See* San Francisco Arts & Athletics v. U.S. Olympic Comm., 483 U.S. 522 (1987) (upholding an injunction which prohibited the use of the word, "Olympic," to promote the "Gay Olympic Games"). Marks may also be hash-tagged words, such as, #RISETOTHRIVE, #TEAMJESUS and #HELMETSARECOOL. *See* Marilesse Sweeney, *Trademark This #Hashtag. Or Is That a #DumbIdea?* LAW.COM, May 29, 2014, *available at* http://webcache.googleusercontent.com/search?q=cache:MO3Yuzfq4LgJ:www.law.com/sites/articles/2014/05/29/trademark-this-hashtag-or-is-that-a-dumbidea/+&cd=2&hl=en&ct=clnk&gl=us (last visited June 15, 2016).

also be registered as a trademark, if its elements in general (1) are nonfunctional, (2) have secondary meaning,[248] and (3) are recognized by the public as an "unmistakable, certain, and primary means of identification,"[249] which would lead to a likelihood of consumer confusion if misused by others. In fact, this concept is so all-inclusive that "nothing ... shall prevent the registration of a mark ... which has become distinctive of [an] applicant's goods in commerce."[250] Examples of trade dress include the shape of the Coca-Cola soft drink bottle, the sewing design on the back pocket of Levi's jeans, the color of Owens-Corning fiberglass insulation, the sound of Harley-Davidson motorcycles, and the red soles on Christian Louboutin women's shoes — but not the shade of purple used on the packaging of British chocolate maker Cadbury's Dairy Milk product.[251]

The basic federal requirement for a trademark or service mark is that it be distinctive,[252] though it may not:[253]

• Be scandalous, immoral, deceptive, or disparaging;

• Consist of a flag or emblem or insignia of any country;

• Resemble a person's name, signature or likeness without consent;

• Resemble any other trade or service mark;

• Be merely descriptive of the product;

• Be primarily descriptive (or mis-descriptive) of the product's geographic origin; or

• Be a surname.

The requirement of distinctiveness in trademark law roughly corresponds to the originality requirement in copyright law.[254] It is also similar to the common law protection against unfair competition available in tort law. In *International News Service v. Associated Press*, for example, the INS was re-distributing news stories the AP had reported, written, sold and disseminated. INS represented the stories as its own work. On the grounds that news stories are quasi-property, the Supreme Court held that the re-distribution — even if the INS rewrote the stories in a different format — created a likelihood of confusion, misleading INS customers, and denied the AP full value for its news-gathering efforts. The INS was "endeavoring to reap where it [had] not sown and ... appropriating to itself the harvest of those who [had] sown."[255]

Context is the key when evaluating potentially disparaging marks, though more recently the First Amendment's protection for offensive language is being weighed against disparagement claims; and the so-called right to offend may finally be determined to be more important — at least the Washington Redskins and the Asian-American rock band, the Slants, would hope so, though it is unclear when a mark is legally inappropri-

---

[248] Such as the Lacoste polo shirt. See Troy Patterson, *When the Polo Shirt Arrived,* N.Y. TIMES MAG., July 12, 2015, at 16. *See also* Wal-Mart Stores v. Samara Bros., 529 U.S. 205 (2000). *But see* Foamation v. Wedeward Enter., 970 F. Supp. 676 (E.D. Wisc., 1997) (where cheese wedge hats worn by football fans did not have secondary meaning and could not be trademarked).

[249] *In re* Swift & Co., 223 F. 2d 950, 955 (Cust. & Pat. App. 1955). *See also* Tatiana Schlossberg, *British Chocolates Won't Cross the Pond,* N.Y. TIMES, Jan. 24, 2015, at A15.

[250] 15 U.S.C. 1052(f) (2016).

[251] *See* Stuart Elliott, *Technology Titans Lead Ranking of Most Valuable Brands,* N.Y. TIMES, Oct. 9, 2014, at B6.; Christian Louboutin v. Yves St. Laurent Am. Holding, 696 F. 3d 206 (2d Cir. 2012). *See also* Benjamin Weiser, *Shoe Designer Can Protects Its "Pop" of Red, Court Says,* N.Y. TIMES, Sep. 5, 2012, *available at* http://www.nytimes.com/2012/09/06/nyregion/court-rules-louboutin-can-enforce-a-trademark-on-its-red-outsoles.html (last visited June 15, 2016). *But see* Michael Safi, *BP Loses Battle to Trademark the Color Green in Australia,* THE GUARDIAN, July 3, 2014, *available at* http://www.theguardian.com/business/2014/jul/03/bp-loses-battle-to-trademark-the-colour-green-in-australia (last visited June 15, 2016); Owen Bowcott, *Cadbury's Attempt to Trademark Dairy Milk Purple Blocked,* THE GUARDIAN, Oct. 4, 2013, *available at* http://www.theguardian.com/business/2013/oct/04/cadbury-dairy-milk-purple-trademark-blocked (last visited June 15, 2016).

[252] 15 U.S.C. 1052 (2016). Lawsuits over "distinctiveness" increasingly involve claims of "trademark bullying" of small businesses by large corporations. *See,* Stephanie Strom, *Battle of the Brands: Trademarked Names Increasingly Vital for Online Search,* N.Y. TIMES, Feb. 21, 2012, at B1, B8; Andrew Martin & Peter Lattman, *P&G Settles Trademark Suit against Start-Up Business,* N.Y. TIMES, Oct. 15, 2011, at B4. They also involve novel questions, such as, can scents be trademarked? *See* Andy Newman, *Small Rival Loses Suit Involving Car Scents,* N.Y. TIMES, Nov. 20, 2015, at A24; Andy Newman, *Pine vs. Palm: Car-Scent Rivals Fight in Trademark Suit,* N.Y. TIMES, Nov. 17, 2015, at A19; Jacob Gershman, *Eau de Fracking? Efforts to Trademark Scents Spread,* WALL ST. J. Law Blog, Apr. 14, 2015, http://blogs.wsj.com/law/2015/04/14/eau-de-fracking-efforts-to-trademark-scents-spread/ (last visited June 15, 2016). There may also be other business reasons to consider adopting new marks. *See* Natalie Grover, *Isis Pharma Changes "Unfortunate" Name to Avoid Confusion,* REUTERS.COM, Dec. 18, 2015, http://www.reuters.com/article/us-isis-pharma-name-change-idUSKBN0U12A720151218 (last visited June 15, 2016); Nikita Steward, *Nonprofits, Aiming for Relevance, Try on New Names,* N.Y. TIMES, Dec. 1, 2015, *available at* http://nyti.ms/21rd29k (last visited June 15, 2016). The "distinctiveness" of trademarks should also be tested before their adoption, something RJ-Metrics failed to do before it introduced a new logo — an orange dodecahedron — that to some looked like a giant pair of men's underpants. *See* Robert Moore, *Logo Underscores Value of Testing,* N.Y. TIMES, May 15, 2014, at B4.

[253] 15 U.S.C. 1052(a) — (e)(4) (2016). In addition, government emblems cannot be registered as trademarks. *See* Rebecca Tushnet, *Unregisterable Means Unprotectable by*

Section 43 as Well, REBECCA TUSHNET'S 43(B)LOG, June 4, 2014, http://tushnet.blogspot.com/2014/06/unregistrable-means-unprotectable-by.html (last visited June 15, 2016). As an example of the challenges facing geographically descriptive and "merely" descriptive marks, *see,* Sheryl Stolberg, *Kentucky Moonshiner in Court Over Trademark, Not the Hooch,* N.Y. TIMES, Apr. 10, 2016, at A1, A13; Tim Worstall, *Apple Loses the iPad Mini Trademark,* FORBES, Mar. 31, 2013, *available at* http://www.forbes.com/sites/timworstall/2013/03/31/apple-loses-the-ipad-mini-trademark/#72f9e2fd6822 (last visited June 15, 2016).

[254] 17 U.S.C. 102(a) (2016). For example, the phrase "three-peat" — which means three consecutive sports championships — has been trademarked by National Basketball Association coach Pat Riley since 1988. *See* Christopher Wade v. Riles & Co. (Trademark Trial & Appeal Board, Sept. 6, 2001), *available at* http://www.uspto.gov/web/offices/com/sol/foia/ttab/other/2001/21869.pdf (last visited June 15, 2016). *See also* Brian Costa, *Pat Riley's Other Master Plan: Trademarking 'Three-Peat',* WALL ST. J., June 4, 2014, *available at* http://www.wsj.com/articles/pat-rileys-other-master-plan-trademarking-three-peat-1401923767 (last visited June 15, 2016). As another example, professional fighter Ronda Rousey is applying for trademark protection for the phrase, "Rowdy Ronda Rousey Is in the House," having previously received trademark protection for the phrase, "F.T.A.", which stands for "F*** Them All." *See,* Tim Bissell, *'Rowdy' Ronda Rousey Seeks Trademark for Unusual Drawing and Slogan,* BLOODY ELBOW, June 2, 2016, *available at* http://www.bloodyelbow.com/2016/6/2/11839976/rowdy-ronda-rousey-seeks-trademark-for-unusual-drawing-and-slogan-ufc-news-mma (last visited June 15, 2016).

[255] 248 U.S. 215, 239-40 (1918).

ate or what rules would be used to make this determination.[256]

Once a mark is registered with the U.S. Patent & Trademark Office, it is good for ten years and may be renewed for unlimited ten-year periods, as long as it is regularly and continually used "in commerce," though a period of three consecutive years of non-use raises the presumption of abandonment.[257] A registered trademark should be noted on the product by ® (the letter "R" in a circle is an indication of official registration). An unregistered mark may use ™ (for trademarks) or ℠ (for service marks) as a notice alerting the public of one's legal claim to the use of the mark.[258]

Under the Trademark Revision Act of 1988, a mark no longer has to be in use before an application for registration is filed. An "intent to use" application gives the requestor at least six months to begin using the mark.[259] The mark is not actually registered until it is placed "in use," but the "intent to use" rules protect it from infringement by someone who has never used the mark nor previously applied for its registration.

Degrees of Protection

The degree of protection varies along a continuum, with fanciful or coined marks receiving the most protection, descriptive marks receiving the least, and generic marks receiving no protection whatsoever,[260] as Figure 4 illustrates.

Fanciful or coined marks are generally created words or designs with no dictionary meaning, such as "Exxon." Arbitrary marks are commonplace words or symbols that do not describe the product of company with which they are associated, such as "Apple" computers. Such "marks convey nothing about the nature of the product except through knowledge of the market."[261] Suggestive marks, on the other hand, are familiar words or phrases that are used to suggest what the product or service really is, such as the Lifetime television network, whose programming is primarily aimed at women, or the Spike television network, whose programming is primarily aimed at men. As might be surmised, descriptive marks actually describe the thing or company, such as *Money*, a personal finance magazine. Proof of some secondary or non-natural meaning is required before descriptive marks may be registered as trademarks.[262]

Generic marks are the names of a product or service and cannot function as trademarks, such as "aspirin," an over-the-counter pain reliever, also known as acetyl salicylic acid. At one time, "aspirin" was a protected trademark of the Bayer Company, but it fell into common usage, no longer distinguishing the particular product of its manufacturer and was invalidated.[263] Similarly, "thermos" was the registered mark belonging to the King-Seeley Thermos Company as the name for its vacuum-insulated containers, before it also began to be commonly used by Aladdin Industries to describe that company's products and

---

[256] *See, e.g., In re* Pamela Geller, No. 2013-1412 (Fed. Cir., May 13, 2014), *available at* http://caselaw.findlaw.com/us-federal-circuit/1666371.html (last visited June 15, 2016) (where the phrase, "Stop the Islamization of America," could not be registered as a trademark as it disparaged a religious group). *See also* Dennis Crouch, *Guest Post: Federal Circuit Blocks Trademark for Being Disparaging to Muslims*, PATENT-LYO.COM, May 14, 2014, http://patentlyo.com/patent/2014/05/circuit-trademark-disparaging.html (last visited June 15, 2016). *See also* Perry J. Viscounty et al., *Watch Your Mark*, WORLD TRADEMARK REV. (Dec.-Jan. 2014), at 56. For more on the lawsuits involving the Redskins and the Slants, *see* Blackhorse v. Pro-Football, No. 92046185 (Trademark Trial & Appeal Board, June 18, 2014), *available at* http://ttabvue.uspto .gov/ttabvue/v?qt=adv&pno=92046185 (last visited June 15, 2016) (where the trademark for the name of the Washington Redskins professional football team was revoked on the grounds that it disparaged indigenous American Indians); Pro-Football v. Blackhorse, No. 1:14-cv-01043-GBL-IDD, (N.D. Va., Jul. 8, 2015), *available at* http://pdfserver.amlaw.com/nlj/ProFootball%20Blackhorse%20opinion.pdf (last visited June 15, 2016) (upholding the trademark board's decision); *In re* Simon Shiao Tam, No. 85472044 (Trademark Trial & Appeal Board, Sep. 26, 2013), available at https://e-foia.uspto.gov/Foia/RetrievePdf?system=TTABIS&flNm=85472044-09-26-2013 (last visited June 15, 2016) (where the board rejected the band's trademark application as disparaging of an ethnic group), No. 2014-1203 (Fed. Cir., Apr. 20, 2015), *available at* http://www.cafc.uscourts.gov/sites/default/files/opinions-orders/14-1203.Opinion.4-16-2015.1.PDF (last visited June 15, 2016) (finding the Lanham Act's disparagement provision unconstitutional). A petition for U.S. Supreme Court review was pending, as of June 15, 2016. *See also* Lee v. Tam, No. 15-1293, SCOTUSBLOG.COM (2016), *available at* http://www.scotusblog.com/case-files/cases/lee-v-tam/ (last visited June 15, 2016). *See also* Ken Belson, *Redskins Lose Round in Battle over Name*, N.Y. Times, July 8, 2015, *available at* http://nyti.ms/1IJI4SX (last visited June 15, 2016); Ken Belson & Edward Wyatt, *Redskins Lose on Trademarks, But Fight Isn't Over*, N.Y. TIMES, June 19, 2014, at B12; Jacob Gershman, *Redskins Look to Punt Trademark Dispute to the Supreme Court*, WALL ST. J., Apr. 26, 2016, *available at* http://on.wsj.com/1rxaycr (last visited June 15, 2016); Adam Liptak, *A Football Team, an Asian-American Band and a Test of Free Speech*, N.Y. TIMES, May 3, 2016, at A15; Richard Sandomir, *Ruling Could Help Redskins' Case: Band Seeking to Register Trademark for Provocative Name Prevails in Appeals Court*, N.Y. TIMES, Dec. 23, 2015, at B1, B13. *See also* Jasmine Abdel-Khalik, *Disparaging Trademarks: Who Matters*, 20 MICHIGAN J. OF RACE & LAW 287 (2015).

[257] 15 U.S.C. 1058 (2016). Trademarks must be used in connection with commerce and are not to be used to protect one's right of publicity or right to privacy. *See, e.g.,* David Lilenfeld, *Trademarks Amid Tragedy*, ATLANTA J.-CONSTITUTION, June 12, 2011, at D2. Non-use of a mark, alone, is not abandonment. *See, e.g.,* Beech-Nut Packing Co. v. Lorillard Co., 273 U.S. 629 (1927).

[258] Trademark processing fees range from $275 to $375 per application. *See* U.S. Patent & Trademark Office, Trademark Fee Information (2016), *available at* http://www.uspto.gov/trademarks/tm_fee_info.jsp (last visited June 15, 2016). Service marks are treated the same as trademarks. 17 U.S.C. 1127 (2016).

[259] 15 U.S.C. 1051(b-d) (2016).

[260] These categories were first distinguished in *Abercrombie & Fitch v. Hunting World*, 537 F.2d 4 (2d Cir. 1976).

[261] MILLER & DAVIS, *supra* note 37, at 176.

[262] *See, e.g.,* Mike Estert, *U.S. Trademark Board Issues Mixed Opinion in Soft-Drink "Zero" Dispute*, NASDAQ.COM, May 27, 2016, http://www.nasdaq.com/article/us-trademark-board-issues-mixed-opinion-in-softdrink-zero-dispute-20160527-00684 (last visited June 15, 2016); Matt Kempner, *Word Grab: Coke Seeks to Keep 'Zero' from Rivals' Use*, ATLANTA J.-CONST., Feb. 21, 2016, at D1, D4; Mike Estert, *Coca-Cola Fights for "Zero" Trademark Rights*, NASDAQ.COM, Feb. 9, 2016, http://www.nasdaq.com/article/cocacola-fights-for-zero-trademark-rights-20160209-01397 (last visited June 15, 2016). *See also* Park 'N Fly v. Dollar Park & Fly, 469 U.S. 189, 205 (1985) (where federal trademark registration creates a presumption that a mark is more than "merely descriptive" and may be used to stop others from using similar signage). Merely descriptive marks may not be registered as trademarks.

[263] Bayer Co. v. United Drug Co., 272 F. 505 (S.D. N.Y. 1921).

CONTINUUM OF TRADEMARK PROTECTION

MOST

Fanciful

Arbitrary

Suggestive

Descriptive

Generic

LEAST

FIGURE 4

thus was subsequently invalidated as a distinct trademark.[264]

Corporations, therefore, are constantly on the look-out for public misuse of their trade and service marks to prevent what has been called "genericide" — the death of trademarks by common or generic use — and regularly place advertisements showing correct trademark usage and write letters to journalists and others who use trademarks incorrectly in the media.

The rule is simple: Trademarks and service marks are proper nouns, which should be capitalized, and not common nouns, verbs or adjectives. The correct usage for trademarks, for example, would be: Xerox® photo-copiers, Egg Beaters® egg substitute food product, Scotch® brand adhesive tape, Play-Doh® modeling compound, Johnson & Johnson's Kleenex® facial tissues, a Jeep Grand Cherokee® sport utility vehicle, Certs® breath freshening mints, Formica® laminated plastic surfaces, U-Haul® truck and automobile trailer rentals, Wham-O's Frisbee® brand plastic flying disc, Chattanooga Bakery's Moon Pie® brand chocolate flavored marshmallow sandwiches, Duraflame® artificial fireplace logs, McIlhenny Company's Tabasco® brand pepper sauce.[265] These companies have introduced new words into common usage through the marketing of their products and have made themselves a lot of money in the process — like Apple's iPad® tablet computer — but also constantly worry about the unintended consequences of "genericization" and "brand deterioration."[266]

Threats to Trademarks

Because the primary purpose of trademarks is to identify and distinguish products and services, making money for their owners while at the same time generating valuable goodwill,[267] trademark owners are very sensitive to any and all threats to their marks,[268] including product confusion they themselves cause.[269] The two most serious threats to trademarks are (1) likelihood of confusion and (2) dilution.[270] All writers and other communicators should therefore be extremely careful when adapting ideas, slogans, images or logos that might be protected by trademark law.[271]

First and foremost, a mark's strength is of critical importance in assessing its likelihood of confusion with another mark.[272] In addition, though there is no exact statutory checklist, courts

---

[264] King-Seeley Thermos Co. v. Aladdin Indus., 321 F.2d 577 (2d Cir. 1963). And DuPont lost control over the trademark, "cellophane," when it was determined that everyone referred to all thin, plastic sheeting (waxed or not) by that name. DuPont Cellophane Co. v. Waxed Products Co., 85 F. 2d 75 (2d Cir. 1936).

[265] See the International Trademark Association's alphabetically searchable database, *Trademark Checklist* (2016), http://applications.inta.org/apps/trademark_check list/ (last visited June 15, 2016).

[266] See Mae Anderson, *Apple's "iPad" Is the Only Tablet People Know*, YAHOO! NEWS, Apr. 9, 2012, http://news.yaho.com/apples-ipad-only-tablet-people-know-124138 038.html (last visited June 15, 2015). This claim is not true in 2016.

[267] The all-important yet fragile nature of "goodwill" is well illustrated by the Internet hoax played on McDonald's in 2011 that purportedly announced a corporate policy charging racial minorities more for their food to offset losses from robberies. The hoax was tweeted and repeatedly re-tweeted, in the face of corporate denials and evidence of its bogus nature (including the toll-free telephone number on the door announcement placard as that of Kentucky Fried Chicken). *See* Zachary Roth, *Racial Hoax Causes PR Headache for McDonald's*, YAHOO! NEWS, June 13, 2011, http://news. yahoo.com/blogs/lookout/racial-hoax-causes-pr-headache-mcdonald-145623383.html (last visited June 15, 2016).

[268] *See* Mrs. U.S. Nat'l Pageant v. Miss U.S. Org., 875 F. Supp. 2d 211 (W.D. N.Y. 2012) (where customer confusion meant that the mark "Miss United States of America" infringed on "Mrs. United States"). *See also* Dave Itzkoff, *Anheuser-Busch Objects to Labels in "Flight,"* N.Y. TIMES, Nov. 7, 2012, at C3. *But see* Jonathan Mahler, *If the Word "How" Is Trademarked, Does This Headline Need a ™?* N.Y. TIMES, Oct. 4, 2014, at A1.

[269] *See, e.g.,* Leon Stafford, *Coke Junks White Cans over Customer Confusion*, ATLANTA J.-CONSTITUTION, Dec. 2, 2011, at A19.

[270] *See, e.g.,* Ringling Bros.-Barnum & Bailey Combined Shows v. Utah Div. of Travel Development, 955 F. Supp. 605 (E.D. Va. 1997) (where the slogan, "the greatest snow on earth" did not dilute the circus' similar slogan); Watchers Int'l v. Stouffer Corp., 744 F. Supp. 1259 (S.D. N.Y. 1990) (where a disclaimer on packages of frozen diet entrees was too small to counter the misleading impression that the food products were associated with the diet program). For recent examples of "likelihood of confusion,. *See, e.g.,* Leigh Beadon, *How Drunk Would You Need to Be to Confuse Jack Daniel's with Cayman Jack?*, TECHDIRT, Apr. 6, 2012, https://www.techdirt.com/articles/20120 405/19034518399/how-drunk-would-you-need-to-be-to-confuse-jack-daniels-with-caym an-jack.shtml (last visited June 15, 2016); Tom Corwin, *School Sues over University Name*, ATLANTA J-CONSTITUTION, Sep. 22, 2012, at B3; Eriq Gardner, *Judge Blocks Release of 'Age of the Hobbits' Movie*, HOLLYWOOD REPORTER, Dec. 10, 2012, *available at* http://www.hollywoodreporter.com/thr-esq/judge-blocks-release-age-hobbits-400062 (last visited June 15, 2016); Michelle Graff, *In Tiffany vs. Costco, the Battle's Just Begun*, NATIONAL JEWELER, Jan. 29, 2014, *available at* http://www.nationaljeweler.com/ majors/market-developments/3013-in-tiffany-vs-costco-the-battle-s-just-begun (last visited June 15, 2015); Margaret Littman, *Hall and Oates Sue Food Company Over Haulin' Oats Granola*, ABA J., July 1, 2015, *available at* http://www.abajournal.com /magazine/article/hall_and_oates_sue_food_company_over_haulin_oats_granola/ (last visited June 15, 2016); David Markiewicz, *Trademark Dispute: Botany Term at Root of Lawsuit*, ATLANTA J.-CONSTITUTION, Feb. 18, 2012, at A12, A13.

[271] *See* MGM-Pathe Commc'ns v. Pink Panther Patrol, 774 F. Supp. 869 (S.D. N.Y. 1991) (where a gay rights organization was held to have infringed on a trademark because ordinary individuals could mistakenly assume that the trademark owners sponsored or otherwise supported activities of the organization).

[272] *See* Golden Door v. Odisho, 437 F. Supp. 956, 967 (N.D. Calif. 1977) (where the use in a market area and goodwill zone of confusingly similar beauty salon names created a likelihood of confusion).

generally consider the following factors:

- Similarity of the marks themselves;[273]
- Similarity of the goods or services identified by the marks;[274]
  - Similarity of trade channels or marketing methods;[275]
- Whether sales promoted by the marks are "impulse buys" or "considered purchases";[276]
  - Strength of the competing marks;
  - Actual confusion;[277]
- The number of similar marks on similar or related goods;[278]
- Length of time of concurrent use of the marks without actual confusion;
- The variety (or range) of goods on which each mark is used.

No single factor is determinative of the likelihood of confusion. Each must be analyzed individually and also must be applied on a case-by-case basis.

In recent years, trademark disputes have been increasing in frequency. For example, Sears' sales of "Bagzilla" garbage bags, "monstrously strong bags," were held not to confuse consumers by suggesting any relation between the bags and Godzilla, the giant radioactive Japanese monster of movie fame.[279] McDonald's Corp. has registered more than thirty trademarks with the prefix "Mc" combined with the name of a food item available at its stores. In U.S. courts, the company has prevented a variety of firms from using the prefix, from "McSleep" (denoting a hotel chain) to "McDental" (denoting a dental practice).[280] But the New York Stock Exchange was not able to stop a gambling casino from using the name "New York $lot [Slot] Exchange" as its trademark, as the court concluded that the public was not

likely to be confused.[281] Nor were the Atlanta Braves professional baseball team able to stop release of the 2012 Walt Disney/Pixar film *Brave*.[282] But how similar is too similar? Does the slogan for a New York coffee shop, Everyman Espresso — "I [coffee mug drawing] N.Y." — violate New York City's own trademarked slogan, "I ♥ N.Y."®?[283] Does such trademark "bullying" really protect the value of the original mark?[284]

Even parodies of trademarks may cause a likelihood of confusion and may be the basis of a lawsuit, even if created in jest. A diaper bag with the words "Gucci Goo," designed to look like the well-known Gucci brand while at the same time allegedly poking fun at it, was held to be infringing on the Gucci trademark,[285] as was the use of the name "A.2." — supposedly used as a pun or play on words on the famous "A.1." steak sauce trademark.[286] Claims of parody are no defense, "where the purpose of the similarity is to capitalize on a famous mark's popularity for the defendant's own commercial gain."[287] Yet, Haute Diggity Dog, the owner and creator of "Chewy Vuiton" dog toys — and the maker of products for dogs, like "Chewnel #5," "Dog Perignon" and "Sniffany & Co." — won a lawsuit brought by Louis Vuitton, in part, because of a parody defense.[288]

Even when there is little likelihood of confusion, there is always the concern that the trademark will lose its power or strength to identify and distinguish the product or service it represents and, as a result, suffer dilution. Generally, this protection is only available to those marks that have acquired strength through prolonged and substantial use. A classic example of the potential for a trademark to be diluted was the sale of a poster with the words, "Enjoy Cocaine," in the flowing red and white type-script used by the Coca-Cola Company,

---

[273] *See, e.g.*, Mead Data Central v. Toyota Motor Sales USA, 875 F.2d 1026 (2d Cir. 1989) (where the similarity of Toyota's Lexus automobile mark was compared with Mead Data's Lexis-Nexis online database mark).

[274] *See, e.g.*, G.D. Searle & Co. v. Chas. Pfizer & Co., 265 F.2d 385 (7th Cir. 1959) (where identical motion sickness medicines were marketed under similar trade names — "Dramamine" and "Bonamine").

[275] *See, e.g.*, Field Enter. Educ. Corp. v. Grosset & Dunlap, 256 F. Supp. 382 (S.D.N.Y. 1966) (where book sales to very young children and to older children were considered to be different marketing methods).

[276] The "discriminating purchaser" theory is often determinative of the outcome when cost of the product, sophistication of the buyer, and probable care involved in the purchase decision are considered. *See, e.g.*, L.J. Mueller Furnace v. United Conditioning, 222 F.2d 755, 757 (Cust. & Pat. App. 1955) (where the similarity of the goods were much less important in light of other factors involved in the decision to purchase room air conditioning units).

[277] *See, e.g.*, Lindy Pen v. Bic Pen, 725 F.2d 1240, 1246 (9th Cir. 1984) (where the court required actual confusion or an implication of "association between the goods or sponsorship of the allegedly infringing goods").

[278] *See, e.g.*, Pure Foods v. Minute Maid, 214 F.2d 792 (5h Cir. 1954) (where customers who bought the same categories of goods — here, frozen foods — could be confused by identical marks on frozen meats and frozen orange juice products).

[279] *See* Toho Co. v. Sears Roebuck & Co., 645 F. 2d 788 (9th Cir. 1981).

[280] McDonald's v. Druck & Gerner, DDS, d/b/a/ McDental, 814 F. Supp. 1127 (N.D. N.Y. 1993); Quality Inns v. McDonald's, 695 F. Supp. 198 (D. Md. 1988).

[281] New York Stock Exchange v. New York, New York Hotel, 69 F. Supp. 2d 479 (S.D. N.Y. 1999).

[282] 'Duk, *The Braves Have a Problem with the Name of Pixar's Latest Film*, YAHOO! SPORTS, Dec. 20, 2011, http://sports.yahoo.com/mlb/blog/big_league_stew/post/The-Braves-have-a-problem-with-the-name-of-Pixar?urn=mlb-wp28853 (last visited June 15, 2016).

[283] *See* Andy Newman, *A Cup Is at the Heart of a Trademark Dispute*, N.Y. TIMES, May 30, 2013, at A16.

[284] *See* Christine Haughney, *Borghese v. Borghese: Battle for a Royal Name*, N.Y. TIMES, June 16, 2013, at A1, A4. *See also* Manny Fernandez, *Not to Be, Um, Trifled With, Texas Guards Its Slogans*, N.Y. TIMES, Sept. 15, 2013, at A12; Matt Flegenheimer, *C Train Café? Transit Agency May Put Up a Fight*, N.Y. TIMES, Aug. 24, 2013, at A1, A16.

[285] Gucci Shops v. R.H. Macy & Co., 446 F. Supp. 838 (S.D.N.Y. 1977).

[286] Nabisco Brands v. Kaye, 760 F. Supp. 25 (D. Conn. 1991).

[287] Hard Rock Café Licensing v. Pacific Graphics, 776 F. Supp. 1454, 1462 (W.D. Wash. 1991).

[288] Louis Vuitton Malletier S.A. v. Haute Diggity Dog, 464 F. Supp. 495 (E.D. Va. 2006). *See also* Cardtoons v. Major League Baseball Players Ass'n, 95 F. 3d 959 (10th Cir. 1996) (where parody trading cards with caricatures of baseball players did not violate MLB trademarks); Steve Baird, *[Subway] Eat Flesh, An Effective Parody?*, DUETSBLOG.COM, Sept. 15, 2014, http://www.duetsblog.com/2014/09/articles/trademarks/subway-eat-flesh-an-effective-parody/ (last visited June 15, 2016).

which asked for and received a court order halting the sale of the poster. More recently, Chick-fil-A sued a Vermont folk artist, claiming that his t-shirts with the slogan, "Eat More Kale," infringed on the company's well-known promotional slogan, "Eat Mor Chikin."[289] Walt Disney's use of Caterpillar construction machinery in the 2003 movie *George of the Jungle 2* resulted in a claim by Caterpillar that the villains' use of its equipment in the movie tarnished its trademark. A court disagreed, concluding that viewers could distinguish between the identity of the film's villains and the equipment they used.[290]

The doctrine of trademark dilution became federal law with the Trademark Dilution Act of 1995,[291] which protected trademarks from other uses that blurred the distinctiveness of the mark, or tarnished or disparaged it. The statute provides for three exemptions from liability:

• Fair use by competitors in comparative advertising or promotion, criticism and parody;

• All forms of reporting and news commentary; and

• Any noncommercial use of a mark.

As an example of the third exemption, the late television actor Andy Griffith filed a trademark dilution lawsuit against a Wisconsin man who had changed his legal name to "Andy Griffith" prior to a try for election to the office of county sheriff that included a "Back to Mayberry" campaign slogan, which was available on clothing, yard signs, condoms and other merchandise. Griffith lost on the grounds that the candidate's use of the "Andy Griffith" trademark name was a noncommercial use, "not to propose a commercial transaction but to seek elective office [which is] fundamental First Amendment protected speech."[292]

In a case involving Victoria's Secret and Victor's Little Secret — retailers whose only similarity was their names — the Supreme Court held that similarity alone is not sufficient to support a claim for trademark dilution. Actual economic harm, it ruled, must be proved, such as loss of sales or profits.[293] The Court's conclusion that federal law required proof of "actual dilution, rather than a likelihood of dilution,"[294] led Congress to revise the statute by enacting the Trademark Dilution Revision

Act of 2006,[295] which lowered the burden of proof required from actual harm to a likelihood of dilution and also defined "dilution by blurring" as impairment of the distinctiveness of the mark and "dilution by tarnishment" as reputational harm to the mark.[296] A simpler solution would be to buy the competing brand name and its associated intellectual assets, as Hobby Lobby Stores did recently.[297]

Increasingly, all trademarks should also have a substantive international component that aims to protect the mark in multinational settings and outside national borders, because — simply put — trademarks and logos and brand names are worth a lot of money. As there is currently no single way to register a trademark and have it legally enforceable worldwide, misappropriated uses of marks abound internationally. This can lead to benign misunderstandings or more to serious situations, as when Apple, Inc., was forced to pay $60 million — down from an initial demand of $400 million — to a Chinese company to which it had already paid $55,000 for the worldwide rights to the name "iPad," after it was threatened with invalidation of its trademark in China on the grounds that it had not initially negotiated "in good faith."[298]

Trademark's Digital Transformation

The Internet has become a battleground for trademarks, since "navigation around the globe's computer networks relies on the special system of domain names, like COCA-COLA.COM."[299] Though these names are actually addresses, they are of critical importance to companies promoting their products and services, blending together, as they do, "features of trademarks, vanity license plates, postal codes, radio-station call letters, and graffiti."[300] The problem, of course, is how to make every name or mark uniquely identifiable using the system. This in itself can create a problem when a domain name, susceptible to misinterpretation, does not perfectly fit the product, as the Newark Nut Company — whose online products include bulk nuts and dried

---

[289] Coca-Cola Co. v. Gemini Rising, 346 F. Supp. 1183 (E.D. N.Y. 1972). *See also* Wilson Ring, *Artist Celebrates Kale Trademark*, ATLANTA J.-CONSTITUTION, Dec. 13, 2014, at A15 (where a Vermont artist could exhort people to "eat more kale," despite the Chik-fil-A slogan).

[290] Caterpillar v. Walt Disney Co., 287 F. Supp. 2d 913 (C.D. Ill. 2003) (where bad intent to confuse the public was not found on the part of Disney, although it was not required to establish likelihood of confusion).

[291] 115 U.S.C. 1125 (2016). Its provisions were subsequently revised and clarified in the Trademark Dilution Revision Act of 2006, 120 Stat. 1730.

[292] Andy Griffith v. William Fenrick, n/k/a, Andrew Jackson Griffith, 486 F. Supp. 2d 848, 853 (W.D. Wisc. 2007). *See also* Rachel Donadio, *There's No Branding a Symbol of Free Speech*, N.Y. TIMES, Feb. 2, 2015, at C3.

[293] Moseley v. V Secret Catalogue, 537 U.S. 418 (2003).

[294] *Id.* at 433.

[295] 120 Stat. 1730 (2006).

[296] 15 U.S.C. 1125(c)(2)(B-C) (2016).

[297] *See* Sarah Max, *Resolving Fight Over Names*, N.Y. TIMES, May 15, 2014, at B4.

[298] Keith Bradsher, *Apple Settles iPad Trademark Dispute with Chinese Company*, N.Y. TIMES, July 2, 2012, *available at* http://www.nytimes.com/2012/07/03/technology/apple-settles-ipad-trademark-dispute-with-chinese-company.html (last visited June 15, 2016). *See also* Neil Gough, *Disney Is Focus of Counterfeiting Crackdown*, N.Y. TIMES, Nov. 6, 2015, at B2.; Dan Levin, *At Chinese Mall, Lost in Translation*, N.Y. TIMES, Dec. 27, 2014, at B1; Julie Weed, *Welcome to the Haiyatt. In China, It's Not the Hotel It Sounds Like*, N.Y. TIMES, Apr. 29, 2014, at B1.

[299] GLEICK, *supra* note 182, at 391.

[300] *Id.* This problem takes on additional dimensions when companies' joint efforts are divided, as when NBC bought Microsoft's interests in MSNBC.com in 2012. *See* Brian Stelter, *Microsoft and NBC Complete Web Divorce*, N.Y. TIMES, July 16, 2012, at B1, B5.

fruits — discovered when it bought NUTS.COM.[301]

But the basic problem with Internet domain names is the difficulty of getting a distinctive name to identify a company or product clearly and specifically — that is, too few words to do too much work, in two senses.

First, many people bought domain names just because they could or because others had neglected to protect their rights.[302] For example, McDonald's Corp. found that journalist Joshua Quittner had registered MCDONALDS.COM before it got around to doing so.

Second, others found that well-known businesses were trying to control names they thought were theirs. As an example, Anand Ramnth Mani (that is, A.R. Mani) of Vancouver, Canada, registered ARMANI.COM and discovered that the fashion empire of Giorgio Armani wanted it, too. From there it's only gotten more complicated. For example, Delta Airlines, Delta Faucets, Delta Financial and some 300 other companies all wanted DELTA.COM. Delta Financial of Woodbury, New York, had it first, though Delta Airlines finally won the "pure" dot-com address — dumping its own DELTA-AIR.COM Internet address — and Delta Faucets settled for DELTAFAUCET.COM. (Delta Financial is now bankrupt, a victim of the 2007 sub-prime mortgage crisis.)

Unsurprisingly, the result of this demand has been "a land grab in trademarks."[303] It has taken on additional historical tones when it became known as "cybersquatting," a reference to earlier land grabs during the periods surrounding settlement of the American West and gold and other mineral discoveries, when "squatters" attempted to wrest control of a claim from its rightful owner by moving in without permission and taking it over.[304] In 2011 the Internet Corporation for Assigned Names and Numbers (known as ICANN) attempted to address this problem by creating more domain names through the introduction of new suffixes as alternatives to *.COM, *.ORG, *.INFO and *.NET — including *.XXX, *.BIZ, *.APP, *.SECURE, *.BLOG, and *.WEB. Nearly 1,000 new domains were added in 2014, including *.TATTOO, *.CEO, *.SHOES, *.COFFEE, *.GUITARS, *.NINJA, and *.FLORIST.[305] The question for

trademark owners concerned about cybersquatting is whether the move has created a new, more flexible "domain name system revolution" or whether all the different suffixes have started a "World War Web."[306] Many trademark owners have already acted defensively, and sometimes at exorbitant cost, to register domain names they have no intention of using simply to protect their name and trademark from misuse.[307]

Some trademark owners have also successfully used the federal Trademark Dilution Revision Act of 2006,[308] which largely supplanted the Trademark Dilution Act of 1995,[309] to stop others from using their trademarks as Internet domain names.

Others have used the Anti-Cybersquatting Consumer Protection Act of 1999,[310] which provides for remedies, including injunctions and monetary damages, to trademark owners who can show (1) the mark was distinctive or famous at the time the accused cyber-squatter registered the domain name and (2) the cyber-squatter acted with "a bad faith" intent to profit from the mark. The statute also lists the following nine factors to help courts determine intent:[311]

• One's trademark or other intellectual property rights in the domain name itself

• Whether the domain name contains the owner's legal name

• The owner's prior use of the domain name in connection with the actual sale of goods or services

• Any lawful, noncommercial use of the trademark in a domain name, such as in comparative advertising, criticism or comment, or parody

• Intent to harm the trademark owner's goodwill which is represented by the mark

• Any offer to sell the domain name to another without having used (or intending to use) it in commerce

• Intentionally providing misleading contact information when applying for domain name registration

• The acquisition or holding of multiple domain names that

---

[301] See Ian Mount, *A Web Retailer Buys the Perfect Domain Name, Then Comes a Letdown*, N.Y. TIMES, Apr. 26, 2012, at B6.

[302] See, e.g., Delia Ephron, *Hey! You Stole My Name*, N.Y. TIMES, Mar. 11, 2012, Sunday Review, at 8.

[303] GLEICK, *supra* note 182, at 392.

[304] See, e.g., *ICANN Makes Historic Changes to Web Domain Names*, SALT LAKE CITY TRIBUNE, June 20, 2011, *available at* http://www.sltrib.com/sltrib/money/52042057-79/icann-names-domain-internet.html.csp (last visited June 15, 2016); Editorial, *Expanding Internet Domains*, N.Y. TIMES, Dec. 26, 2011, at A20.

[305] See Karen Klein, *The Latest Domain-Name Gold Rush*, BLOOMBERG-BUSINESSWEEK, June 4, 2012, http://www.businessweek.com/articles/2012-06-04/the-latest-domain-name-gold-rush (last visited June 15, 2016); Nicole Perlroth & Eric Pfanner, *Imagining Dot Magic in a Name*, N.Y. TIMES, June 14, 2012, at B1, B2; Mike Snider, *Heads Up, .Com and .Net! You've Got Company*, USA TODAY, Feb. 5, 2014, at B1.

[306] Nicole Perlroth, *Seeking Security in Domain Switch*, N.Y. TIMES, May 21, 2012, at B8; Natasha Singer, *When You Can't Tell the Suffixes Without a Scorecard*, N.Y. TIMES, Aug. 18, 2013, Sunday Business, at 3.

[307] See, e.g., Vikas Bajaj, *The Trouble with "Sucks,"* N.Y. Times, Apr. 13, 2015, *available at* http://nyti.ms/1H1aEw6 (last visited June 15, 2016); Paul Barrett, *The New Republic of Porn*, BLOOMBERG-BUSINESSWEEK, June 21, 2012, *available at* http://www.businessweek.com/articles/2012-06-21/the-new-republic-of-porn (last visited June 15, 2016); Glenn Chapman, *Non-Porn Players Rush to Grab .XXX Websites*, INQUIRER .NET, Dec. 14, 2011, http://technology.inquirer.net/6847/non-porn-players-rush-to-grab-xxx-websites (last visited June 15, 2016).

[308] 15 U.S.C. 1125 (2016).

[309] 109 Stat. 985 (1995).

[310] 15 U.S.C. 1125(D) (2016).

[311] 15 U.S.C. 1125(d)(1)(B) (2016). *See also* Charles Runyan, *Domain Name Disputes*, KEYTLAW.COM, 2014, http://www.keytlaw.com/urls/acpa.htm (last visited June 15, 2016); Martin Samson, *The Anticybersquatting Consumer Protection Act: Key Information*, INTERNET LIBRARY OF LAW & COURT DECISIONS, Sept. 9, 2005, *available at* http://www.internetlibrary.com/publications/anticybsquattSamson9-05_art.cfm (last visited June 15, 2016).

are confusingly similar to well-known, distinctive marks

• The extent to which a mark incorporated into a domain name is distinctive or famous

In the first appellate examination of the new law, *Sporty's Farm v. Sportsman's Market*, the appellate court found bad faith and a violation of the statute when "Competitor X of Company Y ... registered Y's trademark as a domain name and then transferred that name to Subsidiary Z, which operates a business wholly unrelated to Y."[312]

Minimally, then, before any mark is used in commerce today, an online trademark search should be conducted to determine if a company in a similar line of business already uses a similar logo or company name or Internet uniform resource locater, sometimes known as a Web address. Failure to do so could lead to a lawsuit seeking to prevent the company from using the logo or mark or domain name in question, even though the mark is already in use by the company and is developing business and goodwill for the company — in addition to a possible tort claim for unfair competition.[313] As an example, a federal court in 2013 forced Jian Yao to give sixteen Internet domain names through which he had sold counterfeit fragrances and accessories to Chanel, Inc., to stop using Chanel trademarks or "any confusingly similar" marks, and not to conduct any business on the Internet for five years.[314]

SUMMARY

The Constitution's protections of intellectual property — video, music, books and other original, artistic works — create the right to profit financially from one's abilities and resourcefulness. To help reach this end, the Constitution gives Congress the power "to promote the Progress of Science and useful Arts, by securing for limited Times to Authors and Inventors the exclusive Right to their respective Writings and Discoveries." Intellectual property consists of copyright, trademarks and patents. Copyright law protects created works of authors and artists. Trademark law protects the symbols and images that signify the authenticity of commercial goods or services. (Patent law protects inventions and discoveries and is beyond the scope of this discussion.) The federal statute which implements the Constitution's grant of power over copyrights is the Copyright Act of 1976; the federal statute which implements the Constitution's grant of power over trademarks is the Trademark Act of

1946, also known as, the Lanham Act.

Copyright protects original works of authorship, but not the idea underlying the expression. Originality has two components: independent creation and creativity. Trademark law protects symbols that identify products and services in a distinctive manner. For a mark — including shapes, colors and sounds — to be valid, it must be used to promote the buying and selling of goods or services.

Copyright attaches to a work at the moment it is fixed in a tangible form and belongs to the creator, unless it was created as part of one's employment, as part of a contract or as a commissioned work-for-hire. Mere ownership of a work does not include the ownership of the copyright. In addition, any sale of the work does not necessarily include the sale of the copyright, without specific terms stating such in a contract. Registration with the U.S. Copyright Office is voluntary, and there is no such thing as "poor man's copyright."

Trademarks must be registered with the U.S. Patent & Trademark Office to be officially valid. They cannot be scandalous, immoral or deceptive; consist of a flag or emblem of a country; resemble any person's name or likeness without consent; resemble any other trademark; be merely descriptive of the product; be primarily descriptive of a product's geographic origins; or be a surname.

Copyrights on works created after January 1, 1978, last for the life of the author, plus seventy years. The Supreme Court upheld this rule in *Eldred v. Ashcroft*. Once registered, a trademark is good for ten years and may be renewed for an unlimited number of ten-year periods, as long as it is used in commerce. Trademarks have different degrees of protection, depending upon whether they are fanciful, arbitrary, suggestive or descriptive with proof of secondary meaning. Generic marks have none.

A copyright owner has the exclusive right to copy the work, to create a derivative work, to distribute the work to the public, to perform the work in public, to display the work in public and to control the digital transmission performance of the work. In essence, copyright is the right to say "no," though the First Sale Doctrine gives copyright owners the right to prohibit others from all distribution of the work prior to its first sale.

Copyright infringement occurs when someone other than the copyright holder appropriates any of the exclusive rights guaranteed copyright owners. Unauthorized copying is the most common form of infringement. It does not matter whether the infringement was intentional. To prove infringement, two elements must be established: ownership and copying. To prove copying, two conditions must be proven: the infringing party's access to the work and that the infringing party's new work is "substantially similar" to the original, copyrighted work, involving at least a "fragmented, literal similarity."

Trademark infringement occurs when someone creates an-

[312] 202 F.3d 489, 496 (2d Cir. 2000).

[313] *See* Thomas Fitzgerald, *Planting Your Flag on a Patch of the Web*, N.Y. TIMES, Sept. 5, 2013, at B7. *See also* MATT HAIG, BRAND FAILURES: THE TRUTH ABOUT THE 100 BIGGEST BRANDING MISTAKES OF ALL TIME (2003).

[314] *See* Chanel Inc. v. Yao (No. 3:07-cv-30032-MAP), Order of Sanctions (D. Mass., Dec. 12, 2013), *available at* http://www.gpo.gov/fdsys/pkg/USCOURTS-mad-3_07-cv-30032/pdf/USCOURTS-mad-3_07-cv-30032-0.pdf (last visited June 15, 2016).

other mark that results in a likelihood of confusion or dilutes the distinctiveness of the original mark.

The only defense to a claim of copyright infringement is found in the Fair Use Doctrine, which may be found in the Copyright Act of 1976. The use of copyrighted works for "criticism, comment, news reporting, teaching ... scholarship [and] research" is permitted by the rule, as is any other use that is determined to be "fair" as a result of the application of the rule's four factors applied on a case-by-case basis: (1) the purpose and character of the use; (2) the nature of the work; (3) the amount of the copyrighted work used; and (4) the use's effect on the market for the work. A parody which creates a transformative use is a fair use, as determined by the Supreme Court in *Campbell v. Acuff-Rose Music*.

Parodies of trademarks may cause a likelihood of confusion and can be prohibited as a result. The Trademark Dilution Act of 1995 and the Trademark Dilution Revision Act of 2006 protect trademarks from other uses that lessen their distinctiveness and generally may take two forms: (1) dilution by blurring; and (2) dilution by tarnishment. There are three exemptions from liability: (1) fair use by competitors in comparative advertising (including parodies); (2) all forms of news reporting and commentary; and (3) any noncommercial use of a mark.

As the transformation of communication moves from printed marks on a page to analog radio waves to digital, binary bits of information, intellectual property law is struggling to keep up with technological innovation. Copyright law is faced with technology's liability for contributory infringement, the problem of the required licensing of digital sampling and mash-ups, the concept of "copyleft" and the new applications of copyright law in cyberspace, while trademark law struggles to distinctively identify entities in an Internet domain name address system that is unable to deal easily with confusingly similar names or those taken by cybersquatters.

Yet the law seems to presume the legal uses of new technology and does not presume technological innovation to be infringing as long as: (1) the technology is capable of substantial noninfringing uses, and (2) the seller's intent is not to induce others to violate the law.

Finally, to protect intellectual property, attorney David Lilenfeld recommends:[315]

• Register your trademarks with the U.S. Patent & Trademark Office;

• Reserve your name and company name as domain names, as well as social media "handles" on Facebook, Twitter, LinkedIn, and other social media sites;

• Register written and other valuable materials with the U.S. Copyright Office;

• Apply for patents judiciously; and

• Monitor your intellectual property for possible infringement.

FOR ADDITIONAL READING

Ginsburg, Jane C., Jessica Litman and Mary Kevlin. *Trademark & Unfair Competition Law: Cases & Materials* (5th ed.). New York: Foundation Press, 2013.

Gorman, Robert A. & Jane C. Ginsburg. *Copyright: Cases & Materials* (8th ed.). New York: Foundation Press, 2011.

LaFrance, Mary. *Copyright Law in a Nutshell* (2d ed.). St. Paul: West Group, 2011.

Lessig, Lawrence. *Code: Version 2.0*. New York: Basic Books, 2006.

Lewinski, Silke von. *Copyright throughout the World*. New York: Thomson West, 2016.

Lisby, Gregory C. "Web Site Framing: Copyright Infringement through the Creation of an Unauthorized Derivative Work," 6 *Communication Law & Policy* 541-55 (2001).

Miller, Arthur R. & Michael H. Davis, *Intellectual Property in a Nutshell* (5th ed.). St. Paul: West Group, 2012.

Nimmer, Melville B. & David Nimmer. *Nimmer on Copyright: A Treatise on the Law of Literary, Musical & Artistic Property, & the Protection of Ideas*. New York: M. Bender, 1978.

Patry, William F. *How to Fix Copyright*. New York: Oxford University Press, 2012.

Patry, William F. *Patry on Copyright*. New York: Thomson West, 2012.

Patry, William F. *Patry on Fair Use*. New York: Thomson West, 2015.

Radin, Margaret, John Rothschild & Gregory Silverman. *Intellectual Property & the Internet*. New York: Foundation Press, 2013.

Sammataro, James G. *Film and Multimedia and the Law*. New York: Thomson West, 2014.

Toula, Christopher M. & Gregory C. Lisby, "Towards an Affirmative Public Domain," 28 *Cultural Studies* 996-1020 (2014).

---

[315] *Biz Voices: Guard Intellectual Property*, ATLANTA J.-CONSTITUTION, Feb. 13, 2011, at D2.

14

Privacy Rights in an Open and Changing Society

By Samuel A. Terilli Jr. and Sigman Splichal

➡ Headnote Questions

- What expectation of privacy do individuals have in American society?
- What kinds of information are private?
- What legal remedies are available for individuals who believe their privacy has been invaded?
- Are any legal remedies available to the news media when they report about private matters?
- Is a right of privacy recognized in the U.S. Constitution?
- Do students have any privacy rights?
- What special privacy issues or concerns do computers and digital technologies raise?

Privacy. The word resonates within American society, its citizens often making social and legal claims based on the belief that they have a fundamental right, as U.S. Supreme Court Justice Louis Brandeis once put it, "to be let alone."[1] New digital technology — from massive databases and social networks to sophisticated search engines and surveillance cameras on streets and in buildings — and new fears ranging from identity theft to terrorist attacks, have combined to make privacy a major concern.[2] In 2016, privacy rights, new media, new technologies and celebrity culture in the United States collided in court and in the headlines with the $140 million verdict against Gawker Media in the case filed by Terry Bollea, who is better known as Hulk Hogan, over the Web site's airing of a brief, grainy sex-tape of Hogan with the then wife of one of his now former best friends.[3] Whatever one may think of Gawker's penchant for posting outrageous news and gossip, the notion that a celebrity who openly bragged about his sex life could convince a jury he was damaged to the tune of $115 million in compensatory damages plus another $25 million in punitive damages, shocked many observers, though the mainstream news media did not feel particularly threatened by this odd case involving an odd story on the Internet.[4]

There is no question digital technology, the Internet, social media and mobile are all affecting societal expectations and legal doctrines regarding privacy. In 2009, more than 90 percent of people surveyed considered online privacy, for example, to be an important issue in society.[5] And, in 2013 and to this day, the ubiquitous search engine, Google, faced precedent setting litigation in the United States over wiretapping allegations related to its Street View project,[6] and in Europe over what has become

---

[1] Olmstead v. United States, 227 U.S. 438, 478 (1928). Actually, Judge Thomas M. Cooley had used the term forty years earlier in his A TREATISE ON THE LAW OF TORTS 29 (2d ed. 1888).

[2] *See, e.g,* Anne Eisenberg, *On the Lookout, With a Digital Security Camera,* N.Y. TIMES, Apr. 12, 2009, at 4BU; Solomon Moore, *F.B.I. and States Vastly Expanding Databases of DNA,* N.Y. TIMES, Apr. 19, 2009, at 1A; Editorial, *Protecting Electronic Data,* N.Y. TIMES, May 25, 2009, at 18A.

[3] *See, e.g.,* Nick Madigan & Ravi Somaiya, *Hulk Hogan awarded $115 Million in Privacy Suit Against Gawker,* Mar. 18, 2016, N.Y. TIMES, *available at* http://www.nytimes.com/2016/03/19/business/media/gawker-hulk-hogan-verdict.html?_r=0; Ravi Somaiya, *Hulk Hogan v. Gawker: A Guide to the Trial for the Perplexed,* N.Y. TIMES, Mar. 18, 2016, available at http://www.nytimes.com/2016/03/18/business/media/hulk-hogan-v-gawker-a-guide-to-the-trial-for-the-perplexed.html.

[4] Paul Callan, *Hulk Hogan verdict body-slams Gawker,* CNN, Mar. 22, 2016, *available at* http://www.cnn.com/2016/03/20/opinions/hulk-hogan-verdict-warning-shot-media-opinion-callan/index.html; Erik Eckholm, *Legal Experts See Little Effect on News Media From Hulk Hogan Verdict,* N.Y. TIMES, Mar. 19, 2016, *available at* http://www.nytimes.com/2016/03/20/business/media/legal-experts-see-little-effect-on-news-media-from-hulk-hogan-verdict.html; Jim Rutenberg, *Drawing the Line on Gossip After the Gawker Trial,* N.Y. TIMES, Apr. 3, 2016, *available at* http://www.nytimes.com/2016/04/04/business/media/drawing-the-line-on-gossip-after-the-gawker-trial.html.

[5] *See* Stephanie Clifford, *Many See Privacy on Web As Big Issue, Survey Says,* N.Y. TIMES, Mar. 16, 2009, at 5B.

[6] *See* David Streitfeld, *Top Court Won't Hear Privacy Case Vs. Google,* N.Y. TIMES, July 1, 2014, at B4.

known as the European "right to be forgotten."[7] While many scholars agree that European countries protect privacy to a greater degree than the United States does, researchers and some critics have found that even Europe's Right to Be Forgotten and stricter standards for online publications have flaws that allow access online to potentially private information and more general objections to the European approach.[8]

On other fronts, privacy concerns have arisen in the context of cellular telephones,[9] drones – private as well as government-operated[10] – and the continuing revelations about the activities of the National Security Agency.[11] The frontiers and legal battle lines over privacy continue to evolve – driven in large part by advances in technology.

Privacy is a social concept as old as the nation, embedded in its beginning, from the first settlers drawn to a new land in search of religious and political freedom in the seventeenth century to revolutionary patriots affronted by England's disregard for the autonomy of their businesses and the sanctity of their homes. The concept of privacy can be found in the liberal theories of Enlightenment philosophers, whose emphasis on individual liberties based on natural rights inspired the Founding Fathers' generation as it began to envision a new nation.[12] Indeed, essential elements of privacy are woven into the nation's most hallowed documents.

While privacy as a social value was apparent during the nation's early years, it remained elusive as the basis for *legal* claims. Only in the last 100 years has it entered the legal mainstream, mainly due to changes in the way Americans live and think. To be understood in an information-driven society – both in social and legal contexts – privacy must be viewed as a value that changes as society tries to balance the rights of individuals with its needs and desires for information. As one appellate court observed, in deciding privacy claims, courts must consider, "[T]he customs and conventions of the community; and in the last analysis what is proper becomes a matter of community

mores."[13]

This chapter looks, first, at the evolution of the concept of privacy. It then focuses on the development of privacy as a legal doctrine and on the four distinct privacy torts courts have identified: (1) publication of embarrassing private facts, (2) physical and technological intrusion, (3) false light invasion of privacy and (4) commercialization. The chapter briefly addresses related torts as well as constitutional and statutory privacy, both of which place limits on government use of personal information – limits that have important implications for journalists, especially in the era of databases, the Internet, social media and reporters' growing reliance on computer-assisted reporting.

THE EVOLUTION OF A RIGHT TO PRIVACY

The general concept of privacy was not unknown in English common law, the dominant legal system in Colonial America. Cases dating to the Norman Conquest recognized a value resembling privacy in individuals' property rights. In 1741, the House of Lords, then England's highest court, invoked a property-rights doctrine to protect contents of personal letters from unauthorized publication.[14] The case, *Pope v. Curl,*[15] is important in the development of privacy in American law because it acknowledged a property right in individuals' retention and control of personal ideas and information in letters sent to others, not only in the letters themselves.

John Locke, an English philosopher whose writings influenced Thomas Jefferson and other founders, argued that government has a duty to protect fundamental rights such as life, liberty and property.[16] These rights were described in the Declaration of Independence, the Constitution and the Bill of Rights. The Supreme Court, almost 200 years later, gleaned from the concept of liberty a constitutional right of privacy.[17]

In his book *Privacy in Colonial New England,* historian David H. Flaherty explored the precursors to modern privacy. He observed that although privacy as a legal doctrine evolved slowly, its underlying values were expressed in colonial customs. Courts, he said, protected privacy values indirectly by enforcing laws against trespass, by limiting government searches and seizures, by hearing defamation cases and by recognizing privileged communications between wives and husbands. Ironically, as Flaherty pointed out, there was little physical privacy – in the modern sense – in most homes and public accommodations. Homes often lacked individual sleeping quarters, and

---

[7] *See* Paul Bernal, *Opinion: Google Privacy Ruling Could Change How We All Use the Internet,* CNN International Edition, May 14, 2014, http://edition.cnn.com/2014/05/13/business/opinion-google-privacy-bernal/index.html; Mark Scott, *Google Fined in France Over "Right to Be Forgotten,"* N.Y. Times, Mar. 25, 2016, at 2B.

[8] *See* Daphne Keller & Bruce Brown, *Europe's Web Privacy Rules: Bad for Google, Bad for Everyone,* N.Y Times, Apr. 25, 2016, *available at* http://www.nytimes.com/2016/04/25/opinion/europes-web-privacy-rules-bad-for-google-bad-for-everyone.html; Mark Scott, *Researchers Uncover a Flaw in Europe's Tough Online Privacy Rules,* N.Y. Times, June 6, 2016, at 3B.

[9] *See* Riley v. California, 134 S.Ct. 2473 (2014).

[10] *See* M. Ryan Calo, *The Drone as Privacy Catalyst,* 64 Stan. L. Rev. 29 (2011); *Domestic Unmanned Aerial Vehicles (UAVs) and Drones,* Electronic Privacy Information Center (2014), *available at* http://epic.org/privacy/drones/.

[11] *See* Byron Acohido, *Analysis: NSA's Data Grab Ought To Boost Privacy Concerns,* USA Today, Oct. 30, 2013, *available at* http://www.usatoday.com/story/cybertruth/2013/10/30/nsas-data-grab-should-boost-privacy-concerns/3 315789/.

[12] *See, e.g.,* John Locke, The Second Treatise on Government (T. Peardon ed., 1952) (1690).

---

[13] Virgil v. Time, Inc., 527 F.2d 1122, 1129 (9th Cir. 1975).

[14] *See* Morris L. Ernst & Alan U. Schwartz, Privacy: The Right to be Let Alone 5-6 (1962).

[15] 2 Atk. 342, 26 Eng. Rep. 608 (1741).

[16] Locke, *supra* note 12, at 55-81.

[17] *See* Griswold v. Connecticut, 381 U.S. 479, 486 (1965).

families congregated in common beds. Communal sleeping arrangements also were common in public inns.[18] Traces of the practice remained as late as 150 years ago: During his early career as a struggling, small-town lawyer, Abraham Lincoln shared a room and bed above his office with a law partner.[19]

Flaherty noted that the concept of informational privacy was officially recognized during Benjamin Franklin's tenure as postmaster general before the American Revolution. Postmasters were required to swear an oath that they would not "wittingly, willingly, or knowingly open ... any letters which shall come into their hands."[20]

Values underlying privacy also were apparent as the Revolutionary War drew near, and they played a central role in the colonists' growing hostility toward British rule. In 1761, Boston lawyer James Otis spoke against the practice of general search warrants: "Now one of the most essential branches of English liberty, is the freedom of one's own house. A man's house is his castle; and while he is quiet he is as well guarded as a prince in his castle."[21] On the eve of the Revolution, each colony drew up a list of grievances against British authorities. On each list was concern about general warrants, which authorized government agents to search premises at will without first presenting evidence of a specific violation of the law. After the colonies won independence, James Madison, a major proponent of a bill of rights spelling out individual liberties, introduced a proposal at the Constitutional Convention in 1789 to limit the scope of government searches. That proposal, which established "the right of the people to be secure ... against unreasonable search and seizures," was later adopted as the Fourth Amendment.

Values supporting privacy also found expression in the writings of nineteenth-century English philosopher John Stuart Mill. He argued in his influential *On Liberty* that the government should have no say in certain kinds of personal conduct, absent a compelling social interest. Expounding on this concept of personal liberty, he wrote: "The only part of conduct of anyone for which he is amenable to society is that which concerns others. In the part which merely concerns himself, his independence is, of right, absolute."[22]

PRIVACY AS A LEGAL RIGHT

Legal claims related to privacy developed slowly during the nation's first century, in part because society was largely agrarian. Land was sparsely settled. This physical distance reduced un-

wanted contacts and intrusions.

The demographics of American society shifted dramatically with the Industrial Revolution. Technological developments such as the steam engine led to manufacturing-based cities populated by factory workers. Physical distance between people shrank as cities grew, and those in foreign lands began a new flow of immigration. In those crowded cities, the barriers of time and space common to rural settings no longer insulated individuals from unwanted contacts.

Dramatic technological developments in the nineteenth century began to threaten privacy. Alan F. Westin traced them in *Privacy and Freedom*, a comprehensive study of privacy issues. He noted that several technological developments in the late nineteenth century "altered the balance between personal expression and third-party surveillance that had prevailed since antiquity."[23] These innovations were the microphone and telephone in the late 1870s, the Kodak camera with its potential for "instantaneous photographs" in the 1880s and the dictograph recorder in the 1890s.

In 1877, the *New York Times* expressed concern about the effect of new technology on privacy. It called the telephone "a nefarious instrument" with "vast capabilities for mischief" that promised to rob individuals of their personal privacy. Responding to a decision by the city to allow telephone wires to be attached to city lamp posts, the *Times* cautioned:

> Every confidential remark made to a lamp-post by a belated Democratic statesman could be reproduced by a telephone connected with any other lamp-post.... Men who had trusted to friendly lamp-posts, and embraced them with the utmost confidence in their silence and discretion, would find themselves shamelessly betrayed, and their unsuspecting philosophies literally reported to their indignant families.[24]

While increased technology spurred the growth of industrial cities and the development of such privacy-altering inventions as the telephone, other innovations — high-speed newspaper presses and advanced photography — spawned an aggressive kind of journalism, a distant cousin to what was espoused by the colonial and revolutionary printers who catered to society's well-read and politically astute. New printing processes reproduced newspapers quickly and cheaply. As a result, a journalism developed that often directed its content at the swelling numbers of city dwellers. The "penny press" era of the mid-nineteenth century later yielded to "yellow journalism," sensationalistic news coverage designed to boost newspaper circulations that reached its peak toward century's end. Newspaper readers,

---

[18] DAVID H. FLAHERTY, PRIVACY IN COLONIAL NEW ENGLAND (1972).
[19] *See* DAVID HERBERT DONALD, LINCOLN 70 (1995).
[20] FLAHERTY, *supra* note 18, at 121.
[21] RICHARD F. HIXSON, PRIVACY IN A PUBLIC SOCIETY: HUMAN RIGHTS IN CONFLICT 13 (1987).
[22] JOHN STUART MILL, ON LIBERTY 13 (Currin V. Shields ed., 1956) (1859).

[23] ALAN F. WESTIN, PRIVACY AND FREEDOM 338 (1967).
[24] Editorial, *The Telephone Unmasked*, N.Y. TIMES, Oct. 12, 1877, at 4.

not so interested in the complexities of politics and other public issues, sought information about misdeeds and travails. This new readership, coupled with journalists armed with cameras intruding into new, heretofore private areas, sometimes brought newspaper practices and privacy concerns into conflict.

In 1890, two former law partners and Harvard Law School classmates took issue with the newspaper practices and technologies of the day. Louis Brandeis and Samuel Warren, upper-crust Boston lawyers, penned "The Right to Privacy" for the *Harvard Law Review*. The seminal article would steer the notion of a legal right of privacy toward the mainstream of American law. Attempting to document what they considered a climate of journalistic excess, the authors said, somewhat hyperbolically: "Instantaneous photographs and newspaper enterprise have invaded the sacred precincts of private and domestic life; and numerous mechanical devices threaten to make good the prediction that 'what is whispered in the closet shall be proclaimed from the house-tops.'"[25] Brandeis and Warren argued that individuals possessed certain attributes, such as sentiments and intellect, over which they exercised rights akin to personal property rights.

In 1895, six years after "The Right to Privacy" was published, the New York Court of Appeals addressed the issue of privacy in *Schuyler v. Curtis*.[26] The family of a prominent woman sued a private organization to halt plans to erect a life-size statue in her memory. The woman had never been a public personality, and the statue was an invasion of privacy, her family argued. The court acknowledged that it lacked clear guidance from previous cases and rejected the family's claim. It focused on the fact the woman was dead and concluded that any privacy interest followed her to the grave, thus stopping short of fully exploring the legal issues.

In some early privacy cases, before psychiatry and psychology had gained credence in legal circles, courts expressed fundamental concerns about awarding damages for mental harm. In 1902, for example, the New York Court of Appeals refused to recognize a right of privacy in *Roberson v. Rochester Folding Box Co.* In *Roberson*, the family of a young girl sued a flour company for using her photograph in an advertisement. The family argued that the ad caused the girl to be "greatly humiliated by the scoffs and jeers of persons who recognized her face and picture."[27] The court, while sympathetic, refused to recognize a legal remedy for an intangible mental harm, fearing such a precedent might trigger similar lawsuits that would clutter the courts. It also expressed concern that privacy liability would place unreasonable burdens on the press, which often used photographs of individuals without permission.

While New York's highest court was hesitant to embrace privacy, the Georgia Supreme Court was not, reaching the opposite result in a similar case, recognizing unauthorized use of a person's identity as a violation of privacy.[28] The ruling prompted Brandeis to write that he was encouraged to see privacy recognized as a legal right.[29]

In addition to promoting privacy as a legal doctrine, Brandeis and Warren may have helped elevate privacy in public discourse. In 1902, the *New York Times* took issue with new photographic technology, which no longer required willing subjects to sit motionless. Echoing Brandeis and Warren, the *Times* complained in an editorial that "Kodakers lying in wait to photograph public figures had become a wanton invasion of privacy that demands legal control."[30]

While Brandeis and Warren nudged the issue of privacy onto the social and legal stage, the development of a unified legal theory remained elusive. In the ensuing decades, the legal contours of privacy developed piecemeal and with many variations. Seventy years after "The Right to Privacy" was published, torts expert William Prosser summarized the extent of the common law development of privacy in an article in the *California Law Review*. Titled simply "Privacy," it dealt with tort law and not with constitutional or statutory questions of privacy. After reviewing some 200 privacy-related cases, Prosser identified four separate torts: (1) disclosure of embarrassing private facts about individuals; (2) intrusion, the physical or technological violation of an individual's privacy; (3) false light, the intentional dissemination of highly offensive false publicity about another; and (4) appropriation, or the use of another person's likeness without permission.[31]

THE PRIVACY TORTS

American law assumes members of society have certain duties toward one another. These duties — derived from customs, mores and values — are often recognized in common law cases and in various statutes; they form the basis of tort law. Under the theory of tort law, when a member of society violates a duty toward another person that results in an identifiable harm, the injured person may recover damages. One class of duties deals with privacy and the harm — usually mental — that results when it is violated. When the news media are involved, courts have balanced individual privacy with other interests, such as the free flow of information about matters of public concern. Since the nature of the harm is usually mental, privacy tort law

---

[25] Samuel Warren & Louis Brandeis, *The Right to Privacy*, 4 HARV. L. REV. 193, 195 (1890).

[26] 42 N.E. 22 (N.Y. 1891).

[27] 64 N.E. 442, 443 (N.Y. 1902).

[28] Pavesich v. New England Life, 50 S.E. 68 (Ga. 1905).

[29] 1 LETTERS OF LOUIS D. BRANDEIS 306 (M. Urofsky & D. Levy eds., 1971).

[30] WESTIN, *supra* note 23, at 338.

[31] William Prosser, *Privacy*, 48 CAL. L. REV. 383-84 (1960).

protects only individuals, not businesses or corporations that exist merely as creatures of law. Businesses and corporations may, though, have claims related to the theft or disclosure of trade secrets and other confidential business information.

Tort law varies from state to state. Any generalizations are based on trends in cases from the various states. Actual application of law in privacy cases may vary from state to state.

Embarrassing Private Facts

Definition: The publication of private information that would be highly offensive to a reasonable person and is not a matter of legitimate public concern.

The common law acknowledges that some information about individuals should remain beyond the reach of neighbors — and the news media — and that disclosures normally would lead to unwarranted embarrassment or humiliation.[32] The embarrassing private facts tort rests on several questions, each of which a plaintiff must answer effectively to advance a privacy claim. As one considers these questions, consider also the facts of the Hulk Hogan dispute with Gawker and 2016 verdict for $140 Million over the sex tape introduced at the beginning of this chapter.[33] Is a sex tape inherently private and its publication online inherently outrageous? Is there ever any possible news value that might protect the airing of such a tape?

What is publication? In libel law, "publication" has a specialized meaning. At a minimum, a libel plaintiff must prove a defamatory communication reached at least one person other than the plaintiff and defendant. Under the embarrassing private facts tort, however, "publication" means "publicity," that is, widespread communication. Publication in a newspaper, magazine or other print medium satisfies this requirement, as does dissemination by broadcast or cable. While laws governing libel and privacy in computer communications are still evolving, it is reasonable to assume that widespread communication of private information *via* a commercial database, social media, bulk e-mail, Web page or similar means would meet this requirement.

Is the information private? As a threshold, a plaintiff must establish that the information in question is, in fact, private. What happens in public, or appears in public records, normally is not considered private. In *Cox Broadcasting Co. v. Cohn,* the Supreme Court held that the news media are not liable for publication of personal information, even if they violate a state statute designed to protect rape victims, if they "merely give further publicity to information about a plaintiff which is al-

ready public."[34] In a California case, a privacy claim failed because the information was gleaned from public records.[35] A person involved in an automobile accident or the victim of a crime, therefore, cannot claim invasion of privacy based on photographs of or stories about the accident. As a Massachusetts court noted: "Many things which are distressing and lacking in propriety or good taste are not actionable."[36] Likewise, a participant in a public rally or parade cannot claim privacy related to those actions.[37] At least one court, however, has said a crime victim's privacy might outweigh newsworthiness and the right to publish even when the name is a matter of public record. In *Times Mirror Co. v. San Diego Superior Court,* a California appellate court reasoned that a crime witness's safety and the state's interest in prosecuting the crime might outweigh the media's right to publish and the public's right to know the name of the witness.[38]

Even intimate personal information cannot normally be the basis for a privacy claim if it is already widely known, as Oliver Sipple learned after he thwarted an assassination attempt on President Gerald Ford. News accounts of Sipple's heroism disclosed that he was a homosexual, a fact already well-known in the San Francisco gay community.[39]

Consent is also a factor in determining whether personal information should be considered public or private. While the question of consent will be addressed later in this chapter, it should be noted that a person cannot normally provide information knowingly to the news media and later claim an invasion of privacy, although in some instances consent might be effectively withdrawn. One can easily envision the relevance of disclosures made on social networking sites. A person who discloses previously private information on a widely accessible social network may be surrendering a degree of his or her privacy.

What kind of information might be considered highly offensive to a reasonable person? A memorable case based on a "Where Are They Now?" story about child prodigy William Sidis offers a good definition. Sidis sued for invasion of privacy based on a 1937 article in *The New Yorker,* which was published more than a quarter century after he made headlines as a preteen math whiz. He claimed that the magazine's delving into his present life was offensive. On appeal, the Second U.S. Circuit Court of Appeals disagreed, holding that to be sufficiently offensive, a private disclosure must "outrage the community's notions of decency."[40] A later California case defined offensiveness different-

---

[32] *See* Trump v. O'Brien, 958 A.2d 85, 96 (N.J. Super. Ct. App. Div. 2008) ("Both privacy and defamation laws seek to protect a person's interest in controlling information written or spoken about him without his consent.").

[33] Somaiya, *supra* note 3.

[34] 420 U.S. 469, 494 (1975).

[35] Briscoe v. Reader's Digest Ass'n, 483 P.2d 34 (Cal. 1972).

[36] Kelley v. Post Publ'g Co., 98 N.E.2d 286, 287 (Mass. 1951).

[37] Sipple v. Chronicle Publ'g Co., 201 Cal. Rptr. 665 (Cal. Ct. App. 1984).

[38] 244 Cal. Rptr. 556 (Cal. Ct. App. 1988).

[39] *Sipple,,* 201 Cal. Rptr. at 666-67.

[40] Sidis v. F-R Publ'g Co., 113 F.2d 806, 809 (2d Cir. 1940).

ly, suggesting the public's legitimate interest in personal information mation ends when a publication forgoes legitimate news values and "becomes a morbid and sensational prying into private lives for its own sake."[41]

What kind of disclosure, then, would outrage a community's sense of decency or constitute sensational prying? Another oft-cited case suggests that stories dealing with medical or other intimate health conditions are most problematic for journalists. Dorothy Barber was dubbed a "starving glutton" in a *Time* magazine article about a bizarre medical condition that caused her to lose weight despite eating large quantities of food. She sued for invasion of privacy after *Time* published a photograph of her in a hospital room. The Missouri Supreme Court, citing the long-standing privacy protection accorded doctor-patient relationships, held that disclosure of the eating disorder was embarrassing and invaded Barber's privacy. The court acknowledged the public's interest in such medical maladies but reasoned that identifying Barber was not necessary to tell the story about the disorder.[42] As a rule, invasive stories or pictures that deal with physical or mental illness, or that expose the intimate parts of the body, require particular caution. The court's reliance on doctor-patient privilege in the Barber case also suggests disclosures that involve information normally protected under common law privileges could be considered highly offensive. *The Restatement of Torts* suggests several problem areas: sexual relations, humiliating illnesses, intimate personal letters, family disputes, details of home life, stolen photos or photos taken in private places, and information from individual tax returns.[43]

A plaintiff must prove the *widespread publicity* of intimately private material that a *reasonable person* would find *highly offensive*, and that the information was *not* related to a *matter of public concern*. In many private-facts cases involving the news media, however, plaintiffs fail because most of what is printed or broadcast is chosen because it *is* newsworthy.

What constitutes a matter of public concern? Even if a plaintiff can establish that disclosure is highly offensive, the likelihood of winning a privacy suit is slim if the plaintiff has become part of a public event or controversy. Information related to traditional news values is likely to deal with matters of public concern. Information about politics, law enforcement, crime, domestic violence, suicide, medical advances and social trends falls within the realm of traditional news.

The 1982 case of Hilda Bridges, who became an unintended celebrity on a very public stage, dramatically underscores the dearth of privacy protection for individuals caught up in news events. She was dragged into a public matter when police offi-

cers — and members of the news media — surrounded her apartment when her estranged husband took her hostage and forced her to undress to prevent her from fleeing. During the standoff, he shot himself, and police rushed the apartment. Bridges fled naked and distraught into the street, clutching only a hand towel. After *Today* newspaper in Cocoa Beach, Florida, published a revealing photograph, she sued for invasion of privacy and infliction of emotional distress.

Satisfied that such publicity was unwarranted and highly offensive, a Florida jury awarded Bridges $10,000. An appellate court, however, unanimously set aside the award, ruling that the law had not been properly followed. The jury erred, the court reasoned, because the events happened in public and because crime was a matter of public concern. Judge James Dauksch noted that individual privacy at some point must yield to the public interest: "Just because the story and photograph may be embarrassing or distressful does not mean the newspaper cannot publish what is otherwise newsworthy."[44] While publication of the photograph raised numerous ethical questions, Bridges' chances of success were virtually nonexistent because she was caught up in a public drama. Years earlier in a similar privacy case, a Florida court had concluded: "Even though the plaintiff's role of 'actor' in an event having news value was not of his own volition ... the fact remains that he was in a public place and present at a scene where news was in the making."[45]

The result was essentially the same when a bystander at a public event thwarted an attempt to assassinate President Gerald Ford during his visit to San Francisco in 1975. As described earlier, Oliver Sipple's act of heroism drew him into the limelight, illuminating his Vietnam War record as well as his homosexuality. Sipple, well known in San Francisco's gay community before the Ford episode, sued the *San Francisco Chronicle* and other newspapers for invasion of privacy. He argued that while his public actions were newsworthy, his private life was not, and that disclosure of his sexual orientation caused him embarrassment because his homosexuality was not widely known. A California appellate court held that both his heroism and his homosexuality were newsworthy, noting that his heroic behavior cut against gay stereotypes.[46]

In Florida, a federal district court judge ruled that a suicidal 16-year-old girl filmed by the Fox Television docudrama *Cops* had no right of privacy because the filming resulted from her call to authorities seeking help. After the call was routed to 911, the film crew, riding with deputies, went to the girl's home, where it videotaped her in an open garage. When televised, the footage intentionally blurred the girl's face. The judge said a

---

[41] Virgil v. Time, Inc., 527 F.2d 1122, 1129 (9th Cir. 1975).

[42] Barber v. Time, Inc., 159 S.W.2d 291 (Mo. 1942).

[43] RESTATEMENT (SECOND) OF TORTS § 652D, comments b, g (1977).

[44] Cape Publ'ns, Inc. v. Bridges, 423 So. 2d 426, 428 (Fla. Ct. App. 1982).

[45] Jacova v. Southern Radio and Television Co., 83 So. 2d 34, 40 (Fla. 1955).

[46] Sipple v. Chronicle Publ'g Co., 201 Cal. Rptr. 665 (Cal. Ct. App. 1984).

person who commits public acts that result in police intervention cannot expect such circumstances to remain private.[47]

While much of what is newsworthy deals with matters of social and political importance, newsworthiness also can be defined as anything out of the ordinary. Unusual occupations, hobbies, talents and other qualities that attract public attention are newsworthy. Two cases are prime examples. The first arose from a story in *Sports Illustrated* about a well-known California body surfer. Michael Virgil sued for invasion of privacy after the magazine included accounts of his unusual personal behavior in a story about his surfing. The information, discussed freely with a reporter, included his eating insects and burning himself with cigarettes, as well as diving headlong down a flight of stairs to impress women. *Sports Illustrated* included the material despite Virgil's request that it not use personal information. Following the guidance of the Ninth Circuit in an appeal in the same case, a federal district court in California rejected Virgil's privacy claim because the court concluded the personal information in the story was a "legitimate journalistic attempt" to give a full portrait of the body surfer.[48]

The second case, *Sidis v. F-R Publishing Corp.*, arose from a *New Yorker* magazine story about a former child prodigy leading a recluse's life in Boston, never having realized his incredible promise. The court rejected Sidis' privacy claim, reasoning that his childhood acclaim gave rise to legitimate public interest in his present activities.[49] While the life of Sidis may not have been a matter of great social or political importance, it was sufficiently out of the ordinary and interesting to be newsworthy.

As implied in *Sidis*, newsworthiness normally stands the test of time in privacy actions. The Kansas Supreme Court reached that conclusion in 1975 after a newspaper republished a story about a police officer fired some ten years earlier. Noting that once "facts are in the public domain they remain there," the court held that republication of a newsworthy event was not an invasion of privacy. It said official government misconduct "is newsworthy when it occurs and remains so for as long as anyone thinks it worth retelling."[50] In *Forsher v. Bugliosi*, the California Supreme Court stated it another way. Quoting tort expert William Prosser, it said, "[O]nce a man becomes a public figure, or news, he remains a matter of legitimate recall in the public's mind until the end of his days."[51]

What about instances when news accounts reveal private information about public officials or public figures? As a rule, most activities of public persons are newsworthy by virtue of their public status. When the *Miami Herald* disclosed that Democratic presidential contender Gary Hart spent the night with a woman who was not his wife, for example, questions were raised about proper bounds of reporting and the *Herald* was criticized; but the legal question of privacy was never seriously raised. Robert Dole, a contender at the time for the Republican presidential nomination, put the privacy issue this way: "Once you stand up and say you're going to be a candidate for president, all bets are off."[52]

Similarly, had former Vice President Al Gore sued the *Star* tabloid magazine for publishing a story in 2010 about his affair with the former wife of Larry David, creator of the *Seinfeld* TV series, he would have had little legal recourse unless the publication was false. The public's interest in his behavior was heightened by the fact that his wife, Tipper, had been a vocal critic of declining social and family values.

The public's interest can be heightened by other factors. In 2007, a federal appeals court held newsworthy a Texas newspaper feature about a husband-wife lawyer team and their scheme to blackmail the wife's former lovers. The court cited the lawyers' prominence, the criminal prosecution and legal ethics as reasons for rejecting the couple's privacy claim, even though the newspaper had obtained and used sealed court records.[53]

Private Facts and Constitutional Protections. The media have some protection under the First Amendment when they publish truthful, lawfully obtained information about matters of public concern. Several cases help define the scope of this protection.

In <u>*Cox Broadcasting Corp. v. Cohn*</u>, parents of a teenage girl who was raped and murdered sued an Atlanta television station for broadcasting the girl's name. The suit was based on a Georgia statute that forbade publication of names of alleged rape victims. The station, WSB-TV, had obtained the victim's name from records provided at an open court hearing. The Georgia Supreme Court upheld the parents' right to pursue the lawsuit, but the U.S. Supreme Court reversed, focusing on the fact that the information was revealed in judicial records. It said the onus should be on government to ensure privacy by keeping certain information out of the public domain. Allegations of crime and the resulting proceedings, the Court said, "are without question events of legitimate concern to the public" that the press has a duty to report.[54]

Similarly, when the *Florida Star*, a small weekly newspaper, published the name of a rape victim as part of its routine police report, copied from a public bulletin board at the Duval County

---

[47] *See* David Kidwell, *Woman Loses Privacy Suit Against TV Crime Show*, MIAMI HERALD, May 13, 1994, at 1B.

[48] Virgil v. Sports Illustrated, 424 F. Supp. 1286, 1289 (S.D. Cal. 1984), *on remand from* Virgil v. Time., 527 F.2d 1122 (9th Cir. 1975).

[49] 113 F.2d 806 (2d Cir. 1940).

[50] Rawlins v. Hutchinson Publ'g Co., 543 P.2d 988, 996 (Kan. 1975).

[51] 608 P. 2d 716, 726 (Cal. 1980).

[52] Deborah Gersh, *Privacy and the Presidency*, EDITOR & PUBLISHER, Oct. 13, 1990, at 15.

[53] Lowe v. Hearst, 487 F.3d 246 (5th Cir. 2007).

[54] 420 U.S. 469, 492 (1975).

Sheriff's Department, the Court held that the report was protected. The rape victim sued the newspaper, claiming that violation of the state criminal statute barring publication of names of alleged rape victims constituted evidence of breach of duty and that she should be awarded civil damages for invasion of privacy. A jury agreed and awarded her $100,000. The Supreme Court overturned the verdict, holding that the Constitution prevents states from punishing the news media — even by allowing civil damages — for publishing truthful, lawfully obtained information. As in *Cox Broadcasting*, the Court reasoned that the government shoulders the burden in protecting such privacy interests and that news media could be punished for publishing truthful information only when the punishment advanced a "state interest of the highest order."[55] The Georgia Supreme Court, citing the *Florida Star* ruling, overturned a jury verdict awarding damages to a sexual assault victim who shot her assailant. The story identified the victim but never said specifically she had been sexually assaulted. The Georgia Supreme Court said both the state and federal constitutions protected the right of the newspaper to "accurately report the facts regarding the incident," including the name.[56]

The inherently public nature of information found in public or governmental records and published by the press arose in the last few years in a variety of interesting contexts, suggesting that courts will strongly protect public disclosure of what some think should be private information when that information relates to or reflects upon government or public policy. For example, in *Lovejoy v. Linehan*, the New Hampshire Supreme Court protected both county officials and a newspaper reporter who disclosed the previously expunged criminal assault record of a candidate running for sheriff.[57] The court stressed that the information, even if expunged, related to a matter of legitimate public concern in the election.

In *Ostergren v. Cuccinelli*, a federal appeals court held that under the First Amendment the state of Virginia could not seek injunctive relief against Betty Ostergren under the state's personal information privacy law for posting online the social security numbers of various public officials.[58] Ostergren, a privacy advocate who had criticized the state and lobbied Virginia legislators over their failure to protect personal information online, had found the numbers in real estate records already put online and made available to the public by the state's various court clerks. To protest and draw attention to the issue she reposted the same documents. The court held that while obvious privacy interests were at stake those interests could not be used to silence this obvious and effective form of criticism.

Perhaps the most interesting reaffirmation of the public nature of public records came in *John Doe v. Sam Reed*, decided by the Supreme Court in 2010.[59] The case was not a press case, but it did involve the public's right to information about individuals. Under Washington's public records act, the names of people who sign citizen petitions calling for a referendum to overturn a state law are available to the public. The petition in question called for a vote on Washington's new law extending some benefits to same-sex couples. The plaintiffs claimed that disclosure of their names would violate their First Amendment rights to free speech and association. The Supreme Court rejected the challenge to the law, which it said served sufficiently important government interests in discouraging fraud, fostering transparency in government and protecting integrity of the state's electoral process. The case was not specifically a privacy case, but privacy interests were obviously close to the core of the plaintiffs' concerns and, yet, were insufficient to strike down that provision of the state's public records law as a general matter.

Consent as a Defense. Normally, individuals may not knowingly and willingly disclose personal information and then claim invasion of privacy. As a rule, the more intimate the information, the more important for the reporter to be sure consent was clearly given, either explicitly or implicitly. Consent is explicit when professional communicators ask for and receive permission to use personal information for publication. Consent must come from someone with the authority or legal capacity to provide the information. A friend cannot give consent for the use of private information about a college roommate. A day-care operator cannot independently give consent for children under his or her care, nor can a hospital official give consent when the privacy of patients is involved. Minor children cannot give legal consent. Consent need not be in written form, but written consent is almost always easier to prove in court than oral consent.

Can explicit consent later be withdrawn? One court has said no — if the person providing information is newsworthy and the private information is used for legitimate journalistic purposes.[60] ABC News took no chance in 2001 and decided not to air portions of a program titled *Tampering With Nature* after some parents of elementary school children interviewed for the program withdrew their consent. In a letter to ABC before the program was to air, parents complained that John Stossel asked the children leading questions.[61] Whether such forms of consent or similar agreements amount to enforceable contracts remains a difficult question.[62]

---

[55] Florida Star v. B.J.F., 491 U.S. 524, 533 (1989).
[56] Macon Telegraph Publ'g Co. v. Tatum, 436 S.E.2d 655, 658 (Ga. 1993).
[57] 20 A.3d 274 (N.H. 2011).
[58] 615 F.3d 263 (4th Cir. 2010).

[59] 561 U.S. 186 (2010).
[60] *See* Virgil v. Sports Illustrated, 424 F. Supp. 1286 (D.C. Cal. 1976).
[61] *See* Associated Press, *Stossel Segment Scrapped,* MIAMI HERALD, June 29, 2001, at 4A.
[62] In a related, but factually different, context, the Supreme Court has limited the

Implied Consent. Reporters frequently talk to sources and use the information without specifically asking for permission. Members of the public generally understand the function of reporters. If journalists identify themselves and sources talk willingly, there should be no problem. Implied consent is problematic, however, if private information is obtained from someone who does not understand that it is likely to be published.[63]

Intrusion

Definition: Intrusion is the invasion of another person's solitude, either physically or by use of technological devices.

The fundamental purpose of the tort of intrusion — to protect a person's solitude — can be traced to many of the nation's early values. But the notion of intrusion has gone beyond the traditional legal doctrine of trespass, or physical intrusion, to mechanical and electronic violations of private space. The means by which intrusion occurs have changed from the "instantaneous photography" that so riled Brandeis and Warren to the miniature video cameras that left ABC's *Prime Time Live* reeling, as explained later, from a $3.5 million verdict in 1996, which, though later reduced to $2, cost the network dearly in terms of legal fees and credibility. The tort of intrusion, whether physical or technological, deals with the *act of gathering information*, not the content of the information gathered.

Privacy in Public and Quasi-Public Places. Under the common law, people in public places have little expectation of privacy with regard to what they do. People engaging in public activities must assume they might be photographed, filmed or recorded. The public sphere almost certainly includes widely accessible Web sites, including many social networks, as well as more traditional, physical spaces.

While people in public places do not forgo all rights to privacy, journalists encounter few legal problems when they photograph or report about them, so long as they report what would reasonably be considered public. A New Jersey court granted a newspaper summary judgment in a suit brought by the owner of a historic house when a photograph appeared in the newspaper. It reasoned that the picture, taken from a public street, simply recorded what any passerby might see.[64] A Kentucky court held that a man photographed stepping fully clothed from a portable toilet on a college campus had no basis for a privacy claim, because he was stepping back into public view.[65] Similar reasoning has been applied to individuals on private property that is customarily open to the public, such as malls, restaurants and businesses. One court has held that a dog trainer waiting backstage to perform his act was in a public place that afforded little expectation of privacy.[66] The Iowa Supreme Court, however, reinstated a lawsuit filed by a woman filmed by a television crew in a pizza restaurant. The restaurant owner had given the crew permission to enter the restaurant. A lower court had dismissed the suit, reasoning that the woman was in public and not cast in a false light, and that the broadcast was for news rather than commercial purposes. The state supreme court disagreed, saying the woman should have an opportunity to present evidence that she was harmed by the telecast.[67]

Courts also have suggested that journalists may be persistent when encountering people in public without invading their privacy, so long as the behavior is not highly intrusive or overzealous. Journalistic behavior that is simply annoying is not necessarily an invasion of privacy.[68] Images come to mind of Mike Wallace doggedly pursuing a reluctant subject across a parking lot or down a public street to get a statement for *60 Minutes*. Persistence in pursuing a story or source is considered a virtue in journalistic circles, but behavior can become legally problematic when it is menacing or harassing. Such was the case with paparazzi Ron Galella and his pursuit of Jacqueline Kennedy Onassis, widow of President John F. Kennedy. A federal court, citing Onassis' right to be left alone, ordered Galella to stay at least twenty-five feet away from her in public. At issue was not Galella's right to photograph Onassis in public, but his overly intrusive efforts to obtain exclusive photographs.[69]

Trespass or Physical and Technological Intrusion. According to *The Restatement of Torts*, anyone who enters private property without consent of the owner or possessor commits a trespass.[70] Everyone has seen "No Trespassing" signs posted to warn away unwanted visitors. Private property is protected from intruders under both the common law and statutes, which define specific penalties for the crime. Entering private property without permission or staying on it after being asked to leave poses legal dangers for journalists, whose rights are normally no different from those of any other private citizen.

As a rule, a visitor on private property must obtain permis-

---

freedom of reporters to change reporter/source agreements that rise to the level of rudimentary contracts. In *Cohen v. Cowles Media*, it said a reporter's promise to keep a source's name private could be treated by states as an oral contract without violating the First Amendment rights of the journalist. Journalists had argued that the source's name was newsworthy and that the ultimate decision to use or not to use newsworthy information should reside with the news media. 501 U.S. 663 (1991).

[63] *See* Prahl v. Brosamle, 295 N.W.2d 768 (Wis. 1980).

[64] Bisbee v. Conover, 452 A.2d 689 (N.J. 1982).

[65] Livingston v. Kentucky Post, 14 Media L. Rep. (BNA) 2076, 2077 (Ky. Cir. Ct. 1987).

[66] People for Ethical Treatment of Animals v. Berosini, 867 P.2d 1121 (Nev. 1994).

[67] Stressman v. American Blackhawk Broad. Co., 416 N.W.2d 685 (Iowa 1987).

[68] *See* Dempsey v. Nat'l Enquirer, Inc., 702 F. Supp. 927 (D. Maine 1988).

[69] Galella v. Onassis, 353 F. Supp. 196 (S.D.N.Y. 1972).

[70] RESTATEMENT (SECOND) OF TORTS 158 (1977).

sion before entry. Permission must be obtained from the possessor of the property, be it the owner or someone with contractual control over the property, such as a renter or tenant. For example, a court held that journalists did not invade the privacy of a farmer when they obtained permission from the caretaker to enter the property and photograph dead cattle.[71]

Consent may be either explicit or implied. Explicit consent occurs when a visitor asks for and is granted permission. A reporter might request an interview at a residence or at a business office, for example. When the purpose of the visit is obscured, however, or when journalists simply lie about their intentions, the question of trespass is much less clear.

Journalists have an array of devices that enhance newsgathering, from telephoto lenses, to sensitive listening devices, to miniaturized video cameras. Technological intrusion is as old as the discussion of privacy. As noted, in 1890, Brandeis and Warren were concerned about a new kind of "instantaneous" photography that no longer required willing subjects to remain perfectly still. Today, the culprit likely would be a mini video camera or even a smart phone. As a rule, the use of technology that enhances viewing or listening is legal as long as the device does not effectively let the journalist hear or see what normally could not be observed. If a device simply allows a journalist to see or hear what might be witnessed in public, there is no intrusion. People who go into public places — streets, parks and college campuses, for example — enjoy very little privacy, as long as they are not menaced or harassed. That is, the zone of privacy they enjoy is very small compared to the privacy they can expect in their homes or other strictly private places.

Several cases involving the same television network show how troublesome the question of lawful access to private property and technological intrusion can be.

In 1997, a North Carolina jury awarded the Food Lion grocery chain $3.5 million in damages after ABC's *Prime Time Live* carried a report, afforded by hidden video cameras, that Food Lion relabeled and restocked meat after its expiration date. The judge had allowed the jury to consider fraud and trespass charges against ABC without considering the veracity of the network's report on Food Lion's business practices. The jury based its award on the fact that *Prime Time Live* producers had committed a trespass by obtaining access to Food Lion facilities through fraudulent job applications.[72] Even though the Food Lion judgment was reduced to $2 on appeal,[73] it illustrates the dangers reporters face in a society increasingly wary of certain reporting techniques.

The Food Lion decision stands in contrast to a ruling by the Seventh U.S. Circuit Court of Appeals. In *Desnick v. ABC*, the court rejected a trespass claim when reporters with hidden cameras posed as patients to investigate claims that a Desnick Eye Center was performing cataract operations unnecessarily. The court drew an analogy between food critics appearing at a restaurant anonymously and unannounced and the undercover reporters' actions, even though they had gained the cooperation of the center by promising not to employ undercover tactics.[74]

ABC didn't fare as well in a subsequent case when it was successfully sued for intrusion after a network reporter went undercover as a telephone psychic and surreptitiously videotaped colleagues discussing their work. The California Supreme Court said that while employee conversations were not completely private, employees did have a reasonable expectation that they would not be videotaped.[75]

ABC prevailed in a later case when its undercover reporters and hidden cameras examined medical laboratories that evaluated women's pap smears and had a high frequency of testing errors possibly caused by pressure on technologists to work too quickly.[76] ABC's *Prime Time Live* used a fictitious health clinic to request tests and obtain interviews as well as a lab tour, but it did not obtain or reveal any personal or private information about patients or the people interviewed. The court emphasized that the ABC crew did not intrude upon the reasonably expected seclusion of the lab's offices or the reasonable expectation of privacy of the owner who was secretly videotaped.

In addition to evaluating the inherent intrusiveness, courts often will consider the actual necessity of the technologically enhanced means of reporting. In *Dietmann v. Time, Inc.*,[77] the court awarded $1,000 damages to an unconventional healer. *Life* magazine reporters gained entry to A. A. Dietmann's home by posing as prospective patients and then secretly photographed and recorded their conversations as he performed his healing ritual. The Ninth U.S. Circuit Court of Appeals rejected media arguments that subterfuge, secret photographing and recordings were essential to telling the story. "We strongly disagree," it said, "that the hidden mechanical contrivances are indispensable tools of newsgathering."[78]

In contrast to *Dietmann*, a Kentucky court rejected an intrusion claim after reporters persuaded a woman indicted on drug charges to secretly record a conversation with her lawyer, who she said had offered to bribe a judge. In *McCall v. Courier Journal & Louisville Times*, the court noted that the woman had not lied to gain access to her lawyer's office and that he had

---

[71] Wood v. Fort Dodge Messenger, 13 Media L. Rep. (BNA) 1614 (Iowa Dist. Ct. 1986). *See also* Lal v. CBS, 551 F. Supp. 356 (E.D. Pa. 1982).

[72] *See* Estes Thompson, *Jury: ABC Committed Fraud to Get Food Story,* MIAMI HERALD, Dec. 21, 1996, at 10A.

[73] Food Lion v. Capital Cities/ABC, 194 F.3d 505 (4th Cir. 1999).

[74] 44 F.3d 1345 (7th Cir. 1995).

[75] Sanders v. American Broad. Cos., 978 P.2d 67 (Cal. 1999).

[76] Med. Lab. Mgmt. Consultants v. ABC, 306 F.3d 806 (9th Cir. 2002).

[77] 449 F.2d 245 (9th Cir. 1971).

[78] *Id.* at 249.

waived his privacy when he continued to talk to her though he suspected he was being taped.[79]

In a 1996 case, a federal court found grounds for technological intrusion when the TV show *Inside Edition* used a shotgun microphone to eavesdrop on conversations inside a home. The court said use of a sensitive directional microphone, which could pick up conversations sixty yards away, was an invasion of privacy. An official of a Pennsylvania health care business had refused requests from the *Inside Edition* journalists to be interviewed for a story on executive salaries. The reporters then waited in a van outside his home and used the shotgun microphone to obtain information.[80] The official sued.

A California court also drew a sharp distinction between photographing or videotaping an accident victim in public versus after the victim was placed inside a rescue helicopter and transported to a hospital. Producers for a reality program arranged to record and videotape inside the helicopter and were sued by the victim for intrusion and disclosure of embarrassing private facts. The California Supreme Court threw out the private facts claim but allowed the case to proceed on intrusion, resulting in an out-of-court settlement.[81]

Cell phones that can take and transmit photographs have raised new privacy concerns, prompting businesses — particularly health clubs — to ban them. Florida made it a crime to secretly record people dressing or undressing when they have a reasonable expectation of privacy. The statute covers both private and commercial distribution of such images and makes "video voyeurism" a felony.[82] Most states now have similar laws. President George W. Bush signed the federal Video Voyeurism Prevention Act of 2004, applicable to improper photographs, film and videotape taken on federal property when an individual has a reasonable privacy expectation.[83]

Similar issues can arise in the context of the paparazzi who photograph celebrities. In 2005, for example, actress Jennifer Aniston filed a lawsuit over topless photographs of her that, she argued, had to have been taken from a great distance and obviously with an intrusive telephoto lens or through trespass or other unlawful means. She and the photographer settled in 2006 — amicably, but confidentially.[84]

While not strictly a privacy case, the litigation against Google over its Street View project, which began in 2007, and the claims that Google violated the wiretapping laws highlights the privacy concerns raised by new, potentially invasive technol-

ogy.[85] The Supreme Court declined to hear an appeal in the case in 2014,[86] meaning the trial could start in the lower court over the data gathered by Google's special cars that photographed homes and streets and, in the process, also on occasion gathered email, passwords and personal information from unencrypted household computer networks. Google has insisted the incidental data collection was unintentional, but this class action could be groundbreaking in the years ahead.[87]

As if strangely outfitted cars were not enough to stir privacy advocates, drones, too, may become a regular sight in domestic skies.[88] Whether drones are used by police or other government agencies, by commercial, private ventures or by journalists, the risks to privacy are obvious, and the demands to create rules are just beginning to be voiced.[89]

Custom and Usage. While explicit consent requires a request of the property owner or possessor, implied consent occurs in a number of ways under what is called the "custom and usage" legal doctrine. A degree of access is implied by custom or typical use of private and quasi-private property. It is customary to cross private property to ring someone's doorbell to solicit contributions or sell a product, absent a locked gate, a "No Trespassing" sign or other warning. It is also customary for shoppers and diners to enter stores and restaurants. This access assumes the visitor does not engage in unwanted activities and leaves when asked.

The Florida Supreme Court accepted the argument that custom and usage justified a news photographer's entry onto private property with government officials. In *Fletcher v. Florida Publishing Co.*, the mother of a teenager killed in a house fire sued the *Florida Times-Union* for invasion of privacy when it published a photograph, over the caption "Silhouette of Death," showing the outline of where the body of the young victim had lain.[90] The mother learned of her daughter's death from the newspaper account. Complicating the case was the fact that fire officials asked the photographer to take the shots, thus also acting in a quasi-official capacity. In court, the newspaper successfully argued that it was customary for journalists to accompany officials onto private property where crimes or disasters oc-

---

[79] 623 S.W.2d 882 (Ky. 1981).

[80] Wolfson v. Lewis, 924 F. Supp. 1413 (E.D. Pa. 1996).

[81] Shulman v. Group W. Prod., 955 P.2d 469 (Cal. 1998).

[82] FLA. STAT., ch. 801.145 (2004).

[83] 18 U.S.C. § 1801 (West 2006).

[84] *See The Daily Dish*, BUFFALO NEWS, Dec. 7, 2005, at C3; *Names & Faces*, WASH. POST, Sept. 4, 2006, at C03.

[85] *See* David Streitfeld, *Court Says Privacy Case Can Proceed vs. Google*, N.Y. TIMES, Sep. 10, 2013, *available at* http://www.nytimes.com/2013/09/11/technology/court-says-privacy-case-can-proceed-vs-google.html?_r=1&.

[86] Google v. Joffe, 746 F.3d 920 (9th Cir. 2014), *cert denied* 134 S.Ct. 2877 (2014)

[87] *See* Streitfeld, *supra* note 6, at B4.

[88] *The Future of Drones: Technology vs. Privacy*, CBS NEWS, Mar. 14, 2014, *available at* http://www.cbsnews.com/news/the-future-of-drones-technology-vs-priva cy/.

[89] Al Tompkins, *2015 MAY BE THE YEAR JOURNALISTS ACTUALLY GET TO USE DRONES*, POYNTER.ORG, Jan. 14, 2015, http://www.poynter.org/how-tos/visuals/30992 1/2015-may-bring-new-drone-regulations-for-journalists/.

[90] 340 So. 2d 914 (Fla. 1976). *See also* Higbee v. Times Advocate, 5 Media L. Rep. (BNA) 2372 (S.D. Cal. 1981).

curred, an argument supported by government officials.

In 1992, however, a federal court in New York emphatically rejected the *Fletcher* reasoning when journalists for CBS's *Street Stories* accompanied Secret Service agents during a search for documents in a credit card fraud investigation. During the raid, based on a search warrant, CBS employees videotaped a suspect's wife and child despite their repeated requests not to be photographed.[91] The Second U.S. Circuit Court of Appeals upheld a lower court ruling against the Secret Service, underscoring the position that law enforcement officials have no authority to allow journalists into private residences without the owners' permission, even when the property is under police control. Flatly rejecting any constitutional defense to justify the presence of CBS, the court found a clear Fourth Amendment violation by the Secret Service based on the presence of the journalists during the search. It concluded that they served no legitimate law enforcement need and that their presence was "calculated to inflict injury on the very value that the Fourth Amendment seeks to protect — the right of privacy."[92]

In *Wilson v. Layne*, the Supreme Court, in 1999, indicated that individuals can win lawsuits on privacy grounds when law enforcement officers take journalists into private homes.[93] The case began when federal marshals and sheriff's deputies from Montgomery County, Maryland, raided the home of Charles and Geraldine Wilson. Officers were looking for the Wilsons' son, Dominic, on charges that he had violated probation. The early-morning raid was part of "Operation Gunsmoke," a program started in 1992 in which law enforcement agencies routinely invited journalists to accompany them in apprehending fugitives. A reporter and photographer from the *Washington Post* accompanied officers on the raid of the Wilson home. The Wilsons sued the officers for violating their Fourth Amendment rights against unreasonable search and seizure by bringing into the home journalists who had no official role in the search.

Chief Justice William Rehnquist, writing for a unanimous court, conceded that reporter ride-alongs were common at the time of the raid and that the law governing the practice was uncertain. Nevertheless, he concluded, the presence of third parties with no legitimate law enforcement roles during the execution of a search warrant violated the Fourth Amendment's core interest in residential privacy.

He rejected the argument that the presence of reporters during raids served a legitimate law enforcement purpose. "It may well be that ride-alongs further the law enforcement objectives of the police in a general sense, but that is not the same as furthering the purposes of the search," he wrote.[94]

He next rejected the argument that the publicity resulting from ride-alongs significantly benefited the government by publicizing efforts to combat crime. The news media play an important role by informing the public about law enforcement activities, he wrote, but Fourth Amendment concerns were paramount in the *Wilson* case. "Surely the possibility of good public relations for the police is simply not enough, standing alone, to justify the ride-along intrusion into a private home," he wrote.[95]

Finally, Rehnquist rejected the argument that the presence of journalists could, in some instances, minimize abuse of suspects and protect the safety of officers. "The *Washington Post* reporters in the Wilsons' home were working on a story for their own purposes," he wrote. "They were not present for the purpose of protecting the officers, much less the Wilsons."[96]

Clearly, consent from the owner is the best defense for journalists who enter private property. Following *Wilson v. Layne*, the FBI's *Law Enforcement Bulletin* cautioned all law enforcement officials not only to avoid inviting media representatives into private areas protected under the Fourth Amendment, but also to use caution when relying on waivers obtained by the media because, "Waivers signed by individuals as law enforcement officials are making an entry into their premises to search for evidence of a crime or to make an arrest are likely to be viewed by courts as contracts under duress and unenforceable."[97]

Recording Conversations with Sources. Journalists often record conversations with their sources to create verbatim records of complicated information and lengthy direct quotes. In many states, this practice poses no legal problem because the law assumes that an exact account of a conversation can only benefit all parties involved. Parties to a conversation are legally allowed to recount a conversation to others, and the law simply extends this reasoning to allow taped conversations.[98] In some states, however, it is illegal to record a conversation without the consent of *all* parties. The reasoning assumes that if a person knows a conversation is being taped, the person might behave or respond differently. Perhaps the source would be more cautious or guarded in his or her comments or say nothing at all. Twelve states require that all parties to a conversation know when the conversation is being recorded. In cases involving personal contact, a journalist may ask for permission or may assume consent if a tape recorder is in full view and turned on. It

---

[91] Ayeni v. CBS, 848 F. Supp. 362 (E.D.N.Y. 1994).

[92] Ayeni v. Mottola, 35 F.3d 680, 686 (2d Cir. 1994).

[93] 526 U.S. 603 (1999).

[94] *Id.* at 612.

[95] *Id.* at 613.

[96] *Id.*

[97] *Supreme Court Cases, 1998-1999 Term*, FBI LAW ENFORCEMENT BULL., Oct. 1999, at 29.

[98] Federal law permits a party to a conversation to record it, so long as the recording is not for criminal purposes. However, the Federal Communication Commission, under penalty of lost phone service, requires all parties to consent. *See* 18 U.S.C.A. § 2511 (West Supp. 1996).

is always a good idea to state before the conversation begins that it is being taped. This creates a record of consent. For telephone conversations, consent should be requested before taping begins and restated at the beginning of the conversation.

The Illinois Supreme Court, in 2014, declared that state's eavesdropping law unconstitutional because it made all nonconsensual recordings illegal regardless of the absence of any privacy interest and thus burdened more speech than necessary.[99] In that case, the defendant surreptitiously recorded three conversations with a court administrator regarding an error in a court transcript. She posted the recordings on her We site. Illinois had been a state that required all parties to agree to recordings, though an earlier court suggested that where privacy is not expected, no such right exists. In *Russell v. American Broadcasting Co.*, a court determined that ABC's *Prime Time Live* did not violate the privacy of a fish market manager when it secretly taped him coaching an undercover reporter about the finer points of selling fish.[100] Because the manager expressed no desire to keep the conversation private, the court reasoned, the taping violated no privacy right. The more recent Melongo decision essentially adopted much of this reasoning.

In 2005, a columnist in Miami stirred up controversy when, without consent, he reflexively recorded a phone call with a county commissioner, who exhibited considerable stress during the call and moments later committed suicide in the newspaper's lobby. The newspaper fired the reporter for violating its policies, and the state attorney initiated a criminal investigation, which it later dropped because the columnist had no intent to violate the law.[101]

The Supreme Court, in 2001, addressed the issue of media liability for publication or broadcast of illegal recordings made independently by third parties and then given to journalists. The case began in 1993 when the chief negotiator for a teachers' union sued public affairs radio commentator Frederick Vopper, who broadcast parts of an illegally recorded cellular telephone conversation sent to him anonymously. The suit alleged that he violated Pennsylvania and U.S. wiretapping laws, which invoke civil and criminal penalties for unlawful intercepts. The Third Circuit of the U.S. Court of Appeals, weighing Vopper's First Amendment claims, reversed the lower court and cited the undue burden that the laws placed on the news media.[102]

The Supreme Court agreed, refusing to apply the so-called "general laws doctrine" applied previously in cases involving reporter's privilege, source confidentiality agreements and news-

room searches. The doctrine states that journalists are not immune from content-neutral laws that apply generally in society and do not unduly burden the news media. The Court concluded that the interest in publication of matters of public concern outweighs privacy concerns, noting that participation in public affairs often results in a loss of privacy. It held the news media blameless so long as the journalists had no role in the illegal recording and obtained it lawfully and the content involved a matter of public concern.[103]

In 2011 and 2012, two important cases underscored the impact of new technology on privacy rights. Each involved issues of constitutional privacy (discussed later in this chapter). In *United States v. Jones*,[104] the Supreme Court held that the government violated the Fourth Amendment protection against unreasonable searches by attaching, without first obtaining a warrant, a Global Positioning System to an automobile parked in a public place to track a drug suspect's movements. In *Glik v. Cunniffe*,[105] a federal appellate court held that Boston police officers lacked qualified immunity from a suit for damages filed by a private person they arrested for filming them in a public space as they arrested a young man in the Boston Common. The police accused the photographer, who used his cell phone to do the filming, of violating the Massachusetts wiretap law and other minor state laws. All the charges were dismissed as baseless. In the photographer's later suit for damages, the lower court held that he was exercising a clear constitutional right to openly film and monitor police. The court of appeals affirmed the ruling and added that the use of a cell phone to do the filming did not lessen that right or in any way make it a secret recording that might have violated the state's law.

Although these cases involved constitutional issues and not tort liability, each demonstrated the court's willingness to adapt basic concepts on privacy to new technologies that record images, voices and even geographic locations and travel.

False Light

Definition: The widespread publication of facts that place a plaintiff in a false light that is highly offensive to a reasonable person and was published with actual malice (at least in stories of public concern).[106]

Newsweek's cover on March 28, 1988, showed a young man, hands clasped behind his head, being frisked by police against a backdrop of flashing patrol-car lights. The headlines read: "The Drug Gangs/Waging War on America's Cities/Anti-Drug Sweep in Los Angeles." On April 25, the photo reappeared on an inside

[99] People v. Melongo, 6 N.E.3d 120 (Ill. 2014).

[100] 23 Media L. Rep. (BNA) 2428 (N.D. Ill. 1995).

[101] *See* Terry Aguayo, *Ex-Columnist Will Not be Tried for Taping Calls*, N.Y. TIMES, Sept. 10, 2005, at A8; Abby Goodnough, *Miami Paper Fires Columnist Adding Own Twist to Tale of Sex, Politics and Suicide*, N.Y. TIMES, July 28, 2005, at A14.

[102] Bartnicki v. Vopper, 200 F.3d 109 (3d Cir. 1999).

[103] Bartnicki v. Vopper, 532 U.S. 514 (2001).

[104] 132 S.Ct. 945 (2012).

[105] 655 F.3d 78 (1st Cir. 2011).

[106] *See, e.g.*, Welling v. Weinfeld, 866 N.E.2d 1051 (Ohio 2007).

page over the small headline "Correction." A caption explained that the man in the photo was released without being charged and that *Newsweek* did not mean to suggest that the man was being arrested. It is not known what transpired between *Newsweek* editors and the young man, but one might logically ask whether the magazine cover had cast him in a false light.

Had the *Newsweek* case resulted in a lawsuit for false light invasion of privacy, the plaintiff would have had some of the same burdens of proof as a libel plaintiff. Consequently, false-light cases are often filed in tandem with libel actions. A plaintiff must prove identification (not always a given in a fictionalization), falsity, and that the publisher was at fault — that material was published recklessly or with knowledge of falsity.

False-light plaintiffs, however, would not allege loss of reputation. They would argue that being cast in a highly offensive false light caused some other kind of harm. Also unlike libel, a false-light plaintiff must prove widespread publication — publicity — not just the legal publication. Some states have refused to recognize false-light claims, citing First Amendment concerns, the similarity to libel claims and even the doctrinal confusion over what false light really means.[107]

False Light and Actual Malice. In the 1967 case of *Time, Inc. v. Hill*,[108] the Supreme Court held that all false-light plaintiffs — not just public officials and public figures, as in libel actions — must prove actual malice if involved in matters of public concern. The *Hill* case began in 1952 when three escaped convicts entered the home of James Hill near Philadelphia and held his family hostage for a day. The ordeal received sensational play in Philadelphia newspapers and was the inspiration for Joseph Hayes' novel *The Desperate Hours*. It was later the basis for a Broadway play and a film starring Humphrey Bogart. In 1955, *Life* magazine published a story titled "True Crime Inspires Tense Play" that purported to describe what actually happened. *Life* carried photos from the Philadelphia tryouts for the play, including one of the sons being mistreated by a "brutish convict." Another photo showed the daughter biting the hand of an abusive convict. Both photos were embellishments, since the real captors did not harass the family.[109] Arguing that *Life* used the family's name and experience for trade purposes, the Hills sued for invasion of privacy. They won at trial in 1963, but the Supreme Court set aside the damages in a 5-4 vote, applying the new legal rule that false-light plaintiffs involved in matters of public concern must prove actual malice. (A point of interest: The Hills' lawyer was Richard Nixon, later U.S. president.)

Courts are most likely to find disclosures highly offensive in

two ways:

1. Fictionalization, which is the embellishment or addition of information to an otherwise factual presentation, a device more common to television or stage dramatizations than to news coverage; and,

2. Distortion, which occurs when elements of a story are deceptively juxtaposed, or when information is omitted, presented out of context or presented in an improper context.

Fictionalizations. The *Time, Inc. v. Hill* case suggests that when a drama or novel is modeled on real events, false-light problems can arise even when names and other facts are changed. Fictionalization also can pose problems when a real person's name is used, but use of a real name normally will not sustain a privacy action unless the person's identity is also appropriated. Both a name and facts are usually necessary for there to be legal problems. The fact that the name used in the publication is coincidentally the same as the name of a real person not intended by the publisher or otherwise related or even similar to the character in the published material will not support a false-light privacy claim.[110] In *Geisler v. Petrocelli*, however, a federal judge held a plaintiff's false light complaint legally sufficient to proceed to the discovery phase because it adequately alleged her resemblance to the author's fictional character.[111] Novels, films and television programs often carry disclaimers, advising readers and viewers that their plots and characters are fictional and that any similarities to real people are coincidental. While disclaimers might prove helpful in marginal cases, they are not a fail-safe way to prevent false-light claims.[112]

Fictionalization also can occur in simple news stories when facts and quotes are created. While such distortions are deplorable as a matter of ethics, they also can result in legal problems. In *Cantrell v. Forest City Publishing*, for example, the widow of an accident victim successfully sued for invasion of privacy after a reporter for the *Cleveland Plain Dealer* wrote a story that implied he had spoken to the woman at her home.[113] She argued that the story held her and her family up for pity and ridicule, humiliating them and causing mental distress. The Supreme Court upheld the verdict, agreeing that the family was knowingly cast in a false light by substantial misrepresentations.

To succeed, a false-light plaintiff must prove the alleged mis-

---

[107] *See, e.g.,* Denver Pub. Co. v. Bueno, 54 P.3d 893 (Colo. 2002); Jews for Jesus, Inc. v. Rapp, 997 So. 2d 1098 (Fla. 2008).

[108] 385 U.S. 374 (1967).

[109] *Id.* at 377.

[110] *See* Botts v. New York Times Co., 2003 WL 23162315 (D.N.J. Aug. 29, 2003) (No. 03-1582) (dismissing false light and intentional infliction of emotional distress claims based on an advertisement for the United Negro College Fund).

[111] 616 F.2d 636 (2d Cir. 1980).

[112] *See, e.g.,* Muzikowski v. Paramount Pictures Corp., 322 F.3d 918 (7th Cir. 2003). A disclaimer stating that a motion picture, though in part inspired by actual events, was a "fictitious story and no actual persons ... have been portrayed" was held to be insufficient to support dismissal of false light claim by well-known little league coach.

[113] 419 U.S. 245, 253 (1973).

representations were significant. Minor falsifications, as in libel cases, will not sustain a false-light privacy claim.

A plainly unbelievable story — one with facts that defy reason and logic — still can be the basis of a successful false-light claim. A 97-year-old Arkansas woman, Nellie Mitchell, won a $1.5 million judgment against *The Sun*, a tabloid published by Globe International, after it pulled a ten-year-old photo of her from company files and used it to illustrate an admittedly contrived story under the headline "World's Oldest Newspaper Carrier, 101, quits because she's pregnant." A federal court held the false publication could reasonably be deemed highly offensive and rejected Globe International's contention that it had a First Amendment right to publish an obviously fake story.[114]

Distortions. Until the upsurge in so-called TV "docudramas" and "infotainment," news organizations were much more likely to find themselves defending false-light lawsuits over instances involving information out of context or inappropriately juxtaposed with other information. The *Newsweek* example is illustrative. The subject, photographed in a public place in the course of a newsworthy event, would have had little recourse if a photo caption simply had said police frisked him during a drug sweep. However, the use of the photo with the various headlines and cutlines implied that the subject of the photo was a suspect in a drug sweep that was part of the war on drugs.

Concern about the relationship of photos to text was evident in a *Miami Herald* series titled "Collars for Dollars." It documented excessive overtime by police officers who attached their names to drunken driving reports so they could earn overtime pay as witnesses. As part of a two-page spread of photos and text, the *Herald* carried this disclaimer: "About the photos. The police officers pictured here were photographed doing their jobs. Some were arresting drunk drivers at roadblocks. Others were at the courthouse, waiting for cases to be heard by a judge. Except where noted, there is no evidence that they are Collars for Dollars cops."[115] Courts will closely scrutinize the accuracy and context of any captions or descriptions of the photographs or other artwork appearing with text. In *Raveling v. HarperCollins Publishers*, the court dismissed the plaintiff's claim that, by including her picture holding her mobster brother-in-law's baby at a christening, a book portrayed her as involved with organized crime.[116] The court found persuasive not only the accuracy of the published description, but the absence of any suggestion that she was somehow involved in organized crime.

The use of file photos and video street scenes is commonplace in most news organizations but can pose problems. Such practices should raise red flags when the subject matter is sensitive or individuals might be identified. Editors should take special care when selecting file photos or footage of auto accidents to illustrate stories on drunken driving or using street scenes for hard-to-illustrate stories. When a Washington, D.C., television station broadcast a story about a treatment for the sexually transmitted disease herpes, for example, it used a street scene to provide visuals. The snippet of tape included a clear view of passer-by Linda Duncan as the reporter was saying the following: "For the twenty million Americans who have herpes, it is not a cure." Duncan sued, and a court refused to dismiss the action.[117] A jury subsequently awarded her $750, an amount she unsuccessfully challenged in court as grossly inadequate.

In a few cases, jurors have found distortions and false light invasions of privacy in stories in which every statement of fact was true. The argument in these cases appears to have been that the order of the sentences or the selection of words might lead some readers to reach — at least momentarily — a false conclusion or impression regarding the plaintiff. One such case is the $18.28 million verdict in 2003 against the *Pensacola News Journal* in a case filed by an influential local businessman, Joe Anderson. In 1998, the paper published an article about his successful paving business and noted that he had shot and killed his wife in 1988.[118] It reported that just days before the shooting he had filed for divorce and that law enforcement officials determined the shooting to be a hunting accident. The article included seven paragraphs about the incident, including Anderson's explanation that a deer ran between him and his wife, leading to the accident. Anderson did not contest the accuracy of the report but claimed the story portrayed him as a murderer through its juxtaposition of facts and use of particular words.

In 2007, a Florida appellate court reversed the verdict by applying a two-year statute of limitations (the one applicable to libel claims in Florida) rather than the four-year general tort (including privacy torts) statute of limitations because, the court held, a false-light claim was indistinguishable from a libel claim.[119] In 2008, the Florida Supreme Court affirmed the reversal of the verdict, but because it had rejected false light as a recognized claim in Florida in a companion case.[120]

---

[114] Peoples Bank & Trust v. Globe Int'l, Inc., 786 F. Supp. 791 (W.D. Ark. 1992). A case that creates an interesting contrast is *Pring v. Penthouse*, 695 F.2d 438 (10th Cir. 1982), in which the court found no basis for the plaintiff's claim that a fictional story might be believed when it suggested a beauty queen was able to make sexual partners levitate during sex.

[115] Lisa Getter, Gail Epstein & Jeff Leen, *Cops Cashing In*, MIAMI HERALD, July 14, 1997, at 8A.

[116] 2004 WL 422538 (N.D. Ill. Feb. 10, 2004) (No. 03 C 7333).

[117] Duncan v. WJLA-TV, 10 Media L. Rep. (BNA) 1395 (D.C.D.C 1984).

[118] *See* Stephen Nohlgren, *Case's Verdict Shows Truth No Certain Shield for Media*, ST. PETERSBURG TIMES, Jan. 4, 2004, at 1B; Reporters Committee for Freedom of the Press, News Media Update: *Jury Awards $18 Million in False Light Lawsuit*, Dec. 16, 2003, http://www.rcfp.org/news/2003/121anders.html.

[119] Gannett Co. v. Anderson, 947 So. 2d 1 (Fla. Ct. App. 2007).

[120] Anderson v. Gannett Co., 994 So. 2d 1048 (Fla. 2008).

Appropriation

Definition: The use of a person's name, likeness or image, without permission, for commercial gain.

Appropriation was one of the first privacy torts to develop, in part, because it resembled property rights — an area of law familiar to nineteenth century courts. But it is also a tort with which courts initially had difficulty because it alleged a mental harm based on unwanted publicity. The field of psychology was not highly developed, and the notion that something as intangible as mental suffering could be quantified for the purpose of monetary damages troubled courts.

The turn-of-the century case *Roberson v. Rochester Folding Box Co.*, discussed earlier, illustrates some early problems that courts had with mental or psychic damages, as well as newspaper concerns about potential problems associated with the use of personal photos in news pages. The case began when a New York company that processed baking flour used a picture of young Abigail Roberson in advertisements for its products. Her family sued for invasion of privacy, saying the unwanted attention the girl received in public caused severe embarrassment and humiliation. The court, by a 4-3 vote, rejected the argument that the mental anguish caused by unwanted publicity could give rise to measurable damages. The majority was concerned about the implications of recognizing damages for such an intangible harm. The court said its understanding of the law "leads us to the conclusion that the so-called right of privacy has not yet found an abiding place in our jurisprudence."[121]

This case of unwanted publicity in turn generated much more publicity, with the public siding with the beleaguered Abigail Roberson. Public sentiment was not lost on the New York legislature, which passed a law prohibiting commercial use of a person's name or likeness without permission.[122]

While the New York court was unwilling to recognize a legal right of privacy, the Georgia Supreme Court was more receptive. In *Pavesich v. New England Life Insurance Co.*, in 1905, it became the first state supreme court to recognize the unauthorized commercial use of one's identity as a violation of privacy.[123] Paola Pavesich sued the insurance company after it used his photograph without permission in a testimonial advertisement that purported to express his sentiments about life insurance. In awarding Pavesich damages, the court focused on the commercial nature of the use. Though private people still sometimes make claims of commercial appropriation, most claims deal with celebrities trying to protect the commercial value of their names and likenesses — a more recent legal development.

A Right to Publicity. One issue the *Roberson* court found troubling was the distinction between public and private individuals. For politicians and celebrities, who seek out publicity, claims of damages based on mental anguish from unwanted attention would be inconsistent with their *intentional* forays onto the public stage. Courts consistently have balked at the notion that people who seek public attention could claim a mental harm based on public exposure.

While courts are not likely to award public persons damages for mental harm in appropriation cases, they have recognized a property-like right when the name or likeness of a celebrity or other public person is used for financial gain without authorization. In some states, this right to publicity can be bartered and inherited. The Georgia Supreme Court blocked the unauthorized sale of plastic models of the Rev. Martin Luther King Jr., holding that the slain civil rights leader's publicity rights could be inherited even if they were not exercised during his lifetime.[124] Similarly, two circuits of the U.S. Court of Appeals have held that Elvis Presley's right of publicity could be exploited exclusively by his heirs.[125]

Most commercial appropriation cases involve advertising or related enterprises, where the defendant has attempted to capitalize on a celebrity's name and identity. For example, an enterprising portable toilet business borrowed the phrase "Here's Johnny," Ed McMahon's nightly introduction from *The Tonight Show With Johnny Carson*, to advertise its product. To capitalize on the link, the firm also advertised itself as "The World's Foremost Commodian." Even though neither his complete name nor likeness was used, Carson won his appropriation claim.[126]

In 2005, a California jury awarded Russell Christoff $15.6 million against Nestle USA for its use of his photograph to advertise Tasters Choice coffee.[127] Christoff had appeared in the company's training videos and been paid, years earlier, a small sum, but he had not signed a release covering the use of his likeness in advertising or on the label of the coffee. He did not even know his likeness was being used until he happened upon a can of the coffee in a drug store. The award amounted to 5 percent of the defendant's profits on the coffee from 1997 to 2003. An intermediate appellate court reversed the verdict on procedural grounds,[128] but the California Supreme Court remanded the case to the trial court to decide if the multiple uses of the likeness over those years amounted to a single publica-

[121] 64 N.E. 442, 556 (N.Y. 1902).

[122] N.Y. Civ. Rights Law §§ 50-51 (McKinney 1992).

[123] 122 Ga. 190 (1905).

[124] Martin Luther King Jr., Ctr. for Soc. Change v. American Heritage Prod., Inc., 296 S.E.2d 697 (Ga. 1982).

[125] *See* Factors, Inc., v. Pro Arts, Inc., 4 Media L. Rep. (BNA) 1144 (2d Cir. 1978); Elvis Presley Enter. v. Elvis Tours, 14 Media L. Rep. (BNA) 1053 (6th Cir. 1987).

[126] Carson v. Here's Johnny Portable Toilets, Inc., 698 F.2d 831 (6th Cir. 1983).

[127] *See* Kevin Fagan, *Teacher in Antioch Wins $15.6 Million From '86 Photo Shoot*, San Francisco Chron., Feb. 2, 2005, at A2.

[128] Christoff v. Nestle USA, Inc., 152 Cal. App. 4th 1439 (Cal. App. 2d Dist. 2007).

tion that might bar Christoff's claims under that state's two-year statute of limitations.[129]

The use of celebrity look-alikes and sound-alikes is common practice in advertising and sometimes results in appropriation lawsuits. A jury awarded singer Bette Midler $400,000 after Ford Motor Co. ran ads in which a singer imitated Midler's distinctive style and voice, an award upheld by the Ninth U.S. Circuit Court of Appeals, an influential authority on celebrity matters. It concluded that "to impersonate her voice is to pirate her identity."[130] A few years later, the Ninth Circuit upheld a $2.5 million judgment for singer Tom Waits, whose raspy voice was imitated in an advertisement for Frito-Lay corn chips. The court held that Waits had a property right "to control the use of his identity as embodied in his voice."[131] It also upheld a portion of the damage award based on mental distress.

Wheel of Fortune letter-turner Vanna White successfully sued an electronics firm for unauthorized use of her likeness. In an advertisement by Samsung Electronics, a well-dressed robot wore a white wig and turned letters on a giant video board. The Ninth Circuit agreed that Samsung had taken White's identity, observing that the identities of stars "are not only the most attractive for advertisers, but the easiest to evoke without resorting to obvious means such as name or likeness or voice."[132]

Among the more interesting and cutting-edge legal battles over publicity rights is Samuel Keller's claim against Electronic Arts, Inc., for its videogames using virtual players who are nearly identical in all but exact facial features to their real-life counterparts. Keller was a quarterback for Arizona State University and the University of Nebraska. In 2010, a federal district court dismissed the NCAA from the case but allowed the case to proceed under California law against Electronic Arts.[133]

As the Keller and similar cases have begun working their way through various courts, many in the sports entertainment world have speculated the stakes could top $1 billion.[134] This speculation gained ground in 2013 as two federal appellate courts rejected the arguments of the video game developer (Electronic Arts) that it had a First Amendment defense against the privacy claims filed by the players.[135] Both courts held that the developer had failed to transform sufficiently each player's identity or likeness in creating the games.

It is not a violation of publicity for a publication to use an individual's name or likeness in reporting news or to promote news content. In *Namath v. Sports Illustrated*, for example, the Supreme Court of New York County held that use of photos of former football star Joe Namath was permissible in promotional ads to establish the news content of *Sports Illustrated*.[136] The Ninth U.S. Circuit Court of Appeals reached a different result when the use of a celebrity's name and photo suggested she endorsed the publication. Actor-singer Cher sued for misappropriation after an interview she granted one publication was sold to another magazine, which used her name and photo for its own advertising. The court upheld a judgment, finding that the advertising implied that Cher endorsed the publication.[137]

A key consideration for courts in these cases is whether the so-called news article is actually incidental to the use of the celebrity's photographs (that is, a mere excuse to publish valuable or embarrassing photographs to obtain a commercial advantage) or whether the photographs are incidental to an article of actual news value.[138]

In the only appropriation case it has decided, the Supreme Court held that the news exemption did not apply in the case of a performer, the "Human Cannonball," who earned his living being shot from a cannon. Hugo Zacchini's entire performance from cannon to net lasted fifteen seconds. When a TV station broadcast his entire act on a news program, he sued for appropriation and won. The Supreme Court refused to block a jury trial on the $25,000 damage claim despite the program's newsworthiness because broadcasting the "entire act poses a substantial threat to the economic value of that performance."[139]

The use of names and likenesses also can pose problems in literary works, films, television and other forms of communication. Obtaining consent or permission is an important defense. In the popular 1997 film *Men in Black*, a spoof on the theory that space aliens reside among us, a television monitor tracks aliens who, disguised as humans, have become celebrities. To avoid legal problems, director Barry Sonnenfeld said, he obtained permission from Dionne Warwick, Danny DeVito, Sylvester Stallone, Newt Gingrich and other celebrities to use their likenesses.[140] Actress Brooke Shields learned belatedly about consent when she tried to prevent publication of nude photographs taken when she was ten years old. Her mother had signed a standard consent agreement that gave the photographer complete control to use or sell the images.[141] Baseball star Orlando Cepeda also learned the hard way that a person's

[129] Christoff v. Nestle USA, Inc., 47 Cal. 4th 468 (Cal. 2009).

[130] Midler v. Ford Motor Co., 849 F.2d 460, 463 (9th Cir. 1988).

[131] Waits v. Frito-Lay, Inc., 978 F.2d 1093, 1100 (9th Cir. 1992).

[132] White v. Samsung Elec. of America, Inc., 971 F.2d 1395, 1399 (9th Cir. 1992).

[133] Keller v. Elec. Arts, Inc., 2010 U.S. Dist. LEXIS 10719 (N.D. Cal. Feb. 8, 2010) (No. C 09-1967 CW).

[134] *See* Darren Rovell, *Electronic Arts Could Lose $1B to NCAA Athletes*, USA TODAY, Aug. 3, 2011, *available at* http://www.usatoday/tech/news/2011-08-02-ncaa-lawsuit-electronic-arts_n.htm.

[135] Hart v. Elec. Arts, Inc., 717 F.3d 141 (3d Cir. 2013); Keller v. Elec. Arts, Inc., 724 F.3d 1268 (9th Cir. 2013).

[136] 363 N.Y.2d 276 (N.Y. Co. Sup. Ct. 1975).

[137] Cher v. Forum Int'l, 692 F.2d 634 (9th Cir. 1982).

[138] Toffoloni v. LFP Publ'g Group, 572 F.3d 1201 (11th cir. 2009).

[139] Zacchini v. Scripps Howard Broad., 433 U.S. 562, 575 (1977).

[140] *See Invasion of the Body Snatchers*, MIAMI HERALD, July 12, 1997, at 2A.

[141] Shields v. Gross, 448 N.E.2d 108 (N.Y. 1983).

identity can be contracted away. He sued Swift & Co. to stop its use of his name and picture, only to discover he had signed a licensing contract lending his name to the meat company.[142]

Most problems are avoided by the use of signed releases or consent forms, but lawsuits still occur. The 2006 documentary-spoof, *Borat: Cultural Learnings of America for Make Benefit Glorious Nation of Kazakhstan*, also spawned several lawsuits, often based on privacy claims though the producers said all people who appeared in the film signed releases.[143]

Definition of Commercial. The potential breadth and definition of what is or is not a commercial use became a hotly contested issue in Florida following the release, in 2000, of the film *The Perfect Storm*. Not only did the surviving family members of the fishermen killed during the storm claim a false light invasion of privacy, they also argued that Warner Brothers' dramatization of the events involving the storm and the crew of the Andrea Gail violated Florida's commercial misappropriation statute.[144] They argued that the film amounted to a commercial use of their deceased family members' names and likenesses without consent. The court of appeals dismissed the false-light privacy claim but certified to the Florida Supreme Court the question regarding the meaning of Florida's commercial misappropriation law. Arguments were heard in 2004.[145] In 2005, the Florida Supreme Court answered that the commercial purpose contemplated by that state's misappropriation statute did not apply because the film did not directly promote a product or service.[146] The case underscored the potential breadth and impact of some states' commercial misappropriation laws.

INTENTIONAL INFLICTION OF EMOTIONAL DISTRESS

The wide berth the First Amendment affords professional communicators makes it difficult for people who feel harmed by the media to succeed in court. Libel law, discussed in Chapter 6, requires plaintiffs to prove not only that information is false, but also that the publishers of alleged defamations were at fault — that publication resulted from either negligent or reckless practices or with outright knowledge of falsehood. False light invasion of privacy typically imposes similar burdens on plaintiffs, and plaintiffs under the embarrassing private facts tort have little chance of recovering damages when involved in matters of

public concern. As a result, lawyers sometimes file other kinds of legal actions, often in tandem with libel or privacy suits, based on general legal doctrines that have largely developed outside the umbrella of First Amendment protections.

One such end-run approach is the tort of intentional infliction of emotional distress, based on something akin to the common law doctrine of malice or ill will.[147] It allows recovery of damages for severe emotional harm or deliberate or reckless conduct that is deemed outrageous and extreme,[148] a judgment normally determined by the sensibilities of the jury.

The leading media case on intentional infliction of emotional distress unfolded in the 1980s after a dispute between pornography mogul Larry Flynt, publisher of *Hustler* magazine, and the Rev. Jerry Falwell, a prominent Virginia-based TV evangelist. The case was the subject of the movie *The People v. Larry Flynt*. Falwell sued Flynt and *Hustler* for libel, invasion of privacy and intentional infliction of emotional distress after the magazine ran a crude take-off of "The first time ..." advertising campaign of Campari Liqueur. The campaign focused on celebrities who recalled their first experiences imbibing the upscale liqueur. Double-entendre in the interviews gave readers the impression — until the end of the ads — that the celebrities were discussing their first sexual experiences. *Hustler* cast Falwell in one of the "first-time" interviews, reporting that his first sexual encounter was with his mother in an outhouse.

Hustler published a disclaimer stating that the page was an advertising parody "not to be taken seriously." The Roanoke, Virginia, jury found in favor of *Hustler* on the libel claim, holding that no reasonable person would believe the parody to be true. The judge dismissed the privacy claim, because only appropriation is recognized as an invasion of privacy action in Virginia, and Falwell's identity had not been appropriated for commercial purposes. But the jury awarded Falwell $200,000 on the emotional distress claim. The U.S. Court of Appeals for the Fourth Circuit upheld the judgment, reasoning that the actual malice standard for public figures in libel cases did not apply to emotional distress.[149] Flynt appealed to the Supreme Court.

The Supreme Court unanimously overturned the lower courts. Citing journalism's long history of caricature in American society and politics, Chief Justice Rehnquist reasoned that allowing public figures to collect damages without proving actual malice would unconstitutionally chill social and political discourse. He noted that the essence of political cartooning often focused on "unfortunate physical traits or politically embarrassing events — an exploration often calculated to injure the feelings of the subject of the portrayal. The art of the cartoonist

[142] Cepeda v. Swift & Co., 415 F.2d 1205 (8th Cir. 1969).

[143] *See* Robert Welkos, *Caution: Sign Now, Sigh Later*, L.A. TIMES, Nov. 20, 2006, at E1.

[144] Tyne v. Time Warner Entm't Co., 336 F.3d 1286 (11th Cir. 2003); FLA. STAT., ch. 540.08 (1998).

[145] *See* Mike Caputo, *Supreme Court: Films' Take on Captain Stirs a Tempest*, MIAMI HERALD, Feb. 5, 2004, at 6B.

[146] Tyne v. Time Warner Entm't Co., 901 So. 2d 802 (Fla. 2005).

[147] *See* William Prosser, *Intentional Infliction of Mental Suffering: A New Tort*, 27 MICH. L. REV. 874 (1939).

[148] *See* RESTATEMENT (SECOND) OF TORTS § 46 comment d (1977).

[149] Hustler Magazine v. Falwell, 797 F.2d 1270 (4th Cir. 1986).

is often not reasoned or evenhanded, but slashing and one-sided." The outrageousness requirement, he noted, was subjective and "would allow a jury to impose liability on the basis of the jurors' tastes or views, or perhaps on the basis of their dislike of a particular expression." To prevail, Rehnquist said, public figures and officials must prove that the communication was false and published with actual malice.[150]

Private individuals fare better in emotional distress cases. Consider again the case of the tabloid newspaper *Sun*, which lost an emotional distress suit in Arkansas after it published the fabricated story about the 101-year-old woman who became pregnant. To illustrate the story, the *Sun* used a photo of a 97-year-old Arkansas woman from its files, believing she had died. Among other things, the jury found the *Sun* guilty of intentional infliction of emotional distress and awarded hefty damages.[151]

Courts typically will not allow plaintiffs to use emotional distress claims to evade the defenses applicable to defamation claims, particularly if the distress claim merely recasts a defamation claim.[152] The Supreme Court confirmed this rule in a case involving the controversial Westboro Baptist Church of Topeka, Kansas, and its anti-gay protests and pickets at the funerals of U.S. soldiers killed in Iraq and Afghanistan. In 2009, a U.S. court of appeals reversed, on free speech grounds, a jury verdict in favor of the father of one fallen soldier and his claims for invasion of privacy and intentional infliction of emotional distress.[153] The Supreme Court affirmed in 2011.[154] As in the *Hustler* case, it held that the speech in question plainly related to matters of public, rather than private, concern, even if the context of the speech (the funeral, for example) was particularly hurtful to the family of the soldier. Consequently, the state could apply reasonable time, place or manner regulations[155] but could not under the First Amendment prohibit or punish the picketers on the basis of the content of the speech, even if the jury deemed the setting outrageous.[156]

A variant of intentional infliction of emotional distress is the tort of outrage, which focuses exclusively on the behavior of the

defendant.[157] For example, in 1988, personnel from a Florida TV station went to a local police department after officials disclosed that skeletal remains found a year earlier were those of a 6-year-old boy reported missing three years before. A police officer removed the child's skull from a drawer in a laboratory. Images of the skull were broadcast as part of a report on crime. After the boy's family watched a newscast showing a dramatic close-up of the skull, they filed an invasion of privacy and outrage lawsuit. Trial testimony centered on callous comments made during the TV station's newsroom debate over whether to air the close-up footage. A Florida appellate court rejected the privacy claim but held that the newscast easily surpassed the outrageousness requirement. In a caustic rebuke of the decision to broadcast the close-up, the court said that if this case "did not constitute the tort of outrage, then there is no such tort."[158]

Plaintiffs also have received damages in some jurisdictions for negligent infliction of emotional distress, which occurs when media behavior exposes individuals to dangers that the media should have reasonably foreseen. For example, a California court held a radio station responsible after a young driver was killed trying to keep up with a disc jockey who traveled about awarding prizes. It said that the accident was a foreseeable consequence of the promotion, which encouraged prize-seekers to rush from place to place.[159] Other courts, however, have been unwilling to hold the media accountable for unforeseeable or speculative consequences, such as copy-cat behavior.[160]

CONSTITUTIONAL AND STATUTORY PRIVACY

The privacy torts do not present the only reasons for special caution when gathering and disseminating information. Constitutional concerns and privacy statutes, which place limits *on government*, have implications for journalists seeking information under government control. Limits on how government uses personal information indirectly affect journalists. And such limits on government use of private information — in this information-soaked era with its headlines about government and private enterprise abuses — are politically attractive to politicians and other policy-makers and records custodians.

Constitutional privacy may prove indirectly relevant to news-

---

[150] Hustler Magazine v. Falwell, 485 U.S. 46, 55-56 (1988).

[151] Peoples Bank & Trust v. Globe Int'l Publ'g, Inc., 20 Media L. Rptr. (BNA) 2097 (1992).

[152] *See, e.g.,* Yohe v. Nugent, 321 F.3d 35 (1st Cir. 2003).

[153] Snyder v. Phelps, 580 F.3d 206 (4th Cir. 2009).

[154] Snyder v. Phelps, 131 S.Ct. 1207 (2011).

[155] For an interesting examination of such regulations, *see* Phelps-Roper v. Koster, 713 F.3d 942 (8th Cir. 2013) (holding state had a significant interest in protecting privacy of funeral attendees for a brief time and limited area, but striking statute to extent it burdened too much speech by defining covered "funerals" broadly to include processions and other activities).

[156] The Court disposed of the intrusion claim by ruling that the family's reliance on the captive audience doctrine to suggest that while at the funeral they were forced to endure offensive and outrageous speech was misplaced because the picketers remained well away from the memorial service while protesting. 131 S.Ct. at 1219-20.

[157] While not specifically an outrage case, the decision in *Marsh v. County of San Diego*, 680 F.3d 1148 (9th Cir. 2012), is relevant and interesting. The court affirmed summary judgment for the defendants under 42 U.S.C. §1983, but agreed that the protected common law right of non-interference with a family remembrances of a decedent and state law were violated when a former district attorney sent an autopsy photograph of a child to the press.

[158] Armstrong v. H&C Commc'ns, Inc., 575 So. 2d 280, 282 (Fla. Ct. App. 1991).

[159] Weirum v. RKO General, Inc., 539 P.2d 36 (Cal. 1975). *See also* Robert E. Dreschel, *Negligent Infliction of Emotional Distress,* 12 PEPP. L. REV. 889 (1985).

[160] *See* Zamora v. CBS, 480 F. Supp. 199 (S.D. Fla. 1979); Olivia v. NBC, 178 Cal. 888 (Cal. App. 1981).

gathering when individuals use these constitutional arguments to bolster privacy claims against the news media, potentially offsetting the presumption favoring publication of private facts about matters of public concern. Statutory privacy designed to protect individuals from government abuse also provides a rationale – sometimes unwarranted – for withholding information from the public and news media.

Constitutional Privacy

Over time, the Supreme Court has defined a range of constitutional privacy protections. Although the word "privacy" appears nowhere in the Constitution, the Court has nonetheless recognized a right to be free from unreasonable governmental intrusion and eavesdropping. For example:

• Reasoning that freedom from intrusion is based on a "zone of privacy" surrounding a person, not a specific place, the Court ruled unconstitutional a government wiretap on a telephone booth.[161]

• In *NAACP v. Alabama*, the Court struck down an Alabama law that required certain organizations, including civil rights groups, to turn over membership rolls to the state.[162] The Court held the rule violated the associational rights of current and potential members of the NAACP, who might not exercise those rights out of fear of government retaliation.

• In *Griswold v. Connecticut*, a case challenging a state law barring dissemination of birth control information, the Court fashioned a right of decisional privacy based on the rights implied in the "penumbra" of various amendments to the Constitution.[163] The case laid the foundation for the controversial *Roe v. Wade* decision that recognized a woman's right to abortion.[164]

Citing its decisions in *Griswold*, *Roe* and related cases, the Supreme Court, in 2003, returned to constitutional privacy in *Lawrence v. Texas*.[165] By a 6-3 vote, it struck down a state statute that made consensual sodomy between adults of the same sex criminal. Writing for the majority, Justice Anthony Kennedy articulated a rationale based on respect for the private lives and intimate choices of the two Texas men who were arrested while in an apartment:

Liberty protects the person from unwarranted government intrusions into a dwelling or other private places. In our tradition the state is not omnipresent in the home. And there are other spheres of our lives and existence, outside the home, where the state should not be a dominant presence. Freedom

extends beyond spatial bounds. Liberty presumes an autonomy of self that includes freedom of thought, belief, expression, and certain intimate conduct. The instant case involves liberty of the person both in its spatial and more transcendent dimensions.[166]

The decision overruled the Court's contrary 1986 holding in *Bowers v. Hardwick*[167] and prompted a stinging dissent from Justice Antonin Scalia, who, together with Chief Justice Rehnquist and Justice Clarence Thomas, questioned the existence of any fundamental constitutional right to engage in homosexual conduct.[168] Thomas added his own dissent in which he questioned the existence of any general constitutional right of privacy.[169]

Most importantly to media professionals, however, has been the recent willingness of the Supreme Court to recognize a constitutional right of informational privacy – the right of individuals to control information about themselves. Concerns about privacy had been raised in several cases addressing government use of computers to gather, store and disseminate information about private individuals.

In 1976, Justice William Brennan expressed concerns about the effects of new information technologies on privacy. In *United States v. Miller*, the Court held that individuals retained no privacy interest in information voluntarily given to a bank. Cautioned Brennan: "Development of photocopying machines, electronic computers and other sophisticated instruments has accelerated the abilities of government to intrude into areas which a person normally chooses to exclude from prying eyes and inquisitive minds."[170]

A year later, the Court acknowledged a right of informational privacy in upholding a New York state practice of compiling and storing in a computer prescription drug records on individuals. Such a practice did not violate individuals' constitutional right of privacy, Justice John Paul Stevens wrote, so long as strict security was in place to ensure the privacy of the information. He wrote: "We are not unaware of the threat to privacy implicit in the accumulation of vast amounts of personal information in computerized data banks or other massive government files."[171] Justice Brennan, in a concurring opinion, echoed concerns about the threat of computers to privacy, noting prophetically: "The central storage and easy accessibility of computerized data vastly increases the potential for abuse of that information, and I am not prepared to say that future developments will not dem-

---

[161] Katz v. United States, 389 U.S. 347 (1967).

[162] 357 U.S. 449 (1958).

[163] 381 U.S. 479, 484 (1965).

[164] 410 U.S. 113 (1973).

[165] 539 U.S. 558 (2003).

[166] *Id.* at 562.

[167] 478 U.S. 186 (1986).

[168] 539 U.S. at 586 (Scalia, J., dissenting).

[169] *Id.* at 605 (Thomas, J., dissenting).

[170] 425 U.S. 435, 451 (1976).

[171] Whalen v. Roe, 429 U.S. 589, 605 (1977).

onstrate the necessity for some curb on such technology."[172]

In *Department of Justice v. Reporters Committee for Freedom of the Press*, the Supreme Court reacted to a long-standing concern about the threat that computers pose to personal privacy; it articulated the practical obscurity doctrine in response to a news media request for information contained in a government database.[173] In essence, the Court reasoned that computers have obliterated traditional barriers of time and space that once afforded individuals a measure of "practical obscurity" — or distance — from their official past. Because of computers, the Court noted, individuals no longer can move to another place to escape past deeds or count on the passage of time to dim official memories. Following this reasoning, it suggested that information compiled in central government computers — even information gathered from various *public* records — regained a privacy interest when brought together in one place. In fact, the Court reasoned, if the information were indeed *public*, reporters should have no need to see a government database.[174] Under the reasoning of the *Reporters Committee* case, public-record information about individuals can be shielded from disclosure simply because it exists in a computer database.[175]

The constitutional privacy issue is particularly thorny in the context of public employees such as teachers and police and what information about them the governmental employer may collect and use. In 2010, for example, the Supreme Court unanimously held that a California police department could constitutionally audit the text messages, some of which were personal and sexually explicit, on a city-issued pager used by a police sergeant.[176] While the decision did not involve private employers or their employees, it did effectively let public employees know that their electronic communications may not have privacy protections if the devices used are issued by the employer and covered by a clear policy stating that the employer has a right to monitor the messages.

Although issues involving searches and seizures are largely beyond the scope of this chapter, the Supreme Court's decision in 2014, in the cellular telephone search case is worth noting. In *Riley v. California*, the Court unanimously held the police violated a gang member-suspect's Fourth Amendment rights when, incident to an arrest, they seized his smart phone, searched its contents and discovered evidence against him.[177] The decision

suggests, among other things, the Court is very aware of the challenges to privacy that new technology creates.[178]

The Freedom of Information Act

Since the Great Depression, government's appetite for information has grown steadily, hitting full stride with the Great Society programs of the 1960s that coincided with the growth of systems analysis — a management technique that depended on vast amounts of data. To balance governmental need for information, much of it personal, statutes were passed to ensure that government gathered information only for specific purposes and that it be used only for those purposes. One of the first such statutes was the federal Freedom of Information Act, passed in 1966 to ensure maximum access to records of federal executive agencies.[179] While the act espouses openness, it also attempts to balance access with competing values. The result was nine exemptions, several of which raise privacy concerns as grounds for withholding information. (The federal Freedom of Information Act is discussed in Chapter 17.)

Exemption 3 applies to records specifically exempted by other federal statutes. For a statute to qualify under the exemption, it must establish criteria or types of matters for withholding and allow no discretion by agency personnel. Laws governing numerous agencies, including the Internal Revenue Act, which handles personal income tax records, fall into this category. The exemption also covers the Census Bureau, the Consumer Products Safety Commission and the Federal Trade Commission.

Exemption 6, which applies to personnel, medical and similar files, shields information that would "constitute a clearly unwarranted" invasion of privacy. Implicit in this language is the understanding that a balancing process must occur to determine whether withholding is warranted. The "similar files" wording has been applied to a range of information. The State Department invoked the exemption to successfully withhold disclosure of the citizenship status of individuals. In *Department of State v. Washington Post Co.*, the Supreme Court supported use of the exemption and said information need not be highly personal to be covered.[180] Information could be withheld, it said, when disclosure could lead to injury or embarrassment. Additionally, the Court upheld the State Department when it argued that the privacy interests of Haitians whose asylum claims were rejected outweighed the public interest in disclosure.[181]

Privacy claims also were successfully raised by the National

---

[172] *Id.* at 607 (Brennan, J., concurring).

[173] 489 U.S. 749 (1989).

[174] *Id.* at 780.

[175] *See* Bursac v. Souzzi, 37 Media L. Rep. (BNA) 1109 (N.Y. Sup. Ct. 2008) (applying the *Reporter's Committee* reasoning to New York's state public records law and ruling that a county official who posted the plaintiff's photograph on a "wall of shame" Web page following her arrest for driving while intoxicated must remove the posting even though the arrest was a matter of public record).

[176] City of Ontario v. Quon, 560 U.S. 746 (2010).

[177] 134 U.S. 2473 (2014).

[178] Tony Perry & Maura Dolan, *San Diego Gang Member's Case Focus of Supreme Court Privacy Ruling*, L.A. TIMES, June 25, 2014, *available at* http://www.latimes.com/local/la-me-riley-impact-20140626-story.html.

[179] 5 U.S.C. § 552 (1966).

[180] 456 U.S. 595 (1982).

[181] Dep't of State v. Ray, 502 U.S. 164 (1991).

Aeronautics and Space Administration in a bid to prevent disclosure of an audio tape of the last communications from the space shuttle *Challenger*, which exploded after takeoff and killed its seven astronauts, including a high school teacher. In *New York Times Co. v. NASA*, the space agency argued that the release of the audiotape, transcripts of which had already been made public, would only add to the anguish of the victims' families.[182] The *Times* argued that background noises and inflections of the astronauts' voices might yield significant information about the tragedy. A federal court rejected that reasoning and adopted the concept of relational privacy that extended protection to family members.

A state judge cited the *Challenger* ruling in the murder trial of Danny Rolling, convicted of killing five young people near the University of Florida in 1990. At the behest of prosecutors, Circuit Judge Stan Morris limited public access to graphic autopsy and crime scene photos — evidence jurors viewed before imposing Rolling's death sentence. The photos were public records under Florida law. Faced with the prospect of the photos appearing in print and further traumatizing victims' families, the judge ordered that they be bound in folders and made accessible to the public only under court supervision. Under the ruling, copies of photos could not leave the courthouse.[183]

In 1998, concern about publication of autopsy photos led a Miami-Dade County circuit judge to seal autopsy photographs in the sensational murder of fashion designer Gianni Versace, who was gunned down on the steps of his Miami Beach mansion. Such photos, notwithstanding the ruling in the Gainesville murder case, were public records. During a brief hearing, with no lawyers for the news media present, a Versace family lawyer said his clients feared photos might appear on the Internet, as happened with the autopsy photos of Nicole Brown Simpson in the O.J. Simpson murder case. The judge sealed the records.[184]

In 2001, in the wake of the death of stock car driver Dale Earnhardt at the Daytona 500 NASCAR race, concerns about publication of autopsy photos prompted the Florida legislature to amend the state's record law to exempt autopsy photos unless a judge approved special disclosure. Initial controversy focused on the *Orlando Sentinel*'s attempts to have a medical expert view the photos to make an independent determination of the cause of Earnhardt's death. The newspaper, focusing on the issue of auto racing safety, expressed no interest in publishing the photos. The legislation restricts both viewing and copying. Violation of the law is a third-degree felony, allowing up to five years in prison and a $5,000 fine. Lawyers for *The Independent Florida Alligator* at the University of Florida and Web-

sitecity.com, a Florida-based Web site, challenged the exemption as unconstitutional. Websitecity.com previously had published autopsy photos of auto racing fatalities. A circuit judge in Daytona Beach, however, upheld the law.[185] In 2002, a state district court of appeals affirmed the trial court's ruling and stated that the statute exempting photographs was not overbroad because it did not apply to written autopsy reports and because it allowed for release upon a showing of "good cause."[186] In 2003, the Florida Supreme Court declined to hear the case.

Exemption 7 covers disclosure of certain law enforcement records, including disclosures that would invade privacy. In the *Reporters Committee* case, the Court recognized privacy interests in certain compilations of criminal records — even records that were public at their original source. For example, if a record is contained in a central government database, such as an FBI computer, it might be considered private. The same record at a courthouse in the jurisdiction where the crime occurred would be a public record. The court said that since the privacy/access balance typically favors withholding records when they are contained in computer compilations, courts don't need to engage in case-by-case balancing with the public interest in disclosure. The simple determination that a record is in a computer compilation was sufficient to withhold it, the court reasoned.

In 2004, the Supreme Court ruled in *Favish v. Office of Independent Counsel*,[187] a case that directly raised privacy and FOIA issues, including the question of the privacy interests of family members of a deceased person. It grew out of requests for photographs taken during the investigation into the death of Vince Foster, a former deputy counsel in the Clinton White House. In 1993, he was found dead in a park in Washington, D.C. The National Park Service, the FBI, committees of the House and Senate, and the Office of Independent Counsel independently investigated. All concluded that his death was a suicide, but rumors and doubts lingered. The District of Columbia Court of Appeals, in 1999, denied the records request of Accuracy in Media, a media watchdog organization, which had requested the photographs from the National Park Service. Allan Favish, a lawyer who had participated in that litigation, renewed the request in California by serving it upon the Office of Independent Counsel, seeking 150 photographs.

The office released more than 100 photos but withheld several for reasons at first not clearly articulated. Favish later dropped twenty-one photos from his request. Eventually the office relied upon the privacy language of Exemption 7. The district court ruled for Favish on one photo and certain issues regarding the quality of the photos but withheld ten to protect the

---

[182] 782 F. Supp. 628 (D.D.C. 1991).

[183] Florida v. Rolling, 22 Media L. Rep. (BNA) 2264 (Fla. Cir. Ct. 1994).

[184] *See* David Lions, *Judge Seals Versace Autopsy Pictures*, MIAMI HERALD, May 1, 1998, at 2B.

[185] *See* Mike Branom, Associated Press, *Judge Upholds Autopsy Photo Law, Denying Bid by Newspaper, Website*, MIAMI HERALD, June 12, 2001, at 5B.

[186] Campus Commc'n, Inc. v. Earnhardt, 821 So. 2d 388 (Fla. Dist. Ct. App. 2002).

[187] 541 U.S. 157 (2004).

privacy interests of Foster's family. The Ninth Circuit Court of Appeals reversed the district court's ruling and held that, though the privacy interests of the family were a valid consideration, they had to be weighed against the public interest in the investigation. Because the court of appeals did not have the photos in question, the case was remanded to the district court for further analysis and the required balancing of the privacy and access interests. On remand, the district court ordered the release of five photos and withheld, on privacy grounds, the other five. The Ninth Circuit affirmed. In 2004, the Supreme Court reversed the appellate court and held that under the FOIA surviving family members have a right to personal privacy regarding the photographic images of the scene of a close relative's death. The Court said such privacy interests outweighed, under the FOIA, the public's interest in disclosure.

In 2011, in *FCC v. AT&T*, the Court in an 8-0 decision emphatically held that corporations, while protected under the Fourth Amendment from unreasonable searches and seizures, are not shielded under the personal privacy language of Exemption 7 (c) from FOIA requests for documents they provided to government because corporations do not have personal privacy rights and the exemption protects only the privacy of individuals, not businesses.[188]

The Privacy Act of 1974

The Privacy Act was meant to create a "Code of Fair Information Practices" to regulate government agencies. The Senate report on the legislation noted that one purpose of the act was "to promote government respect for the privacy of citizens" by ensuring that executive branch agencies follow certain rules regarding the gathering and disclosing of information.[189] The Privacy Act is most likely to affect requests for information that is not clearly covered by the legislation. In such cases, custodians of records tend to be very cautious because the Privacy Act imposes penalties on custodians who release protected information. Withholding information that should be disclosed, on the other hand, may violate the federal Freedom of Information Act, but that legislation poses no penalties for wrongly withholding information.

Other Privacy Concerns

A number of other federal and state statutes raising privacy concerns can erect barriers to information gathered and kept by government and, in some cases, private institutions. A few key examples are discussed below.

Driver's Privacy Protection Act. Driver's license records have long been a source of useful information for journalists, more so in recent years with the growth of computer-assisted reporting. In 1991, for example, the *Miami Herald* used a computer analysis of state Division of Motor Vehicle records to show that many drunken drivers were being put back on the road. In 1997, however, federal legislation began limiting access to such records. The law, passed in 1994, was partly in response to the slaying of California actress Rebecca Schaeffer by a fan who located her address through driver records obtained through a private investigator. The intent of the law is to inhibit stalkers and anyone else who might harm an individual after linking a name with an address.[190] The federal legislation contains a provision that allows states to disclose such information if they enact a provision notifying drivers that they have an option to withhold personal information.

Several states challenged the law, arguing that Congress had overstepped its authority in attempting to regulate a state practice. The Seventh and Tenth Circuits of the U.S. Court of Appeals upheld the law. The Fourth Circuit, however, sided with South Carolina, which argued the law was unconstitutional because state driver's license information constituted internal state activity and lay beyond the scope of congressional jurisdiction.[191] The Supreme Court, in *Condon v. Reno*, reversed the Fourth Circuit.[192] The unanimous opinion by Chief Justice Rehnquist held that the release or sale of drivers' license information constituted interstate commerce, thereby giving Congress regulatory authority.

In 2015, a federal appellate court upheld the law's prohibition of access to and publication of unlawfully obtained driver's license information about police officers in a controversial case involving the *Chicago Sun-Times* and its investigation into a homicide investigation involving those officers.[193]

The Buckley Amendment. Enacted as the Family Educational Rights and Privacy Act, the Buckley Amendment requires educational institutions receiving federal money to keep certain student records private. Directory information such as names, addresses and majors is not covered. Academic records, including non-criminal disciplinary records, are. Before 1992, the Department of Education was advising institutions that campus crime records should be considered student disciplinary records under the Buckley Amendment — a position that was frustrating many media organizations, most notably campus newspapers. A 1992 amendment, however, specifically states that crime reports are not educational records and cannot be withheld as

---

[188] FCC v. AT&T, 562 U.S. 397 (2011).

[189] 5 U.S.C. § 552a (1974).

[190] Driver's Privacy Protection Act of 1994, 18 U.S.C.S. § 2721 (1994).

[191] Condon v. Reno, 155 F.3d 453 (4th Cir. 1998).

[192] 528 U.S. 141 (2000).

[193] Dahlstrom v. Sun-Times Media, 777 F.3d 937 (7th Cir. 2015).

disciplinary records.[194]

Rape Shield Laws. Whether to publish the name of a rape victim is a controversial topic, both legally and ethically. Rape shield laws were designed to encourage victims to come forward by preventing the additional trauma of publicity. Some courts have upheld such laws.[195] In Florida, however, the state supreme court, in 1994, upheld a ruling that the state's law was unconstitutional in a case spawned by the William Kennedy Smith rape trial.[196] The court relied heavily on *Florida Star v. B.J.F.*, which held the news media should not be punished for publishing truthful, lawfully obtained information about matters of public concern absent a state interest of the highest order.[197] The Georgia Supreme Court, also citing *Florida Star*, overturned a verdict against a state newspaper in a civil case based on disclosure of the name of a sexual assault victim.[198]

Juror Shield Laws. Much has been said and written about protecting jurors' privacy, particularly since the Rodney King police brutality trial and the O.J. Simpson murder trial. Since the Supreme Court's ruling in *Press-Enterprise v. Superior Court,*[199] jurors' selection and identity have been presumptively public matters. But after the King and Simpson cases, and the Timothy McVeigh trial in the Oklahoma City bombing, the tide appears to be changing. Citing privacy, judges appear to be routinely impaneling anonymous juries, a practice once reserved for the trials of organized crime kingpins when juror safety was a factor.[200] Texas is the one state that has passed a law allowing anonymous juries. The law creates a presumption that juries will be anonymous in all criminal trials. Robert Dawson, a University of Texas criminal law professor, believes the 1993 statute was responsible for the growing number of private juries: "Before, a judge would have to go out on a limb to justify such a ruling. Now, he doesn't have to."[201] Jane Kirtley, former executive director of the Reporters Committee for Freedom of the Press, says the concept of juror privacy "has become almost epidemic." It is not a question of "media access or exploitation," she says. "It's the notion of public oversight of the system."[202]

Computer Privacy. Journalists depend increasingly on information contained in computer databases and from other computer-based sources, such as the World Wide Web and Internet. Indeed, going online is allowing journalists greater speed and access to more information. Many significant news stories are based on an analysis of government databases. Most laws dealing with computer privacy are designed to place limits on government. The Computer Matching and Privacy Act of 1988, for example, limits the ability of government to routinely cross-reference information in various government databases.[203] The Electronic Communications Privacy Act of 1986 made the interception of computer communications a crime,[204] and the Computer Crime Act of 1986 made it unlawful to access or disclose certain records in computer form.[205] Many of the laws, reflecting some of the constitutional and statutory concerns discussed previously, treat computerized information as more threatening to privacy than similar information in paper files. Such laws can be vague or over-inclusive in ways that inhibit legitimate journalists.

The computer/privacy debate also has begun to focus on private-sector information practices. One survey of Internet users found that 55 percent favored privacy limitations.[206] In 1997, the Federal Trade Commission held four days of hearings that suggested support for the self-regulation of privacy in computer communications. In 2000, after conducting a series of Web site surveys, the FTC abandoned its long-standing policy supporting self-regulation. Instead, it announced support for federal legislation to protect online consumers, much to the dismay of the Online Privacy Alliance, an informal industry coalition that included some of the biggest online companies. FTC officials recommended that Congress establish "Basic standards of practice for the collection of information online."[207] More recent controversies have focused on the search information, email and personal identifiers retained by companies such as Google (including YouTube) and various cellular telephone providers.[208]

In 2014, the Pew Research Center published a new study that indicated most people are generally not worried about the collection of their search information and receipt of targeted advertising if that's the price for getting certain online services at no cost, though many also indicated some concerns about tracking geographic locations through mobile devices.[209]

---

[194] 20 U.S.C.S. § 1232g(a)(4)(B)(ii) (1995).

[195] *See, e.g.,* Nappier v. Jefferson Standard Life Ins. Co., 322 F.2d 502 (4th Cir. 1963).

[196] Florida v. Globe Commc'n Corp., 648 So. 2d 110 (Fla. 1994).

[197] 491 U.S. 524 (1989).

[198] Macon Tel. Publ'g Co. v. Tatum, 436 S.E.2d 655 (Ga. 1993).

[199] 464 U.S. 501 (1984).

[200] *See* Tony Mauro, *Trend to Press Restriction Escalates in Denver*, FIRST AMENDMENT NEWS, May 1997, at 1.

[201] Wendy Benjaminson, *Shroud of Secrecy Increasingly Veils Trials in Texas*, HOUSTON CHRON., Mar. 13, 1994, at 1.

[202] Mauro, *supra* note 200, at 6.

[203] 5 U.S.C. § 552a (1988).

[204] 18 U.S.C. § 2510 (1986).

[205] 18 U.S.C. § 1030 (1986).

[206] *See* Dan Harrison, *Computer Users Back Net Privacy Law*, DM NEWS, June 16, 1997, at 3.

[207] Deborah Branscum, *Guarding Online Privacy*, NEWSWEEK, June 5, 2000, at 77.

[208] An excellent resource on such matters can be found at http://www.eff.org, the Web site of the Electronic Frontier Foundation.

[209] Rick Edmonds, *New Pew Study Finds Most People OK Trading Privacy for Valued Digital Services*, POYNTER.ORG, Dec. 18, 2014, http://www.poynter.org/news/ mediawire/309055/new-pew-study-finds-most-people-ok-trading-privacy-for-valued-digital

A growing privacy concern involves the posting of diary entries and other information by individuals on online social networking sites such as Facebook and LinkedIn.[210] Many students and others have found that once information is posted and widely shared, the expectation of privacy lessens. Employers, government agencies and others have used these sites to gather information about individuals. In 2007, Facebook triggered substantial public criticism with its Beacon advertising program that transmitted users' online purchasing information to their friends on the social network. Facebook ultimately changed the program, added an opt-out feature, and apologized to its users.[211] Of course, these issues with Facebook, Twitter and other social media sites as well as search engines continue to arise here and elsewhere in the world as the technology changes.[212]

Social media sites, search engines, business interests and individual consumers have increasing engaged in online conduct that may erode or at least alter societal expectations and norms regarding personal privacy. Facebook's various privacy policies and controversies, Google's Buzz and retention of search histories and user information, cell phone tracking capabilities, and even cable companies and other companies that can read, block or track certain types of messages all stand to change traditional notions about what is private and what is not.[213]

In 2012, Facebook entered into a $9.5 million settlement with a class of its members who had sued over the site's Beacon program (started in 2007) that effectively gathered and disseminated information about Facebook members' online activities without their consent.[214] In addition to the payment, which went to attorney's fees and to set up a new foundation dedicated to user education and protection of online identities, Facebook agreed to end the Beacon program.

The conflict over what privacy rules or laws apply to the online collection of personal information by commercial sites is likely to continue as new government agencies enter this arena and as more people look for ways to control their own data.[215]

In a reminder that the world is shrinking, Google, in 2014, hit the so-called "right to be forgotten" wall in Europe when the European Court of Justice ruled that it must comply with local law on such a right and thus will have to remove, after a process, certain items from its search results.[216] The results are potentially dramatic not only for the giant search engine's business model, but for fundamental notions of public access to information as well, showing once again that on privacy matters Europe and the United States are two related, but very different legal worlds.[217]

Health Insurance Privacy. The privacy rules under the Health Insurance Portability and Accountability Act of 1996[218] took effect in 2003. They do not directly apply to the media,[219] but they do affect many businesses, including hospitals. They probably are more likely to refuse to release information about patients or even to confirm that an accident victim has been admitted. In addition, the law may influence the tone and direction of future privacy legislation.

The HIPAA rules limit the use and disclosure of individuals' health information by doctors, hospitals, health-care clearinghouses, insurance plans, their business associates and many employers who provide health care or coverage. For example, employers may not use the information to make personnel decisions, and any covered entity may only disclose the information for purposes related to treatment, payment and health care operations, unless the individual has provided a clear, voluntary authorization permitting disclosure. The rules also require that each covered business adopt privacy procedures and train a designated privacy official to assure compliance.

-services/.

[210] See, e.g., Moreno v. Hanford Sentinel, Inc. 172 Cal. App. 4th 1125 (Cal. Ct. App. 2009). See also Sam Terilli, The Internet: Privacy Matters, MIAMI HERALD, June 29, 2006, at 27A.

[211] See Louise Story, Apologetic Facebook Changes Ad Program, N.Y. TIMES, Dec. 6, 2007, at C4.

[212] See, e.g., Miguel Helft & Jenna Wortham, Facebook Bows to Pressure Over Privacy, N.Y. TIMES, May 26, 2010, available at http://www.nytimes.com/2010/05/27/technology/27facebook.html?scp=5&sq=facebook+privacy+helft&st=nyt; Claire Cane Miller & Ravi Sumaiya, Free Speech on Twitter Faces a Test, N.Y TIMES, May 22, 2011, available at http://www.nytimes.com/2011/05/23/techno logy/23twitter.html?_r =1&scp=13&sq=privacy+press&st=nyt; Brad Stone, Twitter Settle F.T.C. Privacy Case, June 24, 2010, N.Y. TIMES, available at http://www.nytimes.com/2010/06/25/technol ogy /25twitter.html?scp=1&sq=twitter+stone+privacy&st=nyt.

[213] See, e.g., Deepa Fernandes, The FCC Will Let It Be, NATION, May 24, 2010, at 5; Michael Isikoff, The Snitch in Your Pocket, NEWSWEEK, Mar. 1, 2010, at 40; Daniel Lyons, The High Price of Facebook, NEWSWEEK, May 24, 2010, at 22; Daniel Lyons, Google's Orwell Moment, NEWSWEEK, Mar. 1, 2010, at 20; Ari Melber, About Facebook, NATION, Jan. 7, 2008, at 22; Lisa Miller, R.I.P. on Facebook, NEWSWEEK, Mar. 1, 2010, at 21; Brad Stone, Google Says it Collected Private Data by Mistake, N.Y. TIMES, May 15, 2010, at B1.

[214] Lane v. Facebook, Inc., 696 F.3d 811 (9th Cir. 2012).

[215] Editorial: Protecting the Privacy of Internet Users, N.Y. TIMES, Mar. 21, 2016, at 20A; Cecilia Kang, FCC Proposes Privacy Rules for Internet Service Providers, N.Y. TIMES, Mar. 11, 2016, at 1B; Natasha Singer & Jeremy Merrill, When a Company is Put Up For Sale, in Many Cases, Your Personal Data Is, Too, N.Y. TIMES, June 29, 2015, at 1B.

[216] Andrew Orlowski, Europe's Shock Google Privacy Ruling: The End of History? Don't be Daft, REGISTER, May 14, 2014, available at http://www.theregister.co.uk/2014/05/14/google_eu_ruling/; David Streitfeld, European Court Lets Users Erase Records on Web, N.Y. TIMES, May 13, 2014, available at http://www.nytimes.com/2014/05/14/technology/google-should-erase-web-links-to-some-personal-data-europes-highest-court-says.html; L. Essers, Google to Tour Europe to Discuss Right-To-Be-Forgotten Ruling, COMPUTERWORLD, July 11, 2014, available at http://www.computerworld.com/s/article/9249674/Google_to_tour_Europe_to_discuss_right_to_be_forgotten_ruling?taxonomyId=14.

[217] Mark Scott, European Tech Companies Play Up Privacy to Challenge Bigger American Rivals, N.Y. TIMES, June 11, 2015, at 9B; Mark Scott, Deal Struck to Balance U.S.-Europe Data Fears, N.Y. TIMES, Feb 3, 2016, at 1B; Mark Scott, Google Takes New Steps to Comply with European Privacy Ruling, N.Y. TIMES, Feb. 12. 2016, at 3B.

[218] 42 U.S.C.A. § 1320d-4 (1996).

[219] See, e.g., Cordero v. NYP Holdings, Inc., 36 Media L. Rep. (BNA) 2269 (N.Y. Sup. Ct. 2008).

The rules do not provide for private lawsuits seeking enforcement but do provide for investigations by the Department of Health and Human Services, which can then seek civil and criminal penalties for violations. Examples of exceptions allowing disclosure, even without authorization by individuals, include public health investigations, law enforcement, emergencies and national security; but there is no exception for any reports to journalists — even for the release of limited information concerning admission and discharge dates of patients.

The law and its consequences took on new importance with the 2014 reporting on the Ebola story, causing journalists to attempt to balance patient privacy with needed reports to the public.[220] Hospitals were typically advised that they could release general information without patient names in an effort to keep people informed about possible risks of exposure.

A recurring problem with HIPAA has been the level of misunderstanding of the law by health care providers that fear claims over disclosures and therefore err on the side withholding too much information — even from close family members of patients.[221] If family members experience these problems, journalists are certain to fare even worse.

Privacy After September 11, 2001

The terrorist attacks that took place on September 11, 2001, have had a far-reaching impact on society, laws and notions of privacy. These matters are still evolving. Interestingly, some government officials responsible for security matters have recently argued that privacy can no longer be equated with anonymity in terms of personal information and private communications.[222] They contend that government must have greater access, particularly to certain telecommunications and financial information, to guard against terrorist and criminal acts and that the focus of privacy advocates should be on the creation of legal safeguards limiting the permissible uses of that information by government.

The USA PATRIOT Act increased federal authority in a number of ways. It relaxed restrictions on the sharing of information between domestic law enforcement agencies and intelligence agencies, enhanced the government's subpoena power to obtain and inspect email records of suspected terrorists, expanded bank record-keeping requirements to track transactions and money laundering, and permitted roving wiretaps of suspected terrorists. More than 300 pages long, the law received virtually no debate or congressional oversight before its passage. The sense of urgency and fear following the attacks and the fact that the law included a provision for its sunset in five years facilitated its quick enactment.

Not long after his reelection in 2004, President George W. Bush began urging renewal of expiring PATRIOT Act provisions as well as expansion of certain powers of government to obtain records without judicial approval.[223] After months of negotiations with Congress and amid media reports of secret government wiretapping of international telephone calls,[224] a compromise was reached in 2006. The act was renewed with a few modifications limiting some government powers to obtain routine library records and providing people served with terrorism-related subpoenas the right to challenge the nondisclosure and gag order requirements of the subpoenas. The renewal, though, made permanent most of the PATRIOT Act's provisions.[225]

In 2008, President Bush and Congress squared off and then compromised regarding a major expansion of government's power to conduct surveillance, including a significant revision of the thirty-year-old Foreign Intelligence Surveillance Act and its rules governing the liability of telecommunications companies that facilitated secret and possibly illegal government wiretaps after the 2001 terrorist attacks.[226] As part of the compromise, Congress included in the new law immunity for the telecommunications companies that had cooperated with the government in conducting warrantless wiretaps, a hotly contested issue that led to prompt but unsuccessful legal challenges.[227] In 2011, President Obama signed a four-year extension of the PATRIOT Act as previously amended.[228] But in 2015 the law and the practice of collecting in bulk data about the telecommunications of Americans hit a legislative and judicial snag as key provisions of the act were challenged and then expired for lack of a legislative deal on revisions and an extension — setting the stage for

---

[220] *See* Al Tompkins, *Journalists Struggle to Balance Reporting on Ebola With HIPAA*, POYNTER.ORG, Oct. 17, 2014, *available at* http://www.poynter.org/news/mediawire/275445/journalists-struggle-to-balance-reporting-on-ebola-with-hipaa/.

[221] *See* Jane Gross, *Keeping Patients' Details Private, Even from Kin*, N.Y. TIMES, July 7, 2007, at A12.

[222] *See, e.g.,* Associated Press, *Official: Private Not Synonymous With Anonymous*, USA TODAY, Nov. 11, 2007, *available at* http://usatoday.com/tech/news/surveillance/2007-11-11-privacy_N.htm?csp=34; James Risen & Eric Lichtblau, *Control of Cybersecurity Becomes Divisive Issue*, N.Y. TIMES, Apr. 17, 2009, at 18A.

[223] *See* Eric Lichtblau, *Plan Would Broaden FBI's Terror Role*, N.Y. TIMES, May 18, 2005, at A19; Editorial, *Patriot Act Redux, and in the Dark*, N.Y. TIMES, June 1, 2005, at A20.

[224] *See* Charles Babington, *White House Working to Avoid Wiretap Probe; But Some Republicans Say Bush Must be More Open About Eavesdropping Program*, WASH. POST, Feb. 20, 2006, at A08; Bob Deans, *White House Steps up Defense of Surveillance Bush's Wiretap Actions Called Legal Safeguard*, ATLANTA J.-CONSTITUTION, Jan. 20, 2006, at 3A.

[225] *See* Charles Babington, *Congress Votes to Renew Patriot Act, With Changes*, WASH. POST, Mar. 8, 2006, at A3; Steve Chapman, *The Surprising Lessons Offered by the Patriot Act*, BALTIMORE SUN, July 10, 2006, at 11A.

[226] 50 U.S.C. § 36 (1978). *See also* Eric Lichtblau, *Senate Approves Bill to Broaden Wiretap Powers*, N.Y. TIMES, July 10, 2008, at A1.

[227] *See* Eric Lichtblau, *Telecom Companies Want Dismissal of Wiretap Suits*, N.Y. TIMES, June 4, 2009, at 17A.

[228] *See* Charlie Savage, *Senators Say Patriot Act Is Being Misinterpreted*, N.Y. TIMES, May 26, 2011, *available at* http://www.nytimes.com/2011/05/27/us/27patriot.html.

continued debate and negotiations during the coming presidential campaign.[229]

During the coming years, the pressure to invest government with new powers and to use computer technology and the Internet to track and prevent terrorism will continue to be strong. The results may include not only a contraction of the privacy rights of individual, but also a contraction of sources of information available to journalists. The controversies that arose in 2013 and 2014 as a result of Edward Snowden's disclosures of data-mining and related activities by the National Security Agency only made more obvious the potential impact — be it positive or negative — of new technology on what once seemed to be settled notions of privacy.[230] While many continue to debate the exact nature of the NSA's data collection and the impact of the Snowden revelations on national security, there is no doubt that the furor over the NSA will fuel privacy debates, new guidelines and a fresh look at government surveillance.[231]

SUMMARY

Despite assaults on their privacy from various quarters — and perhaps in part because of those assaults — Americans remain strong in their belief in the right to be let alone. Privacy concerns are manifested in constitutions, statutes and common law cases that attempt to balance individual rights with competing values, including the right of the news media to publish and the right of the public to be informed. It is to be expected that the rights of individuals and of a free and vigorous press often will clash. The balance has generally tilted toward the press because of the bedrock principle that a democratic society works best when information flows freely.

Journalistic excesses are not lost on the public, whose declining opinion of journalism has been reflected in some polls. The results of declining confidence can be seen in the outcome of some court cases such as the Food Lion case. Lack of public confidence in the news media also can embolden politicians to pass laws limiting press freedoms in the name of privacy.

FOR ADDITIONAL READING

Coleman, A.D. "Private Lives, Public Places: Street Photography Ethics," 2 *Journal of Mass Media Ethics* 60 (Spring /Summer 1997).

Glasser, Charles, ed. *International Libel & Privacy Handbook.* New York: Bloomberg Press, 2006.

Flaherty, David H. *Privacy in Colonial New England.* Charlottesville: University Press of Virginia, 1972.

Halstuk, Martin E. and Chamberlin, Bill F. "The Freedom of Information Act 1966-2006: A Retrospective on the Rise of Privacy Protection Over the Public Interest in Knowing What the Government's up To," 11 *Communication Law & Policy* 511 (2006).

Hixson, Richard F. *Privacy in a Public Society: Human Rights in Conflict.* New York: Oxford University Press, 1987.

Pember, Don. *Privacy and the Press.* Seattle: University of Washington Press, 1972.

Prosser, William. "Privacy," 48 *California Law Review* 383 (1960).

Rule, James B. *Privacy in Peril: How We Are Sacrificing a Fundamental Right in Exchange for Security and Convenience.* New York: Oxford University Press, 2007.

Smith, Jeffery A. "Moral Guardians and the Origins of the Right to Privacy," 10 *Journalism and Communications Monographs* 63 (2008).

Thomason, Tommy, ed. *Newspaper Coverage of Rape: Dilemmas on Deadline.* Fort Worth: Texas Christian University Press, 1994.

Warren, Samuel D. and Louis D. Brandeis. "The Right to Privacy," 4 *Harvard Law Review* 220 (1890).

Westin, Alan F. *Privacy and Freedom.* New York: Atheneum, 1967.

Woo, Jisuk. "The Right Not to be Identified: Privacy and Anonymity in the Interactive Media Environment," 8 *New Media Society* 949 (2006).

---

[229] *See* Erin Kelly, *Patriot Act Provisions Expire as Senate Compromise Comes Late,* USA TODAY, June 1, 2015, *available at* http://www.usatoday.com/story/news/nation /2015/05/31/nsa-cia-data-collection/28259481/. *See also* ACLU v. Clapper, 2015 U.S. App. LEXIS 7531 (2d Cir. May 7, 2015)(No. 14-42-cv)(holding organizations had standing to assert First and Fourth amendment challenges to bulk collection by NSA of telephone metadata and text of law did not authorize the metadata program).

[230] *See, e.g.,* James Risen, *Privacy Group to Ask Supreme Court to Stop N.S.A. Phone Spying Program,* N.Y. TIMES, July 8, 2013, at 9A; Charlie Savage, *Nation Will Gain by Discussing Surveillance, Expert Tells Privacy Board,* N.Y. TIMES, July 10, 2013, at 16A. *See also* Clapper v. Amnesty Int'l USA, 133 S.Ct. 1138 (2013) (holding plaintiffs lacked standing to challenge government interception of foreign communications of certain domestic entities and persons).

[231] Barton Gellman, *NSA Broke Privacy Rules Thousands of Times Per Year, Audit Finds,* WASH. POST, Aug. 15, 2013, *available at* http://www.washingtonpost.com/ world/national-security/nsa-broke-privacy-rules-thousands-of-times-per-year-audit-fin ds/2013/08/15/3310e554-05ca-11e3-a07f-49ddc7417125_story.html; Press Release, National Security Agency, NSA Announces New Civil Liberties and Privacy Officer (Jan. 29, 2014), *available at* http://www.nsa.gov/public_info/press_room/2014/civil_liber ties_privacy_officer.shtml.

Confidential Sources and Information

By Anthony L. Fargo

➡ **Headnote Questions**

- How is the constitutional journalist's privilege limited?
- To what extent is a journalist's work product protected from disclosure?
- In what ways have recent cases cast doubt on the future of the constitutional privilege?
- What common characteristics do state shield laws have? How do they differ?
- What are the advantages and disadvantages of shield laws?
- What is the status of attempts to pass a federal shield law?
- What issues do newer media raise in regard to the journalist's privilege?
- What are the potential legal ramifications of voluntarily revealing a confidential source?
- How did Congress respond to a Supreme Court decision on newsroom searches?

Some journalists go through their entire careers without using a confidential source, while others rely on such sources daily. Reporting on politics, national security and financial markets may require journalists to navigate complex relationships with sources who provide deep background information that cannot be published, or who agree to be quoted only anonymously or with ambiguous monikers.

The use of confidential sources carries significant ethical baggage. Journalists are supposed to tell their audiences the truth, but using a confidential source requires hiding some part of the truth. They must be careful not to put such sources in danger by being careless with their identities, but they also must guard against being used for unsavory purposes by people to whom they have pledged confidentiality. The complexity of the ethical relationships between journalists and sources is reflected in the ethics code of the Society of Professional Journalists. It discourages journalists from relying on confidential sources, while admonishing them to keep their promises of confidentiality.[1]

This same ambiguity is evident in the law regarding journalists and their sources. A journalist who receives a subpoena to appear before a grand jury or in a courtroom to name a confidential source faces being found in contempt of court and fined or jailed for refusing to cooperate. The extent to which a journalist is protected from that fate varies widely, based on whether the agency issuing the subpoena is federal or state and where it is located. The U.S. Supreme Court's sole attempt to clarify the law in 1972 backfired because of a sharp divide among the justices. Further complicating things are varying degrees of legal protection for journalists' non-confidential work product, such as unpublished photographs and unaired video images, and new challenges posed by digital media.

Journalists who voluntarily reveal sources, meanwhile, may find they are liable for damages to their sources for breaking promises of confidentiality. They also have to be concerned that police may get search warrants allowing officers to rummage through files for evidence related to criminal acts.

The tension between journalists and those who seek their testimony and work product arises from conflicting views of journalists' duties. Reporters argue that if they reveal their sources, those and other potential sources will stop going to the press with important information. That, in turn, will harm the press' ability to act as a watchdog, or check, on government and corporations.[2] Critics of a privilege for journalists argue that journal-

---

[1] Society of Professional Journalists, Code of Ethics, *available at* www.spj.org/ethicscode.asp (last visited June 28, 2016).

[2] *See* Vincent Blasi, *The Checking Value in First Amendment Theory*, 1977 Am. Bar

ists are no different from other citizens who have a duty to testify when they have relevant and important information about a legal controversy. Journalists who refuse to obey valid orders to appear before grand juries or in court are putting themselves above the law, which no person has a right to do.[3]

Faced with powerful challenges to what they see as a professional obligation to protect sources, journalists have turned to the First Amendment for shelter. That has not proved entirely successful, leading press organizations to seek statutory protection in most state legislatures and from Congress. The media have been successful in getting legislation approved in the states, but the statutes carry their own limitations.

CONSTITUTIONAL PRIVILEGE

Although the First Amendment was ratified in 1791, reporters did not claim that it protected them from revealing sources until the middle of the twentieth century. However, the first prominent case involving someone who would fit the modern definition of a reporter protecting the identity of a news source arose in 1848. A *New York Herald* reporter wrote a story about a treaty intended to be secret. The Senate held him in contempt when he refused to name his source and jailed him in the Capitol for ten days. When it became apparent he would not talk, he was released.[4]

The standoff between the reporter and the Senate was typical of the occasional skirmishes that arose between journalists and authorities until the 1950s.[5] A newspaper would publish a controversial story, leading authorities to issue a subpoena to the publisher or writer demanding to know the source. The journalist would refuse to cooperate, citing professional obligations. The reporter would be held in contempt, or authorities would give up, or the information would be revealed some other way.

It is not clear from the historical record why journalists did not seek protection under the First Amendment during the nineteenth and early twentieth centuries, but there are several possible explanations. Many of the cases involved state court proceedings, and the Supreme Court did not rule that the First Amendment restrained state abridgement of speech and press rights until the 1920s.[6] Also, it would be two more decades before opinions from the Supreme Court began laying the groundwork for a more robust protection for speech and press rights.[7]

Furthermore, legal experts viewed privileges suspiciously — and perhaps none so suspiciously as the journalist's privilege. Although privileges protecting attorneys, medical doctors, mental health workers and pastors from testifying against clients, patients and congregants had existed through statutory or common law for many years, they were seen as impediments to the legal system's search for truth. John Henry Wigmore, a leading expert on evidence law in the early 1900s, who is still cited frequently, wrote that a privilege should only be recognized if a communication was conducted in confidence, confidentiality was essential to the relationship between the communicators, society considered the relationship important, and the harm of disclosing the communication outweighed the benefit. Wigmore found that most privileges, including the journalist's privilege, lacked one or more of the four elements he described.[8]

It was not until 1958 that a reporter claimed that the First Amendment protected her right to conceal her source. Marie Torre, an entertainment columnist for a New York newspaper, quoted a CBS executive as blaming singer and actress Judy Garland for delays in bringing a variety show starring Garland to television. Garland sued CBS for libel and breach of contract and demanded that Torre reveal her source. Torre refused, claiming the First Amendment press clause protected her. But in an opinion written by Judge Potter Stewart, who would soon join the Supreme Court, the Second U.S. Circuit Court of Appeals ruled against Torre. The court determined that while there might be circumstances in which journalists should have a right to conceal sources, Torre's information went to the heart of Garland's suit and had to be disclosed.[9] Torre served ten days in jail for contempt but never revealed her source.[10]

Conflicts between the press and authorities over sources remained rare until the late 1960s. One study of subpoena cases involving the press showed that the number of subpoenas served on the media jumped from a total of about one or two per year nationwide to more than seventy per year.[11] Sociologist Michael Schudson has provided a logical and concise explanation for the growing tensions between the press and the government in the 1960s. Journalists became less likely to take government pronouncements at face value after catching the government in lies about the Bay of Pigs invasion of Cuba and about the war in Vietnam, he wrote. Younger journalists in particular were more open to non-traditional sources, such as the leaders of various social movements who often did not want to

---

FOUND. RES. J. 521.

[3] *See* Randall D. Elisason, *Leakers, Bloggers, and Fourth Estate Inmates: The Misguided Pursuit of a Reporter's Privilege,* 24 CARDOZO ARTS & ENT. L.J. 385 (2006).

[4] *See* Aaron David Gordon, Protection of News Sources: The History and Legal Status of the Newsman's Privilege 185-88 (1971) (unpublished dissertation, University of Wisconsin) (copy on file at Indiana University Herman B. Wells Library).

[5] *Id.* at 184-287.

[6] *See* Gitlow v. New York, 268 U.S. 652 (1925).

[7] *See, e.g.,* Bridges v. California, 314 U.S. 252 (1941) (striking down contempt citation

---

for commenting on pending court case).

[8] 8 J. WIGMORE, EVIDENCE § 2285 (McNaughton ed. 1961).

[9] Garland v. Torre, 259 F.2d 545 (2d Cir. 1958).

[10] *See* Stephen Bates, Garland v. Torre *and the Birth of Reporter's Privilege,* 15 COMM. L. & POL'Y 91 (2010).

[11] *See* Achal Mehra, *Newsmen's Privilege: An Empirical Study,* 59 JOURNALISM Q. 560 (1982).

speak to the media on the record but wanted to get publicity for their causes.[12] Law enforcement officials, frustrated that the news media seemed to know more about potentially dangerous organizations than they did, and no longer able to count on co-operation from journalists, began seeking subpoenas to force journalists to turn over source names, tapes, notes and other information about the groups and their members.[13]

Branzburg v. Hayes

In 1971, the Supreme Court agreed to weigh in on the growing controversy about confidential sources by consolidating cases involving three reporters who had refused to cooperate with grand juries investigating alleged crimes committed by their sources. The Court issued its opinion in *Branzburg v. Hayes* in 1972.[14]

The first of the three reporters was subpoenaed by grand juries twice because of stories about drug traffic in Kentucky. Paul Branzburg wrote a story about two hashish dealers in Louisville he called "Larry" and "Jack" who told him about their lives in the drug trade.[15] He wrote another story that included interviews with several drug users in Frankfort, the state capital. The sources ranged from a 14-year-old student to a state employee.[16] Both stories resulted in grand jury subpoenas seeking Branzburg's testimony about his sources, which he resisted, citing Kentucky's shield law for reporters.

In 1970, the Kentucky Court of Appeals, then the state's highest court, ruled 5-1 against Branzburg.[17] It noted that Kentucky's shield law barred courts, grand juries and other government bodies from forcing a journalist to reveal the "source of any information" obtained in the course of his or her work as a journalist.[18] However, the court determined that Branzburg could not claim the statutory privilege's protection for what he saw because his personal observation, not his sources, was the "information."[19] The court denied a rehearing in the Louisville case[20] and ruled against Branzburg in the Frankfort case.[21]

The second reporter, Paul Pappas, worked for a Massachusetts TV station and covered an outbreak of apparently racially

motivated violence in New Bedford.[22] He recorded a man reading a statement outside a store that was also a Black Panthers headquarters. The Black Panthers told Pappas he could return later with his camera as long as he agreed not to report on anything except an anticipated police raid. Pappas returned and was allowed to enter, but the raid did not happen while he was there, and he filed no story.[23]

However, authorities learned he was in the headquarters building and subpoenaed him to appear before a state grand jury. Pappas answered some questions before the grand jury but nothing about what or whom he saw. He moved to quash the subpoena, but a superior court judge denied the motion.

On appeal, the Massachusetts Supreme Judicial Court ruled against Pappas. Noting that Massachusetts had no statutory privilege, it held that to create one by constitutional or common law "would be engaging in judicial amendment of the Constitution or judicial legislation."[24]

The third reporter, Earl Caldwell, was a correspondent for the *New York Times* in Oakland, California, and covered the Black Panthers. In a 1969 story, David Hilliard, the Black Panther Party's chief of staff, told him the party's goals included the "overthrow of the government by way of force and violence."[25] Hilliard was being investigated for a speech before the story appeared in which he allegedly threatened President Richard Nixon's life. Caldwell was subpoenaed to appear before a federal grand jury to testify and surrender his interview notes.[26]

A federal district court agreed that Caldwell could refuse to testify about his sources' identities but ruled that he had to enter the grand jury room and answer all other questions.[27] Caldwell, fearing an appearance in the grand jury room would end his relationship with the Black Panthers, appealed to the Ninth U.S. Circuit Court of Appeals. In 1970, a Ninth Circuit panel ruled that Caldwell not only did not have to identify his confidential sources but also did not have to appear before the grand jury at all. It noted that Caldwell swore that he had no information for the grand jury beyond his published stories except that covered by the district court's protective order. In the narrow circumstances of this case, the court held, "[T]he public's First Amendment right to be informed" had to be balanced against any compelling interest the government could show for a witness' appearance before a grand jury. The court said it saw no real public interest in Caldwell's appearance given the probable

---

[12] MICHAEL SCHUDSON, THE SOCIOLOGY OF NEWS 80-82 (2d ed. 2011).

[13] *See* Margaret Sherwood, Comment, *The Newsman's Privilege: Government Investigations, Criminal Prosecutions and Private Litigation*, 58 CAL. L. REV. 1198 (1970).

[14] 408 U.S. 665 (1972).

[15] Paul M. Branzburg, *The Hash They Make Isn't to Eat*, COURIER-JOURNAL, Nov. 15, 1969, at A1.

[16] Paul M. Branzburg, *Rope Turns to Pot: Once an Industry, Kentucky Hemp Has Become a Drug Problem*, COURIER-JOURNAL & TIMES, Jan. 10, 1971, at A1.

[17] Branzburg v. Pound, 461 S.W.2d 345 (Ky. 1970).

[18] *Id.* at 346 (citing KY. REV. STAT. § 421.100).

[19] *Id.* at 347-48.

[20] *Id.* at 345 (noting that petition for rehearing was denied on Jan. 22, 1971).

[21] Branzburg v. Meigs, 503 S.W.2d 748 (Ky. 1971).

[22] *Shooting, Fires Flare in New Bedford*, BOSTON GLOBE, July 30, 1970, at 1.

[23] *In re* Pappas, 266 N.E.2d 297, 298 (Mass. 1971).

[24] *Id.* at 302.

[25] Earl Caldwell, *Declining Black Panthers Gather New Support from Repeated Clashes with Police*, N.Y. TIMES, Dec. 14, 1969, at 69.

[26] *Times Reporter Gets a Subpoena*, N.Y. TIMES, Feb. 3, 1970, at 20.

[27] *In re* Caldwell, 311 F. Supp. 358, 360 (N.D. Cal. 1970).

damage to the First Amendment his appearance would cause.[28]

Branzburg and Pappas appealed to the Supreme Court, as did the government in Caldwell's case. The three consolidated cases gave the Court the chance to rule on privilege questions in a state with a shield law, in a state without a shield law and in a federal proceeding.

Justice Byron White's opinion for the 5-4 majority began by asserting that the Court recognized that newsgathering needed to be protected by the First Amendment. "[W]ithout some protection for seeking out the news, freedom of the press would be eviscerated," he wrote.[29] But that protection did not exempt reporters from providing evidence about crimes to grand juries. The Court said that neither common law nor constitutional law favored the type of privilege the reporters were seeking, and most states at that time, as well as Congress, had declined to provide reporters with statutory protection.[30] The Court also found insufficient evidence for the claim that lack of a privilege would harm relationships between reporters and sources, for instances of reporters being forced to testify were rare and were unlikely to deter sources.[31] It also noted that the press had flourished throughout American history without a common law or constitutional privilege, and it dismissed the concern that the number of subpoenas had increased in recent years, saying that such concerns were "treacherous grounds" on which to build a constitutional privilege.[32]

Justices also were concerned by practical aspects of the reporters' claims to a First Amendment privilege. For one thing, how would lower courts determine who would be entitled to it? The "liberty of the press is the right of the lonely pamphleteer who uses carbon paper or a mimeograph just as much as the large metropolitan publisher who utilizes the latest photocomposition methods."[33] Justice White wrote that press freedom is an individual right that does not belong just to the institutional press. The functions that newspaper and TV reporters perform, he said, are "also performed by lecturers, political pollsters, novelists, academic researchers, and dramatists."[34] The majority also worried that the type of qualified privilege the reporters sought would force courts to engage in complicated calculations about whether government interests were compelling or evidence was relevant. Such issues not only would bog down the courts but raise serious questions about judges second-guessing

legislatures about which crimes were most important.[35]

Although the majority rejected a constitutional privilege that would protect journalists who witnessed crimes from testifying before grand juries, it noted that Congress and the state legislatures were free to create such a right by statute. Also, the majority said it had no power to prevent state courts from recognizing a privilege under the free-press guarantees in state constitutions. The Court concluded with a warning to prosecutors and judges that the decision did not mean that it was open season on journalists and their sources: "We do not expect courts will forget that grand juries must operate within the limits of the First Amendment as well as the Fifth."[36]

In what proved to be a pivotal concurring opinion, Justice Lewis Powell, who had voted with the majority, said he wanted "to emphasize what seems to me to be the limited nature of the Court's holding."[37] He favored a case-by-case balancing of the competing interests between law enforcement and journalists. Such balancing should occur, he wrote, when a journalist is called to provide testimony "bearing only a remote and tenuous relationship to the subject of the investigation," or if the journalist reasonably believed the testimony would not fulfill "a legitimate need of law enforcement."[38]

In a strongly worded dissenting opinion, Justice William O. Douglas advocated an absolute privilege that would bar the government from subpoenaing a journalist unless the reporter was suspected of a crime, in which case the Fifth Amendment would protect the journalist from self-incrimination. Justice Douglas argued that a free press was essential to self-government and that the majority opinion would interfere with the public's right to know. "The press has a preferred position in our constitutional scheme, not to enable it to make money, not to set newsmen apart as a favored class, but to bring fulfillment to the public's right to know," he wrote.[39]

Justice Potter Stewart, writing in dissent for himself and Justices William Brennan and Thurgood Marshall, complained that the majority had adopted a "crabbed view of the First Amendment." He wrote that the majority opinion would allow government officials "to undermine the historic independence of the press by attempting to annex the journalistic profession as an investigative arm of government." Also, he wrote, the majority opinion would interfere with "the broad societal interest in a full and free flow of information to the public."[40]

"Simple logic," Justice Stewart wrote, showed that confidential sources were necessary to the press' proper functioning.

[28] Caldwell v. United States, 434 F.2d 1081, 1089 (9th Cir. 1970).

[29] Branzburg v. Hayes, 408 U.S. 665, 681 (1972).

[30] Id. at 685-89. The Court listed seventeen states that had shield statutes in place at the time it decided the case. Id. at 689 n.27.

[31] Id. at 693-94.

[32] Id at 698-99.

[33] Id. at 704.

[34] Id. at 704-05.

[35] Id. at 705-06.

[36] Id. at 709.

[37] Id. (Powell, J., concurring).

[38] Id. at 710 (Powell, J., concurring).

[39] Id. at 721 (Douglas, J., dissenting).

[40] Id. at 725 (Stewart, J., dissenting).

Journalists could not gather news without informants, he wrote, and confidentiality was necessary to maintain relationships with informants. An unchecked government subpoena power, he added, not only would deter sources from talking to reporters but also would deter reporters from pursuing certain stories that likely would land them in front of grand juries.[41]

Although Justice Stewart shared many of Justice Douglas's concerns about the impact of the majority opinion, he did not go so far as to advocate an absolute privilege. Instead, he argued that the government's subpoena power in regard to the press should be limited by requiring the government to show, before enforcing a subpoena, that[42]

• There is probable cause to believe the reporter had "clearly relevant" information about a crime

• The information could not be obtained elsewhere

• The government had a "compelling and overriding interest in the information."

Aftermath of Branzburg

One result of the Supreme Court's *Branzburg* ruling was a sharp increase in the number of subpoenas served on the news media. A series of surveys of news organizations conducted from the late 1980s through 2001 found that the responding news organizations reported between 820 and 4,500 subpoenas per year, depending upon how many media outlets responded to the survey.[43] A more recent study by a Brigham Young University law professor had similar findings, with news organizations reporting more than 3,000 subpoenas nationwide in one year.[44]

However, only 3 to 5 percent of the subpoenas issued to news organizations sought the names of confidential sources, according to the Reporters Committee for Freedom of the Press, which conducted the earlier studies. Most subpoenas sought copies of stories already published or aired.

There is no record to indicate that any of the reporters in the *Branzburg* case ever testified before a grand jury.

Caldwell predicted shortly after the Court issued its decision that it would mean the end of investigative reporting because no source could ever trust that a reporter would protect his identity.[45] But soon afterward, the Watergate scandal that forced President Nixon to resign in 1974 broke open with the help of *Washington Post* reporters Carl Bernstein and Bob Woodward and their confidential sources, to whom they dedicated their book *All the President's Men*.[46] They were able to protect the identity of their most famous source, known as "Deep Throat," for more than thirty years before former FBI deputy director Mark Felt voluntarily identified himself.[47]

While Watergate would seem to vindicate the Supreme Court majority's view that the press would continue to flourish without a constitutional privilege, something more complicated was actually going on. Lower federal courts began ruling, within months of the *Branzburg* decision, that the decision created, or allowed the creation of, a qualified constitutional or common law journalist's privilege. For example, the Second U.S. Circuit Court of Appeals ruled in 1972 that a journalist did not have to reveal his source for a story about shady real estate deals to one of the parties involved in a civil lawsuit over the deals. The appellate court in *Baker v. F & F Investments* determined that *Branzburg* was not directly controlling because it dealt with grand jury subpoenas rather than a civil dispute. The appellate panel wrote that the First Amendment did not allow either direct or indirect stifling of the press absent a "compelling concern" that did not exist in the case.[48]

In an attempt to explain how *Branzburg* could be a victory for the press, First Amendment lawyer James Goodale wrote in 1975 that the Douglas and Stewart dissents and Justice Powell's call for a case-by-case balancing of interests, particularly if the information sought was irrelevant to an investigation, amounted to a plurality endorsement of a qualified journalist's privilege except in cases where grand juries sought eyewitness testimony about criminal activity.[49] Similarly, Justice Stewart, in a 1974 law school speech that was published in 1975, suggested that the Powell concurrence created a "four and a half to four and a half" decision, leaving its interpretation open.[50]

Another development in 1975 further complicated lower courts' attempts to determine journalists' rights to protect sources. Congress approved a new evidence code for the federal courts that included a rule about how courts should determine the legitimacy of a privilege claim by a prospective witness. Instead of specifically adopting most of the privileges commonly recognized by state laws, Congress instead instructed the fed-

---

[41] *Id.* at 728 (Stewart, J., dissenting).

[42] *Id.* at 743 (Stewart, J., dissenting).

[43] REPORTERS COMMITTEE FOR FREEDOM OF THE PRESS, AGENTS OF DISCOVERY: A REPORT ON THE INCIDENCE OF SUBPOENAS SERVED ON THE NEWS MEDIA IN 2001 (2003). Other reports were issued in 1993, 1995, 1999 and 2001.

[44] The study was described in two law journal articles: RonNell Andersen Jones, *Media Subpoenas: Impact, Perception, and Legal Protection in the Changing World of American Journalism*, 84 WASH. L. REV. 317 (2009); RonNell Andersen Jones, *Avalanche or Undue Alarm: An Empirical Study of Subpoenas Received by the News Media*, 93 MINN. L. REV. 585 (2008).

[45] Earl Caldwell, *Ask Me. I Know. I Was the Test Case*, SATURDAY REV., Aug. 5, 1972,

at 5.

[46] CARL BERNSTEIN & BOB WOODWARD, ALL THE PRESIDENT'S MEN 7 (1974) (dedicating book "[t]o the President's other men and women — in the White House and elsewhere — who took risks to provide us with confidential information. Without them there would have been no Watergate story told by the *Washington Post*.").

[47] BOB WOODWARD, THE SECRET MAN (2005).

[48] 470 F.2d 778, 785 (2d Cir. 1972)

[49] James C. Goodale, Branzburg v. Hayes *and the Developing Qualified Privilege for Newsmen*, 26 HASTINGS L. J. 709 (1975).

[50] Potter Stewart, *"Or of the Press,"* 26 HASTINGS L. J. 631, 635 (1975).

eral courts to adhere to "the principles of the common law as they may be interpreted by the courts of the United States in the light of reason and experience."[51] Rule 501 left the question of whether journalists had a privilege allowing them to protect sources up to the courts to decide on a circuit-by-circuit basis.

As a result, most federal appellate circuits have recognized a qualified privilege grounded in the First Amendment when journalists are subpoenaed to testify in civil or criminal cases. Federal courts generally have agreed, however, that there is no privilege when a journalist is subpoenaed by a properly convened grand jury investigating a specific crime. The Third Circuit has grounded the privilege its judges have recognized in common law rather than the First Amendment,[52] and the Sixth has flatly rejected the existence of a constitutional privilege, saying that the Supreme Court in *Branzburg* foreclosed any recognition of such a privilege.[53] The Seventh Circuit, in a 2003 case to be discussed in more detail later in this chapter, rejected a privilege for non-confidential information and expressed skepticism about a privilege for confidential material as well.[54]

The development of the qualified constitutional privilege in the federal appellate circuits has been uneven at best, but it is possible to identify some common questions that have arisen in litigation over reporters' rights. These questions deal with who may claim the privilege, how the privilege is qualified, in what types of proceedings does the privilege apply, and what types of information are protected.

Who Is a Journalist?

Surprisingly, given the concern that the *Branzburg* court expressed about defining who would be protected by a journalist's privilege, the issue has rarely arisen in federal appellate courts. To the extent that it has, the courts have developed a requirement that those claiming the privilege to show that they gathered the information being subpoenaed for the purpose of disseminating it to the public and while engaged in "investigative journalism." The federal circuits have found that the privilege could protect the sources and work of a nonfiction book author and a documentary filmmaker.[55] The courts have rejected privilege claims by the host of a hotline about professional wrestling who admitted he was more entertainer than journalist and a woman who gathered information to help her partner's defense in a criminal trial before later deciding to write a book.[56]

How Is the Privilege Qualified?

Appellate courts generally have used Justice Stewart's three-part *Branzburg* test in balancing the interests of journalists and those seeking the names of confidential sources. It requires someone subpoenaing the press to show that the information is relevant to the legal question at hand, important to resolving the question and unavailable from other sources.

The third part of the test has led to disagreements among the circuits. The Second Circuit has indicated that a party seeking to unmask a confidential source must first exhaust all other sources for the information before seeking it from a reporter.[57] The District of Columbia Circuit Court of Appeals, however, has said that a litigant must only exhaust all *reasonable* alternative sources.[58] In a 2005 case, a former government scientist seeking the identities of federal employees who leaked information about him to the press persuaded the D.C. Circuit to allow him to depose reporters who wrote about the espionage case against him. The court ruled for Wen Ho Lee, who faced nearly sixty charges before the government dropped all but one for lack of evidence, even though he had only been able to depose twenty of the hundreds of possible sources for the stories about him. The court found that twenty was a reasonable number because many of the possible sources had claimed that national security or other considerations prevented them from testifying.[59]

In What Types of Proceedings Does the Privilege Apply?

Federal appellate courts are more likely to find that a qualified constitutional privilege exists when journalists are subpoenaed to testify in civil instead of criminal cases. The Sixth Amendment guarantees criminal defendants the right to a fair trial, and the government's interest in protecting citizens against crime is a strong counter-argument to a journalist's desire to protect sources. While the Seventh Amendment protects the right to a jury trial in civil cases, its protection does not extend as far as the Sixth Amendment and does not set up the same type of conflict with the journalist's privilege.

The number of privilege cases heard since *Branzburg* varies widely from circuit to circuit. So in some circuits an appellate court might never have been asked to decide if a privilege applied in a particular type of proceeding. Privilege has been recognized in civil cases by the First, Second, Third, Fourth, Fifth, Eighth, Ninth, Tenth and District of Columbia circuits.

The Second, Third, Eleventh and District of Columbia circuit

---

[51] FED. R. EVID. 501 (1975).

[52] Riley v. City of Chester, 612 F.2d 708 (3d. Cir. 1979).

[53] *In re* Grand Jury Subpoena (Storer Comm., Inc., 810 F.2d 580 (6th Cir. 1987).

[54] McKevitt v. Pallasch, 339 F.3d 530 (7th Cir. 2003).

[55] Shoen v. Shoen, 5 F.3d 1298 (9th Cir. 1993); Silkwood v. Kerr-McGee Corp., 563 F.2d 433 (10th Cir. 1977).

[56] von Bulow v. von Bulow, 811 F.2d 136 (2d Cir. 1987); *In re* Madden, 151 F.3d 125

(3d Cir. 1998).

[57] *In re* Petroleum Prods. Antitrust Litig., 680 F.2d 5 (2d Cir. 1982).

[58] Zerilli v. Smith, 656 F.2d 705 (D.C. Cir. 1981).

[59] Lee v. U.S. Dep't of Justice, 413 F.3d 53 (D.C. Cir. 2005).

courts have recognized a constitutional privilege in criminal cases. One example is *United States v. Burke*,[60] a 1983 case in which the Second Circuit, using the Stewart three-part test, determined that a criminal defendant had failed to show a need for documents from *Sports Illustrated* related to a story about his alleged part in a college basketball point-shaving scheme.

There is some disagreement among the circuits about whether a journalist may rely on the privilege in a libel suit if the journalist or the journalist's employer is the defendant. In 2000 the First Circuit held the plaintiff might have been able to prove actual malice because of the defendant's failure to reveal a source, but the question was moot because the jury determined that the plaintiff had not proven that the statements about him were false and defamatory.[61] However, the Fourth Circuit, in 1986, applied the Stewart three-part test in a libel case against NBC and denied a politician's subpoena for the names of sources the network used, finding he had not exhausted alternative ways to find the information.[62]

Further complicating the law in regard to libel cases is *Herbert v. Lando*,[63] a 1979 Supreme Court decision in which the justices held that libel defendants do not have a First Amendment right to refuse to testify about their state of mind or editorial process in the preparation of an allegedly defamatory story. A good rule of thumb would be to assume that a court will be reluctant to give defendants a major advantage by allowing them to conceal their sources for potentially libelous material.

What Types of Information Are Protected?

There is general consensus among most federal appellate circuits that journalists have the limited right to conceal confidential sources from civil litigants, criminal prosecutors, criminal defendants or all three. There is less consensus regarding non-confidential materials such as unpublished photographs, unaired videotape or digital television footage and notes.

In 1988, in *United States v. LaRouche Campaign*, the First Circuit Court of Appeals ordered NBC to comply with a subpoena from a criminal defendant for outtakes of its interview with a leading witness in a pending criminal case. Although the court ruled against the network, it agreed that four of NBC's arguments for refusing to turn over non-confidential material were valid. NBC argued that disclosure would[64]

• Raise the threat of government interference in the news-gathering process

• Make NBC appear to be an investigative arm of the court

• Serve as a disincentive for networks to gather and maintain unaired material

• Place an undue burden on employees' time and resources.

The court acknowledged that there was a "lurking and subtle threat" to journalists if forced disclosure of their materials became the norm, but it determined that the defendant's due process and fair trial rights overcame NBC's objections.[65]

NBC's arguments in *United States v. LaRouche Campaign* neatly summarize the concerns journalists and their employers have raised in fighting disclosures of their work products. Federal appellate circuits have split almost evenly in determining whether the First Amendment protects non-confidential material from disclosure. The Second, Third and Ninth circuits agree that non-confidential material is protected, although to a lesser extent than confidential material. The Second Circuit is the only federal appellate court that has developed a specific test for determining whether non-confidential material must be disclosed. In *Gonzales v. NBC*,[66] the court held that when non-confidential material is subpoenaed, a court should weigh whether the information is of likely relevance to the underlying case and is not reasonably obtainable elsewhere.[67] This differs from the Stewart three-part test requiring a clear showing of relevance and the exhaustion of alternative means of obtaining the information, which the Second Circuit has adopted in cases involving confidential sources.

The Fifth and Seventh circuits have held that subpoenas for non-confidential information raise no First Amendment concerns in criminal cases. In a 1998 case, a Fifth Circuit panel rejected a television station's attempt to quash subpoenas from both the prosecution and defense for outtakes of interviews with an arson suspect, finding that there was no threat that sources would dry up if the material was disclosed.[68]

The Fourth Circuit rejected reporters' arguments against disclosure in a criminal case involving a state senator accused of taking bribes who had given interviews to the reporters, finding that no legitimate First Amendment concerns were implicated.[69] However, a Fourth Circuit panel one year later upheld a lower court's decision in a civil suit to quash a subpoena for reporters' notes from an interview with a named source.[70]

Cracks in the Privilege

Since the early 2000s, journalists have lost several high-profile

---

[60] 700 F.2d 70 (2d Cir. 1983).

[61] Gray v. St. Martin's Press, 221 F.3d 243 (1st Cir. 2000).

[62] LaRouche v. NBC, 780 F.2d 1134 (4th Cir. 1986).

[63] 441 U.S. 153 (1979).

[64] 841 F.2d 1176, 1181 (1st Circ. 1988).

[65] *Id.* at 1182.

[66] 194 F.3d 29 (2d Cir. 1999).

[67] *Id.* at 36.

[68] United States v. Smith, 135 F.3d 963 (5th Cir. 1998).

[69] *In re* Shain, 978 F.2d 850 (4th Cir. 1992).

[70] Church of Scientology Intern'l v. Daniels, 992 F.2d 1329 (4th Cir. 1993).

attempts to protect confidential source identities. The cause of the losing streak is debatable but can most likely be traced to a combination of bad facts and increasing judicial impatience with uncooperative journalists.

The first case involved a terrorism trial in Northern Ireland. Three reporters who had interviewed an American informant in the Real IRA group for newspaper stories and a potential book fought a subpoena for their interview tapes. Michael McKevitt, the leader of the Real IRA, was facing trial for his alleged role in a bombing that killed twenty-eight people, and the informant was expected to be the star witness against him. McKevitt's attorneys hoped that statements to reporters by the informant, whose identity had been published, would impeach his testimony at trial.[71]

A U.S. district court judge in Chicago ordered the reporters to comply with the subpoena, and they subsequently lost their appeal to the Seventh Circuit. Influential federal appellate Judge Richard Posner wrote in the Seventh Circuit's 2003 opinion that the reporters had no First Amendment interests to protect given that the source was known and did not object to the tapes being used at trial.[72]

The opinion went further, however, and also questioned the wisdom of recognizing any type of journalist's privilege under federal law in the wake of *Branzburg*. Judge Posner wrote that federal courts that had recognized a constitutional privilege for confidential sources had acted surprisingly and audaciously, given the ruling in *Branzburg*. Those that had extended the privilege to non-confidential material were, according to Judge Posner's opinion, "skating on thin ice."[73]

A year later, Providence, R.I., TV station WJAR aired a tape showing a city official accepting a bribe. An undercover informant had recorded the tape, which was part of the federal government's evidence in an upcoming corruption trial involving the mayor and other officials. A special prosecutor subpoenaed reporter James Taricani to testify about his source for the tape, which was supposed to remain sealed until the trial. Taricani refused to cooperate and was found in civil contempt and ordered to pay $1,000 a day until he named the source.[74]

The First Circuit Court of Appeals denied Taricani's appeal, determining that the special prosecutor's investigation into the leak was similar enough to a grand jury investigation that *Branzburg* precluded any privilege.[75] The station continued paying the fine for nearly three months before the district court judge recalled Taricani for a hearing on whether he should be found in criminal contempt. While Taricani was awaiting the hearing, his source, an attorney for one of the corruption defendants, came forward and admitted supplying the tape to Taricani. Although the source's identity had become known, the judge still found Taricani guilty of criminal contempt and sentenced him to six months of house arrest.[76]

The case that garnered the most attention in the post-McKevitt era involved *New York Times* reporter Judith Miller and *Time* magazine reporter Matthew Cooper. The case began after Joseph Wilson, a former American ambassador to Iraq, wrote an op-ed column in the *Times* saying that the government had sent him to Africa to check out reports that Iraq was attempting to obtain yellow cake uranium, an ingredient used to make nuclear weapons. Wilson wrote that he found no evidence to back up the reports, but the Bush administration nevertheless cited the reports in justifying the decision to invade Iraq in 2003.[77]

After Wilson's column appeared, conservative syndicated columnist Robert Novak wrote that two administration officials told him that Wilson was married to a CIA operative named Valerie Plame.[78] The motive for the leak was not entirely clear, although Wilson claimed that the administration ruined his wife's career at the CIA to get back at him for questioning the motives for the Iraq invasion.[79] What was clear was that the leak of an undercover intelligence operative's name to the press was a possible violation of federal law.[80] A special federal prosecutor was named to look into the leak, which went to other journalists besides Novak.

Miller, who never wrote about Plame, and Cooper eventually were subpoenaed to testify about who gave them Plame's name, but they refused to cooperate. Eventually, a three-judge panel of the D.C. Circuit Court of Appeals ruled unanimously that no common-law privilege would protect the two reporters from testifying, although the three judges differed on whether such a privilege might exist under other circumstances.[81] The Supreme Court denied *certiorari*.[82]

Cooper and Miller continued to refuse to testify; but on the day that they were to be sentenced to jail for contempt, *Time* editor Norman Pearlstine gave the court Cooper's notes and email messages regarding his source. Pearlstine had decided that it was futile to keep fighting after the Supreme Court re-

[71] McKevitt v. Pallasch, 339 F.3d 530 (7th Cir. 2003).

[72] *Id.* at 532.

[73] *Id.*

[74] *In re* Special Proceedings, 373 F.3d 37 (1st Cir. 2004).

[75] *Id.* at 44-45.

[76] *In re* Special Proceedings, C.A. No. 01-47 (D.R.I. Dec. 9, 2004).

[77] Joseph C. Wilson IV, *What I Didn't Find in Africa*, N.Y. TIMES, July 6, 2003, Sec. 4 (Week in Review), at 9.

[78] Robert Novak, *Mission to Niger*, WASH. POST, July 14, 2003, at A21.

[79] *See* Scott Shane, *Private Spy and Public Spouse Live at Center of Leak Case*, N.Y. TIMES, July 5, 2005, at A1.

[80] Intelligence Identities Protection Act of 1982, 50 U.S.C. § 421 (2000).

[81] *In re* Grand Jury Subpoena, Judith Miller, 397 F.3d 964 (D.C. Cir. 2005).

[82] Cooper v. United States, 545 U.S. 1150 (2005); Miller v. United States, 545 U.S. 1150 (2005).

fused to hear the case.[83] Miller continued to resist, however, and served eighty-five days in jail before her source, Vice President Dick Cheney's chief of staff I. Lewis "Scooter" Libby, released her from her promise not to name him.[84] Libby was eventually convicted of lying to investigators about his role in the leak of Plame's identity, but President Bush commuted his prison sentence. Novak, who died in 2009, identified his sources to authorities as Deputy Secretary of State Richard Armitage and Karl Rove, a political adviser to President Bush. Neither was charged with a crime.[85]

The only person who served jail time was Miller.

At about the same time that the Miller case was capturing headlines, the Wen Ho Lee case mentioned earlier in this chapter was playing out in the federal courts in Washington, D.C. After being cleared of espionage charges that he had sold nuclear secrets to China while working at the Los Alamos weapons laboratory in New Mexico, Lee sued the Department of Justice and Department of Energy for violating the Privacy Act of 1974[86] by leaking information about him to the press. After failing to get anyone at either agency to admit to being the source of the leaks, he subpoenaed reporters from several news organizations to learn the identities of their sources.

Five reporters were found in contempt of court and ordered to pay fines of $500 a day until they complied, with the imposition of the fines delayed while they appealed.[87] In 2005, the District of Columbia U.S. Court of Appeals dismissed the contempt citation against Jeff Gerth of the New York Times, finding he had no relevant evidence, but upheld the citations against James Risen of the Times, Bob Drogin of the Los Angeles Times, Josef Hebert of the Associated Press and Pierre Thomas of ABC. The appellate court determined that Lee had exhausted all other reasonable sources for the information.[88] A sixth reporter, Walter Pincus of the Washington Post, lost his challenge to a subpoena from Lee in a district court ruling after the other reporters' appeal had failed.[89] However, Lee reached a financial settlement with the government and, in an unusual move, also with the news organizations employing the subpoenaed reporters, ending his need for the reporters' testimony.[90]

Judith Miller was a player in another case involving government subpoenas. After someone in federal law enforcement told her and Times reporter Philip Shenon that the government was investigating several Islamic charities in the United States with suspected ties to terrorists, a federal prosecutor subpoenaed a telephone company for Times phone records to learn who Miller and Shenon had talked to. The Times challenged the subpoenas, but the Second Circuit Court of Appeals ruled in 2006 that the newspaper had no standing to challenge a subpoena to a phone company, at least in this situation.[91]

Also in 2006, a freelance video journalist in San Francisco lost in his attempt to avoid jail time for contempt after he refused to comply with a federal grand jury subpoena for outtakes of footage he shot at a political protest. The grand jury hoped Joshua Wolf's unaired video would help identify protesters who injured a police officer and tried to set fire to a police car.

The Ninth Circuit Court of Appeals, in rejecting Wolf's appeal, sidestepped the question of whether he would qualify as a "journalist" under the constitutional privilege. Instead, the court noted that he was resisting a grand jury subpoena, which meant that he had no privilege under Branzburg and Ninth Circuit precedent.[92] Wolf ended up serving the longest jail term for contempt of any reporter in history — nearly seven and a half months — before he and prosecutors reached a deal in which he would turn over his outtakes in exchange for not being forced to testify before the grand jury.[93]

Two other Bay Area reporters fared somewhat better, but only because their source came forward. Mark Fainaru-Wada and Lance Williams had written about steroid use among baseball players for the San Francisco Chronicle and in a book. Part of their reporting, however, was based on grand jury testimony from a federal investigation into the Bay Area Laboratory Cooperative, or BALCO, an alleged source of illegal steroids. A special prosecutor subpoenaed the reporters to learn the source of the grand jury transcripts, which were supposed to remain secret. A district court judge, in 2006, ruled against the reporters in their challenge to the subpoena, noting that no other persons could identify the leaker.[94]

While the reporters' appeal to the Ninth Circuit was pending, the source of the grand jury transcript stepped forward — an attorney for one of the people indicted in the case against BALCO, who admitted he hoped the leak would cause a mistrial in his client's case.[95] The reporters' testimony was no longer re-

---

[83] See Adam Liptak, *Time Inc. to Yield Files on Sources, Relenting to U.S.,* N.Y. TIMES, July 1, 2005, at A1.

[84] See David Johnston & Douglas Jehl, *Times Reporter Free from Jail; She Will Testify,* N.Y. TIMES, Sept. 30, 2005, at A1.

[85] See Douglas Martin & Jacques Steinberg, *Robert Novak, Pugnacious Columnist, Dies at 78,* N.Y. TIMES, Aug. 19, 2009, at A24.

[86] 5 U.S.C.S. § 552a (LEXIS 2014).

[87] Lee v. U.S. Dep't of Justice, 287 F. Supp. 2d 15 (D.D.C. 2003).

[88] Lee v. U.S. Dep't of Justice, 413 F.3d 53, 55-60 (D.C. Cir. 2005).

[89] Lee v. U.S. Dep't of Justice, 401 F. Supp. 2d 123 (D.D.C. 2005).

[90] See Adam Liptak, *News Media Pay in Scientist Suit,* N.Y. TIMES, June 3, 2006, at A1.

[91] New York Times v. Gonzales, 459 F.3d 160 (2d Cir. 2006).

[92] In re Grand Jury Subpoena, Joshua Wolf, 201 Fed. Appx. 430 (9th Cir. 2006) (unpub.).

[93] See Bob Egelko & Jim Herron Zamora, *The Josh Wolf Case: Blogger Freed After Giving Video to Feds,* S. F. CHRON., Apr. 4, 2007, at B1.

[94] In re Grand Jury Subpoenas to Fainaru-Wada and Williams, 438 F. Supp. 2d 1111 (N.D. Cal. 2006).

[95] See Bob Egelko & John Koopman, *Lawyer Enters Guilty Plea as BALCO Leaker,* S.F. CHRON., Feb. 16, 2007, at A1.

quired, and the subpoenas were withdrawn.

In a case similar to that of Wen Ho Lee, a former reporter subpoenaed in another Privacy Act lawsuit briefly faced the possibility of financial ruin before a timely settlement was reached. Toni Locy, formerly of *USA Today,* refused to testify about her government sources for stories about Steven Hatfill, who was suing the government for leaking information about him to the press. Attorney General John Ashcroft publicly identified the scientist as a "person of interest" in the investigation into mailings of anthrax in 2001 to various politicians and journalists, resulting in five deaths. Hatfill was eventually cleared and sued the government for leaking information about him. After Locy refused to identify her sources for stories she wrote about the anthrax investigation, a federal judge ordered her to pay progressively higher fines that would total $45,000 in three weeks. Judge Reggie Walton, in an unusual twist, also ordered that she pay the fines personally, rather than having her former employer do so.[96] While Locy's appeal was pending, however, Hatfill and the government reached a multi-million dollar settlement, ending the need for her testimony.[97]

While the losses, jail sentences and threats of heavy fines greatly concerned journalists, the outcomes of the cases likely were affected by questionable behavior by the sources and the journalists involved. The sources in the Taricani and BALCO cases turned out to be attorneys who were among those under court order not to reveal evidence in pending cases. The sources in the Miller and Cooper case violated federal law, possibly for political gain, in revealing the identity of an undercover intelligence officer. The sources who leaked information to reporters about the Lee and Hatfill investigations did considerable damage to each man's reputation while hiding their own identities.

Also, it should be noted that several of the cases involved grand jury or special prosecutor subpoenas, which fall under the holding in *Branzburg.* In the Lee and Hatfill cases, judges used the Stewart three-part test to weigh the competing interests, and while the test often favors journalists subpoenaed in civil cases, it is not a guarantee of victory.

National Security and the Privilege

National security issues were involved in several of the cases mentioned in the previous section, including the two involving Judith Miller. It should come as no surprise that national security issues have become particularly sensitive since the terrorist attacks of September 11, 2001, making it harder for journalists to fight subpoenas for sources of leaks of classified information.

In 2012, Attorney General Eric Holder announced that he was naming two federal prosecutors to look into leaks of classified information to the press about the death of terrorist leader Osama bin Laden and other clandestine operations. The *New York Times* noted that the Obama administration had in three years already prosecuted more government employees for leaking information to the media than all other administrations combined.[98] In 2013, former CIA operative John Kiriakou became the first representative of that agency to go to jail for leaking information to a reporter.[99]

So far, only one journalist has been subpoenaed in relation to the leak prosecutions. James Risen, a *New York Times* reporter and author of the book *State of War,*[100] was subpoenaed to testify in the trial of former CIA employee Jeffrey Sterling, who was suspected of being a source for Risen's book chapter about a clandestine operation to sabotage Iran's suspected nuclear weapons development.[101] Risen fought the subpoena, but the Fourth Circuit U.S. Court of Appeals ruled that there was no privilege when a reporter witnessed criminal activity (in this case, revealing classified information), citing *Branzburg.*[102] The Supreme Court denied certiorari.[103] Holder told reporters after the Fourth Circuit decision that "no reporter who is doing his job is going to jail" while Holder was in office.[104] The government and the defense later dropped attempts to force Risen to testify at Sterling's trial.[105] Sterling was convicted of disclosing classified information and sentenced to forty-two months in prison.[106]

The fact that more reporters have not been subpoenaed in the Obama leak investigations is somewhat surprising because journalists are often the most direct witnesses to leaks. Some press advocates fear that the relative lack of journalists being subpoenaed in recent years only means that the government no longer needs to subpoena them. Lucy Dalglish, then executive director of the Reporters Committee for Freedom of the Press, told an interviewer in 2012 that she believed the government had honed its ability to track emails, phone calls and other communications and thus no longer needed to subpoena reporters in leak investigations because it could find out to whom they

---

[96] Hatfill v. Mukasey, 539 F. Supp. 2d 96 (D.D.C. 2008).

[97] *See* Scott Shane & Eric Lichtblau, *Scientist Is Paid Millions by U.S. in Anthrax Suit,* N.Y. TIMES, June 28, 2008, at A1.

[98] *See* Charlie Savage, *2 Inquiries Set to Track Down Paths of Leaks,* N.Y. TIMES, June 9, 2012, at A1.

[99] *See* Scott Shane, *From Spy to Source to Convict,* N.Y. TIMES, Jan. 6, 2013, at A1.

[100] JAMES RISEN, STATE OF WAR: THE SECRET HISTORY OF THE CIA AND THE BUSH ADMINISTRATION (2006).

[101] United States v. Sterling, 724 F.3d 482, 488-90 (4th Cir. 2013).

[102] *Id.* at 492.

[103] Risen v. United States, 134 S.Ct. 1361 (2014).

[104] *See* Charlie Savage, *Holder Hints Reporter May Be Spared Jail in Leak,* N.Y. TIMES, May 28, 2014, at A13.

[105] Matt Apuzzo, *Reporter Wins a 7-Year Fight Not to Testify,* N.Y. TIMES, Jan. 13, 2015, at A1.

[106] Matt Apuzzo, *Ex-C.I.A. Officer Gets Prison Term for Leak to a Times Journalist,* N.Y. TIMES, May 12, 2015, at A14.

were talking without their testimony.[107] Later revelations about the National Security Agency's widespread ability to tap the phone calls and Internet traffic of citizens seemed to bear out those concerns.[108]

In 2013, the Associated Press learned that federal investigators had secretly examined the records of twenty phone lines used by reporters and editors at the news agency, apparently in response to a story about the CIA's successful operation to stop a terrorist attack on an airliner. The Associated Press said the seizure of the phone records was a "serious interference with A.P.'s constitutional rights to gather and report the news."[109]

At about the same time, Fox News expressed outrage that Justice Department investigators had conducted expansive surveillance of Fox reporter James Rosen and had named him as a possible leak co-conspirator in the affidavit it used to request access to email records of Rosen and his alleged source from the FBI. The affidavit noted that Rosen and his alleged source in the State Department, who was allegedly giving Rosen information about North Korea's nuclear program, often entered and left the source's office building at around the same time.[110]

State Common Law and Constitutional Privileges

Eleven states have no statutory privileges, but state appellate court rulings in all but Mississippi, South Dakota and Wyoming have found that there is a qualified journalist's privilege based on the courts' interpretations of the First Amendment, state constitutions, common law or some combination of the three.[111]

Courts in Iowa and New Hampshire have stated that the qualified privilege in those states was rooted in the free press guarantees of their state constitutions.[112] Missouri, Virginia and Vermont courts have based their findings on the First Amendment.[113] The Idaho Supreme Court found support for the privilege in both the federal and state constitutions,[114] while the

Massachusetts privilege is based on the Supreme Judicial Court's interpretation of state common law.[115] Hawaii had a statutory privilege from 2008 to 2013.

STATUTORY PRIVILEGE

Because the U.S. Constitution is the supreme law of the land, one who asserts a right to do or not do something would naturally prefer to have that right enshrined as constitutional. The supremacy of the Constitution accounts to some extent for the continued insistence of journalists that their right to refuse to comply with subpoenas is protected by the Constitution despite the holding in *Branzburg*.

If a right has no constitutional basis or an unsettled one, the next best solution is often a statute. For journalists, seeking legislation that gives them a right to protect their sources and work product has a long tradition. Maryland passed the first state shield law in 1896, and while other states were slow to follow suit, the *Branzburg* decision and recent controversies such as the Judith Miller cases have led thirty-six states and the District of Columbia to follow Maryland's lead. Two states, New Mexico and Utah, have established the same protection through the adoption of formal court rules. Hawaii's legislature passed a shield law in 2008 but let it expire without renewal in 2013.[116] There also have been numerous efforts over the years to pass a federal shield law, so far all unsuccessful.

Shield laws have both advantages and disadvantages in relation to constitutional privileges.

Advantages:

• Legislatures can define classes of persons — such as journalists — to favor, as long as by doing so they do not strip others of their constitutional rights.

• Courts can often take years, even decades, to fully develop the parameters of constitutional rights. Legislatures can move much more quickly, if they choose to do so.

• Legislatures can amend shield laws to take account of new technologies or controversies more quickly than the courts can react to the same issues.

Disadvantages:

• Courts tend to interpret shield laws narrowly because they conflict with the need to present all relevant information in trials and other legal proceedings. This makes it unlikely that a court will protect a journalist in a way that the legislature did not anticipate when it wrote the statute.

• The ability of legislatures to amend shield laws quickly

---

[107] *See* Michael Calderone & Dan Froomkin, *"Reporter's Privilege" Under Fire Amid Broader War on Leaks,* HUFFINGTON POST, May 18, 2012, http://www.huffington-post.com/2012/05/18/reporter's-privilege-obama-war-leaks-new-york-times_n_1527748.html.

[108] *See, e.g., The NSA Files,* GUARDIAN, *available at* http://www.theguardian.com/world/the-nsa-files (last visited July 28, 2014).

[109] Charlie Savage & Leslie Kaufman, *Phone Records of Journalists Seized by U.S.,* N.Y. TIMES, May 24, 2013, at A1.

[110] *See* Christine Haughney, *Press Sees Chilling Effect in Justice Dept. Inquiries,* N.Y. TIMES, May 25, 2013, at A13.

[111] The South Dakota Supreme Court has said that a privilege exists but did not state the constitutional or common-law basis for that privilege. Hopewell v. Midcontinent Broadcasting Corp., 538 N.W.2d 780 (S.D. 1995).

[112] *See* Winegard v. Oxberger, 258 N.W.2d 847 (Iowa 1977); Opinion of the Justices, 373 A.2d 644 (N.H. 1977).

[113] *See* State ex. rel. Classic III, Inc. v. Ely, 954 S.W. 2d 650 (Mo. Ct. App. 1997); State v. St. Peter, 315 A.2d 254 (Vt. 1974); Brown v. Commonwealth, 204 S.E.2d 429 (Va. 1974).

[114] *In re* Contempt of Wright, 700 P.2d 40 (Idaho 1985).

[115] Sinnott v. Boston Ret. Bd., 524 N.E.2d 100 (Mass. 1988).

[116] Jack Komperda, *Hawaii Shield Law Will Expire After Lawmakers Unable to Reconcile Competing Bills,* REPORTERS COMM. FOR FREEDOM OF THE PRESS, May 3, 2013, http://www.rcfp.org/browse-media-law-resources/news/hawaii-shield-law-will-expire-after-lawmakers-unable-reconcile-compe.

could also work against journalists if lawmakers come under pressure from police or other citizens to limit journalists' rights for some reason.

• A statutory privilege generally will give way to a conflicting constitutional right, such as the Sixth Amendment right to a fair trial for a criminal defendant, instead of being balanced on a case-by-case basis.

State shield laws vary widely, as might be expected, but all of them share three basic characteristics. They define:

• Whom the laws protect,

• What the laws protect, such as confidential source identities and unpublished non-confidential information, and

• How the protection is qualified, sometimes by omission.

JURISDICTIONS WITH SHIELD LAWS

Alabama	Alaska	Arizona	Arkansas	California
Colorado	Connecticut	Delaware	District of Columbia	Florida
Georgia	Illinois	Indiana	Kansas	Kentucky	Louisiana
Maine	Maryland	Michigan	Minnesota	Montana
Nebraska	Nevada	New Jersey	New Mexico	New York
North Carolina	North Dakota	Ohio	Oklahoma	Oregon
Pennsylvania	Rhode Island		South Carolina	Tennessee
Texas	Utah	Washington	West Virginia	Wisconsin

Who is protected? Shield laws generally define "journalist" or similar terms by what the covered person does, what type of entity the person works for, or both. Some states are not specific about who is protected. For example, Michigan's shield law defines a covered person as a "reporter or other person who is involved in the gathering or preparation of news for broadcast or publication."[117] Connecticut, on the other hand, defines a covered person as someone working for

> any newspaper, magazine or other periodical, book publisher, news agency, wire service, radio or television station or network, cable or satellite or other transmission system or carrier, or channel or programming service for such station, network, system or carrier, or audio or audiovisual production company that disseminates information to the public, whether by print, broadcast, photographic, mechanical, electronic or any other means or medium.[118]

The shield laws in Delaware, Florida, Indiana, Texas and

West Virginia require that the person claiming protection must be earning income from journalism. The Indiana statute, for example, states that a covered person is someone "who receives or has received income" from engaging in journalistic activity.[119] Such a requirement could make it difficult for bloggers, freelancers and student journalists to claim protection under the statute. By contrast, Maryland's legislature recently changed that state's shield law to protect student journalists specifically.[120] West Virginia's relatively new law has an exception to its income requirement for student reporters who meet all other qualifications for the statute's definition of "reporter."[121]

How a shield statute defines who is protected by the law can be problematic if the definition is too narrow, which may explain both why some states define "journalist" broadly and others very specifically. As new media emerge, broad definition may give courts more leeway in deciding who qualifies. A specific definition can avoid courts defining the covered person too narrowly, however, as long as the list of eligible media employees is inclusive.

The narrowness of some statutory definitions of covered persons has led to bizarre outcomes. In 1986, the Michigan Court of Appeals ruled that a television reporter was not protected by the shield law as then written (it was later amended) because it referred only to print media reporters.[122] More recently, the Eleventh U.S. Circuit Court of Appeals, in a diversity jurisdiction case, ruled that a writer for *Sports Illustrated* was not protected by the Alabama shield law because the law did not specifically mention magazines.[123]

What is protected? Twelve of the forty shield laws refer only to confidential sources or information in the statutory language. Those twelve are in Alabama, Alaska, Arizona, Arkansas, Illinois, Indiana, Kentucky, Maine, New Mexico, Ohio, Pennsylvania and Rhode Island. Fairly typical is the Kentucky shield law, which states that "[n]o person shall be compelled to disclose … the source of any information procured or obtained" through journalistic work.[124]

In the other states and the District of Columbia, journalists are protected not only from having to disclose the names of confidential sources but also from having to disclose other information obtained through newsgathering activities. Again, the definitions vary widely from the broad to the specific. The Tennessee statute, for example, simply states that a journalist does not

---

[117] MICH. COMP. LAWS § 767.5a (1) (Lexis 2015).
[118] CONN. GEN. STAT. § 52-146t (2)(A) (Lexis 2015).

[119] IND. CODE ANN. § 34-46-4-1 (1)-(2) (Lexis 2015).
[120] MD. CTS. & JUD. PROC. CODE ANN. § 9-112 (b)(3) (Lexis 2015).
[121] W.VA. CODE § 57-3-10 (a) (Lexis 2015).
[122] *In re* Contempt of Stone, 397 N.W.2d 244, 246 (Mich. Ct. App. 1986).
[123] Price v. Time, Inc., 416 F.3d 1327 (11th Cir. 2005).
[124] KY. REV. STAT. § 421.100 (Lexis 2015).

have to disclose any information.[125] At the other extreme, the Colorado shield law defines protected "news information" as "any knowledge, observation, notes, documents, photographs, films, recordings, videotapes, audiotapes, and reports, and the contents and sources thereof." However, the Colorado statute excludes information gathered at a news conference, published or broadcast, or based on a journalist's personal observation of the commission of a crime.[126] Like the Colorado statute, most shield laws either explicitly or implicitly exclude published or broadcast materials from protection.

How is the protection limited? About a quarter of the shield laws are written in such a way that they could be read as absolute prohibitions on forcing journalists to reveal sources or other information. Statutes in Alabama, Arizona, California, Indiana, Kentucky, Montana, Nebraska, Nevada, New York (for confidential material only), Oregon, Pennsylvania and Texas (for civil cases only) have no qualifying language.

However, the fact that a shield law does not have qualifying language does not mean that reporters in that state will never be ordered to testify or turn over information they have gathered. Even absolute shield laws can be balanced against other statutes or constitutional rights. In California, for example, the state supreme court, in 1990, determined that a reporter and photographer who witnessed an arrest had to testify for the defense at the subsequent trial. Although California is the only state in which the shield law is also part of the state constitution,[127] the court said that in this case the defendant's Sixth Amendment rights outweighed the reporters' rights.[128] In the same year, however, the California Supreme Court ruled that reporters had an absolute right to refuse to testify or provide evidence in a civil case.[129]

Most states with shield laws and court rules protecting reporters use some variation on the Stewart three-part test to provide exceptions to the right to protect sources and work product. Arkansas, however, protects reporters unless it is shown that information from the source was published "in bad faith, with malice, and not in the interest of the public welfare."[130] Alaska's shield law says the privilege can be overcome if it is shown that withholding the information would "result in a miscarriage of justice or the denial of a fair trial" or would "be contrary to the public interest."[131]

Several shield laws have provisions that make it difficult for a journalist to protect a source while relying on information from that source as a defense in a defamation case. Shield laws in Colorado, Louisiana, Minnesota, Oklahoma, Oregon and Tennessee say that a journalist may not simultaneously claim she got defamatory information from a reliable source and then refuse to identify that source.

In Massachusetts, which does not have a shield law, a judge entered a default judgment against the *Boston Globe* in a defamation and invasion of privacy suit when the paper refused to reveal its confidential sources to the plaintiff. The Massachusetts Supreme Judicial Court affirmed the $2.1 million award to a doctor implicated by the paper in the chemotherapy overdose death of a *Globe* columnist.[132]

Are bloggers journalists? One question that has arisen is whether non-traditional communicators, such as bloggers and people who publish online magazines, or e-zines, may claim the same rights as mainstream journalists, including rights conveyed by shield laws. The answer is still unclear, in part because not many courts have dealt with the question directly.

In 2006, the California Court of Appeals ruled that the publishers of an online news magazine devoted to Apple electronic products did not have to comply with subpoenas from Apple seeking the identities of people who leaked information to the e-zines about upcoming products. The court in *O'Grady v. Superior Court* found there was no "theoretical basis" for treating e-zine publishers differently than print media publishers protected by the state shield law.[133] The New Hampshire Supreme Court came to a similar conclusion in regard to its state constitutional privilege, finding that a Web site that monitored mortgage lenders was a "reporter" for the purpose of the privilege.[134] In Illinois, a judge in a case similar to the facts of *O'Grady* initially ruled that a Web site could not protect its source for images of an upcoming smartphone before reversing himself and finding that the site was eligible for shield-law protection.[135]

However, courts in New Jersey and Oregon have found that bloggers who claimed protection under shield laws in those states did not qualify as news media or journalists under the statutes' definitions.

The New Jersey Supreme Court determined that a blogger being sued for libel over allegations of illegal activity by a company that provided services to pornographers did not have a sufficient journalism background or affiliation to claim protec-

---

[125] TENN. CODE ANN. § 24-1-208 (a) (Lexis 2015).

[126] COLO. REV. STAT. § 13-90-119 (1)(b) & (2) (a)-(d) (Lexis 2015).

[127] CALIF. CONST. ART. I, § 2.

[128] Delaney v. Superior Court, 789 P.2d 934 (Cal. 1990).

[129] New York Times Co. v. Superior Court, 796 P.2d 811 (Cal. 1990).

[130] ARK. CODE ANN. § 16-85-510 (Lexis 2015).

[131] ALASKA STAT. ART. 3 § 09.25.310 (b)(1)-(2) (Lexis 2015).

[132] Ayash v. Dana-Farber Cancer Inst., 822 N.E.2d 667 (Mass. 2005).

[133] 139 Cal. App. 4th 1423 (Cal. Ct. App. 2006).

[134] Mortgage Specialists, Inc. v. Implode-Explode Heavy Indust., Inc., 999 A.2d 184 (2010).

[135] Johns-Byrne Co. v. TechnoBuffalo LLC, No. 2011 L 009161 (Ill. Cir. Ct. July 13, 2012), *available at* http://www.dmlp.org/sites/citmedialaw.org/files/2012-07-13-order %20on%20motion%20for%20reconsideration.pdf.

tion under the state shield law.[136] In a similar case, a federal district court judge in Oregon found that a blogger who was sued for defamation by a financial services company and one of its employees she criticized was not affiliated with the types of media covered in the shield law. Also, the court noted that the shield law specifically barred journalists from its protection when they were defendants in a libel case.[137] The Ninth Circuit reversed and remanded parts of the lower court decision dealing with libel privileges but not the shield law ruling.[138]

Cases like the ones in California, Illinois, New Jersey and Oregon are real-world examples of a philosophical debate about what constitutes "journalism" in a rapidly changing media landscape and who qualifies as a journalist and may claim privilege protection. One concern among commentators is that extending protections designed for traditional media employees to bloggers and other citizen journalists would make the privilege so broad that courts and legislators would be tempted to limit or eliminate it. Commentators have responded to the concern by either recommending that the privilege be limited to those who fit a somewhat narrow normative definition of "journalist"[139] or extended to all of those who inform the public about important issues, including bloggers and other nontraditional journalists.[140]

Anonymous comments. A related debate has arisen about whether people who post anonymous comments on news organization Web sites should be protected by shield laws. The question has come up in a number of cases since 2008 in which potential libel plaintiffs, prosecutors and defense attorneys subpoenaed media Web sites for identifying information on people who commented on stories appearing online.

Newspapers, like Web site operators, are considered "Internet Service Providers" protected from liability for their users' actions under Section 230 of the Communications Decency Act.[141] Courts have developed tests to determine when ISPs must provide identifying information about their anonymous users, such as the Internet Protocol numbers of their computers or subscriber information. The tests that are most often cited were de-

veloped in *Dendrite International v. Doe*[142] and *Doe v. Cahill*.[143] Both tests require someone wishing to force an ISP to unmask an anonymous user to notify the user that his or her identity is being sought and show that the libel case being considered is viable. Additionally, courts are expected to weigh the plaintiff's need for the information against the user's First Amendment right to engage in anonymous speech.

In cases that arose starting in 2008 in Florida, Illinois, Indiana, Montana, North Carolina and Texas, however, newspapers subpoenaed by libel plaintiffs, prosecutors and criminal defense attorneys claimed their state shield laws protected their users' identities. For the most part, trial courts agreed with the newspapers that their users' identities were the types of information protected under the statutes or that the newspaper employees subpoenaed were "journalists" as defined by the shield laws.[144]

However, a trial judge in Illinois determined that the shield law in that state probably did not apply to the identities of five commenters who responded to a story about the slaying of a child. Despite the judge's doubts, however, he determined that the *Alton Telegraph* would have to identify only two of the commenters, who appeared from their comments to have direct knowledge about the crime's suspect that prosecutors had a right to ask them about.[145]

In the only case decided by a state appellate court, the Indiana Court of Appeals ruled that the state shield law did not apply to the identities of anonymous commenters. However, it said the trial judge in the libel case, in which the *Indianapolis Star* was not a party, should have used the *Dendrite* test before ordering the paper to identify a commenter.[146]

Critics of this use of the shield law argue, similar to critics of extending shield law protection to bloggers, that extending the definition of confidential source to include readers who comment on stories invites harsh reactions from legislators.[147] Other critics, including some journalists and media attorneys, argue that it is wrong to equate the often uninformed or crude comments of readers with the type of information provided by confidential sources for investigative stories. It probably is also ethically unnecessary because most Web site user agreements warn comment posters that the Web site operator will not protect them from legal consequences of their posts.[148] The counter-

---

[136] Too Much Media LLC v. Hale, 20 A.3d 364 (N.J. 2011).

[137] Obsidian Finance Group, LLC v. Cox, 2011 U.S. Dist. LEXIS 137548 (D. Or. Nov. 30, 2011).

[138] Obsidian Finance Group LLC v. Cox, 740 F. 3d 1284 (9th Cir. 2014).

[139] *See* Laurence B. Alexander, *Looking Out for the Watchdogs: A Legislative Proposal Limiting the Newsgathering Privilege to Journalists in the Greatest Need of Protection for Sources and Information*, 20 YALE L. & POL'Y REV. 97 (2002).

[140] *See* Joseph S. Alonzo, Note: *Restoring the Ideal Marketplace: How Recognizing Bloggers As Journalists Can Save the Press*, 9 N.Y.U. J. LEGIS & PUB. POL'Y 751 (2005/2006); Linda L. Berger, *Shielding the Unmedia: Using the Process of Journalism to Protect the Journalist's Privilege in an Infinite Universe of Publication*, 39 HOUS. L. REV. 1371 (2003); Mary-Rose Papandrea, *Citizen Journalism and the Reporter's Privilege*, 91 MINN. L. REV. 515 (2007).

[141] Protection for Private Blocking and Screening of Offensive Material, 47 U.S.C. § 230 (c) (Lexis 2015).

[142] 775 A.2d 756 (N.J. Super. Ct. App. Div. 2001).

[143] 884 A.2d 451 (Del. 2005).

[144] *See* Jason A. Martin, Mark R. Caramanica & Anthony L. Fargo, *Anonymous Speakers and Confidential Sources: Using Shield Laws When They Overlap Online*, 16 COMM. L. & POL'Y 89 (2011).

[145] Alton Telegraph v. Illinois, No. 08-MR-548 (Ill. Cir. Ct. May 15, 2009).

[146] *In re* Indiana Newspapers, Inc., 963 N.E.2d 534 (Ind. Ct. App. 2012).

[147] *See* Ashley I. Kissinger & Katharine Larsen, *Shielding Jane and John: Can the Media Protect Anonymous Online Speech?*, COMM. LAW, July 2009, at 4.

[148] *See* Jane E. Kirtley, *Mask, Shield and Sword: Should the Journalist's Privilege Protect the Identity of Anonymous Posters to News Media Websites?*, 94 MINN. L. REV.

argument is that journalists who value the First Amendment should not be in the business of withholding its protections from people they invite to their sites to enhance the public forum.[149] At the least, some have argued that news organizations should protect the identities of posters whose comments have contributed materially to the reporting of a story, while directing other posters to the protection offered by the *Dendrite* test.[150]

A Federal Shield Law?

Because of the inconsistencies among federal appellate circuits about the level of protection journalists enjoy under the constitutional privilege, Congress on multiple occasions has considered passing a shield law. Efforts to pass legislation picked up steam in the years immediately following the *Branzburg v. Hayes* decision, when dozens of bills were introduced. However, disagreements among senators, representatives and journalists over the scope of the privilege and whether it was necessary derailed the efforts.[151]

Interest in passing a shield law also increased in the wake of the Judith Miller cases and similar decisions. In the 111th Congress, a bill that would have created a qualified journalist's privilege passed in the House by a wide margin.[152] However, the Wikileaks Web site's disclosure of classified military and diplomatic communications raised fears that the shield law could protect sites like Wikileaks, leading to calls to amend the Senate version of the bill to exclude such sites from protection.[153] Although Senate sponsors promised to amend the bill to allay administration concerns, it died without a vote. Under congressional rules, a bill that is not passed by both houses during a two-year session of Congress dies and must start the legislative process from scratch in the next session.

A new version of the House bill was introduced in the 112th Congress but never got to a subcommittee vote.[154] After news reports about the government's seizure of Associated Press phone records and about the surveillance of a Fox News reporter, mentioned earlier in this chapter, versions of a federal shield law bill were introduced in the House and Senate in May 2013. The House bill would have protected persons who earned some portion of their incomes from gathering and reporting news. It would have exempted from protection anyone who pos-

sessed information that would threaten national security, reveal a trade secret or protected private information about a person, or that was needed to prevent serious injury or death.[155] The Senate version would not have required someone to earn income from journalistic activity to be protected and contained fewer exemptions, although it also exempted persons with information about credible threats to national security or information that could prevent death or serious injury.[156] Both versions of the bill would also have protected journalists from subpoenas for their phone and Internet use records. Neither version passed during the 113th Congress, and no bills were introduced on the subject in the 114th Congress (2015-16).

Other Sources of Protection

Journalists, like all other persons, are protected under federal law from abusive or unreasonable subpoenas. Federal Rule of Criminal Procedure 17 (c), for example, allows courts to quash subpoenas if compliance would be "unreasonable or oppressive."[157] Federal Rule of Civil Procedure 26 (c) allows federal courts to issue protective orders for witnesses if compliance with a subpoena would cause them "annoyance, embarrassment, oppression, or undue burden or expense."[158] These and similar rules in the states can protect journalists even if the courts rule that the First Amendment does not.

In addition, the U.S. Department of Justice adopted guidelines in 1970 that are designed to make it harder for the department to subpoena journalists. The rule requires department attorneys to exhaust other sources before turning to the media and requires the attorney general's approval before a member of the news media is subpoenaed.[159] The guidelines were amended in 2014 after media uproar over the AP phone records and Rosen incidents to make it harder for government attorneys to subpoena journalists and to require that the attorney general approve more of the subpoenas to journalists rather than lower-level Department of Justice officials.[160]

LIABILITY FOR REVEALING A SOURCE

As we have seen, journalists often fight hard to avoid being forced to reveal confidential sources, even going to jail. But what happens when the opposite scenario occurs and journalists voluntarily reveal their sources after promising not to do so?

1478 (2009-2010).

[149] *See id.* at 1512.

[150] *See* Martin, et al., *supra* note 144, at 123-24.

[151] *See* Jason M. Shepard, *After the First Amendment Fails: The Newsmen's Privilege Hearings of the 1970s,* 14 COMM. L. & POL'Y 373 (2009).

[152] 155 CONG. REC. H4209 (daily ed. Mar. 31, 2009) (reporting voice vote on H.R. 985).

[153] *See* Charlie Savage, *After Afghan War Leaks, Revisions in a Shield Bill,* N.Y. TIMES, Aug. 4, 2010, at A12.

[154] Free Flow of Information Act, H.R. 2932 (112th Cong. 2011).

[155] Free Flow of Information Act, H.R. 1962 (113th Cong. 2013).

[156] Free Flow of Information Act, S. 987 (113th Cong. 2013).

[157] FED. R. CRIM. PROC. 17 (c) (2015).

[158] FED. R. CIV. PROC. 26 (c) (2015).

[159] 28 C.F.R. § 50.10 (2015).

[160] *See* Charlie Savage, *Holder Tightens Rules on Getting Reporters' Data,* N.Y. TIMES, July 13, 2013, at A1.

In *Cohen v. Cowles Media Co.*[161] the Supreme Court determined that the First Amendment did not bar sources from suing news organizations for revealing their identities.

The source in the case, Dan Cohen, was a public relations professional working for a candidate for governor in Minnesota. After he gave reporters documents revealing that the opposing candidate for lieutenant governor had been arrested twice, reporters at the two major newspapers in the Twin Cities determined that the charges were minor and had been expunged from the candidate's record. Editors at the *Minneapolis Star-Tribune* and the *St. Paul Pioneer Press* then ordered the reporters to shift the focus of the story to Cohen's attempt to smear the candidate on the eve of the election and to name him as the source. Cohen was fired from his job after the stories appeared.[162] He sued the newspapers for fraudulent misrepresentation and breach of contract and won $700,000 in damages at trial. However, the Minnesota Court of Appeals and Minnesota Supreme Court reversed the trial court judgment. The Minnesota Supreme Court also speculated on whether Cohen could have prevailed on a legal theory known as *promissory estoppel* but also rejected that idea, finding that the First Amendment would bar holding the press liable for an editorial judgment as to what it should print.[163]

The U.S. Supreme Court reversed. While the newspapers argued that a judgment against them would violate the protections for publishing lawfully acquired, truthful information, the Court said it had doubts about whether Cohen's identity was lawfully obtained because the newspapers broke their promises of confidentiality. It also noted that the First Amendment does not immunize the press from "the incidental, and constitutionally insignificant" burdens associated with enforcing generally applicable laws, such as fraud and breach of contract.[164]

Perhaps because breaking a promise of confidentiality to a source raises serious ethical as well as legal issues, there have not been a large number of similar cases. In 1993, relying on *Cohen,* the Eighth U.S. Circuit Court of Appeals reinstated a lawsuit against a magazine publisher over a broken promise to a source. In *Ruzicka v. Conde Nast Publications, Inc.,*[165] a woman sued after a writer promised to protect her identity if she agreed to be interviewed for a story about patients sexually abused by their therapists. Although her name was not used, she argued that she was still recognizable to her friends and co-

workers because of details the writer included in the story. In Georgia, a state appellate court upheld a judgment against a television station in 1994 after it promised to digitally hide an AIDS victim's appearance in a story about the disease but failed to do so adequately to hide his identity.[166]

Although the issue has apparently never been litigated, it would seem unlikely that a journalist could be sued successfully for identifying a source under court order and threat of a contempt citation.

SEARCH WARRANTS

While journalists regard subpoenas demanding that they reveal their sources or turn over unpublished information to be nuisances at best and threats to the First Amendment at worst, subpoenas generally provide enough time for challenges in court. Search warrants are more ominous. If a police officer arrives at the door with a valid search warrant, the warrant usually gives the officer the right to search physical and digital files immediately. Journalists fear that search warrants might be used for fishing expeditions through their files in search of source information.

In 1978, the Supreme Court ruled that nothing in either the First Amendment or the Fourth Amendment, which protects citizens against unreasonable searches and seizures, protects the news media from valid warrants. In *Zurcher v. Stanford Daily*,[167] police in California served a search warrant at the Stanford University student newspaper looking for photographs and negatives from the paper's coverage of a violent protest at the university hospital that injured several police officers. The paper sued the police, arguing that the search violated the First and Fourth Amendments, especially in light of the fact that no one at the paper was suspected of being involved in the protest. But the Supreme Court rejected the paper's arguments, finding that the Fourth Amendment does not bar searches of places unassociated with criminal suspects if police reasonably believe evidence is there. That includes newsrooms, the First Amendment notwithstanding.

Alarmed, press groups lobbied Congress to pass a law barring law enforcement agencies from searching newsrooms. Congress responded by passing the Privacy Protection Act of 1980, which generally bars law enforcement agencies from searching or seizing the possessions of someone engaged in "public communication."[168] The law limits the power of authorities to search or seize work products, defined as impressions, conclusions, opinions or theories of the communicators, and documentary mater-

---

[161] 501 U.S. 663 (1991).

[162] *Id.* at 665-69.

[163] *Id.* at 666-67. Promissory estoppel is "[t]he principle that a promise made without consideration may nonetheless be enforced to prevent injustice if the promisor should have reasonably expected the promisee to rely on the promise and the promisee did actually rely on the promise to his or her detriment." BLACK'S LAW DICTIONARY 591 (8th ed. 2004).

[164] *Id.* at 669-71.

[165] 999 F.2d 1319 (8th Cir. 1993).

[166] Multimedia WMAZ, Inc. v. Kubach, 443 S.E.2d 491 (Ga. Ct. App. 1994).

[167] 436 U.S. 547 (1978).

[168] 42 U.S.C. § 2000aa(a) (LEXIS 2015).

ial, which includes notes, photographs, film, negatives, video-tapes, audio tapes and computer records.

There are exceptions, however. Police are allowed to search and seize work product and documentary materials if

• The communicator is suspected of a crime

• The material is needed immediately to prevent serious injury or death

• There is reason to believe that the material in question would be destroyed, altered or hidden in response to a subpoena

• A subpoena has been issued, all appeals have been exhausted and any further delay would interfere with the interests of justice.

Not surprisingly, it is rare to hear of a newsroom being the subject of a police search.

PRACTICAL TIPS

How can journalists navigate the complicated legal and ethical terrain associated with the use of confidential sources? Here are a few tips:

• Become familiar with the federal and state law in your region regarding the protection of journalists from forced disclosure of their sources and work product.

• Make sure you are aware of your employer's policies regarding the use of confidential sources and anonymous quotations.

• Get an editor's or news director's approval, if possible, before agreeing to keep a source's identity secret.

• Never enter into a confidentiality agreement with a source unless you are clear on the source's motives for providing information.

• When possible, persuade sources to go on the record or direct you to a document or someone who will agree to be quoted by name.

• Find out whether the source would be willing to be identified if you face jail time or heavy fines for protecting the source's identity.

• Never voluntarily provide anyone with the name of a confidential source without that source's permission, preferably in writing.

• For sources who work in highly sensitive government or private sector jobs, avoid using cell phones, emails and other electronic communication if possible. Meet in person and communicate by paper.

SUMMARY

There have been confidential sources nearly as long as there have been reporters. These sources often provide valuable information to journalists, but there are ethical and legal risks to entering into confidential relationships. The sources may be engaging in illegal or unethical behavior by talking to the press, and quoting them anonymously requires reporters to hide part of the truth of a story from the audience.

Despite the ethical concerns, journalists have continued to use confidential sources. On occasion, grand juries have sought the identities of sources, and journalists often resist those demands. They fear that identifying sources will discourage those and other sources from going to the media with information the public should know. Also, professional codes admonish journalists not to break promises to their sources.

It was not until the 1950s that journalists began arguing that the press clause of the First Amendment should be interpreted as protecting their right to conceal sources from discovery. As the number of subpoenas rose in the late 1960s and early 1970s, the Supreme Court accepted the cases of three reporters who had resisted efforts to get them to name their sources to grand juries investigating crimes.

The Supreme Court's 1972 decision in *Branzburg v. Hayes* held that the First Amendment did not give journalists a right to refuse to testify to grand juries when the reporters had direct evidence of criminal activity involving their sources. The Court expressed concern that recognizing such a privilege would create considerable trouble for the lower courts. For example, how would courts define who was protected by the privilege, given that anyone can claim to be a journalist? Also, the justices were concerned that the privilege would bog down the courts in determining which subpoenas were proper and which were not.

Four justices dissented. Justice Douglas called for an absolute privilege protecting journalists from answering all subpoenas. The other three justices, led by Justice Stewart, advocated the recognition of a qualified privilege, which would protect journalists from testifying unless the government could show that the information it sought was important to the case, relevant to the case and unavailable elsewhere.

The pivotal opinion in the *Branzburg* case turned out to be Justice Powell's concurrence, which emphasized the limited nature of the majority opinion and also seemed to agree with some parts of Justice Stewart's dissent. Because Justice Powell was the fifth vote for a 5-4 majority, his confusing concurrence left lower courts somewhat baffled about how to interpret the decision. The Supreme Court has accepted no other journalist's privilege case to resolve the confusion.

As a result, the federal appellate circuits have developed a qualified constitutional privilege along the lines suggested by Justice Stewart. The privilege varies from circuit to circuit, however, with most circuits adopting a privilege that protects journalists in some cases from being forced to testify in civil cases. Several circuits also protect journalists from being forced to disclose sources in criminal cases.

Three circuits have extended protection to non-confidential work products, such as unpublished photographs, unaired video or notes, on the theory that forcing journalists to disclose those materials also interferes with their rights under the First Amendment. Non-confidential information gets less protection than confidential material, however. Three other circuits have expressly refused to protect journalists from disclosing non-confidential information in criminal cases.

After a 2003 decision in the Seventh Circuit cast doubt on whether other circuits had been right to recognize a privilege, journalists lost a series of high-profile cases in which special prosecutors, grand juries and civil litigants sought the names of their sources. The losses led journalists and members of Congress to call for the passage of a federal shield law, which would give journalists limited protection from subpoenas in federal courts, but so far Congress has been unable to pass such a law.

Shield laws are much more common in the states. Thirty-nine states and the District of Columbia have statutes or formal state court rules that give widely varying degrees of protection to journalists. About a fourth of the shield laws protect only confidential sources or confidential information, but the rest also protect non-confidential work product.

The state shield laws vary widely in how they define who is protected, as well as what is protected and to what extent. Ten of the laws are written in absolute terms, but state courts have ruled that even absolute statutory privileges must give way if the journalist's statutory right conflicts with someone else's constitutional right.

In recent years, there has been much debate about whether shield laws should protect bloggers and other nontraditional journalists as well as mainstream media employees. Courts have been divided on the question, and the small number of cases so far does not provide a clear answer. Likewise, the jury is still out on whether shield laws protect the identities of people who post anonymous comments on news organization Web sites. Several state trial courts have said yes; but there have been few cases, and the one case decided by a state appellate court ruled against the newspaper on the shield law question.

In addition to finding their way through the unsettled nature of privilege law, journalists must also be aware that voluntarily identifying their sources may make them liable for damages if the disclosure harms a source. And, in rare situations, journalists may find themselves on the receiving end of search warrants, although an act of Congress limits the government's power to use that device on newsrooms.

Given the ethical and legal issues in regard to confidential sources, the best advice for a journalist might be to avoid using such sources whenever possible. If you do enter into an agreement with a source to protect her identity, however, be prepared to keep that promise, even if it means jail or fines. If a story does not seem worth that price, do not make the promise.

FOR ADDITIONAL READING

Buchanan, Kelly. "Freedom of Expression and International Criminal Law: An Analysis of the Decision to Create a Testimonial Privilege for Journalists," 35 *Victoria University of Wellington Law Review* 609 (2004).

Fargo, Anthony L. & Paul McAdoo, "Common Law or Shield Law? How Rule 501 Could Solve the Journalist's Privilege Problem," 33 *William Mitchell Law Review* 1347 (2007).

Fargo, Anthony L. "The Year of Leaking Dangerously: Shadowy Sources, Jailed Journalists, and the Uncertain Future of the Federal Journalist's Privilege," 14 *William & Mary Bill of Rights Journal* 1063 (2006).

Jones, RonNell Andersen. "Rethinking Reporter's Privilege," 111 *Michigan Law Review* 1221 (2013).

Kielbowicz, Richard B. "The Role of News Leaks in Governance and the Law of Journalists' Confidentiality, 1795-2005," 43 *San Diego Law Review* 425 (Summer 2006).

Kimball, Michele Bush. "The Intent Behind the Cryptic Concurrence That Provided a Reporter's Privilege," 13 *Communication Law and Policy* 379 (2008).

Jason A. Martin & Anthony L. Fargo, "Rebooting Shield Laws: Updating Journalist's Privilege to Reflect the Realities of Digital Newsgathering," 24 *University of Florida Journal of Law & Public Policy* 47 (2013).

Packer, Cathy. "The Politics of Power: A Social Architecture Analysis of the 2005-2008 Federal Shield Law Debate in Congress," 31 *Hastings Communication/Entertainment Law Journal* 395 (2009).

Reporters Committee for Freedom of the Press, "The Reporter's Privilege," http://www.rcfp.org/reporters-privilege.

Smith, Dean C. "The Real Story Behind the Nation's First Shield Law: Maryland, 1894-1897," 19 *Communication Law & Policy 3* (2014).

Smith, Dean C. "*Price v. Time* Revisited: The Need for Medium-Neutral Shield Laws in an Age of Strict Construction," 14 *Communication Law and Policy* 235 (2009).

Ugland, Erik. "Demarcating the Right to Gather News: A Sequential Interpretation of the First Amendment," 3 *Duke Journal of Constitutional Law & Public Policy* 113 (2008).

Youm, Kyu Ho. "International and Comparative Law on the Journalist's Privilege: The *Randal* Case as a Lesson for the American Press," 1 *Journal of International Media & Entertainment Law* 1 (2006).

Access to Courts

By Derigan Silver

➡ **Headnote Questions**

- How might media coverage of the criminal justice system interfere with a defendant's right to a fair trial?
- What remedies are available to judges to compensate for prejudicial publicity?
- Under what circumstances may a judge impose a gag order on the media?
- What might be the consequences of disobeying a judicial gag order?
- Under what circumstances may a judge impose a gag order on attorneys' or other trial participants' extrajudicial statements?
- What test do courts use to determine if a journalist can be held in contempt for commentary on or coverage of the judicial process?
- What test do courts apply to determine if the media may be punished for publishing information?
- When may a court proceeding be closed to the press and public?
- Do the press and public have a right of access to judicial records?
- What types of judicial records are considered confidential?
- Does the U.S. Constitution prohibit cameras in courtrooms? Does it require courts to admit cameras?

Every day the news is filled with stories related to the judicial system. Whether it's a celebrity charged with murder, a movie star's messy divorce, charges of rape against a sports star, or a hearing for a suspected terrorist, the courts generate news that affects and interests the public. The trials of football player Aaron Hernandez for murder, Casey Anthony for the murder of her daughter Caylee, George Zimmerman for the death of teenager Trayvon Martin, and the high-profile murder case of James Holmes, the Colorado man accused of killing twelve and wounding fifty-eight people at an Aurora, Colorado, movie theater, are simply a few recent examples of sensational court cases that have attracted massive media attention. Exhaustive coverage of sensational police investigations and court cases, however, often result in concerns about the effects of press coverage on trial fairness and allegations of "trial by media."

Free press-fair trial issues present a conflict between rights guaranteed by two amendments to the U.S. Constitution: the First Amendment right of freedom of the press and the Sixth Amendment right of a criminal defendant to a fair trial. Some argue that allowing unrestrained media coverage of crimes, arrests, pretrial proceedings and trials seriously threatens defendants' Sixth Amendment rights and that restrictions must be placed on the media to ensure the proper operation of the crim-

inal justice system. Others contend that the First Amendment cannot be subordinated to the Sixth Amendment, that a free press plays a critical role in ensuring the proper functioning of the judicial system.

The U.S. Supreme Court has adopted a balancing approach in dealing with free press-fair trial conflicts, consistently instructing trial judges to take steps to vigorously protect the rights of defendants without limiting the rights of journalists to attend court proceedings and report on crime and the operation of the court system. In general, the Court has held that restrictions on the media may be imposed only as the last resort if all else fails to ensure the defendant's right to a fair trial. Of course, this does not mean that judges do not still attempt to restrict the media and trial participants, seal records or close courtrooms. In 2012, for example, the Colorado judge in the Holmes case issued a gag order barring reporters from discussing certain aspects of the case and initially sealed all of the documents related to the case.[1] In 2014, however, the same judge wrote an eloquent opinion championing journalists' role in the proper

---

[1] *See* Amanda Simmons, *Colo. Judge Upholds Majority of Sealing and Gag Orders in Aurora Theater Shooting Case*, AI.COM, Aug. 14, 2012, http://www.rcfp.org/browse-media-law-resources/news/colo-judge-upholds-majority-of-sealing-and-gag-orders-aurora-movie-thea.

functioning of the judicial system.[2]

THE NATURE OF THE PROBLEM

Although recent developments in the use of social media by jurors and reporters have complicated issues, generally the conflict between freedom of the press and the right to a fair trial is manifested in three ways:

(1) *Pretrial publicity* may make it difficult to find impartial jurors who have not made up their minds about the defendant's guilt — or, in unusual cases, innocence — before the trial begins.

(2) *During-trial publicity* may taint a sitting jury, causing jurors to base a verdict on what they read, see or hear in the media or information that gather *via* the Internet, rather than solely on the evidence presented at trial.

(3) *The presence of journalists* and their equipment in the courtroom may cause physical and/or psychological distraction and disruption.

Let's consider each of those three potential problems and look at some Supreme Court cases dealing with them.

Pretrial Publicity

Jurors are supposed to arrive at a verdict based solely on the evidence presented to them in the courtroom. Therefore, the rules of evidence under which courts operate prevent certain types of information from being presented to the jury. Anyone who has watched a courtroom drama on TV — real or fictional — knows that such things as hearsay or the opinions of non-experts are usually ruled inadmissible. But, of course, the media don't follow court rules of evidence in deciding what to publish or broadcast. Thus, considerable information that will never reach the jury in the courtroom could reach potential jurors as they watch TV or read newspapers.

The Supreme Court has made it clear that jurors need not be "totally ignorant of the facts and issues involved" in a case to be considered impartial. Exposure to "information about a ... defendant's prior convictions or to news accounts of the crime with which he is charged" is not, standing alone, enough to disqualify a potential juror.[3] The Supreme Court has held that so long as a juror does not have "strong and deep impressions which will close the mind against the testimony that may be of-

fered in opposition to them"[4] the juror can be considered impartial.

The trick, of course, is to determine what types of publicity can result in "strong and deep impressions" that may render jurors biased. Numerous court decisions, especially those in which criminal convictions have been overturned on appeal, have discussed the types of news stories that can cause prejudice. In addition, the American Bar Association and voluntary bench-press-bar committees in several states have developed guidelines to help identify potentially prejudicial material. Most of the guidelines recognize that reporting the following types of information can create a danger.

Prior Criminal Records. Prior criminal charges and convictions are usually part of the public record, and journalists may believe it is important for the public to be informed of a defendant's past. But normally a criminal record is not admitted as evidence at trial since the jury is supposed to base its verdict on evidence relating to the *current* charge only. Officially keeping information about a defendant's record from jurors may be fruitless if they have already unofficially been informed of it through the media. It's important to recall, however, that the Supreme Court has said knowledge of a defendant's prior criminal record *alone* is not enough to disqualify a potential juror.

Confessions or Other Admissions by a Defendant. Criminal defendants sometimes make statements to the police that are declared inadmissible at trial because of the Fifth Amendment's protection against forced self-incrimination or for some other reason, such as law enforcement failing to inform a suspect of constitutional rights. As with criminal records, jurors who have heard or seen media reports of a confession, or even references to the existence of a confession, may have a hard time forgetting those reports when they deliberate.

The Results of Investigative Procedures or Tests. The admissibility of test results can be the basis for a key battle in a criminal case, and such information is often kept from a jury. In addition, reporting that the accused refused to submit to a test or procedure could leave the impression that the defendant had something to hide.

Opinions Regarding the Character, Personality, Guilt or Innocence of the Accused. As numerous cases have shown, the media attach derogatory nicknames to suspects, report alleged character flaws, unusual lifestyles or suspicious behavior, or conduct on-the-street interviews about a defendant's guilt or innocence. These so-called "trials by media" can result in widespread per-

---

[2] People of the State of Colorado v. James Eagan Holmes, No. 12CR1522, Order In Regards to Defendant's Request to Close Jury Selection to the Public (D-154-a2), Jun. 11, 2014, *available* at http://www.courts.state.co.us/userfiles/file/Court_Probation/18th_Judicial_District/18th_Courts/12CR1522/007/Order%20Regarding%20Defendants%20Request%20to%20Close%20Jury%20Selection%20to%20the%20Public%20%20D-154-a-2.pdf.

[3] Murphy v. Florida, 421 U.S. 794, 799-800 (1975).

---

[4] United States v. Burr, 25 F. Cas. 49, 50-51 (D. Va. 1807).

ceptions of guilt regardless of evidence introduced at trial.

Speculation on Evidence or Witnesses. Prospective witnesses who tell journalists what they intend to say in court may change their minds or be prevented from making certain statements before the jury. Police officers and lawyers may often be the source of leaks about potential evidence or witnesses, adding a ring of authority to the speculation.

In addition to those five categories, any sensational coverage of a crime and its aftermath is potentially prejudicial. Three important cases in which the Supreme Court considered claims that pretrial publicity robbed defendants of their rights to impartial juries provide examples of prejudicial coverage as well as an understanding of the types of publicity that may constitute grounds to overturn a conviction.

Irvin v. Dowd,[5] decided in 1961, marked the first time the Supreme Court overturned a state criminal conviction solely because of prejudicial publicity. Leslie "Mad Dog" Irvin, as the media dubbed him, was charged with the murder of Whitney Wesley Kerr, one of six victims in a series of murders in the vicinity of Evansville, Indiana. Although Irvin was tried for only one murder, the police, prosecutor and media all made it clear they believed he was responsible for all six. The Supreme Court described the publicity surrounding the trial as "a barrage of newspaper headlines, articles, cartoons and pictures." News stories revealed Irvin's juvenile record, his prior convictions for arson and burglary, and his court-martial on AWOL charges during World War II. The media also reported that he had confessed to the six murders and offered to plead guilty if promised a ninety-nine-year sentence. One report characterized Irvin as "remorseless and without conscience."[6]

The effects of this publicity were evident during jury selection. The court excused 268 of 430 prospective jurors "as having fixed opinions" of Irvin's guilt. Almost 90 percent of the potential jurors "entertained some opinion as to guilt — ranging in intensity from mere suspicion to absolute certainty." Of the twelve jurors finally chosen, eight admitted they thought Irvin was guilty although all twelve said they would be fair and impartial. In reversing Irvin's conviction and death sentence, the Supreme Court wrote: "

With his life at stake, it is not requiring too much that [Irvin] be tried in an atmosphere undisturbed by so huge a wave of public passion and by a jury other than one in which two-thirds of the members admit, before hearing any testimony,

to possessing a belief in his guilt.[7]

Irvin was retried and again found guilty of murder. He was sentenced to life imprisonment.

Two years later, the Supreme Court again reversed a conviction, this time based on the pretrial broadcasting of the defendant's confession. Wilbert Rideau was arrested and charged with bank robbery, kidnapping and murder.[8] Without being informed of his right to remain silent and to have an attorney, Rideau confessed to the crimes — both on and off camera. A twenty-minute interview with Rideau, during which he was "flanked by the sheriff and two state troopers," was broadcast for three consecutive days to estimated audiences of 24,000, 29,000 and 53,000 in Calcasieu Parish, Louisiana, with a population of about 150,000. Rideau's motion for a change of venue was denied, and the trial was held with a jury that included three persons who admitted they had seen the televised confession. Rideau was convicted and sentenced to death.

The Supreme Court ruled that the judge's refusal to move the trial to a community in which Rideau's confession had not been televised violated the defendant's due process rights. On retrial Rideau was once again convicted, and the Louisiana Supreme Court upheld that second conviction.

Among lawyers, judges and journalists, *Sheppard v. Maxwell*[9] has become synonymous with prejudicial publicity. The Supreme Court's reversal of Samuel Sheppard's conviction in 1966 was based on all three free press-fair trial problems listed earlier in this chapter, but the focus here will be on the nature and extent of the pretrial coverage.

In the early morning of July 4, 1954, Marilyn Sheppard was beaten to death in her bed in her home in Bay Village, a suburb of Cleveland, Ohio. Her husband, Samuel, a surgeon and member of a wealthy, prominent family that ran an osteopathic hospital, said he had fallen asleep on the couch downstairs and was awakened by his wife's cries. Sheppard testified that when he ran upstairs, he saw what he called "a form" by his wife's bed and was struck on the back of the neck and knocked unconscious. After he came to, he said, he went downstairs, saw someone run out the door and pursued the person to the lake behind his home, where a struggle ensued and he was again knocked unconscious. When he awoke, he returned to the house, checked his wife and determined she was dead. He then called a neighbor, who called the police.

The pretrial publicity that followed was relentless and, according to the Supreme Court, virulent. Within days of the murder, Cleveland newspapers began emphasizing Sheppard's al-

---

[5] 366 U.S. 717 (1961).

[6] *Id.* at 725-26.

[7] *Id.* at 727-28.

[8] Rideau v. Louisiana, 373 U.S. 723 (1963).

[9] 384 U.S. 333 (1966).

leged lack of cooperation with the police — which the Supreme Court later indicated was untrue — and his refusal to take a lie detector test or be injected with truth serum. Front-page editorials charged "Somebody's Getting Away with Murder" and demanded an inquest. The inquest, which was called the next day, was held in a school gymnasium and broadcast live. During and after the inquest, news stories emphasized incriminating evidence, much of which was never presented at the trial. The media also focused on Sheppard's personal life, especially his admitted affair with one woman and alleged — but never admitted or proven — affairs with others. A few days after the inquest, a front-page editorial asked, "Why Isn't Sam Sheppard in Jail?" and demanded, "Quit Stalling — Bring Him In." At about 10 p.m. the day the editorial appeared, Sheppard was arrested for his wife's murder.

Between July 5, when the murder was first reported in the media, and July 30, the day Sheppard was arrested, the *Cleveland Plain Dealer* ran a page-one story about the case twenty-five of the twenty-six days, with twelve of those stories under banner headlines. The *Cleveland Press* ran a page-one story each of the twenty-three days it published during the same period and printed three page-one editorials.[10]

In its opinion overturning Sheppard's conviction — eleven years after the jury verdict — the Supreme Court listed numerous examples of prejudicial and sensational coverage. For example, before jury selection, all three Cleveland papers published the names and addresses of the prospective jurors. "As a consequence, anonymous letters and telephone calls, as well as calls from friends, regarding the impending prosecution were received by all of the prospective jurors," the Court wrote. Despite this, Judge Edward Blythin, who was running for reelection, refused to move the location or delay the start of the trial, despite the fact that all but one of the twelve jurors selected admitted reading about the case in the newspapers.[11]

Despite the massive, prejudicial pretrial news coverage, the Supreme Court said that alone did not constitute a denial of due process. Instead, the Court said its reversal of Sheppard's conviction was based on the "totality of the circumstances," including juror exposure to publicity during the trial and disruptions the media caused.[12]

In 2010, in *Skilling v. United States*, the Court laid out a number of factors that have to be considered before the publicity can be deemed prejudicial. First, the Court wrote, it is important to consider "the size and characteristics of the community in which the crime occurred."[13] In large diverse communi-

ties, it is highly unlikely that unbiased jurors would not be available. Second, the Court held that to be prejudicial, stories about a defendant must contain a confession or some other blatantly prejudicial information "of the type readers or viewers could not reasonably be expected to shut from sight."[14] Third, courts should consider the amount of time that had passed between a widely reported crime and the trial for that crime. Finally, the Court noted that it is important to consider whether a jury provided an "overwhelming victory" for the prosecution. The Court concluded this consideration was of "prime significance" as it "would be odd for an appellate court to presume prejudice in a case in which jurors' actions run counter to that presumption."[15]

During-Trial Publicity

The same types of stories that could prejudice potential jurors if published before a trial can also taint a sitting jury. The Supreme Court has said that the effect of highly prejudicial information "may indeed be greater" when it reaches jurors through the media rather than through testimony in court "for it is then not tempered by protective procedures."[16]

The Supreme Court has considered several cases involving prejudicial during-trial media coverage. In 1959, in *Marshall v. United States*, the Court reversed the federal criminal conviction of Howard R. Marshall, who was charged with illegally dispensing drugs to an undercover Food and Drug Administration inspector. During the trial, two potentially damaging newspaper articles appeared. One reported Marshall had two prior felony convictions, had written prescriptions for dangerous drugs, and, while serving a forgery sentence in Oklahoma, had told a legislative committee he practiced medicine with a $25 mail-order diploma. The article also stated that Marshall "acted as a physician and prescribed restricted drugs for Hank Williams before the country singer's death." The second article said Marshall had been arrested with his wife, who was convicted of drug charges and sentenced to jail.[17]

The judge had refused to admit as evidence much of the information published in the two articles, specifically because of its highly prejudicial nature. After the articles were published, the judge questioned each juror and learned that seven had seen at least one story. The jurors assured him they could be impartial, however, and the judge denied Marshall's motion for a mistrial. The jury brought in a conviction, which the Supreme Court overturned because of the jurors' exposure to the prejudi-

---

[10] *See* ALFRED FRIENDLY & RONALD L. GOLDFARB, CRIME AND PUBLICITY 14 (1967).

[11] 384 U.S. at 342, 354 n.9.

[12] *Id.* at 352.

[13] 561 U.S. 358, 361 (2010).

[14] *Id.* at 382.

[15] *Id.* at 383.

[16] Marshall v. United States, 360 U.S. 310, 313 (1959).

[17] *Id.* at 311-12.

cial information.

As noted above, publicity during the trial also played a major role in the reversal of Sam Sheppard's conviction in 1966. The jury was not sequestered until it began deliberations, and the judge failed to give adequate instructions regarding juror exposure to the media. He suggested and requested that jurors avoid media coverage of the case, but he never ordered them to do so. Several times throughout the trial Sheppard's attorney requested that the judge question jurors about their exposure to specific, highly prejudicial coverage. The judge refused all but once. That one instance resulted from a television and radio broadcast in which Walter Winchell reported that a woman arrested in New York for robbery said she was Sheppard's mistress and the mother of his child. Two jurors admitted hearing the broadcast — despite the judge's suggestions and requests. After the jurors assured him that the broadcast would not affect their decisions, the judge "merely asked the jury to 'pay no attention whatever to that type of scavenging.... Let's confine ourselves to this courtroom, if you please.'" The Supreme Court considered such admonitions insufficient to protect the jury from outside influence.[18]

The Effects of Publicity

While there is widespread agreement about the types of publicity that are prejudicial, there is significantly less agreement about the actual *effects* of such publicity on jurors. As noted, the Sixth Amendment does not guarantee a defendant freedom from inflammatory publicity; it guarantees a trial by an "impartial jury." The key question, then, is whether news coverage of a case — either pretrial or during trial — actually affects jurors' impartiality. Opinions and evidence are mixed. In all of the cases discussed previously, the jurors told the judges that, despite the publicity, they could be impartial. However, Justice Tom Clark, who wrote the Court's opinion in *Irvin v. Dowd*, was skeptical: "No doubt each juror was sincere when he said that he would be fair and impartial," but "[w]here so many, so many times, admitted prejudice, such a statement of impartiality can be given little weight."[19]

Numerous efforts to measure the effects of publicity on jurors during the past six decades have proved inconclusive. As one study concluded, "[A]fter 50 years of scientific research on juries and juror decision making, there are still many gaps in understanding how factors such as pretrial publicity ... influence juries."[20] A key problem with empirical studies is that they gener-

ally involve mock trials and juries — experimental simulations — rather than real jurors deciding real cases.[21] Real juror deliberations are conducted behind closed doors, and courts fear that allowing researchers to tape deliberations might improperly influence jurors. Jurors in the experiments are often exposed to news stories after which the trial immediately begins. This ignores the fact that, in real life, exposure to prejudicial coverage may go on for months before the trial actually starts. Real jurors have the time to either forget much of what they saw in the media or, perhaps because of repeated references, they become convinced of its accuracy. Furthermore, in the experiments, all jurors are exposed to the same news stories, another unrealistic circumstance that may, in fact, affect the studies' results.

Despite their drawbacks, experimental research and studies of public reaction to news stories are the main sources of data for lawyers, judges and scholars trying to determine the effects of prejudicial publicity. An article in the *Stanford Law Review* summarized the results of empirical studies:

> Experiments to date indicate that for the most part juries are able and willing to put aside extraneous information and base their decisions on the evidence. The results show that when ordinary citizens become jurors, they assume a special role in which they apply different standards of proof, more vigorous reasoning and greater detachment.[22]

This confirms what many judges and lawyers firmly believe: Individuals called to jury duty generally take their responsibility very seriously; they listen to and obey the judge's instructions; they recognize that a human being's liberty and perhaps life are in their hands; and they want to make the right decision based on the evidence and the law.

In the landmark 1966 study *The American Jury*, not one of 555 judges who had presided over 3,576 criminal cases mentioned publicity as a factor affecting a jury's decision.[23] That's largely due to the fact that most criminal cases receive little publicity. While trials that are particularly scandalous or shocking or involve famous defendants such as O.J. Simpson, Michael Jackson or Kobe Bryant may receive a great deal of media attention, these trials can make us lose sight of the fact that "pre-

---

[18] 384 U.S. 333, 348-58 (1966).

[19] 366 U.S. 717, 728 (1961).

[20] Tarika Daftary-Kapur, Rafaele Dumas & Steven D. Penrod, *Jury Decision-Making Biases and Methods to Counter Them*, 15 LEGAL & CRIMINOLOGICAL PSCHOL. 133 (2010).

[21] *See, e.g.*, Geoffrey P. Kramer, Norbert L. Kerr & John S. Carroll, *Pretrial Publicity, Judicial Remedies and Jury Bias*, 14 LAW & HUM. BEHAV. 409 (1990); Robert Riedel II, *Effects of Pretrial Publicity on Male and Female Jurors and Judges in a Mock Rape Trial*, 73 PSYCHOL. REP. 819 (1993); Jerry Shaw & Paul Skolnick, *Effects of Prejudicial Pretrial Publicity From Physical and Witness Evidence on Mock Jurors' Decision Making*, 34 J. APPLIED SOC. PSYCHOL. 2132 (2006).

[22] Rita J. Simon, *Does the Court's Decision in* Nebraska Press Association *Fit the Research Evidence on the Impact on Jurors of News Coverage?*, 29 STAN. L. REV. 515, 528 (1977).

[23] HARRY KALVEN JR. & HANS ZEISEL, THE AMERICAN JURY (1966).

judicial publicity is often only a factor in the rare, sensational case; elsewhere it appears to be close to nonexistent."[24] A 1999 study reported that of 134 federal, first-degree murder cases, 65 percent received little or no newspaper coverage. The study also found no significant relationship between the amount of publicity a case received and the verdict. Conviction rates in cases that generated high levels of publicity were virtually identical to those in cases involving no publicity.[25] Thus, although some research has found that potential jurors are more affected by television coverage of very sensational crimes than they are by print coverage,[26] most cases warrant little or no coverage at all by either print or broadcast journalists.

Disruption in the Courtroom

Publishing or broadcasting prejudicial material isn't the only way in which the media might interfere with a fair trial. The presence of journalists and their equipment in a courtroom could physically disrupt the proceedings, perhaps distracting jurors and trial participants or creating an atmosphere inconsistent with fairness and calm, reasoned deliberation. Some people, including Supreme Court justices, have argued that the presence of cameras in courtrooms causes psychological disruption sufficient to violate a defendant's rights.

The trial of Bruno Hauptmann in 1935 for kidnapping Charles and Anne Morrow Lindbergh's 18-month-old son is often cited as an early example of journalists disrupting the judicial process and as the reason the American Bar Association recommended in 1937 that cameras be banned in all courtrooms.

Because of the international popularity of Charles Lindbergh, the first person to fly solo across the Atlantic Ocean, journalists from around the world crowded into the small town of Flemington, New Jersey, where the trial was held. Estimates of the number of media members present ranged from about 200 to nearly 1,000. While the Hauptmann trial may have been the impetus for the camera ban, the evidence indicates most journalists obeyed the judge's ban on photographing while court was in session. And, while the case has been repeatedly cited as evidence of press misbehavior, various accounts of the proceedings seem to indicate that court officials and the general public contributed to the lack of decorum as much as, if not more than, the media.[27] Regardless of who was actually to blame for what occurred in the courtroom, the trial became a prominent example of media interference with the judicial process.

By the 1960s, when Texas financier Billie Sol Estes went on trial for swindling, only two states — Colorado and Texas — permitted televising trials under some conditions. From the outset, Estes' attorney objected to broadcasting the proceedings, but the judge allowed both radio and television to broadcast the pretrial hearing live. According to the Supreme Court, twelve cameramen moved around the courtroom; cables and wires were "snaked across" the floor; three microphones were set up on the judge's bench; and "others were beamed at the jury box and the counsel table."

During the trial itself, four cameras — one for each of the three major networks and one for a local station — and camera operators were confined to a booth specially constructed at the rear of the courtroom and painted to blend into the walls. Only the state's opening and closing arguments and the delivery of the jury's verdict were broadcast live with sound. Other portions of the trial, however, were filmed, without sound, and broadcast during regular newscasts.

In the light of the exhaustive, nearly twenty-four-hour coverage of recent trials, all of this seems relatively tame and nonthreatening. Nonetheless, the Supreme Court voted 5-4 to overturn Estes' conviction, saying he had been deprived of "that judicial serenity and calm to which [he] was entitled."[28] Justice Clark, for the Court, contended that televising trials caused both physical and psychological disruptions and could negatively impact the jury, judge, witnesses and defendant.

The *Sheppard* case provides the classic example of disruptions resulting from media presence in the courtroom. Journalists filled most of the seats in the 26-by-48-foot room. The judge allowed about twenty newspaper and wire service reporters to sit at a temporary table inside the bar directly behind Sheppard and his attorney, making "confidential talk [between them] ... almost impossible.... They frequently had to leave the courtroom to obtain privacy." The journalists' frequent movement in and out "caused so much confusion that, despite the loud-speaker system installed in the courtroom, it was difficult for the witnesses and counsel to be heard." The media were permitted to install private telephone lines and telegraphic equipment in all of the rooms on the floor where the courtroom was located. In addition, a radio station set up broadcasting facilities in a room on the third floor next to the jury room. Cameras were not permitted in the courtroom, although "[i]n the corridors outside the courtroom there was a host of photographers and television personnel with flash cameras, portable lights and motion picture cameras." Jurors, witnesses, attorneys and the defendant were repeatedly filmed as they en-

---

[24] FRIENDLY & GOLDFARB, *supra* note 10, at 69.

[25] Jon Bruschke & William E. Loges, *Relationship Between Pretrial Publicity and Trial Outcomes*, J. COMM., Dec. 1999, at 104.

[26] *See* James R. P. Ogloff & Neil Vidmar, *The Impact of Pretrial Publicity on Jurors: A Study to Compare the Relative Effects of Television and Print Media in a Child Sex Abuse Case*, 18 LAW & HUM. BEHAV. 507 (1994).

[27] *Id.*

[28] Estes v. Texas, 381 U.S. 532, 536-37 (1965).

tered and exited the courtroom.[29]

The Supreme Court summarized the situation this way: "The fact is that bedlam reigned ... during the trial and newsmen took over practically the entire courtroom, hounding most of the participants in the trial, especially Sheppard."[30] The existence of this "carnival atmosphere," coupled with the prejudicial publicity that saturated the community before and during the trial, led the Court to reverse Sheppard's conviction. When retried a few months later, Sheppard was found not guilty.

Despite changes in technology that have greatly reduced the intrusive nature of cameras and recording equipment, as discussed below, allowing cameras and portable electronic devices such as smartphones that allow journalists to tweet from the courtroom continues to be a contentious issue.

COMPENSATING FOR PREJUDICIAL PUBLICITY

There are two broad categories of remedies designed to deal with problems created by media coverage of trials:

1. Measures designed to compensate for the existence of prejudicial publicity.

2. Measures designed to prevent, or at least diminish, prejudicial publicity and to control the presence and/or activities of journalists in the courtroom.

The key difference between the two types of remedies is that the former seeks to mitigate or lessen the *effects* of media coverage without restricting it. Therefore, use of the first category of remedies does not raise First Amendment concerns because no interference with the operations of the press occurs. In contrast, the remedies in the second category are designed to control journalists, prevent access to courtroom proceedings and limit coverage of trial proceedings and thus raise serious First Amendment issues.

The Supreme Court has repeatedly declared that the trial judge has the responsibility to protect a defendant's right to a fair trial. In *Sheppard*, *Estes*, *Rideau* and *Irvin*, although the Court indicated its disapproval of and disenchantment with the press' performance, it focused on what the judges should have done to safeguard the defendants' rights. Here we will focus on the traditional tools that judges can use to compensate for the effects of publicity without restricting access or publication.

Change of Venue

When a trial is moved to a new location, it's called a "change of venue." The new location is one in which the publicity has not been as intense and, therefore, potential jurors are less likely to

have been influenced by pretrial coverage. Change of venue requires, however, that a defendant give up another Sixth Amendment right — the right to be tried in the "district wherein the crime shall have been committed." Generally, however, this presents no problem since the motion for a venue change comes from the defense attorney.

Whether a change of venue will be effective in mitigating the impact of prejudicial publicity depends on several factors, one being how far the trial is moved. In *Irvin v. Dowd*, the judge agreed to move the trial from Vanderburgh County, Indiana, to neighboring Gibson County. Considering that 90 percent of the prospective jurors questioned said they believed Irvin was guilty, it would appear that moving the trial such a short distance did little to protect Irvin's right to an impartial jury.

If a case is subject to nationwide publicity it's unlikely that moving it anywhere would make a difference in prospective jurors' exposure to media coverage. Defense lawyers tried to get the trial of Enron executives Kenneth Lay and Jeffrey Skilling moved out of Houston, citing a pretrial survey showing more than 80 percent of potential jurors believed the two were guilty. U.S. District Court Judge Sim Lake, however, refused, saying adequate safeguards existed to ensure the fairness of a Houston jury.[31] As noted above, on appeal, the Supreme Court created a test to determine when a change of venue is warranted.

While a change of venue may make it easier to find unbiased jurors, it also increases the costs and inconveniences associated with a trial. A major objection to moving the 1995 trial of Oklahoma City bombers Terry Nichols and Timothy McVeigh to Denver was the hardship the move caused for survivors and victims' families who wanted to attend the proceedings. In response, Congress passed a law requiring closed-circuit televising of a federal trial when it is moved from its original location out of the state and more than 350 miles away so that victims and their relatives can view the televised proceedings.[32]

Change of Venire

"Venire" refers to the pool of potential jurors from which a trial jury will be selected. To change the venire is to import jurors from another community. The tool is much less common than change of venue. As with change of venue, a change of venire only works if the publicity has been confined to the location in which the crime occurred. It also can be an expensive option since it requires the state to pay for transporting, housing and feeding jurors for the duration of the trial.

---

[29] 384 U.S. 333, 333-44 (1966).

[30] *Id.* at 355.

[31] *See* Skilling v. United States, 561 U.S. 358, 358 (2010).

[32] Antiterrorism and Effective Death Penalty Act, 42 U.S.C. § 10608(a) (Supp. 1999).

Continuance

To continue a trial is to delay it. Like change of venue, it requires a defendant to sacrifice a constitutional right — the right to a speedy trial — in the hope of enhancing juror fairness. Postponing a trial may be an effective remedy if publicity surrounding an arrest and trial can reasonably be expected to diminish over time. Studies have shown that people forget much of what they read in newspapers or saw on television news; and, especially in large cities, a continuance may mean another crime will have taken over the headlines by the time the trial begins.[33] Of course, there's always the possibility that publicity will flare up again once a trial starts. In addition, for defendants who are not granted bail or are unable to pay it, delaying a trial means they must remain in jail longer awaiting trial.

Voir Dire

"Voir dire" is the term for the process at the beginning of a trial when potential jurors are questioned to determine if they can be impartial. It is a crucial part of the trial and, in highly publicized, sensational trials, it can take weeks, with hundreds of jurors questioned. In the murder trial of O.J. Simpson, 304 prospective jurors were questioned in a voir dire that took eleven weeks. In the trial of Jeffrey Skilling, the court sent a seventy-seven-question, fourteen-page document to 400 perspective jurors that asked about their source of news, exposure to Enron-related stories and their opinions regarding the defendants prior to conducting face-to-face questioning.[34] The jury selection process for the Aurora theater shooting case was one of the longest and most complex on record. The court summoned 9,000 potential jurors, 403 of whom were asked face-to-face questions over thirty-eight days.[35]

Both the prosecution and defense may challenge an unlimited number of jurors for cause. The judge then determines if there is sufficient reason to believe a potential juror is biased or for some other reason unsuited to sit on the jury. Attorneys for both sides also can dismiss a limited number of jurors with peremptory challenges. An attorney does not need to provide a reason for using a peremptory challenge. The number of peremptory challenges available to each side differs depending on the type of case and jurisdiction.

Judges, including the Supreme Court justices, have placed a great deal of faith in the voir dire process and believe that, if correctly used, it can effectively weed out biased jurors.[36] Critics, however, note that potential jurors can and do hide the truth, whether consciously or unconsciously.

Admonitions to the Jury

A judge may order jurors not to read, watch or listen to any coverage of or commentary on the trial, not to discuss it with anyone except other jurors and then only when deliberations begin, and not to use the Internet or research the case. These admonitions are intended to impress upon them their responsibility to decide the case solely based on the law and evidence presented in court. Failure to follow the orders can result in removal from the jury, citation for contempt of court or both. For example, in the Aurora theater shooting case, the judge released four jurors because one had discussed media coverage of the trial with the other two.[37] Whether jury admonitions actually prevent juror exposure to media coverage of the trial is uncertain; but, as with voir dire, most judges say they believe that admonitions are effective in most cases.

Sequestration

Sequestration is the most extreme, costly and seldom-used remedy designed to shelter jurors from prejudicial publicity. Sequestration means isolating the jury for the duration of the trial. It entails housing the jurors in a hotel, screening their phone calls and monitoring their use of mass media to ensure that they do not see or hear any media coverage of the trial. While sequestration can be very effective in preventing jury exposure to prejudicial publicity, it is a remedy that also has many drawbacks. It adds significantly to the cost of the trial because the state must transport, house, feed and guard the jurors. Perhaps more importantly, though, sequestration creates significant disruptions to jurors' lives and effectively eliminates from juries people who cannot leave their families or jobs for weeks or even months. In addition, keeping jurors away from family, friends and normal routines for an extended period of time may have unintended psychological effects, causing jurors to resent the defendant and blame him or her for disrupting their lives.

---

[33] See, e.g., Daftary-Kapur et al., supra note 20; Geoffrey P. Kramer, Norbert L. Kerr & John S. Carroll, Pretrial Publicity, Judicial Remedies and Jury Bias, 14 L. & Hum. Behav. 409 (1990).

[34] Skilling, 561 U.S at 359.

[35] See John Ingold, Aurora Theater Shooting Jury Pool Cut Down to 115 Names, Denver Post, Apr. 10, 2015, available at http://www.denverpost.com/news/ci_278917 92/aurora-movie-theater-shooting-jury-pool-cut-down.

[36] See, e.g., Skilling, 561 U.S. at 386 (writing that trial court judges conducting voir dire are very capable of ascertaining a juror's impartiality through the juror's "inflection, sincerity, demeanor, candor, body language, and apprehension of duty" and trial courts' use of voir dire should be given "wide discretion" by appellate courts).

[37] See Jordan Steffan & John Ingold, Aurora Theater Shooting Judge Releases Three Jurors for Misconduct, Denver Post, Jun. 9, 2015, available at http://www.denverpost.com/theater-shooting-trial/ci_28281114/aurora-theater-shooting-gunmans-sister-ca uses-stir-court.

PREVENTING OR DIMINISHING PUBLICITY

Despite the existence of the remedies discussed above, trial judges sometimes try to control what information journalists have access to or prevent the media from publishing or broadcasting information they have obtained. These efforts raise significant First Amendment implications, and during the past twenty years the Supreme Court has severely limited their use, although in high profile cases judges still frequently attempt to restrict the press. Remedies aimed at eliminating or reducing prejudicial publicity and media interference with fair trial rights fall into six categories: (1) restrictive orders (also called "gag orders") aimed at the media, (2) restrictions on trial participants, (3) post-publication sanctions, (4) court closures, (5) denials of access to court records and (6) bans or limits on the use of cameras or portable electronic devices in the courtroom.

Gag Orders on the Media

While in *Sheppard v. Maxwell* the Supreme Court provided a list of tools trial judges could use to protect defendants' rights, it never suggested judges issue restrictive orders prohibiting the media from publishing information that might be prejudicial. Nonetheless, that's exactly what some judges did in the wake of the Court's decision.

In 1976, the Supreme Court put a halt to the indiscriminate use of press gag orders. The landmark case *Nebraska Press Association v. Stuart*[38] began on October 18, 1975, when police arrived at the Henry Kellie home in Sutherland, Nebraska, a town of 850 people, to find six family members with shotgun wounds to their heads. Five were already dead, and the sixth died later that night. The next day Erwin Charles Simants, a neighbor of the Kellies, was arrested and charged with the murders. He admitted to police that he had killed the Kellies and was arraigned. Reporters learned of his confessions and publicized the information, along with speculation — later confirmed by autopsies — that Simants had sexually assaulted some of the victims after murdering them.

Both geography and Nebraska law complicated protecting Simants' right to a fair trial. The court in which Simants was to be tried was in North Platte, population 19,000, the county seat of Lincoln County, just twenty miles east of Sutherland. Publicity about the crime had, of course, been as widespread in North Platte, the largest city in southwest Nebraska, as in Sutherland. Nebraska law restricted the use of continuance and change of venue by requiring that the accused be brought to trial within six months and also allowing a change of venue to an adjoining county, all of which were smaller than Lincoln County.

The county attorney proposed a solution to Judge Ronald Ruff — a gag order prohibiting publication of potentially prejudicial material. The next day Judge Ruff barred publication of testimony and evidence presented during the preliminary hearing. In addition, he ordered journalists to abide by the Nebraska Bar-Press Guidelines, a set of voluntary recommendations for minimizing prejudicial publicity.[39]

The media immediately appealed to District Court Judge Hugh Stuart. Finding that there was a "clear and present danger that pre-trial publicity could harm the defendant's right to a fair trial," Judge Stuart vacated Judge Ruff's order and entered his own, which also incorporated the bar-press guidelines and prohibited publication of specific information — including the existence and contents of Simants' confession and information relating to the sexual assaults — until after a jury had been impaneled. His order also prohibited the media from reporting on the exact nature of the gag order itself.[40]

Although the Supreme Court granted *certiorari*, it denied a motion to expedite review or stay the order during the trial. Thus, it was not until five months after Simants was tried, convicted and sentenced to death that a unanimous Court held that Stuart's gag order was a prior restraint that violated the First Amendment. Incidentally, Simants' conviction was eventually overturned on the ground that a sheriff had tried to influence the sequestered jury. On retrial Simants was found not guilty by reason of insanity, which was his original plea.

In *Nebraska Press Association*, all nine justices agreed that the gag order was unconstitutional. However, they did not all agree on the reasons. Chief Justice Warren Burger, joined by four other justices, took a balancing approach, using a variation of the clear and present danger test, which had been developed in the context of sedition cases. After acknowledging that prior restraints "are the most serious and the least tolerable infringement on First Amendment rights," Burger said the constitutionality of a gag order had to be determined by looking at the circumstances of a particular case and deciding whether "'the gravity of the "evil," discounted by its improbability,'" justified a gag order.[41] To determine this, Burger said three factors must be considered:

(1) the nature and extent of pretrial news coverage,

(2) whether other measures would be likely to mitigate the effects of unrestrained publicity, and

(3) how effectively a restraining order would operate to prevent the threatened danger.[42]

Judges still use this three-part test to decide whether restric-

---

[38] 427 U.S. 539 (1976).

[39] *Id.* at 542.

[40] *Id.* at 543-44.

[41] *Id.* at 559, 562 (quoting United States v. Dennis, 183 F.2d 201, 212 (2d Cir. 1950), *aff'd*, 341 U.S. 494 (1951)).

[42] *Id.* at 562.

tive orders can be imposed on the media.

Burger said Judge Stuart was correct in concluding there would be intense and pervasive pretrial publicity. However, he failed to consider whether alternative measures might have protected Simants' right to a fair trial. Furthermore, Burger voiced doubts about the effectiveness of the gag order. Noting the crimes took place "in a community of 850 people," he wrote: "It is reasonable to assume that, without any news accounts being printed or broadcast, rumors would travel swiftly by word of mouth. One can only speculate on the accuracy of such reports, given the general propensities of rumors; they could well be more damaging than reasonably accurate news accounts."[43] Thus, Stuart's order failed Burger's balancing test and was declared unconstitutional.

Three justices — William Brennan, Thurgood Marshall and Potter Stewart — were willing to go even further, saying gag orders on the press would always be unconstitutional. Two other justices — Byron White and John Paul Stevens — indicated they might agree to an absolute ban on gag orders at a later date.

A year after *Nebraska Press Association*, the Supreme Court struck down an order prohibiting publication of the name and picture of an 11-year-old charged with murder. The juvenile court judge had allowed journalists to attend the detention hearing for the accused boy but then banned publication of the child's name and a photo that had been taken outside the courthouse. By the time the judge issued the gag order, the boy's name and picture had already been widely published and broadcast. In *Oklahoma Publishing Co. v. District Court*,[44] the Supreme Court said that once the judge permitted journalists to attend the hearing, he could not prohibit them from publishing the information they gathered while in attendance.

Nebraska Press Association and *Oklahoma Publishing Co.* have made it extremely difficult for a trial judge to justify gagging the press. Judges still try, but their orders are frequently struck down on appeal. For example, appellate courts have struck down gag orders prohibiting publication of jurors names,[45] evidence presented in open court but outside the presence of the jury,[46] videotapes made during the government's in-

vestigation of alleged drug trafficking,[47] the identities of juvenile offenders and victims,[48] and defendants' prior criminal records and nicknames, such as "Quapaw Quarter rapist" and "Sugarhouse rapist."[49]

"Docudramas" based on sensational crimes have led a number of defendants to seek to prevent such broadcasts. One of the best known of these cases involved an attempt by Lyle and Erik Menendez to prevent the broadcast in Los Angeles County of *Honor Thy Father and Mother: The True Story of the Menendez Murders* while the brothers awaited retrial on charges of murdering their parents. The Menendez brothers, who ultimately were convicted, claimed that airing the program in the county would make it impossible to find an unbiased jury. Applying the *Nebraska Press Association* test, a California federal district court disagreed, holding that the trial judge could adequately protect the defendants' fair trial rights by implementing *voir dire* and jury instructions.[50]

In 1996, the Sixth U.S. Circuit Court of Appeals declared unconstitutional an unusual gag order issued in a civil case involving Procter & Gamble Co. and Bankers Trust Co. An attorney who represented Bankers Trust provided a *Business Week* reporter with copies of documents relating to the lawsuit that had been sealed by the trial judge. Hours before the story based on the documents was to go to press and without holding a hearing or giving *Business Week* a chance to protest, the judge issued a gag order barring publication. A few weeks later, Judge John Feikens unsealed the documents on which the story was based. Amazingly, however, he still refused to rescind his order barring the magazine from publishing its original article. The Sixth Circuit court of appeals called this a "classic case of a prior restraint" in violation of the First Amendment. The trial judge had failed to demonstrate that publication would cause irreparable harm to a substantial government interest and had not provided McGraw-Hill the opportunity to argue the merits of the gag order, the appellate court wrote.[51]

---

[43] *Id.* at 567.

[44] 430 U.S. 308 (1977).

[45] *See* Capital Cities Media v. Toole, 463 U.S. 1303 (Brennan, Circuit Justice, 1983); Times Publ'g Co. v. Florida, 632 So. 2d 1072 (Fla. Dist. Ct. App. 1994); Des Moines Register & Tribune Co. v. Osmundson, 248 N.W.2d 493 (Iowa 1976); State v. Neulander, 801 A.2d 255 (N.J. 2002); New Mexico *ex rel.* New Mexico Press Ass'n v. Kaufman, 648 P.2d 300 (N.M. 1982); Ohio *ex rel.* Chillicothe Gazette, Inc. v. Ross County Court of Common Pleas, 442 N.E.2d 747 (Ohio 1982); Pennsylvania v. Genovese, 487 A.2d 364 (Pa. 1985).

[46] *See* Florida *ex rel.* Miami Herald Publ'g Co. v. McIntosh, 340 So. 2d 904 (Fla. 1976).

[47] *See* CBS v. Dist. Court, 727 F.2d 1174 (9th Cir. 1984) (involving an FBI sting operation targeting car manufacturer John DeLorean, who was ultimately acquitted).

[48] *See* Arkansas Democrat-Gazette v. Zimmerman, 20 S.W.3d 301 (Ark. 2000); KGTV Channel 10 v. Superior Court, 32 Cal. Rptr. 2d 181 (1994); Lesher Commc'ns, Inc. v. Alameda County Superior Court, 22 Media L. Rep. (BNA) 1383 (Cal. Ct. App. 1994); San Bernardino County Dept. of Pub. Soc. Servs. v. Superior Court, 283 Cal. Rptr. 332 (1991); Sarasota Herald-Tribune v. J.T.L., 502 So. 2d 930 (Fla. Dist. Ct. App. 1987); *In re* a Minor, 537 N.E.2d 292 (Ill. 1989); Minneapolis Star & Tribune Co. v. Schmidt, 360 N.W.2d 433 (Minn. Ct. App. 1985); Minneapolis Star & Tribune Co. v. Lee, 353 N.W.2d 213 (Minn. Ct. App. 1984); New Jersey *ex rel.* H.N., 632 A.2d 537 (N.J. 1993).

[49] Arkansas Gazette v. Lofton, 598 S.W.2d 745 (Ark. 1980); KUTV v. Conder, 668 P.2d 513 (Utah 1983).

[50] Menendez v. Fox Broad. Co., 22 Media L. Rep. (BNA) 1702 (C.D. Cal. 1994). *See also* Hunt v. NBC, 872 F.2d 289 (9th Cir. 1989); Goldblum v. NBC, 584 F.2d 904 (9th Cir. 1978); Corbitt v. NBC, 20 Media L. Rep. (BNA) 2037 (N.D. Ill. 1992); Clear Channel Commc'ns, Inc. v. Murray, 636 So. 2d 818 (Fla. Dist. Ct. App. 1994); Zamora v. Adams, 25 Media L. Rep. (BNA) 1638 (Tex. Dist. 1997).

[51] Procter & Gamble Co. v. Bankers Trust Co., 78 F.3d 219, 225 (6th Cir. 1996).

Since *Nebraska Press Association*, only a few gag orders on the media have been upheld on appeal. For example, in 2004, the Colorado Supreme Court affirmed in part a gag order in the Kobe Bryant rape case.[52] Eventually, the charge against the NBA star was dropped when his accuser refused to continue participating in the case.

Before that, however, the trial judge issued a gag order prohibiting seven media outlets from publishing information from transcripts of closed proceedings they had received erroneously. Because of the massive media interest in the case, the trial court had set up an email list to disseminate public proceeding transcripts. Inadvertently, the court reporter emailed transcripts of closed hearings held to determine the admissibility of evidence relating to the accuser's prior and subsequent sexual conduct. The trial judge ordered anyone who had received the transcripts "to delete and destroy any copies and not reveal any contents thereof."[53] Holding that preventing public disclosure of irrelevant information about the accuser's sexual history was a compelling interest, the Colorado Supreme Court narrowed the order by striking the requirement that recipients must delete and destroy all copies and limiting the ban on disclosure to just those portions deemed "not relevant and material" to the case under the state's rape shield law.[54]

QUESTIONS A TRIAL JUDGE MUST CONSIDER BEFORE ISSUING A GAG ORDER ON THE PRESS

1. Has there been intense and pervasive publicity that is likely to affect the fairness of the trial?
2. Are there no alternatives to a gag order that would protect the defendant's fair trial rights?
3. Is a gag order likely to be effective?

Only if the answers to all three questions are "yes" may a judge gag the media.

In 1990, the Eleventh U.S. Circuit Court of Appeals refused to lift a temporary gag order prohibiting CNN from disseminating the contents of tape recordings of conversations between deposed Panamanian dictator Manuel Noriega, who was in jail in Miami awaiting trial on federal drug charges, and his lawyers. Jail officials had allegedly made the tapes, and CNN had obtained them legally. On a motion from Noriega's attorneys, a

U.S. district judge issued a temporary restraining order prohibiting CNN from broadcasting the tapes and ordered the network to submit the tapes to him so he could decide whether their dissemination would present a "clear, immediate, and irreparable danger" to Noriega's fair trial rights and, therefore, should be permanently banned.[55] The next day the judge limited his order to material that was privileged. CNN appealed the order but also disobeyed it by continuing to air the excerpts from the tapes it had broadcast prior to the issuance of the gag order.

The court of appeals refused to lift the district court's order, saying CNN's failure to allow the judge to inspect the tapes had made it impossible for the court to balance the network's First Amendment rights against Noriega's Sixth Amendment rights.[56] The Supreme Court denied *certiorari*, despite vigorous dissent from Justices Marshall and Sandra Day O'Connor, who said the trial judge's order could not be reconciled with *Nebraska Press Association* and the Pentagon Papers case.[57] CNN eventually turned the tapes over to the district judge, who, after reviewing them, concluded that broadcast of the remaining unaired portions would not violate Noriega's rights.[58]

Despite the fact that the gag order was ultimately lifted, CNN was found in contempt of court for airing portions of the tapes while the temporary restraining order was in force. CNN was given the choice of paying a "substantial" fine or airing an apology and paying a smaller fine. CNN choose to pay an $85,000 fine and broadcast the apology.[59] This case illustrates an important point that journalists must keep in mind: Even if a court order is eventually declared unconstitutional, a person who violates the order while it is in effect can be found guilty of contempt of court and subject to fines and/or imprisonment. This is known as the "collateral bar rule," which states that a person who disobeys a court order may not collaterally challenge the constitutionality of the order as a defense to the contempt of court charge. The reasoning behind the rule is simple and generally sound: The effectiveness of the entire judicial system would be severely hampered if individuals were free to make their own decisions as to which court orders they would obey

[52] People v. Bryant, 94 P.3d 624 (Colo.), *stay denied sub nom.* United States v. District Court, 542 U.S. 1301 (Breyer, Circuit Justice 2004).

[53] *Id.* at 626.

[54] *Id.* at 637. *See also* KUTV v. Wilkinson, 686 P.2d 456 (Utah 1984) (upholding an order prohibiting the media from reporting a criminal defendant's alleged ties to organized crime).

[55] United States v. Noriega, 752 F. Supp. 1032, 1034-35 (S.D. Fla.), *aff'd sub nom. In re* Cable News Network, Inc., 917 F.2d 1543 (11th Cir.), *cert. denied,* 498 U.S. 976 (1990). *See also In re* State Record Co., 504 S.E.2d 592 (S.C. 1998), *cert. denied,* 526 U.S. 1050 (1999) (upholding a gag order prohibiting media coverage of a secretly recorded conversation between a defendant in a murder trial and his attorney).

[56] *In re* Cable News Network, Inc., 917 F.2d 1543, 1544 (11th Cir. 1990).

[57] New York Times Co. v. United States, 403 U.S. 713 (1971).

[58] United States v. Noriega, 752 F. Supp. 1045 (S.D. Fla. 1990).

[59] United States v. CNN, 865 F. Supp. 1549 (S.D. Fla. 1994). Beginning at 6 p.m. on Dec. 19, 1994, CNN broadcast an apology every hour for twenty-two hours. The statement said, in part: "CNN realizes that it was in error in defying the order of the court and publishing the Noriega tape while appealing the court's order. We do now and always have recognized that our justice system cannot long survive if litigants take it upon themselves to determine which judgments or orders of court they will or will not follow."

and which they would ignore. Under many circumstances, waiting for appellate review of a court order imposes little or no hardship on the individual subject to the order. But the situation changes when gag orders are imposed on the media since timeliness is the essence of news and waiting for an appellate court ruling could change news into history.

A 1972 case decided by the U.S. Court of Appeals for the Fifth Circuit illustrates the strict application of the collateral bar rule. In *United States v. Dickinson*,[60] two Baton Rouge, Louisiana, reporters were held in contempt and fined $300 each for disobeying a federal judge's order not to report on what took place during a hearing that was open to the public. The hearing was held to investigate the state's motives in prosecuting a federal volunteer worker charged with conspiring to murder the Baton Rouge mayor. The volunteer contended the charges were brought to harass him because of his civil rights activities. Because the volunteer might later be tried on the criminal charges, the U.S. district judge ordered that there be no media coverage of what occurred at the hearing. On appeal, the Fifth Circuit struck down the gag order as unconstitutional but sustained the contempt convictions of the reporters. It wrote:

> We begin with the well-established principle in proceedings for criminal contempt that an injunction ... *must be obeyed*, irrespective of the ultimate validity of the order. Invalidity is no defense to criminal contempt.... "People simply cannot have the luxury of knowing that they have a right to contest the correctness of the judge's order in deciding whether to willfully disobey it.... Court orders have to be obeyed until they are reversed or set aside in an orderly fashion."[61]

While the court recognized that "[t]imeliness of publication is the hallmark of 'news,'" it added, "But newsmen are citizens, too.... They too may sometimes have to wait."[62] It is somewhat ironic that having recognized the importance of timeliness in news reporting, the Fifth Circuit itself took five months to issue an opinion in the case.

More than a decade later, the First U.S. Circuit Court of Appeals adopted a more flexible approach, ruling that a "transparently invalid" gag order could be violated with impunity as long as the publisher first made "a good faith effort" to have an appellate court reverse the order. The case resulted from the *Providence Journal*'s violation of a judge's order prohibiting publication of information the paper had received from the FBI. The information, which the FBI had gathered through illegal wiretaps in the 1960s, related to reputed organized crime leader Raymond L.S. Patriarca, who had died in 1985. In 1976, the *Journal* had sought access to transcripts of the wiretaps under the federal Freedom of Information Act. The FBI denied the request, and a federal court upheld the denial, ruling that release of the transcripts would violate Patriarca's privacy. However, after his death, the FBI released the transcripts to the *Journal* as well as other news organizations. After a Providence radio station aired some of the information from the transcripts, Patriarca's son sued to prevent further publication, claiming dissemination of the information would violate his privacy.[63]

On November 13, 1985, Judge Francis Boyle issued an order barring publication of the wiretap information. The next day the *Journal* published an article in direct disobedience of that order. Though Judge Boyle vacated his order on November 19, acknowledging that it was likely unconstitutional, in 1986, he found the *Journal* and editor Charles Hauser in contempt, fining the paper $100,000, giving Hauser an eighteen-month suspended sentence and ordering him to perform 200 hours of community service. The *Journal* appealed, and a three-judge panel of the First Circuit reversed the convictions. While it recognized that the collateral bar rule is the "general rule," it emphasized that the case involved a prior restraint on speech, which, it said, represents "an unusual class of orders because they are presumptively unconstitutional." It held the *Nebraska Press Association* test was the standard that applied to evaluating the constitutionality of Boyle's gag order and that it was "patently clear" the order did not meet that test. In fact, Boyle had failed even to consider two prongs of the test. Furthermore, the court noted that the purpose of a temporary restraining order, such as Boyle issued, is to preserve the status quo while the court considers the case. However, for newspapers, the court said, the status quo "is to publish news promptly that editors decide to publish. A restraining order disturbs the status quo and impinges on the exercise of editorial discretion."[64]

A few months later, the First Circuit reheard the case *en banc*, affirmed the three-judge panel's ruling but modified it. It said that in the future a publisher had to "make a good faith effort to seek emergency relief from the appellate courts" before violating an invalid gag order. "If timely access to the appellate court is not available or if [a] timely decision is not forthcoming," the publisher may go ahead and publish in violation of the order, subsequently challenging its constitutionality as a defense to a contempt citation.[65]

The Supreme Court failed to reconcile the apparent conflict

---

[60] 465 F.2d 496 (5th Cir. 1972).

[61] *Id.* at 509 (quoting Southern Railway Co. v. Lanham, 408 F.2d 348, 350 (5th Cir. 1969) (Brown, C.J., dissenting)).

[62] *Id.* at 512 (citation omitted).

[63] *In re* Providence Journal, 820 F.2d 1342, 1353 (1st Cir. 1986), *modified*, 820 F.2d 1354, 1355 (1st Cir. 1987) (en banc).

[64] *Id.* at 1346-53.

[65] *Id.* at 1355.

between the Fifth and the First circuits when it dismissed the appeal from the government in the *Providence Journal* case on procedural grounds.[66]

In attempting to understand these two cases, it's important to keep in mind that *Dickinson* is binding precedent only in the Fifth Circuit and *In re Providence Journal* only in the First Circuit. In addition, both cases are federal cases, and individual states are free to devise their own rules regarding application of the collateral bar rule when state court judges issue gag orders. Some courts have chosen to follow the First Circuit's lead. For example, in 1998, the Mississippi Supreme Court unanimously overturned the contempt conviction of a *Delta Democrat Times* reporter who had disobeyed a trial judge's order not to report on a criminal defendant's juvenile record, which was discussed in open court. The state high court noted that the trial judge did not consider the *Nebraska Press Association* test.[67]

VIOLATING COURT ORDERS & CONTEMPT OF COURT

The *Collateral Bar* Rule:
A journalist must obey a court order, even an obviously unconstitutional gag order, until an appellate court overturns it.

The *Providence Journal* Rule:
A journalist may violate a "patently invalid" gag order after making a "good faith effort" to get an appellate court to overturn it.

In contrast, in 2002, a New Jersey trial judge held four *Philadelphia Inquirer* reporters in contempt and fined them $1,000 each for printing the name of a juror in a high-profile murder trial even though two months earlier the New Jersey Supreme Court had struck down the order prohibiting publication of jurors' names.[68] Thus, despite some successes in challenging contempt convictions resulting from disobeying gag orders, many attorneys still advise journalists to obey such orders until they are reversed on appeal or, at the very least, to make a sincere effort to obtain appellate review before disobeying an order.

---

[66] 485 U.S. 693 (1988). The special prosecutor who was handling the government's case had failed to obtain the U.S. Solicitor General's authorization to petition the Supreme Court for *certiorari*.

[67] Jeffries v. Mississippi, 724 So. 2d 897, 900 (Miss. 1998). The judge who found the reporter in contempt and jailed her for seventy-two hours was found guilty of misconduct by the Mississippi Supreme Court in 2000, primarily because of her handling of the *Jeffries* case. The judge, who had already been defeated in her bid for reelection, was publicly reprimanded and fined. Mississippi Comm'n on Judicial Performance v. Byers, 757 So. 2d 961 (Miss. 2000).

[68] *See* Phillip Taylor, *Colliding With Contempt*, NEWS MEDIA & L., Summer 2002, at 4.

Restrictions on Trial Participants

Judicial gag orders on trial participants became front-page news in 2005 when a gag order temporarily barred *Tonight Show* host Jay Leno from telling jokes about Michael Jackson during the singer's child molestation trial. The judge in the case had issued a sweeping order prohibiting all trial participants, including witnesses, from speaking publicly about the case. Leno, who had received a phone call from Jackson's accuser a few years earlier during which the boy had asked for money to help with his cancer treatments, was subpoenaed by the defense and, thus, fell within the provisions of the gag order. After Leno called in surrogate comedians to deliver his Jackson jokes, the judge clarified his order, saying it did not prevent Leno from joking about the case but only from discussing his part in it.[69]

While *Nebraska Press Association* made it very difficult for judges to gag the media, it is easier for them to restrict the flow of information to the media by issuing gag orders aimed at trial participants, especially attorneys. Generally, courts view gag orders on trial participants as less distasteful under the First Amendment because they do not prevent the media from disseminating information but simply make it more difficult for journalists to obtain information. In addition, courts have greater power over trial participants, especially lawyers, than they do over non-participant journalists. Newsgathering, however, does receive some First Amendment protection, and trial participants have their own First Amendment rights to speak. Thus, there are limits on judges' gag powers. Before considering how those limits apply to the typical gag orders aimed at attorneys, witnesses, defendants and jurors, a somewhat unusual situation — a gag order aimed at newspapers that were themselves participants in the case — will be addressed.

In *Seattle Times Co. v. Rhinehart*, the Supreme Court said the strict *Nebraska Press Association* test did not apply when the media themselves were parties to the litigation and had obtained information through the pretrial discovery process.[70] The *Seattle Times* and *Walla Walla Union-Bulletin* were defendants in a libel and invasion of privacy lawsuit that Keith Rhinehart, head of the Aquarian Foundation, a religious group, brought. The newspapers wanted information on the foundation's members and donors, but the foundation refused, arguing that publication of such information would violate the members' and donors' First Amendment rights. A Washington state trial judge ordered the group to release the information but issued an order prohibiting the newspapers from publishing what they learned as parties to the lawsuit.

---

[69] *See* Lisa de Moraes, *For Jay Leno, Michael Jackson Jokes Are in Order*, Mar. 12, 2005, *available at* http://www.washingtonpost.com/wp-dyn/content/article/2005/03/25/AR2005032507531.html.

[70] 467 U.S. 20 (1984).

The Supreme Court unanimously upheld the judge's order, saying it was not a "classic prior restraint that requires exacting First Amendment scrutiny." Preventing abuse of the discovery process was a substantial governmental interest sufficient to justify the order, the Court concluded. However, it noted that the papers could publish the same information if they obtained it through some other way.[71]

Seattle Times v. Rhinehart was an unusual case. Usually restrictive orders prohibit attorneys or witnesses from making statements that might prejudice the outcome of a trial. These rules are important to know, as attorneys and jurors can be great sources for legal reporters.

One of the most recent examples of a gag order being challenged comes from the 2015 criminal trial against Donald Blankenship, former CEO of Massey Engery Co., who was facing criminal charges for the Upper Big Branch Mine explosion in 2010 that killed twenty-nine people. The trial judge issued a sweeping order restricting access to court documents and prohibiting extrajudicial statements by lawyers, victims' family members, and others who were subject to the order. On appeal, the Fourth Circuit Court of Appeals applauded the trial court's efforts to ensure Blankenship had a fair trial. However, with little discussion of the First Amendment principles involved in the case, it ruled the order was unconstitutional.[72]

Attorneys. The American Bar Association's Model Rules of Professional Conduct provide that an attorney should not make extrajudicial, public statements that "have a substantial likelihood of materially prejudicing" a pending case. While not expressly prohibiting any particular types of comments, the rules list certain subjects likely to cause prejudice, including statements about the character, credibility, reputation or criminal record of a party, suspect or witness; the existence or contents of a confession or a suspect's refusal to make a statement; the results of examinations or tests or the refusal of a suspect to take a test; opinions as to a defendant's guilt or innocence; or even that "a defendant has been charged with a crime, unless there is included therein a statement explaining that the defendant is presumed innocent until and unless proven guilty."

In 1994, amidst the massive publicity surrounding the O.J. Simpson murder trial, the ABA amended its rules to add a right-of-reply for defense lawyers. The provision says that an attorney "may make a statement that a reasonable lawyer would believe is required to protect a client from the substantial undue prejudicial effect of recent publicity not initiated by the lawyer or the lawyer's client." At the same time, the ABA added language directing prosecutors to "refrain from making extrajudi-

cial comments that have a substantial likelihood of heightening public condemnation of the accused."[73]

About forty states have adopted rules governing attorney statements. Most follow the ABA's model, allowing an attorney to be disciplined for making prejudicial statements even if the judge hasn't issued an order limiting extrajudicial statements. In *Gentile v. State Bar of Nevada*, Nevada's rules were challenged by a lawyer who was disciplined for holding a press conference during which he declared his client was innocent and questioned the integrity of the grand jury witnesses.[74] In 1991, the Supreme Court ruled that the "substantial likelihood of material prejudice" standard, used in Nevada's and most other states' rules, did not violate the First Amendment. Chief Justice William Rehnquist, noting that lawyers are "officers of the Court," justified applying a different standard to attorneys than to the media and general public. "Because lawyers have special access to information through discovery and client communications," he wrote, "their extrajudicial statements pose a threat to the fairness of a pending proceeding since lawyers' statements are likely to be received as especially authoritative."[75]

Whether a state has adopted specific rules limiting attorneys' extrajudicial statements, a trial judge has the inherent power to issue gag orders aimed at attorneys. One of the key criticisms of Judge Lance Ito's conduct of the O.J. Simpson murder trial was his failure to regulate the attorneys' out-of-court comments. Ito justified his approach by noting that California had not adopted a rule limiting attorney speech; but most commentators agreed that Ito, as the trial judge, did not need a bar association or state supreme court rule to give him the power to prohibit lawyers' prejudicial statements. In fact, during the subsequent civil lawsuit brought against Simpson by the families of the victims, Judge Hiroshi Fujisaki imposed a wide-ranging gag order on all trial participants, including the lawyers.

If an attorney violates a gag order, the result can be a contempt of court conviction, just as when a journalist violates a court order. For example, in 1995, the Second U.S. Circuit Court of Appeals upheld the criminal contempt conviction of Bruce Cutler, attorney for alleged organized crime boss John Gotti, because he violated a trial court order prohibiting extrajudicial statements by attorneys if there was a "reasonable likelihood" that statements would interfere with a fair trial. The trial court found that Cutler knowingly and willfully violated its order by repeatedly speaking to journalists.[76]

---

[71] *Id.* at 33-35.

[72] *See In re* The Wall Street Journal, No. 15-1179 (4th Cir. Mar. 5, 2015).

[73] MODEL RULES OF PROF'L CONDUCT R. 3.6 cmt., and R. 3.8(g) (1994).

[74] 501 U.S. 1030 (1991).

[75] *Id.* at 1074.

[76] United States v. Cutler, 58 F.3d 825, 828 (2d Cir. 1995). This case provides an excellent example of the collateral bar rule at work. The appeals court upheld Cutler's contempt conviction but refused to consider the constitutionality of the gag order since Cutler had violated it without first seeking appellate review.

Gag orders on lawyers have been struck down when they were overbroad or when the trial judge failed to consider alternative measures for protecting the defendant's right to a fair trial. In a case resulting from the trial of the people accused of bombing the World Trade Center in 1993, the Second Circuit vacated a gag order prohibiting the attorneys from publicly discussing any aspect of the case. The trial judge had issued the blanket order without considering whether less restrictive means were available to protect the defendants' fair trial rights, the appeals court held.[77] In 1986, a New York appeals court overturned as "vague and overbroad" a sweeping order prohibiting attorneys from "any discussion of this case with the news media," including telling reporters what time court would convene.[78] The following year, a trial judge's order banning "any public statement" to the media during a sensational murder trial was declared invalid.[79]

Witnesses. As the Jay Leno incident illustrated, occasionally judges issue gag orders aimed at witnesses. Just as with restrictions on attorney speech, such orders will be upheld if they are necessary to protect a defendant's right to a fair trial and alternative measures are not available. In 1984, a U.S. district judge in North Carolina issued an order prohibiting all potential witnesses in a murder trial from making "any extrajudicial statement relating to the testimony in this case that such potential witnesses may give, or relating to any of the parties or issues such potential witnesses expect or should reasonably expect to be involved in this case, or relating to the events leading up to and culminating" in the crime. The order specifically forbade potential witnesses from giving interviews to the press. The case involved the trial of Ku Klux Klan and Nazi party members for the shooting deaths of five people in Greensboro. In upholding the gag order, the U.S. Court of Appeals for the Fourth Circuit noted that there had already been tremendous publicity and that many of the potential witnesses were relatives of the victims. The appellate court agreed with the trial judge that alternative remedies, such as change of venue, jury admonitions or sequestration, would be ineffective or impractical.[80]

In 1990, the Supreme Court upheld the right of a grand jury witness to publish his own testimony after the grand jury term had ended. A grand jury investigates but does not decide a person's guilt or innocence. Instead, it determines if there is suf-

ficient evidence to indict, or formally charge, someone with a crime. Grand juries meet in secret, and grand jurors themselves are prohibited from revealing what goes on during the proceedings. Florida law took the traditional grand jury secrecy even further, however, by prohibiting witnesses from disclosing their own testimony.

Because of articles he had written, Michael Smith, a reporter for the *Charlotte Herald-News*, was called to testify before a grand jury investigating alleged wrongdoing in the State Attorney's Office and Sheriff's Department in Charlotte County. After the grand jury term ended, he wanted to use his testimony in his writing and claimed he had a First Amendment right to do so. Noting that the information related to government misconduct and thus constituted "speech which has traditionally been recognized as lying at the core of the First Amendment," the Supreme Court unanimously held the Florida law unconstitutional.[81] Its opinion was narrow, however, restricted solely to a witness publishing his *own* testimony *after* the grand jury term ended.

Defendants. Occasionally judges also try to gag defendants, with mixed results. Some appellate courts have struck down such gag orders using the same test applied to the media in *Nebraska Press Association* while others have upheld restrictions on defendants' speech by applying the *Gentile* standard. Saying it saw no "legitimate reasons" for treating "individuals, including defendants" differently than the press, the Sixth Circuit used the *Nebraska Press* test to strike down a gag order that prohibited a congressman, on trial for mail and bank fraud, from commenting publicly on his own case outside of Congress.[82]

In contrast, the Fifth Circuit upheld a sweeping gag order in a high profile, federal corruption and racketeering case involving former Louisiana Gov. Edwin W. Edwards, state Insurance Commissioner James Harvey Brown and others. The trial court had prohibited parties, lawyers and witnesses from giving "any extrajudicial statement or interview" to "any public communications media" that "could interfere with a fair trial or prejudice any defendant, the government, or the administration of justice," including statements "intended to influence public

[77] United States v. Salameh, 992 F.2d 445 (2d Cir. 1993).

[78] NBC v. Cooperman, 501 N.Y.S.2d 405 (App. Div. 1986).

[79] Connecticut Magazine v. Moraghan, 676 F. Supp. 38 (D. Conn. 1987). *See also In re* New York Times Co., 878 F.2d 67 (2d Cir. 1989); Levine v. United States Dist. Court, 764 F.2d 590 (9th Cir. 1985); United States v. Marcana Garcia, 456 F. Supp. 1354 (D.P.R. 1978); Breiner v. Takao, 835 P.2d 637 (Haw. 1992).

[80] *In re* Russell, 726 F.2d 1007, 1008-10 (4th Cir. 1984). *See also* South Bend Tribune v. Elkhart Circuit Court, 691 N.E.2d 200 (Ind. Ct. App. 1998) (upholding a gag order on participants in a murder trial).

[81] Butterworth v. Smith, 494 U.S. 624, 632 (1990). In a similar case, the Third U.S. Circuit Court of Appeals ruled that reporters who testified about the alleged misconduct of a Pennsylvania Supreme Court justice before a state judicial review board could not be prohibited from revealing their own testimony. They could, however, be barred from revealing the testimony of other witnesses or information they overheard during their appearances before the board. First Amendment Coalition v. Judicial Inquiry & Review Bd., 784 F.2d 467 (3d Cir. 1986).

[82] United States v. Ford, 830 F.2d 596, 598-99 (6th Cir. 1987). *See also* United States v. Krzyske, 836 F.2d 1013 (6th Cir.) (striking down a judge's ruling that a defendant could go free on bail as long as he promised not to discuss his views on income taxes with anyone other than his attorney); Ohio *ex rel.* Dispatch Printing Co. v. Golden, 442 N.E.2d 121 (Ohio Ct. App. 1982) (striking down a municipal judge's gag order on the defendant, as well as members of the defendant's immediate family and counsel).

opinion regarding the merits of the case."[83] Commissioner Brown appealed the gag order to the Fifth U.S. Circuit Court of Appeals, which upheld it, saying that if a trial court

> determines that there is a "substantial likelihood" (or perhaps even merely a 'reasonable likelihood,' a matter we do not reach) that extrajudicial commentary by trial participants will undermine a fair trial, then it may impose a gag order on the participants, as long as the order is also narrowly tailored and the least restrictive means available.[84]

A few weeks later, former Governor Edwards was fined $1,700 — $100 per word — for violating a similar gag order in a related case by discussing allegedly exculpatory evidence with reporters outside the courtroom.[85]

Jurors. Jurors, of course, are always prohibited from discussing the trial in which they are involved while it is going on, just as they are prohibited from reading, viewing or listening to news reports about the trial. More recently, courts have had to deal with jurors posting updates on social media sites such as Facebook and Twitter during a trial or jury deliberation or using Google to research cases, activities which are also not allowed. Such during-trial restrictions on jurors are considered essential to preserving the integrity of the jury process. Concerns arise, however, when judges impose restrictions on post-verdict juror speech. The two most common reasons for post-verdict restrictions are to protect jurors' privacy and to ensure the secrecy of jury deliberations.

The Supreme Court has never ruled on the constitutionality of restrictions on post-verdict juror interviews, but a number of lower courts have upheld narrowly tailored restrictions. For example, the New Jersey Supreme Court upheld a ban on contacting jurors who had been dismissed after failing to reach a verdict until after a new trial was held.[86]

If the ban on juror interviews is overly broad, however, it is unlikely to survive. In 1991, the Ohio Supreme Court declared an order prohibiting anyone, including journalists, from discussing a highly publicized murder case with jurors unconstitutional.[87] More than a decade earlier, the U.S. Court of Appeals for

the Ninth Circuit had struck down a similar order requiring everyone, including the media, to "stay away from the jurors."[88]

Sometimes restrictions on juror interviews will be modified or upheld in part by appellate courts in an attempt to balance the interests at stake. In 1994, the Third U.S. Circuit Court of Appeals upheld a trial judge's order informing jurors that they were under no obligation to speak to journalists and also banning journalists from asking a juror about the votes or statements of other jurors. However, the court struck down a ban on repeated requests for an interview from any one juror and a requirement that a reporter immediately stop asking questions if a juror asks to end an interview.[89]

In 1995, two federal district courts in California declared unconstitutional state laws designed to prevent jurors and witnesses from selling their stories to the media. California's legislature had enacted the laws in response to publicity surrounding the O.J. Simpson trial. One law made it a misdemeanor for a juror or ex-juror to accept a benefit of more than $50 to talk or write about his or her jury service until ninety days after the trial concluded. It also prohibited anyone from paying a juror or ex-juror more than $50 for the juror's story. The other law prohibited crime witnesses from accepting payment for their stories until one year after the crime had occurred or, if a criminal prosecution had begun, until a final verdict was reached.

Michael Knox, an original juror in the Simpson case who was dismissed part way through the trial, challenged the juror gag law. He wanted to write a book about his experiences, and the Los Angeles district attorney informed him and his publisher they would be prosecuted if they entered into a publishing agreement in violation of the California law. The federal court ruled that the law was a content-based prior restraint and was not narrowly tailored to serve a compelling government interest. Furthermore, it said the law was unconstitutionally overbroad and vague.[90] In the other case, a coalition of media organizations challenged the witness gag law as unconstitutional. The court agreed, holding that it violated both the U.S. and California constitutions.[91]

Post-Publication Sanctions

Just as the Supreme Court established constitutional limits on judges' powers to gag the media, so too it set up First Amendment barriers to post-publication punishment of the press for reporting about and commenting on the operation of the judicial

[83] United States v. Brown, 218 F.3d 415, 418-19 (5th Cir. 2000).

[84] Id. at 428.

[85] See S.L. Alexander, A Reality Check on Court/Media Relations, 84 JUDICATURE 146 (2000).

[86] State v. Neulander, 801 A.2d 255 (N.J. 2002). See also United States v. Harrelson, 713 F.2d 1114 (5th Cir. 1983) (upholding an order prohibiting journalists from asking jurors about the votes of other jurors and repeatedly attempting to interview jurors who had said they did not want to be interviewed).

[87] Ohio ex rel. Cincinnati Post v. Court of Common Pleas, 570 N.E.2d 1101 (Ohio 1991). See also In re Express-News Corp., 695 F.2d 807, 810 (5th Cir. 1982) (striking down an order prohibiting juror interviews without prior permission of the court).

[88] United States v. Sherman, 581 F.2d 1358, 1360 (9th Cir. 1978).

[89] United States v. Antar, 38 F.3d 1348 (3d Cir. 1994).

[90] Dove Audio v. Lungren, No. CV 95-2570 RG (JRX), 1995 WL 432631 (C.D. Cal., June 14, 1995).

[91] California First Amendment Coal. v. Lungren, No. C 95-0440-FMS, 1995 U.S. Dist. LEXIS 11655 (N.D. Cal., Aug. 9, 1995).

system. Post-publication sanctions can be divided into two categories: contempt of court citations issued by judges and criminal penalties imposed by statutes for the publication of certain types of information.

Contempt of Court. Judges have the power to find people in contempt if they disobey court orders, show disrespect for the court or otherwise engage in conduct that interferes with the administration of justice. A contempt of court citation can result in a fine, imprisonment or both. Judges have a great deal of power to summarily punish someone for any act of disobedience or disrespect; and some judges have used their powers to punish criticism of and commentary about their own actions and the judicial process. In the 1940s, however, the Supreme Court effectively put an end to judges' use of contempt of court to punish critics. It ruled that out-of-court commentary could not be punished as contempt unless it presented a clear and present danger of interfering with the fair administration of justice.

The first such case to reach the Supreme Court was a joinder of two appeals, *Bridges v. California* and *Times Mirror Co. v. Superior Court*.[92] In one case, labor leader Harry Bridges was held in contempt after he publicly called a judge's ruling in a labor dispute outrageous and threatened to tie up the docks on the Pacific coast if the judicial order was enforced. In the second case, the *Los Angeles Times* was held in contempt for a series of anti-union editorials, which, the trial court concluded, were aimed at influencing judicial decisions in pending labor disputes. Ironically, the Supreme Court used the same opinion to strike down the contempt convictions of both militant labor leader Bridges and the anti-union *Los Angeles Times*.

Writing for a five-member majority, Justice Hugo Black summarily dismissed the argument that the contempt powers held by judges were an appropriate tool for preserving public respect for the courts. "The assumption," he wrote, "that respect for the judiciary can be won by shielding judges from published criticism wrongly appraises the character of American public opinion.... [A]n enforced silence ... would probably engender resentment, suspicion, and contempt more than it would enhance respect."[93] Resurrecting the old clear and present danger test, which the Court had first used in World War I sedition cases,[94] Black wrote that judges could punish commentary on pending cases only if such publications presented an imminent and extremely serious threat to the fair administration of justice.

Just what a formidable obstacle the clear and present danger test presented to judges attempting to punish critical journalists

was demonstrated in 1946 and again in 1947 when the Supreme Court struck down contempt citations against the *Corpus Christi Caller-Times* and the *Miami Herald*.[95] *Bridges* and the two cases that followed have virtually eliminated the ability of judges to punish criticism or general commentary on the judicial system. It's important to remember, however, that none of those cases involved efforts to influence jury decisions, disobedience of court orders, in-courtroom disruptions of judicial proceedings or disrespectful behavior. Judges can and do continue to use their contempt powers to punish such conduct, whether the perpetrator is a journalist or not.

State Statutes. It is not unusual for state laws to declare certain information relating to the justice system — such as juvenile offender, adoption and involuntary commitment records — confidential. Such laws generally prohibit government officials from releasing the information to unauthorized individuals, including journalists. Some states, however, have tried to go even further in protecting confidentiality by enacting laws that penalize the media for publishing certain information relating to the courts. In two cases in the 1970s, the Supreme Court ruled such state laws unconstitutional, holding that government could not punish the publication of truthful information that had been lawfully obtained unless there was a compelling need to do so.

In the first case, the *Virginian Pilot* was fined $500 for violating a state statute that made it a crime to publish information about the confidential proceedings of the Virginia Judicial Inquiry and Review Commission, which heard complaints about judges' misconduct or disabilities and conducted its proceedings in secret to encourage the public to file complaints and to protect judges from the reputational harm that could result from unwarranted complaints. The *Virginian Pilot* identified a judge who was being investigated and accurately reported that the commission had not filed a formal complaint against him. Acknowledging that the commission could meet in secret and keep its records confidential, a unanimous Supreme Court said in *Landmark Communications v. Virginia*, that imposing criminal sanctions on the publication of such information, which "lies near the core of the First Amendment," was unconstitutional.[96]

The following year, the Court struck down a West Virginia law that made it a crime for newspapers to publish the names of youths charged as juvenile offenders unless they first obtained written approval from the juvenile court. Two Charleston papers were indicted for identifying a 14-year-old who had shot and killed a classmate. His name was obtained through interviews with witnesses, the police and an assistant prosecuting at-

---

[92] 314 U.S. 252 (1941).

[93] *Id.* at 270-71.

[94] *See* Abrams v. United States, 250 U.S. 616 (1919); Schenck v. United States, 249 U.S. 47 (1919)

[95] Craig v. Harney, 331 U.S. 367, 374-75 (1947); Pennekamp v. Florida, 328 U.S. 331, 346 (1946).

[96] 435 U.S. 829, 839 (1978).

torney. Once again the Supreme Court unanimously ruled in favor of the press. The newspapers had argued that the statute imposed a prior restraint on publication since it required a judge's permission to publish a juvenile's name. In *Smith v. Daily Mail Publishing Co.*, the Court said it didn't matter whether the law was labeled prior restraint or not since "First Amendment protection reaches beyond prior restraints."[97]

Relying on its decision the previous year in *Landmark Communications*, the Court found that publication of lawfully obtained, truthful information could be punished only "to further a state interest of the highest order." While protecting the anonymity of juvenile offenders to enhance their chances of rehabilitation was an important interest, the Court held it was not sufficient to justify the infringement of First Amendment rights caused by imposing criminal sanctions for the publication of true information. It noted that while every state had a law providing for the confidentiality of juvenile proceedings, only five states "impose criminal penalties on nonparties for publication of the identity of the juvenile." Finally, the Court said the statute didn't even accomplish its goal since it only punished newspaper publication of juveniles' names. Radio stations in the area had broadcast the youth's name but were not indicted because the statute did not prohibit broadcasts.[98]

Court Closures

As noted, the Supreme Court in *Sheppard v. Maxwell* did not suggest that gag orders on the press be used as a remedy for prejudicial publicity. Nor did it suggest closing the courtroom door to the press and public. In fact, in *Sheppard* the Court specifically reiterated its antipathy toward judicial secrecy.[99] But, like gag orders, court closures became popular with judges seeking to avoid the problems they believed trial coverage caused.

Criminal Trials. In 1980, the Supreme Court began limiting judges' ability to close access to their courtrooms by ruling in *Richmond Newspapers v. Virginia*[100] that the press and public have a First Amendment right to attend criminal trials. It may seem odd that the Court used the First Amendment's guarantee of freedom of the press as a source of access rights, especially since the Sixth Amendment specifically provides for public trials. But the Court had earlier ruled that the Sixth Amendment's guarantee of a public trial, like its other guarantees of a

speedy trial by an impartial jury in the district in which the crime was committed, was a *defendant's* right.[101] If the defendant agreed to give up his constitutional right to a public trial, then the press or members of the public could not claim a Sixth Amendment violation.

In 1978, John Paul Stevenson, charged with murdering a hotel manager, did waive his right to a public trial. The prosecutor had no objections. So Circuit Court Judge Richard Taylor agreed to conduct Stevenson's trial behind closed doors. It's easy to understand why the judge and attorneys all wanted a closed trial. This was to be Stevenson's fourth trial on the same charge. The Virginia Supreme Court had overturned his 1976 conviction because of the use of inadmissible evidence. A second trial ended in a mistrial when one of the jurors had to be excused for illness and no alternate was available. A third trial, which Judge Taylor also agreed to close, ended in a mistrial when one prospective juror told others about Stevenson's previous trials.

After Judge Taylor ordered the fourth trial closed, Richmond Newspapers protested and asked for a hearing, which Taylor conducted in secret. At the conclusion of the hearing, he stuck by his decision that the extraordinary circumstances justified a closed trial. The next day he dismissed the jury, ruled the state had not presented sufficient evidence to justify a guilty verdict and declared Stevenson not guilty. The decision was reported in a two-sentence order; and, because the trial had been conducted behind closed doors, there was no way for the public to determine if Taylor's conclusion was justified.

Richmond Newspapers appealed the trial closure to the Virginia Supreme Court, which refused to overturn Taylor's decision. The U.S. Supreme Court, however, ruled 7-1 that the closure was unconstitutional. (Justice Lewis Powell, a Virginian, did not participate in the decision because he was acquainted with some of the people involved in the case.) As in *Nebraska Press Association*, the justices in *Richmond Newspapers* were divided over their reasoning. The majority of seven produced six different opinions, with no opinion garnering the endorsement of more than three justices.

Chief Justice Burger, joined by Justices White and Stevens, rested his opinion on the history of open trials in the Anglo-American justice system. Contending that trials had been open "to all who care to observe" since before the Norman Conquest, Burger wrote open trials discouraged perjury and official misconduct, inspired public confidence in the justice system, and have "significant community therapeutic value," helping to defuse community outrage over crime. Although the First Amendment contains no express language regarding access to criminal proceedings, Burger wrote that the guarantees of freedom of speech and press and the rights to assemble and petition the

---

[97] 443 U.S. 97, 101 (1979).

[98] *Id.* at 103-05. Since *Smith v. Daily Mail*, at least two other state laws prohibiting the publication of juvenile offenders' names have been declared unconstitutional. *See* Florida Publ'g Co. v. Morgan, 322 S.E.2d 233 (Ga. 1984); *In re* Johnson, 5 Media L. Rep. (BNA) 2512 (S.C. Fam. Ct. 1980).

[99] 384 U.S. 333, 349-50 (1966).

[100] 448 U.S. 555 (1980).

[101] Gannett Co., Inc. v. DePasquale, 443 U.S. 368 (1979).

government all "share a common core purpose of assuring freedom of communication on matters relating to the functioning of government. Plainly it would be difficult to single out any aspect of government of higher concern and importance to the people than the manner in which criminal trials are conducted." The public right of access to a criminal trial can be overcome only by "an overriding interest," Chief Justice Burger concluded, only if the trial judge finds that "alternative solutions" are inadequate to ensure fairness. Burger expressly declined to provide examples of overriding interests that might justify closure, only saying Judge Taylor had "made no findings to support closure [and] no inquiry ... as to whether alternative solutions would have met the need to ensure fairness."[102]

In a concurring opinion, which later became very influential in the development of a test for determining when courtrooms could be closed, Justice Brennan, joined by Justice Marshall, stressed the structural value of open courts, that is, the role openness plays in self-government. "[P]ublic access to trials acts as an important check, akin in purpose to the other checks and balances that infuse our system of government," Brennan wrote. Open trials, he reasoned, "play a fundamental role" in ensuring defendants receive fair trials and in assuring the public that "procedural rights are respected, and that justice is afforded equally. Closed trials breed suspicion of prejudice and arbitrariness, which in turn spawns disrespect for law."[103]

Two years after *Richmond Newspapers*, the Supreme Court ruled 6-3 that a blanket rule requiring courtroom closure during the testimony of minor victims in sex crime cases violated the First Amendment.[104] A trial judge in Norfolk County, Massachusetts, had closed the trial of a man charged with raping three girls, two 16-year-olds and one 17-year-old. The judge interpreted a state statute as *mandating* closure of the entire trial. On appeal, the Supreme Judicial Court of Massachusetts interpreted the statute more narrowly, holding that it only required closure during the testimony of minor sex crime victims. The *Boston Globe* appealed to the Supreme Court.

In *Globe Newspaper Co. v. Superior Court*, Justice Brennan, for the majority, wrote that closure of criminal trials had to be determined case by case on the basis of a "compelling governmental interest" and had to be "narrowly tailored to serve that interest." While Brennan conceded that protecting "minor victims of sex crimes from further trauma and embarrassment" was a compelling interest, it did not justify a *mandatory* closure law since such a measure was not narrowly tailored. Case-by-case determinations were needed to consider such factors as "the minor victim's age, psychological maturity and understand-

ing, the nature of the crime, the desires of the victim, and the interests of parents and relatives." Brennan questioned the state's second justification for the law — that closure encouraged minor victims to come forward and testify — because there was no empirical evidence to support the claim that mandatory closure accomplished that goal. Furthermore, since trial transcripts were open to the public, there was no way to guarantee a victim's testimony would remain secret.[105]

Continuing the trend of opening courtrooms to the press and public, the Supreme Court ruled in 1984 that jury selection is an integral part of a criminal trial and, therefore, is subject to the First Amendment presumption of access. *Press-Enterprise Co. v. Riverside County Superior Court* (which is known as *Press-Enterprise I* to distinguish it from a later case of the same name) began when a California judge closed almost six weeks of the *voir dire* — jury selection proceedings — in a rape and murder trial involving a teenage victim. After the defendant was convicted and sentenced to death, the judge still refused to release the transcript of the *voir dire*, saying, "[S]ome of the jurors had some special experiences in sensitive areas that do not appear to be appropriate for public discussion."[106] After failing to obtain relief from the California appellate courts, the *Press-Enterprise* petitioned the Supreme Court to grant *certiorari*, which it did.

The Court unanimously ruled that closure of the *voir dire* violated the First Amendment. Chief Justice Burger, who wrote the opinion of the Court, used both the historical arguments he had articulated in *Richmond Newspapers* and the structural/functional arguments of Justice Brennan. The "historical evidence," he wrote, indicates that, "since the development of trial by jury, the process of selection of jurors has presumptively been a public process with exceptions only for good cause shown." As for the functional argument, he wrote: "The open trial thus plays as important a role in the administration of justice today as it did for centuries before our separation from England.... Openness ... enhances both the basic fairness of the criminal trial and the appearance of fairness so essential to public confidence in the system."[107]

Just as Justice Brennan had held in *Globe Newspaper Co.*, Chief Justice Burger in *Press-Enterprise I* said the presumption of open *voir dire* proceedings "may be overcome only by an overriding interest based on findings that closure is essential to preserve higher values and is narrowly tailored to serve that interest." Furthermore, the trial judge must present specific, written findings to justify closure and demonstrate that alternatives to closure are not available to protect the interests at stake. In

---

[102] 448 U.S. at 564-81.

[103] *Id.* at 595-96 (Brennan, J., concurring).

[104] Globe Newspaper Co. v. Superior Court, 457 U.S. 596 (1982).

[105] *Id.* at 607-10.

[106] 464 U.S. 501, 504 (1984).

[107] *Id.* at 505, 508.

this case, the trial judge failed to present findings supporting his conclusion that closure was necessary to protect the defendant's fair trial rights and the jurors' privacy rights. Furthermore, the judge "failed to consider whether alternatives were available to protect the interests of the prospective jurors."[108]

Despite these rulings, judges still sometimes attempt to close jury selection. For example, in 2010, Judge Warren Wilbert ruled that jury selection in the trial of Scott Roeder, who was accused of murdering a late-term abortion provider in Kansas, would be closed. "[T]he dissemination of information from the juror selection process," he reasoned, "would create a real and present danger of the defendant's ability to receive a fair trial." When several media outlets sued, the Kansas Supreme Court ordered Wilbert to reconsider his ruling, holding that court closures must balance the defendant's right to a fair trial and the public's and media's right to access judicial proceedings.[109]

In 2014, the Colorado judge in the trial of James Holmes for the 2012 shooting at the midnight premier of *The Dark Night Rises* wrote a memorable opinion explaining why it was important to keep *voir dire* open to the press and the public.[110] Holmes' attorneys moved to close the entire jury selection process in order to preserve their client's Sixth Amendment right to a fair trail. At a hearing considering the motion, the prosecution partially joined the motion, arguing for closed introductory jury selection sessions and closed individual *voir dire*. A conglomeration of media organizations, however, filed an objection opposing any closure. Citing the experience and logic test, Justice Brennan's concurrence in *Nebraska Press Association*, and *Press-Enterprise I*, Judge Carlos A. Samour Jr. denied the parties' request for closure, reasoning that the presence of the press would ensure a fair trial. The final two sentences of Samour's opinion sums up what many believe to be true:

> Contrary to the parties' speculation, openness and public pressure will ensure that suspicions of potential juror misconduct are publicized and will discourage those inclined to abuse the system. Hence, the presence of the public and the

watchful eye of the media will enhance the fairness and effectiveness of the jury selection process.[111]

Other Criminal Proceedings. In 1986, the Supreme Court extended the First Amendment presumption of openness to a criminal pretrial proceeding, specifically a preliminary hearing. In some states a preliminary hearing is known as a "show-cause" hearing; it is designed to determine if the government has sufficient evidence to bind a defendant over for trial. *Press-Enterprise v. Riverside County Superior Court*, known as *Press-Enterprise II*, resulted from the closure of a forty-one-day preliminary hearing in the case of Robert Diaz, a nurse accused of murdering twelve patients by administering massive doses of a heart drug.[112]

As he had in *Press-Enterprise I*, Chief Justice Burger, writing for the majority, combined the historical justifications he relied on in *Richmond Newspapers* with Justice Brennan's concern for the structural value of openness to establish a two-pronged test for deciding when a constitutional right of access attaches to a particular type of judicial proceeding. The preliminary hearing at issue in *Press-Enterprise II* passed the so-called test "of experience and logic." First, the Court said, "there has been a tradition of accessibility to preliminary hearings of the type conducted in California," and second, "preliminary hearings are sufficiently like a trial" to justify the conclusion that openness was necessary for the proper functioning of the process. The chief justice noted that the preliminary hearing was often the "final and most important" criminal proceeding since so few cases proceed to trial and, therefore, often presented the only opportunity for the public to observe the criminal justice system. Furthermore, the absence of a jury at a preliminary hearing made public and press attendance even more important to protect "'against the corrupt or overzealous prosecutor and against the compliant, biased, or eccentric judge.'"[113]

Deciding that a First Amendment right of access attached to the preliminary hearing was only the first step in the analysis, however. The Court had noted in earlier cases that the right of access was qualified and could be overcome by an overriding or compelling interest. Therefore, before closing a proceeding a trial judge must provide "specific, on the record findings" that "'closure is essential to preserve higher values and is narrowly tailored to serve that interest.'" Furthermore, the Court said that, if the overriding interest to be served by closure was the defendant's right to a fair trial, a judge had to find that there was "a substantial probability" of prejudice resulting from an open proceeding, that closure would prevent the harm and that

---

[108] *Id.* at 510-11. In 2010, the Supreme Court reiterated its robust support for open juror voir dire. Although the case was a Sixth Amendment case because the challenge was brought by the defendant, the Court relied upon *Press Enterprise I* to conclude, "Absent consideration of alternatives to closure, the trial court could not constitutionally close the voir dire." Presley v. Georgia, 558 U.S. 209, 214 (2010) (quoting *Press-Enterprise*, 464 U.S. at 511).

[109] Wichita Eagle v. Wilbert, No. 103,666 (Kan. Jan. 12, 2010). *See also*, *In re Main Today Media, Inc.*, 59 A.3d 499 (Me. 2013)(holding that concerns over a lack of juror candor during voir dire because of the presence of the media was insufficient to deny access to the process).

[110] People of the State of Colorado v. James Eagan Holmes, No. 12CR1522, Order In Regards to Defendant's Request to Close Jury Selection to the Public (D-154-a2, Jun. 11, 2014), *available* at http://www.courts.state.co.us/userfiles/file/Court_Probation/18th_Judicial_District/18th_Courts/12CR1522/007/Order%20Regarding%20Defendants%20Request%20to%20Close%20Jury%20Selection%20to%20the%20Public%20%20D-154-a-2.pdf.

[111] *Id.* at 29.

[112] 478 U.S. 1 (1986).

[113] *Id.* at 10-13 (quoting Duncan v. Louisiana, 391 U.S. 145, 156 (1968)).

reasonable alternatives to closure would be unable to protect the defendant's rights.[114]

Although more complicated, the closure test articulated by the Court in *Press-Enterprise II* is similar to the gag order test it used in *Nebraska Press Association*. Both emphasize the judge's responsibility to evaluate the effectiveness of the order and to try all other alternatives before infringing on First Amendment rights. In the years since *Press-Enterprise II*, lower courts have applied the closure test to a variety of different types of proceedings.

In a highly publicized case, the Ninth U.S. Circuit Court of Appeals ruled, in 1988, that closing a pretrial detention hearing violated the First Amendment.[115] Stella Nickell was charged with murdering her husband and a woman whom she did not know by placing poison in Excedrin capsules on store shelves to make her husband's death appear to be a random product-tampering murder. The hearing was to determine whether she would be released pending trial.

Applying the first portion of the *Press-Enterprise II* test, the Ninth Circuit acknowledged that pretrial detention hearings were relatively new proceedings and thus there was no history of public access. However, it said the arguments in favor of openness were sufficient to support a constitutional right of access to them. It concluded that there was inadequate evidence that an open detention hearing would prejudice Nickell's right to a fair trial and that the trial judge had not sufficiently considered alternatives to closure.

Based on both the First Amendment right of access and a state constitutional provision guaranteeing open courts, a North Carolina trial court, in 1994, refused to close pretrial evidence suppression hearings in the case resulting from the murder of Michael Jordan's father.[116] Evidence suppression hearings present special problems since their sole purpose is to determine whether certain evidence will ever be presented to a jury. If evidence, say an allegedly coerced confession or the results of an allegedly illegal wiretap, is declared inadmissible during a public hearing, the media are free to report on its existence. The fear, then, is that potential jurors will learn about the evidence, remember it and perhaps be influenced by it even though it was never used in court.

On the other hand, evidentiary hearings are often crucial to the outcome of a criminal trial because they can determine the strength of the prosecution's case. If, for example, a judge refuses to suppress a particularly damaging piece of evidence, such as a confession or the results of laboratory tests, the case

against the defendant may be so strong that he or she decides to plead guilty and no trial is ever held. Furthermore, evidentiary hearings often deal with allegations of police and prosecutorial misconduct, which are important to bring to public attention.

In 1979, the Supreme Court held that the Sixth Amendment did not provide the press and public with a right to attend pretrial evidence suppression hearings.[117] That case, however, preceded *Richmond Newspapers* and was not based on the First Amendment. Since the Supreme Court began articulating a broad First Amendment right of access to judicial proceedings, many lower courts have reached the same conclusion as did the North Carolina trial court in the James Jordan murder case and have recognized a constitutional right of access to pretrial evidentiary hearings.[118]

Courts have also held that a constitutional right of access attaches to numerous other types of criminal proceedings, including plea and sentencing hearings,[119] bail hearings,[120] post-trial examinations of jurors about potential misconduct,[121] hearings on a motion to compel a defendant to give a blood sample for an HIV test,[122] hearings on a criminal defendant's recusal motion (asking the judge to remove himself from the case),[123] and contempt-of-court hearings for a juror accused of disobeying a court order.[124] However, some types of criminal proceedings, most notably grand jury proceedings, have historically been conducted behind closed doors, and courts continue to rule that the First Amendment presumption of openness does not apply.[125] The D.C. Court of Appeals underscored this point in 1998 when it ruled that the media did not have a right of access to court proceedings and documents related to the grand jury investigation of the Monica Lewinksy-President Clinton affair.[126]

Juvenile Proceedings. Juvenile proceedings historically were

---

[114] *Id.* at 13-14 (quoting Press-Enterprise v. Riverside County Superior Court (I), 464 U.S. 501, 510 (1984)). *See also* El Vocero de Puerto Rico v. Puerto Rico, 508 U.S. 147 (1993) (per curiam).

[115] Seattle Times v. United States Dist. Court, 845 F.2d 1513 (9th Cir. 1988).

[116] North Carolina v. Demery, 22 Media L. Rep. (BNA) 2383 (N.C. Super. Ct. 1994).

[117] Gannett Co. v. DePasquale, 443 U.S. 368 (1979).

[118] *See, e.g.*, United States v. Klepfer, 734 F.2d 93 (2d Cir. 1984); Gannett Westchester Rockland Newspapers v. Lacava, 551 N.Y.S.2d 261 (Ct. App. 1990); New York v. Franklin, 22 Media L. Rep. (BNA) 1255 (N.Y. Crim. Ct. 1993); Ohio v. Nobles, 21 Media L. Rep. (BNA) 1500 (Ohio Ct. Cm. Pls. 1993).

[119] *See* United States v. Cardenas-Guilen, No. 10-40221 (5th Cir. May 17, 2011); United States v. Eppinger, 49 F.3d 1244 (7th Cir. 1995); United States v. Soussoudis, 807 F.2d 383 (4th Cir. 1986); United States v. Byrd, 812 F. Supp. 76 (D.S.C. 1992); Baltimore Sun Co. v. Colbert, 593 A.2d 224 (Md. 1991); New York Times v. Demakos, 529 N.Y.S.2d 97 (App. Div. 1988); Washington v. Campbell, 21 Media L. Rep. (BNA) 1895 (Wash. Super. Ct. 1993).

[120] *See In re* Globe Newspaper Co., 729 F.2d 47 (1st Cir. 1984); United States v. Chagra, 701 F.2d 354 (5th Cir. 1983).

[121] *See* United States v. Simone, 14 F.3d 833 (3d Cir. 1994). *But see* United States v. Edwards, 823 F.2d 111 (5th Cir. 1987).

[122] *See* Florida v. Jenkins, 21 Media L. Rep. (BNA) 2159 (Fla. Cir. Ct. 1993).

[123] *See* Glen Falls Newspapers, Inc. v. Berke, 614 N.Y.S.2d 628 (App. Div. 1994).

[124] *See* Riley v. Gibson, No. 2010-CA-000947-OA (Ky. Sup. Ct. May 19, 2011).

[125] *See, e.g., In re* Subpoena to Testify Before Grand Jury, 864 F.2d 1559 (11th Cir. 1989); *In re* Multicounty Grand Jury Proceedings, 847 P.2d 812 (Okla. Crim. App. 1993).

[126] *In re* Dow Jones & Co., 142 F.3d 496 (D.C. Cir. 1998).

closed to the public. The primary goal of the juvenile justice system was considered rehabilitation rather than punishment. State laws, therefore, often provided for closed hearings and confidential records to avoid stigmatizing minors by making their identities and crimes known to the public. Prompted by a rash of high profile, serious crimes by juveniles during the 1990s, however, many states have now opened their juvenile proceedings and records to the public and press, especially when the crimes involved would be felonies if committed by adults.

WHEN MAY A JUDICIAL PROCEEDING BE CLOSED?

A judge must follow a specific path to determine whether a judicial proceeding may be closed:

First, the judge must determine whether a First Amendment right of access attaches to the particular type of proceeding. The Supreme Court has held that there is a right of access to criminal trials and preliminary hearings, but if a judge is evaluating a closure motion for a different type of proceeding, the judge must consider the following:
  • whether this type of proceeding has historically been open to the public (the experience test), and
  • whether public access plays a significant positive role in the functioning of the particular proceeding in question (the logic test).

Second, if the judge decides, as a result of the experience and logic tests, that a right of access exists, the judge must determine whether that right can be overcome by a compelling interest. To close the courtroom, the judge must issue specific, written findings that
  • closure is essential to preserve higher values, such as the defendant's fair trial rights or jurors' or victims' privacy rights; and
  • the closure is narrowly tailored, that is, as brief as possible to serve the interest.

Third, if the overriding interest justifying closure is the defendant's right to a fair trial, the judge must find that
  • there is a substantial probability that an open proceeding will interfere with that right,
  • closure will be effective in protecting the right, and
  • there are no reasonable alternatives to closure.

The Supreme Court has not ruled on whether the First Amendment right of access applies to juvenile proceedings. However, because there is a history of secrecy associated with juvenile proceedings and because many people who work with juvenile offenders believe confidentiality plays an important role in rehabilitation, several courts have held that the First Amendment right of access does not apply to such proceedings. For example, in 1981, the Vermont Supreme Court flatly declared, "[A] juvenile proceeding is so unlike a criminal prosecu-

tion that the limited right of access described in *Richmond Newspapers* does not govern."[127]

On the other hand, some courts have found a constitutional right of public and press access to juvenile proceedings — either based on the First Amendment or on state constitutional provisions. For example, the Tennessee Supreme Court ruled that the public has a qualified First Amendment right to attend hearings at which juvenile court judges determine whether youths charged with crimes will transfer to adult court for trial,[128] and both the Oregon and South Carolina supreme courts have interpreted their state constitutions to provide a qualified right of access to juvenile proceedings.[129]

State statutes have become increasingly important as a source of access rights as more state legislatures have enacted laws declaring that juvenile proceedings shall be open to the public.[130] Some states — Florida and Colorado are two — provide that a judge can close a proceeding only "when the public interest and the welfare of the child are best served by so doing"[131] or "the best interest of the child or of the community" requires closure.[132] About one-third now require public proceedings when minors are charged with crimes that would constitute felonies by adults or with certain enumerated serious, violent crimes, such as street gang activity, murder, rape, kidnapping and arson.[133] A few states base openness on the age of the juvenile.[134] Illinois has a unique provision declaring juvenile hearings closed "except for the news media and the crime victim." The law also says that the court may prohibit anyone in attendance at a hearing from disclosing the juvenile's identity.[135] De-

---

[127] *In re* J.S., 438 A.2d 1125, 1128 (Vt. 1981). *See also In re* T.R., 556 N.E.2d 439 (Ohio 1990); Sherman Publ'g Co. v. Goldberg, 443 A.2d 1252 (R.I. 1982); *In re* N.H.B., 769 P.2d 844 (Utah Ct. App. 1989).

[128] Tennessee v. James, 902 S.W.2d 911 (Tenn. 1995). *See also* Florida Publ'g Co. v. Morgan, 322 S.E.2d 233 (Ga. 1984).

[129] Oregonian Publ'g v. Deiz, 613 P.2d 23 (Or. 1980); *Ex parte* Columbia Newspapers, Inc., 333 S.E.2d 337 (S.C. 1985).

[130] *See, e.g.,* COLO. REV. STAT. § 19-1-106(2) (2008); MICH. COMP. LAWS § 712A.17(7) (2008); MONT. CODE ANN. § 41-5-1502(7) (2007); NEV. REV. STAT. § 62D.010 (2007); N.C. GEN. STAT. § 7B-2402 (2008); N.M. STAT. ANN. § 32A-2-16(B) (2008); TEX. FAM. CODE ANN. § 54.08 (2007); WASH. REV. CODE § 13.40.140(6) (2008).

[131] FLA. STAT. ANN. § 985.035 (2007).

[132] COLO. REV. STAT. § 19-1-106(2) (2008).

[133] *See, e.g.,* CAL. WELF. & INST. CODE § 676 (2008); DEL. CODE ANN. tit. 10, § 1063(a) (2008); GA. CODE ANN. § 15-11-28(c) (2007); IDAHO CODE § 20-525 (2008); IND. CODE § 31-32-6-3 (2008); LA. CHILD. CODE ANN. art. 879(b) (2008); ME. REV. STAT. ANN. tit. 15, § 3307(2) (2008); MASS. GEN. LAWS ANN. ch. 119, § 65 (2008); MO. REV. STAT. § 211.171(6) (2008); PA. CONS. STAT. ANN. tit 42, §6336 (2008); S.D. CODIFIED LAWS § 26-7A-36 (2008); TENN. CODE ANN. § 37-1-153 (2008); UTAH CODE ANN. § 78A-6-114 (2008); VA. CODE ANN. § 16.1-302 (2008).

[134] *See, e.g.,* KAN. STAT. ANN. § 38-2353 (2007) (judge can close hearing for a juvenile under 16 if an open hearing is not in the child's best interests); S.D. CODIFIED LAWS § 26-7A-36 (2008) (open if juvenile was 16 and the crime was violent or a drug felony); TEX. FAM. CODE ANN. § 54.08(c) (2007) (closed if juvenile is under 14 at the time of the hearing); UTAH CODE ANN.§ 78A-6-114 (2008) (open if juvenile is 14 and charged with a felony or is a repeat offender).

[135] 705 ILL. COMP. STAT. 405/1-5(6) (2008). *See also* ALASKA STAT. § 47.10.070 (2008)

spite the trend toward openness, about a quarter of the states still provide that juvenile proceedings be closed or permit judges to exclude the press and public at their discretion.[136] In some of those states, though, the judge has the discretion to permit individuals to attend the proceedings if they have "a proper interest in the case or in the work of the court."[137]

Because the law is not uniform across jurisdictions, journalists who wish to report on juvenile proceedings should acquaint themselves with the law on the topic in the state or federal district in which they work.

CHALLENGING A COURTROOM CLOSURE

Journalists need to be familiar with their First Amendment rights of access and be prepared and willing to protest closure motions. If faced with a motion to close a judicial proceeding, you should do the following:

- Raise your hand, stand and identify yourself as a reporter.
- Formally object to the closure.
- Request the judge hold a hearing at which your news organization's attorney can appear.
- Immediately call your editor so he or she can contact your attorney.
- Be sure to remain respectful as you are registering your objection.

Here's the statement the North Carolina Press Association recommends journalists use in protesting a closure motion:

Your honor, I respectfully request the opportunity to register on the record an objection to the motion to close this proceeding to the public, including the press. Our legal counsel has advised us that standards set forth in recent U.S. Supreme Court decisions regarding the constitutional right of access to judicial proceedings recognize the right to a hearing before the courtroom is closed. Therefore, I respectfully request such a hearing and a brief continuance so I can call our counsel to come to explain our position.

Civil Proceedings. Although the Supreme Court has not ruled that civil trials are subject to the same First Amendment right of access as criminal proceedings, numerous lower courts, both state and federal, have held that the press and public enjoy a right of access to civil proceedings. In addition, in 2011, the Judicial Conference of the United States, which sets policy for the

federal courts, adopted a national policy that encourages federal courts to limit instances in which they seal entire civil case files. The conference, a body comprised of senior circuit court judges, concluded that federal judges should seal civil case files only when statutory law requires or extraordinary circumstances justify sealing.[138]

Some courts have based this right of access on the First Amendment, following the Supreme Court reasoning in *Richmond Newspapers* and its progeny; others have found a common law or state constitutional basis for access; and still others have used a combination of constitutional and common law.

One of the most frequently cited cases involving access to civil proceedings is *Publicker Industries v. Cohen*,[139] decided by the U.S. Court of Appeals for the Third Circuit in 1984. Reporters for the *Philadelphia Inquirer* and *Wall Street Journal* appealed when denied access to hearings in a lawsuit resulting from a corporate proxy fight. The Third Circuit recognized both constitutional and common law rights of access to civil proceedings, saying that "the public's right of access to civil trials and records is as well established as that of criminal proceedings and records."[140] Other courts have followed the Third Circuit's lead, finding a right of access to an array of civil proceedings.[141]

Not every type of civil proceeding, however, is open to the press and public. Like grand jury and juvenile proceedings, some civil hearings traditionally have been closed and remain closed under state statutes. Involuntary commitment and adoption proceedings are two of the most commonly closed civil proceedings. Furthermore, just as with criminal proceedings, judges sometimes find that even when a right of access exists for a particular type of civil proceeding, a compelling interest can overcome that right as long as the closure is narrowly tailored. Two of the most common interests used to justify closing proceedings are preventing the disclosure of trade secrets and protecting individual privacy, especially if the litigation involves a child.[142]

Civil discovery proceedings have generated a number of ac-

(prohibiting those attending an open juvenile hearing from disclosing the juvenile's identity).

[136] ALA. CODE § 12-15-65(A) (2008); CONN. GEN. STAT. ANN. § 46B-122 (2008); D.C. CODE ANN. § 16-2316(E) (2008); KY. REV. STAT. ANN. § 610.070(3) (Michie 2007); MISS. CODE ANN. §43-21-203(6) (2007); N.H. REV. STAT. ANN. § 169-B:34 (2008); N.D. CENT. CODE § 27-20-24(5) (2007); OKLA. STAT. ANN. tit. 10, § 7003-4.1 (2008); R.I. GEN. LAWS § 14-1-30 (2007); S.C. CODE ANN. § 20-7-755 (2008); VT. STAT. ANN. tit. 33. § 5523(c) (2008); W. VA. CODE 49-5-2(I) (2008); WIS. STAT. § 48.299 (2008); WYO. STAT. § 14-6-224(b) (2008).

[137] ALA. CODE § 12-15-65(a) (2008). *See also* KY. REV. STAT. ANN. § 610.070(3) (Michie 2007); N.D. CENT. CODE § 27-20-24(5) (2007); VT. STAT. ANN. tit. 33. § 5523(c) (2008).

[138] *See* Conference Approves Standards & Procedures for Sealing Civil Cases, *Third Branch News*, (Sept. 13, 2011), http://www.uscourts.gov/News/NewsView/11-09-13/Conference_Approves_Standards_Procedures_for_Sealing_Civil_Cases.aspx.

[139] 733 F.2d 1059 (3d Cir. 1984).

[140] *Id.* at 1066.

[141] *See, e.g.*, Newman v. Graddick, 696 F.2d 796 (11th Cir. 1983) (pretrial and posttrial hearings in a class action suit charging overcrowding in a state prison); NBC Subsidiary (KNBC-TV), Inc. v. Superior Court, 980 P.2d 337 (Cal. 1999) (proceedings held outside the jury's presence in a civil lawsuit against actor Clint Eastwood by his former companion); Barron v. Florida Freedom Newspapers, Inc., 531 So. 2d 113 (Fla. 1988) (divorce proceeding); In re Brown, 18 Media L. Rep. (BNA) 1460 (Fla. Cir. Ct. 1990) (child custody hearing); Bingham v. Struve, 591 N.Y.S.2d 156 (1992) (libel trial); Hutchinson v. Luddy, 18 Media L. Rep. (BNA) 1071 (Pa. Super. Ct. 1990) (pretrial proceedings in a civil suit against a Catholic priest charged with sexual misconduct).

[142] *See, e.g.*, Woven Elec. Corp. v. Advance Group, Inc., 19 Media L. Rep. (BNA) 1019 (4th Cir. 1991); *In re* Iowa Freedom of Info. Council, 724 F.2d 658 (8th Cir. 1983); Doe v. Indep. Sch. Dist., 933 F. Supp. 647 (S.D. Tex. 1996); Morgan v. Foretich, 528 A.2d 425 (D.C. 1987); Milo v. Milo, 6 Media L. Rep. (BNA) 2524 (Ohio Ct. C.P. 1981).

cess lawsuits. Discovery is the pretrial phase of a lawsuit during which the litigants attempt to collect the information they need from one another and from third-party witnesses. Traditionally, discovery in civil litigation has not been open to the press and public. In fact, it is usually conducted in attorneys' offices rather than in public courthouses. Because there is no history of public access and because so much of the information gathered during discovery never becomes part of the official court record, judges often rule that there is no right of access to discovery proceedings during which depositions are taken.[143] There have been exceptions, however. In one case a federal district court held that representatives of the media should be allowed to attend sessions when depositions from the New York mayor and a former police commissioner were being taken in a lawsuit against the city.[144] During the antitrust suit the federal government filed against Microsoft in 1998, the D.C. Court of Appeals ruled that journalists were entitled to attend the depositions from several Microsoft employees, including CEO Bill Gates. It based its decision on a little-known 1913 statute, which provided that depositions taken as part of Sherman Antitrust Act lawsuits "shall be open to the public as freely as are the trials in open court."[145] In addition, as discussed later in this chapter, some courts have ruled there is a right of access to discovery documents.

Denials of Access to Court Records

Since *Richmond Newspapers*, many lower courts have presumed that the First Amendment right of access to court proceedings extends to the documents filed in connection with those proceedings. Indeed, the Supreme Court in deciding *Press Enterprise I* and *II* didn't distinguish between access to a judicial proceeding itself and access to at least one type of court record — the transcript of the proceeding. In *Press Enterprise II*, Chief Justice Burger wrote, "Denying the transcript of a 41-day preliminary hearing would frustrate what we characterized as the 'community therapeutic value' of openness."[146]

The Constitution, however, is not the only source of a right of access to court records. Many states have access statutes.[147] In addition, both state and federal courts have long recognized a common law right of access. Two years before it decided *Rich-*

mond Newspapers, the Supreme Court, in *Nixon v. Warner Communications, Inc.*, acknowledged that the common law created a "presumption ... of access to judicial records."[148]

Courts have ruled that this general right of access applies to a wide array of both criminal and civil court records. In 2012, the District of Columbia Court of Appeals ruled the First Amendment right of access to the *voir dire* process established in *Press-Enterprise Co.* extended to questionnaires filled out by the sixteen jurors and alternates impaneled in the murder trial of the man who was convicted of killing former congressional intern Chandra Levy.[149] This followed a similar decision to release the questionnaires of jurors administered during the trial of baseball player Barry Bonds for perjury and obstruction of justice.[150]

In 1983, the Ninth U.S. Circuit Court of Appeals ruled that the pretrial motions and documents filed in the John DeLorean drug prosecution had to be available to both the press and public. "There is no reason to distinguish between pretrial proceedings and the documents filed in regard to them," the court declared in finding a constitutional right of access.[151] The same court also held that there is a right of access to post-conviction records, including pre-sentencing reports and post-sentencing documents filed in connection with a motion to reduce a sentence.[152] In civil cases, courts have found a right of access to pleadings, documents filed in connection with pretrial motions, summary judgment papers, and settlement agreements.[153]

Some types of court records, however, are not generally available to the press and public. For example, grand jury proceedings are closed, as are most grand jury records, including transcripts and evidence. However, when a grand jury hands down an indictment, it becomes a public record even though sometimes a court may seal an indictment until an arrest has been made. Adoption and involuntary commitment records are additional types of documents that are often declared confidential by state law and, therefore, unavailable to the press and public.

Research suggests that patent trials are another area where

---

[143] *See* Amato v. Richmond, 157 F.R.D. 26 (E.D. Va. 1994); Kimberlin v. Quinlan, 145 F.R.D. 1 (D.D.C. 1992); Fort Myers Broad. Co. v. Nelson, 460 So. 2d 420 (Fla. Dist. Ct. App. 1984).

[144] Estate of Rosenbaum v. New York City, 21 Media L. Rep. (BNA) 1987 (E.D.N.Y. 1993). *See also* United States v. Didrichsons, 15 Media L. Rep. (BNA) 1869 (W.D. Wash. 1988); Avirgan v. Hull, 14 Media L. Rep. (BNA) 2136 (D.D.C. 1987).

[145] United States v. Microsoft Corp., 165 F.3d 952, 953 (D.C. Cir. 1999).

[146] 478 U.S. 1, 13 (1986).

[147] *See Judicial Records: A Guide to Access in State & Federal Courts*, NEWS MEDIA & L., Summer 1995, at 1.

[148] 435 U.S. 589, 602 (1978).

[149] *In re* Access to Juror Questionnaires No. 10-SP-1612 (D.C. Cir. Jan. 19, 2012), *available at* http://www.rcfp.org/sites/default/files/docs/20120119_152115_levy.pdf. *See also* Beacon Journal Publ'g Co. v. Bond, 781 N.E.2d 180 (Ohio 2002).

[150] Order re: Access to Completed Juror Questionnaires, United States v. Bonds, No. C07-0073251 (N.D. Cal. Mar. 14, 2011), *available at* http://www.rcfp.org/newsitems/docs/20110318_125315_bonds_opinion.pdf.

[151] Associated Press v. United States Dist. Court, 705 F.2d 1143, 1145 (9th Cir. 1983).

[152] United States v. Schlette, 842 F.2d 1574 (9th Cir. 1988); CBS v. United States Dist. Court, 765 F.2d 823 (9th Cir. 1985).

[153] *See* Leucadia, Inc. v. Applied Extrusion Techs, Inc., 998 F.2d 157 (3d Cir. 1993); Rushford v. New Yorker Magazine, Inc., 846 F.2d 249 (4th Cir. 1988); Bank of Am. Nat'l Trust & Sav. Ass'n v. Hotel Rittenhouse Assocs., 800 F.2d 339 (3d Cir. 1986); Resolution Trust Corp. v. Dean, 854 F. Supp. 626 (D. Ariz. 1994); Soc'y of Prof'l Journalists v. Briggs, 675 F. Supp. 1308 (D. Utah 1987); Willie Nelson Music Co. v. Comm'r, 85 T.C. 914 (1985); Shenandoah Publ'g House, Inc. v. Fanning, 368 S.E.2d 253 (Va. 1988); Goldberg v. Johnson, 485 So. 2d 1386 (Fla. Dist. Ct. App. 1986).

documents are routinely filled under seal with no redacted versions available to the press or the public.[154] In addition, this is frequently done with little judicial oversight and many of the filings do not contain trade secrets or other information that needs to be protected. As one court noted in a high profile patent case, the result is that "many patent trials ... contain mountains of sealed exhibits."[155]

Juvenile Records. Just as access to juvenile proceedings has increased during the past few years, so, too, has access to juvenile court records. While most states still consider most juvenile records confidential, some permit access to records of cases involving felonies or specific serious, violent offenses.[156] In addition, several courts have recognized at least a qualified right of access to juvenile records.[157] Sometimes judges allow the press access to redacted versions of records. For example, in a case involving the Federal Juvenile Delinquency Act, the judge prohibited access to proceedings but did permit release of records that had been edited to hide the identities of the defendants.[158]

Discovery Documents. As previously indicated, access to civil discovery is sometimes an area of controversy. Journalists not only have sought to be present during the actual taking of depositions but also have tried to obtain access to deposition transcripts and documents obtained as part of discovery. They have enjoyed the most success when seeking access to discovery documents that have been filed with a court but are less likely to be granted access to unfiled materials.

A 1988 D.C. Court of Appeals case, *Mokhiber v. Davis*,[159] illustrates this distinction. Russell Mokhiber, an investigative reporter, sought access to a variety of discovery documents from a civil lawsuit that had settled four years earlier. The court held that Mokhiber had no right to see materials that had never been submitted to the court but did have a right of access to "papers submitted to the court for decision," including those obtained *via* discovery.[160] Likewise, in an antitrust case, a federal district court in California held that a common law right of access attached to documents as soon as they were filed with the

court in either civil or criminal cases.[161]

In 2009, the Connecticut Supreme Court issued a detailed ruling involving sealed documents filed in twenty-three actions alleging sexual abuse by Roman Catholic clergymen. The Court ruled that there was a presumptive right of public access to "judicial documents" or "any document filed that a court reasonably may rely on in support of its adjudicatory function."[162] Although the cases had been settled and withdrawn in 2001, in 2002, four newspapers filed motions seeking permission to intervene in the cases and an order vacating the sealing of the documents. Although the court recognized there was a split as to whether discovery related documents should be considered public, the court concluded that because "discovery proceedings can have a significant impact on the eventual resolution of disputes" those documents should be public in order to advance the public interest in judicial monitoring.[163]

In other instances, courts have ruled that there is no right of access to discovery materials until the trial has begun or the documents have been introduced at the trial.[164]

Additionally, some courts have agreed to seal certain discovery documents to protect personal privacy. The Sixth U.S. Circuit Court of Appeals ruled that protecting the associational privacy rights of non-parties was sufficient cause to justify sealing a list of Ku Klux Klan members that had been obtained as part of discovery in a civil lawsuit resulting from the fire-bombing of a black couple's home.[165]

Other reasons frequently given for denying access to discovery materials filed with a court are to protect trade secrets and to ensure the efficient functioning of the judicial process. A 2001 case involving discovery documents filed in a lawsuit brought against Bridgestone/Firestone, Inc. for the death of an 18-year-old football player from West Virginia University is a good example of a court protecting trade secrets. When four media companies sued to unseal nine discovery documents and ten pages excerpted from legal briefs, the Eleventh Circuit ruled that under the "good cause" standard Bridgestone/Firestone's interest in keeping trade secrets confidential had to be balanced against the press' contention that disclosure would serve the public's interest in health and safety.[166] A good example of a

[154] *See* Bernard Chao & Derigan Silver, *A Case Study in Patent Litigation Transparency*, 89 J. OF DISP. RESOL. 87 (2014).

[155] Order Granting-In part and Denying-In-Part Motions to Seal at 3, Apple Inc. v. Samsung Electronics Co. et al., No. 11-CV-01846-LHK, 2012 WL 3536800.

[156] *See, e.g.,* ARK. CODE ANN. § 9-27-309 (2008); CAL. WELF. & INST. CODE § 676 (2008); IND. CODE § 31-39-2-8 (2008); OKLA. STAT. tit. 10, § 7307-1.2 (2008); TENN. CODE ANN. § 37-1-153 (2008); UTAH CODE ANN. § 78-3a-206 (2008).

[157] *See, e.g., In re* K.F., 559 A.2d 663 (Vt. 1989); Orange County Publ'ns v. Sawyer, 14 Media L. Rep. (BNA) 1766 (N.Y. Sup. Ct. 1987); *In re* Richmond Newspapers, Inc., 16 Media L. Rep. (BNA) 1049 (Va. Cir. Ct. 1988).

[158] United States v. Three Juveniles, 862 F. Supp. 651 (D. Mass. 1994), *aff'd*, 61 F.3d 86 (1st Cir. 1995).

[159] 14 Media L. Rep. (BNA) 2313 (D.C. Cir. 1988).

[160] *Id.* at 2327.

[161] *In re* Coordinated Pretrial Proceedings in Petroleum Products Antitrust Litigation, 101 F.R.D. 34 (C.D. Cal. 1984).

[162] Rosado et al. v. Bridgeport Roman Catholic Diocesan Corp., 970 A.2d 656, 682 (Conn. 2009).

[163] *Id.* at 683.

[164] *See In re* Reporters Comm. for Freedom of the Press, 773 F.2d 1325 (D.C. Cir. 1985); Tavoulareas v. Washington Post, 724 F.2d 1010 (D.C. Cir. 1984); Booth Newspapers, Inc. v. Midland Circuit Judge, 377 N.W.2d 868 (Mich. Ct. App. 1985); *appeal denied* (Apr. 28, 1986), *cert. denied* 479 U.S. 1031 (1987).

[165] Courier-Journal v. Marshall, 828 F.2d 361 (6th Cir. 1987).

[166] Chicago Tribune Co. v. Bridgestone/Firestone, Inc., 263 F.2d 1304, 1314-15 (11th Cir. 2001).

court protecting the effective functioning of the legal system is a decision of the U.S. District Court for Arizona, which denied access to unfiled discovery materials in a class action suit resulting from savings and loan association failures. The court said that access would impede the progress of the case and create administrative burdens for both the court and parties.[167]

While most courts have refused to recognize a right of access to unfiled discovery documents, a few judges have ruled in favor of openness and declined to seal discovery materials except upon a showing of "good cause." The "good cause" standard is based on Rule 26(c) of the Federal Rules of Civil Procedure, which requires a party in a civil lawsuit to show good cause as to why documents should be sealed, and similar provisions in state rules of civil procedure.[168] For example, a Minnesota trial court, in 1992, denied a motion from a St. Paul City Council member who was a defendant in a civil lawsuit to seal all discovery materials on the grounds that disclosure would cause her public humiliation and reputational harm. The court said there was a common law and statutory presumption of openness and, therefore, rejected the closure request as overbroad. However, it did agree to temporarily seal unfiled materials relating to medical, financial and psychological records.[169]

Courts have traditionally been reluctant to make records available as a result of the criminal discovery process open to the media or the public. The criminal discovery process involves the exchange of materials the prosecution will use to secure a conviction and material the defense will use to achieve an acquittal. In criminal cases, prosecutors are not required by law to turn over all evidence gathered in a criminal investigation to the defense, although prosecutors must share with the defense evidence that may exonerate the defendant.[170] This material may or may not eventually be submitted as evidence at trial.

Like civil courts, criminal courts typically make a distinction between material that is filed with the court or used to support a motion and material that is not with most courts unwilling to attach a common law or First Amendment right of access to unfilled discovery material. A 2010 study found no examples of a federal court attaching a First Amendment or common law right of access to material disclosed during criminal discovery unless the material was later filed with the court. The same study concluded that Florida is the only state to specifically allow access to all criminal discovery records by state statute, while Rhode Island is the only state to specifically allow some access to criminal records through a judicial opinion.[171] Under Florida public-records law, records provided to a defendant in a criminal case are accessible, although a court may order specific information be maintained as confidential.[172] In 1985, in *State v. Cianci*, the Rhode Island Supreme Court developed a four-part test based on the Supreme Court judicial access decisions to determine when closure of discovery materials was justified.[173]

Audio-visual Records. As the use of audio-visual materials in the courtroom has increased, so too have efforts by journalists, especially broadcasters, to obtain copies of them. Sometimes the parties to litigation and judges are reluctant to allow broadcasters to copy audio-visual records because they fear the airing of such tapes will invade privacy, interfere with fair trial rights, implicate innocent third parties and/or sensationalize and distort the judicial process. Some judges have argued that the right of access to court records is met by simply allowing journalists to see or hear audio-visual evidence when it is used in the courtroom or by providing reporters written transcripts of tapes. Broadcasters who want to air portions of tapes are seldom satisfied with such limited access and claim a right to copy as well as to see and hear audio-visual records.

The Supreme Court addressed the issue in 1978 when it denied media requests to copy former President Richard Nixon's Watergate audiotapes. As noted previously, in *Nixon v. Warner Communications* the Court recognized a common law presumption of access. However, Justice Powell, writing for the Court, noted that "the right to inspect and copy judicial records is not absolute."[174] In this case, the Presidential Recordings and Materials Preservation Act, passed by Congress within weeks of President Ford's pardon of Nixon for his part in the Watergate scandal, superseded the common law presumption of access. That act gave the Administrator of General Services the responsibility for overseeing public access to the tapes.[175]

Since *Richmond Newspapers*, lower courts have generally recognized either a constitutional or common law right to inspect and copy audio-visual records. That right, however, like all of the other access rights discussed thus far, is not absolute and can be outweighed by other interests. Several good examples of how courts balance the interests for and against access came in the early 1980s, when two FBI sting operations, known as ABSCAM and BRILAB, resulted in four different access-to-tapes lawsuits. During ABSCAM, the FBI videotaped govern-

[167] *In re* Am. Continental Corp./Lincoln Sav. & Loan Sec. Litig., 18 Media L. Rep. (BNA) 2303 (D. Ariz. 1991).

[168] *See also In re* Alexander Grant & Co. Litig., 820 F.2d 352, 356 (11th Cir. 1987) (discussing the operation of umbrella protective orders that postpones the necessary showing of "good cause").

[169] Baloga v. Maccabee, 20 Media L. Rep. (BNA) 2201 (Minn. Dist. Ct. 1992). *See also* Glenmede Trust Co. v. Thompson, 56 F.3d 426 (3d Cir. 1995).

[170] Brady v. Maryland, 373 U.S. 83 (1963).

[171] Brian Pafundi, *Public Access to Criminal Discovery Records: A Look Behind the Curtain of the Criminal Justice System*, 21 U. FLA. J.L. & PUB. POL'Y 228 (2010).

[172] FLA. STAT. § 119.011(3)(c)(5)(2008).

[173] 496 A.2d 139, 144-45 (R.I. 1985).

[174] 435 U.S. 589, 598 (1978).

[175] Pub. L. No. 93-526, 88 Stat. 1695 (1974).

ment officials allegedly accepting bribes from undercover agents. In BRILAB, the tapes were of Texas officials allegedly accepting bribes in the awarding of state employee insurance contracts. Understandably, broadcasters wanted to obtain copies of those tapes to show on the air.

In the first case, resulting from the trial of former Congressman Michael Myers, the Second U.S. Circuit Court of Appeals allowed the media to copy the tapes. Once the evidence was introduced in court, it reasoned, "[I]t would take the most extraordinary circumstances to justify restrictions on the opportunity of those not physically in attendance at the courtroom to see and hear the evidence, when it is in a form that readily permits sight and sound reproduction." The court considered the impact that copying of tapes might have on the fair trial rights of Myers and future ABSCAM defendants but concluded that the risks were not sufficient to justify "curtailing the public's right of access to courtroom evidence." It added that: "Defendants, as well as the news media, frequently overestimate the extent of the public's awareness of news."[176]

In the other two ABSCAM cases, the Third and D.C. Circuits also granted broadcasters the right to copy the tapes despite claims that airing the tapes would interfere with the defendants' fair trial rights and invade the privacy of unindicted third parties.[177] The D.C. Circuit, however, told the trial judge that he could edit the tapes before releasing them to eliminate portions that might harm innocent third parties.

In contrast, in the BRILAB case, the Fifth Circuit upheld the trial court's refusal to allow copying of the FBI sting tapes.[178] First, it said the media's right of access was satisfied when journalists were allowed to view the tapes as they were played in open court and were provided transcripts of the contents. While the court acknowledged that there was a common law right of access to the tapes, it said the fair trial rights of a defendant who had not yet been tried outweighed the access right.

Media have continued, with mixed results, to try to obtain copies of audio-visual materials used in the courtroom. For example, in 1996, the Eighth U.S. Circuit Court of Appeals followed the approach taken by the Fifth Circuit in the BRILAB case and denied media access to the videotape of President Bill Clinton's testimony in the Whitewater-related fraud trial of James McDougal. The tape had been played in an open courtroom, and transcripts were released to the public. The court said the press and public "were given access to the information contained in the videotape," and this met First Amendment requirements.[179] Similarly, in 2013, in a case involving the trial of

a former police officer who was convicted of rape and indecent assault on a minor, the Massachusetts Supreme Court ruled that documentary filmmaker Steve Audette did not have a First Amendment or common law right of access to an audiotape "room recording" of trial proceedings made by a court reporter because the recording was "not the official record of the trial" and was never filed with the court. The court further held that Audette's right of access was satisfied by the official typed transcript of the proceedings, which is a public document.[180]

Terrorism-Related Secrecy

In the wake of the September 11, 2001, attacks on the World Trade Center and Pentagon, new access controversies arose as the government sought to close proceedings and seal records in cases with connections to terrorism. The first such controversy began just ten days after the attacks when Chief Immigration Judge Michael J. Creppy issued a directive mandating closure of all "special interest" immigration hearings. "Special interest" cases are those in which sensitive or national security information may be presented, including any information related to terrorist investigations.

In December, a Michigan immigration judge held a closed hearing to decide if Rabih Haddad, who had overstayed his tourist visa and was suspected of having connections to al-Qaeda, could be deported. Several media organizations, along with members of Haddad's family and the public, sued, contending the closed proceeding was unconstitutional. Both a federal trial court and the U.S. Court of Appeals for the Sixth Circuit agreed that the First Amendment right of access established in *Richmond Newspapers* applied, even though the immigration hearings were not actually court proceedings but administrative, quasi-judicial proceedings. The courts held that the Creppy directive requiring blanket closure of all "special interest" hearings was unconstitutional.[181]

A few months later, in a case involving closed deportation hearings in Newark, N.J., the Third Circuit issued a contradictory decision, ruling 2-1 that there was no constitutional right of access to such proceedings.[182] In 2003, the Supreme Court refused to hear an appeal in the case, thereby failing to resolve the conflict between the two circuits.[183]

The proceedings involving convicted 9/11 conspirator Zacarias Moussaoui offered numerous examples of secrecy. U.S. District Judge Leonie Brinkema prohibited the release of jurors' names in the sentencing hearing due to "the intense media and

[176] United States v. Myers, 635 F.2d 945, 952-53 (2d Cir. 1981).

[177] *In re* Application of NBC (Criden), 648 F.2d 814 (3d Cir. 1981); *In re* Application of NBC (Jenrette), 653 F.2d 609 (D.C. Cir. 1981).

[178] Belo Broad. Corp. v. Clark, 654 F.2d 423 (5th Cir. 1981).

[179] United States v. McDougal, 103 F.3d 651, 659 (8th Cir. 1996).

[180] Commonwealth v. Winfield, 985 N.E.2d 86, 88-89 (Mass. 2013).

[181] Detroit Free Press v. Ashcroft, 195 F. Supp. 2d 948 (E.D. Mich. 2002), *aff'd*, 303 F.3d 681 (6th Cir. 2002).

[182] North Jersey Media Group, Inc. v. Ashcroft, 308 F.3d 198 (3d Cir. 2002).

[183] North Jersey Media Group, Inc. v. Ashcroft, 538 U.S. 1056 (2003).

public interest in this case,"[184] blocked release of a Justice Department report on the FBI's handling of intelligence information about the 9/11 attacks,[185] and allowed scores of documents to be filed under seal or heavily redacted.[186] Even at the appellate court level, portions of oral arguments were closed and the documents sealed.[187]

The basis for most of the secrecy in the Moussaoui proceedings, as well as other terrorism-related cases, was the Classified Information Procedures Act, which establishes procedures for the handling of classified information in criminal cases.[188] Among other things, CIPA provides that if the U.S. attorney general certifies that an open hearing will result in the disclosure of classified information, the hearing must be closed and records sealed.[189] In one of several appeals during the Moussaoui case, the Fourth Circuit acknowledged, "There can be no question that the First Amendment guarantees a right of access by the public to oral arguments [before] this court." However, the court also recognized the requirements of CIPA and declared that "the Government's interest in the security of classified information is a compelling one" sufficient to overcome the right of access.[190] To assure that the closure was narrowly tailored, though, the court bifurcated the oral argument into open and closed portions and gave the government five days to edit a transcript of the closed portion for public release.[191]

In 2004, the Supreme Court denied *certiorari* in another terrorism-related case in which every document, including the dockets, were sealed and all parties and attorneys were gagged.[192] Mohamed Kamel Bellahouel, an Algerian married to a U.S. citizen, was detained in Florida in 2001, initially for overstaying his student visa. He was held for five months, during which time he was transported to Virginia to testify before the grand jury that indicted Moussaoui.[193] Bellahouel filed a *habeas corpus* petition challenging his deportation proceedings with a U.S. district court in Florida. The court kept the case off the public docket, sealed all records and prohibited the parties

and their attorneys from speaking publicly about the case.[194] Bellahouel appealed to the Eleventh Circuit Court of Appeals, where a clerk briefly and inadvertently listed the case on the public oral argument calendar, prompting news coverage of the extreme secrecy surrounding the case.[195] The court of appeals upheld the secret proceedings, and Bellahouel appealed to the Supreme Court, which on its docket used only the initials M.K.B. to identify the petitioner. It released a heavily redacted version of Bellahouel's petition for *certiorari* but kept the government's brief in opposition secret.[196]

Although journalists had been allowed to cover previous hearings at Guantánamo Bay, those involving fourteen so-called "high value" detainees, including confessed 9/11 mastermind Khalid Sheikh Mohammed, were conducted in secret beginning in 2007.[197] Known as Combatant Status Review Tribunals, they were to determine if detainees qualified as enemy combatants and thus could be tried by the military. The government also refused to release the audiotape of Mohammed's hearing, at which he confessed to involvement in thirty-one terrorist plots including 9/11. However, a censored transcript was made public, as well as an audiotape of the hearing for alleged senior al-Qaeda leader Abu Faraj al-Libi.[198]

The Supreme Court's 2008 ruling that foreign detainees at Guantánamo Bay have the right to challenge their imprisonment in civilian courts opened the door for more battles over government secrecy.[199] In more than 100 cases brought as a result of the ruling, the Justice Department filed unclassified documents under seal, thereby restricting access to judges, lawyers and government officials. The secrecy, the government said, was necessary because some unclassified documents mistakenly contained classified information. On June 1, 2009, a federal district judge ruled the wholesale sealing of unclassified documents violated the public's First Amendment and common law right of access to judicial records.[200] "Public interest in Guantanamo Bay generally and these proceedings specifically has been unwavering. The public's understanding of the proceedings, however, is incomplete without the factual returns. Publicly disclosing the factual returns would enlighten the citizenry and improve perceptions of the proceedings' fairness," Judge Thomas

---

[184] *Court Will Not Release Names of Jurors in Moussaoui Case*, WASH. POST, Feb. 3, 2006, at A20.

[185] Dan Eggen, *Judge in Moussaoui Case Blocks Release of Sept. 11 Report*, WASH. POST, Apr. 30, 2005, at A2.

[186] *See generally* Reporters Committee for Freedom of the Press, *Behind the Homefront*, *available at* http://www.rcfp.org/behindthehomefront/search.php?srch=Moussaoui.

[187] *See, e.g.*, United States v. Moussaoui, 65 Fed. App'x 881, 31 Media L. Rep. (BNA) 1705 (4th Cir., 2003).

[188] 18 U.S.C.A. app. 3 §§ 1-16 (West 2000 & Supp. 2003).

[189] *Id.* at § 6.

[190] *Moussaoui*, 65 Fed. App'x, at 890.

[191] *Id.* at 890-91.

[192] M.K.B. v. Warden, 540 U.S. 1213 (2004).

[193] *See* Meliah Thomas, *The First Amendment Right of Access to Docket Sheets*, 94 CAL. L. REV. 1537, 1548 (2006).

[194] Petition for Writ of Certiorari at 23-24, *M.K.B.*, 540 U.S. 1213 (No. 03-6747).

[195] *Id.* at 7.

[196] Thomas, *supra* note 193, at 1549-50.

[197] *See* Associated Press, *Pentagon to Bar News Coverage of Hearings for Terror Suspects From CIA Prisons*, Mar. 6, 2007, http://www.iht.com/articles/ap/2007/03/06/america/NA-GEN-US-Guantanamo-Prisoners.php.

[198] *See* Associated Press, *U.S. Fears Release of Guantanamo Hearing Tape Could Aid Terrorists*, May 31, 2007, http://www.lawinfo.com/index.cfm/fuseaction/News.story/msgID/0E8899E9-C2E3-40CA-9251-E48E2C519A74.

[199] Boumediene v. Bush, 553 U.S. 723 (2008).

[200] *In re* Guantanamo Bay Detainee Litigation, 630 F. Supp. 2d 1 (D.D.C. 2009).

Hogan wrote.[201] He gave the government until July 29 to make public the unclassified documents or request continued secrecy for specific words or lines highlighted in colored marker with an explanation of why the material should be protected.[202]

In December 2009, U.S. District Judge Gladys Kessler held the Department of Defense in contempt because it disobeyed a court order to videotape the release hearing of a Guantanamo Bay detainee, Mohammed Al-Adahi. Kessler previously had ruled that while the hearing could be conducted in secret to protect national security information, to "afford the public and the press an opportunity to observe the greatest possible portion" of the defendant's testimony the government was to videotape the testimony.[203] In January 2010, the *New York Times* reported that Naqib Jaji, the uncle of indicted terror suspect Najibullah Zazi, who was accused of plotting to bomb New York City subways, was secretly indicted and arrested for felony charges under the name John Doe.[204] Zazi's guilty plea to terrorism charges, meanwhile, was the subject of controversy when the Associated Press and *Newsday* wrote a letter asking a federal judge to unseal it in order to determine if Zazi's relatives were threatened with prosecution in order to compel Zazi to testify.[205] Finally, in April 2010, Chief Judge David Sentelle of the U.S. Court of Appeals for the District of Columbia abruptly closed the courtroom during a habeas corpus hearing for detainee Adham Awad despite the fact that both his lawyer and the Justice Department had both consented to a public hearing.[206]

Although in 2010 the Pentagon received praise from news organizations that had protested Guantánamo policies as unduly restrictive when the Department of Defense revised its rules for reporters covering military trials at Guantánamo,[207] these incidents raise numerous important questions about the balance of power between the government, the people and the press.

---

[201] *Id.* at 7.

[202] *Id.* at 9. *See also* Parhat v. Gates, 532 F.3d 834 (D.C. Cir. 2008) (ordering the government to specifically explain why protected status is required for the information it sought to keep secret).

[203] *See* Al-Adahi v. Obama, 672 F. Supp. 2d 114 (D.C. Cir. 2010).

[204] William K. Rashbaum, *Uncle Who Vouched for Terror Suspect Arrested*, N.Y. TIMES, Jan. 28, 2010, at A27.

[205] *See* Deepti Hajela, *News Outlets Ask Judge to Unseal Terror Plea Deal*, NEWSDAY, Feb. 25, 2010, at A17.

[206] *See* Nadia Tamez-Robledo, *D.C. Appeals Court Suddenly Closes Guantanamo Detainee Hearing*, http://www.rcfp.org/newsitems/index.php?i=11353.

[207] *See* Rosemary Lane, *Pentagon Relaxes Reporter Guidelines at Guantánamo Bay*, REPORTERS COMMITTEE FOR FREEDOM PRESS, Sept. 14, 2010, http://www.rcfp.org/newsitems/index.php?i=11555 (noting that new guidelines allowed media organizations to use edited photos and videos, narrowed the definition of "protected information," and provided for an appeals process in which organizations could challenge decisions to classify information as "protected"). *See also* U.S. DEPARTMENT OF DEFENSE, MEDIA GROUND RULES FOR GUANTANAMO BAY, CUBA (Sept. 10, 2010), http://www.defense.gov/news/d20100910groundrules.pdf.

CAMERAS IN COURTROOMS

In 1976, only two states — Texas and Colorado — allowed cameras in courtrooms; in 2010, every state allowed at least some camera coverage. A key reason for this shift was technological advances that eliminated the need for obtrusive flashes, bulky cameras and electrical cords snaking across courtroom floors. Also important were changing public and judicial attitudes. At the same time courts were recognizing the importance of allowing public and press access to the judicial process, video cameras were becoming part of everyday life for most Americans. People became accustomed to being videotaped as they did their shopping and banking, rode on elevators and attended weddings and parties. Today, many people videotaped seemingly mundane events in their life in order to post them on social media sites.

The situation was significantly different earlier in the twentieth century when cameras were obvious and intrusive, and their presence in the courtroom was viewed as inconsistent with judicial dignity and decorum. The first official bans on cameras in the courtroom followed the 1935 trial of Bruno Hauptmann for the kidnapping of the Lindbergh baby. In 1937, the American Bar Association adopted Canon 35 as part of its Canons of Professional and Judicial Ethics. Canon 35, which declared that cameras "detract from the essential dignity of the proceedings, degrade the court and create misconceptions with respect thereto in the mind of the public," recommended that cameras be banned in all courtrooms. That recommendation, which was amended in 1952 to specifically include television cameras, was followed by most states for more than four decades.

When the Supreme Court heard its first cameras-in-the-courtroom case, *Estes v. Texas*, it agreed with the ABA that TV cameras intruded upon "the solemn decorum of court procedure." Justice Clark, writing for the Court, held that jurors could be distracted by the equipment and by the mere knowledge that the trial was being televised. "Not only will the juror's eyes be fixed on the camera," he wrote, "but also his mind will be preoccupied with the telecasting rather than with the testimony." The judge, Clark continued, had enough to do supervising the trial without also worrying about supervising television crews. Witnesses, he wrote, "may be demoralized and frightened, some cocky and given to overstatement; memories may falter, as with anyone speaking publicly, and accuracy of statement may be severely undermined. Embarrassment may impede the search for truth, as may a natural tendency toward over-dramatization." Finally, for the defendant, the presence of TV cameras "is a form of mental — if not physical — harassment, resembling a police line-up or the third degree," Clark wrote.[208]

---

[208] 381 U.S. 532, 546-49 (1965).

Chief Justice Earl Warren, in a concurring opinion, referred to the noise and disorder of television equipment but was most concerned about the psychological effects, concluding that the real evil was "the trial participants' awareness that they are being televised."[209] Justice John Marshall Harlan also wrote a concurring opinion in which he shared his colleagues' fears about television's potential for causing "serious mischief" but also speculated that someday television might become "so commonplace ... in the daily life of the average person" that its disruptive influence would disappear.[210]

By the 1980s, Harlan's prediction had nearly come true. In its second cameras-in-the-courtroom case, *Chandler v. Florida*, the Supreme Court, in 1981, held that "no one has been able to present empirical data sufficient to establish that the mere presence of the broadcast media inherently has an adverse effect on that process."[211] Florida was one of several states that had begun experimenting with allowing cameras in its courtrooms in the 1970s. In *Chandler*, which involved two Miami Beach police officers charged with burglarizing a restaurant, the judge allowed a television camera in the court despite the defendants' objections. Although only about three minutes of the trial were ultimately broadcast, the officers appealed their conviction, claiming that the televising of trials was "inherently a denial of due process."

Writing for a unanimous Court, Burger — who throughout his tenure as chief justice steadfastly opposed the introduction of cameras into federal courts — declared that the mere presence of cameras did not automatically deprive a defendant of a fair trial. He wrote that broadcast coverage might, in some cases, violate a defendant's constitutional rights, but the mere possibility of prejudice did not justify a ban on televising trials. Instead, a defendant would have to prove that "the presence of cameras impaired the ability of the jurors to decide" the specific case. "To demonstrate prejudice in a specific case a defendant must show something more than juror awareness that the trial is such as to attract the attention of broadcasters."[212]

While *Chandler v. Florida* permits states to open their courtrooms to cameras, it does not require them to do so. The Supreme Court did *not* say that photographers have a First Amendment right to take their equipment into courtrooms. Instead it simply said that states were free to experiment with television coverage of trials. This point was underscored just two years later in another case out of Miami. U.S. District Judge Alcee Hastings, who was charged with accepting a bribe, asked to have his trial televised and was joined by news media

organizations in challenging the ban on cameras in federal courts. After the trial court denied the motion, the media appealed to the Eleventh U.S. Circuit Court of Appeals, which upheld the lower court ruling, saying there was no constitutional right, under either the First or Sixth Amendment, to bring cameras into courtrooms.[213]

The Federal Rules of Criminal Procedure have prohibited televising of federal criminal trials for more than fifty years. In 1983, in *United States v. Hastings*, the United States Court of Appeals for the Eleventh Circuit affirmed that Federal Rule 53 did not violate the First Amendment.[214] In *Hastings*, several media organizations and the defendant in the case wanted the trial court to televise proceedings. Discussing *Globe Newspapers*, the court concluded the right to attend criminal trials could not be extended to the right to televise, record, or broadcast trials.

Although cameras are still banned in most federal courtrooms and in District of Columbia courts, despite the lack of empirical evidence that the mere presence of the broadcast media has an inherently negative effect on the judicial process,[215] there have been multiple attempts to experiment with cameras in federal courts. In the early 1990s, limited television coverage of civil proceedings was tried under an experimental program authorized by the Judicial Conference of the United States, which, as mentioned above, sets policy for the federal courts. An evaluation of the program by the Federal Judicial Center found that judges became more favorable toward cameras in the courts after the experiment began; judges and court personnel believed the guidelines governing the program were workable and that journalists were generally cooperative; and judges and attorneys reported minimal or no effects of cameras in the courtrooms. Despite such favorable reactions, the Judicial Conference, in 1994, voted 19-6 to terminate the program.

In 2010, the Supreme Court barred a federal district court from broadcasting a non-jury trial in a case involving Proposition 8, which amended the California Constitution to include a section providing that the state would only recognize marriage between a man and a woman as valid. *Hollingsworth v. Perry* began when the Ninth Circuit Judicial Council decided to begin a pilot program allowing the limited use of cameras in federal district courts in the Circuit.[216] Cases would be selected for participation by the chief judge of the district court in consultation with the chief circuit judge. Judge Vaughn R. Walker of the District Court for the Northern District of California announced

---

[209] *Id.* at 570 (Warren, C.J., concurring).

[210] *Id.* at 597 (Harlan, J., concurring).

[211] 449 U.S. 560, 578-79 (1981).

[212] *Id.* at 581.

[213] United States v. Hastings, 695 F.2d 1278 (11th Cir. 1983). *See also* Conway v. United States, 852 F.2d 187 (6th Cir. 1988).

[214] 461 U.S. 499 (1983).

[215] *See* MARJORIE COHN & DAVID DOW, CAMERAS IN THE COURTROOM: TELEVISION AND THE PURSUIT OF JUSTICE 62-64 (1998).

[216] 558 U.S. 183 (2010).

that under the pilot program the lawsuit involving a challenge to California's Proposition 8 would be streamed live to courthouses in other cities and recorded for broadcast on the Internet. Wishing to block the recording and broadcasting of their testimony, supporters of the proposition filed an application for a stay of the decision with the Supreme Court. In a *per curiam* opinion, the Court held that, while it was not "expressing any views on the propriety of broadcasting court proceedings generally," the district court had not properly amended its local rules to allow for broadcasting of the trial in accordance with federal law.[217] Thus, although the trial was recorded, it was never broadcast or streamed via the Internet.

In 2011, the Judicial Conference decided to conduct a three-year pilot program to evaluate the effects of cameras on federal courtroom proceedings. Under the program, which began in July 2011, cameras controlled by judges were placed in fourteen volunteer federal district courts. Only civil proceedings are recorded, and both parties and the judge must consent to the recording, with the proceedings being available on a Web site at a later time. In addition, the presiding judge is allowed to terminate recordings in the interest of justice, to protect the dignity of the court and the rights of the parties and witnesses, or for any reason the judge considers "necessary or appropriate."[218]

Although federal courts themselves have not always been open to broadcasting their proceedings, during the past few years Congress has repeatedly considered legislation to permit federal judges, both trial and appellate, to open their courtrooms to cameras. In 2011, a U.S. Senate Judiciary subcommittee met to hear testimony over a bill, the Cameras in the Courtroom Act of 2011,[219] that would have required the U.S. Supreme Court to televise its public proceedings. The hearing included testimony from a witness who offered numerous quotes from past and present justices who have opposed allowing cameras into the Court. The bill was sent to the House, where it was referred to committee. As of summer 2016, no camera-access bill had ever managed to pass both houses.

While the Supreme Court has also been reluctant to allow cameras to tape its hearings, in 2000, in *Bush v. Gore*, for the first time it released audiotapes of oral arguments immediately after the arguments were completed.[220] Since *Bush*, the Court has occasionally released expedited audio of oral arguments in high profile cases at the request of media. The 2010 term marked the first time in four years it did not release any expedited audio.[221] In 2012, it declined media organizations' requests to tape arguments in three cases challenging the Patient Protection and Affordable Care Act (sometimes referred to as "Obamacare") but agreed to release same-day audio recordings of the arguments, which lasted nearly six hours over three days.

All fifty states allow some camera coverage. However, the extent of coverage permitted, as well as the rules journalists must follow, differs greatly among the states, and journalists are well advised to study their individual state rules regarding trial and appellate proceedings carefully before taking a camera, tape recorder or smartphone into a courtroom. The best sources for information about cameras-in-the-courtroom rules in the fifty states is the Web site of the Radio-Television News Directors Association.[222]

At one end of the spectrum is Florida, where the Casey Anthony trial was heard, where there is a presumption of camera access that can be overcome only by a finding that electronic coverage of a trial would have a "qualitatively different" effect than other types of media coverage.[223] In California, broadcasting is permitted by the written order of the judge, although recording jurors, jury selection, and conferences between participants is prohibited. At the other end of the spectrum are Alabama and South Dakota, where the consent of all parties and attorneys is needed. In New York, appellate courts coverage is permitted with the permission of the court. Consent of the parties is not needed, and coverage will only be barred upon a showing of good cause.

Like California and New York, many states require the consent of the presiding judge, and many place restrictions on the photographing of jurors and certain types of trial participants, such as juveniles, victims of sex crimes and undercover officers. Most states also limit the number of cameras allowed in the courtroom and specify where cameras may be placed. State rules often require pooling agreements among the various media. Practicing journalists should know the rules in their state as journalists who violate the rules governing electronic coverage can be found in contempt of court.

Despite some recent trials receiving gavel-to-gavel coverage, cameras in the courts continue to be a contentious issue, and judges often decide to ban coverage of highly publicized trials. For example, in 2004, a California trial judge prohibited camera coverage of the murder trial of Scott Peterson, accused of killing his wife, Laci, and their unborn child;[224] and, a year later, another California judge banned cameras during the child moles-

---

[217] *Id.* at 184.

[218] Judicial Conference Committee on Court Administration and Case Management Guidelines for the Cameras Pilot Project in the District Courts, *available at* http://www.uscourts.gov/uscourts/News/2011/docs/CamerasGuidelines.pdf.

[219] H.R. 3572 (2011).

[220] 531 U.S. 98 (2000).

[221] See *High Court Denies Broadcasters Access to Audio Recordings*, Apr. 16, 2010, http://www.rcfp.org/newsitems/index.php?i=11378.

[222] *See* https://www.rtdna.org/content/cameras_in_court#.Ue2kYxbxnFI.

[223] Florida v. Green, 395 So. 2d 532, 536 (Fla. 1981).

[224] *See Judge Bars Cameras from Peterson Courtroom*, Feb. 2, 2004, http://www.cnn.com/2004/LAW/02/02/peterson.case/.

tation trial of pop star Michael Jackson.[225] In contrast, on the other side of the country in North Carolina, another Peterson — this one Michael, a novelist and former newspaper columnist and mayoral candidate — was convicted of murdering his wife in a trial broadcast live on Court TV.[226]

PORTABLE ELECTRONIC DEVICES AND SOCIAL MEDIA

More recently, judges have also had to consider to what extent they will allow trial observers and participants to engage in microblogging from the courtroom as services such as Twitter attract more journalists and private individuals. Most federal courts have not addressed the issue of Twitter, although some have begun to confront the issue — with differing results. In 2009, U.S. District Judge J. Thomas Marten became the first federal judge officially to allow a journalist to use a Blackberry device to update his Twitter account when he granted Ron Sylvester, a reporter for the *Wichita* (Kansas) *Eagle*, permission to use the site to cover a federal racketeering trial. While Sylvester had been tweeting from the courtroom since 2007, Marten's decision was the first official order from a federal judge allowing this form of coverage.[227] Not long after Marten's order, however, U.S. District Judge Clay Land wrote that Rule 53 of the Federal Rules of Criminal Procedure should be interpreted as banning tweeting. According to Judge Land, the rule's prohibition on the "broadcasting of judicial proceedings" included "sending electronic messages from a courtroom that contemporaneously describe the trial proceedings and are instantaneously available for public viewing."[228] To date the U.S. Circuit Courts of Appeals have remained silent on the issue of tweeting or using wireless communication devices.

In addition, many states have yet to consider the question of whether updating a Twitter feed is "broadcasting." However, even states that have traditionally been camera friendly may have trouble adjusting to new media such as Twitter. For example, in Florida, as mentioned above, electronic media and still photography coverage of proceedings is allowed. In early 2010, however, the Standing Committee on Rules of Practices and Procedures considered a statewide ban on electronic devices in courthouses, although the proposal was voted down.[229]

In 2013, Utah's rules about electronic coverage of courtroom proceedings underwent drastic changes to allow more coverage of judicial proceedings. While Utah's prior rules had only allowed cameras in appellate courts under tight restrictions and banned them in trial courts, under new rules cameras, live streaming, live blogging and tweeting are allowed in all courts unless a judge provides a specific compelling reason to deny coverage. In 2014, however, Utah revised its rules regarding video, reversing the presumption that recording is allowed and, instead, letting individual judges use a large number of factors to determine when taping is allowed. Portable electronic device may be used inside a courtroom, but may not be used to record or transmit images or sound of court proceedings.[230]

Because most state judicial systems have yet to adopt a uniform approach to live blogging and tweeting, state judges, like federal judges, have reached conflicting decisions. While some courts are allowing Twitter, others have banned it — particularly in high profile cases. In 2012, for example, Judge Charles Burns of Illinois banned all spectators, including journalists, from tweeting during the trial of William Balfour, who was charged with the murder of singer Jennifer Hudson's mother.[231] The same year, Judge John Cleland banned all "electronic-based communications from the courtroom during the trial of former Penn State football coach Jerry Sandusky for sex abuse.[232] Like federal judges who have interpreted Rule 53 to prohibit tweeting, Cleland interpreted Pennsylvania state court laws that ban broadcasting of court proceedings to prohibit live tweeting from the trial. Although Cleland originally interpreted the rule to only prohibit the tweeting of direct quotes, when members of the media including the Associated Press and ESPN filed a motion seeking clarification, he modified his ruling to ban all tweeting from the trial.[233]

Most courts appear to be taking an ad hoc approach and there is no broad consensus about whether to let journalists use portable electronic devices to do live updates during trails, with many jurisdictions considering the issue on a case-by-case basis. Even when cameras are allowed in courtrooms or media organizations are allowed to broadcast video from closed circuit cameras in a courtroom, judges still sometimes ban the use of port-

[225] *See* Tina Susman, *Wheels of Justice Turn Secretly*, June 13, 2005, http://www.newsday.com/news/nationworld/world/ny-usjack134302689jun13,0,7754064.Story.

[226] *See* http://www.courttv.com/trials/novelist/.

[227] *See* Ahnalese Rushmann, *Courtroom Coverage in 140 Characters*, NEWS MEDIA & L., Spring 2009, at 28, *available at* http://www.rcfp.org/news/mag/33-2/courtroom_coverage_in__characters_28.html.

[228] United States v. Shelnutt, 2009 U.S. Dist. LEXIS 101427, *4 (M.D. Ga., Nov. 2, 2009).

[229] *See* Tricia Bishop, *New Rules Could End Tweets From Trials Statewide*, BALTIMORE SUN, Feb. 22 2010, *available at* http://articles.baltimoresun.com/2010-02-22/news/bal-md.twitter22feb22_1_cell-phones-trials-tweets.

[230] *See* Rule 4-401.01, Electronic Coverage of Media Proceedings, *available at* http://www.rcfp.org/sites/default/files/docs/20140617_161413_utah_rule_revision.pdf.

[231] *See* Ameet Sachdev, *Judge Bans Tweets From Reporters in Hudson Trial*, CHICAGO TRIBUNE, Apr. 26, 2012, *available at* http://articles.chicagotribune.com/2012-04-26/business/ct-biz-0413-chicago-law-martin-20120413_1_tweets-murder-trial-cook-county-courtrooms.

[232] Court Order, Commonwealth of Pennsylvania v. Gerald A. Sandusky, No. Cp-14-CR-24212011 (Penn. Ct. Com. Pl. June 4, 2012), *available at* http://www.rcfp.org/sites/default/files/docs/20120604_141047_june_4_memo_and_order.pdf.

[233] *See* Emily Miller, *Judge Changes Mind, Prohibits Tweeting and Other Electronic Communication in Sandusky Trial*, REPORTERS COMMITTEE FOR FREEDOM OF THE PRESS, June 4, 2012, *available att* http://www.rcfp.org/browse-media-law-resources/news/judge-changes-mind-prohibits-tweeting-and-other-electronic-communica.

able electronic devices in a courtroom. A study conducted by the Reporter's Committee for Freedom of the Press concluded that different jurisdictions are adopting a plethora of rules and no preferred approach has taken root.[234] Therefore, before covering a proceeding, reporters in states that have not adopted clear rules about using social media in courtrooms should consult with court personnel or know the presiding judge's individual preferences. Before tweeting from a judge's courtroom, check the court's standing orders and see if the court's electronic device policy is posted. If it's unclear how the court will apply rules designed to deal with traditional electronic media to live-blogging or what a judge's individual preference might be, journalists should contact the court's public information officer.

SUMMARY

While concern about press coverage of crimes and trials dates back at least two centuries, debate over the so-called free press-fair trial issue escalated during the 1960s when the Supreme Court overturned several murder convictions on the grounds that prejudicial publicity had deprived the defendants of their Sixth Amendment right to a fair trial. Televised and often sensationalized coverage of the O.J. Simpson trial in 1995 again brought the controversy to the forefront of public attention; and high-profile twenty-first century cases, such as the highly publicized Casey Anthony and George Zimmerman trials in Florida, have kept the debate going. The perceived conflict between the First and Sixth Amendments can occur in three ways: pretrial publicity can make it difficult to find impartial jurors; during-trial publicity can influence a sitting jury; and the presence of journalists and/or their equipment in the courtroom can cause physical or psychological disruption.

Two broad categories of remedies are available to judges. First are the traditional remedies designed to compensate for — but not eliminate — publicity. The most commonly used of such remedies are change of venue, continuance, *voir dire* and jury admonitions. The second category consists of remedies aimed at reducing or eliminating publicity. They are much more problematic since they directly affect the media's ability to obtain and report information related to the judicial system; and, beginning in the 1970s, the Supreme Court began placing First Amendment restrictions on their use.

In 1976, in *Nebraska Press Association v. Stuart*, the Supreme Court said gag orders on the press constituted prior restraints and could be used only if there were pervasive publicity that was likely to interfere with a fair trial, no other remedies

were available, and a gag order would be effective in preventing prejudicial publicity. This test made it difficult for a trial judge to justify gagging the media and greatly reduced the number of gag orders issued and upheld on appeal. Journalists must keep in mind, however, that if a judge *does* issue a gag order, violating it can result in a contempt of court citation even if subsequently the order is struck down on appeal. While some appellate courts have ruled that journalists can violate a patently invalid gag order if timely relief is not available from an appeals court, others have enforced the collateral bar rule, which says that a person cannot disobey a judicial order and then challenge its constitutionality as a defense to contempt of court.

Gag orders aimed at trial participants generally are not subject to the same rigorous test of constitutionality as gag orders aimed at the media. In *Gentile v. State Bar of Nevada*, the Supreme Court said it was permissible to punish an attorney who made extrajudicial statements that posed a "substantial likelihood" of interfering with a fair trial. While trial judges have greater leeway in restricting the speech of lawyers and other trial participants, there are First Amendment limits. A gag order cannot be overbroad and cannot be issued unless necessary to protect a defendant's right to a fair trial and no other alternative measures are available.

In addition to restricting the use of prior restraints on media coverage of the courts, the Supreme Court has also applied the First Amendment to limit the use of post-publication sanctions. In the 1940s, it ruled that judges could not use their contempt of court powers to punish coverage of and commentary on the judicial process unless such publications presented a clear and present danger of interfering with the fair administration of justice. This stringent standard has virtually eliminated the practice of judges citing for contempt journalists and others who criticize the courts. Three decades later the Court strengthened the media's protection against post-publication punishments when it ruled that the media could not be punished for publishing lawfully obtained, truthful information unless necessary to serve a compelling governmental interest.

In a series of cases in the 1980s, the Supreme Court also put a halt to the widespread use of court closures as a means of controlling publicity when it ruled that the press and public enjoyed a First Amendment right of access to criminal proceedings. The Court established a multi-part test for determining when a hearing could be closed, which requires a judge to issue written findings that, among other things, closure is essential to serve higher values and is as narrowly tailored as possible. While the Supreme Court has not ruled directly on whether a constitutional right of access exists to civil proceedings, lower courts that have considered the issue have found a qualified First Amendment right of access and have used the same test the Court mandated for closing criminal proceedings.

---

[234] *See* Tom Isler, *Tweeting From Courts Still Slow in Catching On: How Courts Across the Country Approach Real Time Reporting*, NEWS MEDIA & L., Spring 2015, at 3, *available at* http://www.rcfp.org/browse-media-law-resources/news-media-law/news-media-and-law-spring-2015/tweeting-courts-still-slow.

Many lower courts have also presumed that the First Amendment right of access extends to judicial records. Even if they recognize a constitutional right of access courts are unanimous that the common law provides both the press and public the right to inspect certain judicial records. However, increasing online access to judicial records is generating concerns about misuse of public information and privacy invasions, prompting some efforts to restrict electronic access. Media attempts to gain access to some types of judicial records — especially juvenile records, discovery materials and audio-visual records — have caused numerous conflicts, and courts have often disagreed about the extent of access rights.

One of the major free press-fair trial battles has involved cameras in courtrooms, especially the televising of trials. In 1965 the Supreme Court overturned a criminal conviction on the grounds that television cameras in the courtroom caused both physical and psychological disruptions inconsistent with the Sixth Amendment's guarantee of a fair trial. In the decades that followed, as cameras became less obtrusive and television became more ubiquitous, some states began to allow video coverage of judicial proceedings, ultimately leading the Court to revise its position. In *Chandler v. Florida* in 1981, it ruled that the mere presence of cameras did not automatically deny a defendant a fair trial. While there is no constitutional right to bring cameras into courts, states are free to experiment with camera coverage; and as of 2009, all fifty states allowed some form of camera coverage of courts. Most federal courts, however, continued to ban cameras despite generally favorable responses to a limited experiment with camera coverage during the early 1990s.

Conflicts between the press and the judiciary are inevitable since each is committed to advancing a different interest and those interests often appear to be at odds with one another. Judges and attorneys see their primary responsibility as ensuring fair trials and the proper functioning of the judicial process. Their key concern is protecting the rights of litigants, witnesses and jurors. Journalists see their primary responsibility as informing the public and serving as a watchdog over government, including the judicial branch. Their key concern is protecting freedom of the press and the public's right to know.

Certainly sometimes less lofty goals motivate both sides, adding problems. The Supreme Court has made it clear, however, that the First and Sixth Amendments are of equal importance in our constitutional scheme. Neither takes precedence over the other, nor can one be used as the justification for infringement of the other. The press has broad First Amendment rights to observe and report on the judicial process; and the judiciary must find ways to respect those rights while at the same time ensuring that trials are fair, jurors are unbiased and the judicial process operates smoothly, effectively and openly.

FOR ADDITIONAL READING

Bunker, Matthew D. *Justice and the Media: Reconciling Fair Trials and a Free Press*. Mahwah, N.J.: Lawrence Erlbaum Associates, 1997.

"The Court of Public Opinion: The Practice and Ethics of Trying Cases in the Media," 71 *Law and Contemporary Problems* (No. 4, Autumn 2008) (contains four articles addressing media coverage of courts).

"Covering the Appellate Courts," 9 *The Journal of Appellate Practice and Process* (No. 2, Fall 2007) (contains four articles on covering appellate courts).

Hengstler, Gary A. "Pressing Engagements: Courting Better Relationships Between Judges and Journalists," 56 *Syracuse Law Review* 419 (2006).

Kramer, Geoffrey P., et al. "Pretrial Publicity, Judicial Remedies, and Jury Bias," 14 *Law and Human Behavior* 409 (1990).

Levine, Raleigh Hannah. "Toward a New Public Access Doctrine," 27 *Cardozo Law Review* 1739 (2006).

Minow, Newton & Fred Cate. "Who Is an Impartial Juror in an Age of Mass Media?" 40 *American University Law Review* 631 (1991).

Silver, Derigan. "Media Censorship and Access to Terrorism Trials: A Social Architecture Analysis." 25 *Notre Dame Journal of Law, Ethics, and Public Policy* 143 (2011).

Terilli, Samuel A., et al. "Lowering the Bar: Privileged Court Filings as Substitutes for Press Releases in the Court of Public Opinion," 12 *Communication Law & Policy* 143 (2007).

Access to Public Documents and Meetings

By Sandra F. Chance

➡ **Headnote Questions**

- Why is access to information important?
- Does the U.S. Constitution guarantee a right of access to government information?
- What laws provide for a right of access to government records and meetings?
- How is the need for access to information balanced with the need for security and government secrecy?
- What is FOIA? Does it apply to state and local records?
- What are the exemptions to FOIA?
- Why is there conflict between the right to privacy and the right of access to information?
- Are computer records covered by access laws?
- How have the September 11, 2001, terrorist attacks and threats of terrorism affected access to information?

From the earliest days of the United States, elected officials, journalists, scholars, attorneys, judges and other citizens have recognized that speech about government is more credible when it is based on information. That information must come, in large part, from the government's own meetings and records. James Madison observed, for example:

> Nothing could be more irrational than to give people power, and to withhold from them information with which power is abused. A people who mean to be their own governors must arm themselves with power which knowledge gives. A popular government without popular information or the means of acquiring it is but a prologue to a farce or a tragedy, or perhaps both.[1]

Despite the logic of observations like that, governments at all levels — national, state and local — have a lengthy tradition of closing their records and meetings to public scrutiny. Madison himself opted to exclude the press and public from the deliberations on the same First Amendment used today to argue for open meetings and records.

Tension between government secrecy and public access to government information runs through U.S. history. Scandals during the administrations of Presidents Ulysses S. Grant and Warren G. Harding, for example, brought demands for specific information about government. But only in comparatively recent times has access become an issue of continuing and widespread interest. Before the Great Depression of the 1930s, people understood their government by reading about the activities in the Oval Office, the legislative bodies — from Congress to town councils — and a few administrative agencies. With the New Deal that followed in the wake of the Depression, however, government surged in both size and complexity. New agencies were established to perform specialized functions once handled, if at all, by elected representatives. Congress, for example, delegated much of its authority over advertising regulation to the Federal Trade Commission.

For all its Byzantine structure and process, Congress is a much easier organization to follow and evaluate than the FTC. Multiply this remote agency by the hundreds of others that were created on the local, state and federal levels, and the sense of frustration that many citizens felt is understandable. Government couldn't be understood, and that loss of understanding was accompanied by a sense of loss of control.

The secrecy precipitated by World War II compounded the problem. Shortly after the war's end, a movement emerged to make government more accessible. At first spearheaded by jour-

---

[1] Letter to W.T. Barry (Aug. 4, 1822), *in* 1 THE WRITINGS OF JAMES MADISON 103 (Gaillard Hunt ed. 1910).

nalists who demanded an enforceable "right to know," the movement gradually broadened to include public interest groups and business interests. Over time it was enormously successful in mobilizing the passage of federal and state access statutes. Today these freedom-of-information or right-to-know laws are the primary legal means by which citizens have access to government meetings and records. But they aren't the only tools. Federal and state constitutions and the common law also play important roles.

A study of access law — or any law — requires an attempt to pinpoint the policy or objectives behind it. Frequently, the purpose of those behind it — whether judges, legislators or the founding fathers — is very different from those who use it.

Some laws, like many state right-to-know laws, often enunciate their rationales. But many others, including the federal Freedom of Information Act, don't. Courts are left to grope for clues in legislative histories and other sources to discover how to guide the interpretation of ambiguous language.

The importance of this search shouldn't be underestimated. If a statute's purpose is, for example, the discovery of truth or self-fulfillment, there just isn't much government information that wouldn't qualify for disclosure in order to foster that policy. If, on the other hand, the objective of a law is to prevent secret rules and regulations — if only final decisions need be made public — it is a narrow right-to-know policy, indeed. Most often, the policy is to permit citizens to participate effectively in government, a standard of openness that comes somewhere in the middle. The benefits of guaranteeing access to government information generally parallel those associated with protecting speech. That is, access to information promotes the discovery of truth, self-government, orderly change and self-fulfillment. Access also enables the press to perform its watchdog function.

In contrast, a government's preference for secrecy has several specific roots.

First, finding and copying public records require time and labor, and providing facilities for public meetings is inconvenient and expensive. Limited resources can best be directed at whatever a particular government agency regards as its primary function, perhaps issuing drivers' licenses or collecting garbage.

Second, opening meetings and records chills creativity and effectiveness in government. If the casual suggestions and give-and-take of frank, brainstorming discussions are open to public examination, and perhaps ridicule, innovators and risk-takers in government won't make bold or daring proposals. The quality of decision-making will suffer.

Third, some interests — national security and personal privacy, for example — are more important than the public interest in access to government information.

And, finally, secrecy prevents disclosure of government waste, incompetence, unfairness and criminal activity.

To these specific objections, advocates of public access respond that providing information is not just an annoying appendage to the duties of government and officials; rather, it is a primary function of government. The public has a need to know what its government is doing if democracy is to work. They also argue that members of the public have good ideas. By excluding them from the early stages of decision-making, government is deprived of a fertile source of imaginative suggestions. And by denying the public access during the formative stages of a proposal, it is being excluded at the very time its input can be most effective. Moreover, access to ideas that are rejected can sometimes be as telling about the governmental processes as those that are accepted.

While most right-to-know advocates concede that there are times when a specific interest, such as the movement of troops, will trump a generalized interest in disclosure, they argue that any exceptions must be specific. Officials may attempt to use a narrow, reasonable exception to a general policy of disclosure as a catchall to hide information that ought to be available.

Keep these policies and attitudes in mind as you read through the survey of constitutional, common law and statutory access issues.

CONSTITUTIONAL ACCESS

In *New York Times Co. v. Sullivan*,[2] the U.S. Supreme Court declared that the "central meaning" of the First Amendment is that it protects discussion about government and officials. Without guarantees of free speech, self-governance is an unobtainable goal. But the Court has been reluctant to extend that guarantee to access to the government information necessary to give content to that speech.

Only in the context of criminal trials has the Court fully considered the access issue. First in *Richmond Newspapers v. Virginia*,[3] and then in *Press-Enterprise Co. v. Superior Court (II)*,[4] it held that the acquisition of newsworthy information was entitled to First Amendment protection. It took pains, however, to limit its holding to a particular kind of access — that of criminal trials. Indeed, at least two justices emphasized this narrow focus in concurring opinions.

But the logic of the case can't be confined to criminal-justice proceedings. The Court based its decision, first, on the premise

---

[2] 376 U.S. 254 (1964).

[3] 448 U.S. 555 (1980).

[4] 478 U.S. 1 (1986). *Press-Enterprise II* involved the question of whether judicial proceedings, other than trials, are required by the First Amendment to be open; the Court held that they are. *Press-Enterprise Co. v. Riverside County Superior Court (I)*, 464 U.S. 501 (1984), involved the question of whether *voir dire* proceedings — the questioning of jurors to determine whether they are competent to sit in a particular trial — must be open to the public; the Court held that they must be. Both cases are discussed in Chapter 16.

that access to criminal trials contributes to the self-governing function and promotes the democratic process. It added that criminal trials are historically open. Whether this latter observation is an independent test or merely evidence of the truth of the first part is unclear, but several lower federal courts have seized on the language to allow access based on the First Amendment.

A federal district court in Ohio, for example, found that the public had a qualified right of access to a city council meeting since such meetings were historically open to the public and the subject matter contributed to the functioning of government.[5] And a district court in Puerto Rico used the same First Amendment analysis to order the governor of Puerto Rico to disclose a record.[6] Both decisions were reversed on other grounds, with the appellate courts expressing skepticism that a broadly based constitutional right of access existed.

On the state level, the New York Court of Appeals adopted the Supreme Court's test but used it to deny access to a dentist's disciplinary hearing since there was no evidence that public access plays a significant role in the functioning of that proceeding.[7]

The reason for the Supreme Court's own reluctance to take the logical next step after the courtroom cases may be the slippery slope problem: Once a court requires some records and proceedings to be open, can a principled, constitutional line be drawn between matters that must be open and those where secrecy is appropriate? Even Justice William Brennan, one of the Court's staunchest free expression advocates, was wary of runaway access. "Analysis is not advanced," he wrote, "by rhetorical statements that all information bears upon public issues [and therefore must be disclosed]; what is crucial in individual cases is whether access to a particular government process is important in terms of that very process."[8]

The Supreme Court decided an important First Amendment case in 1999. *Los Angeles Police Department v. United Reporting Publishing Corp.*[9] illuminates the growing conflict between open records and a citizen's right to privacy. The Court ruled that a California law limiting who could get access to police records listing names and addresses of arrested suspects did not, on its face, violate the First Amendment. The California law limits access to names and addresses of arrestees and crime victims to those who seek the information for "scholarly, journalistic, political or governmental purposes." The law bars businesses from using the information "to sell a product or service."[10]

Writing for the majority, Chief Justice William Rehnquist said the case was not one "in which the government is prohibiting the speaker from conveying information that the speaker already possesses." The law merely requires that if a company "wishes to obtain the addresses of arrestees, it must qualify under the statute to do so." According to the Court, the California law did not abridge anyone's right to engage in speech but simply regulated access to information in the government's hand.[11]

State constitutions may also provide access rights to government information. Five states provide explicit constitutional provisions concerning the public's right to know. The constitutions of Florida, New Hampshire, North Dakota, Louisiana and Montana all guarantee access to government meetings and records.[12] The Montana Constitution, for example, provides that "[n]o person shall be deprived of the right to examine documents or to observe the deliberations of all public bodies or agencies ... except in cases in which the demand of individual privacy clearly exceed the merits of public disclosure." Montana's is unusually explicit, but most state constitutions have provisions paralleling the First Amendment that can be employed in the right circumstances.

Claims based on either federal or state constitutions face uncertain prospects. The law continues to emerge, with issues related to electronic access helping to define the constitutional parameters. In 1998, for example, a federal district court in Tennessee ruled against a newspaper's claim that the First Amendment provided a right to the Web browser history and so-called "cookie" files of a government employee.[13] The newspaper wanted to know what Web sites the employee had visited online.

Courts of last resort often move with great caution. Edicts based on the constitution have no appeal short of the unwieldy task of amending the constitution itself. When courts err in interpreting statutes, on the other hand, Congress or state legislatures can easily make adjustments, at least in theory. Without finding a workable rule that can be applied to each of the millions of records and meetings whose openness they would otherwise have to resolve on a case-by-case basis, courts won't rush into this complex area.

Constitutional change may thus seem to move with the speed of glaciers. But the law will never be developed on that level if those seeking access don't make and pursue claims based on First Amendment theories. It was more than three decades af-

---

[5] WJW-TV v. Cleveland, 686 F. Supp. 177 (N.D. Ohio 1988), *rev'd on other grounds,* 878 F.2d 906 (6th Cir. 1989).

[6] El Dia, Inc. v. Colon, 783 F. Supp. 15 (D.P.R. 1992), *rev'd on other grounds,* 963 F.2d 488 (1st Cir. 1992).

[7] Johnson Newspaper Corp. v. Melino, 564 N.E.2d 1046 (N.Y. 1990).

[8] *Richmond Newspapers,* 448 U.S. at 589 (Brennan, J., concurring in judgment).

[9] 528 U.S. 32 (1999).

[10] CAL. GOV'T CODE § 6254(f)(3) (1995).

[11] 528 U.S. at 40.

[12] FLA. CONST. art. I, § 24 (1992); N.H. CONST. Part I, art. 8 (1976); N.D. CONST. art. XI, § 5 (1974); LA. CONST. art. XII, § 3 (1974); MONT. CONST. art II, § 9 (1972).

[13] Pitman Pit, Inc. v. City of Cookeville, 23 F. Supp. 2d 822 (M.D. Tenn. 1998).

ter Justice William Douglas declared in 1947 that "a trial is a public event" before the Court declared that the Constitution requires courtrooms to be open.[14]

COMMON LAW ACCESS

Under the common law of England — the traditional, judge-made law passed from generation to generation — access to public information was limited. The doors of legislative bodies were usually closed to the public, and citizens were allowed to inspect or copy public records only if they were able to show what was called a "proper interest." Just what formed a "proper interest" was uncertain for citizens then and historians now.

Virtually all reported judicial decisions describe controversies over records, not meetings. Evidently there was no right of access to meetings. After the American Revolution, meetings of legislative bodies on both sides of the Atlantic became much more open, without judicial prodding. The outcomes in the great majority of these older common law cases turned on whether an interest — a need to see the record — was so important that the record would be available in a lawsuit. If a citizen, say, wanted to see all the town's utility bills out of personal curiosity, his interest wasn't proper. If, on the other hand, access to the record was essential to proving that he had paid his own bill, then the interest was proper and access was granted.

These cases have long captured the attention of scholars and litigants. But largely forgotten are those cases in which citizens sought access, not to serve a personal or private interest, but to serve the general or public welfare. Given the common law's bad reputation, it may be surprising to learn that those who claimed to represent the public interest were often successful.

By the middle of the nineteenth century, for example, English courts were regularly opening the financial records of municipalities for taxpayer inspections. They often reasoned that citizens were like shareholders in a corporation; they had a right, limited though it was, to review the records of their enterprise, in these cases, their government. In the leading case, *Rex v. Guardians of Great Farrington*,[15] an English court held flatly that municipal financial records could no longer be withheld because a taxpayer failed to prove any special interest.

In the United States, as in England, most of the reported decisions concerned the demands of individuals seeking to serve private purposes. Sometimes the interest was merely curiosity; sometimes it was financial. A century ago, for example, title companies — companies that insured the ownership of land — found they could abstract information from deeds and other land records, repackage it and resell it at a profit. Officials,

fearful of losing both income and control of what they perceived as their property, frequently resisted these incursions. Often requests for these purposes were unsuccessful. There are similar conflicts today between government and resellers of government information — on-line services, for example.

There were only a few reported cases where plaintiffs, usually newspapers, claimed their business was to represent the public interest. It's not clear why there weren't more. It may be that media seldom requested records or that they got them whenever they did. On the other hand, it is also possible that when access was denied, cases were not contested in court. The media won almost every case that they did contest. Courts typically recited the common law's narrow, historical "proper interest" restrictions and then declared that the "public interest" was a "proper interest." In a leading case, the Michigan Supreme Court concluded in 1928: "If there is any rule of English common law that denied the public the right of access to public records, it is repugnant to the spirit of our democratic institutions. Ours is a government of the people."[16]

A 1994 decision illustrates how the common law of access functions today. In *Washington Legal Foundation v. United Sentencing Commission*,[17] a public interest group sought access to records the commission used in formulating recommendations. The threshold question was whether the records were "public records" under the common law. Not every document contained in a government file qualifies. Common law records are generally only those that record official actions or are vital to the functioning of government. Even if a record is a "public record," it may still be withheld if, the court said, its "specific interests favoring secrecy outweigh the general and specific interests favoring disclosure."[18] This means the broad public interest in knowing about government may be insufficient to force disclosure. A particular public might also be necessary. It wasn't necessary to do the balancing in this case, however, for the threshold test wasn't met. The records sought were held to be "predecisional" and thus were public records under the common law.

Despite its limitations, the common law can be a highly effective access tool. In one case, for example, a common-law-based suit forced a government official to create a record that did not exist, something a statute never does. A sheriff had negotiated a settlement with a discharged deputy but kept no documents relating to the settlement. He said the law did not require any. A newspaper filed suit under the state freedom of information act and under the common law. The state supreme court ruled that no statute obligated the sheriff to create or maintain records of

---

[14] Craig v. Harney, 331 U.S. 367, 373 (1947).

[15] 109 Eng. Reprint 202 (1829).

[16] Nowack v. Fuller, 219 N.W. 749, 750 (Mich. 1928).

[17] 17 F.3d 1446 (D.C. Cir. 1994).

[18] *Id.* at 1451.

the settlement agreement. As a result, there was no record to be demanded under the state's right-to-know law.

But the common law claim fared better. The court held that the common law required a record to be made:

Whenever a written record of the transaction of a public officer, in his office, is a convenient and appropriate mode of discharging the duties of his office, it is not only his right but his duty to keep that memorial, whether expressly required to do so or not; and when it is kept it becomes a public document.[19]

The common law required the sheriff first to create a record that he then was ordered to disclose.

In another case, a newspaper that had been excluded from a meeting of the Atlantic City Convention Center Authority demanded access to audiotapes recorded at the meeting. The newspaper's claim was based on the New Jersey right-to-know law and the common law. The statutory claim was dismissed since the meeting was taped only to make the drafting of minutes easier and more accurate, and, therefore, the tapes weren't public records under the state's narrow right-to-know law. On the common law claim, however, the New Jersey Supreme Court held that the records were indeed public records since recording was a "convenient, appropriate or customary method" of documenting official action.[20]

Access to records not available otherwise may be possible through requests based on a common-law theory. Legislative bodies, for example, typically exclude themselves from the reach of right-to-know statues. In *Schwartz v. Department of Justice*,[21] however, a federal district court noted that all three branches of government are subject to the common law right of access, and it ordered records of Peter A. Rodino Jr., then chairman of the House Judiciary Committee, released.

These decisions, of course, are binding only in jurisdictions where the rulings were made, but they represent some creative or last-resort uses to which the common law can be put.

The use of common law is limited, however. Its answer to the question of what is a public record is narrow — generally confined to documents that memorialize some official transaction such as a deed or minutes of a meeting. Even when a document is clearly a public record and the requester's purpose proper, a custodian may withhold it if disclosure is outweighed by some other interest, such as personal privacy.

The discretionary aspect of the common law can frustrate the usual judicial remedy: a writ of mandamus. A writ of mandamus is a court order for an official to comply with the law. Since the common law permits discretion, some courts are reluctant to overrule a custodian who has exercised that discretion in good faith, however wrong the custodian may have been on the primary issue.

In the everyday world, a demand based on the common law is so unusual that it is likely to be met by an official with a puzzled or blank look. It will probably only be pursued to a conclusion when more conventional means, such as access statutes, are unavailing; and it will almost certainly entail a time-consuming and expensive suit with an uncertain outcome. Still, given the right circumstances, the common law can be exploited to fill the cracks left by constitutions and statutes.

THE FEDERAL FREEDOM OF INFORMATION ACT

The Fourth of July 2016 marked the fiftieth anniversary of the federal Freedom of Information Act.[22] The law is, in several respects, the most important access tool today. The FOIA is certainly the most visible and most analyzed right-to-know law, governing access to the country's largest group of records. As the Internet has revolutionized the way information is collected, stored and shared, the law and those charged with providing access to government information have struggled to keep up.

A study of the policies and issues of the federal act will also provide insights into comparable state laws, since it provides a framework for analyzing in detail each of the fifty state right-to-know laws, an individual analysis that is beyond the scope of this book.

The FOIA is the outgrowth of the Administrative Procedures Act of 1946. That act was, in turn, a response to the explosive growth of government that began in the 1930s. The emergence of highly specialized, independent regulatory agencies, like the Federal Trade Commission, and the activities of agencies of the executive branch, like the Department of Labor, triggered fears not just about secrecy but about incomprehensibility. Each of the agencies had its own rules and procedures, causing many to feel out of touch with government.

The Administrative Procedures Act attempted to restore a sense of order to government by standardizing the procedures used to adopt and enforce rules and by making sure those procedures were accessible to the public. Though this was a considerable improvement, particularly for those regularly doing business with an agency, in another sense it failed because of its focus on how things were done, rather than on what was being done and why. And agencies remained largely their own judges of how well they complied with the act.

In response to these problems and the swelling interest in the

---

[19] Daily Gazette Co. v. Withrow, 350 S.E.2d 738, 747 (W.Va. 1986).

[20] Atlantic City Convention Ctr. Auth. v. South Jersey Publ'g Co., 637 A.2d 1261, 1267 (N.J. 1993).

[21] 435 F. Supp. 1203 (D.C. 1977), *aff'd* 595 F.2d 889 (D.C. Cir. 1979).

[22] 5 U.S.C. § 552 (1966).

public's right to know, in 1966, the Freedom of Information Act amended the Administrative Procedures Act. For the first time, the public had a clear right of access to records of the executive and administrative agencies of government. In contrast to the common law, the legal burden was on the government to justify withholding, not on the requester to justify release. The law is now forty-eight years old and has provided access to extraordinarily important information about governmental operations.

However, some agencies adopted tactics to undermine the law: The exemptions were given sweeping interpretations; fees for finding, copying and segregating exempt from non-exempt material were exorbitant; long delays became routine; and agencies claimed they couldn't find the requested information. As a result, the act was extensively amended in 1974. The changes sought to ensure compliance, for example, by limiting the fees agencies could charge to actual costs, expediting the scheduling of FOIA cases and allowing a wrongly denied requester to recover attorney's fees from the agency. The act was again amended in 1976 and in 1986.

How well it works, of course, isn't measured strictly by what it says or how courts interpret it. The attitude of government leadership can be a powerful influence on the practical, day-to-day functioning of the FOIA. In contrast to its predecessors, the Clinton Administration did a lot, at least on paper, to encourage agencies to comply with the spirit, as well as the letter, of the FOIA. In 1995, for example, President Bill Clinton issued a long-awaited executive order that sharply reduced the number of documents that may be classified for national security. He said his order would "lift the veil" from millions of documents and keep others from ever becoming classified. The *New York Times* characterized it as the least secretive policy on government records since the beginning of the Cold War.[23]

Despite this "presumption of openness," the government, four years later, succeeded in keeping a document secret, taking the case all the way to the Supreme Court.[24] By granting *certiorari* and ruling on the substantive issues, the Court was poised to interpret the national security exemption to FOIA for the first time. In an unusual decision, it vacated the appellate court's ruling before the oral arguments were even heard. As a result, it deferred to the government's claim that national security would be damaged and set the tone for increased governmental discretion over release of information.

This ruling continued a line of cases narrowing what the act is meant to do and, thus, the kinds of records it makes available. In a key FOIA case, for example, Justice John Paul Stevens wrote for the majority:

[T]he basic purpose of the Freedom of Information Act [is] to open agency action to the light of public scrutiny.... Official information that sheds light on an agency's performance of its statutory duties fall squarely within that statutory purpose. That purpose, however, is not fostered by disclosure of information about private citizens that is accumulated in various government files but that reveals little or nothing about an agency's own conduct.[25]

For many, this view is unsupported by the language of the statute. Justice Ruth Bader Ginsburg observed in another leading case that the "'core purpose' limitation is not found in FOIA's language. A FOIA requester need not show that ... disclosure would serve any public purpose, let alone a 'core purpose' of 'opening agency action to the light of public scrutiny' or advancing 'public understanding of the operations of activities of the government.'"[26]

Advocates of an expansive interpretation of the FOIA argue that the law's purpose is the discovery of truth. The more restrictive view is often based on the argument that the purpose of the FOIA is only to disclose the final actions of government. The law itself contains no statement of purpose, leaving plenty of room for interpretation.

In an effort to eliminate this confusion and strengthen FOIA, Congress passed the OPEN FOIA Act of 2009.[27] The law requires Congress to state clearly and explicitly its intention to create statutory exemptions.[28] The law "provide[s] a safeguard against the growing trend towards FOIA exemptions."[29]

In 2009, on his first full day in office, President Barack Obama indicated a new era of openness would begin. "For a long time now, there's been too much secrecy in this city," he said. He pledged to make government transparency a touchstone of his presidency.[30] One of his first acts was to change the way FOIA requests would be handled, saying that, under his administration, "there would be a presumption of openness."[31] For the first time in history, visitor logs would be available online. "Americans have a right to know whose voices are being heard in the policymaking process," he said.[32]

---

[23] *See* Douglas Jehl, *Clinton Revamps Policy on Secrecy of U.S. Documents,* N.Y. TIMES, Apr. 18, 1995, at A1.

[24] *See* United States v. Weatherhead, 528 U.S. 1042 (1999).

[25] Dep't of Justice v. Reporters Comm. for Freedom of the Press, 489 U.S. 749, 772 (1989).

[26] Dep't of Defense v. Fed. Labor Relations Auth., 510 U.S. 487, 507 (1994).

[27] 5 U.S.C. § 522 (2009).

[28] S. 612, 111th Cong. (2009).

[29] Press Release, U.S. Sen. Patrick Leahy, Leahy Marks 43rd Anniversary of Freedom of Information Act (June 25, 2009), http://leahy.senate.gov/press/200906/062509b.html.

[30] Sheryl Gay Stolberg, *On First Day, Obama Quickly Sets a New Tone,* N.Y. TIMES, Jan. 21, 2009, at A1.

[31] Memorandum for the Heads of Executive Departments and Agencies, *available at* http://www.whitehouse.gov/the_press_office/TransparencyandOpenGovernment.

[32] Christi Parsons, *Obama Opens Visitor Logs,* L.A. TIMES, Sept. 5, 2009, at A20.

Advocates were encouraged in 2009 when Obama ordered national security officials to study whether the government is classifying too much information and to make recommendations for changing the current system.[33] The administration also issued an Open Government Directive, directing agencies to create open government plans.[34]

However, studies varied on how much government secrecy had changed. A 2011 study, for example, said that federal agencies had improved FOIA performance during President Obama's administration,[35] while a 2012 study found that agencies had rejected 50 percent more requests for public records during Obama's presidency than they did during President Bush's administration.[36]

The current White House has been called "more restrictive" and "more dangerous" to the press than any other in history.[37]

The public's interest in learning more about U.S. drone strikes, the raid that killed Osama bin Laden, terror threats, the IRS's scrutiny of conservative organizations, and government's secret surveillance programs has highlighted the competing values of transparency and national security.

To better understand the issues, it's important to understand the law.

Overview of the FOIA

In general, the FOIA requires federal government agencies to make their records available for inspection and copying unless the records fall into one of nine categories. The act does not apply to Congress, the courts or the president's staff.

Some information must be published by an agency — statements of its organization, functions, procedures and rules, for example, and steps one must take to obtain information, including copies of decisions. Many agencies, including all those of special interest to communications law, have public reading rooms where this and other information is available.

Other agency records must be specifically requested. The FOIA does not define "agency record," but judicial interpretations are so broad as to include almost anything containing information, so long as it was created by and is under control of the agency. Audio tapes and computer disks, as well as written materials, are agency records. Some records — appointment books, calendars and telephone logs, for example — may exist only for the convenience of individual employees. They aren't agency records. And the FOIA does not require an agency to create a document that does not exist.

The FOIA requires that a record be "reasonably described" by a requester so it can be located. An agency can charge reasonable search and copying fees. There are standard fee schedules, but individual requirements vary, so a requester needs to ask for an estimate of costs. The law authorizes waivers for educational and non-commercial scientific institutions and for the news media when the requested information will "contribute significantly to public understanding of the operation or activities of Government." To qualify for consideration, a requester will have to explain the purpose of the request, something not otherwise required.

Though the FOIA requires a quick response to a request, substantive compliance — the production of the record or specific grounds for denial — can take months or even years. Some federal agencies are overwhelmed by requests.

If a request is ultimately refused, the FOIA provides for an administrative appeal to the head of the agency and then to U.S. district court. There are hundreds of judicial decisions resolving FOIA disputes. The legal burden of justifying secrecy is on the agency. A court can — but is not required to — order the government to pay attorneys' fees if a requester "substantially prevails."

FOIA Exemptions

An agency may withhold a record under the FOIA only if it is covered by at least one of the act's nine exemptions. Even in those cases, the law doesn't require a record to be withheld. The exemptions are discretionary; although other laws may require secrecy, the FOIA never does. Moreover, if part of a document is legitimately exempt from required disclosure and the remainder is not, the custodian must release the non-exempt portion if, in the words of the law, it is "reasonably segregable."

Exemption 1: National Security. This exemption authorizes the president to make and enforce rules to keep information secret in the interest of national defense or foreign policy. The rules are established by executive order without congressional involvement. While the president has leeway to decide what documents should be protected, the order must make plain both the procedures for classifying and declassifying and the underlying criteria for determining whether a specific document should be classified.

The exemption has become one of the most important weap-

---

[33] *See* Carrie Johnson, *Review of Government Secrecy Ordered*, WASH. POST, May 28, 2009, at A3.

[34] Open Government Directive, *available at* http://www.whitehouse.gov/omb/assets/memoranda_2010/m10-06.pdf (Dec. 8, 2009).

[35] Glass Half Full: 2011 Knight Open Government Survey Finds Freedom of Information Change, But Many Agencies Lag in Following Obama's Order, *available at* http://www.gwu.edu/~nsarchiv/NSAEBB/NSAEBB338/KnightOpenGovtSurvey2011.pdf (Mar. 14, 2011).

[36] Government Secrecy Increases Under Obama, *available at* http://www.judicialwatch.org/blog/2010/03/govt-secrecy-increases-under-obama/ (Sept. 26, 2012).

[37] *See* http://www.washingtonpost.com/blogs/erik-wemple/wp/2014/10/27/usa-todays-sus (Oct. 27, 2014).

ons in the war on terrorism, as the federal government has instituted rules and presidents have issued executive orders classifying large amounts of information in the name of national security. However, some argued that the orders covered more than national security matters. For instance, many people do not associate national security with trade agreements, but under this executive order, any document received from a foreign government "is presumed to cause damage to the national security" and are not subject to release.[38] This is not unexpected. Administrations since that of George Washington have withheld information because of national security concerns. Even the most outspoken advocates of public access concede that the release of certain information would be devastating for the country. But critics claim that national security has also been used to shield misconduct or incompetence from public view.

The national security exemption was used to block access to photographs and video of Osama bin Laden's death in 2011. "A picture may be worth a thousand words. And perhaps moving pictures bear an even higher value. Yet, in this case, verbal descriptions of the deal and burial of Osama Bin Laden will have to suffice," according to a federal district court ruling in 2012.[39]

As originally enacted, the exemption gave the executive branch virtually blanket authority to classify information in the interest of national security or foreign policy. In 1973, for example, the Supreme Court held that the mere fact that the administration had classified a document was enough to justify withholding the document.[40] The FOIA, it ruled, just did not allow a national security classification to be challenged. Partly in response to that decision, Exemption 1 was amended in 1974 to permit a court to examine a document in private to determine whether it should be released. The amendment also allowed courts to order the release of non-classified portions of otherwise properly classified documents, that is, segregating portions of a document.

Courts today scrutinize agency actions closely to see whether the government follows its own procedures to classify documents. But they remain reluctant to overrule government experts as to whether the release of a particular document would threaten national security. Given the potential consequences of a mistake, the line between information that is safe and that is harmful may be too fine for courts to draw with confidence. The Clinton Administration, for example, refused to disclose details of a $25 million telephone system at the White House. Would disclosure expose national secrets? Or extravagance? Or both.

Exemption 2: Administrative Documents. This exempts from required disclosure routine and insignificant matters that are "related solely to the internal personnel rules and practices of an agency." And, though the decisions of lower courts are not uniform, the exemption also protects agency manuals and rules — such as law enforcement manuals — if their release would help people dodge the law. (Materials like these are often also exempt under Exemption 7, law enforcement records.)

The exemption protects routine administrative documents, such as rules about lunch hours or sick leave, because it's considered burdensome for an agency to have to assemble and maintain the material for public inspection, and the public wouldn't reasonably be expected to have an interest.

Federal agencies often use this exemption to prevent the release of documents they consider sensitive. However, in 2011, the Supreme Court overruled thirty years of case law that agencies had used to deny access using this exemption and significantly narrowed the scope of the exemption.[41]

Exemption 3: Other Laws. This exempts records that are "specifically exempted from disclosure by statute ... provided that such statute (a) requires that matter be withheld from the public in such a manner as to leave no discretion on the issue, or (b) establishes particular criteria for withholding or refers to particular types of matters to be withheld." An example is 50 U.S.C 403(g), under which the Central Intelligence Agency is not required to disclose its organization, functions, names, official titles, salaries or number of personnel employed. There are probably hundreds of statutes that authorize withholding information from disclosure.

The exemption applies only to statutes and not to agency rules and regulations. Thus, an agency can't exempt itself; only Congress can do that. Similarly, an agency can't invoke the exemption because a state law may protect certain records. A federal appellate court has held that state juvenile records in possession of federal authorities could not be withheld under this exemption because the federal law protected only federal juvenile delinquency proceedings from disclosure.[42] A record exempt from disclosure under state law may be available under the FOIA. The opposite may also be true.

In recent years, a number of educational institutions have invoked student privacy rights as grounds for withholding records under FOIA's Exemption 3. The Family Education and Rights Protection Act[43] helps protect students' right to privacy in their educational records. However, many schools around the country have used this law to deny access to information on criminal ac-

[38] Exec. Order No. 13,292, 68 C.F.R. 15,315 (2003), *available at* http://www.white house.gov/news/releases/2003/03/20030325-11.html.

[39] Judicial Watch v. U.S. Dep't of Defense, 857 F. Supp. 2d 44 (D.C. Cir. 2012).

[40] Environmental Protection Agency v. Mink, 410 U.S. 73 (1973).

[41] Milner v. Dep't of the Navy, 562 U.S. 562 (2011).

[42] McDonnell v. United States, 4 F.3d 1227 (3rd Cir. 1994).

[43] 20 U.S. C. §1231g(b)(1) (2006).

tivities on campus, the use of influence and political clout in the admissions process, and athletic program misconduct.[44]

Exemption 4: Trade Secrets. This exemption protects "trade secrets and commercial or financial information" that individuals and businesses supply to the government. For Exemption 4 to apply, the information must be commercially valuable, actually used in a trade or business and maintained in secret.

The idea is to protect the competitive positions of those who submit confidential information to the government. If companies that voluntarily submit information cannot depend upon it being held in confidence, they may refuse to cooperate, impairing the government's ability to get information. When the government compels production of the information, the rationale becomes strained; and this exemption would seem not to apply.

This distinction was muddied, however, by a 1992 case in which the Court of Appeals for the District of Columbia held that when a company submits information voluntarily, even if the government could have compelled disclosure, the information enjoys exempt status.[45] This decision has been criticized, for it seems to invite collusion between an agency and a business when neither wants the information to be made public. An agency and a business simply agree to voluntary submission, undermining a line of cases that refused to recognize an agency's pledge of confidentiality as a substitute for meeting the standards of Exemption 4. Whether the other circuits will follow this court's lead is unknown. But because of the number of FOIA cases it decides due to its location in the District of Columbia, and the expertise it has developed in this area, the FOIA decisions of the D.C. Circuit merit special attention. They are highly influential.

Businesses themselves sometimes try to protect their interests in secrecy through "reverse FOIA" suits. In these, a business that has provided information to the government sues the government to stop it from making the information public. Reverse FOIA suits involve only information that falls into an exempt category, usually Exemption 4, and that the government has the discretion to release. These suits challenge the release as an abuse of discretion.

Exemption 5: Inter- and Intra-Agency Memoranda. The use of this exemption to deny access to information has skyrocketed in recent years.[46] Designed to allow employees to candidly express their ideas and positions, this exemption is now being referred to as the "withhold it because you want" exemption.[47]

While President Obama instructed agencies that information should not be withheld merely because "public officials might be embarrassed by disclosure, because errors and failures might be revealed, or because of speculative or abstract fears" in 2009,[48] access advocates argue this is precisely how the exemption is being used and are calling for Congress to include a balancing test.[49]

This exemption is intended to protect agency memoranda or letters and reflects several common law privileges. Under the common law, some communications are privileged, that is, protected from forced disclosure by a court. These privileges seek to protect some larger purpose. The attorney-client privilege, for example, was created to make the criminal justice system function better, even though it may create injustices in a particular case by denying access to some evidence. Similarly, this exemption protects agency communication and encourages cooperation between various agencies and their employees.

Because of the privileges, Exemption 5 is probably the most complex and most important exemption: More than 95 percent of all documents are inter- or intra-agency memoranda.

The exemption also protects the deliberative process of government that leads to a decision — candid advice and recommendations or the open exchange of ideas — in what is called "executive privilege." The exemption doesn't apply to the final decisions and opinions themselves, and it doesn't apply to statements of policy and instructions to staff that affect the public.

In deciding whether the privilege is applicable, courts examine whether a particular "predecisional" document is "so candid and personal in nature that public disclosure is likely in the future to stifle honest and frank communication within the agency," whether it is in the form of a recommendation or a draft and whether it considers the "pros and cons ... of one viewpoint or another."[50]

The Supreme Court decided an important FOIA case involving Exemption 5 in 2001. In *Department of the Interior v. Klamath Water Users Protective Association*,[51] it unanimously ruled in favor of public disclosure of correspondence between American Indian tribes and the Department of the Interior. The

---

[44] *See* Chicago Tribune Co. v. Univ. of Illinois Bd of Trustees., 781 F. Supp. 2d 672 (N.D. Ill., 2011); Press-Citizen Co., Inc. v. Univ. of Iowa, 817 N.W.2d 480 (Iowa 2012); News & Observer Publ'g Co. v. Baddour, No. 10 CVS 1941, slip op. at 2 (N.C. Sup. Ct. May 12, 2011 (order) Orange Cty. Super Ct. Apr. 19 2011), *available at* http://www.splc.org/pdf/BaddororderMay2011.pdf.

[45] Energy Project v. NRC, 975 F.2d 871 (D.C. Cir. 1992) (en banc).

[46] *See* Ted Bridis, *Administration Sets Record for Withholding Government Files,* ASSOCIATED PRESS, Mar. 18, 2015, http://bigstory.ap.org/article/ab029d7c6251493481 43a51ff61175c6/us-sets-new-record-denying-censoring-government-files.

[47] *See* Nate Jones, *The Next FOIA Fight: The B(5) "Withhold It Because You Want To" Exemption,* https://nsarchive.wordpress.com/2014/03/27/the-next-foia-fight-the-b5-withhold-it-because-you-want-to-exemption/.

[48] *See* http://www.justice.gov/oip/blog/foia-post-2009-creating-new-era-open-government (July 8, 2015).

[49] *See* Jones, *supra* note 47.

[50] Coastal States Gas Corp. v. Dep't of Energy, 644 F.2d 854, 866 (D.C. Cir. 1980).

[51] 532 U.S. 1 (2001).

case involved a dispute over water rights in the Klamath River Basin in Oregon and California.

Water users, competing with a handful of American Indians tribes for water-use rights, filed FOIA requests for documents the tribes had turned over to the Bureau of Indian Affairs in the Interior Department. The government denied the request, saying the papers were inter-agency memoranda and should be withheld from the public under Exemption 5. The Court reiterated several of its earlier FOIA rulings, stating that the "limited exemptions do not obscure the basic policy that disclosure, not secrecy, is the dominant objective of the Act."[52] It also pointed out that FOIA mandates a "general philosophy of full agency disclosure," which would "help ensure an informed citizenry, vital to the functioning of a democratic society."[53]

In addition to executive privilege, Exemption 5 incorporates several other common law privileges, including attorney-client confidences and a lawyer's work product — documents prepared by attorneys as part of their representation. But courts also have cited lesser-known privileges, including, for example, one that protects commercial information created by government itself if its disclosure would put the government at a competitive disadvantage in, say, contract negotiations.

Exemption 6: Personal Privacy. This exemption protects "personnel and medical files and similar files the disclosure of which would constitute a clearly unwarranted invasion of personal privacy." Congress enacted the exemption to protect intimate and personal details in government files. No specific kinds of files are categorically exempt, though some are more likely to contain the sort of highly intimate, personal information the exemption is designed to protect. The term "similar files" has been interpreted broadly. One appellate court, for example, held that the voice recordings of the crew in the space shuttle Challenger was a "similar file" since the tape revealed personal information about particular individuals.[54] The tapes contained the final radio transmissions before the shuttle exploded, killing everyone on board.

Some recent decisions, however, have hardly concerned the sort of items usually associated with medical and personnel records. In *Department of Defense v. Federal Labor Relations Authority,*[55] for example, two unions sought certain federal employees' home addresses. The privacy interest at stake was that of individuals not wanting to be bothered at home with work-related matters.

The Supreme Court reversed a lower court that had ordered

release of the addresses. It balanced the competing interests and found that if the privacy interest of the employees was slight, the weight on the public interest side of the judicial balance beam was even slighter. Disclosure of home addresses would not shed appreciable light on government operations or activities. With this case, the Court has instructed lower courts to consider only the broad purpose of the FOIA in striking a balance — to what extent does disclosure enlighten the public about the operations of government? The particular purpose of the requester is irrelevant.

In a 2011 decision, the U.S. Supreme Court ruled that corporations have no right of personal privacy under this exemption.[56] In rejecting AT&T's claim that corporations should be defined as "persons," Chief Justice John Roberts wrote, "We trust that AT&T won't take it personally."[57]

Exemption 7: Law Enforcement Records. The purpose of this exemption is to protect law enforcement records and other information whose disclosure would jeopardize investigations. The exemption can apply to the details of a specific investigation or of general investigative techniques or policies. The exemption also protects the physical safety of officials, informants and others in the criminal justice system.

As originally enacted, the exemption applied to "investigatory files compiled for law enforcement purposes." Courts interpreted that to give a blanket exemption to any file that met the threshold test of being "investigatory." In one case, a court ruled that, even though there was no on-going or contemplated law enforcement proceeding, an analysis of the bullet that killed President John F. Kennedy was exempt because it remained part of an "investigatory" file.[58]

Congress narrowed the exemption in 1976 to avoid results like that. First, it limited withholding only to situations where release would cause any of several specific kinds of harm, such as, for example, disclosure of the identity of a confidential source. Second, it allowed only the withholding of certain records, not entire files. Authorities had often withheld an entire file even if only one record in it contained exempt material. One result of this amendment was to give historians and others access to a wealth of important material — such as that related to executed spies Julius and Ethel Rosenberg — that had remained sealed for decades as an "investigatory file." Agencies complained that the amendment went too far in the other direction and no longer gave adequate protection to some sensitive law enforcement information, particularly training manuals and other non-investigatory materials. So the exemption was again

---

[52] *Id.* at 8 (quoting Air Force v. Rose, 425 U.S. 352, 361 (1976)).

[53] *Id.* at 16 (quoting NLRB v. Robbins Tire & Rubber Co., 437 U.S. 214 (1987)).

[54] New York Times Co. v. NASA, 920 F.2d 1002 (D.C. Cir. 1990) (*en banc*).

[55] 510 U.S. 487 (1994).

[56] FCC v. AT&T, 562 U.S. 397 (2011).

[57] *Id.* at 409.

[58] Wiesberg v. Dep't of Justice, 489 F.2d 1195 (D.C. Cir. 1973).

amended in 1986.

For a record to be exempt from required disclosure, a two-part test must be met. First, it must be determined that the records or information were compiled for "law enforcement purposes." This includes more than investigatory records; training manuals, for example, are exempt.

The Supreme Court answered one crucial question in 1989: Could an agency invoke Exemption 7 to deny access to information that was originally compiled for a purpose other than law enforcement but was later assembled for a criminal investigation? A majority of the Court said it could, for the statute's language did not require the original purpose of the information to be considered.[59] Justice Antonin Scalia dissented, arguing that the majority focused too tightly on the words of the law. He complained that the decision allows the policy behind the exemption to be "readily evaded (or [made] illusory) if it requires nothing more than gathering up documents the government does not wish to disclose, with a plausible law-enforcement purpose in mind. This is a hole one can drive a truck through."[60]

Whether the information is compiled for law enforcement purposes is only the first part of the test. For the exemption to apply, it must also be shown that release of the information "could reasonably be expected to cause" one of six specific kinds of harm. Four are noncontroversial and have received little judicial attention. They are:

- withholding of records when disclosure would deny a person a right to a fair trial or impartial adjudication,
- withholding of information that would "endanger the life or physical safety" of an individual,
- withholding of records that would disclose law enforcement techniques, guidelines and procedures "if such disclosure could reasonably be expected to risk circumvention" of the law, and
- withholding records that protect the identities of confidential sources so long as there is a mutual expectation of a confidential relationship.

The remaining categories produce much litigation and confusion. One allows withholding if disclosure could "interfere with enforcement proceedings." If enforcement proceedings are over, however, or if none are on the horizon, this exemption shouldn't apply. Nonetheless, some agencies claim the exemption on the basis that a case may arise or be reopened.

Records or information may also be withheld if their release could "reasonably be expected to constitute an unwarranted invasion of personal privacy." This exemption is similar to Exemption 6 in that a balancing of the privacy interest and the public interest is required. A comparison of the wording of the two ex-

emptions suggests that privacy interests should receive greater weight here. Before the privacy interest prevails in Exemption 6, the intrusion must be "clearly unwarranted." Here it must only be "unwarranted." In *Department of Justice v. Reporters Committee for Freedom of the Press,* the Court held that a request for information about a person's criminal history was unwarranted since it shed little light on "public understanding of the operations or activities of government."[61]

The case is important, not just for an explanation of the substantive test to be used, but for the insights it provides about the Court's attitude toward electronic data. Most of the records the Reporters Committee sought were available in one place or another in the form of accessible, traditional, paper records. Getting them would require a lot of legwork. The federal government had them all in one place — a computer. But the Court said the records, in electronic form, were qualitatively different; the power of the computer to assemble and manipulate the data held vastly greater potential to violate personal privacy.

In 2004, the Supreme Court decided another important FOIA case involving the conflict between access and privacy and ruled in favor of "survivor privacy" in *National Archives and Records Administration v. Favish.*[62] California attorney Allan Favish sued for access to photos taken at the death scene of Vince Foster, former top aide to President Clinton. The Court held exemption 7(C) allowed the government to withhold documents that "could reasonably be expected to constitute an unwarranted invasion of personal privacy."[63] It ruled that survivors of a deceased person could assert a privacy interest in "their own piece of mind and tranquility."[64]

The government interpreted this decision broadly and advised federal agencies to "take heed of the Court's explicit recognition in *Favish* that unfortunately today's 'sensation-seeking culture' breeds the potential for 'unwarranted public exploitation' of FOIA-disclosed records."[65]

Exemption 8: Records of Financial Institutions. This exemption applies to records related to government supervision of financial institutions such as banks and savings and loans. The purpose is to protect the security and integrity of financial institutions.

Exemption 9: Geophysical Data. An exemption to "geological and geophysical information and data, including maps, concerning wells," it protects oil well data.

---

[59] John Doe Agency v. John Doe Corp., 492 U.S. 146 (1989).

[60] *Id.* at 163 (Scalia, J., dissenting).

[61] 489 U.S. 749, 775 (1989).

[62] 541 U.S. 157 (2004).

[63] *Id.* at 171.

[64] *Id.* at 166.

[65] U.S. Dept. of Justice FOIA Post, *available at* http://www.usdoj.gov/oip/foiapost/2004foiapost12.htm.

Statutes and case law provide the framework for FOIA and the applications of exemptions. Equally important is the commitment to openness by the governmental officials who establish and enforce agency rules regarding access to information. President Obama promised a new era of openness and transparency, and while there has been some improvement over the Bush administration, open government advocates insist more needs to be done.[66]

THE ELECTRONIC FOIA

The access guaranteed by the FOIA, however, has not kept pace with this electronic revolution. Some government agencies used their conversion to computerized record-keeping as a way not to release information to the public and the press. They argued that the new formats make reproducing information too expensive or unwieldy, or that the FOIA does not require releasing electronic data. In addition, agencies under pressure to raise revenue began charging fees for data that would have been free in paper form.

To solve some of these problems, Congress passed the Electronic Freedom of Information Act Amendments in 1996.[67] The EFOIA guarantees that records maintained in computer databases are as accessible as paper records. It requires that agencies make regulations, opinions, policy statements and similar information available on-line, on CD-ROM or on computer disc. It also requires agencies to provide information in the format requested whenever possible.[68] And it allows reporters expedited access if they can demonstrate a "compelling need" for the federal records they request under FOIA.[69]

Agencies are required to respond faster in two situations: (1) when failure to obtain records can pose an imminent threat to an individual's life or physical safety and (2) when a request is made by a person "primarily engaged in disseminating information ... to inform the public concerning actual or alleged federal government activity."[70] Expedited access requests must be processed within ten days. In addition, the law changes the time limit for other requests from ten to twenty days.

Under the EFOIA, agencies must make reasonable efforts to search for requested records in electronic form, except when a search would significantly interfere with agency information. Programming created to facilitate a database search does not amount to the creation of records.[71]

Commentators believe that the legislative history surrounding the law may ultimately provide broader access to governmental information and limit the Supreme Court's problematic ruling in *Department of Justice v. Reporters Committee*.[72] In *Reporters Committee*, the Supreme Court limited access to governmental records that revealed information relevant to the agency's "core purpose." Access advocates, including those in Congress, disagreed with the Court's decision. Congressional leaders indicated they crafted this FOIA amendment to address this restrictive view of access to public records.

According to the findings of the Senate: "The purpose of the FOIA is to require agencies of the federal government to make records available to the public through public inspection and upon the request of any person for any public or private use."[73] With this finding, Congress challenged the Supreme Court's narrow interpretation of the purpose of FOIA in *Reporters Committee*.

In language intended to clarify the FOIA's purpose, one of the bill's sponsors, Senator Patrick Leahy of Vermont, said:

> The purpose of the FOIA is not limited to making agency records and information available to the public only in cases where such material would shed light on the activities and operations of government. Efforts by the courts to articulate a "core purpose" for which information should be released imposes a limitation on the FOIA that Congress did not intend and that cannot be found in its language, and distorts the broader import of the Act in effectuating government openness.[74]

DO FOIA AND EFOIA WORK?

Many access advocates have been disappointed with the government's response to the FOIA and its amendments. It is not unusual to wait for months or even years for a response.

Agencies say they do the best they can with their resources. The government spent a record $480 million responding to 713,168 FOIA requests in 2015, an increase of $50 million from the previous year.[75] It also spent $31 million on legal fees fighting to keep records secret. The government censored or denied a record 45 percent of the time.[76] Contrary to a popular belief,

---

[66] *See* http://www.rcfp.org/newsitems/index.php?i=11319 (last visited June 22, 2011).

[67] 5 U.S.C. § 552 (1996).

[68] This provision was intended to overrule a 1983 federal district court decision, *Dismukes v. Dep't of the Interior*, 603 F. Supp. 760 (D.D.C. 1984), which held that agencies had no obligation to accommodate a requester's preference for computer access as long as the information was available in a reasonably accessible form.

[69] 5 U.S.C. § 552 (a)(6)(vi) (1996).

[70] 5 U.S.C. § 552 (a)(6)(E)(v)(II) (1996).

[71] 5 U.S.C. § 552(a)(3)(C) (1996).

[72] 489 U.S. 749 (1989).

[73] 5 U.S.C. § 522 (a)(2)(a) (1996).

[74] S. Rep. No. 104-272 (additional views of Sen. Patrick Leahy, at 23).

[75] *See* Summary of Annual FOIA Reports for Fiscal Year 2015, *available at* https://www.justice.gov/oip/reports/fy_2015_annual_foia_report_summary/download (last visited Aug. 24, 2016).

[76] *Id.*

journalists use the FOIA relatively infrequently. According to the latest study of federal reports, most FOI requests come from individuals, not from the news media. These requests are from people seeking personal information from the Department of Veterans Affairs, the Department of Health and Human Services and the Social Security Administration. [77] A 2006 study found that FOIA is a critical tool for businesses seeking government information. According to the study, 60 percent of requests from other agencies come from commercial interests. [78]

Many agencies meet the time limits to respond to requests. Some do not. For example, three agencies that handle complex and security-related issues — the State Department, the CIA and the National Science Foundation — responded fully less than 20 percent of the time. [79]

Inspired at least in part by the frustrations over backlogs and delay, Congress passed an act called the Openness Promotes Effectiveness in our National Government Act, which President Bush signed on New Year's Eve 2007. [80]

The first major change to the law in a decade, the act established the Office of Government Information Services and an FOIA ombudsman to mediate disputes, review federal agencies' policies and compliance, and recommend policy changes to the president and Congress. [81] The OPEN Government Act restored meaningful deadlines for agency action under FOIA and the imposition of real consequences on federal agencies for missing FOIA's twenty-day statutory deadline for responding to requests. The amendments also contain useful language making it clear that FOIA applies to government records held by outside private contractors and establishing a FOIA hotline service for all federal agencies. [82]

While the EFOIA has triggered major reforms in electronic information processing, including the development of numerous government-agency Web pages filled with useful information, the courts and executive branch have ignored the amendment's findings intended to broaden FOIA's use to serve "any public or private purpose." After more than a decade, agencies have basically ignored EFOIA, according to one study. [83]

In 2016, Congress passed, and President Obama signed the FOIA Improvement Act. [84] Government agencies must now be more transparent and make it easier for journalists, historians, and the public to gain access to documents.

The new law amends FOIA by codifying the "presumption of openness" that has often been used by federal agencies when deciding whether to disclose information to the public. Agencies may refuse to disclose information "only if the agency reasonably foresees that disclosure would harm an interest protected by an exemption ... or disclosure is prohibited by law." [85]

While using the FOIA and EFOIA takes patience and many of its promises have yet to be fulfilled, many of the nation's most important stories, including numerous Pulitzer Prize winners, have come from government documents accessed through the FOIA. Such stories have focused on human rights violations, official corruption, workplace and aircraft accidents, bridge safety, cocaine trafficking, unsafe consumer products, serious health hazards and questionable research programs on humans. [86]

In 2015, the Associated Press used FOIA to show that Nazi war criminals continued to receive Social Security payments after leaving the country, that Marine Corps armored vests failed to protect against bullets and needed to be recalled and that firefighter safety equipment failed to work properly. [87]

FEDERAL OPEN MEETINGS LAWS

To supplement the Freedom of Information Act, Congress enacted the Sunshine Act in 1976. [88] The law requires the meetings of high-level decision-makers in about fifty executive-branch agencies to be open. Information available under the FOIA often represents only what was done, sometimes in a general or cursory way. The Sunshine Act lets the public observe how and why an agency makes the decisions it does.

The act has limited impact. Only agencies that are subject to the FOIA are affected. Thus, groups as important as the President's Council of Economic Advisors and the Board of Governors of the Federal Reserve aren't covered. Moreover, for the law to apply, the agency must be headed by a body of two or more members. Others are exempt on the premise that when an agency is headed by an individual, the need to observe give-and-take discussion among equals is absent.

[77] *See* Coalition of Journalists for Open Government, A Review of the Federal Government's FOI Act Performance, 2006, *available at* http://www.cjog.net/documents/Combined_reports.pdf.

[78] *See* Coalition of Journalists for Open Government, Frequent Filers: Businesses Make FOIA Their Business, July 3, 2006, *available at* http://www.sunshineweek.org/files/cjogfoiarpt06.pdf.

[79] *See* Rebecca Carr, *Open Government Advocates Push for FOIA Reform*, COX NEWS SERVICE, May 11, 2005 (LEXIS).

[80] 5 U.S.C § 522 (2007).

[81] *About OGIS,* http://www.archives.gov/ogis/about/html (last visited July 10, 2010). *See* The FOIA Ombudsman, *available at* http://blogs.archives.gov/foiablog/about-2/.

[82] *See* Charles N. Davis, *Good News for FOIA: Recent Update Covers Private Contractors, Attorney Fees and More*, IRE J., Mar. 2008, at 15.

[83] *See* The National Security Archive, File Not Found: 10 Years After E-FOIA, Most Federal Agencies Are Delinquent, The Knight Open Government Survey 2007, FOIA Web Sites: Missing Links, *available at* http://www.gwu.edu/~nsarchiv/NSAEBB/NSAEBB216/foia_web.htm.

[84] S.337, 114th Cong., (FOIA Improvement Act of 2016) (2016).

[85] *Id.*

[86] *See* FOI-Based Journalism, QUILL, Sept. 1997, at 34-36.

[87] Caroline Little, *Why Strengthening the FOI Act Is So Important,"* available at http://www.brechner.org/reports/2015/05may2015.pdf.

[88] 5 U.S.C. § 522(b) (1996).

The law is evaded regularly. Staff members, who aren't subject to the act, present the views of their bosses to staffers of other agency heads, who then pass the information to their bosses. In agencies where a quorum for a meeting is larger than two, members can meet two at a time and discuss public matters. Some acknowledge that this isn't an efficient way to work, but many agency heads argue that complying is just as inefficient. In 1995, fifteen current and former agency heads asked Congress to amend the Sunshine Act to allow "broad outlines of policy" to be discussed in closed meetings.[89]

As it stands, the law requires that meetings be announced at least one week in advance and that the announcement include the time, place and subject of the meeting. It prohibits informal discussions and decision-making. The meetings opened by the Sunshine Act "are not intended to be merely reruns staged for the public after agency members have discussed the issue in private and predetermined their views," one Senate report concluded. "The whole decision-making process, not merely the results, must be exposed to public scrutiny."[90] (The act does not give the public a right to participate in the meetings.)

The act allows, but does not require, portions of meetings to be closed when the subject matter falls into one or more of ten exemptions. If an exemption applies, the agency must balance the public interest in openness against the particular interest the exemption is designed to protect before closing a meeting.

Seven of the Sunshine Act's ten exemptions parallel those of the FOIA. The act has nothing like FOIA Exemption 5 (inter- and intra-agency memoranda) or Exemption 9 (geological or geophysical data). Instead, the act's Exemption 5 protects agency discussions that "involve accusing any person of a crime, or formally censuring any person." A general discussion doesn't qualify. It must focus on a specific person and, if it concerns a crime, a specific charge.

Exemption 9 shields two kinds of discussions: those that might jeopardize the stability of a financial institution or might trigger significant speculation in financial instruments, and those that might "significantly frustrate implementation of a proposed agency action." One court has limited the exemption to matters whose disclosure would allow someone to profit at government expense or allow an agency regulation to be evaded.[91] Exemption 10 of the Sunshine Act permits closure when discussions concern a subpoena or participation in a civil action or proceeding, such as arbitration or adjudication.

While the Sunshine Act governs the conduct of government agencies, the Federal Advisory Committee Act, enacted in 1972, governs the advisory committee process and opens "to public scrutiny the manner in which government agencies obtain [information] from private individuals."[92] Whether called a "council," "task force," "commission" or something else, an advisory committee is a private group that a statute created or the executive branch either established or utilizes to obtain advice.

FACA was passed to expose waste of government funds on committee meetings that serve no useful function and to allow the public to observe any undue influence of lobbyists and special interest groups on federal decision-makers. In addition to opening deliberations, it provides for public access to all committee records, reports, transcripts, appendices, working papers, drafts, studies, agenda or other documents that were prepared by or made available to the advisory committee. FACA is complex and riddled with qualifications, but it can be useful.

ACCESS IN AN AGE OF TERRORISM

The terrorists' attacks on September 11, 2001, in New York City and Washington, D.C., had an immediate impact on federal freedom of information laws and access to information. Following the attacks, the federal government adopted numerous measures that increased government secrecy and restricted the public's right to know. It became more difficult to get information from federal agencies under FOIA, access information from governmental websites and review presidential records.

A month after the attacks, Attorney General John Ashcroft issued an official memorandum directing agencies to withhold information from FOI requesters if there were any "sound legal basis."[93] This action reversed a policy adopted during the Clinton administration that created a presumption of "maximum responsible disclosure of information."[94] Clinton's attorney general, Janet Reno, had instructed federal agencies not to use discretionary exemptions to FOIA unless they could point to a "foreseeable harm" that would occur from disclosure.[95] As a result, the presumption of openness to federal records was reversed, and agencies were encouraged to withhold many types of information formerly available to the public.[96]

[89] Cindy Skrycki, *Getting a Little Burned Up About the Sunshine Act,* WASH. POST, Apr. 28, 1995, at F1.

[90] ALLAN ROBERT ADLER, LITIGATION UNDER THE FEDERAL OPEN GOVERNMENT LAWS 316-17 (1993) (quoting Senate Report No. 354, 94th Congress, 1st Session).

[91] Common Cause v. NRC, 674 F.2d 921 (D.C. Cir. 1982).

[92] Nat'l Anti-Hunger Coalition v. Executive Comm. of the President's Privacy Sector Survey on Cost Control, 711 F.2d 1071, 1072 (D.C. Cir. 1983).

[93] U.S. Dept. of Justice, Memorandum for Heads of All Federal Department and Agencies, *available at* http://www.usdoj.oip/foiapost/2001foiapost19.htm. *See also* Don Wycliff, *Top Secret: Just Whose Government Is It?,* CHICAGO TRIB., Jan. 17, 2002, at 23.

[94] Eric Sinrod, *Defanging the Freedom of Information Act,* N.Y. L.J., Jan. 22, 2002, at 5.

[95] Office of the Attorney General, Memorandum for Heads of Departments and Agencies, *available at* http:///www.fas.org/sgp/clinton/reno.html. *See also* Tamara Lytle, *White House Clamps Down on Information,* ORLANDO SENT., Mar. 10, 2002, at A22.

[96] *See* Jane Kirtley, *Hiding Behind National Security,* AM. JOURN. REV., Jan.-Feb. 2002, at 62.

In 2002, Congress passed and President Bush signed the Homeland Security Act.[97] Senator Patrick Leahy, a Democrat who voted against the bill, claimed it was "the most severe weakening of the Freedom of Information Act in its thirty-six-year history."[98] The act provides mandatory confidentiality for information submitted to the government by business. The section is designed to protect information about the vulnerabilities of the country's critical infrastructure. The act criminalizes agency disclosure of critical infrastructure information without the consent of the business. Companies that voluntarily share information with the government are guaranteed that the government will keep the information secret. In addition, they become immune from civil liability if the information reveals wrongdoing and immunity from antitrust suits for sharing the information with the government and each other.[99]

Citizen activists, public interest groups and environmental groups insisted that the FOIA already protected against any legitimate risk of harmful disclosure. The groups argued, unsuccessfully, that knowing about vulnerabilities is the first step to correcting them.[100]

A number of public interest groups filed suit to force the government to disclose information about potential terrorists and their supporters, including the names of potential detainees arrested after September 11.[101] The federal appellate court reversed a lower court's decision, ruling that the government did not have to release the information. "Both the Supreme Court and this Court have expressly recognized the propriety of deference to the executive in the context of FOIA claims which implicate national security," the court ruled.[102]

Information available on the Internet was also limited following the terrorist attacks. A number of federal agencies removed information from their Web sites, posting notices that the information had been removed because of its possible usefulness to terrorists.[103] "The atmosphere of terror induced public officials to abandon this country's culture of openness and opt for secrecy as a way of ensuring safety and security," wrote Lucy Dalglish, then executive director of the Reporters Committee for Freedom of the Press. "No one has demonstrated however, that an ignorant society is a safe society."[104]

In 2001, President Bush also issued an executive order restricting access to presidential papers.[105] The order reversed the policy of increased openness in presidential records following the Watergate scandal of the 1970s. It modified the Presidential Records Act of 1978,[106] signed into law by President Jimmy Carter, which made presidential records public property and created a mechanism for the records to be released over a specific period of time. Under the act, papers from Ronald Reagan's presidency should have been released in 2001. Bush's order gave the president the authority to order the National Archives to withhold records. It also allows a former president to control the release of his records, keeping them secret if he wishes. President Obama has not rescinded the order.

STATE RIGHT-TO-KNOW LAWS

All states have laws requiring government records and meetings to be open to the public. In addition, states have specific statutes applicable to particular kinds of records. For example, Florida's public records law played a critical role in the 2000 post-presidential election process. Florida is the only state that provides for immediate access to ballots.[107] Newspapers and other groups used the law to review the state's ballots in an effort to determine who really received most of the votes for president in Florida. Other state statutes provide access to land deeds or voter registration records or to particular kinds of meetings.

Citizens are more likely to use these state laws than the federal laws, there are more state and local records, and there are more state and local issues.

In 2013, the Supreme Court unanimously ruled that states may constitutionally limit access to state public records to in-state residents. While most states make their public records available to anyone who requests them, a few states, including Virginia, limit access to residents.[108]

In *McBurney v. Young*, the Court upheld Virginia's FOIA provision restricting access to residents, saying it "has repeatedly made clear that there is no constitutional right to obtain the information provided by FOIA laws."[109]

---

[97] P.L. 107-296 § 214 (2002).

[98] Dan Morgan, *Disclosure Curbs in Homeland Bill Decried; Information From Companies at Issue*, WASH. POST, Nov. 16. 2002, at A13.

[99] Homeland Security Act of 2002, Pub. L. No. 107-296; 116 Stat. 2135 (2002) (codifying various new surveillance and security measures and creating the Department of Homeland Security).

[100] *See* HOMEFRONT CONFIDENTIAL: HOW THE WAR ON TERRORISM AFFECTS ACCESS TO INFORMATION AND THE PUBLIC'S RIGHT TO KNOW 55 (3d ed. 2003), *available at* http://www.rcfp.org.

[101] Ctr. for Nat'l Sec. Studies v. United States Dep't of Justice, 215 F. Supp. 2d 94 (D.D.C. 2002).

[102] Ctr. for Nat'l Sec. Studies v. United States Dep't of Justice, 331 F.3d 918, 927 (D.C. Cir. 2003).

[103] *See* Kevin Galvin, *Wary Agencies Stem Flow of Information*, SEATTLE TIMES, Dec. 11, 2001, at A1.

[104] *White House Embarked on Path of Secrecy After Sept. 11, Report Says, available at* http://www.rcfp.org/2002/0315report.html (Mar. 15, 2002).

[105] Exec. Order No. 13,233, 66 Fed. Reg. 56,025 (Nov. 1, 2001), *available at* http://www.whitehouse.gov/news/releases/2001/11/20011101.12.html.

[106] 44 U.S.C. § 2201 (1978).

[107] FLA. STAT. ch. 119.07(1)(c)(2009).

[108] States with similar laws are Arkansas, Delaware, Missouri, New Hampshire and Tennessee.

[109] 133 S.Ct. 1709, 1718 (2013).

TIPS ON GETTING ACCESS TO STATE PUBLIC RECORDS AND MEETINGS

1. Be prepared.

Do your homework. Know the law. Understand how the process works. Be aware of possible exemptions.

2. Understand the agency you are investigating.

Identify the official responsible for the records or meetings you want and be as specific as possible with your requests.

3. Be nice AND firm.

Most frequent requestors strongly recommend you ask nicely. In addition, you may have to remind public officials of their obligations under the law. Explain the law when necessary, but be polite. If this approach doesn't work, see tip number 10.

4. Put your request in writing.

Even if a written request is not required by your state, this serves as an official record of the request. In many states, it triggers the law requiring an official response.

5. Don't give up when you hear "no."

Many records custodians use the initial denial as a test and count on you giving up. Also, most states require an agency to document denials, citing appropriate exemptions and explaining the appellate process.

6. Report the story.

When you get shut out of a meeting or are denied a record, that's news; report it.

7. Don't explain why you want the information.

Keep your request formal and your description of why you want the information broad. Explaining the purpose of your request can sometimes alert the records custodian, making it more difficult to get your information.

8. Be prepared for some delays.

This is especially true when you ask for a lot of information or access to sensitive documents. Remember tip number 5.

9. Understand how they use computers.

Most government information is now stored on computers. This is often the cheapest and the most efficient way to get records. Ask how officials store information and the least expensive way for you to get access. Take a flash drive with you so you can download the record on the spot.

10. Consider calling your lawyer.

When records custodians deny your request and clearly violate the law, you need to consider your legal alternatives. Individuals need to consider whether they're willing to pay a lawyer for advice. Journalists typically make these decisions in consultation with editors and station managers.

It's important, therefore, to have a working knowledge of your state's open government laws.

For reporters, such knowledge is never more true than with meetings. If access to a record is denied, a requester will almost always have plenty of time to find help and consider the next step. No law requires that a record be handed over immediately; officials are given time to find and deliver it.

Meetings, however, are timely, and decisions have to be made on the spot. When the city council orders the public to leave the room so that "financial matters" can be discussed, for example, an observer must quickly answer several questions. Does the open meetings law allow secrecy when "financial matters" are discussed? Has the city council taken the required procedural steps, like taking a vote to close the meeting? If there are violations of the law, should the observer object immediately or file some kind of complaint? Or do nothing?

Answers to these questions require a working knowledge of the law, a feel for the workings of the particular governmental body and, sometimes, an understanding of what the observer's boss will authorize — like paying a lawyer to file an action.

Each state right-to-know law is unique. Each differs, not only in its language, but in its political setting and judicial arena. There is no substitute, then, for becoming acquainted with state law. In most states, there are several sources of help, and some suggestions for finding help will be offered later in this chapter. Still, some general observations can be made.

As with any law, a good starting point is the policy behind the law. Precisely what did a legislature attempt to accomplish when it enacted the statute? Many state freedom of information statutes begin with a statement of policy. Some may not be particularly helpful. Kentucky, for example, says only that: "It is declared to be the public policy of this state that public records shall be open for inspection by any person."[110] Others have a richer texture. Michigan, for example, declares:

It is the public policy of this state that all persons are entitled to full and complete information regarding the affairs of government and the official acts of those who represent them as public officials and public employees.... The people shall be informed so that they may fully participate in the democratic process.[111]

When a custodian or court must decide whether to release information or open a meeting whose subject matter falls into a gray area, a statute like Michigan's is immensely more helpful to the analysis and may prove persuasive.

The nuts and bolts of the state right-to-know laws share sim-

---

[110] KENTUCKY REV. STAT § 61.870 (1994).

[111] MICHIGAN COM. LAWS ANN. § 15.231 (1993).

ilarities. They generally declare that all records and meetings are open to the public unless exemptions apply. Some states follow the federal lead and exempt only a few broad categories. This broad approach makes for a tidy-looking statute but probably causes more litigation because of the case-by-case balancing that inevitably goes with it.

Other states opt for specific, narrow exemptions, and, over the years, many have built a rather lengthy list. Virginia, for example, exempts some 100 types of records. Because of its length and apparent complexity, this narrow, specific approach results in an ugly looking law, but one that often works surprisingly well day-to-day because of its precision in describing what is accessible and what is not.

Many policy and legal issues are common to the federal FOIA and state right-to-know statutes. The decisions of federal courts in interpreting the FOIA, of course, are in no way binding on state courts interpreting their own laws. But the experience of federal courts in freedom of information issues may provide persuasive reasoning for states. So a careful review of the federal FOIA is not a bad place to acquire a background to understand local law.

Electronic records raise special issues that courts and legislatures are struggling to deal with. Right-to-know laws were passed in an era of paper, folders and filing cabinets. Today many records are kept in electronic databases, accessible only through computers. Many states have amended their laws to accommodate this change, broadening the definition of "record" to include information on computer disks and tapes. For example, in Florida, "public records" mean "all documents, papers, letters, maps, books, tapes, photographs, films, sound recordings, data processing software, or other material, regardless of the physical form, characteristics, or means of transmission."[112]

Florida was one of the first states to amend its public records statute to reflect changing technology. Florida law, in its statement of policy, says:

> The legislature finds that given advancement in technology, providing access to public records by remote electronic means is an additional method of access that agencies should strive to provide to the extent feasible. If an agency provides access to public records by remote electronic means, then such access should be provided in the most cost-effective and efficient manner available to the agency providing the information.[113]

The revisions also include a statement regarding accessibility of electronic records. It reads:

The legislature finds that providing access to public records is a duty of each agency and that automation of public records must not erode the right of access to those records. As each agency increases its use of and dependence on electronic recordkeeping, each agency must ensure reasonable access to records electronically maintained.[114]

However, keeping pace with technology remains the biggest challenge for most states.

First, there are physical complications. In earlier days, a request for a record required a custodian to locate and retrieve a specific piece of paper from a filing cabinet. The law, not unreasonably because of the labor needed, did not require a custodian to create a record that did not already exist or to abstract or manipulate data from those that did.

Requesters usually get the same information they received when records were on paper. But there is a serious problem with the borderline requests — those that require more than minimal personnel intervention with the computer. At what point does programming, because of the quantity or quality of the data manipulation required or because of the novelty of the finished product, cross the line between the routine (which is required) and the extraordinary (which isn't)? No legislative body has developed a satisfactory answer. Finding and describing that point, at the federal and state levels, is a pressing legal challenge.

As a matter of public policy, many state and local governments sell computer-generated data to pay for computer systems and to provide a regular stream of additional revenue. Commercial interests, direct-mail firms and utilities, for example, are willing to pay well for this data. But if state law requires an agency to provide information virtually free to all comers, it can hardly expect to profit from the data. So many states have either amended or are trying to amend their right-to-know laws to allow them to enter the business of selling government information. The inevitable result is that less data in less powerful forms is available to the public.

Local, state and national governments are conducting an extraordinary amount of government business *via* the computer and through emails. While only a handful of states explicitly include email in their open records statutes, most email communication regarding government business is considered a public record.[115]

Although email is not directly addressed in the open record

---

[112] Fla. Stat. ch. 119.01(1) (2010).

[113] Fla. Stat. ch. 119.01(2) (2010).

[114] Fla. Stat. ch. 119.01(3) (2010).

[115] *See* Reporters Committee for Freedom of the Press, Open Government Guide, http://www.rcfp.org/ogg, (last visited July 15, 2010); Tom Hester Jr., *State Officials Keep E-Mail from View,*" USA Today, Mar. 15, 2008, *available at* http://www.usatoday.com/tech/news/internetprivacy/2008-03-15-emails_N.htm?loc=Interstitialskip.

statutes of most states, their statutory definitions of records could include email.[116] Oklahoma, for example, includes in its definition of a public record "data files created by or used with computer software, computer tape, disk ... or other material regardless of physical form or characteristic."[117] In Florida, whose public record statute does not directly address email, the supreme court in 2003 held that though email can be a public record, private emails of public employees are not subject to the public record law.[118]

However, confusion still reigns over how to handle email in many states. The lack of a specific statute in Michigan allowed two agencies to develop radically different email practices: The University of Michigan made email private to the "fullest extent permitted by law"; Washtenaw County, where the university's Ann Arbor campus is located, adopted a policy that makes the county's email open to the public.[119]

New technology, including text messages, instant messages, and the widespread use of smart phones, is the newest challenge to open records. As more and more government officials Tweet, instant message, text and post on Facebook, a number of local and state governments are considering limits on using this new technology to conduct government business.[120]

In 2010, the Supreme Court considered the issue of text messages that police officers created on their government-issued phones and whether they had a right to privacy in their personal messages sent while working. In *City of Ontario v. Quon*, the Court ruled that the police department had the authority to review the messages and did not violate the officers' privacy.[121]

As the *Quon* case demonstrates, the same power that makes electronic information so valuable raises grave privacy concerns to others. In many states, privacy advocates are successfully arguing that because computers can acquire, manipulate and store vast amounts of information, the right to privacy is threatened.

In 1994, Congress, concerned about protecting privacy, passed legislation that controls access to state government records. The Drivers Protection Privacy Act is a complex federal statute that prevents public access to personal information in state drivers'

records.[122] The act is filled with irony. Congress passed it following the 1989 death of Rebecca Schaeffer, who was killed by an obsessed fan. The fan hired a private investigator to obtain the actress' address by accessing her California motor vehicle record. The irony is that private investigators continue to have access to this information under the relatively new federal law.

The Supreme Court upheld the Drivers Protection Privacy Act in 2000, ruling in *Reno v. Condon*[123] that Congress has the authority to tell state governments not to release certain records otherwise available under state law. The attorney general of South Carolina had challenged the federal statute. He argued that it violated the Tenth Amendment to the Constitution. That amendment prohibits the federal government from intruding on the right of states to govern themselves. The Court ruled that the DPPA was a valid exercise of congressional power. As a result, federal law trumps state law, and even states that want to keep the records open must obey the federal mandate.

Finally, access to public records and meetings may rest on the statutory enforcement provisions. Despite the statutory directive to open their processes to public scrutiny, agencies often try to hide behind exemptions for records and meetings. Government attorneys, funded with taxpayer money, often litigate with the hope of establishing a precedent of closure.

Some states vest enforcement power with the local prosecutor, who has the power to investigate and file charges against public officials for violating open government laws. Florida law, for example, authorizes state prosecutors to file civil or criminal complaints against public officials who knowingly violate the public records law. Those officials can be removed from office and face criminal penalties of up to a year in jail and $1,000 fines.[124]

For the first time in Florida's history, a public official who was convicted of a criminal violation of the state's public records law was actually sent to jail in 1999. Vanette Webb, a school board member, spent seven days in jail before being released, pending an appeal. A jury convicted Webb of knowingly violating the law. The judge sentenced her to eleven months and fifteen days in jail. The governor also suspended her from office.[125] In 2003, a former Florida Speaker of the House, W.D. Childers, was sentenced to sixty days in jail for violating the state's open meetings part of its Sunshine Law.[126]

In most cases, however, officials who violate the law face no penalties. Research shows that almost 70 percent of prosecutors

---

[116] Statutory definitions of public records could be interpreted to include email in Alaska, Arkansas, Connecticut, Delaware, District of Columbia, Florida, Georgia, Hawaii, Idaho, Indiana, Illinois, Iowa, Kansas, Kentucky, Louisiana, Maine, Maryland, Michigan, Minnesota, Mississippi, Missouri, Nebraska, New Mexico, New York, North Carolina, North Dakota, Ohio, Oklahoma, Oregon, Rhode Island, South Carolina, Texas, Vermont, Virginia, Washington, West Virginia, Wisconsin and Wyoming.

[117] OKLA. STAT. tit. 51, § 24A.3 (2004).

[118] State v. City of Clearwater, 863 So. 2d 149 (Fla. 2003).

[119] REPORTERS COMMITTEE FOR FREEDOM OF THE PRESS, ACCESS TO ELECTRONIC RECORDS: A GUIDE TO REPORTING IN THE COMPUTER AGE (1998), *available at* http://www.rcfp.org/elecaccess.

[120] *See* John Waters Jr., *State Lawmakers Want to Limit Text Messages and E-mails*, WEEKLY CALISTOGAN, *available at* http://www.weeklycalistogan.com/articles/2010/03/25/news/local/doc4baaae084c98d411108338.txt.

[121] 560 U.S. 746 (2010).

[122] 18 U.S.C. § 2721-2725 (1994 & Supp. IV. 1998).

[123] 528 U.S. 141 (2000).

[124] FLA. STAT. ch. 119.02 (1909).

[125] Associated Press, *School Board Member Free*, PALM BEACH POST, May 22, 1999, at A24.

[126] *See* Ginny Graybiel, *Childers Gets 60 Days; Bass Avoids Jail Time*, PENSACOLA NEWS J., May 13, 2003, at 1A.

across the nation charged with enforcing their states' open meetings laws never initiated an investigation into an alleged violation.[127] Even where state statutes allow private citizens to file civil suits to enforce the law, the high costs of litigation discourages many people. Citizens, who make far more complaints about open government than the news media, know that fighting City Hall can be an expensive, time-consuming process. As a result, major media organizations have historically borne the burden of filing lawsuits to enforce the law.

More freedom of information lawsuits were brought against the federal government in fiscal year 2014 than in any year since at least 2001, according to a new analysis of court records by the Transactional Records Access Clearinghouse.[128]

On the state level, however, as newsroom budgets shrink, there is less money for investigative journalism and fewer FOI fights. Not only has the number of FOI requests dropped sharply, but the number of lawsuits has also plummeted.[129] This is a pressing concern for access advocates who believe that shrinking newsrooms and fewer FOI requests will inevitably result in more government corruption.[130]

SUMMARY

Access to government records and meetings is essential to meaningful participation in government. As vital and as obvious as that axiom is, only recently has there been a widespread and sustained effort to guarantee citizen access to governmental information.

The federal Constitution and some state constitutions provide limited access, particularly in the criminal justice system. Viewed optimistically, the decisions hint at a broader, emerging right of access, but only after a workable rule can be crafted that will draw a sharp, easily applied line between those things that need to be public and those that don't. This can take years.

The common law can supplement other access tools, mainly statutes. The elastic quality of the common law, one of its historic weaknesses, is an asset to exploit when a tool must be found to reach information inaccessible by other means.

Federal and state statutes — freedom of information or right-to-know laws — are the front-line means of access. Federal laws include the Freedom of Information Act and a federal meetings law (the Sunshine Act). Access to federal electronic records is covered in the Electronic Freedom of Information Act. Each state has its own counterpart to the federal laws, and many states are including access to electronic records, as well. As a group, these laws give each citizen the right to inspect and copy government documents or attend government meetings.

Some agencies and, in fact, entire branches of government, typically the judicial branch and the Congress, are exempt. Each statute also identifies kinds of records or subjects of meetings that are exempt from required disclosure. In most, but not all of these exempt categories, secrecy is not required. The government may open the record or meeting if the public interest in access outweighs the competing interest of the exception.

Finally, it's important to note that much of the world is catching up to, and even surpassing, the United States in terms of transparency and providing access to government information. For example, the U.S was ranked forty-fourth out of 102 countries in the latest Global Right to Information World Wide Index.[131]

FOR ADDITIONAL READING

There are many sources of practical help for gaining access to meetings and records, but a few stand out:

Federal Access Law. The National Archives website has links to several helpful publications, including the FOIA Reference Guide. The guide is available on the Archives Web site: http://www.archives.gov/foia/foia-gude.html. The Office of Government Information Services' Federal FOIA Ombudsman's website features the "Requester Best Practices: Filing a FOIA Request, https://ogis.archives.gov/for-foia-requesters/requester-best-practices---filing-a-foia-request.htm. The Reporters Committee for Freedom of the Press publishes "How to Use the Federal FOI Act," a detailed guide to using the Freedom of Information Act. It is available at http://www.rcfp.org/foiact/index.html.

State Access Law. The Reporters Committee also publishes "Tapping Official's Secrets," a guide to open government in the fifty states. It's available on the RCFP Web site: http://www.rcfp.org. Written for and by lawyers, these publications are important resources for information about specific state laws. In addition, most state press associations are willing, even eager, to help with understanding local, right-to-know laws.

Electronic Access. The Sunlight Foundation uses technology to make government more accountable by creating tools, open data, and policy recommendations. They focus on the use of technology to require real-time, online transparency for all government information. http://www.sunlightfoundation.com.

---

[127] *See* Charles Davis, Sandra Chance & Bill Chamberlin, *Constant Fight for State Records,* QUILL, Oct. 1996, at 50.

[128] *See* http://foiaproject.org/2014/12/22/foia-suits-jump-in-2014 (Dec. 22, 2014).

[129] *See* Michelle Rydell, *No Money to Fight,* QUILL, Oct. 2009, at 35.

[130] *Id.* at 36.

[131] *See* http://www.rti-rating.org/country-data (July 19, 2015).

Sunshine Week. The American Society of News Editors promotes Sunshine Week, which typically occurs around James Madison's birthday, March 16. Sunshine Week is a national effort to focus on the importance of open government. The Web site features stories, studies, research, editorials and editorial cartoons focused on access to information. The resource material can be found at http://www.sunshineweek.org.

OpenTheGovernment.org. This coalition of journalists, consumer and good government groups, environmentalists, library groups and labor organizations researches open government issues and produces a yearly government secrecy report card. Its Web site is: http://openthegovernment.org.

The Society of Professional Journalists. SPJ provides a wealth of helpful information, resources and training material on its site: http://www.spj.org/foi.asp.

18

Newsgathering

By Charles N. Davis

➡ Headnote Questions

- To what extent does the First Amendment protect the right to gather news?
- What restrictions can constitutionally be placed on journalists covering newsworthy events in public places?
- Where has the battle to gather news in public places been most successfully fought?
- Do reporters have a First Amendment right to interview prisoners, view executions and gather news at schools or private businesses?
- Do reporters have a First Amendment right to enter private property to gather news?
- Does the First Amendment protect journalists who violate the law?

Information is the lifeblood of news. Journalists report on what happens in city halls and in the halls of Congress, in local courthouses and in the U.S. Supreme Court, in statehouses and in the White House. Their reports help broaden the public's understanding and help citizens make decisions vital to maintaining a democracy. To get the information they need from all those venues, reporters must have access to meetings, to places and to government documents at the federal, state and local level.

The Supreme Court has steadfastly ruled that the First Amendment protects the right to disseminate information, news and opinions. And in *Branzburg v. Hayes*, it recognized the press' First Amendment right to gather information because, "without some protection for seeking out the news, freedom of the press could be eviscerated."[1] But the level of First Amendment protection for newsgathering activities is unclear. In that same *Branzburg* decision, the Court held that "the First Amendment does not guarantee the press a constitutional right of special access to information not available to the public generally."[2]

While the Court has acknowledged that the First Amendment protects newsgathering activities, the extent of that protection remains uncertain. The September 11, 2001, terrorist attacks renewed the age-old debate over the news media's ability to gather news of military conflict abroad and at home.

NEWSGATHERING IN PUBLIC PLACES

Newsworthy events occur in public, and journalists are free to gather news from any places where activities "could be observed by passers-by."[3] As one court held, once an individual is exposed to public observation, the person "is not entitled to the same degree of privacy that she would enjoy within the confines of her own home."[4]

Streets, sidewalks, parks and similar places are known as "traditional public forums," and the public and the press enjoy a general right of access to them and activities that occur there. In addition, the government often makes other property available for public use. Those places are known as "dedicated public forums." In most circumstances, the government may not limit or deny access to traditional or dedicated public forums, but may impose reasonable time, place and manner restrictions on activities that go on there.

Reporters, like other citizens, do not have free rein to go wherever they want whenever they want. Access to people and places — even public places — is often restricted. There are restrictions, for example, on how and when reporters may gather news in prisons, at disaster scenes, on military installations and in other public places.

---

[1] 408 U.S. 665, 681 (1972). *See also* California First Amendment Coal. v. Calderon, 150 F.3d 976 (9th Cir. 1998).

[2] *Id.* at 684.

[3] Forster v. Manchester, 189 A.2d 147, 150 (Pa. 1963).

[4] *Id.*

Judicial Proceedings

The battle over the First Amendment right to gather news in public places has been most successfully fought in the area of access to judicial proceedings. In 1980, the Supreme Court acknowledged a First Amendment right of public access to judicial proceedings. In *Richmond Newspapers v. Virginia*,[5] it held that the First Amendment provided the public and the press with a right to attend trials. That "watershed decision"[6] laid the groundwork for the evolving First Amendment right of access to other judicial proceedings,[7] as well as to other governmental activities. Access to courts is covered in depth in Chapter 16.

Disaster, Accident and Crime Scenes

When a train derails or a school bus wrecks, cameras and news crews are not far behind. And, while reporters have an "undoubted right to gather news from any source by means within the law,"[8] officials have, in the interest of safety or administrative efficiency, the authority to restrict access to public property when a disaster occurs. Indeed, the Supreme Court noted in *Branzburg*, "newsmen have no constitutional right of access to the scenes of crime or disaster when the general public is excluded."[9] So, if a crime or disaster occurs on private property or a police or fire department restricts admittance to the scene, generally there is no First Amendment right of access. Journalists have been arrested for refusing to obey officials' orders to leave disaster scenes.

Some courts, however, have acknowledged a First Amendment right for journalists to cover news at accident scenes, so long as there is no interference with emergency activities.[10] In addition, at least three states — California, Ohio and Virginia — have statutes that specifically recognize a right of press access to emergency and disaster scenes.[11] "Members of the news media must be afforded special access to disaster sites in order that they may properly perform their function of informing the public," a California appeals court held.[12] But even in California, authorities may curtail access where law enforcement offi-

cials are investigating a crime.[13]

In addition to state laws allowing access to disaster scenes, access might be granted through the doctrines of implied consent and custom and usage. In *Florida Publishing Co. v. Fletcher*,[14] reporters entered a fire-ravaged house and photographed a silhouette left on the floor after a victim's body was removed. The victim's mother, who was out of town at the time of the fire and learned of her daughter's death from the news report, was outraged and sued the paper.

The Florida Supreme Court ruled that there was a "longstanding custom and practice throughout the country" that protected the media in such situations.[15] It ruled that it was customary for journalists to accompany officials onto private property and that the photographer was asked to take photographs for the fire officials; therefore, the journalists were protected. That reasoning, however, has not been widely adopted.

NEWSGATHERING ON PUBLIC PROPERTY

While journalists are generally free to gather and report on news that occurs in public forums, newsgathering activities can be restricted on government property not open for general public use, that is, in nonpublic forums.

Prisons

The Supreme Court outlined some of the limitations of the First Amendment right of access to prisons and prisoners in three cases in the 1970s. In *Pell v. Procunier*,[16] *Saxbe v. Washington Post*[17] and *Houchins v. KQED*,[18] it declared that the First Amendment does not guarantee the press access to correctional facilities or specifically identified prisoners.

In *Pell*, the Court upheld California's correctional rules that restricted the ability of media representatives to interview specific prisoners. While the First Amendment prohibits the government from interfering with a free press, the Court held, the Constitution doesn't guarantee the press more access to correctional facilities than the average citizen. In *Saxbe*, decided the same year, the Court upheld the constitutionality of a federal prison regulation that, like the California rule, prohibited interviews with specific prisoners. Finally, in *Houchins*, four years later, it held that, because the First Amendment does not require the release of information within the control of govern-

---

[5] 488 U.S. 555 (1980).

[6] *Id.* at 582-83 (Stevens, J., concurring).

[7] *See, e.g.,* Press-Enter. Co. v. Riverside County Superior Court, 478 U.S. 1 (1986); Press-Enter. Co. v. Riverside County Superior Court, 464 U.S. 501 (1984); Globe Newspaper Co. v. Superior Court, 457 U.S. 596 (1982).

[8] City of Oak Creek v. King, 436 N.W.2d 285, 292 (Wis. 1989).

[9] 408 U.S. 665, 684-85 (1972).

[10] *See, e.g.,* Connell v. Town of Hudson, 733 F. Supp. 465 (D.N.H. 1990).

[11] CAL. PENAL CODE § 409.5(a), (d) (2006); OHIO REV. CODE ANN. § 2917.13(B) (2006); VA. CODE §§ 15.2-17.14 and 27-15.5 (1950).

[12] Leiserson v. City of San Diego, 184 Cal. App. 3d 41, 51-52 (Cal. 1986).

[13] *Id.* at 51.

[14] 340 So. 2d 914 (Fla. 1976).

[15] *Id.* at 918.

[16] 417 U.S. 817 (1974).

[17] 417 U.S. 843 (1974).

[18] 438 U.S. 1 (1978).

ment, it does not require a sheriff to grant journalists access to a county jail.

In this triad of cases, the Court balanced the responsibility of prison officials to maintain order and provide a secure environment against the right of journalists to gather news in volatile environments, and it ruled in favor of the government. The decisions gave officials considerable latitude in restricting access to prisons and prisoners. According to a study sponsored by the Society of Professional Journalists, many state correctional systems have seized upon the Court's rulings to restrict inmates' access to the outside world. Some regulations include outright bans on face-to-face interviews, others discriminate between so-called "legitimate" and "entertainment media," and still others ban the use of electronic equipment within a prison.[19] The restrictions at issue in *Pell* pale in comparison to such bans.

California, responding to complaints from officials about an overwhelming number of requests from reporters to interview so-called "celebrity" prisoners, such as Charles Manson and the Menendez brothers, was the first state to embrace new, more restrictive policies designed to prevent high-profile criminals from becoming celebrities. The restrictions, which prohibit face-to-face interviews, make it almost impossible for reporters to cover other important prison-related stories, such as allegations of beatings, rapes and administrative abuses. Prisoners have even been punished in California for contacting the news media to report possible abuses.[20]

Executions

Executions usually occur in prisons. So access to these events, particularly by broadcasters and photographers, is also subject to government fiat.

In 1994, talk show host Phil Donahue tried unsuccessfully to get permission to televise the execution of a convicted murderer in North Carolina. The prison warden refused, and the state's Supreme Court ruled that the First Amendment did not require officials to allow taping of executions.[21]

In 2001, two Internet companies lost a lawsuit in which they sought the right to broadcast the execution of Oklahoma City bomber Timothy McVeigh over the Internet. A federal judge in Terre Haute, Indiana, said there is no First Amendment right to broadcast an execution from within a prison.[22]

In addition, a federal appeals court ruled that California officials may bar the public and press during the preparation of inmates for execution.[23] The court acknowledged that executions are "unquestionably matters of great public importance" and that "more information leads to a better informed public,"[24] but it ruled that officials were justified in barring public access out of concern for the anonymity of execution team members. The ruling overturned a federal judge's decision that the public and press have a First Amendment right to attend executions.[25]

Military Bases, Operations and War Zones

Neither military bases nor battlefields are public forums.[26] During the 1960s and 1970s, the press enjoyed broad access to battlefields. In fact, media reports on the Vietnam War are often credited with changing Americans' feelings about the war. During the 1983 invasion of Grenada, however, the press was much more controlled by the military. Reporters whom military escorts accompanied on battlefields complained of attempts to censor their reports. As a result, an inquiry by a special panel of the Joint Chiefs of Staff concluded that "it is essential that the U.S. news media cover U.S. military operations to the maximum degree possible consistent with mission security and the safety of U.S. forces."[27]

Despite the military's position on providing access to the media following Grenada, eight years later journalists again complained about restrictions during Operation Desert Storm. A group of journalists maintained in a special report to the Department of Defense that the military restrictions "made it impossible for reporters and photographers to tell the public the full story of the war in a timely fashion."[28] In a report to the Defense Department, executives representing seventeen of the country's major news organizations — including ABC, CBS, NBC, CNN, the *Washington Post* and the *New York Times* — formally protested about the pool system that limited the number of journalists allowed to cover certain stories and the long delays in getting copy to newsrooms in the United States.[29] They also charged that reporters' copy was altered during military security reviews.[30] Ultimately the Defense Department, key press associations and representatives from twenty news organizations agreed that "open and independent reporting" will

---

[19] *See* Charles N. Davis, *Access to Prisons,* QUILL, May 1998, at 19-28.

[20] *See id.* at 22.

[21] Lawson v. Dixon, 446 S.E.2d 799 (N.C. 1994).

[22] Entm't Network v. Lappin, 134 F. Supp. 2d 1002 (S.D. Ind. 2001).

[23] California First Amendment Coal. v. Calderon, 150 F.3d 976 (9th Cir. 1998).

[24] *Id.* at 982.

[25] California First Amendment Coal. v. Calderon, 956 F. Supp. 883 (N.D. Cal. 1997).

[26] *See* United States v. Albertini, 472 U.S. 675 (1985).

[27] CHAIRMAN OF THE JOINT CHIEFS OF STAFF MEDIA-MILITARY RELATIONS PANEL 3 (1984).

[28] REPORT OF 17 NEWS EXECUTIVES TO SECRETARY RICHARD CHENEY, COVERING THE PERSIAN GULF WAR 2 (June 14, 1991).

[29] *See* Jane DeParles, *17 News Executives Criticize U.S. for "Censorship" of Gulf Coverage,* N.Y. TIMES, July 3, 1991, at A4.

[30] *See* Paul McMasters, *Free Press Falls Victim to War,* QUILL, Oct. 1991, at 7.

be the "principle means" by which U.S. wars are covered.[31]

The conflict in Afghanistan precipitated by the terrorist attacks of September 11, 2001, also was marked by access debates and tight controls on battlefield journalists. The escalation of U.S. forces before the October 7, 2001, attacks on al-Qaeda and the Taliban generally occurred without a media presence; and press restrictions early in the conflict constrained coverage so severely that American reporters learned second-hand about the fall of Mazar-e-Sharif, a strategic gateway to U.S. troops based in nearby Uzbekistan.[32]

Defense officials have described the war in Afghanistan as a different kind of war, one that required restrictions on journalists so that military operations and soldiers' lives would not be endangered. The compromises reached after the Gulf War did not hold, and journalists struggled to provide full coverage.

Strained relations between the military and reporters have been a staple of the war on terror. *Washington Post* reporter Doug Struck claimed that a U.S. soldier, whom he did not identify, threatened to shoot him if he went near the scene of a U.S. Hellfire missile strike in 2002. The military denied that a troop leader would knowingly threaten an American citizen, a response that Struck asserted was "an amazing lie."[33] In February 2002 — when the war was more than four months old — the Pentagon began allowing journalists to accompany ground troops in combat, but only after the reporters agreed to delay filing their reports until military officials gave them permission.[34]

Journalists can do little more than negotiate with the Defense Department and complain when access to military operations limits the amount of independent reporting that the press can do. Legal challenges to restrictions on press access to military operations have been unsuccessful.

The beginning of hostilities in Iraq in 2003 ushered in a new form of reporting, and with it a new word in the lexicon: embedding. Responding to the criticism of the first Gulf War conflict, the Pentagon launched an embedding policy that placed journalists within military units in the field. Reporters traveled, ate and slept alongside soldiers, in a carefully planned system that resulted in compelling images of live firefights and U.S. bombing runs as well as its share of criticism for tight controls on the movements of reporters.

Polling Places

Newsgathering near polling places has become controversial in recent years, which anyone who has witnessed presidential elections can attest. Critics of exit polls claim they interfere with the election process, influencing undecided voters and discouraging potential voters from casting their ballots. Pollsters, however, assert that political speech about the electoral process is core First Amendment speech and must be protected.

Although the Supreme Court has not ruled on the issue of exit polling,[35] a federal appellate court has. In 1988, the Ninth U.S. Circuit Court of Appeals struck down as unconstitutional a Washington law prohibiting exit polling within 300 feet of polling places. It said the law was a content-based restriction on voters' First Amendment rights to discuss their political views and the press' right to gather news. It acknowledged the state's compelling interest in preserving peace, order and decorum at polling places; but as one judge wrote, the law "restricts the media's right of access to information crucial to the political process, and for that reason, violates the principles embodied in the First Amendment."[36]

Though not ruling on exit polling, the Supreme Court has upheld a law restricting campaign activities near polling places. In *Burson v. Freeman,* it upheld a Tennessee law prohibiting solicitation of votes and regulating the display and distribution of campaign material within one hundred feet of a polling place.[37] The Court acknowledged that the law regulated core political speech but found that it satisfied the strict scrutiny test, because the "restricted zone is necessary in order to serve the state's compelling interest in preventing voter intimidation and election fraud."[38]

Schools

Taxpayers own public schools. When school business is being conducted, however, schools are usually not open to the public. Journalists who want to gather news on school property, therefore, generally need permission from school officials. In addition, reporters and photographers need to be aware that minors cannot legally waive their rights, meaning they cannot legally consent to interviews or be photographed. Many schools are sending standard photograph releases home, asking parents to give permission for their children to be photographed while

---

[31] Howard Kurtz & Barton Gellman, *Guidelines Set for News Coverage of Wars,* WASH. POST, May 22, 1992, at A23.

[32] *See* REPORTERS COMMITTEE FOR FREEDOM OF THE PRESS, HOMEFRONT CONFIDENTIAL: HOW THE WAR ON TERRORISM AFFECTS ACCESS TO INFORMATION AND THE PUBLIC'S RIGHT TO KNOW 23 (2005), *available at* http://www.rcfp.org/homefrontcon fidential/covering.html.

[33] *Id.* at 25.

[34] *Id.* at 22.

[35] *But see* Mills v. Alabama, 384 U.S. 214, 218 (1966), in which the Court indicated that a state may have power to regulate conduct in and around polls to maintain peace, order and decorum.

[36] Daily Herald Co. v. Munro, 838 F. 2d 380, 389 (9th Cir. 1988) (Reinhardt, J., concurring).

[37] 504 U.S. 191 (1992).

[38] *Id.* at 206.

at school.

The First Amendment, however, protects the right of reporters and photographers to cover events on school property from adjacent public property, such as sidewalks and streets.

NEWSGATHERING ON PRIVATE PROPERTY

When owners of private property and journalists clash over journalists' efforts to gather news on that property, courts frequently focus on whether the journalists had consent to enter the property. Reporters and photographers often don't have permission. Sometimes they enter over the objections of property owners; other times, a property owner is not present to grant permission.

Some states recognize a common law right for journalists to enter private property to gather news. In other states, however, entry without an owner's permission is trespassing, and both criminal and civil penalties could attach. In any event, remaining on private property after being ordered to leave by a property owner or a custodian of the property is almost always considered trespassing.

Ride-Alongs

A popular genre of TV shows involves journalists accompanying and recording the activities of law enforcement officers and emergency personnel. Police agencies sometimes encourage these so-called "ride-alongs" because they tend to put officers in a human, and sometimes heroic, light. And journalists argue that the practice serves a significant public interest by enabling public oversight of law enforcement, deterring crime and danger to police, and curbing potential police misconduct. All that may be true, but the practice still has come under increased scrutiny.

It has also been threatened by legal action. In 1999, the Supreme Court, in two unanimous opinions, struck a blow against ride-alongs. In both cases, the targets of searches sued law enforcement officials, claiming that, by inviting the press to accompany them on raids, the officials violated Fourth Amendment rights against unreasonable searches. The Court agreed, ruling in *Hanlon v. Berger*[39] and *Wilson v. Layne*[40] that police may be sued for allowing journalists to accompany them onto private property.

In *Layne,* U.S. marshals and county sheriff's deputies allowed a reporter and photographer from the *Washington Post* to join their early-morning raid of a home where they expected to find a fugitive. He was not there, but his parents were rousted from bed in full view of the journalists. The photographs, one show-

ing Charles Wilson in his underwear with an officer's gun to his head, were never published; but the couple, claiming an invasion of privacy, sued the officials.

In *Berger*, CNN crews accompanied U.S. Fish and Wildlife agents onto a Montana ranch in search of eagles that may have been poisoned by pesticides. The ranch owners sued the agents who had invited the journalists along.

Writing for the Court, Chief Justice William Rehnquist held that the public interest benefit of ride-alongs did not justify the Fourth Amendment violation. "Surely the possibility of good public relations for the police is simply not enough, standing alone, to justify the ride-along intrusion into a private home," he wrote. "And even the need for accurate reporting on police issues in general bears no direct relation to the constitutional justification for the police intrusion into a home in order to execute a ... warrant."[41]

The legal liability for members of the news media who accompany police on ride-alongs remains unclear.

Private Businesses Open to the Public

Reporters and photographers often face access problems when they cover events in places that are privately owned but open to the public, like restaurants and shopping malls. In 1968, the Supreme Court held that a shopping mall is the modern equivalent of a downtown business district.[42] It retreated from that position in 1972, however, when it ruled that property does not "lose its private character merely because the public is generally invited to use it for designated purposes."[43]

So, the First Amendment does not require owners of private businesses, including malls, to permit reporters to gather news on their property. But some states have laws that protect free speech rights on such property. California's constitution, for example, protects the rights to speak, write and publish; and the state's supreme court has interpreted these rights to apply to activities at malls. The Supreme Court affirmed that interpretation.[44]

Restricting Paparazzi

In 1997, Princess Diana of England was killed in an automobile accident. Reports of the accident indicate that it might have been caused, in part, because Diana's driver was attempting to elude cars driven by celebrity photographers — called "papa-

---

[39] 526 U.S. 808 (1999).

[40] 526 U.S. 603 (1999).

[41] *Id.* at 620.

[42] Amalgamated Food Employees Union Local 590 v. Logan Valley Plaza, Inc., 391 U.S. 308 (1968).

[43] Lloyd Corp. Ltd. v. Tanner, 407 U.S. 551, 569 (1972).

[44] *See* Robins v. Pruneyard Shopping Ctr., 592 P.2d 341 (Cal. 1979), *aff'd* Pruneyard Shopping Ctr. v. Robins, 447 U.S. 74 (1980).

razzi." As a result of the accident, an outcry arose for laws restricting the activities of paparazzi. Lawmakers responded to the outcry.

Legislation was adopted in California, for example, that severely limits the use of telephoto lenses and other electronic equipment to gather news.[45] The law creates a civil cause of action against photographers who trespass on private property in order to obtain photographs or who "technologically trespass" by employing enhancement devices, including telephoto lenses or high-powered microphones. The law establishes liability when a person

> attempts to capture, in a manner that is offensive to a reasonable person, any type of visual image, sound recording, or other physical impression of the plaintiff engaging in a personal or familial activity under circumstances in which the plaintiff had a reasonable expectation of privacy, through the use of a visual or auditory enhancing device, regardless of whether there is a physical trespass, if this image, sound recording, or other physical impression could not have been achieved without a trespass unless the visual or auditory enhancing device was used.

In the wake of Princess Diana's death, Congress considered three separate bills — the so-called "paparazzi bills" — that would provide punishment for harassment by photojournalists.[46] After several hearings, at which some celebrities testified about their lack of privacy, the bills died.

The controversy was rekindled in 2005 when a photographer rammed his minivan into Disney star Lindsay Lohan's Mercedes Benz. Spurred by Justin Timberlake, Cameron Diaz and others, Los Angeles police and prosecutors opened a criminal investigation into what they describe as a hyper-aggressive new breed of paparazzi willing to go to almost any lengths to get photographs.[47] California lawmakers responded in 2005 by toughening the previous law, greatly increasing the amount of damages possible when an individual commits an assault while trying to get a photograph or video.[48]

LEGAL AND ILLEGAL NEWSGATHERING TECHNIQUES

How far may a journalist go to gather news? What behavior constitutes a newsgathering tort? Does the First Amendment protect a journalist from misleading a source? Can he use stolen documents? Can she conduct ambush interviews? Can a journalist secretly tape conversations?

The answers to these questions, and others like them, have, in recent years, driven the discussion about newsgathering, about how much journalists can push beyond traditional boundaries and about the use of new technologies. The Supreme Court has never ruled on a reporter's liability for publishing information from illegally obtained documents. In general, if a reporter lawfully acquires information about matters of public concern, states may not punish publication of the information absent a compelling interest.[49] But a reporter, of course, may be punished for illegal activities.

In 1998, a reporter for the *Cincinnati Enquirer* learned this lesson the hard way. Michael Gallagher admitted to gaining access illegally to Chiquita Brands International's corporate voicemail system.[50] The newspaper fired him, and the state prosecuted him on multiple counts of violating Ohio's electronic communication privacy law and for unauthorized access to a computer. He pleaded guilty to two counts and was sentenced to five years of probation and 200 hours of community service work.[51] Chiquita also sued him for defamation and for breaking into its voice mail system. Gallagher settled that lawsuit in 1999, and the terms were not released.[52]

The *Cincinnati Enquirer* also suffered from the experience. It renounced the stories about Chiquita's business practices, apologized and paid more than $10 million to the company to avoid a lawsuit.[53] A former lawyer for Chiquita — the reporter's source for the original story — did sue the newspaper. He accused the newspaper of breach of contract, fraud and negligence for breaking a promise by identifying him.[54] Indeed, the Supreme Court has held that liability can be found when journalists break promises to sources.[55] The *Cincinnati Enquirer* has called the entire episode "one of the most unfortunate, and em-

[45] CAL. CIV. CODE § 1708.8(b) (2008).

[46] Personal Privacy Protection Act, S. 2103, 105th Cong. (1998); Privacy Protection Act of 1998, H.R. 3224, 105th Cong. (1998); Protection from Personal Intrusion Act, H.R. 2448, 105th Cong. (1997).

[47] *See* David M. Halbfinger & Allison Hope Weiner, *As Paparazzi Push Ever Harder, Stars Seek a Way to Push Back,* N.Y. TIMES, June 9, 2005, at A1.

[48] *See* Reporters Committee for the Freedom of the Press, *Governor Takes Three Steps Against Free Speech Interests* (Oct. 13, 2005), *available at* http://www.rcfp.org/news/2005/1013-new-govern.html.

[49] *See* Florida Star v. B.J.F., 491 U.S. 524 (1989); Smith v. Daily Mail Publ'g Co., 443 U.S. 97 (1979); Landmark Commc'ns, Inc. v. Virginia, 435 U.S. 829 (1978).

[50] *See* Ben Kaufman, *Former Chiquita Lawyer Sues Paper,* CINCINNATI ENQUIRER, Sept. 28, 1999, at B2.

[51] *See* Dan Horn, *Former Reporter Given Probation,* CINCINNATI ENQUIRER, July 17, 1999, at B1.

[52] *See Reporter Gets Probation in Chiquita Case,* July 20, 2000, *available at* http://www.freedomfreedom.org/professional/1999/7/16chiquita.ap.

[53] *See* James C. Goodale, *Why Did the "Enquirer" Pay $10 Million?,* N.Y. L.J., Aug. 7, 1998, at 3.

[54] *See* Dan Horn, *Enquirer Denies It Divulged a Source,* CINCINNATI ENQUIRER, Nov. 30, 1999, at B2.

[55] *See* Cohen v. Cowles Media Co., 501 U.S. 663 (1991).

barrassing, failures of modern investigative journalism."[56]

Another hotbed of controversy in newsgathering involves tape-recorded conversations. In a highly anticipated 2001 decision, the Supreme Court held that the First Amendment protects the release of illegally tape-recorded conversations when neither the source nor the reporter plays a role in the unlawful interception. In a 6-3 decision, it held in *Bartnicki v. Vopper*[57] that the First Amendment rights of the media outweigh a federal wiretapping statute designed to prevent interception of private conversations.

The case involved the dissemination of an illegal tape recording of a cell phone conversation between Gloria Bartnicki, the chief negotiator for a teacher's union in Wyoming Valley West School District in Pennsylvania, and Anthony Kane, the union's president. The tape included Bartnicki's complaints about the school board's reluctance to approve a proposal for a three-percent pay raise and a discussion about blowing up the front porches of uncooperative school board members. An unknown person gave a copy of the tape to Jack Yocum, the leader of the group opposed to the union's wage proposals. Yocum passed a copy of the tape to Frederick Vopper, a radio talk show host, who played it repeatedly on his show.

Justice John Paul Stevens, writing for the majority, held that although the privacy of communications and the minimization of harm to those whose communications were illegally intercepted represented strong government interests, these interests did not outweigh the First Amendment right to publish matters of public concern.

Although they signed on to the majority's opinion, Justices Stephen Breyer and Sandra Day O'Connor concurred in a narrower opinion, written by Breyer, stating that the publication was protected because the recording was of public interest and the speakers were public figures.[58] Breyer and O'Connor were swayed by the fact that the federal statutes were broader than necessary to deter the relevant bad conduct and that the publication concerned a potential threat to public safety, decreasing the speaker's legitimate interest in maintaining the privacy of the communication.

Chief Justice Rehnquist, joined by Justices Antonin Scalia and Clarence Thomas, dissented, citing concern for privacy in electronic communications.[59]

Journalists have also been successfully sued for breaching a duty of loyalty. In 1997, Food Lion sued Capital Cities/ABC,

Inc., for an undercover report on the grocery store's food-handling policies.[60] Reporters assumed false identities to get the jobs at Food Lion stores and used hidden cameras to expose practices in the grocer's delicatessens. Food Lion claimed intentional misrepresentation, deceit, fraud, negligent supervision, trespass, breach of fiduciary duty, civil conspiracy, violation of federal wiretap statutes, unfair and deceptive trade practices and violations of the Racketeer Influenced and Corrupt Organizations Act. A jury awarded Food Lion $1,500 in compensatory damages and $5.5 million in punitive damages, which the trial court reduced to $315,000.[61] ABC appealed the decision, and the Fourth U.S. Circuit Court of Appeals cut the verdict to $2: $1 for trespass and $1 for breach of loyalty.[62]

While some lower courts have allowed lawsuits against the media for engaging in fraud to obtain stories or footage, courts typically dismiss fraud claims where the claim is an alternative to a libel claim.[63]

SUMMARY

The Supreme Court has noted that the First Amendment protects newsgathering. Specifically, both the First Amendment and the common law provide for the right of journalists to gather news from traditional public forums. In addition, the Court has interpreted the First Amendment to ensure a right of access to criminal judicial proceedings.

But the Court has also said that the First Amendment does not guarantee an unrestricted right to gather news on all public property and in all public places. Not all government-owned properties are public forums. Military bases and public schools are two examples. In addition, activity around polling places — including newsgathering — may be restricted. Legislative bodies also have passed laws restricting some newsgathering activities of paparazzi.

In 1999, the Supreme Court ruled on two cases involving journalists accompanying police on raids, known as "ride-alongs." It unanimously held that law enforcement officials violate the Fourth Amendment protections against unreasonable searches by allowing television crews and other journalists to accompany them.

The First Amendment does not require private businesses, including shopping malls and restaurants, to allow reporters unfettered access to their property. As a result, reporters do not have a right to remain on private property after being told to leave, and in some jurisdictions it may be illegal to enter the

---

[56] *See* Dan Horn, *Gannett: Suit Dodges Blame,* CINCINNATI ENQUIRER, June 21, 2000, at B2 (Former editor Lawrence Beaupre sued Gannett for fraud, breach of contract, attorney malpractice and conspiracy to injure his reputation. Gannett has denied the allegations.).

[57] 532 U.S. 514 (2001).

[58] *Id.* at 535 (Breyer, J., concurring).

[59] *Id.* at 541 (Rehnquist, C.J., dissenting).

[60] Food Lion, Inc. v. Capital Cities/ABC, Inc., 887 F. Supp. 811 (M.D.N.C. 1995).

[61] Food Lion, Inc. v. Capital Cities/ABC, Inc., 984 F. Supp. 923 (M.D.N.C. 1997).

[62] Food Lion, Inc. v. Capital Cities/ABC, Inc.; 194 F.3d 505 (4th Cir. 1999).

[63] *See, e.g.,* La Luna Entm't, Inc. v. DBS Corp., 74 F. Supp. 2d 384 (S.D.N.Y. 1999).

property at all without first gaining the permission of the property owner. Shopping malls and restaurants are considered private property.

While successful journalists have to be cunning and persistent, sometimes gaining access to information and people in unconventional ways, they must remember that the First Amendment will not protect them when they commit a crime, such as trespassing. The media have also been held liable for fraud, breach of promise of confidentiality and breach of duty of loyalty to employers when reporters pose as employees to gain access to nonpublic areas.

FOR ADDITIONAL READING

Alexander, Marc C. "Attention, Shoppers: The First Amendment in the Modern Shopping Mall," 41 *Arizona Law Review* 927 (1992).

Carney, Damian. "Self-regulation of unlawful newsgathering techniques," 13:3 *Communications Law: Journal of Computer, Media and Telecommunications Law* 767-81 (2008).

Davis, Charles N. "Access to Prisons," *Quill,* May 1988, p. 14.

Dyk, Timothy B. "Newsgathering, Press Access, and the First Amendment," 44 *Stanford Law Review* 927 (1992).

Jones, Merrit. "First Amendment Protection for Newsgathering: Applying the Actual Malice Standard to Recovery of Damages for Intrusion," 27 *Hastings Constitutional Law Quarterly* 539-562 (2000).

LeBel, Paul A. "Symposium: Undercover Newsgathering Techniques: Issues and Concerns: The Constitutional Interest in Getting the News: Toward a First Amendment Protection from Tort Liability for Surreptitious Newsgathering," 4 *William & Mary Bill of Rights Law Journal* 1145 (1996).

Lee, W. E. "Probing Secrets: The Press and Inchoate Liability for Newsgathering Crimes," 36:2 *American Journal of Criminal Law* 129-178 (2009).

Levine, Lee & C. Thomas Dienes. *Newsgathering and the Law.* New Providence, N.J.: LexisNexis/Matthew Bender, 2011.

Millar, Gavin. *Newsgathering: Law, Regulation and the Public Interest.* New York: Oxford University Press (2016).

Reporters Committee for Freedom of the Press, *Homefront Confidential: How the War on Terrorism Affects Access to Information and the Public's Right to Know,* 6th ed. Arlington, Va.: Reporters Committee for Freedom of the Press, 2005.

Sager, Kelli L. & Karen N. Frederiksen. "People v. Simpson: Perspectives on the Implications for the Criminal Justice System: Televising the Judicial Branch: In Furtherance of the Public's First Amendment Rights," 69 *Southern California Law Review* 1519 (1996).

Sharkey, Jacqueline E. "The Television War," *American Journalism Review,* May 2003, p. 18.

Smolla, Rodney A. *Suing the Press.* New York: Oxford University Press, 1986.

The Constitution of the United States of America*

We the People of the United States, in Order to form a more perfect Union, establish Justice, insure domestic Tranquility, provide for the common defence, promote the general Welfare, and secure the Blessings of Liberty to ourselves and our Posterity, do ordain and establish this Constitution for the United States of America.

Article I

Section 1

All legislative Powers herein granted shall be vested in a Congress of the United States, which shall consist of a Senate and House of Representatives.

Section 2

The House of Representatives shall be composed of Members chosen every second Year by the People of the several States, and the Electors in each State shall have the Qualifications requisite for Electors of the most numerous Branch of the State Legislature.

No Person shall be a Representative who shall not have attained to the Age of twenty five Years, and been seven Years a Citizen of the United States, and who shall not, when elected, be an Inhabitant of that State in which he shall be chosen.

[Representatives and direct Taxes shall be apportioned among the several States which may be included within this Union, according to their respective Numbers, which shall be determined by adding to the whole Number of free Persons, including those bound to Service for a Term of Years, and excluding Indians not taxed, three fifths of all other Persons.][1] The actual Enumeration shall be made within three Years after the first Meeting of the Congress of the United States, and within every subsequent Term of ten Years, in such Manner as they shall by Law direct. The Number of Representatives shall not exceed one for every thirty Thousand, but each State shall have at Least one Representative; and until such enumeration shall be made, the State of New Hampshire shall be entitled to chuse three, Massachusetts eight, Rhode-Island and Providence Plantations one, Connecticut five, New-York six, New Jersey four, Pennsylvania eight, Delaware one, Maryland six, Virginia ten, North Carolina five, South Carolina five, and Georgia three.

When vacancies happen in the Representation from any State, the Executive Authority thereof shall issue Writs of Election to fill such Vacancies.

The House of Representatives shall chuse their Speaker and other Officers; and shall have the sole Power of Impeachment.

Section 3

The Senate of the United States shall be composed of two Senators from each State, [chosen by the Legislature thereof,][2] for six Years; and each Senator shall have one Vote.

Immediately after they shall be assembled in Consequence of the first Election, they shall be divided as equally as may be into three Classes. The Seats of the Senators of the first Class shall be vacated at the Expiration of the second Year, of the second Class at the Expiration of the fourth Year, and of the third Class at the Expiration of the sixth Year, so that one third may be chosen every second Year; [and if Vacancies happen by Resignation, or otherwise, during the Recess of the Legislature of any State, the Executive thereof may make temporary Appointments until the next Meeting of the Legislature, which shall then fill such Vacancies.][3]

No Person shall be a Senator who shall not have attained to the Age of thirty Years, and been nine Years a Citizen of the United States, and who shall not, when elected, be an Inhabitant of that State for which he shall be chosen.

The Vice President of the United States shall be President of the Senate, but shall have no Vote, unless they be equally divided.

The Senate shall chuse their other Officers, and also a President pro tempore, in the Absence of the Vice President, or when

---

*The Constitution was adopted in 1788.

[1] Changed by section 2 of the Fourteenth Amendment.

[2] Changed by the Seventeenth Amendment to elections by the people of each state.

[3] Changed by the Seventeenth Amendment to an election process.

he shall exercise the Office of President of the United States.

The Senate shall have the sole Power to try all Impeachments. When sitting for that Purpose, they shall be on Oath or Affirmation. When the President of the United States is tried, the Chief Justice shall preside: And no Person shall be convicted without the Concurrence of two thirds of the Members present.

Judgment in Cases of Impeachment shall not extend further than to removal from Office, and disqualification to hold and enjoy any Office of honor, Trust or Profit under the United States: but the Party convicted shall nevertheless be liable and subject to Indictment, Trial, Judgment and Punishment, according to Law.

Section 4

The Times, Places and Manner of holding Elections for Senators and Representatives, shall be prescribed in each State by the Legislature thereof; but the Congress may at any time by Law make or alter such Regulations, except as to the Places of chusing Senators.

The Congress shall assemble at least once in every Year, and such Meeting shall be on [the first Monday in December,][4] unless they shall by Law appoint a different Day.

Section 5

Each House shall be the Judge of the Elections, Returns and Qualifications of its own Members, and a Majority of each shall constitute a Quorum to do Business; but a smaller Number may adjourn from day to day, and may be authorized to compel the Attendance of absent Members, in such Manner, and under such Penalties as each House may provide.

Each House may determine the Rules of its Proceedings, punish its Members for disorderly Behaviour, and, with the Concurrence of two thirds, expel a Member.

Each House shall keep a Journal of its Proceedings, and from time to time publish the same, excepting such Parts as may in their Judgment require Secrecy; and the Yeas and Nays of the Members of either House on any question shall, at the Desire of one fifth of those Present, be entered on the Journal.

Neither House, during the Session of Congress, shall, without the Consent of the other, adjourn for more than three days, nor to any other Place than that in which the two Houses shall be sitting.

Section 6

The Senators and Representatives shall receive a Compensation for their Services, to be ascertained by Law, and paid out of the Treasury of the United States. They shall in all Cases, except Treason, Felony and Breach of the Peace, be privileged from Arrest during their Attendance at the Session of their re-

spective Houses, and in going to and returning from the same; and for any Speech or Debate in either House, they shall not be questioned in any other Place.

No Senator or Representative shall, during the Time for which he was elected, be appointed to any civil Office under the Authority of the United States, which shall have been created, or the Emoluments whereof shall have been encreased during such time; and no Person holding any Office under the United States, shall be a Member of either House during his Continuance in Office.

Section 7

All Bills for raising Revenue shall originate in the House of Representatives; but the Senate may propose or concur with Amendments as on other Bills.

Every Bill which shall have passed the House of Representatives and the Senate, shall, before it become a Law, be presented to the President of the United States; If he approve he shall sign it, but if not he shall return it, with his Objections to that House in which it shall have originated, who shall enter the Objections at large on their Journal, and proceed to reconsider it. If after such Reconsideration two thirds of that House shall agree to pass the Bill, it shall be sent, together with the Objections, to the other House, by which it shall likewise be reconsidered, and if approved by two thirds of that House, it shall become a Law. But in all such Cases the Votes of both Houses shall be determined by yeas and Nays, and the Names of the Persons voting for and against the Bill shall be entered on the Journal of each House respectively. If any Bill shall not be returned by the President within ten Days (Sundays excepted) after it shall have been presented to him, the Same shall be a Law, in like Manner as if he had signed it, unless the Congress by their Adjournment prevent its Return, in which Case it shall not be a Law.

Every Order, Resolution, or Vote to which the Concurrence of the Senate and House of Representatives may be necessary (except on a question of Adjournment) shall be presented to the President of the United States; and before the Same shall take Effect, shall be approved by him, or being disapproved by him, shall be repassed by two thirds of the Senate and House of Representatives, according to the Rules and Limitations prescribed in the Case of a Bill.

Section 8

The Congress shall have Power To lay and collect Taxes, Duties, Imposts and Excises, to pay the Debts and provide for the common Defence and general Welfare of the United States; but all Duties, Imposts and Excises shall be uniform throughout the United States;

To borrow Money on the credit of the United States;

To regulate Commerce with foreign Nations, and among the several States, and with the Indian Tribes;

---

[4] Changed by section 2 of the Twentieth Amendment to January 3.

To establish an uniform Rule of Naturalization, and uniform Laws on the subject of Bankruptcies throughout the United States;

To coin Money, regulate the Value thereof, and of foreign Coin, and fix the Standard of Weights and Measures;

To provide for the Punishment of counterfeiting the Securities and current Coin of the United States;

To establish Post Offices and post Roads;

To promote the Progress of Science and useful Arts, by securing for limited Times to Authors and Inventors the exclusive Right to their respective Writings and Discoveries;

To constitute Tribunals inferior to the supreme Court;

To define and punish Piracies and Felonies committed on the high Seas, and Offences against the Law of Nations;

To declare War, grant Letters of Marque and Reprisal, and make Rules concerning Captures on Land and Water;

To raise and support Armies, but no Appropriation of Money to that Use shall be for a longer Term than two Years;

To provide and maintain a Navy;

To make Rules for the Government and Regulation of the land and naval Forces;

To provide for calling forth the Militia to execute the Laws of the Union, suppress Insurrections and repel Invasions;

To provide for organizing, arming, and disciplining, the Militia, and for governing such Part of them as may be employed in the Service of the United States, reserving to the States respectively, the Appointment of the Officers, and the Authority of training the Militia according to the discipline prescribed by Congress;

To exercise exclusive Legislation in all Cases whatsoever, over such District (not exceeding ten Miles square) as may, by Cession of particular States, and the Acceptance of Congress, become the Seat of the Government of the United States, and to exercise like Authority over all Places purchased by the Consent of the Legislature of the State in which the Same shall be, for the Erection of Forts, Magazines, Arsenals, dock-Yards, and other needful Buildings; []And

To make all Laws which shall be necessary and proper for carrying into Execution the foregoing Powers, and all other Powers vested by this Constitution in the Government of the United States, or in any Department or Officer thereof.

Section 9

The Migration or Importation of such Persons as any of the States now existing shall think proper to admit, shall not be prohibited by the Congress prior to the Year one thousand eight hundred and eight, but a Tax or duty may be imposed on such Importation, not exceeding ten dollars for each Person.

The Privilege of the Writ of Habeas Corpus shall not be suspended, unless when in Cases of Rebellion or Invasion the public Safety may require it.

No Bill of Attainder or ex post facto Law shall be passed.

No Capitation, or other direct, Tax shall be laid, unless in Proportion to the Census or Enumeration herein before directed to be taken.[5]

No Tax or Duty shall be laid on Articles exported from any State.

No Preference shall be given by any Regulation of Commerce or Revenue to the Ports of one State over those of another: nor shall Vessels bound to, or from, one State, be obliged to enter, clear, or pay Duties in another.

No Money shall be drawn from the Treasury, but in Consequence of Appropriations made by Law; and a regular Statement and Account of the Receipts and Expenditures of all public Money shall be published from time to time.

No Title of Nobility shall be granted by the United States: And no Person holding any Office of Profit or Trust under them, shall, without the Consent of the Congress, accept of any present, Emolument, Office, or Title, of any kind whatever, from any King, Prince, or foreign State.

Section 10

No State shall enter into any Treaty, Alliance, or Confederation; grant Letters of Marque and Reprisal; coin Money; emit Bills of Credit; make any Thing but gold and silver Coin a Tender in Payment of Debts; pass any Bill of Attainder, ex post facto Law, or Law impairing the Obligation of Contracts, or grant any Title of Nobility.

No State shall, without the Consent of the Congress, lay any Imposts or Duties on Imports or Exports, except what may be absolutely necessary for executing its inspection Laws: and the net Produce of all Duties and Imposts, laid by any State on Imports or Exports, shall be for the Use of the Treasury of the United States; and all such Laws shall be subject to the Revision and Controul of the Congress.

No State shall, without the Consent of Congress, lay any Duty of Tonnage, keep Troops, or Ships of War in time of Peace, enter into any Agreement or Compact with another State, or with a foreign Power, or engage in War, unless actually invaded, or in such imminent Danger as will not admit of delay.

Article II

Section 1

The executive Power shall be vested in a President of the United States of America. He shall hold his Office during the Term of four Years, and, together with the Vice President, chosen for the same Term, be elected, as follows

Each State shall appoint, in such Manner as the Legislature thereof may direct, a Number of Electors, equal to the whole Number of Senators and Representatives to which the State may be entitled in the Congress: but no Senator or Representa-

---

[5] But the Sixteenth Amendment allowed for the collection of income taxes.

tive, or Person holding an Office of Trust or Profit under the United States, shall be appointed an Elector.

[The Electors shall meet in their respective States, and vote by Ballot for two Persons, of whom one at least shall not be an Inhabitant of the same State with themselves. And they shall make a List of all the Persons voted for, and of the Number of Votes for each; which List they shall sign and certify, and transmit sealed to the Seat of the Government of the United States, directed to the President of the Senate. The President of the Senate shall, in the Presence of the Senate and House of Representatives, open all the Certificates, and the Votes shall then be counted. The Person having the greatest Number of Votes shall be the President, if such Number be a Majority of the whole Number of Electors appointed; and if there be more than one who have such Majority, and have an equal Number of Votes, then the House of Representatives shall immediately chuse by Ballot one of them for President; and if no Person have a Majority, then from the five highest on the List the said House shall in like Manner chuse the President. But in chusing the President, the Votes shall be taken by States, the Representation from each State having one Vote; A quorum for this Purpose shall consist of a Member or Members from two thirds of the States, and a Majority of all the States shall be necessary to a Choice. In every Case, after the Choice of the President, the Person having the greatest Number of Votes of the Electors shall be the Vice President. But if there should remain two or more who have equal Votes, the Senate shall chuse from them by Ballot the Vice President.][6]

The Congress may determine the Time of chusing the Electors, and the Day on which they shall give their Votes; which Day shall be the same throughout the United States.

No Person except a natural born Citizen, or a Citizen of the United States, at the time of the Adoption of this Constitution, shall be eligible to the Office of President; neither shall any Person be eligible to that Office who shall not have attained to the Age of thirty five Years, and been fourteen Years a Resident within the United States.

[In Case of the Removal of the President from Office, or of his Death, Resignation, or Inability to discharge the Powers and Duties of the said Office, the Same shall devolve on the Vice President, and the Congress may by Law provide for the Case of Removal, Death, Resignation or Inability, both of the President and Vice President, declaring what Officer shall then act as President, and such Officer shall act accordingly, until the Disability be removed, or a President shall be elected.][7]

The President shall, at stated Times, receive for his Services, a Compensation, which shall neither be encreased nor diminished during the Period for which he shall have been elected, and he shall not receive within that Period any other Emolument from the United States, or any of them.

Before he enter on the Execution of his Office, he shall take the following Oath or Affirmation:□ "I do solemnly swear (or affirm) that I will faithfully execute the Office of President of the United States, and will to the best of my Ability, preserve, protect and defend the Constitution of the United States."

Section 2

The President shall be Commander in Chief of the Army and Navy of the United States, and of the Militia of the several States, when called into the actual Service of the United States; he may require the Opinion, in writing, of the principal Officer in each of the executive Departments, upon any Subject relating to the Duties of their respective Offices, and he shall have Power to grant Reprieves and Pardons for Offences against the United States, except in Cases of Impeachment.

He shall have Power, by and with the Advice and Consent of the Senate, to make Treaties, provided two thirds of the Senators present concur; and he shall nominate, and by and with the Advice and Consent of the Senate, shall appoint Ambassadors, other public Ministers and Consuls, Judges of the supreme Court, and all other Officers of the United States, whose Appointments are not herein otherwise provided for, and which shall be established by Law: but the Congress may by Law vest the Appointment of such inferior Officers, as they think proper, in the President alone, in the Courts of Law, or in the Heads of Departments.

The President shall have Power to fill up all Vacancies that may happen during the Recess of the Senate, by granting Commissions which shall expire at the End of their next Session.

Section 3

He shall from time to time give to the Congress Information of the State of the Union, and recommend to their Consideration such Measures as he shall judge necessary and expedient; he may, on extraordinary Occasions, convene both Houses, or either of them, and in Case of Disagreement between them, with Respect to the Time of Adjournment, he may adjourn them to such Time as he shall think proper; he shall receive Ambassadors and other public Ministers; he shall take Care that the Laws be faithfully executed, and shall Commission all the Officers of the United States.

Section 4

The President, Vice President and all civil Officers of the United States, shall be removed from Office on Impeachment for, and Conviction of, Treason, Bribery, or other high Crimes and Misdemeanors.

---

[6] Changed by the Twelfth Amendment.

[7] Changed by the Twenty-Fifth Amendment.

Article III

Section 1

The judicial Power of the United States, shall be vested in one supreme Court, and in such inferior Courts as the Congress may from time to time ordain and establish. The Judges, both of the supreme and inferior Courts, shall hold their Offices during good Behaviour, and shall, at stated Times, receive for their Services, a Compensation, which shall not be diminished during their Continuance in Office.

Section 2

The judicial Power shall extend to all Cases, in Law and Equity, arising under this Constitution, the Laws of the United States, and Treaties made, or which shall be made, under their Authority; ☐ to all Cases affecting Ambassadors, other public Ministers and Consuls; ☐ to all Cases of admiralty and maritime Jurisdiction; ☐ to Controversies to which the United States shall be a Party; ☐ to Controversies between two or more States; [☐ between a State and Citizens of another State;][8] ☐ between Citizens of different States, ☐ between Citizens of the same State claiming Lands under Grants of different States, [and between a State, or the Citizens thereof, and foreign States, Citizens or Subjects.][9]

In all Cases affecting Ambassadors, other public Ministers and Consuls, and those in which a State shall be Party, the supreme Court shall have original Jurisdiction. In all the other Cases before mentioned, the supreme Court shall have appellate Jurisdiction, both as to Law and Fact, with such Exceptions, and under such Regulations as the Congress shall make.

The Trial of all Crimes, except in Cases of Impeachment, shall be by Jury; and such Trial shall be held in the State where the said Crimes shall have been committed; but when not committed within any State, the Trial shall be at such Place or Places as the Congress may by Law have directed.

Section 3

Treason against the United States, shall consist only in levying War against them, or in adhering to their Enemies, giving them Aid and Comfort. No Person shall be convicted of Treason unless on the Testimony of two Witnesses to the same overt Act, or on Confession in open Court.

The Congress shall have Power to declare the Punishment of Treason, but no Attainder of Treason shall work Corruption of Blood, or Forfeiture except during the Life of the Person attainted.

Article IV

Section 1

Full Faith and Credit shall be given in each State to the public Acts, Records, and judicial Proceedings of every other State. And the Congress may by general Laws prescribe the Manner in which such Acts, Records and Proceedings shall be proved, and the Effect thereof.

Section 2

The Citizens of each State shall be entitled to all Privileges and Immunities of Citizens in the several States.

A Person charged in any State with Treason, Felony, or other Crime, who shall flee from Justice, and be found in another State, shall on Demand of the executive Authority of the State from which he fled, be delivered up, to be removed to the State having Jurisdiction of the Crime.

[No Person held to Service or Labour in one State, under the Laws thereof, escaping into another, shall, in Consequence of any Law or Regulation therein, be discharged from such Service or Labour, but shall be delivered up on Claim of the Party to whom such Service or Labour may be due.][10]

Section 3

New States may be admitted by the Congress into this Union; but no new State shall be formed or erected within the Jurisdiction of any other State; nor any State be formed by the Junction of two or more States, or Parts of States, without the Consent of the Legislatures of the States concerned as well as of the Congress.

The Congress shall have Power to dispose of and make all needful Rules and Regulations respecting the Territory or other Property belonging to the United States; and nothing in this Constitution shall be so construed as to Prejudice any Claims of the United States, or of any particular State.

Section 4

The United States shall guarantee to every State in this Union a Republican Form of Government, and shall protect each of them against Invasion; and on Application of the Legislature, or of the Executive (when the Legislature cannot be convened) against domestic Violence.

Article V

The Congress, whenever two thirds of both Houses shall deem it necessary, shall propose Amendments to this Constitution, or, on the Application of the Legislatures of two thirds of the several States, shall call a Convention for proposing Amendments, which, in either Case, shall be valid to all Intents and Purposes, as Part of this Constitution, when ratified by the

---

[8] Changed by the Eleventh Amendment.

[9] Changed by the Eleventh Amendment.

[10] Changed by the Thirteenth Amendment.

Legislatures of three fourths of the several States, or by Conventions in three fourths thereof, as the one or the other Mode of Ratification may be proposed by the Congress; Provided that no Amendment which may be made prior to the Year One thousand eight hundred and eight shall in any Manner affect the first and fourth Clauses in the Ninth Section of the first Article; and that no State, without its Consent, shall be deprived of its equal Suffrage in the Senate.

Article VI

All Debts contracted and Engagements entered into, before the Adoption of this Constitution, shall be as valid against the United States under this Constitution, as under the Confederation.

This Constitution, and the Laws of the United States which shall be made in Pursuance thereof; and all Treaties made, or which shall be made, under the Authority of the United States, shall be the supreme Law of the Land; and the Judges in every State shall be bound thereby, any Thing in the Constitution or Laws of any State to the Contrary notwithstanding.

The Senators and Representatives before mentioned, and the Members of the several State Legislatures, and all executive and judicial Officers, both of the United States and of the several States, shall be bound by Oath or Affirmation, to support this Constitution; but no religious Test shall ever be required as a Qualification to any Office or public Trust under the United States.

Article VII

The Ratification of the Conventions of nine States, shall be sufficient for the Establishment of this Constitution between the States so ratifying the Same. Done in Convention by the Unanimous Consent of the States present the Seventeenth Day of September in the Year of our Lord one thousand seven hundred and Eighty seven and of the Independence of the United States of America the Twelfth In witness whereof We have hereunto subscribed our Names.... [The names of signers follow.]

The Bill of Rights*

Amendment I

Congress shall make no law respecting an establishment of religion, or prohibiting the free exercise thereof; or abridging the freedom of speech, or of the press; or the right of the people peaceably to assemble, and to petition the government for a redress of grievances.

Amendment II

A well regulated militia, being necessary to the security of a free state, the right of the people to keep and bear arms, shall not be infringed.

Amendment III

No soldier shall, in time of peace be quartered in any house, without the consent of the owner, nor in time of war, but in a manner to be prescribed by law.

Amendment IV

The right of the people to be secure in their persons, houses, papers, and effects, against unreasonable searches and seizures, shall not be violated, and no warrants shall issue, but upon probable cause, supported by oath or affirmation, and particularly describing the place to be searched, and the persons or things to be seized.

Amendment V

No person shall be held to answer for a capital, or otherwise infamous crime, unless on a presentment or indictment of a grand jury, except in cases arising in the land or naval forces, or in the militia, when in actual service in time of war or public danger; nor shall any person be subject for the same offense to be twice put in jeopardy of life or limb; nor shall be compelled in any criminal case to be a witness against himself, nor be deprived of life, liberty, or property, without due process of law; nor shall private property be taken for public use, without just compensation.

Amendment VI

In all criminal prosecutions, the accused shall enjoy the right to a speedy and public trial, by an impartial jury of the state and district wherein the crime shall have been committed, which district shall have been previously ascertained by law, and to be informed of the nature and cause of the accusation; to be confronted with the witnesses against him; to have compulsory process for obtaining witnesses in his favor, and to have the assistance of counsel for his defense.

Amendment VII

In suits at common law, where the value in controversy shall

---

* The first ten amendments to the Constitution were ratified effective December 15, 1791.

exceed twenty dollars, the right of trial by jury shall be preserved, and no fact tried by a jury, shall be otherwise reexamined in any court of the United States, than according to the rules of the common law.

Amendment VIII

Excessive bail shall not be required, nor excessive fines imposed, nor cruel and unusual punishments inflicted.

Amendment IX

The enumeration in the Constitution, of certain rights, shall not be construed to deny or disparage others retained by the people.

Amendment X

The powers not delegated to the United States by the Constitution, nor prohibited by it to the states, are reserved to the states respectively, or to the people.

A Short Glossary of Legal Terms

absolute privilege – an immunity from DEFAMATION* suits that attaches to government officials protecting those officials from actions based on speech or writings made within their official capacities.

absolutism – the belief that the First Amendment pronouncement that no law should be made restricting free speech or a free press is absolute and, therefore, that there may be no restrictions on expression.

acquit – in criminal law, to find a defendant not guilty; in contract law, to release from an obligation.

act – STATUTORY LAW; used interchangeably with "law."

actionable – giving rise to a CAUSE OF ACTION.

actual damages – a monetary award in a lawsuit for actual injury or loss, such as harm to reputation, emotional distress or mental suffering; also called COMPENSATORY DAMAGES.

actual malice – knowledge of falsity or reckless disregard for whether material is true or false; this standard, sometimes called "*New York Times* actual malice," which all public officials and public figures must prove in order to prevail in libel actions, was first enunciated by the U.S. Supreme Court in *New York Times Co. v. Sullivan.*

adjudication – giving or pronouncing a judgment or decree; also, the judgment itself.

advance sheet – a pamphlet form of a decision issued at the time the decision is delivered.

allegation – a charge or declaration made in a lawsuit which the plaintiff is required to prove.

all-purpose public figure – in a libel or privacy action, a person of widespread fame or notoriety; a person of special prominence within society or of pervasive power and influence; a "household name."

amicus curiae – literally, "friend of the court"; a person, organization, company or government that provides information to a court – in the form of a BRIEF or argument – who is not a party in the case being litigated.

appeal – a plea to a higher court to alter or overturn a judgment of a lower court because of errors of law.

appellant – the party who appeals a court's decision, requesting that a higher court review the ruling or rulings of the lower court.

appellate court – a court that has jurisdiction to hear cases on appeal.

appellee – the party against whom an appeal is taken; that is, the party who won the case in the lower court.

appropriation – in privacy law, the use of a person's name, image or likeness without permission for trade purposes.

arraignment – a judicial proceeding at which a criminal defendant is formally informed of the charges against him or her and to which the defendant enters a plea.

Articles of Confederation – the first constitution of the United States; it was replaced by the constitution of 1787, which is still in force.

---

* Terms appearing in SMALL CAPITAL LETTERS appear as separate entries in the glossary.

406

B

bad tendency test – a judicial test that allows restrictions on expression when a court finds that the speech might have even the slightest tendency to cause harm.

bail – money or property that will be forfeited if a criminal defendant does not appear at a judicial proceeding.

bail bond (or bond) – a signed obligation with collateral attached to assure the appearance in court of an individual.

bait-and-switch – a sales technique whereby an item is advertised at a very low price, but shoppers are pressured to buy a more expensive item; in some cases, the low-priced item is not available or is available only on a very limited basis.

balancing – a court's weighing of competing interests guaranteed by law to determine which rights must give way.

Bill of Rights – the first ten amendments to the U.S. Constitution.

black letter law – an informal term indicating the basic principles of law generally accepted by the courts and/or embodied in the STATUTES of a particular jurisdiction.

Bluebook – the popular name of *A Uniform System of Citation,* the standard reference work for legal writing; the *Bluebook* was originally developed by the *Harvard Law Review,* but, now in its 18th edition, is produced by the law reviews at Harvard, Columbia, Yale and the University of Pennsylvania.

bootstrapping – an attempt by a media libel defendant to elevate a plaintiff to PUBLIC FIGURE status as a result of the attention brought to the plaintiff by the defendant's coverage of the lawsuit.

brief – a written argument prepared by attorneys involved in an appeal, supporting the attorneys' positions. It contains a summary of the facts, the pertinent law and an argument of how the law applies to the facts. Briefs are prepared by counsel for both sides, but often *AMICUS CURIAE* briefs will also be filed. A BRIEF should not be confused with a CASE BRIEF, which is a synopsis of an opinion.

burden of proof – the elements a plaintiff must prove in order to prevail in a CIVIL ACTION, or that a prosecutor must prove in order to successfully convict a criminal DEFENDANT.

C

case brief – a synopsis of an opinion, generally only one or two pages long, highlighting the facts, question, holding and rationale of the opinion.

CATV – community antenna television; the early name for cable television, reflecting the perception that cable was a regional service designed to expand the reach of broadcast television.

cause of action – those facts which give rise to a right to sue.

censorship – the halting of expression at its source by the government; also called PRIOR RESTRAINT.

certiorari – the name of a WRIT issued by the U.S. Supreme Court when it agrees to review a case; it is an order to the lower court to send up the records. Some state supreme courts also use the term.

change of venire – the transfer of a jury pool from a distant jurisdiction to a location in which a crime was committed in order to seat jurors who have not been biased by publicity about the case.

change of venue – the moving of a trial to a location other than that in which the crime was committed in order to seat jurors who have not been biased by publicity about the case.

child pornography – material containing depictions of children in sexually explicit situations; it is not protected by the First Amendment; also called "kiddie porn."

citation – a notation indicating the location of legal authority. Also called a "cite."

civil action – a lawsuit alleging a private wrong, as opposed to a criminal wrong.

clear and present danger test – a test first enunciated by Justice Oliver Wendell Holmes in 1919 allowing restrictions on speech and press when the expression would cause substantive, immediate harm.

code – a classified arrangement of public laws in effect. Also called "compiled statutes" or "revised statutes."

collateral bar rule – the rule that a person who disobeys a court order may not challenge the constitutionality of the order as a defense to a CONTEMPT OF COURT charge.

colloquium – a libel plaintiff's proof of special circumstances in establishing that a defamatory statement is about or understood to be about the plaintiff.

commercial speech – communication intended to promote a business or service or sell a product.

common carrier – the regulatory category traditionally applied to service providers - like telephone services - that must provide universal, nondiscriminatory service to all on a first-come-first-served basis and may not control the messages they carry.

common law – court-created law; in modern usage, case law as opposed to statutory law; in theory, the common law was "discovered" rather than created by historical Anglo-Saxon courts. The discovery was based on the common customs of the times, thus the term "common." "Common" law was also distinguished from "ecclesiastical" or church law.

common law malice – ill will, hatred or spite.

compelling government interest – an overriding interest advocated by the government that must be proved in order for a regulation aimed at suppressing expression to be found constitutional. In such cases - which require STRICT SCRUTINY - the government must also prove that the regulation is narrowly tailored.

compensatory damages – a monetary award in a lawsuit for actual injury or loss, such as harm to reputation, emotional distress or mental suffering; also called ACTUAL DAMAGES.

complainant – the person bringing a legal complaint; the PLAINTIFF.

complaint – the first legal argument filed by a plaintiff.

constitution – a document outlining the organization of a government, specifying the rights, responsibilities and limits of that government.

contempt of court – willful disobedience of a lawful order of a court or any act calculated to embarrass, hinder or obstruct a court in the administration of justice.

content neutral restrictions – restrictions that are not related to the content of expression, but on circumstances related to the TIME, PLACE OR MANNER of the expression.

continuance – a judicial order that a criminal or civil action be delayed.

copyright – protection for the ownership of an original work that has been fixed in a tangible medium of expression.

copyright infringement – copying the form or expression of an idea without permission; punishable by a civil or criminal action or both.

criminal libel – a malicious publication that exposes or tends to expose a living person or the memory of a deceased person to hatred, contempt ridicule or obloquy in violation of a statute; a prosecutor brings the criminal charges against the publisher of the publication.

cross-ownership – an array of FCC rules and statutory provisions aimed to protect diversity of ownership and content by preventing consolidation of media ownership.

D

damages – compensation recovered by a PLAINTIFF from a DEFENDANT.

DBS – direct broadcast satellites; they operate in GEOSYNCHRONOUS ORBITS to create a stable broadcast imprint or coverage area for transmission of messages and programming to receiving dishes eighteen to twenty-four inches in diameter.

de novo – a second time; totally new.

defamation – communication that injures another's reputation, that is, that holds one up to scorn, ridicule or spite; SLANDER is oral defamation; LIBEL is written defamation.

defendant – the party against whom a lawsuit is brought.

demurrer – an allegation by a defendant that even if the facts alleged by a plaintiff are true, they do not state a sufficient CAUSE OF ACTION.

deposition – a formal interview by an attorney of a witness who answers questions under oath, but not in open court; also, the transcript of the interview.

deregulation – a policy of eliminating laws and regulations in favor of market pressures.

dictum – technically *obiter dictum,* this is an incidental comment in an opinion; a comment not necessary to the determination of the issue at hand; it is not binding precedent. The plural is *"dicta."*

digital sampling – converting sounds from existing songs to digital bits and then manipulating and combining notes to create a new song.

discovery – a proceeding through which parties in a case are informed of facts known by the adversarial parties.

diversity of citizenship action – a civil action in which the parties are residents of different states; the U.S. Constitution allows federal district courts to hear such cases, even if the subject matter of the suit is one of state law, as long as the amount in the controversy exceeds $75,000.

docket number – the numerical designation assigned to each case by a court; it is used to identify the case as it progresses through the judicial system.

DTH – direct-to-home; the services send video signals to home dishes or receivers in the United States, including the relatively high-power DBS systems and lower-power HSD systems.

DTV – *see* HDTV.

due process – a term used to describe the proper operation of legal proceedings according to the rules and principles that have been established to protect the rights of individuals.

E

effective competition – the standard that allows cable systems to operate without rate regulation; it exists when substantial overlap of services offered by cable and other providers exists.

en banc – a session in which the entire court — rather than a panel — hears and participates in the determination of a case.

enjoin – to require, by a judicial action, an individual to perform or refrain from performing some act.

equity – justice administered according to fairness as contrasted with the strict, formulated rules of COMMON LAW; it renders the administration of justice more complete, by affording relief where courts of law are incompetent to give it or enforce it.

erotica – sexually explicit material; generally "erotica" is a neutral term that refers to material that can be distinguished from PORNOGRAPHY or OBSCENITY; erotica is protected by the First Amendment.

exemplary damages – a monetary award designed to punish a defendant in a lawsuit for some action; the same as PUNITIVE DAMAGES.

ex parte – by, for or on behalf of one party.

F

fair comment and criticism – a COMMON LAW defense against a defamation claim in which the defendant avows a right to express an opinion, based on well-known or truthfully stated facts, without COMMON LAW MALICE against a person who has entered the public sphere.

fair use – a provision in copyright law that allows copying of protected material for use in certain specific circumstances.

false light – the privacy tort which protects individuals from the publication of material that is not necessarily defamatory but is false and offensive.

fault – culpability; it must be proved in order for an individual to prevail in a libel action; the most common types of fault are NEGLIGENCE and ACTUAL MALICE.

felony – a serious crime punishable by imprisonment in a penitentiary, or more serious punishment.

fighting words – language that is likely to cause an immediate, violent response; it lies outside First Amendment protection.

first sale – the doctrine that permits a copyright owner to collect royalties the first time each copy of a work is sold. The purchaser may then rent or resell that copy without permission, but may not make derivative works, reproduce or publicly perform the work.

franchise agreement – the contract between local authorities and cable operators that imposes conditions on cable systems in exchange for permission for them to string their cables along public rights-of-way.

G

gag order – an order by a court not to speak or write about matters before the court.

geosynchronous orbit – an orbit that enables a satellite to maintain its position relative to the earth.

grand jury – an investigatory panel; a panel whose duty is to hear the state's evidence in a criminal case and determine whether there is probable cause to believe a crime has been committed and whether the accused should stand trial; the grand jury does not determine guilt or innocence.

group libel – a DEFAMATION aimed at a group rather than an individual; if the group is large, members of the group are precluded from bringing libel actions because they are not sufficiently identified.

H

habeas corpus – literally, "you have the body"; a WRIT through which a person can be brought before a court to determine whether the person has been denied liberty without DUE PROCESS of law.

HDTV – high definition television or digital television (DTV); it uses digital technology and a new transmission standard to improve picture and sound quality and to provide an image area shaped more like a movie theater screen than a traditional television screen.

headend – the control center of a cable system, where the cable operator brings together programming from diverse sources before distributing it to subscribers.

headnote – a summary of legal principles in a case, printed immediately before the text of the opinion in a REPORTER; a case may be preceded by a number of headnotes, depending upon the findings of the court.

holding – the declaration in an OPINION of the conclusion of law reached by a court.

HSD – home satellite dish services; they are more properly called "fixed satellite services" and require a receiving dish approximately four to eight feet in diameter to receive their low-power signals.

I

implied consent – consent that is not explicit, but may be available based on the facts of the case.

in camera – in private; in a judge's chambers.

incorporation – in constitutional law, the process by which portions of the BILL OF RIGHTS, including the First Amendment, have been applied to the states *via* the Fourteenth Amendment's due process clause.

indict/indictment – a written accusation by a GRAND JURY charging a person with a crime.

inducement – a libel plaintiff's allegation that extrinsic facts make a statement defamatory although it is not defamatory on its face.

infra – a signal indicating that further information appears later in the text or footnotes.

injunction – a court order halting some activity or commanding someone to undo a wrong.

inter alia – literally "among other things."

interconnection rules – the rules that govern the ability of communication service providers to link up with and use the network facilities of a competitor.

Internet – an international network created by high-speed, broadband connections and satellite links.

interrogatory – a list of written questions posed by a party in a lawsuit to the opposing party.

J

judgment – the HOLDING of a court in a case.

judgment n.o.v. – a judgment rendered in favor of one party in a case, notwithstanding a verdict in favor of the opposing party; that is, the overruling of a jury verdict by a judge.

jurisdiction – the area over which a court has authority; the power and authority of a court to hear and determine a judicial proceeding; the area may be geographic or based on the subject matter of the case. If a court does not have jurisdiction, it may not render a legal decision in the matter.

K

Key Number – a permanent number assigned to a specific point of law in a case, as developed by the West Publishing Company, to aid in the discovery of material on the same topic of law in other cases.

L

leased-access channels – channels provided by cable systems for commercial lease, which, when not leased, cable operators may use to carry cable programming.

liable – responsible or answerable for some action.

libel – written communication that damages a person's reputation, that is, that holds a person up to hatred, ridicule or scorn; a type of DEFAMATION.

libertarianism – a governmental theory allowing absolute and unrestricted liberty, especially of thought and speech.

licensing – a governmental policy under which express permission must be granted before material may be published.

likelihood of confusion – grounds for legal action to protect a TRADEMARK from being confused with another trademark; courts compare the two marks on a variety of factors to determine whether consumers are likely to be confused as to the source, sponsorship or approval of a product.

limited-purpose public figure – in libel law, a person who voluntarily injects himself or herself into a public controversy in order to influence the outcome; also known as a "vortex public figure."

lock boxes – television set-top devices that can be programmed to eliminate certain channels or content.

M

malice – *see* COMMON LAW MALICE, ACTUAL MALICE.

mandamus – an order by a court directing a lower court or government official to do something.

marketplace of ideas theory – the theory that the government should exercise minimal control on speech, based on the notion that when all ideas are allowed to be expressed - that is, are allowed in the "marketplace of ideas" - truth will prevail.

misdemeanor – a criminal offense that is not serious enough to warrant a prison sentence; penalties are usually fines and community service or a sentence to a local jail.

moot – the absence of a genuine controversy or contention of law. Courts will rarely decide "moot" points of law unless there is an indication that the point of law is likely to recur in another case.

MSO – multiple system operator; a person who runs cable systems in several geographically dispersed locations.

multiplexing – a technology that enables the transmission of up to four television signals on one channel.

must-carry rules – a series of FCC rules requiring cable systems to carry all local broadcast signals.

N

negligence – a standard of FAULT in TORT law; an act or omission that a reasonably careful person would not take; in libel law, it is acting other than in a manner in which a reasonably careful or ordinarily prudent person would act or failure to follow accepted professional practices or standards.

network nonduplication rules – rules that allow television stations affiliated with a broadcast network to demand that a cable system black out network programming being carried on an imported station.

nonsuit – termination of an action without adjudicating the issues on the merits.

O

obscenity – pornographic material that has been determined by a court to meet the Supreme Court's test for obscene material articulated in *Miller v. California* and, therefore, lies outside First Amendment protection.

opinion – an explanation of the rationale for a judicial decision, that is, the holding of a court and the rationale for that holding; in libel law, a communication that cannot be proved to be true or false and, therefore, cannot be the subject of a successful libel action.

overbroad/overbreadth – a term used to refer to a law that prohibits or punishes legal as well as illegal conduct or speech.

P

parallel citation – a citation reference to the same case printed in a different REPORTER. (See definition of "reporter.")

PEG channels – cable television channels reserved by law for public, educational and government access.

per curiam – an opinion "by the court"; that is, an unsigned opinion.

peremptory challenges – rights by which an attorney may dismiss potential jurors without providing a reason; the number is generally limited based on the nature of the trial.

petit jury – a panel whose function it is to decide the facts of a case, that is, to determine guilt or innocence in a criminal suit and the party that prevails in a civil suit.

petitioner – the party who starts an EQUITY proceeding or the party who appeals a judgment to a higher court.

plaintiff – the party who brings a lawsuit.

pleading – a legal argument, filed in writing, outlining the contentions of a party in a lawsuit.

pocket supplement – also called a "pocket part," a supplement found in the back of a legal source book, updating the information contained within the book.

pornography – sexually explicit material that is in some way demeaning; it is protected by the First Amendment.

precedent – legal authority that must be followed, absent a sound legal basis for variance; previous cases on the same point of law.

preliminary injunction – a temporary order, generally to stop a person from doing something.

preponderance of evidence – the standard of proof in a civil action, determined by balancing the evidence and determining which allegations or contentions are more likely to be true.

prima facie case – a case that unless contradicted would likely prevail before a reasonable jury.

primary authority – mandatory legal authority; that is, judicial precedent or legislative enactment; authority that must be followed or contended with.

prior restraint – the prohibition of expression at its source by the government; also called CENSORSHIP.

promissory estoppel – a legal doctrine similar to contract law that holds that when a clear promise is intended to and does induce a specific action, that promise is binding if injustice can be avoided only by enforcing it.

publication – in libel law, the exposure of material to a third party.

public domain – material no longer protected by COPYRIGHT falls into the public domain, meaning that it is available for anyone to use without authorization.

public figure – *see* ALL-PURPOSE PUBLIC FIGURE and LIMITED-PURPOSE PUBLIC FIGURE.

public official – a government employee who has or appears to have substantial responsibility for or control over the conduct of government affairs.

punitive damages – a monetary award designed to punish a defendant in a lawsuit for some action; the same as EXEMPLARY DAMAGES. The U.S. Supreme Court has said that libel plaintiffs must prove ACTUAL MALICE in order to recover punitive damages.

Q

qualified privilege – a privilege to report information that appears in absolutely privileged *fora*, if certain conditions or qualifications are met, that is, if the report is accurate, fair and made without COMMON LAW MALICE.

quash – to vacate, abate or annul.

R

ratio decidendi – the rationale of a decision; that is, the legal point in the case which leads to the result.

reckless disregard – extreme indifference as to the truth or falsity of a defamatory statement; indifference that is tantamount to conscious, deliberate or intentional ignoring of the truth or falsity of a statement.

remand – to send back to a lower court for further proceedings, usually based upon the findings of a higher court.

report – to publish a decision of a court.

reporter – one in a series of books in which legal decisions are published; to publish the decisions.

reporter's privilege – the right of a journalist to keep the identities of sources or other information confidential.

respondent – in an EQUITY case, the party who answers the PETITIONER's bill of particulars; in appellate practice, the party who contests or opposes an APPEAL.

retraction – a published statement acknowledging that a publication was in error; "taking back" an incorrect statement.

S

scienter – guilty knowledge; prior knowledge.

scope note – a short note identifying and limiting the content of a topic; it appears immediately after the topic's heading in a legal reference work.

search warrant – an order issued by a magistrate or other officer of the court authorizing law enforcement officials to search for and seize evidence of a crime.

secondary authority – persuasive but not mandatory (PRIMARY) authority; supporting material; it may include legal encyclopedias, treatises, law journal articles or text books.

sedition – attacks on the government punishable by law because they could cause unrest.

seditious libel – harsh criticism of the government.

sequestration – the isolation of members of a jury during the taking of evidence and/or the deliberations on the facts of a case.

service mark – any word, name, symbol or device, or any combination thereof, adopted and used by a manufacturer or merchant to identify its services and distinguish them from services provided by others.

session laws – published laws of a state, as enacted by each assembly in each session; laws listed in chronological, rather than topical, order.

Shepardizing – to use a *Shepard's* citator index to locate all subsequent references to or uses of a case or other legal authority.

shield law – a statute providing journalists a testimonial privilege.

slamming – the illegal practice of switching a person's long-distance service provider without permission.

slander – oral communication that damages someone's reputation, that is, that would tend to hold a person up to scorn, ridicule or hatred; a type of DEFAMATION.

SMATV – also known as "private cable," a cable system within a single apartment building or bloc of buildings that does not use public rights-of-way; the system collects local television signals through antennas and satellite signals through receiving dishes and transmits them through the buildings.

special damages – a monetary award for financial or pecuniary loss.

standing – the right to bring a legal action.

star paging – a pagination scheme in reprint editions of court reporters, showing on its pages where the pages of the official text begin and end.

stare decisis – literally, "let the decision stand"; the legal doctrine of precedent; the tendency to follow, rather than overrule, precedent, i.e., the doctrine that a court will follow the principle established by a previous court when the facts of the cases are substantially the same.

statute of limitations – the time period in which a civil or criminal action must be brought.

statute/statutory law – law adopted by legislative bodies.

stay – a court order stopping some judicial action or order.

strict liability – the doctrine that a person is LIABLE for an act even if that action was unintentional and without FAULT.

strict scrutiny – a test to determine whether a regulation is constitutional; the test is used when the regulation is directed at the suppression of expression; under the test, the regulation is constitutional if it meets a COMPELLING GOVERNMENT INTEREST and is narrowly tailored.

subpoena – a command to appear in court at a certain time to testify about a certain matter; a **subpoena duces tecum** requires that the subpoenaed party bring certain documents or other materials to the hearing.

summary judgment – a ruling by a judge that there is no dispute of material fact between the two parties in a case, and that one party should win the case as a matter of law.

supra – a signal indicating that further information on a point or case is provided earlier in the text or footnotes.

syllabus – a summary of the case and the court's holding, prepared by the publisher of a REPORTER.

syndicated exclusivity – an FCC rule that prohibits cable companies from importing syndicated programs to which television stations possess exclusive contracts.

T

temporary restraining order – a court order to temporarily prevent an action.

time, place and manner restrictions – restrictions on expression based on the circumstances surrounding the expression rather than the content of the expression.

tort – a civil wrong by one person against another.

trade name – any name used by a person to identify his or her business or vocation.

trademark – a word, name, symbol or device or any combination thereof used to identify goods and distinguish them from those manufactured or sold by others.

trademark dilution – using a famous trademark in ways that blur its distinctiveness or tarnish or disparage it.

transformative – among the factors used to determine whether a use of copyrighted material is a FAIR USE or a COPYRIGHT INFRINGEMENT; courts examine whether the secondary use added value to the original copyrighted work.

V

vagueness – a rationale for finding a law unconstitutional because the law is not specific enough to give fair warning as to the parameters of the law.

venire – the potential jurors in a trial.

venue – the place in which a trial occurs.

voir dire – literally "to see, to say"; the process through which attorneys and a judge question potential jurors to determine whether they are qualified to serve.

W

wireless cable – a system licensed and regulated by the FCC that includes multi-point distribution services and multi-channel distribution services. It sends up to thirty-three channels by microwave signals to small antennas on subscribers' homes but does not cross public rights-of-way, so it does not require a local franchise.

work made for hire – intellectual property created as part of one's employment so that the employer, rather than the creator of the work, owns the COPYRIGHT; there are two types: (1) work done by an employee for an employer within the scope of employment; (2) a work specially commissioned or ordered for inclusion in a collective work if a work-for-hire agreement is signed.

writ – an order by a court requiring some action or giving authority and commission to that act.

The Authors

Sandra F. Chance is a professor in the College of Journalism and Communications at the University of Florida and is McClatchy Professor in Freedom of Information. She is also Executive Director of the Brechner Center for Freedom of Information. She teaches law of mass communication at the undergraduate and graduate levels and was named the Scripps-Howard National Journalism Teacher of the Year in 2005. She practiced media law with one of the country's largest law firms before joining the faculty at Florida. She has published articles in *Communication Law and Policy, Journal of Broadcasting & Electronic Media, Journalism & Mass Communication Quarterly, Journal of Law and Public Policy, UALR Law Review, Quill, Editor & Publisher* and other journals. She is on the board of directors of the First Amendment Foundation and is Sunshine Chair for the Society of Professional Journalists. She is a past head of the Association for Education in Journalism and Mass Communication Law Division and an active member of the Florida Bar's media and communications law committee. She has traveled to Brazil and Jamaica and participated in a videoconference with Chinese journalism students at the request of the U.S. State Department to speak about freedom of information. She has also worked in Peru, Chile and Guatemala on FOI issues. She won AEJMC's Baskett Mosse Award in 2003. She holds B.A., M.A. and J.D. degrees from the University of Florida. Her e-mail address is schance@jou.ufl.edu.

Charles N. Davis is the dean of the Henry W. Grady College of Journalism and Mass Communication at the University of Georgia. He worked as a journalist in Georgia, Florida and Ireland for nearly ten years after graduating from North Georgia College. He received a master's degree from the University of Georgia and a Ph.D. degree from the University of Florida, where he assisted reporters and others with freedom of information questions for the Brechner Center for Freedom of Information. He taught at Georgia Southern University and was department chair at Southern Methodist University before joining the faculty at the University of Missouri. He edited *Access Denied: Freedom of Information in the Information Age,* his first book, for Iowa University Press. His e-mail address is cndavis@uga.edu.

Anthony L. Fargo is an associate professor in the School of Journalism at Indiana University and director of the Center for International Media Law and Policy Studies. He holds a bachelor's degree in English and journalism from Morehead State University and master's and doctorate degrees in mass communication from the University of Florida. He has taught at the University of Nevada, Las Vegas and the University of Rhode Island in Kingston. His research has been published in *Communication Law and Policy, Free Speech Yearbook, Cardozo Arts & Entertainment Law Journal, Newspaper Research Journal,* the *Journal of Broadcasting and Electronic Media,* the *William & Mary Bill of Rights Journal,* the *William Mitchell Law Review,* the *University of Arkansas Little Rock Law Review,* the *Harvard Journal of Law & Public Policy, Journalism and Mass Communication Monographs,* and the *Journal of Media Law* (UK). He is on the board of the Indiana Coalition for Open Government and writes a monthly column about transparency and good government for the *Indianapolis Business Journal.* His email address is alfargo@indiana.edu.

Karla K. Gower is director of the Plank Center for Leadership in Public Relations and a professor in the Advertising and Public Relations Department of the College of Communication and Information Science at the University of Alabama, where she teaches public relations courses. She has published a book on the relationship between journalism and public relations since World War II and two books on communication law topics. In addition, her articles have appeared in *Journalism and Mass Communication Quarterly, Journalism History, Communication Law and Policy* and other journals. Her research focuses on legal issues affecting corporate communication and the history of public relations. She received her bachelor's and law degrees from the University of Western Ontario, Canada, her master's degree from Arizona State University and her doctorate from the University of North Carolina at Chapel Hill. Her e-mail address is gower@apr.ua.edu.

Steven Helle is a professor emeritus and former head of the Department of Journalism at the University of Illinois in Urbana-Champaign. He is co-author of *Last Rights: Revisiting Four Theories of the Press* and has published numerous articles on communication law in, among others, *Duke Law Journal, Journalism and Mass Communication Quarterly, Villanova Law Review, University of Illinois Law Review,*

Iowa Law Review, Illinois Bar Journal, Journalism and Mass Communication Educator and *DePaul Law Review*. A former head of the Law Division of the Association for Education in Journalism and Mass Communication, he has been named to the editorial boards of the *Illinois Bar Journal, Journalism Monographs* and *Communication Law and Policy*. He is past chair of the Media Law Committee and the Human Rights Section Council of the Illinois State Bar Association. He is the only person to receive the Campus Award for Excellence in Undergraduate Teaching at the University of Illinois on three occasions, most recently in 2010. He was also selected Freedom Forum Journalism Teacher of the Year in 1998. His J.D. and M.A. degrees are from the University of Iowa. His e-mail address is steveh@illinois.edu.

W. Wat Hopkins is a professor of communication at Virginia Tech, where he teaches journalism and communication law courses. He has published three books and a number of articles on First Amendment topics and is editor of *Communication Law and Policy,* the research journal of the Law Division of the Association for Education in Journalism and Mass Communication. He is a past head of the Law Division and is on the editorial board of *Journalism & Mass Communication Quarterly*. He is also past president of the Virginia Coalition for Open Government and was a founding member of Virginia's first Freedom of Information Advisory Council, an advisory and educational group established by the Virginia General Assembly. He was the Roy H. Park Distinguished Visiting Professor in the School of Journalism and Mass Communication at the University of North Carolina at Chapel Hill for the spring 2010 semester. He received his bachelor's degree from Western Carolina University and his master's and Ph.D. degrees from UNC-CH. His e-mail address is whopkins@vt.edu.

Matt Jackson is an associate professor and head of the telecommunications department in the College of Communications at Pennsylvania State University. He teaches telecommunications regulation and policy, programming, management and communication law. He has published articles in *Journal of Broadcasting & Electronic Media, Federal Communications Law Journal, Communications Law and Policy, Hastings Communication and Entertainment Law Journal* and other journals. His research focuses on the evolution of intellectual property law and its impact on communication networks and free speech. He received his bachelor's and master's degrees from the University of Florida and his doctorate from Indiana University at Bloomington. His e-mail address is mattj@psu.edu.

Robert Kerr is a professor in the College of Journalism and Mass Communication at the University of Oklahoma. He is also a member of the affiliated faculty of Oklahoma's Institute for the American Constitutional Heritage. He teaches undergraduate and graduate courses in the law of mass communication, and students have twice voted him recipient of his college's annual teaching award. His research focuses primarily on First Amendment issues involving corporate political media spending, commercial speech, and sports media. He has published two books. His most recent — *The Corporate Free-Speech Movement: Cognitive Feudalism and the Endangered Marketplace of Ideas* (2008) — foreshadowed the 2010 Supreme Court ruling in *Citizens United v. FEC* as well as the recent economic crisis in global markets. His articles have appeared in *Journalism and Communication Monographs, Journalism and Mass Communication Quarterly, Communication Law and Policy, The First Amendment Law Review, American Journalism* and *The Journal of Media Law and Ethics*. He is a recent winner of the National Communication Association's Franklyn S. Haiman Award for Distinguished Scholarship in Freedom of Expression. He received his bachelor's degree from Southern Arkansas University, his master's degree from the University of Oklahoma, and his doctorate from the University of North Carolina at Chapel Hill. He worked as a journalist for twenty years in Memphis, Las Vegas, and Texarkana. His email address is rkerr@ou.edu.

Dan V. Kozlowski is an associate professor in the Department of Communication at Saint Louis University, where he teaches free expression, journalism and media courses. He also holds a secondary appointment in SLU's law school. His research has appeared in *Communication Law and Policy, Journalism & Mass Communication Quarterly, Journal of Media Law & Ethics, Free Speech Yearbook, The International Encyclopedia of Communication* and other places. His research interests include student speech rights, judicial decision-making, comparative law, and journalism and culture. He has twice won the Laurence R. Campbell Research Award from the Scholastic Journalism Division of AEJMC for the top faculty paper at the annual conference. He received his master's degree from Saint Louis University and his doctorate from the University of North Carolina at Chapel Hill. He is former newspaper copy editor and page designer and has been a sports producer for WNBC-TV in New York City. His email address is dkozlows@slu.edu.

Jeremy Harris Lipschultz is Isaacson Professor in the School of Communication, University of Nebraska at Omaha. He is Reviews Editor for *Journalism & Mass Communication Educator*, PRSA Nebraska Ethics Chair and a blogger for *The Huffington Post* and *ChicagoNow*. His newest book is *Social Media Communication: Concepts, Practices, Data, Law and Ethics* (2015), and he is leading a team in developing the UNO Social Media Lab in the Community Engagement Center —

one of the first of its kind. Lipschultz is Senior Fellow in the Center for Collaboration Science. He is @JeremyHL on Twitter. His email address is jeremy.lipschultz@gmail.com.

Greg Lisby is a professor of communication at Georgia State University, where he teaches mass communication law and policy, and communication ethics. In addition to serving as a member of the editorial board of *Communication Law and Policy*, he has had articles published in *Journalism Monographs, Communication Law and Policy, Communications and the Law, Journalism Quarterly, Journal of Communication Inquiry, Newspaper Research Journal* and *Georgia Historical Quarterly.* The sixth edition of his book *Mass Communication Law in Georgia* was published in 2011. He was executive producer of a PBS documentary on film censorship in 2000. He is past head of the Law Division of the Association for Education in Journalism and Mass Communication and a past member of the editorial board of *American Journalism.* He was the 2003 recipient of the American Journalism Historians Association's book of the year award, the 2000 recipient of the *Georgia Historical Quarterly's* article of the year award, and the 1990 recipient of the Henry W. Grady Prize for Research in Journalism History. He received his bachelor's degree from Auburn University, his master's degree from the University of Mississippi, his doctorate from the University of Tennessee and his law degree from Georgia State University. He is a member of the State Bar of Georgia. His e-mail address is glisby@gsu.edu.

Mike McGregor is a professor of telecommunications and adjunct professor of law at Indiana University, where he teaches electronic media law and policy courses and introductory telecommunications courses. His research, which focuses on telecommunications policy making, the effects of policy decisions and e-government, has been published in *Communication Law and Policy, Journalism and Communication Monographs, Federal Communications Law Journal, COMM/ENT, Journalism Quarterly, Journal of Broadcasting and Electronic Media* and *Telecommunications Policy.* He has been a staff attorney at the Cable Television Information Center of the Urban Institute and has been an attorney/advisor in the Mass Media Bureau of the Federal Communications Commission. He received his bachelor's degree in history from Purdue University and his J.D. from Georgetown University Law Center. His e-mail address is mcgregom@indiana.edu.

Kathleen K. Olson is an associate professor in the Department of Journalism and Communication at Lehigh University. She has a Ph.D. in mass communication from the University of North Carolina at Chapel Hill and a law degree from the University of Virginia. She practiced law in Washington, D.C., and helped start the online version of the *Austin American-Statesman* in Austin, Texas. She co-authored *Mass Communication Law in Pennsylvania* and has published in *Communication Law and Policy, Journalism and Communication Monographs, Free Speech Yearbook* and other journals. Her research interests include intellectual property issues and the First Amendment. Her email address is kko2@lehigh.edu.

Derigan Silver is an assistant professor in the Department of Media, Film and Journalism Studies at the University of Denver. He is the director of the joint MA/JD program and teaches graduate and undergraduate courses on the First Amendment, media law, Internet law and political communication. He is the author of *National Security in the Courts: The Need for Secrecy vs. the Requirement of Transparency* and has published articles on national security information law and policy, access to government information, defamation, social architecture theory, judicial decision making and student press rights at public universities. He received his bachelor's degree from the University of California at Santa Barbara, his master's degree from the Walter Cronkite School of Journalism and Mass Communication at Arizona State University and his doctoral degree from the School of Journalism and Mass Communication at the University of North Carolina at Chapel Hill. His e-mail address is derigan.silver@du.edu.

Sigman L. Splichal is an associate professor in the School of Communication at the University of Miami, where he teaches media law and ethics, and is director of undergraduate and graduate journalism programs. He began his journalism career in 1971 and was a newspaper writer and editor in Georgia, Florida and Virginia. He received his bachelor's, master's and Ph.D. degrees from the University of Florida. He is co-editor of *Access Denied: Freedom of Information in the Information Age* and is author of numerous law and academic journal articles on legal and ethical topics. His e-mail address is sig@miami.edu.

Samuel A. Terilli is an assistant professor in the School of Communication at the University of Miami, where he teaches media law, ethics, reporting and related courses. He is also a practicing attorney and has represented and advised a variety of media organizations for twenty-two years. He received his bachelor's degree from the State University of New York at Albany and his juris doctorate from the University of Michigan. His e-mail address is sterilli@Miami.edu.

John C. Watson is an associate professor at the American University School of Communication in Washington, D.C. He holds a J.D. from the Rutgers School of Law and a Ph.D. from the University of North Carolina at Chapel Hill. He is the co-author of "Herman Lynn Womack: Pornographer as First Amendment Pioneer" in *Journalism History*, and is the author of *Journalism Ethics by Court Decree: The Supreme Court on the Proper Practice of Journalism.* His research and commentary have been published in *Communication Law and Policy, the Journal of Mass Media Ethics, Journalism History* and other refereed, scholarly journals. He is the author of book chapters and encyclopedia entries on communication law and has been published in the *Rutgers Race and the Law Review* and the *Thomas M. Cooley Law Review.* Watson has 21 years of experience as a daily newspaper reporter and city editor. He has been interviewed on communication and law issues by correspondents for NPR, NBC, CBS, CNN, ABC, BET, KBS (Korean Broadcasting System) and Fox News networks as well as *The New York Times, Washington Post* and *The Christian Science Monitor.* His e-mail address is jwatson@american.edu.

Kyu Ho Youm is a professor and Jonathan Marshall First Amendment Chair in the School of Journalism and Communication at the University of Oregon. He has published scholarly articles on communication law subjects in major U.S. and foreign academic journals, including *Journalism & Mass Communication Quarterly, Hastings Communication/Entertainment (COMM/ENT) Law Journal* and the *International and Comparative Law Quarterly* of London. His articles have been cited by American and English courts, including the House of the Lords (the United Kingdom equivalent of the Supreme Court) and the High Court of Australia. A former head of the AEJMC Law Division and a former chair of the Communication Law and Policy Group of the International Communication Association, he serves on editorial boards of thirteen communication law journals in the United States and England. He is the president of AEJMC. He received his bachelor's degree in South Korea and his master's and doctoral degrees from Southern Illinois University. He holds master of law degrees from the Yale Law School and Oxford University. His e-mail address is youm@uoregon.edu.

AUTHORS EMERETI

Dorothy Bowles, a professor at the University of Tennessee, has taught communications law at the graduate and undergraduate levels for thirty years. She is the author of *Kansas Media Law Guide* and *Media Law in Tennessee,* as well as numerous journal articles. She is an emeritus member of the board of directors of the Student Press Law Center and has held several offices in the Association for Education in Journalism and Mass Communications. She has worked as a newspaper reporter and editor and is co-author of one of the leading editing textbooks. In 2005, she received The Jefferson Prize, a top faculty award at the University of Tennessee. Her bachelor's degree is from Texas Tech University, her master's from the University of Kansas and her Ph.D. from the University of Wisconsin.

Thomas Eveslage is a professor of journalism in Temple University's

School of Communications and Theater. He has directed the Master of Journalism program and chaired the Department of Journalism, Public Relations and Advertising. He holds an M.A. degree in journalism from the University of Minnesota and a Ph.D. in journalism from Southern Illinois University at Carbondale. He has served on the board of directors of the Student Press Law Center, the Pennsylvania School Press Association and Quill and Scroll Society. He has written a column on student press law issues for more than ten years and has received the Lawrence Campbell Research Award three times from the Scholastic Journalism Division of the Association for Education in Journalism and Mass Communication. A member of Temple University's Teaching Academy, he was named Journalism Teacher of the Year in 2003 by AEJMC's Scholastic Journalism Division. He is a former copy editor and university news director.

F. Dennis Hale was an emeritus professor and former director of the School of Mass Communication at Bowling Green State University at the time of his death in 2008. He had published more than eighty book chapters, convention papers and journal articles, many about mass media law. He was a former head of the Law Division of the Association for Education in Journalism in Mass Communication and had received research grants from the U.S. Justice Department and the Newspaper Research Council. His Ph.D. degree was from Southern Illinois University.

Louise Williams Hermanson was a professor in the Department of Communication at the University of South Alabama, until her death in 2001. She taught law, ethics, print journalism and media history. Her research interests focused on alternative dispute resolution in conflicts between media and the public. She had published numerous journal articles and book chapters. Her bachelor's and master's degrees were from the University of South Carolina, and her Ph.D. was from the University of Minnesota. She had worked as a professional journalist in South Carolina.

Robert L. Hughes is an attorney in Richmond. He taught law for nineteen years at the Virginia Commonwealth University School of Mass Communications. Before that, he was a reporter and editorial writer for newspapers in Charlotte and West Palm Beach. He has a B.A. degree from Davidson College, an M.J. degree from the University of Missouri and a J.D. degree from the University of Florida.

Paul E. Kostyu is a senior outreach and education specialist for the Office of the Ohio Consumers' Counsel, a state agency that advocates on behalf of residential users of public utilities. He is a former Ohio statehouse bureau chief and business writer for newspapers in Ohio, Michigan and North Carolina and at *National Geographic* magazine. He is also an adjunct associate professor of journalism at Ohio Wesleyan University, where he has taught courses in reporting, editing, journalism history and communication law. His bachelor's degree is from Heidelberg College, and his master's and Ph.D. degrees are from Bowling Green State University. In 2005 he was a Kiplinger Fellow in Public Affairs Journalism at Ohio State University. He has published in *Communication and the Law, American Journalism,* the *Journal of Mass Media Ethics* and *News Photographer* magazine.

Arati R. Korwar has taught courses in media law, visual communication and online journalism, most recently Louisiana State

University. Her research in communication law and First Amendment issues has been published in *Communication Law and Policy, Journalism and Mass Communication Monographs* and other journals, and by the Freedom Forum First Amendment Center. As an American Society for Newspaper Editors fellow, she worked at *The New York Times on the Web*. She also worked at *The Times of India* as a reporter and copy editor. She received a bachelor's degree from the University of Massachusetts at Amherst and master's and doctorate degrees from the University of North Carolina at Chapel Hill.

Cathy Packer is the W. Horace Carter Distinguished Professor in the School of Journalism and Mass Communication at the University of North Carolina at Chapel Hill. She is also co-director of the UNC Center for Media Law and Policy. She teaches media law and Internet law and is the author of *Freedom of Expression in the American Military: A Communication Modeling Analysis*. A former newspaper reporter, she is co-editor of *The North Carolina Media Law Handbook,* to which she contributes the chapter on access to state and local records. She has published articles in *Journalism & Mass Communication Quarterly, Mass Comm Review, Carozo Arts & Entertainment Law Journal, Communication Law and Policy* and *Hastings Communications and Entertainment Law Journal*. She received her doctoral degree from the University of Minnesota.

Michael Perkins was chair of the Department of Communication at Brigham Young University until 2003 when he was killed in a kayaking accident. He taught primarily mass communications law and ethics. He had also taught at Drake University and the University of Costa Rica. His research, which focused on mass communication law internationally as well as in the United States, has been published in *Journalism and Mass Communication Quarterly, Communication Law and Policy, Journal of Mass Media Ethics, Gazette* and *Newspaper Research Journal*. He was the head of the AEJMC Law Division at the time of his death.

Milagros (Millie) Rivera-Sanchez teaches telecommunication courses at the National University of Singapore. She has published articles in *Journalism and Mass Communication Monographs, Journalism and Mass Communication Quarterly, Journalism History, The Federal Communications Law Journal, Communications and the Law, Hastings Communications* and *Entertainment Law Journal* and other journals. Her research interests include regulation of the electronic media in the United States and in Latin America. She holds a bachelor's degree from the University of Puerto Rico and master's and doctorate degrees from the University of Florida. She spent the summer of 1999 in Chile as a Fulbright Scholar.

Susan Dente Ross is an associate professor at Washington State University. She teaches media law, First Amendment theory, access to public records and journalism skills courses. In addition to conducting research on the regulation of emerging communication technologies, she examines the application of the First Amendment to speech and studies how media coverage frames marginalized groups and affects social change.

Joseph Russomanno is an associate professor at Arizona State University. His articles have appeared in a variety of journals. He worked as a television news journalist — primarily as a producer and executive producer — for ten years. He received his his doctorate from the University of Colorado.

Thomas A. Schwartz recently retired from School of Journalism and Communication at Ohio State University where he teaches reporting, mass communication law and legal research. He is a former newspaper and magazine editor, reporter and photographer. His recent research emphasizes the U.S. Supreme Court and the First Amendment and South African freedom of expression. He is past editor of the journal *Communication Law and Policy.*

Robert Trager teaches at the University of Colorado at Boulder. He holds a Ph.D. in journalism and mass communication from the University of Minnesota and a J.D. from the Stanford Law School. He has practiced law in Washington, D.C., and with Time Warner Cable. He is also the founding editor of *Communication Law and Policy.*

Ruth Walden is the emeritus James Howard and Hallie McLean Parker Distinguished Professor in the School of Journalism and Mass Communication at the University of North Carolina at Chapel Hill. She has held academic positions in Utah and Wisconsin-Madison and was a newspaper reporter in Wisconsin and Illinois. She was also assistant director of judicial education for the Wisconsin Supreme Court. She is the author of *Insult Laws: An Insult to Press Freedom* and *Mass Communication Law in North Carolina* and has published a number of articles on media law and First Amendment theory. A former head of the Law Division of the Association for Education in Journalism and Mass Communication, she serves on the editorial boards of *Journalism & Mass Communication Quarterly* and *Communication Law and Policy*. She holds B.A, M.A. and Ph.D. degrees from the University of Wisconsin.

Case Index

Subject Index

Bono, Sonny, 250
Boorstin, Daniel J., 49
Borat, 308
Bork, Robert, 107
Bose Corporation, 97
Bosley, Karen, 134
Boston Globe, 331, 355
Boyle, Francis, 348
Brandeis, Louis, 18, 59, 60, 61, 106, 291, 294, 299, 300
Branzburg, Paul, 321-22
Brennan, William J., 10, 26, 31, 38, 40, 72, 73, 74, 82, 96, 106, 310, 322, 346, 355, 356, 373
Breyer, Stephen G., 19, 82, 156, 245, 250, 397
Bridges, Harry, 353
Bridges, Hilda, 296
Bridgestone/Firestone, 361
Bright Tunes Music, 271
BRILAB, 362-63
Brinkema, Leonie, 363
Brinkley, John R., 185
Broadcast Decency Enforcement Act, 80
broadcast formats, 191
broadcast indecency, 79-81
broadcast licenses
　applications, 187
　fees, 188-89
　public input, 188
　renewals of, 188
　requirements, 186-87
　transfers of, 188
　See also broadcasting, cross-ownership rules
Broadcast Music Inc. (BMI), 267
　See also copyright
broadcast networks, 189, 191
broadcast spectrum, 180, 182-83
broadcast station ownership, 189-91
broadcasting
　alcohol advertising, 198
　children's programming, 193-94
　cigarette advertising, 198
　hoaxes, 198
　impact of, 183
　indecent programming, 192-93
　lotteries, 197-98
　pervasiveness, 183
　political, 195, 197
　public interest, 180, 185-86
　public trustees, 182-83
　See also broadcast licenses, cross-ownership rules, fairness doctrine, safe harbors
Brown, James Harvey, 351-52
Bryant, Kobe, 347
Buckley Amendment, *see* Family Educational Rights and Privacy Act (FERPA)
Buckley, James L., 132
Bunker, Matthew, 62
Burger, Warren, 29, 43, 60, 73, 74, 115, 345-46, 354-55, 360, 366
Burnett, Carol, 98
Bush, George W., 18, 45, 80, 137, 301, 316, 327
Bush, George, 237, 383, 385
Business Executives Move for a Vietnam Peace, 182
Business Week, 63-64, 66, 346

C

Cable Communications Policy Act of 1984, 204, 205, 206, 210, 211, 212, 213-14, 222, 223, 234

cable information services, 215, 216
Cable News Network, *see* CNN
cable telecommunications services, 215, 216
cable television
　a la carte pricing, 223-24
　copyright, 220-21
　franchises, 203-04, 213-14
　leased-access channels, 210-11
　must-carry rules, 208-10
　network nonduplication rules, 220-21
　open access, 214-15
　ownership regulations, 206-07
　privacy, 222
　public, educational and governmental (PEG) access channels, 210, 211-12
　rate regulation, 205-06
　retransmission rules, 209-10
　sexually explicit programming, 219
　subscribers, 201
　telephone service, 221-22
　See also cross-ownership rules
Cable Television Consumer Protection and Competition Act of 1992, 204, 205, 206, 207, 209, 210, 211, 212, 213, 239, 240
Cablevision, 205, 223-24
Cablevision of Boston, 235
Caldwell, Earl, 321-22, 323
California courts, 63, 70, 79, 88, 98, 93, 113, 124, 167, 295, 296, 297, 300, 301, 306, 309, 331
California, David John, 276
California Law Review, 294
California State University, 130
Caligula, 76
campaign contributions/expenditures, 166
Campbell, Luther, 273
Camperi Liqueur, 308
CAN-SPAM, 233
Canada, 117, 118
candidates for public office, 183, 195-97
Capital Cities/ABC, 397
Carlin, George, 79, 81, 192
Carnal Knowledge, 75
Carson, Johnny, 306
Carter-Mondale Committee, 195
Carter, Jimmy, 385
Carter, Patricia, 129
Case Western Reserve University, 65
Castle Rock Entertainment, 266, 275
Cat NOT in the Hat, The, 274
Catcher in the Rye, 276
Catherine, Queen of England, 50
Catholics, *see* Roman Catholic Church
Caxton, William, 26
CBS, 80, 112, 182, 195, 198, 302, 320
censorship, *see* gag orders; prior restraint
Central Connecticut State University, 134
Central Hudson test, 152-54, 155, 156, 157, 163-64, 172
　See also Case Index, Central Hudson Gas & Electric Corporation v. Public Service Commission of New York
Central Intelligence Agency, *see* CIA
Cepeda, Orlando, 307
Chafee, Zechariah, 59
Challenger, 312
change of venire, 343
change of venue, 343
Chaplinski, Walter, 43

Charlotte Herald-News (Florida), 351
Charter Communications, 225
Cheney, Dick, 327
Cher, 307
Cherry Sisters, 108
Chevalier, Erik, 158
Chicago Tribune, 94
Child Online Protection Act (COPA), 81, 125, 139, 242, 243-44
child pornography, *see* pornography, child
Child Pornography Prevention Act (CPPA), 242, 248-49
Childers, W.D., 388
Children's Advertising Review Unit, 163
Children's Internet Protection Act (CIPA), 81, 139, 242, 245-48
Children's Online Privacy Protection Act (COPPA), 232
Children's Television Act, 194
Chinn, Denny, 114
Chiquita Brands International, 396
Christensen, F.M., 150
Christoff, Russell, 306-07
Chronicle of Higher Education, The, 131
Chumley, Libby Sue, 94
Church of England, *see* England, Church of
CIA, 326, 328, 329
Cincinnati Enquirer, 396
Cinderella-96, 76
Clark, Dorothy, 94
Clark, Russell, 130
Clark, Tom, 73, 341, 342, 365
Clarke, Arthur C., 239
Class of '74, 80
Classified Information Procedures Act, 364
clear and present danger test, 29, 59, 60, 345
Clearview Junior High School (New Jersey), 140
Cleland, John, 368
Cleveland Plain Dealer, 304, 340
Cleveland Press, 340
Clinton, Bill, 18, 33, 243, 249, 312, 357, 376, 381, 384
Clinton, Hillary, 167
CNN, 62, 66, 347, 395
Cochran, Jonnie L., 62-63, 88
Code of Federal Regulation, 266
Cohen, Dan, 334
Cohen, Paul, 70
Cohen, Paul Robert, 42-43
Coke, Lord, 89
Cole, R. Guy, 128
Colgate-Palmolive, 159
collateral bar rule, 347-48
College Campus Press Act (Illinois), 135, 144
Collegian (Kansas State University), 134
Collins, Ronald, 149
Colorado courts, 45, 347
Columbine (Colorado) High School, 121, 138
Comcast, 205, 216-17, 222, 224, 230
Commentaries on the Law of England, 2, 49, 51
　See also Blackstone, William
commercial speech, defined, 150, 165
　See also advertising, First Amendment and advertising, public relations
Commission on Obscenity and Pornography, 71
Committee to Defend Martin Luther King and the Struggle for Freedom in the South, 96
common carriers, 231